PRESIDENTIAL PROFILES
THE CARTER YEARS

Burton I. Kaufman

AMAZON, 3rd (Lib-Pol. Sci)

12/11

Presidential Profiles: The Carter Years

Facts On File, Inc.
An imprint of Infobase Publishing
132 West 31st Street
New York NY 10001

Library of Congress Cataloging-in-Publication Data

Kaufman, Burton I.
The Carter years/Burton I. Kaufman.
p. cm.—(Presidential profiles)
Includes bibliographical references and index.
ISBN 0-8160-5369-3 (hc : alk. paper)
1. Politicians—United States—Biography. 2. United States—Politics and government—1977–1981. 3. Carter, Jimmy, 1924– —Friends and associates. 4. United States—History—1969– —Biography. 5. United States—History—1969– I. Title. II. Presidential profiles (Facts On File, Inc.)
E840.6K38 2006
973.926092—dc22 2005034657

Facts On File books are available at special discounts when purchased in bulk quantities for businesses, associations, institutions, or sales promotions. Please call our Special Sales Department in New York at (212) 967-8800 or (800) 322-8755.

You can find Facts On File on the World Wide Web at http://www.factsonfile.com

Text design by Mary Susan Ryan-Flynn
Cover design by Nora Wertz

Printed in the United States of America

VB Hermitage 10 9 8 7 6 5 4 3 2 1

This book is printed on acid-free paper.

CONTENTS

INTRODUCTION

In 1974, former governor James Earl Carter, Jr., of Georgia decided to run for U.S. president. Although his political career consisted of two terms as state senator and one term as governor and he was virtually unknown outside of Georgia, he believed he could win the Democratic presidential nomination and go on to win the presidency by entering all the primary contests and campaigning as a political outsider. By doing so, he and his advisers were persuaded they could take advantage of the national backlash against Washington as a result of the Watergate affair and the Vietnam War. Running as a moderate, Carter promised new ideas without upsetting more conservative voters. Chalking up victories in the early primaries in 1976, he was able to gain the Democratic nomination and then defeat President Gerald Ford narrowly in November, receiving 40.8 million votes to Ford's 39.1 million votes.

Yet Carter was more frenetic than forthcoming, and his campaign was more one of style than of substance. As one political commentator observed, Carter had "given heart, mind, soul and smile to winning the presidency." But he never made clear for what ends and to what purpose. Indeed, the new president's entire campaign for office had been dogged with charges that he was "fuzzy" on the issues, and few voters knew exactly what to expect from a Carter administration except that the new president would never lie to them, that he would run an open administration, that his foreign policy would reflect his commitment to human rights, that he would reform and cut the size of government, that he would make it more responsive to the people, that he would

President Carter in the oval office, 1977 *(Jimmy Carter Library)*

seek tax reform, and that he would take measures to cut the nation's high rate of unemployment (running at a little more than 7 percent in the summer of 1976).

On specifics of these programs or how he would go about implementing them (for example, how he promised to pay for the cost of a national health insurance program or what federal agencies he proposed to eliminate), Carter remained silent. Because he also chose to make the central issue of his campaign the need for a spiritual reawakening on the part of the American people, his campaign speeches dealt far more with questions of national values than with specific programs and policies.

Because Carter was unusually abstruse, political commentators who, at the beginning of Carter's run for the presidency, used to ask "Jimmy Who?" increasingly asked, "Jimmy What?" Indeed, the only humor in an otherwise humorless campaign had to do with the candidate's "fuzziness." One story that circulated in Washington had young Jimmy responding when asked by his father whether he had chopped down the family's peach tree, "Well, perhaps." The historian C. Van Woodward delighted at "Carter's remarkable propensity ... for fusing contradictions and reconciling opposites," remarking that the result was an "unusual assortment of unified ambiguities and ambiguous unities."

The fact that he was not a particularly effective speaker also hurt Carter, the candidate. Former senator Eugene McCarthy referred to him as an "oratorical mortician [who] inters words and ideas beneath piles of syntactical mush," while the political columnists Rowland Evans and Robert Novak, suggested that he was "allergic to all efforts of eloquence." One expert on political forensics characterized his speaking as "containing no applause lines, little detail on issues [and] no rhetorical flourishes," and still another remarked that Carter's "visions of America the beautiful [had] the quality of gilded figurines bought in penny arcades."

Carter was vague, however, not only on specific issues, but on his overall sense of national purpose and national direction, the very issues he emphasized during the campaign. Except in the broadest generalities, Carter offered the nation no blueprint to follow, no structure to build. An engineer by training, he was more a problem solver than a program planner. Lacking a sense of mission or clearly defined vision (again, except in the most general terms), he had no points of reference toward which he could guide his administration or which might inform his style of leadership; in this sense, he failed both in terms of substance *and* style. Indeed, Carter was the only 20th-century Democratic president up to that time who did not attempt to attach to his legislative program some overall theme, such as the New Freedom, the New Deal, the Fair Deal, the New Frontier, or the Great Society. In itself, this was not particularly important, but in the view of many political observers, it was symptomatic of what went wrong with the Carter presidency.

When the new president entered the White House, he faced problems that were arguably more complex than those faced by other peacetime presidents. A national sense of despair and even cynicism (in considerable part a result of the Watergate affair and the Vietnam War), which had helped get him elected in the first place, would have greatly complicated the task of any administration, not just Carter's. And there were other problems, such as the breakdown of the historically strong party system, changes in the congressional system of seniority, the appearance of hundreds of political action committees (PACs), and a rejection of modern liberalism and a movement toward more conservative political, cultural, and social values that posed problems for the Georgian that earlier presidents had not had to face in the same way or to the same extent.

Within months after Carter took office, his administration seemed to self-destruct. First, the president cut from the budget a series of water projects being promoted on Capitol Hill. Although most of these projects were clearly wasteful, such pork-barrel politics had been sacrosanct for decades, and Carter's unilateral action, taken without first consulting Congress, stunned and angered Capitol Hill. Then the president announced that he had decided against a $50 rebate for every American taxpayer, even though he had made that a campaign promise. This was followed by a series of statements and actions on such matters as the Central Intelligence Agency (CIA), welfare costs, and cuts in the White House staff, all of which suggested that Carter was not fulfilling the pledges he had made during the election.

Finally, toward the end of Carter's first year in office, came the revelations that the president's closest friend and political ally, OMB director Bert Lance, had engaged in unsavory business practices while a banker in Georgia (including running up huge overdrafts on the Calhoun National Bank that his family controlled) and that someone within the administration had attempted to halt the investigation into Lance's financial dealings. Instead of asking for Lance's resignation, the president stood loyally by him, declaring publicly that Lance was "a man of honesty, trustworthiness, [and] integrity" and that he was "proud" of the OMB director. The Lance affair, which dominated the headlines for weeks, struck at the very credibility of the administration and damaged Carter severely on Capitol Hill. In losing one of the president's closest advisers—a man who had a better sense of how to operate as a Washington insider than any of Carter's other most trusted aides—the Lance affair was a crushing blow to the new administration from which it never recovered.

President Carter addressing a Joint Session of Congress, 1977 *(Jimmy Carter Library)*

In the three years that followed, the administration's real achievements were overshadowed by the growing problems of energy, inflation, and rising unemployment; by the increasing public estrangement between Congress and the White House, including the crushing defeat of President Carter's proposal to establish a consumer protection agency; by the controversy over developing a neutron bomb; by a scandal involving the writing of illegal prescriptions for drugs by a White House physician; by the alleged escapades of the president's top aide, Hamilton Jordan, including accusations that had thrown ice cubes down the dress of a woman in a Washington, D.C. bar; by open splits within the administration, most notably between Secretary of State Cyrus Vance and National Security Advisor Zbigniew Brzezinski; the January 1979 overthrow a year earlier of the shah of Iran, Mohammad Reza Pahlavi, whom only a few months before the president had toasted as an "island of stability in one of the more troubled areas of the world"; by the summary firing that same year of a number of top administration officials and members of his cabinet; by the tripling of oil prices to $35 a barrel; by long lines at the gas pumps; by the taking of American hostages in Tehran in November 1979; and, finally, by the December 1979 Soviet invasion of Afghanistan.

In all, the events of 1977–80 projected an image of a hapless (and helpless) administration in total disarray. The nation witnessed a presidency increasingly divided, lacking in leadership, ineffective in its dealings with Congress, incapable even of defending the United States's honor abroad, and unclear as to its priorities, both foreign and domestic.

It was, however, the administration's failure to direct its efforts toward any specific goal—other than some vague notion of restoring goodness and trust to government and basing foreign policy on a commitment to human rights—that was at the core of many of these other problems, particularly those having to do with establishing short- and long-term priorities.

By 1980, a growing number of Americans, even within the Democratic Party, were ready for a change of leadership. At first, it appeared that that alternative might be Senator Edward Kennedy of Massachusetts. But an interview with a television correspondent, Roger Mudd, in which Kennedy could not articulate a reason why Americans should elect him over Carter, undermined his candidacy and resulted in Carter's renomination by the Democrats in August 1980. Carter's opponent was former California governor Ronald Reagan.

More charismatic than Carter and better able to face the cameras, Reagan was a formidable opponent. Often using the phrase "there you go again" in response to Carter's answers during his single debate with the president a week before the election, Reagan turned a contest that had been regarded as a tossup before the debate into a trounce when he asked the penultimate question of the campaign: "Are you better off today than you were four years ago?" On November 4, the voters answered with a resounding "no" by electing Reagan, who received 51 percent of the vote to Carter's 41 percent. Republican Congressman John Anderson received 7 percent of the vote.

Despite Carter's defeat and notwithstanding the many problems he faced when he entered office, he was able to point to a number of significant achievements by the time he left office in 1981. Among the most important of these were: the Panama Canal Treaties of 1977; a nuclear nonproliferation treaty; strip-mining legislation; a measure setting aside a large area of the Alaskan wilderness as a permanent part of the federal domain; a major reform of the civil service system; and, of course, the Camp David accords of 1978.

As president, Carter also deserves credit for the quiet manner in which he furthered the earlier efforts of President Gerald Ford to restore to the Oval Office the dignity lost as a result of the Vietnam War and Watergate affair. Personally, Carter was intelligent and thoughtful, with an abiding commitment to ethical principles and human rights. Unlike Lyndon Johnson, he was not ill-tempered or mean-spirited. Unlike Richard Nixon, he was not insecure and conspiratorial. Both privately and publicly, he was courteous, gracious, and self-possessed.

Yet it remains hard to reach any conclusion other than that the Carter presidency was a mediocre one. He had been elected to office mainly because he offered the American people new hope and a real change of leadership and by promising to clean house and bring in an outside team more in tune with what the voters wanted. Once he became president, however, he failed to establish the same kind of political ties on Capitol Hill or to engage in the same types of power-brokering that successful presidents from Franklin Roosevelt to Lyndon Johnson (prior to Vietnam) had done. At the same time, he presented Congress with a package of programs that even the most politically astute presidents would have had difficulty getting through the House and the Senate. Furthermore, the president undercut his own campaign image of openness and integrity by his steadfast loyalty to the ol' Georgia clique even when serious questions, such as during the controversy surrounding the director of the Office of Management and Budget Bert Lance, were raised about the moral and ethical rectitude of some of its members. The result was that during his four years as president, he alienated much of the American public as well as lawmakers on Capitol Hill. More important, he failed to achieve such important parts of his legislative program as welfare and urban reform and a program of national health insurance.

Aaron, David L.

(1938–) *deputy assistant for national security affairs, deputy director of the National Security Council*

David L. Aaron served as deputy assistant for national security affairs and deputy director of the National Security Council (NSC) during the Carter administration (1977–81). A career diplomat, he was highly respected by both National Security Advisor ZBIGNIEW BRZEZINSKI and Secretary of State CYRUS VANCE and was involved in virtually every major foreign policy initiative of the Carter presidency.

Aaron was born in Chicago on August 21, 1938. A graduate of Occidental College (B.A., 1960) and Princeton University (M.A., 1962), he entered the foreign service in 1962 and gained a number of increasingly responsible postings and assignments. The last of these was from 1969 to 1972 as a member of the U.S. delegation to the first Strategic Arms Limitations Talks (SALT I). From 1972 to 1974, he served as a senior staff member on the NSC.

In 1974, Aaron left the NSC to accept a fellowship with the Council on Foreign Relations. Soon thereafter, Senator WALTER MONDALE (D-Minn.), who was contemplating running for president in 1976 and realized he needed to broaden his knowledge of foreign policy, asked Aaron to serve as his legislative assistant and staff adviser on foreign policy. A lifelong Democrat, Aaron accepted the offer, and over the next 10 years he was instrumental in educating Mondale about international relations.

Following the Carter-Mondale victory in the 1976 presidential election, Mondale helped Aaron to secure his position on the NSC as deputy to National Security Advisor Zbigniew Brzezinski. The two officials, who had known each other earlier, developed a good working relationship. Brzezinski later described Aaron as "an energetic and competitive official [who] was especially persuasive in arguing that I insist on controlling crisis management." Aaron shared Brzezinski's concern about the importance of power in diplomacy and the need to develop a strategic framework in order to analyze international events and exercise power, but he tended to be more of an optimist and a coalition builder than Brzezinski. His loyalty both to Mondale and Brzezinski sometimes placed Aaron in an awkward position since the vice president and National Security Advisor had differing views on Soviet foreign policy objectives and how to deal with Moscow.

As Brzezinski's deputy, Aaron took on a number of tasks, including serving as confidential presidential emissary to Europe, the

Middle East, Africa, Latin America, and Asia. His main areas of responsibility, however, were arms control and consultations with Europe. In 1977, he played a significant role in persuading President Carter to seek deeper cuts in strategic weapons—specifically the Soviet Union's heavy missiles—than those negotiated in 1974 at Vladivostok by then-President GERALD FORD and Soviet president LEONID BREZHNEV. In doing so, he later acknowledged that he was guilty of hubris and naïveté. It would have been far better, he conceded, to have first gauged the Soviets' likely response to a comprehensive proposal before laying it on the table without prior notice, as Secretary of State Cyrus Vance did during his trip to Moscow in March 1977.

In 1978, Carter sent Aaron to Europe to ascertain the position of the United States' European allies on the development and deployment of the neutron bomb. That same year, he accompanied Vice President Mondale to Beijing as part of the White House's effort at normalizing relations with China. The next year, he played a leading role in the administration's ill-fated effort to find an alternative to leftist guerillas in Nicaragua, known as the Sandinistas, who had recently overthrown the country's longtime dictator, ANASTASIO SOMOZA DEBAYLE, following a two-year civil war. During the crisis leading to the overthrow of the shah of Iran, MOHAMMAD REZA PAHLAVI, in January 1979, Aaron was responsible for convening a series of mini-meetings of the NSC's Special Coordination Committee to oversee contingency planning by various agencies in the event of the shah's fall from power. In 1980, he was one of a group of advisers whom the president invited to Camp David to discuss foreign affairs and the relationship of the White House to the State Department. Throughout much of the Carter administration, Aaron also acted as a watchdog for the NSC, protecting its turf against encroachments from the Department of State.

In September 1980, Aaron was accused of being responsible for exposing the cover of an American spy in the Soviet Union who was subsequently arrested and executed. The Senate Intelligence Committee investigated the anonymous accusation and found it baseless. Later, the *New York Times*, which had reported on the story, attributed the charge to the Madison Group, a group of ultraconservative Republican staffers on Capitol Hill who had acquired their name because they met once a week for lunch at the Madison Hotel.

In 1981, Aaron was awarded the National Defense Medal for his service in government. Two years later, he resigned to become vice president for mergers and acquisitions at Oppenheimer and Company, a major investment banking firm. He also served at the National Democratic Institute and the International League for Human Rights and remained a long-term member and contributor to the Council on Foreign Relations. Beginning in 1987, he used his experience as a diplomat to write a series of well-reviewed spy novels.

In 1993, President Bill Clinton named Aaron as the United States' permanent representative to the Organization for Economic Cooperation and Development. Three years later, Clinton appointed him as the nation's special envoy for cryptography, with responsibility for promoting and assuring the security of international electronic commerce and communication. In 1997, the president appointed him as undersecretary of commerce for international trade.

Abourezk, James George
(1931–) *member of the Senate*

As U.S. senator during the first two years of the Carter presidency, James Abourezk (D-

S.Dak.) is best known for his efforts on behalf of Native Americans and Arab Americans. He was also at the center of considerable controversy because of his confrontational style, even with fellow Democrats on Capitol Hill.

Abourezk was born to Lebanese immigrant parents on February 24, 1931, on the Rosebud Sioux Indian Reservation, where his father ran a general store. After graduating from high school, Abourezk served in the navy (1948–52) and worked as a rancher, bartender, and car salesman before earning a degree in civil engineering from the South Dakota School of Mines (B.S., 1961) and a law degree from the University of South Dakota (LL.B., 1966). As an attorney with his own law practice, he did a considerable amount of pro bono work for Native Americans and became interested in politics. In 1968, he worked for Robert F. Kennedy's presidential campaign. That same year, he ran unsuccessfully for the position of state attorney general, but two years later he won an upset victory in a congressional race in which he stressed his opposition to the Vietnam War and his concern for the small farmer.

Serving only one term in the U.S. House of Representatives (1971–73) before running successfully in 1972 for the U.S. Senate, Abourezk played a leading role in establishing the Senate Select Committee on Indian Affairs Committee and was author of the Indian Child Welfare Act and the Indian Self-Determination Act. He was also an outspoken critic of the Bureau of Indian Affairs, which he referred to in his memoirs as "a bureaucracy that has designed programs to insure that Indians will fail."

A curmudgeon with a populist streak, Abourezk was widely known in Washington for his distrust of moneyed interests and his disdain for symbols of privilege. He repeatedly criticized the CIA for its covert operations, which he described as "nothing more than the president's private hit squad, available to rub out anybody who makes the president politically uncomfortable." He also antagonized many of his fellow lawmakers on Capitol Hill by ridiculing the manner in which they conducted their business, remarking that there was "a collective cowardice at work that prevents Congress from ever challenging a strong president."

In 1977, Abourezk gained national notoriety for calling President Carter a liar on the Senate floor. A key critic of the president's proposal to deregulate natural gas, he held up final approval in 1978 of the administration's energy program with a three-day filibuster. He ended the filibuster only after he realized that he was angering colleagues anxious to return home to campaign.

No issue stirred more controversy, however, than Abourezk's unwavering support in the Senate for the Arab cause. A year after being elected to the Senate, he visited his father's birthplace in Lebanon for the first time and then traveled to a number of other Arab states in the region. Troubled that what he saw and heard on the trip "didn't seem to fit in at all with what I had been hearing in Washington," he became one of the leading spokesmen for the Arab view in the United States. He repeatedly attacked the pro-Israeli lobby on Capitol Hill and the military and financial assistance the United States provided Israel. He ridiculed suggestions that his opposition to Israel reflected anti-Semitism on his part. He also railed against the media for what he termed its biased reporting of the Arab-Israeli conflict and for fostering anti-Arab sentiment in the United States.

Unhappy with what he referred to as the Senate's "clublike" nature and the "vicious" pro-Israeli lobby on Capitol Hill, and concerned that his career was taking a toll on his marriage and family, Abourezk decided not to seek reelection in 1978. Instead, two years later, he organized the American-Arab Anti-Discrimination Committee (ADC), which he formed after the national exposure in February 1980 of an FBI sting operation, named Abscam, in which agents posed as wealthy Arabs trying to bribe lawmakers. The ADC soon became the nation's largest Arab-American civil rights organization; Abourezk chaired the committee for the next 15 years.

Author of *Advise and Dissent: Memoirs of South Dakota and the U.S. Senate* (1989), Abourezk has lectured widely and served as adjunct professor of international politics at American University. He currently practices law in Sioux Falls, South Dakota.

Abzug, Bella Savitsky

(1920–1998) *member of the House of Representatives; cochair, National Advisory Committee on Women*

A member of the House of Representatives from 1971 to 1977, Bella Abzug (D-N.Y.) was known for her brashness, tough-mindedness, and flamboyancy, including her penchant for large, wide-brimmed hats, which became her trademark. Abzug was also one of the leaders of the feminist and gay rights movements when they were still in their infancy in the late 1960s and 1970s. In 1976, she was one of 50 feminist leaders who met with Jimmy Carter at the Democratic convention in New York to discuss a proposal they were pushing that provided for women to have 50 percent of the delegates at the party's convention in 1980. Carter persuaded Abzug and other women's leaders to settle for a compromise in the party platform. In lieu of the quotas the women wanted, Carter promised to promote equality at the convention and, as president, to promote the Equal Rights Amendment and appoint more women to high positions in his administration, two promises he later tried to keep. Meeting with the press afterward, Abzug stated that just as former president Lyndon Johnson wanted to eliminate legal barriers against blacks, Carter would strive to eliminate legal barriers against women.

A large and imposing figure physically, Abzug was born on June 20, 1920, and grew up in the Bronx, the daughter of Jewish immigrants from Russia. After graduating from Hunter College (B.A., 1942), where she was student body president, and Columbia University Law School (LL.B., 1947), where she was editor of the *Law Review*, she practiced labor law and worked as a lawyer for the American Civil Liberties Union (ACLU). She also represented clients caught up in the Red Scare of the 1950s. In the 1960s, she became active in the antiwar and feminist movements, helping to found the Women's Strike for Peace, and cofounding the National Women's Political Caucus with Gloria Steinem and Shirley Chisholm.

First elected to the House of Representatives in 1970, Abzug represented New York City's 19th district, which stretched from Greenwich Village to the Upper West Side of Manhattan. In 1974, she introduced the first gay civil rights bill, which would have amended the Civil Rights Act of 1964 to include the category of sexual orientation as a protected class. She continued to reintroduce the bill each year until she left Congress in 1977, but it never made its way through the House.

In 1977, Abzug presided over the first National Women's Conference in Houston. She was then appointed by President Carter as chair of the National Advisory Commission on the observance of International Women's Year and later as cochair of his National Advisory Committee on Women (NACW). By this time she had been named in a Gallup Poll as one of the 20 most influential women in the world. But almost from the time the Carter administration took office, she had been a thorn in its side. In contrast to the White House, Abzug viewed NACW as a voice of the women's movement rather than as an agency of the administration. Accordingly, she had no qualms about attacking the White House when she thought its policies conflicted with what she considered the women's agenda, As early as November 1977, she publicly reviled the "white-dominated White House" and demonstrated against Secretary of Health, Education, and Welfare JOSEPH CALIFANO for the administration's position on funding abortions only when a women's life was threatened or a pregnancy was the result of rape or incest. As a founding member of Women Strike for Peace, she also criticized the president's decisions to increase defense spending while cutting back the domestic budget.

In 1979, Carter decided to fire Abzug after he learned that the NACW was about to release a report highly critical of him for cutting back on funding for women's programs. The president's senior staff had already decided that she needed to be fired, but Carter delayed her termination until after a meeting with the NACW at the White House. He then asked HAMILTON JORDAN and legal counsel, ROBERT LIPSHUTZ, to inform Abzug that she was being dismissed.

Their meeting with Abzug was stormy. After first denying that she was about to release the report in question and stating that she was being falsely slandered, she became defiant, claiming she was being made a Jewish scapegoat, a comment that angered Lipshutz, who was also Jewish. Abzug threatened, nevertheless, to organize her large constituency of women against the administration. Half of the other members of the NACW resigned with her. Even feminists who disliked Abzug's aggressive style and personality felt that the president had made a mistake in firing her.

In 1976, Abzug had made an unsuccessful run for the U.S. Senate. After running unsuccessfully the next year for mayor of New York and then three more times for the House, she withdrew from elective politics, though she remained a strong advocate of gay and women's rights and the environment. In 1991, she founded the Women's Environment and Development Organization (WEDO). In 1995, she traveled to Beijing to attend an international conference on women. She died in 1998 of complications following heart surgery.

Adams, Brock

(Brockman Adams)

(1927–1993) *secretary of transportation*

As transportation secretary for the first three years of the Carter administration, Brockman (Brock) Adams took on a number of powerful interests and instituted important initiatives in all the major areas of transportation. But his firmly held views did not always coincide with those of the administration and led eventually to President Carter's decision to dismiss him in July 1979 as part of a major shakeup of his cabinet.

A naval veteran of World War II (1944–46), Adams was born in Atlanta, Georgia, on January 13, 1927, but he grew up on the West Coast. After graduating from the University of Washington with a degree in economics (B.S., 1949) and then from Harvard Law School (LL.B., 1952), he established a law practice in Seattle and taught law at the American Institute of Banking from 1954 to 1960. In 1961, he was appointed U.S. attorney for the western district of Washington State. In 1964, he ran successfully as a Democrat for the U.S. House of Representatives and was reelected six times before being named by Carter in 1977 as secretary of transportation.

What brought Adams to Carter's attention was his service as the first chairperson of the House Budget Committee, which, together with the Senate Budget Committee and the Congressional Budget Office, had been established by Congress in 1974 in order to regularize the process by which lawmakers considered the president's budget requests. A liberal Democrat, he had a keen knowledge of finance and a growing expertise on transportation. Highly regarded on Capitol Hill, he had even been briefly considered by Carter as a possible running mate.

As transportation secretary, Adams came into conflict with automakers almost immediately. In 1977, he announced new regulations requiring all new cars sold in the United States to have installed, by 1984, front airbags or passive safety belts that fastened automatically. The next year, he put into place new fuel economy standards for the nation's motor vehicles as part of President Carter's larger effort to reduce energy consumption in the United States. Adams also challenged manufacturers to improve their products, remarking that in recent years the American automobile industry "has acquired a reputation for imitation, not innovation. The companies have been collaborators, not competitors."

In 1978, Adams supported passage of a highly controversial measure, the Inland Waterways Revenue Act of 1978, which authorized the Army Corps of Engineers to construct new 1,200-foot locks and a dam at Altoona, Illinois, in order to break major logjams in barge traffic on the Mississippi River from Chicago and Minneapolis. The measure required, for the first time, commercial users of the nation's inland waterways to pay modest user fees into a new Inland Waterways Trust Fund similar to the Highway Trust Fund. The final legislation was a much-watered-down version of an earlier measure that would have had waterway users pay the full costs of federal expenditures to operate and maintain the waterways and most of the cost of new water projects. After the barge industry, which was most impacted by the new fee structure, was able to whittle the measure down, Adams said he would recommend vetoing the bill. The legislation was also strongly opposed by railroads and environmentalists who believed the trust fund would be a catalyst for future projects. But after strong pressure from farmers, electrical and rural co-ops, and other groups dependent on reliable river traffic, Adams was forced to retreat from his earlier position, and the president signed the measure into law.

In 1978, Congress approved the Airline Deregulation Act, which opened the airline industry to greater competition and set a precedent for similar deregulation in the motor carrier and railroad industries. In contrast to President Carter, who strongly supported deregulation of transportation as part of his effort to make government more efficient and less costly, and even some fellow liberals on Capitol Hill, such as Senator EDWARD KENNEDY (D-Mass.), who had been championing the cause of deregulation since the early 1970s, Adams expressed concerns that the administration was moving too hastily to deregulate one of the nation's most vital sectors. But he was overruled by the president, who signed the measure into law with considerable fanfare.

Other measures Adams supported as transportation secretary included one to replace the crumbling West Side Highway in New York City and another to improve screening at the nation's major airports following a string of hijackings. But by summer 1979, he had become deeply worried about the state of the administration and his place in it. On July 3, President Carter cancelled a television address to the nation on energy and retreated instead to Camp David for eight days of meetings with prominent Americans; the meetings were part of the events leading up to the president's so-called malaise speech of July 15. Concerned about the president's mental stability, Adams tracked down Carter's close friend and former director of the Office of Management and Budget, BERT LANCE, who was in San Francisco, to tell him that president was in deep trouble. "[H]e thinks everything is falling apart for him," Adams remarked to Lance. "You need to call him and find out what's going on. I think he's having real problems."

By this time, however, the president had lost all confidence in Adams, with whom he had never been ideologically or personally close. Adams was also not well liked among staffers at the White House, where he was known for having an unbridled tongue and for being disloyal to the president. Derogatory remarks about Adams were sometimes leaked to the press from the White House, including one that he was too interested in the Senate race in his home state of Washington to run his department effectively or to serve the administration well.

On July 17, 1979, after refusing to follow a directive from the White House to fire his top assistant, Adams was forced to resign as transportation secretary. He did not leave his post quietly. A few weeks after being fired, he remarked about Carter, "I think one of the problems is ... there's a difference between campaigning and governing. Governing takes a different kind of person. You can't govern being against government."

After resuming his law practice in Seattle, Adams ran successfully for the U.S. Senate in 1986 but quit his bid for reelection in 1992 after being accused by the *Seattle Times* of sexual misconduct toward eight former female employees and political associates. On September 10, 2004, he died of Parkinson's disease at his home in Stevensville, Maryland.

Albright, Madeleine Korbel

(1937–) *congressional liaison officer, National Security Council*

Future U.S. ambassador to the United Nations and secretary of state Madeleine Korbel Albright served from 1978 to 1981 as a staff member on President Carter's National Security Council (NSC) as well as a White House staffer. Her primary responsibility was as a congressional liaison officer.

Albright was born on May 15, 1937, in Prague, Czechoslovakia. Her father, Josef Korbel, had been a member of Czechoslovakia's diplomatic service. Following the communist seizure of the Czech government in 1948, he fled with his family to the United States. Granted political asylum, he accepted an academic position with the University of Denver, where he established a graduate school in international relations. Despite the fact that his daughter Madeleine was 11 years old when she came to the United States, by the time she graduated high school, she could speak English without an accent. She attended Wellesley College, from which she graduated with honors in political science (B.A., 1959).

Shortly after graduation, Madeleine Korbel married Joseph Medill Patterson Albright, scion to a family newspaper dynasty. Moving to Washington, D.C., when her husband was made Washington bureau chief of the family-owned magazine, *Newsday*, she subsequently had three daughters. Despite her family responsibilities, she managed to earn both her M.A. (1968) and Ph.D. (1976) degrees in international affairs and Soviet studies from Columbia University, where she studied under ZBIGNIEW BRZEZINSKI. She also did graduate work at Johns Hopkins University's School of Advanced International Studies.

Already enjoying an extensive and influential network of friends and social contacts, Albright began her political career in 1976 as a campaign fund-raiser and adviser to Senator EDMUND MUSKIE (D-Maine) during his unsuccessful bid for the Democratic presidential nomination. From 1976 to 1978, she served as chief legislative assistant on Capitol Hill for Muskie, whom she later described as her mentor. In 1978, Carter's National Security Advisor and her former professor at Columbia, Zbigniew Brzezinski, appointed her as congressional liaison officer for the NSC. In this capacity, she worked with the administration's chief congressional lobbyist, FRANK MOORE; she later recalled that he did not seem to have a rapport with lawmakers or consult with them in the manner expected of congressional lobbyists.

Although there is little to indicate that Albright played a formative or decisive role in any major foreign policy decisions while she was a member of the Carter administration, Brzezinski describes her in his memoirs as one of the NSC's key advisers and credits her with improving White House coordination with Congress. Vice President WALTER MONDALE's chief of staff, Richard Moe, commented later that Albright succeeded in her job because she worked twice as hard as her male counterparts.

When President Carter appointed Senator Muskie to replace CYRUS VANCE, who had resigned as secretary of state in protest of the failed Iranian hostage rescue mission of April 1980, Albright found herself in the difficult position of trying to mediate between her former mentor, Muskie, and her former professor, Brzezinski. Since both men were of Polish descent, she described their difficult relationship as "Poles Apart" in her memoirs.

Albright was stung by Carter's defeat in the 1980 presidential election. Leaving the White House, she accepted a fellowship at the Woodrow Wilson International Center for Scholars, where she wrote what was to be her first book, *Poland: The Role of the Press in Political Change* (1983). In 1982, she became a professor of International Relations at Georgetown University and director of its Women in Foreign Service program. In contrast to her success professionally, however, was the breakup of her marriage of 24 years to Joseph Albright.

Albright returned to her political career in 1984 when she joined the presidential campaign of Walter Mondale and worked closely with his choice for vice president, Geraldine Ferraro, on foreign policy issues. Although the Democratic ticket of Mondale-Ferraro lost in its bid to unseat President RONALD REAGAN, Albright established her reputation among Democrats as an expert on foreign policy, especially with respect to the Soviet Union and Eastern Europe. Four years later, she worked as senior foreign policy adviser to Democratic presidential candidate Michael Dukakis in his unsuccessful bid for the White House against Republican GEORGE HERBERT WALKER BUSH. From 1989 to 1992, she was president of the Center for National Policy, a nonprofit organization based in Washington, D.C.

During the 1988 campaign, Albright met the young Arkansas governor, Bill Clinton, who already had presidential ambitions. When Clinton was elected president in 1992, he selected Albright to be the United States' ambassador to the United Nations. She had strong academic and political connections, was already known to be a tough negotiator, and was fluent in English, Czech, Russian, Polish, and French. She also served as a member of Clinton's cabinet and the National Security Council. As UN ambassador, Albright emphasized the need for the United States to take a more vigorous stand in resolving international disputes left over from the end of the cold war, fighting force with force, as she often stated. She acted on this belief in helping to persuade President Clinton to take forceful action to bring down the regime of Yugoslav president Slobodan Milošević, whom the administration accused of acts against humanity in the province of Kosovo (now recognized as an autonomous province in Serbia).

Following President Clinton's successful bid for reelection in 1996, he named Albright to replace WARREN CHRISTOPHER as secretary of state, making her the first woman to hold that office and the highest-ranking woman in the nation's history to date. As secretary of state, Albright was a strong advocate of democracy and human rights and encouraged the expansion of American trade and finance abroad. Among her most notable accomplishments were the expansion and modernization of NATO; successful efforts to end the practice of ethnic cleansing in Kosovo; the promotion of peace in Northern Ireland and the Balkan states; improved relations with Russia; and the expansion of democracy throughout Europe, Asia, Africa, and Latin America. She also made it one of her personal priorities to focus global attention on the condition of women in foreign countries.

Since leaving government service in 2001, Albright has served as the first Michael and Virginia Mortara Professor in the Practice of Diplomacy at Georgetown University's School of Foreign Service. She also is the first distinguished scholar of the William Davidson Institute affiliated with the University of Michigan. She chairs the nonprofit National Institute for International Affairs and is founder of The Albright Group LLC, a firm that deals with strategic global issues.

Although Albright was raised as a Catholic, she learned in 1997 that her family had been Jewish and that her grandparents had died during World War II in German concentration camps. Her father had raised his family as Catholics in order to avoid a similar fate for them. Since learning this news, she has spent considerable time becoming more acquainted with her heritage. In 2003, she published her memoirs, *Madame Secretary.*

Allon, Yigal

(1918–1980) *Israeli minister of foreign affairs*

Israel's minister of foreign affairs from 1974 to 1977 and chair of the Knesset's (Israel's parliament) Committee on Foreign Affairs from 1977 to 1980, Yigal Allon was best known during the Carter administration for his proposal (the Allon Plan) to divide the West Bank, seized during the 1967 Six Day War, in such a way as to increase Israel's security along its narrow and highly populated waist.

Born in 1918 in what was then the British mandate of Palestine, Allon was one of the founders of the Palmach, the military unit of the Haganah, the Jewish underground organization seeking the end of British rule of Palestine and the establishment of a Jewish state. During World War II, he fought alongside the British, heading an underground intelligence and sabotage unit in Syria and Lebanon and later participating in those countries' occupation by the Allies.

As commander of the Palmach, Allon helped prepare Jewish forces for the first Arab-Israeli War following the establishment of the state of Israel in 1948. During the war, he headed Israeli forces along the southern front, driving Arab forces from the whole of the Negev desert and part of the Sinai Peninsula. By the end of the war, he was widely regarded as one of Israel's most experienced field commanders. In 1950, after the dissolution of the Palmach, Allon retired to civilian life, devoting much of the next 10 years to academic studies and politics. In a number of publications that he wrote between 1948 and 1967, however, he formulated the doctrine of "anticipatory initiative" (preemptive military engagement) that was applied in the Six Day War of 1967.

In 1954, Allon was elected to the Knesset. From 1961 to 1968, he served as Israel's minister of labor. A founding member of the Labor Party, he was also a member of the inner war cabinet during the Six Day War, during which he proposed what became known as the Allon Plan. The plan, which became the basis for much of the negotiations that were to follow over the division of Arab territories seized during the war, specifically the West Bank, called for the establishment of new borders between Israel and its Arab neighbors that would provide Israel with maximum security and a minimal Arab population.

From 1969 to 1974, Allon served as deputy prime minister and minister of education and culture. In 1974, he was named minister of foreign affairs. As foreign minister, he engaged in difficult talks with U.S. secretary of state HENRY KISSINGER over the disengagement of Israeli forces from the Sinai Peninsula seized from Egypt during the Yom Kippur War, which had begun in October 1973. He also defended Israeli occupation and settlement of the West Bank. At the same time, he raised the possibility with Kissinger that Israel might be willing to recognize the Palestine Liberation Organization (PLO) should the PLO recognize the legitimacy of the state of Israel and be willing to negotiate on the West Bank settlements and other issues preventing peace in the Middle East.

Because Allon and other leaders of the Labor government, including Prime Minister Yitzhak Rabin, seemed open to negotiations with Egypt and other Arab states, the incoming Carter administration was hopeful that a peace agreement could be reached in the Middle East. President Carter's National Security Advisor, ZBIGNIEW BRZEZINSKI, who had met with Allon in summer 1976, was impressed by his moderation and what he considered his subtle and incisive mind. In February 1977, Secretary of State CYRUS VANCE also met with Allon along with other Israeli leaders. During their meeting, Allon recognized the need to resolve the Palestinian problem and even hinted once more that Israel might acknowledge the PLO if it accepted Israel's existence. In May 1977, however, the Likud Party won a stunning victory in national elections, bringing to power a more hard-line government led by MENACHEM BEGIN.

Following the defeat of the Labor government, Allon lived out his remaining years as a member of the Knesset, serving as a member of its Committee on Foreign Affairs and chairing its subcommittee on Lebanon. From 1978 until his death in 1980, he was also chairman of the World Labor Zionist movement. He died on February 29, 1980.

Amin, Hafizulah

(1929–1979) *Soviet-installed president of Afghanistan*

Hafizulah Amin, leader of the Knaig, a political group made up mostly of Pashtuns, the dominant ethnic community of Afghanistan, became the second Soviet-picked Afghan president in September 1979. Before becoming president he served in the government led by Nur Muhammad Taraki, whom he later overthrew. His failure to bring stability to Afghanistan led to the massive Soviet invasion of 85,000 troops into Afghanistan in 1979. The invasion had a severe impact on Soviet-American relations during the last year of the Jimmy Carter administration.

Amin was born in the Peghman district of Kabul, the capital of Afghanistan, on August 21, 1929. The son of a civil servant, he had studied at Kabul University and became a high school teacher and principal. In 1957, he won a scholarship to Columbia University's School of Education, in New York City. While studying at Columbia, he became involved in the Associated Students of Afghanistan and grew interested in communist doctrine. After returning to Afghanistan in 1965, he joined the Marxist People's Democratic Party of Afghanistan (PDPA) and became a prominent member of its Khalq (People) faction. Thirteen years later, Amin helped lead a coup that overthrew the Afghan government of Mohammed Daoud Khan. He became one of two top deputy prime ministers in a government led by President Nur Mohammad Taraki, who was also the PDPA's secretary general.

The next several months saw conditions in Afghanistan deteriorate, as Afghans expressed growing opposition to the efforts of the Taraki government to impose communist reforms on the country. Kabul lost control of much of the countryside. This prompted Taraki to turn to the Soviet Union for help. Moscow provided Kabul with military equipment and advisers but it grew increasingly alarmed as the situation in Afghanistan worsened and Taraki and Amin seemed to Moscow to be turning a deaf ear and blind eye to what was occurring in their country. "I also want to raise another question," Soviet Premier Alexei Kosygin remarked in a meeting of the Politburo on March 17, 1979, "Amin and Taraki alike are concealing from us the true state of affairs. We still don't know exactly what is happening in Afghanistan."

At first, the Soviets made no distinction between Amin and Taraki, and the two men seemed to work well together. But as early as March 1979, a rift had developed between the two men, as Amin gained considerable control within government circles. By September, the power struggle was widespread. The Soviets, who sided with Taraki and had even plotted with him in the spring to remove the deputy prime minister, considered mediating the dispute. By September 13, however, the Kremlin concluded that it was too late because "all the levels of real power" were in Amin's hands. After Taraki made a belated attempt to remove Amin from power, Amin struck back on September 14 by overthrowing Taraki. Amin's government announced shortly thereafter that Taraki had died of an illness, though evidence suggests that Amin had had him executed.

Although Amin worked to broaden his base of support, his regime proved nearly as unpopular as the Taraki regime before it. Amin purged the PDPA of his enemies and dealt harshly with the ongoing insurgency against his Marxist government. In November 1979, he launched a major military operation against the insurgents at Sayd Karam in Paktia Province, killing as many as 1000 resistance fighters. Many Afghans fled to Pakistan. Amin's conduct of government greatly concerned the Soviet Union, and matters in Iran only added to that anxiety. A revolution against the strongly pro-American shah of Iran, MOHAMMAD REZA PAHLAVI, had led him to flee that nation in January 1979. A new government, led by the anti-American AYATOLLAH RUHOLLA KHOMEINI, assumed power. The Iranian Revolution meant not only that the United States had lost an ally in the strategically important Middle East, but one next door to the Soviet Union, from which Washington had conducted intelligence operations against the Soviets.

Officials in Moscow understood the significance of the Iranian Revolution to the United States. They feared that the White House would try to make up for its loss in Iran by attempting to establish closer relations with the Amin government. The Kremlin had good reason to believe this. Egypt, which had previously been pro-Soviet, had developed a close friendship with the United States; what was to prevent Afghanistan from doing the same? A nationalist as well as a Marxist, Amin also displayed a streak of independence that greatly troubled the Kremlin. Moreover, in October 1979, Moscow learned of meetings between American officials and Amin. Unsubstantiated rumors also spread that Amin was even a CIA agent.

In the meantime, U.S.-Soviet relations had grown worse. Soviet activities in Cuba and in Africa had upset U.S. officials; simultaneously, Moscow had become concerned with growing American ties to China. The possibility of closer U.S.-Afghan relations only added to Soviet concerns. The Soviet secret police, the KGB, warned that if Afghanistan became a U.S. ally, it would allow the White House once again to place intelligence-gathering equipment along the Soviet border.

By November 1979, therefore, Kremlin leaders, such as Defense Minister Dmitri Ustinov and KGB chief Yuri Andropov, were willing to support a military intervention in Afghanistan. They began an intense campaign to convince doubters in the Politburo and, more important, Soviet Premier LEONID BREZHNEV of the importance of moving fast. Their efforts succeeded. On December 8, 1979, Brezhnev agreed that intervention was necessary. "In spite of the fact that the people of Afghanistan and their armed forces have been repelling the armed interference of imperialist and reactionary forces for a long time now, the dangers that threaten them to continue to grow," members of the Politburo remarked a few weeks later. "This to a considerable degree is connected to the fact that Amin and the narrow group on which he relies undertook a brutal and criminal removal of the leader of the Afghan revolution." With the acquiescence of the Politburo, the stage was set for an attack late that month. Amin and 200 of his elite guards were killed by the Soviet-backed Parchame Communist Party on December 27, 1979, after elements of the KGB Spetsnaz (Alpha Group), in Afghan uniforms, stormed the presidential palace. They also blew up Kabul's communications center, paralyzing the Afghan military command, and seized the Afghan military command. According to the Soviets, they were only complying with the 1978 Treaty of Friendship, Cooperation and Good Neighborliness they had signed with former President Taraki. Amin was replaced by a puppet government headed by Babrak Kamal, who had been living in exile in Moscow.

Anderson, Jack

(Jackson Northman Anderson)
(1922–2005) *syndicated columnist*

In the view of President Carter's press secretary, JODY POWELL, Jack Anderson, a syndicated columnist for more than 50 years, was the worst example of unfair, and even shameless, media reporting of the Carter presidency. Other targets of Anderson's reporting shared similar views of the columnist, and he was held in low regard even by many of his own colleagues. Yet he was a winner of the Pulitzer Prize for his investigative reporting, and his ability to obtain leaked and confidential materials added a level of credibility to his widely read column, which remained a major concern for the White House throughout Carter's four years in office.

Born on October 19, 1922, in Long Beach, California, but raised in Utah, Anderson began his journalistic career working for his local newspaper, the *Murray Eagle.* At age 18, he became a journalist for the *Salt Lake City Tribune.* His major break came when he was recruited by investigative reporter Drew Pearson to work with him for the *Washington Post.* At first, Anderson's role was primarily investigatory, checking out stories and working on leads for Pearson's hard-hitting and nationally syndicated column, *The Washington Merry Go Round.* Eventually he shared the byline for the column with Pearson. Together, they vehemently criticized such well-known figures as Joseph McCarthy, J. Edgar Hoover, and Mafia figure Lucky Luciano.

By 1969, when Pearson died, *The Washington Merry Go Round* was syndicated in more than 650 newspapers, making it the most widely read column in the United States. What accounted for this was Pearson's and Anderson's ability, through their sources, to acquire confidential and even highly classified information not available to other journalists. How they were able to do this is still not entirely clear.

Following Pearson's death, Anderson took over the column and expanded its syndication to 800 newspapers. In 1972, he was awarded the Pulitzer Prize in journalism for revealing the fact that the RICHARD NIXON administration was aiding Pakistan while claiming neutrality in the India-Pakistan War. That same year, his earlier charge that the Justice Department had, at the request of Deputy Attorney General Richard Kleindienst, held up an antitrust lawsuit against International Telephone and Telegraph Co. (ITT) delayed Kleindienst's confirmation to replace John Mitchell as attorney general.

During the 1976 presidential campaign, Anderson exposed an effort by campaign aides of President GERALD FORD to link Jimmy Carter to a sex scandal. According to Anderson, the aides even provided him with the name of a woman who had allegedly had an affair with the Democratic presidential candidate; later they provided four additional names. Although Anderson denied ever leaking the names or the charges, word got out (probably from Republican sources) that he was about to break a major sex scandal involving Carter. A journalistic feeding frenzy followed. After conducting his own investigation into these charges, Anderson reported that there was no truth to any of them. But the presidential candidate remained furious both at both the Republican campaign for its alleged effort at dirty politics and at Anderson for giving leverage to the allegations made against him.

As president, Carter—who, not unlike many of his predecessors, came increasingly to disdain the White House press corps—continued to be riled by leaks of confidential information, including the minutes of cabinet meetings that Anderson was able to obtain and publish. In response, the president limited the distribution of the minutes to the cabinet secretaries only. He also ordered that they be treated as highly classified documents. But Anderson continued to obtain the documents.

Particularly galling to the White House were two stories that Anderson published in 1978. The first involved the columnist's allegation that the president's mother, Lilian Carter, was furious with presidential brother BILLY CARTER for supposedly neglecting the family's peanut farm while traveling throughout the world. What made this story insidious from the White House's point of view was that it involved the president's mother, who was so distraught over the charge that she wrote Anderson a letter calling him a liar. The story also came at a time when Billy Carter was being hauled over the coals by the media for allegedly anti-Semitic remarks he made after returning from a trip to Libya, where he had been the guest of the Libyan government.

More serious, though, were charges that Anderson made in September 1978 on ABC's *Good Morning America* that Carter's senior aide, HAMILTON JORDAN, and his closest friend, CHARLES KIRBO, were involved in a scheme to keep fugitive financier Robert Vesco from being extradited to the United States. In response to the claims, the Department of Justice impaneled a special grand jury. After an 11-month investigation, it exonerated both men of Anderson's charges, but not without harmful publicity for them and for the White House.

Anderson continued to make serious allegations against the administration. Following Carter's renomination for president in August 1980, the columnist published a series of stories charging the administration with planning an invasion of Iran in October, ostensibly to rescue the American hostages seized by the Iranians during their revolution a year earlier, but intended also to assure Carter's reelection. These accusations seemed so baseless that the *Washington Post*, which normally carried his column, and most other newspapers and magazines refused to publish them. Notwithstanding his claims that he based his stories on reliable sources, Anderson seems to have been motivated at least in part by personal disdain for what he came to regard as the president's unctuous sanctimony and hypocrisy after having voted for him in 1976. As the columnist later acknowledged, "I have never been more saddened than I was when Carter left me stuck in the muck. ... Throughout his term, Carter believed that his heart was pure. But I saw in him an excessive need to prove that purity to himself and to others by wearing his piety on his sleeve." A devout Mormon himself, Anderson found Carter's excessive piety galling.

Following Carter's defeat in 1980, Anderson continued to write his syndicated column as well as his autobiography and several other books of science fiction and nonfiction. His column rans in 200 papers, and he also wrote occasionally for *Meridian,* a magazine of news and commentary affiliated with the Mormon Church. He died on December 17, 2005, of complications from Parkinson's disease. He was 83.

Anderson, John Bayard

(1922–) *member of the House of Representatives, independent candidate for president in 1980*

John B. Anderson ran for president in 1980 on the National Unity Party ticket. Although widely regarded throughout much of the campaign as a major threat to the reelection of President Carter, he received only 7 percent of the vote. While still a sizeable percentage for an independent candidate, the plurality of which were probably liberals disenchanted with Carter but unwilling to vote for Republican challenger RONALD REAGAN, the outcome of the election would have been the same were Anderson's name not on the ballot.

A World War II veteran and a graduate of the University of Illinois (LL.B., 1946) and Harvard Law School (LL.M., 1949), Anderson was born in Rockford, Ohio, on February 15, 1922. While completing his degree at Harvard, Anderson served on the faculty of Northeastern University School of Law. From 1952 to 1956, he was an economics reporting officer on the staff of the United States High Commissioner for Germany. In 1956, he was elected state's attorney of Winnebago County, Illinois, a position he held until he was elected as a Republican to the U.S. House of Representatives in 1960.

A political moderate and highly respected on Capitol Hill, Anderson was reelected nine times and served as chair of the House Republican Conference before he decided to run for president in 1980. Concerned about the conservatism of Ronald Reagan, the leading candidate for the Republican nomination, he challenged Reagan and other Republican candidates by running as a centrist. In his campaign, he emphasized decentralized government, a hands-off economic policy, and a return to traditional values. Although few political observers took his candidacy seriously, he began to attract support for his willingness to take politically unpopular position on such issues as a 50-cents-a-gallon tax on gasoline in order to conserve energy.

After Reagan trounced Anderson in the primaries, the Illinois lawmaker withdrew from the race, but he was encouraged enough by the response to his quixotic campaign that he decided to run as a third-party candidate on the National Unity Party ticket. Seeking to exploit the widespread public dissatisfaction with the two major parties and their candidates, Reagan and Carter, he attacked the Republican Party for being too socially conservative and intolerant, and he took issue with Democrats for their deficit spending and what he regarded as their excessive social welfare agenda. He also attacked Reagan for his proposals to increase defense spending and cut taxes, while he accused Carter of not dealing adequately with the oil crisis and the attendant long gasoline lines and high inflation. Instead, he called for business tax cuts and incentives, measures to shore up the financially troubled Social Security Fund, and the 50-cents-a-gallon tax on gas.

For Anderson, just getting on the ballot in all 50 states was a major achievement; at one time, he was involved in nine different lawsuits. But polls conducted in the summer of 1980 showed Anderson garnering as much as 20 percent of the votes in November, the plurality of which came from voters who might otherwise have cast their ballots for Carter. On August 25, moreover, Anderson chose as his running mate former Democratic governor Patrick Lucey of Wisconsin. His selection of a disaffected Democrat gave Anderson's campaign more viability and threatened to cut even further into Carter's Democratic base.

Anderson's campaign complicated President Carter's bid for reelection in another way as well. In September, the League of Voters sponsored a three-way presidential debate between Carter, Reagan, and Anderson. The president wanted to debate Reagan one-on-one. He also did not want to add to Anderson's stature as a serious candidate, believing him to be a creature of the media. Carter refused, therefore, to participate in the debate. His decision left Reagan and Anderson to debate each other and subjected the president to widespread criticism.

As the November elections neared, however, Anderson's poll numbers began to drop. Part of the reason for this was the drift back to party regularity characteristic of most elections as election day nears. Another was the lack of financial resources Anderson needed to sustain a national campaign. More important was that many of the issues on which he had campaigned, such as the 50-cent gasoline tax and cutbacks in defense, came back to haunt him.

On election day, Anderson received nearly 6 million votes. This, however, was less than what Alabama governor GEORGE WALLACE had received in 1968, and he did not win any electoral votes. Although he collected enough votes in 24 states to prevent the successful candidate from winning a majority, his largest impact was in the Northeast and far West. Only in New York, where Reagan beat Carter by a margin of 2.7 percent, did Anderson possibly play the role of a spoiler.

Following his defeat, Anderson remained active as a lecturer; as a commentator on such networks as the BBC, NPR, and C-SPAN; and as a visiting professor at a number of universities. He also served as president of the Center for Voting and Democracy and as president and chief executive officer of the World Federalist Association. In the year 2000, he considered running for president on the Reform Party ticket but decided against becoming a candidate.

Andrus, Cecil Dale
(1931–) *secretary of the interior*

Cecil D. Andrus was serving his second term as governor of Idaho when he was selected by President-elect Carter in 1976 to be his secretary of the interior. Although never within the inner circle of Carter's closest advisers, Andrus developed a reputation as a commonsense conservationist who was skilled at resolving often conflicting demands on the nation's natural resources, such as offshore oil leasing and lumbering rights in national forests. He was known for his direct and frank manner.

Andrus was born in Hood River, Oregon, on August 25, 1931, grew up in Oregon logging country, and worked as a lumberjack in Idaho. He later told stories about skidding logs down streambeds because it was the easiest way to move them. At the time, he said, no one paid much attention to the environmental damage of such practices. "Those of us

Secretary of the Interior Cecil Andrus and President Carter conduct a briefing on new water proposals, 1978. *(Jimmy Carter Library)*

logging in those good old days simply did not know any better. We were too engrossed in the everyday effort of earning a living to consider the long-term damage," he commented.

Although he failed to graduate college, Andrus spent two years at Oregon State University before serving in the U.S. Navy during the Korean War. After the war, he helped operate a saw mill in Idaho, but he was inspired to enter politics by the young and handsome Democratic candidate for president, John F. Kennedy. He ran successfully for the Idaho State Senate in 1960, spending all of $11 on his campaign and becoming, at age 29, the youngest senator in Idaho history. He was reelected four times before being elected Idaho's governor by a small margin in 1970; he was reelected in 1974 with 70 percent of the vote. In 1977, he stepped down as governor to be sworn in as secretary of the interior.

Andrus's appointment to head the Department of the Interior was generally well received. The first Idahoan to serve in a presidential cabinet, he was also a close friend of Idaho's powerful Democratic senator and fellow liberal, FRANK CHURCH. He was already widely respected by the environmental community for his efforts as governor to protect the environment, including his opposition to the development of a molybdenum mine in the White Cloud Mountains of central Idaho, the issue on which he had successfully run for governor in

1970. He had also been lauded for saving peregrine falcons, one of which he later brought to Washington. He was nonetheless well liked by ranchers, timber interests, and other users of the public lands whose interests often conflicted with those of environmentalists.

As interior secretary, Andrus played an important role in the passage of such legislation as the National Surface Mining Act of 1977 and local land-use planning laws and in developing standards for offshore oil. Along with Senator Church, he also championed protection of wild and scenic rivers, including the Frank Church of No Return Wilderness Area, the Snake River Birds of Prey Area, and the Hells Canyon National Recreation Area.

Andrus will best be remembered, though, for his effort in winning congressional approval of the Alaska National Interest Lands Conservation Act (ANILCA) of 1980, passage of which President Carter made his highest legislative priority that year. Providing for the designation of 104 million acres (or about one-third of Alaska's land) as a wilderness area closed off from development, ANILCA doubled the size of the country's national park and refuge system, tripled the amount of land designated as wilderness, and created 10 new national parks. A similar measure had been on the environmentalists' agenda since the 1960s, after passage of the Wilderness Act. But the powerful Alaskan delegation led by Republican senator Ted Stevens had been able to stop each attempt to get the legislation through Congress. Prior to final passage of ANILCA in 1980, however, Andrus had withdrawn 40 million acres of Alaskan land from development under authority given to the Interior Department in 1976. He said he would rescind his withdrawal, which provided even stricter protection of this acreage than the legislation before Congress, only after an Alaskan lands bill was approved. In this way, he effectively outmaneuvered the wilderness opponents who would need a bill to override Andrus's withdrawal.

Some environmental groups were unhappy with provisions of the ANILCA. They complained about the lack of protection afforded calving grounds for caribou and habitats for migratory birds. They also spoke out against allowing seismic exploration of certain parts of Alaska's North Slope, believed to hold millions of barrels of oil. The measure has been widely recognized, however, as one of the Carter administration's most important achievements.

Andrus was one of the cabinet members Carter decided to retain following his cabinet shake-up of 1979, and he stayed in office for the remainder of the president's term. White House staffers thought highly of him. According to the president's senior assistant and chief of staff, HAMILTON JORDAN, "His views were largely compatible with Carter's on environmental and resource questions. He was a good manager. He was sensitive to the President's political interests. He was good on [Capitol] Hill. He was good at dealing with constituent groups and most importantly, he kept his problems over at the Department of Interior." He was, in short, "a big plus for the President."

After returning to Idaho following Carter's defeat for reelection in 1980, Andrus ran successfully for governor in 1987 and was reelected in 1991, making him the first person in the history of Idaho to be elected governor for four terms. As governor in 1988, he closed Idaho's borders to nuclear waste destined for storage in the state. He also became involved in a series of contentious and unsuccessful efforts to designate wilderness in Idaho during the 1980s and early 1990s. He was criticized for pressing the development of an air force training range at Mountain Home Air Force Base near a wild scenic river and wilderness area. In response, Andrus argued that he had won as many concessions as possible, and because the air base was Idaho's second largest employer, he could not afford to lose it.

Since leaving the governorship, Andrus has continued to be an active environmentalist, speaking out on such issues as the extinction of Idaho salmon, the breaching of dams, and the preservation of wilderness. In 1995, he founded the Andrus Center for Public Policy at Boise State University. The Center has sponsored conferences on western public land issues, national fire policy, endangered species issues, and the economy of the rural west. Andrus is a board member of several major Idaho and northwest corporations.

Arafat, Yasser

(1929–2004) *chairman, Palestine Liberation Organization*

Considered by some a terrorist, by others a national hero, Yasser Arafat was the chairman of the militant Palestine Liberation Organization (PLO). Dedicated to the establishment of a Palestinian homeland and the destruction of the state of Israel, Arafat vigorously opposed the Camp David accords of 1978, generally acknowledged as one of Jimmy Carter's greatest achievements as president. Vilified even by other Arab leaders, he nevertheless made the establishment of a Palestinian homeland one of the central demands of the Arab states and the crucial provision of any agreement to end the Arab-Israeli dispute.

Arafat was born on August 24, 1929, to a Palestinian family living either in Cairo or Jerusalem. His early years are murky. It is known, however, that his mother, from a prominent Sunni family in Jerusalem, died when he was five years old. He became estranged from his father, a textile merchant in Cairo who moved to Jerusalem following his wife's death, remarried when Arafat was eight years, and then moved back to Cairo. Arafat never talked about his father, nor did he attend his funeral in 1952. Apparently he was brought up by his maternal uncle in Jerusalem and an older sister living in Cairo. He considered Jerusalem his home and the place where he wanted to be buried when he died.

Even as a youth, Arafat was a Palestinian nationalist. As a teenager, he smuggled arms to Arabs in Palestine to fight against the British and the Jews seeking to carve a Jewish state out of the Palestinian mandate. When the state of Israel was established in 1948, he left Cairo University to join Arab forces in the first Arab-Israeli War. Devastated by the Arab defeat, he applied for a visa to study at the University of Texas. He decided, however, to finish his degree at Cairo University, where he also spent much of his time organizing Palestinian students.

After completing his degree in civil engineering in 1956, Arafat resettled in Kuwait, where he prospered running his own contracting firm. But he contributed much of his wealth and his time to the cause of a Palestinian homeland. In 1958, he and some friends founded a secret organization committed to the destruction of Israel that became one of the constituent groups of the new Palestinian nationalist movement known as Al Fatah (meaning "armed struggle"). In 1964, Arafat left Kuwait to return to Egypt and then Jordan, where he became the leader of Al Fatah and a full-time revolutionary, leading raids from Jordan into Israel. In 1969, Al Fatah seized control of the PLO, which the Arab states had established in 1964, and named Arafat as its chairman.

Henceforth the PLO, which until now had been something of a puppet organization of the Arab states and had not engaged in direct action against Israel, became an independent nationalist organization, engaged in a military struggle against the Jewish state. By 1970, it had become such a powerful force in Jordan that King HUSSEIN, fearing for his monarchy, forced the PLO to leave Jordan for Lebanon, where it remained until driven out by the Israelis in 1982. During this time, Arafat, wearing his trademark checkered keffiyeh draped carefully over his shoulder to represent the shape of a map of Palestine, became an icon of the Palestinian cause.

Although it had been forced out of Jordan, the PLO enjoyed some of its greatest power in the 1970s. Splintered into several groups, Al Fatah remained dominant within the PLO, and Arafat continued as its leader. Following the October 1973 Arab-Israeli War, the PLO hinted that it might accept a two-state solution to the Palestinian problem but at the same time made clear that its purpose remained a Palestine-wide secular state. In 1974, the Arab League recognized the PLO as the "sole legitimate representative of the Palestinian people." That same year, Arafat was invited to deliver a speech before the UN General Assembly. The PLO was also granted observer status at the United Nations.

During the Carter administration, Arafat tried to capitalize on the new president's interest in reaching a settlement in the Middle East by becoming a voice in any peace discussions regarding the Middle East. He even held indirect talks with the United States using secret channels about Palestinian representation at a reconvened peace conference in Geneva, which had been dormant since 1973. Carter responded by speaking out on a number of occasions in favor of some kind of Palestinian homeland or entity, perhaps federated with predominantly Palestinian Jordan, but short of an independent Palestinian state. The president also issued a joint communiqué with the Soviet Union, which had participated in the 1973 meeting, calling for a new Geneva conference and even making reference to "the legitimate rights of the Palestinian people." Washington had in the past always referred to Palestinian "interests" rather than "rights." By employing this new term, which had been used by the PLO to justify their struggle against Israel, the president seemed to be signaling to the Palestinians his sympathy for the establishment of a Palestinian homeland. He was forced, however, to jettison his plans for a Geneva conference as a result of strong opposition in the United States to his inclusion of the Soviet Union, which had just been thrown out of the Middle East, and to having Palestinian representation at the meeting. Israel would not attend a Geneva meeting with the PLO, while Arab states would not go without it. Any remaining possibility of a Geneva meeting was pushed to the side by Egyptian leader ANWAR EL-SADAT's dramatic three-day trip to Jerusalem in November 1977 and his address to the Knesset (the Israeli parliament) in which he talked about the need to break down the barriers to peace.

For Arafat, as for most Arab leaders, Sadat's visit to Israel represented a betrayal of Arab unity and the cause of a Palestinian state. For the remainder of Carter's presidency, Arafat and Israel remained sworn enemies. In March 1978, the PLO attacked along the Israeli coast, killing 35 people. The Israelis responded by invading southern Lebanon, leaving more than 1,000 dead and 100,000 homeless. Although the president tried to pressure Israeli prime minister MENACHEM BEGIN into withdrawing from the West Bank and allowing the Palestinians living there to determine their own fate, short of establishing an independent Palestinian state, Begin refused to budge on the issue of withdrawal from the occupied territories.

The much-vaunted Camp David accords of September 1978, which provided for an Egyptian-Israeli peace treaty and an ambiguous "framework for peace" for the Middle East, were rejected out-of-hand by Arafat and most other Arab leaders. Sadat and Begin were able to reach an agreement by largely finessing the question of Israeli withdrawal from the occupied territories and the establishment of a Palestinian state. The "framework for peace" provided for a transitional period of no more than five years during which Egypt, Israel, and Jordan would determine the final status of the West Bank and Gaza Strip but assure the inhabitants of the two areas "full autonomy" and a "self-governing authority." This was hardly the guarantee of an independent Palestinian state that Arafat demanded.

As for the Carter administration, while it had maintained indirect and unofficial contact with the PLO, State Department regulations explicitly prohibited official contacts with the organization. When it was revealed in the press in 1979 that ANDREW YOUNG, the U.S. ambassador to the United Nations, had met secretly with Zehdi Labib Terzi, the UN observer for the PLO, he was forced to resign from his position.

From Arafat's perspective, however, the 1970s, and especially the four years of the Carter presidency, were productive ones. If the decade had begun with the PLO being driven out of Jordan, it ended with Arafat in firm control of the organization, which was recognized by all the Arab states as the legitimate representative of the Palestinian people and had been granted observer status at the United Nations. In addition, an American president had committed the United States to the establishment of some form of Palestinian homeland. Even the Camp David accords, which Arafat and other Arab leaders rejected, incorporated the concept of an Israeli withdrawal from the occupied territories and a Palestinian autonomy plan in the West Bank and Gaza as foundational to a Middle East settlement.

In contrast, the early 1980s were some of the worst years for the Palestinian leader, even forcing him to modify his position with respect to a peace agreement with Israel, something he had considered beyond the pale just a few years earlier. After a series of PLO raids from southern Lebanon into Israel, the Israelis responded in 1982 by launching an attack into Lebanon that became a full-scale invasion in which the Israelis drove into the suburbs of Beirut and encircled Arafat. Saved by American diplomacy and heavy Israeli losses, Arafat was forced to leave Lebanon and establish his new headquarters in Tunisia. In 1982, the PLO's ruling body, the Palestinian National Council (PNC), decided to pursue a reconciliation with Egypt and Jordan as a first step toward suing for peace with Israel. In February 1985, King Hussein of Jordan and Arafat agreed to a confederation between Jordan and a Palestinian entity comprised of the West Bank and Gaza. Plans were drawn up by which the PLO would agree to UN Resolution 242 passed by the Security Council in 1967 and calling for Israel to withdraw from the territories it had seized during the Arab-Israeli War of that year in return for Arab guarantees of peace with Israel.

In 1986, Hussein broke off talks with Arafat, citing the PLO's refusal to compromise. Arafat's support of Iraq's leader, Saddam Hussein, during the Gulf War of 1991 also hurt him financially and diplomatically. The countries of the oil-rich Persian Gulf cut off financial and political aid to him. In 1993, however, Arafat saved his political career by signing the Declaration of Principles on Interim Self-Government Arrangements with Israeli prime minister Yitzhak Rabin. The Oslo accords, as they were called, provided for limited Palestinian self-rule in the West Bank city of Jericho, the Gaza Strip, and, eventually, the remainder of the West Bank. In return, the PLO recognized the right of Israel to exist as a nation. In 1996, Arafat was elected president of the new Palestinian National Authority. Arafat, Rabin, and Israeli foreign minister Shimon Perez, who had also participated in the negotiations of the Oslo accords, were awarded the Nobel Peace Prize for reaching this agreement, which was supplemented in 1996 by the Hebron Agreement removing Israeli forces from the last occupied city in the West Bank. In return, Arafat agreed to amend the Palestinian National Charter (adopted in 1968) to eliminate the provision calling for the destruction of Israel.

Israel's decision to build additional homes in Jerusalem, however, resulted in a wave of terrorism that undermined the fragile agreements of 1993 and 1996 and continued unabated for most of the remainder of Arafat's life. Efforts by President Bill Clinton to broker a peace failed in 2000. During the last two years of his life, Arafat was under virtual house arrest in his compound in the Gaza city of Ramallah. Suffering from an indeterminate illness, he was allowed by the Israelis to be flown to Paris for medical treatment. He died at a military hospital outside of Paris on November 11, 2004, at the age of 75 from complications stemming from a blood disorder. He was accorded an official funeral in Cairo before his body was flown by helicopter back to Ramallah, where his coffin was placed in marble tomb.

Ashley, Thomas Ludlow

(1923–) *member of the House of Representatives*

Thomas Ludlow Ashley of Ohio was a Democratic member of the House of Representatives who headed the ad hoc committee on energy created in 1977 by House Speaker TIP O'NEILL to speed passage of the energy legislation submitted by President Carter through Congress. He was also one of O'Neill's closest allies in the House until his defeat for reelection in 1980.

Ashley was born on January 11, 1923, in Toledo, Ohio, into a rich, old Republican family. His great-grandfather, James M. Ashley, had served in Congress and was an abolitionist who participated in the Underground Railroad before the Civil War. During World War II, Thomas Ashley served in the Pacific theater as a corporal in the United States Army. After the war, he attended Yale University (B.A., 1948), where he was a member of the Skull and Bones Society and became a lifelong friend of future president GEORGE HERBERT WALKER BUSH. He obtained his law degree from Ohio State University Law School (LL.B., 1952) and worked for two years for Radio Free Europe. In 1952, he narrowly defeated Frazier Reams, Sr., who had served two terms as an independent representing Ohio's ninth district, a heavily industrial and ethnic area that included most of Toledo. Ashley served in Congress for the next 26 years.

As a member of the House, Ashley established his liberal credentials by being only one of six lawmakers in 1961 to vote to cut off funds for the House Un-American Activities Committee. A member and eventual chair of the House Banking and Currency Subcommittee on Housing and Community Development, he worked to convert existing housing into low-cost living quarters for the poor. He also developed an impressive liberal voting record supporting all the major Great Society programs of the Lyndon Johnson administration. In both 1968 and 1970, he won a 100 percent rating from the liberal Americans for Democratic Action (ADA) for his voting record. He was an early opponent of the war in Vietnam.

Elected to Congress two years after Tip O'Neill, Ashley became good friends with the future Speaker of the House, with whom he shared similar political views. Occasionally he attended House Speaker John McCormack's breakfast table with O'Neill, who was impressed by Ashley's intelligence. In 1976, Ashley also did a great favor for O'Neill, who was slated to become House Speaker, by changing his vote for O'Neill's replacement as majority leader from PHILLIP BURTON of California, whom O'Neill personally disliked and distrusted but who enjoyed strong support among liberal Democrats, to JIM WRIGHT of Texas, who won the election by a single vote.

In 1977, when President Carter sent Congress a comprehensive and complex energy proposal, at the heart of which was a tax on all domestic oil production and a standby gasoline tax, O'Neill decided to establish a special ad hoc committee on energy to consider and report out the massive measure in its entirety rather than have its many sections parceled out to different committees. To head the 37-member committee, which included the most influential members of the authorizing committees, he selected Ashley. Although not one of the more well-known members of the House, Ashley was well-liked by his colleagues and had barely lost a race for the chairmanship of the newly established Budget Committee. He had voted with the energy industry to postpone clean-air standards, but he had also voted in 1975 for a higher gas tax. Above all, O'Neill trusted his competency. "His talent was like a light hidden under a bushel, and when it came to the surface, it shone brilliantly," the Speaker later wrote.

Ashley, who was grateful for the appointment, proved worthy of O'Neill's trust. The Speaker had set a deadline of having the ad hoc committee submit an omnibus energy package by July and the House completing work on the package before the August recess. "We will not go home without an energy bill," the Speaker told the House Rules Committee. With O'Neill's help, Ashley met the deadline for getting the energy bill onto the House floor, where the key battle was over deregulation of natural gas. In committee, he allowed generous natural gas-pricing rules for independent producers of new gas. He and O'Neill gambled that by doing this, they could win over enough lawmakers from southern and border states without alienating Democrats from non-gas–producing states to get the measure through the House.

In order to appear fair to lawmakers from energy-producing states, who wanted to deregulate all new natural gas, Ashley and O'Neill allowed a floor amendment providing for total deregulation. Despite intense lobbying by the energy industry, the decontrol amendment was defeated, and the energy measure, as reported out by Ashley's committee, was approved largely intact. "This was a remarkable exhibition of leadership by the Speaker, Chairman Ashley, and the others who worked with them," President Carter later wrote.

Unfortunately for the White House, the measure was largely gutted by the Senate. Ashley was bitterly disappointed. "As the Senate moves along in consideration of the energy bill," he wrote O'Neill in fall 1977, "it is becoming increasingly clear that only the bare skeleton of a national energy policy will emerge from that body. And that skeleton will save very little oil or natural gas."

Although Ashley had worked closely with O'Neill and the president to get the energy bill through the House, like other liberal lawmakers he was critical of the White House. There was too little coordination, he believed, between the administration and the House in getting measures through Capitol Hill. He also had little regard for the Georgians who surrounded the president. Referring to Carter's chief aide, HAMILTON JORDAN, he remarked to O'Neill in 1979, "The poor bastard. ... [H]e's the right-hand man to a Democratic president, and he doesn't even know that the Speaker of the White House is a great storyteller. No wonder we're having problems."

The Toledo congressman soon had his own problems. In the 1980 Reagan election landslide, he was defeated for reelection by a relatively unknown Republican, Edward Weber. Following his defeat, he established a legal and congressional consulting firm in Washington. Ironically, his relationship with Vice President-elect and then President George Bush grew closer. In 1993, just two weeks before leaving office, President Bush gave him a recess appointment to the Board of Governors of the U.S. Postal Service, but it was later struck down by the courts. Bush also made him a member of the Board of Directors of the George Bush Presidential Library Foundation. He is president of a legal and consulting firm.

Assad, Hafez al-
(1930–2000) *president of Syria*

Syrian president Hafez al-Assad was courted by President Jimmy Carter as one of the three Arab leaders who were key to a Middle East peace settlement; the others were ANWAR EL-SADAT of Egypt and King HUSSEIN of Jordan. Yet of these Arab leaders, Carter found Assad the most confounding and least likely to reach a peace agreement with Israel.

Assad was born on October 6, 1930, in the rural, mountainous village of Qardaha. The ninth of 11 children, his family was of the Alawi sect, a poor, underprivileged, nonsectarian community that comprised about 12 percent of Syria's population. Because his village did not have a secondary school, Assad was sent to Latakia on the Mediterranean Coast, where he became the first of his family to graduate from high school. Unable financially to attend a university, he enrolled in the Syrian Military Academy and later attended the new Air Force Academy in Aleppo, where he graduated as a combat pilot in 1955 at the top of his class. He also received training with the Soviet air force, learning to fly MIG-15s and MIG-17s as part of the armed forces of the newly formed United Arab Republic (UAR). The UAR brought Egypt and Syria into a confederation that was nominally of equals but in fact was dominated by Egypt's Gamal Abdel Nasser. Assad was assigned to Cairo and quickly came to despise the subordinate role of Syria to Egypt within the UAR.

While serving in the military, Assad became active politically, joining a secret group of other Syrian officers known as the Military Committee and loosely connected to the Ba'ath Party, a secularist, socialist group encompassing all Arabs that preached the overthrow of Western imperialism in the Middle East. Assad had been a member of the Ba'ath Party since 1947. In a series of coups and countercoups beginning in 1963, the Military Committee broke up the Syrian-Egyptian confederation, took control of the Ba'ath Party, and appointed Assad commander of the Syrian air force. In a countercoup that followed, Assad was on the winning side, becoming minister of defense and the number two man in the regime.

Syria continued to remain politically unstable as different faction within and outside the Ba'ath Party, including nationalist and pro-Soviet Marxist groups, vied for power. Finally, in 1972, Assad engineered another coup that overthrew the existing regime and put him in power. He then proceeded to execute or imprison the leaders of the former Ba'ath Party and established a new Ba'ath Regional Command, which elevated him to the presidency in 1971. Needing Soviet military assistance, he strengthened ties with Moscow.

As a pan-Arabist who had sought to emulate Nasser in the 1950s and 1960s, Assad formed the short-lived Federation of Arab Republics, which included Egypt and Libya. In 1973, he joined in the ill-fated October 1973 Yom Kippur War, which, after some initial success, brought Israeli forces close to Damascus before a cease-fire was arranged and the Israel withdrew its troops. Assad blamed Egyptian leader Anwar Sadat for losing the war by digging in along the eastern shore of the Sinai Desert, after taking the Israelis by surprise, instead of advancing immediately into the Sinai. He believed that Sadat had purposely stopped his advance as a means of seeking a limited victory that would restore Egypt's image as leader of the Arab world and, more importantly, attract American patronage. Following the Yom Kippur War, Assad tried to improve relations with the United States even as he remained committed to turning Syria into a strong regional military and political power. His hope was to obtain the return of the entire Golan Heights, which Israel had seized during the 1967 Arab-Israeli War. Able to gain only a partial return of the Heights, he still refused to negotiate with Israel.

This remained the major stumbling block in relations with Syria after Jimmy Carter took office. In February 1977, one of Carter's first actions as president was to send Secretary of State CYRUS VANCE to the Middle East to meet with the major Arab leaders. He decided to wield American influence to resolve the Arab-Israeli conflict even if it meant placing himself at odds with Israeli leaders and the American Jewish community.

Vance and Carter were encouraged by the reception the secretary of state received during his trip to the Middle East, especially from Sadat. But even Assad, whom Vance described as the "hardest" of the Arab leaders, appeared willing to make compromises. He indicated, for example, that he might be prepared to accept something less than full autonomy for the Palestinians. This seemed a major concession since the establishment of an independent Palestinian state had always been a sine qua non of any settlement with Israel insofar as Arab leaders were concerned. Syria also appeared to be the special protector of the Palestinians. In 1970, it had briefly sent tanks into Jordan after King Hussein suppressed the Palestinian fedayeen, who had tried to assassinate him, and then driven the Palestine Liberation Organization (PLO) into neighboring Lebanon.

The optimism of February soon faded, however. In March, Carter began a series of meetings with Arab heads of state, even flying to Damascus to meet with Assad, who greatly impressed the president with his intelligence, self-confidence, humor, and even flexibility. "Assad was obviously doubtful about the success of my efforts to bring disputing parties together around a negotiating table," Carter later remarked. "But he was willing to consider a broad range of options on how we might reconvene the so-called Geneva conference under U.N. Resolution 338." The resolution had been adopted by the United Nations after the Yom Kippur War and provided for peace negotiations under the joint chairmanship of the United States and the Soviet Union. Assad also raised the possibility that secure borders between Syria and Israel might be achieved through the establishment of demilitarized zones, perhaps manned by international forces, and, most important, through an ending of the state of belligerency between Israel and Syria.

The president left Damascus pleased by the outcome of his talks with the Syrian leader. "In Assad, I observed a man who spoke simply for himself and his country, without self-doubt and with little consideration of how his views might conflict with those of anyone else," the president wrote. "Many other Arab leaders seemed to follow almost a party line, but some of Assad's views sounded original, thought out from his own contemplation."

Any optimism that Vance and Carter might have derived from their talks with Assad, however, was quickly dampened. For one thing, Assad's position on the Palestinians was ambiguous and might not have been all that conciliatory even when he seemed willing to compromise on the Palestinian question in his meeting with Vance. The fact was that in 1970 he had defied the orders of Syrian president Saleh Jadid to use Syrian air forces in support of the PLO in Jordan, and he had seized power in Syria after being condemned for this action by Syria's leaders. Although he raised the Palestinian question again in his meeting with Carter and insisted that the Palestinians needed to be guaranteed the right of return to their homeland or be compensated, he did not trust the Palestinians and despised the PLO leader, YASSER ARAFAT. Instead of a Palestinian homeland, he preferred some kind of confederation with Jordan. As even Carter later acknowledged, "Assad's position was consistent with his belief that Arab unity of purpose (as defined in Damascus) was more important than Palestinian nationalism."

Assad became livid, moreover, after he learned of the decision by Egypt's Sadat to follow his own course, beginning with his visit to Israel at the end of 1977, in order to reach a separate Egyptian peace settlement with Israel. Just before going to Jerusalem in November 1977, Sadat had gone to Damascus to encourage Assad to follow Egypt's lead with Israel. Assad refused. Not only did the Egyptian leader's decision fly in the face of a united Arab front, which the Syrian president claimed was essential in dealing with the Arab-Israeli dispute, it also challenged Assad's quest to be the leader of the Arab world. At the same time, by joining Prime Minister MENACHEM BEGIN in signing the Camp David agreements of 1978, which established a "framework for peace" in the Middle East and provided for a peace settlement between Egypt and Israel, Sadat allowed Israel, in Assad's view, to neutralize its strongest military foe and gain worldwide approval as a peacemaker while at the same time increasing the likelihood of an Israeli attack on Syria. Assad never forgave Sadat for what he considered his "betrayal" of the Arab case.

Accordingly, Assad denounced the Camp David accords of 1978 and, like other Arab leaders, refused to become involved in the peace process that President Carter had hoped would follow the accords. Instead, the Syrian leader joined other Arab nations in imposing an economic embargo against Egypt. He also strengthened his hold in Lebanon, where he had first sent troops in 1976 to protect the Maronite Christians against terrorist attack from Palestinians in an ongoing civil war in the country. In June 1982, Syrian forces clashed with Israeli forces, which had launched a strike deep into Lebanon against the Palestinians. In 1983, Carter went to Syria as a private citizen and met with Assad, who refused to budge in his opposition to Israel or in his criticism of the United States for its economic and military support of the Israelis. Washington's support of Israel, he said, made possible Israeli aggression in Lebanon. He insisted to the former president that the only way to deal with Israel was through an international forum with a single Arab delegation that included Palestinian participation and Soviet involvement—in other words, a resumption of the Geneva peace process of the early 1970s. In 1993, Assad attacked the secret Oslo peace agreement between Israel and the PLO, led by Arafat. "Nobody expects us to raise banners of happiness and pleasure with such a clandestine agreement held behind our backs," he remarked in an American television interview.

During the 1980s, Syria obtained massive amounts of Soviet military equipment to replace the weapons it had lost during the Israeli invasion of 1973. Syrian forces also brought about a shaky end to the civil war in Lebanon, driving out more militant PLO groups from northern Lebanon and remaining in the country in large numbers until an uprising by the Lebanese against their control forced them to leave the country in 2005.

Domestically, Assad maintained tight control over Syria even though the country was nominally a democracy with an elected parliament and there were growing signs of opposition to his rule because of Syria's backwater economy. The country suffered from a crumbling industrial base, the lack of a single major export commodity, a backward banking system, and an inadequate educational system. It was also the last state in the Middle East to introduce fax machines and the Internet. In 1982, Assad killed at least 10,000 residents of the town of Hama to end a growing Islamic-led insurgency against his rule.

Only in his last years in power did Assad begin to modernize the economy and loosen some of his control over the country. A gaunt figure who had been ill for a number of years, he had, however, begun to prepare for his succession by naming his son Bashar, an ophthalmologist inexperienced in politics, to succeed him. Assad died of a heart attack on June 11, 2000, at the age of 69.

B

Baker, Howard Henry, Jr.

(1925–) *member of the Senate, minority leader*

Minority leader of the U.S. Senate during the Carter presidency, Howard H. Baker, Jr. (R-Tenn.), a moderate, supported the administration on a number of key issues and even risked his political career to vote in favor of the Panama Canal Treaties in 1978. However, for political reasons, he took an increasingly borderline position on other measures supported by the administration and came out in opposition to the second Strategic Arms Limitation agreement (SALT II).

Baker was born in Huntsville, Tennessee, on November 25, 1925. After graduating from high school in 1943, he immediately enlisted in the U.S. Navy and he served during World War II. As a candidate in the navy's V-12 officer training program, he studied engineering at the University of the South (Sewanee) and at Tulane University. After military service, he earned his law degree from the University of Tennessee Law College (LL.B., 1949) and went to work in the law firm his grandfather had founded. He also became a millionaire by engaging in various business ventures. In 1950, he managed the successful campaign of his father, Howard H. Baker, Sr., for the U.S. House of Representatives. In 1951, he married Joy Dirksen, daughter of Senator Everett Dirksen (R-Ill.).

Following his father's death in 1964, Baker was expected to run for the senior Baker's seat in the House. Instead, he ran in a special election to fill the seat in the U.S. Senate vacated by the death of its incumbent, Estes Kefauver (D). Running as a conservative in a year in which the Republican ticket headed by Barry Goldwater was trounced, Baker was also defeated. Taking a more moderate stance, he ran again in 1966, this time for a full six-year term, and was elected. He became the first popularly elected Republican senator from Tennessee.

In 1972, Baker was reelected to the Senate. The next year, he served as vice chairman of the Senate committee investigating President RICHARD NIXON's role in the 1972 break-in at the Democratic headquarters in the Watergate office building and its subsequent coverup by the White House. During the televised hearings, he gained national attention by asking the penultimate question of the hearings: "What did President Nixon know about the break-in and when did he know it?" Although a friend and adviser to the president, Baker won considerable bipartisan support for his even-handed conduct, objective demeanor, and probing questions throughout the hearings. It was during the hearings that he first raised the idea for an office of public prosecutor in the Justice Department to investigate cases then handled by the independent counsel.

Baker continued to gain national prominence when he was chosen the keynote speaker at the 1976 Republican convention. In January 1977, he was elected Senate minority leader. As the ranking Republican on Capitol Hill, Baker opposed President Carter on a number of issues, including Carter's decisions to cut production of the B-1 bomber, defer production of the neutron bomb, and begin a phased withdrawal of U.S. troops from South Korea. He was also dubious about the president's intent in 1978 to hold the Camp David summit on the Middle East that brought together Israeli leader MENACHEM BEGIN and Egyptian president ANWAR EL-SADAT. On a more personal level, Baker and Carter did not get along well; there simply was a lack of chemistry between the two men.

For the most part, however, Baker tried to work with the White House during the president's first two years in office. Despite Republican opposition to Carter's nomination of JOSEPH CALIFANO to be secretary of health, education, and welfare because of Califano's views on abortion, Baker supported the nomination. He also supported the Clean Air Act and worked with the Democratic leadership in 1977 to end a filibuster by Senator JAMES ABOUREZK (D-S.Dak.) against natural-gas price deregulation. Most important, in 1978 he proved indispensable in winning Senate approval of one of the most divisive issues of the Carter administration, the Panama Canal Treaties.

Having expended considerable political capital in getting the treaties through the Senate and looking toward running for president in 1980, Baker assumed more of the role of opposition leader during Carter's last two years in office. Nevertheless, widely regarded as a moderate Republican, he continued to back the White House on a number of matters, including hospital cost-containment legislation and a compromise welfare reform bill, which he cosponsored with Senate Republicans Henry Bellmon (Okla.) and John Danforth (Mo.) and Democrat ABRAHAM RIBICOFF (Conn.).

Baker rebuked the president, however, for his handling of the Iranian hostage crisis in 1979. He also took a hard stand against ratification of the Strategic Arms Limitation Talks agreement (SALT II) restricting the strategic arsenals of the Soviet Union and the United States. In June 1979, he shocked the White House when he announced that he would reject the agreements unless significant changes were made, including a requirement that the Soviets dismantle all their huge SS-9 and SS-18 missile launchers. Baker's position, however, was consistent with his record of always endorsing a strong military defense. He was worried that the provision allowing the Soviets to keep their mammoth weapons would place the United States at a distinct disadvantage to the Soviet Union in terms of their respective nuclear delivery systems. Without Baker's support, the Senate would most likely have rejected the agreement. But the president avoided that embarrassment by withdrawing the treaty from consideration following the Soviet invasion of Afghanistan in December 1979.

In 1980, Baker ran for the Republican nomination for president, emphasizing foreign policy and the need for a strong defense. Appealing to the conservative base of the party, he also advocated tax cuts, reduced federal spending, and limited government controls. But he did poorly in the early primaries and withdrew from the race.

Baker became the Senate majority leader following RONALD REAGAN's sweeping victory over Carter for the presidency in 1980 and the Republican capture of the Senate for the first time since 1950. He held the position until he retired from the Senate at the end of his third term in 1985. Intending to run for president again in 1988, he gave up that idea when President Reagan asked him, in the midst of the Iran-contra scandal, to serve as his chief of staff. Helping to quell the public furor over the scandal, Baker stayed in the position until the end of Reagan's presidency and generally received high marks for the manner in which he ran White House operations.

In 1989, Baker resumed his law practice in Washington. In 1993, his wife Joy died of cancer. Three years later, he married former senator Nancy Kassebaum (R-Kans.). In 2001, President George W. Bush appointed Baker the U.S. ambassador to Japan. As ambassador, he was sometimes critical of Washington, such as when the administration tried to pressure the Japanese to quickly clean up their nonperforming loans as part of Japan's economic recovery. He reminded the White House that the Japanese had their own way of doing things.

Baker remained as ambassador to Japan until the beginning of President Bush's second term in 2005. He currently divides his time between Washington and Tennessee.

Baker, James Addison, III

(1930–) *campaign manager for President Gerald Ford, chair of George Bush presidential campaign*

Although he has never run for political office himself, James A. Baker has been one of the most prominent national political figures in the Republican Party since the early 1970s. Born in Houston, Texas, on April 28, 1930, he is a graduate of Princeton University (B.A., 1952) and the University of Texas Law School (LL.B., 1957). He also served in the United States Marine Corps (1952–54). After graduating from law school with honors, he practiced law in the Austin firm of Andrews and Kurth from 1957 to 1975.

While practicing law, Baker became active in the fast-growing Republican Party in Texas. In 1970, he ran GEORGE HERBERT WALKER BUSH's unsuccessful campaign for the U.S. Senate against Lloyd Bentsen. In 1975, President GERALD FORD appointed him undersecretary of commerce. The next year, Ford named him as deputy chairman in charge of delegate operations for Ford's national presidential campaign. In that capacity, he acted as the president's principal spokesman on campaign matters and was responsible for rounding up enough wavering delegates to the Republican National Convention in Kansas City to narrowly beat back a tough challenge for the nomination from California governor RONALD REAGAN. Following the convention, after first asking former Texas governor John Connally, who declined the offer, Ford named Baker to serve as national chairman of his presidential campaign. He replaced the ailing Rogers Morton, who was held responsible by Ford's advisers for the close call in Kansas City.

During the campaign against Carter, Baker worked closely with Ford's chief of staff, Richard (Dick) Cheney, who served as liaison between the White House and the campaign; Cheney's assistant, Stuart Spencer, who was the campaign's chief political strategist; and Robert Teeter, the campaign's chief pollster. Together they worked off a 120-page campaign plan that Cheney and Spencer had developed and Baker and Teeter had refined. The strategy was based on the assumptions that President Ford was not a good campaigner; that the American people nevertheless respected his human qualities; and that his opponent, Jimmy Carter, was vulnerable on the issues of vagueness, duplicity, and trustworthiness. The plan called for a frontal media assault on the Democratic nominee while making Ford look presidential by keeping him close to the White House and limiting his campaign appearances.

The campaign seemed to work brilliantly as the gap in the polls, which at one time in September showed Carter leading Ford by as much as 15 percent was almost erased: on the eve of the election, most polls showed the outcome too close to call. Ford also proved to be a better and more active campaigner than his advisers had anticipated. Aside from a gaffe he made in the second of three scheduled debates with Carter, during which he denied that there was any Soviet domination of Eastern Europe, he may have won the election; certainly that ill-chosen remark by Ford on October 6 disrupted the momentum of his campaign while galvanizing his opponent's effort. But the slim margin by which Carter won (50.1 percent to Ford's 48 percent) makes it impossible to attribute Ford's defeat to a single cause or event.

During the campaign, Baker committed his own gaffe by sending a telegram to 400 African American ministers suggesting that Carter had not shown leadership in integrating the Plains Baptist Church where he was a member. The telegram followed an incident in which a black minister, Clennon King, who had his own church 40 miles from Plains and was well known in the area as a political eccentric and a longtime foe of Carter, was denied membership in the church and turned away from worshiping there. The incident attracted national media attention. Although the Democratic candidate had supported integration of the church, in his telegram Baker questioned whether Carter could lead the nation if he was unable to influence the decisions of his own church. The telegram backfired when such black leaders as JESSE JACKSON and Congressman ANDREW YOUNG came to Carter's defense, pointing to his strong record as governor of Georgia on matters of race and suggesting that Reverend King had been used by Republicans to embarrass the Democratic candidate and raise doubts about his commitment to racial integration. Baker later denied that the Republican Party had instigated the King incident but acknowledged that it had been a mistake to send the telegrams.

Despite this blunder and Ford's defeat in November, Baker received high marks from political commentators and professionals for almost bringing victory to a political party that had been badly divided at its national convention and a candidate who had trailed far behind his opponent in the polls at the beginning of the campaign. Widely regarded now as an extremely savvy political strategist, Baker headed George Bush's campaign for president in 1980. Although Bush was defeated for the Republican nomination, he did better in the primaries than many political observers had anticipated. Ronald Reagan then chose Bush to be his running mate and Baker as one of his senior advisers in the Reagan-Bush campaign.

Following Reagan's victory over Carter in 1980, the president-elect named Baker as his chief of staff. In 1984, Baker chaired the campaign that led to Reagan's landslide victory over former vice president WALTER MONDALE, and in the 1988 presidential race, he managed Vice President Bush's impressive victory over Michael Dukakis. In between elections, he served as secretary of the treasury (1985–88) and secretary of state (1989–92). He stepped down as secretary of state in August 1992 to head Bush's unsuccessful reelection campaign. For the remainder of Bush's term, he served as the president's chief of staff and senior counselor. In 2001, President George W. Bush appointed Baker ambassador to Japan, where he served until 2005. In March 2005, he joined Citigroup as an adviser to senior management on international affairs.

Bakke, Allan Paul

(1940–) *litigant in Regents of the University of California v. Bakke*

Allan Bakke was the litigant in a landmark Supreme Court case involving the constitutionality of affirmative action. Bakke, a white person, brought his case against the Board of Regents of the University of California (UC) after being denied admission to the medical school at its campus at Davis (UC-Davis). He won the case, but the Supreme Court upheld the principle of affirmative action.

Born in Minneapolis on February 4, 1940, Bakke graduated from the University of Minnesota with a degree in engineering (1962) and a 3.5 grade point average out of a possible 4.0. Following graduation, he served for four years in the U.S. Marine Corps, where he learned about space medicine and began to think about combining his knowledge of mechanical engineering with medicine. Returning to civilian life in 1967, he worked for NASA at its Ames Research Center in Sunnyvale, California, and received a master's degree in engineering from Stanford University in 1970.

Having decided to pursue a medical career, Bakke applied in 1972 to the medical schools at Northwestern University and the University of Southern California, but he was denied admission. The next year, he applied to 12 medical schools, including the one at UC-Davis. He was denied admission to all of them despite his high academic average, the fact that he had done well on the Medical College Admission Test (MCAT), and evidence that he had apparently performed well in his personal interviews. After he threatened to take legal action against UC-Davis, he was encouraged by a member of its admissions committee to reapply the next year. But when he was rejected a second time, Bakke sued the UC Board of Regents. He maintained that his rights under Title VI of the Civil Rights Act of 1964 and the equal-protection provision of the Fourteenth Amendment had been violated because he had been denied admission even though his test scores were higher than the 16 various minorities admitted under a special program that reserved 16 of 100 spaces each year for minority students.

In filing his lawsuit, Bakke appears to have had as his purpose the limited one of gaining admission to UC-Davis's medical school. As the case wound its way through the appeals process, however, it attracted national attention as the most important civil rights case since *Brown v. Board of Education of Topeka* (1954) declared the doctrine of "separate but equal" to be unconstitutional. The California Superior Court ruled that race could not be used as a factor in admissions decisions, but it did not force Bakke's admission because the Court could not determine if he would have been admitted had there been no 16-seat set-aside for minorities. Bakke appealed to the California Supreme Court, which found in his favor, maintaining that it was the university's responsibility to prove that Bakke would not have been admitted without the special program, and ordered his immediate admittance. The Board of Regents then took the case to the U.S. Supreme Court, which suspended Bakke's admittance pending its decision on the case.

Given the magnitude of the *Bakke* case and the national split over affirmative-action programs, especially ones with racial quotas, the case presented the Carter administration with a complicated judicial and political problem. On the one hand, President Carter had established a solid civil rights record as governor of Georgia and recognized that previous patterns of racial discrimination needed to be addressed. On the other hand, while he and the majority of his supporters backed the purpose of affirmative-action programs, they had major concerns about racial quotas. As a matter of principle, the president opposed quotas of any kind. To complicate matters even more, most African American leaders, who had played a decisive role in getting the president elected, wanted the administration to support the position taken by the Board of Regents against Bakke. Other Democrats, especially within the influential American Jewish community, vehemently opposed racial quotas. On the essential question of how far an affirmative-action program could go to redress past racial discrimination and segregation, therefore, there was a real division even within the president's own party.

In August 1977, Attorney General GRIFFIN BELL presented the president with a brief on the *Bakke* case, assuring Carter that while the Justice Department supported affirmative action, it opposed the Davis plan because it established separate admissions procedure for whites and minorities. It also maintained that racial classifications, even those that appeared ostensibly benign, were suspect and even pernicious. Other administration officials, however, including the president's domestic adviser, STUART EIZENSTAT, and his counsel, ROBERT LIPSHUTZ, attacked the brief, maintaining that it contradicted the administration's firm commitment to affirmative action. Instead of asking the Supreme Court to declare the UC-Davis Medical School's admission policy unconstitutional, they urged the White House to firmly endorse affirmative-action programs while delineating between racial goals and quotas. The president weighed in on their side, requiring the Justice Department to rewrite its brief in a way consistent with both his support of affirmative action and his opposition to racial quotas.

Although the Justice Department filed its brief in September 1977, the Court did not make its ruling until the following June. By a vote of 5 to 4, it ruled in favor of affirmative-action programs but found that the UC-Davis Medical School had employed an unconstitutional quota in denying Bakke's application for admission. It ordered that Bakke be admitted with the school's next class. In making its ruling, the nine justices filed six separate opinions, each with nuances. Key to the final outcome in the *Bakke* case was Justice LEWIS POWELL. In his opinion, Powell sided with Chief Justice WARREN BURGER and Justices WILLIAM REHNQUIST, POTTER STEWART, and JOHN PAUL STEVENS in declaring the UC-Davis Medical School's special admission-quota system unconstitutional. At the same time, Powell sided with Justices WILLIAM BRENNAN, HARRY BLACKMUN, BYRON WHITE, and THURGOOD MARSHALL in upholding the use of racial classifications when necessary to promote a substantial state interest, including special admissions programs using an explicit racial classification.

As a result of the Supreme Court's decision, Allan Bakke was admitted in 1978 to the UC-Davis Medical School at the age of 38. He graduated four years later and then completed a residency in anesthesiology at the Mayo Clinic in Rochester Minnesota. He was not entirely able, however, to escape the public limelight. In 1995, journalist Nicholas Lehmann published an article in the *New York Times Magazine* comparing Bakke's career with that of Patrick Chavis, one of five black students who had been admitted in 1975 to the UC-Davis Medical School under its special admissions program. Defending affirmative-action programs, Lehmann noted that Bakke's medical career had been unimpressive while Chavis had had a thriving career in obstetrics and gynecology, serving poor people in a ghetto suburb of Los Angeles.

As it turned out, however, and as opponents of affirmative action publicized widely, in 1998 the California Medical Board revoked Chavis's license to practice medicine because of gross negligence in the cases of three patients, one of whom died after he had performed a liposuction procedure on her. On July 23,

2002, Chavis was murdered during a robbery at a local convenience store in Los Angeles. As for Bakke, he remains a practicing anesthesiologist in Minnesota.

Ball, George Wildman
(1909–1994) *presidential adviser*

A consummate Washington political insider and widely regarded as one of the "wise men" of U.S. foreign policy during much of the cold war period, George Ball served the Carter administration primarily as an unofficial adviser to the president during the Iranian revolution of 1978–79.

A native of Iowa, Ball was born on December 21, 1909, the third son of a schoolteacher and a vice president of Standard Oil of Indiana. He attended Northwestern University, where he received his undergraduate and law degrees (B.A., 1930; LL.B., 1933). After working in the Farm Bureau and the Treasury Department in Washington, D.C., he accepted a position as a tax lawyer in Adlai Stevenson's Chicago law firm. During World War II, he followed Stevenson to Washington and served in the Office of Lend Lease Administration until 1944, when he moved to London and became director of the U.S. Strategic Bomb Survey. While in Europe, he met French statesman Jean Monnet, one of the architects of postwar European unity. For the rest of his career, Ball made a strong Atlantic community a guiding principle of his foreign policy.

After the war, Ball founded his own law firm, which represented the European Common Market and the European Coal and Steel Company. He was also the chief volunteer in Stevenson's two unsuccessful campaigns for president in 1952 and 1956, and campaign manager for Stevenson's unsuccessful attempt in 1960 to gain the Democratic Party's nomination a third time. Despite Ball's support for Stevenson, President-elect John F. Kennedy appointed him undersecretary of state for economic affairs and then, in November 1961, as undersecretary of state (the second-ranking position at the State Department). Objecting to the United States's growing involvement in Vietnam, Ball also became increasingly critical of the nation's pro-Israeli policy in the Middle East. In September 1966, he left the State Department to join the investment banking firm of Lehman Brothers, where he remained until his retirement in 1982.

Ball continued, however, to write and comment extensively on foreign affairs. He remained outspoken in his views, especially with respect to the Middle East. He continued to call for a more balanced American position in the Arab-Israeli dispute and criticized unlimited arms sales to Iran. In 1976, he sent Democratic presidential nominee Jimmy Carter a copy of his new book, *Diplomacy for a Crowded World: An American Foreign Policy* (1976). Carter asked several of his advisers, including his future National Security Advisor, ZBIGNIEW BRZEZINSKI, whether Ball should be invited to join a small group preparing a transition paper on foreign policy should Carter win in November. Brzezinski advised against an invitation, pointing to people in the campaign who were opposed to Ball because of his anti-Israeli views. Instead, Ball was asked to write a separate report that involved him less directly with the campaign.

Following the November elections, Ball was briefly considered for the positions of secretary of state and secretary of the treasury in Carter's cabinet. But neither Carter nor Brzezinski were enthusiastic about having Ball in the new administration. Brzezinski was wary of his close ties to the State Department and questioned whether he would be a good team player.

After Carter entered the White House, Ball, who viewed himself as a pragmatic realist in matters affecting foreign policy, quickly became frustrated by what he regarded as the president's moralistic approach to diplomacy and failure to understand the nuances embedded in the conduct of foreign policy. By fall 1977, Ball had joined a group of other, mainly Democratic, members of the foreign-policy establishment who privately questioned whether the president was up to the job. He also questioned the value of Carter's human rights campaign.

In November 1978, however, Secretary of the Treasury W. MICHAEL BLUMENTHAL recommended that Ball be brought into the White House to develop a long-term program for Iran, where opposition was growing against the country's ruler, Shah MOHAMMAD REZA PAHLAVI. Brzezinski supported the recommendation, and Ball was hired as a consultant to the National Security Council (NSC), but the two men clashed almost immediately. The former undersecretary of state believed that Brzezinski, who favored a strong military regime under the shah, was part of the problem in Iran. The National Security Advisor was convinced that Ball was leaking misinformation to the State Department. Brzezinski even ordered Ball not to talk with the head of the Iran desk at State, HENRY PRECHT.

On December 14, Ball delivered his report on Iran to President Carter. He had vetted it three days earlier with the Special Coordinating Committee, an interagency crisis management team chaired by Brzezinski, which had been established at the beginning of the administration as a means of bringing about interagency coordination and cooperation in foreign policy crises like the one unfolding in Iran. The main recommendation of Ball's report was that the shah yield his power to a Council of Notables representing the various political and religious factions in Iran.

As Brzezinski later commented, discussion of the report became largely a debate between him and Ball over the timing of any advice to the shah. They argued over whether the Iranian ruler should be encouraged to establish a civilian government immediately or impose a firm military government that would restore law and order and move toward a civilian form only as the threat of revolution ebbed. On this issue the president reserved his position, believing it would be inappropriate for the United States to be excessively involved in Iran's internal affairs. But he did agree to send the shah a list of questions designed to force him to review his options carefully.

Having delivered his recommendations to the administration, Ball returned to private life. As the revolution in Iran unfolded, President Carter became increasingly agitated with the State Department, which he accused of not following out his orders to support the shah and of leaking misinformation. Whatever standing Ball had with the White House was gone; he was not called again to advise the administration. Instead, he spent much of the rest of his life working with his son, Douglas, on a book, *The Passionate Attachment: America's Involvement with Israel, 1947 to the Present* (1992), in which the two authors criticized the power of the Jewish lobby on Capitol Hill and the United States's unwavering support of the state of Israel. Ball died in New York City on May 26, 1994, at the age of 83.

Bayh, Birch Evans, Jr.

(1928–) *member of the Senate*

First elected to the Senate in 1962, Birch Evans Bayh, Jr., ran unsuccessfully for the Democratic presidential nomination in 1976. One of the most influential members of the Senate during the Carter presidency, he was also known for his liberal views on most issues. For that reason, he was successfully targeted by Republicans in his bid for reelection in 1980.

Bayh was born on January 22, 1928, in Terre Haute, Indiana. After majoring in agriculture at Purdue University (B.S., 1951), he farmed on 340 acres of land outside of Terre Haute. In 1954, he won election as a Democrat to the largely Republican Indiana House of Representatives. Serving as minority leader, he became Speaker of the House when the Democrats were able to capture the state legislature in 1958. While serving in the legislature, he earned his law degree from the Indiana School of Law (J.D., 1960). With the strong support of the state AFL-CIO, he was able to win an upset victory to the U.S. Senate in 1962, defeating the incumbent, Homer Capehart, a conservative Republican who was running for a fourth term.

As a freshman senator, Bayh supported most of the legislative package of President John F. Kennedy's New Frontier and Lyndon Johnson's Great Society. He also developed a reputation as one of the Senate's foremost experts on constitutional law. As a member of the Senate Judiciary Committee and chair of its Subcommittee on Constitutional Amendments, he wrote and sponsored the Twenty-fifth Amendment on presidential and vice-presidential succession (ratified in 1967) and the Twenty-sixth Amendment lowering the voting age from 21 to 18 (ratified in 1971). He also wrote and sponsored two other amendments approved by Congress but never ratified: the Equal Rights Amendment (ERA) and an amendment giving representation in Congress to the District of Columbia. Another amendment Bayh supported would have abolished the electoral college. Although the amendment passed the House of Representatives, it was filibustered in the Senate by lawmakers from smaller states. Reelected to the Senate in 1968, Bayh led the opposition in 1969 and 1970 against President RICHARD NIXON's nomination of Clement F. Haynsworth and G. Harrold Carswell for the Supreme Court. He also authored Title IX of the Higher Education Act (1972) mandating equal opportunity for women students and faculty.

A popular and highly respected lawmaker on Capitol Hill identified with the more liberal wing of the Democratic Party, Bayh had been preparing to run for president in 1972 when his wife was diagnosed with breast cancer, causing him to withdraw from the race. Although he entered the race for the Democratic nomination in 1975, his bid was short-lived. In the early caucuses in Iowa, Jimmy Carter beat Bayh by almost a three-to-one margin, receiving 29.1 percent of the vote in a large field to 11.4 percent for the Indiana senator, who came in a distant second. A few weeks later, he ran a distant third in the New Hampshire primary behind Carter, who won 29.4 percent of the vote, and Arizona Congressman MORRIS UDALL, who received 23.9 percent to Bayh's 16.2 percent. In both Iowa and New Hampshire, Carter was able to take advantage of the fact that his more liberal opponents split much of their natural constituency while he was able to co-opt the political center and more conservative wings of the party. Bayh withdrew his candidacy a week later, following a humiliating defeat in Massachusetts in which he came in seventh in a crowded field and received only 5 percent of the vote. Not until May, however, did he throw his support behind Carter.

After Carter's close victory over GERALD FORD and a solid victory of Democrats over Republicans in both houses of Congress in November, Bayh wielded considerable clout on Capitol Hill. As chairperson of the Senate Select Committee on Intelligence (1977–80), he helped reform the intelligence-gathering community. A senior member of the Senate's Public Works Subcommittee on the Environment, he worked to improve the nation's air and water quality. He also continued to champion the Equal Rights Amendment to the Constitution and an amendment replacing the electoral college with a popular vote for the presidency; the amendment also provided for a runoff election between the two candidates receiving the highest vote if no candidate on the ballot won at least 40 percent of the vote. Although the president supported the amendment, Congress failed to act upon it.

Bayh fell victim in 1980 to the country's increasingly conservative mood, exemplified by RONALD REAGAN's landslide victory over Carter. Despite spending almost $2.8 million in his bid for reelection, Bayh lost to Congressman Dan Quayle, who had spent $2.4 million. Along with a number of other lawmakers on Capitol Hill, the National Conservative Political Action Committee had successfully targeted Bayh for defeat because of his liberal views.

After leaving Congress, Bayh became a partner with a practice in public policy advocacy at Venable, Baetjer, Howard, and Vivillet, one of Washington, D.C.'s most respected and influential law firms. In 1995, he was appointed by President Bill Clinton to the J. William Fulbright Scholarship Board.

Bayh's son, Birch Evans Bayh III, has followed his father into Indiana politics. After serving two terms as governor (1989–97), he was elected to the U.S. Senate in 1998 and reelected in 2004.

Begin, Menachem Wolfovitch

(1913–1992) *prime minister of Israel*

Prime minister of Israel during and following the presidency of Jimmy Carter, Menachem Begin was a leader whose personality and life were marked by contradiction, inconsistency, and irony. "The world does not pity the slaughtered. It only respects those who fight," he once remarked to the *Times* of London. Yet he was a cowinner of the Nobel Peace Prize along with Egypt's ANWAR EL-SADAT. A prime minister who caused President Carter more anguish than any other foreign leader, he was nonetheless responsible for one of Carter's greatest achievements as president. Having brought great world acclaim to his country in 1979, he opened it to international calumny and renunciation just three years later. Passionate and even fanatical in his oratory, he was usually cautious and careful in his statesmanship and courteous in his conduct. A public figure most of his life, he slid into seclusion after 1983 and died a recluse.

Key to understanding Begin in later life was his fervor and despair as a youth. He was born on August 16, 1913, in Brest-Litovsk (now Belarus), Poland. His father, a businessman, was also a Zionist. Attending the University of Warsaw, where he received his law degree (1935), Begin became a follower of Vladimir Zee Jabotinsky, the founder of the biblical Revisionist Zionist Movement—as opposed to the secular Zionism of Theodore Herzl and David Ben-Gurion—and eventually headed the Polish branch of Betar, the Revisionist Zionist Youth Movement, with 70,000 members. When Germany invaded Poland in 1939, Begin fled to the Soviet Union, where he was imprisoned for his Zionist activities. Freed in 1941 after serving only one year of an eight-year sentence because he was a Polish citizen, he was drafted into the Free Polish army and was sent to British Palestine as an interpreter. Meanwhile, he learned that his entire family, except for one sister, had been killed by the Nazis.

In 1943, Begin was released from the Polish army and took command of the Irgun, a militant underground organization committed to the expulsion of the British from Palestine and the establishment of a Jewish state. In the years that followed, the Irgun carried out a series of terrorist activities, the most notorious of which was the July 1946 blowing up of the King David Hotel in Jerusalem, which had been serving as the British headquarters, leaving hundreds of civilians killed or wounded. The British offered a reward of $50,000 for Begin's capture, and the Irgun was repudiated by the more moderate Haganah led by David Ben-Gurion. The Irgun and Haganah fought together in the first Arab-Israeli war following the establishment of the state of Israel in 1948. But when the Irgun refused to abide by the terms of an Arab-Israeli cease-fire in June, Prime Minister Ben-Gurion ordered the shelling of an Irgun ship carrying a consignment of arms and 900 resistance fighters, including Begin.

With the dissolution of the Irgun, Begin established the strongly nationalist Herut Party and for the next 30 years was its leader in the Knesset (Israeli parliament). During the Six-Day War of 1967, he joined the cabinet as a minister without portfolio. In 1969, he resigned in opposition to an Arab-Israeli peace plan worked out by the United States that called for a return of Arab territories seized in the 1967 war. Instead, he formed the Likud Party, a rightist segment of Herut.

Regarded at first as a fringe party, Likud gained in political strength in part because of its appeal among the Sephardim, immigrants to Israel from the Middle East and North Africa who were attracted to its commitment to build Jewish settlements in the occupied territories, and in part because of complacency and corruption in the Labor Party that had governed Israel since its establishment. But Likud also gained in strength because of the fiery oratory and political acumen of its leader, Begin, who was able to forge alliances with ultranationalist religious parties that were also part of Israel's political landscape. In parliamentary elections in 1977, Likud surprised most political observers by securing a mandate to form a new government led by Begin, Israel's first nonsocialist leader. One of Begin's first decisions as prime minister was to visit the United States in order to confer with its new president, Jimmy Carter.

Carter had been shocked to learn that Begin would be Israel's new leader. Labeled a "superhawk" by *Time*, Begin referred to the West Bank and Gaza Strip, seized from the Arabs during the 1967 war, as "liberated territories, part of the land of Israel" and even called the West Bank by its biblical names of Judea and Samaria. In the president's view, Begin's election did not bode well for the peace process he wanted to achieve in the Middle East. But Carter was pleasantly surprised by his two days of talks on July 19 and 20, 1977, with the Israeli leader. Begin proved to be an intelligent, courteous, and even charming man who listened attentively both to the president's reassurances that he would not impose a peace plan on Israel and to his objections about the building of Israeli settlements in the occupied territories. In response, the prime minister expressed his desire for a Geneva conference. He also stressed that all issues were negotiable at Geneva and that the deliberations should be based on United Nations Resolutions 242 and 338 calling for the withdrawal of Israeli troops from the occupied territories in return for Arab recognition of the state of Israel.

While the Carter-Begin talks did much to dispel the president's fears about Begin's inflexibility, major differences still existed between the Israeli prime minister and the American president. Begin interpreted UN Resolutions 242 and 338 to mean withdrawal of Israeli forces from *some* of the occupied territories; Carter construed the resolution to mean from *all* the territories. Under no circumstances would Begin give up the West Bank, parlay with the Palestine Liberation Organization (PLO) led by YASSER ARAFAT, begin talks in Geneva with a combined Arab-Palestinian delegation, agree to a Palestinian homeland, or stop the construction of Israeli settlements in the occupied territories.

Soon after returning to Israel, the prime minister announced plans at the end of July for a large number of new settlements on the West Bank. Despite Carter's best efforts, his talks with Begin had failed to make any progress toward resolving the Middle East crisis. Worse, the Israeli prime minister was outraged when, in October 1977, the president issued a joint communiqué with the pro-Arab Soviet Union calling for a new Geneva conference. Seeming to bring Moscow back into the Mideast peace process, the joint statement produced a storm of protest in Israel and in the United States.

Yet the next month, Begin invited Egyptian leader Anwar Sadat to visit Israel and speak to the Knesset. Sadat had taken the courageous step of asking to be invited to Israel in an effort to reach a settlement of the 25-year-old Arab-Israeli dispute, and Begin had boldly extended the invitation. Egypt wanted the return of the Sinai captured in the 1973 Yom Kippur War; Israel wanted secure borders.

Although Sadat's visit to Israel and Begin's return visit to Egypt were widely hailed as first steps toward resolving the Arab-Israeli conflict, the peace process foundered on Begin's unwillingness to stop the settlements in the occupied territories or agree to the establishment of a Palestinian state. Instead, he proposed granting the Palestinians limited home rule in the West Bank and Gaza Strip for a five-year period, during which Israel would "hold

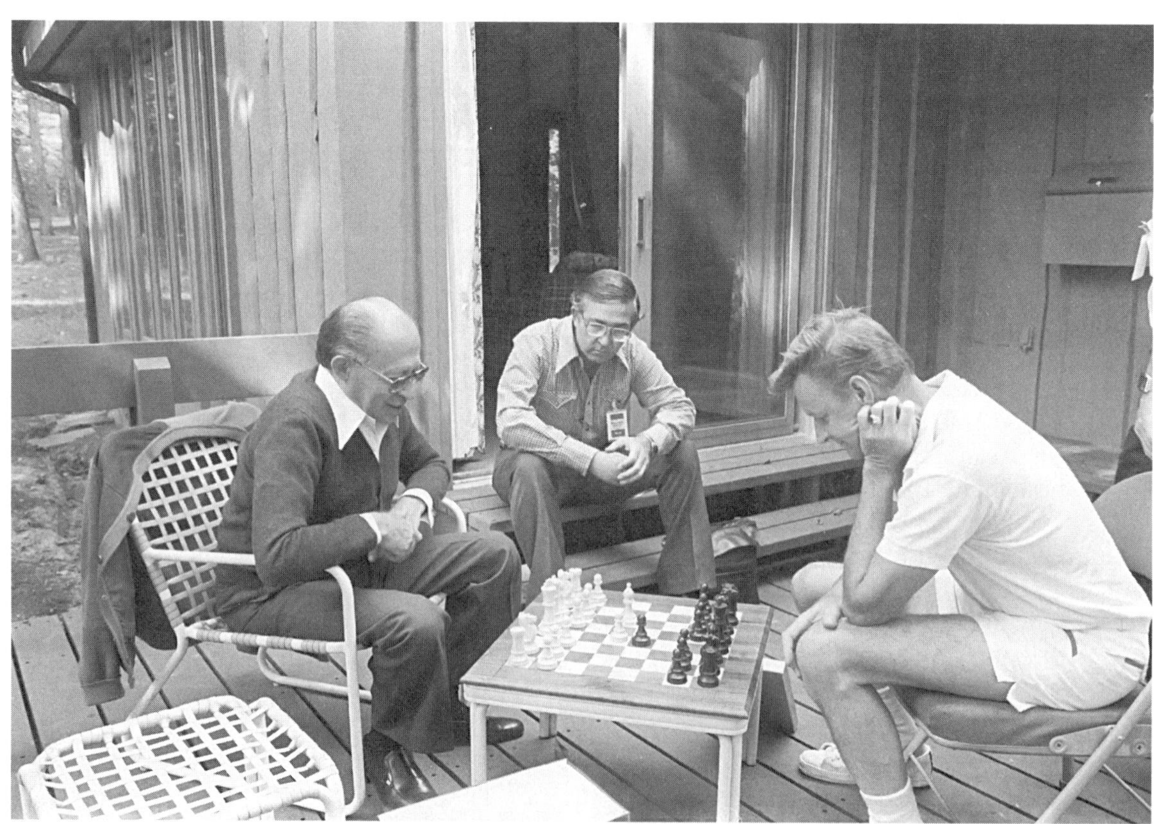

Prime Minister Menachem Begin of Israel playing chess with National Security Advisor Zbigniew Brzezinski at Camp David, 1978 *(Jimmy Carter Library)*

in abeyance" its claim to sovereignty over the region. After five years, Israel would decide whether to continue or modify the arrangement. In the months that followed, Begin continued to refer to the "rights of Jews to acquire land and settle in Judea, Samaria, and Gaza."

When the Israeli prime minister came to Washington in spring 1978 at Carter's invitation, the president could barely contain his disdain for Begin, who, in his mind, had become the major roadblock to peace in the Middle East. In a last-ditch effort to save the peace process that had begun with Sadat's visit to Israel, Carter decided to invite both Begin and the Egyptian leader to the presidential retreat at Camp David in September 1978. In the 13 days of negotiations that followed, Begin displayed the stubbornness of conviction and attention to detail that both impressed and dismayed the American president. Yet just when it seemed that the negotiations at Camp David were about to end in failure, Begin consented to the Framework for Peace in the Middle East at Camp David, which the president had prepared a week earlier. Pending approval of the Knesset, Israel agreed to remove its settlements in the Sinai, which it would return to Egypt. Sadat agreed to sign a peace treaty with Israel.

Begin achieved far more from the Camp David accords, as the agreement became known, than his Egyptian counterpart. The accords delayed any final agreement on Israeli withdrawal from the West Bank and Gaza or the establishment of a Palestinian state. In return for agreeing to an ambiguous "framework for peace" and giving up the Sinai, which he never considered a rightful part of Israel or territory essential for its security in the same way that he did the West Bank or Gaza, the Israeli prime minister achieved a peace agreement with Egypt essential to Israel's security. Rightfully hailed, nevertheless, as a major breakthrough in the Arab-Israeli dispute, the Camp David accords won the 1978 Nobel Peace Prize for Begin and Sadat.

The agreements reached at Camp David represented the high point of the Carter presidency. They also were the high mark of Begin's leadership of Israel. In fact, after Begin returned from the United States, Israel announced construction of new settlements on the West Bank in violation of the spirit of the accords. It took President Carter's personal intercession and more frosty meetings with the prime minister before Begin and Sadat signed the Egyptian-Israeli peace treaty at the end of March 1979.

By the time Carter left office in 1981, the Camp David agreements had reached a dead end. Despite repeated affirmations by both Egypt and Israel of their solid commitment to the Camp David peace process, they made little progress in resolving the Arab-Israeli dispute. The immediate problem remained Palestinian autonomy in the West Bank and Gaza Strip. Although the Camp David accords had called for an agreement on self-rule by May 26, 1980, Prime Minister Begin held steadfastly to a definition of Palestinian autonomy limited largely to municipal affairs. Under no circumstances would he permit Palestinian self-determination, which was what Sadat had intended. Carter tried in a number of ways, including meeting again with Begin, to bridge this difference. But Begin would not budge from his frequently declared positions on either Palestinian independence or the building of Israeli settlements in the occupied territories.

In 1982, Begin made the tragic mistake of sending Israeli forces across Israel's border with Lebanon, from where the PLO was sending guerrilla raids into Israel. What had been intended as a short-term occupation of southern Lebanon with limited armed forces turned into a major military expedition as far north as the outskirts of Lebanon's capital of Beirut. For 10 weeks, Israeli forces shelled and trapped the PLO and threatened their complete destruction unless the PLO agreed to a swift and unconditional withdrawal. The expedition, however, proved extremely costly to the Israelis in terms of casualties and world opinion, which turned markedly against them.

Worse, what was already a major disaster for Lebanon turned into a horrible and unremitting human tragedy when Lebanese Christian militia (the Phalangists) took vengeance on the Palestinians by attacking, apparently with Israeli acquiescence, two Israeli camps for Palestinian refugees at Sabra and Shatila, slaughtering an estimated 800–1,000 men, women, and children. There was universal outrage at the massacre, and world opinion blamed Israel for allowing it to happen. The United States demanded that Israeli forces withdraw immediately from Lebanon.

Eventually Israel did leave Lebanon, but not before suffering additional casualties as Israeli forces fell victim to snipings, ambushes, car bombings, and other terrorist activities. As the casualty lists grew, so did the opposition from within Israel to its occupation of Lebanon. Stunned by Israeli losses, disheartened by the opposition, and distraught over the recent death of his wife, Begin went into a deep depression and ordered a withdrawal of Israeli forces from the Shuf Mountains overlooking Beirut to the Awali River south of the city.

On September 15, 1983, Begin unexpectedly resigned from office and went into seclusion in Jerusalem. Only rarely was he seen in public, usually at memorial services for his wife. A sick man who had suffered a series of heart attacks, he died of heart failure on March 9, 1992. He was buried on the Mount of Olives overlooking Jerusalem.

In reminiscing about Begin, President Jimmy Carter later recalled that his meetings with the Israeli prime minister were characterized by "a series of sometimes highly emotional confrontations with strongly felt opposing opinions. . . . I would spend months negotiating with Begin, often with his own advisers being more amenable to agreement than he was." Yet Carter also called Begin "an extremely courageous man who made decisions for the well-being of Mideast peace that sometimes were in contravention of longstanding political alignments."

Bell, Griffin Boyette
(1918–) *attorney general*

One of Jimmy Carter's close friends, Griffin Bell was born in Americus, Georgia, on October 31, 1918. After receiving his law degree from Mercer University Law School (LL.B., 1947), Bell worked in several firms before joining the prestigious Atlanta law firm of King and Spaulding. In 1958, Governor-elect S. Ernest Vandiver appointed him as his chief of staff. Two years later, Bell cochaired the Georgia state presidential campaign of John F. Kennedy. In October 1961, President Kennedy nominated him for a judgeship on the U.S. Fifth Circuit Court of Appeals, where he served until 1976.

Judge Bell's record as a jurist on the Fifth Circuit, where some of the most contentious cases of the Civil Rights movement were heard, became a matter of considerable controversy when Carter nominated Bell to be his attorney general. On the one hand, Bell won considerable plaudits for his decisions in support of civil rights for African Americans in a number of landmark cases. These included one in 1962 when he joined with the majority of the court in forcing the University of Mississippi to admit James Meredith as the first black student in the school's 114 year history, and another in 1966 when he issued a desegregation order putting the school system of Taliaferro County, Georgia, into federal receivership after local officials closed down the county's only white school and made arrangements for its students

Griffin Bell is sworn in as attorney general, 1977. *(Jimmy Carter Library)*

to attend schools in adjoining counties. On the other hand, Bell strongly opposed forced busing as a way to end de facto segregation in the South, believing it was a form of social engineering that had nothing to do with the equal-protection clause of the Fourteenth Amendment, on which much of the case for integration had been based. To the extent that busing might bring about greater integration, he thought it should be voluntary.

In 1976, Bell decided to leave the bench and return to his former law firm of King and Spalding. That same year, he also joined the Carter campaign for president. Bell had known Carter as a childhood acquaintance and was a distant cousin of ROSALYNN CARTER. He also served on the three-person panel of the Fifth Circuit that cleared the way for Carter to run for the Georgia State Senate in 1962 by ruling the county unit system for electing the Georgia legislature unconstitutional and forcing its replacement with representation based on population (one man, one vote). It was, however, one of Bell's law partners and Carter's closest confidants, CHARLES KIRBO, who brought Bell into the Carter campaign. Ironically, Bell had first recommended Kirbo to represent Carter in his successful challenge to the fraudulent results of his 1962 campaign.

Bell played only a limited role in the 1976 presidential campaign. His most significant contribution was the preparation of a questionnaire for each of the six candidates the former Georgia governor was considering at the Democratic convention as his running mate. Nevertheless, President-elect Carter admired his role in bringing about electoral change in Georgia and his moderate record on civil rights, including even his views on busing as a means to integrate southern schools. Largely on this basis, Carter decided to appoint Bell as attorney general. The appointment stirred a wave of protest, though, precisely because of Bell's record on the Fifth Circuit and the fact that he had membership in two segregated social clubs. The transition team at the Justice Department recommended against the nomination, urging that the president-elect appoint someone more respected by minority leaders. But Carter refused even to meet with civil rights leaders to discuss the appointment.

As attorney general, Bell was an effective administrator in such areas as criminal justice reform and intelligence reform. He also helped restore the integrity and public approval of the FBI, which had been lost in the wake of the Watergate scandal, and he oversaw the selection of 152 new federal judges, including a higher percentage of blacks, Hispanics, and women than any administration up to that point.

The most controversial issue that Bell faced as attorney general, however, was the Carter administration's position on affirmative-action programs. In the landmark case *Regents of the University of California v. Bakke*, involving the establishment of racial quotas and a separate admissions committee for minority applicants to the University of California–Davis Medical School, the Justice Department prepared an amicus curiae brief that seemed to take a position against affirmative-action programs by challenging the separate admissions procedures for minority students. Despite Bell's reassurances that the Justice Department still supported affirmative action, the brief was harshly criticized within the administration because its language on affirmative action seemed murky. Special assistant for domestic affairs STUART EIZENSTAT, legal counsel ROBERT LIPSHUTZ, and Secretary of Health, Education and Welfare JOSEPH CALIFANO were especially outspoken in their opposition to the brief. Under considerable pressure from the White House, the Justice Department was forced to rewrite the brief to include an unequivocal statement of support for affirmative action. In its 1978 decision on the *Bakke* case, the Supreme Court declared racial quotas unconstitutional but upheld the principle of affirmative action as a means of promoting diversity.

Although civil rights leaders later pointed to the Justice Department brief as one of the administration's major contributions to the cause of civil rights, Bell remained disenchanted by the rifts that the *Bakke* case had revealed. He later complained about the hurdles he encountered as attorney general, attributing them to liberals within the administration, in particular Vice President WALTER MONDALE, and to competing centers in the Executive Branch such as the Office of the White House Counsel. In July 1979, Bell resigned as attorney general. Although his resignation was viewed by some political observers as part of a presidential shake-up of the administration that included the resignations of five cabinet secretaries, Bell had intended to resign even before the shake-up.

After leaving Washington, Bell returned to a highly lucrative practice at King and Spaulding, an increasing part of which concerned matters related to corporate crime. In 1982, he published his memoirs, *Taking Care of the Law.* He also continued to be active in public service, including serving as cochairman of the Attorney General's National Task Force on Violent Crime (1981) and as a member of the Secretary of State's Advisory Committee on South Africa (1985–87).

Although Bell has denied that he has switched political allegiance to the Republican

Party, he has more recently supported Republican candidates for President, including Vice President GEORGE HERBERT WALKER BUSH in 1992, Senator ROBERT DOLE in 1996, and Texas governor George W. Bush in 2000. He was also chairman of the first President Bush's Commission on Federal Ethics Law Reform (1989) and, more recently, has been serving as a member of an ad hoc committee established by Secretary of Defense Donald Rumsfeld to develop rules governing military tribunals.

Bergland, Robert Selmer

(1928–) *secretary of agriculture*

Robert Selmer Bergland was born on July 22, 1928, in Roseau, Minnesota. A farmer who had studied agriculture at the University of Minnesota for two years, Bergland had worked in the U.S. Department of Agriculture's (USDA) Stabilization and Conservation Service (1963–68) before entering politics. An unsuccessful Democratic candidate for Congress in 1968, he ran successfully in 1970 and served four terms before being appointed by President Carter as secretary of agriculture. Even though Bergland and Congressman Paul Simon (D-Ill.) had tried unsuccessfully to start a draft campaign for HUBERT HUMPHREY before the 1976 Democratic convention, he had been chosen for the position by Carter on the recommendation of Bergland's friend, Vice President-elect WALTER MONDALE.

As agriculture secretary, Bergland was well known both as a strong defender of farm interests and as a consumer advocate, even though these interests sometimes conflicted, as, for example, in the case of tobacco supports. Although Bergland understood the health implications of cigarette smoking, he nevertheless supported tobacco subsidies. In contrast, he favored a ban on sodium nitrates used as a preservative in about 7 percent of the nation's food supply, including bacon, meats, fish, and cold cuts, because they were suspected of being carcinogenic, although evidence for this suspicion was later shown to be inconclusive.

Although Bergland was not part of the cabinet shake-up of July 1979 that included the forced resignations of Health, Education and Welfare (HEW) secretary JOSEPH CALIFANO, energy secretary JAMES SCHLESINGER, Treasury secretary W. MICHAEL BLUMENTHAL, and transportation secretary BROCK ADAMS, and the planned and voluntary resignation of Attorney General GRIFFIN BELL, his relations with the president and the White House were often rocky in the four years that he served as agriculture secretary. Bergland had reservations, for example, about the low price supports for agriculture in the farm bill that Carter sent to Congress in March 1977. He maintained that view even after the president agreed to higher target prices for wheat, cotton, corn, and rice. On his part, Carter expressed to the agriculture secretary his "disappointment" about the way "farm bill costs ha[d] apparently skyrocketed" for 1978. Even after the president admonished Bergland, Carter's head of the domestic policy staff, STUART EIZENSTAT, and his director of the Office of Management and Budget (OMB), JAMES MCINTYRE, complained that Bergland still made commitments on price supports for 1978 without going through the proper budgetary vetting process.

More generally, Bergland was unhappy about the lack of authority the president gave him to coordinate the administration's farm policy and the consequent bickering that took place within the administration over the size of price supports. In 1978, Carter criticized him again for his efforts on Capitol Hill to maintain the food stamp program in the Department of Agriculture rather than having it transferred into the welfare program in HEW as the president and HEW secretary Califano wanted. During the Iranian hostage crisis of 1979–80,

Bergland thought the president focused too much on the crisis and not enough on the other business of government. He also termed the foreign policy views of Carter's National Security Advisor, ZBIGNIEW BRZEZINSKI, as "nutty."

After leaving the Department of Agriculture in 1981, Bergland became president of Farmland World Trade (1981–82) and then vice president and general manager of the National Rural Electric Cooperatives Association, a position he retained until his retirement in 1993. He has also served on the boards of numerous organizations, including the National Center for Appropriate Technology, the Agricultural Utilization and Research Institute, and the University of Minnesota Board of Regents. He is president of Communicating for Seniors, an advocacy group that has supported legislation establishing drug coverage under the Medicare program.

Biden, Joseph Robinette, Jr.

(1942–) *member of the Senate*

One of the youngest members ever to serve in the U.S. Senate, Joseph Biden (D-Del.) became quickly recognized for his oratorical skills and candor. During the Carter administration, he was best known for his opposition to busing to achieve school integration and for his support of increased defense spending. Yet on most issues, including civil rights, he was widely regarded as one of the strong liberal voices in the Senate.

Acknowledged by his colleagues as a fierce competitor, Biden was born on November 20, 1942, in Scranton, Pennsylvania. Growing up in Delaware, he used to jump motorcycles and play rugby and football as a teenager. A graduate of the University of Delaware (B.A., 1965) and Syracuse University College of Law (J.D., 1968), he always had political ambitions. Following law school, he opened a law practice in Wilmington. In 1972, he was elected to the New Castle County Council and almost immediately began to plan his campaign for the U.S. Senate. In 1972, he challenged the incumbent, J. Caleb Boggs, who had held office in Delaware for 26 years and was so popular that no other Democrat wanted to challenge him. Running a grass-roots campaign and displaying a mastery of the issues, Biden was able to defeat Boggs by about 3,000 votes. At the age of 29, he was the youngest popularly elected senator to date.

Shortly after being elected, Biden suffered a personal tragedy when his wife and infant daughter were killed and his two sons seriously injured after the automobile they were driving in was hit by a truck. Biden almost resigned his seat before even being sworn into office. Majority Leader Mike Mansfield (D-Mont.) was able to persuade him to change his mind. He took his oath from his sons' hospital room and began a practice—which he still continues—of commuting four hours daily in order to be with his family and not disrupt their normal routine.

Although Biden was only in his first term, Mansfield gave him choice committee assignments. He was appointed to the powerful Senate Committees on Foreign Relations and the Judiciary and Select Committee on Intelligence. The Delaware senator quickly developed a reputation for his candor and lively debating skills. Before running for public office, he had been a successful trial lawyer, and he carried his oratorical abilities to the Senate floor. Following Jimmy Carter's selection as the Democratic candidate for president in 1976, Biden was one of 14 persons whom Carter's campaign manager, HAMILTON JORDAN, recommended that Carter telephone personally and ask to campaign for him in the fall.

Although a liberal Democrat, Biden was not a doctrinaire ideologue. He numbered among his closest Democratic friends in the Senate both the liberal EDWARD KENNEDY (Mass.) and the conservative Fritz Hollings (S.C.). He also opposed federal funding of abortions and endorsed harsh penalties for drug use.

A strong supporter of civil rights, Biden was nonetheless offended by the practice of using busing to achieve school integration. Title VI of the Civil Rights Act of 1964 gave the Department of Health, Education and Welfare (HEW) the authority to require school districts to bus children to schools in order to achieve racial integration if the school districts refused to bus voluntarily. Failure to comply with Title VI, even if that meant sending children to institutions other than neighborhood schools, could result in the termination of federal funds or referral to the Justice Department for litigation. As Title VI was implemented in the 1970s in cities like Boston and Chicago, with strong ethnic neighborhoods, opposition to the legislation mounted and turned violent. In 1974, Congress adopted the Esch Amendment to the Equal Opportunities Act of the same year, prohibiting any agency of government, other than the federal courts, to require the transportation of any student to a school "other than the school closest to or the next closest to his place of residence" providing the appropriate grade level.

In 1977, Biden and Senator Thomas Eagleton (D-Mo.) introduced a similar amendment to Title VI. In making the case for the legislation, Biden maintained only a "duly constituted federal court" and not some "mindless bureaucrats" at HEW should decide when busing should be required. In that form, Congress approved the legislation, which President Carter signed into law in December. Although the president understood the backlash among black voters that the Eagleton-Biden amendment might generate and believed that busing could legitimately be used as a last resort to bring school systems into compliance with Title VI, he accepted the argument that that decision should be left to the courts and not to an administrative agency. The effect of the legislation was, nevertheless, to kill Title VI since it eliminated HEW's enforcement mechanism and replaced it with a litigation process that, prior to 1964, had been ineffectual.

As a member of the Foreign Relations Committee, Biden led a group of senators in 1979 to Beijing, where they met with Chinese leader DENG XIAOPING as part of the administration's efforts to normalize relations with the People's Republic of China. At their meeting, Deng agreed to provide intelligence collection facilities to help monitor a Strategic Arms Limitation Talks agreement being negotiated between the United States and the Soviet Union (SALT II) as long as the facilities were staffed by the Chinese. His decision was in response to a growing rift between Moscow and Beijing over China's recent military attack against Vietnam (whose government the Soviet Union supported) in response to Vietnam's incursion into Cambodia (whose government the Chinese supported). The rift threatened to escalate into a major military confrontation between the two communist powers as China sought to play the American card against the Soviets. Although there was significant press coverage of the Biden delegation's visit to China and Deng's offer to the United States, nothing tangible resulted from the meeting.

Later that year, while hearings were underway on Capitol Hill over the SALT II agreement, Biden led another Senate delegation to Moscow, where he met with Soviet foreign minister Andrei Gromyko. At their meeting, Gromyko reaffirmed an agreement he had made earlier with Secretary of State CYRUS VANCE, stipulating that a protocol on short-term limits on the deployment of cruise missiles would not establish a negotiating precedent for extended or permanent limits on cruise missile deployments. On this basis, Biden supported the SALT II treaty. He also generally supported increased spending for defense and backed the development of the MX missile.

In 1978, Biden was reelected to the Senate and has since been reelected four more times. In 1988, he ran for the Democratic nomination for president but withdrew from the race after charges were made that he had plagiarized one of his speeches. Notwithstanding these charges, Biden remains widely respected in the Senate. He is the ranking Democratic member of both the Foreign Relations Committee and the Judiciary Subcommittee on Crime and Drugs. He appears frequently as a commentator on Sunday news shows and is best known for his directness in responding to questions.

Blackmun, Harry Andrew

(1908–1999) *associate justice, U.S. Supreme Court*

Most widely known for writing the majority decision in the landmark Supreme Court case, *Roe v. Wade* (1973), upholding the constitutional right of women to choose abortions, Associate Justice Harry Blackmun also figured prominently in the case of *Regents of the University of California v. Bakke* (1978), which upheld affirmative-action programs but declared unconstitutional racial quotas to achieve affirmative-action goals. He was born on November 12, 1908, in Nashville, Illinois. A summa cum laude graduate of Harvard College with a major in mathematics (B.A., 1929) and Harvard Law School (LL.B., 1932), Blackmun began his career in a prominent Minneapolis law firm in 1934 after clerking for two years for Judge John B. Sanborn of the U.S. Court of Appeals, Eighth Circuit. He also taught at St. Paul College of Law and at the University of Minnesota Law School.

In 1950, Blackmun accepted a position as legal counsel for the Mayo Clinic and Mayo Foundation, where he remained until 1959, when he was appointed by President Dwight Eisenhower to succeed Sanborn on the Court of Appeals, Eighth Circuit. In 1970, he was elevated by President RICHARD NIXON to the Supreme Court to replace resigning justice Abe Fortas after the Senate rejected Nixon's earlier nominations of Clement H. Haynsworth and G. Harrold Carswell.

In appointing Blackmun, Nixon thought he had appointed a judicial conservative as part of his effort to undo what he regarded as the Court's liberal bias. In fact, Blackmun increasingly found himself siding with his more liberal colleagues, especially in cases involving an individual's right to privacy and protection of the rights of minority and other disadvantaged groups. Although the word *privacy* did not even appear in the Constitution, Blackmun believed the constitutional right to privacy was inherent in the Bill of Rights and elsewhere in the Constitution. "In a line of decisions … going as far back as [1891]," he wrote, "the Court has recognized that a right of personal privacy, or a guarantee of certain areas or zones of privacy, does exist under the Constitution." As the author of the majority opinion in the case of *Roe v. Wade*, he maintained that privacy included the right of a women to have an abortion in the first trimester of a pregnancy (before a fetus was able to survive outside its mother's womb) or later if the mother's life or health was threatened.

In the *Bakke* case, the question before the Supreme Court was not one of privacy but rather the constitutionality of affirmative-action programs, especially those involving racial quotas. In an earlier case involving many of the same issues, Blackmun had sided with the majority in ruling the case moot because the original plaintiff, a Caucasian who claimed he had been denied admission to the University of

Washington Law School because of its special admissions program for minorities, had subsequently been admitted and was about to graduate by the time the Court ruled on the case.

Ill and recovering from prostate cancer when the Supreme Court took up the *Bakke* case, Blackmun did not render his opinion until May 1, 1978, thereby delaying the divided Court's decision until June. But he had agonized over the case for months. Although he voted with the majority in striking down racial quotas in affirmative-action programs, he upheld the constitutionality of these programs, arguing that Title VI of the Civil Rights Act of 1974 did not prohibit race-conscious special admissions programs. Challenging the argument of other justices that the Constitution should always be "color-blind," he also said this was impossible in the real world. "In order to get beyond race," he wrote, "we must first take account of race." Since the equal-protection clause of the Fourteenth Amendment was intended to affirm rather than to deny racial equality, it should also not be used to prohibit programs established for that very purpose. "It is the unconstitutional use of race that is prohibited," he remarked, "not the constitutional use."

Blackmun continued to hold to this position throughout the remainder of his tenure on the High Court. In a 1986 Michigan case involving the layoff of white teachers even though they had greater seniority than some minority teachers who were kept on the job, he took the position that layoff plans could include race as a consideration if it was related to an important governmental objective such as easing racial tensions. In all, Blackmun wrote more than 30 opinions addressing constitutional and statutory issues in the area of race discrimination. In other cases, he defended private consensual homosexual conduct and reaffirmed a women's legal right to an abortion.

In a 1994 case involving the death penalty, Blackmun attracted national attention once more when he announced that he would no longer "tinker with the machinery of death." A firm defender of the death penalty when he had been appointed to the Supreme Court, he had voted with the minority in 1972 when the Court declared the death penalty, as then administered, amounted to cruel and unusual punishment. In 1976, he sided with the majority in reinstating the death penalty. In the years that followed, however, he changed his mind as he found no legal formulas or procedural rules—such as two phased jury trials in capital murder cases—which could be applied without violating the due-process and equal-protection guarantees of the constitution. By challenging the fairness rather than the legitimacy or morality of the death penalty, he provided its opponents with an argument that resonated even among those who viewed the death penalty as constitutionally and morally valid.

Blackmun retired from the Court in August 1994. In 1997, in the movie *Amistad*, he had a cameo role as Justice Joseph Story, who read the Supreme Court decision allowing African mutineers to be freed. He died in 1999 at age 90 from complications following hip-replacement surgery. He was widely eulogized by pro-choice and civil rights organizations.

Blumenthal, W. Michael

(Werner Michael Blumenthal)
(1926–) *secretary of the Treasury*

Never one of President Jimmy Carter's inner circle even though he served in one of the administration's key cabinet positions, W. Michael Blumenthal's responsibilities as secretary of the Treasury were never clearly defined. Although he chaired the advisory Economic Policy Group (EPG), he was never able to chart the administration's economic course or be recognized as its chief economic spokesman. Instead, he had to share this role with persons closer to the president, such as Office of Management and Budget (OMB) director BERT LANCE, Council of Economic Advisers (CEA) chairman CHARLES SCHULTZE, and, later, anti-inflation czar ROBERT STRAUSS. Not only did this cause confusion within business and financial circles as to who was the White House's authoritative voice on economic, financial, and monetary matters, it weakened Blumenthal's effectiveness as Treasury secretary. The EPG itself proved to be so unwieldy and ineffectual that the president considered abolishing it altogether. Leaks on confidential matters, such as privileged conversations in cabinet meetings, that were reported to have come from the Treasury Department also undermined the president's confidence in the secretary and led to Blumenthal's forced resignation in 1979.

Born on January 3, 1926, in Oranienburg, Germany, and of Jewish descent, Blumenthal escaped with his family in 1939 from Nazi Germany to Shanghai, where they were interned by the Japanese during World War II. In 1947, he came to the United States, where he became a U.S. citizen in 1952. Graduating in 1951 from the University of California at Berkeley with a B.S. degree in international economics, he attended Princeton University, where he received a Master of Arts and Master of Public Affairs (1953) and a Ph.D. in economics (1956). In addition to a successful business career, Blumenthal had a long record of public service, serving as deputy assistant secretary of state for economic affairs during the John F. Kennedy administration (1961–63) and then as deputy special representative for trade negotiations with ambassadorial rank under Presidents Kennedy and Lyndon Johnson (1963–67). He was chief executive of the Bendix Corporation at the time that Jimmy Carter asked him to serve as Treasury secretary.

Blumenthal had first met Carter in 1975 while both men were attending a meeting of the Trilateral Commission in Japan. During the presidential campaign, the Democratic nominee invited the Bendix executive to meet with him at his home in Plains as part of a series of meetings he was holding with well-respected figures in areas such as international economic policy. As with other members of his cabinet, the president-elect chose Blumenthal as his Treasury secretary not so much because he regarded him as an innovative thinker or theorist but because of his managerial talent and negotiating skills. Carter also thought he could rely on Blumenthal for sound advice.

Early into the administration, Blumenthal complained, along with other high-level officials, that he had no opportunity to comment on the White House's highly complex energy program, which had been drafted in secret by Carter's special assistant for energy, JAMES SCHLESINGER, and a small group of his assistants. Later Blumenthal made the same complaints about the development of the administration's welfare program. During the so-called Lance affair, a controversy involving Bert Lance, director of the OMB and Carter's close friend, Lance accused Blumenthal of leaking information about an earlier investigation conducted by the GERALD FORD administration concerning Lance's management of the National Bank of Calhoun.

Blumenthal also clashed with Carter's special assistant for domestic policy, STUART EIZENSTAT, over tax policy. Eizenstat chaired the Domestic Policy Staff (DPS), an agency responsible for analyzing and coordinating domestic policy. In May 1977, in response to the president's instructions to develop a tax reform and simplification measure, Blumenthal submitted a plan that seemed to Eizenstat to favor the rich by eliminating taxes on dividends and reducing the highest bracket in income taxes from 70 to 50 percent while reducing the lowest bracket from 14 to 13 percent. Under prodding from the president, Blumenthal modified the plan by cutting the lowest tax bracket to 12 percent and tightening allowable business reductions. Still, Eizenstat and CEA chairman Schultze continued to complain that the tax breaks favored business. For his part, Blumenthal thought the DPS was ill-informed on tax policy. He was also annoyed that Eizenstat and Shultze, whose views on spending issues were more moderate than his own, seemed to be the ones the president looked to the most for economic advice—this despite the fact that the secretary's call for major budget cuts and a deficit of no more than $30 billion in the 1980 budget prevailed over their warnings that such a draconian budget could lead to a recession.

Blumenthal's recommendation for drastic budget cuts was in response to the growing inflation rate in the United States, which had soared from an already high 7 percent at the beginning of 1978 to over 11 percent by the fall. The inflation rate weakened the dollar in international markets and threatened a further slowing down of an already anemic global economy. In an article appearing in *Foreign Affairs* in July 1978, Blumenthal urged Japan and West Germany, the United States's major industrial competitors whose currencies were appreciating rapidly against the dollar, to grow their economies faster through increased levels of government spending. Stressing the

National Security Advisor Zbigniew Brzezinski, Secretary of the Treasury Michael Blumenthal, President Carter, and Secretary of State Cyrus Vance aboard Air Force One, traveling to London for the G7 Economic Summit, 1977 *(Jimmy Carter Library)*

importance of balancing national with international needs, he also called for a liberalization of rules inhibiting foreign trade and direct foreign investment.

Europeans accused Blumenthal of purposefully "talking down the dollar" to improve the United States' balance of trade. They also complained about America's excessive dependence on foreign oil, which, they said, was driving oil prices up and contributing to the worsening global economy. At a summit meeting of the leading industrial powers in Bonn in July, German chancellor HELMUT SCHMIDT agreed to a stimulus package of up to 1 percent of the German gross national product. Japan also agreed to cut taxes in order to stimulate its economy. In return, President Carter promised to increase domestic oil prices to world prices by the end of 1980. He made that commitment without any prior agreement with Blumenthal or his other economic advisers as to how his administration would carry out such a pledge. The Treasury secretary and other advisers concerned with foreign economic policy generally favored the decontrol of oil prices in order to meet the president's commitment while protecting the dollar in international trade. Eizenstat and Vice President WALTER MONDALE, however, were more concerned with the domestic political ramifications of rising oil prices. What confounded all the president's economic advisers was that an increase in oil prices was incompatible with the administration's other goal of reducing inflation.

On November 1, 1978, Blumenthal announced new measures to deal with inflation, including increasing the discount rate by a full percentage point to 9.5 percent and reserves of foreign currencies by $30 billion and stepping up monthly gold sales. By tightening credit and stockpiling foreign reserves, the Treasury secretary and the president, who had summoned reporters to the White House for the announcement, hoped to make clear to the international community the administration's determination to stop inflation and protect the dollar even at the risk of recession.

Neither these measures nor those announced earlier did much, however, to halt the long-term fall of the dollar: by the end of December, the dollar had given up half of the gains it had made following Blumenthal's announcement just a month earlier. Nor did they do much to stop the growth in the inflation rate, which still ended the year at about 9 percent. Furthermore, the nation slid into recession and the rate of unemployment grew. By the summer of 1979, inflation was running at an annual rate of almost 14 percent, while the unemployment rate in some of the nation's hardest-hit cities, like Detroit, was approaching 25 percent.

Much of these economic woes had to do with another sharp increase in oil prices by the Organization of Petroleum Exporting Countries (OPEC) over which the White House had little control, notwithstanding the president's commitment to reducing the United States' dependence on foreign oil. But as the economy deteriorated, public confidence in the president and the administration's confidence in Blumenthal diminished. Even some of the cabinet began to complain openly about the budget cuts the secretary had supported. Within the White House, Schultze and Eizenstat remained at odds with the more conservative Treasury secretary. His reputation for arrogance and aloofness also did not sit well with other members of the president's staff, including Carter's senior administrative assistant, HAMILTON JORDAN.

In early July 1979, President Carter went to Camp David, where he spent 11 days meeting with invited experts and reflecting on the status of his administration. Returning from Camp David, he delivered a televised address on July 15 in which he spoke of a "crisis of spirit" in the country and outlined measures to deal with the nation's energy crisis. The next day he asked each member of his cabinet and his senior staff members to submit a letter of resignation. Having concluded that Blumenthal was not able to work harmoniously with other officials in the administration and with Congress, he accepted the Treasury secretary's resignation along with four other cabinet officials.

Following his forced resignation, Blumenthal returned to the private sector, where he accepted a position as vice chairman of the board of the Burroughs Corporation, a manufacturer of computer systems. When Burroughs merged in 1986 with the Sperry Corporation, another computer manufacturer, to form the Unisys Corporation, Blumenthal became chairman and CEO of Unisys. The merger was unsuccessful, though, as customers of Unisys's mainframe computers switched to smaller, less-expensive versions. In 1990, Blumenthal resigned from Unisys to accept a position as a limited partner with Lazard and Frares & Company, a private international investment bank, where he remained as a senior adviser and cochair of its international coordinating group until his retirement in December 1996.

Blumenthal has written extensively on issues having to do with international business and finance. A convert to Presbyterianism who has regained an interest in his Jewish heritage, he is author of *The Invisible Wall: Germans and Jews, a Personal Exploration* (1998), a history of German Jews and gentiles. His extensive record of public and private work includes service as president and chief executive of the Berlin Jewish Museum, the largest Jewish museum in Europe.

Bolling, Richard Walker

(1916–1991) *member of the House of Representatives*

Richard Bolling was a senior member and then chairman of the House Rules Committee (1979–81) as well as one of the intellectual giants of the House of Representatives during the Carter administration. Along with PHILLIP BURTON of California, he was also one of the leaders of the reform movement that liberalized the governance of the House in the early 1970s. He despised the abrasive Burton and was himself widely disliked for his brusqueness and intellectual arrogance. But because of his intellect, his efforts in reshaping the House, and his position as chair of the Rules Committee, he wielded considerable clout in the lower chamber. He was highly critical of the president in many respects, especially with regard to his energy plan, yet unlike many other House Democrats, he had good things to say about Carter, especially in terms of his efforts to increase American productivity through industrial deregulation.

Bolling was born in New York City on May 16, 1916, but as a teenager he moved to Huntsville, Alabama. The son of a successful surgeon, he attended Phillips Exeter Academy and then received an undergraduate degree magna cum laude and Phi Beta Kappa in English and classical French literature and a graduate degree in English literature from the University of the South (B.A., 1937; M.A., 1939). He also worked on his Ph.D. degree at Vanderbilt University (1939–40) but never completed it. An educational administrator by profession, he taught at Sewanee Military Academy (1938) and served as assistant to the head of the department of education at Florence State Teacher's College in Alabama (1940). In April 1941, he entered the U.S. Army as a private and served until he was discharged as lieutenant colonel in July 1946. During World War II, he served in the South Pacific and in Japan, where he was an assistant to General Douglas MacArthur's chief of staff. He was awarded both the Legion of Merit and the Bronze Star.

After the war, Bolling became director of student activities and veteran affairs for the

University of Kansas City (now the University of Missouri at Kansas City) and was midwest director of the liberal Americans for Democratic Action (ADA). Riding the coattails of President Harry S. Truman, who swept Missouri in 1948, he defeated the Republican incumbent, Albert L. Reeves, Jr. He remained a member of the House until his retirement in 1982.

Thanks to the president and his own intelligence, Bolling was recognized early as one of the more promising junior members of the House and became the protégé of legendary House Speaker, Sam Rayburn, who in 1955 put him on the powerful Rules Committee after only six years in Congress. As a member of the Rules Committee, Bolling engaged in an ongoing conflict with another legendary lawmaker, the highly conservative chair of the committee, Howard W. Smith of Virginia, who for many years controlled the committee with an iron fist and blocked all civil rights and other liberal legislation.

Bolling developed into a supreme tactician and parliamentarian, however, and with Rayburn's help, he was able to win House passage of the Civil Rights Act of 1957, the first such bill since Reconstruction. With Rayburn's aid again and that of President John F. Kennedy, he helped win expansion of the Rules committee from 12 to 15 members in order to allow more liberal lawmakers to serve on it. In 1964, he helped gain passage of the even more meaningful Civil Rights Act of 1964, which outlawed discrimination in public places and strengthened voting rights for blacks in the South.

Following Speaker Rayburn's death in 1961, Bolling considered briefly running for majority leader but deferred to Carl Albert (Okla.). In 1965, however, he published *House Out of Order*, followed three years later by *Power in the House*, in which he called for major modifications of the seniority system by which southern conservatives still controlled the House leadership. In particular, he proposed replacing the seniority system with an election of committee chairpersons and open committee meetings. "I believe it is possible," he wrote, "to restore representative government to the people of the United States." *House Out of Order* became a primer for new members of the lower chamber and an inspiration for more liberal and independent members of the body whose presence was being felt in growing numbers by the early 1970s. Among these newer members of Congress were the Democrats MORRIS UDALL (Ariz.), JOHN BRADEMAS (Ind.), THOMAS FOLEY (Wash.), and DAVID OBEY (Wis.). Each would make his own mark in the House.

Between 1970 and 1976—but especially after the election of the freshman class of 1974, which included a number of highly educated, liberal, and independent-minded legislators—Democratic liberals were able to institute a number of major reforms along the lines first suggested by Bolling in *House Out of Order*. These included the election of committee chairpersons, an increase in the number of subcommittees and their staffing so as to give more authority to junior members, and assurance of at least one important committee assignment to each House member. Liberals also stripped the lower chamber's most powerful committee, Ways and Means, of some of its authority, including the selection of committees. Among Democrats, there was a strong sense of fealty to Bolling for helping to bring about these changes.

At the same time, however, Bolling was intensely disliked by southern conservatives and more traditional Democrats who believed in the seniority system and against whom he directed many of his harshest barbs. The Missouri lawmaker's acerbic style, intellectual arrogance, haughty demeanor, and personal ambition also alienated even House liberals.

Among these, the most notable was the chair of the Democratic Caucus, Phillip Burton. As abrasive and ambitious as Bolling and as instrumental as his colleague in bringing about internal reform of the House, Burton detested the Missourian.

Matters between Bolling and Burton came to a head in 1976 when the Democrats had to select a new majority leader to replace TIP O'NEILL (Mass.), who had been chosen to be the new Speaker of the House following the retirement of the incumbent Speaker, Carl Albert. The two leading candidates for the position were Burton and Bolling, with another candidate, the more moderate JIM WRIGHT (Tex.), considered to be a decided underdog. But because Burton and Bolling split the liberal vote between them and each had created enemies, Wright emerged the winner. For both Bolling and Burton, defeat was a bitter loss from which neither ever fully recovered. Most pundits agreed that had Bolling been more direct in asking his Democratic colleagues to vote for him, he could have won the election. But his haughty demeanor prevented him from doing this, and he was incapable of engaging in glad-handing.

In 1977, Bolling suffered a heart attack and had to undergo quadruple-bypass heart surgery, which kept him bedridden for several months. As a senior member of the House Rules Committee, however, he still wielded considerable power during the Carter administration, which grew even greater when he became chair of the committee during Carter's last two years as president. As he later made clear in *America's Competitive Edge: How to Get Our Country Moving Again*, which he coauthored with John Bowles in 1982, one of the issues that most concerned Bolling was what he believed to be the United States' lagging productivity compared to its industrial competitors and the nation's growing dependence on foreign oil. Although he offered a multidimensional explanation and solution for the problem, he believed energy independence and industrial deregulation were important parts of the solution to the nation's competitive problems. To the extent that President Carter identified these needs and sought to deal with them, he had high praise for the president.

Indeed, Bolling was a strong supporter of the president's efforts at deregulating industry and backed the administration in bringing about deregulation of the airline and trucking industries. In March 1978, Carter also issued an executive order that was the beginning of a program to analyze the cost of regulation. The Missouri lawmaker believed this was one of the most important steps taken by any recent president to free the productive potential of American industry. Although it was defeated by Congress, Bolling was also a strong supporter of the president's Regulatory Cost Accounting Act of 1980. "The proposed act," he wrote in 1982, "would have created a systematic body of data on the costs of complying with federal regulations which would identify key problems of regulation and if properly used by policymakers, bring the regulatory process into balance with other national objectives."

Even with respect to energy issues, Bolling gave President Carter considerable credit for recognizing the seriousness of the United States' dependence on foreign oil, his awareness of the need to develop alternative energy sources, and his willingness to ask the American people to make sacrifices in order to wean the nation off its dependence on imported oil. In 1979, when gas prices soared from $13 to $34 a barrel following the Iranian Revolution and more than 100 Democrats deserted Carter by killing a standby gas-rationing plan, Bolling called them "gutless" and stood by the president.

Nevertheless, Bolling believed that Carter lacked the patience and political skill to effect needed change. The president "was intelligent enough to understand the underlying problems," he later wrote. "But he did not take time to diagnose the interrelationship of the institutions of our government. He rushed to take command. And in the end he left, as he had come, without an understanding that our greatest need was to revitalize the spirit of cooperation, compromise, and consensus in America."

With respect to the energy issue, for example, Bolling believed Carter made major mistakes from the very time he assumed office in 1977. Instead of laying the groundwork for an energy plan the American people could understand and accept, the president had his energy adviser, JAMES SCHLESINGER, develop a highly complex energy plan without any prior consultation or effort to build consensus behind it. "The result of his effort was the exact antithesis of the process that had produced the Marshall Plan," Bolling remarked. Because the president did not take the time to prepare the ground for an energy plan when it was presented to the American people at the end of April 1977, 80 percent of Americans found that it proposed unfair remedies for a crisis that was not all that bad, in their view.

Perhaps because he came from a state with considerable coal supplies, Bolling also believed that the White House should have built an energy plan around a coal-export program that he thought would break OPEC's "stranglehold on the energy pricing mechanism." Instead, the administration's plan was predicated on weaning the American people and business away from the use of oil and natural gas through a crude equalization tax supplemented by various conservation measures and alternative energy initiatives. Although he did not object to these proposals in principle, Bolling still believed that the only way to break the back of spiraling OPEC prices would have been to develop more coal production and the infrastructure to get it to market and make it environmentally safe.

In 1981, Bolling announced that he would not seek another term in office. His health was not good, he was an alcoholic, his first wife had died a few years earlier, and he had remarried. After retiring from Congress in 1982, he served as a visiting professor of political science at the University of Missouri at Kansas City and taught politics at Boston College. On April 21, 1991, he suffered a heart attack and died at the age of 74.

Bourne, Peter Geoffrey

(1939–) *special assistant to the president for health issues, director of the Office of Drug Abuse Policy, Carter biographer*

Peter Bourne was special assistant to the president for health issues and director of the Office of Drug Abuse Policy from 1977 to 1978. A physician with a special interest in mental health issues, he had headed Georgia's drug-abuse program during Jimmy Carter's governorship. He was also one of the first persons to urge Carter to run for president. One of the most liberal members of the Carter administration but never one of the president's closest advisers, he was forced to resign under a cloud of controversy as a result of writing a prescription for quaaludes, a powerful sedative, for one of his assistants, who tried to fill the prescription using a fictitious name. News of what Bourne had done embarrassed Carter, who turned what might still have been a back-page news story into a first-page headline by dodging questions at a news conference about other prescriptions Bourne might have written for the president's family. Matters became even more damaging to the administration when Bourne claimed that substance abuse, including the use of cocaine, was prevalent among White House staffers.

Born in Oxford, England, on August 6, 1939, and a naturalized citizen of the United

States, Bourne was the son of a prominent Australian scientist, Geoffrey Bourne, who directed the internationally known Yerkes Primate Research Center at Emory University. While a student at Emory University in the late 1950s, Peter Bourne had become active in the Civil Rights movement. He was one of a small group of white students who joined with African-American students from Morehouse and Spellman Colleges to picket lunch counters in downtown Atlanta.

After obtaining his M.D. from Emory in 1962, Bourne interned in psychiatry and then served in the army, including a tour of duty in Vietnam, where he won several medals including the Bronze Star. After his discharge in 1966, he became active in the antiwar movement and helped to found Vietnam Veterans Against the War. He also attended Stanford University, where he completed a residency in psychiatry and received an M.A. in Anthropology in 1969. Committed to public service, he returned to Atlanta, taught at Emory, and, in 1970, founded and directed the Atlanta South Central Community Mental Health Center, whose clientele was mainly alcoholics and drug abusers. His work in mental health caught the attention of Jimmy Carter, who was preparing to run a second time for governor and asked Bourne to advise him on health policy.

Following Carter's election in 1970, the new governor appointed Bourne as director of Georgia's Narcotic Treatment Program with responsibility for setting up a statewide drug-treatment program. In this capacity, he worked closely with ROSALYNN CARTER, who made mental health and drug-abuse problems her primary interest. In 1972, Bourne joined with a small group of other Georgians close to the governor, including HAMILTON JORDAN, GERALD RAFSHOON, and Atlanta lawyer Landon Butler in urging the governor to seek the Democratic nomination for president in 1976.

Bourne's success in establishing methadone treatment programs throughout Georgia had, in the meantime, attracted national attention. Oddly enough, given his liberal credentials and activity in Democratic politics (he was an alternate to the Democratic Convention in 1972), he was extended an offer, which he accepted, to serve in RICHARD NIXON's administration as assistant director of the White House's newly established Special Action Office for Drug Abuse. Bourne became the proverbial fox in the chicken coop because even as he worked for the Nixon White House, he helped plan Carter's anticipated run for the presidency, returning to Atlanta on weekends to map out campaign strategy.

In 1974, Bourne left the White House and took a consultancy position with the Drug Abuse Council in Washington. When Carter announced his candidacy for president in December 1974, he asked Bourne to serve as the campaign's deputy manager. Over the next two years, Bourne devoted most of his time to the campaign, opening up and running its Washington office. In the summer of 1976, however, he was reassigned to lesser duties by Hamilton Jordan, the national campaign manager. Furthermore, despite his early support for Carter and his close personal ties with the candidate and his wife, Bourne was never to become the prominent figure in the Carter White House that he had seemed destined to be.

The reasons for Bourne's declining influence within Carter's inner circle of Georgians are still not entirely clear, but certain facts stand out and others can be inferred. In the first place, the prominent play that Bourne received in the press annoyed others of the Georgian cadre, including the two persons closest to Carter, Hamilton Jordan and JODY POWELL. In particular, they resented a story in the *Washington Post* of June 21, 1976, that portrayed Bourne as the candidate's closest friend and the one most responsible for persuading him to run for president. Bourne's mild temperament, style of dress (striped ties and tweed coats), and British accent and mannerisms also set him apart from the other Georgians. If the predicate of the Carter campaign was an outsider running against the Washington establishment, Bourne was increasingly identified by those within the Carter camp as part of that establishment, given the cachet of Georgetown acquaintances with whom he sometimes mingled. Finally, Bourne's political views seemed too liberal for those close to Carter. An article he wrote in 1974 in which he referred to cocaine as an "exciting, euphoria-producing recreational drug which posed only a minimal health hazard" placed him very much to the political left of those Georgians closest to Carter. There was, in other words, a political and cultural gap within Carter's ranks.

By summer 1976, stories from unidentified sources critical of Bourne's performance in the campaign began to appear in the media. Within a month of the appearance of these stories, he was ousted as Carter's representative in Washington, D.C. Following Carter's victory in November, he was appointed special assistant to the president on health issues and drug abuse and director of the Office of Drug Abuse Policy (ODAP), but he was relegated to a basement office in the White House with only a small staff. In summer 1977, the ODAP was phased out, even though Bourne had already hired several people, including the police chief of Berkeley, California, to work for the office. Bourne was mortified by the decision to eliminate the ODAP. "[T]he announcement of its abolition," he wrote the president in July, "has been interpreted in the press and in agencies as a setback for me that leaves me essentially impotent in the White House structure."

Bourne's diminished status within the administration was evident in other ways as well. He regularly wrote memorandums to the president, for example, recommending an expanded effort by the United States in the areas of world hunger and malnutrition and mental illness, but he had little success in getting more funding for these programs. And while he also supported vigorously the administration's plan for national health insurance (NHI), his was a marginal role at best in the titanic conflict over NHI between President Carter, Secretary of Health, Education and Welfare JOSEPH CALIFANO, and Senator EDWARD KENNEDY (D-Mass.).

Bourne also stirred public controversy. His acknowledgement before a Senate Committee in May 1977 that he had smoked marijuana while serving in Vietnam caused the White House considerable public flack. Although the administration did not consider the use of marijuana a significant health problem, and President Carter had supported the decriminalization of marijuana during the campaign, the fact that the nation's drug czar should admit to having used a drug, however benign, seemed to many Americans outrageous. Making matters worse for Bourne among the senior White House staff was his close association with the National Organization for the Reform of Marijuana Laws (NORML), a liberal organization that advocated the nationwide decriminalization of the use of marijuana. NORML's effort to get the president's son, Chip Carter, to testify before a committee of the New Mexico state legislature in support of decriminalization infuriated even the first lady.

Bourne had alienated a number of senior White House officials, therefore, even before his 1978 indiscretion in writing a prescription for quaaludes for an assistant using a false name. Furthermore, the syndicated columnist JACK ANDERSON published a story claiming that at a party given by NORML in December 1977, Bourne had smoked marijuana and snorted cocaine. According to Bourne, he had told the director of NORML, Keith Stroup, at an earlier event that he could not be in charge

of drug policy and have people visibly breaking the law in his presence. As soon as he realized that drug use was taking place at the December party, he left. But Anderson claimed that he had witnesses who could support his story of what had actually taken place at the December party. Pressure grew on Capitol Hill and in the White House for Bourne to resign in order to save the administration further embarrassment. It increased even more after Bourne indiscreetly told the *New York Times* about the widespread use of drugs among the White House staff.

The mounting pressure for Bourne's resignation happened about the same time that the White House was trying to deal with the problem of growing inflation. President Carter also had to cope with another serious political problem involving the country's controversial ambassador to the United Nations, ANDREW YOUNG. Remembering the damage that had been done to his administration by his unsuccessful effort a year earlier to save his close friend BERT LANCE, director of the Office of Management and Budget, the president felt he could not risk another national uproar by trying to save Bourne's job for him. So when Bourne offered his resignation, Carter accepted it immediately.

Bourne bore no grudge against Carter and continued to support him both privately and publicly. His remarks to the *New York Times*, however, caused considerable harm to the administration, especially to Hamilton Jordan, who was identified in the media as one of those allegedly using drugs.

Following his resignation from the White House, Bourne accepted a position as assistant secretary-general of the United Nations Development Program (1979), where he established and ran a program to improve the quality of drinking water worldwide and launched another highly successful program to eradicate the disease caused by the guinea worm. In 1981, he left the United Nations to enter the private sector, founding his own firm to promote the establishment of private enterprise in developing countries.

Bourne has also been an adviser to Co
gressman (now Governor) Bill Richardsor
New Mexico on Third World issues and
served on numerous nonprofit boards m
dealing with health matters in devel
countries. In addition, he has been vice
cellor of St. George's University (1998
and has held numerous other academ
tions at Stanford, Emory, Harvard,
University of California at San Die
the author of a number of books ar
including biographies of Fidel Ca
and Jimmy Carter (1996), both of
been well-received by book reviev
torians. He divides his time betw
ton, D.C., and Tregaron, Wales.

Brademas, John W.

(1927–) member of the Hous
Representatives, majority whi

A liberal Democrat from In
mas was House majority
Carter presidency. Harv
Rhodes scholar, he was ar
also well-versed in con
having survived a bitte
eral wing of the Demo
liberals in the Hous
increasingly alienate
istration because of
political ineptness
vative fiscal polici
views cost him re
landslide of that
The son of a
was born in Mi
Bend, on Mar
in the navy (1

University, where he graduated magna cum laude (B.A., 1949) and won a Rhodes Scholarship to Oxford University. After earning a doctoral degree in social studies from Oxford (Phil.D., 1954) he began his political career, running unsuccessfully for Congress in 1954 and 1956 and working as an assistant to Democratic presidential candidate Adlai Stevenson, before being elected to the U.S. House of Representatives in 1958.

From the time he entered Congress, Brademas took a special interest in education and the arts. As a member of the House for nearly 20 years, he helped write much of the federal
egislation in support of higher education and
lmost all the legislation that promoted librar-
es, museums, the arts, and the humanities. He
as one of the original cosponsors of the leg-
ation creating the National Endowment for
e Arts (NEA) and the National Endowment
the Humanities (NEH), and for 10 years
chaired the committee that had jurisdiction
r both. With varying success, he fought
rts to limit the funding of both institutions.
lso coauthored both the Arts and Artifacts
mnity Act, which covered the insurance
of transporting art from other countries
United States, and the Museum Services
hich provided modest grants to museums,
nd botanical gardens, both in 1975.

ademas also cosponsored the Elemen-
d Secondary School Act of 1965, which
doubled the amount of federal assis-
education, and he led the floor fight
Head Start program (launched 1965).
the Nixon-Ford years, he sponsored
ronmental Education Act of 1970 and
Abuse Education Act of 1970, and
e architect of the National Institute
tion in 1972. A 1975 poll of 4,000
d university presidents and others
n higher education named Brade-
the four most influential leaders of
cation in the United States.

On Capitol Hill, Brademas was one of the leaders of the movement, begun in the 1960s and continuing into the 1970s, to reform the rules of the House of Representatives by challenging the seniority system that gave control of the chamber's most important committees to southern conservatives and limited opportunities for newly elected members of the House. With the election of more liberal Democrats to the House in the 1960s and 1970s—culminating in 1974 with the election of a large group of mostly young, liberal, and independent-minded Democrats, a number of whom had never held political office before—the reformers were able to change the House rules in ways that limited the seniority system and opened leadership positions to the more recently elected lawmakers.

The reform movement was most closely associated with Congressman PHILLIP BURTON (D-Calif.), a brilliant political strategist. But Burton's abrasive and often garish behavior alienated other liberal reformers, including the more intellectual Brademas and Majority Leader TIP O'NEILL (Mass.). Since 1973, Brademas had been serving under O'Neill as a deputy whip. The climax of the struggle among House Democrats came in December 1976 when O'Neill was elected Speaker of the House and Burton was defeated by JIM WRIGHT of Texas (quietly backed by the new Speaker) to replace O'Neill as the new majority leader. O'Neill then named Brademas to majority whip, the third top leadership position among House Democrats.

At the beginning of the Carter administration, the majority whip generally acted in tandem with the House Speaker, which meant that he tried to support the White House. At the end of the first session of Congress in 1977, Brademas acknowledged that while the president had made mistakes in his dealings with lawmakers, relations between the White

House and Capitol Hill were improving. With respect to meetings between the president and congressional leaders, he remarked that there had been "a gradual metamorphosis. At first there was a reserve; everyone was taking each other's measure. Now these meetings are very pointed, very frank. [The president] is learning that the left hand washes the right hand and they both wash the face."

Yet Brademas never had the same personal relationship with the president as the House Speaker, and he was more of an ideologue than O'Neill. As a result, he became more outspoken in his opposition to the president as his liberal views clashed with the administration's more conservative perspective. Even at the beginning of the administration, when he was on his best terms with the White House, he became annoyed when it let languish a list of names he had submitted soon after the election for appointment to the new Institute for Museum Service, created under legislation he had sponsored to make grants to help museums defray operation costs.

Similarly, Brademas became angry when the White House failed to consult him about the reorganization of the Rehabilitation Services Administration in the Department of the Health, Education and Welfare (HEW), which affected many of the programs he monitored. "If the reorganization is good enough," he argued with his friend, HEW secretary JOSEPH CALIFANO, "you should be able to convince us in advance, consult in advance." Later he was critical of HEW for not instituting regulations for compliance with Section 504 of the Rehabilitation Act of 1973, which prohibited discrimination against the disabled, including assuring accessibility or accommodation in such public places as schools, libraries, hospitals, and museums. Developing appropriate guidelines proved to be a major undertaking for HEW.

One issue that came increasingly to bother the Indiana congressman was the president's leadership style. He felt Carter resorted too much to threats and bombast with lawmakers. In Brademas's opinion, the president would have been more successful if he had relied on the force of his arguments to gain congressional majorities for his programs. When Brademas learned that Senate majority leader ROBERT BYRD (W.Va.) had suggested the same thing to Carter, he quipped, "If Carter does that, he will truly have been born again politically."

Most of the congressman's differences with the administration, however, were over budget and spending priorities, a point that Carter acknowledged in his diary. "The congressional leadership breakfast was devoted almost entirely to expressions on the part of the liberal members, Tip O'Neill, Shirley Chisholm [of New York] and John Brademas that we were neglecting social programs in order to try to balance the budget in four years," the president remarked on May 3, 1977. As a liberal Democrat, Brademas was concerned with protecting entitlement programs from what he considered excessive budget cuts. This did not mean that he was indifferent to budget concerns. He joined other Democratic leaders, for example, in opposing efforts to increase veterans' benefits by nearly $1 billion. He also spoke out against a national program of health insurance because he believed no one wanted "a program of medical insurance that will run into the same cost problem as Medicare and Medicaid." Similarly, he fought to keep big spenders in his party from increasing the size of the president's $532 billion budget for 1980.

Brademas believed, however, that government had a responsibility to provide basic social needs for its citizens and that the welfare of Americans could not be sacrificed on the altar of budget cuts and a balanced budget. In

1978, therefore, he warned the White House that if it did not provide a tuition tax credit or some other break for middle-class Americans faced with college tuition costs, Congress would take the initiative in doing so. This led the administration to increase the amount a family could earn and still remain eligible for student grants and loans. Like other Democratic leaders, Brademas also lashed out at a proposal the administration floated in 1979 to cut social security benefits. "They're going to run into a buzzsaw if an effort is made to eliminate major benefits in the social security system," he remarked with reference to the White House.

Brademas was also critical of Carter's foreign policy. As the son of a Greek immigrant with strong ties to Greece, he objected vigorously when the White House made the decision in the summer of 1978 to end the 42-month arms embargo on Turkey, imposed when Turkish forces invaded the island of Cyprus. Earlier he had agreed to a one-year suspension of the embargo if Turkey would take positive steps to resolve the Cyprus stalemate. But the president rejected the proposal on the grounds that it would offend Turkey. If the president had put as much effort into his tax plan as he had into lifting the Turkish embargo, the Indiana congressman responded, his tax plan might have passed. In 1979, Brademas was also instrumental in blocking House approval of a $50 million military grant to Turkey, even though Secretary of State CYRUS VANCE had referred to Turkey as "the southeastern anchor of the American security system."

The White House's response to Soviet and Cuban activities in Angola and the Horn of Africa involving Cuban forces and Cuban-trained exiles also drew Brademas's attention. The president's harsh rhetoric in reaction to developments in Africa, he suggested in 1978, "might be an attempt to appear decisive in order to reverse his decline in the polls."

One issue that was only tangentially related to foreign policy but tinged Brademas was a scandal dubbed "Koreagate" by the media. Koreagate involved influence peddling by a South Korean rice broker, Tongsun Park, who entertained lavishly and contributed generously to a group of lawmakers, including Brademas and House Speaker O'Neill. Besides being a businessman, Park had also been a clandestine agent of the Korean government. Brademas acknowledged receiving $4,650 in campaign contributions from Park. But while the House Ethics Committee eventually took disciplinary action against four Democratic lawmakers because of their dealings with Park, in July 1978 it absolved Brademas, O'Neill, and seven other congressmen of ethical misconduct.

In 1980, the Indiana congressman was one of a group of Democratic lawmakers who refused to endorse President Carter's campaign for a second term in office. At a time when Carter was engaged in a battle for the Democratic nomination against EDWARD KENNEDY (Mass.), Brademas merely announced that he would support the Democratic nominee for president. Of more immediate concern to Brademas than presidential politics was his own campaign for reelection to Congress. Targeted by the Republican Party and vulnerable because of his liberal voting record at a time when the country was becoming more conservative, Brademas was one of a score of liberal Democrats who lost in the Republican landslide in November. His Republican opponent, John Hiler, a businessman, successfully blamed Brademas and the Democratic-controlled Congress for the high unemployment rate in a district that included one county where unemployment was nearly 16 percent.

After serving for 22 years in Congress, Brademas began a new career as president of New York University (NYU), a position in which he served from 1981 to 2002. During that time, he turned a largely regional commuter school into one of the nation's most respected research universities with 46,000 students. He also increased its endowment by over $1 billion.

Brademas has served as chairman of the Federal Reserve Bank of New York, director of the Rockefeller Foundation, and member of various corporate boards. In 1994, President Bill Clinton appointed him chairman of the President's Committee on the Arts and the Humanities. As chairman, he oversaw the development of a report, "Creative America," which set forth more than 50 recommendations to the president about how to reinvigorate the arts in the United States. The report called for increasing the per capita amount Americans pay in taxes in support of the arts from 36 cents to about $2.

President emeritus of NYU since 2002, Brademas remains active as one of the nation's leading educational figures promoting the arts and the humanities.

Brennan, William Joseph, Jr.

(1906–1997) *associate justice, U.S. Supreme Court*

At the dedication of the Brennan Center for Justice at New York University School of Law in 1995, Abner J. Mikva, a former federal appeals court judge, who was then serving as the White House counsel, stated that he was coining a new word, *Brennanist*, which he defined as "one who influences his colleagues beyond measure." In his 34 years as a Supreme Court justice, which spanned eight presidential administrations and encompassed a swing in judicial philosophy on the Court from highly liberal to conservative, William J. Brennan, Jr., developed a reputation as one of the most influential and effective justices in U.S. history. He became known for his defense of individual rights and the dignity of the individual and for his many landmark decisions that brought about sweeping social change, assured a voice for the underrepresented in America, and shifted the nation's political power from rural to urban regions. During the Carter administration, he and Justice THURGOOD MARSHALL were the liberal activist wing of the Court, voting alike in almost all cases before them.

Brennan was born in Newark, New Jersey, on April 25, 1906, the second of eight children. His immigrant father was a brewery worker who became involved in union and local politics and eventually became New Jersey's commissioner of public safety. A Roman Catholic, Brennan attended parochial and public schools and graduated from the University of Pennsylvania's Wharton School of Finance magna cum laude (B.S., 1928) and, later, Harvard Law School (LL.B., 1931), where he finished in the top 10 percent of his class. Following his graduation, he took a position with one of New Jersey's top law firms, Pitney, Hardin, and Skinner, specializing in labor law. Curiously enough considering his background and future decisions on the Supreme Court, he defended mostly management in labor cases.

During World War II, Brennan served in the army, handling labor disputes on the staff of the undersecretary of war. After the war, he returned to his law firm, where he developed a thriving practice; the firm's name was eventually changed to Pitney, Hardin, and Brennan. In 1949, however, he gave up a lucrative income to accept a position as a superior court judge. A year later, he became an appellate judge for the superior court, and in 1952 he was named to the state Supreme Court, where he became nationally known for instituting various procedural reforms to reduce unfair delays. The reforms made the New Jersey judicial system one of the nation's most progressive. Brennan also became a leader in a national movement to modernize the courts.

In 1956, a presidential election year, a seat opened on the U.S. Supreme Court as a result of the retirement of Justice Sherman Minton.

A speech Brennan had given in May at the Justice Department on court congestion and delay had brought him to the attention of President Eisenhower, who was seeking to fill the Court vacancy with a Roman Catholic from the Northeast. He therefore nominated Brennan—the first time that a Republican president had appointed a Democrat to the Supreme Court in nearly 25 years. The only senator to vote against his confirmation was Joseph McCarthy of Wisconsin. Later Eisenhower lamented that the two greatest mistakes of his presidency were his appointments of Earl Warren and William Brennan to the Court.

Brennan became Chief Justice Warren's closest colleague and, many Court observers believed, the intellectual driving force behind the famously liberal Warren Court of the 1950s and 1960s. Unassuming and accommodating, he sought compromise and crafted language to meet the objections of his colleagues without sacrificing the basic legal and constitutional principles on which he based his decisions. As a result, he was able, in 13 years of service on the Court before Warren's retirement in 1968, to fashion many of its landmark decisions in First Amendment and privacy cases and in cases involving the rights of criminals, minorities, and the poor.

In *New York v. Sullivan* (1964), Brennan extended the First Amendment freedom of the press with his majority opinion that the press could not be held liable for false statements except when they were made intentionally and published in reckless disregard of the truth. In *Fay v. Noia* (1963), he wrote the majority opinion that state preclusion of court review in criminal cases did not preclude federal court review of the conviction in habeas corpus proceedings. In *Malloy v. Hogan* (1964), he again wrote the majority opinion in a 5-4 decision stating that the Fourteenth Amendment protected a state witness's Fifth Amendment guarantee against self-incrimination in a criminal proceeding. In *Griswold v. Connecticut* (1965), he joined with the majority in protecting the right of marital privacy against state restrictions on a couple's ability to be counseled on the use of contraceptives. In the landmark case *Miranda v. Arizona* (1966), he joined once more with the majority in a 5-4 decision holding that prosecutors could not interrogate individuals without notifying them of their right to counsel and their protection against self-incrimination. And in *Katzenbach v. Morgan* (1966), he wrote the majority opinion upholding a section of the 1965 Voting Rights Act guaranteeing the right to vote to non-English-speaking Puerto Ricans.

Brennan also was the driving force behind legislative reapportionment predicated on the principle of one person, one vote. The landmark case in this regard was *Baker v. Carr* (1962), in which he wrote the majority opinion holding that federal courts could decide cases involving legislative apportionment. Chief Justice Warren later called the case "the most important ... that we decided in my time." The majority opinion began a lengthy process of reapportionment of state legislative and congressional districts that over time shifted political power from rural to urban areas and, following the cases of *Lucas v. Forty-Fourth General Assembly of Colorado* (1964) and *Reynolds v. Sims* (1964), extended that principle to include state senates as well as houses.

Although one of the most devout members of the Court, Brennan also became one of the strongest proponents of the doctrine of separation of church and state. In what he regarded as perhaps his most difficult cases, *Abington Township v. Schempp* and *Murray v. Curlett*, which were decided together in 1963, he wrote a 70-page concurring opinion striking down state laws requiring public-school students to participate in classroom religious exercises, including bible reading and recitation of the Lord's Prayer.

As the Supreme Court became increasingly more conservative following the resignation of Chief Justice Earl Warren in 1968 and President RICHARD NIXON's appointment the following year of WARREN BURGER to replace him, Brennan found himself increasingly in the minority. In most of the Court's terms after 1970, he ranked second only to Justice William O. Douglas in the number of dissents he wrote. Until Douglas's retirement in 1975, he was identified with Brennan and Thurgood Marshall as part of the liberal activist wing of the Court that protested majority rulings in criminal cases, the death penalty, reapportionment, racial discrimination, and free expression.

Yet Brennan was still able to put together majorities and craft decisions on important cases. In several decisions, he opened the courthouse doors to parties that had been excluded in the past. In *Bivens v. Six Unknown Named Agents* (1971), for example, individuals were given the right, for the first time, to sue government officials directly under the Constitution. And in *Goldberg v. Kelly* (1970), which Brennan appeared to cherish above all others, he wrote for the majority in a 7-2 decision that a state's termination of public aid, without affording the beneficiary a hearing prior to termination, violated the due-process clause of the Fourteenth Amendment. The opinion proved to be a watershed for other due-process cases that protected ordinary citizens against the arbitrary and capricious use of governmental power.

Brennan also continued to extend private rights. His opinion in *Eisenstadt v. Baird* (1972) expanded upon *Griswold v. Connecticut* by striking down a Massachusetts law making it a felony to distribute contraceptives to unmarried men or women. "If the right of privacy means anything," he wrote for the majority, "it is the right of the individual, married or single, to be free from unwarranted governmental intrusion into matters so fundamentally affecting a person as the decision to whether to bear or beget a child." In the landmark case *Roe v. Wade* (1973), he joined with the majority in extending this decision to include the right of women to legalized abortions.

Brennan also took a broad view of the equal-protection clause and voted to overturn laws that discriminated against the poor, illegal aliens, and illegitimate children. In *United States Department of Agriculture v. Moreno* (1973), he was able to attract enough other justices to uphold a challenge to a provision of the Food Stamp Act of 1971 denying food stamps to a household containing nonfamily members as a way of avoiding fraud. "[T]he denial of federal food assistance to *all* otherwise eligible households containing unrelated members," he wrote for the majority, "[does not constitute] a rational effort to deal with [potential fraud]." In *Labine v. Vincent* (1971), however, he was in the minority in a case in which the Court rejected a challenge to a Louisiana statute denying illegitimate children the right to inherit where there was no will. Since a marriage primarily signified "a relationship between husband and wife, not between parent and child," he argued unsuccessfully, "the rights of illegitimate and legitimate children should be equal."

In First Amendment cases, Brennan continued to vote in favor of individual rights, holding patronage of public employees to be a violation of their rights of freedom of belief and association, and further expanding the protection of the press from libel judgments. In *New York Times Co. v. United States* (1970, the famous Pentagon Papers case), the question before the Court was whether the Nixon administration's efforts to prevent publication of what it termed "classified information" violated the First Amendment. Concurring with the majority, Brennan said it did, reasoning that since publication would not imperil the safety of American forces, prior restraint was unjustified.

A lifelong opponent of the death penalty, Brennan had little luck in persuading the Court that it violated the Eighth Amendment prohibition against cruel and unusual punishment. In *Witherspoon v. Illinois* (1968), the Court held that dismissal of potential jurors because of their "conscientious scruples" against the death penalty violated the Sixth Amendment's guarantee of an "impartial jury" and the Fourteenth Amendment's guarantee of due process. In *Furman v. Georgia* (1972), opponents of the death penalty seemed to win an even greater victory when the Court struck down a death-penalty verdict because of what it viewed as the capricious and discriminatory manner in which the verdict had been applied. Only Brennan and Marshall, however, believed the death penalty was unconstitutional in all cases. Following the decision, states rewrote their procedures in capital cases to provide for separate trials for those found guilty of a capital crime to determine whether they should be put to death. In a series of fives cases decided in 1976—*Gregg v. Georgia*, *Jurek v. Texas*, *Robert v. Louisiana*, *Profitt v. Florida*, and *Woodson v. North Carolina*—the Court approved the constitutionality of these statutes.

The most important—and divisive—case before the Court during Jimmy Carter's administration was *Regents of the University of California v. Bakke* (1978), involving a special admissions program for minorities at the University of California–Davis's School of Medicine that included racial quotas. In its ruling on *Bakke*, the Court upheld the principle of affirmative action (race could be one of several factors in making decisions in admissions cases) while rejecting the use of quotas. There was, however, no single majority opinion. Four of the justices, including Brennan, who wrote the opinion for his group, believed that the Davis plan was constitutional in every respect and that the California Supreme Court opinion should be reversed in its entirety. The majority of the Court found racial quotas unconstitutional. The question, then, was whether race could be used as one of several factors in making decisions on admissions. Eight of the justices were evenly divided on the issue. The question was how Justice LEWIS POWELL, who had not made clear his view on the use of race as part of an affirmative-action program, would vote. Brennan invited him to write an opinion striking down racial quotas while upholding the principle of affirmative action. Powell immediately accepted Brennan's suggestion, and his opinion became the decisive one validating the inclusion of race as one of several factors in affirmative-action programs. In a subsequent case, *United Steelworkers of America v. Weber* (1979), Brennan was even able to persuade the Court to sanction an affirmative-action program at Kaiser Steel to increase the number of the company's black skilled workers by setting aside 50 percent of the places in a training program for black workers.

In other cases decided during the Carter presidency, Brennan continued to be consistent with earlier cases involving equal protection, due process, and First Amendment rights. He dissented, for example, in a case in which the Court stated that notice and hearings were not constitutionally required before imposition of corporal punishment in public schools (*Ingraham v. Wright*, 1977); voted with the majority in a 5-4 decision striking down an Illinois law allowing legitimate children to inherit by intestate (without a will) succession from either their mothers or fathers but allowed illegitimate children to inherit by intestate succession only from their mothers (*Trimble v. Gordon*, 1977); joined in a dissenting opinion written by Marshall that would have struck down a New York law requiring state police to be U.S. citizens (*Foley v. Connelie*, 1978); and voted in the minority in two cases (*Houchins v. KQED*, 1978, and *Gannett Co. v. DePasquale*, 1979) to uphold the constitutional right of access to information by the press. In an important case involving foreign policy (*Goldwater v. Carter*, 1979), Brennan dissented from a majority opinion made without oral argument upholding President Carter's right to abrogate a mutual-defense treaty with Taiwan without first obtaining the consent of Congress. Brennan wanted to hear the case.

Brennan remained an unwavering force on the Court until he was forced to retire on July 20, 1990, after suffering a stroke at the age of 84. In one of his last major decisions (*Texas v. Johnson*, 1989), he found that a state statute criminalizing the desecration of religious objects was in violation of freedom of speech after the law was applied against an individual who had burned the American flag. He recognized the "special place reserved for the flag in this Nation," but, he went on, "we do not consecrate the flag by punishing its desecration, for in doing so we dilute the freedom that this cherished emblem represents."

In 1987, Brennan described his vision of the Constitution, especially the due-process clause of the Fourteenth Amendment. The Constitution, he said, existed to guarantee "the essential dignity and worth of each individual." He remained consistent in this belief, notwithstanding the Court's growing conservatism. After his retirement in 1990, only one liberal activist from the Warren Court, Justice Marshall, remained on the bench, and he retired the next year, in part because he had lost his closest colleague on the Court.

Following growing ill health, Brennan died on July 24, 1997, in Arlington, Virginia, at the age of 91.

Brezhnev, Leonid Ilyich
(1906–1982) *leader of the Soviet Union*

General secretary of the Communist Party during the Carter presidency, Leonid Ilyich Brezhnev led the Soviet Union longer than any man except Joseph Stalin. Although not an autocrat in the manner of Stalin, he ruled with a heavy hand at home and was intolerant of political liberalization in Eastern Europe. Responsible for a significant improvement in the standard of living of the Soviet people, he allowed the Soviet economy to deteriorate badly in the last years of his rule. He was also responsible for a massive Soviet military buildup in order to put the Soviet Union on strategic parity with the United States. Even as he pursued an adventurous policy in places like Africa and the Middle East, he sought a policy of détente with the West and looked to lessen the chances of a nuclear war through arms agreements with the United States. Although in declining health, he joined President Carter in Vienna on June 16, 1979, to sign the Second Strategic Arms Limitation Talks treaty (SALT II) placing caps on various types of nuclear missile heads. Just a few months later, however, Soviet forces invaded Afghanistan, leading to the most serious crisis in Soviet-American relations since President RICHARD NIXON had placed American military forces on a high state of alert in the aftermath of the Yom Kippur War of 1973.

The son of a Soviet factory worker, Brezhnev was born on December 19, 1906, in Kamenskoye (later renamed Dneprodzerzhinsk), Ukraine. In 1921, his family moved to Kursk, and the following year he took a job as a factory worker. Over the next 17 years, Brezhnev went from obscure work in a factory to membership in the Communist Party (1931), a graduate degree in metallurgical engineering from the Metallurgical Institute in Dneprodzerzhinsk (1935), and his appointment as party secretary in Dneproderzhinsk responsible for the city's defense industries.

Brezhnev was able to further his career during World War II. Joseph Stalin's purge of 1937–39 opened opportunities for middle- and senior-level party members. During the war, Brezhnev became the commissar (chief) of the Political Department of the Eigheenth Army, which in 1943 was merged into the Ukranian Front. The senior political commissar of the front was Nikita Khrushchev, who became Brezhnev's patron. By the time the war was over, Brezhnev was political commissar of the 4th Ukrainian Front with the rank of major general. The massive destruction inflicted on the Soviet Union as a result of the conflict made a lasting impression on him.

After the war, Brezhnev continued to rise within the ranks of the Communist Party. At the time of Stalin's death in 1953, he was working under Stalin in the powerful Secretariat of the Central Committee of the Communist Party. Because of his association with Stalin, his star fell briefly following the dictator's death, and he was assigned to lesser responsibilities away from Moscow. But as Khrushchev consolidated his power as the new leader of the Kremlin, he brought his protégé back to Moscow to serve again in the Secretariat. With Khrushchev's support, Brezhnev rose to become second secretary of the Central Committee in 1959. The next year, he was chosen as chairman of the Presidium, more an honorary office than one with power, but nevertheless a prestigious position, that allowed him to travel abroad, where he acquired a taste for fine clothes and expensive western automobiles.

Brezhnev remained steadfastly loyal to Khrushchev as he eliminated still-strong Stalinist elements struggling for control of the party. When, however, it became apparent by 1964 that Khrushchev was acting erratically and that his agricultural policy was a disaster, Brezhnev changed sides and allied himself with dissidents in the Kremlin. In October that year, they were able to remove Khrushchev from office while he was on a holiday in the Crimea. After a short time during which he shared power with Alexi Kosygin as party first secretary, Brezhnev became the undisputed leader of the Soviet Union. Although he did not have the power that Stalin and Khrushchev were able to exercise, adroit political moves enabled him to strengthen his control over the ruling Politburo. In 1966, he took the title of general secretary of the Communist Party. In 1977, he assumed the added title of state president, becoming the first person to hold both titles.

In 1968, Brezhnev ordered Soviet troops to invade Czechoslovakia in response to the liberalization of the Czech government under Alexander Dubček and enunciated the so-called Brezhnev Doctrine, proclaiming the right of the Soviet Union to intervene in the domestic affairs of any Soviet bloc nation if communist rule was at risk. He also cracked down on Soviet dissidents, restoring much of the power of the notorious KGB.

At the same time, Brezhnev favored closer relations with the West. He became an ambassador of détente, meeting in 1970 with West Germany chancellor Willy Brandt and French president Charles de Gaulle. In 1972, he invited President RICHARD NIXON to visit Moscow, where they signed the SALT I agreement establishing parity in nuclear weapons between the two superpowers. In 1974, he met with President GERALD FORD at Vladivostok, where they agreed that at the next round of SALT negotiations, each side would be allowed the same number of missile launchers—2,400 each—with a sublimit of 1,320 for missiles with multiple independently targeted reentry vehicles (MIRVs). At Helsinki in 1975, Brezhnev and Ford met again at the 35-nation Helsinki Conference on Security and Cooperation in Europe. Along with other world leaders, they signed the Helsinki agreements accepting the postwar boundaries of eastern and central Europe in exchange for a Soviet commitment to human rights.

With the Vladivostok and Helsinki agreements, Brezhnev was at the zenith of his power internationally. In essence, the West formally accepted Soviet occupation of its East European satellites in exchange for a vague Soviet commitment to human rights, which it soon breached by arresting a number of Soviet dissidents. At both Vladivostok and Helsinki, Brezhnev had shown himself to be a tough and truculent bargainer who did not take kindly to criticism about the Soviet Union's internal affairs.

This almost assured that he would clash with President Carter. Even before he took office, Carter had attacked Moscow for its violations of human rights. After he entered the White House, he continued his assault, even sending a personal note to the Soviet dissident, Andrei Sakharov, pledging his support for human rights worldwide. Brezhnev was infuriated. In his view, Carter had broken an unwritten agreement between the two powers not to comment on each other's internal affairs.

Furthermore, Carter wanted to negotiate much larger cuts in the nuclear arsenals of the two powers than had been agreed upon by Brezhnev and Ford at Vladivostok. German chancellor HELMUT SCHMIDT tried to warn the White House that someone who continually compromised the Soviet leadership by waging a human rights campaign could hardly hope to persuade the Soviets to go beyond the old agreements reached at Vladivostok. The president's way of thinking remained mysterious to them, and they were distrustful of his intentions.

In fact, when Secretary of State CYRUS VANCE visited Moscow in March 1977 and laid out the administration's proposals for arms reductions, Brezhnev rejected them out-of-hand, especially since the major cutbacks being proposed were in weapons categories in which the Soviets held an edge. Following a meeting with Vance, during which Brezhnev offered no counterproposals, he cancelled the rest of the negotiating sessions scheduled during the secretary of state's visit.

Despite the failure of the first Moscow meeting, both sides were still willing to return to the bargaining table. Brezhnev wanted a formal conclusion to the Vladivostok agreement of 1974, while the United States was under increasing pressure domestically and from its allies to recover some of the ground lost as a result of the March fiasco. By the end of 1978, the negotiations at the arms limitation talks were close to agreement on the broad outlines of a new SALT II accord that would run through 1985. Although months of negotiations followed over such issues as encryption and a definition of new types of Intercontinental Ballistic Missiles (ICBMs), a final agreement was reached in June 1979. It provided for new limits on weapons development while at the same time allowing both sides to develop one new missile system. For millions of television viewers who watched the ceremony, Brezhnev's and Carter's signing of the agreement in Vienna symbolized a new rapprochement between the United States and the Soviet Union.

Such was hardly the case. Various issues, including Soviet support of Cuban troops in the Horn of Africa, disagreements over the issue of Jewish emigration from the Soviet Union, the consequent failure of the United States to ease trade restrictions with the Soviets, Washington's normalization of relations with China, Carter's ongoing human rights campaign, and conflicting interests in the Middle East, especially following the Iranian Revolution of 1979, led to a deterioration in Soviet-American relations. This was exacerbated by the growing influence in the administration of Carter's National Security Advisor, ZBIGNIEW BRZEZINSKI, who advocated a hard-line policy toward the Kremlin, and by the enfeeblement of Brezhnev, whose apparent ill health was visible at the SALT II signing ceremony in Vienna, where he seemed to doze at times and needed assistance in walking.

As the revolution in Iran began to unfold in late 1978, Brezhnev issued a warning against "outside interference, especially military interference" by the United States. About the same time, he began to tighten his hold on Afghanistan, the historic barrier against invasion from the south. The Soviet leader signed a 20-year economic and military treaty with the country's new pro-Soviet government. By fall 1979, the United States was receiving reports of growing Soviet troop movements into Afghanistan.

When, in December, Brezhnev ordered a full-scale invasion of 85,000 Soviet forces into Afghanistan, President Carter interpreted the move as a first step by the Kremlin to take advantage of the chaos in the Middle East resulting from the Iranian revolution. He responded with a series of measures that included postponing Senate consideration of the SALT II agreement, imposing a grain embargo on the Soviets, barring the Soviet Union from access to American high technology, and instituting a boycott of the summer Olympic Games in Moscow. He also issued the so-called Carter Doctrine, warning that any assault on the Persian Gulf by outside forces would be regarded as an attack on the United States' vital interests and would be repelled by any means necessary, including the use of military forces.

In May, Secretary of State EDMUND MUSKIE met in Vienna with Soviet foreign minister Andrei Gromyko in the first high-level contact between the countries since the beginning of the Afghan crisis. But the talks were unproductive. For the remainder of Carter's administration, neither Washington nor Moscow evinced much interest in improving relations between the two countries. The Soviet Union gave no indication that it was preparing to withdraw its troops anytime soon from Afghanistan, and the White House continued to pursue Brzezinski's hard-line policy toward Moscow. In July 1980, President Carter even signed Presidential Directive 59 (PD-59) authorizing the largest arms-procurement program in 30 years.

How much Brezhnev was in control of the Kremlin in the last few years of his life is a matter of speculation, although he appeared to rely more heavily on such aides as Yuri Andropov, Konstantin Chernenko, and Mikhail Gorbachev. During a visit to Bonn in 1982, he was in charge only at the beginning of meetings and thereafter left all discussions to Foreign Secretary Gromyko or other aides.

In March 1982, Brezhnev suffered a stroke; on November 10, he died of a heart attack. The Soviet people learned of his death the next day, Armistice Day. Writing in the *New York Times*, the columnist James Reston commented on the symbolism of the day, remarking that whatever else might be said against Brezhnev, "even when he was drifting into the shadows at the end of his life, he was still muttering vaguely about the importance of avoiding a third world war."

Brown, Harold
(1927–) *secretary of defense*

The first scientist to serve as secretary of defense, Harold Brown was appointed to that position because of President Carter's desire to have someone at the Pentagon with the scientific and technological expertise necessary to bring about significant cost efficiencies in defense spending. As secretary, Brown was responsible for major changes in defense organization and strategic modernization. He also figured prominently in arms-control negotiations even as he emphasized the importance of upgrading U.S. military forces and improving collective security arrangements. When he became defense secretary in 1977, he was generally perceived as a moderate in terms of U.S. relations with the Soviet Union. However, he grew increasingly bothered by his perception of Secretary of State CYRUS VANCE as a person who seemed to consider any decision possibly involving the use of force as inherently a mistake. As a result, Brown often found himself aligned with the more hard-line position of Carter's National Security Advisor, ZBIGNIEW BRZEZINSKI. Together with Brzezinski, he helped draft Presidential Directive 59 (PD 59), an approach to nuclear strategy that emphasized a "countervailing strategy" predicated on responding to intermediate levels of Soviet aggression in place of the prevailing doctrine of assured destruction.

Brown was born in New York City on September 19, 1927. Gifted intellectually, he received his undergraduate degree from Columbia University (B.A., 1945) at the age of 18 and his doctorate in physics (Ph.D., 1949), also at Columbia, at the age of 21. Between 1947 and 1960, Brown held positions at the Stevens Institute of Technology, Columbia University, the E.O. Lawrence Laboratory of the University of California at Berkeley, and its newly formed offshoot, the Lawrence Livermore Radiation Laboratory. In 1960, he was appointed as the new director of the Livermore facility, succeeding the renowned nuclear scientist Edward Teller. While at Livermore, Brown also served as a member of the Air Force Scientific Advisory Board (1957–61) and the President's Scientific Advisory Committee (1958–61), and also as a senior science adviser to the Geneva Conference for the Discontinuance of Nuclear Tests (1958–59).

In 1961, Secretary of Defense Robert McNamara appointed Brown as director of defense research and engineering for the Defense Department. As one of the experts dubbed the "whiz kids" whom McNamara brought with him to the Pentagon, Brown made such an impression on the defense secretary for his work on weapons research and modernization and on intra-service coordination of weapons systems that in 1965 President Lyndon Johnson appointed him secretary of the air force. In 1969, Brown resigned his position to become president of the California Institute of Technology, where he remained until 1977, when he accepted President-elect Carter's offer to join his cabinet as secretary of defense. During this time, he also served as a member of the U.S. delegation to the Strategic Arms Limitation Talks (SALT) that resulted in the signing of the SALT I nuclear limitations treaties in May 1972 and in ongoing negotiations for a more extensive SALT II agreement.

As secretary of defense, Brown maintained his ongoing interests in the Defense Department's peacetime efficiency and in arms control. But he coupled these interests with his conviction that the United States must not appear inferior to the Soviet Union in terms of either strategic nuclear forces or conventional military forces. "Unless it is grossly unequal," he later remarked, "the strategic balance can no longer be used by either side as a substitute for conventional military forces in a regional or global conflict." This required, in his view, maintaining the triad of intercontinental ballistic missiles (ICBMs), submarine-launched ballistic missiles (SLBMs), and strategic bombers. It also required upgrading U.S. military forces and weapons. While he joined President Carter in opposing costly new weapons systems like the B-1 bomber because studies he had ordered raised questions about its cost effectiveness, he recommended upgrading the existing fleet of B-52 bombers and equipping them with air-launched cruise missiles.

Brown also endorsed the development of stealth technology and the MX missile. Meant to give the United States the same capacity to launch a first strike against Soviet ICBMs as the Soviets were believed to possess against the

United States, the MX was also to be the single new missile system permitted under the SALT II agreement. Although President Carter considered development of the MX "a nauseating prospect to confront," Brzezinski and Brown persuaded him that without the MX trade-off, the Senate would never ratify the SALT II agreement.

Given Brown's involvement in the negotiations for the SALT I agreement and in preliminary discussions for a SALT II treaty prior to becoming secretary of defense, it is not surprising that, as secretary, he made arms control an integral part of his national security policy. In discussions within the administration over the posture to adopt with respect to negotiating with the Soviets, he sided more with Zbigniew Brzezinski's hard-line posture toward Moscow than with Cyrus Vance's more conciliatory approach. According to Brzezinski, Brown adopted an even tougher negotiating position than the National Security Advisor because of the secretary's need to placate the Joint Chiefs of Staff. Brzezinski has even maintained that Brown's insistence on an expanded allowable range for America's air-launched cruise missiles was the reason the Soviets broke off talks in Moscow in March 1977 when Secretary of State Vance presented the United States' proposal for a comprehensive SALT agreement, including deeper cuts in its land-based ICBMs.

Once the SALT II agreement was approved in Vienna in June 1979, Brown played a major role in lobbying for its approval by the Senate. In testimony before the Senate Armed Services Committee in July, he pointed to the reduction in Soviet strategic forces the agreement would bring about while pointing at the same time to the United States' enormous advantage in the number of aircraft capable of launching nuclear weapons against the Soviet Union. In addition to aircraft already in a position to launch sorties against the Soviets, he remarked that the United States could, with appropriate warning, "double the number of nuclear capable aircraft forward based in a position to strike the Soviet Union." But he emphasized that the purpose of the SALT agreement was not to give the United States an advantage over the Soviet Union in case of a nuclear war: rather, it was to reduce the likelihood of such an Armageddon by bringing enhanced predictability and stability to the Soviet-U.S. nuclear relationship. He also stated that compliance with the treaty was verifiable despite the loss of monitoring stations in Iran as a result of the Iranian revolution.

Brown remained concerned, however, about the basing system for the MX missile. He was worried that the MX, which was to replace the increasingly vulnerable Minuteman and Trident missiles, would itself remain exposed to Soviet attack if based in hardened silos. Accordingly, he was attracted to the concept of a "racetrack," shuttling the missiles between 4,600 underground "protective shelters" (23 for each of 200 MXs) in Nevada and Utah so that the Soviets would not be able to identify the missiles' locations at any one time. But the costs of such a system and the environmental damage it might cause kept it from being approved. Brown regretted later that he was never able to resolve the MX basing problem.

Integrally related to Brown's involvement with the SALT II agreement and development of the MX missile system was the Pentagon's preparation of PD 59, the presidential directive in which was articulated the strategy of "countervailing" force. In 1974, JAMES SCHLESINGER, who was then was secretary of defense under President GERALD FORD, initiated a review of the United States' strategic policy. Concerned that the Soviet Union was seeking to achieve nuclear weapons superiority, Schlesinger was anxious to develop a strategic nuclear doctrine more flexible than mutual assured destruction (MAD), one that allowed for selective retaliatory options. In the summer of 1977, Brzezinski encouraged the president to issue a directive calling for a comprehensive review of the nation's defense strategy.

In formulating his response to the president's order, Defense Secretary Brown assumed that the Soviets had reached nuclear parity with the United States and that the policy of mutual assured destruction failed to take into account the possibility of intermediate levels of Soviet attacks. Although not ruling out the approach of MAD, he remarked that "such destruction must not be automatic, our only choice, or independent of any enemy's attack. Indeed, it is at least conceivable that the mission of assured destruction would not have to be executed at all in the event that deterrence failed."

On July 25, 1980, President Carter approved PD 59. In explaining the significance of the president's action, the secretary of defense emphasized that the new directive was not so much a new strategic doctrine as a "refinement, a codification of previous explanations of our strategic policy." Nevertheless, PD 59 represented the first public declaration that the United States was moving away from the concept of massive retaliation against urban and industrial targets and toward a more limited one of retaliation against the enemy's highest-value targets, specifically military targets and war-related industries. The United States, the defense secretary made clear, had not replaced a policy of deterrence predicated on MAD, but it had made it more flexible.

Besides confronting broad issues of national security, Brown dealt with a number of other more immediate issues of national concern. He supported the Panama Canal Treaties of 1977 returning the canal to Panama by the year 2000, insisting that the agreements were essential to the security and operations of the waterway. In July 1977, he traveled to Seoul to deliver a personal letter from President Carter to President Park Chung Hee reaffirming the United States' defense commitment to South Korea, notwithstanding Carter's decision to withdraw more than 30,000 troops from the country.

During the war between Somalia and Ethiopia in fall 1977 and spring 1978, Brown sided with Cyrus Vance in opposing Brzezinski's recommendation to send an American carrier fleet to the Indian Ocean as a show of force against further Soviet-Cuban involvement in the Horn of Africa. Brown was concerned that American naval power might lose its credibility in future crises if the dispatch of the fleet had no specific goal other than to show the flag. The defense secretary also gave his approval to the ill-fated effort in April 1980 to rescue the American hostages seized at the American embassy in Iran in November 1979. When it became apparent that the rescue mission was going to fail because of mechanical failures on two of the helicopters essential to the mission, it was Brown who had to recommend to the president that the mission needed to be aborted. The next year, he became the first secretary of defense to visit the People's Republic of China, where he and Beijing officials discussed joint strategy against Soviet aggression in the Middle East.

In assessing Brown's stewardship of the Pentagon, HAMILTON JORDAN and his deputy, Lance Butler, later criticized the defense secretary for being ineffective in explaining the administration's defense policy to the American public. According to Brzezinski, President Carter also grew increasingly annoyed with Brown during his last two years in office because of the secretary's requests for increased defense spending. In terms of his relationship with other members of the administration, Brown could be, at different times, aloof, introspective, argumentative, and overbearing. But his intelligence commanded respect, and both Jordan and Butler acknowledged that they could not imagine the president having had a better person at the Pentagon.

Certainly the president had great respect for Brown and was grateful for his support on such matters as the B-1 bomber. In his memoirs, Carter pointed out that most of the polls in the Washington news media ranked Brown as his best cabinet officer. Carter also wrote that while he never engaged in the ranking game, there were no other members of his cabinet better than Brown. Unlike other cabinet members, Brown's job never appears to have been in jeopardy.

Following his departure from the Pentagon in 1981, Brown taught at the Johns Hopkins University School of International Studies, first as a visiting professor and then as chairman of the John Hopkins Foreign Policy Institute. He also published *Thinking about National Security: Defense and Foreign Policy in a Dangerous World* (1983). He has been affiliated with a number of research organizations and serves on the boards of a number of corporations.

Brown, Jerry

(Edmund Gerald Brown, Jr.)

(1938–) *governor of California; presidential candidate, 1976 and 1980*

Jerry Brown was one of the most unconventional political figures of the 1970s and a late entrant in the 1976 campaign for the Democratic presidential nomination. His success in the late primaries revealed, as did Jimmy Carter's own successful campaign for the presidency, that the American people were looking for a leader who was outside the Washington establishment and seemed to offer them something new and novel. Had Brown entered the race earlier, he might have presented a formidable challenge to Carter for the Democratic nomination. The fact that from 1974 to 1982 he was extremely popular as governor of California even though much of his message was the same as Carter's message to the American people offers insights into how the president might have been more successful as the nation's 39th leader.

Born on April 7, 1938, in San Francisco California, Brown enjoyed a privileged upbringing. He was the only son and namesake of Edmund Gerald Brown, Sr., known as Pat Brown. One of California's most popular politicians, Pat was elected governor in 1958 and easily defeated his Republican opponent, RICHARD NIXON, for reelection in 1962. Jerry Brown, a deeply thoughtful and introspective person, studied for the Catholic priesthood at the Sacred Heart Novitiate for four years (1956–60) before deciding he was not meant to be a priest. Instead, he attended the University of California, Berkeley, graduating with a major in classics (B.A., 1961), and then earned his law degree from Yale Law School (LL.B., 1964). After clerking for a year for a California Supreme Court justice and then working for a top-rated Los Angeles law firm, Tuttle & Taylor, Brown became attracted to public service and politics. In the late 1960s, he organized migrant workers and antiwar groups and was Southern California's vice chairman and treasurer for Senator Eugene McCarthy's 1968 campaign for president. In 1969, he won an elected seat on the Los Angeles Community College District Board of Trustees, and in 1970 he was elected California's secretary of state, the only Democrat to survive a Republican sweep of state offices that year. Although his position was normally one without much political clout, he used it to initiate highly publicized and popular suits against major corporations for violating the state's laws on campaign contributions. He also tightened the state's campaign disclosure laws. In 1974, he ran for governor. Not taken seriously at first by most political observers because of his youth and inexperience, and relying solely on his own political resources, he won an upset victory in the primaries and then the general election in November.

Although a liberal as governor, Brown gained a reputation for austerity and innovation. He also emphasized environmental and educational reform, development of innovative technology, and jobs training for unskilled and unemployed workers. Like Jimmy Carter after he became president, Brown rejected the trappings of his office. He dispensed with elaborate inauguration ceremonies and drove himself in a Plymouth from the state vehicle pool rather than being driven in the traditional chauffeured limousine. He refused even to live in the huge new governor's mansion, preferring instead to live in a modest apartment. He also cancelled a salary increase for himself, and he reduced the salaries of his staff.

At the same time, Brown helped to make California the world leader in solar and wind technologies. He enacted into law the California Coastal Protection Act and pushed successfully for the country's first building and appliance energy standards. He created the highly successful California Conservation Corps (CCC), which trained and provided 50,000 jobs for young men and women; more than 25 percent of the nation's new jobs were created in California in Brown's first two years as governor. Brown increased the number of women and minorities in state government, including the first woman, African American, and Latino on the California Supreme Court. He also pushed through legislation giving farm workers the right to collective bargaining. Even though he expanded the role of state government, he reduced taxes and vetoed what he regarded as large and wasteful spending. "I was a man of great details," he later told *Newsweek.* "I knew the budget better than any governor in the history of the state."

In short, Brown was able to combine traditional liberal programs with conservative fiscal policies and anti-establishment ways. His theme of limited governmental powers and his image of thrift and austerity made him popular with the state's voters, as did his heavy law-and-order stance and the fact that he dated the pop singer Linda Ronstadt. In December 1975, Californians gave him an approval rating of 84 percent, making him one of the most popular politicians in the country.

In 1976, even though it was late to launch a presidential campaign and Jimmy Carter was well on his way to gaining the Democratic presidential nomination, Brown decided to enter a number of the late primaries about the same time that Senator FRANK CHURCH of Idaho made the same decision. Their rationale was similar. Jimmy Carter had momentum, but there were lingering doubts about him, especially among liberal voters. If Senator HUBERT HUMPHREY (Minn.) decided to enter the race, which still seemed a possibility, he could win over labor leaders and party regulars who might otherwise support Carter. The focus of the primaries was moving to the western states where Brown (and Church) could do well. If Carter could be stopped in these states and some of the late primaries in the East and Midwest, like Maryland, New Jersey, Ohio, and Michigan, he would not be able to come to the convention in New York in July with the nomination sewed up. This would open the way for a candidate like Brown to win the nomination on the second or third ballot.

In March, following Carter's defeat in the Massachusetts primary, Brown decided to enter the race. About the same time, Church also decided to run. The first big contest for Brown came in Maryland, where he was able to win the unannounced backing of the state's governor, Marvin Mandel, as well as a number of other local leaders. Brown blitzed the state and became the darling of the media as he explained his frugal lifestyle and long working hours as governor. Again, his message was not all that different from that of the former governor from Georgia: "I'm not going to overpromise or kid anybody, but times are tough and they may just get even tougher still. … I've lived a certain way and I've done that all my life and I don't see any reason why I should change. … I don't see why the governor ought to live any better than the people he represents." On May 18, Brown resoundingly defeated Carter, winning 49 percent of the vote to just 37 percent for Carter. That same night, Congressman MORRIS UDALL (Ariz.) nearly beat Carter in Michigan, gaining 43 percent of the vote to Carter's 44 percent. A week earlier, Church had defeated the Georgia governor in Nebraska. Suddenly Carter seemed stoppable, and Brown's chances had improved mightily.

In subsequent weeks, Brown did extremely well. Even in Oregon, where he had to run as a write-in candidate, he still managed to get 23 percent of the vote while Carter, whose name was on the ballot, got only 28 percent of the vote and the winner, Church, received 35 percent. In Nevada and Rhode Island, Brown won handily, while Church managed additional victories in Idaho and Montana. In every state they had entered against Carter, Brown and Church had beaten him.

What Brown (and Church) had ignored, however, was the fact that delegates were chosen on a basis proportional to the votes that a candidate received, so that even in the states Carter lost, he still continued to pick up delegates. Furthermore, every week of the primary season, he was able to claim at least one victory, including those in the border states of Kentucky, Tennessee, and Arkansas. As his delegate count mounted, political operatives got onto the Carter bandwagon by announcing their support for the former Georgia governor.

As a result, although Brown managed to win impressive victories in New Jersey and California on June 8, often dubbed Super Tuesday, Carter won in Ohio, where Brown was not running, gaining 52 percent of the vote against 21 percent for Udall and only 14 percent for Church. Carter's victory in Ohio assured his nomination in July. Mayor Richard Daley of Chicago announced his support for Carter, and, one by one, other former candidates threw their support behind the front-runner.

Brown still refused to give up. Why he stayed in the race is still an enigma. "One of the things you've got to remember," his campaign manager, Mickey Kantor, remarked, "is that Jerry Brown's great strength is in not being the same, in being different, in not playing the game. We were concerned that if he just dropped out, he'd look like everybody else." Brown did eventually drop out after making a costly national telecast. He endorsed Carter but did not campaign for him in any major way. Instead, he returned to California, and in 1978, he was reelected governor by the largest margin in the state's history.

After his victory in 1978, things began to unravel for Brown. He was called "Governor Moonbeam" by a growing number of critics because of his proposal, which later proved to be visionary, for California to launch its own satellite into orbit to provide emergency communications for the state. In 1980, he decided to pursue the Democratic nomination again, but his campaign was far more quixotic than that of President Carter's only real rival for the nomination, Senator EDWARD KENNEDY (Mass.). Following Carter's victories over Kennedy in the Wisconsin primary and the Kansas caucuses, Brown gave up the race. But his harsh criticism of the president during the campaign was regarded by some Democratic leaders as contributing to RONALD REAGAN's landslide victory over Carter in November. In 1982, Brown decided to run for the U.S. Senate but was badly beaten by the popular Republican mayor of San Diego, Pete Wilson.

Following his defeat, Brown vanished briefly from the U.S. political scene, spending six months in Japan studying Buddhism and then working briefly with Mother Teresa in India before returning to the United States. He practiced law in Los Angeles and, in 1989, became chairman of the state Democratic Party in California. Although he resigned that position in 1991, expressing disgust with the growing influence of money in politics, he ran again for president in 1992. While he was regarded by now as well outside the mainstream of American politics—plagued, some political observers said, by the "weirdo factor"—and not considered a serious contender for the Democratic nomination, he surprised these political pundits by how well he did with limited resources. Refusing to take contributions larger then $100, eschewing paid consultants and speechwriters, depending on appearances on news and talk shows for publicity, and displaying an 800 number to raise funds, he was able to raise more than $2 million in contributions, Running on a platform calling for a complete reform of the tax system, including a flat tax in place of the nation's income tax and a value-added tax, he won primaries in 13 states. He was the only candidate other than Governor Bill Clinton of Arkansas to have enough voter support to continue until the Democratic National Convention, by which time Clinton was assured of the Democratic nomination. Brown gave grudging support to the Clinton campaign, which kept him at arm's length, and he was not offered a position with the new administration after Clinton was elected president.

In 1994, Brown started his own radio talk show, "We the People," in which he interviewed prominent individuals on matters ranging from the environment to philosophy. In 1998, he ran successfully for mayor of Oakland, California, capturing close to two-thirds of the votes in the primary. He proved to be a popular and successful mayor, attracting a number of biotech companies to the city and working to reduce Oakland's infamous crime rate. In 2001, *Newsweek* featured Oakland as one of nine cities in the world that have become important players in the information age.

Never comfortable with traditional liberal views, Brown became a proponent of such measures as charter schools and school vouchers; a downtown development zone exempt from sections of the California Environmental Quality Act, or CEQA review; and "Operation Beat Feet," which allows police officers to confiscate the vehicles of suspected drug peddlers and buyers. In 2002, he was reelected for a second term as mayor. In addition to serving as mayor of Oakland, Brown gives frequent interviews and appears often on television news shows.

Brzezinski, Zbigniew Kazimierz
(1928–) *National Security Advisor*

President Carter chose Zbigniew Brzezinski as his National Security Advisor because he wanted someone in the White House who could think in broad conceptual terms. As such, he sought a person whose skills extended beyond the National Security Advisor's normal functions of gathering, collating, and interpreting national security data for the president's morning briefings. Relishing the opportunity to be the president's principal adviser on matters of national security and foreign policy, Brzezinski took full advantage of the broad flexibility Carter gave him. Not only did this lead to a power struggle between Brzezinski and Secretary of State CYRUS VANCE over who was primarily responsible for foreign policy, but as Brzezinski prevailed over Vance, it resulted in an increasingly confrontational policy with the Soviet Union.

The son of a Polish diplomat, Brzezinski grew up in Canada, where his father had been

National Security Advisor Zbigniew Brzezinski, 1977 *(Jimmy Carter Library)*

posted in 1938. After receiving his B.A. (1949) and M.A. (1950) degrees from McGill University and his Ph.D. in political science from Harvard University (1953), where he specialized in Soviet studies, he taught at Harvard (1953–61). In 1958, he became a U.S. citizen, and in 1961 he moved to New York, where he headed Columbia University's new Institute on Communist Affairs. Besides his academic responsibilities, Brzezinski advised officials in the administrations of John F. Kennedy and Lyndon Johnson and was foreign policy adviser to Vice President HUBERT HUMPHREY during his unsuccessful bid for the White House in 1968. From 1966 to 1968, Brzezinski was also a member of the Policy Planning Council for the Department of State. A strident anticommunist, he was known for his hard-line positions toward the Soviet Union and his advocacy of closer ties to the countries of Eastern Europe.

In 1973, Brzezinski became the first director of the Trilateral Commission, an organization established by the chairman of the Chase Manhattan Bank of New York, DAVID ROCKEFELLER. The commission's purpose was to bring together highly influential figures in government, business, finance, academia, and the media from North America, Western Europe, and Japan in order to promote mutual understanding and closer cooperation among the world's major industrial democracies. Rockefeller had established the Trilateral Commission because he was concerned that the United States was no longer the singular power it had been since the end of World War II. In an increasingly interdependent world, Rockefeller believed new forms of international cooperation were essential to counteract political and economic nationalism. At the time he appointed Brzezinski as its first director, the young academic had already defined the Trilateral Commission's major concerns. In his book *Between Two Ages: America's Role in the Technocratic Era* (1970), Brzezinski argued that the changing nature of the world as a result of new technology and electronics made it imperative for the United States and the other industrially advanced nations of the world to steer change along constructive paths.

One of the original members of the Trilateral Commission was Jimmy Carter, whom Rockefeller and Brzezinski had invited to become a member because of his reputation as a progressive southern leader who, as governor, had opened up trade offices for the state of Georgia in Brussels and Tokyo. Through his involvement in the commission, Carter got to know Brzezinski, and soon after he decided to run for president, he asked him to serve as an adviser on foreign relations. After the election,

Carter appointed Brzezinski as his National Security Advisor. In selecting Brzezinski for this position, the president-elect clearly wanted someone who thought in broad geopolitical terms and could provide him with a comprehensive overview of international developments. He regarded the Columbia University professor as an individual with a penetrating mind——brash and sometimes wrong-headed but always able to grasp and clarify the fundamental interrelationships of global policy. These were particularly important attributes for a president who did not hold the State Department in high regard and intended very much to direct foreign policy from the White House. For his part, Brzezinski was attracted to the position because it allowed him daily contact with a president who, he believed from his contact with him on the Trilateral Commission, would make issues of foreign policy among his highest priorities.

Invariably Brzezinski found himself at odds on a number of issues with Secretary of Sate Cyrus Vance. In dealing with the Soviet Union, for example, Vance preferred quiet diplomacy while Brzezinski, still passionately distrustful of the Soviet Union, favored a more direct and confrontational approach. On the issue of arms control, both men saw an opportunity for the new administration to go beyond the Strategic Arms Limitation Talks (SALT I), agreement of 1972, which was due to expire in 1977, and the Vladivostok interim agreement of 1974, which set limits on both the United States and the Soviet Union of 2,400 nuclear missile launchers with a ceiling of 1,320 for multiple independently targeted warheads (MIRVs). But while both officials favored deep cuts on existing warheads and limits on the development of new missiles, Brzezinski preferred a more comprehensive proposal than Vance, who feared correctly that the Soviets would reject the more comprehensive approach. Furthermore, Brzezinski wanted to link arms control to other security issues, such as normalization of relations with the People's Republic of China (PRC) and the development of a new weapons system (the MX mobile missile). Vance opposed linkages.

On the question of normalizing relations with the PRC, while both Brzezinski and Vance favored the idea in principle, the National Security Advisor took the lead in 1978 in promoting the move as a means of striking a common front against the Soviet Union. He even proposed in the spring to travel to China in order to meet with Chinese leaders to discuss a strategic-military relationship. In contrast, Vance, who had already met with Chinese leaders the previous August, thought the United States needed to develop a more nuanced and detailed position, in consultation with Congress, before moving toward normalization. Vance also objected strongly—and unsuccessfully—to the president about Brzezinski's proposal to go to China, arguing that it would raise doubts about who spoke for the United States on foreign policy. In this regard, the secretary of state resented the National Security Advisor's increasing public posture, including hiring his own press spokesman, holding frequent press briefings, and appearing frequently on television interview shows. On his part, Brzezinski accused the State Department of leaking secret and confidential materials to the press.

At first, Brzezinski and Vance were able to keep their differences private and work together in a reasonably collegial manner. On such matters as negotiating new agreements on ownership and control of the Panama Canal (1977), widely recognized as one of the great achievements of the young administration, Brzezinski gave most of the credit to the State Department and the president, although he took responsibility for helping to sell the agreements to the American public. On relations in the Middle East and the Camp David accords of 1978, he acknowledged that his role was essentially one of complementing the secretary of state, primarily by underscoring the importance of peace in the region to all the participants, but especially to Israel.

On other issues, however, such as what policy to follow in Rhodesia, where a white minority government, led by Ian Smith, was trying to hold on to power against the black Patriotic Front, on U.S. policy toward the Soviet Union, or on the United States' response to the Iranian revolution of 1979, relations between Brzezinski and Vance became increasingly strained. In the case of Rhodesia, for example, the National Security Advisor supported a plan proposed by Smith that Brzezinski thought would allow a transition to a moderate black government but which the secretary of state argued was only a subterfuge to keep whites in power. In the case of the Soviet Union, Brzezinski thought the State Department was too focused on concluding a SALT II agreement with Moscow while ignoring what he referred to as Soviet "adventurism" in the Horn of Africa, Angola, and Afghanistan.

On no issue, however, were Brzezinski and Vance more at odds than on the overthrow by Islamic fundamentalists in January 1979 of the shah of Iran, MOHAMMAD REZA PAHLAVI, and the seizure in November of the American embassy in Tehran along with the taking of 66 American hostages (of whom 15 were later released). In contrast to Vance, who sought a diplomatic solution to the Iranian crisis involving the establishment of a moderate Islamic government, Brzezinski favored a more hard-line approach, including support for the shah and, when it became apparent that the shah was about to be toppled from power, the establishment of a military government that would crack down on the militants.

As the crisis in Iran deepened, the differences between Brzezinski and Vance came to a head. Always suspicious of the bureaucracy he associated with the State Department, Carter accepted Brzezinski's claim that the department, particularly the U.S. ambassador to Iran, WILLIAM SULLIVAN, had not given the shah the type of diplomatic support he needed to remain in power. In April 1980, he ordered a military mission to rescue the hostages, which Vance had opposed but Brzezinski had advocated. Following the unsuccessful mission, Vance resigned as secretary of state.

Carter's decision to order the rescue operation was only one indication of Brzezinski's growing dominance over the formulation of foreign policy. Increasingly distrustful of the Soviet Union, the president became persuaded by Brzezinski's hard-line arguments against the Kremlin, especially following the Soviet Union's decision at the end of 1979 to send 85,000 troops into Afghanistan in order to quell an insurrection against a Marxist-controlled government. Although Brzezinski had warned the president that the Soviets might invade the country as part of their effort to access the Persian Gulf region, Carter had been caught off guard by the invasion. In response, the president took a number of measures proposed or endorsed by his National Security Advisor, including the imposition of a grain embargo on the Soviet Union; cancellation of American participation in the forthcoming Olympic games in Moscow; and, most important, enunciation of what became known as the Carter Doctrine, a warning to the Kremlin that any move against the Persian Gulf region would be repelled by the United States, even if this meant using military force. The president also asked the Senate to table consideration of the SALT II agreement, which he and Soviet leader LEONID BREZHNEV had signed in Vienna in June 1979. The agreement provided for new limits on weapons development while at the same time allowing both sides to develop one new missile system (in the case of the United States, this would be the MX).

Most of Brzezinski's last year as National Security Advisor was taken up by the ongoing Iranian hostage crisis; the Soviet invasion of Afghanistan; and, together with Secretary of Defense HAROLD BROWN, the development of a new strategic nuclear directive (Presidential Directive 59, or PD 59) approved by the president in July. PD 59 proposed to target military installations as well as population centers, thereby breaking away from the doctrine of mutual assured destruction, which had been the basis for much of the nation's strategic planning.

In February 1981, a month after he left office, Brzezinski gave an interview in which he concluded that he had been most effective as National Security Advisor in normalizing relations with the People's Republic of China; forcing a review of the United States' strategic posture doctrine, including pushing through approval of the new MX mobile missile system; and initiating a regional security framework for the Persian Gulf.

Since leaving the White House, Brzezinski has been active as a private consultant, author, lecturer, and commentator. He has also been a counselor at the Center for Strategic and International Studies and a professor of American foreign policy at the School for Advanced International Studies at Johns Hopkins University. He has served as a member of the National Security Council–Defense Department Commission on Integrated Long-Term Strategy (1987–88) and the President's Foreign Intelligence Advisory Board (1987–89), and he was cochair of the Bush National Security Advisory Board (1988).

Burger, Warren Earl

(1907–1995) *chief justice, U.S. Supreme Court*

Chief justice of the Supreme Court during the Carter administration, Warren E. Burger was born in St. Paul, Minnesota, on September 17, 1907. One of seven children from a working-class family, Burger received his law degree by taking extension courses at the University of Minnesota and then night courses at St. Paul College of Law while working as a life-insurance salesman. This was in contrast to most justices of the Court, who receive their undergraduate and law degrees from the nation's most prestigious colleges and universities. After earning his LL.B. magna cum laude (1931), Burger joined the highly respected St. Paul firm of Boyesen, Otis & Fairey, where he made partner in 1935. During this time, he also became active in politics, helping to organize the Minnesota Young Republicans in 1934.

In 1938, Burger worked in the successful gubernatorial campaign of his friend Harold Stassen, a rising star in the Republican Party. Rejected for military service during World War II because of a spinal injury, Burger served as a member of Minnesota's Emergency War Labor Board from 1941 to 1947. After the war, he was Stassen's floor manager at the Republican Party Convention in 1948 and 1952. When it became apparent in 1952 that Dwight D. Eisenhower was going to win the nomination, Burger switched his support to Eisenhower. The following year, President Eisenhower appointed Burger to head the Justice Department's Civil Division. Two years later, the president nominated him to the U.S. Court of Appeals for the District of Columbia, where he served for the next 13 years.

As a justice on the Court of Appeals, Burger gained a reputation as a law-and-order judge, a judicial conservative who, in criminal cases, interpreted the law in favor of prosecutors over defendants. In a speech in 1967 that was reprinted in *U.S. News and World Report*, Burger maintained that even the most enlightened nations of Europe did not extend the same rights to defendants as the United States.

He even raised questions about a defendant's right against self-incrimination under the Fifth Amendment to the Constitution.

Burger's reputation as a hard-line conservative and his 1967 speech attracted the attention of RICHARD NIXON, who was already planning to run for president in 1968 on a platform that included judicial restraint and an end to coddling criminals. Following the resignation of Chief Justice Earl Warren in 1969, President Nixon seized the opportunity to reorient the Supreme Court in a more conservative direction by appointing Burger as the nation's 15th chief justice. He was sworn in on June 23, 1969.

Many liberals feared that Burger would undo many of the historic decisions of the Warren Court. In criminal cases, he did live up to Nixon's expectations, permitting exceptions to the *Miranda* decision of 1966, validating confessions gained under duress, and allowing seizure of property obtained through unlawful entry. In other areas, however, no counterrevolution occurred. In fact, in one of the Burger Court's most important decisions, *Roe v. Wade* (1973), he voted with the majority, defying strongly held conservative values by upholding the right of women to have abortions. The Court also established busing as a tool to end segregation, and it adopted a narrow definition of pornography.

In the landmark civil rights case decided during the Carter presidency, *Regents of the University of California v. Bakke* (1978), the Court upheld the principle of affirmative action. In this case, in which Burger voted with the minority, ALLAN BAKKE, an applicant denied admission to the University of California–Davis Medical School, brought suit against the university claiming that he was a victim of reverse discrimination because minorities less qualified than he was had been admitted to the medical school on the basis of reserving 16 of 100 spaces each year for minority students.

Two other important cases that came before the Burger court during the Carter presidency involved matters of foreign policy. In *Goldwater v. Carter* (1979), the Court ruled that President Carter, who as part of his effort to normalize relations with the People's Republic of China had acceded to its insistence that the United States abrogate its mutual-defense treaty with Taiwan, had upheld his authority to take this action without first obtaining the consent of Congress. In ruling in the president's favor, Burger argued that the Court had to defer to the executive on matters involving foreign affairs, particularly since Congress provided no clear guidelines on the issue. In *Narenji v. Civiletti* (1979), the Court refused to hear a lower court ruling upholding the president's action in ordering the deportation of all Iranian students at American universities following Iran's seizure of the American embassy in Tehran in 1979 and the taking of 52 American hostages.

In a third, related case, *Dames and Moore v. Regan* (1981), not decided until after Carter had left office, the Court upheld the president's executive order transferring Iranian assets in the United States, seized by the government in 1979, to a newly established Iran–United States Claims Tribunal as part of an agreement with Iran to secure the release of the American hostages. The plaintiffs argued that the executive order was unconstitutional since it violated a court order attaching $3 million in Iranian assets to settle their claims against Iran. Joining with the Supreme Court's majority in upholding the executive order, Burger stated that the International Emergency Economic Power Act (IEEPA), which allowed President Carter to regulate transaction in national currencies during a national emergency, gave the president "express Congressional authority" to transfer the assets free of any liens.

Much to President Carter's disappointment, his administration was one of the few in the nation's history when not a single vacancy occurred on the Court. Accordingly, he was denied the opportunity to influence its decisions on cases through the appointments he might have made. In contrast, President RONALD REAGAN was able to have a major influence on the Court by appointing three new justices and a chief justice.

Overall, the Burger Court proved to be less significant historically than the Warren Court. Burger did not provide the Court with the strong leadership that Chief Justice Warren had provided. He was not an especially distinguished jurist, although he had taught contract law for 12 years at his alma mater and published a number of articles in law reviews. He preferred judicial restraint to judicial activism and pragmatism to judicial theory. Yet he did not share Warren's talent for consensus building.

Burger was also temperamental, sometimes overbearing, and frequently abrasive with his colleagues. The open and obsequious manner in which he conferred with President Nixon prior to his break with the president over the Watergate affair raised questions about his integrity that followed him throughout his tenure on the Court. He also intruded far more into the political arena than was normally the case with justices of the court. In 1978, he joined Justice HARRY BLACKMUN in warning Solicitor General Wade H. McCree that news leaks about divisions within the Carter Administration over the *Bakke* case had offended and displeased the Court. In 1979, he urged Secretary of Health, Education and Welfare JOSEPH CALIFANO to remain tough in his antismoking campaign.

In fact, Burger's greatest accomplishment as chief justice was not as a jurist but through his efforts to reform the administration of the nation's judicial system. He made the Supreme Court one of the most computerized courts in the nation and established the National Center for State Courts, the Institute for Court Management, and the National Institute for Corrections, all of which were intended to better prepare people involved in the judicial process. He persuaded many courts to hire professional administrators, encouraged states to mandate continuing legal education for attorneys and jurists, and improved coordination between the federal and state courts.

In 1986, Burger surprised President Reagan by resigning from the Court to head the commission planning the bicentennial of the Constitution and Bill of Rights; this reflected his lifelong interest in the history of the Constitution. After stepping down as chief justice, he also founded the Supreme Court Historical Society and served on the boards of the National Geographical Society and the Smithsonian Institution. In 1988, he received the Presidential Medal of Freedom. Burger died on June 25, 1995, in Washington, D.C., at the age of 87.

Burns, Arthur Frank

(1904–1987) *chair, Federal Reserve Board*

Arthur F. Burns was chair of the Federal Reserve Board (Fed) from 1970 to 1978, when President Carter decided not to reappoint him for a third four-year term, a decision that was widely attacked in the business and financial communities. A nominal Democrat who served mostly under Republican presidents, Burns waged a lifelong fight against big government, deficit spending, and inflation. He regarded budget deficits as the principal source of inflation, and inflation as the scourge of healthy and sustainable economic growth. Yet he eschewed strict rules in the conduct of monetary policy, and he was sometimes criticized by fiscal and monetary conservatives for his interventionist policies as the Fed's chairperson.

Born in Stanislau, Austria, on April 27, 1904, Burns immigrated to the United States with his parents, who were Austrian, grew up in Bayonne, New Jersey, and attended Columbia University, where he received his B.A. (1921), his M.A. (1925), and his Ph.D. in economics (1934). His dissertation, a highly detailed study of production trends in the United States since 1934, helped land him an academic position with Columbia University, where he later met former General Dwight D. Eisenhower while Eisenhower was serving as the university's president. When Eisenhower was elected president of the United States in 1952, he named Burns as chair of his Council of Economic Advisers (CEA), a body he had originally wanted to eliminate but Burns persuaded him to keep. Twice during Eisenhower's two administrations, the first as chair of the CEA and then as a private citizen, Burns recommended stimulating the economy through tax cuts and increased spending on national security in order to avoid a recession. Both times he was turned down, and both times a recession followed.

Burns resigned as the CEA chair at the end of Eisenhower's first term to return to Columbia and to serve as president of the National Bureau of Economic Research. During the 1960s, he took on temporary assignments for Presidents John F. Kennedy and Lyndon Johnson. President RICHARD NIXON appointed him as counselor to the president in 1968 and two years later nominated him to be chairperson of the Fed. Burns continued to serve in this position under President GERALD FORD.

In appointing Burns as Fed chairperson, Nixon made clear his intention that the Federal Reserve Board serve the interests of his administration. Once Burns was confirmed as chair, however, he made clear that he had no intention of subordinating the Board to the interests of the White House. "You know," he told the president's special assistant, John Ehrlichman, "the idea that I would ever let a conflict arise between what I think is right and my loyalty to Dick Nixon is outrageous." He had little interest in being a team player. The Fed's independence was always sacrosanct to him.

At the time of Burns's appointment, the United States was experiencing what came to be referred to as stagflation (high unemployment and high inflation). To deal with this double threat to the economy, Burns proposed a policy of seeking to limit wage increases to increased labor productivity; the president incorporated this into his New Economic Policy. Burns also unsuccessfully opposed Nixon's decision to take the United States off the gold standard (eliminating the convertibility of dollars into gold in international transactions), thereby effectively devaluing the dollar against the Japanese yen and the German mark.

Although Burns pursued a pragmatic approach to fiscal and monetary policy as chair of both the CEA and the Fed, at the time that Jimmy Carter entered the White House in 1977, Democrats still widely regarded Burns as a fiscal conservative. Certainly he believed that it was the government's responsibility to fight inflation. An unusually forceful leader, he was determined to do this as head of the Fed by pursuing a policy of maintaining tight control of the nation's money supply and by advocating fiscal restraint, which he thought was also necessary to rebuild lagging business confidence in the economy. At the same time, he sought to legitimate the Fed as a nonpartisan institution responsible for monetary and credit policy independent of any intervening political authority. Reviewing other countries' experiences with central banks (although the Fed was not technically a central bank, it acted like one), he commented upon "the need for a strong monetary authority to discipline the inflationary tendency inherent in modern economies."

As a candidate for the White House, Carter had proposed that the president be given the authority to select his own chairperson of the Fed by having that person "serve a term coterminous with the President's." Once in the White House, he pursued a different policy, rarely criticizing the Fed publicly. Yet almost from the time he took office, he found himself at odds with Burns. The most pressing economic problem his administration faced was recovery from recession, which he proposed to achieve through a modest economic-stimulus package that included a $50 tax rebate for every American, tax cuts for individuals and businesses, and a $4 billion increase over two years in the authorization for government jobs. Concerned, however, that even this modest increase in government spending was too much at a time when business confidence in the economy was still fragile, Burns opposed these recommendations. Testifying before the Joint Economic Committee in February, he warned that "the increase in the Federal budget [was] stirring up new fears and expectations of inflation that in some degree may turn out to be a self-fulfilling prophecy." Were the administration to pursue a tax cut, he urged that it be weighted toward business since that "would encourage positive business attitudes and willingness to take investment risks."

To stave off inflation, Burns pursued a policy of gradually raising interest rates as a means of slowing economic growth. The chair of Carter's Council of Economic Advisers (CEA), CHARLES SCHULTZE, worried that the Fed might be slamming on the brakes too rapidly because the velocity, or turnover rate, of the money supply was several times greater than its actual expansion. For precisely the same reason, other economists later argued that the Fed should have been more restrictive in curbing economic growth through higher interest rates and tighter control of the nation's money supply, and that the Fed's failure to do this contributed to the rapid acceleration in interest rates beginning in 1978.

As chairperson, Burns also had to contend with efforts by Congress to restrict the Fed's independence. In September 1977, Representative HENRY REUSS of Wisconsin introduced legislation that would increase the Fed's accountability to Congress and the president's authority over the institution by: (1) requiring the Fed to disclose its money targets; (2) requiring Senate confirmation of both the chair and vice chair of the Board; (3) broadening the composition of the boards of the 12 regional reserve banks so as to have less banker and more public representation on their boards; and, most important, (4) coordinating the terms of the Fed chair and vice chair with that of the president. Although most of these provisions were included in the Federal Reserve Reform Act of November 1977, Burns was able to suppress making the appointment of the Fed's chair and vice chair coterminous with the president's new term in office. With that provision, therefore, the legislation proved to have little impact in limiting the independence of the Fed chairperson.

Almost from the time Carter took office, Burns made it clear to the new administration that he wanted to be reappointed to a third term as Fed chair when his second term expired in 1978. Although Burns enjoyed strong support within the business and financial communities, the Fed's apparent inability to contain inflation worked against his reappointment. Even more important, most of Carter's economic advisers agreed with CEA chair Schultze and Treasury Secretary W. MICHAEL BLUMENTHAL that Burns's outspoken views on the economy, which were often critical of the White House, and his almost myopic concentration on inflation, to the exclusion of reducing unemployment, did not warrant his reappointment. Carter agreed. "I didn't get along very well with Chairman Burns," he acknowledged after leaving office. To replace Burns at the Fed, the president nominated G. WILLIAM MILLER, the chief executive of Textron and a person regarded by the president's advisers as a team player.

Following the president's decision not to reappoint him for another term, Burns accepted a position as distinguished scholar at the American Enterprise Institute, a conservative think tank. In 1981, President RONALD REAGAN nominated him as ambassador to the Federal Republic of Germany where he served until 1985. On June 26, 1987, he died from complications following triple-bypass heart surgery. He was 83 years old.

Burton, Phillip

(1926–1983) *member of the House of Representatives*

The best description of California Democrat Phillip Burton was the one he gave of himself: "I am a fighting liberal." A masterful political infighter with seemingly inexhaustible energy and a fiery temper, Burton was abrasive, profane, and ambitious. Known for wreaking vengeance on those who, he felt, had betrayed him, he had much of his power stripped in 1977 after he lost his bid to be House majority leader by one vote. He also frequently clashed with House Speaker TIP O'NEILL (Mass.), who regarded Burton as a political rival and had quietly campaigned against his bid to be majority leader. But through his chairmanship of the House Subcommittee on National Parks and Insular Affairs and his mastery of legislative and political strategy, Burton engineered the most sweeping national-parks legislation in the nation's history.

Born in Cincinnati on June 1, 1926, and raised in Milwaukee, Burton had a neglected childhood. His father Thomas decided at the age of 36 to go to medical school at the University of Illinois while leaving his family in Milwaukee. His mother Mildred could barely make ends meet and had little time for Phillip and his two younger brothers. Yet Phillip was greatly influenced by his civil libertarian father's commitment to leftist causes and social and economic justice for the underprivileged. It provided the basis for his own passionate liberalism.

In 1939, Phillip moved with his family to San Francisco, where his father's medical practice was established. In 1944, he enrolled at the University of Southern California (USC) while enlisting in the U.S. Navy under a program that prepared naval officers during World War II. Following the war, he completed his studies at USC (B.A., 1947). He then worked selling oil leases while taking night classes at Golden Gate University's School of Law. After receiving his law degree (LL.B., 1952), Burton became active in politics and ran unsuccessfully for the state assembly in 1954 before winning election to that body two years later. He served for eight years in Sacramento supporting liberal causes, including greatly liberalizing California's welfare system. His overpowering and intimidating demeanor made him a feared political rival of the Speaker of the General Assembly, Jesse Unruh, one of California's most powerful political figures.

In 1964, Burton was elected to Congress from San Francisco's liberal eastern district in a special election to fill the vacancy caused by the resignation of John F. Shelly. In November, he won the regular election and he was subsequently reelected nine times. On Capitol Hill, he became a champion of President Lyndon Johnson's Great Society programs and an expert on labor and welfare legislation. He was also one of the earliest lawmakers to speak out against the war in Vietnam. At the 1968 Democratic Party convention in Chicago, he presented the minority platform position against the war.

During the administrations of Presidents RICHARD NIXON and GERALD FORD, Burton continued to champion liberal causes, including cosponsoring the Federal Coal Mine Health and Safety Act (1969) and promoting the Occupational Safety and Health Act (1970). He also supported public-works programs and helped get through Congress an increase in the minimum wage for nonfarm workers from $1.30 an hour to $2.20 by 1976, only to have the legislation vetoed by President Nixon. He continued to oppose the war in Vietnam and pushed for cuts in defense spending. In 1972, he supported the antiwar candidacy of GEORGE MCGOVERN for the Democratic presidential nomination.

Burton also became a Democratic leader and power broker on Capitol Hill. In 1971, he was chosen to chair the Democratic Study Group, and three years later he was elected chairman of the House Democratic Caucus. In 1975, following the election of a number of freshman liberals to the House, Burton led a successful fight to liberalize the seniority system by which chairmen of committees and subcommittees were appointed; the result was greater power for the younger members of the House. He also promoted changes in the House rules that made it easier to get legislation out of committee and onto the floor for consideration by the full House.

A master at organizing unlikely coalitions, Burton had a way of putting together congressional alliances on seemingly unrelated issues. For example, he extracted votes for issues like minimum wage and black-lung benefits, from southerners who supported high farm subsidies, and in turn he extracted votes on farm subsidies from liberals. He was widely regarded on Capitol Hill as one of the brightest and most politically astute members of either the House or the Senate. He was also considered the lawmaker most likely to succeed the incumbent Democratic majority leader, Tip O'Neill, when O'Neill became Speaker of the House at the opening of the 95th Congress (1977).

Burton's abrasive, and often insulting, manner and personality worked against him, however. The derisive attitude he adopted toward lawmakers who did not join with him, the threats of political retaliation against those who opposed his legislative agenda, and his sometimes coarse behavior toward colleagues, even in social settings, alienated many important Democrats in the House, including the presumptive House Speaker. Unwilling to have as his principal deputy someone whom he distrusted and disliked, O'Neill quietly threw his support behind JIM WRIGHT (Tex.) as majority leader while other Democrats backed the two other candidates for the position, John McFall (Calif.) and RICHARD BOLLING (Mo.). After McFall and Bolling were eliminated in the preliminary rounds of balloting, Wright, who had been a long shot for the position behind Bolling, was able to defeat Burton by a single vote, 148 to 147.

Instead of then giving Burton the position of party whip, which was a nonelective position and would have kept Burton in the House leadership, O'Neill and Wright named JOHN BRADEMAS (Ind.) as whip and DAN ROSTENKOWSKI (Ill.) as deputy whip. Burton had suffered a devastating and humiliating defeat. "In the final analysis," Mary Russell of the *Washington Post* wrote, "Burton was seen as too driven, too ambitious, too manipulative, too contentious—despite the fact that his liberal credentials are impeccable, he had support from some in labor and environmentalists, and his reputation as a 'reformer' is good."

Within a short time after losing to Wright as majority leader, Burton began planning to challenge him again in the 95th Congress (1979–81). His strategy was to use his position as chair of the House Subcommittee on National Parks and Insular Affairs to obtain political obligations from lawmakers by engaging in what his biographer has labeled "park barrel" politics: incorporating into legislation pet projects of lawmakers that fell within the purview of his subcommittee. To assure passage of this legislation, he also intended to package the measures into a single omnibus bill so large and complex that lawmakers would have difficulty deciphering, much less amending, it.

More was involved than politics, however, in the interest Burton took in major new land legislation. A smoker and drinker who preferred a cocktail lounge to the outdoors and whose single lifelong obsession was politics, he was not the stereotypical environmentalist or conservationist. But during a trip to California a year before his family moved there permanently, he had seen the scenic beauty of the West and had been awed by the giant size of California's redwood trees. As a young congressman, he established a special relationship with Dr. Edgar Wayburn, president of the San Francisco–based Sierra Club and helped win passage of legislation establishing the Golden Gate Recreational District, which extended on both sides of the entrance to San Francisco Bay. As chair of the Subcommittee on National Parks and Insular Affairs, he pushed through legislation in March 1978 extending the size of the Redwood National Park to prevent environmental degradation of the redwoods within the park's existing borders. The timber, mining, and other interests that often found themselves opposing such environmental groups as the Sierra Club were also the same interests against which he had fought as a liberal lawmaker, so that he was predisposed to align with the environmentalists regardless of political considerations, even though these were always uppermost in his mind.

Employing his uncanny political skills, Burton was able to get through Congress the $1.4 billion National Parks and Recreation Act of 1978, one of the most sweeping pieces of environmental legislation in the nation's history, tripling the national trails system, doubling the wild and scenic river system, and more than doubling the wilderness in national parks. Among its provisions were funds for the establishment of 11 new national parks, historic sites, and national seashores as well as development funds for an additional 34 parks, sites, and seashores and additions to eight wild and scenic rivers and four national trails. In all, the measure incorporated 90 percent of President Carter's preservation programs, combining 150 projects in more than 200 congressional districts in 44 states. As the chairman of the Interior Committee and his close ally, MORRIS UDALL (D-Ariz.), commented about Burton after passage of the legislation, "[h]e unscrewed the inscrutable." He preserved the nation's natural wonders.

President Carter signed the measure, which was in accord with his own interest in preserving and expanding the nation's public lands, into law on November 10, 1978. Earlier that year, after Burton won expansion of Redwood National Park and had helped win a measure increasing the minimum wage from $2.30 an hour to $3.35 an hour by 1981, the president had written to congratulate him on his achievements: "Your efforts as Chairman of the Subcommittee on National Parks," Carter wrote, "contributed to today's passage of the bill expanding Redwood Park. Your work with the Speaker helped to shape the most significant minimum wage bill since 1935."

Burton and the president were not natural allies, however. The congressman's passionate liberalism was at odds with Carter's fiscal conservatism. Even the Redwood Park legislation contained a labor-compensation provision inserted by the congressman that the president strongly opposed. Besides environmental matters, Burton's legislative agenda also included expansion of such social welfare programs as supplemental social security, black-lung benefits to miners, and federal unemployment insurance that were unacceptable to the White House.

The president was also well aware of the lawmaker's ability to get his way on Capitol

Hill. As the president's assistant for congressional liaison, FRANK MOORE, advised Carter as early as March 1977, Burton did this "by knowing in a way that few policymakers in either the executive or legislative branch do—the ins and outs of virtually all the major benefit entitlement programs with their now well-known budget-breaking potential."

Passage of the National Parks legislation proved to be Burton's last major achievement. Although he was able to build on this 1978 milestone by gaining legislative approval of additional land preservation projects, his strategy of "park barrel" politics failed in its objective of unseating Jim Wright as majority leader in the 96th Congress. Following the midterm elections of 1978, Burton concluded that he did not have enough votes to unseat an incumbent majority leader. The election results showed a swing away in Congress from the ultraliberalism associated with the California congressman toward the more moderate views identified with Wright.

The House leadership also remained on guard against Burton, and Democratic lawmakers became increasingly annoyed with the internecine war taking place within their ranks. Although still a power broker who dominated the California delegation in the House and was able to strike terror in those who crossed him, Burton's influence on national affairs during the Carter administration remained largely confined to what he could accomplish in his position as chairperson of the Subcommittee on National Parks and Insular Affairs.

Once RONALD REAGAN took office in 1981, Burton gave up his national parks subcommittee in order to chair the labor-management subcommittee. He had been persuaded to make the change by labor leaders in order to keep the new president from gutting labor programs such as pension benefits, workers' compensation, and occupational health and safety. But his role was largely defensive rather than offensive in terms of developing any new legislative programs.

In California, however, House Speaker Willie Brown made Burton congressional point man for the state's reapportionment plan, which, reflecting the 1980 census, provided for two additional congressional seats for the state. Burton seized the opportunity to craft a plan almost single-handedly. In 1982, the plan resulted in a Democratic gain of six seats in California, nearly one-fourth of the party's national pickup of 26 seats that year. Although the reapportionment plan caused an uproar among state Republican leaders, who targeted Burton for defeat in 1982 by fielding and heavily funding their top San Francisco vote-getter, state senator Milton Marks, Burton was reelected by a comfortable margin of 58 percent to 40 percent for Marks.

On April 11, 1983, while visiting his congressional district in San Francisco, Burton collapsed and died of a ruptured abdominal artery; a secondary cause was heart disease. At the time of his death at age 56, he was contemplating challenging Jim Wright again for House majority leader. His wife Sala was elected to fill his seat.

Bush, George Herbert Walker

(1924–) *candidate for Republican presidential nomination, Republican vice-presidential nominee*

Having served in various political and government posts, George Herbert Walker Bush proved to be an unexpectedly strong candidate for the 1980 Republican Party presidential nomination. Although he lost the nomination to the more conservative former governor of California, RONALD REAGAN, he was selected by Reagan to be his vice-presidential candidate, in large measure because of his moderate credentials.

Born into a wealthy family in Milton, Massachusetts, near Boston on June 12, 1924, Bush was the son of Prescott Bush, a managing partner in a Wall Street investment firm and U.S. senator from Connecticut from 1952 to 1962. He pursued the family tradition of attending the exclusive Phillips Andover Academy, where he played basketball and was senior-class president, but delayed enrollment at Yale University following his graduation from Phillips in order to enlist in the navy during World War II. The youngest fighter pilot in the navy at the time, he received his commission in 1943 and flew more than 50 missions in the Pacific. He was shot down during one mission and had to spend a night at sea before being rescued by a submarine. He later received the Distinguished Flying Cross.

After the war, Bush married Barbara Pierce, the daughter of the publisher of *Redbook* and *McCall's*, and enrolled at Yale, where he majored in economics and graduated Phi Beta Kappa (B.A., 1948). He was also a member of the Skull and Bones Society and captain of the baseball team. Instead of taking a position with his father's firm after graduation, Bush moved to West Texas and began a career in the oil industry. In 1953, he cofounded his own oil- and gas-drilling firm, the Zapata Petroleum Corporation, and became a millionaire in his own right. In 1955, he moved the corporate headquarters to Houston, where he raised his family of five children (a sixth child died of leukemia at the age of three).

Sharing his family's interest in politics, Bush became chairman of the Harris County (Houston) Republican Party. Running as a BARRY GOLDWATER Republican opposed to the Civil Rights Act of 1964 and calling for the withdrawal of the United States from the United Nations, Bush ran unsuccessfully for the U.S. Senate against the liberal Democratic incumbent, Ralph Yarborough. Two years later, however, he was elected to the House of Representatives from Houston's wealthy seventh congressional district and won reelection in 1968. Encouraged by President RICHARD NIXON to run again for the Senate, he gave up his House seat to oppose Lloyd Bentsen, a former conservative congressman from southern Texas who had defeated Yarborough in the Democratic primary. Facing another conservative candidate rather than the liberal Yarborough, whom he might have defeated in an increasingly conservative state, Bush was again defeated for the Senate by his Democratic opponent, who portrayed Bush as a transplanted, liberal Ivy Leaguer from the East.

Even without an elected office, Bush became increasingly well-known nationally because of a series of appointed positions he held over the next 10 years. In return for his loyalty and because he still considered Bush a rising star who needed foreign policy experience, President Nixon appointed him as the U.S. ambassador to the United Nations. There Bush unsuccessfully opposed the effort to admit the People's Republic of China (Communist China) in place of Taiwan, offering instead the administration's "two Chinas" proposal, whereby Taiwan and Communist China would both be given seats in the General Assembly. Gaining the admiration of other delegates because of his low-key diplomatic style and access to the White House, Bush served at the United Nations until 1973, when he was named chairman of the Republican National Committee. In that position, he had the difficult job of defending the president during the Watergate scandal, but he remained loyal to the president while distancing the party from Watergate and avoiding becoming tainted by the scandal himself.

Also recognizing the loyalty that Bush always displayed both to the Republican Party and the people for whom he worked, President GERALD FORD named him in 1974 as head of the U.S. Liaison Office in the People's

Republic of China. The next year, the president appointed him as the new director of the Central Intelligence Agency (CIA), replacing William Colby at a time when the agency was under investigation for its covert operations, including snooping on U.S. citizens at home and attempting assassinations of foreign leaders. He proved to be an effective director, defending the agency against efforts to curtail its covert operations and restoring the morale of its personnel. Bush remained at the CIA until Jimmy Carter was elected president in 1976.

Having developed an impressive résumé of public service, Bush decided to seek the 1980 Republican nomination for president. Although he had a conservative voting record while in Congress, he presented himself as an attractive moderate alternative to the leading candidate for the Republican nomination, Ronald Reagan. Taking a cue from Carter's 1976 campaign strategy, Bush campaigned hard in Iowa, which Reagan largely ignored because early polls showed him with a commanding lead over Bush in the state and because his campaign manager, John Sears, thought it was necessary to concentrate on New Hampshire. The upshot was that Bush won an upset victory over Reagan in the Iowa caucuses.

Bush's victory made New Hampshire all the more important to both him and Reagan. With the Reagan camp bitterly divided as a result of what had happened in Iowa and momentum seeming to work in Bush's favor ("Big Mo," as his momentum was called in the press), it seemed at first that Bush might also be able to win in New Hampshire, making him the front-runner for the Republican nomination. In the first of two scheduled debates among Republican candidates, Bush was the clear winner. But, campaigning hard in the Granite State, Reagan began to pull even with Bush in the polls. His victory became assured when in the second of two debates, scheduled to be a one-on-one between two leading candidates, Reagan, who had agreed to fund the event, insisted at the last moment that the four other candidates running in the primary participate in the debate. A hapless Bush objected, and when the moderator of the debate, Jon Breen, tried to cut off Reagan's microphone, Reagan grabbed the microphone, stating, "I *paid* for this microphone, Mr. Green [sic]." Reagan had taken command of the moment in front of the television cameras and won over those watching the proceedings. He then went on to win an impressive victory in New Hampshire.

Bush never recovered from his loss in New Hampshire. In the months that followed, he attacked Reagan's proposal for a 30 percent cut in personal income taxes over three years, calling it "voodoo economics." He also assailed his opponent's suggestion that the United States might blockade Cuba in response to the Soviet invasion of Afghanistan, and he tried to make an issue of Reagan's age, pointing out that Reagan was 69 years old, while he was only 56 and jogged three miles a day.

Notwithstanding the urging of his advisers, however, Bush refused to attack Reagan harshly. Nor did he emphasize other important differences he had with the former California governor over issues such as an equal-rights amendment (which Bush favored and Reagan opposed) or a constitutional amendment prohibiting abortion (which Reagan favored and Bush opposed). Despite their differences and Bush's reputation as a moderate, moreover, their views on most issues were similar. They both favored tax cuts, they both opposed big government, and they both favored increased spending for defense and a hard-line policy toward the Soviet Union.

Unwilling or unable to distinguish himself from Reagan, Bush undermined his own strategy of making himself a moderate alternative to a political figure already enjoying a deep base of support within the Republican

Party. As a result, while Bush continued his campaign until June and won six primaries, including those in such key states as Massachusetts, Pennsylvania, and Michigan, even before Bush won Michigan in May, it was clear to most political observers that Reagan would be the Republican nominee for president.

According to some of Bush's advisers, in fact, he had entered the race not intending to win the presidential nomination but to position himself for the second spot on the ticket. Whatever the validity of these claims, which Bush denied, Reagan had reservations about putting him on the ticket. Both he and his wife Nancy, who wielded considerable political influence with her husband, regarded Bush as an effete political snob and questioned his political toughness. For a time at the Republican convention, it appeared that former president Ford would be Reagan's running mate in what political commentators referred to as "the dream team." But when Ford insisted on a role for himself in a Reagan administration equivalent to that of a copresident, the "dream team" idea fell apart. Instead, Reagan turned immediately to Bush as his choice for vice president.

From the beginning of the Republican campaign to defeat President Carter in his bid for reelection, Bush made clear that his role in a Reagan administration would be totally supportive of the president. Even during the campaign, Bush played a modest role, filling in where needed, making regional headlines, appearing on local TV news shows, and defending Reagan, whose own campaign was often characterized by inauspicious remarks, which Carter ridiculed. Attacking the president on what came to be referred to in the media as the "meanness issue," Bush said he was "appalled at the ugly, mean little remark Jimmy Carter made." *Time* magazine characterized Bush's campaign effort as "the model of self-effacement" and remarked that he said so little of national interest that reporters covering his activities were often left on hold by their editors. In contrast to Bush, Carter's running mate, Vice President WALTER MONDALE played a much more active role trying to assuage the liberal wing of the Democratic Party.

As Bush promised, he remained totally loyal to Reagan after their victory over Carter and Mondale, completely subordinating his own preferences to those of the president. No Reagan adviser ever remembered Bush arguing his own position on an issue during the Reagan presidency. Although Bush and Reagan had never been close, they came to enjoy each other's company. A number of Bush's campaign staff became key members of the administration. Of these the most notable was Bush's campaign manager, JAMES BAKER, who became Reagan's chief of staff and, later, secretary of the Treasury.

Following Reagan's reelection in 1984, Bush decided to run for president in 1988. Although he had difficulty defining a rationale for his candidacy other than the fact that he had been Reagan's vice president, he was able to capitalize on the weaknesses of his principal opponent for the Republican nomination, Senator ROBERT DOLE (Kans.) and his Democratic opponent, Massachusetts governor Michael Dukakis. At the beginning of the campaign, Dukakis had been favored to beat Bush, but he proved to be an uninspiring and ineffective candidate. Dukakis allowed Bush to put him on the defensive by a series of negative political advertisements (the infamous "Willie Horton" ads) that made him look weak on crime. For some inexplicable reason, Dukakis refused to respond to these attacks and suffered a humiliating defeat.

As president, Bush seemed unbeatable for reelection following the 1991 Persian Gulf War, in which the United States had formed an international military coalition that quickly drove Iraqi forces, who had invaded Kuwait, back above the border in an operation known as Desert Storm. But Bush reneged on a promise he had made in 1988 of "no new taxes." This and other factors—a worsening economy; the independent candidacy of Ross Perot, who won 19 percent of the popular vote; and a poor performance by Bush during his campaign against one of the smartest political strategist in recent history, Arkansas governor Bill Clinton, in which Bush often seemed distracted and unfocused and Clinton ebullient and on message—led voters to reject Bush in 1992.

Unlike many losing candidates, however, Bush seemed almost relieved to be able to leave high office after almost 30 years of increasingly responsible public service. Since leaving the White House, he has been content to spend much of his time enjoying his grandchildren; vacationing at his summer home in Kennebunkport, Maine; and watching the political careers of his sons, Florida governor Jeb Bush and President George W. Bush. In 1997, at the age of 72, he became the first American president to parachute out of an airplane. In 2004, he celebrated his 80th birthday by repeating the stunt.

Bush is the author of two recent books, *A World Transformed* (1998), a memoir of his foreign policy as president; and *All the Best, George Bush* (1999), his autobiography, told through letters. The George Bush Presidential Library and Museum has been established at Texas A&M University in College Station, Texas.

Byrd, Robert Carlyle

(1917–) *member of the Senate, majority leader*

Robert Byrd of West Virginia is one of the towering figures of the U.S. Senate. He is the only member of the House and Senate to have earned both his undergraduate and law degrees while a member of Congress, receiving first his law degree from American University in 1963 and then, 21 years later, his B.A. degree from Marshall University. No member of the Senate has held as many leadership positions. He is the acknowledged master of Senate rules and one of the upper chamber's leading experts on its history. Throughout most of his career, he has maintained an abiding interest in protecting what he considers the Senate's prerogatives.

As Senate majority leader during the Carter administration, Byrd had a strained relationship with the president. Generally he tried to be supportive of the White House, but like other members of Congress, he was more often than not frustrated, finding the president and his staff inexperienced and indifferent to congressional concerns. For its part, the administration found Byrd to be vain and arrogant. Byrd's uncanny ability to win hundreds of millions of dollars for public-works projects in West Virginia also clashed with President Carter's determination to end what he regarded as pork-barrel politics. Recognizing his leadership on Capitol Hill and the awe that other senators had for him, the White House took his advice and warnings seriously and tried to be as accommodating as possible. Relations between the president and the Senate majority leader, however, were not much better when Carter left office than they had been during his first year in the White House.

Byrd's life was a classic one of overcoming personal hardship to become one of the nation's most powerful leaders. He accomplished this through sheer pluck and intellect. He was born on November 20, 1917, in North Wilkesboro, North Carolina. Orphaned when he was only one year old, he was raised by an aunt and uncle. His new family moved him to West Virginia, where he was valedictorian of his high school class, but in the midst of the Great Depression, he lacked the resources to go to college. Instead, he became a meat cutter and then a welder in a shipyard during World War II.

In 1946, Byrd won his first election as a delegate to the West Virginia House of Delegates. This was followed by successful bids for the West Virginia Senate (1950), the U.S. House of Representatives (1952), and, finally, the U.S. Senate (1958). In 1971, he outmaneuvered and then ousted EDWARD KENNEDY (Mass.) as Democratic whip in the upper chamber. In 1976, after briefly considering a run for the presidency, Byrd ran unchallenged as a favorite son candidate in West Virginia's Democratic presidential primary, the only primary in which the Carter campaign decided not to compete.

In 1977, Byrd replaced the retiring Mike Mansfield (D-Mont.) as Senate majority leader. Relations between President Carter and the West Virginia senator, both new to their respective positions, got off to a rocky start. Within a week after Carter took office, the president read reported complaints from Byrd and Speaker of the House TIP O'NEILL (Mass.) that they were not being adequately consulted by the White House. Aware that he was still regarded as a Washington outsider, Carter invited the two congressional leaders to dinner at the White House. The dinner went well enough, and subsequently Carter found in the affable O'Neill someone with whom he could work well. Of particular importance in this regard was the Speaker's effort in August 1977 to assure speedy House passage of the administration's long and complex energy bill by establishing one omnibus committee, stacked with O'Neill loyalists, instead of dividing it into five separate measures. In this way, he prevented the measure from being emasculated in committee. In the Senate, however, the situation was much different, in part because the rules of the upper chamber placed greater restraints on the power of the leadership by making it possible for a small group of senators to block legislation or to amend it to death, but in part also because Byrd was defensive of Senate prerogatives.

The majority leader was also furious over Carter's decision, in one of his first acts as president, to kill a series of 19 water projects that the president regarded as pork. What bothered Byrd was not only the fact that he had been enormously successful in obtaining projects of this kind for his state, but that by his action the president was violating the normal process of White House notification and consultation with lawmakers before decisions of this kind were made. "I can't tell you, Mr. President, how much damage the water project list is doing," Byrd told Carter in April. But the president ignored his advice.

Carter's about-face on a $50-per-person tax rebate, first pressuring Byrd to twist arms to get it passed and then changing his mind nine days later further incensed the majority leader. On two occasions, Byrd asked the White House's liaison to the Senate, Dan Tate, whether the president and his advisers really recognized that a president could not deal with Congress in the same fashion that a governor dealt with a state legislature.

Byrd was not inclined, therefore, to help the president with his energy bill. At a breakfast meeting of congressional leaders with the president in April, he complained that senators had not been brought into the energy-planning process, a point that even the president conceded. Instead of bending Senate rules and establishing one ad hoc committee to consider the energy bill as O'Neill had done, Byrd divided the measure into six individual bills that would be reported separately to the Senate floor. He then warned Carter to "let the Senate work its will," remarking that the upper chamber was "a place of shifting moods."

The result was that final action on the measure, which bitterly divided lawmakers in the Senate, was delayed until the end of 1978. Also, the legislation that was finally approved excluded the increased tax on oil that the president wanted. Instead, it provided for a gradual deregulation of gas and crude oil, which was expected to increase energy prices by making them more responsive to market demands.

Byrd was also critical of the White House for its Summer 1977 plans to send to Capitol Hill another highly complex and controversial measure to reform the nation's tangled and almost unintelligible welfare system, especially since it was clear that the administration was nowhere near agreement on a reform measure. When, instead of submitting a plan to Congress, the White House issued a statement of principles on which it would base a reform measure, the majority leader responded that "welfare reform [would] simply have to wait" given the legislative agenda already before the Senate.

Similarly, the West Virginia senator protested against President Carter's plan during the summer of 1977 to sell AWACS (*A*irborne *W*arning *a*nd *C*ontrol *S*ystem) aircraft to Iran without giving Congress sufficient time to review, and possibly disapprove, the sale as provided by law. Byrd believed that the United States had already sold the shah of Iran, MOHAMMAD REZA PAHLAVI, too much sophisticated military equipment, that the advanced technology of the AWACS might somehow find its way into the hands of the Soviet Union, and that the sale would have a destabilizing effect in the Middle East. When the president failed to respond in writing to a letter he had written outlining his objections to the sale, instead sending Secretary of State CYRUS VANCE to meet with Byrd, the Senate majority leader went before the Senate Foreign Relations Committee and, as a matter of personal privilege, insisted that it vote to disapprove the sale. It did so, as did the House International Relations Committee. But before Congress took final action, the president withdrew the proposal. Although Carter resubmitted it and won congressional approval for the sale in September, the way the White House handled the matter only frustrated Byrd all the more.

Byrd's record with respect to supporting the Carter White House was by no means one-sided. Although he was not interested in being too closely identified with what he regarded as an inept and bungling White House, the senator wanted the president to look to him for advice and support in the Senate in the same way that Carter looked to O'Neill in the House. In fact, another point of contention with the president was Byrd's belief that he was not treated with the same respect accorded to the Speaker.

Byrd tried to be helpful to the president, but in the manner of an instructor teaching a student. For example, during the BERT LANCE affair involving questionable banking practices on the part of Carter's director of the Office of Management and Budget, Byrd lent a sympathetic ear to Lance. Much to the chagrin of Carter's Georgia advisers, however, he advised the president that, despite Lance's strong defense of his business practices, the matter would not go away and that the presidency was more important than any individual.

Byrd also generally supported the president's fight against inflation and his budget proposals, and he was particularly helpful to the White House in the realm of foreign policy. In 1978, for example, he lent his strong support to ratification of the Panama Canal Treaties and to the normalization of diplomatic relations with the People's Republic of China. The next year, he supported the Strategic Arms Limitation Talks (SALT II) agreement with the Soviet Union. He also played an important role in resolving a potentially dangerous dispute between Moscow and Washington over the presence of a Soviet combat brigade in Cuba, which, for a time, nonplussed the White House. In conversation with the president, Byrd made clear that to him the issue was a red herring since Soviet troops had been in Cuba since 1962. When matters seemed to be spinning out of control, he went to see Soviet ambassador Anatoly Dobrynin to tell him that ratification of the SALT II treaty was in jeopardy unless the Soviets were more accommodating.

Dobrynin responded that his government could not do anything because the issue of the Soviet brigade was a phony one. Relaying that message to President Carter, Byrd now told the president that the United States would have to cool its rhetoric if SALT II was to be saved. Impressed by what Byrd said to him, Carter decided to deliver a message to the nation on October 1 in which he stated that the Soviet presence in Cuba posed no direct threat to the United States. His address effectively killed the national angst that had been building over the Soviet brigade. But it was not enough to save the SALT agreement, which fell victim to the Soviet invasion of Afghanistan in December.

While Byrd proved he could be an important ally of the White House, he remained distrustful, even disdainful, of the administration throughout its four years in office. The White House clearly understood this. Although it tried hard to reach out to the proud and vain majority leader, both publicly and privately it began to express its own displeasure toward him and its other opponents on Capitol Hill. When it appeared in June 1980 that the House and Senate were about to vote against Carter's proposal for a 10 cent increase in the gasoline tax, the president shot back. "The charge by Senator Byrd that we have not made an effort to educate Senators and Congressmen on this issue is just not true," the president remarked on June 4 at a congressional leadership breakfast.

The fact that Byrd privately supported Edward Kennedy in his bid for the presidency in 1980 and that Kennedy was even considering Byrd as his running mate did not help matters. In a fair assessment of the problem that Byrd posed for the White House, the president's congressional liaison, FRANK MOORE, and his deputy, Dan Tate, wrote to Carter on June 10, 1980: "Senator Byrd does not fear you politically. He is much more powerful in the Senate than you. He is able ... to reward friends and punish enemies far more easily than you. ... In short, if a Senator must choose between your wishes and Byrd's, he will go with Byrd." Whether things might have gone better for the White House on Capitol Hill had Byrd not been the Senate majority leader is, of course, speculative. But what is not in doubt is that the West Virginia senator's contempt for the Carter White House complicated matters enormously for the president on Capitol Hill.

Byrd outlasted Carter and the three presidents that followed him. He has continued to be returned to the Senate by overwhelming margins delivered to him by his grateful West Virginia constituency. As he has grown older, he has relinquished most of his leadership positions. But he remains the ranking Democratic member of the powerful Appropriations Committee and among the most powerful and respected members of the Senate.

Caddell, Pat

(Patrick H. Caddell)
(1950–) *pollster, political consultant*

Founder and chief executive of the Cambridge Research Group, a test-marketing and polling firm for political and business clients, Patrick "Pat" Caddell was one of the principal architects of Jimmy Carter's 1976 presidential campaign and one of his leading advisers and strategists. Although not one of the circle of Georgians whom Carter brought with him to the White House, his detailed and thoughtful analyses of public opinion, while often critical of the administration, were carefully read by the president and his closest staff.

Pat Caddell was born on May 19, 1950, in Rock Hill, South Carolina. Something of an intellectual prodigy, Caddell attended Harvard University but did not graduate, later commenting that he "went to one statistics class [at Harvard] and lasted five minutes. I discovered that whatever they were doing and I was doing had nothing in common." Although only 22 years old in 1972, he was already the pollster for Democratic presidential candidate GEORGE MCGOVERN (S.Dak.). At the Democratic National Convention in New York that year, HAMILTON JORDAN and GERALD RAFSHOON tried to persuade him to consider Carter as McGovern's running mate. Caddell, however, was unimpressed by the polling data purporting to show how the Georgia governor would make the strongest vice-presidential candidate on the McGovern ticket.

In 1975, while Carter was campaigning in Iowa, more than a year after announcing his presidential candidacy, Caddell agreed to join the campaign. Based on polling his company had conducted in 1974, he was impressed by what he regarded as Carter's instinctive sense of the major issues concerning Americans. "Even today," he remarked after Carter had left the White House, "it is hard to imagine how a peanut farmer and one-term governor from Georgia with no national experience could become president. But by figuring out what Americans were looking for—and giving it to them—Carter did just that."

Caddell was instrumental in defining the candidate's campaign appeal to the American people. Driving Americans the most, he had found in his 1974 polling, was a sense of alienation from the increasingly partisan political process and a desire to return to traditional values. What the American people wanted as president, he concluded, was someone with whom they could identify, whom they could trust, and who would be moderate and nonideological in governing the nation. These findings meshed with his own sense of a disconnect between American politics and the American people and the need to recast the Democratic Party along more populist, antiestablishment lines.

Caddell's conclusions also resonated nicely with Carter's perception of the national mood. The values-oriented themes of decency, honesty, trust, and governmental transparency helped carry Carter through the presidential campaign and into the White House. Throughout the campaign, Caddell remained close to the future president, constantly evaluating the public mood and honing his fundamental message accordingly. In the process, he boosted Carter's own self-confidence.

Once elected, Carter continued to rely heavily on Caddell as part of his inner political circle. In a 55-page memorandum, the political consultant warned the president-elect of the opposition awaiting him on Capitol Hill. He took his harshest aim at such liberal Democrats as Senator EDWARD KENNEDY (Mass.), Representative MORRIS UDALL (Ariz.), and even George McGovern, for whom he had worked just four years earlier, referring to them "in many ways ... as antiquated and anachronistic a group as are conservative Republicans." Caddell recommended that the president-elect "Carterize" the Democratic National Committee and make it "a political wing of the White House." Carter referred to the report as "excellent" and ordered that it be read by his other political advisers.

Although not holding any office within the administration, Caddell was hired as a pollster by the Democratic National Committee. Throughout Carter's four years as president, he continued to conduct surveys and make recommendations on a wide spectrum of issues. In fact, Caddell's responsibilities as private political consultant and unofficial adviser to the president expanded upon a development first begun by President RICHARD NIXON. During his administration, Nixon used private pollsters on an ongoing basis for the first time. But Carter elevated the role of the private consultant even further by the influence he allowed Caddell to assume within the administration and by making him one of the three main public spokesmen for the White House along with Press Secretary JODY POWELL and Gerald Rafshoon.

Under Nixon and GERALD FORD, moreover, political pollsters had been hired mainly to gauge public opinion on presidential image or performance. In contrast, Caddell conducted policy-related surveys on at least 20 important issues ranging from energy to consumer protection, government reorganization to race relations, and American attitudes toward Israel to the Iranian hostage crisis. For his efforts, he was paid roughly $2.1 million, compared to approximately $330,000 that Ford's political consultants had received from the Republican National Committee. Data collected from Caddell's surveys were distributed to the president's other top advisers and provided the basis for many White House discussions on major policy matters.

More generally, Caddell was able—often to the chagrin of such other key advisers as Vice President WALTER MONDALE and Special Assistant for Domestic Affairs STUART EIZENSTAT—to reinforce the president's own conviction about the alienation of the American people from the political process and their quest for a redemptive presidency. Carter's most notable address to the nation—his so-called malaise speech of July 15, 1979, in which the president warned of a "crisis of spirit" that was sapping the nation's ability to deal with an energy crisis—was predicated on Caddell's conclusion that a "sense of crisis" was the most serious problem facing the nation. Caddell had also persuaded the president to postpone a speech on energy planned for July 5 and go to Camp David, where he met with leaders representing a wide cross section of the American people, before returning to Washington to give his July 15 address.

That Caddell was able to assume such an important role in the Carter administration was due in large measure to his talents as a pollster and political consultant. But his position also reflected broader trends in the American political process. These included the declining influence of the two major political parties in determining presidential candidates and their agendas, the breakdown of party discipline on Capitol Hill, and increased competitiveness between Congress and the White House, all of which created the administration's need for frequent and detailed analysis of the public mood. Caddell was also the first political consultant to recognize what has come to be referred to as the "permanent campaign"—the view that maintaining public support and gaining congressional approval of a legislative agenda required an ongoing political effort akin to a political campaign. As Caddell wrote to Carter even before he took office, "Essentially it is my thesis that governing with public approval requires a continuing political campaign." He held to that view throughout the four years that followed.

Caddell had the unpleasant responsibility of telling President Carter, as Air Force One flew back to Andrews Air Force Base on the eve of the 1980 election, that the president was going to be beaten soundly the next day by his Republican opponent, RONALD REAGAN. Following Carter's defeat, Caddell remained active in Democratic politics, first serving as political consultant to Colorado senator Gary Hart in the 1984 presidential primaries and then to Walter Mondale after Hart bowed out of the race. In 1988, he backed the unsuccessful candidacy of Delaware senator JOSEPH BIDEN.

Caddell, however became increasingly disenchanted by what he considered the "moral bankruptcy" of the political left. In 1992, he voted for the independent candidate, Ross Perot, over the Democrat, Bill Clinton. After Clinton was elected, Caddell became outspoken in his opposition to the president, urging the Democratic Party in 2000 to purge itself of Clinton's influence and to return the party to its principles. In the 2000 election, he voted for the Green Party candidate, Ralph Nader, and even accused Democrats of trying to steal the election in Florida rather than having it stolen from them as most Democratic leaders believed.

Caddell also changed careers, moving from political polling and consulting to serving as a consultant and screenwriter for the highly successful television show *The West Wing*. He appears occasionally on political talk shows, including CNN, FOX, and MSNBC's *Hardball*, hosted by former Carter speechwriter Chris Matthews.

Califano, Joseph Anthony, Jr.

(1931–) *secretary of health, education and welfare*

As secretary of the Department of Health, Education and Welfare (HEW) from 1977 until July 1979, when he was fired by President Carter, Joseph A. Califano, Jr., was arguably the most able, and certainly one of the most contentious, members of the Carter administration. A former adviser to President Lyndon Johnson and an unreconstructed liberal, his views on social spending often conflicted with those of the president and his White House staff. What led to his firing, however, was his outspoken views on a number of controversial issues, most notably his antismoking campaign, and what Carter's closest advisers considered his lack of loyalty to the president.

Califano was born in New York City on May 15, 1931. The son of a working-class family, he grew up in Brooklyn during the Great

Depression and developed a hard-driving work ethic and ambition for success that stayed with him throughout his career. Raised a Catholic, he graduated from Holy Cross College (B.A., 1952) and then Harvard Law School, magna cum laude (LL.B., 1955), where he served as an editor on the *Harvard Law Review*. He then became a Wall Street lawyer who impressed those around him with his sense of commitment, energy, and obvious intelligence. He left private practice to serve in the Pentagon (1961–65), becoming Secretary of Defense Robert McNamara's assistant and main troubleshooter. He also caught the attention of President Lyndon Johnson's press secretary, Bill Moyers, who had been in charge of the president's domestic agenda before taking on his new job and was preparing to return to private life as a newspaper editor and journalist. On Moyers's recommendation, Johnson brought Califano to the White House and gave him primary responsibility for preparing and coordinating domestic legislation.

Although Johnson was a difficult and demanding boss, Califano developed a deep devotion to the president and to the Great Society programs that influenced his own career in government. Johnson's work ethic, his skills as a deal maker, his willingness to take risks, and his commitment to the poor and the underprivileged resonated with Califano. As for the president, he confided in his young special assistant and considered him one of his most trusted advisers.

After Johnson left office in 1969, Califano returned to the private sector, where he became a high-powered Washington lawyer, representing the *Washington Post*, serving as general counsel of the Democratic National Committee, and socializing with the likes of *Post* publisher Katherine Graham, *Post* editor Ben Bradlee, columnist Art Buchwald, president of the Motion Picture Association of America Jack Valenti, and law partner Edward Bennett Williams. As a private citizen, he entertained the idea of one day returning to public service as secretary of HEW, the only job, he said later, that he would be interested in accepting. He wanted to show that the enormous bureaucracy of HEW could be managed effectively and that the much-maligned programs of the Great Society could work.

Given Jimmy Carter's persistent attacks on Washington insiders during his campaign for the Democratic nomination in 1976, Califano thought that his appointment as HEW secretary was unlikely. But he was a personal friend of Senator WALTER MONDALE (Minn.), whom Carter chose as his running mate after winning the nomination in July. Mondale arranged a meeting between the two men at which the Democratic nominee expressed his concern about the decline of the American family and asked Califano to prepare a report on the family. Knowing that Califano was a devout Catholic, he discussed the politics of the Catholic vote with him and asked him to consult widely with Catholics in preparing his report.

Following Carter's victory in November, Mondale continued to press the case for Califano. Although the president-elect still had doubts about Califano's ability to run such a huge and complex department as HEW and told him so during an interview in early December, he offered him the position two weeks later. Califano accepted it immediately.

It was a choice Carter later regretted. Califano was an unreconstructed liberal who believed passionately in the Great Society and remained convinced of the beneficence of strong government. The incoming president was more concerned about the efficient operation of HEW and the need to rein in what he considered its untamed bureaucracy and ever-increasing budget, which was the third largest in the world behind the United States and the Soviet Union. While the new president was committed to giving cabinet secretaries ample autonomy in running their agencies, he also expected them to operate as a team and to apprise him on a weekly basis of their major initiatives. Califano was too independent-minded and too much of an infighter to fit easily into the Carter mode. And while Carter relied heavily on his inner circle of advisers from Georgia, Califano remained the quintessential Washington insider.

The secretary's first major initiative at HEW, however—restructuring its lumbering bureaucracy—meshed perfectly with the new president's own interest in improving the process of governmental operations by streamlining and making them more efficient. In fact, Califano chided what he referred to as "the liberal establishment" for sometimes forgetting that while government needed to be compassionate, it also had to be competent and efficient. This was not the case at HEW, in his view. When he took office, he was surprised to learn that 50 people reported directly to him; he considered this "a preposterous scam." He also objected to the way in which HEW was organized—along political rather than functional lines—so that Medicare and Medicaid, for example, were broken up and administered separately even though they both provided health care. Medicare was approved in 1965 as an amendment to the Social Security system because it was basically buying health care for the elderly. Medicaid was hooked to the welfare system because that was the only way it could get through Congress. Yet because they were both health programs, they needed, in Califano's view, to be administered together. Accordingly, he established the Health Care Financing Administration (HCFA), which brought the two programs under one administrative umbrella.

Characteristically, Califano established the new agency and made other major organizational changes at HEW within eight weeks after taking office. But he also did so in great secrecy and without informing the White House of what he was doing until a few days before he was ready to brief the president. Carter welcomed the news enthusiastically since it represented a telling example of what he was trying to accomplish in Washington. Yet this same veiled approach to administering HEW was already getting the secretary in trouble with White House staffers close to the president. In particular, Carter's chief assistant, HAMILTON JORDAN, was angry that Califano had not sought White House approval of his pick for undersecretary of HEW, Hale Champion, before announcing it publicly, especially since Champion had opposed Carter in the Massachusetts presidential primary.

In Califano's view, the major issue in Champion's appointment and in other high-level appointments he made was the degree of autonomy he would have in running HEW. But it was not the only issue. The secretary also objected to what he believed were news leaks from White House staffers alleging the president's displeasure with him over Champion's appointment because of the latter's support of Congressman MORRIS UDALL (Ariz.) during the Massachusetts primary. Despite the president's assurance that there was no substance to the stories and that he would not talk to Califano through the newspapers, the secretary was not entirely persuaded Carter was being candid with him. He also wondered about the administration's ability to leave the campaign behind it and get on with governing the nation.

Also worrisome to Califano was the president's approach to welfare reform. Like Carter, Califano recognized the need to make more cost efficient the labyrinthine welfare system administered by a patchwork of federal agencies serving a multitude of constituencies dependent on one or more income maintenance programs, such as Aid to Families with Dependent Children (AFDC), Supplemental Security Income

(SSI), food stamps, and the earned income tax credit (EITC) for the working poor. But the flip side of efficiency, in Califano's view, was compassion for welfare recipients and provisions for the working poor: this was consistent with his own commitment to the Great Society. It meant additional funding for such alternatives as guaranteed public service jobs for the unemployed, a negative income tax, a guaranteed minimum income, and health and family planning services. Furthermore, Califano was concerned that the president did not recognize the political complexities of welfare reform. Any major reform of a system so bureaucratically and politically inclusive would require the political wisdom of a Solomon, the courage of a Daniel, and the resilience of a Job.

But the president, who was committed to balancing the budget and cutting inflation, insisted on welfare reform at no additional cost to the federal budget. Having campaigned on the promise of a complete overhaul of the welfare system, Carter also insisted that Califano and Secretary of Labor RAY MARSHALL have a program ready for him by May 1, 1977, even though fashioning it at zero additional cost resulted in sharp differences between HEW and the Labor Department over which programs would receive preferential funding. HEW favored replacing the existing system of nine separate programs with a negative income tax, or direct cash payments to the poor based strictly on need. Labor favored more jobs.

The May 1 deadline for a welfare reform plan passed without HEW and Labor able to resolve their differences. Instead of submitting to Congress a comprehensive welfare reform program, the White House issued a statement of principles on which reform would be based. Submission of a welfare package was now put off until August. Both the president and his HEW secretary were by this time frustrated, the president because he had not met his own May deadline, Califano because the president, in contrast to Lyndon Johnson, seemed almost totally indifferent to the politics of welfare reform, much less to getting a package through Congress.

When the package was finally presented to the House and Senate in August 1977, it had such little support that House Speaker TIP O'NEILL (Mass.) announced that he was putting off consideration of welfare reform for the remainder of the session. In 1979, the House did finally pass a $5.7 billion program. By this time, however, Carter had lost interest in trying to reform the welfare system, and the measure became stalled in Senate committee, effectively killing any chance for liberalizing or simplifying the system at a time when the number of Americans living below the poverty line was growing.

Califano also found himself at odds with members of the administration on other major issues. These included the administration's handling of *Regents of the University of California v. Bakke*, an affirmative-action case before the Supreme Court involving 16 slots set aside for minority students seeking admission to the medical school at the University of California at Davis (UC-Davis). The HEW secretary was angered by the Justice Department's first brief on the case prepared by Attorney General GRIFFIN BELL, in which the department seemed to take the side of the plaintiff, ALLAN BAKKE, who had been denied admission to UC-Davis's Medical School and was challenging its policy of reserved admissions for minority students. After reading the brief, Califano wrote a lengthy memorandum to the president attacking the position taken by the Justice Department.

Carter's special assistant for domestic affairs STUART EIZENSTAT and counsel ROBERT LIPSHUTZ also took strong exception to the document. The president responded by ordering the Justice Department to rewrite the brief to include an unequivocal statement of support for affirmative action. But Eizenstat and Lipshutz expressed great displeasure at what they regarded as Califano's meddling in the matter. For his part, the secretary was struck by how uninvolved the president had been in the *Bakke* case, particularly when compared to Lyndon Johnson, who had helped to launch the first federal affirmative-action programs in 1965. Califano also noted the "sea change" he believed had taken place among lawyers in the Justice Department since the 1960s.

Nor did Califano agree with President Carter's decision to establish a separate Department of Education, something the National Education Association (NEA) had pushed for and had been promised by Carter in return for the NEA's support of his candidacy for president. In Califano's view, a separate department was not needed since it would mostly distribute money and oversee grants rather than have any policy function or purpose. It also posed the danger of federal intrusion into higher education on such matters as academic standards and excellence.

On health issues, the secretary, who was widely recognized as the most liberal member of the cabinet and was on good terms with Senator EDWARD KENNEDY (Mass.), acted as the administration's point man in opposing Kennedy's proposal for a program of national health insurance. At the Democratic Party's midterm convention in 1978, he even debated Kennedy, arguing that, like the senator, President Carter was committed to a national health plan but, because of budgetary issues, could not establish a firm date for its implementation, as Kennedy was demanding. Nevertheless, Califano sensed that the president found his relationship with the senator too close for his political comfort.

Even more disturbing to the White House, however, was the secretary's antismoking campaign. At one time a chain-smoker who had gone through four packs a day, Califano had weaned himself off smoking in 1975. After becoming HEW secretary, he decided to make smoking HEW's leading health issue, although he also gave high priority to such other health-related matters as substance abuse, child immunization, and alcoholism prevention. Following months of quiet planning and without consulting the White House, he announced on January 11—the 14th anniversary of the surgeon general's report on smoking and health—an aggressive antismoking campaign for which he labeled smoking "Public Health Enemy Number One."

Even before the announcement, newspaper leaks had begun to circulate about the campaign. Carter's special assistant on health issues, PETER BOURNE, tried to distance the president from it by stating that smokers should not be treated as social outcasts. But as soon as the campaign was launched, lawmakers from tobacco-producing states and lobbyists representing the cigarette industry complained loudly to the president, warning him that if the campaign was not stopped, he would lose much of the South in his bid for reelection in 1980. The governor of North Carolina, Jim Hunt, urged Carter to fire Califano.

The president declined to take any drastic action against his cabinet member and even pointed out to him that Carter's own father was a heavy smoker who had died of pancreatic cancer. But he made clear to the secretary that he did not want the White House tied to the antismoking campaign. Members of the White House staff were even more direct, letting it be known through the press that, in their view, the antismoking campaign represented another example of Califano's lack of loyalty to Carter.

By late summer 1979, the issue of loyalty to the president had assumed particular importance for the White House. At a time when the administration was clearly in political trouble because of high energy prices, a troubled economy, and the Iranian hostage crisis, and on the eve of the president's bid for reelection, it ill behooved the administration to have a member of the cabinet who was not loyal to the president or whose own agenda could harm the president politically. Unfortunately for Califano, that was how he was being perceived at the White House. Even the president's wife Rosalynn believed he should be fired.

The president reached a similar conclusion. On July 15, 1979, after spending 11 days in seclusion at Camp David and then making a televised speech on a "crisis of confidence" in the United States, the president asked for resignation letters from all his staff and cabinet members. The next day, he told Califano he was accepting his resignation.

The news shocked the HEW secretary, all the more so because his marriage of 23 years was in the process of breaking up. Califano attributed his firing to the power of the tobacco interests in Washington. Despite his deserved reputation for toughness as both an attorney and public official, he became deeply depressed by his firing and even shed tears when he announced his resignation to an assembly of HEW employees. He did not leave his position quietly. Instead, he entered into a public dispute with the president over whether Carter had told him on the day he accepted his resignation that he was the best secretary HEW had ever had, something Califano claimed and the president denied.

In 1981, Califano published *Governing America*, a highly unflattering account of his experiences as a member of the Carter administration. In the book, he pointed out the ethical and moral issues he faced as a devout Catholic whose position required him to deal with such public health issues as abortion rights and care of the dying.

After leaving HEW, Califano considered seeking elective office running for either the U.S. Senate from New York or governor of New Jersey. But he was dissuaded from doing so because of the time and fund-raising involved in elective politics. Instead, he founded his own law firm, Califano, Ross, & Heineman, with two colleagues from HEW and built up a lucrative practice representing prominent Washington figures and major corporate clients. Reflecting his ongoing interest in health-care delivery and cost containment, Califano has also consulted and lectured widely on the United States' health-care system. In 1992, he established the National Center on Addiction and Substance Abuse (CASA) at Columbia University; he serves as its president and chairman. He has received numerous honorary degrees and has authored nine books.

In 1982, Califano divorced his wife Trudy after being assured that he could continue to receive Catholic communion. The next year, he married Hilary Paley Byers, whom he had met two years earlier and who was the daughter of CBS Chairman William Paley. They live in New York City.

Callaghan, James

(Leonard James Callaghan)
(1912–2005) *British prime minister*

Of all the European leaders with whom he dealt during his administration, President Jimmy Carter felt most comfortable with the British prime minister James Callaghan. In contrast to his sometimes adversarial relationship with the leaders of Western Europe's two other major powers, West Germany's HELMUT SCHMIDT and France's VALÉRY GISCARD D'ESTAING, Carter found Callaghan to be generally accommodating on such matters as sanctions against Rhodesia and missiles in Europe. On a more prickly question having to do with the treatment of Catholics in Northern Ireland, the two leaders largely finessed the question by making self-serving statements and then ignoring the problem. Callaghan's defeat in the British elections in 1979 and his replacement by Margaret Thatcher as prime minister, whose agenda differed dramatically from that of her predecessor, was a disappointment, therefore, for the American president.

Born in Portsmouth, England, on March 12, 1912, Leonard James Callaghan was the son of a chief petty officer in the Royal Navy. When he was nine years old, his father died, and his family was thrown into poverty until the Labour Party took office in 1931 and began paying small pensions to families like the Callaghans. "After that we were Labour for life," Callaghan later recalled.

Although Callaghan never completed his education, he was able to secure a job as a clerk for the Internal Revenue Service. At age 24, he became an official of the Association of Officers of Taxes, which he had been instrumental in establishing. Two years later, he was assistant secretary of the Inland Revenue Staff Federation and being considered by the Labour Party as a candidate for Parliament. In 1939, he joined the Royal Navy, and he served as an intelligence officer in the Far East during World War II.

After the war, Callaghan began his political career when he was elected to Parliament for South Cardiff in the general election that threw out the Conservatives under Prime Minister Winston Churchill and brought the Labour government into power under Clement Attlee.

Prime Minister of the United Kingdom James Callaghan and President Carter, 1977 *(Jimmy Carter Library)*

In the years that followed, he rose steadily through the Labor ranks, becoming a national figure and spokesman for Labour. From 1956 to 1964, while the Conservatives were in power, he served in Labor's shadow government. He also vied unsuccessfully for leadership of the party following the death of Hugh Gaitskell.

Following Labour's narrow victory in 1964, Prime Minister Harold Wilson made Callaghan chancellor of the exchequer, an unfortunate appointment since he had to oversee a sluggish economy, which he tried to remedy through severe budget cuts. He also approved some of the most controversial tax measures in British history, including the corporation and selective employment taxes. In 1967, he acceded to the inevitable by devaluating the pound by over 14 percent—from $2.80 to $2.40—following a run on the British pound as a result of the Six-Day War in the Middle East and a London dock strike.

With the British economy in disarray and a growing call for Callaghan's resignation, he swapped positions with Roy Jenkins and served as home secretary until 1970, when the Conservatives were returned to power under Edward Heath. As home secretary, Callaghan had to deal with an upswing of violent attacks by Protestants against the Catholic minority in Northern Ireland. At the request of the Northern Ireland government, he sent British troops into Northern Ireland to protect the Catholics.

When Harold Wilson was returned to power in 1974, he appointed Callaghan as foreign secretary. Callaghan's main task was to renegotiate the terms of Britain's entry into the European Economic Community (or Common Market). In 1976, when Wilson resigned unexpectedly as prime minister following his 60th birthday, Callaghan was chosen by the Labour Party to replace him. He was the first prime minister to have held all three major cabinet positions—chancellor of the exchequer, home secretary, and foreign secretary—prior to becoming prime minister.

As prime minister, Callaghan had to lead from a position of political weakness since his was a minority government dependent on support from the Liberal Party to remain in power. Furthermore, he was faced with many of the same problems that President Carter faced in the United States—inflation and high unemployment exacerbated by rising oil prices over which he had little control. Also, the Labour Party was divided between its more radical and more conservative wings, just as the U.S. Democratic Party was split between its more liberal and more moderate factions. Following a vote of no confidence in 1979, Callaghan was forced to call for new elections that returned the Conservatives, led by Margaret Thatcher, to power, just as Carter lost a year later in his bid for reelection to his conservative opponent, RONALD REAGAN.

In the years that they led their respective countries, Callaghan and Carter worked well together. Part of the reason was the similarity of the problems they shared. Unlike Schmidt and Giscard d'Estaing, who blamed many of the world's economic problems during the second half of the 1970s on the profligacy of the United States, especially its huge consumption of oil, rather than on the need to stimulate their own economies, Callaghan, faced with problems similar to his American counterpart, was far less accusatory.

Callaghan also sought to align British interests with Washington's rather than with those of Europe. For this reason, he seems to have made a concerted effort to be on good terms with President Carter. He wrote frequent notes to the president, talked to him often on the telephone, and in a cordial manner tried to explain to him the intricacies of interallied politics. According to National Security Advisor ZBIGNIEW BRZEZINSKI, "Callahan literally co-opted Carter in the course of a few relatively brief personal encounters."

Like the United States' other European allies, the British prime minister urged President Carter at the beginning of his administration to be more forthcoming with the Soviet Union on the Strategic Arms Limitation Talks (SALT). He also raised questions about the president's outspoken criticisms of the Soviet Union's treatment of its political dissidents. But he did so in a less critical way than other European allies.

British treatment of Catholics in Northern Ireland presented a thornier question for the two leaders. The president was under intense pressure from Irish-American leaders in the United States, including House Speaker TIP O'NEILL and Senator EDWARD KENNEDY of Massachusetts and Governor Hugh Carey and Senator DANIEL PATRICK MOYNIHAN of New York, to speak out against violence against innocent Catholics by British troops sent to Northern Ireland to protect them in the sectarian war between Protestants and Catholics. Given the United States' historical relationship with Britain and Carter's own high profile on human rights, this placed the president in an awkward position, all the more so because during the 1976 campaign he had worn a campaign button during the St. Patrick's Day parade in New York proclaiming "Get Britain out of Ireland." Furthermore, in the week before the election, he had proclaimed the Democratic Party's commitment to Irish unity. As president, Carter would have liked to have avoided the issue of Northern Ireland altogether. Under pressure from Irish-American leaders, however, he was compelled to issue a statement in August 1977 urging the Irish and British governments to work toward a solution in Northern Ireland and raising the possibility of U.S. economic assistance to help rebuild the strife-torn province. Nonetheless, for the next two years, he failed to put any pressure on the British to resolve the situation in Northern Ireland. To the contrary, he stated that the British were fully aware of his position on human rights and that to make a statement urging Britain to promote "a comprehensive bill of rights for Northern Ireland," as was being proposed by some lawmakers on Capitol Hill, would constitute undue interference in British affairs.

Not until six days before the 1978 election did the president issue another statement, this time calling for an "international commission on human rights in Northern Ireland." But again, the administration failed to apply any pressure on the Callaghan government to further this proposal other than to tacitly support a ban on the sale of arms to the Royal Ulster Constabulary (RUC). As for Prime Minister Callaghan, his government launched protests whenever the United States raised the issue of the treatment of Catholics in Northern Ireland. Like the president, however, he finessed the matter by not raising it as a major agenda item in British-American relations.

On two other issues, Callaghan and Carter worked together closely. The first of these concerned maintaining sanctions against the all-white minority government of Ian Smith in Rhodesia until arrangements could be worked out for majority rule. Despite demands by right-wing Republicans in the United States for lifting sanctions against Rhodesia following elections that were unacceptable to the majority of blacks in that country, both Callaghan and Carter were committed to maintaining sanctions until a more satisfactory political settlement could be reached. Their efforts were complicated by growing pressure on the British government to extricate Britain from the Rhodesian quagmire and in the United States to accept the results of the elections that had taken place in Rhodesia and lift the economic sanctions. Because Rhodesia was a break-away colony from Britain, Callaghan asked the president in a telephone conversation to be able to "move on his own," and Carter agreed to the request.

When British efforts to bring the various Rhodesian parties together for an all-parties conference failed, however, London and Washington issued a joint statement urging that such a conference be called. In an effort to ward off demands in the United States to accept the results of the elections that had taken place in Rhodesia, the White House endorsed the 1978 Case-Javits Amendment, which provided for the lifting of sanctions by December 31, 1978, on the condition that the Rhodesian government agreed to attend an all-parties conference and that a new government was installed following internationally supervised free elections. Nevertheless, at the time that James Callaghan was replaced by Margaret Thatcher in 1979, the British and Americans were still striving together to bring about a final settlement in Rhodesia.

Callaghan and Carter were in general agreement about the neutron bomb. No matter caused West German chancellor Schmidt more apoplexy, however, than Carter's indecision on the bomb, even though Schmidt failed to acknowledge his own vacillation on the issue. The weapon was intended to deter a Soviet attack in Europe by destroying enemy personnel in tank concentrations without destroying nearby population centers through the explosion of a shell that emitted high concentrations of radiation without the blast or heat caused by other weapons. The morality of a weapon that killed people but did little damage to property weighed heavily on the president's mind, as it did for opponents of the weapon throughout Europe. For that reason, none of the European powers, including Germany, were willing to have the weapon on their soil, which was one reason the president decided not to go forward with its development.

Carter's announcement that he was deferring production of the neutron bomb nevertheless created a tempest throughout western Europe. In West Germany, Schmidt charged the president with indecision and betrayal. In contrast, Prime Minister Callaghan was one of those who persuaded the president not to go forward with the development of the nuclear device. "He said it would be the greatest relief in the world if we announced that we were not going to go ahead with [development of the neutron bomb]; that it would be a very difficult political issue for him to handle in Great Britain," the president noted in his diary after meeting with the British prime minister on March 23, 1978.

Callaghan was also supportive of the president's position on the deployment of theater nuclear forces (TNF) in western Europe. This was another problem that came between Schmidt and Carter. At issue was the superiority of the Soviet Union in medium-range nuclear weapons, not covered in the SALT talks, capable of hitting much of western Europe but not the United States. All the European leaders emphasized the need for countermeasures. At a summit meeting of the Western allies in 1979 at Guadeloupe in the French West Indies, the president agreed to place intermediate-range ballistic missiles and ground-launched cruise missiles in Europe.

Nevertheless, Schmidt continued to be confrontational about the TNF issue, insisting that he would allow the deployment of additional missiles on his soil only if the other European countries agreed to do the same. Although Callaghan took the position that it was necessary to include the European medium-range systems in SALT III, his demeanor was quite different from that of the German leader. According to National Security Advisor Brzezinski's account of the Guadeloupe meeting, "Callaghan displayed good political sense, was quite vigorous, and spoke very sensibly." In contrast, Schmidt "gave us a rather elementary lecture on nuclear strategy."

German chancellor Helmut Schmidt, President Jimmy Carter, President of France Valéry Giscard d'Estaing, and Prime Minister of the United Kingdom James Callaghan at the Summit Meeting of Western Allies in Guadelope, 1979 *(Jimmy Carter Library)*

In one unexpected way, the meeting at Guadeloupe helped to bring down the Callaghan government. In the previous year, Britain had showed signs of recovery from its economic slump. This was evident in the polls as the Labour Party began to close the gap between it and the Conservative Party. Most political observers had anticipated that Callaghan would take advantage of the improving political climate by calling for national elections, but instead he decided to wait.

Meanwhile, in what has since become known as the "winter of discontent," British trade unions went on strike after failing to get the large wage increases they were demanding. Factories closed, services came to a halt, garbage collected in the streets, water supplies were threatened, and families were unable to bury their dead. When asked about the crisis upon his return from Guadeloupe, a well-tanned Callaghan responded, "Crisis? What crisis?" Although his careless remark was not the primary reason for Labour's crushing defeat at the polls—a number of noneconomic as well as economic issues worked against the Labour Party—it added to the British public's general disgruntlement. Following a vote of no confidence in the House of Commons, Callaghan was forced to call an election. As expected, the Conservatives, led by Margaret Thatcher, were swept into office.

Callaghan stayed on as the Conservatives' leader until September 1980, when a party conference changed the way its leaders were selected. In 1983, he became Father of the House as the longest continuously serving member of the Commons. He remained a member of Parliament until 1987, when he retired after 42 years. Shortly thereafter, he was elevated to the House of Lords. On February 14, 2005, he became the longest-lived British prime minister.

Callaghan died on his farm in East Sussex on March 26, 2005, on the eve of his 93rd birthday, just 11 days after the death of Audrey, his wife of 67 years.

Carter, Billy
(William Alton Carter III)
(1937–1988) *brother of President Carter*

Widely regarded as an embarrassment to his brother, President Carter, Billy had a tragic life. While his older brother was in the world's spotlight, Billy was left to run the family business in Plains, Georgia. Considered a redneck and buffoon by many, a reputation that he encouraged for his own purposes, he was, in fact, an intelligent person and avid reader who suffered from a serious problem with alcohol made worse by his own sudden fame. During the most serious political crisis involving him and his brother's administration, Billy comported himself with great dignity, although his reputation as a sorrowful clown continued to follow him until his death from cancer at a young age.

Jimmy Carter was already 13 years old when William Alton Carter III was born in Plains on March 29, 1937. Billy's life was full of disappointments. While his brother was serving in the navy, Billy left high school to take care of his terminally ill father, Earl, and to run the family's peanut warehouse business. Billy later admitted that he was "mad as hell" when his brother Jimmy took over the business, which he had expected to fall to him.

After Earl died of cancer, Billy graduated from high school, but he had been a mediocre student who finished near the bottom of his class. Immediately after graduation, he joined the Marine Corps, and as soon as he finished basic training, he married. He never went to college. Every job he tried on his own was unsuccessful, although by the time his brother became governor of Georgia, he was doing a good job running the Carters' peanut warehouse. In 1976, he had another disappointment when he lost his bid to be mayor of Plains.

After Jimmy won the Democratic nomination for president, Billy became a celebrity in his own right, which would create problems for him later. From a gas station he owned across the street from Carter campaign headquarters in Plains, he often talked with reporters visiting the small town. He was strikingly different from his straight-laced older brother, and reporters found his self-effacing jokes and down-home personality engaging. When once asked about his family, he remarked, "My mother went into the Peace Corps when she was 68. My one sister is a motorcycle freak, my other sister is a Holy Roller evangelist, and my brother is running for president. I'm the only sane one in the family."

After Jimmy Carter became president, Billy's good-natured humor and his willingness to laugh at himself were so well-received by the American public that he became a popular guest on talk shows. Seeking to capitalize on his notoriety, he awarded prizes at beauty contests, served as the pitchman for local businesses, and made appearances at public events, receiving as much as $10,000 an appearance. Known for his fondness for beer, he even allowed a line of beer to be named after him.

Matters changed dramatically for Billy after he returned in September 1978 from a trip to Libya, which Washington considered a renegade nation that encouraged terrorism. He had gone there as a guest of the government after being informed by Atlanta businessman Mario Leanza, who had Libyan connections, that Libya wanted to develop trade with the United States. In January 1978, Billy had held a lavish reception in Atlanta with a group of Libyans to discuss a trading partnership between their two countries. Asked why he was involved with a renegade government, he responded, "[T]he only thing I can say is there is a hell of a lot more Arabians than there is [sic] Jews. He also said that the "Jewish media [tore] up the Arab countries full-time," and he defended Libya against charges of state-sponsored terrorism, remarking that a "heap of governments support[ed] terrorism and [Libya] at least admitted it."

The public outcry to Billy's remarks was an embarrassment for President Carter, who could only tell the American public that he could not be responsible for his brother's actions. But for Billy, the response was personally devastating. His self-mockery, which the public had found endearing, was turned against him. His paid public appearances dried up, and his beer venture proved short-lived. A large acreage that he had purchased and a house he had built on it in Buena Vista—in part to escape the tourists that had flocked to Plains after his brother's election—were attached by creditors and the Internal Revenue Service (IRS), which claimed Billy owed back taxes on unreported earnings. Having had a drinking problem since he was a teenager, even consuming beer with breakfast, he began to drink more heavily as his financial problems grew worse. Finally, he committed himself to an alcoholic addiction treatment facility in California for seven weeks.

Although sober, Billy was still without a meaningful income. Using bad judgment, he turned to his Libyan friends for help; they were happy to accommodate the brother of the American president. Libya advanced him $220,000 as the first installment of a $500,000 "loan" for oil sales being worked out between Libya and a Florida oil company. As news leaked of this "loan," the Justice Department asked Billy, because of his close association with Libya, to register as a foreign agent as required by law. He refused on the grounds that he had never acted as an agent for Libya. Lacking evidence to the contrary, the Justice Department began an investigation into his affairs. In May 1980, the $220,000 loan was discovered. On July 14, Billy agreed reluctantly to register as a foreign agent and filed a report showing the $220,000 he had received as compensation.

The news that Billy Carter had registered as an agent for Libya created a political firestorm that the White House clumsily turned into a hurricane in the midst of the presidential election. Although the president and his brother denied truthfully that any influence peddling had taken place at the White House, they made unintentionally erroneous statements or overlooked matters that brought into question the veracity of their denials and led the media and Republicans to refer to Billy Carter's relationship with Libya as "Billygate." It was revealed, for example, that both National Security Advisor ZBIGNIEW BRZEZINSKI and First Lady ROSALYNN CARTER had asked Billy if he could get the Libyan government to assist in gaining the freedom of the 52 Americans being held hostage in Iran. A denial and then subsequent retraction by Attorney General BENJAMIN CIVILETTI and President Carter that they had not discussed Billy's case prior to July even raised questions about Civiletti's role in the fast-growing scandal.

The White House's inept handling of Billy's relationship with the Libyan government raised so many questions about possible cover-ups and influence peddling that the Senate decided to hold hearings into the matter. In response, the president announced that he would waive executive privilege and furnish whatever documents the Senate requested. But the star witness at the hearings was Billy Carter himself. In nine hours of testimony spread over two days in August, he succeeded in putting an end to the whirlwind the White House—and his own actions—had created. Denying that he was "a buffoon, a boob, or a wacko," Billy described himself as "a common citizen with uncommon financial and family problems." He also disputed charges that he had pandered for Libya. "I have not asked anything of Jimmy Carter or of any U.S. Government representative on behalf of the Libyan government," he said. Rather than profiting from being the brother of the president, Billy also maintained that he had suffered financially from the connection. Ten separate investigations into his affairs, including several by the IRS, had meant enormous legal fees, while negative publicity about his ties with Libya had cost him as much as $500,000 a year in public appearances.

Instead of the beer-guzzling clown often depicted by the news media, Billy proved to be an articulate, courteous, even sympathetic witness. His testimony, moreover, supported the president's claims that he knew nothing about his brother's $220,000 loan and that the White House had not extended special treatment to Billy. On October 2, the Senate investigation concluded with a report criticizing the president for trying to involve his brother in an attempt to free the Iranian hostages but acquitted him of any other charges. Nevertheless, "Billygate" tarnished the administration's image and added to the growing public displeasure with the Carter presidency.

After President Carter lost his bid for reelection in 1980, Billy Carter remained out of the public limelight. He had to auction off much of his property, including the gas station he owned in Plains that had become such a tourist attraction, in order to pay off $70,000 in federal tax arrears and $30,000 owed to local bankers. After the auction, Billy moved to Alabama, where he took a job as a public relations and sales representative for Tidwell Industries, a manufacturer and refurbisher of mobile homes and an outfitter of private airplanes. Later, he took a position as vice president of Scott Housing System, Inc., of Waycross, Georgia.

On September 25, 1988, Billy Carter died of pancreatic cancer, the same disease that had killed his father and two sisters. He was 51 years old.

Carter, Jimmy

(James Earl Carter, Jr.)
(1924–) *39th president of the United States*

James Earl Carter, Jr.—better known as Jimmy Carter—was born on October 1, 1924, in Plains, Georgia, a community of about 500 in the southwest part of the state approximately 190 miles west of Savannah and 120 miles south of Atlanta. The oldest of four children, he was the first president to be born in a hospital. He grew up on the family's 350-acre farm in Archery, a predominantly black community a few miles from Plains. His father, James Earl Carter, Sr., known as Earl, was a successful local businessman and farmer, who owned a considerable amount of real estate and operated a warehouse and brokerage in peanuts.

President Carter waving from Air Force One, 1977 *(Jimmy Carter Library)*

His mother, Lillian Gordy, was a registered nurse. Jimmy also had two sisters—Gloria, born in 1926, and Ruth, born in 1929—and a much younger brother, BILLY CARTER, who was born in 1937, when Jimmy was already a teenager.

As Carter has recounted in *An Hour Before Daylight: Memories of a Rural Boyhood* (2001), he had a childhood typical of a white youngster growing up in the rural South whose father was a successful—but by no means wealthy—member of the community. A loyal supporter of the Talmadge dynasty that dominated Georgia politics and an ardent foe of the New Deal, Earl believed totally in the southern system of segregation, but, according to his son, he treated his black workers with great respect and dignity. Lillian, who often cared for African Americans when other health providers would not, was more liberal in her racial views. The family home, a shotgun cottage set back about 50 feet from the dirt road on which it fronted, was comfortable. Jimmy had his own room, and there was even a dirt tennis court next to the house. But until he was 11 years old, there was no indoor plumbing, electricity, or telephone. The bathroom was the outdoor privy. When the family wanted to listen to the radio, it used a battery. Most of its food was homegrown. Electricity finally reached Archery when Jimmy was 13.

Most of Jimmy's neighbors either worked for the nearby Seaboard Airline Railroad or were sharecroppers or field hands on his father's land. On Sundays he attended the Plains Baptist Church, which, like all social institutions in the South, was segregated. But once a year his family would be invited by one of his neighbors, Bishop William Decker Johnson, to attend services at St. Mark African Methodist Episcopal Church (AME).

Carter's playmates as a young boy were the black youngsters who lived nearby. They hunted, trapped, explored, and fished together and played at each other's houses. He often ate

Jimmy Carter with his dog Bozo, 1937 *(Jimmy Carter Library)*

and slept at their homes, and for much of the time while his mother was working, he was brought up by a young black woman, Rachel Clark, whose husband, Jack, was foreman of Earl Carter's farmhands. Rachel would live to see Carter become president.

Occasionally Jimmy and his closest black friend, A. D. Davis, would get on the local train and go to nearby Americus to see a movie together. But his friend would have to sit in a separate section of the train and the balcony of the theater reserved for blacks only. "I don't remember ever questioning the mandatory racial separation, which we accepted like breathing or waking up in Archery every morning," Carter later recalled.

What Carter did remember was how obsessed he was with hunting and fishing, which was ingrained in every rural youngster. But like other such youngsters, he had his daily chores, the worst of which, he recalled, was taking buckets of drinking water as much as two miles from the spring where the water was drawn to the workers in the fields during the hot Georgia summers.

Carter did not become aware of the full system of southern segregation until he was about 14 years old when, as was the southern custom, he continued with his schooling while his black friends did not. Wanting to be on the varsity basketball team and having an interest in girls, he developed closer ties with the white community. Commenting on the separation that developed between him and his black friends, he later wrote: "We were still competed equally while on the baseball field, fishing, or working in the field, but I was not reluctant to take advantage of my new stature by assuming, on occasion, the authority of my father. Also, we were more inclined to go our separate ways if we had an argument, since I was increasingly involved with my white friends."

Finishing high school in 1941, Carter spent the next two years studying science at Georgia Southwestern College in nearby Americus and Georgia Institute for Technology in Atlanta before being admitted to the U.S. Naval Academy, which had been his goal since he was six years old. Rushing through accelerated wartime courses, he worked hard, excelled in his studies, and received high grades, finishing 59th out of a class of 820. Aside from his good academic record, there was little else noteworthy about his term at the academy. After graduating from Annapolis in 1946, Jimmy married Rosalynn Smith, who was also from Plains and was his sister Ruth's best friend.

Carter spent the next seven years in the navy. His first assignment was as radar officer on the USS *Wyoming*, an old battleship that was decommissioned in 1947. In 1951, he was assigned to what he regarded as "the finest Navy billet available to any officer of my rank—the development of the first atomic submarine." Before he received the assignment, he had to be screened by the person most responsible for the navy's atomic submarine program. Captain (later Admiral) HYMAN RICKOVER, a brilliant but demanding naval officer. As the lengthy interview was ending, Rickover asked the junior officer whether he had done his best at Annapolis. After reflection, Carter said that he had not, to which Rickover countered, "Why not?"

The interview had a profound and lasting impact on Carter. "Why Not the Best?" would be the theme of his drive for the presidency and the title of his campaign autobiography. A perfectionist, Carter saw Rickover's question as a challenge that demanded an ongoing process of self-examination. Rickover always remained bigger than life for Carter, a figure who would haunt him long after he left the navy. Even as governor of Georgia, more than a dozen years later, he would break out in a cold sweat whenever he was told that Admiral Rickover was on the telephone waiting to speak to him.

Carter had intended to make the navy his career. For Jimmy, and especially ROSALYNN CARTER, the U.S. Navy offered the opportunity to break from the confines of small-town rural America and to see the world and experience life in a way they could only have dreamed about growing up in Plains. Carter also enjoyed his work as a submarine officer. During his 11 years in the service, he proved that he was a good officer—intelligent, resourceful, able to carry out difficult assignments with a minimum of direction. If he had a career goal, it was to achieve the rank of chief of naval operations.

Then word came from Plains that Jimmy's father was dying, and his life abruptly changed. The next few years were a traumatic period for him and, even more, for Rosalynn, who did not want to return to Plains. But Carter felt obliged to take over the family business and assume the leadership role that his father, who in 1952 had been elected to the Georgia

House of Representatives, had always played. He felt he had deserted his roots to follow his own ambitions. The more he compared his life with his father's, the more he was convinced his father's way had been the more satisfying one.

After Carter returned to Plains, he learned that his father's warehouse peanut business was faltering, and it took several years of hard work by both him and Rosalynn before the business began to turn around. By 1960, however, the business was flourishing and Carter started to take an interest in politics. When some of his friends encouraged him to run for office, he needed little persuasion. In 1962, he ran for the state senate. On election day, he lost by 139 votes to the candidate of a county political machine, Homer Moore. But with the help of two lawyers, GRIFFIN BELL and CHARLES KIRBO, both of whom would figure prominently in Carter's later political career, he was able to go to court and prove widespread voting fraud, giving him the primary victory. In the regular election, he won by a comfortable margin.

Carter served two terms in the senate, during which he established a record as an industrious and hard-working legislator who supported "good government" measures and educational reform. He lashed out at lobbyists for special-interest groups, and he stressed the importance of caring for the poor, the underprivileged, and the underrepresented in government. By 1965, Carter was named in a Georgia newspaper poll as one of the state's most influential legislators. Spurred by this, he decided to seek higher office in 1966. Although first announcing that he intended to run for Congress, he changed his mind and decided instead to run for governor.

Virtually unknown outside his own district, Carter conducted a grueling campaign, traveling throughout the state and meeting an estimated 300,000 Georgians. Although political pundits initially gave him little chance of winning the election, he only narrowly lost in the primary to the segregationist LESTER MADDOX. The outcome of the election was another defining moment for Carter. Deeply depressed, he went through a spiritual reawakening that put religion at the very core of his existence. His renewed Christian faith intensified his commitment to public service. He accepted theologian Reinhold Niebuhr's aphorism that "the sad duty of politics is to establish justice in a sinful world."

At peace with himself and convinced that he had good work to do, Carter decided to run for governor again in 1970 and to win whatever the cost. The result was a campaign that even his own advisers would later regret, as he won by appealing to segregationist elements in the state. But after assuming office, Carter established a reputation as a racial moderate and reform leader. In his inaugural address, he surprised his listeners by promising to steer Georgia into a new era of racial equality and economic and social justice. "No poor, rural, weak, or black person," he declared, "shall ever again have to bear the additional burden of being deprived of the opportunity for an education, a job, or simple justice."

As part of that commitment, Carter increased the number of black state employees from 4,850 to 6,684. He also signed into law legislation mandating equal distribution of state aid to poor and wealthy areas of Georgia, and he worked successfully for environmental protection; for tax, welfare, and judicial reform; and for consumer protection—all programs that would receive similarly high priority during the Carter presidency. He also instituted the practice of "zero-based budgeting," a system requiring an annual review of budgetary priorities as a means of promoting and measuring efficiency.

Carter's first priority as governor, however, was the reorganization of state government in order to improve its operation and cost-effectiveness. A reorganization measure was approved, and the governor was able to reduce the number of state agencies from 300 to 22. In getting the measure approved by the state legislature, Carter encountered stiff resistance in the senate and made many of the same strategic and tactical mistakes that he would make as president. He unnecessarily antagonized powerful state officials by his stubbornness and combativeness, turning the battle over reorganization into a morality play in which he was the guardian of the public welfare and his opponents were tools of special interests. As one reporter remarked, "Carter feels he's right and he's got a lot of integrity, but he just doesn't communicate." Much of the reorganization that took place also amounted to little more than a reshuffling of responsibilities or eliminating agencies that never met. Nevertheless, the overall outcome was a more effective and responsive state government than had existed before.

In 1974, Carter announced his intention to run for president. Although no candidate from the South had been elected president for more than a century and the Georgia governor was scarcely known outside his own state, he believed he could win by campaigning as a political outsider. In fact, he had begun to consider running for president as early as 1972. Meeting a number of Democratic leaders at the executive mansion in Atlanta, including potential candidates for the party's nomination in 1976, he was convinced that he was as qualified as they were to be president. Several of his closest advisers had encouraged him to seek the office. One of them, HAMILTON JORDAN, had drawn up a detailed plan for winning the nomination that included running as an outsider on a platform of restoring honesty and trust to government. Jordan's 72-page memorandum became the blueprint for Carter's campaign. In fact, the only major difference between Jordan's recommendations and the strategy adopted was Carter's decision to enter as many primaries as possible instead of running in a carefully chosen few as Jordan had advised. "Our strategy was simple," Carter later recalled, "make a total effort all over the country."

The strategy worked brilliantly. Wherever he traveled, Carter remained intentionally vague on the issues—stating publicly, for example, that he could not support an antiabortion constitutional amendment (already a heated campaign issue) but allowing that he might back a "national statute" limiting abortions. Since Carter's message was the failure of government to be worthy of the character and principles of the American people, he could reap the fallout from the Watergate scandal and RICHARD NIXON's subsequent resignation in August 1974. Among a large group of candidates vying for the nomination, he was able to position himself as the most moderate and centrist, giving him the broadest appeal of all the candidates. He also developed the best organization and was meticulous in keeping track of potential supporters. Chalking up victories in the early primaries in 1976, he lost in some important states, among them California and some of the other late-primary states. But even in those states where he lost, he picked up delegates because of the proportional manner in which delegates were selected. By the time the Democrats gathered in New York in July to select their presidential nominee, Carter was assured a first-ballot victory.

Carter's campaign against the Republican nominee, President GERALD FORD, proved more difficult. Beginning with a substantial lead over Ford in the polls, he squandered most of it through a number of tactical errors, including an interview he gave to *Playboy* magazine in which he used risqué language and said that he had "committed adultery in [his] heart many times." The story exposed him to ridicule and raised questions about his judgment in granting an interview to *Playboy* in the first place. More serious was Carter's vagueness on the issues, which allowed Ford to use Carter's "fuzziness" against him effectively. The momentum of the campaign turned in Carter's favor, however, when, during the two candidates' second televised debate, Ford stated that Eastern Europe was not under Soviet control and would never be during his administration. In November, Carter narrowly defeated his Republican opponent, receiving 40.8 million votes to Ford's 39.1 million votes.

Elected president mainly because he offered the American people new leadership, Carter almost immediately alienated Congress by cutting from the federal budget a series of water projects that had strong support on Capitol Hill. He also presented Congress with an overly ambitious legislative agenda, which included welfare reform, a comprehensive energy program, hospital cost-containment legislation, tax reform, and Social Security reform. By August 1977, every one of these initiatives had become stalled on Capitol Hill. Meanwhile, a sluggish economy, which had begun to recover in the first half of 1977, started downward once more. The fact that Carter was more concerned with attacking inflation through budgetary restraint than with dealing with high unemployment through fiscal stimulus alienated many Democratic constituencies.

Besides domestic issues, Carter devoted considerable attention to foreign policy. In March 1978, he won a major victory when,

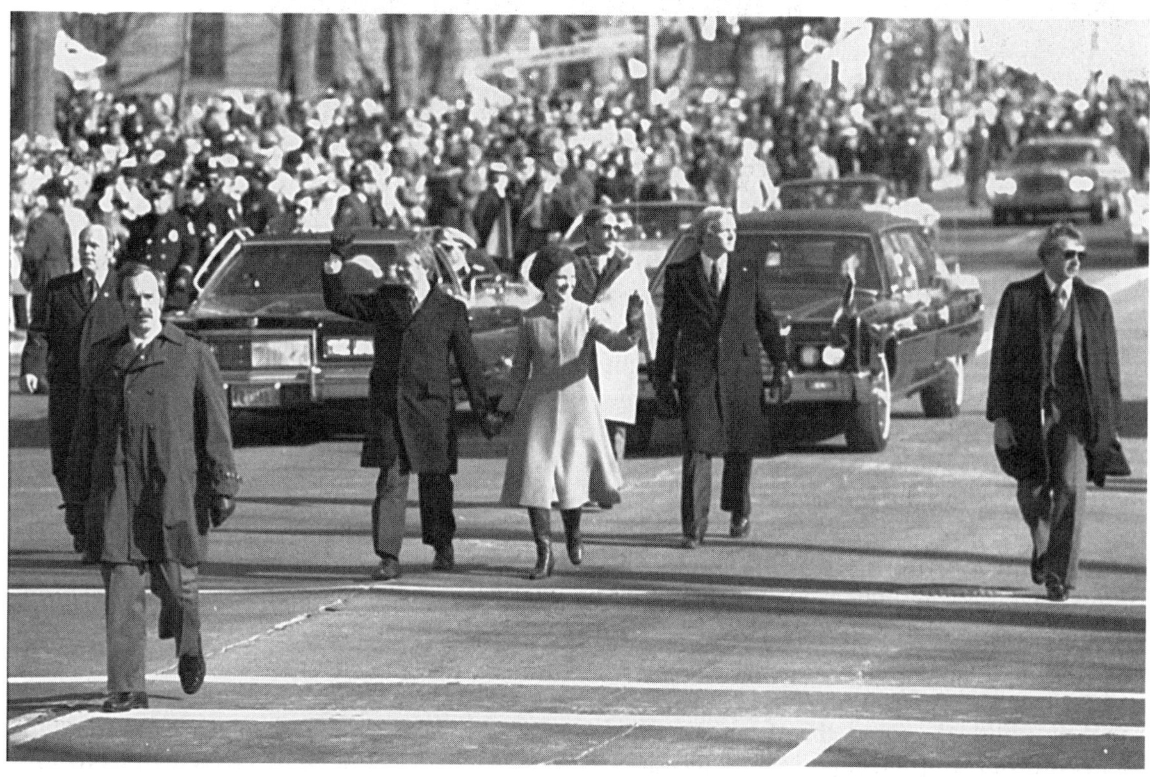

President Jimmy Carter and first lady Rosalynn Carter walk down Pennsylvania Avenue on his inauguration day, 1977. *(Jimmy Carter Library)*

President Carter addresses the nation on the energy crisis from the Oval Office, 1977. *(Jimmy Carter Library)*

over strong opposition, the Senate ratified the Panama Canal agreements turning over ownership and control of the canal to Panama by the year 2000. Six months later, Egyptian president ANWAR EL-SADAT and Israeli prime minister MENACHEM BEGIN signed the Camp David accords, ending their nations' long conflict and providing the framework for a settlement of the entire Arab-Israeli dispute. Carter won plaudits worldwide for brokering the Camp David accords. The next month, he won an important legislative victory when lawmakers finally approved his energy program, which had been stalled in Congress for 18 months.

The political capital that Carter gained as a result of Camp David and his success on Capitol Hill was, however, short-lived. As the nation experienced slow economic growth, high unemployment, and high inflation fed by dramatic increases in fuel costs, the president's approval ratings spiraled downward. Public discontent with Carter intensified in July 1979 when he fired five members of his cabinet after delivering a speech on energy in which he talked about a "crisis of spirit" in America. Carter fell so low in the polls that many political observers thought the Democrats would turn to Massachusetts senator EDWARD KENNEDY as their presidential nominee in 1980.

The political landscape was dramatically changed by two events. The first was the taking of the American embassy in Tehran and the seizure of 52 American hostages in November 1979, by followers of the AYATOLLAH RUHOLLA KHOMEINI, a fundamentalist Muslim cleric who had overthrown the shah of Iran, MOHAMMAD REZA PAHLAVI, the previous January. The second was the Soviet invasion of Afghanistan in order to prop up a Marxist regime in that country. Carter responded to the seizure of the American hostages by trying to gain their release through diplomatic means. He responded to the Afghan invasion by imposing a grain embargo on the Soviet Union and asking the Senate to delay consideration of the Strategic Arms Limitation Talks agreement (SALT II), which he had signed with Soviet leader LEONID BREZHNEV on June 18, 1979. As a result of his handling of these two crises, Carter was able to fend off the Kennedy challenge and win the Democratic presidential nomination.

Yet the hostage crisis, together with the slumping economy, ultimately helped defeat Carter's bid for reelection. A failed military mission to rescue the hostages in April 1980 became another entry in the list of failures that many Americans attributed to the president. At the same time, the economy remained in the doldrums. Although Carter managed to stay even with his Republican opponent, RONALD REAGAN, for most of the campaign by raising questions about Reagan's fitness to be president, the former California governor was able to win an overwhelming victory after dispelling doubts about his presidential timber during a televised debate with Carter. The Republican then returned to the two issues—the economy and America's position in the world—that most concerned American voters. On November 4, they gave Reagan 51 percent of the vote to Carter's 41 percent. An independent candidate, Republican Congressman JOHN ANDERSON of Illinois, received 7 percent of the vote.

After leaving office in January 1981, Carter returned to Plains, not fully recovered from the shock of his defeat, particularly the dimension of Reagan's victory. For several years, he was considered a political pariah by many Democrats. He did not attend the 1984 Democratic Convention and took no part in that year's presidential election. He also made few public appearances.

But then Carter began to turn matters around. He attracted considerable national attention by building houses for the Christian charity Habitat for Humanity. Following a brainstorming meeting with his closest advisers in 1982, he established the Carter Center, dedicated to the advancement of peace and human rights. One of the principal tasks undertaken by the Carter Center was to monitor and help resolve conflicts around the world. Carter personally supervised elections in such places as Haiti, Panama, Ethiopia, and Nicaragua. Following elections in Nicaragua in 1990, he persuaded Daniel Ortega, the leader of the Sandinista movement that had run the government since 1979, to concede defeat to his opponent, Violeta Chamorro. In 1988, the Carter Center also established the International Task Force for Disease Eradication, dedicated to ending such diseases as Guinea worm, river blindness, and polio found in Africa and other poor places of the world.

Not all the humanitarian work Carter did was well received. In 1990, he was criticized in Israel and the United States for meeting in Paris with Palestinian leader YASSER ARAFAT in an attempt to get him to accept Israel's right to exist as a preliminary step toward peace in the Middle East. In 1994, he was criticized again for negotiating, with the help of former chief of the Joint Chiefs of Staff Colin Powell and Georgia senator SAM NUNN, an agreement with a Haitian military junta to return to office the country's elected president, Jean-Bertrand Aristide, whom the junta had ousted from power. Carter drew further criticism for allowing the leaders of the junta to stay in Haiti instead of being exiled. In 1994, Carter also angered the Clinton White House and many political commentators by traveling on his own to North Korea and negotiating with its leader, Kim Il Sung, for a freeze in its nuclear program after it had been learned that North Korea had acquired the ability to produce the plutonium needed for an atomic bomb. By 2002, it had become clear that North Korea had violated the agreement. Even before then, the former president was accused of naïveté in believing he could deal successfully with such a ruthless regime. Finally, in May 2002, he was rebuked for traveling to Cuba and meeting with its leader, Fidel Castro.

Despite these criticisms, Carter has become widely regarded as the nation's best ex-president, a person who, along with his wife, has dedicated his life to world peace and human justice. In recognition of his work, the former president has received a number of major awards, including, in 1999, the Presidential Medal of Freedom, the nation's highest civilian honor. But no honor has been more prestigious than the Nobel Peace Prize he received in 2002. In making the award, which some commentators have charged was also intended as an expression by the prize committee of its opposition to the war in Iraq, the Norwegian Nobel Committee said, "In a situation currently marked by threats of the use of power, Carter has stood by the principles that conflicts must as far as possible be resolved through mediation and international cooperation based on international law, respect for human rights, and economic development."

Characteristic of the grueling schedule he has followed throughout his life, Carter has also found time since leaving the White House to write more than a dozen books on topics ranging from his recollections of growing up in rural Georgia, to the central importance of faith in his life, to a book of poetry, and even an historical novel set in revolutionary America. He has also become an expert maker of furniture in his fully equipped workshop in Plains, and he has found time to hunt, fish, and teach Sunday school at his church.

Finally, Carter has continued to speak out on issues of concern to him, most recently in opposition to the war in Iraq and in favor of shutting down the Guantánamo Bay prison because of alleged human rights violations of prisoners detained at Guantánamo. In March 2004, he roundly condemned the Bush administration for carrying on a war "based on lies and misinterpretations" in order to oust Saddam Hussein.

Carter, Rosalynn
(Eleanor Rosalynn Smith Carter)
(1927–) *first lady*

President Jimmy Carter's wife, Rosalynn, became one of the most influential first ladies in 20th-century U.S. history. Desirous of being more than a traditional first lady who limited her role to overseeing White House dinners and parties, Mrs. Carter acted as her husband's partner, adviser, and confidante. She gave numerous speeches in support of his presidency, represented him on missions abroad, attended cabinet meetings, advised him on a variety of policy matters, and became only the second first lady in the nation's history to testify before Congress. Her activism generated controversy, with critics charging that she had too much power and supporters arguing that she represented the modern American woman.

The eldest of four children, Eleanor Rosalynn Smith was born on August 18, 1927, in Plains, Georgia. Her father, Edgar, worked as a mechanic, while her mother, Allethea (Allie), stayed at home with the children. They instilled in their children a strong sense of hard work and religious devotion. Though she was from a relatively poor family, Rosalynn did not remember feeling deprived, and by all accounts, her early childhood was happy. When she was 13, however, her father passed away from leukemia, and the small inheritance he left was not enough for the family to live on. Rosalynn therefore took care of her sister and two brothers, while Allie mended clothes and worked at the local post office. When she was old enough, Rosalynn took a job as a beautician. Although she tried to appear strong for the benefit of her siblings, Rosalynn admitted that she "felt very weak and vulnerable." She also felt that she was not doing enough to help her mother, which added to her self-doubt.

Underneath Rosalynn's insecurities were characteristics that would make her an active and powerful first lady. She was driven to do a good job, both in helping to take care of the family and in school. Her parents had encouraged her to get good grades, and it was her father's wish before he died that she attend college. She graduated as her high school's valedictorian and then took two years of classes at Georgia Southwestern College. She planned to attend Georgia State College for Women to study interior design but left school in order to marry Jimmy Carter.

Rosalynn Carter, 1977 *(Jimmy Carter Library)*

There were close ties between the Carter and Smith families. Jimmy's sister Ruth was Rosalynn's best friend, and his mother Lillian, who was a nurse, had taken care of Edgar Smith during his last months. Jimmy, who was three years older than Rosalynn, had left Plains to attend the U.S. Naval Academy. After seeing a picture of him in uniform, Rosalynn developed a crush on him. With Ruth's help, Rosalynn and Jimmy went on their first date in 1945; they wed the following year.

Between 1946 and 1953, Jimmy Carter was stationed in Virginia, Hawaii, and Connecticut. Because he was often away at sea, Rosalynn had to assume new responsibilities, including overseeing the family finances. She also had to care for three children, born between 1947 and 1952: John Carter, James Earl Carter III, and Donnel Jeffrey Carter. Yet the future first lady enjoyed the independence she gained by running much of the family's affairs on her own.

Upon learning in 1953 that his father was dying, Jimmy decided to resign his commission from the navy and return to Plains. Rosalynn strongly opposed the idea, leading to the first serious crisis in their marriage. But she soon found herself with new responsibilities, including overseeing the accounting books of the family's peanut warehouse and giving Jimmy advice on how to run the business. For Rosalynn Carter, these duties marked the development of what would become a full-fledged partnership between her and her husband.

That partnership fully blossomed following Jimmy Carter's successful bid for the Georgia state senate in 1962. His new job required him to be in Atlanta three months out of each year, and consequently Rosalynn had to take on even more responsibilities. Yet she embraced them. "I felt very, very important because he couldn't have done it all if I hadn't managed the business," she later remarked. In 1966 and 1970, Jimmy ran for the governorship, losing in 1966 but winning in 1970. In both campaigns, he enlisted the family's support. For Rosalynn, going on the campaign trail caused problems, both because of a new family member—Amy Carter, born in 1967—and because she was insecure about her speaking ability. Seeing herself as her husband's partner, however, she left Amy in her mother's care and traveled around the state to speak, oftentimes on her own. Taking her husband's advice that she write down a few key points on note cards to help her gather her thoughts when giving a speech, Rosalynn developed into an increasingly confident and skillful speaker.

As first lady of Georgia, Mrs. Carter became her husband's full-fledged partner. Her experiences with the Carter family business and on the campaign trail had made her more self-assured. Furthermore, she wanted to maintain the independence she had come to enjoy. With one of her sons at college and the other two working for the administration, and with a nanny taking care of Amy, Rosalynn focused on a personal agenda that included promotion of the Equal Rights Amendment (ERA) and improvements in mental health care. Her support for the ERA developed from her belief that women should have the right to choose to be more than housewives and mothers. Her concern for mental health was influenced in part by the fact that Jimmy Carter had two first cousins who were mentally ill and another who was mentally retarded. In addition, during the 1970 campaign, she had been asked by a mother of a mentally retarded child if there was anything that Carter could do for her child. The new governor put his wife in charge of the Governor's Commission to Improve Services to the Mentally and Emotionally Handicapped. The commission's recommendations led to an increase in the number of state community health centers from 23 to 134.

During Jimmy Carter's bid for the presidency in 1976, Rosalynn again went on the campaign trail. She often stumped on her own or with her friend, Edna Langford. Her days were grueling, lasting as long as 18 hours, but she made certain to be back in Plains each weekend so that she could spend time with Jimmy and Amy. Observers noted the partnership that had developed between Jimmy and Rosalynn. It was not uncommon for her to refer to "we" when talking about her husband's campaign. She convinced Jimmy to run in all the nation's primaries, and she promised to use her influence to get her husband, if elected, to give women a greater voice in government. It was during the 1976 campaign that she received the nickname of the Steel Magnolia: she appeared calm and sweet on the outside, but according to campaign aides, she was a tough, ambitious individual who wanted to be first lady just as much as her husband wanted to be president.

As first lady, Rosalynn Carter was determined to open up the White House to as many people as possible while maintaining her family's privacy. The family's quarters, therefore, were kept off limits to the media and to visitors, and reporters were kept away from Amy, who attended a public school near the White House. With the help of her social secretary, Gretchen Poston, Rosalynn planned dinners for foreign guests and particularly enjoyed choosing the entertainment for those dinners.

But Rosalynn declared she had no intention of being a traditional first lady of the United States. She resolved to develop her own agenda and to continue acting as her husband's surrogate, advocate, and adviser. Domestically, her agenda focused on four goals: improving the nation's mental health system, trying to secure passage of the ERA, promoting volunteerism, and getting more help for the elderly. The latter two goals developed out of her work

First lady Rosalynn Carter chairs a meeting in Chicago for the President's Commission on Mental Health, 1977. *(Jimmy Carter Library)*

for the mentally ill. She had been inspired by programs where volunteers helped those with mental health problems, and she had learned that the elderly, more than any other age group, suffered from mental illnesses. She hoped that if she achieved these four goals, they would lead to a single larger objective, which was the creation of "a more caring society."

To promote this agenda, Rosalynn established a "Projects, Issues and Research Office" in the East Wing of the White House. It had a staff of nearly 20 individuals, including a chief of staff who received the same pay as the White House chief of staff (following President Carter's decision to appoint HAMILTON JORDAN to that post). The first lady fought mandatory retirement for the elderly; her advocacy helped lead passage of the Age Discrimination Act, which increased the mandatory retirement age in the private sector from 65 to 70. Additionally, she volunteered to help revitalize Washington, D.C.'s General Hospital; supported volunteer organizations such as Cities in Schools, which was designed to keep children from large-city ghettos from dropping out of school; lobbied state legislators to ratify the ERA; and, with her husband's support, was appointed honorary chair of his Commission on Mental Health, the job of which was to examine the state of the mental health-care system in the country and to make recommendations to improve it.

In what Mrs. Carter would later call one of her greatest disappointments, the ERA failed to be approved (the deadline for ratification expired on June 30, 1982). In Congress, however, lawmakers approved the Mental Health Systems Act, which she considered her greatest success. The mental health commission had held hearings in several cities throughout the country. In 1978, it issued its report, making more than 100 recommendations in such areas as health coverage, protecting the rights of the mentally ill, and community support for those with mental health problems. The following year, Rosalynn became only the second first lady in U.S. history to testify before Congress when she appeared before the Senate's Resource Committee's Subcommittee on Health and Scientific Research and lobbied for what would become the 1980 act.

Seeing herself as her husband's advocate and partner, the first lady believed that such successes as the passage of the Mental Health Systems Act would reflect well on him. To further support him, she made numerous speeches advocating his policies. She also lobbied lawmakers in support of the 1978 Panama Canal Treaties and went on the stump for Democratic lawmakers during the 1978 midterm campaign. In 1980, she came under criticism for her suggestion to use her brother-in-law BILLY CARTER's connections to Libya in an effort to get the American hostages out of Iran.

Rosalynn also acted as her husband's representative abroad. Commenting that his wife was an "extension of myself," President Carter sent her on missions in his name. During 1977, she traveled to 18 foreign nations including a multination trip to Latin America, during which she visited Jamaica, Costa Rica, Peru, Brazil, Venezuela, and Colombia. She held talks with the leaders of each of those countries on topics ranging from human rights to conventional arms sales, nuclear proliferation, U.S.–Latin American trade relations, and illegal drug trafficking. In 1979, she traveled to Thailand to examine camps where Cambodian refugees had fled to escape fighting in their country between the government of Pol Pot and invading Vietnamese troops. Upon returning home, the first lady successfully lobbied for millions of dollars in private and U.S. government aid for the refugees. Between 1978 and 1980, she also traveled, alone or with her husband, to India, Italy, Portugal, and West Germany.

The first lady also believed it was important that she have an understanding of what was happening in the administration. President Carter therefore had her attend cabinet meetings, and she joined many of the daily foreign policy briefings given the president by National Security Advisor ZBIGNIEW BRZEZINSKI. Carter also scheduled weekly luncheon meetings with her during which they discussed matters ranging from family to policy. Believing she had a better sense of people than he did, Carter oftentimes sought her advice on the loyalty of possible political appointees and had her travel around the country to learn what was on the mind of the U.S. public.

The first lady was also prepared to critique and even criticize her husband, urging him to adopt certain policies, suggesting alterations to his speeches, and offering her assessments of whom to appoint to administration positions. For instance, she convinced her husband to scrap his July 5, 1979, speech on energy and replace it with a broader message on the energy crisis. She also took part in the debate over the subsequent purge of the cabinet, seeing it as a chance to get rid of Health, Education and Welfare Secretary JOSEPH CALIFANO, whom she had come to oppose because of his lukewarm support for mental health funding; however, she did not favor the mass resignation that the president eventually decided upon.

The first lady acknowledged her influence within the administration. However, she was careful to qualify such statements by declaring that she limited it to those issues about which she had knowledge, such as mental health. Otherwise, she acted solely as a sounding board for her husband. There was no doubt that she was well-informed as to what was happening in the White House. The president himself commented that "aside from a few highly secret and sensitive security matters, she knew all that was going on." The perception that her influence was greater than she herself admitted was widespread, even within the administration. As the president's chief aide, Hamilton Jordan, stated, "Whenever I think the President is pursuing an unwise course of action and I strike out with him, I try to get her on my side."

Although Jordan and others in the West Wing saw Mrs. Carter as a potential ally in achieving their goals, relations between the East and West Wing staffs were tense. Mrs. Carter's press secretary, Mary Hoyt, and White House press secretary JODY POWELL did not get along. "The relationship between Rosalynn's staff and Jimmy's staff," reported one White House aide, "is hate. Hate. Kill. Kill." It was this poor relationship that reportedly led to the appointment of Edith (Kit) Dobelle as Rosalynn's chief of staff. The appointment, however, failed to overcome the ongoing disaffection between the two wings.

Not only was there antagonism between the two staffs, questions were also raised about the very idea of an active, influential first lady. Critics believing in a more traditional role for the president's wife disapproved of her activism and involvement in policy making, urging her to focus on issues more befitting her office, such as hosting dinners. Questions were also raised in the media as to why she needed so many staff members, including her own chief of staff, and why they received pay equivalent to those individuals who worked in the West Wing. Others wondered why the president would send her as his representative abroad rather than Secretary of State CYRUS VANCE or other high-level administration officials. "Who elected *her*?" became a common refrain. But the first lady also had her defenders, who stated that she was doing what any wife should do: support and advise her husband.

For feminists in particular, the first lady was an enigma. On the one hand, they regarded her as the personification of what women could accomplish and praised her support of the ERA and of appointing women to high-level government offices. On the other hand, they disliked her opposition to abortion and were dismayed by her seeming inability or unwillingness to adopt positions at variance with her husband. "She never appears to say anything separate from him," Gloria Steinem declared.

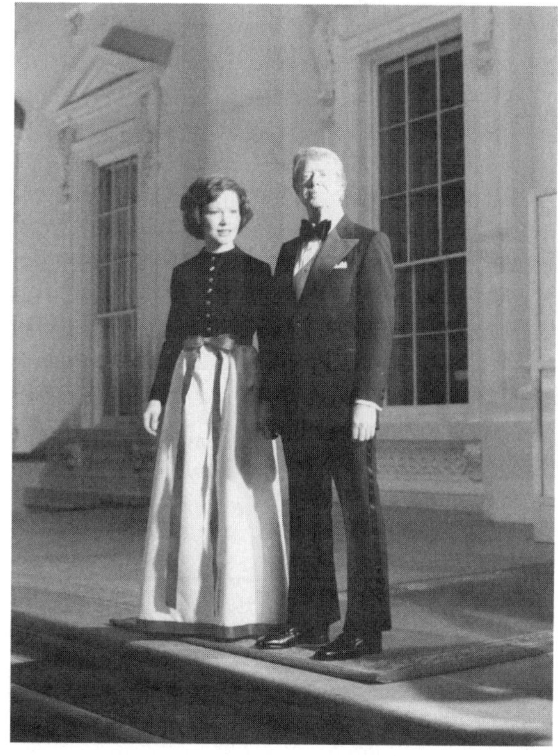

Jimmy and Rosalynn Carter, 1977 *(Jimmy Carter Library)*

"More than any other president's wife I have seen there is no independent thought or phrasing separate from his." Mrs. Carter responded to such criticism by stating that while she was opposed to abortion, she also opposed a constitutional amendment banning it. As for not publicly disagreeing with her husband, she declared that to do so would undermine any influence she might have on his decision making. However, this did not assuage feminists who felt that Rosalynn was more worried about getting her husband reelected than supporting women's issues.

During the 1980 presidential campaign, Mrs. Carter again was largely on her own, as the president decided to stay in the White House to oversee the effort to achieve the release of the American hostages being held in Iran. The hostage crisis, the Soviet invasion of Afghanistan, and the nation's economic troubles all played their part in the president's failure to defeat his Republican challenger, RONALD REAGAN, that November.

Since leaving the White House, Mrs. Carter has remained active. Continuing their partnership, she and her husband have worked together building homes for Habitat for Humanity, developing the Carter Center in Atlanta, and traveling around the world in an effort to fight disease and promote world peace. She has persevered in championing the causes of mental health and care for the elderly, and has written a book on each topic: *Helping Yourself Help Others: A Book for Caregivers* (1994) and *Helping Someone with Mental Illness: A Compassionate Guide for Family, Friends, and Caregivers* (1998). In 1995, she and her husband coauthored a book on life after the White House—*Everything to Gain: Making the Most of the Rest of Your Life*—which, ironically, nearly destroyed their marriage, as their memories of the past conflicted. ("I accused him of destroying my memories," she later commented.) She is currently cochair of the Carter Center where, among her other responsibilities, she heads the Carter Center Mental Health Task Force.

Christopher, Warren Minor

(1925–) *deputy secretary of state*

By the time Jimmy Carter appointed Warren Christopher as deputy secretary of state, Christopher had already become part of the Democratic foreign policy establishment. Later secretary of state during the administration of Bill Clinton, Christopher was best known during the Carter presidency for helping to negotiate the release of 52 American hostages from Iran just as Carter was about to turn over the reigns of leadership to President-elect RONALD REAGAN. For his efforts in gaining the hostages' release, he was awarded the Medal of Freedom, the nation's highest civilian award.

Christopher was born on October 27, 1925, in Scranton, North Dakota, the fourth of five children. After his father died of a stroke in 1937, his mother moved the family to California. He graduated from high school in 1942 and thereafter served as an ensign in the naval reserves (1943–46) with active duty in the Pacific theater. He then attended the University of Southern California (B.A., 1945) and the Stanford University School of Law, where he was president of the *Law Review* and graduated with honors (LL.B., 1949). Following law school, he took a coveted position as clerk to U.S. Supreme Court justice William O. Douglas. After working for Douglas, he was offered a position with the staunchly conservative California law firm of O'Melveny and Myers, where he was made partner in 1958 after serving as counsel to a number of large corporate firms.

At Stanford, Christopher had come under the influence of its young dean, Carl Spaeth, an internationalist who had worked in the State Department and had attended the first meeting of the United Nations in San Francisco. Spaeth kindled in Christopher his lifelong interest in a global order based on international law. He was also influenced deeply by his experience working for the liberal and social-minded Douglas.

In 1958, Christopher joined the gubernatorial campaign of Pat Brown, whom he followed to Sacramento as special counsel when Brown was elected governor of California. In 1965, he was named to a commission to investigate the rioting and looting that had broken out in the predominantly middle-class black Los Angeles area of Watts. President Lyndon Johnson was impressed enough by Christopher's efforts to appoint him in 1967 as deputy attorney general under Ramsey Clark. After touring Detroit that same year with Deputy Secretary of Defense CYRUS VANCE, his future boss during the Carter presidency, he recommended sending in troops to stop the looting taking place in the city. The next year, he and Vance worked together again to quell the disturbances in Washington that broke out after the assassination in April of Martin Luther King, Jr.

After Johnson left office in 1969, Christopher returned to his law firm but continued to remain active in Democratic political circles. When his former colleague and friend Cyrus Vance was appointed secretary of state by President-elect Carter, Vance lured Christopher, whom he later described as his "alter ego," to Washington as his deputy secretary of state. Whenever Vance was away from Washington, Christopher was fully in charge of the department.

As Vance's top deputy, Christopher was also a key player in many of the major diplomatic initiatives undertaken by the Carter administration. Christopher had not been President Carter's first choice for deputy secretary of state; that choice had been W. MICHAEL BLUMENTHAL. But when the president decided to make Blumenthal his Treasury secretary, he followed Vance's recommendation in selecting Christopher for the second top spot at the State Department.

Already known for his quiet manner, keen and analytical mind, unflappable demeanor, and persuasive powers, Christopher's first major assignment was helping get the Panama Canal Treaties of 1977 through the Senate. To do this, he needed to win over wavering Democrats, like SAM NUNN (Ga.) and especially DENNIS DECONCINI (Ariz.), who the president's top aide, HAMILTON JORDAN, said held "the fate of the treaties in his hand." Christopher worked closely with Nunn and DeConcini in last-minute wordings of reservations having to do with the possibility of a future U.S.–Panamanian agreement allowing U.S. forces to remain in Panama and giving the United States the right to intervene militarily to reopen the canal if it should ever become necessary (in exchange for which the United States agreed not to intervene in Panama's internal affairs).

Christopher also played an important role in normalizing relations with the People's Republic of China in 1979. The major opening to the Beijing government had occurred in May 1978 when, much to the chagrin of the State Department, National Security Advisor ZBIGNIEW BRZEZINSKI had traveled to China before a detailed position had been developed about moving toward normalization. In the months that followed Brzezinski's visit, Christopher spearheaded the normalization of relations with China, working closely with LEONARD WOODCOCK, the chief of the Beijing Liaison Office.

Unquestionably, though, Christopher's most important assignment as deputy secretary of state was negotiating, in the waning days of the Carter presidency, the successful release of the American hostages held by Iran following the seizure of the U.S. embassy in Tehran in November 1979. In December 1978, during the early months of the revolution before the shah of Iran, MOHAMMAD REZA PAHLAVI, fled the country, Christopher had joined Vance and other State Department officials in support of a policy that would have tried to work out some kind of compromise between the shah and the revolutionaries. But they lost out to the more hard-line position of Brzezinski, who urged the establishment of a military government that would suppress the revolutionaries. In April 1980, just before the failed military effort to rescue the American hostages, President Carter had telephoned Christopher in an unsuccessful effort to get Vance to support the rescue attempt.

Following Vance's resignation, many leading political observers in Washington expected that the president would appoint Christopher to replace him. Instead, Carter named Maine senator EDMUND MUSKIE as his new secretary of state. Although the president had developed great trust in Christopher and believed that he knew more about foreign policy than Muskie, the president thought the senator could help him more politically. Had Muskie not accepted his offer, Carter would have offered the position to Christopher, who agreed at his request to remain as Muskie's deputy. In fact, Christopher handled most of the high-level daily business at the department while Muskie acted more as the administration's spokesman on foreign policy.

Accordingly, it fell to Christopher to work closely with Jordan and the president's counsel, LLOYD CUTLER, in negotiating and coordinating the complicated details of the hostages' release. Secret negotiations for their release had begun in February 1980 when Hamilton Jordan met secretly in Paris with two men believed to have close ties with Iran's Revolutionary Council. For a time, it seemed that an agreement might be reached for their release, but the plan was thwarted by the Islamic leader of Iran, AYATOLLAH RUHOLLA KHOMEINI. In early September, however, the Iranians signaled their willingness to negotiate the release of the hostages under certain conditions, the most important being the unfreezing of Iranian assets in the United States. Carter assigned Christopher responsibility for conducting negotiations with the Iranians. By October, it appeared that the release of the hostages must be imminent, which led some Republicans, in the midst of a presidential campaign, to talk of an "October Surprise," suggesting that the Carter White House was seeking to use the release of the hostages for its own political advantage.

There was, however, no October Surprise. On October 27, Christopher, Muskie, and Brzezinski informed the president that the Iranians had postponed any decision on the release of the hostages and might release only some of the hostages to test whether the United States was living up to its part of the bargain. On November 2, the Majlis (the Iranian parliament) voted on the conditions for the release of the hostages. Reports that buses had been assembled outside the American embassy where the hostages had been seized a year earlier raised expectations at the White House that their release was about to happen. But Christopher then received news from German intermediaries who had met with top Iranian officials that a resolution to the crisis was not imminent.

Christopher and Cutler continued to negotiate with the Iranians. On November 10, Christopher traveled to Algeria, which had assumed the role of mediator between Washington and Tehran. Over the next month, Christopher performed a kind of shuttle diplomacy traveling back and forth between the United States and North Africa. Working through the Algerians, he was able finally to broker a complex deal for the release of the hostages in return for most of Iran's assets in the United States and the lifting of punitive sanctions. But much to his annoyance, the Iranians were bent on humiliating the president again by delaying the release of the hostages until after the nation's new president, RONALD REAGAN, had taken the oath of office. Not until 11 A.M. on inauguration day did airplanes holding the hostages lift off from Algeria. The Iranians made sure that the hostages did not leave Iranian air space until after the oath of office had been administered to Reagan.

After leaving the State Department in 1981, Christopher returned to private practice with his own law firm, O'Melveny and Myers. In 1991, however, he was asked by Los Angeles mayor Tom Bradley to head a commission to investigate police brutality and racism following the national scandal over the videotaped beating of an African American, Rodney King. Christopher's commission recommended significant reforms of the Los Angeles Police Department.

In 1992, Governor Bill Clinton of Arkansas asked Christopher to head a search committee for his vice-presidential candidate. After Clinton was elected president, he looked to Christopher once more to help select members of his new cabinet and to serve as director of the presidential transition team. A little later, he nominated Christopher to be his secretary of state. The appointment came as little surprise to most Washington observers. Since gaining the release of the Iranian hostages in 1981, Christopher had often been mentioned in the media as a likely candidate to head the Department of State should a Democrat be elected president. He had the credentials and experience for the position, and it was one he coveted. He also engaged in considerable networking while the Democrats were out of office.

Yet Christopher served only four years as secretary of state. During that time, he had to deal with such critical matters as establishing some degree of order in Somalia, peace negotiations in the Middle East, and an ongoing genocidal war in the Balkans involving Serbia, Bosnia, and Kosovo. Although he succeeded in achieving a peace accord between Israel and the Palestine Liberation Front (PLO), his tenure as secretary of state was dogged by events in Somalia and the Balkan states.

Following Clinton's reelection in 1996, Christopher resigned from the administration and returned to his law firm in Los Angeles. Since 1997, he has also served as a member and then president of the Board of Trustees of Stanford University and director and vice chairman of the Council on Foreign Relations. He remains active in civic and political affairs.

Church, Frank Forrester

(1924–1983) *member of the Senate, presidential candidate*

Frank Church of Idaho was a liberal Democrat from a strongly conservative Republican state who was elected to the Senate in 1956 and then reelected three times before he was narrowly defeated for a fifth term in 1980. His political longevity was due in considerable measure to his ability to stick to his basic political principles, such as in the areas of civil rights and the environment, while being keenly sensitive to the concerns of his constituency, such as protecting the rights of ranchers and lumbermen and restoring Amtrak service to southern Idaho. But his success was also the result of his intelligence, his oratorical skills, and his charisma, which made him one of the most powerful members of the Senate. The compromises that Church had to make between his liberal principles and the demands of his constituency, however, were evident during the Carter administration.

Church was born on July 25, 1924, in Boise, Idaho. His interest in politics began while he was still in junior high school. Even as a boy, his hero was William Borah, a Republican senator from Idaho for 33 years and one of the nation's leading political figures. It was Borah's example, Church later claimed, that led him to pursue a political career. After graduating from high school in 1942, where he was student body president and won a national debate championship, Church entered Stanford University. A member of the army reserves, he was called to active duty in 1943. He served as an officer in military intelligence in the China-Burma-India theater of operations and received the Bronze Star for his reports on Japanese troop movements in southern China's Yunnan Province. Discharged from the service in 1946, he returned to Stanford University, where he received his undergraduate degree in political science (B.A., 1947) and his law degree (LL.B., 1950). Already married and with two children, he was diagnosed with terminal cancer while still at Stanford Law School. Through a radical treatment of radiation, he was able to make a complete recovery, but doctors predicted that the treatment would probably shorten his life expectancy by as much as 15 years.

Following his graduation from Stanford, after working briefly for the Idaho Office of Price Stabilization in Boise, Church began a law practice and became active in state Democratic politics. Although he lost his first bid for election in 1952, for a seat in the Idaho Legislature, he was able four years later to defeat the incumbent in the United States Senate, Republican Herman Welker, making Church, at age 32, the fifth youngest person ever to serve in the Senate. In 1959, after serving on three relatively minor Senate committees, he was appointed to the Foreign Relations Committee, the first Idaho senator to serve on that committee since Borah.

Already known on Capitol Hill for his rhetorical skills, Church was chosen in 1960 to give the keynote address at the Democratic National Convention. A rising star in the Democratic Party, he supported the New Frontier and Great Society programs of John F. Kennedy and Lyndon Johnson, in particular the Civil Rights Act of 1964 and the Voting Rights act of 1965. But he was an early and outspoken opponent of the Vietnam War, taking the floor of the Senate in February 1965 to speak out against the conflict at the same time that Johnson was making his first major commitment of ground troops to the war.

Church was also a leading environmentalist on Capitol Hill before environmentalism turned into the major national movement it became after 1970. His vote on the National Wilderness Act of 1962 alienated mining, cattle, and lumber interests in Idaho and almost cost him his reelection in 1962. Church was able, however, to balance his liberal and environmental voting record with a good record of support for the needs of his constituents. He voted against gun control, for example, and blocked a measure to divert the waters of the Snake and Columbia Rivers from Idaho to the Southwest with a 10-year ban on federal aid for such projects. He also became chair of several subcommittees important to Idaho interests, in particular the subcommittee on public lands.

In the years between 1968 and 1976, Church continued to increase his reputation as one of the major figures on Capitol Hill. But it was his chairmanship of the Select Committee to Study Governmental Operations with Respect to Intelligence Activities, which uncovered abuses of power by the CIA and FBI, that brought him into the national limelight. Accusations that the FBI had used illegal wiretaps against such figures as Martin Luther King, Jr., Adlai Stevenson, and Justice William O. Douglas and that the CIA had been involved in plots to assassinate or overthrow such world leaders as Cuba's Fidel Castro and Chile's elected Marxist president, Salvador Allende, captured the headlines. They also stoked Church's presidential ambitions and led to a brief fling for the Democratic presidential nomination in 1976. Late in the primary campaign, he entered and won contests for the Democratic nomination in Nebraska, Idaho, Montana, and Oregon. Aware that his chances of gaining the Democratic nomination were slim, he pinned his hopes on a brokered convention in July in which he would emerge the winner. But when it became clear that this was not going to happen, he threw his support behind Jimmy Carter.

By 1977, Church had become the ranking member of the Senate Foreign Relations Committee. At President Carter's request and at considerable political risk to himself as a senator from a highly conservative state, he undertook a goodwill mission to Cuba that year. In 1978, he was the floor leader for ratification of the Panama Canal Treaties. Without his considerable political skills in shepherding the agreements through a floor debate that was characterized by countless "killer" amendments and parliamentary questions, they may never have been ratified. He also backed the second Strategic Arms Limitation Talks agreement (SALT II) that the United States had negotiated in 1979 with the Soviet Union. For the most part, Carter could look to Church to support his foreign policy.

Yet like many other congressional leaders, Church felt uncomfortable with the president and his staff. Almost immediately after Carter took office, the *Washington Post* published a story that the CIA had been secretly paying Jordan's King HUSSEIN millions of dollars over more than two decades. Given that he had just headed an investigation on abusive intelligence practices by federal agencies, Church was startled by the fact that when he confronted the president with the *Post*'s story, Carter seemed more concerned that news of the payments had been leaked than that they had been made in the first place. Offended by the president's reaction, the Idaho senator published an essay chastising the White House for its "draconian response."

Church also found Carter and most of those around him withdrawn and pedestrian in their thinking. "I feel no closeness with those people at the White House," he remarked more than once. On a number of occasions, he returned from the White House commenting on how mediocre Carter was as a president. As evidence of the political ineptness of the White House staff, he pointed to its insensitivity to protocol, including inviting opinion leaders from Idaho to the White House without first consulting him or keeping him apprised of developments. Long a supporter of the state of Israel, he split openly from the White House by voting in the Foreign Relations Committee against the president's proposal to sell 60 F-15 jets to Saudi Arabia.

More to Church's discredit than to Carter's, however, was the issue of a Soviet brigade in Cuba, which brought matters to a head between the two men in 1979. Having won a narrow victory for reelection in 1974, Church, now chairman of the Foreign Relations Committee, knew that he would be facing a difficult bid for reelection in 1980. He was also aware that the flip side of his growing national prominence was a sense in Idaho that the senator had lost touch with his constituents' interests. With the polls showing a tight race, Church was looking for an issue that might galvanize support for him in Idaho. The issue he found was the revelation of a Soviet brigade in Cuba.

Actually, some Soviet troops had remained in Cuba in a training capacity since the end of the missile crisis in 1962. President John F. Kennedy knew about the forces, but he did not regard them as a threat to the United States. Having come close to a nuclear war with the Soviet Union over the missiles in Cuba, Kennedy also did not want to reignite the crisis by challenging Moscow about the remaining troops. He asked the Soviets to remove the troops. Receiving no response, the subject was dropped.

Responding to a review of Soviet military activities in Cuba ordered by National Security Advisor ZBIGNIEW BRZEZINSKI, the National Security Agency (NSA) revealed in 1979 what it had known since the end of the missile crisis: the Soviets were maintaining a military force of 2,000–3,000 personnel in Cuba. Because a force of that size usually had a combat mission, the NSA referred to it as a "combat brigade." Whether, in fact, Soviet military personnel in Cuba had increased substantially in numbers in recent years or had been organized into a combat force from their earlier training mission was still not clear, although new intelligence in August concluded that there was a Soviet motorized rifle brigade in Cuba that had recently conducted field maneuvers.

News of the intelligence had already been leaked to *Aviation Week and Space Technology* magazine, which was waiting for confirmation before running with the story. Because of the sensational impact the news would have if it were also leaked on Capitol Hill before the administration had a chance to defuse it, the White House decided to brief key congressional leaders on what it knew. Among those briefed were members of the Senate Foreign Relations Committee, which was considering ratification of the SALT II agreement.

Known for his dovish views on the Vietnam War, which were still not popular in Idaho, Church called a press conference in which he attacked the White House for allowing the Soviet troops to remain in Cuba and announced that further consideration of the SALT II agreement would be postponed until the Soviets withdrew their forces from Cuba. In an unusual juxtaposition of views, Secretary of State CYRUS VANCE stated categorically that the United States must insist that the Soviets withdraw their forces, while the more hardline Brzezinski warned that to do so would only embarrass Moscow and prove counterproductive. (In fact, what Brzezinski wanted was a more generalized statement by President Carter condemning Soviet adventurism worldwide. What Vance wanted was to confine the issue to Cuba so as not to undermine the SALT II agreement.) The president seemed to side with Vance when he remarked that the "status quo" in Cuba was unacceptable. Meanwhile, the Soviets made clear that they would not negotiate over the withdrawal of their troops from Cuba even as Church continued his barrage on the White House.

Despite having instigated the dispute over the Soviet brigade, Church still supported the SALT II agreement, but he warned the president that there was "no likelihood whatever that the Senate would ratify the SALT treaty" until after the Soviet forces left Cuba. With the administration divided over what policy to pursue with respect to the Soviet brigade and with other lawmakers on Capitol Hill, including those opposed to the SALT II treaty, joining the Idaho senator in demanding action, President Carter decided to address the nation. In a speech on October 1, 1979, he declared that the Soviet brigade, while a serious issue, posed no immediate threat to the United States.

By his speech, the president effectively diffused a potentially explosive issue in Soviet-American relations. But the message did nothing to save the SALT treaty. The next day the Senate voted not to consider the agreement until the president assured them that the Soviet troops in Cuba were not engaged in combat. Whether the Senate would have voted to ratify the treaty absent the flap over the Soviet brigade is speculative. After December 25, when Soviet forces invaded Afghanistan, the question became moot, as the treaty was effectively dead.

Church's public campaign against the Soviet brigade failed to prevent him from losing, by less than one percent of the vote, his bid in 1980 for a fifth term in the Senate in a Republican tide that accompanied RONALD REAGAN's landslide victory for the White House over President Carter. It was ironic that a political figure hitherto able to win reelection in a politically conservative state despite his liberal voting record and his early and outspoken opposition to the Vietnam should go down to defeat taking a hard-line position on an issue, the Soviet brigade in Cuba, that he almost certainly would have opposed under other circumstances.

Following his defeat, Church remained in Washington practicing with the international law firm of Whitman and Ranson, traveling, and lecturing on international affairs. His life was cut short, however, on April 7, 1984, when he died of cancer in Bethesda, Maryland, at the age of 59.

Civiletti, Benjamin Richard

(1935–) *assistant attorney general, attorney general*

Benjamin Civiletti was attorney general during the last two years of the Carter administration. During that time, he and the Department of Justice were involved in a number of high-profile cases, including alleged cocaine use by Carter's chief of staff, HAMILTON JORDAN, and the connections of the president's brother, BILLY CARTER, with the Libyan government. He also argued before the International Court of Justice on behalf of the 52 Americans held as hostages by Iran.

Born on July 17, 1935, in Peeksill, New York, Civiletti received his undergraduate degree from Johns Hopkins University (B.A., 1957) and his law degree from the University of Maryland Law School (LL.B., 1961). After serving as a clerk for two years for William Calvin Chestnut, a U.S. district court judge from Maryland, Civiletti took a position as an assistant U.S. attorney (1962). In 1964, he joined the well-known Baltimore law firm of Venable, Beatjier and Howard, specializing in criminal and civil trial litigation. He made partner in 1969.

Following Jimmy Carter's election as president in 1976, the new attorney general, GRIFFIN BELL, looking for lawyers with criminal trial experience to oversee federal prosecutions, appointed Civiletti as assistant attorney general in charge of the criminal division of the Justice Department. Civiletti had been recommended to Bell by the attorney general's former law partner and the president's close friend, CHARLES KIRBO. Very quickly, Civiletti became Bell's trusted lieutenant, although he tended to be more liberal on social issues than the more conservative attorney general. A year later, Bell promoted Civiletti to deputy attorney general.

During Senate hearings on Civiletti's appointment as deputy attorney general, questions were raised about his involvement in the so-called Marston affair, which involved Bell's firing of Republican David Marston as U.S. attorney for Philadelphia, normally a patronage job, after Marston refused to resign voluntarily. The reasons for the firing came under a cloud of suspicion when it was revealed that Bell and Carter had been urged to dismiss Marston by Congressman Joshua Eilberg of Philadelphia, whose law firm was being investigated by Marston's office. In a sworn statement, a Civiletti aide stated that he had twice passed news about Marston's investigation of Eilberg on to Civiletti. But the assistant attorney general responded that he did not gather from the first conversation that Eilberg was himself under investigation and that he did not remember any subsequent conversation with his aide about Eilberg. This was enough for

New York Times columnist WILLIAM SAFIRE to write that either Civiletti or his aide was lying. But Safire's comment had no traction, and Civiletti was easily confirmed by the Senate.

When Bell decided to resign from the administration in 1979, he recommended Civiletti as his replacement, and the nomination was easily confirmed by the Senate. Not long afterward, Civiletti had to deal with a scandal involving Hamilton Jordan's alleged cocaine use. In 1978, Congress had passed the Ethics in Government Act, which was in part a Watergate-inspired measure and in part a response to the president's own call for higher ethical standards in government. The act provided for the establishment of a special prosecutor whenever allegations of misconduct were made against a senior government official unless the attorney general found the charges to be so unsubstantiated as to warrant no further investigation.

In 1978, one of the co-owners of the trendy New York nightclub Studio 54, Steve Rubell, who had been convicted of tax evasion, stated that Jordan had snorted a small amount of cocaine at his club. Rubell's story was corroborated by two other shady characters, one a drug dealer and the other a publicist. All three men leveled their charges against Jordan on ABC's television show *20/20.* Having doubts about the truthfulness of two convicted felons, one of whom (Rubell) was seeking to make a deal to get his sentence reduced, Civiletti was reluctant to pursue the case. Even if the accusations were true, he did not believe the amount of cocaine allegedly involved (two snorts) warranted a major criminal investigation. As he told President Carter, he thought the charges were outrageous, and he found no reason to prosecute Jordan on the basis of the evidence turned up so far. But he felt he had no choice under the Ethics in Government Act other than to call for a special prosecutor. "But for the act," a Justice Department official remarked, "this would never have gone beyond an Assistant U.S. Attorney."

A special federal court appointed New York City attorney Arthur H. Christy as special prosecutor. As a young prosecutor in 1959, Christy had won convictions against two notorious underworld figures, Frank Costello and Vito Genovese. In a six-month investigation that was extended to include other accusations of drug use by Jordan and other members of the Carter administration, Christy was able to undermine the veracity of the charges made against Jordan. All three of his accusers backed off from their stories that they had seen Jordan snorting cocaine. As it turned out, Rubell's lawyer had been attempting to trade derogatory information on Jordan for a reduced sentence on his tax-evasion conviction. On May 21, 1980, a grand jury convened by Christy voted, on his recommendation, not to bring any charges against Jordan.

Civiletti felt sorry that Jordan had been unnecessarily maligned (although Jordan himself acknowledged later that he had set himself up for trouble by not being more circumspect about where he went and with whom he associated). He believed, however, that his hands were tied not only by the law but by the fact that he and the administration would have been pilloried by the press if it ignored the legal requirements of the Ethics in Government Act the first time they were tested. As Civiletti explained to Christy, who never wanted to go forward with the investigation, "Look, it's an allegation that's in the public eye now, we've got this act, how can I just decline to prosecute?"

A more troublesome problem for Civiletti was a 1980 investigation by the Justice Department into whether President Carter's brother Billy was acting illegally as an unregistered lobbyist for the Libyan government. Warmly portrayed at one time in the media as a caricature of the southern redneck, Billy had lost much of this public affection by 1980 because of a highly publicized trip he had made to Libya in 1978 and alleged anti-Semitic remarks he had made following his return to the United States. A recovering alcoholic with serious financial problems, he had turned to his Libyan friends for assistance. In January 1980, they advanced him $20,000, followed in April by $200,000, as the first installments of a $500,000 "loan" from the Libyan government. Although this business deal eventually fell through because of a cutback in Libyan oil production, Billy Carter could have made as much as $5 million annually in helping to procure an additional 100,000 barrels per day of high-grade Libyan oil for a Florida business concern, the Charter Oil Company.

Because of Billy Carter's close association with Libya, the Justice Department asked him in 1979 to register as a foreign agent under a 1933 law requiring all persons who did political or public relations work for a foreign government to list their activities and pay with the department. Carter ignored the request on grounds that he had never acted as an agent for Libya, and the department began an investigation into his affairs. In April 1980, Attorney General Civiletti learned from "highly sensitive" intelligence reports that Billy might be about to receive a large sum of money from the Libyan government, and the next month the Justice Department discovered his $220,000 loan. Two weeks later, Billy agreed to be questioned by Justice officials. On July 14, 1980, he registered as a foreign agent and filed a report showing the $220,000 he had received as compensation.

News that Billy Carter had accepted $220,000 from Libya and was listed as a foreign agent produced a political storm of allegations about influence-peddling reaching into the White House. Sensing a scandal, the news media began to refer to Billy's connection with Libya as "Billygate" and asked questions as to what Billy had done to earn the Libyan largesse. Billygate dominated the news for a good part of the summer, adding further problems to Jimmy Carter's troubled campaign for reelection.

At a news conference on July 24, 1980, while Billygate was still front-page news, Civiletti denied that he had discussed the Billy Carter case with the president. But two days later, after both he and the White House had repeatedly denied that President Carter had been involved in any way with the Justice Department's investigations into Billy's affairs, the attorney general disclosed that "in an informal" and brief exchange on June 17, he had told the president that it was foolish for Billy not to register as a foreign agent and that he would not be prosecuted if he did so even at this late date. At the same time, he acknowledged that he had learned as early as April about the large sum of cash Billy was about to receive from Libya but did not tell anyone about it until June, by which time other investigators had learned of the payments Billy had received.

The Billy Carter case raised so many questions about possible cover-ups and influence peddling at the White House that the Senate decided to hold hearings into the matter. On the day before Civiletti was scheduled to testify in September, Joel S. Lisker, a career Justice official who had led the investigation into Billy Carter's affairs and had discovered the April payment to him, testified that Civiletti had asked him not to disclose the information to anyone for 10 days. He also said that one reason the attorney general might have requested the delay was to consult with the president.

When Civiletti testified before the Senate committee, he cited two main reasons why he had withheld from his department's investigators the information he had had for a month about Libyan payments to Carter. First, he had feared compromising the intelligence sources and methods that were the basis of the information. Second, he said it would have improved the department's case against Billy Carter if the transfer of money had occurred. As to Lisker's testimony a day earlier, Civiletti said he did not remember asking him to delay action for 10 days, but that if he did make such a request, it was not to delay the investigation or give him time to talk to the president.

As for his discussion with the president on June 17, Civiletti said he had thought about going to the president as early as April about Billy's dealings with Libya but had decided against it because he did not believe there were serious foreign policy implications involved in the arrangement. After Billy acknowledged the financial transactions in June, Civiletti decided to inform President Carter, but he did so just in passing during a more lengthy conversation with the president. He acknowledged that he had told Carter that his brother ought to register as a lobbyist and would probably not be prosecuted if he did so, but Civiletti denied telling the president about the substance of the case.

Finally, the attorney general acknowledged that he had made a mistake in denying on July 24 that he had had no discussions with the president about Billy Carter. He said that he had drawn a "close, lawyer-like distinction" between a thorough discussion and the brief discussion he had had with President Carter; he had realized his error that same evening and corrected it immediately. In sum, he told the senators, he was "comfortable with and proud" of the way he and his associates at the Justice Department had dealt with the Billy Carter case.

Senators were by no means satisfied with Civiletti's testimony, and there were a few calls from Republicans for his resignation. The *New York Times* columnist William Safire again accused Civiletti of lying. Other aspects of the case, including the president's denial, and then acknowledgment, that he had talked to his attorney general about his brother prior to July and revelations that Billy Carter had been asked earlier by National Security Advisor ZBIGNIEW BRZEZINSKI to use his Libyan connections to help secure the release of the American hostages being held by Iran, made the whole relationship between Billy Carter and the Libyans appear tawdry and odious.

After July, however, the White House adopted a policy of open frankness about the case. In nine hours of testimony before the Senate committee, moreover, Billy Carter proved an excellent witness, denying that he had asked anything of his brother or of the government and remarking that, rather than profiting from his relationship with Libya, he had suffered financially as a result of 10 separate investigations into his affairs. Most important, his testimony supported the president's claim that he knew nothing about the $220,000 Billy had received from Libya and that the White House had extended no special treatment to his brother.

On October 2, 1980, the Senate investigation concluded with a report criticizing the president for trying to involve his brother in an attempt to free the Iranian hostages but acquitting him or other officials within the administration, including Civiletti, of any other charge. As for the attorney general, Billygate was an acute embarrassment for him, but he felt he had done nothing wrong, other than misstating on July 22 what he had told the president, an error that he had quickly corrected. He saw no reason to resign his position, which he held until the end of the administration.

In addition to Civiletti's involvement in the Marston affair, charges about cocaine use by Hamilton Jordan, and Billygate, there were a number of other controversial matters that he had to confront as the attorney general. He had to deal, for example, with an ongoing investigation into the affairs of President Carter's friend and former director of the Office of Management and Budget, BERT LANCE, who was indicted by a federal grand jury in May 1979 for alleged violation of banking laws. Lance was acquitted of these charges one year later. Similarly, Civiletti's office had to devote considerable time and energy to investigating allegations of efforts by South Korean officials to bribe members of Congress, allegations of illegal methods used by the Federal Bureau of Investigation in the conduct of its affairs, allegations that the fugitive Robert Vesco had tried to bribe the Carter administration in 1977, and obstruction of justice charges against former CIA director Richard Helms. Not since the Watergate affair of the early 1970s, in fact, had the Justice Department been called on to handle more allegations of alleged criminality at the senior levels of government than during the two years that Civiletti served as attorney general.

Complicating matters for Civiletti was the fact that he was heavily involved in the negotiations for the release of the American hostages who had been seized by Iranian students at the U.S. embassy in Tehran in November 1979. Not only was he responsible for arguing the American case before the International Court of Justice at The Hague, he also had to fashion the legal case for U.S. embargoes on Iran and the seizure of Iranian assets in the United States, He also had to fend off efforts by National Security Advisor Brzezinski to punish Iranian diplomats in the United States. At the same time, he was responsible for deportation operations against illegal Iranian immigrants, and after the shah of Iran, MOHAMMAD REZA PAHLAVI, was allowed into the United States for emergency medical treatment in October 1979, he was the only cabinet member involved in the hostage crisis to support Brzezinski's unsuccessful plea to the president that the deposed monarch be allowed to remain in the United States.

Following President Carter's defeat for reelection in 1980, Civiletti returned to the law firm of Venable, Baetjer & Howard, where he is a trial lawyer and chair of Venable LLP. He has also served on many Maryland state task forces and committees and has chaired the American Bar Association's Litigation Section and the Task Force on an International Criminal Court.

Conyers, John, Jr.

(1919–   ) *member of the House of Representatives*

One of the founders of the Black Caucus and the first African-American member of the House Judiciary Committee, John Conyers, Jr., of Michigan was one of the most influential members of Congress when Jimmy Carter became president in 1977. A liberal Democrat who was serving in his seventh term in Congress, he was one of the key sponsors of the Humphrey-Hawkins Bill, intended to guarantee a full-employment economy. Disappointed by Carter's lukewarm support for this legislation, he sought to replace Carter as the Democratic candidate for president in 1980.

The son of an official of the United Auto Workers (UAW), Conyers was born on May 16, 1929, in Detroit, Michigan, where he was raised. Bored by high school and unable to afford college, he enlisted as a private in the U.S. Army in 1950. After attending officers candidate school, he was commissioned a lieutenant and saw action in the Korean War. Following the war, he used his veteran's benefits to attend Wayne State University, where he received both his undergraduate and law degrees (B.A., 1957; J.D., 1958). A practicing attorney, he was general counsel for the Trade Union Leadership Council, an organization of black trade unionists. He also served as legislative assistant to Representative JOHN DINGELL (1959–61) and was appointed referee of Michigan's Workmen's Compensation Department

(1961). In 1963, President John F. Kennedy appointed him to the National Lawyers Committee for Civil Rights under Law, an organization intended to promote greater racial tolerance in the legal profession.

In 1964, Conyers ran for Congress in a new, predominantly black congressional district. After a tough primary campaign, he defeated Richard H. Austin in the Democratic primary by 45 votes and won easily in the November election. Appointed to the Judiciary Committee, he soon established a reputation as one of the most liberal members of Congress, supporting the entirety of Lyndon Johnson's Great Society programs but taking a special interest in legislation to advance civil liberties. A cosponsor of the Voting Rights Act of 1965, he was also a leading proponent of universal health insurance. An early opponent of the Vietnam War, he voted as early as 1965 against additional funding for the conflict.

As an African-American member of Congress, Conyers was especially attentive to what he regarded as racism and police brutality. In 1965, he helped organize a group of congressmen to go to Selma, Alabama, where Martin Luther King had taken his civil rights campaign, in order to observe conditions there. As the only black member of the special committee appointed in 1967 to investigate charges of misconduct against Harlem Congressman Adam Clayton Powell, whom he admired, Conyers helped frame a compromise resolution that refrained from censuring Powell but fined him $25,000 for misuse of funds and stripped him of his seniority in the House. In 1967, following rioting in his district, Conyers joined other black political leaders to demand an investigation of charges of police brutality during the rioting.

During RICHARD NIXON's administration, Conyers made the president's "enemies list" by his outspoken opposition to most of the president's domestic and foreign policies, including revision and extension of the Voting Rights Act of 1965, welfare reform, and Nixon's conduct of the Vietnam War. He also helped lead the opposition to the president's nominations of Clement Haynsworth and G. Harrold Carswell for the Supreme Court. In 1971, he opposed Carl Albert (D-Okla.) for the position of Speaker of the House, but lost.

During the 1976 campaign for the Democratic presidential nomination, Conyers was disappointed at how many black leaders decided to support Jimmy Carter following the early primaries. He joined two other leaders, Julian Bond and John Lewis of SNCC, the Student Nonviolent Coordinating Committee, in calling Carter's strength with African Americans a failure in black leadership.

Like other Democratic liberals in Congress, Conyers became increasingly disenchanted by what he regarded as President Carter's economic conservatism and his attempt to deal with the problem of inflation after 1978 by cutting entitlement programs. Speaking at the Democratic miniconvention in Memphis in 1978, he told a group of 100 black delegates that the president's anti-inflation policies "will flatly result in his defeat in 1980." "He owes us the presidency," Conyers added. "If you like your president and want to keep him, you'd better knock some sense in his head about a program of full employment, housing, and national health insurance."

Conyers's opposition to the White House extended to its oil and energy policy. Representing a district that was home to the nation's automobile industry, he was opposed to any program of legislation that sought to conserve energy by raising gasoline prices. He also took issue with the president's claims that the world lacked enough energy to meet demand. Rather, he blamed oil shortages and soaring oil prices on the major oil companies who, he claimed, were in collusion with the Organization of Petroleum Exporting Countries (OPEC).

Commenting on the president's speech of July 15, 1979, on the energy crisis (the so-called malaise speech), the Detroit congressman remarked: "His lack of any reference to the role of the oil industry, alongside the OPEC cartel, in engineering shortages ... and in promoting exorbitant prices is a glaring evasion."

The issue on which Conyers was most outspoken, however, was the Humphrey-Hawkins full-employment bill. The legislation empowered the government to provide "last resort" jobs to guarantee full employment. For Conyers, as for other members of the Congressional Black Caucus, who accused the Carter administration of abandoning African Americans although he owed his election to the black vote, Humphrey-Hawkins became important not only because it promised full employment but because it symbolized the extent of the president's commitment to a black agenda in Congress. The president had supported the measure, but he did so only after considerable prodding from African-American leaders and organized labor. Carter also insisted on provisions that took into account the need to deal with inflation.

In September 1978, leaders of the Black Caucus met with the president. During the meeting, they chastised Carter for not throwing his full weight behind the Humphrey-Hawkins legislation. Carter and Vice President WALTER MONDALE told the group that the president had always regarded full employment as a "top priority" but that there were other urgent matters, such as producing an energy bill and curbing inflation. The caucus members warned that the White House would be blamed if Congress failed to pass Humphrey-Hawkins. When Carter and Mondale heatedly challenged that assertion, Conyers stalked out of the meeting in anger. After Conyers left, the chairman of the Congressional Black Caucus, Parren J. Mitchell of Maryland, and Ron Dellums of California took up the argument.

Surprised by what had taken place, both Mitchell and the White House tried to patch up their differences. On October 15, the Senate approved the Humphrey-Hawkins legislation, but the final product was a bitter disappointment to its original proponents. Although the goal of reducing unemployment was intact, the Senate added another goal of lowering the rate of inflation to 3 percent by 1983 and eliminating it entirely by 1988. Backers of the bill feared that the inflation objective would undermine the measure's primary purpose of stemming unemployment. Many black leaders were grateful for the White House's assistance in forcing senatorial action on the bill, but a number of them, including Conyers, were also resentful that the administration had not worked earlier and harder on behalf of the legislation.

By summer 1979, Conyers was ready to support someone other than Carter for the Democratic presidential nomination. In June that year, he joined four other congressmen to form the Coalition of Democratic Alternatives to oppose Carter's renomination, although, unlike the others, he refrained from endorsing Senator EDWARD KENNEDY (Mass.) for the nomination. He became even angrier with the White House when, in the summer, the administration forced the resignation of the U.S. ambassador to the United Nations, ANDREW YOUNG, one of the leaders of the Civil Rights Movement in the 1960s and the administration's most prominent black member. This action was taken after Young's meeting with an official of the Palestine Liberation Organization (PLO), which was in violation of U.S. policy. To Conyers, Young's resignation as UN ambassador was a "point-blank firing."

In 1978, Conyers commented on how the increasing responsibilities of being a congressman were leading a growing number of lawmakers not to seek reelection. "Congress used to be a lifetime career," he stated. "You died in

Congress, or you tried to become Governor or Senator. On a clear day, some guys even saw the White House. Now members are cashing in early. Congressmen are being watched more closely, criticized more, and prosecuted more." Nevertheless, in 2004, Conyers was reelected to his 21st term, making him the second most senior member of the House.

Despite the conservative tide that came to dominate American politics in the years after Carter left office in January 1981, Conyers has remained a committed liberal; the *National Journal* has called him one of the two most liberal members of Congress. He has continued to speak out against police brutality, as in the Rodney King case of 1992, when four Los Angeles policemen were caught on tape beating the black motorist. But he also wrote the Public Safety Officers Benefit Act of 2004, which doubled the benefits for families of police officers and firefighters killed during duty. Convinced that increased defense spending came at the expense of needed domestic programs, such as affordable health care, he was a harsh critic of RONALD REAGAN's military buildup in the 1980s and his Strategic Defense Initiative (SDI), or "Stars Wars" program.

A partisan Democrat, even though he believes the party needs to field more black candidates for high political office, Conyers has not always agreed with its selections for president—for example, the 1988 candidate, Massachusetts governor Michael Dukakis, whom Conyers considered too conservative. In 1998, he attacked the Republican effort to impeach President Bill Clinton. Questioning the motives of the independent counsel, Kenneth Starr, in pursuing his investigation of Clinton, Conyers called Starr "a modern day equivalent of Senator Joe McCarthy" and sought evidence of partisan motives in his investigation. Most recently, Conyers has been an opponent of the war in Iraq, appearing at antiwar protests and proposing a reintroduction of the draft, which would include women and not provide for college exemptions.

Costanza, Midge

(Margaret Costanza)

(1932–) *special assistant to the president for public liaison*

The daughter of immigrant parents from Sicily, Margaret "Midge" Costanza was born on November 28, 1932, in LeRoy, New York, and grew up in Rochester. In contrast to many other leaders of women's causes, Costanza did not attend college. Instead, she held various clerical jobs after graduating from high school, finally landing a position as an administrative assistant to a Rochester real-estate developer that allowed her to become involved in many community organizations.

Beginning with Averill Harriman's campaign for New York governor (1954), Costanza became increasingly involved in Democratic state and national politics. In 1965, she became the county executive director of Robert F. Kennedy's Senate campaign. In 1972, she was appointed to the Democratic National Committee, a position she held until moving over to the Carter White House in 1977. In 1973, she was elected for an at-large seat on the Rochester City Council by the largest number of votes in the election. Although it was traditional for the largest vote-getter to be named mayor, the position was given to a man. She had to settle for the largely ceremonial title of vice mayor, a slight she never forgot. She also served on Governor Hugh Carey's state task force on public authorities. During this time, she established a record as a champion of gay and lesbian rights.

HAMILTON JORDAN and Jimmy Carter met Costanza in 1974 when she ran an unsuccessful campaign against the long-entrenched Republican congressman Barber Conable. Impressed by her effort, Jordan put in her charge of the 1976 Carter campaign for upstate New York. Later, she seconded Carter's nomination for president at Madison Square Garden.

After his election, President-elect Carter pledged to put a woman in a high-profile White House position for the first time and to make a concerted effort to involve women in other high places within his administration. Carter's efforts were unprecedented. Unfortunately for him, the high profile that Costanza generated as special assistant for public liaison, which also involved representing the administration to national women's organizations, was not what he had in mind.

Costanza was the only non-Georgian of the president's top seven White House aides. The Office of Public Liaison (OPL) that she headed was begun when President RICHARD NIXON's aid, Charles Colson, organized a small staff to target potentially supportive groups such as labor unions and white ethnics. During the Nixon and Ford administrations, the size of the OPL staff ranged from a high of 17 to a low of 12. Although President-elect Carter's transition team recommended eliminating the OPL staff entirely, the president decided to maintain the office with 12 staffers. He also placed Costanza's office close to the Oval Office and mandated that the OPL "pay particular attention … to enhancing communications with groups and interest[s] which traditionally have not had access to the White House, Cabinet, or sub-Cabinet levels of government."

What the president had in mind were such groups as the poor, disabled, and the elderly. But Costanza allowed her liberal ideology to cloud her understanding of what the president intended, and she included as part of her mandate such other controversial groups as supporters of draft amnesty, abortion rights, and gay and lesbian rights—an outreach effort, in other words, that raised the hackles of more

Special Assistant to the President for Public Liaison Midge Costanza, 1977

conservative interests, including business interests that Carter wanted to cultivate. The president was especially embarrassed when Costanza organized a gay-lesbian conference at the White House led by Jean O'Leary, the co-executive director of the National Gay Task Force, who had worked with Costanza in an unsuccessful effort to insert a gay-rights plank into the 1976 Democratic Party platform. "We are highly optimistic that [the conference] will soon lead to complete fulfillment of President Carter's pledge to end all forms of federal discrimination on the basis of sexual orientation," O'Leary remarked at the small conference, putting the president in a highly uncomfortable position. Similarly, he was angry when Costanza came out strongly for other public causes that he did not fully embrace, such as abortion rights.

Furthermore, Carter and his chief assistant, Hamilton Jordan, who distrusted Costanza's commitment to advocacy and was particularly disturbed that she was using her staff to promote the pro-choice side of the abortion issue, became annoyed by the insistent complaints of feminist leaders that the president was not doing enough for women's causes and was relegating women he hired to less-significant positions than they deserved. Although Carter had done more than any president before him to place women in high-level jobs within his administration, including three cabinet positions, a coalition of 60 women's groups met with Carter in March 1977 to complain that the numbers of women in policy-making positions remained "shockingly low." This was too much for the frustrated president, who responded that his cabinet officers were complaining that "no matter what we do, we get nothing but criticism."

Although Costanza tried to defend the president against these charges, Jordan reassigned many of her duties and moved her office to the White House basement, thereby virtually cutting her off from all contact with the president. A comment she had made to the *Washington Post* in the first week of the Carter presidency proved prophetic: "Either I will function as a window to the President or I won't be in Washington." Realizing that she had become unwanted within the White House, especially after she called for BERT LANCE, the president's close friend and director of the Office of Management and Budget (OMB) to resign during the so-called Lance affair, she resigned her own position, causing an uproar from the very women's groups that the president had sought to embrace.

Following Costanza's departure from the White House, she served as executive director of the actress Shirley MacLaine's Higher Self Seminars and as a vice president of Alan Landsburg Productions (1985), producing films and advertisements for commercial clients. All the while, she remained active in the gay rights movements and in politics, serving on the board of the National Gay Rights Alliance, as campaign coordinator for California Senator Barbara Boxer (1992), and as San Diego County campaign manager for Kathleen Brown's failed run for governor in California (1994). In 2001, she was appointed by Governor Gray Davis of California as his liaison for women's groups and issues, a position she retained until the end of his administration in 2003.

Presently Costanza is working with San Diego State University, where she had taught a course on the presidency, and the University of California at San Diego to establish the Midge Costanza Institute, intended to make available an extensive archive of documents through the Internet.

Cranston, Alan MacGregor

(1914–2000) *member of the Senate, majority whip*

Majority whip of the U.S. Senate during the Carter presidency, Alan Cranston of California was a liberal activist who disagreed with the White House on a number of issues yet remained one of its strongest defenders on Capitol Hill during Jimmy Carter's first two years in office. By 1978, however, he began to speak more critically of the president, and in 1980 he refused to support Carter's second bid for the Democratic presidential nomination. Cranston's own career ended in shame in the early 1990s when he was reprimanded by the Senate for accepting campaign funds in return for political favors from a California banker, Charles Keating.

The son and grandson of successful real-estate developers, Cranston was born on June

19, 1914, in Palo Alto, California. A journalism major at Stanford University (B.A., 1936), he worked after graduation as a correspondent in Europe and Ethiopia. Experiencing firsthand the growing threat to world peace posed by Adolf Hitler and Benito Mussolini, Cranston became frustrated by the United States' indifference to developments in Europe. Returning to the United States, he published an unabridged and unauthorized English edition of Hitler's *Mein Kampf*, which he sold for 10 cents a copy after he saw a watered-down English version that was intended to make Hitler appear more benign to Americans. He sold half a million copies of the book and was later successfully sued by the Third Reich for copyright violation.

During World War II, Cranston worked in the Office of War Information, where he came up with the idea of naming an Illinois town, Lidice, for a Czechoslovakian village that had been destroyed by the Nazis. In 1944, he enlisted as a private in the army. The war had a profound effect on Cranston. "I finally decided I didn't want to just write about all these problems but to be able to do something about them," he later remarked. In 1945, he published *The Killing of Peace*, an indictment of the U.S. Senate for defeating U.S. membership in the League of Nations after World War I. He also became involved in the world peace movement, first as a director of Americans United for World Government and then as president of its successor, the United World Federalists.

Tall, bald, craggy-looking, and gawkish, Cranston hardly fit the profile of many of the successful postwar politicians who won national office. After the overwhelming victory of Dwight D. Eisenhower in the 1952 elections, Cranston helped start, and then headed, the liberal California Democratic Council, a statewide movement that mobilized tens of thousands of volunteers at a grassroots level to elect Democrats to office. In 1958, he won election as the state's first Democratic controller in 72 years. Four years later, he was reelected by a landslide. In 1964, he ran unsuccessfully for the Democratic senatorial nomination, losing to John F. Kennedy's former press secretary, Pierre Salinger. Four years later, however, he won the primary for California's other senatorial seat and then went on to defeat his Republican opponent, Max Rafferty. He was reelected by California voters three times.

Although Cranston maintained a generally low profile during his first term, he developed a reputation as an energetic, loyal, and popular senator. Democrat Dale Bumpers (Ark.) spoke for many of his colleagues when he described Cranston as "intense, sincere, hardworking and well liked" and added that "you can trust his word on how he is going to vote." He managed to be on good terms even with those who, like Senator BARRY GOLDWATER (R-Ariz.), were ideologically his polar opposite. As the presidency of RICHARD NIXON began to fall apart as a result of the Watergate scandal, Cranston joined with Goldwater in asking that the charge of a special prosecutor appointed to look into the scandal be broadened to cover allegations of corruption beyond the Watergate break-in.

In 1977, when Majority Whip ROBERT BYRD (W.Va.) was chosen as the Senate's new majority leader, Cranston was elected without opposition to replace him in the whip's position. The two leaders proved to be a good combination. Byrd was the master of logistics and parliamentary procedure; he was respected more than liked. The affable Cranston was concerned more with policy matters. In his quiet way, he was also a persuasive advocate who knew how to count votes.

Because Cranston remained unabashedly liberal in his politics, he often clashed with the more fiscally conservative President Carter over spending priorities and budget deficits.

As chairman of the Veteran's Committee, for example, the California senator took issue with the administration's proposal to cut veterans' benefits. "It's a little tough on veterans," he complained, "to have to start worrying about the size of the budget deficit." In May 1977, he criticized Carter's gas-guzzler tax, which sought to finance rebates to small-car owners. He was even more critical when the president announced the same month that his top priority was a balanced budget by 1981. "We can't sacrifice everything to a balanced budget," Cranston remarked. "Government programs should not only stress a balanced budget and fighting inflation, but also reducing unemployment and fighting for those who need help."

Cranston's emphasis, however, was one of working with and supporting the president. He led the fight on the Senate floor, for example, in the highly controversial battle to confirm PAUL WARNKE as both director of the Arms Control and Disarmament Agency and chief negotiator of the Strategic Arms Limitation Talks (SALT) with the Soviet Union. While both Democrats and Republicans were highly critical of Carter's lobbyist on Capitol Hill, FRANK MOORE, for not returning their telephone calls and otherwise being inattentive to their interests, the California senator defended Moore, remarking that he was "doing a fine job" and adding, "I find him affable, intelligent and concerned and effective on matters I've dealt with him on."

In contrast to many other lawmakers, Cranston also defended the president's handling of the so-called Lance affair involving the resignation of the president's close friend and director of the Office of Management and Budget, BERT LANCE, due to his questionable banking practices as president of the Calhoun National Bank and National Bank of Georgia. "The Carter administration has faced, and resolved, its first major crisis," Cranston remarked after Lance tended his resignation. "It ... should be stronger for the experience."

Cranston's support for the president was even stronger on foreign policy. In June 1977, he prepared a letter, later signed by eight other senators, stressing their support of Carter's efforts to arrange a Middle East peace settlement. He was also one of the floor leaders rounding up votes in 1978 in favor of the Panama Canal Treaties. Later he was a strong proponent of the SALT II agreement.

Notwithstanding his strong support for President Carter, however, Cranston began to have growing doubts about the administration's effectiveness. When he was asked at the end of 1977 to give a report card on how well the president had done in his first year in office, Cranston gave Carter generally high grades. But he also acknowledged that the president had made mistakes, trying, for example, "with perhaps a lack of total wisdom" to resolve all the nation's problems in a single year. "In the context of the turmoil our country has been through in recent years," Cranston added in what might have been an oblique slap at the White House, "the fact is no President has been able to lead to the degree that we expect a President to lead for 16 years now."

Over time, despite his strong support for the Panama Canal Treaties and the SALT II Treaty of 1979, Cranston's defense of the administration became increasingly muted. In June 1978, he joined 23 Democrats and 36 Republicans in cosponsoring a measure, which the president opposed, to cut the capital gains tax. During the debate in 1979 over the president's standby gas-rationing plan, the California senator employed the most strident language he had used against the White House since Carter took office. He called the president's plan "a shambles" and urged the dismissal of Secretary of Energy JAMES SCHLESINGER. To Cranston, as to many congressional leaders, the president seemed never able to grasp the mantle of strong leadership. "He's basically making good decisions,"

Cranston commented in March 1979, "but somehow his leadership qualities don't come across."

Besides responding to the White House's legislative and foreign policy agenda, Cranston undertook a number of his own initiatives. He worked with the White House soon after Carter took office to establish a nonpartisan panel to recommend people for appointment as federal judges and prosecutors in California. He was one of the leading proponents of a Senate reorganization plan intended to reduce the number of standing committees and the maximum number of committee assignments for each senator. In July 1977, he cosponsored a bill with EDWARD KENNEDY (Mass.) to extend public financing of elections to include senate races. When lawmakers rejected the president's proposals for welfare reform in the summer of 1978, Cranston and Senator DANIEL PATRICK MOYNIHAN (D-N.Y.) introduced a $5 billion "no frills" measure for direct federal relief of state and local welfare spending. In October 1979, he cosponsored a measure with WILLIAM PROXMIRE (D-Wis.), chairman of the Senate Banking Committee, authorizing interest-bearing checking accounts and lowering from $10,000 to $1,000 the minimum amount required to buy six-month money-market certificates, which had been first introduced in mid-1975.

By 1980, Cranston had decided that he could not support Jimmy Carter's bid for the Democratic presidential nomination because the president lacked leadership qualities and could not control his own administration. Cranston even considered running for the nomination himself but decided, instead, to concentrate his efforts on his own reelection. Although he was one of the liberal Democrats targeted for defeat by the conservative right-wing of the Republican Party, he was one of the few liberals to survive RONALD REAGAN's landslide victory in November, actually receiving more votes in California than the former California governor.

In 1983, Cranston decided to run for the 1984 Democratic presidential nomination. Identifying himself as "the peace candidate" and making nuclear freeze the focus of his campaign, he won straw-poll victories in Wisconsin, Alabama, and California, and finished second place in Massachusetts. But he was never able to get his campaign off the ground and withdrew from the contest in early 1984. This was the beginning of his political trajectory downward. In 1986, he was narrowly reelected to a fourth term as senator.

Throughout his career, Cranston had been a highly effective fund-raiser, even though he had been one of the leading proponents of campaign-finance reform. Although as much as half the money he raised in California went to voter registration drives nationwide, his quest for campaign funds proved to be his undoing. In the late 1980s, he received nearly $1 million from a constituent, Charles H. Keating, Jr., at the same time that he intervened with the Federal Home Loan Bank Board in an effort to save Keating's Lincoln Federal Savings and Loan Association from collapse during the unfolding savings and loan (S&L) scandal that rocked the Reagan and Bush administrations.

Four other senators were also identified as having extensive dealings with Keating; together with Cranston, they became known as the "Keating Five." In a Senate investigation, Cranston's involvement with Keating was revealed to have been the most extensive and dubious of the lawmakers. Although he tried to defend himself by arguing that he had done nothing improper in exchange for political contributions and that he only performed for Keating the same help he would have provided for any contributor, in 1991 the Senate Select Committee on Ethics formally rebuked him for "an impermissible pattern of conduct."

Embittered and facing almost certain defeat, Cranston decided not to seek reelection in 1992. Instead, he devoted his efforts to eliminating nuclear weapons. He served first as chairman of the Gorbachev Foundation and then as president of the Global Security Institute, which he founded. On December 31, 2000, Cranston died of cancer at his home in Los Altos Hills, California. He was 86 years old.

Cutler, Lloyd Norton

(1917–2005) *counsel to the president*

Widely regarded as the consummate Washington insider, Lloyd Cutler was brought into the White House in summer 1979 as counsel to the president, replacing ROBERT LIPSHUTZ in that position. His appointment was part of a general shakeup of the administration that President Jimmy Carter made that summer and was intended to bring seniority and experience to the White House. A founding partner of a large Washington law firm who knew Carter as a fellow member of the Trilateral Commission, Cutler had in the past combined public service with private practice. As counsel to the president, he was involved in a number of high-profile events, including completion of the second Strategic Arms Limitation Talks (SALT II) treaty, the U.S. response to Soviet invasion of Afghanistan and the Iran hostage crisis, and the investigation into a scandal surrounding the president's brother Billy's connections to the Libyan government.

Cutler was born in New York City on November 10, 1917. He received both his undergraduate and law degrees from Yale University (B.A., 1936; LL.B., 1939), where he was editor in chief of the law journal. Following graduation, he joined the prestigious New York law firm of Cravath, Swaine & Moore, but after Japan's attack on Pearl Harbor on December 7, 1941, he gave up a promising career with Cravath to work for the Lend-Lease Administration. In 1942, he enlisted in the army and subsequently became a code breaker and intelligence analyst.

Following the war, Cutler opened his own law practice in Washington, D.C., in partnership with three other lawyers. Seventeen years later, his firm merged with another law firm to form Wilmer, Cutler & Pickering. By the 1970s, it had become one of the most prominent firms in the nation with about 230 lawyers. It handled a wide variety of cases, sometimes defending corporate interests under government investigation and at other times working with indigent clients on a pro bono basis; in fact, the firm became known for the large number of pro bono cases it handled. A Democrat, Cutler helped build his firm by networking with a wide circle of influential friends, including publishers, journalists, and politicians, both Republicans as well as Democrats.

In 1960, Cutler worked in the presidential campaign of John F. Kennedy. After Kennedy's election as president, he assisted the president-elect's brother, Bobby, in choosing people to serve in the Justice Department. Following the Bay of Pigs disaster in April 1961, Cutler helped to arrange the release of Cuban exiles taken prisoner in exchange for medicines from pharmaceutical companies, some of which were his firm's clients. In 1968, he was appointed by President Lyndon Johnson as executive director of the National Commission on the Causes and Prevention of Violence (known as the Byron Commission), formed as a result of the assassinations that year of Martin Luther King, Jr., and Bobby Kennedy. Following the night of rioting after King's murder, Cutler's firm provided counsel to dozens of detainees arrested during the riot.

Cutler first met Jimmy Carter in 1974 during one of the Trilateral Commission's meetings; Carter informed Cutler then that he was running for president. The next year, Cutler accompanied the presidential candidate on a trip to Japan. Nevertheless, he was not one of Carter's early supporters. Cutler respected Carter and found him compassionate, highly intelligent, and sincere, but he never campaigned actively for the candidate. Following Carter's victory, Cutler wrote a few papers for his transition team, but as he later commented, he had "no really, active relationship" with the president-elect and he was never asked to join the administration.

In the spring of 1979, however, Secretary of Defense HAROLD BROWN asked Cutler if he would be interested in being undersecretary of defense for policy, a newly created post that would place him in the third-highest position in the Defense Department. Not wanting to join the administration so late into its term and fearful that he would become involved in bureaucratic infighting at the Pentagon, Cutler declined the offer. However, having an interest in arms control and worried that the Senate might reject the recently concluded SALT II treaty, he expressed an interest in a position with the Defense Department that might help achieve ratification of the agreement. A few weeks later, he received a call from Secretary of State CYRUS VANCE asking him to assume responsibility for shepherding the treaty through the Senate. Cutler accepted the offer with the understanding that he could continue his law practice at Wilmer, Cutler & Pickering.

What was intended as a part-time position for the express purpose of gaining Senate ratification of the SALT agreement became a full-time position at the White House when, in August, the president asked Cutler to be his special counsel. Putting aside whatever reservations he had about joining the administration so late into its first term, Cutler accepted the offer, which meant that he would have an office in the West Wing of the White House and direct access to the president. Soon after accepting his new position, Cutler also asked to attend meetings of the National Security Council (NSC) and Friday breakfast meetings with the president's National Security Advisor, ZBIGNIEW BRZEZINSKI. Except for NSC meetings dealing with the most sensitive national security matters, Carter gave Cutler the access he requested.

Although the president still expected that Cutler's main responsibility would be achieving ratification of the SALT II treaty, and he seemed to be making good progress in gaining support for it on Capitol Hill, unexpected events later in the year changed Cutler's duties dramatically. Revelations in August 1979 of a Soviet combat brigade in Cuba and the invasion of Soviet forces into Afghanistan the following December undercut support for the treaty and led to President Carter's decision in January 1980 to withdraw the agreement from further consideration by the Senate.

On the matter of the Soviet brigade in Cuba, Cutler tried unsuccessfully to separate the issue from ratification of the SALT treaty by supporting Secretary of State Vance's contention that while the Soviets had to withdraw their forces from Cuba (where they may have been since the end of the Cuban missile crisis in 1962), their presence was not part of a pattern of Soviet global meddling, as Brzezinski maintained. Over Brzezinski's objections, Cutler even persuaded the president to call a meeting of senior statesmen to advise him on the brigade issue, and he played an important role in softening a speech that Carter delivered to the nation on October 1 on the Soviet presence in Cuba. The speech had the effect of defusing a potentially explosive incident, but it was not enough to save the SALT II agreement.

Any remaining chance that the Senate would ratify the treaty disappeared after the Soviets invaded Afghanistan in December 1979. Once again, Cutler played a significant part in developing the U.S. response to the

Soviet action. In contrast to his view of the brigade in Cuba, which, he believed, had probably been there since 1962 and did not pose a threat to American interests, he viewed the invasion of Afghanistan as naked aggression and a new departure for Moscow that posed a strategic threat to every nation bordering the Soviet Union and to U.S. oil interests in the Persian Gulf. The invasion, in his view, demanded a tough but calculated response from the White House. With this in mind, he sided again with Vance in opposing Brzezinski's recommendation that the administration use the invasion as an opportunity to establish a U.S.-Chinese defense relationship. He believed such a move would set back U.S.-Soviet relations indefinitely. At the same time, he supported the president's imposition of a grain embargo against the Soviet Union. He also assumed a leading role in pressuring the U.S. Olympic Committee to support the president's decision to boycott the 1980 Olympics in Moscow.

Coinciding with the Soviet invasion of Afghanistan was the ongoing hostage crisis in Iran that began in November 1979 when a group of Iranian students seized the American embassy in Tehran and took more than 60 American hostages. In the months that followed, Cutler had responsibility for coordinating the legal defense of the White House's decision to freeze Iranian assets in the United States, including assets held in the country by foreign countries, and the application of economic sanctions against Iran in April 1980. He also had to deal with numerous other complex issues, such as how to handle demands for the deportation of Iranian students in the United States and how to respond to anti-Iranian demonstrations that might provoke violence and produce a boomerang effect in Tehran. In each case, Cutler had to confront such complicated constitutional issues as due process and free speech as well as questions of international law. He also worked side by side with Deputy Secretary of State WARREN CHRISTOPHER throughout the negotiations leading to the final release of the Iranian hostages just as Carter left office on January 20, 1981.

Meanwhile, even though the hostage crisis continued to take up much of his time, Cutler had to confront another matter much closer to home. This involved allegations that the president's brother, BILLY CARTER, had taken $220,000 from the Libyan government, in the guise of a loan but actually as payment for representing Libyan interests in the United States without registering as an agent for a foreign government, as required by law. When Billy finally registered as a foreign agent in July 1980, questions were asked in the media as to why he had refused earlier Justice Department requests that he register and what he had done to earn his fees from Libya.

Although President Carter denied any knowledge of his brother's involvement with Libya, much less being involved himself, the clear implication of the charges was that Billy had been attempting to peddle to Libya his access to the Oval Office. Further adding to the drama were revelations that Billy and a Libyan representative had met at the White House with Brzezinski to discuss the possibility of using Libya to help win the release of the Iranian hostages, and that the president knew of his brother's representation of Libya in the sale of its high-grade oil to a Florida oil company. All this led some journalists to characterize the growing scandal surrounding Billy's dealings as Billygate, an obvious reference to the Watergate scandal that had destroyed the Nixon presidency. The Senate appointed a special committee to look into the matter.

President Carter was able to defuse the issue, which threatened to distract public interest from the forthcoming Democratic Convention, by holding a news conference on August 4 during which he denied any improprieties in his relationship with his brother and then backed up his assertions by releasing thousands of official documents and excerpts from his diary. In two days of testimony before the Senate committee investigating his affairs on August 21 and 22, Billy Carter proved to be a stellar witness in his own defense, and almost overnight, Billygate ceased to be a major campaign issue. On October 3, the special Senate committee issued its report criticizing the president for trying to influence Iran through Libya with his brother acting as intermediary but acquitting him of any other charge.

As the president's legal counsel, Cutler had been the one responsible for investigating the charges made against the president and for preparing his defense. He also had to defend his own actions when the *Washington Star* disclosed on July 16 that he had earlier advised Billy, who had sought his counsel, to "get a lawyer immediately." In response to the charges made against him and the president, Cutler drafted, on the president's instructions, an executive order prohibiting any executive-branch employee from associating with a member of the president's family under circumstances that might suggest improper influence. For Cutler, the attention given to Billy Carter's relations with Libya had been a major distraction throughout the summer from his other responsibilities, especially the negotiations taking place for the release of the American hostages in Iran.

Following Carter's defeat in November 1980, Cutler returned to his firm of Wilmer, Cutler & Pickering, but he continued to combine public with private service. In 1983–84, he was the senior consultant to the President's Commission on Strategic Forces (the Scowcroft Commission). In 1989, he served as a member of the President's Commission on Federal Ethics Law reform. In 1994, President Bill Clinton, then under attack as a result of the Whitewater investigation, appointed him as special counsel to the president, the same position he had held during the Carter presidency. In agreeing to the appointment, Cutler stipulated that he would serve in the position for only 180 days. In 1999, Clinton appointed him senior White House representative on U.S.-Canada salmon negotiations. In that capacity, he was also White House liaison to the governors of Alaska, Washington, and Oregon, the 24 treaty Indian tribes, and Congress. In 2004, Cutler was appointed to the Iraq Intelligence Commission tasked with investigating U.S. intelligence with respect to the existence of weapons of mass destruction in Iraq. He died on May 8, 2005, of complications from a broken hip. He was 87.

In his memoirs, *Taking Care of the Law* (1982), former attorney general GRIFFIN BELL maintains that during his tenure in the White House Counselor's Office, Lloyd Cutler transformed what had been a position with limited authority and duties into one of the power centers of the White House. Clearly there is merit to Bell's argument.

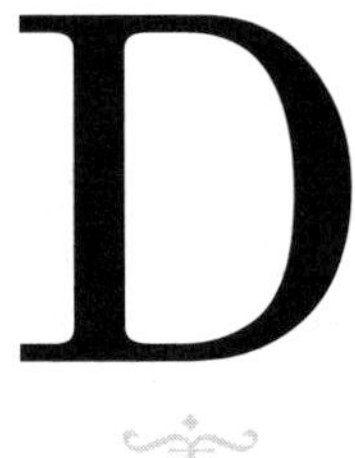

DeConcini, Dennis Webster
(1937–) *member of the Senate*

Although only elected to the U.S. Senate the same year Jimmy Carter was elected president, Dennis DeConcini of Arizona played a role far beyond that normally associated with a newcomer to the upper chamber. He was one of a handful of senators whose vote was decisive in President Carter's 1978 effort to win Senate approval of the Panama Canal Treaties of 1977. But as one of the last undecided senators, he demanded a reservation, which was embarrassing to the president but which DeConcini considered essential, before agreeing to vote in favor of the agreements. This proved characteristic of the freshman senator's relationship with the president. Although a loyal Democrat, he manifested a streak of independence throughout the Carter presidency that often put him at odds with the White House and led *Time* magazine to refer to him in 1980 as a gadfly.

DeConcini was born on May 8, 1937, in Tucson, Arizona, the son of Evo DeConcini, a wealthy real-estate speculator who became Arizona attorney general and then served as justice of the Arizona Supreme Court (1949–53). He attended the University of Arizona, where he majored in political science (B.A., 1959) and the University of Arizona Law School (LL.B., 1959). Following law school, he served in the army and army reserve (1959–66) and managed his family's vast real-estate holdings in Arizona and California. He also spent two years (1965–66) as special legal counsel and administrative assistant to Arizona governor Sam Goddard. In 1968, he established a law firm with his father and a colleague, John R. McDonald, which eventually became one of Arizona's 10 largest law firms.

DeConcini's political career began in 1973 when he was elected attorney of Pima County (1973–76). He attracted statewide attention by launching an investigation that led eventually to the conviction on obstruction of justice charges of the former reputed Mafia boss, Joseph "Bananas" Bonnano, who had spent considerable time in Tucson in the 1950s and lived there in retirement since the 1960s. (Curiously, DeConcini's father had at one time been on friendly terms with Bonnano and had even been a character witness on his behalf when the federal government sought to deport him in 1954.) As a county attorney, DeConcini made it his business to win the friendship of law enforcement officers and labor leaders, both of whom played an important role in his election to the U.S. Senate in 1976.

In 1976, although DeConcini had served only one term in an elected office, he was able to win the Democratic nomination for the Senate in the three-way primary when more well-known Democrats, like Representative MORRIS UDALL, decided not to run. Although Udall was challenging Carter for the party's presidential nomination, he still could have filed for the Senate seat after the nominating convention, but he decided to remain in the House. A nasty primary contest for the Republican nomination to succeed retiring senator Paul Fannin split the Republican Party, so that in November DeConcini was able to defeat his Republican opponent, Congressman Sam Steiger, who during the primary had been erroneously linked with the gangland slaying of an Arizona reporter.

Almost immediately, DeConcini showed his independent streak and made his presence felt at the White House by remaining on the fence in a key vote on whether to lift federal controls on the price of newly discovered natural gas that was sold across state lines. The White House supported increasing the price of new gas but favored continued regulation. Although the House of Representatives had passed an administration-backed energy bill that contained this provision, the outcome of separate legislation to deregulate natural gas was in doubt in the Senate due to the uncertainty of four Democrats, including DeConcini, who was invited to confer with the president. "There may be a key vote on this," Carter told him, "and the Secretary [of Energy James Schlesinger] and I wanted to talk to you a little about it." Nevertheless, DeConcini voted in favor of the immediate deregulation of natural gas, helping to narrowly pass the measure by a vote of 50 to 46, which ultimately delayed passage of the president's entire energy program by a year.

The same independent streak and fence straddling that brought DeConcini to the White House's attention over energy legislation had a similar result when the Senate took up consideration in the spring of 1978 of the first of the two Panama Canal Treaties (the Neutrality Treaty) that the president had negotiated with Panama in September 1977. According to this agreement, the United States had the right to defend the canal's neutrality after it was ceded to Panama by the year 2000. Like a number of senators, DeConcini had serious reservations about relinquishing control of such a vital waterway after the year 2000. He introduced a strongly worded amendment to the treaty that would give the United States the right to intervene militarily to reopen the canal if it should ever become necessary.

The administration maintained that the right to keep the canal open was implied in the agreement. By making it explicit, however, the Senate would be insulting Panamanian national pride. President Carter therefore realized that if the Senate approved the amendment, it would effectively kill the canal agreements. Not only would they have to be renegotiated, but the Panamanians would never approve a treaty provision that seemed to give the United States the power to interfere militarily in Panama whenever it deemed intervention was necessary to keep the waterway open to U.S. commerce. Given these circumstances and how close the vote on the treaty was expected to be, the White House felt it was imperative to work out an agreement with DeConcini in which he would not introduce his proposed amendment and yet would vote for the treaties.

Although the administration had a similar problem with another amendment proposed by Senator SAM NUNN of Georgia that would allow the United States to station troops in Panama after December 31, 1999, under certain circumstances, DeConcini posed the greater challenge to the president. After considerable negotiation, the Arizona senator agreed to substitute for his amendment a reservation (an understanding written into the treaty that was less likely to lead to renegotiation of the treaty than a more formal agreement), which was less likely to require renegotiation of the treaty. (Nunn had agreed to do the same with his amendment.)

The State Department was still worried that the reservation was too strong. "They wanted more from me, but I said no," the senator later remarked. Instead, he asked to meet with the president at the White House, where he persuaded Carter to support his reservation. "Next time I get into one of these confrontations," the president told DeConcini afterwards, "I would like to have you on my side earlier." On this basis, DeConcini voted for the treaty, and it passed, 68-32—one more vote than the required two thirds. Although the Panamanians were offended by the reservation, Panama's strongman, OMAR TORRIJOS, agreed to accept it and the Nunn reservation, maintaining that Panama had still achieved its fundamental objectives.

Throughout the remainder of the Carter presidency, DeConcini continued to be an irritant to the White House. In 1977, for example, he voted against the president's proposal to reform the Social Security system. In 1980, he threatened a Senate investigation after the Customs Service refused to release the records of a 1977 incident in which the president's son, Chip Carter, had been hustled away from a bar in Panama City, Florida, by the Secret Service while talking with the owner of a boat about to be involved in a major drug bust. Although Chip appeared innocent of any involvement in the bust and the Treasury Inspector's General Office later looked into the matter and found nothing wrong, DeConcini demanded answers to questions about the raid, including payments to informants prior to the bust and the location of records having to do with the operation. Despite the senator's threats, however, no Senate investigation into the matter was undertaken.

DeConcini served three terms in the Senate. During this time, he was a member of a number of important committees including Judiciary, Appropriations, Veterans, and Indian Affairs. In 1993, he became chairman of the Senate Select Committee on Intelligence. On the state level, his priority was funding of the Central Arizona Project, implemented in the 1980s to deliver Colorado River water to Phoenix and Tucson. Nationally, he proposed the congressional veto, a balanced-budget amendment, campaign reform, and congressional term limits. In 1978, he authored the Bankruptcy Reform Act of 1978, the first reform of bankruptcy courts and law in four decades. Internationally, he served on the U.S. Helsinki Commission on human rights. Although he traveled throughout the world, his efforts concentrated on Africa, where he heard testimony on the plight and persecution of refugees.

A recurrent theme throughout DeConcini's career were issues related to children. A Roman Catholic pro-life advocate (although he never ran as a pro-life senator), he advocated affordable, quality child care in the workplace and wrote legislation that provided for tax incentives for employers who provided child care. He also fought child pornography; secured funding for outreach immunization programs; and, in 1990, cosponsored the National Child Search Assistance Act, which required police officers to take an immediate report in missing-child cases. He also helped to establish the National Center for Missing and Exploited Children.

In the 1990s, DeConcini was implicated in a scandal involving him and four other senators, known as the "Keating Five," who intervened with federal regulators investigating the financial dealings of Charles Keating, the president of Lincoln Savings and Loan, in return for financial support. Keating had donated thousands of dollars to DeConcini's senate campaigns. The question was not whether the senators had intervened in the investigation of Keating's affairs, but whether they had done so improperly. All five senators affirmed their innocence, but after an investigation by the Senate Ethics Committee, DeConcini was chastised by the Senate for his behavior. As a result, in 1994 the Arizona senator decided not to seek reelection to a fourth term. Instead, he opened a Washington office of his law firm.

Continuing his interest in children's affairs, DeConcini also agreed to serve on the board of directors for the Center for Missing and Exploited Children. In 1995, he became the board's chairman. That same year, President Bill Clinton appointed him to the board of directors of Federal Home Loan Mortgage Corporation.

Deng Xiaoping

(Teng Hsiao-ping)
(1904–1997) *leader of the People's Republic of China*

Deng Xiaoping became the leader of the People's Republic of China (PRC, or Communist China) in the late 1970s after a brief period of consolidation following the death of Mao Zedong in 1976. In 1979, he helped normalize relations between the United States and the PRC. As the undisputed leader of China for almost 20 years, Deng was also responsible for the creation of a market-like economy, including a budding generation of entrepreneurs, even as he maintained tight communist political control of the nation.

Deng was born on February 19, 1904, to a prosperous landowner in Guangan, Sichuan Province, in south-central China. Although little is known about his childhood, he had an older sister and two younger brothers who later played roles in the Chinese Revolution. He also studied in a modern middle school due to abolishment of the traditional civil service system in 1905. Already a committed nationalist and socialist by 1919, he went to France as part of a work-study program and remained there for five years. During this time, he met other young Chinese radicals and joined a faction of the Chinese Communist Party (CCP) led by future foreign minister Zhou Enlai, who remained his friend throughout his career. He then studied in Moscow for eight months at Sun Yat-sen University.

Sometime in the late 1920s, Deng began to work for the underground CCP in Shanghai, and in 1929 he was sent to the southwestern province of Guangxi, where he helped to establish a rural communist party and a military force. After suffering a series of military defeats, he was ousted from power in the first of three crises that he would experience during his career as a leader of the CCP. A year later, however, he made a comeback, joining the fabled Long March in 1934 and then fighting against the Japanese. During this time, he rose steadily in the military ranks and came to command the 129th Division. In 1945, he was elected to the CCP Central Committee.

After the end of World War II, the 129th Division became the Second Field Army, which, under Deng's command, participated in the military campaign of 1948–49 that overthrew the Nationalist regime of Chiang Kai-shek. Although only five feet, two inches tall, Deng had developed a reputation by 1949 as a tough and fierce fighter. Following the Communist victory, he became the ranking party leader in southwest China. He continued to rise in the CCP leadership hierarchy, serving briefly as finance minister and then, in 1954, as secretary-general of the Central Committee and vice premier of China. In 1955, he was elected to the Politburo and then to the position of secretary-general of the party.

In 1967, Deng went through the second and longest of the three crises in his career. At one time close to China's leader, Mao Zedong, who liked Deng's sardonic humor and respected his toughness, Deng distanced himself from Mao during the Great Leap Forward (1958–61), Mao's efforts to establish agricultural communes throughout China. A wily pragmatist, Deng criticized the movement, remarking that the color of a cat was unimportant as long as it caught mice. In the Cultural Revolution that Mao instituted in 1966 to remove all vestiges of antirevolutionary sentiment, Deng was disgraced, paraded through the streets of Beijing wearing a dunce cap, denounced for his "capitalist policies," forced to wait tables at a CCP school, and then exiled to a tractor factory in Jiangxi province in southeastern China where he wound wire for generator coils.

By 1973, however, opposition to the Cultural Revolution had mounted because of the domestic turmoil it had caused. Deng's longtime acquaintance, Foreign Minister Zhou Enlai, who was suffering from cancer, brought him back into the party leadership. By 1975, Deng held leadership positions in the party, the nation, and the military, yet once more he was deposed by more radical elements in the CCP who opposed his more pragmatic approach to problems before him. This time, though, his fall from grace was short-lived. In 1976, Mao Zedong, who had been ill and retained only a modicum of the power he once possessed, died. After a brief power struggle, Mao's wife, Jiang Qing, and the so-called Gang of Four, who wanted to continue the Cultural Revolution, were arrested. With wide support from the Chinese populace, Deng was reinstated to most of his posts by the summer of 1977. He alone among the leaders of the group that had overthrown the Gang of Four had both a history of long service as a party functionary and as a military leader of the Chinese Revolution.

Deng's return to power effectively ended the Cultural Revolution and began a new era in Chinese life. Deng began to reinterpret Maoism and criticized many of its excesses. By the end of 1978, he was the paramount leader of China, although Chairman Hua Guofeng was the ostensible head of government. Working with his protégés, Hua Yaobang and Zhao Ziyang, Deng developed a pragmatic economic modernization program. One of his first reforms was to abolish Mao Zedong's rural agricultural communes and allow Chinese peasants to cultivate family gardens, the produce from which they could sell in free markets. He also encouraged the development of a class of entrepreneurs to develop and sell their own goods, and he courted international investment as a way of bolstering the nation's industrial productivity.

In terms of foreign policy, Deng decided to normalize relations with the United States as part of his long-standing concern about the Soviet Union, whose forces along the Sino-Soviet border presented a real threat to China. In his mind, the United States was a card to play against the Soviets. Deng's economic policies also required opening China to the rest of the world in order to encourage foreign investment from the world's industrial powers.

For its part, the Carter administration, clearly under the influence of National Security Advisor ZBIGNIEW BRZEZINSKI, who favored a hard-line policy against the Soviet Union, was anxious to normalize relations with China. Thinking in much the same way as Deng, who was then serving as vice premier, Brzezinski viewed China as a card to play against Moscow.

On May 20, 1978, Brzezinski traveled to Beijing in order to begin negotiations about normalizing relations with China. Following his visit, Deng, and President Carter, who as a young submarine officer had participated in naval operations off the coast of China in 1949, conducted intense negotiations. The big stumbling block was the United States' treaty with Taiwan, which the PRC considered part of China. On December 15, 1978, however, Carter was able to announce to the American people that he had decided to grant full diplomatic status to the PRC. He also announced that Deng would be visiting the United States. The news surprised even lawmakers on Capitol Hill. The Chinese insisted that before full diplomatic relations could be restored, the United States had to terminate its defense pact with Taiwan and not sell any more arms to Taiwan. In response, the White House stated that it could not abrogate its defense pact with Taiwan and not sell Taiwan any more arms. The Chinese accepted the president's terms.

Normalization of relations with the United States was a major achievement for Deng, providing him with insurance against the Soviets and paving the way for American investment in China. To encourage American businessmen to help jump-start China's economy with technology, knowledge, and capital, Deng visited the United States in January 1979. His trip was widely regarded as a big success. Traveling the country and courting the business community, he was portrayed in the press as a new type of Chinese leader, ready to lead China out of its isolationism. Affable and charming, he even posed for a picture in a cowboy hat at a Texas barbeque.

Many Americans remained distrustful of China, however, and felt that the United States had betrayed Taiwan. At the end of February 1979, China's invasion of Vietnam confirmed their worst fears. Vietnam had attacked Cambodia, driving its odious leader Pol Pot and his Khmer Rouge forces into the mountains and then renaming the country Kampuchea. China was determined to punish Vietnam for its invasion of Cambodia. During his visit to the United States, Deng told the president of his plan for a punitive strike across China's borders into Vietnam. Carter tried to dissuade him, maintaining that such military action would refute one of the administration's best arguments for normalization—that it would contribute to peace and stability in Asia. But Deng rejected his advice; Vietnam had to learn that it could not attack one of its neighbors with impunity.

The invasion was a failure. Chinese forces drove 25 miles into Vietnam and withdrew after only 17 days. Vietnamese forces fought the Chinese to a standstill, and casualties were heavy; each side lost about 30,000 men. The conflict exposed weaknesses in the Chinese army that sparked a drive to rebuild China's military hardware.

In 1980, Deng decided to give up most of his official titles, including resigning as chief of staff of the army and as vice premier. According to some sources, his move was intended to elicit resignations from other aging leaders. But he still remained China's unquestioned leader. During the 1980s, he improved relations with the Soviet Union and, in 1984, secured the long-cherished Chinese goal of recovering the British colony of Hong Kong through an agreement to be implemented in

De facto leader of the People's Republic of China Deng Xiaoping and President Carter shake hands after signing diplomatic agreements between the United States and China. *(Jimmy Carter Library)*

1997. Under Deng's leadership, the Chinese economy began to recover from the excesses of the Cultural Revolution and developed into one of the fastest-growing economies in the world. Agricultural production increased dramatically as the communal labor system was virtually eliminated. Light industry and trade also increased markedly in response to freer markets, an emphasis on exports, and a movement of China's rural population into its burgeoning cities.

Although he was a modern economic reformer, Deng imposed an iron will on China's population. Determined to deal with China's population problem, he set a limit of one or two children per family, with forced abortions and severe cutbacks in benefits for families violating those limitations. (Deng himself had five children—three daughters and two sons.) Committed to suppressing any opposition to communist political rule even as China moved toward a more capitalist economy, he brutally suppressed student protesters in Tiananmen Square in 1989. Hundreds of students and bystanders were believed to have been killed and hundreds of others arrested, thereby tarnishing China's image in the world.

Suffering from Parkinson's Disease, Deng had given up all his offices and titles by 1990. Even so, he was still able to exert considerable influence in selecting China's new leadership, passing his mandate to Jiang Zemin, China's president and general secretary of the CCP. On February 19, 1997, Deng died in Beijing at the age of 92.

Derian, Patricia Murphy

(1929–) *human rights and humanitarian affairs coordinator, assistant secretary of state*

The coordinator of the State Department's Bureau of Human Rights and Humanitarian Affairs and later assistant secretary of state for human rights during the Carter administration, Patricia Derian was a strong advocate of promoting human rights in American foreign policy. She encountered firm opposition, however, to her effort to incorporate human rights considerations into U.S. foreign-aid decision making. Frustrated by what she regarded as a losing battle, she nearly resigned her post in 1980.

Born on August 12, 1929, in New York City, Patricia "Pat" Murphy was raised near Danville, Virginia, and attended nursing school at the University of Virginia. While attending the university, she met and married Paul Derian, who graduated with a degree in orthopedics; the couple moved to Mississippi. In 1959, Patricia Derian joined the Civil Rights movement despite threats against her life from the Ku Klux Klan. In 1964, she gathered signatures to put Lyndon Johnson's name on the ballot in Mississippi. Four years later, she helped organize the biracial Mississippi Democratic Freedom Party, which challenged the all-white Mississippi state delegation at the Democratic National Convention in Chicago.

In 1976, Derian served as deputy director of Jimmy Carter's presidential campaign and was a member of Carter's transition team. Her strong support for civil rights, combined with a desire by the new president to appoint women to high positions in government, led Carter to designate her coordinator of the Bureau of Human Rights and Humanitarian Affairs (HA). Established by Congress in 1976, HA had a number of responsibilities, including coordinating and advocating the human rights policy within the State Department and giving nongovernmental organizations—such as Amnesty International—a voice within the department.

Upon her appointment, Derian made clear that she intended to make her voice heard. "If you want a magnolia to decorate foreign policy," she told Carter's nominee for deputy secretary of state, WARREN CHRISTOPHER, "I'm the wrong person. I expect to get things done." Indeed, it appeared early in the administration that she would play a significant decision-making role. Carter had declared in his inaugural address that his commitment to human rights would be "absolute." The implication was that the United States would punish any country, friend or foe, that violated the rights of its people. The president attended Derian's swearing-in ceremony, suggesting that he intended to give her his full support.

In April 1977, at the initiative of National Security Advisor ZBIGNIEW BRZEZINSKI, the National Security Council (NSC) established the Interagency Group on Human Rights and Foreign Assistance. Also known as the Christopher Group because it was chaired by Deputy Secretary of State Christopher, it was made up of representatives from all government departments as well as the NSC, the Export-Import Bank, and HA. Its job was to examine all military and economic assistance proposals and to decide whether to grant the aid in question. Derian therefore had input in all U.S. foreign-assistance decisions. Finally, in August 1977, with the support of both Christopher and lawmakers on Capitol Hill, the president elevated Derian's position from coordinator to assistant secretary of state for human rights, further suggesting that she would have considerable influence within the administration.

A number of White House decisions, however, undermined these early indications of an influential Bureau of Human Rights. The process had begun on January 31, 1977, when Secretary of State CYRUS VANCE announced that, rather than take an "absolute" position on human rights, the Carter administration would adopt a case-by-case stance. This meant that nations such as South Korea and the Philippines, which were run by repressive governments but were also strategically important to the United States, would not receive the same level of criticism or aid reductions as other countries. In addition, for political or security reasons, the United States adopted cautious approaches toward such nations as Egypt, Indonesia, China, Saudi Arabia, North Yemen, and Iran.

There was also infighting within the administration over the extent to which human rights should be made a consideration in the provisioning of foreign assistance. Although Brzezinski had worked to establish the Christopher Group, he was wary of overemphasizing human rights, arguing that it could lead to a backlash against the United States. He warned, for example, that criticizing Brazil might not only threaten U.S. relations with that country but also undermine the president's nuclear nonproliferation policy. At the time, the White House was trying to keep Brazil from acquiring nuclear technology from West Germany, and Brzezinski worried that an antagonistic government in Brasilia would be less willing to cooperate with Washington if the United States assailed Brazil for its human rights violations.

Other governmental departments and bureaus also successfully fought Derian and HA. This was evident by the restrictions placed on the role of the Christopher Group. By the middle of 1978, the Defense Department's military assistance and security supporting assistance programs, the Food for Peace program and export credits from the Commodity Credit Corporation (CCC), both administered by the Department of Agriculture, the Overseas Private Investment Corporation, and the International Monetary Fund had successfully removed themselves from the purview of the Christopher Group. In some cases, HA did not fight the agency involved. For instance, Derian agreed that Title II of the Food for Peace Program should not be covered by human rights considerations because Title II was humanitarian in nature. But HA failed to have Title I, CCC export credits, military assistance, and security supporting assistance remain under the Christopher Group's authority. As a result, the bureau found its responsibilities limited largely to aid from the multilateral development banks (such as the World Bank and Inter-American Development Bank).

There was also opposition to HA within the Foreign Service. Not only was Derian an outsider with no experience within the Beltway, but foreign service officers felt that she and her bureau were tainted by myopia, focusing solely on human rights and failing to take into account the broad range of issues that affected U.S. relations with other countries. By far the strongest opposition in the State Department came from Assistant Secretary of State for East Asian and Pacific Affairs Richard Holbrooke and Undersecretary of State for Inter-American Affairs Terence Todman. After Derian traveled to the Philippines in early 1978 and criticized Philippine president Ferdinand Marcos, Holbrooke persuaded the White House to send Vice President WALTER MONDALE to Manila to smooth matters over with the Philippine leader. Todman, for his part, censured the administration's human rights policy in a February 1978 speech, arguing that it endangered America's relations with its southern neighbors. Carter responded by assigning Todman as ambassador to Spain.

Even when Derian turned to the White House or Congress for help, it was not always forthcoming. Vance left final decisions regarding the Christopher Group to Christopher, and both he and Carter had to weigh human rights against other foreign policy considerations. The president believed, moreover, that the best way to deal with countries violating human rights was through a carrot-and-stick approach, employing a combination of sanctions and incentives to promote change. Carter refused, for example, to approve new military aid to Chile and Uruguay in 1977 and 1978 and cut military assistance to Argentina in 1977 to $15 million because of human rights violations. These restrictions, however, did not cover goods in the "pipeline" (items already ordered but not yet delivered). Additionally, the president permitted the sale of spare parts and support equipment (including trucks and unarmed aircraft) to countries such as Paraguay, Uruguay, and Argentina, even though they were run by repressive authoritarian governments.

Lawmakers, for their part, were divided over the extent to which human rights in U.S. foreign policy should be emphasized. Although Democrats controlled Congress, some senators, like EDWARD KENNEDY (D-Mass.) and JAMES ABOUREZK (D-S.Dak.), felt Carter's human rights policy was not strong enough, while others, including Representatives William Moorhead (D-Pa.) and Joseph Minish (D-N.J.), felt it was too tough. Such divisions could be seen as early as 1977, when Kennedy proposed a bill that would have cut all military aid to Argentina, including that in the pipeline. Democratic senator HUBERT HUMPHREY (Minn.) proposed, at the request of the White House, a substitute amendment that would free up the pipeline and permit a presidential waiver. Lawmakers passed the Humphrey bill. The following year, Congress, aware of growing tensions between Romania and the Soviet Union, granted most-favored-nation (MFN) status to the government in Bucharest. Derian had objected to granting MFN status to Rumania, pointing to the repressive policies of Rumania's leader, Nicolae Ceauşescu.

The restriction of the Christopher Group's purview and the lack of a sympathetic hearing in the executive or legislative branches frustrated Derian. In March 1977, she warned against "send[ing] a double message" to repressive nations. She later declared her opposition to a carrot-and-stick approach, saying that "it doesn't work. I don't think you can buy people out of jail without insuring and guaranteeing that the next time whatever it is you bought them with is wanted."

During 1979, crises in Nicaragua, Iran, and Afghanistan led the president to place more emphasis on strategic concerns and less on human rights. Derian, in turn, grew increasingly discouraged. In 1979, Pol Pot, the leader of Cambodia who had killed at least 1 million of his own people, was ousted from power by invading Vietnamese troops. He immediately sought UN recognition for his government-in-exile. Over Derian's objections, the Carter administration supported Pol Pot's claim. China, a nation with which the United States sought to improve relations, had backed Pol Pot, and the administration did not want to anger Beijing.

Also in 1979, Derian failed to kill an Iranian request for crowd-control equipment, including tear gas. She made her frustration clear to Congress, telling the House Committee on Foreign Affairs in spring 1980: "I often find myself in the decision-making process, not in the majority." When the Carter administration, desirous of improving relations with Argentina, began discussions on renewing military aid to that country, Derian threatened to resign; she changed her mind after the White House decided against the military aid. The fact was, however, that HA had become largely powerless in an administration worried more about the United States' strategic position in the world and less about promoting human rights.

After Carter left office, Derian was an outspoken critic of the human rights policy of President RONALD REAGAN. She continues to work with organizations that seek to protect human rights abroad.

Dingell, John David, Jr.

(1926–) *member of the House of Representatives*

John D. Dingell, Jr., is the longest-serving member of the U.S. House of Representatives. Because of Dingell's lifelong commitment to a single-payer national health insurance plan and to other social welfare programs, the columnist Michael Barone has described him as an "old-fashioned social Democrat." But he is also widely recognized as one of the House's most adept legislators, assertive turf-fighters, toughest negotiators, and staunchest defenders of the institutional prerogatives of Congress. Some of those who have crossed paths with Dingell have included President Jimmy Carter's secretary of the interior, CECIL ANDRUS, and his former secretary of health, education and welfare, JOSEPH CALIFANO. Califano later called Dingell a "congressional bully" for challenging the ethics one of his clients, John Shad, RONALD REAGAN's nominee for chairperson of the Securities and Exchange Commission.

Born on July 8, 1926, in Colorado Springs, Colorado, Dingell has spent almost his entire life in politics. He was only six years old when his father, John Dingell, Sr., a former newspaperman, businessman, and labor leader, was elected to the U.S. Congress from Detroit. During his terms in office, the elder Dingell was a New Dealer who helped draft and pass the legislation establishing the Social Security system and later worked for passage of a national health insurance plan.

John Dingell, Jr., grew up in the Washington, D.C., area and, as a boy, served as a congressional page from 1938 to 1943. After serving in the army during World War II (1944–46), he attended Georgetown University, where he received both his undergraduate and law degrees (B.S., 1949; J.D., 1952). Working briefly as a forest ranger and an assistant prosecuting attorney, he won a special election in 1955 to fill the vacant seat in the House created by the death of his father, who had been serving his 12th term in Congress.

As a young congressman, Dingell supported most of President Lyndon Johnson's Great Society programs. In 1965, he presided over the House as it approved legislation establishing Medicare, and he accompanied Johnson to the Harry S. Truman Library in Independence, Missouri, for the signing of the new Medicare measure. "It's hard to believe that there was no Social Security or Medicare," he later remarked. But Dingell also broke with the administration on several occasions. While he supported Johnson's civil rights bill, for example, he opposed mandatory busing to end de facto segregation in Detroit's white neighborhoods. As a member of the National Rifle Association (NRA), he also opposed gun control and referred to agents of the Alcohol, Tobacco, and Firearms Agency as "jack-booted thugs."

Dingell also had a mixed record on other matters important to the 1960s and 1970s, such as feminism and the environment. A Polish Catholic, he took a moderately conservative position on abortion, voting for a ban on "partial-birth" abortions. On the environment, he was an avid hunter and outdoorsmen who authored the Endangered Species Act of 1973 and engaged in various projects to save the Potomac River, including the Dyke Marsh, a resting place for migrating ducks just down the river from the National Airport. However, since he represented a district whose economic base was the automobile industry, and he was also married to a former lobbyist for General Motors and an heiress to the Fisher Body fortune, he opposed air-pollution bills that could drive up the cost of automobiles and fought off attempts to strengthen safety and fuel-efficiency standards.

During Carter's administration, Dingell was a senior member of the Energy and Commerce Committee and chair of its Energy and Power Subcommittee, established by the 94th Congress (1975–76) to deal with developing energy problems. Having already developed a reputation as one of a select group of House members who could make things happen, he was largely responsible for the creation of the Energy and Power Subcommittee, and he was able to amass considerable power over important energy issues. As a result, he played a key role in congressional enactment of energy legislation, one of the administration's highest priorities during the Carter presidency.

Dingell went along with Speaker TIP O'NEILL's insistence that the House include the administration's complex energy proposal in 1977 in one omnibus package, but he sided clearly with the automobile industry in energy legislation affecting the industry. He opposed deregulation of natural gas, one of the president's key energy measures, believing that deregulation would drive prices beyond what was necessary for increased supply and could lead to inflation and recession. Dingell made that point forcefully when JAMES SCHLESINGER, who prepared the administration's energy bill and would later serve as the first secretary of energy, appeared before his committee. He also opposed deregulation of oil prices, warning in 1980 that deregulation could mean gasoline prices of $2 a gallon, not including inflationary increases, and he fought against the administration's proposed gas-guzzler tax, maintaining that it was unnecessary and would not achieve its purpose. More generally, Dingell argued that many of the programs contained in the White House's energy proposals, such as appliance standards, efficiency standards for new buildings, and the establishment of a Strategic Petroleum Reserve Program, were already contained in the Energy Policy and Conservation Act of 1975. At the same time, he was a strong supporter of alternative energy sources, and he berated the president in 1980 when the administration abandoned its demand that the proposed Energy Mobilization Board, whose purpose was to cut through the red tape that often strangled nascent projects for new energy sources, be empowered to override federal and state laws.

In every year of the Carter administration and throughout the 1980s and 1990s, Dingell continued to introduce legislation for a program of national health insurance. This made him sympathetic to Carter's chief political foe within the Democratic Party, Senator EDWARD KENNEDY (Mass.), who led the fight in the party for a comprehensive health-insurance program and had the support of most of organized labor, including the United Auto Workers.

In 1983, Dingell became chairman of the Committee on Energy and Commerce. Already a power broker in the House, he developed a reputation for excluding from conference committees lawmakers whom he felt had been disloyal to him. He also took pride in the control he was able to assert over his committee. "Either you were with him, or in the doghouse," one member of the committee remarked after being berated by the chairman. Dingell was also known for having a highly qualified staff and for doing his homework on bills before his committee.

For most of the time that he served in Congress, Dingell's seat was widely regarded as a safe one for Democrats, but the increasing conservatism of Detroit's white suburbs made it more competitive for Republicans. In 2002, his district was reapportioned by the Republican-controlled Michigan legislature, and he had to run against a fellow Democratic incumbent, Lynn Rivers of Ann Arbor. Although both Rivers and Dingell had solid liberal voting records, Rivers was considered the more liberal of the two. Not surprisingly, organized labor and the NRA supported Dingell, while the Sierra Club supported Rivers. Dingell beat Rivers by a 59 to 41 percent margin, larger than most observers had expected. As Michael Barone reported on the primary, labor outweighed feminism, and environmentalism and gun control were not winners.

Dole, Robert Joseph

(1923–) *member of the Senate, Republican vice-presidential candidate*

Known for his sharp tongue and sardonic wit, Robert Dole was a U.S. senator from Kansas and President GERALD FORD's running mate against Jimmy Carter and WALTER MONDALE in the 1976 presidential election. Throughout Carter's four years in office, Dole remained a relentless and outspoken foe of the administration, opposing the president on virtually every major legislative initiative and his foreign policy agenda from the Panama Canal treaties to the second Strategic Arms Limitation Talks (SALT II) agreement.

Poor farm boy, high-school athlete, decorated and badly wounded veteran of World War II, U.S. senator, vice-presidential candidate, and presidential candidate, Dole epitomized the virtues and values of what some writers have referred to as "America's greatest generation." He was born on July 22, 1923, in the farming community of Russell, Kansas. His father ran a grain elevator; his mother sold Singer sewing machines. After living briefly in the one-room home where Robert was born, the Doles moved to a larger house. During the Great Depression, they had to rent the house while they lived in the basement.

A star athlete while in high school, Dole also delivered newspapers and worked as a soda jerk at the local pharmacy. He was able to attend the University of Kansas only because a local banker loaned him $300 to help pay for his tuition. He expected to be a physician, but in December 1942, he signed up for the Army Enlisted Reserve Corps. After various postings in the United States, including completion of officers' training, he was sent to the Po Valley in northern Italy, where, on April 14, 1945, he was badly wounded just two weeks before the war in Europe ended. Dole lost a kidney and was temporarily paralyzed from the neck down; his condition was so critical that it was unclear whether he would even live. Nevertheless, although he lost permanent use of his right arm and regained only limited feeling in his left fingers, he was able to recover fully enough to attend the University of Arizona and then Washburn University in Topeka, Kansas, where he received both his undergraduate and law degrees (B.A., 1949; LL.B., 1952). For his service during World War II, he won two Purple Hearts and the Bronze Star with Cluster.

Even before completing law school, Dole ran successfully as a Republican for the state legislature (1950–52). After serving one term, he was elected Russell County attorney, a position he held for eight years before being elected to the U.S. House of Representatives in 1960. After serving four terms in the lower chamber, he ran in 1968 for the Senate seat being vacated by longtime Kansas senator Frank Carlson. Following a grueling campaign in which he spent 11 months crisscrossing the state, Dole was elected with 60.5 percent of the vote.

As a congressman from a rural conservative district, Dole opposed most of the legislation associated with John F. Kennedy's New Frontier and Lyndon Johnson's Great Society. He was also against abortion rights and court-ordered busing and was a strong supporter of the war in Vietnam, but he voted for the Civil Rights Act of 1964 and the Voting Rights Act of 1965. A fiscal conservative, he was concerned mostly with protecting the agricultural interests of his constituency. Except for his sardonic attitude and the special attention he gave to the rights of the disabled, there was very little to distinguish him from other lawmakers representing similar constituencies.

Dole's biting tongue, sharp wit, and loyalty to the Nixon administration, however, caught the attention of the White House. In 1971, President RICHARD NIXON asked him to be chairman of the Republican National Committee. Later, Dole commented humorously how fortunate it was for him that despite his new responsibilities, he was "cut out of the action": fortunate in the sense that he might otherwise have wound up in jail. But he found the Watergate affair no laughing matter. "What angered me was the callousness of a White House staff that demanded loyalty but failed to return it," he later remarked.

In 1974, Dole narrowly escaped being defeated in his bid for reelection to the Senate, beating Democratic congressman and physician Bill Roy by less than 14,000 votes. During the campaign, Dole accused Roy of being an abortionist, and his campaign workers distributed graphic photos of aborted fetuses in Topeka neighborhoods. One result of this, however, was to make Dole an attractive candidate to the right wing of the Republican Party who wanted President Gerald Ford to dump his liberal vice president, Nelson Rockefeller, in favor of a conservative. Having narrowly defeated former California governor RONALD REAGAN for the Republican presidential nomination, Ford bowed to their wishes and selected Dole as his running mate.

Most political observers agree that Dole hurt, rather than helped, the Republican ticket in 1976. Recalling later that he was assigned the task of being "the tough guy" in the campaign, the Kansas senator seemed to take on that responsibility with relish. In contrast to the pleasant and even cheerful demeanor of the Democratic vice-presidential candidate, Walter Mondale, Dole came across as mean-spirited and nasty, and his prickly and barbed remarks seemed graceless and unbecoming a candidate for high office. The low point of his campaign occurred during his debate with Mondale, the first debate between vice-presidential candidates in campaign history, when Dole seemed to suggest that Democrats were alone responsible for leading the United States into war. "I figured out the other day," he commented "if we added up the killed and wounded in Democrat wars in this century, it would be about 1.6 million Americans, enough to fill the city of Detroit." Surprised by Dole's remarks, Mondale responded, "I think that Senator Dole has richly earned his reputation as a hatchet man tonight." Even Dole realized the mistake he had made. At the annual Gridiron Club dinner the next year, he quipped that the person wounded most by his razor tongue "was me."

With Gerald Ford's defeat in November, Dole returned to the Senate, where he became one of the Carter administration's most caustic critics. As a wounded veteran of World War II, Dole opposed President Carter's nominee for director of the Central Intelligence Agency (CIA), THEODORE SORENSEN, the former speechwriter for President Kennedy, because of his well-known pacifist background. (Sorensen had been a conscientious objector during the Korean War.) Dole also spoke out sharply when President Carter carried out his campaign promise to pardon Vietnam War draft evaders as a way of healing the wounds left from the Vietnam conflict. "It's distressing," he told lawmakers on Capitol Hill, "to see conscious disobedience condoned on a blanket basis." Similarly, he rebuked the administration for supporting the admission of Vietnam to the United Nations as part of an effort to normalize relations with Hanoi, stating that such a step should not have been taken "until the Vietnamese have been more responsive in accounting for the Americans missing in action" in Vietnam.

As a member of the Senate Agriculture Committee, Dole strongly opposed the administration's four-year farm plan that it sent to Congress in March 1977. Although Carter had made the farm crisis a campaign issue, accusing former presidents Nixon and Ford of causing farm income to drop and promising new legislation to assure support prices at least equal to the cost of production, the president discovered after he took office that his promise conflicted with his higher commitment to a balanced budget by 1981. As a result, his farm program, which Secretary of Agriculture ROBERT BERGLAND sent to Congress at the end of March, contained support prices even lower than existing prices. Referring to President Nixon's agriculture secretary, Earl L. Butz, Dole commented to Bergland, "if Earl Butz had offered this, he would have needed a bodyguard to get out of here." Eventually the White House had to agree to a farm bill significantly exceeding the price supports favored by the administration.

Dole was also a strong opponent of the president's 1977 fiscal-stimulus program, favoring increased tax reductions and tax credits in lieu of the White House's $50 tax rebate proposal. When even Democrats balked at the tax rebate, the senator remarked with characteristic wit that Republicans should delay floor action on the measure since it could lead to more Democratic defections due to the lawmakers spending more time with their constituents.

Critical of what he regarded as the sanctimony of the Carter presidency, Dole was at the forefront of Republicans calling for the resignation of BERT LANCE, the director of the Office of Management and Budget (OMB) and the president's closest friend in the administration, after it was revealed that Lance had been involved in questionable banking practices as president of the Calhoun National Bank and the National Bank of Georgia. While most Republicans, as well as Democrats, were relieved when Lance announced at the end of September 1977 that he was resigning his position as OMB director, Dole was not. Instead, he called for the investigation to continue into Lance's financial dealings before taking office "so that the public will know the truth, as they did in Watergate."

The Kansas senator was also one of the leading opponents of the 1977 Panama Canal

Treaties handing over ownership of the canal and the Panama Canal Zone to the Panamanians by the end of the century. Working closely with other opponents of the canal pacts, Dole tried unsuccessfully to defeat the agreements by proposing six amendments and two reservations that he knew would be unacceptable to the Panamanians. Similarly, he strongly opposed the White House's Middle East peace initiative in October that involved a joint statement by the United States and the Soviet Union calling for a Geneva peace conference, possibly by the end of the year. The prospect of an imposed peace settlement that involved the pro-Palestinian Soviets was anathema to American Jewish leaders as well as to most lawmakers on Capitol Hill. Dole termed the joint statement on the Middle East by Washington and Moscow "an abdication of Mideast leadership by President Carter." The opposition to the joint statement in the United States was so strong that the White House quickly abandoned the concept of a Geneva conference involving Moscow.

Dole's strong opposition to most proposals emanating from the White House continued throughout the remainder of the administration. His criticisms were frequent, barbed, and eminently quotable in the media. He accused Carter's economic plan of fiscal restraint, announced in the 1978 State of the Union message, of being built on quicksand, contending that the rate of inflation had doubled since Carter had taken office and that the nation seemed "headed for double digit inflation and a recession during the coming year." Dole fought against the administration's efforts to raise Social Security taxes in order to deal with the system's funding problems. When the president intervened in February 1978 to resolve a lengthy coal strike that was having a rippling effect on the nation's economy, causing scattered layoffs, school closings, and shortened workweeks in affected regions, the Kansas senator put out a lengthy statement saying that the administration had waited too long and "contributed to the worsening situation." When reports circulated in March that an associate of the U.S. ambassador to Saudi Arabia, John C. West, was lobbying on behalf of the sale of jet aircraft to Saudi Arabia, Dole asked for an investigation of the reports. When Attorney General GRIFFIN BELL appointed a special counsel rather than a special prosecutor to look into charges that a bank controlled by Bert Lance had made questionable loans of $7 million to the Carter family peanut business, Dole said that a special prosecutor should have been appointed so as to assure the independence of the investigation.

In terms of social-welfare legislation, Dole followed a generally conservative line on such matters as welfare reform and aid to urban areas. Reflective of his concern for the disabled and the handicapped, however, he broke with many of his conservative colleagues in favoring a program of national catastrophic health insurance. He also supported school-lunch programs, although that could be attributed to the benefits the programs brought to his agricultural constituency.

By 1979, Dole was considering running for the presidency and had formed a campaign committee to explore whether he should seek the Republican presidential nomination. In 1980, he made a brief run for the White House but withdrew from the race after an early poor showing. As part of his possible presidential candidacy, Dole mellowed his slashing wit, but he did not lessen his attacks on the Carter administration. He spoke out strongly, for example, against the Strategic Arms Limitation Talks agreement (SALT II) that the United States had signed with the Soviet Union in 1979. Earlier, in April 1979, he joined 11 other Republican senators in announcing that they would attempt to amend the SALT agreement or attach reservations to it. He also attacked the president's second energy program calling for the decontrol of oil and a windfall profits tax on oil producers, remarking that the proposals amounted to "an admission that his original energy proposal was totally misdirected." Dole came out against the administration's effort to keep a complex 1976 tax provision changing the cost basis of inherited assets for later tax purposes from their value at the time of the inheritance to their original cost. When the White House threatened to veto any repeal of the 1976 tax provision, he attached the repeal amendment to the windfall-tax bill so that should the windfall tax be approved (as it was), the president would be unable to veto the repeal unless he vetoed the windfall-profits tax (which he did not).

As the 1980 election neared, Dole sat on a special committee looking into charges that the president's brother, BILLY CARTER, had improperly taken money from Libya without registering as a foreign agent. Dole pressed the investigation, which made headline news for several months and embarrassed the White House, with unusual vigor, even though it exonerated Billy Carter of any criminal liability. When one of Billy Carter's associates, who had helped to arrange a loan from Libya for him, became involved indirectly in a drug inquiry, Dole wanted to pursue the drug investigation to learn whether the president's brother was involved with drugs. Despite the fact that the drug inquiry was entirely separate from the investigation into Carter's ties with Libya, Dole claimed it opened a "whole new dimension in this increasingly complex case." Nevertheless, the Senate committee declined to pursue the matter further.

As a result of Ronald Reagan's decisive victory in November 1980, the Republicans not only won the White House, they captured the Senate. Dole then became chair of the powerful Senate Finance Committee. In this role, he figured prominently in the tax cuts and budget reductions that became known as Reaganomics. In 1982, he played a key role in extending the Voting Rights Act for 25 years. In 1985, he became Senate majority leader, a position he held from 1985 to 1987, when the Democrats recaptured the Senate, and then again from 1995 to 1996, when he resigned from the Senate to run for president. In the years when the Democrats controlled the Senate, he served as minority leader.

Most political observers believed that Dole was an effective leader in the Senate. In 1985, he worked out a carefully crafted budget deal to cut the deficit, which President Reagan never fully grasped and turned down. Many Republicans, Dole among them, believed that Reagan's failure cost the Republicans control of the Senate in the 1986 elections. As a result, the senator was furious with the president.

In 1988, Dole ran again for the Republican presidential nomination but lost in the primaries to GEORGE HERBERT WALKER BUSH. Remaining in the Senate, he played a decisive role in winning approval of the Americans with Disabilities Act. Although he won the Republican nomination in 1996, he was forced to give up his Senate seat to campaign. He then ran a lackluster race and was solidly defeated by President Bill Clinton in his bid for a second term.

After the election, Dole worked for a Washington, D.C., law and lobbying firm, did consulting work, and appeared frequently on television as a commentator and spokesperson for such products as Viagra and Pepsi-Cola. In 1997, he was awarded the Presidential Medal of Freedom. From 1997 to 2004, he was chairperson of the National World War II Memorial. In 2005, he published *One Soldier's Story: A Memoir*, an account of his experiences during World War II, including his three-year struggle to recover from the battle wounds that nearly killed him. Dole currently lives in Washington, D.C. with his wife, U.S. senator Elizabeth Dole (R-N.C.).

Donovan, Hedley Williams

(1914–1990) *newsmagazine editor, senior adviser to the president*

After retiring as editor in chief of Time Inc., Hedley Donovan served as senior adviser to President Carter from August 1979 to August 1980. His appointment was part of a reorganization of the White House staff and shakeup of the cabinet that the president instituted in summer 1979 in response to the American public's growing lack of confidence in his presidency. Not having any specific responsibilities, Donovan was expected to advise the president, on a one-on-one basis, on any problem he deemed pressing.

From a comfortable middle-class background, Donovan was born in Brainerd, Minnesota on May 14, 1914, and grew up in Minneapolis. He attended the University of Minnesota, where he graduated magna cum laude in history (B.A., 1934) and won a Rhodes Scholarship to attend Oxford University. While at Minnesota, he also developed an interest in journalism and became editor of the campus paper, the *Minnesota Daily.*

After graduating from Oxford in 1937 with a B.A. in modern history, Donovan settled in Washington, D.C., where he worked until 1942 as a reporter for the *Washington Post.* From 1942 to 1946, he served as a naval intelligence officer whose job entailed reading classified documents. Following the war, he moved to New York, where he began his long and highly successful career with Time Inc., first as a political and financial writer for *Fortune*, the business magazine owned by Time, and then gradually working his way up the ranks until he became managing editor of *Fortune* in 1953 and editorial director of Time Inc. in 1959. When the founder of Time Inc., Henry Luce, had to step down in 1964 because of illness, he named Donovan to succeed him as editor in chief, a position Donovan held until his retirement in 1979. In the publishing world, he was widely respected for his shrewdness, managerial skills, and fair-mindedness, all qualities that President Carter felt his troubled administration could use in the summer of 1979.

The president had known Donovan since his term as governor of Georgia, when Donovan had paid a call on Carter at the governor's mansion. They were also both members of the Trilateral Commission, the organization established by New York banker DAVID ROCKEFELLER to promote closer ties among the United States, Canada, the industrial powers of Western Europe, and Japan. It was not surprising, therefore, that Carter asked Donovan to join his administration in 1979 or that Donovan accepted even though the Luce enterprises, which he had led for 15 years, was closely identified with the right wing of the Republican Party. Certainly Donovan did not regard himself as a right-winger. Although a self-described fiscal conservative and hard-liner in foreign policy, he considered himself a political independent who had voted for Lyndon Johnson in 1964 and for Carter in 1976. As far as both he and the president were concerned, there was no incompatibility between their positions on most issues.

Yet in his new position, Donovan came to share a number of the same views about the president that many of the administration's critics were already making. He was struck by Carter's intelligence, diligence, decency, unflappability, compassion, and courtesy. He was also impressed by the president's memory and attention to detail. At the same time, he was troubled by Carter's lack of vision and what Donovan referred to as Carter's inability even to "visualize contingencies," such as the fall of the shah of Iran, MOHAMMAD REZA PAHLAVI, or the Soviet invasion of Afghanistan in 1979. What concerned Donovan was not that the president failed to foresee these specific developments or even acted unwisely as events unfolded—in fact, he later remarked that the "mechanisms of decision making and follow-through were generally efficient" in both instances—but that the White House had failed even to contemplate their possibility. He attributed part of Carter's problem to his disinterest in history (beyond biblical history) and his consequent lack of understanding about historical change. But he was also worried about the president's failure to resolve the differences between his National Security Advisor, ZBIGNIEW BRZEZINSKI, and his secretary of state, CYRUS VANCE. As someone inside the administration, Donovan found these differences even more acute than he had as an outsider.

Because of the fault line within the administration between Brzezinski and Vance and a lack of presidential direction, Donovan thought that problems such as the 1979 discovery by the CIA of a Soviet military brigade in Cuba were manufactured needlessly into crises. Indeed, he later wrote about "a surplus of secretaries of state" within the administration. When Vance resigned in April 1980 following the failed attempt to rescue the American hostages who had been seized by Iran in November 1979, Donovan urged Carter to give his successor, EDMUND MUSKIE, a clearer charter than Vance had been allowed. He was disappointed that the president failed to do so.

In the realm of domestic politics, Donovan was again disturbed by Carter's lack of vision and, on a more immediate level, by his unwillingness to cultivate close ties, much less friendships, with congressional leaders, creating what he later referred to as a "siege mentality" at the White House. In response to the first of these concerns, the president asked Donovan, shortly after he joined the administration, to establish a commission in order to examine the question of the dire national mood and how some sense of common purpose and optimism might be restored. This resulted in the establishment of the President's Commission on a National Agenda for the Eighties, chaired by President William McGill of Columbia University. In December 1980, the commission delivered its report, in which it made a number of legislative recommendations, including the complete federalization of the nation's welfare system and a comprehensive national health insurance program. Another of its recommendations, against making massive amounts of federal assistance available to the beleaguered cities of the Northeast, stirred up a hornet's nest among northeastern mayors and congressmen. But by the time the commission delivered its report, Carter had been defeated in his bid for reelection, and the incoming administration of RONALD REAGAN had no interest in its agenda for the country.

Although much of the flak created by the commission's report was directed at Donovan because he had been responsible for organizing the body and was thought to be a Republican, he had taken little interest in its proceedings once the commission had been formed. Of far more interest to him was the work of another group in which he was heavily involved. His concern about the lack of contingency planning in foreign policy had become acute as a result of developments in Iran and Afghanistan. In response to what was happening in that part of the world, he proposed to the president in February 1980 that he (Donovan) bring together a group of experts to engage in systematic thinking about foreign policy options and objectives. Carter agreed, and over the next several months, 25–30 experts, drawn mostly from academia and government, were brought together at different times in order to discuss and map out different foreign-policy scenarios. Donovan later referred to the group as "a think tank of my own." The result of the group's deliberations was a study Donovan prepared in which he took a hard line toward the Soviet Union, pointing to a fundamental conflict between Soviet and American values and stressing the nation's need to position itself as the world's preeminent superpower. As a corollary, he emphasized the need for the United States to achieve military superiority over the Soviet Union rather than to accept parity and to enhance its intelligence and propaganda capabilities. In making his recommendations, Donovan acknowledged that his views were even more hard-line than those of the administration. But he was convinced the president needed to think in these terms.

The recommendations of the Donovan group had much the same fate as the President's Commission on a National Agenda for the Eighties. By the time the group completed its work in August, the White House was directing most of its efforts to resolving the Iranian hostage crisis and getting Carter reelected. Donovan had also decided to resign his position at the White House in order to avoid becoming involved in the campaign and because he had become disappointed in the Carter administration. Although the president told Donovan in October that he intended to turn to his report in establishing his agenda for his second term, he was denied that opportunity by the voters in November.

Following Donovan's return to private life, he published two books, the first of which, *Roosevelt to Reagan: A Reporter's Encounters with Nine Presidents* (1985), described in detail his brief experience as a member of the Carter administration. The second, *Right Places, Right Times: Forty Years in Journalism, Not Counting My Route* (1989), told about his experiences at Time Inc. Donovan also wrote articles for *Time* and *Fortune* and conducted a seminar on the press and society at Harvard's John F. Kennedy School of Government. He died on August 13, 1990, at the age of 76 after a long illness.

Duncan, Charles William, Jr.

(1926–) *deputy secretary of defense, secretary of energy*

President of the Coca-Cola Corporation in Atlanta and deputy secretary of defense during the Carter presidency, Charles W. Duncan, Jr., was appointed to replace JAMES SCHLESINGER as secretary of energy in 1979 as part of a shake-up of President Carter's administration. Known for his skills as an administrator and his ability across the negotiating table, Duncan brought to the Department of Energy precisely those skills that had been lacking under Schlesinger's leadership. He proved adept in getting the president's second energy bill through Congress, and he conducted key negotiations on energy matters with the world's leading oil-producing countries. Negotiators frequently compared Duncan's give-and-take method of negotiation favorably to the more one-sided and haughty manner in which Schlesinger conducted business. Duncan was threatened by Congress, however, with a contempt citation for not agreeing to hand over to a congressional committee documents having to do with oil import-fee data. The incident proved to be a tempest in a teapot, as President Carter invoked executive privilege, and no contempt citation was issued.

Duncan was born on September 9, 1926, in Houston, Texas, into a wealthy family who owned Duncan Foods Co. He attended Rice University, graduating with a degree in chemical engineering (B.S., 1947). During the summers, while attending Rice and after his graduation, he worked as a roustabout in the Texas oil fields. He also studied management at the University of Texas and served in the U.S. Air Force before entering the family business. In 1958, he became president of Duncan Foods. He moved to Coca-Cola after the beverage company purchased the business, becoming the Atlanta-based company's president in 1971. In 1974, he left Coca-Cola to head the Houston-based banking concern Rotan Mosle Financial Concern.

Duncan came to the attention of Jimmy Carter through J. Paul Austin, chairman of Coca-Cola and an early financier of the Carter campaign. As a businessman, Duncan developed a reputation for being hard-nosed, fair, and practical—just the type of administrator that President-elect Carter was seeking for his cabinet. Ultimately having to choose between HAROLD BROWN and Duncan to be his secretary of defense, Carter decided to offer the position to Brown on the condition that Brown would ask Duncan to serve as his deputy. With that understanding Brown agreed to head the Pentagon, and Carter and Brown were able to persuade Duncan to be deputy defense secretary.

So impressed was Carter with Duncan's management and administrative skills that, beginning in 1977, the president's aides began looking for ways to expand his role in the administration. Once the president decided to fire Schlesinger as secretary of energy in 1979, the only person that he considered seriously as a replacement was Duncan. As Carter later remarked, with Duncan's "outstanding management capability and fresh approach, we were ready to tackle the energy problems—specifically oil—with renewed vigor."

As secretary, Duncan brought significant changes to the manner in which the Department of Energy (DOE) operated. As Steven Rattner of the *New York Times* later wrote, under Schlesinger's stewardship, the department was like the man himself, "aggressive, often brilliant, but also disorganized and steeped in controversy and confrontation." Under Duncan, the DOE became more even-tempered and businesslike. Instead of propounding intricate and ambitious new policies, the department became more concerned with matters of organization and order, establishing guidelines to carry out and evaluate existing programs before developing new ones. What had been one of the president's most contentious and controversial government agencies became almost bland and, to the extent possible, out of the media spotlight. That was the way the White House wanted it to function.

Duncan got much of the credit for the changes that took place at the DOE, but he was also criticized on the very same grounds. There was "at least a feeling that those in charge don't want anything done," one senior official who worked for both Schlesinger and Duncan commented. "The thing you could say for Schlesinger was that at times he was brilliant, at times maddening." Energy officials regularly faulted Duncan for having a limited knowledge of the energy field and for being reluctant to make decisions on controversial matters such as changes in pricing regulations for Alaskan oil. For his part, Duncan appeared satisfied with the changes that took place at the department, although he regretted that it had not done enough to pursue environmental controls.

Duncan was fortunate in the sense that he became energy secretary when Carter's first energy program had been enacted into law and energy shortages had begun to lessen. Yet he continued to worry about future shortages even after gasoline stocks reached an 11-month high in January 1980. In his first major speech as energy chief, Duncan told oil executives at the American Petroleum Institute that "the most reliable projections currently available indicate that in 1980 and 1981 world oil demand and supply will be in a very tight balance." In contrast to his predecessor, who often used such occasions to discuss in detail the administration's energy policies, Duncan spoke only in generalities. He also generated none of the acrimony sometimes evident when Schlesinger spoke before similar groups.

As energy secretary, Duncan expended considerable effort in negotiations with oil-producing countries like Canada, Mexico, and Saudi Arabia. Again he received generally favorable reviews as a diplomat, especially when compared to his predecessor. In April 1980, for example, he held two days of talks with Mexican officials on a broad range of questions, setting the stage for closer cooperation between Mexico and the United States. Mexican officials described the negotiations as "low-key" and "diplomatic" as compared to the sometimes abrasive style of Schlesinger, who had angered the Mexicans with his public criticism of its energy policies.

In May 1980, Duncan refused to hand over to a House investigations subcommittee 12 DOE documents on an oil-import fee of $4.62 a barrel that the president had imposed as a means to discourage gasoline consumption and cut imports by 100,000 barrels a day. The surcharge would also raise $10 billion and was an integral part of Carter's anti-inflation program. Although the president pledged that the fee would be applied only against oil meant to be refined into gasoline, consumer organizations feared it would also be applied to heating oil. They sought the documents to bolster their case. When Duncan refused to give the subcommittee the required documents they threatened to cite him for contempt. The president invoked executive privilege, however, and in June both the House and the Senate passed, by overwhelming margins, a resolution killing the surcharge.

In 1980, Duncan helped push President Carter's second energy program through Congress. Among other things, it provided for the decontrol of natural gas and oil prices, a $227 billion windfall-profits tax, and the establishment of a Synthetic Fuels Corporation—albeit as part of a new Energy Security Corporation rather than of DOE—with authority to spend up to $88 billion over the next 10 years developing alternative energy sources.

Following Carter's defeat for reelection in November 1980, Duncan became president and principal of the Warren-King Companies, a Houston-based group of 11 energy-related companies. He was also elected to the boards of a number of major corporations, including United Technologies and American Express.

Eastland, James Oliver
(1904–1986) *member of the Senate*

President pro tempore of the Senate, longtime chairperson of the Judiciary Committee, and an archconservative, James Oliver Eastland of Mississippi completed his last two years in the Senate during Jimmy Carter's first two years as president. During these years, President Carter secured Eastland's agreement to the establishment in each federal judicial circuit of a presidentially appointed nominating committee responsible for recommending to Carter the names of qualified individuals to fill judicial openings. This was an historic agreement effectively shifting the power to name circuit judgeships from members of the president's own party in the Senate to the Oval Office. The change added to the strained relations that existed throughout Carter's presidency between Capitol Hill and the White House. An effort to obtain a similar system for the appointment of district judges was rebuffed by Eastland and a number of other senators.

Eastland was born on November 28, 1904, in Doddsville, Mississippi, but grew up in Forest. His father, a lawyer, was also a powerful state politician and cotton plantation owner, part of the aristocracy of the Mississippi Delta. In 1922, Eastland enrolled at the University of Mississippi. After three years, he transferred to Vanderbilt University for one semester and then to the University of Alabama from 1926 to 1927. He never received an undergraduate degree, but after passing the bar exam in 1927, he returned to Forest, where he opened a law practice.

Encouraged by his father, Eastland ran successfully for the Mississippi House of Representatives, where he served from 1928 to 1932. In June 1941, he was appointed by Governor Paul B. Johnson to the United States Senate to fill the vacancy caused by the death of Pat Harrison. Eastland, a Democrat, accepted the appointment with the understanding that he would not run in the special election for the seat later in the year, which was won by Wall Doxey. Even as an interim senator, Eastland was able to block an attempt by the Office of Price Administration (OPA) to establish a ceiling price on cottonseed oil, thereby endearing him to cotton farmers who would have had their profits cut in half by the ceiling.

Although Eastland had agreed not to run in the special election, he enjoyed his experience on Capitol Hill enough that in 1942 he successfully challenged Doxey for his seat in the regular election, running on an anti-Roosevelt platform. Over the next 36 years, Eastland was easily reelected five times. In the seniority system that prevailed on Capitol Hill, this assured his place as one of the Senate's most influential members. He served as chair of the Judiciary Committee from 1956 until his retirement in 1978.

A racist and arch-segregationist, Eastland made his position clear on race relations using unusually inflammatory language. Following the landmark case of *Brown v. Board of Education of Topeka* (1954), he accused the Supreme Court of destroying the U.S. Constitution and told his fellow Mississippians that they were not obligated "to obey the decisions of any court which are plainly fraudulent [and based on] sociological considerations." At a mammoth meeting of the White Citizens' Council in 1956, he described blacks as being "slimy, juicy, unbearably stinking" and said that all methods should be used "to abolish the Negro race, Among these are guns, bows and arrows, slingshots and knives."

As the youngest senator ever to chair the Senate Judiciary Committee, Eastland used his authority arbitrarily, exercising virtual veto power over judicial nominations and civil rights legislation. Liberals decried the fact that in his first 10 years as chairperson, he bottled more than 120 civil rights measures in the committee. As chairperson also of the Internal Security Subcommittee and a great admirer of the red-baiting senator from Wisconsin, Joseph McCarthy, Eastland linked the Civil Rights movement with communism and became the Senate's most notorious communist hunter following McCarthy's death in 1957. He claimed that communists sought to subvert states' rights as a first step toward overthrowing the federal government. He also had significant veto power over crime and gun-control legislation.

Eastland's most positive contributions came in the area of farm legislation. As a senior member of the Agricultural and Forestry Committee and an adviser to the Appropriations Committee on agricultural programs, he proved effective in restoring funds for agricultural research, supported school lunch programs, and protected minimum cotton allotments for small farmers (although he also opposed capping subsidies at $55,000, which, as a large plantation owner, would have adversely affected him).

During the 1960s, as the Civil Rights movement gained support throughout much of the nation and as Eastland (and Mississippi) became symbols of the bigotry and backwardness of the South, more liberal Democrats were able to invoke the Senate practice of cloture (closing a debate to force a vote) to pass the Civil Rights Act of 1964 and the Voting Rights Act of 1965. Increasingly the Mississippi senator and other ardent segregationists found themselves fighting a rearguard action. In his last years in the Senate, Eastland avoided incendiary remarks and disassociated himself from racist groups because of increasing black political power in the South.

As chair of the Judiciary Committee, Eastland remained a powerful figure on Capitol Hill when Jimmy Carter became president in 1977. Early in the presidential campaign, Eastland had supported Senator Lloyd Bentsen (Tex.) for the Democratic nomination. After Carter won the nomination in July, Eastland nonetheless seemed proud that the Democratic nomination had gone to a southerner. Although he did not participate actively on Carter's behalf during the campaign, he and Mississippi's other U.S. senator, JOHN STENNIS, attended a luncheon for congressional candidates hosted by FRANK MOORE, who was managing the Carter campaign in what was essentially the Old Confederacy. In November, the Democratic nominee won the state.

One of the pledges that Carter had made as a candidate was to reform the system by which federal court judges were appointed. He wanted to replace the patronage system, which gave senators control over who was appointed from their states, with a merit system by which prospective judges would be recommended by a presidentially appointed commission based solely on their professional qualifications. Barely four weeks into his administration, the new president established, by executive order, a Circuit Judge Nominating Commission, with each circuit having its own panel. The panels were mixed in terms of race and gender and included lawyers and nonlawyers. They were charged with providing within 60 days the names of five qualified persons for a Court of Appeals seat whenever one became vacant. Intended to reduce politics as much as possible from the nominating process, the executive order meant an historic transfer of power over judicial appointments from the Senate to the president, who decided which persons approved by the panels to forward to the upper chamber for confirmation. Over time, the change in process resulted in a broader spectrum of highly qualified judges including women and minorities.

Although the president was able to institute this change by executive order, Eastland could easily have obstructed its implementation by rallying the Judiciary Committee and such interest groups as the American Bar Association against it. But he did not do this, and why he agreed to the change is not entirely clear. Part of the reason may have been the fact that his committee still had to approve the nominations submitted by the president. The fact that President-elect Carter and his future attorney general, GRIFFIN BELL, who later described Eastland as his "strongest supporter on the [Judiciary Committee] and in the Senate," met with Eastland a month after the election to discuss their reform proposals with him was also crucial. Although the Mississippi senator tried to maintain senatorial prerogatives, he agreed to help persuade senators to accept the commission concept and establish merit selection commissions in their states for the federal circuit courts of appeal. He and other key senators, however, refused to extend the merit system to include district court judges or U.S. attorneys.

Told that the increased black political power in Mississippi would keep him from being reelected, Eastland decided not to seek a seventh term in the Senate in 1978. Instead, he retired to his vast Delta cotton plantation, which he continued to manage almost until the time he died of multiple medical problems in Greenwood on February 19, 1986.

Eizenstat, Stuart Elliot

(1953–) *executive director of the White House domestic policy staff*

One of the Georgians (the so-called Georgia Mafia) that President Carter brought with him to Washington in 1977, Stuart Eizenstat became widely respected, both inside and outside the White House, as one of the ablest members of the administration. Probably no member of the administration dealt with more issues at one time than Eizenstat. His thoughtful and detailed memorandums, which he often coauthored with other members of the administration, were carefully read by the president, and his recommendations were usually followed. Although he may not have enjoyed quite the same rapport with the president as Carter's senior assistant, HAMILTON JORDAN, or even his press secretary, JODY POWELL, no one played a more influential role with the president on domestic issues than his director of the domestic policy staff.

Born in Chicago on June 15, 1943, Eizenstat moved to Atlanta when he was just a few months old. He graduated with honors from the University of North Carolina at Chapel Hill, where he majored in political science (B.A., 1964), then attended Harvard Law School (LL.B., 1967). Immediately following graduation, he took a position with the Johnson administration writing domestic policy papers. During the presidential campaign of 1968, he did much the same thing for the Democratic nominee, HUBERT HUMPHREY. Following Humphrey's defeat in November that year, Eizenstat returned to Atlanta, where he served as a law clerk for a federal judge and then joined the law firm of Powell, Goldstein, Frazer and Murphy.

Eizenstat met Jimmy Carter in 1969 through a friend and practicing attorney, Henry Bower, Jr., when Carter was a state senator running for governor. What impressed Eizenstat most about the future governor and president was Carter's apparent ability to bridge the gap between rural Georgia and urban Atlanta. He joined the campaign as Carter's issues coordinator while still maintaining his own private practice. In 1973, anticipating his appointment as chairperson of the 1974 Congressional Democratic campaign, Carter asked Eizenstat to write a series of issue papers for the use of congressional candidates. During a meeting with the governor just before the elections, Eizenstat raised the possibility of Carter running for president in 1976, not knowing that the future president had already decided to seek the Democratic nomination. Carter asked Eizenstat to join his fledging campaign, and the young attorney agreed.

During the campaign that followed, Eizenstat assumed a role similar to what he had done in Carter's campaign for governor and what he would do in the future as the new president's chief adviser for domestic affairs. Still maintaining his law practice, he established an issues staff of mostly student volunteers. He also spent many hours with the governor, fleshing out and refining his views on likely campaign issues and helping to put together position papers and speeches.

By 1976, Eizenstat's campaign responsibilities had become so extensive that he took a leave of absence from his law firm to work on the campaign full-time. Before the convention in July, when it became clear that Carter was going to be the Democratic nominee, Eizenstat recruited a more professional staff, drawing heavily from Capitol Hill. He also served as Carter's representative on the convention's Platform Committee, where he worked out a compromise with more liberal Democrats seeking to include a provision for a blanket pardon for opponents of the Vietnam War as part of the Democratic platform. The provision would have included deserters and those who had fled to Canada to avoid the draft, but the amendment that was approved merely called for the president to consider pardons on a case-by-case basis.

Following Carter's victory in November 1976, the president-elect appointed Eizenstat as director of policy planning for the transition. This caused considerable difficulty with another of Carter's inner circle of advisers, JACK WATSON, whom the president-elect had asked to perform a similar role and who had prepared extensive briefing books for him on the transition. In a power struggle that followed between Watson and HAMILTON JORDAN, who had been Carter's campaign manager and was his most trusted confidant, over who would be responsible for staffing the new administration and be in charge of White House personnel, Eizenstat sided with Jordan. Jordan returned the favor by recommending him to be Carter's special assistant for domestic affairs and head of the Domestic Policy Staff (DPS), a position he wanted and for which he was obviously well qualified. Consistent with Carter's commitment to frugality in the conduct of government business, the president-elect instructed Eizenstat to limit his staff to 3 percent less than that of his predecessor, Jim Cannon.

In contrast to President GERALD FORD's domestic staff, whose role was mostly reactive since Ford saw his main function being one of fighting off Democratic measures the administration opposed, Eizenstat intended his staff to be much more proactive in vetting and sending forward measures to the Democratically controlled Congress. But he also meant the DPS's responsibility to be more one of coordination between different departments and agencies and the presentation to the president of options on major legislative issues than one of developing and implementing policy. Unfortunately, the boundaries between these responsibilities often proved to be less sharp than he or the president envisioned.

In fact, throughout the Carter presidency, Eizenstat proved to be one of the president's closest advisers and the DPS one of the most visible and important offices in the White House. He sometimes had strong differences with such cabinet members as Treasury Secretary W. MICHAEL BLUMENTHAL over budgetary issues; with Attorney General GRIFFIN BELL over the Justice Department's handling of the *Bakke* case involving racial quotas and affirmative-action programs in higher education; or with Carter's energy adviser, JAMES SCHLESINGER, over his energy program. Nevertheless, Eizenstat was highly respected throughout the administration as well as on Capitol Hill, a person known for his high intelligence, thoughtfulness, and civility.

In addition Carter rarely questioned Eizenstat's judgment or his advice. An exception early in the administration was the president's 1977 decision to sign a compromise measure on water projects, his first major confrontation with Congress. In sharp contrast to the House and Senate, most of whose members had a particular project for their districts contained in the legislation or regarded such public-works projects as a normal way of getting reelected, the new president threatened to veto the measure because it was replete with pork. Instead, Carter agreed to a compromise that cut back the number of water projects. Still, Eizenstat advised against signing the legislation because several dam projects that he thought were economically and environmentally unsound were kept in the measure. Over Eizenstat's objections, the reluctant president signed the legislation, but he later stated that he rued the day he did so. Eizenstat's willingness to disagree with the president on such a politically contentious issue only increased the respect Carter had for his special assistant.

One of the most difficult issues Eizenstat faced during his four years in the White House was the huge increases in energy prices resulting from escalating energy consumption in the United States and cartel-like pricing and production practices on the part of the Organization of Petroleum Exporting Countries (OPEC). During the Senate debate over Carter's first energy plan, which the House had packaged into one omnibus measure and then approved without any major changes, Eizenstat warned the president that the public would judge his first year in the White House on his success in getting Congress to approve his energy plan. Despite a concerted lobbying effort on the part of the administration to get the Senate to approve the House measure, the upper chamber gutted the legislation, rejecting the president's proposal to bring intrastate natural gas prices under federal control. Instead, the senators approved a measure providing for deregulation of gas prices within two years. They then eliminated the centerpiece of the plan, a wellhead tax on domestic oil production intended to force consumers to conserve energy by raising oil prices to world levels. Finally, the Senate locked horns with the House in conference committee over their very different energy measures.

Eizenstat responded to this major setback for the administration by stressing the urgency of swift passage of an energy compromise acceptable to both chambers on Capitol Hill as well as to the White House. Later he expressed regret that the White House had not coupled decontrol of both oil and natural gas with a windfall-profits tax to capture some of the huge increase in profits the gas and oil companies would make as a result of attendant higher energy prices. Had the president sent this relatively simple package to the Congress rather than the massive measure he did send, containing more than 100 separate but interlocking provisions, Eizenstat believed it might have won early congressional approval.

Instead, months of negotiations followed after the House and Senate reconvened in January. During this time, the administration offered several compromise proposals on energy, but each of them became unglued at the last moment. Meanwhile, the White House came under growing attack from Capitol Hill over such other matters as refinancing the ailing Social Security system and reforming the nation's tax structure. Questions were even raised on Capitol Hill and in the media about the president's ability to cope with these matters. Once more Eizenstat warned the president that his performance as president would be judged by the outcome of his national energy plan.

It took until May before the conference committee was able to agree on a compromise on deregulation and then another three months before the legislative language could be written and the conferees could finally send a measure to the full House and Senate. Even then, it was not until October, after an intense struggle in both chambers and a three-day filibuster in the Senate, that Congress was able to send an energy program to the president. The final measure was far different from what the White House had proposed nearly 20 months earlier. Instead of an energy program based on conservation through taxation, as the White House had recommended, the program passed by the Congress and approved by the president was a far more limited one whose major provisions were the deregulation of natural gas and the establishment of a single price structure for intra- and interstate gas. Although the legislation also contained conservation and tax credits for expanding the use of nonfossil fuel and represented a major effort by the administration to deal with a problem that only promised to grow worse if left unintended, Eizenstat viewed the measure as an "utter and tragic catastrophe."

Another major issue that confronted Eizenstat and his staff was a proposal by Senator EDWARD KENNEDY (D-Mass.) for a program of national health insurance (NHI). This was Kennedy's highest priority in 1978 and had been a major priority of the more liberal wing of the Democratic Party since Carter took office. As a candidate, Carter had promised to recommend a program of comprehensive health insurance without saying how comprehensive the insurance would be or how it would be financed. But fearing that even Congress would question Carter's commitment to cutting inflation and restraining the budget if he proposed any major new health insurance initiative, Eizenstat advised the president to agree only to a statement of principles on which NHI should be based and to delay any actual legislation until the next session. At the same time, Eizenstat, whose staff and that of Secretary of Health, Education and Welfare JOSEPH CALIFANO had been engaged in lengthy but largely fruitless negotiations with Senator Kennedy and his staff over an NHI plan, urged the president to meet a final time with the senator to see if they could arrive at some kind of compromise.

Carter held the meeting, but it proved a disaster. Kennedy was willing to accept a phase-in of NHI but insisted on implementation of a comprehensive program regardless of economic and budgetary circumstances. On this the president could not agree, and the split between him and the senator, which had been festering for months over this issue, became public, dooming the chances of an NHI program anytime soon.

Undoubtedly the most nagging issue that Eizenstat faced during the administration's last two years, however, was a new spike in energy prices as a result of the overthrow of the shah of Iran, MOHAMMAD REZA PAHLAVI, in January 1979, which virtually shut down Iran's oil fields, as well as a decision by OPEC to raise the price of oil by nearly 15 percent. In response, the president directed Eizenstat to head a multiagency task force responsible for developing a new energy program. As the crisis over energy worsened, the president met with his closest advisers at Camp David and then, in April 1979, announced a new energy plan to the nation, the centerpieces of which were a phased-in decontrol of oil prices under authority he had from the Energy Policy and Conservation Act of 1975 and the windfall-profits tax that Eizenstat regretted not having sent to Capitol Hill two years earlier.

Still, there was no relief at the White House as both prices at the gas pumps and opposition to the president continued to rise. The president responded by canceling, without explanation, another national address on energy, planned for July 5, 1979, and then holding a wide-ranging series of meetings at Camp David intended for the president to hear a diversity of views on the nation's ills.

After 11 days, Carter returned to Washington, where, on July 15, he delivered a major address to the nation in which he commented on a sense of crisis that seemed to be sapping the American will. (This message has often been referred to, inaccurately, as the president's "malaise" speech, even though he never used that term.) In his address, the president also proposed several additional measures to cope with the energy crisis, including limits on oil imports, establishment of an Energy Security Corporation (ESC) to develop synthetic fuels, and formation of an Energy Mobilization Board (EMB) to cut through the red tape that often strangled nascent energy projects. Two days later, he shook up his administration by accepting the resignations of five cabinet members.

Eizenstat, who regarded the energy crisis and an inflation rate approaching 13 percent by July as one and the same and wanted to blame both on OPEC, had been opposed to cancellation of the July 5 speech, most of which he had written. He was also taken aback by the tone and tenor of the president's address of July 15 and by the cabinet shake-up that followed, both of which he thought were ill-advised politically. Although the president's speech was well-received, even by some die-hard opponents of his earlier energy proposals, whatever political benefits he might have realized were forfeited by his cabinet shake-up, which raised new questions about Carter's capacity to govern.

Furthermore, the economy began to slide into recession even as the oil and gas industries reported record earnings. As this happened, opposition to Carter's plan to decontrol oil and establish a windfall-profits tax mounted once more on Capitol Hill. Only after months of debate—during which Democrats from consuming states accused the administration of caving in to the oil lobbyists over decontrol and Republicans from producing states attacked the tax as hampering the production of new oil—did Congress approve, in March 1980, a $227 billion windfall-profits tax. Separately, it also passed legislation establishing a Synthetic Fuels Corporation with authority to spend up to $88 billion over the next 10 years to develop alternative energy resources.

For Eizenstat, who had been involved in every phase of the struggle over energy, these measures amounted to major victories, which, with earlier measures deregulating natural gas and phasing-in the decontrol of domestic oil, represented the most sweeping energy legislation in the nation's history. As he later lamented, however, the political costs to the White House were enormous, perhaps dooming the president's bid for reelection in November 1980. This was particularly galling for someone who had expended so much time and effort in the fight over energy and thought the cause was so urgent.

Although Eizenstat's area of responsibility was domestic policy, he sometimes involved himself with issues of foreign policy, in particular, becoming a leading advocate within the administration of a strong human rights policy. In fact, he had been attracted to Carter in part because of the president's own strong advocacy of human rights. Of the Jewish faith, Eizenstat was profoundly moved by the Holocaust of World War II and the failure of the Franklin Roosevelt administration to respond to the genocide taking place in Germany. While in the White House, he recommended to President Carter the establishment of a presidential commission, headed by Elie Wiesel, to plan for a permanent memorial for victims of the Holocaust. Although Carter and Congress approved the proposal, no money was authorized to implement it until 15 years later. However, honoring Holocaust victims and preventing more genocide became two of Eizenstat's lifelong commitments.

After leaving the White House in 1981, Eizenstat returned to the law firm of Powell, Goldstein, Frazer and Murphy as partner and vice chairman and served as adjunct lecturer at Harvard University and guest scholar at the Brookings Institution. In 1993, he was appointed by President Bill Clinton as U.S. representative to the European Union. He then served as undersecretary of commerce for international trade (1996–97) and as undersecretary of state for economic, business and agricultural affairs (1997–98). He is presently a partner in the law firm of Covington and Burling, where he heads its international practice.

Eizenstat has also remained active in Jewish affairs, serving on numerous boards and committees of Jewish organizations. While in the Cinton administration, he was instrumental in exposing the extent to which the Swiss National Bank had been implicit in the financing of the German war effort during World War II and in getting Swiss banks to pay reparations to descendants of Holocaust victims whose bank accounts had remained dormant because of the lack of death certificates. He has recounted these efforts in his book *Imperfect Justice: Looted Assets, Slave Labor and the Unfinished Business of World War II* (2003).

Fallows, James Mackenzie

(1949–) *chief speechwriter*

James Fallows was President Carter's chief speechwriter from 1977 to 1978. As he later acknowledged, he probably had less influence within the White House than almost any other person holding that position in recent administrations. In 1978, however, he resigned his post, and the next year he gained national notoriety by publishing in *The Atlantic Monthly* a long article, "The Passionless President," which was highly critical of Carter.

Fallows was born in Philadelphia on August 2, 1949, but his family soon moved to Redlands, California. After growing up in southern California, he attended Harvard College, where he was president of the college's daily newspaper, the *Crimson*. He graduated Phi Beta Kappa from Harvard (B.A., 1970) and then spent two years studying economics at Oxford University as a Rhodes scholar. Afterward, he served as a staff member and editor of the *Washington Monthly* (1972–74) and the *Texas Monthly* (1974–76) and wrote freelance articles for a number of magazines. He also wrote *The Water Lords* (1971), an exposé of corporate power and indifference to the environment in Savannah, Georgia, and coauthored *Who Runs Congress* (1972), a best seller about the power of moneyed interests in politics.

Fallows was attracted to Jimmy Carter because he found the Georgian different from the other candidates running for president or the types of persons he wrote about in his articles and books. He agreed to serve as one of Carter's speechwriters because, as a political journalist, he thought he should experience firsthand how the nation's political system worked. At age 27, he was elevated to chief speechwriter following the resignation of Patrick Anderson, who had served in that position during the campaign but who left the White House less than a year later over policy differences with the president.

Much the same thing happened with Fallows, although he remained in the White House for two years. As he explained later in his 1979 article for the *Atlantic Monthly* and in a follow-up article the next month, he had great respect for Carter as a person. He especially admired the president's moral values, his intellect, and even his magnetism. But he found Carter to be a chief executive without a clearly defined set of priorities or a plan for achieving them. "I came to think," he wrote, "that Carter believes fifty things, but not one thing." Fallows believed the president was frivolous with his time and energy, worrying about small-scale matters while neglecting more important leadership responsibilities. Notwithstanding Carter's high ethical standards and deep religious beliefs,

Fallows also thought he was guilty of the sin of pride, which left him stubborn, even arrogant, and reluctant to make necessary choices. As for the president's inner circle of advisers, according to Fallows, they knew how to win elections but not how to govern; worse, they seemed unwilling to learn.

Fallows later claimed that in writing his article, his purpose was not so much to disparage the administration as it was to suggest changes in strategy for a faltering, but not yet failed, administration. But as he has also acknowledged, the article left hard feelings and permanent wounds. According to Fallows, the complaints against him by members of the administration were not ones of accuracy but of disloyalty. In trying to help Carter, he only hurt a man who had taken him into his trust.

Whatever Fallows's intention, that was certainly its effect. At a time when confidence in the administration was at new lows as a result of an ongoing energy crisis, inflation, and economic stagnation as well as charges that part of the proceeds of a loan to the Carter family peanut business had been illegally diverted to the president's campaign in 1976, the publication of Fallows's critique received widespread attention. For many Democrats as well as Republicans, it confirmed their worst fears about the administration. A Yankelovich poll published about the time the article appeared found that only 23 percent of the people interviewed believed that things were going well in the country, while 64 percent believed that the nation was in serious trouble. For the conservative journalist of the *New York Times*, WILLIAM SAFIRE, who had written numerous columns highly critical of the Carter White House, Fallows's article provided new ammunition to attack the president, who, Safire stated, wanted to be president without any idea of what he wanted to do as president. Safire's refrain became a common theme used against Carter.

The reason why Fallows published his article in the *Atlantic Monthly* was because he had accepted a position with the highly respected publication after leaving the White House. He remained there for the next 18 years as a correspondent and Washington, D.C., editor. From 1996 to 1998, he held a similar position at *U.S. News and World Report*, but in 1998 he returned to the *Atlantic Monthly*, where he remains as its national correspondent. Since 1987, he has also been a frequent commentator on National Public Radio. In addition to his distinguished career as a journalist, he is author of eight books on a wide range of social and political issues, one of which, *The National Defense* (1981), won a National Book Award.

Fallows has had a particular interest in the societal changes brought about by the technological, informational, and communications revolution of the last 25 years. In 1999, he worked for six months at Microsoft, designing software for writers. Since 2001, he has been executive producer of Agenda, an annual high-level conference for technology industry leaders. He has been especially critical of the transformation of journalism from "journalism for the public interest" to "journalism as entertainment." Fallows lives in Washington, D.C.

Foley, Thomas Stephen
(1929–) *member of the House of Representatives*

Chairperson of the House Agriculture Committee and a future Speaker of the House, Thomas "Tom" Foley (D-Wash.) was one of the most influential members of Congress during the Carter administration. He was tied personally, politically, and ideologically to a number of the president's staunchest Democratic foes on Capitol Hill, including Senator HENRY JACKSON (D-Wash.), who was Foley's mentor, and Congressman PHILLIP BURTON

(D-Calif.), who was elected to the House the same year he was and was part of Foley's weekly poker game. In contrast to Jackson and Burton, however, Foley was neither driven by vaunted ambition nor clamorous in pushing a personal agenda. Instinctively judicious, he was a pragmatist who had to balance his liberal beliefs with the need to get reelected every two years from a marginally Republican district as well as a consensus builder who was a facilitator more than a partisan. He concentrated on what was important to his district, which mainly had to do with agriculture, while otherwise maintaining a low profile.

Foley was born in Spokane, Washington, on March 26, 1929. His family was well-known and respected in the area; one of his grandfathers was a wealthy landowner and grain-elevator operator. His father, a Spokane County prosecutor when he was born, became a Superior Court judge in 1940 and remained on the bench for the next 35 years, the longest sitting judge in the state's history.

After attending Gonzaga University, a Jesuit institution in Spokane, Foley transferred in his senior year to the University of Washington, where he received both his undergraduate and law degrees (B.A., 1951; LL.B., 1957). He then practiced law briefly with a cousin before taking a position for two years as Spokane County deputy prosecutor (1958–60), the same position his father had once held. That was followed by one year as an assistant attorney general for the state of Washington (1960–61).

After approaching Senator Warren Magnuson (D-Wash.) about being appointed U.S. attorney in eastern Washington and being turned down because Magnuson considered him too young, Foley was hired by Senator Jackson, a family friend, as special counsel to the Senate Interior and Insular Affairs Committee. In 1964, Jackson urged Foley to run for Congress. Hesitant to challenge the long-term Republican incumbent, Walt Horan, in a largely rural and conservative district, he thought about waiting two years in order to raise enough money to run a serious campaign. But on the last day before the filing deadline, he ran into one of his potential backers at lunch, Joe Drumheller, who gave him a virtual ultimatum to run in 1964 or forget about a race two years later. Foley entered the contest. With the strong support of Jackson, Magnuson, and organized labor, he became part of the Lyndon Johnson landslide of 1964, winning by a narrow 3 percent margin. "I am morally certain," Foley recounted later, "that if Joe Drumheller hadn't come to lunch on July 16, 1964, I wouldn't be a member of Congress." It was not the last time that chance would play an important role in his career.

As a new member of Congress, Foley was appointed to the Agriculture Committee and the Interior and Insular Affairs Committee, where he had served as a staff member. His appointment to the Agriculture Committee was another piece of good fortune for Foley. Not only was it an important committee for a lawmaker from a rural district, but because of the number of freshmen lawmakers on the committee, making it necessary to draw names out of a hat, he immediately became a high-ranking member of the committee.

Once in Congress, Foley backed most of President Johnson's Great Society programs. However, he showed an independent streak by opposing a rent-supplement program, which Johnson wanted but which Foley thought had been ill-examined. In what was a difficult decision for him, he also voted against an anticrime bill enacted by the House following the assassinations of Martin Luther King, Jr., and Robert Kennedy in 1968. He thought the wiretapping provisions were too loose and subject to abuse.

Foley also became one of a growing number of reform-minded liberals, led by Phillip

Burton and RICHARD BOLLING (D-Mo.), who wanted to change the House rules to modify the seniority system by which committee and subcommittee chairs were chosen. Other aims of the reformers included making it easier to move legislation from committee to the House floor for consideration and enhancing the speaker's power by granting him exclusive authority to select the Democratic members of the powerful Rules Committee. In 1974, Foley was elected chairperson of the Democratic Study Group (DSG), which served as the strategy and research arm of liberal and moderate Democrats and had become the driving force behind these internal reforms.

In 1974, the movement for reform of the rules received a major impetus with the election of 43 reform-minded Democrats, dubbed the "Watergate babies" as a result of the scandal that had helped get them elected. Since being narrowly elected in 1964, Foley had himself been reelected with relative ease. In 1974, he won with 64 percent of the vote, running against a local member of the John Birch Society. As chairperson of the DSG, Foley's role was to serve as its intermediary with the new class of 1974.

Although things did not always go the way Foley wanted, they managed again to work to his advantage when he was elevated to chairperson of the powerful Agriculture Committee. The incumbent chairperson, 75-year-old W. R. Poage of Texas, who had been in Congress for 40 years, was one of three long-term conservative southern chairpersons targeted for removal by the new class of House reformers. Although Foley had supported the change in rules by which committee chairs were elected by secret ballot, he respected Poage and nominated him for reelection. But Poage lost, and the Democratic Caucus promoted Foley to replace him. Appreciating the fact that Foley had stood by him, Poage returned the lawmaker's favor by nominating him to be the new chair.

At age 45, Foley was the youngest chairperson of a major House committee and the first westerner to chair the Agriculture Committee. He was also a respected member of the reform coalition in the House, someone who had not alienated conservative Democrats or even split reform Democrats like Burton and Bolling because of their abrasive demeanors. As a measure of the high regard in which he was held by members of his party, he was elected in 1976 as head of the Democratic Caucus.

During the 1976 campaign for the Democratic nomination for president, Foley supported and campaigned for his fellow Washingtonian, Henry Jackson. He was somewhat more conservative in terms of his commitment to New Deal liberalism and less of a defense hawk than Jackson. Earlier, he had also had more doubts about the Vietnam War and had consistently voted against authorizing the draft because he felt it disadvantaged the working class. But he had continued to support the Vietnam War longer than most liberal Democrats and, like Jackson, had a strong liberal voting record.

After Jimmy Carter became president, Foley shared some of the same concerns as other Democratic moderates and liberals about the administration's lack of competence, but he chose to work with the White House. A case in point was the 1977 farm bill, the issue that most concerned Foley after Carter took office. The president had threatened to veto the measure, which included renewal of major crop-support programs and the food-stamp program. The president's own proposals provided for lower support prices than even the existing ones. Instead of publicly attacking the White House as being uncaring, however, as did some other House members, Foley fashioned a compromise, which Carter still did not like because it provided for increases in price supports and a significant increase in the food-stamp program, but which he signed because of an inevitable veto override.

As chair of the Agriculture Committee, Foley also proved to be a masterful coalition builder, painstakingly bringing together lawmakers from rural districts interested in higher price supports for farmers with urban liberals eager to expand food stamps and lunch programs. Of all his legislative accomplishments, he later stated that the growth of the food-stamp program was his proudest achievement.

With respect to other legislation, Foley followed the lead of Henry Jackson in the Senate in supporting military spending programs the White House opposed, such as the antiballistic missile and supersonic transport programs. This led some in the House to refer to him as a "Jackson Democrat." But even though he was head of the Democratic Caucus, Foley was not an activist. Instead, he acted on the premise that the president initiated policy, which Congress reviewed and reshaped, especially when the president was a member of one's own party. On major measures like energy legislation, government deregulation, or hospital cost containment, Carter could, therefore, count on Foley's support. One measure in which he broke openly with the president, however, was Carter's decision to impose a grain embargo against the Soviet Union following its invasion of Afghanistan in 1979. The embargo simply hurt his wheat-growing constituency too badly.

One reason why Foley may have chosen to occupy himself primarily with matters important to his district rather than seek the national limelight was that his seat in the House was by no means assured despite his growing power in Congress. Although he had easily won reelection in 1974, he had a more difficult time in 1976 running against a stand-in candidate, Duane Alton, following the death of his original Republican opponent and his family in a plane crash. Alton attacked Foley's liberal voting record and his pro-choice position on abortion. While Foley still won with 56 percent of the vote, it was his lowest margin in years.

Two years later, Alton ran again. This time the Republican National Campaign Committee (RNC) targeted Foley's district and made his liberal voting record a campaign issue. Republicans also accused Foley of ignoring his local constituents in his rise to national power, of taking a $500 campaign contribution from Korean rice dealer Tongsun Park, and of leading an extravagant life style in Washington. Although Foley won the campaign, he received only about 48 percent of the vote, with the rest going to Alton and an independent candidate who won about 8 percent.

The undercurrent of the campaign was that Foley's national prominence was not necessarily an advantage in his conservative district and that it behooved him to appear less liberal than many of his closest Democratic allies in Washington. At a time, therefore, when the Carter administration was coming under increasing attack by liberal Democrats because of its fiscal conservatism, it was good politics for Foley to remain reticent. As he explained prior to his 1980 campaign, "What I've always said is that every member of Congress has a responsibility to give the most respectful and serious attention to the views of the people they represent." In 1980, he won with 52 percent of the vote despite RONALD REAGAN's landslide and the defeat of a large number of Capitol Hill's most liberal lawmakers in both the House and Senate. He was the only House Democrat from Washington State to win election that year.

One of the casualties of the Reagan landslide was the liberal JOHN BRADEMAS (Ind.), who had been the Democratic whip. As a result of Foley's victory and Brademas's defeat, the Washington state lawmaker was chosen by Speaker of the House TIP O'NEILL (Mass.) to replace Brademas as Democratic whip. When O'Neill decided to retire from Congress in

1986, Majority Leader JIM WRIGHT (Tex.) replaced O'Neill as speaker, and Foley was elected by acclamation as the new majority leader.

In 1989, Wright was forced to step down as House Speaker and then resign from Congress because of a series of scandals. To replace Wright, the Democrats turned to Foley. In contrast to the former Speaker, who was partisan and aggressive and disliked by many Democrats as well as Republicans, the fair-minded and unpretentious new House Speaker, whom the *New Yorker* described "as a major player in spite of himself," was well-liked on both aisles of the House. Within a few months after being elected House Speaker, he brought back a sense of comity and collegiality to what had been a fractious body.

In the summer of 1991, Foley and Senate majority leader George Mitchell (D-Maine) agreed reluctantly to conduct an investigation of allegations made by former National Security Council staff member GARY SICK that the Reagan campaign in 1980 had stolen the election in November by getting Iran's AYATOLLAH RUHOLLA KHOMEINI to delay the release of American hostages seized in Tehran in November 1979 until after the election. Republicans charged that the investigation was politically motivated and intended to embarrass President GEORGE HERBERT WALKER BUSH, who in 1980 was Reagan's vice-presidential running mate and allegedly knew of the hostage scheme. The investigation failed to substantiate Sick's allegations. Most Republicans still regarded the inquiry as a waste of the taxpayer's money and part of a Democratic vendetta against Bush, but they also believed it had been conducted fairly and openly.

Foley differed on many issues with President Bush. These included his proposal for a constitutional amendment to ban the burning of the American flag, a cut in the capital gains tax, and the president's decision to go to war against Iraq in 1991 following Iraq's invasion of Kuwait the previous summer. But the House Speaker worked with the White House on a budget compromise in 1990 that included budget cuts and tax increases.

Foley's tenure as Speaker proved shortlived. Although popular among most Democrats and respected by Republicans for his fair-minded rulings and evenhandedness on legislative and parliamentary matters, there were still a number of Democratic lawmakers who wanted a more powerful and partisan leader, one who would demand greater party discipline in the House and be more of a public figure, like former House Speaker Tip O'Neill. Foley's poor handling of a scandal involving the overdrafts of some congressmen's checking accounts with the House bank hurt him with these and other House members, as did another scandal involving the trading of stamps for cash at the House post office by several members of Congress. By 1992, some Democrats were even calling for Foley to step down as Speaker, claiming that he had sat on the scandals for three years, thereby allowing them to fester and grow.

Even more important, Foley still had to contend with the voters in his largely Republican district. Throughout the 1980s, he had continued to be reelected to Congress by comfortable margins. Facing only token opposition in 1988, he received 70 percent of the vote against his Republican opponent. But the voters in his district turned against him in the 1990s when he filed a lawsuit opposing term limits for members of Congress after a term-limit ballot initiative was approved by the state's voters in 1992. The voters were also angered by Foley's support of a ban on assault weapons and by the scandals in the House being widely covered in the media. In the "Republican Revolution" of 1994, Foley lost in a narrow race to his Republican challenger, George Nethercutt, who promised not to seek more than three terms if elected to the House. In losing, Foley became the first Speaker defeated for reelection since 1862.

In November 1997, President Bill Clinton nominated Foley to be U.S. ambassador to Japan. He remained ambassador until 2001, when he joined a Washington, D.C., law firm. In 1999, he coauthored, with his former press secretary Jeffery R. Biggs, *Honor in the House: Speaker Tom Foley*, a combination of biography and memoir.

Ford, Gerald Rudolph

(1913–) *thirty-eighth president of the United States*

When Jimmy Carter won the Democratic nomination for president in 1976, most political observers predicted that he would defeat his likely Republican opponent, either Gerald Ford or RONALD REAGAN, by a considerable margin. Even after Ford narrowly defeated Reagan for the Republican nomination, Carter remained the odds-on favorite. But on the eve of the election, the outcome was viewed as too close to call. Although Carter won a narrow election victory, he might have lost had Ford not made a bad stumble during the second of three presidential debates.

The first American president not to have faced a national electorate, Gerald R. Ford was born in Omaha, Nebraska, on July 14, 1913. He was raised in Grand Rapids, Michigan, by his mother and stepfather, a local businessman who had married his mother following her divorce from his father and then adopted her only child. A star athlete, Ford played football at the University of Michigan, where he graduated in 1935. Turning down offers to play professionally, he accepted a position as an assistant football coach at Yale. In 1938, he was admitted to Yale Law School, where he graduated in the top third of his class (LL.B., 1941).

After serving in the U.S. Navy during World War II, Ford returned to Grand Rapids and practiced law until 1948, when he was elected to the House of Representatives. He was reelected 12 times, always by majorities of more than 60 percent. Hardworking and well-liked, an internationalist on most foreign-policy issues and a conservative on most domestic issues, Ford was elected House minority leader by his fellow Republicans in 1965. A Nixon loyalist, he stirred a hornet's nest when, acting for the administration, he tried unsuccessfully to have Supreme Court justice William O. Douglas impeached in retaliation for the Senate's rejection of two Nixon nominees to the Court, Clement Haynesworth and G. Harrold Carswell. But this action was not characteristic of his service in the House.

In 1973, following the forced resignation of Nixon's vice president, Spiro Agnew, who pleaded no contest to charges of having taken bribes when he was governor of Maryland, Nixon chose Ford as his new vice president. What made Ford's selection so important was a growing belief among political observers that, because of the growing Watergate scandal, Nixon might be forced to resign as president or be impeached.

For most of the eight months between Ford's appointment and Nixon's resignation, the vice president remained in the background, continuing to believe in Nixon's innocence and thinking that the president would serve out his full term. When it became apparent that Nixon would be forced to resign or face impeachment, most political analysts anticipated that Ford would be a caretaker president, serving only until a new president was elected in 1976.

They were not entirely correct. In the two years that he was president, Ford signed into law a $25 billion aid to education measure, a campaign-reform act providing public funding for presidential campaigns, consumer-protection legislation, an extension of unemployment benefits, and a $4.8 billion measure to improve mass-transit facilities. He also used his veto power 66 times and had only 12 of them overturned by a two-thirds vote in Congress.

Yet the Ford presidency was characterized by generally indecisive leadership, political miscalculation, bad judgment, and lack of vision. In fairness to Ford, he lacked the three-month transition period a president-elect normally has between election and inauguration. He had no time to select a staff and cabinet of his own or to plan a coherent program. But by merely adding Nixon's senior staff to his own staff, he almost assured the administrative disarray that encumbered his presidency.

More important, though, was Ford's decision to offer clemency—but not amnesty—to Vietnam-era draft evaders and deserters and to grant Nixon a pardon from Watergate-related crimes. These decisions were part of Ford's effort to bring an end to two of the most nightmarish events in the nation's history. Despite later charges to the contrary, no political deal was involved in Ford's decision to pardon Nixon. Although Nixon's chief of staff, Alexander Haig, had floated the idea of a pardon with Ford just before Nixon resigned, Ford decided on the pardon for the reasons he later claimed: he felt Nixon had been punished enough, and he wanted to get on with the nation's other business. Nevertheless, Ford handled the pardon issue poorly, failing even to insist that Nixon give up his presidential papers and tapes or issue a statement of contrition. The pardon, moreover, destroyed Ford's honeymoon with the American people, millions of whom were already infuriated by his decision to grant clemency to Vietnam-era draft evaders.

In addition, in a period of both high unemployment and high inflation, Ford vacillated between a tax cut to promote economic growth and budgetary restraint to curb inflation. He also badly mishandled the incident in which 15 marines were killed and eight U.S. helicopters downed in rescuing the crew of the American merchant ship *Mayaguez*, which had been captured by the Khmer Rouge when it allegedly sailed into Cambodian waters. Not only were more lives lost in the rescue mission than the number of crew rescued, but the administration had rejected the option of negotiations prior to the rescue mission. More generally, Ford failed to develop a coherent foreign policy.

Realizing that his opponent in the 1976 presidential election, former Georgia governor Jimmy Carter, had won the Democratic nomination in part by basing his campaign on an appeal to values rather than by taking clearly defined positions on specific issues, Ford's advisers adopted a strategy of attacking the Democratic candidate on his vagueness. Unknowingly, Carter played into this strategy by defining "trust in the people" as the campaign's major issue. Ford responded by accusing his opponent of "fuzziness." The Republican strategy seemed to work. In August, Carter had a 15 percent lead over the Ford, but less than a month later the gap was clearly closing, helped in part by Carter's uninspiring rhetoric, which was rarely eloquent and sometimes seemed ambiguous and contradictory. Polls conducted by the Ford campaign showed that the Republican candidate was gaining ground in southern states, including Texas, Mississippi, Virginia, and Louisiana. Another poll revealed that although Carter still had a 6–8 percent lead over Ford in California, his support was soft.

By the end of September, the campaign's momentum had shifted in Ford's favor. Dick Cheney, the president's strategist, informed Ford at the end of September that the most recent polls showed him "closing the gap in the South." A member of the White House staff,

Doug Bailey, remarked that the "President's major opportunity to win the election" was the second presidential debate scheduled for October 6 in San Francisco. The first debate had been on the domestic economy, and most observers concluded that the president had more than held his own against his opponent. The second debate was to be on foreign policy and defense issues, which seemed to give Ford a decided advantage over Carter, whose exposure to these matters was limited. Ford's staff anticipated, therefore, that the second debate would be the trump card of the president's campaign. He would describe his foreign policy as one of peace through strength. Because of the military might of the United States and its allies, Ford's administration had succeeded in lowering the level of tensions with the Soviet Union. The danger of war in Central Europe had been greatly reduced, Berlin was no longer a threat to world peace, and limitations had been placed on the size of the Soviet nuclear arsenal. All of this would make the president seem like the more statesmanlike of the two candidates.

The debate did not follow the Republican script. Predictably, Carter was much more aggressive in the second debate than he had been in the first one, accusing the president of a lack of leadership and vision. Ford countered by charging that his Democratic opponent would cut the defense budget by $15 billion. But then Ford made what proved to be the greatest gaffe of the campaign. In response to a question about Eastern Europe, he said that there was "no Soviet domination of Eastern Europe, and there never will be under a Ford administration."

The question about Eastern Europe was not unexpected. Anticipating that it would be raised at some point in the debate, the president's staff had carefully prepared a response for him. "The peoples of Europe," he was told to say, "have a right to freedom and national independence, and the United States has not, and will not abandon them." However, in longhand, Ford had added the following note to the briefing remarks he received: "No Soviet sphere of influence in Eastern Europe. Agreement borders cannot be changed by force." Apparently, Ford had simply misread or misinterpreted the information provided by his staff.

Ford's mistake disrupted the momentum of his campaign. Immediately after the debate, polls showed Ford beating Carter decisively (54 to 36 percent). As reporters pressed Ford to clarify his remarks, however, the seriousness of his blunder became apparent. When his pollsters conducted another survey the next night, they found the challenger leading the president by the same margin (54 to 37 percent) that he had trailed a day earlier. Democrats (but not Carter) portrayed Ford as not being smart enough to be president. The president's remarks cost him heavily among ethnic Catholics, many of whom still had families in Eastern Europe. Ford's comments also galvanized the Carter campaign.

In the remaining weeks of the election, the president was able to recover most of the ground he had lost in the second debate by hammering away at the issue of Carter's fuzziness on the issues. "He wavers, he wanders, he wiggles, and he waffles and he shouldn't be President," Ford said repeatedly with great effectiveness. As the campaign drew to a close, the polls indicated a virtual dead heat. "The vast number of voters," commented Jerald ter Horst, a Ford campaign staffer, "have looked at the two men and see no practical difference."

As the polls predicted, the election proved to be one of the closest in he nation's history. Carter won with about 41 million popular votes (51 percent) to Ford's 39 million (48 percent). In electoral votes, Carter received 297 to Ford's 240. Notwithstanding the margin of defeat, however, the first nonelected president failed to be returned to office by the voters.

Over time, Carter and Ford became friends, even touring on the lecture circuit together after Carter suffered his own defeat at the polls in 1980. But the intensity of the campaign left bruises between the outgoing president and the president-elect. During the Carter administration, the president met occasionally with Ford at the White House for private conversation, and he talked more frequently with him on the telephone. Ford also played a crucial role, at Carter's request, in rounding up Republican votes to win approval of the Panama Canal Treaties in 1978. For the most part, however, the relationship between the president and former president was cordial but formal and distant.

In 1979, Ford published his memoirs, *A Time to Heal: The Autobiography of Gerald R. Ford.* In 1980, he was almost Ronald Reagan's vice-presidential running mate, but in the end, Ford's insistence that he have a role resembling that of a copresident if the Republican nominee were elected proved unacceptable to Reagan. During the 1980 election, Ford campaigned actively for Republican candidates and was featured in numerous fund-raising events.

Following the 1980 campaign, Ford prospered by being active on the lecture circuit, serving as a consultant to various businesses, and being on the board of directors of a number of major firms. By 1996, he was reported to have amassed a fortune of close to $300 million with homes in Vail, Colorado, and in Los Angeles. In 1998, he joined with former presidents GEORGE HERBERT WALKER BUSH and Jimmy Carter in urging voters to reject referendums on state ballots to legalize marijuana for medical purposes. The next year, President Bill Clinton awarded Ford the nation's highest civilian honor, the Presidential Medal of Freedom.

Now in his 90s, Ford has cut back on most of his activities and travel, although he gave an interview to Larry King in June 2004, attended the funeral of former president Ronald Reagan the same month, and spoke at ceremonies commemorating the 30th anniversary of his swearing-in in August 2004. Believed to be in frail health, he resides with his wife Betty in Rancho Mirage, California.

Giscard d'Estaing, Valéry
(1926–) *president of France*

Valéry Giscard d'Estaing was president of France from 1974 to 1981. A right-wing Gaullist who nevertheless came to an accommodation with the social liberalization evident in much of the Western world in the 1960s and with the need to modernize the French economy, Giscard sought to achieve his ends in part by working closely with German chancellor HELMUT SCHMIDT, whose experience in government was similar to Giscard's and who came to power the same year he did. Together they shared a common goal in strengthening the European Union both for internal economic and political reasons and as a counterforce to the United States' economic and political dominance over the Atlantic alliance. As a Gaullist, Giscard opposed subservience to any foreign power. The two leaders also shared a common antipathy toward President Jimmy Carter, whom Giscard believed lacked international experience and was seeking to subordinate Europe's legitimate national interests to those of the United States. Like Schmidt, Giscard was especially dismissive of Carter's international economic and monetary policies and what he considered the president's ill-conceived response to the Soviet invasion of Afghanistan in December 1979.

Giscard was born on February 2, 1926, in Koblnez, Germany, then part of the occupied Rhineland, into an aristocratic family; his father was of noble lineage. As a teenager, he attended exclusive schools in Paris, but at the age of 16, he joined the French resistance against the German occupation of France during World War II, and he later served in the French army. For his wartime service he received the Croix de Guerre.

After the war, Giscard rose rapidly through the French governmental bureaucracy. He entered France's prestigious engineering school, the École Polytechnique in Paris, graduating second in his class. He received additional training at the École Nationale d'Administration, attended by those identified as prospective high-level government bureaucrats, and graduated third in his class. He later spent a year at Harvard Business School. After completing his education, Giscard joined the prestigious Inspectorate of Finance and began his meteoric rise through the bureaucracy. Committed to modernizing the French economy even though he came from the "old France" of the nobility and small-town politics, he came to the attention of Prime Minister Edgar Faure. In 1955, Faure made Giscard deputy director of his personal staff. In 1956, Giscard was elected to the French parliament from his home department in central France. A reform-minded Gaullist, he joined General Charles de Gaulle's first government of the Fifth Republic in 1959, being named deputy minister of finance. He was the youngest member of the cabinet.

Over the next 15 years, Giscard was appointed to several critical posts, including minister of finance and economic affairs from 1962 to 1966. Forced out of that position after splitting from the Party of Independents and Peasants (CNIP) and forming a separate party, the Independent Republicans, a centrist Gaullist party, he became chair of the National Assembly Finance Committee (1966–68). In 1962, the support of the Independent Republicans for the direct election of a president had been critical in establishing the first stable parliamentary majority in French republican history. In 1969, it also helped elect Georges Pompidou president of France, and in return for that support, Pompidou reappointed Giscard as minister of finance and economic affairs. When the ailing Pompidou died of cancer in 1974, Giscard ran successfully to succeed him, defeating the socialist candidate, François Mitterand.

As president, Giscard tried, with some initial success, to respond to the movement for social liberalization that had been evident in France since the 1960s. He also called for a more open, pluralistic society, supported expansion of social services, lowered the minimum voting age from 21 to 18, established a secretariat for women, approved laws facilitating abortion and divorce, lifted controls over broadcasting, made secondary education more egalitarian, and favored protection for the environment. But he was best known for his efforts to transform France's backward economic system, with its heavy emphasis on agriculture and small business, into one of Europe's most dynamic economies, even using state funds and other incentives to encourage large industrial growth. Yet by the end of Giscard's presidency in 1981, France's economy had entered into a serious recession, caused in part by rising world oil prices, leading to inflation and high unemployment, and in part by his own liberalization reforms. Political scandals also wracked the later years of his presidency, as did internal bickering between his backers and those supporting his ambitious prime minister and political rival, Jacques Chirac. In 1981, Giscard was defeated by François Mitterand in an election that left him bitter.

During his seven-year presidency, in addition to his concern with domestic economic and social reform, Giscard pursued France's interest as part of the European Economic Community (EEC, or Common Market). He held regular summit meetings with European leaders, but he developed a particularly close relationship with German chancellor Helmut Schmidt, whose technocratic orientation and background in economics and finance were similar to Giscard's own. Together, France and Germany dominated the EEC. Under Giscard, France strengthened its historic relationship with Africa, with which it maintained strong interests in trade and oil. Committed to maintaining stability in Africa, the French president intervened twice during a civil war in Chad and acted in Zaire to prevent destabilization in that resource-rich country. This included sending paratroopers into the country in 1977 after rebel forces moved across the border from pro-Soviet Angola. He acted even though Zaire had been in Belgium's political orbit rather than France's. He was later criticized by the Belgian press for his willingness to cooperate with the dictatorial Zairian government of Joseph Mobutu. He also followed an independent policy in the Middle East, supporting the Palestinian cause and supplying the oil-producing Arab countries with substantial military and technological assistance.

As was the case with Helmut Schmidt, Giscard's relations with the United States were rocky. On the one hand, the G-7 conferences—a series of summits of the major industrial nations, begun by Giscard in Rambouillet in 1975 during GERALD FORD's administration and continuing in London (1977), Bonn (1978), Tokyo (1979), and Venice (1980)—produced some notable achievements among the leaders on such matters as trade and currency problems as well as economic policy coordination. On the other hand, not everyone was happy with the results of the G-7 meetings, and there were differences over whether the summits should be institutionalized. Both Giscard and Schmidt perceived the conferences initially as occasional events with limited attendance and attention, devoted primarily to economic and financial matters. Both the Ford and Carter administrations took a more trilateralist conception of the meetings, envisioning them as ongoing and more broadly representative forums concerned with a range of economic and political issues. That view ultimately prevailed.

Beyond differences over the question of summitry, there were other strong differences between the United States and France during Carter's administration. Giscard's policies in the Middle East, for example, ran contrary to the United States' strong backing of Israel. In opposition to American policy, France also continued to act as the primary supplier of military equipment to South Africa and disregarded UN sanctions levied against Rhodesia (later Zimbabwe).

Like Schmidt, Giscard also disparaged President Carter's human rights campaign against the Soviet Union, fearing, quite correctly, that the White House would attempt to undermine the domestic policies of the Soviet government. Already angry with Carter for not revoking the New York Port Authority's ban on the Concorde supersonic airliner, Giscard gave a magazine interview in which he accused the president of having "compromised the process of détente" by being clumsy in his dealings with Soviet leader LEONID BREZHNEV. He joined Schmidt and the leaders of all the Common Market countries in urging Carter to moderate his campaign on behalf of human rights.

In addition to taking issue with the American president on his human rights policy, Giscard also criticized Carter for allegedly expecting Europe to follow every twist and turn of American foreign policy. He and Schmidt, for example, joined together to promote a common European monetary system because they were irritated by what they perceived as President Carter's management of the dollar to obtain a low energy bill. Giscard also wanted a European monetary union that combined Germany's historic anti-inflation discipline with a strong franc without subordinating Paris to the Bundesbank's fear of inflation.

Like other European leaders, Giscard also sought a more balanced American approach to the Middle East, one that took into account Europe's heavy dependency on Persian Gulf oil. Similarly, he urged a more reasoned response to the Soviet invasion of Afghanistan, which reflected western Europe's close proximity to the Soviet Union.

In May 1980, the French president met privately in Warsaw with Soviet president Brezhnev. Plans for the five-hour session had been kept secret from the United States. About the same time, rumors spread around Washington that the annual summit of the Western leaders, scheduled for Venice in July, would be the occasion of a European demand that the Palestine Liberation Organization (PLO) be allowed to participate in all future negotiations on the Middle East and that UN Resolution 242, the heart of most long-range peace formulas for the Middle East, be revised to remove its reference to the Palestinians as mere "refugees." President Carter's new secretary of state, former senator EDMUND MUSKIE (D-Maine), became livid when he learned of the Brezhnev-Giscard summit and the plans afoot to pressure the United States and Israel into accommodation on the Palestinian question. While in Vienna to attend a foreign ministers meeting, Muskie had been scolded by French foreign minister Jean François-Poncet on the failure of the United States to consult with its allies, but the minister himself had neglected to mention Giscard's forthcoming meeting with Brezhnev. When he finally learned of the Soviet-French conference, therefore, Muskie, who was known for his fiery temper, did not mince words about French hypocrisy. "I'm concerned that when I was being given a lecture on consultation, the lecturer was not inclined to practice what he was preaching," he commented caustically to reporters. In a thinly veiled reference to the allies, he also attacked what he referred to as meddling in the Middle East "from the sidelines."

By the time Carter left for the Venice summit in July 1980, so much distrust had emerged among the Western powers and so much scorn heaped upon the American president that many political observers feared the meeting would be a disaster. Although the allies agreed on most strategic issues, they remained sharply at odds on a peace prospectus for the Mideast, on the proper response to the crises in Iran and Afghanistan, and on a unified policy for dealing with the nuclear threat posed by the Soviet Union. Giscard refused, for example, to honor the president's request to boycott the Summer Olympics in Moscow or impose economic sanctions against the Soviets.

These differences in Franco-American relations continued well past Carter's defeat for reelection in 1980. Giscard himself lost in his bid for reelection less than a year later. Although embittered by his defeat, Giscard followed the former American president's example of remaining active on the world scene rather than slipping into a state of permanent seclusion. He continued his career in politics, becoming chairman of the Commission on Foreign Affairs of the French National Assembly in 1987 and president of the European Union after 1989. In 1999, he also helped to win approval of the Euro, a single currency now used widely throughout Europe.

Moving toward the right politically, Giscard played a major role in establishing the Union for France (UPF) in 1990. He has also worked with leading business and political leaders to promote regional economic development and to respond to the challenges of the global marketplace.

Goldschmidt, Neil Edward

(1940–) *secretary of transportation*

Neil Goldschmidt was secretary of the Department of Transportation during the last two years of the Carter administration, replacing BROCK ADAMS, who had been forced to resign. A second-term mayor of Portland, Oregon, at the time of his appointment, he was selected by President Carter for the position because of his success in revitalizing downtown Portland, including the first designs for light rail. As transportation secretary, he was best known for his efforts to revive the ailing automobile industry. He also encouraged efforts to deregulate the airline, trucking, and railroad industries.

Goldschmidt was born in Eugene, Oregon, on June 16, 1940. The son of a working-class Jewish family, he attended the University of Oregon, where he majored in political science (B.A., 1963) and the University of California, Berkeley's Boalt School of Law (J.D., 1967). While at the University of Oregon, he was elected student body president. In 1964, he served as an intern in Washington, D.C., for Senator Maurine Neuberger and participated in the Freedom Summer voter registration campaign in Mississippi.

After graduating from law school, Goldschmidt served as a legal aid attorney in Portland (1967–69). In 1971, he began his political career by being elected to the city commission. A Democrat, he ran successfully in 1973 for mayor of Portland, becoming the nation's youngest big-city mayor at age 32. In 1977, he was reelected for a second term. Glib, humorous, and charismatic, he won considerable national attention for his success in rejuvenating downtown Portland, especially the creation of TriMEt (Tri-County Metropolitan Transit District of Oregon) and a downtown transit mall, which became a model for other cities of light-rail mass transportation. He also created new downtown housing and revitalized downtown office spaces. He was popular across a wide spectrum of Portland's voters. While mayor, he also served as president of the United States Conference of Mayors.

In 1976, Goldschmidt worked for the Carter presidential election campaign in Oregon. Impressed by his record in the area of mass transportation and wishing to repay a political debt, President Carter appointed the mayor of Portland in 1979 as secretary of transportation to replace Brock Adams, whom he had fired as part of a major shake-up of his cabinet. Goldschmidt quickly proved to be a loyal member of the administration. When, for example, Chicago mayor Jane Byrne announced in October 1979 that she was supporting Massachusetts Senator EDWARD KENNEDY for the Democratic presidential nomination in 1979, Goldschmidt made it known publicly that Chicago would receive less federal aid for transportation. "I've got a lot of pink slips [telephone messages] stacked up on my desk," he told reporters. "Hers would not be the first one I'd answer." Although Byrne cried foul, the secretary's action had its intended result. As *Newsweek* later commented, "the message would not be lost on other local officials."

As transportation secretary, Goldschmidt also expressed an interest in government industrial policy, especially the Chrysler Corporation Assistance Program, an effort worked out largely by the Treasury Department to save Chrysler, which was faced with a surplus of gas-guzzler cars as a result of rising oil prices, from insolvency. The bankruptcy of Chrysler—the nation's third largest automaker and the 17th largest company in the country, employing 134,000 workers, mostly in the Detroit area—would have been the biggest in the country's history. Accordingly, President Carter agreed in 1979 to provide up to $1.5 billion in loan guarantees as long as Chrysler won $2 billion in concessions from banks, suppliers, and unions. After Congress drafted the Chrysler Loan Guarantee Act of 1979, which included the secretary of transportation as a nonvoting member of the board administering the loan guarantee program, Goldschmidt authored a lengthy study of the automobile industry's problems, "U.S. Automobile Industry, 1980," which he submitted to the White House. There is no evidence, however, that anything came about as a result of the report.

During Goldschmidt's term as transportation secretary, both the Staggers Rail Act (1980) and the Motor Carrier Regulatory Reform and Modernization Act (1980) became law, deregulating the railroad and trucking industries, respectively. The Staggers Rail Act replaced the regulatory structure that had been in existence since the 1887 Interstate Commerce Act. The Motor Carrier Regulatory Reform and Modernization Act decontrolled trucking only partially but, together with a supportive Interstate Commerce Commission (ICC), substantially freed the industry from uncompetitive regulation.

While Goldschmidt was secretary, the Department of Transportation also issued regulations on child restraints and established the Office of Small and Disadvantaged Business Utilization (OSDBU). The OSDBU was intended to provide policy guidance for minority, women-owned, and disadvantaged businesses taking part in the department's procurement and federal financial assistance efforts.

At the end of the Carter administration, Goldschmidt returned to Oregon, where he became an executive with Nike, the sneaker company. In 1986, he became head of its Canadian subsidiary, Nike Canada. That same year, he entered the state gubernatorial race, narrowly defeating the Republican candidate, former Oregon secretary of state Norma Paulus, by one of the closest margin's in the state's history. As governor, Goldschmidt once again proved to be enormously popular, turning Oregon's moribund economy around by placing more emphasis on economic growth than on environmental protection (an historic concern of Oregonians). He improved the business climate through a series of regulatory reforms, initiated an investment strategy to repair the state's deteriorating infrastructure, poured money into schools and higher education, and promoted the state as a good place to live.

Although most political observers believed the state's dynamic governor could easily win reelection, Goldschmidt announced that he would not seek another term in office, citing marital difficulties. Instead, he opted to open his own consulting firm, which soon became enormously successful. His clients included Nike, Bechtel Enterprises, and Texas Pacific Group. Even though he had apparently turned his back on politics, Goldschmidt also remained popular in the state. In 1991, he helped create the Oregon Children's Foundation and another program that put 10,000 volunteers into Oregon schools to read to children. A number of his former aides won election to state office, including the governor's office, and there was frequent talk that he would make a political comeback, perhaps running for governor again or even the Senate.

At the same time, there were rumors that while married to his first wife, Goldschmidt had been a philanderer and that this was why he had decided to leave politics. No one was prepared, however, for his public admission in spring 2004 that when he was mayor of Portland in 1975, he had carried on a lengthy sexual affair with a 14-year-old girl who had been his family's babysitter. He also admitted his concern that his sexual abuse of a minor, a felony in Oregon, would be uncovered and that this was a factor in his decision not to run for reelection as governor or to seek other political office.

For nearly 30 years, Goldschmidt had managed to keep the affair a secret, telling it only to his second wife, Diana Snowden, a senior vice president at PacifiCorp at the time he met her. In 1994, he and his wife agreed to pay the unidentified victim, now a 44-year-old woman, $250,000 in return for a confidentiality statement. In 2004, however, he was informed that the weekly *Willamette Week*, founded by a former aide, was about to reveal the details of the sordid affair. In ill health with a heart condition and referring to the Jewish holiday of Yom Kippur, the day of atonement, he made his statement of apology, stating that he had lived with "enormous guilt and shame" for 30 years. It was later revealed that he had been helped in keeping his affair a secret by a business associate whose bid to extend a houseboat moorage on the Willamette River Goldschmidt had unsuccessfully supported as governor.

Although the statute of limitations had expired for prosecuting Goldschmidt's act of sex with a minor, he voluntarily gave up his Oregon license to practice law, resigned his position with the Oregon Board of Higher Education, and withdrew from the board of a firm trying to acquire Oregon's largest utility from the bankrupt Enron Corporation. Despite the fact that Goldschmidt has been roundly condemned in his state, a number of Oregonians still expect him to make a political comeback.

Goldwater, Barry Morris
(1909–1998) *member of the Senate*

Senator Barry Goldwater of Arizona has often been referred to as "Mr. Conservative" because of his leadership in reviving the conservative movement in the United States in the last half of the 20th century. Despite his overwhelming defeat as the Republican candidate for president in 1964, Goldwater was still a highly respected figure in national politics in the 1970s. He was also an inveterate foe of President Carter, whom he genuinely disliked and whom he opposed on almost every issue. In 1979, he even went to the Supreme Court in an unsuccessful effort to block the president's effort to abrogate the United States' mutual-defense treaty with Taiwan as part of the administration's effort to normalize relations with the People's Republic of China (PRC, or Communist China).

The son of a wealthy businessman who was a partner of a family-owned chain of department stores, Goldwater was born in Phoenix, Arizona, on January 1, 1909. Although an indifferent student, he had leadership skills, and was elected president of his freshman class in high school. Because of low grades, however, he transferred to the Staunton Military Academy in Virginia, where he won a medal as best all-around cadet and developed a lifelong interest in the military. Although he wanted to attend the U.S. Military Academy at West Point, his father insisted that he enroll at the University of Arizona.

When his father died in 1929, Goldwater dropped out of university to enter the family business. He proved to be an adept businessman and innovative entrepreneur, rising from junior clerk to president of the firm by 1937 and introducing such innovations as a five-day workweek, employee health insurance and profit sharing, and new product lines. He was also the first Phoenix merchant to hire black salespersons. By the end of the 1930s, the Phoenix branch of the family's chain was the city's premier department store. Goldwater had also become a respected community leader. But his efforts came at a high personal cost, including two nervous breakdowns and a drinking problem.

During World War II, Goldwater, who had learned to fly in the 1920s, enlisted in the U.S. Army Air Force. Denied a combat mission, he flew aircraft with supplies in the India-Burma theater and across the Atlantic. After the war, he helped to establish the Arizona Air National Guard, eventually achieving the rank of major general in the Air Force Reserve.

Goldwater began his political career in 1949 when he ran successfully in the nonpartisan election for the Phoenix City Council. Already an outspoken conservative and opponent of the New Deal and Fair Deal, both of which he believed stymied free enterprise and self-initiative, Goldwater helped reorganize the moribund Republican Party in what was a heavily Democratic state. In 1950, he managed the successful gubernatorial campaign of Howard Pyle. Two years later, he decided to run for the U.S. Senate, challenging the incumbent, Senate majority leader Ernest McFarland (D). Taking advantage of President Dwight D. Eisenhower's popularity and an overconfident opponent who barely defended his seat, and campaigning against wasteful federal spending, a "no-win" policy in the Korean war, and a weak foreign policy toward the Soviet Union, Goldwater squeaked out a narrow victory.

Goldwater's election proved to be a turning point in the conservative movement. It showed that a conservative Republican could do well in what had been a Democratic stronghold and brought to the Senate an attractive figure willing to challenge even a popular president and leader of his party, Eisenhower, because of his accommodation with the New Deal. It also introduced into the national limelight a

Republican prepared to engage in battle with the traditional moderate leadership of his party, drawn mostly from the Northeast. This, together with his stand in favor of states' rights and opposition to integration (even though he was not himself a racist or bigot) prepared the way for a conservative takeover of the Republican Party and a realignment of politics that turned the South and Southwest from Democratic to Republican bastions of power.

This shift in the nation's political alignment did not happen at once and was not even fully apparent until California governor RONALD REAGAN, an early advocate of Goldwater's brand of Republicanism, almost defeated President GERALD FORD for the Republican presidential nomination in 1976. But by attacking even President Eisenhower in the 1950s for embracing New Deal statism and deficit spending, by opposing the Supreme Court's 1954 landmark decision in *Brown v. Board of Education of Topeka* and the use of federal troops to integrate Little Rock's Central High School in 1957, and by adopting strongly nationalistic and fervently anticommunist foreign-policy positions, Goldwater was able to appeal to strongly held values in small-town and rural America and even among urban Democratic Catholics from Eastern Europe opposed to communist control of their former homelands.

In 1964, Goldwater's supporters were able to seize control of the Republican Party from its traditional leadership and nominate the Arizona senator for president. Although the strident extremism of Goldwater and his supporters contributed to the overwhelming defeat of Republicans in the election, the conservative takeover of the party prepared the way for Reagan.

In 1968, Goldwater was able to reclaim the seat in the Senate that he had forfeited in his run for the presidency in 1964. He championed RICHARD NIXON's policy with respect to the Vietnam War and defended him throughout most of the Watergate scandal that increasingly consumed the presidency in 1973 and 1974. But Goldwater opposed Nixon's domestic spending programs and had serious doubts about his policy of détente with the Soviet Union and his approach to the People's Republic of China (PRC) in 1972. In August 1974, when Goldwater heard incontrovertible evidence that Nixon had known about the Watergate break-in during the 1972 election and had participated in its cover-up, he was one of three Republicans who went to the White House to tell the president that only 15 Republicans would support him in the Senate if he were impeached by the House and put on trial by the Senate. The next day, Nixon announced his resignation as president.

Notwithstanding Ronald Reagan's conservative views and the stirring speech he had given in support of Goldwater's nomination in 1964, which had marked the beginning of his national political career, Goldwater supported President Gerald Ford's campaign for the Republican nomination in 1976 and campaigned for him against Jimmy Carter. Exactly when he began to develop his personal disdain for Carter is not entirely clear, but Carter's decision soon after he took office to honor a campaign promise to pardon Vietnam War draft evaders infuriated the Arizona senator, who later described Carter's action as "the most disgraceful thing that a President had ever done."

Goldwater was also upset by Carter's negotiation of the 1977 Panama Canal Treaties, which he described as giving away an American-owned possession vital to the nation's security. In a letter to the president, he tried to dissuade Carter against his carefully orchestrated campaign to win Senate approval of the treaties, even making the strange argument that the president was not responsible for the agreements with Panama. "I suggest to you, with all respect," he wrote Carter in September, "that you not get too excited about this Treaty. It is not something you originated."

It was Carter's decision to abrogate the United States' mutual-defense treaty with Taiwan as part of his effort to normalize relations with Communist China, however, that most upset the Arizona senator. The president knew how Goldwater would react to his decision to normalize relations with the PRC at the expense of Taiwan. According to Carter, in fact, he had delayed taking any action toward normalization until after ratification of the Panama Canal Treaties in the faint hope that he might yet gain the senator's vote for the agreements.

Support of the Nationalist government of China against the Communists had been an essential part of the Republican Party's right-wing mantra since before the 1940s. Many Republicans, including Goldwater, regarded the "loss" of China to the Communists in 1949 as evidence of an internal American communist conspiracy, an accusation that gained national attention as a result of the distortions and fabrications of Senator Joseph McCarthy (R-Wis.), who made the word *McCarthyism* a synonym for political demagoguery. Goldwater had been only one of 22 senators who defended McCarthy when he was censured by the Senate for his scurrility at the end of 1954.

Already alienated from the Carter administration, Goldwater regarded the president's decision to abrogate the nation's mutual-defense treaty with a longtime ally as part of a deal with a regime he hated as just the latest evidence of the president's spineless behavior. On the Senate floor, he termed the president's decision on China "one of the most cowardly acts ever performed by a President of the United States." Unwilling to stop with this verbal assault on the president, Goldwater, joined by like-minded senators and representatives, went to the Supreme Court to challenge the constitutional right of the chief executive to unilaterally abrogate a treaty approved by the Senate without the prior consent of the upper chamber. The Court refused to give Goldwater the declaratory judgment that he sought. Four of the justices found that the case involved a political question, making it beyond the bounds of the Court to render a judgment; they were unwilling to second-guess the president on matters related to foreign relations. Justice WILLIAM BRENNAN, one of the Court's most liberal members, however, went to the case's merits, concluding that Carter had acted within his authority in abrogating the treaty with Taiwan.

Following Reagan's victory over Carter in 1980, Goldwater grew increasingly disenchanted with the conservative movement within his party because of its growing emphasis on cultural and social issues rather than on the brand of political conservatism that he had always espoused. He had little regard for the movement known as the Moral Majority and even spoke out in defense of abortion rights and gays in the military. "You don't need to be 'straight' to fight and die for your country," he stated in a letter to the *Washington Post.* "You just need to shoot straight."

In 1987, Goldwater retired from the Senate, by now a highly respected statesman known for his blunt and outspoken honesty, commitment to principle, and willingness to defy conventional politics. In 1996, the former senator suffered a stroke. A year later, he was diagnosed with Alzheimer's disease. On May 29, 1998, he died of natural causes at his home in Paradise Valley, a suburb of Phoenix. He was 89 years old.

Griffin, Robert Paul

(1923–) *member of the Senate*

Despite having failed to be reelected as minority whip in the U.S. Senate and having announced that he would not seek reelection to the upper chamber in 1978 (a decision that he later reversed), Senator Robert P. Griffin of Michigan was a leading Republican critic of President Carter until he was defeated in his bid for reelection in 1978.

The son of a factory worker, Griffin was born in Detroit, Michigan, on November 6, 1923, and attended public schools in Garden City and Dearborn, Michigan. During World War II, he enlisted in the U.S. Army and spent 14 months in Europe. After the war, he attended Central Michigan College (B.A., 1947) and the University of Michigan Law School (LL.B., 1950). He opened a law practice with a partner in Traverse City, in the northwest part of Michigan's lower peninsula, and in 1956 ran successfully as a moderate Republican for the U.S. House of Representatives, defeating his more conservative rival in the party primary. He was easily reelected to the succeeding four Congresses.

In his second term as a congressman, Griffin attracted national attention when, as a member of the Education and Labor Committee, he helped win passage in 1959 of what became known as the Landrum-Griffin Labor Reform Law. The measure aimed at curbing racketeering in union organizations by guaranteeing workers the secret ballot on matters of union representation and protecting union finances. Between 1963 and 1965, Griffin also led a revolt of "young Turks" against the staid Republican leadership in the House, leading eventually to the unseating of Minority Leader Charles Halleck of Indiana in favor of his Michigan colleague, GERALD FORD.

In May 1966, Governor George W. Romney appointed Griffin to the Senate to fill the vacancy caused by the death of Democrat Patrick V. McNamara. That fall, Griffin was elected to a full six-year term, defeating former governor G. Mennan Williams; he was reelected in 1972. As a junior senator, Griffin again attracted national attention when, in June 1968, he led a successful filibuster against President Lyndon Johnson's nomination of Supreme Court justice Abraham Fortas to be chief justice of the Court. In attacking the Fortas nomination, Griffin raised issues of conflict of interest, revealing that Fortas had accepted an unusually high salary for teaching a summer course at American University Law School that had been paid for by his former business associates and clients. Ultimately Fortas withdrew his name from consideration and later resigned from the Court.

Having developed a reputation as a "giant killer," Griffin ran successfully in 1969 for minority whip in the Senate. He proved to be a strong and effective whip whose unassuming physical appearance belied his feisty skills in floor debate. During the administrations of RICHARD NIXON and Gerald Ford, he voted along moderate-conservative lines, generally supporting both presidents but occasionally dissenting on such matters as Nixon's failed nomination to the Supreme Court of Clement Haynsworth (though later voting in support of the nomination of G. Harrold Carswell, which also failed) or funding for the supersonic transport (SST). Griffin supported Nixon throughout most of the Watergate scandal, but on August 3, 1974, he warned the president that if he defied a Senate demand for tapes in an expected impeachment trial, he (Griffin) would vote for Nixon's conviction. Two days later, Griffin went on television to urge the president to resign; behind the scenes, he told Vice President Ford to prepare himself for the presidency. He became part of the transition team when it became clear after the release of the tapes on August 5 that Nixon would have to resign.

In 1976, Griffin played an important role in Ford's campaign against RONALD REAGAN for the Republican presidential nomination. He was a key adviser, for example, in the Michigan primary, urging Ford to appeal to Democrats to cross over in the primary in order to vote for him instead of making the usual appeal to Republican voters. On primary day, the president won a resounding victory over Reagan, beating him by a margin of nearly two to one and changing the direction of the campaign, which had seemed to be moving in Reagan's favor. At the party convention in Kansas City, Griffin was Ford's floor manager.

Because of his closeness to Ford, Griffin was disappointed by the president's defeat in November 1976. He was in line to be minority leader in January 1977 but was unexpectedly defeated for the position, losing by one vote to HOWARD BAKER of Tennessee. A major reason for his defeat was his close association with Ford and the desire by Republicans for a new face and more forceful opposition voice now that the Republicans no longer controlled the White House. Disheartened by the results of the November election and by his own defeat for minority leader, Griffin announced in April 1977 that he would not seek reelection in 1978.

Instead of withdrawing into the background, however, the Michigan senator proved to be a relentless foe of President Carter on Capitol Hill. A member of the Foreign Relations Committee, he was openly hostile to Carter's nomination of PAUL WARNKE as the nation's chief arms negotiator because of what he regarded as the president's dovish views toward the Soviet Union. He was only one of two members of the committee to vote against the nomination, which was even more strongly opposed by Republicans and Democrats in the Senate Armed Services Committee. Although Warnke was confirmed by the Senate, the vote of 58 to 40 fell short of the broad demonstration of support the Carter administration was seeking and short of the two-thirds vote needed to ratify any arms agreement that Warnke might negotiate with Moscow. Denying on the Senate floor that he had tried to cripple Warnke's effectiveness as an arms negotiator by opposing his nomination so strongly, Griffin stated that the opposition was "not trying to cripple Mr. Warnke. He is already crippled because of self-inflicted wounds."

Griffin also helped kill President Carter's proposal to allow voters to register on Election Day, forcing the White House to release a Justice Department memorandum that said the bill had a "tremendous potential for fraud." Representing the nation's major automobile manufacturing state, Griffin additionally helped win a delay in the imposition of stricter control of automobile fuel emissions after failing to win approval of an amendment that would have weakened the standards permanently. Similarly, he tried unsuccessfully to win Senate approval of a resolution that would have nullified a Department of Transportation decision to require air bags or other passive safety devices in all new automobiles by the 1984 model year.

In the Senate Commerce Committee, Griffin spoke out against the administration's cargo-preference bill raising the percentage of U.S. oil imports required to be carried by American-flag ships. He challenged the White House's contention that the measure was necessary for national security reasons. Suggesting instead that the president was influenced by a political campaign commitment to the maritime unions and industry, which would benefit by the increased tonnage carried on American-flag ships, he called the legislation a rip-off of American consumers to benefit special-interest groups in the maritime industry.

Despite former President Ford's strong lobbying efforts in support of the Panama Canal Treaties that President Carter had signed in 1977, relinquishing U.S. ownership of the Panama Canal and Panama Canal Zone by 1999, Griffin was outspoken in his opposition to the agreements. He promised the president that he would not introduce any killer amendments to the treaties and would not join any so-called "truth squads" campaigning around the country for their defeat. Nevertheless, he led the fight in the Foreign Relations Committee against the treaties, remarking that the Senate should advise the president to have his negotiators "go back to the drawing board." He was the only member of the committee to vote against the treaties before they were sent to the full Senate for debate. When the upper chamber approved the treaties, Griffin warned on the Senate floor that the treaty giving up the canal was "a dangerous step, a gamble for the United States and the security of the United States."

Although Griffin had announced a year earlier that he would not run for reelection in 1978, Republican leaders in Michigan persuaded him to change his mind. This, however, angered a number of Republicans who had hoped for his support in the race to replace him. It also prompted a primary challenge in which a central issue was the assertion by his opponents that Griffin had lost the will and the energy to represent Michigan and should be retired. The senator won an easy primary victory, but his Democratic opponent, Carl Levin, a former president of the Detroit City Council, used the same issue with great effectiveness, pointing to a number of Senate votes that Griffin had missed and arguing that Michigan needed some "new blood" in Congress. In November, Levin defeated Griffin handily.

Following his defeat, Griffin became a senior fellow at the American Enterprise Institute, a conservative think tank. In 1987, he became a justice of the Michigan Supreme Court, a position he held until his retirement in 1994.

Harris, Patricia Roberts

(1924–1985) *secretary of housing and urban development; secretary of health, education and welfare; secretary of health and human services*

Patricia Harris was secretary of the Department of Housing and Urban Development (HUD) at a crucial period insofar as the development of a national urban policy was concerned. Previous administrations since at least the Franklin Roosevelt administration had enacted programs and policies to assist the nation's urban areas. HUD itself had been established as a cabinet-level agency during the Lyndon Johnson administration. Not until the Carter administration, however, was the first attempt made to develop a comprehensive federal policy to respond to the growing plight of the nation's urban areas, especially the so-called rust belt cities of the Northeast and Midwest. HUD became the agency leading this effort, partially due to its officials' attempts to stake out a central role in what promised to be one of the highest priorities of the incoming Carter administration, and partially a reflection of Secretary Harris's determination to do something about the growing urban crisis.

In contrast to the ambitious recommendations of the task force that Harris headed, however, the president never intended any major new spending for the cities. Instead, he promoted an urban program predicated on public-private partnerships and community-based planning at little cost to the federal government. Disappointed by the president's response to her task force's proposals, Harris nevertheless remained loyal to the president. When Carter fired Secretary of Health, Education and Welfare (HEW) JOSEPH CALIFANO in 1979 as part of his purge of his cabinet, he named Harris to replace him. As HEW secretary, she watched over the restructuring of the department into the Department of Health and Human Services.

Harris was born on May 31, 1924, in Mattoon, Illinois. Her life became one of firsts: first in her graduating class from George Washington Law School (LL.B., 1960); first African-American woman ambassador; first black woman to serve as a director of a major United States corporation (IBM, 1971); and first African-American woman to hold a cabinet position. A summa cum laude graduate of Howard University (B.A., 1945), she had also done graduate work at the University of Chicago and American University. Always interested in politics and political activism, she became assistant director of the American Council on Human Rights in 1953. In 1955, she married attorney and namesake, William Harris, who encouraged her to earn a law degree.

After graduating from George Washington University Law School, Harris worked for a year at the Department of Justice before accepting a position at Howard University as associate dean of students and lecturer in the Howard School of Law. In 1962, she was asked by President John F. Kennedy to cochair the National Women's Committee for Civil Rights, an umbrella organization of 100 women's groups throughout the United States. In 1965, President Lyndon Johnson appointed her ambassador to Luxembourg. Two years later, she returned to Howard University School of Law as a professor and, for a brief period in 1969, as dean of the school, before resigning amidst student and faculty conflicts. Entering private law practice, she remained active in the Civil Rights movement and served on the executive board of the NAACP Legal Defense Fund from 1967 to 1977, when she was asked by President-elect Carter to be his secretary of housing and urban development.

During Harris's confirmation hearings, Senator WILLIAM PROXMIRE of Wisconsin questioned whether she could properly serve as a representative of the poor, being herself part of the black middle class and out of the mainstream of black America. In a poignant response, the blunt-spoken nominee replied that the senator did not understand who she was: a black woman who was raised by a single mother, a person who needed a scholarship to go to school, and an African American who as recently as eight years earlier would not

Secretary of Housing and Urban Development Patricia Harris, President Jimmy Carter and New York Mayor Abraham Beame tour the South Bronx, 1977. *(Jimmy Carter Library)*

have been able to buy a house in some parts of the District of Columbia because of her skin color. She had not forgotten her background, she said.

Harris took office as HUD secretary at a time of mounting crisis for the nation's urban areas. All the demographic changes that had been evident since at least the end of World War II—white flight from the cities to the suburbs, population shifts from the North to the South and Southwest, and a declining revenue base—were complicated by racial strife; single-parent families; growing welfare rolls; increased crime rates; and a backlash against civil rights, welfare, and increased taxes. New York City was bankrupt, and other older major metropolitan areas like Boston, Cleveland, Detroit, and St. Louis teetered on insolvency.

Although HUD had been established by President Lyndon Johnson in 1965 in order to deal with urban problems, prior to 1977 there still had not been a single, comprehensive national urban policy that would make explicit the federal government's responsibility to confront the growing urban crisis in all of its complexities. Typically, Carter made vague promises during the campaign to develop such a policy, even referring to the cities as "America's number one economic problem" in a June 1976 address to the U.S. Conference of Mayors. After his victory in November that year, the president-elect continued to indicate the high priority he intended to give to urban problems. On the day before his inauguration, he sent eight cabinet-level members of his new administration to meet with a group of mayors in Washington to discuss their concerns. Less than a month after taking office, he paid a ceremonial visit to HUD to underscore his concern for cities in distress.

Sensing the urgency of the moment as well as an opportunity for Harris to define her stewardship of HUD, her staff persuaded the secretary to seek authority from the president to convene and lead a working group with representatives from all appropriate agencies to develop a national urban and regional policy. In a memorandum of March 21, 1977, sent to the secretaries of the Treasury, commerce, labor, HEW, transportation, and HUD, Carter gave Harris the authority she requested. A week later, Harris convened the first meeting of the Urban and Regional Policy Group (URPG).

What the president had in mind, however, was something different from what the URPG recommended. Ever since the establishment of HUD, three essential principles of most urban programs had been (1) federal-local cost-sharing, (2) public-private partnerships, and (3) community-based programs. In 1977, Secretary Harris argued forcefully and successfully for amendments to the Urban Development Action Grant Program (UDAG) of 1974 that would further public-private partnerships and local government control in urban redevelopment and recovery programs. This type of shared power and funding appealed to President Carter's antibureaucratic and fiscally conservative inclinations. What he sought from the URPG were the cost efficiencies and improved delivery of services that he anticipated would result from reorganization and better coordination of existing urban programs, including eliminating overlapping and duplicative programs, reducing paperwork, and streamlining administrative procedures. Furthermore, he expected the URPG to submit its recommendations to him by early summer.

For a number of reasons, this did not happen. In the first place, the size of the URPG made it unwieldy. Second, bureaucratic infighting and jurisdictional disputes continued unabated. For example, Secretary Harris strongly resisted efforts by HEW secretary Joseph Califano to fold $1 billion or more of HUD's housing subsidies into a comprehensive program of cash payments to poor families as part of his effort at reforming the nation's welfare system, another high priority of the Carter administration. Third, even within HUD, there were competitive pressures between program offices—in particular, Housing and Community Planning and Development—to lead the urban-reform effort. Critics even questioned Harris's ability to lead HUD because of this internecine warfare.

As a result, URPG failed to deliver on its mandate to present recommendations to Carter by early summer 1977 for developing a national urban and regional policy. Meanwhile, the president came under mounting criticism by such groups as the National Urban League to develop the urban policy he had promised. Under increasing pressure from the White House and from lawmakers on Capitol Hill representing urban interests, the URPG was reorganized in August 1977, with the White House assuming a more active role in its proceedings. URPG deputies were assigned specific tasks and deadlines. The URPG/HUD staff was given a September 1 deadline to come up with an analysis of urban problems, a December deadline for a preliminary report and recommendations, and a date of March 1978 for a final report and list of recommendations.

Instead of recommending a coherent national urban and regional urban policy predicated largely on reorganization and coordination of existing programs to achieve cost efficiencies, as Carter wanted, what the URPG delivered in December was a 150-page draft report that called for adding $8–12 billion to the $50 billion in aid that cities and towns already received. This was simply unacceptable to the White House. In contradiction to the URPG draft report, STUART EIZENSTAT, the head of Carter's domestic policy staff, recommended to the president a much more restrained and less costly role for Washington that was more in accordance with the president's own thinking. Unlike the Harris task force, which still believed that well-conceived federal programs could produce urban revitalization, Eizenstat argued that Washington could act more responsibly by promoting public-private partnerships at the local level and encouraging greater involvement by neighborhood and citizen's groups.

Carter agreed with Eizenstat. "Don't tell me we'll spend more money all around and then we'll call it an urban policy," he said angrily at a meeting with the URPG in December. "Give me something worth funding if you want more money." The next day, he instructed the director of the Office of Management and Budget (OMB), JAMES MCINTYRE, not to include any urban initiatives in the 1979 budget.

Aside from its price tag, the president had good reason to reject the URPG's report and to send the task force back to the drawing board. Many of its recommendations were conceptually flawed. Its much-touted proposal for an urban development bank, for example, assumed that low-cost credit, which the bank would presumably make available to investors, would spur economic development in distressed areas. But the URPG did not carefully analyze the other critical factors affecting investment, such as operating costs, the availability of land and skilled labor, government regulations, and crime rates.

In deciding not to include any additional funding for cities in the budget, the president also displayed considerable political courage. As he had anticipated, his action angered urban interests whose support was essential to his presidency. A spokesman for the U.S. Conference of Mayors stated that if the president failed to provide more aid to cities, his administration would "be viewed as a traitor to urban America." Rather than being intimidated by such warnings, Carter made it clear that his urban policy would stress the role of state and local governments and of neighborhood and voluntary groups, not just the spending of federal dollars.

Indeed, for the remainder of his administration Carter gave relatively little attention to the cities. He also rejected any effort to increase significantly the level of federal spending in urban areas. With much ballyhoo, the president announced, in March 1978, "The New Partnership to Conserve America's Communities." But this "comprehensive" urban initiative rang hollow. Although calling for many of the proposals in the URPG's preliminary report in December, it stressed Carter's emphasis on a "partnership" involving federal, state, and local governments, the private sector, and community. It also emphasized repeatedly that the changes being recommended could be enacted with little or no cost to the federal government.

Secretary Harris was disappointed by the president's response to the URPG's recommendations and, more generally, by his urban policy. She could not have felt otherwise given the fact that her staff and she had hoped that formation of the task force would heighten HUD's role in the administration as well as her own. Yet she remained stoically quiet about her disappointment, although she was not ordinarily reticent about expressing her views in cabinet meetings and elsewhere. At HUD, in fact, she had developed a reputation for being abrasive. Nevertheless, she was also respected for being hardworking, focused, and determined to address the problems of the poor. Even Secretary Califano, with whom she had clashed over housing subsidies for the poor, characterized her as "tough and unimpeachable."

Harris believed strongly, however, that as a member of the cabinet, she represented the president. At one cabinet meeting in 1979, discussing alleged White House leaks to the press, including some directed at her, she expressed annoyance with White House staffers for what she regarded as their "we all–you all mentality," that it was only they, and not the cabinet, who spoke for the president. So while she understood her responsibilities to the constituencies that HUD served, she also believed that her first allegiance was to the president even when she disagreed with him strongly.

The president appreciated this type of loyalty. After he accepted the forced resignation of HEW Secretary Califano precisely because he considered him disloyal to the administration, Carter appointed Harris to replace him. In the short time that she served as the department's secretary, she was not able to accomplish much other than to watch over the reorganization of HEW to the Department of Health and Human Services and the establishment of a new cabinet-level Department of Education, all of which became effective as of May 4, 1980.

Following Carter's loss to RONALD REAGAN in the 1980 presidential election, Harris returned to George Washington University Law School as a full-time professor. In 1982, she ran for mayor of Washington, D.C., but lost badly to Marion Barry, who was widely liked for his civil rights activism in the 1960s while Harris was regarded by African-American voters as the candidate of both the white and African-American middle class. Shortly after the election, she was diagnosed with cancer; she died on March 23, 1985.

Haskell, Floyd Kirk

(1916–1998) *member of the Senate*

A former Republican turned Democrat, Floyd Kirk Haskell served as U.S. senator from Colorado from 1973 to 1979. A moderate liberal who supported President Carter's comprehensive energy plan, he was roundly defeated for reelection in 1978 despite Carter's strong endorsement and personal campaigning on his behalf. His defeat, along with the defeat of several other moderate liberal Democrats in an election campaign that *Time* magazine characterized as a "referendum" on the Carter presidency, was a harbinger of even more stunning defeats in the 1980 presidential election, including Carter's own failed bid for reelection.

Haskell was born on February 7, 1916, in Morristown, New Jersey. He received his undergraduate degree (B.A., 1937) from Harvard College and his law degrees (LL. B., 1941) from Harvard Law School. During World War II, he served in the United States Army (1941–45), attaining the rank of major. In 1946, he was admitted to both the New York and Colorado bars and began practicing law in Denver. He did not enter politics until 1965, when he was elected as a Republican to the Colorado House of Representatives. Reelected in 1967, he served as the assistant majority leader. While a state legislator, however, he became strongly opposed to the war in Vietnam. After leaving the legislature in 1968, he took an active role in the antiwar movement and switched his party allegiance from Republican to Democrat.

In 1972, Haskell decided to run as an antiwar candidate for the U.S. Senate against the three-term incumbent Republican, Gordon Allcott. Given practically no chance of winning the election by political pundits, he won a stunning upset in a close election, in part because of growing public dissatisfaction in Colorado with President RICHARD NIXON's handling of the war in Vietnam.

Haskell's own standing on Capitol Hill grew following the 1974 elections, which increased the numbers of liberal Democrats in both houses on Capitol Hill and led to major changes in the seniority system by which committee chairs had been historically appointed. His own legislative accomplishments were modest, however, and had mainly to do with obtaining federal funding for countries with large acreages of nontaxable federal lands and gaining tax breaks for small businesses hiring more employees.

During the first two years of the Carter presidency, Haskell generally supported the president on such matters as his national energy plan and the Equal Rights Amendment. He also backed controls on auto emissions, supported the Panama Canal Treaties, and opposed right-to-work legislation. He was considered a tax reformer on the Senate Finance Committee and a specialist on nonpetroleum sources of energy on the Energy Committee.

Because of Haskell's support of the White House, President Carter threw his strong support behind the Colorado Senator's reelection effort in 1978 and was the principal speaker at a fund-raising dinner in Denver on his behalf. But the president's backing actually proved to be an embarrassment to Haskell. As the president often did, he engaged in hyperbole, referring to the one-term senator as a "national treasure" and "one of the great senators of all times." The *Denver Rocky Mountain News* referred to the president's comments as "purple praise" and "preposterously insincere compliments." Haskell's enemies were amused and his supporters flabbergasted.

Adding to Haskell's troubles was the fact that he was not a particularly good campaigner. Laid-back and shy in the presence of people he did not know, he was also tied to Carter's flagging popularity and raging inflation; opposed by one of Colorado's best campaigners, Republican Congressman Bill Armstrong; attacked for his spending and tax policies; and accused of accepting a flight back to Washington on an $890-per-hour jet provided by the administration in order to vote on the Equal Rights Amendment. Consequently, he lost badly to Armstrong, who won nearly 60 percent of the vote.

Haskell was only one of four liberal Democratic senators to be defeated in 1978, the others being Richard Clark of Iowa, Wendell Anderson of Minnesota, and Thomas McIntyre of New Hampshire. Following his defeat, he became a successful lobbyist and consultant in Washington. He also worked with a bipartisan group of retired senators and senior politicians in trying to break congressional stalling, including modifying the filibuster. In 1984, he suffered an accident after slipping on ice and slamming his head on the curb, which required three brain operations. He never fully recovered from the accident. Haskell died of pneumonia on August 25, 1998, while vacationing in Maine with his wife, National Public Radio reporter Nina Totenberg. He was 82 years old.

Helms, Jesse Alexander, Jr.
(1921–) *member of the Senate*

One of the most conservative senators in recent history, Senator Jesse Helms received the nickname of "Dr. No" from his colleague for his efforts to reject nominees for important government positions and legislation that he believed violated essential American principles. Although there were few other senators who supported Helms's ultraconservative positions on Capitol Hill, he worked closely with STROM THURMOND of South Carolina on a number of issues. Helms also used his mastery of the legislative process to make himself one of the most powerful members of the Senate. During the Carter administration, he opposed most of the president's legislative programs, which, he argued, severely weakened the United States. Although Helms always faced tough opposition in his bids for reelection, through the support he drew from outside the state and his appeals to rural and suburban North Carolinians, he was able to be reelected four times before he decided to retire from office in 2004.

A seventh-generation citizen of the small town of Monroe, North Carolina, Helms was born on October 18, 1921. His father was both the town's chief of police and chief of the fire department. He attended Wingate Junior College and Wake Forest College but never graduated. Instead, he began a career in journalism, serving as city editor of the *Raleigh Times*. During World War II, he served in the navy, mainly as a recruiter. After the war, he turned to broadcast journalism as news and program director of WRAL in Raleigh.

In 1950, Helms began his career in politics by serving as an adviser to Willis Smith in his successful bid for the U.S. Senate in what was widely reported as one of the most virulently racist campaigns in North Carolina history. From 1951 to 1953, he worked as an aid for Smith in Washington and then briefly for Senator Alton Lennon. Returning to North Carolina, Helms served from 1953 until 1960 as executive director of the North Carolina Bankers Association.

Helms won his first elected office to the Raleigh City Council, on which he served from 1957 to 1961. From 1960 to 1972, he was executive vice president and then vice chairman of the board of the Capital Broadcasting Company. He was also chairperson of the board of the Specialized Agricultural Publications. He used his prominent place in the media to broadcast and write daily editorials challenging what he referred to as the "consistent bias in national television network news," especially concerning the Civil Rights movement in the South. He filed hundreds of bias cases against the three major television networks. He also called the Civil Rights Act of 1964 "the single most dangerous piece of legislation ever introduced in Congress," referred to the University of North Carolina as "The University of Negroes and Communists," and charged Martin Luther King, Jr., with being a communist. He attacked welfare recipients, judicial coddling of criminals, and academic freedom. In 1972, he even attacked President RICHARD NIXON for "appeasing Red China" by visiting Beijing.

At one time, over 200 newspapers carried Helms's editorials and over 70 radio stations read them on the air. His ultraconservative and antiliberal message resonated with rural and suburban North Carolinians among whom he was able to build a base of strong support. Switching from the Democratic to the Republican Party in 1972, he ran for the U.S. Senate and easily beat his Democratic opponent, Nick Galifianakis, becoming the first Republican to represent North Carolina in the 20th century.

Never afraid to express his beliefs publicly or to take extreme positions, Helms used the Senate as a forum to attack busing, communists, gays, abortion, gun control, federal campaign subsidies, elimination of school prayer, and "useless government spending." A hawk in his support of the war in Vietnam, he voted against reducing troop commitments abroad, foreign aid, and the ban on importing Rhodesian chrome. In 1974, he sought to rescind by constitutional amendment the 1973 Supreme Court decision in *Roe v. Wade* upholding the right of women to have an abortion. A leading supporter of RONALD REAGAN for the 1976 Republican presidential nomination, he spoke out strongly against the proposal to return the Panama Canal to Panama. In his first term in office, the conservative Americans for Constitutional Action gave him a 100 rating, while liberal journalists and magazines became livid in their opposition to Helms and targeted him for defeat in 1978. Conservative senator HERMAN TALMADGE of South Carolina quipped, "Jesse Helms was so conservative he made me look like a left-winger by comparison. He got a lot of people riled up by taking the most extreme position in any issue."

President Carter's first major battle with Helms came over the Panama Canal Treaties ceding the canal to the Panamanians by the year 2000. After negotiations were completed on the agreements, but before they were signed in September 1977, the president sent a message to all the senators urging them not to speak out against the treaties until they knew more about the details. "Apparently [the letter] worked with most of [the senators] except a few nuts like Strom Thurmond and Jesse Helms," Carter later commented. Together with Thurmond, Helms flaunted a poll conducted in August 1977 by the Opinion Research Corporation showing that 78 percent of American favored keeping the canal, while only 14 percent were willing to cede it to Panama.

Even before the Senate began consideration of the treaties, Helms made several speeches attacking SOL LINOWITZ, who had helped negotiate the agreements. In his remarks, Helms suggested a conflict of interest because Linowitz sat on the board of the Marine Midland Bank, which was part of an investment syndicate that had made a $200 million loan to Panama, even though Linowitz had already resigned from the board to avoid any conflict of interest. (In his 1984 bid for reelection to the Senate, Helms made an issue of the fact that his Democratic opponent, Governor Jim Hunt, was supported by Linowitz and was, by association, an enthusiast for the surrender of the waterway.) When the agreements were before the Senate for final ratification, Helms was scathing in his comments. "The decision to give away the Panama Canal," he said, "was based on purely political pressures in total disregard of the defense and economic consequences of that decision."

The next year, Helms joined Strom Thurmond in helping to lead the fight against a labor reform bill that would amend the 1935 National Labor Relations Act by making it easier for unions to organize workers. The measure, which the House had already approved and which had the backing of more than 50 senators, would authorize the National Labor Relations Board (NRLB) to set wages for newly unionized workers if the NRLB determined that an employer had not bargained in good faith. It would also give workers fired for union or organizing activities time and a half in back pay and reduce the legal organizing period from 45 to 30 days, so as to give management less time to fight unionization. "This bill," declared Helms, "is designed to unionize the South by federal force." Notwithstanding the backing of a majority of the Senate, a threatened filibuster by opponents of the measure, who argued that it would be inflationary and would bankrupt many small nonunion firms, was enough to derail the legislation before it could be approved and sent to Carter for his consideration.

Helms also worked closely with Thurmond and other conservative senators on an attempt to lift sanctions against the import of chrome from Rhodesia before it agreed to fair elections that would replace the minority white government of Ian Smith. Since taking office, Carter and his advisers had called repeatedly for black majority rule in South Africa and Rhodesia. On Capitol Hill, right-wing Republicans led by Helms responded by arguing that the United States needed to support the friendly governments of these two African nations. They also lashed out at both UN ambassador ANDREW YOUNG and Vice President WALTER MONDALE because of their public stance against the minority white governments and apartheid policies of the two countries.

At the beginning of 1978, Smith offered to begin sharing political power with blacks immediately and to hold free elections, based on universal adult suffrage, by December 31. A number of Rhodesia's more moderate black nationalists found Smith's proposal acceptable. The militant black Patriotic Front, however, wanted immediate majority rule. After Secretary of State CYRUS VANCE failed to broker a compromise, Smith announced "an internal settlement" that provided for a new government and included black moderates. But Smith would remain prime minister and whites would be assured enough seats in the parliament to prevent any constitutional changes. Predictably, the Patriotic Front denounced the plan and intensified its five-year guerrilla war against the Rhodesian goverment.

Smith's proposal for an internal settlement split the White House and exposed the differences between National Security Advisor ZBIGNIEW BRZEZINSKI, who thought the proposal was a worthwhile one, and Vance, who thought it was a sham intended to maintain white control of the country. Although the president leaned toward Brzezinski's position and ordered the American delegation at the United Nations to abstain on a resolution condemning the plan, Vance was able to persuade him to continue the sanctions against Rhodesia until a final settlement was reached in the country.

The president's decision angered liberal lawmakers on Capitol Hill and black leaders at home who thought the U.S. abstention at the United Nations amounted to a tacit endorsement of Smith's internal settlement. But it also enraged conservatives, and even some moderates, who believed the continuation of sanctions favored the Patriotic Front at the expense not only of Smith but also of black moderates. As far as Helms was concerned, the Patriotic Front was a coalition of Marxist forces that should not be allowed to come to power under any circumstances. Leading the movement in the Senate to lift the sanctions against Rhodesia, he sponsored a bill demanding that the embargo be ended unconditionally by the end of the year.

Helms came within six votes of getting his measure approved by the Senate. Instead, the administration accepted a compromise amendment empowering the president to lift sanctions after December 31, 1978, if he had determined that the Rhodesian government had negotiated in good faith at an all-parties conference and then had yielded power to a government chosen in internationally supervised elections participated in by all parties.

As Secretary of State Vance later commented, the administration's difficulty in turning back Helms's proposal and the necessity of a compromise amendment were an indication that sentiment in the country was moving "to the Right in angry frustration at the seemingly insoluble economic problems at home and growing turbulence abroad." The North Carolina senator was able to capitalize on this movement to the right. In 1978, President Carter targeted Helms for defeat in his bid for reelection to the Senate and traveled to the state in support of his friend John Ingram. Helms, however, was able to raise $6.7 million, a record for a Senate race, as compared to only $300,000 for Ingram, who sought to make an issue of the huge sums that Helms received from fellow conservatives across the country. Nevertheless, by labeling Ingram a liberal and blanketing the state with media and mail advertisements, Helms was able to defeat him in a tight race. This was the process Helms repeated in four more elections before he decided to retire in 2002.

Helms owed his success on Capitol Hill to his mastery of parliamentary procedure. In 1979, he nearly killed the administration's measure to establish a new Department of Education by attaching a school-prayer amendment to the legislation. It took the skillful maneuvering of Senate majority leader ROBERT BYRD, himself a master of parliamentary procedure, to remove the amendment and save the legislation. Helms also frustrated the White House repeatedly by holding up its nominations for political office, a practice that he had employed during GERALD FORD's presidency and that he would also use during President Ronald Reagan's administration.

After becoming a member of the Senate Foreign Relations Committee in 1979, Helms tried to promote his own ultraconservative foreign policy by seizing upon Senate reorganization rules that allowed the minority members of a committee to have their own budget and office space. Outflanking the ranking minority member on the committee, JACOB JAVITS of New York, Helms was able to put together a staff that served his interests. This became apparent during the committee's finalization of the Strategic Arms Limitation Talks treaty of 1979 (SALT II) between the United States and the Soviet Union, which Helms strongly opposed. According to one observer, the relationship between the majority and minority staffs became so adversarial that the situation resembled that of a courtroom.

Between the time Carter left office in 1981 and Helms's decision in 2002 not to seek reelection, his power on Capitol Hill continued to grow. From 1981 to 1987, he was chair of the Agriculture Committee. He was the ranking Republican member of the Foreign Relations Committee from 1987 to 1995 and, beginning in 1995, chair of the committee. There were indications that he had begun to soften his ultraconservatism in his last years in the Senate, befriending Secretary of State MADELEINE ALBRIGHT during the Clinton administration as well as rock singer Bono, and agreeing to debt relief for poor countries and—in a turnaround for the senator—funding for AIDS research and prevention in Africa. Nevertheless, he showed little deviation from the positions he had taken before and during the Carter presidency. He continued to make statements, for example, that most government officials found outrageous. After a raucous reception during a visit to Mexico in 1986, he remarked, "All Latins are volatile people. Hence, I was not surprised at the volatile reaction." Commenting on providing help to African countries to deal with an AIDS epidemic, he commented the next year, "The only way to stop AIDS is to stop the disgusting and immoral activities that continue to spread the disease." And, noting

President Bill Clinton's unpopularity in North Carolina in 1994, he stated, "Mr. Clinton better watch out if he comes down here. He'd better have a bodyguard."

Helms also forced a reorganization that consolidated the Arms Control and Disarmament Agency and the U.S. Information Agency into the State Department. He won approval of the Helms-Burton Act of 1996 that tightened the U.S. embargo against Cuba by penalizing third-party nations for pursuing trade with Cuba. In 1997, he single-handedly prevented the appointment of former governor William Weld (R-Mass.) as ambassador to Mexico by refusing to hold a hearing on the nomination after noting that Weld was soft on drugs. Helms also attempted to eliminate the National Endowment for the Arts (NEA) because he believed many of the beneficiaries of NEA grants were contemptuous of traditional moral standards, and he fought against increased funding in the United States to fight AIDS on the grounds that such federally supported programs encouraged homosexual behavior.

By the time Helms left the Senate in January 2003, he was in declining health, having recently undergone open-heart surgery to replace a heart valve. In recent years, he has been diagnosed with prostate cancer and Paget's disease, a rare bone disease. He recently published his memoirs, *Where I Stand* (2005).

Hufstedler, Shirley Mount

(1925–) *secretary of education*

Shirley Mount Hufstedler was the first secretary of the new Department of Education, which was established during the Carter presidency. A federal judge from California, she was appointed to the position by President Carter because he liked her judicial decisions on bilingual education. She agreed to accept the post because Carter said she would be his first appointment to the U.S. Supreme Court. Unfortunately for her, the president never had the opportunity to make an appointment to the Court.

Hufstedler was born in Denver, Colorado, on August 24, 1925. The daughter of a construction worker and a schoolteacher, she received her undergraduate degree in business administration from the University of New Mexico (B.B.A., 1945) in two and half years. She then worked briefly for the actors Paulette Goddard and Burgess Meredith before enrolling at Stanford University Law School, where she graduated 10th in her class (LL.B., 1949). She was also the first woman to be elected to the *Stanford Law Review*. After graduating from Stanford, she practiced law in Los Angeles until 1960, when she was appointed special legal counsel to the state's attorney general. Her work involved mainly issues relating to the diversion of water from the Colorado River. The complex litigation ended in a suit before the U.S. Supreme Court.

In 1961, California governor Edmund "Pat" Brown appointed Hufstedler to the bench of the Los Angeles Superior Court, a position to which she was elected in 1962. In 1966, Governor Brown elevated her to the California Court of Appeals. In 1968, President Lyndon Johnson named her to the U.S. Ninth Circuit Court of Appeals, a position she held until 1979, when President Carter appointed her secretary of education. She was described by her colleagues as a vivacious person and able jurist who usually took a liberal position in the more than 100 decisions she wrote each year. She has described herself as "independent minded" and not "a political creature."

During the 1976 election, candidate Carter had promised that, if elected, he would establish a new Department of Education, something that the powerful National Education Association (NEA), which had endorsed Carter for president, had been wanting for years. In 1975, the NEA joined forces with other unions to form the Labor Coalition Clearinghouse to lobby on behalf of the new cabinet-level agency. Its purpose would be to bring disparate programs scattered throughout the government under one administrative agency and thereby make those programs more efficient. Senator ABRAHAM RIBICOFF (D-Conn.) had been working on the formation of a department since the 1960s, when he was secretary of health, education, and welfare (HEW), under President John F. Kennedy.

There was, however, strong opposition to establishing a separate Department of Education. Within the administration, HEW secretary JOSEPH CALIFANO strongly opposed taking the expanse of educational programs that his department administered and putting them in a separate agency. He was also against establishing a national testing program by which the achievement of elementary and secondary school children would be measured. "My concern with both these proposals stemmed from a fear that they threatened to breach the healthy limits of federal involvement in education," he later wrote. "I also thought they gave insufficient weight to the wisdom, in a diverse democracy, of keeping primary responsibility for elementary and secondary education on states and local communities."

On Capitol Hill, many lawmakers considered a new education agency an additional and unnecessary layer of bureaucracy in the federal government and a threat to local and state control of education. Carter had similar misgivings although he decided after much deliberation to make good on his campaign promise by endorsing department status for education. But even with his support, it was not until 1979 that both the House and the Senate were able to pass the implementing legislation.

In announcing his appointment of Hufstedler as his first secretary of education, the president said he wanted "a strong, creative thinker and someone not a creature of the education lobby in Washington." His announcement of an individual with no experience in education or administration met a lukewarm reception. "She is rather a curious choice, but we are going to keep an open mind," commented Phyllis Franck of the American Federation of Teachers. Officials of the NEA said they would take a "wait-and-see position." The chairman of the Senate Subcommittee on Education, Claiborne Pell of Rhode Island, wondered whether she had "management and organization" skills to administer a department of 17,000 employees and a budget of $14.2 billion. In response to her critics, Hufstedler insisted that her "lifelong interest" in education qualified her for the position.

Taking office as the first secretary of education on November 30, 1974, Hufstedler had by law only six months to get the new department up and running by its official establishment date of May 4, 1980. She also had to set the agency's agenda. In line with the president's goal of streamlining government, she reduced the red tape for all federal programs to local schools. In a message intended for the NEA, she made clear that she intended to focus on the students' needs and not on special interest groups' requests. She also made clear that the new department would not replace local educational practices and objectives with federal goals. Instead, she sought to foster the establishment of local-level coalitions to identify and promote "local success models" that could be applied across the country. Hufstedler was also a strong proponent of bilingual education, although she did concede that efforts at bilingualism, which consisted of a series of initiatives at all levels of government to cope with the 3.5 million schoolchildren who came from families in which English was not the primary language, needed improvement. Along these lines, she stressed the need for all branches of education to change with the new needs of their students, and she envisioned the Department of Education as an agency that would be proactive rather than reactive. "The education institutions of the U.S.," she stated, "*must* change in response to the changing needs of the nation."

Following Carter's defeat in the 1980 election, Hufstedler established a private law practice in Los Angeles. From 1992 to 1997, she served as chair of the U.S. Commission on Immigration Reform, established by the U.S. House Subcommittee on Immigration and Claims. The commission's major conclusion was that there was a need to consolidate the diffusion of responsibility for immigration that was scattered across federal agencies into fewer agencies without creating a new cabinet-level department or super-agency on immigration affairs.

In 1995, Hufstedler became the first woman to receive the American Bar Association's ABA Medal, the organization's highest award. She is senior counsel with the law firm of Morrison and Foerster.

Humphrey, Hubert Horatio

(1911–1978) *member of the Senate*

One of the dominant political figures in U.S. politics from the end of World War II until his death in 1978, former vice president and Democratic presidential nominee Hubert H. Humphrey was a valuable ally of President Carter in the U.S. Senate during the last year of Humphrey's life. Fearing the Minnesota senator as a possible rival for the Democratic presidential nomination in 1976, Carter delivered political barbs against him as a candidate. But Humphrey became one of the president's closest friends and most candid advisers on Capitol Hill, and his death from cancer deprived Carter of what might have been a valuable resource in his dealings with a contentious Congress.

The son of a druggist, Humphrey was born in Wallace, South Dakota, on May 27, 1911, and grew up in Doland, South Dakota. Valedictorian of his high school class, he seemed destined to follow in his father's footsteps when the Great Depression forced him to leave the University of Minnesota in order to take a six-month course in pharmacy at Capitol College of Pharmacy in Denver and then work in his father's store in Huron, South Dakota. But he decided after five years to return to the University of Minnesota and complete his college degree, hoping for a career in higher education.

After graduating magna cum laude (B.A., 1939) and then doing graduate work in political science at Louisiana State University (M.A., 1937), Humphrey went back to the University of Minnesota to teach and work on his Ph.D. in political science. He never finished his degree. Married and soon to become a father for the first time, he instead went to work for the War Production Administration.

Humphrey had a passion for politics. His father had been active in South Dakota Democratic politics, he had been a star debater in high school and college, and he had written his master's thesis on "The Political Philosophy of the New Deal." With little prodding from his professors, he became active in the Democratic Party and established ties with the state's more radical Farm-Labor Party. In 1943, he narrowly lost the mayoral race in Minneapolis. Following the race, he convinced Democrats to merge with the Farm-Laborites to form the Democratic-Farmer-Labor Party (DFL), and in 1944, he became the state campaign chairman of the united party.

Over the next five years, Humphrey became one of the rising stars of the Democratic Party. Elected mayor of Minneapolis in 1945 and reelected by the largest majority in the city's history to that time, he was one of the founders in 1947 of Americans for Democratic

Action (ADA), an organization of largely Democratic liberals like himself. He also helped purge the DFL of its procommunist elements. At the 1948 Democratic Party Convention in Philadelphia, he delivered a stirring speech in defense of a minority plank on civil rights that propelled him into the national limelight. As a result of his speech, in which Humphrey spoke about the need to replace "states' rights with human rights," the delegates voted to substitute for the party's timid majority plank his much stronger minority plank. This led to a walkout of southern delegates from the convention hall and the formation of the Dixiecrat Party, but it contributed to President Harry Truman's victory in 1948. It also helped get Humphrey elected to the U.S. Senate that same year.

At first ostracized by southern conservatives for his performance at the Democratic Convention and by other senior lawmakers offended by the talkative Minnesotan who did not seem to know his place as a junior senator, Humphrey's jocularity and conviviality began to win over even those opposed to him ideologically. A fellow member of the talented class of 1948, RUSSELL LONG (D-La.), became a close friend and helped him break the ice with other southerners. In the Senate, Humphrey introduced measures that spanned the gamut of liberal legislative priorities for the next 20 years. Among the measures he introduced were proposals for national health insurance, food stamps, a nuclear test ban, arms control, civil rights legislation, increased Social Security benefits, aid for school construction, an accident-prevention bureau in the Department of Labor, and expansion of the Social Security system.

In 1960, now recognized as a leader of the liberal wing of the Democratic Party, Humphrey ran for president but was outmaneuvered and outspent by the handsome and telegenic junior senator from Massachusetts, John F. Kennedy, who went on to win the presidency against RICHARD NIXON. Much of Kennedy's legislative agenda, such as the Peace Corps, Food for Peace, the Jobs Corps, and the Limited Nuclear Test Ban Treaty were ideas first pioneered by Humphrey. Reelected to the Senate in 1960, Humphrey was appointed Democratic whip in 1961. In 1964, he was able to cajole enough Republican senators to break the southern filibuster against the 1964 Civil Rights Act, which he considered his greatest achievement. That same year, President Lyndon Johnson named Humphrey as his running mate on the Democratic presidential ticket.

The next four years were difficult ones for Humphrey. Although elected vice president as a result of Johnson's smashing 1964 victory, he was treated disparagingly by the president, who demanded absolute loyalty from his vice president. Yet Johnson largely ignored Humphrey and, on occasion, humiliated him after he spoke out against unleashing U.S. airpower against the communists in North Vietnam in 1965. Having learned his lesson, Humphrey became a staunch public defender of the war in Vietnam.

Although the growing unpopularity of the Vietnamese conflict led Johnson to decide in April 1968 not to seek reelection, his heir apparent, the vice president, still had to contend with a serious challenge for the Democratic nomination from New York senator Robert Kennedy and from his fellow Minnesota senator, Eugene McCarthy. Even though Kennedy's assassination in June 1968 virtually assured the nomination for Humphrey, the growing antiwar movement threatened to undermine the vice president's chances to replace Johnson in the Oval Office. In August, the disastrous convention in Chicago—when police chased down antiwar protesters with police sticks, and tear gas penetrated into the convention halls—seemed to undermine any chance Humphrey had of beating the Republican presidential candidate, former vice president Nixon.

In a speech in Salt Lake City on September 30, however, Humphrey promised to stop the bombing of North Vietnam and institute a cease-fire if elected. The campaign turned around, and an energized Humphrey closed the gap separating him from Nixon. On the eve of the election, the outcome was a toss-up, but the next day Nixon won by one of the smallest majorities in any presidential election, 43.4 percent for Nixon, 42.7 percent for Humphrey, and 13.5 percent for Alabama governor GEORGE WALLACE, who ran as the candidate of the American Independent Party.

Following the election, Humphrey taught at the University of Minnesota and Macalaster College. At first he decided not to seek office again, but he changed his mind when Eugene McCarthy announced that he would not seek reelection to the Senate. In 1970, Humphrey won the DFL nomination and then went on to win McCarthy's seat. In 1972, he ran again for the Democratic nomination for president, but changes in the party rules increased the importance of the primaries in selecting delegates to the party convention. He therefore lost the nomination to South Dakota senator GEORGE MCGOVERN, who beat him in several of the primaries, including the crucial one in California. That November, McGovern was crushed by President Nixon.

Although defeated three times for president, Humphrey's standing never was higher among Democrats and his colleagues on Capitol Hill than it was in the last five years of his life. Always undaunted, upbeat, and optimistic, he remained throughout his career a crusader for the oppressed, the neglected, and the poor. The sincerity of his commitment to the underprivileged was unquestioned even by those who opposed him ideologically.

For that reason, in 1976 the liberal wing of the Democratic Party looked to Humphrey to challenge Jimmy Carter, whose drive for the nomination seemed unstoppable following his victory over Washington senator HENRY JACKSON in the Pennsylvania primary in April. Warily awaiting a Humphrey challenge in the New Jersey primary, Carter took some strong stabs at the Minnesota senator, referring to him as a has-been and loser whose brokered nomination in 1968 had left the Democratic Party in disarray. After considerable hesitation, however, Humphrey decided not to enter the race, saying a fourth try for the presidency would be "ridiculous—and the one thing I don't need at this stage of my life is to be ridiculous." Deprived of the office he had always wanted, he nonetheless took great pride when, after the Democrats chose Carter as their nominee, the Georgian decided on Humphrey's protégé, Senator WALTER MONDALE of Minnesota, as his running mate.

By the time Humphrey decided not to run in the New Jersey primary, he was already suffering health problems. In 1976, he had to have surgery to remove a cancerous bladder that had first been diagnosed and apparently treated successfully in 1973. Later he had to have another serious operation. Despite the two surgeries, he was easily reelected to the Senate in November 1976. By the time he began his new term in January 1977, Humphrey was gaunt and terminally ill with cancer. Recognizing how sick he was, his Senate colleagues created a new post for him, deputy president pro tem of the Senate, which carried with it an increase in salary, a limousine, and a Capitol office.

During his last year of life, Humphrey drew unusually close to Carter, whom he had first met while he was vice president. He became, in fact, the president's most valuable ally in the Senate, a place where Carter had few friends and allies. "You know we hated this fellow," Carter's chief aide, HAMILTON JORDAN, commented. "Now we love him. This is the greatest man alive."

The irony of the alliance was that Humphrey represented precisely the old-style type of Washington politics and the very kind of social entitlement programs against which Carter had campaigned. The senator, moreover, did not retreat from his lifelong liberal beliefs. At the first leadership breakfast at the White House, Humphrey bombarded the president with memos on foreign aid, energy, more schools for Native Americans, and even one on relief for honey producers. He also objected to the White House's concerns about congressional spending and the dangers of inflation.

Humphrey's approach to the president, however, was that of one friend speaking to another, and Carter responded with deference, frequently calling him on the telephone to ask for his advice. In April 1977, Humphrey was able to persuade Carter to retract the $50 tax rebate that he had proposed. As deputy president pro tem of the Senate, he also kept Carter out of trouble on a number of other pieces of legislation, and he pushed through an unpopular and embattled foreign-aid measure. In addition, he battled frequently with Federal Reserve Board chairman ARTHUR BURNS, on whom he blamed the nation's economic ills. "Every time you get the economy moving," he told the president, "Arthur Burns raises interest rates and slams on the brakes." Humphrey's protests were one reason why Carter decided not to keep Burns on as chairman.

In October, Carter stopped in Minnesota to pick up Humphrey in Air Force One after another operation for cancer and return him to Washington. He also joined in a large dinner for the projected Hubert Humphrey Institute of Public Affairs. Out of respect for the Minnesota senator, the president invited him (the weekend of December 10–11) to Camp David, where the two men spoke for more than two hours, the first time Humphrey had ever been to Camp David.

On December 22, Vice President Mondale took Humphrey back to Minnesota on Air Force Two. On January 13, 1978, Humphrey died in his home in Waverly at the age of 66. His body was returned to Washington to lie in state in the Capitol's rotunda. At his funeral, President Carter delivered one of many eulogies. "It was not in his nature to forget how to love," the president said. "He has given me freely what I need: the support and understanding of a close and true friend, the advice of a wise and honest counselor."

Hussein I
(Hussein ibn Talal Ibn Hussein)
(1935–1999) *king of Jordan*

King Hussein I ruled Jordan for 46 years, the longest reigning monarch of recent times prior to his death in 1999. Although President Carter greatly admired Hussein, he was disappointed when the Jordanian king not only refused to participate in the peace process begun with the Camp David accords of 1978 but broke off relations with Egypt following its peace treaty with Israel in 1979.

Hussein was born in Amman, Jordan, on November 14, 1935. Although most often known simply as King Hussein I of Jordan, his full name was Hussein ibn Talal Ibn Hussein. The scion of an illustrious Hashemite family and supposedly descended from the Prophet Mohammed, Hussein was the grandson of King Abdulllah, who was one of the first Arab leaders to fight against the Turkish army during World War I. Afterward, he established the Hashemite kingdom of Transjordan. In 1946, Transjordan gained its complete independence from Britain and was renamed Jordan. When Abdullah was killed outside the Al Aqsa mosque in Jerusalem in 1951, Hussein's father briefly held the throne, but he was forced to step aside because of a mental illness. At age

15, Hussein was named Jordan's new monarch, but because of his age, Jordan was actually run by a regency council. As a young man, Hussein was educated at Harrow and the famed Royal Military Academy at Sandhurst in Britain, where he learned military principles and attitudes.

On May 2, 1953, Hussein assumed his position as king. At the time he took over the monarchy, he had the reputation of being a playboy. "The King and country were alike," wrote John Newhouse in a *New Yorker* profile in 1983, "young, inexperienced, poor, and unpromising." Yet Hussein proved to be a skillful political leader who managed to survive 12 separate assassination attempts on his life. His early years on the throne were spent trying to win the support of his countrymen, especially the Bedouin, and staving off personal threats to his life by would-be assassins. He also had to navigate through the dangerous shoals of Arab politics. Making his task even more difficult were his efforts at strengthening ties with the West, especially with the United States, Israel's strongest supporter and therefore maligned throughout much of the Arab world.

In 1967, Hussein made what he later regarded as a major blunder by participating with other Arab countries in the Six-Day War with Israel. Warned by Israel not to engage in the conflict and knowing Jordan was not fully prepared militarily for war, Hussein nevertheless feared that unless he joined with other Arab leaders against Israel, he might provoke civil war in his own country. Accordingly, the Jordanians went to war against Israel and lost the whole west bank of the Jordan River and East Jerusalem. Afterward, Hussein helped formulate UN Resolution 242 calling for Israeli withdrawal from all the occupied territories in return for Arab acknowledgment of Israel's right to exist as a nation with secure and recognized boundaries. Although failing to get the Israelis to withdraw from the occupied territories, UN Resolution 242 became the basis for all subsequent efforts at peace in the Middle East.

The years that followed the end of the Six-Day War continued to be dangerous ones for Hussein. In a nation that was predominantly Palestinian, he had to endure repeated attacks after 1970 by fighters organized as the Palestine Liberation Organization (PLO), headed by YASSER ARAFAT and supported by Syrian troops and tanks. In a civil war known as Black September, however, Hussein was able to drive the Palestinians out of Jordan and into neighboring Lebanon. During the Yom Kippur War of 1973, Hussein provided only limited support to Egypt and Syria. In response, the Arab League decided to recognize the PLO as the sole representative of the Palestinian people.

In the years that followed the end of the war, Jordan enjoyed an economic boom fed in part by moneys brought into the country by Jordanians providing military and technical support to the oil-rich Arab countries, whose own fortunes swelled during these years. Hussein also received grants and financial concessions from these same oil-laden nations. Yet he remained a leader torn in two directions. Educated in England, well versed in Western culture, and realizing the support that Israel enjoyed in Europe and the United States, he sought to maintain good relations with the West and to reach an accommodation with Israel along the lines of UN Resolution 242. An Arab himself, head of a country the majority of whose population was Palestinian, and dependent on his Arab friends for economic support, however, he needed to be acutely sensitive to how his actions would be perceived by other Arab states.

The difficult road Hussein had to follow ultimately disappointed President Jimmy Carter, who, when he took office, regarded Hussein as the most moderate of the Arab leaders and anticipated working closely with

President Carter, King Hussein of Jordan, Shah of Iran Mohammad Reza Pahlavi, and Shahbanou of Iran Farah Pahlavi, 1977 *(Jimmy Carter Library)*

him to bring about a settlement of the decades-old Arab-Israeli conflict. Even when it became clear that Egypt's ANWAR SADAT, and not Hussein, would take the initiative in trying to end the Arab-Israeli dispute, Carter still looked to Hussein to back Egypt's efforts to reach a Middle East settlement and sign a peace treaty with Israel. At the end of December 1977, he traveled to the Middle East and met with Hussein in Amman. Although Carter had hoped to involve the Jordanian leader in the peace process begun by Sadat, the king made it clear that he would not participate in negotiations until Israel withdrew from the occupied lands and agreed to Palestinian autonomy.

Hussein held to this position even after Sadat and Israeli prime minister MENACHEM BEGIN signed the 1978 Camp David accords establishing a "framework for peace" in the Middle East. Even more frustrating to Carter was Hussein's reaction after Cairo signed its historic peace agreement with Israel in spring 1979. The Jordanian leader held an emergency meeting of his cabinet and then called for implementation of economic measures against Egypt. He was also the first Arab leader to break his country's diplomatic ties with Egypt. The White House responded by refusing to sell Jordan 300 American tanks equipped with a special, highly advanced technology for night-vision targeting.

This marked a new low in Jordan's relations with Washington. When Hussein came to the United States at the end of September 1979 in order to address the United Nations, he refused even to come to Washington to see the president. For the remainder of Carter's administration, he continued to hold to the position that he would not enter the peace process until Israel returned the West Bank and East Jerusalem, a condition that the Israelis would never accept.

Even after Carter left office in 1981, Hussein remained torn in two directions. In 1994, he finally signed a peace treaty at the White House with Israeli prime minister Yitzhak Rabin, ending Jordan's 46-year state of war with Israel. He also acknowledged that the Six-Day War with Israel in 1967 had been a mistake. At the same time, he did not object when Saddam Hussein, who had been a close personal friend, attempted to take over Kuwait in 1990. Although he remained neutral at the beginning of the Persian Gulf War that followed, he openly supported Hussein during the conflict.

Although King Hussein's opposition to the 1991 Persian Gulf War tarnished his image in the United States, he still remained, after Sadat's assassination in 1981, the most popular Arab leader among Americans. This was partly due to his marriage to a young and beautiful American woman, Queen Noor, the former Lisa Halaby, a graduate of Princeton University who was Hussein's fourth wife. He also distanced himself from Saddam, stating that it was time for the Iraqis to embrace Democratic rule and end Saddam's dictatorship.

In 1992, Hussein was stricken with non-Hodgkin's lymphoma. He spent six months in 1998 at the Mayo Clinic in Rochester, Minnesota, undergoing an unsuccessful bone marrow transplant. He also spent the last months of his life trying to advance peace between Israel and the Arab world and preparing for his succession. In a surprise move, he named his 37-year-old son Abdullah as his successor over his 51-year-old younger brother Prince Hassan. In a bitter letter to Hassan that became public, he said his brother's supporters had tried to "destroy Jordan" by spreading vicious gossip about his wife and children.

Hussein died on February 7, 1999. He was 63 years old.

Jackson, Henry Martin

(Scoop Jackson)
(1912–1983) *member of the Senate, candidate for the Democratic presidential nomination*

A quintessential liberal, an unreconstructed cold warrior, an unflinching defender of the prerogatives of Congress, and a deep believer in human rights, Henry M. "Scoop" Jackson was one of the last of the powerful Democrats on Capitol Hill to support both interventionism abroad and social welfare at home. He was also one of President Carter's harshest critics within the Democratic Party, accusing the president of pursuing a disastrous policy of "moralism, malaise, and retrenchment."

Jackson spent almost his entire adult life in politics and never lost an election. Born in Everett, Washington, on May 31, 1912, the son of Norwegian immigrants, he attended Stanford University briefly before graduating from the University of Washington, where he received his law degree (LL.B., 1935). Three years later, he was elected prosecuting attorney of Snohomish County, and in 1940, after developing a reputation as a hard-bitten prosecutor, he won in his first bid for the U.S. House of Representatives. He was reelected five times by wide margins before running successfully for the U.S. Senate in 1952 despite a Republican landslide in the country.

As a member of the House, Jackson had quickly established his liberal credentials, voting for social-welfare measures and against the creation of the House Un-American Activities Committee. He became interested in the peacetime and military uses of atomic energy and was appointed in 1949 to the Joint Atomic Energy Committee. He also became an advocate of the nation's fledging missile program. In 1955, now Senator Jackson, he criticized President Dwight D. Eisenhower for allowing a "missile gap" to develop between the Soviet Union and the United States.

Although Jackson was elected from an historically isolationist district, World War II and his visit to the Nazi concentration camp at Buchenwald 11 days after its liberation made him an ardent internationalist and one of Capitol Hill's strongest supporters of Israel. Henceforth he practiced a type of moral realism that synthesized power and principle, infusing U.S. foreign policy with an unequivocal commitment to basic American values and demanding a constant vigilance against threats to its core beliefs; in the context of the developing cold war, this meant the Soviet Union. Believing that sometimes there was no substitute for the use of military power, he became an early proponent of the development of a hydrogen bomb, preferring to rely more on the nation's nuclear arsenal than Soviet forbearance to contain communist expansion.

While in the Senate, Jackson became close friends with another Democrat elected to the upper chamber in 1952, John F. Kennedy (Mass.). Jackson was more dedicated to his job than his friend and compiled a more liberal voting record. His primary interests, however, remained national security and foreign policy. Although a strident anticommunist himself, he helped lead the successful movement in 1954 to censure the red-baiting senator from Wisconsin, Joseph McCarthy, whose name became synonymous with demagoguery. At the same time, Jackson played a key role in developing the nuclear-powered navy. One of the few things that the Washington senator later found he had in common with Jimmy Carter was their profound respect for the father of the nuclear navy, Admiral HYMAN RICKOVER, whose naval career Jackson helped save.

Throughout the 1950s and 1960s, Jackson was reelected to the Senate by wide margins. He also continued to gain a national reputation as one of the Senate's leading liberals and experts on national security matters. At the same time, he began to feel increasingly marginalized even within his own party. Despite the fact that he was selected in 1960 by his close friend President-elect Kennedy to be chairperson of the Democratic National Committee, he felt ignored by Kennedy, who had chosen Texas senator Lyndon Johnson over Jackson as his running mate and then rarely consulted with Jackson on national security or foreign policy issues. He nearly broke with the White House and most other Democrats by almost voting against the 1963 nuclear test-ban treaty before agreeing reluctantly to support it. During the Johnson administration (1963–68), his unwavering backing for the Vietnam War made him a pariah among antiwar New Left Democrats.

Jackson continued to pursue a hard-line policy during President RICHARD NIXON's first term (1969–72). Remaining steadfast in his support of the war, he opposed Nixon's policy of détente toward the Soviet Union. In 1972, he established the Coalition for a Democratic Majority (CDM), a union of Democrats favoring a strong military to counter the Soviet threat. In 1974, he shepherded the Jackson-Vanik Amendment through the Senate, which tied the easing of trade barriers against Moscow to freer passage of Jews out of the Soviet Union. Finally, he opposed the first Strategic Arms Limitation Talks agreement (SALT I) until an amendment was inserted into the pact guaranteeing in future negotiations U.S. parity with the Soviets in land-based missiles. These positions made him even more unpopular among the Democratic left. Their takeover of the party in 1972 left him without a political mooring.

Not understanding the sea change taking place within his own party, Jackson sought the Democratic nomination for president in both 1972 and 1976. Of the two campaigns, the latter was the more viable. In 1972, he was still not that well-known nationally and the Democrats had not yet experienced the repudiation of their nominee, Senator GEORGE MCGOVERN (S.Dak.), whose liberal views were regarded as extremist even among Democrats. Because Jackson had gained considerable national exposure since 1972 as a result of his ongoing campaign against President Richard Nixon's détente policy, and McGovern had been overwhelmingly rejected by the voters, Jackson had reason to believe that his second effort at gaining the Democratic nomination would be more well-received. He saw in McGovern's overwhelming defeat an opportunity to rebuild the Democratic Party along time-honored liberal lines. Expecting considerable support from traditional Democratic constituencies, including strong backing from organized labor, white ethnics, and the influential Jewish community in highly populated states like Massachusetts, New York, and Florida because of his strong support of Israel, Jackson announced his candidacy in February 1975.

Early in the race, Jackson was perceived by some political pundits as the front-runner for the Democratic nomination; certainly that seemed the case if Senator EDWARD KENNEDY (Mass.) decided not to run. A Gallup poll ranked the Washington senator among the 10 most admired people in the world for 1973, and President GERALD FORD thought Jackson would be his strongest challenger. The senator was featured in stories by the nation's leading news magazines and journals of opinion.

Jackson, however, was never able to translate his popularity in his home state into a comparable national following. Many of the same obstacles that had confronted him in 1972 faced him again in 1976. He did not understand the importance of television in a modern campaign. His unassuming appearance lack of charisma, and dry, poorly cadenced delivery did not go over well even when he appeared on television. He depended too much on his own senatorial staff to help run the campaign, and his reputation as a cold warrior continued to follow him. Furthermore, his message of traditional Democratic liberalism did not resonate with a more fiscally conservative, antiauthoritarian generation of voters who worried about large budget deficits and the strong arm of government and were more concerned with personal and social values than with social-welfare programs and entitlements—in short, those voters who supported Jimmy Carter's candidacy. As a result, while Jackson was able to win primary victories in Massachusetts and New York, he failed to win in the key primary states of Florida and Pennsylvania. Following his loss to Carter in Pennsylvania in April 1976, he withdrew from the campaign.

After Jackson bowed out of the race, he and Carter tried to put the difficult primary campaigns, in which they had exchanged bitter barbs, behind them. Jackson refused, for example, to participate in a "Stop Carter" movement following his defeat in Pennsylvania. At the Democratic convention in New York in July, he released his delegates to Carter, and Jackson was one of six names that Carter considered for his vice-presidential candidate. After Carter was elected in November, he invited Jackson to Plains for a series of meetings on energy policy and followed his recommendation to establish a new Department of Energy headed by JAMES SCHLESINGER, who had worked with Jackson in his struggle against détente during the Nixon and Ford administrations. As the chair of two important committees (Government Operations and Energy and Natural Resources) and a leading member of a third (Armed Services), and as the Senate's leading expert on national defense, Jackson expected to play an influential role during the Carter administration and to be consulted frequently by the White House.

Of the nine presidents, from Franklin Roosevelt to RONALD REAGAN, under whom Jackson served, however, his worst relationship was with Carter. Notwithstanding the efforts by both men to get along after the senator gave up his quest for the presidency, Jackson still held Carter in low regard. In private conversations with Jackson, whose nomination he had seconded at the Democratic convention in 1972, Carter had excoriated McGovern. But after McGovern received the nomination, the governor called Jackson to solicit his help in getting Carter the vice-presidential nomination. Jackson never forgot, nor forgave, Carter for what he considered his duplicitous character and venal ambition.

To the extent that Jackson was part of the very Washington political establishment against which the new president had run, moreover, the two leaders were bound to clash. Little effort was made by the White House in the first few months of the administration to cultivate good relations with Jackson or other top Democrats, most of whom found Carter's staff to be arrogant and aloof. The president's decision to kill 19 water projects because he considered them pork annoyed most lawmakers on Capitol Hill, but especially those from the West, like Jackson, for whom plentiful supplies of water were essential to their states' economies.

Most important, the president and the senator were ideologically and politically opposites. In contrast to Jackson's commitment to traditional liberal values and programs, Carter was determined to cut government spending at the expense of entitlement programs. Unlike the president, Jackson's solution for rising unemployment rates was to use federal dollars to create jobs programs akin to the Works Progress Administration of the 1930s. On the energy crisis that plagued the administration through most of Carter's four years in office, Jackson blamed the crisis not on cheap oil and the lack of alternative energy resources, as the White House did, but on the big oil companies. His solution, therefore, was not to drive the price of energy higher in order to conserve fuel but to urge price controls and a federal bureaucracy to administer them.

On national security policy, Jackson fought unrelentingly against what he regarded as the administration's neglect of military preparedness. He was annoyed that Carter rejected all but two of a list of 53 candidates for office in national security affairs that the CDM, which he and senator DANIEL PATRICK MOYNIHAN (D-N.Y.) cochaired, had delivered to the White House. He denounced the president's decision, soon after taking office, to reduce U.S. forces in South Korea by 32,000 ground troops. He responded in a similar way to Carter's firing of General John K. Singlaub, the third-ranking army officer in Korea, for criticizing that decision.

Similarly, Jackson spoke out against the president's announcement in June 1977 that he was scrapping the B-1 bomber program, which had been intended to replace the nation's aging fleet of B-52s. In 1978, Jackson and SAM NUNN (D-Ga.) tried unsuccessfully to reverse Carter's decision to forego the neutron bomb, which was intended to destroy Soviet tanks in Western Europe in case of an attack without causing extensive civilian damage. They charged that the president's decision not to deploy the weapon undermined the United States' credibility with its West European allies. Also in 1978, Jackson expressed disgust when UN ambassador ANDREW YOUNG defended the role of Cuban troops on the African continent on the grounds of providing a degree of order and stability in that troubled region. The Washington senator was equally troubled by the president's decision in August 1978 to veto the fiscal year 1979 military authorization bill that had provided funding for an additional nuclear aircraft carrier.

A strong advocate of human rights, Jackson took the administration to task for not applying its human rights policy uniformly, enforcing it in the case of right-wing governments in Latin America but ignoring what he felt were more serious human rights violations by the Soviet Union. He believed in this regard that Carter and Secretary of State CYRUS VANCE had failed to grasp the interplay of power and ideals. He described Vance as "the closest thing to a pacifist the U.S. had ever had as secretary of state, with the possible exception of William Jennings Bryan."

Not surprisingly, Jackson found his own views on national security and foreign policy much closer to those of the president's National Security Advisor, ZBIGNIEW BRZEZINSKI, the title of whose memoirs, *Power and Principle*, perfectly matched Jackson's own thoughts on the subject. Like Brzezinski, the senator was a strong advocate of normalizing relations with the People's Republic of China (PRC) as a foil to Soviet expansionism. (Jackson had been advocating improving relations with the PRC since as early as 1966, and his death in 1983 came just two weeks after he had returned from his fourth visit to China, where he had met with China's leader, DENG XIAOPING.)

The great divide between Jackson and Carter, however, was over the SALT II negotiations and agreement. From the time that PAUL WARNKE was nominated by the president in 1977 to be the chief negotiator in arms talks with the Soviet Union, the Washington senator kept up an unremitting drumfire against a second SALT agreement on the grounds that it would weaken the United States' defense posture An adviser to McGovern on national security issues during the 1972 campaign, Warnke represented, in Jackson's view, the flaccid underbelly of U.S. foreign policy, a diplomat who blamed the arms race on the United States and not the Soviet Union, who dismissed nuclear superiority as not all that consequential as long as either superpower maintained a minimal nuclear deterrent, and an official who argued that the best way to assure Soviet nuclear restraint was for the United States to serve first as a model of restraint.

As chair of the Armed Services Subcommittee on Arms Control, Jackson monitored the negotiations for a SALT II treaty and strongly criticized the resulting document, which, he maintained, was dangerously disadvantageous to the United States. The agreement provided for a beginning cap of 2,400 strategic launchers (to be phased down by 10 percent to 2,160 over the term of the proposed treaty) and 1,320 multiple independently targetable reentry vehicles (MIRVs). These were the same figures that resulted from a meeting between former president Gerald Ford and Soviet president LEONID BREZHNEV at Vladivostok in 1974. But what Jackson objected to were the subceilings that limited the number of air- and sea-launched cruise missiles (ALCMs and SLCMs, the United States's operational missiles of choice) while doing virtually nothing to reduce the Soviets' advantage on MIRVd heavy land-based missiles. In particular, he was taken aback by the cut of more than 50 percent in the number of ALCMs. This meant a reduction in the number of deliverable warheads from between 3,000 and 5,000 before SALT II to between 1,440 and 2,400 if the Senate ratified the agreement. Although President Carter withdrew the treaty from Senate consideration following the Soviet Union's invasion of Afghanistan in December 1979, it is quite probable that opponents of the pact, led by Jackson, Nunn, and John Tower (R-Tex.) would have been able to defeat it even without the Afghan invasion.

When Jackson died unexpectedly on September 1, 1983, of a massive heart attack, his health had seemed excellent, but his influence had been on the wane. His presidential ambitions shattered by age and by his two unsuccessful bids for the Democratic nomination, he made his influence felt on the national stage by his leadership role on Capitol Hill. But, stripped of chairing important Senate committees as a result of the Republican landslide in 1980, his influence was greatly diminished. The term *liberal*, with which he had always been proud to identify, had become a term of scorn and rebuke.

Oddly enough, Jackson's views on national security received a warmer reception during the Reagan years than they had during the Carter administration. President Reagan, in fact, adopted many of Jackson's ideas and some of his people. Former Jackson Democrats, relabeled "neoconservatives," who served the Reagan administration included UN ambassador Jeane Kirkpatrick, Undersecretary of Defense Richard Perle, and Undersecretary of

State Elliot Abrams. On June 14, 1984, President Reagan awarded Jackson the Presidential Medal of Freedom posthumously.

Jackson, Jesse Louis

(1941–) *civil rights leader, minister*

Although Jesse Jackson did not become the nation's foremost African-American political activist until the 1980s, he was by 1976 already an accomplished civil rights leader and major figure among African Americans. He played an important role in helping Jimmy Carter get elected president in 1976 and enjoyed considerable influence within the administration.

Jackson was born in Greenville, South Carolina, on October 8, 1941, the illegitimate son of a poor teenage mother. At the age of two, however, he was adopted by Charles Jackson, who married his mother, Helen Burns, and gave the boy his surname. Jackson was an excellent student and athlete. He graduated at the top of his high-school class and won a football scholarship to the University of Illinois, but after learning that blacks were not eligible to be quarterbacks, he returned to the South to complete his education at North Carolina Agricultural and Technical College (North Carolina A&T), graduating with a degree in sociology (B.S., 1964). An historically African-American college in Greensboro, North Carolina, A&T attracted national attention in 1960 when four of its students launched what became a series of sit-down demonstrations at Woolworth lunch counters throughout the South. While there, Jackson became active in the Civil Rights movement and was elected student body president. In 1963, police arrested him after he led a protest march in Greensboro. That summer, he also participated in the March on Washington, where Martin Luther King, Jr., delivered his famous "I have a dream" speech.

Following graduation, Jackson was named field representative for the southeast region of the Congress on Racial Equality (CORE). In fall 1964, he decided to attend the Chicago Theological Seminary on a Rockefeller grant, but he left before graduation to work with Martin Luther King's Southern Christian Leadership Conference (SCLC). In 1965, he marched alongside King in Selma, Alabama. He also headed the Chicago branch of Operation Breadbasket, an effort to get white businessmen to promote jobs for blacks in Chicago by boycotting businesses that exploited blacks. In 1966, King appointed Jackson as the national director of Operation Breadbasket. Jackson was also with King on April 4, 1968, when the civil rights leader was assassinated while standing on the balcony of the Hotel Lorraine in Memphis, Tennessee.

The day after the assassination, Jackson appeared on national television describing how he had held the bloodied head of the dying King and heard his last words. He even held a turtleneck jersey covered in blood that he said he was wearing when King died. Many believed that Jackson would replace King as the nation's foremost African-American leader. Jackson was driven, ambitious, charismatic, and had a flair for oratory in the mode of King. But King's closest friend, Ralph Abernathy, and his assistant, ANDREW YOUNG, who were also with King, disputed Jackson's account of what had happened in Memphis. Young said Jackson had been with him in the parking lot of the hotel where King was staying when he was shot and that it was Abernathy who cradled King's head at the time of his death. This dispute over the events of April 4 followed Jackson throughout his career and was pointed to by his many future critics, even within the Civil Rights movement, as evidence that Jackson's driving ambition and ego sometimes trumped the truth.

Whatever happened at Memphis, Abernathy—not Jackson—replaced King as the head of the SCLC, and relations between the two men became strained. Jackson wanted to emphasize jobs for blacks in the North, while other SCLC leaders preferred to focus on race relations in the South. Despite these differences, Jackson stayed on as head of Operation Breadbasket. In June 1968, he was also ordained as a Baptist minister, but in December 1970, he resigned from the SCLC after a dispute with Abernathy, taking with him much of the SCLC's staff and its financial backing. By this time, Jackson had become recognized as one of the nation's major civil rights figures.

No longer a part of the SCLC, Jesse Jackson continued forward with his own plans, which soon included politics. He founded Operation PUSH (People United to Save Humanity) to secure jobs for minorities. Traveling around the United States, his influence within the black community continued to grow. Remaining committed to nonviolence, he drew lessons, nevertheless, from some of the more militant black groups. These included overt efforts to promote racial pride, self-help efforts, and a militant stand in demanding greater economic opportunity for minorities from the nation's largest corporations. PUSH also organized yearly expositions (EXPOS) to promote minority businesses and was not above flexing its political muscle to support candidates for office. It financed its operations through donations and generous grants from corporate America. Jackson's critics accused him of being a puppet of the very white-dominated economic and political establishment he criticized. The *New York Times* offered a different analysis: "Jackson is militant but non-violent, good copy but safe copy; radical in style, not in action."

Regardless, Jackson remained among the nation's most visible and influential African-American leaders at the start of the 1976 presidential campaign. Like other black leaders, he was astonished by remarks that Jimmy Carter, seeking the Democratic nomination for president, made in April 1976 about maintaining the "purity" of ethnic neighborhoods and preventing "alien intrusions." He called Carter's views "a throwback to Hitlerian racism." But the Georgian apologized for his remarks, and a number of black leaders, including Jackson, threw their support behind Carter, launching massive voter registration drives in black communities. Their influence with African-American voters helped Carter win the presidency in 1976.

Members of the new administration, including Secretary of Health, Education and Welfare (HEW) JOSEPH CALIFANO, who had earlier been criticized by Jackson for remarks he had made in opposition to job quotas for minorities, were greatly impressed by Jackson's emphasis on self-help and jobs for blacks. Of special note was a new program, Push for Excellence (EXCEL), which had received a $200,000 grant from the Ford Foundation and was featured on CBS's popular news program *60 Minutes* in 1968. EXCEL emphasized overcoming cultural and generational gaps by bringing parents, students, and teachers together in a common pursuit of educational excellence through hard work and mastery of basic academic skills. "I say to our young," Jackson remarked in explaining the purpose of EXCEL, "that we must turn off that television for at least three hours a night. Mental development becomes a certain kind of pressure and discipline is the key." Former vice president HUBERT HUMPHREY, a Democratic icon dying of cancer, telephoned Califano after watching the *60 Minutes* segment to express his support of EXCEL. HEW was soon awarding lucrative contracts to PUSH and EXCEL; the total amount of grants for the programs eventually totaled $5.6 million. By 1978, 500 public school districts had also invited Jackson to help them institute EXCEL programs.

In 1979, President Carter sent Jackson to South Africa, where he attracted huge crowds and denounced apartheid. He also toured the Middle East, but he offended many Americans, especially American Jews, by embracing the exiled leader of the Palestine Liberation Organization (PLO) YASSER ARAFAT, still considered a terrorist by the American government. Conversely, Jackson joined about 200 other black leaders, including representatives from the SCLC and the National Association for the Advancement of Colored People (NAACP), in condemning the firing in August of UN ambassador Andrew Young after Young met secretly with Zehdi Labib Terzi, the UN observer for the PLO, even though the State Department explicitly prohibited official contact with the PLO. In their statement, the black leaders took aim at the American Jewish community for its rigid support of Israel and charged it with abandoning blacks on the issue of affirmative action.

Jackson's greatest impact on the American political scene, however, came after Carter was defeated for president in 1980 by RONALD REAGAN, who drastically cut back federal support for Operation PUSH, arguing accounting irregularities in PUSH's books and poor evaluations of its programs. In 1984, Jackson decided the time had come for an African American, representing the needs of the African-American community, to run for president. Although even many of his closest friends and advisers discouraged him from running, he did surprisingly well, arousing his audiences with stinging attacks on the Reagan administration for cutting back on programs for minorities and the poor and winning an impressive 3.5 million votes in the primaries.

After the campaign, Jackson formed a new organization, the National Rainbow Coalition, a diverse social justice group representing people left out of the American mainstream. In 1988, he made an even more serious presidential bid. With the help of the Rainbow Coalition, the civil rights leader won 15 primaries and caucuses and 6.7 million votes, capturing not only 95 percent of the African-American vote but about 12.5 percent of the white vote, and winning nearly a third of the delegates to the national convention.

Although Jackson lost the nomination to Massachusetts governor Michael Dukakis, he electrified the delegates with one of the great convention speeches in recent history and made clear that it was possible for an African American to win a presidential nomination. Interestingly, former president Carter's old friend and former director of the Office of Management and Budget, BERT LANCE—who had been booed at the 1984 Democratic convention and felt slighted by the party's nominee that year, former vice president WALTER MONDALE—served as an unofficial adviser to Jackson in 1988.

Although Jackson decided not to run a third time for the Democratic nomination in 1992, supporting instead Governor Bill Clinton of Arkansas, his showing in the 1984 and 1988 primaries established him as the most formidable African-American leader since Martin Luther King, Jr. In subsequent years, he helped win the release of a number of hostages after Iraq's invasion of Kuwait in 1990 and lobbied for statehood for the District of Columbia. He also continued to remain politically active through his Rainbow Coalition. He led a massive voter-registration drive among African Americans, served as an adviser to President Clinton, and traveled extensively throughout the country and around the world, emphasizing economic and racial justice not only for all Americans but for oppressed groups throughout the world. In 1997, Clinton made him special envoy and secretary of state for the promotion of democracy in Africa. In 1999, he won the release of three American soldiers held as prisoners of war in Yugoslavia. In 2000, he was awarded the Presidential Medal of Freedom, the nation's highest civilian honor.

Despite his humanitarian work, a cloud has continued to hang over Jackson. He has always traveled first class; earned a large yearly income, the sources of which have not always been clear; and lived comfortably—too comfortably, claim his critics who have even accused him of taking bribes from potential targets of his operations. His meeting with Arafat in 1979, offensive remarks he made in 1984 about Jews (for which he later apologized), his close ties to Louis Farrakhan, the Nation of Islam leader who has also spoken disparagingly about Jews, and his characterization of Jews in the 1988 presidential campaign as "Hymies" and New York as "Hymietown" have all raised questions about whether Jackson harbors anti-Semitic feelings. His critics have also maintained that personal ambition and a quest for self-aggrandizement, more than humanitarianism or concern for the downtrodden or oppressed, have always been Jackson's primary motivations.

These are not mutually exclusive goals, however, and the fact remains that for over 30 years, Jackson has been an influential public figure. Notwithstanding his faults, moreover, his concern for the less fortunate and for those who cannot speak for themselves has been inspirational for millions of Americans and others across the world. It is not surprising, therefore, that for the past 10 years Jackson has been on the Gallup list of the 10 most respected Americans.

Jackson, Maynard Holbrook, Jr.

(1938–2003) *mayor of Atlanta*

Mayor Maynard Jackson of Atlanta was one of three African Americans elected in 1973 as mayors of three of the largest cities in the nation (the others being Tom Bradley of Los Angeles and COLEMAN YOUNG of Detroit). As mayor of Atlanta, he did more than anyone to transform it from a growing, but still sleepy, southern city into a dynamic center of business, finance, and commerce with the nation's busiest airport and huge convention facilities. Like other black leaders, Jackson also endorsed Jimmy Carter's candidacy for president, but unlike Young and Bradley, he did so without great enthusiasm. And while his fellow Georgian, former President Carter, eulogized Jackson at his funeral, the two did not have a close relationship, and there is no indication that Carter ever considered Jackson for a position in his administration as he did for other black leaders.

Jackson was born in Dallas, Texas, on March 23, 1938, the son of a prominent African-American minister and a college language teacher. When he was seven years old, his parents moved to Atlanta, where his father took over as minister of the Friendship Baptist Church. From a solidly middle-class family and intellectually gifted, Jackson entered prestigious Morehouse College at the age of 14 as a Ford Foundation Early Admission Scholar and graduated four years later with a major in history and politics (B.A., 1956). After working in Cleveland for the state of Ohio and then for an encyclopedia company where he rose to become district sales manager, he enrolled in the School of Law at North Carolina Central University, where he graduated cum laude (J.D., 1964).

Returning to Atlanta, Jackson worked as an attorney for the National Labor Relations Board and the Emory Community Legal Services Center. In 1968, he decided to challenge Georgia's venerable U.S. senator, HERMAN TALMADGE, in the Democratic primary for the Senate, using $3,000 of his own money to help finance his campaign. He said that Dr. Martin Luther King, Jr.'s assassination in 1968 had led him to enter politics and that he did not think Talmadge should be elected unopposed. Although he lost by a vote of more than three to one in this David vs. Goliath battle, the fact that a young and unknown African American had entered the primary late and could win more than 200,000 votes—including those of poor white farmers and organized labor, who liked his call for repeal of portions of the hated Taft-Hartley Act—gave Jackson's fledging political career significant momentum.

Taking advantage of this momentum, Jackson ran the next year for vice mayor of Atlanta and easily defeated the white incumbent of 13 years, in the process gaining one-third of the white vote. While vice mayor, Jackson founded and became the senior partner of Jackson, Patterson & Parks, the first firm of African-American attorneys in Georgia's history. He also spent much of his time preparing to run for mayor of Atlanta in 1973 against the white incumbent, Sam Massell. Although Massell resorted to racial tactics in a runoff against Jackson, he lost handily. Jackson received 59.1 percent of the vote, and Atlanta had its first black and, at age 35, youngest mayor. Jackson had suddenly become a political star. In 1977, he was easily reelected to a second term in city hall.

As mayor, Jackson insisted that small black contractors be included in all contracts involving the city. He even threatened that "tumbleweeds would run across the runaways" of the Hartzfeld International Airport if black contractors were not included in its construction. His tactics worked. At his insistence, 71 of the 200 contractors working on the facility were African Americans. By 1978, black business owners were also getting nearly 39 percent of the city's contracts as compared to 1 percent just five years previously, and Hartzfeld Airport was on its way to becoming one of the country's busiest airports and a boon to Atlanta's economic growth.

As mayor, Jackson was also responsible for the development of Metropolitan Atlanta Rapid Transportation (MART), one of the country's most efficient rapid-transit systems. In addition, he revamped the city charter, doing away with the existing board of alderman system and replacing it with an 18-member biracial city council. He also divided the city into 24 planning districts, each of which was assured input into urban planning.

Outspoken in his determination to provide opportunity to all the city's citizens, including minorities and the poor, Jackson offended the white corporate structure of Atlanta who were critical of what they called his "black involvement-at-any-cost" attitude. His efforts to fire the white police chief, John Inman, whom he accused of discriminating against African Americans, his appointment of black activist A. Reginald Eaves, and his aggressive and outspoken personality did not help matters. But as the Hartzfeld project was completed on time and as the city began a period of rapid economic expansion, the white opposition against his administration eased, although it never entirely dissipated.

Jackson became mayor of Atlanta just at the time that his fellow Georgian, Governor Jimmy Carter, was calling for a new era of racial relations in the South predicated on equal treatment and respect of all races and was reaching out to the black community in his state. This fact might seem to have assured that the two political leaders would be close political allies, but such was not the case. At the 1972 Democratic convention, when Carter was interested in being GEORGE MCGOVERN's running mate, Vice Mayor Jackson told reporters that the vice-presidential candidate should be someone from the South—Jimmy Carter. But on a number of occasions after the Georgia governor decided to run for president, he tried unsuccessfully to get Jackson to endorse his candidacy. During the flap in April 1976, when the presidential candidate talked about maintaining the ethnic purity of neighborhoods, he urged Jackson to lend him the same support he was receiving from Mayor Coleman Young of

Detroit, but without much success. "Jackson can kiss my ass, and you can tell him that," he said to his campaign aid STUART EIZENSTAT. "I'm through calling him." Publicly, Jackson pondered whether there was any white politician he could trust.

Not until the end of April, following Carter's impressive victory in the Pennsylvania primary, Washington senator HENRY JACKSON's announcement that he was withdrawing from the race, and Senator HUBERT HUMPHREY's announcement that he would not actively campaign for the Democratic nomination, did the Atlanta mayor jump on the Carter bandwagon, calling the Georgian candidate "a president for all the people." Once Carter became the Democratic presidential nominee, Jackson campaigned actively on his behalf.

During Carter's presidency, Jackson was close to UN ambassador ANDREW YOUNG and to his (Jackson's) former high-school classmate, VERNON JORDAN, who was executive director of the National Urban League and the president's strong ally. Jackson also conferred occasionally with the president on such matters as maintaining the embargo on aluminum from white-dominated Rhodesia. Still, he was not among the pantheon of African-American leaders with whom the White House stayed in close and regular contact. There is little evidence to indicate anything more than that the relationship between the two leaders was cordial. But in 1980, Jackson was one of the early black leaders to make clear his support of Carter as a way of thwarting the candidacy of Senator EDWARD KENNEDY (Mass.).

Jackson was limited by statute to serving only two consecutive terms as mayor. So strong was his base of political support, however, that he was able to handpick his successor, Andrew Young. Yet Atlanta's white business community still did not embrace him, and none of the city's law firms offered him a job. Instead, he established an office as a bond dealer for a Chicago law firm, Chapman and Cutler, which eventually made him a millionaire.

In 1989, after Young had completed his second term as mayor of Atlanta, Jackson ran for a third term and received an overwhelming 79 percent of the vote. By all indications, however, he had lost some of the enthusiasm for the job he had displayed in his first two terms. Although he helped secure the 1996 Summer Olympics for Atlanta, the problems he faced—the AIDS crisis, homelessness, drugs, and rising crime—were not as exciting for him as those of economic development. In 1994, he decided not to seek another term, although he remained active in the Democratic Party. In 2001, he ran unsuccessfully for chairman of the Democratic National Committee, but he served as its national development chair and led its Voting Rights Institute. In 2000, President Bill Clinton appointed Jackson to the Federal National Mortgage Association (Fannie Mae).

Although six foot, three inches in height, Jackson weighed more than 300 pounds, and he began to have serious health problems, including major bypass heart surgery in 1992. He died on June 23, 2003, after suffering a severe heart attack. At his funeral, former President Carter remarked, "Maynard Jackson was one of the rare political leaders in the history of this country, who has been able … profoundly to impact for the better the people whom he served."

Jarvis, Howard Arnold

(1902–1986) *businessman, leader of nationwide tax revolt*

In 1978, Howard Jarvis was a successful 75-year-old California businessman who was responsible for the passage of a tax initiative that cut property taxes drastically throughout the state and led to similar tax initiatives in other states. The maestro of what became dubbed the "tax revolt of 1978," Jarvis touched into a nationwide sense of discontent against big government, high taxes, and inflation that sharpened right-wing attacks against Democratic liberals and spurred on the growing conservative movement in the United States that helped elect Ronald Reagan president in 1980.

Jarvis was born on September 22, 1902, in Magna, Utah. The son of a farmer who went to law school and then became a state judge and state legislator, Jarvis attended the University of Utah (B.A., 1925) with the intention of being a lawyer like his father. Instead, he entered the publishing business, buying the local town newspaper and eventually 10 other weekly papers in surrounding towns. He also became active in politics and ran unsuccessfully for the state legislature. In 1932, he was press officer on President Herbert Hoover's campaign train. In 1934, he met future California governor Earl Warren, who persuaded the young entrepreneur to move to California, where he became a successful businessman and founder of Femco Corporation, a manufacturer of aircraft and missile parts.

After retiring from business in 1962, Jarvis joined a small citizen's group in Los Angeles, United Organization of Taxpayers (UOT), that monitored spending by local governments and advocated lower property taxes. Blunt-spoken and self-described as a "Jack Mormon"—a Mormon who liked to drink vodka, smoke a pipe, and "play a little golf on Sundays"—Jarvis became a principal spokesman for the group. He also became a regular figure at tax hearings and developed a reputation as a demagogue, a nuisance, and even an anarchist. But although he tried to get initiatives on the ballot to cut taxes, he was never able to get the requisite number of signatures. He also ran unsuccessfully for mayor of Los Angeles in 1977.

In fact, Jarvis attracted little public notice until 1978, when he joined forces with Paul Gann, another retired businessman from the Sacramento area heading a group seeking to curb rising property taxes. Together, they collected 764,000 signatures to force a referendum on a proposal—Proposition 13—that would slash property taxes an estimated 57 percent and place tight lids on the power of local government to raise revenues by other means. Because he was the more colorfully outspoken of the two men, Jarvis quickly overshadowed Gann in the campaign that followed. The Jarvis-Gann initiative was opposed by Governor JERRY BROWN, most of the state's other political leaders, union leaders, and major newspapers, which pointed out that the measure would primarily help commercial property owners and cause massive social dislocations. A less drastic measure, Proposition 8, which promised smaller (30 percent) property-tax cuts to homeowners but not to commercial and industrial property owners, was also put on the ballot.

On June 6, however, California voters stunned the nation by approving Proposition 13 by almost a two-to-one margin while defeating Proposition 8. "It was as though millions of the state's taxpayers had thrown open their windows like the fed-up characters in the movie *Network* and shouted in thunderous unison: 'I'm mad as hell—and I'm not going to take it anymore,'" reported *Time* magazine.

The tax revolt Jarvis had led in California spread quickly to more than 20 other states from Maine to Alaska. A number of these states passed referenda similar to Proposition 13 or placed lids on property taxes and state spending. The tax revolt reached its peak in 1980 when liberal Massachusetts, the only state to vote for the Democratic presidential nominee, GEORGE MCGOVERN, in 1972 and a state that Jimmy Carter carried in 1976, passed Proposition 2½, limiting property taxes to 2½ percent of a property's assessed value.

The movement ignited by Jarvis, however, had political repercussions that extended beyond changes in property taxes and state-spending lids. It gave common cause to and legitimized disparate conservative groups, including neoconservatives, evangelical Christians, and social and cultural conservatives. It also introduced new and effective methods of campaigning, including petition drives and mass mailings. In November 1978, five Democratic liberals in the Senate—Dick Clark of Iowa, FLOYD HASKELL of Colorado, Wendell Anderson of Minnesota, Thomas McIntyre of New Hampshire, and William Hathaway of Maine—were defeated in their bids for reelection. Although Democrats remained in firm control of both houses of Congress, the complexion of both the House and the Senate was decidedly more conservative. Conservatives increased their gains in 1980 when RONALD REAGAN was elected president and Republicans captured the U.S. Senate for the first time since 1952. Seven more liberal Democrats, including the party's standard-bearer in 1972, George McGovern, went down to defeat. Republicans also picked up 33 seats in the House and, on the state level, finished with a net gain of four governorships.

Howard Jarvis enjoyed less fortune after 1978. In the aftermath of his victory in California, he founded the American Tax Reduction Movement, which pushed new antitax measures at the state level and sought to reduce federal spending by $100 billion and federal income taxes by 40 percent over four years. Jarvis remained as blunt and cantankerous as ever. Speaking to a group of businessmen in New York in 1984, he remarked, "Businessmen have two great attributes. One is stupidity, and the other is abject cowardice." Most of his ideas, however, were not realized. Even in California, his new initiatives to reduce state income taxes and plug loopholes in Proposition 13 were defeated at the polls.

On August 12, 1986, Jarvis died at the age of 83 of complications from a blood disease that had left him in failing health for several months. While his fame was fleeting, he had caught the crest of a national wave of discontent whose repercussions survived into the 21st century.

Javits, Jacob Koppel
(1904–1986) *member of the Senate*

In almost every respect, the voting record of Jacob Koppel Javits, who served in the U.S. Senate as a Republican from New York (1957–81), was more mainstream Democratic than it was Republican. This was one of the reasons why he was never fully embraced by his Republican colleagues in the Senate. His curt and plucky personality—and more than a whiff of anti-Semitism in the Senate chamber—also did not help. As the ranking minority member of the Senate Foreign Relations Committee during the Carter presidency, however, he wielded considerable influence on Capitol Hill. A staunch defender of Israel, he was often at odds with the administration over its policy with respect to the Middle East. He also had issues with the White House over its effort in 1979 to normalize relations with Communist China and over the second Strategic Arms Limitation Talks treaty (SALT II) it had negotiated with the Soviet Union. For the most part, however, his emphasis was on working with the administration in a bipartisan manner rather than against it. As a result, he proved to be a useful ally for the Carter administration on the other side of the aisle.

Javits owed his successful career as a lawyer and politician to a combination of intelligence and hard work. Born on May 18, 1904, the son of Jewish immigrants on the Lower East Side of New York City, he worked as a traveling salesman and attended night classes at Columbia University before obtaining his law degree from New York University (LL. B., 1926). Over 20 years following law school, he built up a successful law practice with his older brother Benjamin specializing in business bankruptcies.

In 1932, Javits joined the Republican Party and supported Fiorello La Guardia, New York's three-term mayor, mainly because he was disgusted with the corruption of Tammany Hall, even though his father had been a ward heeler (canvasser) for the powerful political machine. He also disliked the influence of southern segregationists in the Democratic Party. After serving in the army in the European and Pacific theaters during World War II, he was given the dubious honor by the Republican Party of being its candidate for the U.S. House of Representatives from Manhattan's heavily Democratic and Jewish Upper West Side. In a major upset in 1946, he became the first Republican to represent the district since 1923.

After serving four terms in Congress, Javits was elected in 1954 as attorney general of New York, easily defeating his Democratic opponent, Franklin D. Roosevelt, Jr. He was the only Republican to win a statewide office that year. Two years later, he won election to the U.S. Senate, beating New York City mayor Robert Wagner, Jr., by almost a half-million votes. Javits was reelected to the Senate three more times between 1956 and 1980.

Although a proven vote-getter from the nation's most populous state, Javits spent almost his entire Senate career as an outsider in the upper chamber. Like his predecessor, Democrat Herbert Lehman, Javits was for a time the only Jew in the U.S. Senate. He was widely regarded, by his detractors as well as his admirers, for his intelligence and his industry. But he could be brusque and quarrelsome, even fighting openly with his Republican colleague from New York, Kenneth Keating. "[T]hey used to race to see who could be first to make a statement on the Senate floor or get his name in the *New York Times*," Georgia's Senator HERMAN TALMADGE later recalled.

Both as a congressman and as a senator, Javits compiled a liberal voting record, which made him a minority member of a minority party. He deplored his party's drift to the right and was horrified by the 1964 nomination of BARRY GOLDWATER as the Republican presidential candidate, openly cursing and booing New York governor Nelson Rockefeller while he was trying to speak at the party's convention. "It chilled me with the thought," Javits commented afterward, "that I might be seeing the beginnings of an American totalitarianism." That year, he refused to back his party's standard-bearer for president.

At a time when the Republican Party was becoming more conservative, Javits remained committed to the belief that "government must do for people what they can't do for themselves." Accordingly, he supported most of the social legislation of John F. Kennedy's New Frontier and Lyndon Johnson's Great Society, and he spoke out strongly in defense of the Civil Rights Act of 1964 and the Voting Rights Act of 1965. In 1974, he was also responsible for legislation, which he had pushed for seven years, protecting the fiscal integrity of private pension funds.

Although he had initially supported the war in Vietnam, Javits was among the first lawmakers to change his mind. As early as 1968, he became one of the Senate "doves" seeking to halt the spread of the war. In 1971, he helped draft what became the Cooper-Church amendment, which stopped all funding for U.S. forces in North and South Vietnam, Cambodia, Laos, and Thailand "except to the extent necessary to withdraw said forces and to protect them from imminent danger as they are withdrawn." In 1973, he wrote the compromise language of the War Powers Act, limiting the president's authority to take the nation into war without congressional approval.

The leitmotif of Javits's entire political career was his defense of Israel. Throughout his career, he fought for increased military aid for Israel, and he spoke out in support of Israel in its several wars with its Arab neighbors. As the ranking minority member of the Senate Foreign Relations Committee during the Carter presidency, he criticized the administration in 1977 for the "imbalance" in the concessions it was asking the Israelis and Arabs to make in order to achieve a settlement in the Arab-Israeli dispute. Israel, he said, was being asked to give up virtually all the territory it had seized during the 1967 war in exchange for a vague hope of peace in the distant future. That, he remarked following a speech Vice President WALTER MONDALE gave to a World Affairs Council group in San Francisco in 1977, was "unrealistic." He also protested in 1978 against a plan that would package the sale of F-15 and F-16 fighter jets to Israel with the sale of F-15s to Saudi Arabia and the older F-5s to Egypt. It was ominous, he said, to make the sale of arms to Israel conditional on supplying comparable weapons to the Arabs.

Yet it would be an oversimplification to label Javits as merely part of the "pro-Israeli" or "American-Jewish" lobby on Capitol Hill. There was, for example, his response to the Jackson-Vanik Amendment of 1974, which tied most-favored-nation (MFN) status for Soviet trade to the liberalization of Jewish emigration from the Soviet Union, much of which would be bound for Israel. Although Javits had worked tirelessly on behalf of Soviet Jews, both to improve their condition as a national group within the Soviet Union and to help them emigrate freely, he expressed reservations about the Jackson-Vanik proposal. He was persuaded by then Secretary of State HENRY KISSINGER, who later referred to Javits as a "Republican foreign policy heavyweight," that it would hurt prospects for détente with Moscow. He and another Jewish senator, ABRAHAM RIBICOFF (D-Conn.), worked out a compromise with HENRY JACKSON (D-Wash.), who was responsible for the amendment, whereby the president could grant MFN status to countries with nonmarket economies for 18 months, after which Congress would have to approve additional extensions by joint resolution.

Javits also recognized the need for Israel to make concessions on the occupied territories. According to National Security Advisor ZBIGNIEW BRZEZINSKI, the New York senator was briefed at the White House in May 1978 about talks that had taken place between President Carter and Israeli prime minister MENACHEM BEGIN. When told that Begin had stated that, notwithstanding the administration's objections, Israel would go forward with building settlements in the territories, Javits was "quite shaken" and urged the president "to stay on course."

Although U.S. policy toward Israel always remained Javits's primary concern as a member of the Senate Foreign Relations Committee, it was not his only interest. He played an important role in working out compromise language to maintain sanctions against the all-white minority government of Ian Smith in Rhodesia until arrangements could be worked out for majority rule. Over the objections of Senator JESSE HELMS (R-N.C.), with whom he clashed when Helms moved onto the Foreign Relations Committee in 1979, Javits worked out with Clifford Case (R-N.J.) the Case-Javits Amendment, which would lift sanctions against Rhodesia by December 31, 1978, provided the president had determined that the Rhodesian government had demonstrated its willingness to attend an all-parties conference and a new government had been installed following free, internationally supervised elections.

Javits also played an important role in winning congressional support for the normalization of relations with the People's Republic of China (PRC, or Communist China). Although he favored normalizing relations with the Beijing government, like a number of senators he was concerned about the fate of Taiwan if the president should abrogate the United States' mutual-defense treaty with the Taiwanese government. He was also irritated by the suddenness of Carter's decision to normalize relations with China and the lack of prior consultation with key members of Congress.

Javits and the chairperson of the Foreign Relations Committee, FRANK CHURCH (D-Idaho), who agreed that the president had mishandled the Taiwan issue and whom Javits greatly admired, helped write compromise language, which the administration reluctantly accepted, that spelled out the United States' concern for Taiwan without unraveling the new ties Washington had established with the PRC. In carefully worded language, the proposal stated that the United States would view anything "other than peaceful means" to unify Taiwan and the mainland "as a threat to the peace and security of the Western Pacific area." Furthermore, the United States would "maintain its capacity to resist" coercive measures that threatened "the security or social or economic system of the people on Taiwan."

On other matters, Javits was only one of two Republicans on the Foreign Relations Committee (the other being CHARLES PERCY of Illinois) to support the SALT II agreement with the Soviet Union, even though he was suspicious of the Soviets and thought the United States needed to do more to improve its own defense. Secretary of State CYRUS VANCE later credited Javits and Church with preventing other members of the committee from attaching to the SALT agreement "killer" amendments that would have made the treaty unacceptable to Moscow.

In contrast to his support of the administration with respect to the SALT II agreement, Javits broke with the White House over its response to the Iranian revolution of 1979. In May that year, at a time when the administration was trying to establish normal diplomatic relations with the regime of the AYATOLLAH RUHOLLA KHOMEINI, Javits introduced a resolution in the Senate expressing abhorrence at the regime's mass execution of its opponents without trial.

Although Javits had been diagnosed with amyotrophic lateral sclerosis (ALS), a fatal neurological disease commonly known as Lou Gehrig's disease, he decided in 1980 to seek a fifth term in the Senate. Facing reports about his health and a national swing toward conservatism, he lost in the Republican primary to Alfonse D'Amato, a Long Island legislator. He stayed in the race, however, as the candidate of the Liberal Party. In November, he siphoned off enough votes from the Democratic candidate, Congresswoman Elizabeth Holtzman, to elect D'Amato.

Following his defeat, Javits became a champion of the disabled and an adjunct professor at Columbia University. In 1981, he published his memoirs, *Javits: The Autobiography of a Public Man*, whose title best summed up his life. In 1983, he was awarded the Presidential Medal of Freedom by RONALD REAGAN. He died in Palm Beach, Florida on March 7, 1986, of complications from ALS. He was 81 years old.

Jordan, Hamilton

(1944–) *senior administrative assistant, White House chief of staff*

Hamilton Jordan was one of the most influential members of the Carter administration. He was also one of its most controversial figures. In the minds of administration critics, he epitomized what was wrong with the Carter presidency—insular, arrogant, uncaring about Congress, and indifferent to the ways of Washington. He was also accused of personal indiscretions, which he denied but made good newspaper copy. At the same time, even Jordan's harshest critics acknowledged that he was the person most responsible for putting an unknown, one-term southern governor into the White House, and that he remained an unusually shrewd political strategist even if his personal political skills were sometimes lacking.

Jordan was born in Charlotte, Georgia, on September 21, 1944, and raised in Albany, Georgia. Outgoing and athletic, he enjoyed the camaraderie of competitive sports and took naturally to politics. His classmates in high school voted him most likely to become governor someday. While a student at the University of Georgia, where he graduated with a major in political science (B.A., 1966), he was president of his freshman class and continued to participate in campus politics while enjoying the school's active fraternity life.

Chief presidential aide Hamilton Jordan,1977 *(Jimmy Carter Library)*

Yet there was a serious, compassionate, and even shy side to Jordan that was not always appreciated by his later critics. Raised in one of the battlegrounds of the Civil Rights movement of the 1960s, Jordan witnessed Dr. Martin Luther King, Jr.'s confrontation with Albany's chief of police, Laurie Pritchett, in 1961. Taken aback by the violence that followed King's refusal to stop a demonstration he was leading, and impressed by the determined commitment of his family's black maid, who had marched behind King, Jordan began to question not only the system of racial segregation in the South but his own social and moral values. In June 1966, he heard and met state senator Jimmy Carter, who was running for governor. In his speech, Carter talked about the need for a more modern and progressive state government. What impressed Jordan was not so much the message itself, which was not especially original, but the apparent conviction and energy of the candidate, which resonated with his own developing idealism and yearning for a new politics in the South. With the help of his uncle, Clarence Jordan, who in the 1940s had established a racially integrated farm known as Koinonia, about nine miles south of Plains in south Georgia, he became youth coordinator for the Carter campaign.

Following Carter's narrow defeat in the Democratic gubernatorial primary, Jordan went to South Vietnam to serve with International Voluntary Services, an organization that sent young volunteers to do community and agricultural work in developing countries. As he later commented, he did this more out of a sense of adventure than out of idealism. Curious about the war in Vietnam, ineligible for military service because of flat feet and a bad knee, and without any career plans, he volunteered for Vietnam. After only six months, however, he had to be sent home with black water fever, a serious tropical disease.

While recovering from his illness, Jordan reestablished contact with Carter, who had decided to run again for governor. Impressed by Jordan's political shrewdness and commitment to the campaign, the candidate appointed him campaign manager. The 1970 campaign itself was not one of the proudest chapters in the future president's career. Believing he had lost in 1966 because he had run as a moderate progressive alternative to the conservative racist candidate, LESTER MADDOX, Carter was determined not to make that mistake again. Accordingly, he ran as a southern conservative appealing to racial and class antagonisms and accusing his most formidable opponent, moderate former governor Carl Sanders, of being part of Atlanta's social and political elite, out of touch with ordinary Georgians. Yet Carter's calls for a competent and progressive government were not all that different from the proposals he had made four years earlier. Jordan therefore believed that Carter still represented the best opportunity for a new and more progressive era in state government.

Following Carter's victory in 1970, the new governor appointed Jordan as his executive secretary, the equivalent of chief of staff, with responsibility for supervising the 30–35 department heads who worked out of the governor's office. He was also responsible, along with FRANK MOORE (who would run the congressional liaison office in the Carter White House) for relations with the General Assembly, and he acted as a political buffer for the governor. These functions made Jordan, at age 26, one of the administration's most influential members and the person with the most daily contact with the governor.

As executive secretary, Jordan proved himself better as a political strategist than as an administrator, a deficiency he would replicate as Carter's senior administrative assistant in the White House. In contrast to his later relations with Congress, but unlike the governor who developed a reputation for being intransigent, Jordan tried to broker deals with lawmakers and sometimes lobbied the governor on their behalf. But because Jordan was the top nonelected official in the governor's office, much of the criticism against the administration was deflected to him and other members of Carter's young staff.

By 1972, Jordan was beginning to think in much more ambitious terms for the governor than getting his programs through the state legislature. Knowing that Carter was constitutionally ineligible to run for reelection in 1976 and would face an uphill fight should he try to challenge incumbent HERMAN TALMADGE for his seat in the U.S. Senate, Jordan did not see much of an immediate political future for the governor in Georgia. Sensing, however, that recent changes in the way Democrats selected delegates to their presidential nominating conventions every four years might make it possible for a virtually unknown candidate like Carter to win the nomination, Jordan began to map out a strategy for a Carter presidential bid. By winning the Iowa caucuses that most presidential candidates had ignored in the past and then using the Iowa victory as a launching pad for a subsequent victory in the important New Hampshire primary a week later, Carter might quickly get enough national exposure to win additional early primaries in the South and industrial Northeast. Thereby establishing himself as a front-runner early in the race and taking advantage of the new rules that apportioned delegates according to the votes each candidate received in a state primary, he could then win enough delegates to gain the nomination.

What this strategy required was an early commitment by Carter to run hard in selected primaries where he could underscore different cores of strength. Working to the governor's advantage would be the fact that, ineligible to run again for governor in 1974, he would have more than a year to devote full-time to the campaign. In what promised to be a crowded field of both liberals (especially if Massachusetts senator EDWARD KENNEDY did not seek the nomination) and conservatives, including Governor GEORGE WALLACE of Alabama, Carter's obscurity could work to his advantage, particularly if he could seem middle-of-the-road. It would be essential, however, to beat Wallace in an early southern primary like the one in Florida, so that he could show the rest of the country that while he was not a regional candidate, he was the region's candidate.

Coincidentally, other Georgians close to the governor were thinking much along the same line. These included PETER BOURNE, who had first met Carter while serving as director of a community health center and was later appointed by the governor as director of Georgia's Narcotic Treatment Program. Following the Democratic nominating convention, Bourne wrote a 10-page memorandum for Carter similar to what Jordan was thinking. Ten days later, Jordan arranged a meeting at the governor's mansion with Bourne and three other Georgians who had participated in the 1970 gubernatorial campaign to discuss a Carter presidential candidacy; these were the governor's press secretary, JODY POWELL, advertising executive GERALD RAFSHOON, and Atlanta businessman Landon Butler.

Even before the meeting, Carter had also begun to give serious thought to running for president. He had been unimpressed by a number of potential candidates he had met, some of whom had stayed overnight at the governor's mansion, and did not believe they were better qualified than he to run for president or could do a better job as the nation's chief executive. He also believed that in the November 1972 elections, the Democratic candidate for president, GEORGE MCGOVERN, would be soundly defeated by RICHARD NIXON, seeking his second term as president.

At the meeting at the governor's mansion, Jordan urged Carter to make the run for president. "We don't know how to say it," he remarked, "other than to say, we think you can be president." The governor responded by telling his executive secretary to put his thoughts on paper. Although Carter still remained noncommittal about running, he met once more with Jordan, Bourne, Rafshoon, and Butler on October 17 and then again following McGovern's overwhelming defeat on November 5. At this last meeting, he also included two of his closest friends, CHARLES KIRBO and BERT LANCE, as well as Philip Alston, senior partner of a major Atlanta law firm.

At the end of the month, Jordan met with Carter to discuss his written plan for winning the presidency. In this 72-page memorandum, he advised Carter to read up on foreign affairs, economics, and defense; cultivate contacts with the "eastern establishment"; and read the major national newspapers each day. He also laid out strategies for beating Kennedy, Wallace, and Senator HENRY JACKSON (Wash.) if they should enter the race. By Christmas, Carter had decided to run using Jordan's plan, except that he intended to enter every primary and caucus rather than selected ones as Jordan had recommended.

Jordan now devoted his full time to preparing for the campaign, which still remained under the political radar screen, even in Georgia. Through Carter, who got himself appointed in 1972 as the national campaign chairperson for the 1974 midterm elections, Jordan was put on the payroll of the Democratic National Committee (DNC) as executive director of its campaign division. He spent the next year traveling the country, putting on workshops for Democratic candidates and identifying potential Carter campaign workers. In November 1974, he resigned from the

DNC to set up the Committee for Jimmy Carter office in Atlanta.

The next month, Carter formally announced his candidacy. Once the campaign began in earnest, it followed closely the blueprint Jordan had prepared in November 1972. First came Carter's early win in January 1976 in the Iowa caucuses, which gave the former governor's campaign credibility. This was followed by a victory in the New Hampshire primary; a crucial win in Florida, which had become a referendum over whether Carter or George Wallace would be the south's candidate; and a victory in Pennsylvania that showed he could win in a northern industrial state. Building on this momentum, Carter was able, by the end of the primary season, to have enough delegates to win the Democratic nomination at the party's New York convention in July. He managed this despite suffering some humiliating losses in early primaries like Massachusetts and New York and in several later primaries in Oregon, Utah, and Nebraska, where two new candidates, Senator FRANK CHURCH (Idaho) and Governor JERRY BROWN (Calif.), had entered the race believing they could still stop Carter.

The election seemed Carter's to win. In contrast to the Democrats, who left their convention united, the Republicans remained badly split between supporters of President GERALD FORD, who won the party's nomination, and those of RONALD REAGAN, who came very close to pulling off a major upset. Because of a number of mistakes on Carter's part, he almost lost the election, but in November, he pulled off one of the great miracles in American politics by narrowly winning with 50.1 percent of the vote to Ford's 48 percent. A virtual unknown a year earlier, he had defeated an incumbent president.

Because Jordan, still only 27 years old, was known as the strategist behind the Carter campaign and was almost certain to have a high position within the White House, probably chief of staff, he gained almost as much celebratory status as the president-elect. He and the other Georgians who had helped elevate Carter to the White House became widely referred to as "the Georgia Mafia," with Jordan as its leader. Though not necessarily intended as a term of derision when Carter took the oath of office, it quickly became one as the Carter staff was held responsible for the miscues that seemed to plague the administration almost from the time the new president entered the White House. As Carter's most senior assistant and the person closest to him on a daily basis, Jordan was often singled out for criticism, just as he had been when the president was governor of Georgia. One early incident had to do with Speaker of the House TIP O'NEILL's complaint that Jordan had purposely given him poor seats for an inaugural gala at the Kennedy Center, a charge that Jordan denied but one that led O'Neill to refer to Jordan as "Hannibal Jerken."

Influential lawmakers on Capitol Hill, Democratic Party professionals, government bureaucrats, and other Washington insiders did not know how to deal with a president and his young staff who defied political pundits by getting the Democratic nomination for Carter in the first place and then by successfully running a campaign whose leitmotif was sweeping change in the way business was conducted in Washington. As Jordan himself later acknowledged, however, there also was an element of arrogance on the part of Jordan and other White House staffers who were boastful about how they had bested the political professionals and were supremely confident in their ability to bring about fundamental change in Washington. "When you're sitting down in south Georgia looking up at Washington, the White House and the Presidency," he remarked in an interview in 1981, "you see all the powers and levers and strings and all the things you can do." This confidence was coupled with paranoia that they would be scornfully regarded as "rednecks," to be tolerated but not welcomed into the inner political and social circles of Washington. Jordan did not help matters by often coming to work at the White House wearing khaki pants and boots and an open shirt without a tie, dressed more like a college undergraduate than one of the nation's most powerful persons.

The most immediate issue confronting Jordan was his responsibilities in the White House. Clearly both he and the president expected him to play a key role. Even before Carter took office, Jordan staked out the central position he expected to have in the administration when, in a power play, he seized control of the appointment process from JACK WATSON, a young attorney who had worked for Carter while he was governor and to whom Carter had given primary responsibility for vetting potential Carter appointees. Intending to be in charge of White House personnel, Jordan accused Watson of trying to undercut him. Eventually the president-elect was forced to intervene in what had become a conflict over power as much as over turf. On November 15, 1976, he announced that Jordan would assume primary responsibility for presidential appointments. Jordan also spent most of the first few months of the new administration working on staffing lower-level positions, something he later acknowledged distracted him from concentrating on more important matters such as helping to set priorities for the president.

Carter would later be criticized for not having a chief of staff, but neither he nor Jordan thought it necessary to have one. Jordan understood his limitations as an administrator, and Carter did not want to repeat the experience of a too-powerful chief of staff, as occurred during Richard Nixon's administration. Rather he wanted his cabinet members and senior staff to have ready access to the Oval Office. Instead of being named chief of staff, therefore, Jordan was appointed senior administrative assistant to the president. Because he had no specific responsibilities, he was able to decide for himself which policy matters to be involved in, which staff meetings to go to, what functions to attend, what memorandums to write or cosign. Yet he had enormous influence. Although he was not chief of staff, he had many of the responsibilities of one. Other members of the White House staff still looked to him to run the White House's daily operations and resolve internal disputes. He also handled the president's political business. He was the person to whom Carter turned when he wanted someone to respond to a close political supporter wanting a favor or having a complaint or to a lawmaker upset at his treatment by the congressional liaison office. Jordan often weighed in on the political implications of a presidential decision, scribbling in longhand his thoughts on the political implications of a recommendation being forwarded for Carter's approval. He helped organize the political campaign to win Senate ratification of the Panama Canal Treaties of 1977 and, beginning in 1978, attended the president's weekly breakfast meetings of senior foreign-policy officials. No member of the administration was more direct with the president than Jordan when he thought Carter was making a bad decision or pursuing a wrong course. Akin to a minister without portfolio, Jordan remained in many ways a shadowy figure in the White House, but one whose power and authority was undisputed.

In 1979, Carter decided finally to make Jordan chief of staff as part of a major reorganization of his administration that also involved the resignations of five members of his cabinet. The reorganization was in response to the president's realization that his administration was in political trouble as a result of a growing sense of crisis in the country and a loss of confidence in the president's ability to deal with such problems as oil shortages and higher prices at the gas pumps, rapidly growing inflation, and high unemployment. His appointment of Jordan as chief of staff was also in response to complaints by critics that Carter needed someone in the White House to run its daily operations and limit intrusions on the president's time. In announcing Jordan's appointment, the president instructed the White House staff to obey his new chief of staff's orders "as if they were the president's own."

After getting off to a bad start by requesting the senior members of the administration to fill out a questionnaire evaluating the performance of their own senior personnel, Jordan proved to be an effective chief of staff, although he delegated the day-to-day administrative chores to his deputy, ALONZO MCDONALD. In the weeks following his appointment, he and the president engaged in controlling damage at the White House caused by the cabinet shake-up. He also developed detailed working plans and established task forces to manage issues of high priority for the administration. Finally, he tried to improve his relationship with House Speaker O'Neill and other lawmakers on Capitol Hill by visiting their offices and seeking advice. In his meeting with O'Neill, Jordan apologized for previous indiscretions, even though he did not believe he had committed any.

Jordan's importance in the administration and the fact that he was such a public figure with a personality that sometimes seemed arrogant (but was often just shyness on his part) also made him one of its most controversial figures. In his four years at the White House, he was accused of making an indecent gesture to the wife of the Egyptian ambassador (1977), spitting a drink on a woman's back in a bar (1978), being anti-Semitic (1978), being implicit in an effort to keep the fugitive financial figure Robert Vesco from being extradited to the United States (1978), and using cocaine at a New York disco (1979). Jordan and Press Secretary Jody Powell, who was also implicated in the last two of these allegations, denied the charges emphatically. Jordan even offered his resignation to the president just before the cocaine charge became public. After nine months, he was cleared by a special prosecutor and grand jury, but the unfavorable publicity he had received in the media added to the impression of a White House staffed by an inner circle of young and inexperienced Georgians who had gone amuck.

Besides his White House responsibilities, Jordan played a major role in the ultimately futile effort by the president to resolve the Iranian hostage crisis before he left office. Fifty-two Americans had been held hostage since they were seized at the U.S. embassy in Tehran on November 4, 1979. In February 1980, Jordan went on a secret mission to Paris, where he met with two men, one a French lawyer and the other an Argentine businessman, who were believed to have close ties to Iran's governing body, the Revolutionary Council. Through these two intermediaries, Abolhassan Bani-Sadr, a political moderate who had been elected Iran's first president, agreed to a plan by which a UN fact-finding mission would travel to Iran to hear its grievances against the United States and then to obtain the release of the hostages. Unfortunately, the negotiations broke down when the Islamic leader of Iran, AYATOLLAH RUHOLLA KHOMEINI, instructed his followers holding the hostages not to hand them over to Bani-Sadr. The way was therefore cleared a few weeks later for a flawed and unsuccessful military rescue of the hostages, a mission to which Jordan gave only lukewarm support.

Jordan's other major responsibility in 1980 was leading Carter's reelection campaign. Given the nation's economic recession and the national sense—so well exploited by Carter's Republican opponent, RONALD REAGAN, in his final debate with the president—that the nation was worse off in 1980 than it had been when Carter took office, Jordan knew he faced an uphill fight. What was surprising was not so much the extent of Carter's defeat in November but how close the election was until the waning days of the campaign. While there were a number of reasons for the tight race throughout the summer and most of the fall, one that still stands out in Jordan's mind was the national uncertainty about Reagan's ability to serve in the Oval Office. These reservations were not resolved until the final debate between Carter and his opponent, who looked far more relaxed and in command than the president and who avoided any major mistakes. In contrast to Reagan, Carter appeared nervous and tense and also seemed to trivialize the issue of nuclear war by referring to it as the most important concern of his young daughter Amy. The debate left Americans persuaded that the former California governor was fit to be president. Together with the White House's failure to secure the release of the hostages before the election, which symbolized the administration's overall impotence, it turned what had seemed a nearly even race into a huge defeat for the president.

Jordan, however, held Massachusetts senator Kennedy just as responsible for Reagan's resounding victory over Carter. In Jordan's view, Kennedy's quixotic effort to continue his campaign right to the convention, when it was clear he could not get the nomination, resulted in fissures within the Democratic Party that could not be repaired. "I deeply resented Ted Kennedy and his millions, coercing all of us to pay off his debt," Jordan later remarked about Kennedy's insistence that the Carter camp help pay off the senator's campaign debt in return for his endorsement of the president.

Since leaving the White House, Jordan has written two books. The first, *Crisis: The True Story of an Unforgettable Year in the White House* (1982), describes in detail the events of 1980, specifically his efforts to free the Iranian hostages and the presidential campaign. The second, *No Such Things as a Bad Day: A Memoir* (2000), reflects on three separate bouts Jordan has had with cancer—lymphoma, skin, and prostate—and also describes his youth in Georgia, his experience as a volunteer in South Vietnam, and his political involvement with Jimmy Carter.

Jordan has also been a successful sports entrepreneur and investor in a number of biotech companies. He is founder of the APT Tour (global men's professional tennis tour) and cofounder of Touchdown Jacksonville, which later became the National Football League franchise team *Jacksonville Jaguars.* In 1986, he ran unsuccessfully for the U.S. Senate from Georgia. Together with his wife Dorothy, who founded Camp Sunshine, a nationally recognized, nonprofit camp for children with cancer or leukemia, he has begun a similar program, Camp Kudzo, for children suffering from juvenile diabetes. Jordan and his wife live in Atlanta.

Jordan, Vernon Eulion, Jr.

(1935–) *executive director of the National Urban League*

Executive director of the National Urban League from 1971 to 1981, Vernon E. Jordan, Jr., supported Jimmy Carter for president in 1976. Like many other black leaders, though, he became quickly disenchanted with the Carter administration for not doing enough for African Americans, most of whom lived in urban areas.

Jordan was born in Atlanta, Georgia, on August 15, 1935, and grew up in a middle-class family in the segregated South. He was educated at DePauw University, the only African American in his class (B.A., 1957) and Howard University Law School (J.D., 1960). He was also a fellow at the Institute for Politics at the

John F. Kennedy School of Government, Harvard University (1969).

Soon after returning to Atlanta to begin a law practice, Jordan became active in the Civil Rights movement. In 1961, he helped organize the integration of the University of Georgia and personally escorted the first African-American student, Charlayne Hunter, through an angry crowd. Over the next 10 years, he engaged in a number of activities related to the Civil Rights movement, including boycotting stores that would not hire blacks, serving as field secretary of the NAACP (1961–63), and participating in the Voter Education Project of the Southern Regional Council (1964–68). In 1970, he was appointed executive director of the United Negro College Fund, which funds historically black colleges. A year later, he was named executive director of the National Urban League following the death of its leader of 10 years, Whitney Young. A civil rights advocacy group and provider of services for African Americans, the National Urban League had experienced large growth under Young's leadership. With a long tradition of self-help, it had also attracted considerable support from the corporate world, private foundations, and the federal government.

Jordan first met Jimmy Carter in 1969 at an interracial fund-raiser for Carter, who was preparing his second run for governor of Georgia. At the time, Jordan was contemplating running for Congress, but he ultimately decided against it. He and Carter became good friends, and Carter came to speak to meetings of the Urban League on a number of occasions. In 1973, Jordan introduced Carter to Peter McCullough, corporate chairman of the Urban League, chief executive officer of Xerox, and treasurer of the Democratic Party. Carter had them spend the night at the governor's executive mansion. After dinner, he startled both of them by telling them that he was going to be the next president of the United States and then went on to explain how it was going to happen. Later that night, Jordan told Carter he could never be president because no one knew him, he would not be in office when he was running, and he was a southerner. But the governor remained unpersuaded.

Over the next two years, Jordan and Carter remained on good terms. Although the National Urban League could not endorse a political candidate, Jordan was one of the first black leaders to unofficially jump on the Carter bandwagon following Carter's announcement in 1974 that he was a candidate for president. On election night, after the networks declared Carter the winner over GERALD FORD, the president-elect called Jordan to remind him of their conversation three years earlier when Jordan had told Carter he could never be elected to the White House.

Following the election, Carter appointed Jordan to an advisory group whose purpose was to review short lists of candidates for high positions in his administration. Carter biographer PETER BOURNE later wrote: "Including blacks in such an influential role was an unprecedented step for any president up to that time." But Carter rejected Jordan's recommendation for what the Urban League director considered to be one of the president-elect's most important selections, a special White House assistant responsible for minority affairs. Though Jordan had strongly endorsed Mayor Richard Hatcher of Gary, Indiana, who was well-known and highly respected both within the black community and the Democratic Party, Carter dismissed him with the remark that Hatcher had not supported him until late in the campaign. Instead, the president-elect appointed a black woman who had worked in his campaign, Bunny Mitchell, even though Jordan, who knew her, said she would be the wrong choice for the job because she lacked political skills and was not well known among black leaders. According to Jordan,

Mitchell proved to be the mistake he thought she would be.

Despite his disagreement with Carter over the Mitchell appointment, Jordan—perhaps even more than other black leaders—still expected the president to undertake major new initiatives for African Americans and for the urban areas where so many of them lived. As he later explained in his memoirs, "I had a literal friend in the highest political office in the land. ... We had delivered and now was the time for the beneficiaries of our show of faith to return the favor."

Jordan was all the more disappointed, therefore, when Carter's programs appeared to provide little relief for the nation's inner cities. At the Sixty-Seventh Annual Urban League Conference in July 1977, the league's director berated the president for having failed to keep his campaign promises. Jordan had prepared his remarks with great care, knowing that, because of his close friendship with the president, who was scheduled to address the conference the next day, his comments would be widely reported and that even other officials of the staid and relatively conservative Urban League might object to what he said. Nevertheless, he decided to deliver what he acknowledged himself was "a blistering attack" on the administration's neglect of the black community. "The sad fact is that ... the list of what his administration has not done for the blacks ... far exceeds its list of accomplishments," Jordan remarked. The president was furious. The next day, he responded that he had "no apologies" for what he had done for African Americans. His relationship with Jordan, who he felt had betrayed him, was never again the same.

Later that summer, Jordan did break with most other black leaders by supporting the president's welfare-reform program, which emphasized uniform, nationwide eligibility standards, minimum levels of income, and jobs for welfare recipients. But his support for even this measure was lukewarm; he merely called the program "an encouraging one." More often, his remarks remained highly critical of the White House. At one point, after Jordan had accused the administration of being "insensitive to the needs of the poor," Carter, clearly frustrated, took Jordan aside to warn him that "erroneous or demagogic statements" would remove "the last hope of the poor" for government help. According to Secretary of Health, Education and Welfare JOSEPH CALIFANO, when Jordan learned in July 1979 that the president had fired the secretary, he left a message with one of Califano's aides to tell him "never to trust a born-again Baptist, especially a Southern White One."

At the same time, the executive director was always careful not to break entirely from the administration and to temper his remarks with recognition of good intentions or positive policies on the part of the White House. Taking advantage of the fact that he still had access to the administration, he organized the Black Leadership Forum, which brought together the heads of all the major national black organizations. Over the course of the Carter presidency, they met several times at the White House for what Jordan described as "constructive discussions." But tension between Jordan and the administration always remained high. When the president's chief of staff, HAMILTON JORDAN, suggested to Vernon Jordan toward the end of Carter's presidency that the black leader had not been constructive in his remarks about the president, Jordan shot back, "If you think I have not given the administration its due when it deserved it, then you are the victim of staff work that would be rotten anywhere, but is especially disturbing when it takes place in the White House."

On May 29, 1980, Jordan was shot in the back by a white supremist out to kill "race mixers." After recuperating, Jordan resigned his position from the National Urban League in 1981 and moved to Washington, D.C., where he assumed a position as senior partner with the law firm of Akin, Gump, Strauss, Hauer and Feld. Over the next 10 years, he built a large and successful practice. He also introduced Bill Clinton, with whom he had worked in Arkansas during the 1970s, to a group of powerful and wealthy individuals who later provided financial support for Clinton's campaign for president in 1992. During the Clinton presidency, Jordan became close friends with Clinton and developed a reputation as one of Washington's leading power brokers.

Jordan is presently a partner in the investment firm of Lazard Frere & Company in New York. In 2001, he published his memoirs, *Vernon Can Read!*

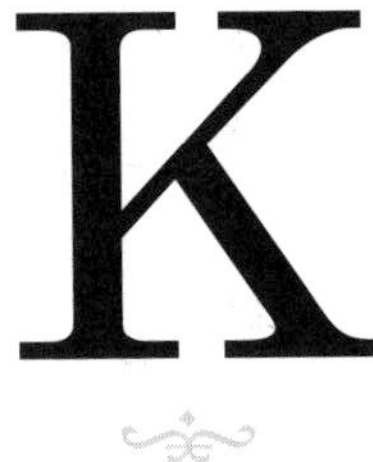

Kahn, Alfred Edward

(1917–) chair, Civil Aeronautics Board; chair, Council on Wage and Price Stability

As chair of the Civil Aeronautics Board and then of the Council of Wage and Price Stability, Alfred Kahn figured prominently in the Carter administration, even more than his titles might suggest. He led the administration's effort to deregulate major industries, beginning with transportation, and then became the White House's leading inflation fighter. More than that, he had a colorful personality and a sharp, analytical mind. With considerable gusto and flair and a wry sense of humor, he was able to raise and respond to complex issues in an understandable and common-sense fashion that turned him into something of a Washington celebrity and always made what he did and said newsworthy. He also developed a public reputation as being irreverent and fiercely independent. Even among the most well-known figures of the Carter presidency, Kahn stood out in the public's mind, usually in a highly favorable way. Yet of the two major tasks he undertook, deregulation and battling inflation, he was successful in the former and unsuccessful in the latter, a record that was reflected in his growing frustration within the administration and his desire to return to the academic life where he had first made his reputation as a nationally respected political economist.

Kahn was born on October 17, 1917, in Paterson New, Jersey. The son of a Russian Jewish immigrant, young Alfred (or Fred, as he was often called) was an intellectual prodigy. After graduating from high school at the age of 15, he attended New York University, where he graduated summa cum laude (B.A., 1936). He then completed a master's degree in economics (M.A., 1937) and studied for a year at the University of Missouri before completing a doctorate in economics at Yale University (Ph.D., 1942). During World War II, he held several government and private positions, including being an assistant to antitrust experts George W. Stocking and Myron W. Watkins (1944–45).

Following the war, Kahn took a position as assistant professor and chairman of the economics department at Ripon College (1945–47). He then moved to the Department of Economics at Cornell University, where he remained until he took leave to become chairperson of the New York Public Service Commission. During his tenure at Cornell, he served as chair of the Department of Economics, a member of the University's Board of Trustees, and dean of the College of Arts and Science. Coauthor of two important books and author of almost two dozen major articles, he was named Robert Julius Thorne Professor of Economics in 1967. In 1970–71, he published his two-volume landmark work, *The Economics of Regulation.* According to one student of the period, "measured by its impact on practitioners—both business executives and commissioners—[the book] remains the most influential work written on the subject."

As chair of the New York Public Service Commission, responsible for regulating 40 industries, from electric utilities to docks and wharves, Kahn gained a national reputation for the innovations he brought to the commission. These included introducing differential pricing in the use of electricity to replace the flat rate then charged for service no matter what season or time of the day. He predicated the pricing scheme on his theory of marginal cost pricing—that is, pegging the price of all goods and services "at the margin," the cost of producing one more unit at a particular time, including such "externalities" as air and water pollution.

In promoting his plan for differential pricing, Kahn often acted like the academic he was rather than as a government bureaucrat. One time he delivered a lecture to an audience of 50–60 public-utility lawyers while lying flat on a table in the middle of a large room in order to rest his bad back. He is even reported to have talked marginal-cost pricing with his staff during his daily swims. He extended his campaign for marginal-cost pricing to the telecommunications industry, eventually winning a difficult battle with consumers over having the New York Telephone Company charge for directory assistance. As chairman of the nation's most powerful state regulatory agency, he made certain to not to accept favors, including free meals with executives of companies he regulated or overnight accommodations while he was in official business, even at homes of personal friends.

In 1977, President Carter invited Kahn to become chairperson of the Civil Aeronautics Board (CAB) with the intention that Kahn would begin the process of deregulating the airline industry. Carter was attracted to Kahn because, unlike Secretary of Transportation BROCK ADAMS, who was not all that interested in deregulation, Kahn and the president believed that it was a way to simplify government and unleash the efficiencies of the marketplace. The airline industry was also ripe for deregulation. The highly regulated industry could not set its own rates, open new routes, or close existing ones without CAB approval. Without competition, costs were kept high. Senator EDWARD KENNEDY (D-Mass.) had held hearings, organized by law professor (and future Supreme Court justice) Steven Breyer, which revealed grossly excessive regulation, with planes flying half-empty and airlines forced to charge fares many could not afford. "We fell heir to some very good work that had been done by the Kennedy subcommittee," CHARLES SCHULTZE, chairman of the president's Council of Economic Advisers, later observed. "It was the distinct strategic, philosophical view of Carter to move in the direction of deregulation." A number of court rulings that challenged the anticompetitive practices of both the CAB and the Interstate Commerce Commission also added to the impetus for deregulation.

Kahn would have preferred to serve on the Federal Communications Commission (FCC); he also readily acknowledged that he knew nothing about airplanes, much less the airline industry. "I don't know one plane from the other," he told executives of Eastern Airlines. "To me they are all marginal costs with wings." But after first refusing and then agreeing to the president's offer to head the CAB, he aggressively took on airline executives, their lawyers, and the airline unions, most of whom still remained reluctant to give up the safety net of regulation. On his own authority, he eased restrictions on fares and airline routes and insisted on clear and well-written regulations. By asking straightforward questions about the reasons for regulations, their costs, and the benefits and harm of deregulation, he was able to bolster the case for deregulation. As one of his former students later commented, he put the term *political* back into *political economy.* Although believing in market principles, he also made clear that economics was not only about efficiency but also about other values, including a fair playing field that incumbents were not allowed to tilt solely on their market power.

In his effort to deregulate the airline industry, Kahn was also not afraid to differ publicly with the president. Although Carter strongly supported deregulation of the airlines, he still sought to maintain control over international routes. When he reversed the CAB's recommendation on an international route, Kahn openly criticized him.

In early 1978, Howard Cannon (D-Nebr.), chairperson of the Senate Commerce Committee, and Senator Kennedy introduced legislation to deregulate the airlines. Although most of the airlines continued to oppose deregulation, the move in that direction, spurred on by the efforts of CAB chairperson Kahn, was too great to be stopped. In October 1978, Congress passed the Airline Deregulation Act, allowing airlines to establish fares and determine their own routes, and providing for freer entry into the airline industry.

Deregulation of the airline industry added impetus to the movement already underway for deregulation of the trucking industry, railroads, and financial institutions, all of which was achieved by 1980. Along with decontrol of oil, the economic deregulation of much of the nation's hitherto regulated enterprise was one of President Carter's major economic achievements. But Kahn deserved considerable credit for making the deregulation movement so successful. As chairman of the CAB, he had led the fight for deregulation of the airline industry. He also played an active role in another capacity in deregulating the trucking industry. More important, through the media attention he received, he was able to generate support for economic deregulation.

In October 1978, as the nation's economy began to spiral downward and inflation began to increase rapidly, with producer prices rising at a yearly rate of 11.4 percent from August to September, Carter asked Kahn to move over from the CAB to chair the Council of Wage and Price Stability (COWPS) and be his chief inflation fighter. The president believed that he had been misled by his economic advisers into not paying sufficient attention to the problem of inflation before it had gotten out of hand. Carter "increasingly felt," Kahn later remarked, "that if he had listened to his own instincts rather than his economic advisers, he would have been better off."

If the president's hope was that Kahn would be as successful in fighting inflation as he had been in promoting the movement for economic deregulation, he was disappointed. In part, the nation's growing inflation was being fed by forces beyond Kahn's or the president's control. These included not only a dramatic increase in oil prices but also the peculiarity of inflation feeding upon itself by encouraging spending and borrowing on the assumption that the dollar would buy less tomorrow than today and that the increased money supply generated by inflation would make debt repayment easier.

Furthermore, the voluntary price and wage guidelines that COWPS had imposed, beginning in 1978, were widely unpopular, especially with organized labor, which was convinced that prices would rise faster than wages. Kahn grew increasingly intolerant of labor's wage demands, but he sought to deal with them by helping to devise a plan of "real wage insurance" by which workers agreeing to limit wage increases to below 7 percent would get a tax rebate if inflation rose more than 7 percent in that year. Finally, as Kahn himself realized, he was only one of a number of economic advisers to the president; they often disagreed among themselves as to the best policy to follow with respect to the economy.

Despite price controls, corporate profits soared by as much as 25 percent between the first quarters of 1978 and 1979. This led labor leaders to demand higher wage hikes than those permitted under the administration's guidelines. Even Kahn recognized that the system of wage and price controls was becoming unglued. He favored a harder line toward spending than Carter's more-moderate economic advisers. After learning of the jump in business profits in April 1979, his verdict was: "A catastrophe." Two months later, he added, "We've got our hands in the dike, and the problems are overflowing anyway." By this time, inflation had reached an annual rate of 14 percent.

Kahn's loose tongue, which also led him to remark that the government could ill afford to rebuild the nation's troubled cities and that decontrol of oil could lead to skyrocketing inflation, was by this time becoming an irritant at the White House. Kahn also did not get along well with COWPS director Barry Bosworth, who favored mandatory wage and price controls. Discouraged by the economic news he was receiving and feeling increasingly isolated at the White House, Kahn wanted to leave the administration and return to Cornell. The president asked him, however, to stay on and even agreed to have a regularly scheduled "inflation breakfast" with his economic advisers under Kahn's aegis.

In 1980, Kahn supported credit controls as a means of stemming the nation's buying frenzy. But increasingly he recognized that he did not have the authority, or the power, to do much to halt the inflationary spiral. In fact, he adopted a monetarist view of the inflationary problem. In conversation with Federal Reserve Board chair PAUL VOLCKER, he concluded that the only way to halt inflation was to cut the money supply drastically, even though that would almost certainly mean a recession or depression and a high rate of unemployment. Beginning in 1979, Volcker instituted this policy, which, during the RONALD REAGAN administration, halted inflation in a dramatic way but not without the consequences that Kahn and others had predicted.

Despite his growing misgivings about the administration's handling of the inflation gripping the nation, Kahn stayed in Washington for the remainder of Carter's term in office. Afterward, he returned to Cornell University, where he continued to write and give media interviews on issues having to do with the deregulation of the airlines and telecommunication industries and, more recently, on the electric-power shortage in California following its deregulation of the power industry. In 1998, he published *Letting Go: Deregulating the Process of Deregulation, or: Temptation of the Kleptocrats and the Political Economy of Regulatory Disingenuousness.* He has also testified before U.S. Senate and House committees, the Federal Power Commission, the Federal Energy Regulatory Commission, and numerous state regulatory bodies. While he continues to be a leading advocate of economic deregulation, he also believes that federal agencies need to do more to assure against anticompetitive policies and mergers, such as those that have taken place both in commercial aviation and telecommunications. Kahn is presently the Robert Julius Thorne Professor Emeritus of Political Economy at Cornell.

Kennedy, Edward (Ted) Moore

(1932–) *member of the Senate, candidate for Democratic presidential nomination*

Edward Kennedy was President Carter's most serious opponent within the Democratic Party.

For a time, he was heavily favored in the polls to defeat Carter for the 1980 Democratic presidential nomination. Although this did not happen, his challenge both reflected and contributed to divisions within the Democratic Party that helped lead to RONALD REAGAN's victory over Carter in 1980.

The youngest of nine children of the multimillionaire Joseph Kennedy, and brother of President John F. Kennedy and Attorney General Robert F. Kennedy, Edward "Ted" Kennedy was born in Brookline, Massachusetts, on February 22, 1932. A graduate of Harvard College (B.A., 1956) and the University of Virginia Law School (LL.B., 1959), he served as manager for his older brother John's successful reelection campaign for the Senate in 1958 and was in charge of his presidential campaign in 1960 in the Mountain and Pacific states. In 1962, Ted Kennedy was elected to the U.S. Senate to fill out the remainder of his brother's term as senator from Massachusetts. He was reelected for a full term in 1964 and has been reelected six times since then. In 1969, he became the youngest person ever to serve as the Democratic whip of the Senate, but he lost that position two years later to the more seasoned ROBERT BYRD (W.Va.).

In 1968, Kennedy was active in the presidential bid of his older brother Robert, who was assassinated in June after successfully winning the California primary. Following the assassination, a movement developed to place Ted Kennedy's name before the Democratic convention, but he refused to be considered for the nomination. An automobile accident on Chappaquiddick Island off Martha's Vineyard in July 1969, involving the drowning death of a young woman, Mary Jo Kopechne, who was traveling with the senator, kept him from running for the presidency in both 1972 and 1976. Kennedy's decision not to run in 1976 paved the way for other liberal candidates to enter the race. By dividing the liberal vote among themselves in key primary states, they helped Jimmy Carter to co-opt the political center and, in this way, gain the Democratic nomination.

As a senator, Kennedy gained a national reputation for championing such causes on Capitol Hill as improved education, better health care, and regulatory reform. Although President Carter also supported these causes, Kennedy's liberal voting record had the potential of putting him at odds with the more moderate and fiscally conservative chief executive. In fact, an abiding distrust of the Massachusetts senator existed among the new president's closest advisers, including pollster and political strategist PAT CADDELL, Press Secretary JODY POWELL, and chief staff aide HAMILTON JORDAN. In a lengthy memorandum to Carter even before he took office, Caddell pointed to Kennedy as one of the biggest obstacles the administration would have to face on Capitol Hill. Powell remained angry at remarks Kennedy had made late into the primary season, when Carter was still being challenged for the Democratic nomination by two latecomers, Senator FRANK CHURCH (Idaho) and Governor JERRY BROWN (Calif.) to the effect that Carter was "intentionally ... indefinite and imprecise" on the issues. Jordan and even the president also regarded Kennedy as Carter's most serious political threat within the Democratic Party.

Despite this distrust of Kennedy, Carter went out of his way to consult with the Massachusetts senator, and Kennedy responded by supporting Carter on such measures as tax reform and hospital cost containment. Long a champion of deregulation, he also helped lead the administration's fight for deregulation of the nation's airline and trucking industries. But the two Democrats locked horns on the issue of national health insurance (NHI). As a candidate for the Democratic nomination, Carter supported a comprehensive program of national health insurance as the price to pay for winning the backing of the United Auto Workers (UAW) in the key primary states of Iowa and Florida and then gaining the backing of the AFL-CIO in the general election in November. Concerned about costs, however, and worried that Congress would question his commitment to cutting inflation and restraining the budget if he proposed an NHI program, Carter purposely left out a timetable for its implementation. In his view, the program should be "phased in ... as revenues permitted." In the interim, he wanted to reorganize the government's health-care system, encouraging alternative delivery systems such as health maintenance organizations (HMOs) and rural group practices and cleaning up scandals within the nation's Medicaid program, all measures which, he believed, could improve access to and delivery of health care at little or no cost to the government.

Senator Kennedy, however, had little interest in anything short of a fully funded program of NHI to be implemented early in the new administration. More than any other cause, he tied his career to passage of a national health insurance program. He and Congressman James Corman (D-Calif.) had introduced such legislation in 1974, but it had not even gotten out committee. Kennedy wanted Carter to throw his support behind the measure, but the president refused. Months of negotiations between the senator and his staff, on the one hand, and Carter's staffs, including Secretary of Health, Education and Welfare JOSEPH CALIFANO and Special Assistant for Domestic Affairs STUART EIZENSTAT, on the other, failed to resolve their differences over NHI. Not only was the president concerned about the price tag of the Kennedy-Corman Bill, which he later estimated would be between $100 and $200 billion, but Hamilton Jordan did not want Kennedy to get primary credit for passage of any health insurance legislation.

Matters came to a head at a meeting between the senator and the president in July 1978 in a final effort by the White House to resolve its differences with Kennedy. Also at the meeting were labor leaders Douglas Fraser of the UAW and GEORGE MEANY of the AFL-CIO. The meeting was a disaster. By the time it took place, a consensus had developed within the administration that the economy and opposition on Capitol Hill would not allow for even a phased-in NHI plan. Even so, Kennedy insisted on implementation of a comprehensive program regardless of economic and budgetary concerns. The meeting ended with each side angry at the other. Afterward, the Massachusetts senator accused the president of "a failure of leadership" that would cripple any national health program from the start.

The months of failed negotiations over NHI left a permanent scar in relations between Kennedy and Carter. Although the senator continued to attend leadership meetings at the White House, called the president to congratulate him on the Camp David accords of 1978, and reaffirmed his intention to support Carter for reelection, it was an open secret by fall 1978 that Kennedy planned to challenge him for the Democratic nomination in 1980. At the Democrats' midterm convention in Memphis in December, the senator delivered a blistering attack against the administration. Evoking traditional Democratic values and accusing the administration of neglecting traditional Democratic constituencies, he once more attacked the administration for its failure on NHI and called its proposals on funding for health programs a sham.

All the polls showed that in a contest between Kennedy and Carter, the Massachusetts senator would win the Democratic nomination by a wide margin, beating the president in the New Hampshire primary, for example, by as much as 50 percent. Kennedy continued to enjoy a lead in the polls through the fall of 1979, when he officially announced his candidacy for the presidency. But already his numbers were beginning to drop dramatically, and his campaign was running into trouble. Despite a well-organized effort by some of his followers in Florida and their prediction that Kennedy would defeat Carter in a straw vote at state party caucuses in October, the president won by a wide margin. In an interview with CBS correspondent Roger Mudd the next month, the Massachusetts Democrat appeared rambling, equivocal, and inarticulate in his responses to questions by Mudd about what had happened at Chappaquiddick 10 years earlier and why Kennedy wanted to be president. Almost all political commentators believed the interview was a disaster for the senator. Hamilton Jordan, who had watched the interview, said he "could hardly contain [his] pleasure."

What really undermined Kennedy's candidacy, however, were two developments abroad. The first was the Iran hostage crisis, beginning with the seizure on November 4, 1979, of the American embassy in Tehran and the taking of 52 hostages. The second was the Soviet Union's invasion of Afghanistan in late December 1979. By remaining close to the White House in order to monitor events in Iran and Afghanistan and foregoing normal campaign activities leading up to the Democratic convention in August, Carter was able to portray himself as a decisive leader staying on top of things in times of trouble, as contrasted with Kennedy, who seemed in his interview with Mudd incapable of articulating how his administration would be different from the present one. Together with lingering doubts about the senator's character as a result of the Chappaquiddick incident, this was enough for Carter to win the Iowa caucuses in January, the senator's neighboring state of New Hampshire a week later, and 24 of the 34 contests in the late winter and spring.

Toward the end of the primary season, Kennedy gained some major victories. On June 3, 1980, Super Tuesday, he won five of the eight primaries, enough to convince the senator, who just 48 hours earlier had contemplated withdrawing from the race, to stay in. Nevertheless, Carter had won enough delegates that day to go over the 2,123 figure needed for the nomination and had a two-to-one lead in delegates. On June 5, the president met with Kennedy at the White House in an effort by Carter to get the senator to bow out, but Kennedy refused. Although he knew that he stood little chance of prevailing over Carter at the August convention, his hope was that he would have enough delegates to help shape the party platform and to be granted a prime-time speech.

From Carter's perspective, Kennedy was seeking to be the spoiler at the convention, wanting it to adopt a liberal platform that challenged the president's efforts at budgetary and fiscal restraint in order to fight inflation. Neither the president nor Kennedy's longtime ally and chairman of the convention, Speaker of the House TIP O'NEILL (Mass.), who had remained quietly neutral during the primary season, were about to let that happen. O'Neill was able to persuade Kennedy to drop most of his demands for changes in the platform in return for a nationally televised address.

The senator's remarks upstaged any other speech made at the convention, including Carter's own acceptance speech. "The work goes on, the cause endures, the hope still lives and the dream shall never die," Kennedy told the convention to thunderous applause. When, at the end of the gathering, President Carter tried to assemble the party's leaders together on the stage in a show of unity, the senator's reluctance to appear alongside Carter was palpable.

During the campaign that followed, the president tried to get Kennedy and his followers, some of whom were defecting to the independent candidacy of Representative

JOHN ANDERSON (R-Ill.), to be more active in supporting his bid for reelection. But while the Massachusetts senator made a few joint appearances with the president, he remained largely uninvolved in the campaign. After Carter's defeat in November 1980, a number of his advisers, including Caddell, Powell, and Jordan, made clear their disdain for Kennedy, believing that his primary challenge to the president, even after he must have known that he could not win the Democratic nomination, had contributed to Carter's defeat.

Since 1980, Kennedy has given up his interest in being president and has instead devoted his career to the Senate. He is now widely respected as one of the nation's leading liberals and one of its most effective lawmakers on Capitol Hill. He has even made strange bedfellows with a number of leading Republican conservatives, including Orrin Hatch (Utah), a close friend, and former senator Alan Simpson (Wyo.). The seventh longest-serving senator in the nation's history, he is currently the ranking member on the Health, Education, Labor and Pensions Committee and also serves on the Judiciary, Armed Services, and Joint Economic committees. Reflecting Kennedy's ongoing interest in health care, he led the fight in 1996 for the Health Insurance Portability and Accountability Act, which allows those who change or lose their jobs to keep their insurance, and the 1997 Children's Health Act, which expanded medical coverage for children through age 18. He also continues to be a leading proponent of educational reform, raising the minimum wage, and strengthening the rights of the disabled.

In the years since 1980, tragedy and scandal have continued to follow Kennedy, including the untimely deaths of his sister-in-law, Jacqueline Onassis Kennedy (1994), and his nephew, John F. Kennedy, Jr. (1999); the arrest of another nephew, William Kennedy Smith, on rape charges (1997); and his highly publicized divorce in 1984 from his wife of 26 years, Joan Bennett. But Kennedy has shown remarkable fortitude and character in dealing with tragedy and family crisis. The events of Chappaquiddick Island in 1969 no longer appear to haunt him. Since 1992, he has been married to Victoria Reggie. Together, they have five children from previous marriages; they live in Hyannis.

Khomeini, Ayatollah Ruholla Mussaui
(1902–1989) *Shi'ite spiritual leader of Iran*

Ruholla Khomeini (more commonly known as Ayatollah Khomeini, or simply the Ayatollah) not only led the movement in Iran resulting in the 1979 overthrow of the nation's shah, MOHAMMAD REZA PAHLAVI, but indirectly played an important—even, as some political analysts believe, decisive—role in the failure of President Jimmy Carter to be reelected in 1980. The frustration and sense of helplessness that Americans felt at the failure of the Carter administration to secure the release of 52 Americans seized by supporters of the ayatollah at the United States' embassy in Tehran on November 4, 1979, and held hostage by the Iranians for exactly one year on the day of the election, was the critical factor, these analysts argue, in RONALD REAGAN's victory over Carter.

Khomeini was, according to most sources, born on September 24, 1902, in Khomeyn, Iran, the son and grandson of mullahs (Shi'ite clerics). (According to a few scholars, he was born on May 17, 1900. No one knows for certain.) His father was killed by a local landlord when he was only five months old, and he was raised by his mother and an aunt, both of whom died when he was about 15 years old. As a young boy of six, he began to study the Koran (Qu'ran; the Muslim holy book) and later was taught Islamic jurisprudence by his older brother, who had the appellation of *ayatollah* (chosen by God) in the holy city of Qom. Khomeini also learned Islamic theology and law (*sharia*) from one of the leading teachers of the time, Ayatollah Abdul Karim Haeri-ye Yazdi, and studied the writings of Plato, whose concept of a philosopher/king influenced his own aspirations. At the age of 32, he was considered by his teachers to be a *mojtahed* (a cleric capable of interpreting Islamic law in all areas of human life). A love of traditional Persian poetry and a mystical sense of God's all-being belied a seemingly sullen and ascetic personality.

Khomeini became a scholar and teacher at the Islamic Institute of Medresseh Faizieh in Qom, where, in both his writings and teaching, he developed in detail his belief in the fundamental interrelationship between faith and social and political practice as prescribed by the Koran. By the early 1960s, he was recognized as an ayatollah and was one of the Shi'ites' most respected and powerful clerics.

Although Khomeini had written in opposition to secular authority as early as the 1940s, he did not begin to campaign actively against the rule of Iran's shah until 1962, when Mohammad Reza Pahlavi instituted the so-called White Revolution. This was an effort to westernize and modernize Iranian society that included granting women the vote (which Khomeini viewed as antithetical to the Koran) and land reforms that stripped the Shi'ite clergy of much of its considerable property holdings. In response to riots against the shah inspired by Khomeini and his followers, thousands of whom came to hear his fiery sermons against the monarch, the Iranian ruler had the ayatollah arrested and exiled, first to Turkey and then to the Shi'ite holy city of Najaf in Iraq.

In Najaf, Khomeini continued to speak out against the shah, investing not only Islamic fundamentalists but nationalists who viewed the shah's 1964 granting of diplomatic privileges and immunities to American military personnel and their dependents as an insult to Iranian independence. Khomeini also taunted the shah for his ties to Israel, warning that the Jews were seeking to take over Iran. Over time, economic corruption, political repression by the shah's notorious security force known as SAVAK, and the more general turmoil of change associated with the process of westernization made Khomeini's message resonate with broad strata of Iranian society.

As opposition to the shah mounted, protesters took to the streets, many waving pictures of Khomeini. Sermons at the mosques denounced tyranny, especially after a fire in a movie theater in Abadan in August 1978 killed 377 persons whose escape was blocked by exit doors that would not open. Khomeini blamed the deaths on the shah. The monarch responded by pressuring Iraq to expel the ayatollah. It was a major mistake. Taking up residence outside of Paris and surrounded by his followers-in-exile, Khomeini attracted the attention of the international media and issued daily sermons encouraging further demonstrations and strikes to shut the country's economy down. Cassettes of his sermons were sold by the thousands in Iran's marketplaces. Despite the shah's imposition of martial law, demonstrations grew larger and became more violent.

Finally, having lost control of the country, the shah and his family fled from Iran on January 16, 1979, after a regency council was established led by Prime Minister Shahpour Bakhtiar, a moderate who had spent time in the shah's prison. On February 1, the ayatollah returned from exile, greeted by millions of adoring Iranians. Khomeini did not attempt immediately to seize power but instead appointed a government headed by one of his advisers, Mehdi Barzagan, promised elections, and retired to his former home in Qom.

Over the next months, however, it became clear that the ayatollah intended to establish a theocracy in Iran. His followers established ruling councils known as *komitehs* throughout the country that took orders directly from a 15-member revolutionary council headed by Khomeini. Barzagan and his cabinet met on a regular basis with the ayatollah at his home and were constrained to carry out his edicts. Thousands of the shah's former supporters or opponents of Khomeini were summarily tried, executed, or given long prison terms. Banks and major industries were nationalized, and opposition newspapers were closed. In March, a referendum was approved turning Iran into an Islamic theocracy. A society based on Khomeini's interpretation of Islamic law was then established. Women were forced to give up western fashion for traditional black robes and were segregated from men in schools below the university level and in most public activities. Alcohol and most forms of music were forbidden. Adulterers were tried and often executed.

The ayatollah had a particular hatred for the United States, which he referred to as the "Great Satan" because of its historic support of the shah and the state of Israel and because of its close association with the westernization of Iran, which Khomeini believed was responsible for the corruption of its society. Throughout 1979, Iranians marched against the United States, burning the American flag and chanting anti-American slogans. The United States ordered Americans out of the country, including most of the personnel at the U.S. embassy in Tehran, which had been seized briefly in February. Iran placed revolutionary guards around the embassy to protect it against unruly crowds.

Matters between the United States and Iran came to a head in October and November 1979, when President Jimmy Carter decided to allow the cancer-stricken shah—who had earlier been refused entry into the United States and had lived in Morocco and Mexico—into the country for emergency medical treatment. At the time, the president had been told by influential friends of the deposed leader, including New York banker DAVID ROCKEFELLER and former secretary of state HENRY KISSINGER, that the shah's own doctors said that he would die unless he received emergency treatment in the United States.

In making his decision, which he did reluctantly, President Carter had informed the Iranian government, which wanted the shah returned to Iran to face charges of torture and mass murders, that he was permitting the former leader into the country purely for humane reasons. While Iran objected to the president's decision, it indicated that it would take no retaliatory measures against the United States. On November 4, however, militant students stormed the embassy in Tehran, taking more than 60 Americans as hostages and seizing thousands of pages of classified documents; police did nothing to stop them. The hostages were blindfolded, and their hands tied behind their backs; eventually some were released, but 52 remained. Outraged at this violation of international law, the United States and most of the international community demanded the Americans' immediate release. The UN Security Council voted unanimously to express its "profound concern" over Iran's detention of the U.S. diplomats.

From Qom, however, the ayatollah, who apparently did not plan the seizure of the embassy, quickly saw it as an opportunity to strengthen his power. Although he was unquestionably the country's most important spiritual and political leader, whose word was virtually tantamount to law, he still had to contend with more moderate rivals. These included believers in parliamentary government, ethnic separatists, secularists, and those who questioned his interpretation of Islamic law. Even Prime Minister Barzagan, who wanted to restore normal relations between the United States and the Tehran government, had fallen from his grace. Also, the economy had failed to return to prerevolutionary levels. Inflation was running at 40 percent and unemployment at 25 percent.

The seizure of the hostages gave Khomeini a perfect opportunity, therefore, to solidify Islamic control over Iran by concentrating popular discontent on his two great demons, the shah and the United States. When Barzagan ordered the militants to withdraw from the embassy and release the hostages, Khomeini refused to back him and, instead, encouraged the militants to hold fast. In despair, Barzagan resigned. The Islamic Revolutionary Council took power, and the ayatollah's control over the country was complete. In December, he proceeded with a referendum for a new constitution. Approved overwhelmingly, it provided for an elected president and parliament (*majlis*) but made them subject to a council of Muslim clerics. Atop the structure was a *faqih* (literally jurisprudent), the leading theologian of Iran who had to approve the president, had veto power over virtually every act of government, and even commanded the armed forces.

As for the hostages, when President Carter sent former attorney general Ramsey Clark and William Miller, a retired foreign service officer who had served in Iran, to Tehran to meet with Khomeini in order to discuss their release, the ayatollah refused even to allow their plane to land. The president responded by stopping imports of oil from Iran and by freezing Iranian assets in the United States. He also ordered the deportation of any Iranian students residing illegally in the country. Days turned into weeks. In April 1980, Khomeini stated that the hostages would have to remain in Iran with their student captors until new elections took place and the *majlis* created by the December 1979 referendum could decide their fate; this meant a delay of at least six or seven months.

In April 1980, Carter ordered a daring rescue mission, but it fell victim to mechanical failure, resulting in the loss of eight American lives. In Khomeini's mind, the president had become Satan himself. For the remainder of the president's term in office, the hostage crisis hang like a shroud over his administration. Despite protracted secret negotiations between the United States and Iran that began in October 1980, the negotiations were not concluded and the hostages not released until after Carter was defeated for reelection and Ronald Reagan took the oath of office as the United States' 40th president on January 20, 1981. Later, Carter wrote that had he been able to secure the hostages' release, he would have won reelection. A number of political analysts agree with that assertion.

During the remainder of Khomeini's life, he sanctioned a somewhat more flexible policy toward the United States, in part because of an eight-year war with Iraq, whose origins are not entirely clear but which left more than a million combatants on both sides killed and the economies of both countries in shambles. One result of the war was the Iran-contra scandal of Reagan's second term, which involved the sale of arms to Iran in exchange for funds that were used in a clandestine operation against the leftist Sandinista government of Nicaragua. Until the end of his life, however, Khomeini remained an inveterate foe of Western ways and a ruthless defender of the faith. In 1989, he provoked international controversy by publicly commanding the killing of Salman Rushdie, a British citizen and author of the novel *The Satanic Verses*, whom Khomeini accused of committing blasphemy because of his unflattering portrait of Islam.

Khomeini died on June 3, 1989, of a heart attack following surgery for stomach cancer. More than a million distraught Iranians thronged his funeral, seizing at his casket and sending his body tumbling into the crowd before it could be rescued and airlifted to the Bahesht-e-Zahra Cemetery, the cemetery of martyrs where thousands of Iranian soldiers killed during the Iraq-Iran War were buried.

Kirbo, Charles Hughes

(1917–1996) *lawyer, Carter friend and unofficial adviser*

Charles Kirbo has often been referred to as President Carter's "one-man kitchen cabinet." Although not holding any government position, he had as much influence on the president as any other individual in the administration. He played a decisive role in launching Carter's political career by representing him in an election-fraud case in his first bid for electoral office in 1962. Kirbo also played a major advisory role in Carter's two campaigns for governor in 1966 and 1970, in his campaign for president in 1976, in his selection of WALTER MONDALE as his running mate in 1976, and in the selection of his White House staff and cabinet following his election. Although declining any position for himself within the administration, Kirbo was, nevertheless, a regular visitor to Washington, staying at the White House about once every two weeks. The president looked to him for advice on staff and personnel problems as well as on legislative and fiscal policy. He was also Carter's closest friend.

A partner during most of his legal career with Atlanta's largest and most prestigious law firm, King and Spalding, Kirbo was born on March 5, 1917, in Bainbridge, Georgia, the sixth of eight children. He graduated from the University of Georgia Law School (LL. B, 1939) and served in the army during World War II. After the war, he began a law practice in Bainbridge. Under the veneer of a soft-spoken and slow-speaking country lawyer in rumpled attire, he had a shrewd legal mind that gained him a statewide reputation as a brilliant trial lawyer. In 1960, King and Spalding invited him to join the firm as a partner.

Kirbo first met Carter in 1962 when the future president was contesting his defeat for the Democratic nomination for the state senate, a nomination that was still tantamount to election in the rural South. Carter believed he had been cheated out of the nomination because 420 ballots were counted in one of the precincts of Quitman County controlled by a local political boss, even though only 333 ballots had been issued. Carter asked Kirbo, who had been recommended to him by a cousin, to represent him. Although the Atlanta lawyer thought Carter had little chance to win, he was impressed by the Plains businessman's determination. He also knew the senatorial district from his earlier law practice in Brainbridge. After some reflection, Kirbo decided to take the case.

The archaic system under which primaries were conducted in the state made it difficult for Carter to turn the election around. But Kirbo had the ballot box in question impounded. In a slow, deliberate presentation, Kirbo then persuaded a superior court judge overseeing the case, Carl Crow, that fraud had, indeed, taken place in Quitman County. When the ballot box was opened, there were 111 ballots clumped together on top of the other ballots. The list of voters and the ballot stubs were also missing. The next day, the judge declared the entire vote from the precinct invalid, thereby changing the outcome of the primary from defeat to victory for the 37-year-old peanut farmer from Plains.

Numerous legal and political problems still had to be overcome before Carter was finally seated in the Georgia Senate in January, including a serious write-in campaign in the general election in November by the candidate Carter had defeated in the primary. Kirbo navigated these difficult waters for the neophyte candidate. "Going to see Charlie Kirbo that day,"

Carter later said of first meeting with Kirbo, "was probably one of the smartest things I ever did in my life."

Over the four years that followed, Carter and Kirbo sealed their friendship. Kirbo helped line up support among his business clients for Carter's first run for the governorship in 1966 and frequented campaign headquarters in Atlanta, where the Carters took up temporary residence. He did much the same during the second bid—this time successful—in 1970. When a seat in the U.S. Senate opened following the death in 1971 of Georgia's much revered U.S. senator, Richard Russell, Governor Carter offered it to Kirbo, who turned it down. Kirbo did agree, however, to serve as chairman of the state Democratic Party. He also offered legal and political counsel to Carter and was even given his own office at the state Capitol. About once a week, he had lunch with the governor.

At the Democratic nominating convention in 1972, a number of Carter's young followers, including HAMILTON JORDAN, GERALD RAFSHOON, PETER BOURNE, and Landon Butler, entertained the notion of getting Carter the vice-presidential spot on the 1972 Democratic ticket headed by GEORGE MCGOVERN. They argued that as a representative of the new generation of progressive governors in the South, who were liberal on racial and other social matters but more conservative on fiscal issues, Carter could bring balance to the Democratic ticket headed by a leader of the party's most liberal wing. He might even help carry some of the southern states. The older and more conservative Kirbo, who backed HENRY JACKSON for the nomination, thought the idea of a McGovern-Carter ticket absurd.

Ultimately the Georgians were rebuffed by the McGovern camp, and Carter wound up making a nominating speech for Jackson. But the differences between Kirbo and the younger Georgians indicated cultural as well as political differences within the Carter camp illustrative of even sharper differences within the Democratic Party that would play themselves out during the Carter presidency. By remaining silent over the question of whether to have his name put forward for vice president on a McGovern ticket, Carter had effectively given the green light to the Georgians to go forward with their effort to secure the second spot on the Democratic ticket for him. Although it ended like a puff of smoke, Carter had made clear that he had been smitten with the idea of holding national office.

Like the other Georgians close to Carter, Kirbo became convinced by the end of 1972 that the governor had his eye on the White House. Furthermore, he was certain that Carter had the demeanor, intelligence, honesty, ethics, knowledge, and sound political sense to be president. As early as 1966, in fact, he had begun to contemplate Carter's presidential potential. A fiscal conservative himself, Kirbo also believed that in fiscal matters Carter was "as conservative as anybody was in a sound way." Once Carter confirmed to his closest friends in December 1972 that he intended to run for president, Kirbo assumed an unofficial role as a political adviser while Hamilton Jordan masterminded the strategy that led to Carter's nomination and election as president.

In 1976, after it became clear that Carter was going to win the Democratic nomination, Kirbo spent most of his time interviewing possible candidates for the vice-presidential spot on Carter's ticket. Even though his responsibility was more in the nature of gathering information on the candidates than giving the former governor his impressions of them, he was not reluctant to express an opinion. He made clear, for example, that his first choice was Washington senator Henry Jackson, whose views, he said, represented a nice balance between those of the liberal and conservative wings of the Democratic Party; he also conceded, however, that Jackson would probably not be the convention's first choice. In addition to Jackson, Kirbo also interviewed Senator EDMUND MUSKIE (Maine) and Senator John Glenn (Ohio), but Minnesota's Walter Mondale emerged, in his view, as the strongest candidate. Kirbo's judgment coincided with Carter's, and the news went out that the former governor's running mate would be the junior senator from Minnesota.

During the presidential campaign, Kirbo was in telephone conversation with the Democratic candidate almost every day, frequently several times a day. In the afternoon, he would also go over to Carter's Atlanta headquarters, where he would work without official title on campaign business. In his conversations with Carter, he joined with Jordan and other campaign strategists in suggesting that the Democratic candidate forego an issue-oriented campaign against his Republican opponent, President GERALD FORD, in favor of one emphasizing core values and the restoration of confidence in government. For the most part, Carter followed this strategy throughout his campaign. What it meant, of course, was that when the former governor entered the White House, the American public did not a have a clear idea of where he stood on the major issues facing the nation.

Following Carter's election as president in November 1976, Kirbo continued to play an important advisory role to the incoming administration, participating once more in the vetting process for the president-elect's cabinet. Among the individuals he discussed with Carter was his friend and former law partner at King and Spalding, Judge GRIFFIN BELL, whom he recommended for attorney general. Because of Bell's earlier decisions on desegregation cases and his membership in two all-white social clubs, his nomination caused considerable unhappiness among liberal Democrats, including even Vice President-elect Mondale. Ironically, Kirbo was later attacked by conservative columnist WILLIAM SAFIRE, who, labeling him the "[Bert] Lance-Carter crony," also accused him of being responsible not only for Bell's appointment but also for all the other major appointments at the Justice Department, including Bell's top deputy, BENJAMIN CIVILETTI. Later, Kirbo conceded that he had recommended Civiletti to Bell but denied that he had been responsible for his selection or for that of any of the other top officials at Justice.

The issues that concerned Kirbo the most after Carter took office were the relative youth and inexperience of the White House staff, the lack of a chief of staff, and the scandal surrounding Office of Management and Budget (OMB) director BERT LANCE. While Kirbo appreciated the role that Carter's closest advisers at the White House, Hamilton Jordan and Press Secretary JODY POWELL, had played in getting Carter elected, he believed they were still "young boys that hadn't fully developed." He was disappointed that another of his partners at King and Spalding, JACK WATSON, who headed the transition team after Carter's election but ultimately lost out to Jordan in a power struggle, was not appointed by the president as his chief aid.

Kirbo also thought the president needed a chief of staff. Carter was willing to have Kirbo serve in that capacity even though the concept of a keeper at the gate, inherent in the position, was contrary to the president-elect's interest in having ready access to the Oval Office for senior staff and cabinet members. So when Kirbo turned the offer down, believing he could not afford the financial sacrifice involved in giving up his law practice and moving his family to Washington, the president did not offer it to anyone else. Kirbo thought Watson would have made an excellent chief of staff, in contrast to Jordan, who lacked both the interest and the attention to detail required by the position. He later regretted that he did not push the case for Watson harder with the president. He said he did not do so because he thought it would harm his effectiveness within the new administration if he attempted to promote his former partner over someone like Jordan, who was much closer to the incoming president and was also known as a tough political infighter.

Tied to what Kirbo believed was the youth and inexperience of a number of Carter's top aids was the Lance affair, the most serious political crisis of Carter's young administration. According to Kirbo, he had always had some concern about Bert Lance's lifestyle and finances, but these were outweighed in his mind by the high regard for Lance within Georgia's banking community, by his good business sense, and by the fact that he was close enough to Carter to be his confidant the way Kirbo would have been had he moved to Washington.

As the scandal involving Lance's finances and questionable banking practices unfolded, however, Kirbo advised the president, together with others of his senior aides, to dismiss Lance in order to avoid further damage to his administration. On September 18, 1977, Carter pressured his OMB director to tender his resignation. Although one of many who had advised the president to ask for Lance's resignation, Kirbo had a better sense than others in the White House of the lasting damage the Lance affair would cause the administration. He also believed it could have been avoided had the White House functioned more efficiently with an ear closer to the ground. Without saying as much, he blamed Jordan for not being on top of things.

On a number of other occasions, Kirbo was called by the White House to put out fires, including a claim by William Safire in October 1979 that the warehouse Carter owned in Plains had been used in 1976 as collateral for a loan to finance Carter's presidential campaign, even though the warehouse was nearly bankrupt. As trustee of Carter's blind trust while he served in the White House, Kirbo denied these charges, and in October 1979 a special investigator appointed by the Justice Department cleared the president and his 1976 campaign committee of wrongdoing.

By then, however, Kirbo was himself an object of unwanted media attention as a result of charges a month earlier by columnist JACK ANDERSON that he and Hamilton Jordan had consorted with the fugitive financier Robert Vesco, who had stolen millions of dollars from an investment firm he had run and then fled to Costa Rica to escape prosecution. According to Anderson, Kirbo and Jordan had attempted to get the Justice Department to stop its efforts to extradite Vesco. As part of this conspiracy, they had purportedly met with one of Jordan's lifelong friends, Spencer Lee, representing Vesco, who had offered them a share of Vesco's vast financial holdings. Both Kirbo and Jordan denied that they had even met with Jordan's friend, and so did Lee.

The only evidence Anderson had to support his allegations were letters, supposedly written by Lee to Kirbo and to Jordan and one by Jordan to Vesco, allegedly on White House stationery but later proved a forgery, discussing their conversations. Nevertheless, Anderson appeared on ABC's *Good Morning America* and went with his story, which also claimed that President Carter had penned a note to Attorney General Bell asking him to see Lee, a note that the president denied writing and the attorney general denied receiving. But because of the seriousness of the charge and its involvement of the Justice Department, Justice was forced to call a special grand jury to look into Anderson's claims. After an 11-month investigation, the administration was exonerated, but not without the type of publicity that hurt the administration and that Kirbo had spent his career trying to avoid.

The last 18 months of the Carter administration was one of the most difficult periods for Kirbo, as it was for the president. In addition to the charges made against the administration by Safire and Anderson, which consumed hundreds of hours of Kirbo's time and raised questions about his own integrity, he also had to deal with a third scandal involving the ties that the president's brother, BILLY CARTER, had with the Libyan government. He was also at Camp David in July 1979 when, for 11 days, Carter held a series of meetings with different groups of Americans as he tried to understand the national angst concerning his leadership. The meetings were followed by an address to the nation on July 15 on the "crisis of confidence" gripping the nation and a shake-up, two days later, of his cabinet and White House staff. In 1980, Kirbo became increasingly involved in the president's campaign for reelection, both the challenge to Carter's nomination by Senator EDWARD KENNEDY (Mass.) and then his loss to his Republican challenger, RONALD REAGAN. Overhanging everything was the shroud of the crisis caused by the November 1979 seizure of 52 American hostages at the U.S. embassy in Tehran, Iran, an ordeal that lasted 444 days.

In reviewing these matters a few years after Carter left office, Kirbo recognized the need for the shake-up of the cabinet and White House staff. Emphasizing the importance of loyalty that any president had a right to expect from those he appointed and were the administration's most senior members, Kirbo believed that the president had been betrayed by Secretary of Health, Education and Welfare (HEW) JOSEPH CALIFANO, Secretary of the Treasury W. MICHAEL BLUMENTHAL, and Secretary of Energy JAMES SCHLESINGER, all of whom had not been loyal to the president and, in Kirbo's view, deserved to be dismissed. At the same time, he noted the president's reluctance to fire anyone, but especially Califano, who, in Kirbo's mind, was the most blatant transgressor but who the president believed had also done an excellent job as secretary of HEW.

Kirbo also welcomed the president's decision to appoint Hamilton Jordan as his chief of staff, an institutional change that he thought was long overdue, and to bring more senior leadership to the White House by his appointments of the journalist HEDLEY DONOVAN as senior adviser and LLOYD CUTLER as counsel to the president.

In recalling the 1980 election, Kirbo made clear his distaste for Edward Kennedy, both the senator's liberal politics and the fact that he refused to withdraw from the race even when it was beyond doubt that the president had the nomination sewed up. He attributed Carter's defeat to a number of factors, including the economy, the president's unwillingness to cower to the special interests of the Democratic Party, and the ongoing hostage crisis. In the final analysis, however, he believed Carter had lost because of an exhaustion of energy, first within the Carter camp but then among the American people, due to the length of the campaign. Americans had just grown tired, he said, of the continuing stream of stories about the election and about Carter. Had Kennedy bowed out of the race in the spring, he believed the campaign would have been shorter, campaign staff and workers would have had time to revitalize themselves, and the American people would have had a much-needed pause in the onslaught of news about the president and the campaign. If Kennedy "had gotten out, when people always got out in the past," he said, "they would have supported Jimmy."

Following Carter's defeat in 1980, he and Kirbo remained close friends. Kirbo also continued to practice law until 1987, when he retired; even then, he retained an office at King and Spalding. He was a fellow in the American College of Trial Lawyers, a trustee of the Carter Center, and a board member of the Christian Church Foundation. He died on September 4, 1996, at the age of 79.

Kissinger, Henry Alfred

(Alfred Heinz Kissinger)
(1923–) *former secretary of state*

National Security Advisor and secretary of state during both the Nixon and Ford administrations, Henry Kissinger has been widely acknowledged as one of the most brilliant and effective individuals to have held either of these positions. Establishing his own consulting firm following Jimmy Carter's election as president in 1976, he remained one of the nation's power brokers, with a network of clients and acquaintances that crossed the country's business, academic, and political communities. During the Carter administration, Kissinger and several of his most influential associates pressured the president in October 1979 to allow the deposed shah of Iran, MOHAMMAD REZA PAHLAVI, into the United States for emergency medical treatment, thereby sparking what became the Iranian hostage crisis, which consumed the last year of Carter's presidency and contributed to his defeat for reelection in 1980.

Kissinger was born Alfred Heinz Kissinger in Furth, Germany, on May 23, 1923. In 1938, his family fled Germany for the United States because of Nazi persecution of the Jews, which had cost his father his job as a teacher in 1935. Because his family, which had settled in New York City, was poor, Henry was forced to attend night school while working in a factory. In 1941, he entered the City College of New York intending to study accounting. The next year, he was drafted into the U.S. Army; he became a naturalized citizen while in the army (1943). Recognizing Kissinger's intelligence and knowledge of Europe, army officials had him lecture servicemen on allied war aims. Another German refugee, Fritz Kraemer, recruited him into army intelligence and became his mentor. After World War II ended, Kissinger remained in Europe, serving first in the military occupation and then as a civilian lecturing army officers on foreign policy at the European Command Intelligence School.

In 1947, Kissinger entered Harvard College, where he became a member of the Phi Beta Kappa fraternity and graduated summa cum laude (B.A., 1950). He also received his master's and doctoral degrees in political science from Harvard University (M.A., 1952; Ph.D., 1954). In his doctoral dissertation—which was later published as a book, *Metternich, Castlereagh and the Restoration of Peace, 1812–22* (1957)—Kissinger emphasized the importance of national self-interest as the guiding force of foreign policy; this became the motif of his own conduct of foreign policy.

After receiving his Ph.D., Kissinger stayed on at Harvard as a faculty member, rising in rank to professor of government in 1962. He also served as director of Harvard's Defense Studies Program (1951–69) and became increasingly active outside of Harvard. A member of the Council on Foreign Relations, he published a report he had prepared for the council, *Nuclear Weapons and Foreign Policy* (1957), a critical analysis of the threatened use of strategic nuclear weapons as a tool of foreign policy, which became a critically acclaimed best seller. He served as a consultant to the Arms Control and Disarmament Agency (1961–67) and to the State Department (1965–69) and as an adviser to the National Security Council (1961–62). He also directed a special project on foreign and domestic policy funded by the Rockefeller Brothers Fund that resulted in another book, *Necessity for Choice: Prospects for American Foreign Policy* (1961), emphasizing the ongoing Soviet threat and calling for a major increase in defense spending.

During the 1960s, Kissinger served as an adviser to New York governor Nelson Rockefeller in his several bids for the Republican nomination for president. In 1969, President RICHARD NIXON surprised many political observers by naming Kissinger as his National Security Advisor and head of the National Security Council (NSC). With Nixon's approval, Kissinger centralized the administration's foreign policy in the White House, effectively making the Department of State, whose bureaucracy Nixon detested, a subordinate agency. As National Security Advisor, he became the architect of the administration's foreign policy and its most influential member next to the president.

A series of brilliantly executed—if later controversial—accomplishments, all fully covered in the media, made Kissinger a national celebrity. These included: a new policy of détente with the Soviet Union; the negotiation of the Strategic Arms Limitation Talks, resulting in the SALT I treaty with the Soviets in 1972; a negotiated settlement of the Vietnam War in 1973; and the opening of a new relationship with Communist China, beginning with a state visit by President Nixon in 1972 that Kissinger secretly arranged.

In 1973, following his reelection, Nixon appointed Kissinger secretary of state, replacing William Rogers in that position even as he continued to serve as the president's National Security Advisor. That same year, Kissinger was awarded the Nobel Peace Prize, along with Vietnam's Le Duc Tho, for helping to end the Vietnam War. In October, he brokered an end to the Yom Kippur War between Israel and its Arab neighbors. He was also seen dating such movie stars as Shirley MacLaine, Candice Bergen, and Jill St. John, which added to his celebrity status. The Gallup Poll listed him as the most admired man in the United States in 1972 and 1973.

Unlike other members of the administration close to the president, Kissinger escaped virtually unscathed from the Watergate scandal that in 1974 brought down the Nixon presidency. Nixon's successor, GERALD FORD, kept him on as secretary of state, but Kissinger's influence began to wane as revelations came out about secret wiretapping of his aides and his role in the overthrow of Chile's elected Marxist president, Salvador Allende. He was also attacked on the right for his policy of détente with the Soviet Union and from the left for his secret diplomacy and his lack of concern about human rights and moral issues. Within a year after Ford took office, rumors spread that the president intended to replace Kissinger as secretary of state. Although Ford denied these rumors, they persisted throughout the remainder of his presidency. In 1975, Ford replaced Kissinger as head of the NSC with his deputy, Brent Scowcroft. Kissinger told the press that he intended to resign after the 1976 election even if Ford were elected to a full term.

The secretary of state was an issue throughout the 1976 presidential campaign. Former California governor RONALD REAGAN, who nearly defeated Ford for the Republican nomination, attacked Kissinger for being "soft" in his dealings with the Soviets and for his effort to work out an agreement with Panama on the future status of the Panama Canal and Panama Canal Zone, while the Democratic candidate, Jimmy Carter, flayed away at his indifference to moral issues and human rights in the formulation of foreign policy and for his closed and secret diplomacy. "Our Secretary of State simply does not trust the judgment of the American people," Carter told the Chicago Council on Foreign Relations in March 1976.

After leaving office following Carter's victory, Kissinger established his own consulting firm and became part of the lecture circuit. He also became a professor of diplomacy in the School of Foreign Service at Georgetown University and signed a five-year contract to do consulting and occasional commentary for ABC Television. Although he had lost some of his popularity in his last two years in office, he remained widely regarded as one of the nation's best secretaries of state and leading minds on foreign policy.

As a private citizen, Kissinger visited President-elect Carter in Plains to discuss the major foreign policy issues he would face when he entered the White House in January 1977. Carter was especially interested in hearing his views on normalizing relations with the People's Republic of China (PRC). In March 1977, Kissinger dined at the White House with the president, Secretary of State CYRUS VANCE, and National Security Advisor ZBIGNIEW BRZEZINSKI. He also provided valuable support in helping President Carter win Senate passage of the Panama Canal Treaties in 1978 and later promised to support the SALT II agreement of 1979. Following the president's successful conclusion of an Israeli-Egyptian peace agreement in the spring of 1979, Kissinger telephoned Carter to congratulate him on his achievement. According to Carter, Kissinger told him that the president was "working [the former secretary of state] out of his career of criticizing the government by not leaving him much to criticize."

In fact, though, Kissinger was highly critical of Carter's foreign policy. There was, of course, his fundamental difference with Carter over the role that moral concerns, as opposed to the role of power and realpolitik, should play in formulating foreign policy. But there were other differences as well. Kissinger had practiced a foreign policy often referred to as "step-by-step diplomacy," resolving one issue at a time, such as the Arab-Israeli dispute or relations with the Soviet Union. The president preferred a "comprehensive" approach to foreign policy, such as in the Middle East or in arms talks with the Soviets. Kissinger also believed foreign policy should pivot around the United States' relations with the Soviet Union. Carter thought the United States should move away from an emphasis on Soviet-American relations in order to focus more on a north-south dialogue and on issues like human rights.

Oddly enough, though, the president and the former secretary of state found themselves taking positions opposite to what one might have expected on the major issue in which Kissinger became involved during the Carter presidency: the question of whether to allow the deposed shah of Iran to enter the United States following the January 1979 revolution in Iran. After fleeing his country, the shah had gone to Egypt and then to Morocco. As it became clear, however, that the former monarch would not be returning to Iran, King Hassan told him that he would have to leave Morocco. The shah wanted to come to the United States, but President Carter was opposed to letting him into the country because the administration was engaged in secret negotiations with Iran to restore normal relations with the new Iranian government and feared for the safety of Americans still in Iran. Carter had also been warned by the CIA that if he permitted the shah to enter the United States, Iranian militants might storm the American embassy in Tehran.

Within the administration, only National Security Advisor Zbigniew Brzezinski believed the White House was morally obligated to give the shah asylum in the United States. Carter instructed Secretary of State Vance to "scout around to help find him [the shah] a place to stay." Undersecretary of State David Newsom even tried to enlist Kissinger's help in persuading the shah to look elsewhere for refuge. Why he thought the former secretary of state would cooperate with the administration in this matter is unclear since Kissinger considered the shah a long and faithful friend of the United States. He also considered the administration's unwillingness to allow one of the nation's most loyal allies to come to the country as just one example of the irresolute and feeble way the White House approached foreign policy. On April 8, 1979, he telephoned Carter, urging him to let the shah into the country; when the president turned him down, Kissinger went public. Speaking that night at the Harvard Business School, he stated that the shah "should not be treated like a Flying Dutchman who cannot find a port of call."

Kissinger was therefore appalled by Newsom's request, remarking that the president's decision not to admit the shah into the United States was "a national disgrace." He would not be a party to the decision. Instead, he helped find the shah a home, first in the Bahamas and then in Cuernavaca, Mexico. At the same time, he continued to pressure the White House on the shah's behalf. In this effort, Kissinger worked closely with his longtime associate, DAVID ROCKEFELLER, the chief executive of Chase Manhattan Bank, and John McCloy, former president of the Chase Manhattan and adviser to Presidents John F. Kennedy and Lyndon Johnson. Rockefeller's bank had made extensive loans to the shah's government, and he was on close terms with the deposed monarch. McCloy's law firm represented Chase and major oil companies operating in Iran. They had some success in their lobbying efforts. Even Vice President WALTER MONDALE joined Brzezinski in urging the president to admit the shah. But until October 1979, Carter remained resolute in his opposition to such a move. "Fuck the Shah," he remarked. "I'm not going to welcome him when he has other places where he'll be safe." All he needed, Carter continued, was to have the shah "here playing tennis while Americans in Tehran were being kidnapped or killed."

In October, however, the president learned that the health of the shah, who had been diagnosed with lymphoma in 1973, had begun to deteriorate. Kissinger and Rockefeller informed the White House that he might die unless he received medical treatment in the United States. The president's chief assistant, HAMILTON JORDAN, warned Carter of the political consequences that might follow if he turned down their request. "[I]f the shah dies in Mexico," he told the president, "can you imagine the field day Kissinger will have ... He'll say that first you caused the shah's downfall and now you've killed him."

According to Jordan, the president responded, "To hell with Kissinger, I am president of this country." For humanitarian reasons, however, Carter did agree to allow the shah to come to New York City for medical treatment. Although he informed the Iranian government of his decision and seemed to have its assurance that it would try to protect the American embassy in Tehran, on November 4, 1979, militant Islamic students seized the embassy and took 52 Americans as hostages, beginning the Iranian hostage crisis that would last for 444 days, consume the president, and contribute to his defeat for reelection in 1980. As for the shah, even with medical treatment, he succumbed to cancer in Egypt on July 21, 1980.

Since the Iranian hostage crisis, there has been considerable scholarly controversy over a number of issues relating to the lobbying effort on behalf of the shah, including even the extent to which Kissinger, Rockefeller, and John McCloy had applied pressure on the administration to allow the shah to come to the United States. Kissinger denied that he had "pressured US officials," but former undersecretary of state GEORGE BALL termed the degree of pressure exerted on the White House as "obnoxious" and stated that but for this, the shah would never have been allowed into the country. According to most accounts, though lobbying by Kissinger and his associates did take place, it did not influence the president's final decision; to the contrary, it was counterproductive since the president deeply resented pressure of this kind.

Since the Ford administration, Kissinger has not played a major role in U.S. foreign policy because his moderate Republicanism and earlier responsibility for the policy of détente with the Soviet Union has been out of favor with the more conservative Republicans who have dominated the party since Ronald Reagan's election in 1980. Following the terrorist attack on the World Trade Center in New York City on September 11, 2001, President George W. Bush named Kissinger to head the commission investigating the attack. But Kissinger chose to step down as commission chair rather than make public his financial records, citing potential conflict of interest with his clients as the reason for his unwillingness to make his records available.

The former secretary of state has also been accused by some of his harshest critics of war crimes growing out of the secret bombing of Cambodia during the Vietnam War; the overthrow of Salvador Allende in Chile in 1973; Operation Condor, an alleged conspiracy of murder and torture organized by a number of Latin American dictators in the 1970s; and his approval of Indonesian president Suharto's 1975 bloody occupation of the former Portuguese colony of East Timor, which led to the slaughter of as many as 200,000 Timorese. At least five countries have issued summonses for Kissinger, seeking information about his role in Operation Condor. He is still considered legally at risk in a number of countries in Europe and South America, and he has avoided travel to these places.

Nevertheless, Kissinger remains a highly respected elder statesman who continues to write, lecture, and provide televised commentary on major foreign policy issues, such as the war in Iraq, which he has strongly supported. He also continues to consult on international affairs.

Klutznick, Philip Morris
(1907–1999) *secretary of commerce*

A leader of the American Jewish community and a successful real-estate developer, Philip Klutznick was secretary of commerce during the last year of the Carter presidency, replacing JUANITA KREPS in that position. As a former envoy to the United Nations and president of the World Jewish Congress at the time of his appointment, he had close ties with both Israeli and Egyptian leaders and had been consulted by President Carter in his quest for a peace settlement in the Middle East. As secretary of commerce, Klutznick was responsible for transferring many of the responsibilities for carrying out trade agreements from the Department of State and other agencies to the Department of Commerce. He also was involved in instituting the economic embargo that the White House imposed on the Soviet Union after the Soviets invaded Afghanistan in December 1979.

The son of Orthodox Jews who had emigrated from eastern Europe and settled in Kansas City, Missouri, at the turn of the century, Klutznick was born on July 9, 1907. A star debater and editor of his high-school newspaper, which during his senior year was judged the best one in the state, he attended the University of Kansas and then the University of Nebraska after his family moved to Omaha. After a year, he transferred to Creighton University, a Jesuit school, where he earned his law degree (LL.B., 1930).

Even as a student, Klutznick became active in American Jewish affairs. As a high-school student, he helped found the second chapter of Aleph Zadik Aleph (AZA), the youth branch of the B'nai B'rith. While a college student, he traveled throughout the country establishing chapters of AZA. In law school, he was executive secretary of AZA and became president of the Omaha chapter of the B'nai B'rith.

After graduating from law school, Klutznick worked as an assistant city attorney for Omaha and became involved in acquiring federal aid for city housing projects. Shortly thereafter, he went into private practice. In 1938, he helped establish the Omaha Housing Authority and served as its general counsel for three years. He also authored the Nebraska Housing Authorities Law and later defended its constitutionality before the state Supreme Court.

As a lawyer specializing in public housing, Klutznick made frequent trips to Washington, D.C., which brought him to the attention of federal officials concerned with providing for the housing needs of workers in the rapidly growing defense industries. In 1941, he became a consultant to the government on federal housing for defense workers. In 1944, President Franklin Roosevelt appointed him federal public housing administrator, a position he held until 1946, when he resigned to return to the private sector. Among the towns he built for the government was Oak Ridge, Tennessee.

Following the end of World War II, the United States was faced with a critical need for new housing to meet not only the needs of returning war veterans but also the growth of population that had taken place since the Great Depression, when housing was either unaffordable or materials to build houses were unavailable. Sensing a business opportunity, Klutznick moved to Chicago, where he joined a partnership to build Park Forest, one of the first totally planned suburbs in the United States. Located 27 miles from Chicago, Park Forest became a huge success and launched Klutznick into a career as a highly innovative and successful real-estate developer. His projects came to include a number of communities and shopping malls around the Chicago area and the famed Water Tower Place in Chicago.

Klutznick's success as a businessman did not keep him from his activities in the Jewish community. With the approval of President Harry Truman, he helped organize an informal campaign to seek contributions from federal employees for the United Jewish Appeal. From 1953 to 1959, he also served as the international president of the B'nai B'rith, and in 1956 he helped establish the Conference of Presidents of Major American Jewish Organizations.

Klutznick's activities in the American Jewish community blended into a return to government service. During the Eisenhower administration, he met on occasion with Secretary of State John Foster Dulles and other State Department officials to protest the administration's increasingly stern policy toward Israel in its ongoing dispute with its Arab neighbors. Relations between the United States and Israel reached crisis proportions following the October War of 1956 when Israel refused to withdraw its forces from Sharm el-Sheik at the mouth of the Straits of Tiran and the Gaza Strip, which it had seized during the war, and the White House responded by threatening to impose economic sanctions. At the height of the crisis in February 1957, Klutznick was one of a small group of Jewish leaders who was invited to the State Department to meet with the secretary of state. The crisis was not settled until a few weeks later, when Israel agreed to withdraw from the territories it occupied in return for U.S. guarantees regarding Israeli navigation through the Straits of Tiran and a UN emergency force was deployed in the Gaza Strip. Klutznick was the only one of the Jewish leaders who subsequently met at the State Department to congratulate the secretary of state on the agreement that had been reached. He also worked closely with the State Department to help arrange a loan from the World Bank in order to build port facilities at Ashdod, a new seaport he was helping to construct south of Tel Aviv. Ashdod later grew into a thriving city of about 200,000.

Although Klutznick was a lifelong Democrat, Secretary of State Dulles invited him to serve as a member of the American delegation to the United Nations during the three-month meeting of the General Assembly. His main responsibility was as a member of the Assembly's sixth (legal) committee. Because he was still president of the B'nai B'rith, he was treated with open hostility by a number of the Arab delegates. However, as a result of his brief service, he nursed a desire to return to the United Nations in a more substantial capacity. In 1961, President John F. Kennedy, for whom Klutznick had raised money and campaigned in 1960, appointed him as ambassador to the UN Economic and Social Council, where he remained until 1963. He also served in various other capacities at the United Nations during the 1970s. As Klutznick later wrote, "nothing quite equaled the emotional charge" he always felt when he addressed the General Assembly and "looked over the sea of faces that reflected all the races and ethnic strains of the world."

Klutznick's commitment to public service was not limited to the United Nations. During Lyndon Johnson's administration, he surveyed housing problems in Brazil for the White House. During GERALD FORD's administration, he served on an advisory committee to facilitate the resettlement of Vietnamese and Cambodians in the United States. He also remained active in the American Jewish community. In 1960, he was elected president of the United Jewish Appeal. In 1977, he was elected president of the World Jewish Congress.

During the Carter administration, Klutznick's activities in the American Jewish community once more blended into public service as he figured prominently in President Carter's efforts to resolve the ongoing Arab-Israeli dispute in the Middle East. As a leader of the American Jewish community who made frequent trips to Israel, Klutznick was on a first-name basis with most Israeli leaders, including the leader of the Likud Party and, after elections in 1977, prime minister, MENACHEM BEGIN. Through his activities at the United Nations, Klutznick also became acquainted with Ashraf Ghorbal, the Egyptian ambassador to the United States.

In February 1978, when Egyptian president ANWAR SADAT came to the United States to meet with President Carter (his second visit to the country since Carter had taken office), Ghorbal asked Klutznick to arrange a meeting between Sadat and a small group of distinguished Jewish leaders. By this time, Sadat had made his historic visit to Israel, where he had addressed the Knesset (the Israeli parliament), and Begin had visited Egypt. Hopes of an Egyptian-Israeli peace agreement that might lead to a broader Middle East settlement involving all the Arab countries, however, had diminished as Israel continued to build settlements on the West Bank. Committed to breaking the Arab-Israeli deadlock, Sadat sought to employ American Jewish leaders in his quest for peace in the Middle East. Nothing specific happened as a result of the meeting, but Klutznick perceived that Sadat came away from it believing that American Jewish leaders would support a peace settlement if it were fair to all parties in the Arab-Israeli dispute, increasing his respect for the Egyptian leader.

In early July, Klutnizk attended another small dinner meeting of American Jewish leaders, this time at the White House and arranged at Carter's request. At the meeting, the Jewish leaders angered the president by taking him to task for selling arms to the Arab countries. Klutznick, however, tried to convey to Carter the same message that had been given to Sadat in February. He also suggested that the president "might want to bring the Israelis and Egyptians together with the Americans in the same proximity, and thrash out what is good for all parties."

After the meeting with Carter, Klutznick stayed behind to talk with Vice President WALTER MONDALE, whom he had known for a number of years. He tried to assure Mondale that while Begin could be a difficult person, he was not totally implacable. Shortly thereafter, Klutznick traveled to Israel, where he explained to the prime minister what had taken place at his White House meeting with Carter. He also repeated previous arguments he had given Begin about the need for more flexibility in Israeli's position with regard to the West Bank and Gaza.

That Kluznick actually played a decisive role in persuading President Carter to hold a meeting between Sadat and Begin at Camp David is doubtful. The almost complete breakdown in the peace process in the summer, including Sadat's expulsion of the Israeli mission from Egypt, was decisive in the president's thinking. At the same time, Klutznick had underscored for the president the support he would have within the American Jewish community for a peace initiative. He had also given the president reason to believe, through his conversation with Mondale, that Begin was not beyond reason. Along these same lines, he may have had some influence in getting the Israeli prime minister to sit down once more with Sadat and show some flexibility in Israeli's negotiating stance, even though he acknowledged that the Israeli leader and he "were far from being of the same mind in the quest for peace."

Klutznick had no further encounters with Carter until the president asked him at the end of 1979 to accept the position of secretary of commerce vacated by Juanita Kreps. He was not Carter's first choice for the position; the president had asked a number of other better-known business leaders before choosing Klutznick. But the Chicago real-estate developer was a successful businessman with worldwide connections and considerable diplomatic experience. Over the years, he had come to know a number of White House and cabinet officials, including Vice President Mondale, Secretary of State CYRUS VANCE, and National Security Advisor ZBIGNIEW BRZEZINSKI. The fact that he was a leader of the American Jewish Community in an election year might also have influenced the president's decision, although Klutznick took umbrage at the suggestion that that was the reason he was chosen for the position.

The president announced Klutznick's appointment in November 1979. At age 72, Klutznick was the oldest member of the cabinet. As secretary of commerce, he oversaw the transfer of operations involving foreign commerce from the Department of State to Commerce. These included the sale abroad of American goods and commercial ideas, in conformity with a new trade bill Congress had passed that had also created the International Trade Administration (ITA). The purpose of the ITA was to promote American business in the growing global marketplace by bringing under one administrative umbrella various commercial, manufacturing, marketing, and compliance services. The object was to make the Commerce Department the key coordinator of U.S. foreign-trade policies.

Another initiative Klutznick undertook as commerce secretary was to establish the Office of Productivity, Technology, and Innovation in order to make American industry more competitive with Japanese industry. He was concerned especially with Japanese competition in steel and automobiles. To the extent permissible under antitrust laws, which he favored amending to make them more flexible, Klutznick encouraged business and industry to carry out joint initiatives as a means of bringing about both greater economic efficiency and innovation. Similar initiatives had already been started by his predecessor, Juanita Kreps. Similarly, he encouraged the National Bureau of

Standards's (NBS) Center for Building Technology, which handled much of NBS's engineering programs, to develop a construction productivity program funded at an annual level of $100 million.

Much of Klutznick's remaining time in office was taken up with heading an interdepartmental committee to develop the regulations and guidelines for carrying out the grain embargo and other export restrictions the president had imposed on the Soviet Union following its invasion of Afghanistan in December 1979. This had resulted in an often disputatious relationship between the president and lawmakers from farm states enraged by the ban on grain shipments to the Soviets. Klutznick also had responsibility for overseeing the 1980 census. He came away from the experience convinced that statistical methods rather than existing door-to-door head counting by census takers would provide a more reliable and less expensive way of providing census information.

Klutznick's experience as a member of the Carter administration left him with great respect for the president's integrity and sense of responsibility. "The President Carter I knew," he later wrote, "was a stranger to the political art of escape and evasion." But he was critical of the president's program of economic austerity and credit controls for dealing with the nation's inflation in 1980, believing such measures would be counterproductive and result in recession and consequent greater budget deficits.

Following Carter's defeat in the 1980 election, Klutznizk returned to his home in Chicago. He remained active in the American Jewish community and in various civic and philanthropic endeavors. He also traveled to the Middle East on numerous occasions and continued to press for a negotiated peace in the region. He even established indirect contact with the leader of the Palestine Liberation Organization, YASSER ARAFAT, and met with Syrian president HAFEZ AL-ASSAD. In 1986 and 1987, he established chairs in Jewish civilization at Northwestern University and Creighton University. In 1991, he published his memoirs (with Sidney Hyman), *Angles of Vision: A Memoir of My Lives*. Klutznick died in Chicago on August 14, 1999 from Alzheimer's disease. He was 92 years old.

Kraft, Tim

(Timothy E. Kraft)

(1941–) *appointments secretary, liaison to the Democratic Party, national campaign manager*

Gifted with a politically shrewd mind, Timothy E. Kraft was given increasingly greater responsibilities during Jimmy Carter's presidential campaign in 1976 and then as a member of Carter's White House staff. In 1980, he served as Carter's campaign manager, but he had to resign following charges that he had used cocaine while a member of the White House staff.

Kraft was born in Noblesville, Indiana, on April 10, 1941. The son of a pediatrician, he was introduced to politics when relatives of his Democratic family were soundly beaten in campaigns for local office in a Republican town. After graduating from Dartmouth College, where he majored in government (B.A., 1963), he spent two years in the Peace Corps, working in Guatemala. He then served as a recruiter for the Peace Corps, did graduate work in Latin American Studies at Georgetown University (1966–67), and became a political nomad. He was a press aide for the Mexican Olympics Committee, worked in Jesse Unruh's unsuccessful campaign for governor in California, managed a losing congressional campaign in Indiana, and became a Democratic fund-raiser in the West.

In New Mexico, Kraft worked for Governor Jerry Apodaca, the state's first Hispanic governor, and became executive director of the state Democratic Party. He also served as regional coordinator for the Democratic National Committee Telethon. In 1975, at Apodaca's invitation, Jimmy Carter visited New Mexico, where he was introduced to Kraft. Carter hired Kraft as a full-time political organizer for the western states, and shortly thereafter, he was given responsibility for organizing the Carter campaign in Iowa.

Moving to Iowa in August 1975, Kraft organized a group of volunteers in each congressional district, a statewide steering committee, similar committees in each congressional district, and even some local committees. Although some of the steering committees never met as a group because their members did not get along, they provided the grass-roots organization that proved pivotal to Carter's victory in the Iowa caucuses in January 1976.

Kraft earned the nickname "Krafty" because of his political cunning. When, for example, he learned that the *Des Moines Register and Tribune* was planning to conduct a straw preference poll of the candidates for president at a fund-raising dinner in Ames in October 1975, he flooded the dinner with Carter volunteers so that Carter won the straw poll with 23.6 percent of the 1,000 votes cast to 12.4 percent for Minnesota senator HUBERT HUMPHREY, who received the second-highest vote.

The Iowa caucuses were lightly attended, and the largest bloc of participants remained uncommitted. But because the former Georgia governor had received twice as many votes as his nearest opponent, Indiana senator BIRCH BAYH, Carter was proclaimed by the media as the winner of the caucuses. This vaulted him into position as a major contender for the Democratic nomination for the first time. "I guess we won't have to send you to Alaska now," Carter told Kraft when he received the news about the results in Iowa.

Because of his success at grass-roots organization, Kraft was given responsibility for the Pennsylvania primary scheduled for April 1976. The primary took on special importance because although Carter had emerged as the leading candidate for the nomination, he had yet to prove that he could win a primary in a northern industrial state. Furthermore, he faced major opposition from Senator HENRY JACKSON (Wash.), who had the support of the state's labor leaders and who had decided to make his last stand in Pennsylvania. Kraft followed much the same strategy he had pursued in Iowa. Working with Jack Sullivan, an Annapolis classmate of Carter's, he fielded 22 organizations throughout the state. Using volunteers from Georgia and Florida as well as Pennsylvania, he canvassed neighborhoods throughout the state. Volunteers rang doorbells, distributed literature, and made 300,000 telephone calls. Carter supplemented Kraft's organization with a media blitz. In April, he won a decisive victory over Jackson, forcing the Washington senator out of the campaign and, according to pollsters, establishing himself as the strongest challenger to President GERALD FORD.

With his credentials clearly established as an effective campaign organizer who had helped Carter win two critical primary victories, Kraft was promoted by Carter to be his national field coordinator. In this role, he selected and took charge of the coordinators who ran the campaign in each state and region. To avoid local political rivalries, Kraft looked in most cases for persons from outside each state with experience as political activists. They were mostly not "big strategists or famous names," he explained. "They have technical ability that they picked up quietly. They're young professionals who can work anywhere." Bill Clinton of Arkansas and his wife, Hilary Rodham, were offered the opportunity to run the Carter operation in Texas.

President Carter with Tim Kraft, 1977 *(Jimmy Carter Library)*

Bill Clinton declined, but his wife joined the campaign as deputy field director.

A laid-back and voluble Hoosier, with a puckish humor, bushy hair, and Pancho Villa mustache, Kraft was not part of Carter's inner circle of Georgians. But he was well-liked, fitted in, and became close friends with the candidate's chief aide, HAMILTON JORDAN, who also became his mentor. Following Carter's victory in November, he was rewarded for his efforts during the campaign by being appointed as the new president's appointments secretary. Despite his easy manner, Kraft was attentive to detail and proved adept at his job of arranging the president's schedule of daily meetings. "My biggest nemesis, and I say that lightly," he remarked in 1978, "was the foreign policy schedule, which seemed to consume an inordinate amount of time. ... In my mind, it's a continuing problem."

By 1978, it had become apparent that Kraft's talents as a political coordinator were not being used to the president's best advantage. The administration, moreover, was under increasing attack from leading Democrats for not being sufficiently responsive to their needs and interests. Accordingly, in April 1978, as part of a reorganization of the White House staff, Kraft was moved to the senior staff and given the task of liaison to the Democratic Party. His job was to mend fences with state party leaders and to help get the president's legislative program through Congress.

Kraft proved a good choice for the job. Talented in the detail of political work, he courted state party leaders by holding a series of White House breakfasts where they had the opportunity to confer with cabinet officials and to meet the president. He took back from cabinet secretaries the authority to appoint persons to second- and third-level jobs in their departments. He also asked each cabinet secretary to schedule at least one speaking engagement a month on behalf of the administration and to give the White House copies of their travel schedules so that political events could be incorporated into the schedules. He had the president make more side trips to congressional districts during fund-raising travels. His office also organized a coalition of Mexicans, Cubans, and Puerto Ricans called the Hispanic American Democrats in an effort to strengthen their ties to the party.

Kraft also acted as troubleshooter to deal with local intra-party disputes. "We're not out to politicize the White House," he explained about his new job, "but we've got to use the political resources we have better than before." By all accounts, his efforts to mend fences had a beneficial effect. "You could get a hearing, sure," remarked Rick Scott, chairman of the Minnesota Democratic Party, about the White House staff prior to Kraft taking charge. "But the guy supposedly listening was always tapping a pencil on the table. Now it's different. They listen."

When it came time to gear up for the 1980 election, Kraft resigned his White House position to become national campaign manager. His job was similar to the one he had in 1976, running day-to-day operations. Hamilton Jordan, with whom he was now sharing a Georgetown house along with Carter's pollster, PAT CADDELL, was in charge of overall strategy for the campaign. The Texan ROBERT STRAUSS, who was chairman of the reelection committee, was responsible for fund-raising and for dealing with the press and party leaders.

The team was able to beat back Massachusetts senator EDWARD KENNEDY's challenge for the Democratic nomination. The Democrats were well ahead in the polls when, in September 1980, Kraft was forced to resign from the campaign while a special prosecutor investigated charges that he had used cocaine. During testimony before a federal grand jury, Evan Dobelle, whom Kraft had replaced as campaign manager, stated that he had seen Kraft use cocaine in New Orleans in 1978. Kraft categorically denied the charges. "Although I am completely innocent of the charges," he said, "I find myself in a very difficult situation and facing a difficult decision."

Having defended Jordan against similar charges less than a year earlier, the White House decided against making a similar effort on behalf of Kraft, especially since Kraft's flamboyant lifestyle had brought him notoriety in Washington. (He had been with Jordan at a Georgetown bar in 1978 when Jordan allegedly spat a drink down a woman's back.) As required by the Ethics in Government Act, a special prosecutor was appointed to examine the Kraft case. No indictment, however, was ever brought against Kraft.

Following his resignation from the campaign and Carter's defeat in November 1980, Kraft ran political campaigns for candidates in Latin America. In 2004, he became active in the presidential campaign of Howard Dean, helping to organize the Dean effort in the Iowa caucuses. Kraft lives in the town of Corrales, New Mexico.

Kreps, Juanita Morris
(1921–) *secretary of commerce*

The first woman and economist to serve as secretary of commerce, Juanita Kreps enjoyed a distinguished career as an educator and administrator at Duke University before being appointed to her cabinet-level position by President-elect Carter. A committed feminist who appointed women to many of the senior positions within her department, Kreps sought to expand opportunities for women within the business world. As commerce secretary, she also sought to play an instrumental role in the the president's urban policy, promote American trade abroad, and save the nation's steel industry from bankruptcy. Despite her credentials, however, she was never included within the circle of President Carter's closest economic policy makers.

The daughter of a coal-mine operator, Kreps was born Juanita Morris on January 11, 1921, in Lynch, in the impoverished coal county of Harlan, Kentucky. She attended Berea College, known for providing a free, quality education to promising students from the Appalachian region who could not otherwise afford a college education. Berea had a profound influence on her. "The spirit of the place," she later recalled, "was one of independence, self-reliance, high-level integrity, and academic excellence. It made a deeper impression on me than my childhood." Graduating Phi Beta Kappa with a major in economics from Berea (B.A., 1944), she received her master's and doctorate in economics from Duke University (M.A., 1944; Ph.D., 1948).

In 1944, she married Clifton H. Kreps, Jr., an economist whom she had met at Berea. Juanita Kreps specialized in labor demographics—the structure and composition of the labor force. After following her husband to various academic positions at Denison and Hofstra Universities and Queens College, she returned to Duke as a part-time instructor. She then began her climb up the academic ladder at Duke, rising from visiting instructor in 1958 to James B. Duke Professor of Economics by 1972. During this period, she wrote two successful books, one on the special problems of working women, *Sex in the Marketplace: American Women at Work* (1971), and the other on the economics of aging, *Lifetime Allocation of Work and Income: Essays in the Economics of Aging* (1971). In 1969, she was also appointed dean of the Women's College and assistant provost (1969–72) and then vice president of the university (1973–77). In addition, she served on the board of directors of a number of the nation's leading corporations, including J. C. Penney and Co., Eastman Kodak, Chrysler Corporation, and AT&T. In 1972, she was appointed the first woman member of the board of directors of the New York Stock Exchange.

Committed to increasing the number of women in high-level federal positions, President-elect Carter asked Kreps to take the position of commerce secretary after former IBM vice president Jane Cahill Pfeiffer took herself out of consideration. This made Kreps not only the first woman to be named secretary of commerce but also the first economist. A feminist with a wry sense of humor, she commented later, "I'd like to get to the point where I can be just as mediocre as a man." Accepting the president's offer, she made her aim as commerce secretary to "encourage business to perform well all tasks that improve human welfare." That included "making a difference in the image of professional women."

A Democrat who said she preferred the liberal MIT (Massachusetts Institute of Technology) economist Paul Samuelson to the University of Chicago's conservative Nobel laureate Milton Friedman, Kreps nevertheless described herself as moderate in economics who preferred, for example, that the marketplace rather than the government resolve the problem of unemployment. At the same time, she believed business had the responsibility to provide flexibility in meeting the needs of working women and in dealing with the problem of early retirement. She was also concerned with the needs of urban areas, pointing out that "the city is where commerce is."

After Kreps took office, she put her strongly held feminist views into action, hiring women for five of the top 10 slots in the department. When President Carter met with Commerce Department employees just three weeks after she became secretary, women thanked him for her appointment. According to one of them, Kreps did "more for our morale ... than all former Secretaries put together." Later, at a cabinet meeting in summer 1977, the president expressed his appreciation to Kreps and Secretary of Housing and Urban Development PATRICIA HARRIS for not attending a meeting organized by female White House staffers to express their views in support of abortion, which were contrary to his own view. Kreps politely and respectfully remarked, "You should not take my absence from the meeting of the women as an indication of support for the administration's position on abortion." Distressed that women owned only 4.6 percent of the nation's 8.5 million businesses, she pushed the president later that summer to establish an Interagency Task Force on Women Business Owners.

Committed to playing a major part in the administration's urban policy, Kreps spurred the Commerce Department's Economic Development Administration to keep industries in cities through such incentives as grants and lower-interest loans to cities. In 1978, she sought to embed her department into the administration's urban policy by taking advantage of the government's "set-aside" program for minority business enterprises (MBEs). In accordance with legislation passed by Congress that year, she established an Office of Small and Disadvantaged Business Utilization to implement MBE programs into the Commerce Department's contracts and grants.

Kreps also took the initiative in getting her department to take a more active role in promoting international trade. In September 1977, she visited Tokyo, where she complained about Japan's huge trade imbalance with the United States and warned of growing protectionist sentiment in the United States against Japan. She urged the Tokyo government to do more to encourage American imports, including stimulating the domestic economy and lifting some of its trade restrictions on imports from the United States. In summer 1978, she headed an interagency task force to put together a package of export promotion measures that included more generous financing for the Export-Import Bank and a new program of loan guarantees by the Small Business Administration for small firms that engaged in exports.

Kreps took issue with National Security Advisor ZBIGNIEW BRZEZINSKI, who sought to use trade policy as a tool of foreign policy. Except in the rarest instances, she opposed the policy of withholding even sophisticated American technology from countries that violated the administration's human rights or diplomatic goals. During the January 1979 visit of Communist China's de facto leader DENG XIAOPING to the United States, she traveled with him as part of an entourage of government and business officials visiting Atlanta, Houston, and Seattle to promote more trade with China. In May 1979, she initialed an historic trade agreement between the United States and China.

While in office, however, Kreps and Secretary of Labor RAY MARSHALL complained to the president that although they were highly respected economists, they had been cut out of economic policy making. They were not invited, for example, to the Thursday economic breakfasts arranged by Secretary of the Treasury W. MICHAEL BLUMENTHAL and also attended by the chair of the Council of Economic Advisers, CHARLES SCHULTZE; the director of the Office of Management and Budget (OMB), JAMES MCINTYRE; and Vice President WALTER MONDALE. Kreps referred sardonically to the meetings as "the boys at breakfast."

Although her demeanor was always pleasant and she remained loyal to the White House, Kreps felt the administration was deficient in consulting with business leaders, and she objected to a number of the White House's economic proposals, such as eliminating the payroll lid for Social Security taxes paid by employers while maintaining a lid on employee taxes. She thought such a proposal would be inflationary. To keep the Social Security system solvent, she preferred raising the normal eligibility age for retirement from 65 to 68.

Kreps also expressed displeasure with such other matters as the way in which the 1977 firing of the first OMB director, BERT LANCE, was handled and the frequency of cabinet meetings, which, she thought, were "fairly useless." If they continued, she told the president, they should be less frequent and should be used by the president to set priorities. She also believed the administration needed to develop a better sense of its priorities. As head, however, of a relatively weak department in the hierarchy of federal agencies, including noncabinet-level agencies, Kreps simply lacked clout within the administration. An example of this was her effort to develop a national industrial policy that would bolster such floundering industries as steel, which was faced with increased competition from the more modern and efficient Japanese steel industry. In an attempt to prevent the American steel industry from falling into bankruptcy, Kreps developed a series of proposals to make American steel more competitive. These included changes designed to improve the patent system and streamline federal and regulatory policy, and a new cooperative program between government and the private sector to develop and promote fundamental technologies of industrial integration and production. Instead of moving in that direction, however, a Special Task Force on Steel, established by President Carter to deal with the plight of the industry and headed by Undersecretary of State Anthony Solomon, opted to establish a "trigger" pricing mechanism, the effect of which was to increase duties on Japanese steel imports and delay the day of reckoning when most U.S. steel would no longer be able to compete against Japanese imports.

In October 1979, Kreps resigned from the administration. Her reasons, however, were personal. Her husband, who had a professorship at the University of North Carolina at Chapel Hill and had not been able to follow her to Washington, D.C., had become depressed and suicidal because of their separation. For the sake of his health, she decided to return to Duke University, where she is presently vice president emeritus and a trustee of the Duke Endowment. From 1985 to 1992, she served as trustee of the Teachers Insurance and Annuity Association and College Retirement Equities Fund (TIAA-CREF).

Laingen, Bruce
(Lowell Bruce Laingen)
(1922–) *chargé d'affaires, U.S. embassy in Tehran*

A career diplomat for 38 years, Bruce Laingen was chargé d'affaires of the U.S. embassy in Tehran when it was seized by Iranian militant students on November 4, 1979. He was the senior American diplomat held captive by the Iranians until the hostages were released immediately following the inauguration of RONALD REAGAN as president on January 20, 1981.

A self-professed farm boy, Laingen was born on August 6, 1922, in Odin Township, Minnesota. During World War II, he served in the navy as a supply officer in the Pacific. Following the war, he graduated from St. Olaf College (B.A., 1947) and studied international relations at the University of Minnesota (M.A., 1949). He then worked as a Scandinavian affairs analyst (1949–50) for the Department of State before joining the Foreign Service in November 1950. His tours of service over the next 25 years included assignments in Germany, Iran, Pakistan, and Afghanistan. Most of his career during this time was unremarkable, dealing with routine economic and political matters in regions of the world that did not receive high priority in Washington. In August 1953, he was sent to Iran after the overthrow of the regime of Mohammad Mossadegh and the restoration to power of the shah of Iran, MOHAMMAD REZA PAHLAVI, in a coup orchestrated by the CIA. As Laingen later described his responsibilities in Iran, "I suppose I wrote one of the most definitive studies of the Iranian cement industry that was ever produced."

Laingen's most striking observation while in Iran and in later postings in nonwestern countries was how little contact the diplomatic corps had with citizens of a country other than those of the upper class—those who had been westernized and spoke English. Even though he spent five months of his tour in Iran in Meshed, a major religious center near Iran's border with the Soviet Union, he never met a senior clerical figure there. Even if he had, he had not been given any training that would have allowed him to discuss with the clerics the role of Islam in Iran. This lack of contact with, or understanding of, much of Iranian society led the American embassy in Iran to overestimate the support the shah had among the Iranian people. The young foreign service officer was also struck in Tehran by the immense size and central locations of the embassies of the major powers—Great Britain, the United States, and the Soviet Union—which became to the Iranians an unwanted symbol of great power intrusion into Iranian affairs.

Laingen's earlier observations were brought home to him by the events of the Iranian revolution. In January 1979, the shah fled Iran following massive demonstrations against his rule. The next month, the leader of the revolution, AYATOLLAH RUHOLLA KHOMEINI, returned to Iran from exile in Paris. That same month, the American embassy in Tehran was seized by Iranian militants and the American ambassador, WILLIAM SULLIVAN, was held captive for about six hours. This led to a decision to evacuate the embassy except for essential personnel who chose to remain on a voluntary basis. In March, Sullivan was recalled to Washington. Replacing him was the senior career officer at the embassy, Charles Naas, who was named chargé d'affaires. When the State Department decided that Naas, having also weathered a difficult period, should also leave, Laingen was sent in his place.

At the time that Laingen was asked to go to Tehran, he was moving up the career ladder. He had recently completed two years as U.S. ambassador to Malta, although at the time of his appointment, he had been disappointed that he had not received a more prestigious posting. Prior to being ambassador to Malta, he had served as acting deputy assistant secretary of state for Near East Asian and South Asian Affairs (NEA, 1973–75) and then as deputy assistant secretary of state for Southern Europe (1975–77) with responsibility for overseeing the desks at the State Department for Spain, Portugal, Italy, and Malta. His move from the NEA to the European bureau came about largely because he had been a participant in Secretary of State HENRY KISSINGER's earlier global outlook policy initiative, intended to broaden the perspective of career officers by moving them among bureaus. "I was a very visible example of that policy," Laingen later remarked.

Laingen was on leave in Minnesota when he received the telephone call from the State Department asking him to go to Tehran for a period of four to six weeks while the department and the White House determined what kind of diplomatic presence to maintain in Iran. Although having the title of chargé d'affaires, Laingen was given the rank of ambassador to make clear to the Iranians that the United States wanted to establish normal relations with them. Besides resuming negotiations with the Iranians, he was also instructed to do what he could to enhance the security of the American compound, including securing the removal of a squad of 30 revolutionary guards that were still on the grounds of the embassy, allegedly to protect the Americans. Furthermore, he was told to try to reach an agreement with Iranian officials on $12 billion in incomplete military supply orders placed by the shah.

Laingen arrived in Tehran on June 16. His temporary assignment of four to six weeks turned into one lasting almost five months prior to the seizure of the embassy on November 4. Yet like most officials at the State Department, Laingen became increasingly optimistic over the summer and fall that normal relations could be restored between Iran and the United States. He found morale at the American embassy high even though the compound was in shambles and there was still considerable uncertainty about the future. In his talks with Iranian officials, he stressed that the United States accepted the outcome of their revolution and did not seek to return the shah to power. Although he was not fondly embraced by the Iranians, he found them to be courteous and polite. He was certain that they wanted a resumption of normal relations with the United States and that he could do business with them.

Laingen was taken aback, therefore, when Secretary of State CYRUS VANCE sent him a note in July, asking for his assessment of the

Iranian government's reaction if the United States decided to allow the shah to take up residency in the United States. Laingen advised strongly against allowing the shah to come to the United States, which, he said, would be prejudicial to U.S. interests in Iran but might be more acceptable later in the fall if progress was made in resolving the power struggle taking place in Iran. More specifically, he wanted any decision on the shah delayed at least until the provisional government was replaced by an elected government. Even then, he was not sure the Iranians would approve having the shah take up residence in the United States. Vance and most other State Department officials agreed with Laingen, and the shah was politely denied access to the United States.

In dealing over the next months with officials of the provisional government, including Prime Minster Mehdi Barzagan and Foreign Minister Ibrahim Yazdi, both of whom were respected and seasoned diplomats, Laingen was well aware that conflict existed between their government and the more militant clerical Revolutionary Council. What he was unable to gauge was the relative influence that Ayatollah Khomeini had on the two competing centers of power. Laingen went on the assumption that Barzagan and Yazdi acted with Khomeini's approval even though Barzagan had expressed his frustration on television about the difficulty he was having in getting his orders implemented. Barzagan was often critical of the revolutionary committees functioning in various sectors of society outside of the normal government. At times, the prime minister even seemed critical of the ayatollah himself.

Notwithstanding the obvious divisions over political power that existed within Iran, conditions between the United States and Iran, as reported by Laingen, seemed promising enough that as late as September 1979, the State Department was giving serious consideration to naming him ambassador to Iran. Much to his later regret, Laingen advised against the move mainly because he wanted to return to the United States as soon as possible. Afterward, he wondered whether the Iranians, if he had been named ambassador, might have interpreted that upgrade of his position as an indication that Washington was seeking a better relationship with Iran, thereby preventing the seizure of the American embassy in November. "Granted that we had not yet seen the Ayatollah and that we were not in direct contact with the Revolutionary Council," Laingen later remarked, "but we and indeed virtually every other embassy in Tehran to which we talked were convinced that things were looking up." Progress had even been made in resolving the complex issues of the incomplete military supply contracts entered into by the shah and existence of large stores of spare parts already in Iran.

It is doubtful, however, whether anything short of returning the shah to Iran would have affected the course of events that followed. By the time Washington announced at the end of October that it was allowing the cancer-stricken shah into the United States for medical treatment, Khomeini was seeking to replace the more secular and prowestern provisional government with the Revolutionary Council in order to establish his dream of an Islamic theocracy led by the mullahs.

On October 21, Laingen and HENRY PRECHT, who was in charge of the Iranian desk at the State Department and happened to be visiting Tehran, went to see Barzagan and Yazdi to explain to them the shah was going to the United States for medical treatment only and to ask for protection of the American embassy. Without making any firm commitment, Barzagan said he would do his best to protect the compound. For the next two weeks, matters were relatively quiet. A large demonstration on November 1 intended for the embassy was diverted away from the compound, apparently on Khomeini's orders, although several thousand protesters still made their way to the embassy, where they shouted slogans at the Americans and displayed pictures of the spiritual leader.

On November 4, however, students swarmed over the walls of the embassy, loudly vilifying Uncle Sam as "The Great Satan," and captured the compound, including large amounts of classified and unclassified documents. They also seized, tied, and blindfolded more than 60 Americans. At the time the embassy was taken, Laingen and two of his aides were at the foreign ministry, where they had gone to discuss diplomatic immunity matters. Although Laingen briefly considered returning to the embassy, he realized that would be unwise since he would be taken captive and important lines of communication with Washington that had been established at the foreign ministry would be lost.

At the time the embassy was seized, apparently no one, including the militant students who had taken the compound, expected that they would hold it for the next 444 days. Embarahim Asgharzadeh, one of the masterminds behind the takeover of the embassy, recalled 25 years later than he had had no calculated plan for taking over the embassy or seizing hostages. "We neither thought of the aspects of this move, nor its implications. We only intended to make the world hear our protest." Similarly, Ibrahim Yazdi, who had just returned from the airport to the Foreign Ministry and was stunned when he heard what had happened at the American embassy, reassured Laingen that the seizure would not last long.

Even Khomeini, residing in the holy city of Qom, about 60 miles south of Tehran, appeared surprised when he was told that students had seized the embassy. At some point, however, he realized that the seizure of the embassy provided him an opportunity to get rid of the moderate secularists with Western ideas who nominally controlled the provisional government, and replace it with the radical Islamic theocracy that he had always wanted in Iran. Therefore, instead of ordering the students to leave the American compound and free their hostages, as Barzagan and Yazdi had asked him to do, he expressed his support for the students holding the embassy. Within 36 hours, both Barzagan and Yazdi resigned their positions. The new foreign minister, Abolhassan Bani-Sadr, was regarded by westerners as a lightweight and figurehead for the ayatollah. At the end of the year, he was replaced by Sadegh Ghotbzadeh, who was anxious to end the hostage crisis but was eventually executed after being accused by his enemies of conspiring to kill Khomeini.

Soon after the hostages were taken, President Carter sent former attorney general Ramsey Clark and William Miller, a retired foreign service officer who had served in Iran, to Tehran in order to meet with the ayatalloh. Khomeini, however, would not even allow their plane to land in Tehran. On November 12, President Carter announced that the United States would stop importing oil from Iran. When Iran announced plans two days later to withdraw its reserves from U.S. banks, Carter froze Iran's assets.

Days turned into weeks. Still, Laingen did not give up hope of a quick settlement to the crisis until April 1980, when Khomeini stated that the hostages would have to remain with their student captors until elections took place and the new legislature (Majlis) could decide their fate. That meant a decision was at least six or seven months off. Since Laingen understood that the ayatollah intended the elections as a way of establishing a theocracy over Iran, he realized there would be no release of the hostages any time soon. In late April, he also learned of the unsuccessful military effort to rescue the captive Americans. The failure of the mission depressed him and the other hostages even more. One result of the failed mission was the dispersal of the hostages throughout Iran, making a second rescue mission improbable.

Early in the crisis, 14 women and African-American hostages had been released. Prior to April, most of the remaining 52 had been held at the American embassy, but Laingen and two of his aides, Victor Tomseth and Michael Howland, remained for most of their captivity in the relatively comfortable quarters of the Foreign Ministry. Laingen expressed regret later that he was not able to be with the other hostages, but he understood that his presence at the ministry, which included accessibility to television and to the telephone, offered a two-way window between Tehran and Washington that was too valuable to sacrifice. Of even greater regret to him, however, was that, as the person in charge of the embassy, he did not do more to destroy the classified and unclassified documents there, which were later used by the Iranian militants against the regime's enemies, who may have had even the most innocent contact with the embassy.

By December 1980, serious negotiations were underway for the release of the American hostages. Iraq had gone to war with Iran in September, Iran needed the release of its assets frozen in the United States, and the hostages no longer served any useful purpose since Khomeini had achieved the Islamic theocracy he wanted for Iran. About the same time, however, Laingen was thrown into prison in solitary confinement for reasons he never fully understood. The three weeks of living in cold, isolated quarters, with little light and inadequate food, was for him the worst part of his captivity.

After a final deal was worked out for the release of the hostages on January 20, 1981, and they were taken to the airport, Laingen instructed the former hostages, a number of whom blamed Jimmy Carter for their captivity, to treat the former president respectfully. Always the career foreign-service officer, he was concerned that the way the former captives conducted themselves over the next weeks and months would reflect well or badly on the foreign service. In his view, the former captives behaved with great dignity.

As for Laingen, he was, for the most part, supportive of Carter's handling of the hostage crisis. "I am often asked," he later recounted, "whether I disagree with the policies that Jimmy Carter followed in the hostage situation in Tehran and my stock answer ... is that I don't think he had many other options other than those he chose, including the seizing of the assets, which any President would have done." A military option would not have been a good one, in his view: "Military force in dealing with terrorists is a very difficult option that doesn't usually work." If he had any criticism of the president's handling of the crisis, it was that Carter did not immediately expel Iran's diplomats from the United States and did not impose sanctions against the country.

Following his release, Laingen served for five years (1981–86) as vice president of the National Defense University, an elite institution for promising mid-career foreign service and military officers. The position of vice president was held traditionally by a senior diplomat, while that of president was held by a general or admiral. In 1987, Laingen retired from the foreign service, having reached the mandatory retirement age of 65. He then served on several national and state commissions concerned with improving the quality of government service, especially on the federal level. In 1992, he also published part of the journals he had kept while a hostage in Iran, *Yellow Ribbon: The Secret Journal of Bruce Laingen.*

Laingen serves as president of the American Academy of Diplomacy and has continued to write critically about U.S. relations with the Middle East, including the United States' decision to go to war with Iraq in 2003.While he was a hostage, his wife, Penelope, put a yellow ribbon around an oak tree outside her home. Soon the yellow ribbon became a national symbol of support for the hostages, with ribbons displayed throughout the country. The original ribbon is now on permanent display at the Library of Congress. Along with the other American hostages, Laigen has filed a class-action lawsuit against Iran for holding them illegally. He resides in Bethesda, Maryland.

Lance, Bert

(Thomas Bertram Lance)
(1931–) *director, Office of Management and Budget*

The resignation in September 1977 of Bert Lance as director of the Office of Management and Budget (OMB) left an indelible mark on the Carter presidency. The events leading up to his resignation brought into question the promise of presidential candidate Jimmy Carter to be worthy of the American people's trust. Just as important, it removed from the administration a close friend whom Carter had described as being like a brother to him. Lance was the only one of Carter's advisers from Georgia who was near in age to him, with whom he was able to engage in frank discussion almost on a daily basis, and who might have acted as a rudder to a president and an administration whose course often seemed aimless.

The grandson of an itinerant Methodist minister and son of a north Georgia college president, Thomas Bertram Lance was born on June 3, 1931, in Gainesville, Georgia. After graduating from Calhoun High School, he attended Emory University for two years and the University of Georgia for one year but did not graduate. Later he took graduate-level courses in banking at Louisiana State University and Rutgers University. In 1950, at age 19, he married LaBelle David. A banker by profession, he began his career as a teller at the Calhoun National Bank, which was owned by his wife's grandfather. By 1963, he was the bank's president and chief executive officer. In 1974, he was elected chairman of the board, a position he held until 1986. In 1975, he also purchased a controlling interest in Atlanta's National Bank of Georgia (NBG).

Lance first met Jimmy Carter in 1966 while attending a business meeting in Rome, Georgia, during Carter's first campaign for governor. Burly and amiable, Lance went over to Carter and introduced himself. Although the future president and the North Georgia banker were polar opposites in many ways, they shared common religious interests that would grow even stronger as Carter went through a spiritual awakening following his defeat in 1966. They were also both energetic individuals who shared in each other's political ambitions in Georgia. By the time Carter was elected governor in 1970, they had become close friends and political allies.

As governor, Carter appointed Lance as director of the Georgia Department of Transportation. Over the next three years, Lance helped reorganize the entire Georgia State Highway Department. Even more important, he was the person to whom the governor turned most often in his own efforts to reorganize state government in Georgia. Lance also acted unofficially as the senior administrative official in planning political and budgetary strategy and in lobbying with state legislators on controversial matters.

Lance began most workdays by meeting with the governor and often ended the day by playing tennis with him. Since Carter could not serve more than two consecutive terms as governor and was planning to run for president in 1976, he helped persuade Lance, who was already considering running for governor, to enter the race. But despite Carter's support, Lance finished a close third in the primaries, behind former governor LESTER MADDOX and State Representative George Busbee, who went on to defeat Maddox in a runoff election.

Given their close ties, it was not surprising that the first person President-elect Carter chose for a cabinet-level position was Lance, whom he nominated to head the OMB. In selecting his friend for this position, Carter wanted someone whom he could trust and who shared his fiscal conservatism. As director of the OMB, Lance rolled back many of the spending proposals recommended by more moderate members of the administration, such as STUART EIZENSTAT, CHARLES SCHULTZE, and JOSEPH CALIFANO. He also shared the president's interest in reducing the size of government and loosening some of the federal controls and regulations that he believed adversely affected the private sector. He remained close to the president personally as well as officially, continuing to play tennis and to talk with him informally, as he had when Carter was governor. The fact that, among the president's most trusted advisers, Lance was nearest in age to Carter only enhanced his personal, almost brotherly, relationship with the chief executive. Easily approachable, as well as influential, he was one of the more well-liked members of the president's inner circle.

Precisely because Lance was so close to Carter, allegations in 1977 about his banking practices as president of the Calhoun Bank turned into a national scandal that rocked the administration, tarred the president, and led to Lance's resignation as OMB director. The episode began innocently enough. In compliance with Carter's directive that his appointees divest themselves of all holdings that might create a conflict of interest, Lance placed his shares of NBG stock, worth $3.3 million, in a blind trust with the promise to sell the stock by the end of the year. The disclosure that the NBG was forced to write off a number of bad loans drove the price of its stock down, cutting the value of Lance's shares almost in half. Furthermore, Lance had used the stock as collateral to help finance a rich and flamboyant lifestyle, including the purchase of a mansion in one of the most prestigious sections of Atlanta. Because he faced financial ruin if he was forced to dump all his stock by the end of the year, which would also drive the price down even more, Lance asked the president for an extension after first offering to resign as OMB director. Instead of accepting his friend's resignation, Carter wrote a letter to the Senate Committee on Governmental Affairs, which had confirmed Lance, asking for an extension beyond the December 31 deadline.

Reports began to circulate in Washington, however, that, contrary to a pledge Lance had made to recuse himself in matters involving banking regulation so long as he held NBG stock, he had lobbied against a proposal being considered by the Senate Banking Committee that would require banks to give priority to local communities in making loans. Even more serious, the *New York Times* columnist WILLIAM SAFIRE accused Lance of peddling his close ties with the president by obtaining a $3.5 million "sweetheart" loan with deferred interest from the First National Bank of Chicago (FNBC). The *Washington Post* reported that the loan was in return for a deposit of $200,000 of NGB funds in a noninterest-bearing account. Other accusations made against Lance included one that he had regularly used a corporate plane to fly to University of Georgia football games. The U.S. Comptroller's Office began an investigation of these charges, and the Governmental Affairs Committee asked Lance to appear before the committee.

In his testimony to the committee, Lance denied the allegations being made against him, pointing out, for example, that he was paying .75 percent interest above the prime rate for his loan with the FNBC and that the loan was fully collateralized. He also stated that the nonbearing account with the FNBC was a long-standing one typical of correspondent accounts that smaller banks maintained with larger financial institutions. He then emphasized that he had done nothing illegal or unethical either before or after he had been appointed OMB director. His testimony seemed to satisfy the committee, which granted him the extension he sought. On August 18, 1977, the Comptroller's Office issued a 394-page report that, at first glance, appeared to vindicate Lance by concluding that he had done nothing illegal. After receiving the report, the president held a news conference in which he stated publicly that he was "proud" of his OMB director.

Instead of settling the controversy over Lance, however, the comptroller's report raised new questions about his probity as a businessman. In particular, it took him to task for allowing sizable overdrafts to be drawn against the NBG by its officers and their relatives. It also found his practice of making loans to local businessmen and farmers without adequate collateral "unsafe and unsound." On September 6, moreover, the Comptroller's Office sent the White House a second report which, it said, showed an inappropriate pattern of borrowing by Lance from other banks similar to the one he had with the FNBC. Comptroller John Heinmann also told the White House that his office was referring Lance's private use of the NBG airplane to the Justice Department and the Internal Revenue Service for investigation.

The findings were sensational. Lance's picture appeared on the front cover of both *Time* and *Newsweek*. Safire tore into Lance's claim before the Governmental Affairs Committee that his loan with the FNBC was fully collateralized. New charges were made against him and even the president, including one that the OMB director had given Carter free use of the NBG plane during his campaign for president and another having to do with the alleged squashing by the Justice Department of an investigation into the manner in which Lance used the Calhoun National Bank to finance his 1974 campaign.

The chairman and ranking minority member of the Governmental Affairs Committee, ABRAHAM RIBICOFF (D-Conn.) and CHARLES PERCY (R-Ill.), notified the White House of the Committee's intention to investigate these charges. Appearing on the White House lawn after meeting with the president on Labor Day weekend, they charged that Lance might have embezzled funds from the Calhoun Bank. On Capitol Hill, pressure mounted for the establishment of a special prosecutor and for Lance's resignation as OMB director. The administration, which had come to office on the promise of transparency and honesty, now found itself under withering questioning on those very issues. Carter's chief aid, HAMILTON JORDAN, and the president's close friend and unofficial adviser, Atlanta lawyer CHARLES KIRBO, both thought Lance should resign.

Lance felt the heat. Sensing that even the president thought he should consider resigning, he asked former defense secretary Clark Clifford, an adviser to Democratic presidents since Harry Truman's administration who was also senior partner in one of Washington's most prestigious law firms, to represent him. In a hastily arranged meeting with Carter on Labor Day, Clifford urged the president not to ask Lance to resign without giving him the opportunity to defend himself against his critics.

Carter readily agreed. Instead of requesting his OMB director's resignation, the president asked lawmakers on Capitol Hill to refrain from judging him until he had an opportunity to testify once more before the Governmental Affairs Committee. On September 15, Lance appeared before the committee in hearings carried on national television. In a two-hour opening statement and then in three days of testimony, he accused members of the committee and others of defaming his character without consideration of due process or fair play. He proved to be a powerful witness, and after his appearance, many observers thought he might be able to keep his job.

They were wrong. After watching Lance's testimony, Jordan, Kirbo, Vice President WALTER MONDALE, and Press Secretary JODY POWELL concluded that while the OMB director had vindicated himself before the committee, he still needed to resign, so strong was the call on Capitol Hill and in the press for his resignation. In a telephone conversation, Senate majority leader ROBERT BYRD (D-W.Va.) told Carter much the same thing, remarking that the presidency was more important than any single individual.

The next day, Carter met with Lance to tell his friend that while he had set back his critics by his testimony, they were regrouping and he should consider resigning. Although Lance told the president later that day that he planned to resign, he also said that he wanted first to speak with his wife, LaBelle. When LaBelle heard what the president had said, she became outraged and urged her husband to stay and fight. But the next day, when Lance met with Carter again, the president told him he had made the right decision the day before. Having little alternative, Lance agreed that afternoon to step down, and Carter announced the resignation a few hours later.

The two months leading to Lance's resignation as OMB director had been a devastating period for him and LaBelle, who remained furious at Carter. She and Lance met with the president in his study a few hours before he made his announcement; there she snapped at Carter for stabbing his friend in the back. In a telephone call to the president later that day, she used harsher language, stating that the president was "joining the rest of the jackals." As for Lance, he was exhausted by his ordeal. Nothing in his experience as a Georgia businessman had prepared him for what had happened over the last two months. Easygoing himself, he had difficulty coping with the type of personal assault that had been made against him.

Even after Lance returned to Georgia, he was never able to escape questions having to do with his business and personal ethics. In January 1978, he paid off his loan to the FNBC and the next day sold his controlling shares in the NBG to Ghaith Pharaon, an Arab and business associate of Agha Hasan Abedi, president of the Bank of Credit and Commerce International (BCCI). In 1979, after an investigation lasting almost two years and involving eight different federal agencies, Lance was indicted for conspiracy and 12 counts having to do with banking irregularities. The presiding judge threw out the conspiracy charge before the trial began, and at his trial Lance was cleared of the remaining charges against him. But to defend himself, he had to pay more than $1.5 million in legal fees.

In 1980, the charges of influence peddling that Safire had made against Lance three years earlier resurfaced when syndicated columnist JACK ANDERSON made similar charges, claiming that Pharaon's purchase of Lance's stock in the NBG was part of a pattern within the Carter administration reaching even to the Oval Office. This pattern of corruption, according to Anderson, also included a loan to Lance of $3.5 million by Abedi about the same time he paid off his debt to the FNBC, the favorable renegotiation by the NGB of an $830,000 loan to the president's peanut farm, and the administration's backing of the sale of F-15 fighter jets to Saudi Arabia.

Anderson's story had little traction and was not picked up by the rest of the media. As a private citizen, Lance was able to regain control of the Calhoun National Bank and to build up an extensive business as a banking consultant. He also returned to nonelective politics. In 1982, he was made chairman of the Georgia Democratic Party, and in 1984 he served as chairman of Walter Mondale's presidential campaign. Four years later, he was one of the leaders of the Reverend JESSE JACKSON's unsuccessful bid for the Democratic presidential nomination. He has also maintained his friendship with former president Carter.

Still, Lance has never been able to put behind him the charges that led to his resignation from the Carter administration and followed him in his return to private life. In the early 1990s, he made the news again when a scandal was instigated by the shutdown of the BCCI, which was reportedly involved in such operations as money laundering, arms trafficking, and support of terrorism. As the scandal broke, Lance was accused of taking millions of dollars in undocumented consulting services from the BCCI. The fact that his lawyer, Clark Clifford, and Clifford's partner, Robert Altman, were closely tied to the BCCI added to the sensational nature of these charges.

Lance never denied that he had worked as a consultant to the BCCI after leaving the administration, but in a book he published, *The Truth of the Matter: My Life In and Out of Politics* (1991), and in testimony before a congressional subcommittee looking into the operations of the BCCI, he maintained that he had no relations with the bank in more than a decade and that he had done nothing illegal or unethical either as OMB director or after leaving government. No new charges were brought against Lance, who lives in Calhoun with his wife LaBelle.

Landrieu, Moon

(Maurice Edwin Landrieu)
(1930–) *secretary of housing and urban development*

In 1979, Moon Landrieu was named by President Carter to replace PATRICIA ROBERTS HARRIS as secretary of housing and urban development (HUD) following a reorganization of the cabinet in which Harris moved over to the Department of Health, Education and Welfare (HEW) to succeed JOSEPH CALIFANO, JR. Landrieu took office at a time when inflation had hit 19 percent, seriously impacting home buying and home-mortgage loans. As HUD secretary, he was more an administrator than a policy innovator as he sought to bring cost efficiencies to the agency because of budgetary limitations imposed by the president.

A native of New Orleans, Landrieu received both his undergraduate degree (B.A., 1952) and law degree (LL.B., 1954) from that city's Loyola University. After serving three years in the U.S. Army, he opened a law practice and taught accounting at Loyola. In 1960, he was elected to the state legislature, where he was one of the few white lawmakers to oppose legislation designed to thwart integration of public schools and public accommodations. In 1966, he was elected councilman-at-large of the New Orleans City Council and successfully pushed for a city ordinance outlawing segregation based on race or religion in public accommodations.

In 1970, Landrieu was elected to the first of two terms as mayor of New Orleans. As mayor, he established an impressive record of opening the top positions of city government to African Americans and of increasing the number of blacks holding civil service positions from 19 percent when he took office to 43 percent when he left city hall. He also focused on expanding the city's shrinking economy and initiated a number of new building projects, including construction of the Superdome. From 1975 to 1976, he served as president of the United States Conference of Mayors.

In naming Landrieu as his new secretary of HUD in July 1979, Carter had appointed someone who was not only respected among his peers but who could potentially have helped him politically with historic Democratic constituencies, including blacks, southerners, and mayors of the nation's major cities. But after presenting in 1978 what the president's domestic adviser, STUART EIZENSTAT, called "the nation's first comprehensive urban policy," Carter had been giving relatively little attention to cities. He had also rejected any effort to increase significantly the level of federal spending to urban areas. As a result, Landrieu's role as HUD secretary during the last 16 months of the Carter presidency was largely one of caretaker and cost-cutter. As he later acknowledged, "My contribution was to get the most out of people there at HUD. … I tried to be a good cheerleader." According to Donna A. Shalala, who served as assistant secretary for policy development and research at HUD from 1977 to 1980, Landrieu even halfheartedly considered having just showers and not bathtubs in public housing projects, until he was reminded by his wife, with whom he had nine children, that people needed bathtubs to wash their young offspring.

After leaving HUD in 1981, Landrieu returned to New Orleans. In 1991, he was appointed judge of the Fourth Circuit Court of Appeals, where he served until his retirement in 2001. He is the father of U.S. senator Mary Landrieu (D-La.).

Linowitz, Sol Myron

(1913–2005) *special representative, Panama Canal Treaties negotiations; negotiator, Middle East talks*

A lawyer and a successful businessman before he became a successful diplomat during the administrations of Lyndon Johnson and Jimmy Carter, Sol Linowitz was born on December 7, 1913, in Trenton, New Jersey. His father was a Jewish fruit importer who built a successful business before being wiped out by the Great Depression. Linowitz attended Hamilton College (B.A., 1935), where he met Elihu Root, an alumnus of Hamilton and former secretary of state under Theodore Roosevelt, who persuaded him to become a lawyer rather than a rabbi because lawyers needed "twice as much religion as a minister or rabbi." Linowitz therefore attended the Cornell University School of Law, where he was editor of the *Cornell Law Review* and graduated summa cum laude (J.D., 1938).

After graduation, Linowitz turned down a lucrative offer from a Wall Street law firm to work for a much smaller concern, Sutherland and Sutherland, in Rochester, New York, at a much lower salary because he did not like the competitive spirit of the large city firms. At the beginning of the United States' entry into World War II, he tried to enlist in the military but was turned down by all the services because of bad eyesight and a leg injury he had sustained while playing sports in college. Instead, he went to the Office of Price Administration for two years (1942–44). One of the persons he worked closely with was RICHARD NIXON, who was the same age as Linowitz and had also been denied a military commission. Both men eventually received naval commissions, although Linowitz was never cleared for sea duty. Instead, he spent his service in the Office of the General Counsel of the Navy, handling the renegotiation of contracts with government suppliers.

After the war, Linowitz returned to Sutherland and Sutherland, where he and a colleague had to virtually rebuild the firm from scratch since one of the two senior partners had retired and the other had gone into teaching. But then he met Joe Wilson, one of the pioneers in the emerging field of photocopying and president of Haloid, a company that sold silver Haloid paper for copying purposes. Together they built what became the Xerox Corporation, with Wilson as president and Linowitz as general counsel and chairman of the board (1959–66). In 1966, Linowitz became chief executive officer. He was also briefly considered as a liberal dark horse for the Democratic nomination for governor of New York. Throughout his career, however, Linowitz always regarded himself more as a lawyer than a businessman or politician.

As part of his responsibilities with Xerox, Linowitz helped set up corporate operations in Latin America, which brought him to the attention of President Johnson. Linowitz had already met Johnson on several earlier occasions when Johnson was still vice president, although they were not close. After Johnson became president, however, he appointed Linowitz as the American representative to the Inter-American Committee on the Alliance for Progress, a position he inherited from the president's special assistant, Walt Rostow. Johnson also started inviting Linowitz to the White House on a regular basis to talk about foreign policy and education. At one point, the president even asked him to serve as secretary of commerce, but Linowitz, by now one of the administration's leading private advisers on foreign aid, was not interested.

Nonetheless, he accepted Johnson's offer to serve as ambassador to the Organization of American States (OAS). According to Linowitz, the president was surprised that he accepted the OAS offer since he had turned down a cabinet position. But he thought the OAS position was more compatible with his growing interests in Latin America. The ambassador spent most of his time at the OAS holding talks on economic development matters with representatives from other OAS countries. The work left him with an ongoing interest in international law, and following the end of the Johnson administration, he accepted a position with Coudert Brothers, then considered one of the world's preeminent international law firms.

During the next eight years, Linowitz was also actively involved in the activities of the International Executive Service Corps (IESC), an organization that he and DAVID ROCKEFELLER of the Chase Manhattan Bank had helped organize in 1964. Patterned after the Peace Corps, the IESC was a voluntary group of businessmen whose purpose was to provide technical and managerial advice to businessmen in developing countries. Momentum for the organization had begun to grow after President Johnson told Congress that the United States should make use of private initiatives to promote economic development abroad. On June 15, 1964, Johnson announced the formation of the IESC at a White House ceremony; Linowitz became its first chairman.

While working with the IESC, Linowitz also became involved in a number of troubleshooting missions for the State Department and the White House, which is how he came to know Jimmy Carter. Shortly before Carter was elected president, Linowitz was chairman of a commission that issued a report on U.S.–Latin American relations. The report concluded that the most important issue facing the United States in Latin America would be the conflict over the Panama Canal. Carter was familiar with the report, and shortly after he assumed office, he and Secretary of State CYRUS VANCE called Linowitz to the White House, where they told him that they wanted him and veteran diplomat Ellsworth Bunker, who had been involved in negotiations with Panama for 14 years, to negotiate a new agreement with Panama over the canal and Canal Zone. The president told Bunker and Linowitz that the treaty should be generous and fair to the Panamanians, but he also made it clear to them that the agreement needed to fully protect U.S. interests in Panama and be acceptable to the United States. Beyond that, he did not provide any guidance as to how these potentially conflicting objectives might be achieved. "In retrospect," Linowitz later recounted, "I'd have to say that assignment was probably the most difficult and exciting challenge of my life."

Although the United States and Panama had completed three draft treaties in 1967 to replace the original 1903 agreement, these had fallen victim to opposition in Panama and the United States. While granting the Panamanians a number of important concessions, they still kept the Canal Zone under effective American control. As a result, they remained so unpopular in Panama that they were never sent to the National Assembly for its approval. In 1968, a junta headed by General OMAR TORRIJOS rejected them outright.

In the United States, feelings also ran strong against "giving away" what seemed to many Americans nothing less than ownership of a strategically and commercially vital piece of real estate that the United States rightfully owned. To many Americans, in fact, the Panama Canal was more than a piece of property: it represented the ingenuity, technical superiority, and, indeed, the superpower status of the United States. Although the administration of President GERALD FORD had worked out many of the details of a new agreement with Panama that would once more transfer ownership of the canal and Canal Zone to Panama, opposition to the waterway's transfer remained so strong that it almost cost Ford the presidential nomination in 1976.

As expected, the talks between the United States and Panama were long, complicated, and frustrating for both sides. Negotiations began on February 14, 1977, but they were almost immediately broken off because of the United States' insistence on retaining the right to use military force if necessary to keep the canal open. The Panamanians were indignant at what they regarded as an infringement of their sovereignty. Complicating matters was Torrijos's demand for a financial package of more than $5 billion, including "reparations" for the years the United States had controlled the canal.

The talks were not resumed until May 1977, when Linowitz and Bunker hit on the strategy of proposing two treaties, one on ownership of the canal, the other on the canal's permanent neutrality and the United States' right to defend it. The Panamanians agreed almost immediately to the U.S. proposal. The first treaty would transfer control of the canal to Panama after 1999; the second would give the United States an indefinite right to defend the canal's neutrality, but only against external threats. Negotiations were not concluded until August, however, a delay caused mostly by Panama's demand for more than $1 billion in a lump sum and $300 million annually until the year 2000. In response, Carter wrote Torrijos a letter stating that that this price tag was out of the question. He also told the Panamanian leader that Linowitz's appointment as the president's special representative was due to expire on August 10 and that his presence as part of the American negotiating team was essential. On August 10, the Panamanians agreed finally to a package of proposals that included an increase in the United States' annual rent to Panama from $2.3 million to $10 million and another $10 million from canal revenues. Panama was also advanced a package of loans of nearly $300 million.

Throughout the protracted negotiations, Linowitz and Bunker worked as a team. As *Time* magazine described the relationship, "Linowitz kept pressing hard, talking fast, rarely letting up. ... More low-keyed and taciturn, Bunker was an inspired contriver of compromises. He also defused arguments by occasionally dozing off—or seeming to." What proved the most difficult obstacle for Linowitz, however, was not the negotiations over the treaties so much as the domestic opposition and vitriolic attacks he faced once an agreement with Panama was concluded in 1977. "The far right was absolutely sure that the nation's security was being damaged, and I bore the brunt of the attacks," he later wrote. "My life was threatened, and my family was threatened."

Knowing that winning Senate approval of the treaties would be difficult, President Carter drafted Linowitz into the effort to win their ratification. Among the people Linowitz briefed were former President Ford, who spoke out in favor of the treaties, and California governor RONALD REAGAN, who had almost defeated Ford for the Republican nomination in 1974 on the basis of his opposition to any agreement returing the canal to Panama. Linowitz met twice with Reagan. During the first meeting, the governor asked questions about the treaties he had prepared on a yellow pad and listened respectfully. At the end of the meeting, Reagan seemed persuaded, saying that Linowitz had answered all of his questions. "I went home elated," Linowitz said. At their second meeting, however, Reagan repeated the ritual of asking questions and taking notes. When Linowitz asked at the end of meeting if he could assume Reagan would support the agreements, the governor said, "Oh, no. I'm gonna be against ya [sic]. But thank you so much for coming and talking to me."

Early in his meetings with Republican leaders, Linowitz had to deal with remarks made at the end of August, shortly after agreement had been reached on the two treaties, by the Panamanian negotiator, Romulo Escobar, to the effect that the agreement giving the United States the right to ensure the neutrality of the Canal did not grant it "the right of intervention." In response, Linowitz obtained assurances that the Panamanian government did not interpret the relevant clauses as Escobar did. In March 1978, after extended and sometimes acrimonious debate, the Senate ratified the first of the two accords (the neutrality treaty) after turning back a series of "killer amendments," which, if implemented, would have required the treaties to be renegotiated. Nevertheless, it became apparent that Escobar had in August represented the government's position accurately when Panama leader Torrijos objected to a "reservation" inserted into the treaty giving the United States the right to intervene militarily to reopen the canal if it should ever become necessary. In response, the Senate agreed to another stipulation inserted into the second treaty transferring control of the waterway to Panama in 2000 explicitly prohibiting the United States from interfering in Panama's internal affairs. This seemed to satisfy Torrijos, and on April 18, the Senate ratified the second agreement. A grateful president thanked Linowitz for the essential role he had played in making the agreements possible.

In March 1980, Carter again asked Linowitz to assume an important assignment, this time to serve as his special negotiator for the Middle East on autonomy talks between Israel and the Palestinians, replacing ROBERT STRAUSS. Like Strauss, however, Linowitz had little luck in moving the talks forward. Although a skilled diplomat, he lacked initimate knowledge about the complex issues involved in Arab-Israeli relations. Some progress was made on the equitable sharing of water rights and Jewish settlements on the West Bank, but not on such other key issues as land, security, and the electoral process for Palestinians. Nevertheless, Linowitz believed enough progress had been made in the negotiations that, had Ronald Reagan pursued the talks after he took office in 1981, an agreement might have been achieved. "But the new administration had other priorities," Linowitz later wrote.

After he returned to the United States from the Middle East, Linowitz devoted much of his time to various charitable and public-service activities. He also wrote his memoirs, *The Making of a Public Man: A Memoir* (1985), in which he described in detail his negotiations on the Panama Canal treaties. In the book, he described Carter as a president so preoccupied with detail that to give him a number "would have been the first step down an endless path" toward even more detailed and irrelevant questions. In 1994, with Martin Mayer, he wrote a second book, *The Betrayed Profession: Lawyering at the End of the Twentieth Century*, in which he berated the law profession for many of its practices, stating, for example, that lawyers were making more money and doing less to earn it than in the past and that large law firms had made billing as many hours as possible an obsession. Linowitz also contributed to professional journals and lectured on the Panama Canal Treaties. In January 1998, he was awarded the Presidential Medal of Freedom, the nation's highest civilian honor, by President Bill Clinton. He died on March 18, 2005, at the age of 91.

Lipshutz, Robert Jerome

(1921–) *counselor to the president*

As counselor to the president from 1977 to 1979, Robert J. Lipshutz played a key senior role in the Carter administration. In his first year alone as senior counsel, he was heavily involved in the affirmative-action case of *Regents of the University of California v. Bakke* and the legal problems of BERT LANCE. In 1979, however, as part of a shake-up of his administration, President Carter decided to replace Lipshutz with a more forceful and assertive public figure, LLOYD CUTLER.

Lipshutz was born on December 27, 1921, in Atlanta, Georgia, where he grew up in a middle-class Jewish family. Because of World War II, he was able to receive both his undergraduate and law degrees in four years from the University of Georgia (LL.B., 1943). After serving as a lieutenant in the army for three years, he returned to Atlanta in 1946 and worked there for one year before opening a law practice with a former classmate, Morris Macey. The firm flourished, and by the time that State Senator Jimmy Carter decided to run for governor of Georgia, Lipshutz had become a prominent attorney in Atlanta's Jewish community.

Lipshutz met Carter through a close mutual friend, Bill Gunter, who had gone to law school with Lipshutz and would later become a state supreme court justice. Impressed by Carter, Lipshutz became a part-time volunteer worker in his campaign. When Carter ran again for governor four years later, he played a more active campaign role. Following Carter's victory, he helped to write the new governor's inauguration address, in which Carter called for a new era in racial relations in Georgia. Although Lipshutz chose not to hold a position in government, he served on the Board of Human Resources and led a grass-roots campaign in support of the governor's efforts to reorganize the state's human resources agencies. He was also one of a small group of Georgians who was told by the governor at the end of 1972 that he intended to run for president in 1976.

By 1974, Lipshutz had become part of Carter's fledging campaign for president, first chairing a political action campaign, which raised funds in support of Carter's activities as cochair of the Committee to Elect Democrats in 1974, and then agreeing to be treasurer of his presidential campaign. The president's choice of Lipshutz for this position reflected his awareness of recent changes in campaign laws. The reform legislation established strict legal accountability in raising campaign funds and created an independent agency, the Federal Election Commission (FEC), to enforce the law. Although Lipshutz participated actively in the fund-raising effort, his main responsibility was making sure that funds were raised and allocated in accordance with the law.

When the campaign became strapped financially, however, especially before the Pennsylvania primary in April, the campaign treasurer engaged in what he later referred to as "creative financing." He had the candidate take out large personal loans with little or no collateral, and the campaign committee itself borrowed heavily using forthcoming matching funds from the FEC as collateral. Concerns were raised by Carter's principal opponent in the Pennsylvania primary, Senator HENRY JACKSON (Wash.), and later in the media and on Capitol Hill about the legality of these methods of financing. But the FEC ruled in Carter's favor, and in 1979 a special investigator appointed by the attorney general found that no laws had been broken by the 1976 Carter campaign committee.

After Carter's election, the president appointed Lipshutz as his legal counsel. In that capacity, Lipshutz headed the Office of the White House Counsel (OWHC), which had been established in the early 1940s during Franklin D. Roosevelt's administration. Although its functions had evolved over the following 35 years, it was still a small office when Lipshutz became legal counsel, with only four lawyers as part of his staff. (Later two more attorneys were added to the staff.) Its main function was to advise the president and the White House staff about legal issues in their conduct of business. Among the tasks of the OWHC were to establish and oversee the vetting process of executive branch nominees, monitor ethical matters, negotiate on the president's behalf with Congress, and interpret the law for the president and his staff.

An issue that confronted Lipshutz during his first year as legal counsel was his relationship with Attorney General GRIFFIN BELL. Both Lipshutz and Bell were among the small coterie of Georgians who had encouraged then-Governor Carter to run for president. Each considered the other a friend, but they never developed an intimate personal relationship. Furthermore, there was an inherent overlap in their responsibilities. While the duty of the attorney general was to interpret the law, the role of the general counsel was to advise the president on the law. It did not necessarily follow that their views on legal matters would always be the same.

Bell also intended that the Department of Justice should be independent of the White House, "a neutral zone in the government," as he later remarked, "where decisions will be made free of political interference." While Lipshutz agreed that the Justice Department should have complete autonomy on criminal matters, he did not believe it could have the same independence on politically controversial civil issues, especially when the law was not clear—as, for example, on the issue of affirmative action. In the case of *Regents of the University of California v. Bakke*, when the Justice Department prepared a brief that seemed to uphold the position of ALLAN BAKKE, who argued that his denial to the University of California–Davis Medical School was unconstitutional because of separate admissions procedures for minority students, Lipshutz joined the president's special assistant for domestic affairs, STUART EIZENSTAT, and Secretary of Health, Education and Welfare JOSEPH CALIFANO in opposing the brief. Under White House pressure, the Justice Department was forced to rewrite the brief to affirm the administration's support of affirmative action.

Another issue that led to conflict between the OWHC and the attorney general concerned the appointment of judges. Historically, the vetting of judges had been ensconced in the Justice Department. Attorney General Bell sought to keep it that way. Lipshutz believed, however, that the White House needed to play a more active role in the vetting process in order to assure that the president's commitment to appoint more women and minorities to the federal judiciary was achieved. "[We] all knew what the president's position was," Lipshutz later commented, "but we found early on that unless someone really got heavily involved ... to do something about affirmative action, it was too easy ... [to] end up with all white males again."

Lipshutz's position collided with that of the attorney general after Congress passed legislation in 1977 establishing 152 new federal judgeships. Lipshutz and his deputy, Margaret McKenna, distributed to various groups representing women and minorities a list of names of nominees for these positions that Bell had compiled; when the president asked the attorney general to make changes to the list, the attorney general considered resigning. Following the intervention of Carter's closest friend and Bell's former law partner, CHARLES KIRBO, Lipshutz and Bell agreed that they would meet together with the president to review prospective nominees. Lipshutz later commented that notwithstanding this and similar disagreements with the attorney general, they still had "a very good genuine rapport." But clearly Bell, who described the president's counsel as a "relatively unassertive, retiring lawyer," did not feel the same way. Rather, he saw Lipshutz yielding to what he regarded as the more liberal wing of the president's advisers.

A major crisis that also confronted Lipshutz during his first year in office was the scandal involving the president's longtime confidant and director of the Office of Management and Budget (OMB), BERT LANCE, whom Lipshutz had also gotten to know during Carter's term as governor. The scandal concerned Lance's questionable financial dealings as a small-town banker in Georgia before he came to Washington.

As the custodian of the transition following Carter's election as president in November 1976, Lipshutz had received FBI reports on prospective nominees for the new administration. Although one of the reports he saw indicated problems with Lance's financial dealings as a banker, Lipshutz had failed to give it proper scrutiny. As he later acknowledged, "I was not as sensitive to that being a potential area of problems as I am today. ... I think my legal analysis was correct. ... I am not sure that I, personally, gave enough attention to the political analysis, either because I wasn't qualified to or because I was a little bit subjective [about Lance]." Once Lance's alleged improprieties made the national headlines in the summer of 1977, Lipshutz compounded his mistake by informing the president, after examining the report of the U.S. Comptroller's Office on Lance's banking practices, that the report gave the OMB director a clean bill of health, even though it did nothing of the sort. This led the president to fly down from Camp David to state publicly that he was "proud" of Lance.

As it became apparent that the comptroller's report was not the vindication they had thought it was, Lipshutz advised the president to protect his office by allowing ongoing investigations into Lance's business affairs to continue without White House interference. He also told Carter to not even discuss any of the specific issues in the report with Lance. Lipshutz continued to believe that Lance had done nothing wrong legally and also agreed with the president and his other close advisers that Lance had defended himself well in September before the Senate Governmental Affairs Committee looking into the charges being made against him. But he concluded along with them that the OMB director should resign. The affair was simply causing too much damage to the president in his opinion. Reluctantly, the president agreed and persuaded Lance to tender his resignation. By this time, the scandal had inflicted a wound on the White House from which it never fully recovered.

Although Lipshutz's function at the White House was that of legal counsel, as a practicing

Jew active in the Jewish community in Atlanta with a strong commitment to the state of Israel, he spent considerable time meeting with National Security Advisor ZBIGNIEW BRZEZINSKI and State Department officials to discuss the situation in the Middle East. On more than one occasion, he clashed with them and with the president over the policy they were pursuing in the region, such as when Carter proposed in 1977 to bring the Soviet Union back into the Middle East negotiating process by reconvening the Geneva talks on the Middle East, and when, later that year, Carter ordered UN ambassador ANDREW YOUNG, to vote in favor of a UN resolution condemning the building of Jewish settlements in the occupied territories.

At the same time, Lipshutz made numerous speeches to Jewish audiences defending what the president was trying to accomplish. To those who argued, for example, that the president's position on the Middle East had shifted toward the Arabs because of his talk in 1977 about Israel's need to recognize the rights of the Palestinian people and to withdraw from the occupied territories, Lipshutz insisted that that impression came about "because the President is taking initiatives out in the open. He's dealing with the questions that have always been vital but have been kept in the backroom."

Lipshutz's proudest day as a member of the Carter administration occurred in September 1978, when Israeli prime minister MENACHEM BEGIN and Egyptian president ANWAR SADAT signed the Camp David accords, a treaty between Egypt and Israel providing a framework for overall peace in the Middle East. Later, when the agreement appeared to be unraveling, Lipshutz accompanied the president to meet with Israeli leaders in a successful effort to salvage it. Back home, he also mobilized Jewish support behind the president. Exhilarated by the events of the past three months, he dictated a memo summarizing his experiences and making clear the respect he had developed for the president. "I personally believe," he wrote, "that [Carter] had taken this on as a 'mission' not only because he is president but because of his personal feelings and concern about the entire situation."

The fact that Lipshutz was Jewish may have been one reason why he was given the unpleasant task in 1979, along with HAMILTON JORDAN, of firing the former congresswoman and outspoken political activist, BELLA ABZUG, who was also Jewish, as cochair of the National Advisory Committee on Women. His meeting with Abzug was extremely unpleasant, especially when Abzug said she was being made a scapegoat. For Lipshutz, the term *scapegoat* had been applied to Jews for 2,000 years. Because Abzug's comment suggested to him that she was being fired because she was Jewish, her remarks deeply offended the White House counsel, especially when she said she was surprised that he would allow himself to be used in this way. Lipshutz regarded his confrontation with Abzug as one of the most unpleasant of his White House career.

In contrast to his unpleasant dealings with Abzug, Lipshutz and Stuart Eizenstat, the director of the policy staff, had been able to persuade President Carter to establish a memorial to honor victims of the Holocaust. They approached the president about the memorial in a memorandum they wrote to him on April 25, 1978, in which they cited his own record on human rights, the growing interest in the Holocaust by Jews and non-Jews alike, and the aging of the remaining Holocaust survivors. Carter approved their memorandum less than a week later. On May 1, in an elaborate ceremony on the South Lawn of the White House attended by Israeli prime minister Begin and 1,000 rabbis from all over the country, the president established a Holocaust Commission. Later he named Holocaust survivor Elie Weisel to head the commission to determined how the Holocaust should be memorialized.

Eventually this led to the establishment of the Holocaust Museum, now one of the most visited sites in Washington.

Although the president was generally satisfied with the job that Lipshutz had done for him as legal counsel, he decided in 1979, as part of a shake-up of his administration, to replace the retiring and unassertive Lipshutz with someone who had a higher profile and a more dynamic personality. Having spent three years in Washington and neglected his law practice, Lipshutz was also anxious to return to Atlanta. Therefore, the president replaced him with Lloyd Cutler, a senior partner in one of Washington's most prominent firms, who was a well-known and highly respected Washington insider.

Just before leaving Washington, Lipshutz commented on the effectiveness of the White House staff during his three years as legal counsel. While giving it generally high marks, he also indicated that he thought it suffered at the beginning of the administration from lack of structure and from having too many Georgians in the White House. "[I]f we had had a little bit more of a structure to begin with," he remarked, "we would probably have been more effective. Also, in retrospect, we probably would have been wiser to have asked the President to bring in a few more at the senior level who we didn't know as well."

Since returning to Atlanta, Lipshutz has been senior partner of Lipshutz, Green, and King, a small law firm of eight lawyers engaged in a general practice. He has also been active in the Atlanta Jewish community and has served as a trustee and member of the Board of Directors of the Carter Center.

Long, Russell Billiu
(1918–2003) *member of the Senate*

The son of Huey Long, one of the most fascinating and controversial individuals in American political history, and heir to the political dynasty that he created, Russell B. Long became a major national political figure in his own right as a result of his nearly 40 years in the United States Senate. Chair of the Finance Committee from 1966 to 1981, he was one of the most powerful lawmakers on Capitol Hill. Long had a flamboyant personality that charmed even his most strident ideological opponents in the Senate. A master of parliamentary maneuvering, his knowledge of the nation's tax code was encyclopedic, and his support was essential to the passage of any tax and energy legislation. The *Wall Street Journal* once called him the fourth branch of government. He used his power to both promote and protect the oil, gas, and sugar interests of his home state. President Carter's difficult congressional struggle over energy legislation was in large measure the result of Long's determination to do no harm to the energy interests he represented.

Long was born in Shreveport, Louisiana, on November 3, 1918. He grew up in politics, being the only U.S. senator whose father and mother had both preceded him in the Senate. He was 10 years old when his father, Huey, was elected governor of Louisiana; he was 16 when Huey, now a U.S. senator thought by political observers to be preparing to challenge President Franklin D. Roosevelt's bid for reelection in 1936, was assassinated. Russell's mother, Rose, filled out the remainder of her husband's term (1935–36). Although Huey was dead, the political dynasty he had created was continued by his colorful brother Earl.

Long received both his undergraduate and law degrees from Louisiana State University (B.S., 1939; LL.B., 1942). As an undergraduate, he was elected student body president on a pledge of five-cent laundry for students. During World War II, he served as a naval officer and saw action during the allied invasion of Sicily. After the war, he opened a law practice in Baton Rouge and worked as a close adviser in his uncle Earl's 1947 gubernatorial campaign. When, in 1948, a U.S. Senate seat opened as a result of the death of the incumbent, John Overton, the well-oiled Long machine helped to get Russell elected to fill out the rest of Overton's term. Long had to wait a few days before taking the seat since he was shy of the constitutional age of 30 required to serve in the Senate. In 1950, he was reelected for the first of six full terms, never facing more than token opposition until his last election in 1980. His maiden speech on the Senate floor was a defense of the filibuster.

First appointed to the Armed Services Committee, Long moved in 1953 to the Finance Committee, which was a better assignment for a senator from a state rich with oilmen looking for tax breaks. He became a strong advocate of tax breaks for business, once remarking, "I have become convinced you're not going to have capital if you're going to spend it." A southerner, Long signed the Southern Manifesto condemning the *Brown v. Board of Education of Topeka* decision (1954) ordering the racial integration of the nation's schools. He also joined in southern filibusters against civil rights legislation.

A gregarious and garrulous figure, with a fund of tales about his Uncle Earl, Long often seemed to barnstorm the Senate, much as he and his father had barnstormed Louisiana politics. He was also as smart and cunning as his father. One of the Senate's icons, Richard Russell, once commented that Long was one of the two smartest senators he had known, the other being his father Huey. Long was also the consummate deal maker. He would often put his arms around a fellow lawmaker while making a deal.

By 1960, Long was one of the inner circle, still mostly of southern Democrats, that controlled the Senate. He was also an unabashed supporter of the oil industry. In 1962, for example, he made a deal with President John F. Kennedy in which he agreed to support the Trade Expansion Act in return for the White House's agreement to continue and, in some cases, strengthen oil imports. He was also chosen by Kennedy to shepherd the administration's tax-reduction plan through Congress.

During the 1960s, Long continued to defend oil and gas interests, becoming the industry's leading advocate on Capitol Hill. He also sought to protect sugar, Louisiana's major agricultural crop. He fought against measures to reduce or eliminate depletion allowances for oil and gas and supported legislation to raise price supports for sugar. His support of President Lyndon Johnson's Great Society was mixed. He filibustered against the civil rights bill of 1964, and, sharing a conservative fear of government interference in medical care, he almost killed Medicare legislation by proposing in its place a program of catastrophic health insurance. Only the president's intervention restored the original measure. Long also opposed Johnson's proposal for an increase in taxes in 1967, and he fought hard against the president's failed effort to elevate Associate Justice Abe Fortas to chief justice of the Supreme Court, even referring to Fortas as "one of the dirty five" who sided with criminals against crime victims.

Yet Long softened his position on civil rights. Although unable for political reasons to vote for the Voting Rights Act of 1965, he spoke out in support of black voting registration, telling a group of Louisiana mayors that "we're going to have to do something about it or have somebody else do something about it" and remarking on another occasion that "one of the things I find hard to speak for as a southerner is to defend situations where a person with no basis whatsoever denies another person a right which is properly his." While trying to scuttle Medicare, he worked ultimately for its eventual passage.

In terms of foreign policy, Long was a steadfast opponent throughout his career of foreign-aid legislation and an advocate of a strong defense, even opposing President Kennedy's 1963 limited nuclear test-ban treaty with the Soviet Union prohibiting atmospheric testing of nuclear weapons. But he supported President Johnson's intervention in the Dominican Republic in 1964, and he remained one of the staunchest defenders of the Vietnam War.

The middle of the 1960s was a period of both personal achievement and crisis for Long. In 1965, he was elected by his fellow Democrats as assistant majority leader (majority whip), even winning the support of liberals despite his record on civil rights and support of business interests. The next year, he became chair of the Finance Committee, thereby assuring his role as a power broker in the Senate. His mastery of the nation's tax laws became legendary. "He knows the tax code as thoroughly as the Pope knows the Lord's Prayer," Senator WILLIAM PROXMIRE of Wisconsin said of him.

About the same time, however, Long began to drink heavily and have marital problems, eventually resulting in his divorce from his first wife, Katherine. He became angry when he had too much to drink, and he was sometimes drunk on the Senate floor, leading some lawmakers to wonder about his emotional balance. Because he was unreliable as assistant majority leader, Democrats replaced the position of assistant majority leader with four whips and, in 1969, replaced him as majority whip with Massachusetts senator EDWARD KENNEDY.

By the early 1970s, however, Long had become a recovering alcoholic and, remarried, soon regained his reputation on Capitol Hill. During the Nixon-Ford years, he used his power as chairman of the Finance Committee to help defeat President RICHARD NIXON's daring and innovative Family Assistance Plan, first proposed in August 1969. The plan, Long concluded, would add 14 million Americans to the welfare rolls. It would also "reward idleness and discourage personal initiative of those who can provide for themselves."

In 1975, however, Long pushed through Congress the Earned Income Tax Credit (EITC), a refundable tax offset for low-income workers. What made the EITC so attractive to the senator was that it seemed to be both an antiwelfare instrument as well as a way to provide for the working poor. Although the Finance Committee chairman was known for the myriad assortment of tax breaks he provided businesses, he always retained some of his father's populist streak and concern for the poor. He was hostile to corporate monopolies, for example, having opposed the 1962 satellite communications bill because he thought it would give American Telephone and Telegraph (AT&T) a monopoly over space communications. In 1966, as the new chair of the Finance Committee, he had attacked the pharmaceutical industry for what he called its "worldwide cartel" to fix prices on antibiotics. As for the poor, former vice president HUBERT HUMPHREY (D-Minn.), ideologically so different from Long but one of his closest friends, commented on their common concern for the working poor. In contrast to the Family Assistance Plan, the EITC was, for the Louisiana lawmaker, an antipoverty device that had the potential to raise the income of all working Americans above the poverty line.

The EITC was retained during the Carter administration, but welfare reform became just one of a number of issues between the president and the Finance Committee chair. Although he had not campaigned for Jimmy Carter in 1976, Long was pleased that someone from the Deep South had been elected to the White House. He credited part of the president's victory to the presidential campaign-reform legislation that he had sponsored, which provided \$21.8 million to each candidate in 1976. But he became annoyed when Carter failed to consult him soon after taking office about a White House proposal for a $50 tax rebate to all taxpayers to stimulate the economy, which the senator thought was wasteful. He was even more annoyed by Carter's decision to pull the plug on the rebate after Long had reluctantly agreed to back it. Worse was the president's proposal to cancel or reduce funding for 23 water projects, including four in Louisiana. Russell termed this decision "dumb, dumb, dumb, dumb," noting that it violated one of his basic political rules: "He was asking for a fight which he didn't have the votes to win to begin with."

As for welfare reform, Long agreed with the president that the nation's current system remained a mess and that welfare needed to be replaced with jobs. But he disagreed sharply on the proposals for welfare reform that the president sent to Congress in August 1977. Illustrating Carter's emphasis on the work ethic, the president's program provided jobs for welfare recipients who could work and a "decent income" for those who could not, such as the disabled and single parents with children. Along with other congressional conservatives, Long expressed alarm at the large number of people who, he maintained, would be added to the welfare rolls. He also had major problems with the projected costs of the program. As far as the senator was concerned, welfare reform was dead on arrival on Capitol Hill.

Long's most serious disagreement with the president, however, was over his energy program. Although the two leaders agreed the United States faced an energy problem and that more needed to be done to identify alternative fuel sources, Carter believed the culprit was over-consumption of energy, to be addressed by imposing higher energy taxes that would be returned to the poor. The Louisiana lawmaker identified the major problem as the lack of oil and gas drilling, to be addressed by tax incentives and the deregulation of oil and natural-gas prices. In his view, the president's strategy of higher energy prices would drive domestic drillers out of business and encourage imports of cheaper foreign oil. He characterized that approach as "an unmitigated disaster."

Although the House passed the president's energy measure largely intact in August 1977, Long used the full weight of his power as chair of the Senate Finance Committee and his skill in parliamentary maneuvering to gut much of the president's plan. The bill that the Senate finally passed in October eliminated most of the energy taxes the president had wanted, including a crude-oil equalization (wellhead) tax, an industrial gas tax, and a tax on gas-guzzling cars. Rather than raising energy taxes in any significant way, the measure provided for $40 billion in conservation tax credits.

Once the Senate measure went to conference committee, Long used delaying tactics to get the House to go along with the Senate version of the energy measure. Bemusedly, the president remarked at a Capitol Hill function, "I came here ... proud of myself for having been elected the first President from the Deep South ... and then I came ... and found that Russell Long had filled that position for a long time." Not until October 1978 did the Congress finally agree on an energy plan. Most of the original proposals, which had been based on the principle of conservation through taxation rather than through deregulation and tax credits, had been either scaled back or, like the wellhead tax, eliminated entirely. In their place, the measure provided for the gradual deregulation of natural gas and the establishment of a single price structure for intra- and interstate gas and the expanded use of nonfossil fuels through various tax credits. There were no provisions for oil pricing. By the time energy legislation passed, moreover, the president had been forced to adjust his position closer to that of the Louisiana lawmaker, rather than the other way around.

In 1979, a new energy crisis developed as a result of gasoline shortages and rising prices. Oil price controls set by the 1975 Energy Policy and Conservation Act were also set to expire in June unless President Carter decided to extend them or gradually phase them out. The president decided to phase them out over three years, assuring additional increases in fuel costs. To prevent oil companies from profiting excessively, he announced a 50 percent windfall-profits tax, the revenues from which would go to an Energy Security Fund to assist low-income families, help fund mass transportation, and promote alternative energy resources. Recognizing the inevitability of some kind of windfall-profits tax, Long decided to support the measure. In committee and on the Senate floor, however, he was able to modify the legislation so that the $227 billion windfall-profits tax Congress approved was considerably less than the president's flat 50 percent proposal. He also won an important provision phasing out the windfall-profits tax if oil prices and revenues increased more rapidly than anticipated. Furthermore, he helped defeat an amendment to apply the windfall-profits tax to income from state-owned oil wells.

After Carter was defeated by RONALD REAGAN in 1980, Long expressed regrets to his wife, Carolyn, that the president had not done more to reach out to him. When she reminded him that the president and Rosalynn had invited them to a private dinner early in his administration, Long said that had not been enough. If the president had approached him in the spirit of trying to reach a mutual accommodation, his relationship with Carter might have been different. But the president never proposed such a deal. "I never knew what I could count on," Long commented. "I never knew if I could count on him or nor."

On one measure, the Panama Canal Treaties of 1978, Long's support had been crucial for the president. The senator became persuaded that voting for the treaties was the correct thing to do and that while his vote would hurt him politically at home, it would not cost him reelection in two years. He was correct on both counts. In 1980, he faced his strongest opponent since being elected to the Senate in 1950, Republican Henson Moore, and he was hurt by Moore's attacks on him for his vote on the canal treaties. But Long's campaign war chest of over $2 million and his popularity with the state's voters was too much for Moore to overcome. Long won with 58 percent of the vote to Moore's 38 percent in Louisiana's unique open primary.

The arduous campaign and Reagan's subsequent landslide victory over Carter, which also resulted in the capture of the Senate by the Republicans and the loss of his Finance Committee chair, made Long less anxious to seek reelection in 1986. Although he continued to play an important role in crafting the major tax-reform legislation of 1986, he shocked his fellow senators by announcing in February 1985 that he would not seek a seventh term in the Senate. Instead, he accepted a lucrative partnership with a major Washington, D.C., law firm. He died in Washington of heart failure on May 9, 2003, at the age of 84.

M

Maddox, Lester Garfield
(1915–2003) *Georgia politician, presidential candidate*

By the time Lester Maddox ran as the presidential nominee of the American Independent Party in 1976, both he and the party had become political anachronisms. But Maddox had been a thorn in Jimmy Carter's side throughout Carter's early political career.

Born on September 30, 1915, in a working-class section of Atlanta, Georgia, Maddox was a high school dropout who held a series of unskilled jobs before opening a small restaurant in 1944 and then selling it three years later to open a larger restaurant, the Pickrick, near the Georgia Tech campus. Outgoing and entrepreneurial, he built the Pickrick, which specialized in fried chicken and nickel hot dogs, into a highly successful establishment grossing more than $1 million a year by the 1960s.

Maddox was a political conservative and segregationist, however, who believed it was his inviolate right to refuse service to whomever he wanted, irrespective of any government edict. When three black students from Georgia Tech tried to enter his restaurant the day after passage of the Civil Rights Act in July 1964, he chased them away brandishing a revolver while his employees waved ax handles at them. Soon Maddox was selling souvenir ax handles, which he called "Pickrick Toothpicks." Rather than serve the public regardless of race, as required by law, he chose in 1965 to close his restaurant. Covered in the national media, these acts of defiance made Maddox a hero to racists and segregationists throughout the South and a potent political force in Georgia.

Maddox had been interested in political office since the early 1950s, when he ran a weekly advertisement in the Atlanta newspapers in which he expressed his own racist and antigovernment views. In 1957 and 1961, he ran unsuccessfully as a white supremacist for mayor of Atlanta and in 1962 for lieutenant governor of Georgia. His political career blossomed, however, after the 1964 incident at his Pickrick Restaurant.

In 1966, Maddox narrowly beat Jimmy Carter for second place in Georgia's first Democratic gubernatorial primary and then won in the runoff election. Although he trailed Republican Howard H. "Bo" Callaway in the general election, write-in candidates kept Callaway from receiving a majority of the votes, thereby leaving the selection of the governor to the state legislature, as required under state law. Heavily Democratic and conservative, the legislature chose Maddox as governor.

As governor, Maddox proved to be more progressive than many of his critics had anticipated. Although he remained a white supremacist, even refusing to close the Capitol in Atlanta during the funeral of Martin Luther King, Jr., in 1968, he hired more blacks to state positions than any previous governor and took an interest in penal reform and higher salaries for teachers. But the fact that Carter had lost the election of 1966 to an avowed segregationist led the future president in 1970 to run a second gubernatorial campaign with decidedly racist overtones that included welcoming the arch-segregationist governor of Alabama, GEORGE WALLACE, into the state and trying to identify himself closely with Maddox. It was a campaign that even Carter's strongest supporters later regretted.

Elected as governor in 1970, Carter still had to contend with Maddox, who was ineligible to run for reelection but had been elected overwhelmingly as lieutenant governor. Presiding over the Senate and having the responsibility under Senate rules to refer bills to appropriate committees, Maddox carried considerable political clout. Because he had also been the largest vote-getter in the last election, Carter sought to reach some kind of accommodation with the lieutenant governor. But Maddox, who still sought to dominate the state by controlling the state legislature, proved an implacable foe. "It's all right for a fellow to grow peanuts," he said of Carter, "but people ought not to think like them." As governor, Carter made reorganization of state government his highest legislative priority. In winning legislative approval of most of his proposals for reorganization, he had to exhaust much of his energy and political capital in fighting Maddox and others opposed to his proposals.

Carter's term as governor ushered in a new period of race relations in Georgia, and increasingly Maddox appeared out of step with the changes taking place in the state and throughout much of the South. Furthermore, some of his political antics, such as riding backwards on a bicycle, made him look like a political buffoon. In 1974, he ran for governor again but lost. Two years later, he ran as the presidential nominee of the American Independent Party, the political organization that Wallace had founded and turned into a powerful political machine. However, by 1976 that, too, had become a relic and Maddox received only a handful of votes.

His political career over, Maddox embarked on a short-lived comedic career with a black man he had pardoned from jail when he was governor; he billed his act as "The Governor and the Dishwasher." Throughout the rest of his life, he remained unrepentant in his racist views and in his distaste for Carter. "I still believe he is the coldest, most deceptive man I have ever met in politics," he said of the former Georgia governor after Carter was elected president. Maddox also continued to rail against government interference in what he believed were the rights and freedoms of individuals. After surviving several bouts with cancer and other illnesses, he died on June 25, 2003, of pneumonia. He was 87 years old.

Marshall, Ray

(Freddie Ray Marshall)
(1928–) *secretary of labor*

Ray Marshall was the only member of President Carter's cabinet who could be regarded as a genuine newcomer to Washington. As secretary of labor, he represented one of the most traditional and important wings of the Democratic Party: organized labor. He shared labor's views on most issues of concern to workers, including jobs, unemployment, wages, and labor law reform. He always believed that his primary function as secretary of labor was to represent the interest of American workers and their organizations. As a result, he was often at odds on policy matters with the White House staff, other members of the administration, and even the president. Being a Washington outsider who had spent most of his life in the South, however, he was able to represent the interests of labor within the administration more effectively than most labor leaders.

Marshall was born on August 22, 1928, in Oak Grove, Louisiana, but lived in an orphanage until he was 15, when he ran away. Lying about his age, he joined the navy and participated with an amphibious unit in the Pacific during World War II. After the war, he attended Millsaps College (B.A., 1949), Louisiana State University (M.A., 1950), and the University of California–Berkeley, where he received his Ph.D. in economics (1955). He then began a successful career in higher education, teaching at the University of Mississippi (1953–57), Louisiana State University (1957–62), the University of Texas–Austin (1962–67), the University of Kentucky (1967–69), and then back to the University of Texas–Austin, where he was professor of economics and director of the Center for the Study of Human Resources (1969–76). During this time, he wrote more than a dozen books on labor economics, industrial relations, labor arbitration, rural development, and the relationship between the labor movement and minorities. In two of his most important works, *The Negro and Organized Labor* (1965) and *The Negro Worker* (1967), he described the underside of organized labor's discriminatory, and sometimes violent, treatment of black workers.

In addition to his academic and scholarly achievements, Marshall served on a number of important national boards and councils. These included membership on the Department of Labor and Health, Education and Welfare (HEW) Committee on Administration of Training Programs (1967–68); the National Manpower Task Force (1969–76); and the Department of Labor Consortium on Rural Manpower Development (1971–75). He was also president of the National Rural Center (1974–77) and cochair of the UN Economic Policy Council's Productivity Panel. As a result, by the time he left the University of Texas in 1977 to accept the position of secretary of labor in the Carter administration, he had become well-networked nationally and was widely recognized as one of the nation's leading authorities on labor economics, the problems of minorities and employment, manpower policy, rural development, international migration of workers, and industrial relations.

Marshall's work had attracted the attention of Georgia governor Jimmy Carter, who had called on Marshall for advice on several occasions. During the 1976 presidential campaign, Marshall wrote a number of position papers on manpower policies, and the academic and the politician from the South struck up a good relationship. Later Marshall said that Carter had appointed him as secretary of labor because he was bilingual ("I also speak Baptist"). The former president recalled that he had asked Marshall to be his secretary of labor "because he successfully bridged the worlds of academia and real folks. He had the unique ability to see and approach every issue from the perspective of the working man."

Marshall was not organized labor's first choice to be secretary of labor. AFL-CIO president GEORGE MEANY would have preferred John Dunlop, who had been labor secretary under GERALD FORD and had resigned his position when Ford vetoed a common situs (picketing by a labor union of an entire construction project as a result of a grievance held by a single subcontractor on the project) bill that labor wanted, which would have lifted the Taft-Hartley Act's ban on construction-site secondary picketing (the picketing of firms that conduct business with an employer against whom an industrial action is being taken). But Meany and other labor leaders considered Marshall sympathetic to labor's needs and were generally pleased with his nomination. Because of his interest in minority issues and his effort to promote blacks within the Department of Labor, he also became one of the more trusted members of the administration among black leaders.

Before accepting Carter's offer to be secretary of labor, Marshall secured the president-elect's agreement that he would have a voice in economic decision making within the administration and be allowed to speak out when he disagreed with the president. He became one of a cacophony of voices that had the ear of the president on economic issues. He usually sided with Carter's more liberal economic advisers.

In addition to the fact that Marshall was from the South and outside the Washington beltway, another reason why President Carter seems to have felt comfortable with his labor secretary was that both men shared a common interest in job training and meaningful job creation, particularly for youth and other targeted groups lacking basic education and job skills. As a result, Marshall was able, in the first few weeks of the new administration, to steer the president to add 415,000 more public-service jobs and to expand jobs training and youth programs under the Comprehensive Employment and Training Act (CETA). Six weeks later, the president sent to Congress a second jobs program that targeted the most disadvantaged sectors of the labor force through extension and expansion of CETA.

The administration proposal became the Youth Employment and Demonstration Projects Act (YEDPA) of 1977, a major effort to employ youth and improve their future economic chances through coordination of existing employment and training projects and development of new and innovative approaches. Congress approved the legislation in May 1977 by creating a new Title VIII to CETA that consisted of three new programs of demonstration projects, the most experimental of which would keep youths in school by guaranteeing a job to any disadvantaged young person who stayed in, or returned to, school. Although the number of new jobs and training was far less than organized labor wanted in order to deal with the 9 percent unemployment rate that the president faced when he took office, it was considerably more than most of Carter's other economic advisers thought desirable, concerned as they primarily were about potential inflation and budget deficits.

Marshall was far less successful in molding to his liking one of the president's highest priorities, welfare reform. Almost everyone involved with the nation's welfare system, including welfare recipients themselves, believed it was a monster in need of taming and reform. The issues were how and at what cost. The president was committed to reforming the system without any additional costs, largely by making it more efficient and taking eligible recipients off the welfare rolls and putting them to work. Marshall also believed that targeted jobs creation was essential to any program of welfare reform.

The problem with this approach to welfare reform was twofold. In the first place, Secretary of Health, Education and Welfare JOSEPH CALIFANO, who had first sunk his teeth into Washington politics as President Lyndon Johnson's principal domestic policy adviser and was the quintessential Washington insider, preferred some kind of guaranteed family income for welfare recipients. He was less enamored with jobs creation than either the president or Marshall. The second was that Carter believed that the economic growth of the post-World War II period, which had sustained the entitlement programs of the New Deal and the Great Society, was at an end and that it would have to be left to the private sector to create most new jobs. In contrast, Marshall felt that jobs creation could not be left primarily to the private sector and that even at the risk of budget deficits and increased inflation, the federal government had the responsibility to create jobs for qualified job seekers.

During the first three months of the new administration, Marshall battled with Califano over the structure of welfare reform—whether it would emphasize jobs or family assistance—and both cabinet members struggled with the president and the majority of his economic advisers over their insistence on welfare reform at no additional cost to the federal budget. The chairman of the Council of Economic Advisers (CEA), CHARLES SCHULTZE, was sent to mediate between Marshall and Califano. He found the task impossible. "I threw up my hands in the sense that there was no way of meeting in between," he later recounted. "They had two fundamentally different views in the way the world ought to work."

As a result, a welfare-reform proposal that Califano and Marshall were supposed to have ready by May 1 had to be put off until August. By the time a proposal was announced in August, incorporating both jobs and family assistance, it had so little support that it was not even brought up for consideration in Congress. Although the House did pass a welfare-reform program in 1979, by that time the president had lost interest in trying to fix the system, and it never got through the Senate.

Marshall had more success with the president in getting the minimum wage increased. By law, the minimum wage had been raised from $2.00 in 1974, to $2.10 in 1975, and to $2.30 in 1976 for all except farm workers. This was still well below its customary relationship to average manufacturing wages. It also put a family of four with one wage earner making the minimum wage below the poverty level. Labor leaders were demanding an immediate increase in the minimum wage to $3.00 an hour. Secretary of the Treasury W. MICHAEL BLUMENTHAL and CEA chairman Schultze argued that such an increase would stimulate inflation and add to unemployment.

By appealing for an increase in the minimum wage on moral as well as economic grounds, noting that it was those at the bottom rung of the labor market rather than more highly paid union members who suffered the most from a low minimum wage, Marshall was able to get the president to agree to an immediate increase to $2.65 an hour with further annual increases until the minimum reached $3.35 by January 1981. The president also took a strong stand against a proposed "split" that would have set a lower minimum for employees not covered by federal minimum wage laws before 1966 (primarily service and farm workers and workers in the retail and wholesale trades). Although labor leaders remained upset that Carter did not agree to a larger hike, the schedule of increases still represented a significant victory for Marshall.

In 1978, Congress passed, and the president signed, the Full Employment and Balanced Growth Act, better known as the Humphrey-Hawkins Act. Drafted with the help of the Labor Department, the law did not create any specific programs but called for government-wide planning and action to achieve reduced unemployment and, eventually, zero inflation. A new Title VII in the 1978 CETA reauthorization bill provided for the establishment of private-industry councils to promote private-sector employment and a targeted tax credit for private businesses that hired disadvantaged workers, Marshall and the White House intended Title VII as a way to make available more private-sector jobs and training programs not only for disadvantaged youth but for such other disadvantaged groups as rural workers, migrant workers, veterans, and Native Americans. Internally, Marshall upgraded the Women's Bureau within the Labor Department, established an Office of Inspector General, and helped bring about a reduction and simplification of the regulations of the Occupational Safety and Health Administration (OSHA).

Most impressively, Marshall completed his term as secretary of labor in 1981 without unduly alienating either the president or organized labor, even though they were barely on speaking terms. High inflation and unemployment—and a White House determined to fight inflation at the cost of jobs and major cuts in entitlement programs—were only part of organized labor's grievances with the administration. Labor leaders also blamed the administration for the failure of labor law reform, specifically repeal of prohibitions on common situs and strengthening of the National Labor Relations Act to expedite union representation elections and strengthen fines for violations of the measure. Even the Humphrey-Hawkins Bill was widely regarded as a sham by labor since it gave the same priority to the elimination of inflation as it did to full employment and provided for no new job programs during periods of high unemployment.

Marshall avoided alienating either the constituency he represented or the president he served by finding a middle ground between the most excessive demands of organized labor and the president's insistence that American workers were going to have to rely less on government and more on the private sector to expand the economy and create new jobs. On the one hand, Marshall remained committed to the proposition that every American who could work was entitled to a job but that jobs creation could not be left primarily to the private sector. On the other hand, he accepted—indeed, helped design—the concept of targeting jobs creation at the most disadvantaged sectors of the labor force. Rather than regard the private sector as the enemy of labor, he agreed with the president on the important role the private sector needed to play in expanding the economy and providing new jobs. Accordingly, he sought an accommodation with business leaders and small-business owners.

Later, looking back at his career as secretary of labor, Marshall commented favorably on the Carter administration's selectively targeted jobs policy and the shift of more of the responsibility for jobs creation to the private sector and more of the responsibility for administering CETA programs to state and local governments. At the same time, he acknowledged that there should have more and better federal oversight of CETA programs. He also expressed regret at the reduction in funding for public-service jobs at a time near the end of the administration when unemployment was approaching 11 percent.

After leaving the Department of Labor in 1981, Marshall returned to the University of Texas–Austin, where he held the Audre and Bernard Rappoport Centennial Chair in Economics and Public Affairs at the Lyndon Baines Johnson School of Public Affairs. He also continued to write, to serve on commissions concerned with labor and economic policy, and to testify before Congress on the need for enforcing tougher standards at home and abroad against sweatshop industries like the garment industry. "In order to extend the protection of labor standards to the global marketplace," he told the House Committee on Education and the Workforce in 1998, "labor standards should be a component of the rules governing international transactions."

Marshall, Thurgood

(1908–1993) *associate justice, U.S. Supreme Court*

The first African-American Supreme Court justice and, before that, one of the nation's greatest civil rights lawyers, Thurgood Marshall was best known during the Carter administration for his strong concurring opinion in the case of *Regents of the University of California v. Bakke*, (1978), upholding the constitutionality of affirmative-action principles but prohibiting numerical quotas in cases involving equity for minorities.

Marshall was born on July 2, 1908, in Baltimore, Maryland. His mother was a schoolteacher in a segregated school system, and his father was a steward in an exclusive all-white yacht club. Though he grew up in a middle-class environment and then attended an all-black college, Lincoln University outside of Philadelphia, Marshall never thought much about racial issues. He said later that fighting segregation was not a burning issue for him as a young person. He was twice expelled for fraternity pranks, but after marrying a student from the University of Pennsylvania, Vivian Burey, during his senior year, Marshall became a more serious student and began to think of a career as a lawyer rather than a dentist, as his mother had wanted. He graduated from Lincoln cum laude with majors in American literature and philosophy (B.A., 1930). He then attended the all-black Howard University Law School in Washington, D.C., where he came under the influence of Charles H. Houston, one of the major figures in the Civil Rights movement of the 1930s and 1940s and the first black lawyer to win a case before the Supreme Court. It was at that point that Marshall made a lifelong commitment to end legal discrimination against minorities and the underprivileged in the United States.

After graduating from Howard at the top of his class (LL.B., 1933), Marshall opened his own law practice in Baltimore, specializing in civil rights and criminal cases. Representing the local National Association for the Advancement of Colored People (NAACP), he negotiated with white businesses who sold to blacks but would not hire them. He also joined John L. Lewis's effort to unionize black and white steelworkers. Although he sometimes took cases on a pro bono basis and his practice struggled, Marshall's first major break came when he successfully argued the right of a black applicant to be admitted to the University of Maryland Law School. His mentor, Charles Houston, joined him in arguing the case, which had special relevance for Marshall since he had wanted to attend the same law school but had been denied admission because it was open only to white students.

Hard work and some luck then began to fashion Marshall's career. In 1936, he was offered a position as assistant special counsel to the NAACP, working for Houston. When Houston decided to return to private practice two years later, Marshall moved into his mentor's position as head special counsel. During the next 20 years, he traveled as many as 50,000 miles a year throughout the South and argued 32 civil rights cases before the U.S. Supreme Court, of which he won 29. At first he followed the NAACP strategy of arguing not against the constitutionality of the doctrine of "separate but equal" but about the inequities existing between white and black facilities. He also argued cases involving college graduates seeking admission into all-white graduate and professional schools, believing that judges were more likely to be sympathetic to college graduates and that it would be prohibitively expensive for states to create "equal" facilities for those still-few black individuals seeking post-graduate education. After winning numerous court cases, Marshall convinced the NAACP's Legal Defense Fund (which had become a separate entity in the 1940s to give it tax-exempt status) to concentrate its attention on public elementary and high schools and on attacking the very constitutionality of segregation.

Marshall's great victory came in 1954, in the historic case of *Brown v. Board of Education of Topeka*, in which the Supreme Court ruled unanimously that the "separate but equal" system of racial segregation was unconstitutional. He later remarked that the *Brown* decision "probably did more than anything else to awaken the Negro from his apathy to demanding his rights to equality." But Marshall also won important cases challenging segregated housing, transportation, and discrimination in voting and jury selection. In 1951, he even went to Japan and Korea to investigate charges of unfair courts-martial against African-American soldiers. He got the sentences of 22 of the 40 men involved in the courts-martial reduced.

Although Marshall continued to head the Legal Defense Fund for 21 years, he became interested in an appointment to the federal bench. In 1961, he made it known to President John F. Kennedy, whom he had advised during the campaign, that he would like to be appointed to a vacancy on the U.S. Second Circuit Court of Appeals. Realizing that the appointment would be opposed by southern Democrats, Kennedy's brother, Attorney General Robert F. Kennedy, tried to persuade Marshall to accept a district court position. Marshall angrily walked out of his office, and the president made the nomination. After a bruising fight and some wheeling and dealing by the White House, the Senate confirmed the nomination. As a justice on the Court of Appeals, Marshall wrote 112 opinions, none of which were overturned by the Supreme Court.

Four years later, Marshall gave up this lifetime judicial appointment after President Lyndon Johnson asked him to accept the position of solicitor general, the litigator for the United States before the Supreme Court and the third-highest position in the Justice Department. As solicitor general, Marshall argued successfully before the Supreme Court in support of the 1965 Voting Rights Act, the reinstatement of indictments in two cases involving conspiracy to murder two civil rights workers, and against a California constitutional amendment prohibiting open-housing legislation. He also argued against electronic eavesdropping involving an illegal trespass, but he defended the right of the government to use informers. Of the 19 cases he argued for the government before the High Court, he won all but five.

When a seat on the Supreme Court opened in 1967, Johnson decided to appoint Marshall as the first African-American Supreme Court justice. In announcing the appointment, the president said that it was "the right thing to do, the right time to do it, the right man, and the right place." Marshall's nomination was, nevertheless, a bold decision on Johnson's part, because he knew it would cost him support in the South, which was still struggling over the end of segregation. As the president anticipated, the appointment led to a hard battle in the Senate before it approved the nomination. (In January 1973, a week before he died, Johnson told Marshall that it was his appointment of blacks to high office that destroyed his chances for reelection in 1968 and kept him from running.)

Aligned, as expected, with the Court's more liberal wing, Marshall proved to be an able, but not exceptional, Supreme Court justice. In contrast to his career as a civil rights attorney, he broke little new constitutional ground. While written in direct and well-crafted language, his decisions were not especially learned, creative, or memorable. They reflected the fact that he had been a practicing lawyer rather than a constitutional theorist or legal expert. Often his dissenting opinions were more powerful than his majority concurrences and were most noteworthy in the areas of his greatest expertise and concern: equal protection, due process, and the First Amendment. Under Chief Justice Earl Warren (1953–69), the Court was decidedly liberal in its opinions, making it a comfortable environment for Marshall. Under

Chief Justices WARREN BURGER (1969–86) and WILLIAM REHNQUIST (1986–2005), the Court became increasingly more conservative, and Marshall felt more and more isolated on the bench, although he retained friendly relations even with the most conservative members of the Court.

In racial discrimination cases, Marshall always voted to expand the civil rights of African Americans. He supported school desegregation cases and busing as a means of integrating white suburban schools. He voted in 1971 to prohibit Jackson, Mississippi, from closing its public swimming pools to avoid desegregation, and he ruled a year later against private clubs using state liquor laws to exclude blacks. In equal-protection cases, he urged the Court to adopt a variable standard to take into account the nature of the classification and of the interests involved in each case. But he took a strong stand against all forms of discrimination, regardless of race. He supported the 1966 *Miranda v. Arizona* ruling requiring suspects in criminal cases to be informed of their rights, including their right to legal counsel, and he was a consistent opponent of the death penalty as an unconstitutional violation of the Eighth Amendment's ban on cruel and unusual punishment. He was equally consistent in opposing government suppression of allegedly obscene material for consenting adults.

In the landmark case of *Roe v. Wade* (1973), Marshall sided with the majority in upholding the right of women to have legal abortions. In 1980, he delivered an eloquent dissent to the Court's decision confirming Illinois's right to restrict the use of public funds for abortion. When SARAH WEDDINGTON, the lead lawyer in the *Roe* case and later an assistant to President Jimmy Carter, learned in 1991 that Marshall had decided to step down from the Court, she remarked that the women of America had "lost a dear friend on the Supreme Court."

During the Jimmy Carter presidency, the most important case to come before the Supreme Court was the 1978 case involving ALLAN BAKKE's legal challenge to a separate-admissions procedure and a set-aside of 16 (out of 100) places for entering minority students at the University of California–Davis Medical School. Bakke was a white student who had been denied admission to the entering class despite being apparently better qualified than some minority students admitted into the program. He claimed that separate-admissions programs and set-asides for minority students were unconstitutional and violated his rights under the due-process clause of the Fourteenth Amendment.

In its decision, while the Court upheld the constitutionality of affirmative-action programs, it struck down racial quotas and ordered Bakke's admission to the medical school. But in an angry 16-page opinion, Marshall went substantially farther than his colleagues on the Court, holding that racial quotas were permissible to redress inequalities for blacks going back to slavery. He also noted the inequities still existing in 1978 between the races: black life expectancy shorter by more than five years than that of a white child, black mothers over three times more likely to die of complications in childbirth, black infant mortality rate twice that of whites, percentage of blacks who live in families with incomes below the poverty level four times greater than that of whites. The Court could not deal, therefore, with the issue of affirmative action in the purely rational, legalistic fashion suitable for an ideal world, he said. "[T]he legality of affirmative action simply could not be resolved without consideration of the historic, legal, and sociological context of past racial policies and practices."

In particular, Marshall directed his anger in the *Bakke* case against Justice LEWIS POWELL, who accepted affirmative action as necessary to redress legitimate historic grievances, but who also said it would be disastrous to give carte blanche to racial preferences. "[T]o argue that the guarantee of equal protection to all persons," Powell maintained, "permits the recognition of special wards entitled to a degree of protection greater than that accorded to others." This statement rankled Marshall, who believed that Powell still maintained a southern gentrified sense of responsibility for the less fortunate and a southerner's instinct for paternalism toward blacks.

In another important case decided by the Court in 1977, *Bounds v. Smith*, Marshall wrote the majority opinion holding that state prison systems were obligated constitutionally to provide inmates with "adequate law libraries and adequate assistance from persons trained in the law."

By the end of the Carter presidency, the White House was anxious to make at least one nomination to the Supreme Court. Rumors began to circulate that Marshall, who was already in ill health and had suffered a heart attack, would step down so that President Carter could appoint a new member to the Court. According to Marshall, he was even approached by two White House aides about retiring, but he made it clear that he had no intention of doing so. In fact, when he did decide to leave the Court in 1991, he surprised even his own colleagues. By this time, however, Marshall's health had deteriorated badly. He was heavily overweight, had difficulty walking, was losing his hearing, and had suffered heart attacks, blood clots, pneumonia, and glaucoma.

Marshall had also become estranged from the Court, which had become increasingly conservative under Presidents RONALD REAGAN and GEORGE HERBERT WALKER BUSH. His closest friend on the Court, WILLIAM BRENNAN, had retired. Never reticent, he became gruff and more tart-tongued on the bench and in his opinions. He also became outspoken in his disdain of the White House, something highly irregular for a Supreme Court justice. He remarked that he would not "do the job of dogcatcher for Ronald Reagan" and later, with respect to Bush, stated in a television interview that he had been taught that if he could not say something good about a dead person, don't say it. "Well, I consider him dead," he remarked. He also told a reporter from *Newsweek* that the actions of the Reagan and Bush administrations reflected a return to the days "when we [blacks] really didn't have a chance."

On January 24, 1993, at the age of 84, Marshall died of heart failure at Bethesda Naval Medical Center. He had been scheduled to administer the oath of office to Vice President Al Gore, but ill health had kept him from doing so.

McDonald, Alonzo Lowry

(Al McDonald)

(1928–) *assistant to the president, White House staff director*

Alonzo McDonald, often known as Al, was assistant to the president and White House staff director during the Carter administration. An expert on administrative management, he was brought into the White House as part of a staff shake-up that led to the appointment of Carter's chief assistant, HAMILTON JORDAN, as chief of staff. Because of Jordan's lack of interest and inexperience in management, McDonald worked alongside him in running the day-to-day operations of the White House staff.

Born on August 5, 1928, in Atlanta, Georgia, McDonald grew up in a rural area outside the city; his father ran an insurance business in Atlanta. After graduating from Emory University with a degree in journalism (B.A., 1948), Al McDonald worked as a reporter and political writer for the *Atlanta Journal* before joining the U.S. Marines in 1950. After his discharge in 1952, he attended Harvard University's School of Business (M.B.A., 1956) and began a business career working for Westinghouse Electric Corporation. After being passed over for a major promotion, he took a position with the international management consulting firm of McKinsey and Co. Over the next 17 years, he occupied a number of key positions in New York, London, Paris, and Zurich, including that of managing director and chief executive officer for the firm's offices worldwide. After he returned to the United States, he settled in Connecticut and was elected McKinsey's managing director in 1973.

McDonald first met Jimmy Carter at a fund-raising dinner given by THEODORE SORENSEN to raise enough money to qualify Carter for the New York primary in 1976. At one time a Republican, McDonald had shifted over time to the Democratic Party because he liked its more-diverse constituencies. Although he found Carter to be an interesting and smart person and contributed to his campaign, he had no interest in politics and did not become involved in the campaign.

Following Carter's election, however, McDonald was contacted by ROBERT STRAUSS, the president's special trade representative. Strauss asked McDonald to join him as his deputy at the forthcoming Tokyo Round of multilateral trade negotiations. McDonald accepted the offer and worked closely with Strauss over the next two years. They were able to negotiate a significant round of trade reductions, which many observers had predicted would never happen. After McDonald signed the final agreement on behalf of the president, he played an instrumental role in winning congressional approval of the trade agreement, testifying in detail before congressional committees and responding quickly to written congressional inquiries. On August 9, 1978, following Strauss's resignation, Carter appointed McDonald to serve as acting special trade representative.

While McDonald was working with Strauss, he became acquainted with Hamilton Jordan. In 1979, after Jordan learned that the president planned to appoint him as chief of staff, he consulted Strauss. According to McDonald, Strauss felt that Jordan did not have the administrative interest or skills to run the day-to-day operation of the White House and that he needed a deputy for that purpose. After talking to several individuals, Jordan offered the position to McDonald, whom Strauss had recommended for the position. "He'll improve our operations and processes, coordinate policy and politics," Jordan remarked in announcing McDonald's appointment. "I plan to give him broad authority. … It'll give me more time to think and plan."

As Jordan's deputy, McDonald applied his experience in corporate management to White House operations. In an interview in August 1979, he described himself as "result oriented" and said he wanted to reduce the "frustration that inhibit[ed] presidential decision making." He also said that Jordan would be "the signal caller" but that others at the White House would have to "run with the ball." He dubbed his blueprint for the White House Operation Matrix Interface.

In six weeks, McDonald changed the layout and operations of the West Wing. Walls and doorways were moved in order to better coordinate operations. Seventy-five people at the White House had their offices moved, in some cases out of the West Wing and into the nearby Executive Office Building on the 17-acre White House complex. Six different offices of the congressional liaison group were brought together. "One of the reasons they could never respond to telephone calls," McDonald later explained, "was that they simply could not find out where their calls had come in. They couldn't respond to correspondence because they couldn't know where the correspondence was, and when they found it they didn't know where to send it."

McDonald also intended changing the layout of the White House offices to be a psychological tool. By rearranging the offices and positioning his own office between those of the president and Hamilton Jordan, he wanted to let the staff know who was in charge and to make clear to the hierarchically oriented personnel that their purpose was to serve the president rather than to enhance their own position. For the same reasons, he appeared frequently with Jordan so that there would be no doubt among White House staffers as to his authority. His intention was that once the White House staff accepted the new organizational arrangements and tighter discipline, he would then become as invisible as possible. "I wanted to go back to the old Roosevelt idea of the good Presidential aide—occasionally seen and rarely heard," he later commented.

McDonald also regularized daily meetings of the senior staff and their deputies, introduced agendas, and established a system of monitoring to make sure that assignments were carried out. He met daily with Jordan and the president and took charge of the speechwriting operation. He insisted on earlier drafts for the president and more input from the senior staff on content. At the same time, Carter's speechwriters were given more access to the president when major policy speeches needed to be written. "Since his advent, I have seen the president more often. I have a better, closer relationship with the president than before," said chief speechwriter Hendrik (Rick) Hertzberg, "and these procedural changes have made my job better and more interesting."

Not everyone was pleased by McDonald's imperious managerial style or changes. Some staffers thought he acted too much from the hip, encouraged stormy sessions on minor details, and ignored the lower-level staff. "Everyone said Carter needed a bastard and he's got one [in McDonald]," a White House staffer remarked. Hamilton Jordan was "the politician," Robert Strauss commented, while McDonald was "the mechanic."

Although McDonald did not resolve all the management problems that had plagued the Carter White House, he brought about a degree of centralized control and administrative order that had not existed prior to 1979. Although some egos were bruised, most White House aides seemed pleased with the new efficiency and hard-nosed management he brought to the administration. "It's much better organized, much more deliberate than before," observed ANNE WEXLER, the president's assistant for public liaison. HEDLEY DONOVAN, who was brought into the White House about the same time that McDonald was hired, later remarked, "McDonald was a first-class administrator, which his boss Hamilton Jordan ... was not." Even critics of the administration expressed regret that someone like McDonald had not been in place in the White House 32 months earlier, at the beginning of the Carter presidency.

Following Carter's defeat for reelection in 1980, McDonald became president and vice chairman of the Bendix Corporation. From 1983 to 1987, he served as a senior counselor to the dean of the Harvard Business School, where he developed and moderated the school's quarterly Senior Executive Seminar for chief executive officers. He is presently chief executive officer of Avenir, a private investment group based in Birmingham, Michigan.

Raised an Episcopalian and devoutly religious, McDonald founded the Trinity Forum in 1991. The organization's purpose is to bring together business leaders to discuss the spiritual dimension of leadership and how their personal beliefs govern their lives and influence the roles they play in society. McDonald presently serves as a trustee and senior fellow of the Trinity Forum. In 1998, he established a distinguished professorship at Emory University dedicated to the study of Jesus and his impact on culture.

McGovern, George Stanley

(1922–) *member of the Senate*

In December 1976, President-elect Jimmy Carter's pollster and political strategist, PAT CADELL—who had performed similar roles in 1972 for the Democratic presidential nominee, Senator George S. McGovern—identified the South Dakota senator, along with Senator EDWARD KENNEDY (Mass.) and Congressman MORRIS UDALL (Ariz.), as among the leading liberals on Capitol Hill who might present the greatest challenges to Carter's policies and presidency. Within months after Carter took office, Caddell's prediction about McGovern began to come true. For the remainder of the administration, McGovern, a champion of the liberal cause throughout his political career, proved to be unrepentant in his criticism of the Carter White House because he thought it had deserted the basic tenets of the Democratic Party.

From the great prairies that bred the populist movement of the late 19th-century America, McGovern was born in Avon, South Dakota, on July 19, 1922. The son of a coal miner turned Methodist preacher, he was taught the virtues of self-discipline, sacrifice, abstinence, and personal integrity. Growing up in Mitchell, South Dakota, McGovern attended nearby Dakota Wesleyan University on a scholarship. He was twice elected class president and won the state oratorical contest on the topic "My Brother's Keeper," an avowal of his belief in one's responsibility to mankind.

McGovern's education was interrupted when he enlisted in 1942 in the United States Army Air Corps. During World War II, he flew 35 combat missions over Europe and received the Distinguished Service Flying Cross. In 2001, his service as a pilot was highlighted in the best-selling *The Wild Blue: The Men and Boys Who Flew the B-24s over Germany*, by the historian Stephen E. Ambrose.

Following his discharge in 1945, McGovern completed his undergraduate education at Dakota Wesleyan (B.A., 1946). Undecided between a career as a minister or a teacher, he attended Garrett Seminary for one year but left to complete a doctorate in history at Northwestern University (M.A., 1950; Ph.D., 1953). His years at Northwestern were a watershed for him. Becoming politically active, he identified himself in 1948 with the political agenda of former vice president Henry Wallace and even served as a delegate to the Progressive Party Convention that nominated Wallace for president. But he was troubled by the fanaticism he encountered at the convention and, in the end, did not vote.

While still working on his doctoral dissertation, McGovern returned to Dakota Wesleyan University as a member of the faculty (1950–55). In 1952, he heard the acceptance speech of the Democratic presidential nominee, Adlai Stevenson, on the radio. Moved to volunteer in the unsuccessful Stevenson campaign, he was asked the next year to become the executive secretary of South Dakota's Democratic Party. Taking a skeleton organization in an overwhelmingly Republican state, he built a structure of volunteers strong enough to increase the Democratic delegation in the state legislature from two to 25 and to get him elected to the House of Representatives in 1956. After serving two terms in the House, he ran unsuccessfully for the U.S. Senate against the incumbent, Karl E. Mundt. Following this defeat, President John F. Kennedy appointed McGovern director of the Food for Peace program, which was intended to help both the

American farmer and the nation's poorer allies by providing them with credits to purchase U.S. surplus crops.

In 1962, McGovern ran for South Dakota's other Senate seat and, despite a bout of hepatitis that kept him on the sidelines for much of the campaign, narrowly defeated his Republican opponent, Joseph H. Bottum, by 597 votes, winning the first of his three terms in the Senate. During the 1960s, he established his reputation as a leading liberal on Capitol Hill, supporting the domestic programs of the New Frontier and Great Society and becoming an early and outspoken opponent of the Vietnam War. In 1968, following the assassination of Robert F. Kennedy, McGovern tried to assume the mantle of the Kennedy presidential campaign, but he came in a distant third to the eventual Democratic nominee, HUBERT HUMPHREY.

Referring to the Vietnam War as a "moral and political disaster—a terrible cancer eating away at the soul of the nation," McGovern coauthored in 1970 and 1971 the unsuccessful McGovern-Hatfield amendments to cut off all funding for the war. In 1971, he also announced that he would again be a candidate for president on an antiwar platform. Given little chance of winning the Democratic nomination, he used the skills he had gained as an organizer in South Dakota to build a network of volunteers throughout the primary states. This and the implosion of the campaign of Senator EDMUND MUSKIE (Maine), the early front-runner, led to a series of primary victories that assured him the Democratic nomination.

McGovern's campaign was flawed from the start. His delegates to the convention, selected under new party rules that had opened the selection process and made it more representative of the party's constituency, proved unruly. Party regulars felt left out of the convention and regarded McGovern as being outside the mainstream of American voters. His acceptance speech was delayed until 3:00 A.M., so few Americans saw or heard it at home. He had to replace his candidate for vice president, Missouri senator Thomas Eagleton, with former president John F. Kennedy's brother-in-law, Sargent Shriver, after it was disclosed that Eagleton had suffered a nervous breakdown requiring electroshock treatments. McGovern's call for a minimum income for all Americans seemed unrealistic, and his anti-Vietnam War platform was outstripped by the efforts already underway by his opponent, President RICHARD NIXON, to end the war. The president's illicit campaign activities, revealed during the Watergate scandal, only aggravated what would have been a losing cause in any case. In 1972, McGovern suffered one of the most humiliating defeats in the nation's history, winning less than 40 percent of the vote and carrying only Massachusetts and the District of Columbia.

Ironically, Jimmy Carter, whom McGovern had visited in Atlanta when Carter was governor, made an effort to be the senator's running mate, only to be rebuffed by Pat Caddell, who thought Carter and his backers "were crazy." Yet his meetings with McGovern and the other presidential aspirants in 1972 convinced the Georgia governor that he was at least as qualified as they were to be president, and McGovern's defeat was one of the factors that figured in Carter's decision to run for president. The South Dakotan's strategy of gaining national status by winning the Iowa caucuses and then gaining an insurmountable lead in delegates by entering the primary states and depending on mostly volunteers to win the election was one to emulate. At the same time, Carter distanced himself from the ideological extremism he associated with McGovern, choosing instead to run a centrist campaign.

Once Carter became president, McGovern's ideological differences with the chief executive soon surfaced. The senator joined with other liberals in defending Carter's nomination of THEODORE SORENSEN as director of the Central Intelligence Agency, remarking that the "ghosts of Joe McCarthy still stalks the land," in reference to right-wing groups seeking to block the nomination. But he was taken aback at a meeting at the White House in May 1977, when the president insisted on the need for a balanced budget and his economic advisers detailed the case for restraint. In one of the earliest and strongest blasts against the president by any Democrat, McGovern remarked at a meeting of the liberal Americans for Democratic Action (ADA): "Last year Jimmy Carter said that full employment was his first priority. Then it should be postponed for a second term. Let us insist that we not balance the federal budget on the backs of the poor, the hungry and the jobless." The senator added, "It sometimes seems difficult to remember who won last fall."

McGovern supported the president's decision in the summer not to go forward with the development of the B-1 bomber, praising him for "prudence, leadership, and courage." Nevertheless, at a convention of the United Auto Workers (UAW) in Los Angeles, he again criticized Carter for his conservative economic and fiscal policies, saying he could see little difference between Carter and a Republican president.

In 1978, McGovern expressed reservations about ratifying the Panama Canal Treaties. Although he believed the canal and Canal Zone should be turned over to Panama and eventually voted for the treaties, he thought proposed reservations by DENNIS DECONCINI (D-Ariz.) and SAM NUNN (D-Ga.), which would have allowed the United States to intervene militarily in Panama after 1999 to keep the canal open, were too loaded against Panama. He joined Edward Kennedy and DANIEL PATRICK MOYNIHAN (D-N.Y.) in threatening to vote against the second of the two agreements unless a "noninterventionist" clarification was added to the agreement. Such language was eventually incorporated into the treaty.

McGovern also opposed a unilateral lifting of the arms embargo against Turkey that was imposed after 1974 when Turkey invaded Cyprus to protect the Turkish minority on the island. Instead, he worked out a compromise with Majority Leader ROBERT BYRD (W.Va.) calling for an end to the embargo but keeping some limits on arms sales to Turkey and requiring the president to certify that any military or economic assistance to that country would contribute to peace in Cyprus. Although an opponent of the Vietnam War, he found the nature of the regime in Cambodia in 1978 so brutal that he suggested armed international intervention there might be necessary.

In the Middle East, McGovern voted for the administration's proposal that packaged the sale of 60 F-15s for Saudi Arabia with 75 F-16s for Israel, but only because he had concluded that the deal was already on the table and would be difficult for the Senate to reject. Privately, he objected strongly to U.S. arms sales and to the timing of Carter's aircraft deal. But he was enthusiastic about the Camp David accords between Egypt and Israel that the president negotiated in September 1978. Commenting on the president's speech to Congress after the deal was announced, with Egypt's president ANWAR SADAT and Israel's prime minister MENACHEM BEGIN in the audience, he remarked that the joint session was "the most dramatic moment in all the years I have been in Washington."

On domestic legislation, McGovern opposed the administration's efforts to deregulate the airline industry because he thought small cities like those in South Dakota would lose service under the bill. Representing a rural state and mindful of his constituencies, he worked closely with his colleague of 17 years on the Agriculture Committee, HERMAN TALMADGE, for higher price supports than the administration wanted. He was also a strong backer of a comprehensive program of national health insurance.

In 1979, McGovern ridiculed the Strategic Arms Limitation Talks agreement (SALT II) that Carter had signed in June in Vienna with Soviet leader LEONID BREZHNEV. Although a leading proponent of disarmament throughout his career, McGovern felt that SALT II did not go far enough in limiting the nuclear arms threat. "I don't think SALT II is worth fighting for," he said. "We ought to just scrap it." About the same time, he announced publicly his support of Edward Kennedy for the 1980 Democratic presidential nomination. Accusing Carter of "moral posturing, public manipulation and political ineptitude," McGovern remarked that Kennedy was "the most logical candidate for our party ... and would be an inspiring president."

Unfortunately for McGovern, his own reelection in 1980 for a fourth term to the Senate was already in doubt. A Democratic liberal in a conservative Republican state, he had always had to fight tight election campaigns, but his attentiveness to his constituents, his affable and pleasant manner, and his skills as an organizer had always allowed him to come from behind to win. Tagged as an "ultra-liberal" by his opponents in an election year when there was evidence of a growing conservative tide, however, he was not able to replicate his previous performances against his Republican opponent, James Abdnor. A popular four-term congressman and wheat farmer, Abnor staked out more conservative positions than McGovern on every issue from abortion and government regulation to federal spending and defense. During the campaign, McGovern became incensed when ultraright groups, who had targeted him for defeat, labeled him everything from "a pawn of Castro" for favoring normalizing relations with Cuba to a "baby killer" for his support of abortion rights.

Although McGovern, who refused to retreat from his liberal credentials, seemed to be closing in in the polls near the end of the race and some political pundits even predicted that he would pull from behind as he had done in the past, Abdnor trounced him on election day. McGovern was only one of a group of liberals in the Senate to be defeated, giving Republicans control of the Senate for the first time since 1954, but the margin of his defeat, 58 to 39 percent, approximated the magnitude of his thrashing for president in 1972.

In 1984, McGovern ran again for president, intending to promote a national health-care system and major cuts in defense spending. With little support, he withdrew shortly after the New Hampshire primary. Dark days followed. Relegated to the political graveyard, he purchased the Stratford Hotel in Connecticut in 1988, fulfilling a lifelong dream of being an innkeeper, but he lost the business less than three years later. In 1992, he considered a third race for the presidency but decided against it. In 1993, his daughter, Terry, who had had a history of alcoholism since she was 13 years old, died tragically after becoming inebriated and freezing to death in the snow near Madison, Wisconsin. Subsequently, McGovern published an account of his daughter's problems, *Terry: My Daughter's Life-and-Death Struggle with Alcoholism* (1996). Ironically, a speech McGovern made about his daughter's experience encouraged Nancy Thurmond, the wife of McGovern's teetotaler Republican foe in the Senate, STROM THURMOND (R-S.C.), to go public about her own alcoholism.

Long regarded as an expert on the politics of food and world hunger, McGovern served from 2000 to 2003 as the U.S. ambassador to the UN Food and Agricultural Organization located in Rome, Italy. In 2000, President Bill Clinton awarded him the Presidential Medal of Freedom, the highest medal awarded a civilian. In 2001 he was appointed UN global ambassador on world hunger. That same year, he published *Ending Hunger in Our Time.*

McGovern has continued to lecture and speak out on public issues. In 2004, he endorsed former NATO commander Wesley Clark for the Democratic Party presidential nomination. A critic of the war in Iraq, he has maintained that the United States needed another "Deep Throat" to expose how President George W. Bush "misled" the United States into the war in Iraq. McGovern maintains a summer home in Stevensville, Montana, near the Idaho border, where he owns a used-book store.

McIntyre, James Talmadge, Jr.

(1940–) *director, Office of Management and Budget*

James McIntyre succeeded BERT LANCE as director of the Office of Management and Budget (OMB) following Lance's resignation from the Carter administration in September 1977. He remained in that position for the rest of the Carter presidency. Although a Georgian who had worked in the administration when Jimmy Carter was governor of the state, McIntyre was not part of the innermost circle of advisers who had accompanied the president to the White House from Georgia. Lacking Lance's gregarious personality, he was more a bureaucrat than a well-known public figure. One of Carter's most fiscally conservative advisers, however, he was often a countervailing force to those in the administration who wanted the president to pursue more liberal spending policies.

Born on December 17, 1940, in Vidalia, Georgia, McIntyre attended Young Harris College, a small two-year Methodist-affiliated liberal arts college in northern Georgia. He then completed his education at the University of Georgia, where he received both his bachelor and law degrees the same year (B.A. and J.D., 1963). During Carter's governorship, he was the director of the Office of Planning and Budget and chief legal counsel for the study of the reorganization of state government. In the latter capacity, he led the team of lawyers from state agencies who wrote the 57-page state reorganization measure that the state legislature eventually approved.

After Carter was elected president, he asked McIntyre to work for the administration at some high-level management position upon which they would mutually agree. One likely possibility was the OMB, but that was to be determined later. The president-elect also asked McIntyre to be involved in the reorganization plans that were being developed by the budget transition team. McIntyre agreed to come to Washington, but he was not well-known even by Carter's closest advisers, who were unclear what his role would be within the administration. Only after Bert Lance gave him the major responsibility of devising the structure for reorganization did his function within the incoming administration become better defined. Subsequently he was appointed assistant director of the OMB under Lance. As McIntyre later defined his and Lance's responsibilities: "My job was to do the overall managing of the agency, relate to the White House, and help Mr. Lance in some of his more visible activities. ... Mr. Lance's role was basically to be an emissary of the President, and to help him in making his policy decisions."

When the president decided to elevate McIntyre to director of OMB following Lance's resignation, he was still not that well-known even among top officials within the administration. Nevertheless, he was totally familiar with the president's economic and political views, and he brought a sense of order to the OMB following the political chaos surrounding Lance's resignation. The president thought that, technically, McIntyre was better qualified to run the OMB and to prepare budgets than Lance.

The contrast in personality and presence between McIntyre and Lance could not have been sharper. Lance was a large, ebullient, and garrulous individual, a mixer and deal maker who genuinely liked people, was liked by them, and had a commanding presence that extended well beyond his close relationship with the president. McIntyre was the epitome of the technocrat and bureaucrat, highly efficient and able but also reserved, short in stature, and without much charisma. Carter's biographer, PETER BOURNE, who also served the president as a special assistant, has portrayed him as a "constrained introvert ... never emotional with a technocratic attachment to government efficiency and a balanced budget." ALFRED KAHN, who became the president's chief inflation fighter, described him simply as "not a powerful, effective person."

Bourne and Kahn may have underestimated McIntyre. The most fiscally conservative of the president's economic advisers, he was one of the administration's earliest and most consistent advocates of targeting inflation rather than unemployment as its highest economic priority and of fighting inflation by balancing the budget, even if it meant sacrificing entitlement programs dear to Democratic constituencies. In policy debates, he played the devil's advocate, frequently reminding his colleagues of the positions that Carter had taken before the election. As a result, McIntyre had major differences with Carter's politically astute director of the domestic policy staff, STUART EIZENSTAT, who believed that the president needed to find a balance between cutting social programs and assuaging Democratic interest groups. According to ANNE WEXLER, Carter's assistant for public liaison, "it was given that on budget and policy issues Jim would take one side and Stu the other." The OMB director's differences with still more liberal members of the administration, such as Vice President WALTER MONDALE and Secretary of Health, Education and Welfare (HEW) JOSEPH CALIFANO, were even more palpable.

McIntyre's financial conservatism was reflected in the preparation of the budget for fiscal 1979. This was the first budget that he had a major hand in preparing, since the budget for fiscal 1978 had been largely prepared by the Ford administration. In December 1977, when he was serving as acting director of the OMB, McIntyre met with a coalition of urban, labor, and education leaders who were urging the administration to live up to its campaign promise to forgo big defense spending increases in favor of domestic spending in the 1979 budget. McIntyre told them that Carter's budget would "go a long way toward resolving the domestic problems" they raised. He also noted, however, that there were many overlapping domestic programs and that the administration was trying to make the existing programs work better.

Just a few weeks later, McIntyre took a harder position. Convinced that the economic-stimulus program the administration had instituted after taking office, when the administration's highest priority was lowering the rate of unemployment, had contributed to an inflation rate approaching double-digit numbers, he urged the president in January 1978 to send Congress a balanced budget even if that meant a recession early in his term. Aware of the uproar that his proposal would create among liberal Democrats, he also recommended that Carter appeal to fiscally conservative middle America. A few months later, as the White House finalized its budget recommendations, he argued against the social spending that Vice President Mondale and other more liberal members of the administration were urging. He maintained that cutting a trillion-dollar budget by even $3 billion or $4 billion would send a message to Congress and the American people that Carter was committed to reducing the deficit and cutting inflation.

McIntyre's impatience with what he regarded as congressional obstructionism was revealed in other ways as well. About the same time that he was arguing against Mondale's budget recommendations, he wrote Carter a memorandum in which he recommended that the president, who had been engaged in difficult fights with Congress that ran the gamut of his legislative program, adopt a tougher policy toward Capitol Hill by making more use of his veto power. "We seem now to consider vetoes as major exercises of Presidential power ... and which, therefore, are almost inappropriate actions by a Democratic President with a Democratic Congress," the OMB director commented. "The Hill perceives our extreme reluctance to use the veto, and predictably, is less willing to negotiate over a wide range of issues." His office drew up a list of 30 objectionable bills as candidates for a presidential veto.

During the Carter presidency, the OMB was used programmatically, not just as an agency to oversee the budget. For example, it became heavily invested in the president's "comprehensive" urban policy initiative, which emphasized a "partnership" between federal, state, and local governments, the private sector, and community groups and was predicated on small-scale, locally administered programs with no overall impact on the budget. As a result, the net effect of the urban initiative was to shift the burden of urban policy from Washington to state and local government and private organizations. The chairman of the president's Council of Economic Advisers, CHARLES SCHULTZE, who worked closely with McIntyre and whose views on budget restraint he came increasingly to share, thought the office could have been used more effectively in terms of program development.

For his part, McIntyre became frustrated with the opposition he met even within the administration to his proposals for budget cuts. In November 1978, he proposed hundreds of individual cuts to the fiscal 1980 budget that HEW secretary Califano had recommended. These included reductions in funds for health maintenance organizations, medical schools, research programs, and preventive health programs. Both Califano and Mondale fought strongly against the cuts, which Senator EDWARD KENNEDY (D-Mass.) had used to embarrass the administration by referring to them (without first consulting Califano or Mondale about his intention) item-by-item at the Democratic Party's midterm convention in Memphis. The OMB director complained to Schultze that that every time he would turn to a target for reduction in the budget, someone in the White House would say, "Well, you can't touch that, you can't touch that."

Despite his frustration, McIntyre remained as director of OMB until the end of the Carter presidency. In that capacity, he continued to emphasize the need to balance the budget in order to fight inflation, which by fall 1980 was approaching 20 percent. After he left the White House, he established the McIntyre Law Firm in Washington, D.C. He also became a member of the Board of Directors of the Committee for a Responsible Budget.

Meany, George
(1894–1980) *AFL-CIO president*

In September 1978, President Jimmy Carter ruminated on individuals with whom he would not like to spend a weekend at Camp David. Among the persons he named was George Meany, president of the American Federation of Labor and Congress of Industrial Organizations (AFL-CIO). Relations between the president and the leader of the nation's most powerful labor organization had never been good, but by fall 1978 they had reached a new low point. Meany had endorsed Carter for president after the 1976 Democratic Party convention, something he had not done in the case of the Democratic nominee, GEORGE MCGOVERN, four years earlier. But Carter had not been Meany's first choice for the Democratic nomination. Within a matter of months, relations between the two men had soured to the point that they were hardly on speaking terms with each other. Although a clash of personalities was part of the problem, more fundamental was Carter's effort to shift the Democratic Party away from its traditional economic and social moorings.

Meany was born into an Irish-Catholic family in New York City on August 16, 1894, and spent most of his boyhood in the Bronx. Organized labor was part of his life since childhood. His father was president of a local plumber's union, and Meany followed in his father's footsteps. Leaving school at the age of 16, he worked as a plumber's apprentice for five years and received his journeyman plumber's certificate in 1915. By 1922, he was business agent of his union local, and by 1934, he was president of the New York State Federation of Labor. In 1939, he was elected secretary-treasurer of the AFL. When William Green stepped down as president of the AFL in 1952, Meany was elected to replace him. In 1955, he unified the labor movement when he combined the AFL with the CIO, which had been created in the 1930s to represent many of the nation's industrial unions. The newly united AFL-CIO named him president, a position he held until he retired in November 1979, two months before his death.

Throughout his career as a labor leader, Meany devoted his efforts to improving the economic and social well-being of union members. This meant higher wages, better benefits, better working conditions, and an enhanced role of government that included such causes as civil rights, public housing, minimum wages, national health insurance, and jobs programs. Meany was also a strident anticommunist and strong supporter of the war in Vietnam. His liberal domestic agenda and conservative foreign policies reflected tensions within the labor movement itself.

Gruff-spoken and blunt, Meany was unhappy at the direction the Democratic Party had taken in the 1960s and early 1970s. Although he championed the Civil Rights movement of the first half of the 1960s, he opposed the disorder, disrespect for established institutions, antiwar activities, and breakdown of traditional values he associated with the youth movement of the period. Changes by which delegates were chosen to the Democratic National Convention had, in his view, led to the capture of the party and the nomination of George McGovern as its standard bearer by the very elements he found intolerable.

A lifelong Democrat, Meany sought a more mainstream candidate in 1976 than McGovern, one who remained committed to the cold war liberal values he associated with the Democratic Party. He preferred either Senator HENRY JACKSON (Wash.), whose hard-line policy toward the Soviet Union and opposition to the policy of détente with Moscow being promoted by President GERALD FORD appealed to Meany, or former vice president HUBERT HUMPHREY, a stalwart liberal and lifelong friend of organized labor. In contrast, he was not enthusiastic about Jimmy Carter, whose rural southern background suggested that he had little familiarity with the concerns of working people. Carter's failure during the campaign to discuss labor issues also troubled the AFL-CIO president. He refrained, however, from endorsing any candidate for president, and when Carter won the nomination, Meany backed him. On election day, organized labor played a major role in getting out the vote in support of the Democratic nominee, revved up by some impolitic remarks about labor from the Republican vice-presidential candidate, Senator ROBERT DOLE (Kans.). When the newly elected president entered office in January 1977, he had organized labor supporting him.

That soon changed. Carter's rejection of special-interest politics and his conviction that inflation was the most serious domestic economic problem facing the United States placed him at odds with organized labor, which was more concerned with unemployment and still believed in the politics of productivity: that a full-employment economy and higher wages were possible through public policies that stimulated economic growth. The personal chemistry between the president and Meany was also bad. Coming from such different backgrounds and having such different perspectves on the economy, they had difficulty communicating with each other. STUART EIZENSTAT, the director of Carter's domestic policy staff, recalled an incident early in the administration when Meany and other AFL-CIO leaders came to the White House for lunch. According to Eizenstat, the president grew upset by the coarse language of his guests. "It was painfully obvious at that point," recalled Eizenstat, "that regardless of what he might do or say, neither was going to feel terribly comfortable with the other."

A number of the president's key economic advisers, including CHARLES SCHULTZE, the chairman of the president's Council of Economic Advisers, had little regard for organized labor, which they held responsible for much of the nation's inflation problem and which, they believed, was becoming an anachronism in an increasingly competitive global economy. "Whenever big management and big labor get together," Schultze remarked, "they normally ... screw the public," with labor causing most of the damage because "management has always been a patsy for large wage increases."

A more specific reason why Schultze and other members of the administration were so annoyed with the AFL-CIO president was Meany's opposition to Carter's proposal for voluntary wage guidelines in 1978. A newly formed Council on Wage and Price Stability (COWPS) had developed the guidelines as the best way to deal with inflation. Meany and other labor leaders were concerned, however, about whether wages would bear the brunt of government intervention; he termed the whole concept of wage and price guidelines "wish-boning." In August 1978, he denounced an agreement with postal workers that kept wage increases within the guidelines. Carter was so infuriated by Meany's remarks, realizing they would assure rejection of the new contract, that he banished Meany from the White House. "I don't want anybody else coming in here and telling me [Meany] is senile and didn't really mean what he said. He knows exactly what he is doing," said Carter.

In an effort to improve relations with organized labor, the White House, with the president's tepid support, backed a labor-reform measure that it had developed in consultation with labor. The legislation would strengthen the National Labor Relations Act to expedite union-representation elections and increase fines for violations of the measure. In speeches before business and civic groups, Carter insisted that the legislation was moderate and modest and only gave "workers the right that was guaranteed them in the Wagner Act of 1935." The president lobbied Congress hard for passage of the measure. Aware that it was going to die in the Senate, Eizenstat advised the president to go down fighting. When the legislation failed, the president made his displeasure public. The measure, he said, had failed because of an "unwarranted outpouring of distortion and political pressure from some business organizations and some right-wing organizations."

Carter's failed effort to win congressional approval of labor-reform legislation hardly satisfied Meany, who remained strongly opposed to the president's program of voluntary guidelines. In October 1978, the president went on national television to announce "phase two" of his anti-inflation program. Wages and fringe benefits, he told the American people, would be limited to 7 percent. In what he called "real wage insurance," he stated that should prices exceed 7 percent, workers whose wages were kept below that level would get a tax rebate during the year. Following his televised address, Carter appointed ALFRED KAHN to head COWPS. Khan was a former professor at Cornell University who, as chairman of the Civil Aeronautics Board, had been instrumental in deregulating many airline operations and making the industry more competitive. Like a number of Carter's other economic advisers, Kahn held organized labor in low regard, blaming much of the nation's inflation problems on labor's unrealistic demands. "I'd love to see the Teamsters to be worse off," he remarked. "I'd love the automobile workers to be worse off."

Kahn thought Meany and his soon-to-be successor, Lane Kirkland, "represented a bankrupt labor movement." In December 1978, however, he agreed to modify the 7 percent cap on wages to exclude automatic increases in health and pension benefits. Even with this concession, many labor leaders remained adamantly opposed to the COWPS guidelines, none more so than Meany. Labor had not been consulted in either the formulation of the guidelines or the appointment of Kahn, despite the recommendation of Secretary of Labor RAY MARSHALL that Meany, in particular, be asked for his input. Meany considered Kahn a lightweight. When asked what Kahn would do to hold prices down, the labor leader quipped, "Make a speech. That's what he does best." Following Carter's announcement of the new guidelines, the AFL-CIO president asked COWPS for a public hearing on the new wage and price standards, but Kahn turned him down.

To the surprise of the White House, Meany then let the administration know that he might be willing to support the new guidelines if the wage level exempted from the cap was raised from $4 an hour to $5 an hour. Even Kahn urged the president to discuss Meany's offer with him, but the president first wanted assurances that the labor leader would support his anti-inflation measures. "Right now Meany looks like shit," he remarked, "and we look good and he knows it."

On January 22, 1979, Marshall reported to the White House that he had concluded an arrangement with the AFL-CIO whereby the administration would consult it on a regular basis on all matters concerning wages and prices. Marshall and Vice President WALTER MONDALE promised to meet monthly with top officials of the AFL-CIO, who would be notified before the administration took actions of any major significance. A short time later, the president announced that organized labor had agreed to abide by his wage and price guidelines.

Carter's announcement proved premature. Still angry that he had been rebuffed earlier by the president when he asked to meet with him at the White House, Meany remained obstreperous in his opposition to the wage and price standards. He and other leaders of the AFL-CIO also distrusted Kahn and Schultze and their continuing influence in setting the administration's economic policy. On February 19, 1979, the AFL-CIO Executive Council denounced real-wage insurance as "a tool to enforce wage controls, not an incentive to encourage voluntary compliance."

In the months that followed, Marshall and Eizenstat tried to patch up the administration's differences with the AFL-CIO leadership. Their task was made easier by the fact that Meany, in ill health for almost a year and confined to a wheelchair since May 1979, turned most of his responsibilities over to his subordinates, especially to the more-accommodating Lane Kirkland, who would succeed him as president of the AFL-CIO. In September 1979, Carter was able finally to announce that the AFL-CIO had agreed to serve on a pay advisory board headed by John Dunlop, who had been secretary of labor under Gerald Ford and had been Meany's first choice to continue as labor secretary under Carter. According to Ray Marshall, Carter's failure to appoint Dunlop as labor secretary had been a major reason why Meany resented the president so much.

In November 1979, Meany announced his resignation as president of the AFL-CIO. Two months later, on January 10, 1980, he died in Washington of cardiac arrest.

In the decade before he died, Meany had been criticized not only by the Carter administration but by other Democrats and labor leaders, as well as by union members, of being too old, senile, out of touch with the times, in office too long, and a hindrance to organizing the young rank and file. While there was much substance to these charges, Meany had nevertheless been a person of great political power who staunchly defended the cause of the 13.5 million members of the organization he led. As Carter discovered, he was never afraid to challenge even the president of the United States. But the president and many of his advisers were also correct in sensing that the golden age of trade and industrial unionism was over. Meany's own death had great symbolism in that respect.

Miller, G. William

(George William Miller)
(1925–) *chair of the Federal Reserve Board, secretary of the Treasury*

Chosen by President Carter to serve in two key positions, first as chair of the Federal Reserve Board and then as Treasury secretary, G. William Miller was never able to win the confidence of the business and financial communities in either position. This was due in part to the fact that he was an industrialist rather than an economist, banker, or financier. But it is also due to the fact that Miller was widely perceived as being largely ineffectual in both positions.

Miller was born in Sapulpa, Oklahoma, on March 9, 1925, but grew up in Borger, Texas. After attending Amarillo College (1941–42), he won an appointment to the U.S. Coast Guard Academy, where he graduated in 1945 with a degree in marine engineering. He served as a Coast Guard officer in the Far East before attending law school at the University of California–Berkeley. After receiving his law degree (LL.B., 1951), he worked for the New York law firm of Cravath, Swaine and Moore. In 1956, he joined Textron Inc., a large conglomerate established in 1923 as a textile firm but consisting of numerous subsidiaries, including (by 1960) Bell Aerospace.

Rising rapidly in the ranks, Miller became the company's chief executive officer (CEO) in 1968, holding this position until he became chair of the Federal Reserve Board (FRB) in 1978. As Textron's CEO, Miller sold off the last of its textile businesses and continued to diversify the company, adding Shaeffer Pens, Bostich, Polaris snowmobiles, and a venture capital firm, American Research and Development. During his career with Textron, Miller also served as chair of President John F. Kennedy's Committee on Equal Employment, as an outspoken member of the National Alliance of Businessmen, a member of the National Council of the Humanities, and the Industry Advisory Commission on Equal Employment Opportunity. Just prior to joining the Carter administration, he was a director of the Federal Reserve Bank of Boston.

Because Miller was an industrialist rather than a banker or an economist, President

Carter's decision in early 1978 to appoint him to head the Federal Reserve Board (FRB) took the financial markets by surprise. The appointment was disturbing to many since Miller would be replacing ARTHUR BURNS, who had been the FRB's chair since 1970 and was widely respected in business circles for his conservative monetary and fiscal views and his insistence on the independence of the Federal Reserve System (Fed).

As the new chairperson of the Fed, Miller was faced with the major challenges of stabilizing the dollar and coping with massive inflationary forces that were exacerbated by the 1979 oil price increases unleashed as a result of the revolution in Iran. In selecting Miller to head the Fed, Carter also wanted someone who would follow a less-independent course than Burns. This was in keeping with the president's belief that, while the Fed was entitled to maintain its independence from the White House, the views of its chairperson should be compatible with his own. In fact, the president selected Miller, a conservative Democrat who had supported his election in 1976, precisely because he and his economic advisers believed Miller would be a "team player." For his part, the Textron executive indicated he would work closely with the administration. "Part of my job," he said on January 18, 1978, during confirmation hearings, "will be to carry on discussion and open communication with the administration, to use my persuasive powers and find common purposes."

Miller lived up to his promise. As the Fed's new chair, he supported the White House's efforts to fight inflation and maintain the stability of the dollar on world currency markets without leading the nation into recession. To deal with the problem of inflation, he tried to place limits on how quickly the nation's money supply was growing by raising the discount rate (the rate the Fed charged banks on overnight loans) from 6.0 to 6.5 percent. To maintain the dollar's value, the FRB and the Treasury Department made up to $35 billion available in foreign currencies to buy dollars. Miller also supported the White House's efforts to decontrol natural gas prices and later domestic oil prices as a means of curbing the nation's appetite for foreign energy resources, a major drain on the nation's foreign exchange balances.

At the same time, Miller refused to take the draconian efforts to halt the monetary growth being advocated by some Wall Street investors. These included increasing the discount rate by several percentage points or using the facilities of the Federal Reserve System's Open Market Desk to sell U.S. Treasury securities, thereby taking dollars out of circulation (measures that Miller's successor at the Fed, PAUL VOLCKER, would use) because he feared that might bring on a recession and increase unemployment. "The Federal Reserve Board," he remarked in December 1978, "is continuing to pursue a monetary policy that aims at a reduction of inflationary pressures while encouraging continued economic growth and high levels of employment." As for unemployment, he rejected the notion being offered by some economists and bankers, including Volcker, that higher unemployment (slack in the workforce) might be needed to wring inflation out of the economy. His belief that drastically restricting demand was not an effective way to reduce inflation led Miller to call for various nonmonetary policies. "[I]t may be necessary," he remarked in February 1979, "to augment monetary and fiscal policies with carefully focused programs to facilitate job placement and to provide skill training."

News that the administration, working in concert with the Fed, had intervened to protect the dollar had the desired effect: the dollar stabilized in world currency markets. Nevertheless, business and financial leaders were unconvinced that the administration's action was enough to stop the dollar's protracted decline, and Miller quickly came under attack for not doing enough to halt inflation or stabilize the dollar abroad.

The attacks on Miller continued unabated as inflation raged and pressure on the dollar again mounted on international markets. As the Organization of Petroleum Exporting Countries (OPEC) doubled the price of oil through 1978 and 1979, inflation reached an annual rate of more than 12 percent by summer 1979. The price of the dollar also began to sink once more against other currencies. Members of Congress joined in the chorus of complaints about Miller's stewardship of the Fed. Senator WILLIAM PROXMIRE (D-Wis.) stated that the FRB chair had earned "a D grade on his report card."

In August 1979, unable to resist the pressures coming from Wall Street investors, Capitol Hill, and Europe's central bankers, and needing to find a replacement for recently fired Treasury secretary W. MICHAEL BLUMENTHAL, the president decided to move Miller over to the Treasury and replace him as Fed chair with Paul Volcker. His appointment of Miller came only after three other prominent businessmen—Reginald Jones of General Electric, Irving Shapiro of Du Pont, and DAVID ROCKEFELLER—had been offered the position but declined it.

As Treasury secretary, Miller strongly opposed the policies of his successor at the Fed to target monetary reserves through open-market sales of Treasury securities as a way of raising interest rates (in effect, letting the market determine rates rather than by having the Fed raise the discount rate, as it had done in the past). Miller complained that such a policy would produce undesirable volatility in interest rates and credit costs that would disrupt the economy and might even exacerbate inflation. Although Volcker promised to consider Miller's objections and others raised by the chairman of Carter's Council of Economic Advisers, CHARLES SCHULTZE, he stayed committed to targeting monetary reserves to raise interest rates.

Miller's tenure as Treasury secretary was not limited solely to monetary differences with the Fed. Following the seizure of the American hostages in Iran in November 1979, he sat on a special coordinating committee that met virtually every morning in response to the hostage crisis. He also worked closely with President Carter's counsel, LLOYD CUTLER, in seizing Iranian assets in the United States. Long committed to a jobs program, he tried to improve relations between the White House and the AFL-CIO, despite the simmering dislike of AFL-CIO president GEORGE MEANY and President Carter for each other. Most important, Miller structured the administration's loan-guarantee program in 1980 to save Chrysler Corporation from going bankrupt, in the process generating about a $300 million profit for the U.S. Treasury. But in Miller's two years at the Treasury Department, he was overshadowed by the imposing figure of Paul Volcker, who quickly made the Fed the fulcrum for dealing with the nation's economic woes.

In January 1981, following RONALD REAGAN's election as president, Miller returned to the private sector as a business and financial consultant. In 1983, he founded G. William Miller and Co., a private merchant-banking firm. Since 2002, he has also been a partner in Blue Water Capital, L.L.C., a leading venture-capital investment firm. He remains active in the corporate world and has testified before a number of congressional committees, most recently in 2002 before the Senate Committee on the Judiciary on the use of criminal sanctions to deter corporate wrongdoing.

Mohammad Reza Pahlavi
(1919–1980) *shah of Iran*

Mohammad Reza Pahlavi was shah of Iran from the time of his father's forced abdication in 1941 until the time he was deposed as monarch in January 1979 during the Iranian revolution. The question of what support to provide the shah as the tide of revolution undermined his rule divided the Carter administration. The issue of whether to allow Pahlavi to seek sanctuary in the United States following his flight into exile proved almost as divisive. President Carter's decision in October 1979 to allow the shah into the United States to seek emergency medical treatment led to the Iranian hostage crisis that consumed the president for the remainder of his administration and contributed to his electoral defeat in November 1980.

Pahlavi's problem—and that of the Carter administration and its predecessors—is that he never fully grasped the nature of the country over which he ruled. Almost from the time he was born on October 26, 1919, in Tehran, Iran, he was trained to rule but sheltered from the society over which he was being prepared to govern. His father, Reza Shah Pahlavi, was an army officer who had seized power in 1921 from the old Qajar dynasty and proceeded to establish a new Pahlavi dynasty, declaring himself shah (monarch) of Iran in 1925. He made his son, Mohammad, crown prince at the age of six. A sickly boy who came close to death at least once, Mohammad was sent to a military elementary school and then for five years to an exclusive boarding school in Switzerland. After he returned to Tehran, he was enrolled in Tehran's Military Officers School, from which he graduated in 1938 with the rank of second lieutenant.

Even the future monarch's marriages were arranged with dynastic purposes in mind. In 1939, he married the daughter of Egypt's King Farouk, the strikingly beautiful Queen Fawzia, with whom he had a daughter before they were divorced. His second marriage to Soraya Bakhtiar also ended in divorce when she failed to produce an heir to the throne. His third wife, Empress Farah Pahlavi, to whom he remained married until his death, bore him two sons and two daughters, the eldest son inheriting the title of crown prince.

As the first of the Pahlavi dynasty, Reza Shah Pahlavi set the direction his son would later follow. He clashed with Shi'ite clerics whose vision of an Islamic theocracy conflicted with his attempt to establish a modern society modeled along Western lines. As part of his efforts at modernization, he stripped the clerics of their judicial and educational responsibilities while developing a modern school system, at the apex of which was the University of Tehran, established in 1930. He also called for the emancipation and education of women, which included a prohibition on the veiling of women in public.

In September 1941, Reza Shah, who was known to be sympathetic to Nazi Germany, was ousted from power by the British and Soviets, who occupied southern and northern Iran, respectively, in order to prevent Iran's rich oil fields from falling to the Germans during World War II. The deposed ruler went into exile in South Africa, where he died three years later. Mohammad Reza Pahlavi was then installed as the new shah of Iran at the age of 21.

From the very beginning of his rule, Mohammad Reza found himself in a tenuous position, caught between the occupying powers on the one hand and, on the other, explosive internal forces that had been bottled up by his father. A large group of nationalists protested against external intervention in Iran. Within this coalition were internal divisions between forces of change and forces of order, between Islamic fundamentalists and those supporting the modernization process begun by Reza Shah, and between fractionalized groups within this broader superstructure. Inexperienced, the shah tried as best he could to balance between these divergent forces within Iranian society. Through the difficult war and postwar years, he was largely successful, in part because of the kaleidoscope of divergent interests within Iran, which made a united opposition against his rule difficult. The onset of the cold war also worked to his advantage. Because of its own immense oil resources and the fact that it stood as a bastion against Soviet expansion toward the oil-rich Persian Gulf, Iran took on geopolitical and economic importance for the United States, which hitherto had not had a major presence in the country. Because Washington regarded the shah as the best guarantor of order and stability within Iran, the United States gave the monarch its strongest backing.

In doing so, Washington locked itself into a special relationship with the shah. In 1951, the National Front Movement, headed by Prime Minister Mohammad Mossadegh and supported by the Iranian Tudeh (Communist) Party, nationalized the British-owned Anglo-Iranian Oil Company, the country's main source of income. The British intelligence service M16 joined with the CIA in a plot, known as Operation Ajax, to oust Mossadegh. When the shah was forced to flee the country in August 1953 following a confrontation with Mossadegh, British and American operatives, led by Kermit Roosevelt, grandson of President Theodore Roosevelt, helped organize mass demonstrations against the wily Iranian prime minister, which restored the shah and forced Mossadegh from office. In this way, the United States sowed the seeds of the intense anti-American feeling that manifested itself in the Iranian hostage crisis of 1979–80.

With U.S. financial support, the shah stabilized the country during the 1950s and 1960s. He also established a secret security force, SAVAK, known for its brutal suppression of dissidents. In 1963, seeking to follow his father's example and under pressure from the Kennedy administration, which was trying to institute economic and political reform in developing countries, the shah instituted the White Revolution, an effort at modernization along Western lines. Included as part of the reform effort were the redistribution of land controlled by the Shi'ite clergy, profit sharing for industrial workers, denationalization of state-owned industries, rural literacy, forest conservation, and women's suffrage.

These Western-styled reforms pleased the United States, but they infuriated Islamic fundamentalists who lost a valuable source of income from land they had rented and who believed women's suffrage was contrary to Islamic law. Among those most angered by the shah's efforts to ape Western ways was one of the Shi'ites' most respected clerics, AYATOLLAH RUHOLLA KHOMEINI, whose own ambition was to establish an Islamic theocracy in Iran. After he incited his followers to lead demonstrations against the shah, whom he vilified as the devil, the monarch had him arrested and exiled.

Khomeini settled in the Shi'ite holy city of Najaf in Iraq, from where he continued to speak out against the shah even as the United States strengthened its ties with the Iranian monarch. As part of the Nixon doctrine intended to reduce American military commitments abroad, and as a guarantor of American interests in the Middle East, Washington made enormous quantities of military weaponry available to Iran. Flush with new oil wealth from rapidly rising oil prices, engineered in part by the shah himself, Iran made huge new purchases of airplanes and other military equipment, mostly from the United States. Between 1972 and mid-1976, the shah, who wanted to make Iran a regional military superpower, ordered $10 billion in military equipment from the United States.

Although the shah also expended billions of dollars on education, food subsidies, and the beginnings of an industrial infrastructure for Iran, he was not able to quell criticism of his regime as a result of economic corruption, a widening gap between rich and poor, repression of dissent by the notorious SAVAK, and the more general turmoil of change associated with the process of westernization. Many Iranians were also outraged that the shah had spent upward of $200 million in 1971 on a garish celebration of Iran's (formerly Persia) 2,500 years as a monarchy. After 1976, matters grew worse when oil revenues began to slacken as a result of decreasing demand abroad, and the government announced that some development plans would have to be delayed and cutbacks made.

Antigovernment feeling among Islamic militants flared into two days of rioting in the holy city of Qom, 90 miles south of Iran. In the months that followed, the shah responded by making his regime more liberal. He freed political prisoners, put restraints on SAVAK, and eased rules on censorship. In summer 1977, he also tried to deal with the nation's acute inflation rate of roughly 50 percent by applying controls on credit. But this only caused the rate of unemployment to grow, and nothing he did was able to stop the criticism of his regime. Yet President Carter, who visited Tehran on New Year's Eve 1977, toasted the shah by remarking that, as a result of his leadership, Iran was "an island of stability in one of the more troubled areas of the world."

As opposition to the shah mounted, protesters took to the streets, many waving pictures of Ayatollah Khomeini. Sermons at the mosques denounced tyranny, especially after a fire in a movie theater in Abadan in August 1978 left 377 people dead. Although no one knew the perpetrator, Iranians held the shah responsible. Riots and protests, some with over 100,000 people, took place throughout the country. The shah declared martial law and banned demonstrations. He also pressured Iraq to expel Khomeini, who took up residence outside of Paris and issued daily sermons encouraging further demonstrations and strikes to shut the economy down. Cassettes of his sermons were sold by the thousands in Iran's marketplaces. Iranians ignored the ban on demonstrations, which grew bigger and more violent, and also shut down the oil fields. From Paris, Khomeini warned that he would call for civil war if the shah did not abdicate.

The shah looked to the United States for advice. The Carter administration, however, was badly divided between Secretary of State CYRUS VANCE, who sought a diplomatic solution to the crisis in Iran involving the establishment of a moderate Islamic government, and National Security Advisor ZBIGNIEW BRZEZINSKI, who favored a more hard-line approach, including strong support for the shah and the establishment of a military government that would crack down on the militants. The U.S. ambassador to Iran, WILLIAM SULLIVAN, even urged the administration to open communication with Khomeini and various opposition groups in case the shah was ousted from power.

Lacking guidance from the White House and having lost control of the country, the shah and his family fled from Iran to Egypt on January 16, 1979. The ruler had already established a regency council led by Prime Minister Shahpour Bakhtiar, a moderate who had spent time in the shah's prisons. As news spread of the shah's exit, Iranians took to the streets in celebration. Within hours, virtually every public square and boulevard once named for the shah had been renamed for Khomeini, who returned to Iran on February 9 to make real his ambition of establishing an Iranian theocracy.

At the time the shah was forced into exile, President Carter invited him to come to the United States, but he decided instead to take up residence in Morocco, hoping that he would still be able to return to Iran. His decision suited the president "fine." As Carter recorded in his diary, he though the shah's presence in a Muslim country was better for the Bakhtiar government in Iran since King Hassan of Morocco might be in a position "to keep Khomeini under control." Carter also believed "the taint of the Shah" being in the United States would not be "good for either us or him." The next month the president decided to rescind the invitation entirely. Following a short-lived seizure of the American embassy in Tehran in February 1979, Vance convinced Carter that if the shah was allowed into the country, American lives in Iran would be endangered. Instead, the administration arranged for the Bahamas and then for Mexico to grant him asylum.

The shah felt betrayed by the Carter administration, believing they had abandoned a loyal ally in time of need. The president did not even "lift up the phone" to talk to him, the shah complained bitterly in his memoirs, published after his death. Influential Americans agreed with the shah, including former president RICHARD NIXON, former secretary of state HENRY KISSINGER, Chase Manhattan Bank chief executive officer (CEO) DAVID ROCKEFELLER, and John McCloy, another former CEO of Chase and a longtime adviser to presidents. In fact, over the years, the deposed monarch had developed an influential coterie of allies in the United States that included highly placed Americans in politics, business, finance, academia, the media, and entertainment, most of whom supported allowing him into the United States. Although he later denied it, Kissinger was the most active of these highly placed persons in lobbying the White House on behalf of the shah. But David Rockefeller, who had met many times with Pahlavi in Iran and whose Chase Manhattan Bank was the lead American financial institution in handling Iran's and the shah's assets, was also active in promoting his cause in the United States. So was McCloy, whose law firm had as clients many of the major oil companies doing business in Iran.

Although most State Department officials—including Deputy Secretary of State WARREN CHRISTOPHER; HENRY PRECHT, the Iranian desk officer at the department; and BRUCE LAINGEN, the chargé d'affaires in Tehran—believed Americans still in Iran would be in danger if the shah were allowed into the United States, the lobbying effort on Pahlavi's behalf had some effect on the administration. In January 1979, only National Security Advisor Brzezinski had favored permitting the shah to live in the United States. Over the summer and fall, he was joined by Vice President WALTER MONDALE and Chief of Staff HAMILTON JORDAN, who emphasized the political backlash that would happen if the president refused to allow the shah into the United States and he died in Mexico.

In October 1979, the president was informed by Kissinger and Rockefeller that the shah was gravely ill with lymphatic cancer and would die unless he could come to New York for emergency medical treatment. Only then did Carter change his mind and agree to allow the shah into the country on humanitarian grounds. Although the president informed Iran of his decision and was given reason to believe that the Iranian government would protect the skeleton crew remaining at the American embassy in Tehran, Iranian militants responded to news that the shah had been allowed into the United States by seizing the embassy and taking more than 60 Americans hostage, thereby beginning the crisis that would last until the end of the Carter presidency on January 20, 1981, and contributed to the president's defeat for reelection.

Following the shah's release from the New York hospital where he had been treated for his cancer, he began a search for a new home. No longer welcome to return to Mexico, he was granted refuge in Panama, where he was forced to pay large sums of money and feared extradition to Iran. Finally, in 1980, he went to Egypt, where he was warmly received by President ANWAR SADAT and lived out the rest of his life. In his last interview, with an Egyptian magazine a month before he died, he remarked that he had made his biggest mistake by listening to the United States; he should not have given Iran so much democracy and progress. He also predicted that Iran would go communist without another revolution.

Mohammad Reza Pahlavi died on July 17, 1980, at the age of 60. Learning of his death, the White House merely expressed its condolences to the shah's family, remarking that "history will record that [the shah] led his country at a time when profound changes were taking place." The message did not mention the shah's close alliance with the United States. Most Americans responded with indifference to news of Pahlavi's death, although a few commentators hoped his passing might lead to the early release of the American hostages. In Tehran, news that the hated former monarch had died was greeted with jubilation and celebration. "The bloodsucker of the century is dead," Iranian radio reported.

In Egypt, Sadat ordered a state funeral for the shah. Although no official delegation from the United States attended the funeral, a number of his American acquaintances and friends did go to Egypt for the ceremonial burial of the former Iranian leader. Among those in attendance was former president Richard Nixon, who denounced the Carter administration's treatment of the shah as "one of the black pages" of American foreign policy.

Mondale, Walter Frederick
(Fritz Mondale)
(1928–) *vice president*

As vice president during President Carter's administration, Walter "Fritz" Mondale transformed the purpose and functions of his office. Before agreeing to run on Carter's ticket, the Minnesota senator insisted that he be actively involved in the administration's decision-making process, that he have an office in the White House's West Wing rather than in the Executive Office Building (as had been customary), and that he have access to the president. He remembered how poorly his friend and mentor, HUBERT HUMPHREY, had been treated as President Lyndon Johnson's vice president, and he wanted no part of the office under those conditions. He also wanted assurances that he would be more than a figurehead in the Carter presidency who took on mostly ceremonial responsibilities.

Carter gave Mondale the assurances he sought, and both men profited as a result. Mondale got the influence he wanted; the president received the insider's knowledge he lacked. No vice president prior to Mondale had played such an important role: vetting potential cabinet members during the transition period from election day to inauguration day; holding weekly luncheon meetings with the president; receiving the same daily intelligence briefings the president received; serving as one of his most influential advisers; acting as the White House's envoy to key Democratic constituencies, in particular African Americans, Jewish groups, and organized labor; and taking on other important assignments for the president. Although not all of his successors would have the same influence within the White House, the trend has been one of building on the precedent established by Carter's vice president.

Born in Ceylon, Minnesota, on January 5, 1928, Mondale was the son of a Methodist clergyman who preached the gospel of helping the poor and needy. A hard worker in school, sports, and debate, his interest in politics began in his freshman year at Macalester College in St. Paul in 1946, when he volunteered as a campaign worker in the successful Minneapolis mayoral campaign of Hubert Humphrey. In 1948, Mondale helped run Humphrey's successful bid for the U.S. Senate. He also became active in the political infighting of the Democratic-Farm-Labor Party (DFL). On campus, he organized Students for Democratic Action (SDA), an offshoot of Americans for Democratic Action (ADA), an influential liberal organization that Hubert Humphrey had helped form.

As Mondale became interested in politics, his interest in school waned. In December 1949, his father died, making it difficult for him and his family to meet tuition costs. When he was offered a position as executive secretary of SDA, therefore, he grabbed it, leaving Macalester one year before graduation and moving to Washington, D.C. His experience at SDA was invaluable for Mondale in terms of establishing ties with present and future lawmakers. It also validated his credentials as a pragmatic liberal. After being in Washington for only one year, however, he decided to return to Minneapolis, where he finished his last year of college at the University of Minnesota, majoring in political science and graduating cum laude (B.A., 1952). He then served two years in the army before entering the University of Minnesota's Law School, where he received his law degree (LL.B., 1956).

Opening a private practice, Mondale maintained his interest in politics. In 1958 and again in 1960, he managed the successful gubernatorial campaigns of Orville Freeman, whom he had known since 1948 when the two had worked together on Humphrey's campaign for the U.S. Senate. In 1960, Freeman appointed Mondale state attorney gen-

Joan Mondale, Vice President Walter Mondale, first lady Rosalynn Carter, and President Jimmy Carter, 1977 *(Jimmy Carter Library)*

Vice President Mondale and President Carter, 1978 *(Jimmy Carter Library)*

eral when the incumbent, Miles Lord, resigned unexpectedly. He was subsequently elected and reelected to two full terms in 1960 and 1962. A similar turn of events awaited Mondale in 1964 when he was appointed by Governor Karl Rolvaag to fill the vacancy in the U.S. Senate caused by Hubert Humphrey's election as vice president. In 1966 and 1972, Mondale was elected and then reelected to full six-year terms in the Senate.

Following in the tradition of Minnesota's DFL, Mondale established a liberal voting record in the Senate, supporting such measures as the 1965 Voting Rights Act, open housing, migrant worker protection, consumer protection, and tax reform. He was perhaps best known as a critic of the National Aeronautics and Space Administration (NASA), which he accused of dangerous practices and wasteful spending of funds that could be better used for social services. Loyal to Humphrey, he did not come out against the Vietnam War until after the vice president had secured the Democratic nomination in August 1968. He later stated that supporting the war so long was his biggest mistake in the Senate.

In 1972, Mondale had become an important enough political figure that he was one of several persons Senator GEORGE MCGOVERN (S.Dak.) asked to be his running mate on the Democratic ticket. But, always a pragmatic politician who understood the likelihood that McGovern would lose to President RICHARD NIXON, Mondale declined the offer, choosing instead to seek reelection to the Senate. In 1974, he explored the possibility of running for president himself in 1976, but he quickly withdrew from the race, maintaining that he did not want to engage in the endless circuit of speeches, fund-raising, and travel involved in a run for the White House.

Mondale's abrupt withdrawal from the 1976 race almost kept Jimmy Carter from choosing him as his running mate. Carter was concerned that the senator might not have the commitment needed to conduct a vigorous campaign, but Mondale gave him the reassurances he needed. The Democratic candidate decided on Mondale mainly because he was a liberal and an insider who, Carter hoped, could balance the ticket and heal any wounds within Democratic ranks left over from the primary campaign. Beyond this consideration, he thought that, as the son of a minister, Mondale would understand his own deep religious feelings. Carter also felt comfortable with the senator, and Mondale's insistence that he be accorded a meaningful and influential role in a Carter administration actually worked to his benefit since the Georgian wanted an activist vice president, someone he could take into his confidence.

That is the role that Mondale played throughout the Carter presidency. More liberal than the president, he had his differences with Carter, particularly when it came to balancing spending for social programs against those for defense. Even before he agreed to run on the Carter ticket, he had been concerned about the former governor's fiscal conservatism. But on what he regarded as the critical question of civil rights, he had been greatly impressed by Carter's record as governor; in Mondale's view, Carter's civil rights record overshadowed any other reservations about the Democratic nominee.

As vice president, however, Mondale grew increasingly frustrated with the president and his more conservative advisers and appointees, none more so than Attorney General GRIFFIN BELL. In a landmark 1978 affirmative-action case before the Supreme Court, the vice president clashed with the attorney general over a Justice Department brief that seemed to side with ALLAN BAKKE, a white man who had challenged as unconstitutional a set-aside program for minority students seeking admission to the University of California–Davis Medical School. Even though Mondale and other more-moderate members of the administration were able to get Carter to have the brief rewritten in such a way as to defend affirmative-action programs in unequivocal terms, the vice president and attorney general remained fierce ideological opponents.

The White House's handling of the Bakke case underscored the deep ideological, philosophical, and bureaucratic divisions that existed within the administration and seemed to get worse rather than better over time. Later Bell blamed the president in his memoirs for caving in to the "liberals" led by Mondale, while the vice president took umbrage with the White House for being unable, in the words of his biographer, Steven M. Gillon, "to understand the relationship between politics and policy."

The fact was that Mondale was an intensely partisan politician who enjoyed being around other politicians and took pleasure in the art of negotiation and compromise. Carter disliked political sparring and believed he had a special obligation to the people who had elected him that transcended political partisanship. Mondale was anchored to traditional New Deal liberalism and appealed to union and other blue-collar workers and to individuals and groups who viewed government as a provider to the needy and disfranchised. Carter had no unifying political philosophy but appealed to a more-affluent and conservative type of voter who regarded big government as intrusive and was more concerned with social values than with social services. Mondale wanted the president to concentrate on a small list of priorities, specifically energy, the economy, and the Strategic Arms Limitation Talks (SALT), and to articulate a coherent vision for his presidency. Instead, Carter rolled out a list of domestic and foreign policy initiatives that overwhelmed Congress and suggested a lack of purpose or direction in the White House.

Mondale, however, always kept private his differences with the president. His reputation in the Senate was also beneficial to Carter, who often infuriated the upper chamber with his political shortcomings. Purposely avoiding any specific assignments, most of which he thought had been dead-end jobs for previous vice presidents, and rejecting even Carter's suggestion that he be chief of staff, Mondale preferred to remain a generalist who could provide advice to the president, serve as an emissary for the administration, and troubleshoot problems as needed.

In these ways, Mondale played a key role in winning passage of the administration's energy bill in 1978. He incurred the wrath of Democratic liberals in the Senate when he worked closely with Majority Leader ROBERT BYRD (D-W.Va.) to end their filibuster against the administration's proposal to deregulate natural gas. He fought hard for labor-law reform, an increase in the minimum wage, and tighter control of U.S. intelligence operations. He also persuaded the president—against the advice of his top aides, who thought Congress would override him—to veto the construction of a $2 billion aircraft carrier; the veto was later sustained. Most of all,

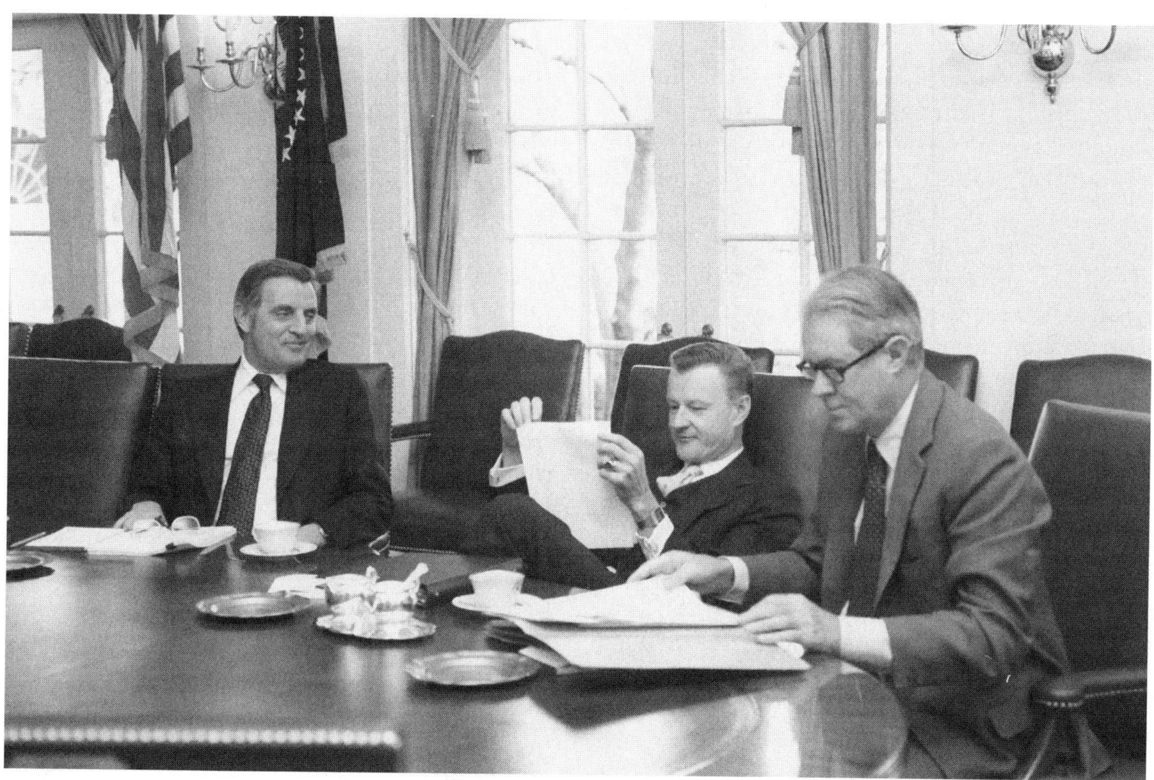

Vice President Walter Mondale, National Security Advisor Zbigniew Brzezinski, and Secretary of State Cyrus Vance, 1978 *(Jimmy Carter Library)*

Mondale sought to bridge the gap between his own liberal expectations and those of his fellow Democrats in Congress and the need for fiscal restraint in a period of slow or no economic growth and rising inflation.

In terms of foreign policy, Mondale undertook 13 foreign assignments, some highly sensitive, to Europe, the Middle East, the Far East, and Africa. One of his first assignments was a nine-day trip to Europe and Japan to reassure the United States' allies that the administration intended to pursue an activist foreign policy and to consult with the allies on substantive issues. On March 7, 1977, Carter announced that the vice president would be in charge of the administration's African policy. In May, he traveled to South Africa, where he told Prime Minister John Vorster, in no uncertain terms, that South Africa's apartheid policies were unacceptable to the United States and that future relations between their two countries would depend on the steps taken by his government to end that policy.

In 1978, Mondale played a key role in winning Senate approval of the Panama Canal Treaties. His trip to the Middle East later that year helped improve the strained relations that had developed between the president and Israeli prime minister MENACHEM BEGIN and to restart the stalled negotiations for a Middle East peace. As part of his effort to win Jewish support at home for the administration's Mideast initiatives, he also got the president to tone down some of his harsh rhetoric toward Begin and to modify his position in support of a Palestinian homeland. In 1979, the vice president made a highly successful trip to China, building on the normalization of relations begun by National Security Advisor ZBIGNIEW BRZEZINSKI during his trip there a year earlier.

In every respect, then, Mondale was the activist vice president that he and President Carter agreed he would be when the Democratic nominee for president asked the Minnesota senator to be his running mate in 1976. Exhausted, however, from three years of trying to keep the peace among Democrats, Mondale almost resigned in 1979 when Carter cancelled a planned speech on energy in July, retreated for 11 days of discussions with prominent Americans at Camp David, and then delivered a national address in which he blamed much of the nation's economic problems on a loss of public confidence in the government. The vice president was convinced that the address was inherently wrong and politically disastrous. As a liberal in the mode of Hubert Humphrey, he was inclined to be optimistic about the nation's future. As a pragmatic politician, he believed that the politics of hope always prevailed over the politics of doom.

Although Mondale stayed on as vice president during Carter's last year in office, he played a less-visible and active role in the administration than he had in the previous three years. In terms of ideology, his views were much closer to Senator EDWARD KENNEDY (Mass.), who decided to challenge Carter for the 1980 Democratic nomination, than they were to the president. Although there was never any concern that Mondale might desert Carter for Kennedy or not accept renomination on a Carter-Mondale ticket—he was too loyal and ambitious for that—the fission in the Democratic Party between those backing Kennedy and those supporting Carter caused the vice president considerable anguish. Not particularly close to Kennedy, whom he viewed as a political rival in the Democratic Party, Mondale's commitment was to the president, even if at heart he remained a liberal.

Following RONALD REAGAN's landslide victory over Carter in November 1980, Mondale accepted a position in the Washington offices of Winston and Strawn, a prestigious

Chicago law firm. By the end of 1981, however, he was back in politics, running for president. After Senator Kennedy took himself out of the presidential race, Mondale became the leading candidate for the Democratic nomination in 1984. A spirited campaign by Senator Gary Hart of Colorado surprised political pundits, but after Hart withdrew from the race following revelations of an extramarital affair on his part, the former vice president won the nomination. It was, however, a pyrrhic victory. Although Mondale took the bold step of nominating Representative Geraldine Ferraro (N.Y.) as his running mate, the first female vice-presidential candidate on a major party ticket, he ran against a popular president during a period of economic recovery from a recession. Mondale's own campaign was hampered by his public commitment to a tax increase if elected and by questionable financial practices on the part of Ferraro's husband. In November 1984, Reagan was reelected in a landslide, losing only in Minnesota and the District of Columbia and winning the electoral college by a margin of 525 to 13 for Mondale.

Since 1984, Mondale has been practicing law and lecturing. In 1987, he returned to Minnesota, where he became a partner in the law firm of Dorsey and Whitney and served as Distinguished University Fellow in Law and Public Affairs at the Hubert H. Humphrey Institute of Public Affairs. From 1986 to 1993, he was also chair of the National Democratic Institute for International Affairs. In 1993, President Bill Clinton appointed him U.S. ambassador to Japan; he served in this role until 1996, when he returned to Dorsey and Whitney. In 2002, he was drafted to run for the U.S. Senate following the death of the incumbent, Paul Wellstone, but he lost in a close election to the Republican candidate, Norm Coleman. Mondale lives in Minneapolis with his wife Joan, to whom he has been married since 1955.

Moore, Frank

(1935–) *assistant for congressional liaison*

As President Carter's principal lobbyist on Capitol Hill, Frank Moore had to bear the brunt of growing congressional displeasure with the White House. Although some of the criticism made against him by lawmakers was probably unavoidable given the contentious relationship that came to exist between the administration and Congress, Moore shared some of the responsibility because of his apparent inattentiveness or insensitivity to just those matters of personal privilege and political patronage that members of the House and Senate found so important.

Moore was born on July 27, 1935, in Gainesville, Georgia. After earning a B.A. degree from the University of Georgia in 1959, he worked as a test marketer for the Quaker Oats Company. Impressed by President Lyndon Johnson's War on Poverty, he decided to leave the private sector and took a position running a Head Start program for 14 counties in northeast Georgia. During this time, he met Jimmy Carter, who was running for governor. Although Moore did not participate in the campaign, the unsuccessful candidate offered him a position in 1967 as a director of a regional planning commission whose executive committee Carter chaired. In 1970, Moore took vacation time to work on Carter's second gubernatorial bid. Following Carter's election, he accepted a position working for the new governor's chief of staff, HAMILTON JORDAN, first as part of a team on the reorganization of state government and then as Jordan's deputy. When Jordan went to work in 1973 for the Democratic National Committee, Carter, who had been impressed by Moore's ability to arbitrate successfully between competing interests, named him to replace Jordan.

In 1975, Moore moved over to the Carter presidential campaign, managing it in what was essentially the former Confederacy and serving as its national finance chairman. Carter also asked Moore to spend part of his time in Washington getting to know members of Congress and the national press. Following Carter's victory in 1976, the president-elect appointed him as his assistant for congressional liaison.

Moore became a lightning rod for congressional displeasure with the president. To a considerable extent this was inevitable, given the fact that he was caught in the middle between an often inflexible White House and a contentious Congress. In addition, Hamilton Jordan and Press Secretary JODY POWELL, the two White House staff members closest to the president, had made a decision even before Carter took office that they would stay off Capitol Hill and direct congressional requests and problems to Moore's office, believing he would know how best to respond to them. But lawmakers, perhaps a majority, felt that Moore was not simply the unfortunate messenger of an impolitic administration indifferent to lawmakers on Capitol Hill. Rather, they were convinced that he and his staff were the cause of much of the difficulty that existed between Congress and the White House.

The claim had merit. In an interview that Hamilton Jordan gave in 1981, a year after Carter had been defeated for reelection by RONALD REAGAN, Jordan maintained that Moore had the best staff of any White House official. "Frank Moore's staff per person was the strongest staff in the White House," Jordan remarked. "It was stronger than [STUART] EIZENSTAT's staff or [ZBIGNIEW] BRZEZINSKI's staff or my staff. Per person it was the strongest group of individuals with the greatest accumulation of knowledge and political skills in the White House." Yet as Carter's representative to Congress and the national press before the former Georgia governor had secured the Democratic nomination, Moore had already developed a reputation for not returning telephone calls or engaging in the social repartee with lawmakers or journalists that was so important to networking in the nation's capital. Even Carter acknowledged this failure on Moore's part, although he attributed it mainly to lack of a staff and budget.

These remained problems throughout Carter's four years in office, but there were other issues as well. Personally, Moore tended to be self-effacing and unassuming, making him an easy target for White House critics. He also made questionable choices in the selection of his staff, including his deputy, Rick Moore, a former aide to House Speaker TIP O'NEILL's rival among House Democrats, PHILLIP BURTON (Calif.), and a person whom the powerful Speaker disliked. Although part of the coterie of Georgians the president had brought with him to Washington, Moore also was never as close to Carter, nor as strong a voice within the administration, as some of the president's other senior staff. As a consequence, he was not able to influence policy in the same manner as Jordan, Powell, Eizenstat, or GERALD RAFSHOON. Finally, Moore shared the president's disdain for gamesmanship, a real deficiency in the hardball politics of Capitol Hill.

The problems Moore faced and his own deficiencies as congressional liaison were underscored in August 1978 when the president approved the firing of Robert Griffin as deputy administrator of the General Services Administration (GSA). A friend of Speaker O'Neill and a fellow graduate of Boston College, Griffin had been passed over by the president to head the GSA despite O'Neill's lobbying on his behalf. Instead, Carter chose to retain Jack Eckerd, a Republican holdover from the Ford administration. After a few months, Eckerd resigned. To replace him, the president named Jay Solomon, a Tennessee real-estate developer and one of Carter's early backers, once again turning Griffin down for the position. Amid accusations of scandal at the GSA, Solomon sought Carter's approval to dismiss Griffin, arguing the need for someone he could trust as his deputy.

Already nursing a host of grievances against the administration going as far back as a dispute over tickets to Carter's inauguration, O'Neill was dismayed, as were other Democrats, at the president's decision to retain a Republican in such a senior position as head of the GSA. He was even more annoyed when the president named Solomon instead of Griffin to head the agency. But he became incensed when the White House then gave its approval to Solomon's request to fire Griffin, with all the implications that had in terms of Griffin's involvement in the alleged fraud.

As these events unfolded, Moore tried his best to avoid a confrontation with O'Neill and the Democratic leadership on Capitol Hill. When he learned that Solomon was planning to fire Griffin, he warned the president that his approval of Griffin's dismissal was fraught with danger and urged him to postpone a decision. At the same time, he informed O'Neill, who had inquired about Griffin's status, that no action was imminent. Believing, however, that it was time for the president to appear tough with Congress, Carter's media adviser, Gerald Rafshoon, urged him to approve Solomon's request to fire Griffin. The next day, the *Washington Post* announced that Griffin would be dismissed.

O'Neill was livid. Having always placed a premium on the importance of trust in personal relationships, he felt deceived by Moore and betrayed by the White House. Furthermore, his friend's character had been besmirched.

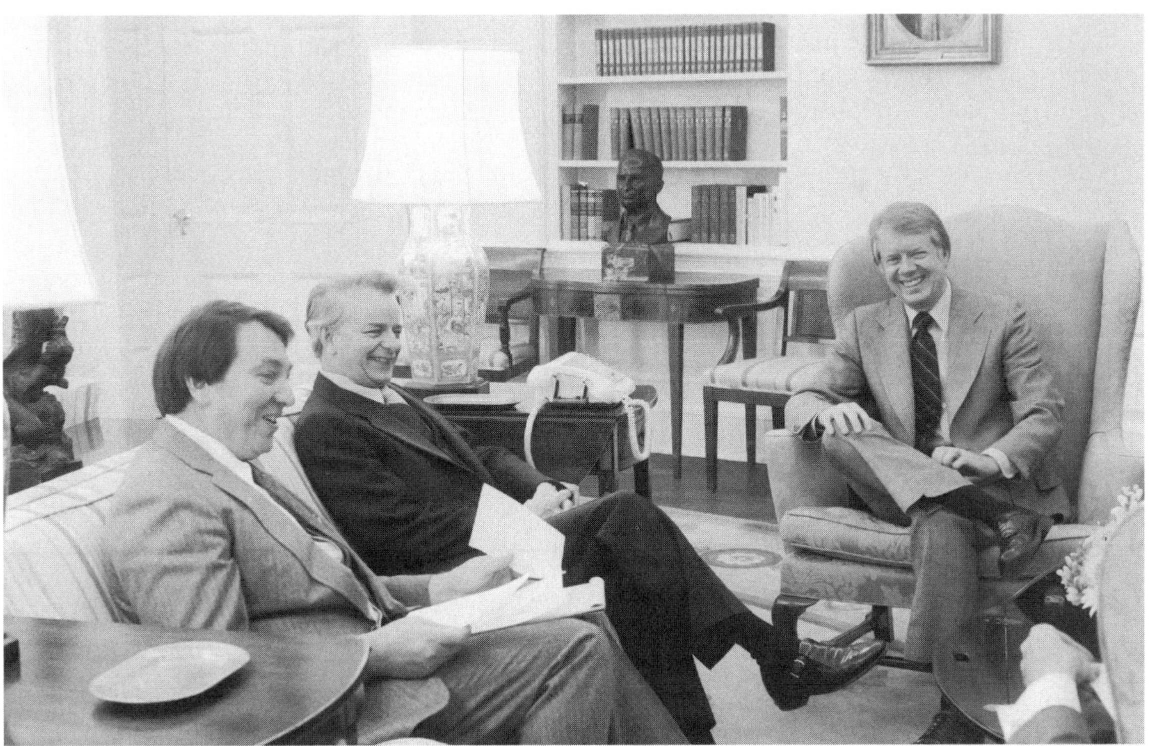

Assistant for Congressional Liaison Frank Moore, Senator Robert Byrd, and President Carter meet in the Oval Office, 1978. *(Jimmy Carter Library)*

In an angry letter to Moore, he called the president's decision "cruel ... one of the worst things I have ever seen." In an effort at damage control, the president invited the Speaker to the White House for breakfast, but O'Neill remained unappeased. In a rare and hastily called meeting of his staff, he gave notice that Moore was to be permanently banished from the Speaker's offices. After Moore wrote a letter of apology to the Speaker and a position was found for Griffin with the U.S. trade representative, O'Neill relented and allowed Moore back into his good graces. But by then the damage had been done. The administration was criticized in the media either for caving in to the Speaker by finding a high-paying position for Griffin or for allowing the incident to happen in the first place. Either way, the White House appeared vacillating, and Moore seemed inept.

Despite his limitations as congressional liaison, Moore could take consolation in what he did accomplish. For one thing, he played an important role in some of the administration's most important legislative achievements, including deregulation of the airlines and trucking industry, approval of the Panama Canal Treaties in 1978, and passage of the Alaska Lands Bill in 1980. For another, his office developed a sophisticated computer program that allowed it to identify voting patterns of each lawmaker on Capitol Hill by almost any marker, from ideological stances to number of terms in state and federal elected office and margins of victory. The program also incorporated the needs and priorities of each congressional district, thereby allowing the administration to concentrate its lobbying efforts on the most likely swing votes on hotly contested legislation.

Following Carter's defeat in 1980, Moore attended the Harvard Business School's Advanced Management Program and then took a position as vice president of government and regulatory affairs with Waste Management Incorporated, where he worked for 15 years. Now retired, he lives with his wife, Nancy, on a farm in Maryland that he and Jody Powell purchased together. They both have homes on the farm separated by about 200 yards.

Moynihan, Daniel Patrick
(1927–2003) *member of the Senate*

Sociologist, educator, government official, and four-term senator from New York, Daniel Patrick Moynihan made his largest impact on national affairs both before and after the Carter administration rather than during it. But as a first-term senator from New York who already enjoyed an illustrious career as a best-selling author, Harvard University professor, assistant secretary of labor under Presidents John F. Kennedy and Lyndon Johnson, special adviser to President RICHARD NIXON, ambassador to India, and ambassador to the United Nations, Moynihan's sharp criticisms of the Carter presidency resonated widely. His flamboyant style and Irish wit added to the poignancy of his comments and were a boon to what was already being considered the neoconservative movement. His later criticisms of the RONALD REAGAN administration made clear, however, that he did not identify himself with any part of the nation's political spectrum.

Although Moynihan was born in Tulsa, Oklahoma, on March 16, 1927, he grew up in poverty in New York City after his father, a former journalist, abandoned his family in 1937. After graduating first in his class from the Benjamin Franklin High School in Harlem and attending the City College of New York, Moynihan enlisted in the navy. He received officer training at Middlebury College and at Tufts University, where, after being discharged from the navy at the end of World War II, he earned his undergraduate degree (B.A., 1948).

He also attended the Tufts Fletcher School of Law and Diplomacy, where he received his doctorate (M.A., 1949; Ph.D.,1961) and did graduate work as a Fulbright fellow at the London School of Economics (1950–51).

Moynihan began his political career working in the mayoral and gubernatorial campaigns of Robert Wagner and Averell Harriman and then as Governor Harriman's chief aide. From 1959 to 1961, he was director of Syracuse University's New York State Government Research Project. While at Syracuse, Moynihan began writing regularly for the *Reporter*, the cold-war liberal magazine whose editor, Irving Kristol, would later be one of the founders of the neoconservative movement.

Never one of President John F. Kennedy's inner circle but stereotypical of the "best and the brightest" minds that came to be associated with Kennedy's New Frontier, Moynihan wrote position papers on urban affairs for the Kennedy presidential campaign in 1960 and was later offered a position as assistant to Secretary of Labor Arthur Goldberg. In 1963, he became assistant secretary of labor for policy planning and research, a position he continued to hold following Kennedy's assassination in November that year. While at the Labor Department, he helped create the Manpower Development and Training Act and served on a working group that conceived the War on Poverty.

The nadir of Moynihan's political career came in 1965 when he was roundly criticized for a Labor Department report he had coauthored with Paul Barton and Ellen Broderick, "The Negro Family: The Case for National Action." The report came to be commonly referred to as the Moynihan Report and was the basis for a speech President Lyndon Johnson gave in June at Howard University. In the report, Moynihan attributed the economic and social plight of the black community to absentee fathers, illegitimate births, and a national welfare system predicated on the breakdown of the two-parent family. He called for an overhaul of the system that would allow more black fathers to remain with their families. Now regarded as prescient by many sociologists, the report was strongly attacked by black leaders and white liberals who believed it was patronizing and even racist because it seemed to attribute the problems of the black community to its own unique social pathology.

In June 1965, Moynihan left the Labor Department to run unsuccessfully for president of the New York City Council. The following year he was named director of the Harvard–M.I.T. Joint Center for Urban Studies. Although active in politics, Moynihan had remained close to the academic community. In 1963, he coauthored, with Nathan Glazer, *Beyond the Melting Pot*, a widely read and highly respected study that challenged earlier arguments on the assimilation of immigrant groups in the United States by arguing against the notion "that the intense and unprecedented mixture of ethnic and religious groups in American life was soon to blend into a homogenous end product." Although Moynihan actually wrote only one chapter of the book, the idea that the United States was not a big ethnic melting pot brought him considerable national attention and gained him academic recognition as a leading urban sociologist.

Moynihan retained his interest in government and Democratic politics, however, opposing the war in Vietnam but eventually supporting Vice President HUBERT HUMPHREY for president in 1968 after New York senator Robert F. Kennedy was assassinated and Minnesota senator Eugene McCarthy failed to wrest the nomination from Humphrey. Because Moynihan was a lifelong Democrat, his colleagues were taken aback when he agreed in 1969 to serve as head of President Richard Nixon's newly created Urban Affairs Council. The new president offered Moynihan the position because, as he later wrote in his memoirs, he found the New Yorker's thinking "refreshing and stimulating" and liked his wry sense of humor. Nixon also identified with Moynihan's humble origins and regarded the New Yorker as an "outsider" like himself.

Over the next two years, Nixon came to regard Moynihan as one of his top aides. He looked to him for advice and defended him when a memorandum Moynihan had written to the president stating "that the time may have come when the issue of race could benefit from a period of benign neglect" was leaked to the press. Moynihan contended that what he meant in the memorandum was that administration officials, in particular Vice President Spiro Agnew, should cease giving opponents of the administration, including militant black leaders, opportunities to attack the White House by cutting back on their own histrionic language. He also thought the administration should focus on job programs rather than race. Civil rights leaders, however, interpreted the memorandum as suggesting that the administration should ignore civil rights issues, a charge Moynihan denied.

The same year that Moynihan was attacked for his remark about "benign neglect," he also lost a fight he had been waging to reform the nation's welfare system by replacing entitlement programs with a guaranteed income for families on welfare, which he believed would be less expensive and more dignified. He won Nixon's support for the program, which the president labeled the Family Assistance Program (FAP) as a way of eliminating the bureaucratic waste inherent in the welfare system and stealing the thunder of liberal Democrats on the issue of welfare reform. But while the House passed the FAP, the measure failed to make its way out of the Senate Finance Committee.

At the end of 1970, Moynihan left the administration to return to Harvard, but after winning reelection in 1972, President Nixon appointed him ambassador to India. As ambassador, Moynihan negotiated an agreement to end India's huge food-aid debt to the United States. He also gained a sophisticated appreciation of foreign cultures and national aspirations that persuaded him that all empires were "bound to crash," including, by extension, the Soviet Union. In addition, he became an outspoken critic of corrupt Third World regimes and their American apologists.

In 1974, President GERALD FORD named Moynihan the nation's permanent representative to the United Nations. One of the more demonstrative ambassadors ever to represent the United States at the UN, Moynihan could charm the delegates with his sardonic humor and puckish charm. At the same time, he condemned Soviet imperialism and obstructionism, lashed out at the General Assembly after it approved a resolution equating Zionism with racism, called Uganda's Idi Amin a "racist murderer," and attacked what he considered the venality and corruption of many Third World countries, writing in *Commentary* that a number of these countries were using their alleged "victimhood" to blackmail the West.

In February 1976, Moynihan resigned his post at the United Nations and returned briefly to Harvard before running successfully for the U.S. Senate against the one-term incumbent, James Buckley, brother of the conservative columnist and intellectual, William H. Buckley, Jr. Although a Democrat and first-term member of the U.S. Senate, Moynihan did not allow either his party affiliation or his lack of seniority to keep him from being a sharp critic of the Carter administration.

Moynihan owed no allegiance to Jimmy Carter. He had supported Senator HENRY JACKSON (Wash.) for the Democratic nomination and figured prominently in Jackson's victory in the bitterly contested New York presidential primary in which Carter had finished a distant fourth. In the Senate, Moynihan aligned himself closely with Jackson and other Democrats who believed that even Republicans had gone soft on communism. Together with Jackson, he cochaired in 1976 the Coalition for a Democratic Majority (CDM), a group of Democrats favoring a strong military to counter the Soviet threat. He was deeply annoyed when the president rejected all but two of 53 names the CDM submitted to him for positions in national security affairs. He regarded Carter as a naïve player in world politics.

Convinced that the president and his administration did not understand how evil the Soviet Union was or the extent of the communist danger in developing countries, Moynihan attacked the Strategic Arms Limitation Talks agreement (SALT II) that the White House had negotiated in 1979 with Moscow as a form of appeasement. More generally, he accused Carter of "trying to divert [the nation's] attention from the central political struggle of our time—that between democracy and totalitarian communism." He also termed the administration's foreign policy "autotherapeutic fantasy." He attacked the White House's foreign policy throughout Carter's four years in office, remarking in 1980 that the president "was unable to distinguish between our enemies and our friends [and] has adopted our enemies' view of the world."

A staunch defender of Israel as well as a harsh critic of the Soviet Union, Moynihan supported the Jackson-Vanik Amendment of 1974, which tied trade liberalization with the Soviets to freer passage of Jews from the Soviet Union. The senator was also furious when Carter's ambassador at the United Nations, Donald McHenry, voted in support of a strongly worded anti-Israeli resolution in the Security Council.

On domestic issues, Moynihan spoke out on the nation's ongoing need to strengthen Social Security, provide tax-tuition credits of as much as $1,000 for elementary and secondary schools, and, especially, reform its costly welfare system. "For much of the third quarter of the twentieth century, Americans, in choices actually made, had more or less opted for more government and less growth," he remarked with respect to welfare reform. "Extrapolated ... these curves could only lead to a condition of no growth and total government." At the same time, he bitterly opposed the president's effort to reform the welfare system without providing additional funding to help relieve some of the welfare burden from state and local governments. "What animates the administration?" he asked in a speech in 1977. "An indomitable innocence or profound cynicism? Are they sending us a program that provides no relief to state and local governments—relief that has been solemnly pledged by the President—such that state and local governments will urge us not to enact it?" When Carter proposed in 1979 to cut welfare costs as part of his anti-inflation program, Moynihan responded by introducing legislation to have the federal government pay a greater share of the Medicaid bill for the indigent and those on welfare.

By spring 1979, as the rate of inflation and unemployment grew in the country and the president's popularity ratings reached new lows, Moynihan was ready to see Carter replaced as the 1980 Democratic nominee. On May 22, 1979, he warned Carter that unless the president acted quickly to take charge of the country, he would be "governing by the sufferance of" EDWARD KENNEDY. When Kennedy made clear that he would challenge Carter for the Democratic nomination, Moynihan threw his support behind the Massachusetts senator. After Carter defeated Kennedy for the nomination, Moynihan gave only tacit support to the president's reelection bid. Moynihan's aid, Elliott Abrams, even suggested that the New York senator would make a good running mate for the likely Republican nominee, Ronald Reagan.

When Carter lost his bid for reelection, Moynihan commented that the president had lost because voters saw a Democratic Party that believed "government should be strong and America should be weak," noting that even Herbert Hoover got more electoral votes in 1932 than Carter got in 1980. He also said that the loss was finalized when the nation's own ambassador at the United Nations voted for a motion that was anti-Israel. If Carter had stood up to the Arab nations, Moynihan added, Carter could have fared better as a president and a politician.

Moynihan's political views in the Senate were welcomed by many Republicans. In the media, he was often referred to as part of the growing neoconservative movement in the United States composed of former cold-war liberal Democrats who were leaving the party because they believed it had lost its moorings on foreign policy and that its reckless spending on entitlement programs was bankrupting the country. They also thought the mindless bureaucracy of the federal government was sapping the sense of individuality and self-reliance that had made the United States great. In fact, Moynihan's views could not be so easily labeled. Although generally supporting a hard-line foreign policy, he was by no means an advocate of increased defense spending. During the Carter administration, he opposed the development of the MX missile and joined with the president in scrapping the B-1 bomber program.

If Moynihan had been a harsh critic of Carter's foreign policy, furthermore, he was equally hard on Carter's successor. He even accused President Reagan of breaking international laws with the 1983 invasion of Grenada, and he denounced the CIA for mining the harbors of Nicaragua in 1984. As for domestic programs, he attacked the wastefulness of the nation's welfare program, but he always remained a liberal in terms of expanding the scope of government to assist the most helpless and indigent of the nation's population. He blasted the administration for cuts in the nation's social-safety net, agreed with critics of supply-side economics who viewed it as "voodoo economics," and even proposed legislation in 1989 to cut Social Security taxes and put the system on a pay-as-you go basis.

Moynihan's hero was Woodrow Wilson, but, unlike Wilson, his career was marked less by lawmaking and more by constructive criticism of existing law. His formidable mind never lacked for new and innovative ideas, ranging from FAP to a proposal for magnetically propelled trains traveling frictionless just above a single rail between the major cities of the East Coast. It was, however, his intellect and his ability to play the role of contrarian and iconoclast—evident again during the presidency of Bill Clinton (1993–2001), whom he regarded as a hubristic product of the 1960s—rather than his sponsorship of any major new legislative program that earned him the admiration of his fellow lawmakers on both sides of the Senate aisle and the respect of the American people.

Although Moynihan could almost certainly have won reelection for a fifth term in the Senate, the New York senator shocked political pundits by announcing that he would not run again in 2000. Instead, he chose to retire to his farm 60 miles west of Albany. Author of 18 books at the time he left the Senate, his plan was to continue to write, but on March 26, 2003, he died of complications from abdominal surgery. Following his death, he was praised across party lines as one of the most important figures of public life. The columnist Michael Barone described him as "the nation's best thinker among politicians since Lincoln and its best politician among thinkers since Jefferson."

Muskie, Edmund Sixtus

(1914–1996) *member of the Senate, secretary of state*

A U.S. senator from Maine and former Democratic candidate for vice president, Edmund S. Muskie was unexpectedly named by President Carter to replace CYRUS VANCE as secretary of state following Vance's resignation in 1980. In this role, Muskie acted mostly as the administration's public spokesman on foreign policy while the department's high-level business, including the negotiations for the release of the 52 American hostages being held by Iran, was conducted by Deputy Secretary of State WARREN CHRISTOPHER.

The son of a Polish immigrant tailor who Americanized his name, Muskie was born in Rumford, Maine, on March 28, 1914. After graduating cum laude and Phi Beta Kappa from nearby Bates College (B.A., 1936) and Cornell University School of Law (LL.B., 1939), he opened a law practice in Waterville, Maine. He interrupted his practice to serve as a naval officer in the Atlantic and Pacific during World War II. After being discharged from the navy at the end of the war, he returned to his law practice and entered politics. A Democrat in an overwhelmingly Republican state, he ran successfully in 1946 for Maine's House of Representatives. Known for his good humor, modesty, and fair-mindedness, he served three terms in the legislature before being elected in 1954 as Maine's first Democratic governor in 20 years and only the second in the century. A popular governor who promoted bipartisanship, economic development, and fiscal conservatism, he helped to rebuild the Democratic Party in the state. After serving two terms as governor, he was elected in 1958 as the state's first Democratic U.S. senator in a century. He served until 1980.

Muskie carried with him to Washington the skills he had developed as a governor having to deal with an overwhelmingly Republican legislature in a fiscally conservative state. Although a liberal who supported most of the domestic programs of the New Frontier and Great Society, he became a leading Democratic advocate of fiscal conservatism and government downsizing. He practiced these principles as the first chairperson of the Senate Budget Committee, which Congress had established as part of the Congressional Budget and Impoundment Act of 1974. Muskie had helped to lead the fight for this legislation, which also created the Congressional Budget Office, in response to President RICHARD NIXON's impoundment of congressionally appropriated funds.

A partisan known by his staff for his volcanic temper, the Maine senator nevertheless gained a reputation in Washington for his civility, high sense of integrity, and bipartisan approach to such legislative initiatives as urban reform and environmental protection. As chair of the Subcommittee on Housing, he was instrumental in the creation of the Department of Housing and Urban Development in 1965, and he was floor leader of the Model Cities Act of 1966.

Muskie also helped to make environmental protection a national issue. As chair of the Senate's new Subcommittee on Air and Water Pollution, he was responsible for the passage of the Water Quality Acts of 1963 and 1965, the Clean Air Act of 1963, and the Clean River Restoration Act of 1966. In addition, he held hearings throughout the country on the need to clean up the nation's air and water and was responsible for the establishment of such agencies as the Federal Water Pollution Control Administration and the Environmental Quality Council, created in 1969 in the Office of the President. He was also a key supporter of the Environmental Protection Agency, established in 1970.

Although respected on Capitol Hill, Muskie was little known nationally until 1968, when the Democratic nominee for president, HUBERT HUMPHREY, selected him as his vice-presidential running mate. The two men had compatible views not only on domestic issues but on the overarching issue of the war in Vietnam. Despite his growing doubts about the war, especially about the bombing of North Vietnam, Muskie generally followed the administration's policy toward the conflict. At the Democratic convention, he joined Humphrey in opposing the platform proposal for an unconditional halt to the bombing of North Vietnam.

During the campaign, the national media noted the differences in character and manner between Muskie and his Republican opponent, Maryland governor Spiro Agnew. In contrast to Agnew's inflammatory rhetoric and rabble-rousing antics, Muskie conducted himself with great dignity, calm, and good humor. A brilliant debater and eloquent speaker with a powerful voice and notable Down East accent, he was a natural crowd pleaser and an imposing figure on television. At six feet, four inches in height, with a big head and craggy appearance, he was compared to Abraham Lincoln so often that he came to hate the adjective *Lincolnesque*.

Although Humphrey narrowly lost to Richard Nixon in November and Muskie returned to the Senate, he became the front-runner for the Democratic nomination in 1972. While campaigning in New Hampshire, however, he seemed to cry in public when he sought to defend his wife, Jane, against the notoriously conservative publisher of the *Manchester Union Leader*, William Loeb, who accused her of using foul language and behaving in a drunken manner. The scene made Muskie look weak and raised questions about his mental stability. He never recovered from the incident. After disappointing results in the early primaries, he withdrew from the race in April 1972.

Muskie did not run for national office again, but he remained one of the Democratic Party's leading spokesmen. In 1976, he was one of Carter's two finalists for the party's vice-presidential nomination. Carter met with him and the other finalist, Senator WALTER MONDALE (Minn.), at his home in Plains. He was impressed with Muskie's sense of independence during their meeting. "He doesn't care if I like him or not," he commented afterwards. But he found Mondale better prepared and more energetic than Muskie. Mondale was also more closely identified with the Democratic Party's liberal wing that Carter needed to court in the general election. On this basis, he selected the Minnesota senator as his running mate.

Despite almost being vice president, Muskie was highly critical of the White House once Carter took office. At the end of February 1977, he joined other prominent Democrats, including the powerful chair of the Finance Committee, RUSSELL LONG (La.), and Majority Leader ROBERT BYRD (W.Va.) in attacking the president for his proposal to cut 19 water projects, including the Dickey-Lincoln Dam in Maine that Muskie wanted, without first consulting the congressional leadership. "No president should have the right to frustrate a policy that has been made a part of a law of this land," he remarked.

Having reworked the entire federal budget as chair of the Budget Committee to accommodate Carter's proposal for a $50 rebate on 1976 income taxes for each personal exemption as a way of stimulating a lagging economy, Muskie also blasted the president in April 1977 when he reversed course and decided that the economy was recovering well enough without the rebate. Muskie "feels that we have … made a fool of him," Carter's congressional liaison, FRANK MOORE, reported to the president. "He believes he went to the wall for us … tearing his Committee apart along party lines."

Yet unlike many of the Democrats in the House and Senate, Muskie genuinely liked the president. "He's got a good mind," he later noted. "He works hard. He doesn't deserve all the harsh treatment he gets." As for Carter, he continued to have great respect for the senator, who was one of the few lawmakers on Capitol Hill with whom he cultivated a warm personal relationship.

Yet Muskie and most political observers in Washington were surprised when the president asked him to be secretary of state after Cyrus Vance resigned from the post in 1980 in response to the unsuccessful rescue mission in Iran to free American hostages. As Muskie commented, Carter had delivered a "blockbuster." Most political pundits had expected that Deputy Secretary of State Warren Christopher, who was well-liked at the State Department and in the White House, would be promoted to head the department. But Vice President Mondale recommended the Maine senator to the president because he believed that National Security Advisor ZBIGNIEW BRZEZINSKI was hurting the president politically. He thought Muskie had the political skills to deal effectively with Brzezinski and could help Carter in his bid for reelection.

Following the strong reaction to the failure of the hostage rescue mission and Secretary of State Vance's resignation, Carter also wanted someone he knew would win quick Senate confirmation. "Ed Muskie seemed the perfect fit," *Newsweek* commented. "a quintessential Washington Democrat who had served 22 honored years in the Senate ... and made a reputation for a tough, flinty, and sometimes Tabasco-tempered independence." Furthermore, the president thought Muskie had the fortitude, self-confidence, and intellectual skills to work well with the United States' allies abroad, seek compromise in places like the Middle East, and not be intimidated by the United States' adversaries, most notably the Soviet Union.

Well aware also of the plagued relationship that had existed between Vance and Brzezinski, Muskie insisted, before he would agree to serve as secretary of state, on a commitment from Carter that he would be the administration's chief spokesman on foreign policy. The president sealed the deal by making the promise. "Ed Muskie doesn't have to come to me to make sure I prop him up," he told reporters. The new secretary would have enough clout "not to be eaten alive by the State Department bureaucracy before his feet are on the ground." After only four hours of hearings, Muskie was confirmed by a vote in the Senate of 94 to 2.

On taking office, Muskie intended to be directly involved in policy making. He also wanted to revive the bipartisanship in foreign policy that had prevailed prior to the Vietnam War and the Watergate scandal. "The way to do it, and the way I did it in the Budget Committee," he said, "is to make clear to the minority that I am interested in their input. They have to be in the takeoffs as well as in the landings."

The new secretary of state had only limited success in achieving his goals since Brzezinski was able to vie successfully with the State Department over control of foreign policy. In July 1980, for example, Carter signed Presidential Directive 59 (PD-59), authorizing the largest arms program in 30 years. Conceived by Brzezinski and Secretary of Defense HAROLD BROWN, PD-59 was predicated on their perception that the buildup of Soviet strategic force and the improved accuracy of its nuclear warheads changed the calculus of the Soviet nuclear threat and required an American response in kind. Carter signed PD-59 without consulting his new secretary of state. Muskie did not even know the details of the directive until he read them in a news story that Brzezinski had leaked to embarrass him, just as he had leaked stories to embarrass Vance. Muskie was simply not a match for Brzezinski. As his deputy, Warren Christopher, later explained, "Muskie's patented style of asking questions as a means of demonstrating substance contrasted dramatically and negatively with Zbig Brzezinski's confident rapid-fire lectures. Muskie also had little experience with executive-branch hardball."

The Soviet Union's invasion of Afghanistan in December 1979 had also convinced the president that his National Security Advisor was correct in advising a hard-line approach toward Moscow. As a senator, Muskie had been just as appalled as the White House by the Soviet action. Before taking office as secretary of state, he told a *Time* magazine correspondent that Moscow had to "know and understand that we must resist and object in the strongest terms to their policy of intervention." Once becoming secretary of state, however, Muskie was less willing than Brzezinski to engage in saber rattling with the Soviets. He even believed it possible to reach an arms agreement with the Kremlin despite the fact that the invasion of Afghanistan had effectively killed whatever chance had existed for Senate ratification of the 1979 Strategic Arms Limitation Talks agreement (SALT II). Muskie's ambivalent attitude toward the Soviet Union, when contrasted to that of Carter's National Security Advisor, led the president to rely increasingly on Brzezinski for advice, just as had happened when Vance was secretary of state. As for Muskie's other goal of making foreign policy more bipartisan, it fell victim to disagreement on Capitol Hill over the SALT process, a sense among Republicans (as well as Democrats) that the president was faltering in his foreign policy, and preelection politics.

In the short time that he was secretary of state, Muskie's major role was that of a spokesman for the administration. For example, he publicly berated the French for reaching a secret agreement with the Soviets to give the Palestine Liberation Organization (PLO) de facto diplomatic status. Although the United States still considered the PLO to be a terrorist organization, the Franco-Soviet agreement would have the PLO participate in all future negotiations in the Middle East. It would also revise UN Resolution 242, the heart of most long-range peace formulas for the region, to remove its reference to the Palestinians as mere "refugees." What galled Muskie was not only the substance of the agreement but the fact that the French had not consulted with the United States about their meeting with the Soviets after having just scolded him for the United States's failure to consult more with its allies. "I'm concerned that when I had been given a lecture on consultation, the lecturer was not inclined to practice what he was preaching," he remarked caustically to reporters.

In May 1980, Muskie met with his Soviet counterpart, Andrei Gromyko, in the first high-level contact between the two countries since the beginning of the Afghan crisis the previous December. The talks were unproductive, however. Moscow dangled the possibility of a pullout from Afghanistan, but Muskie dismissed the proposal as cosmetic. He later met with European leaders at a NATO meeting, where he told them that they would have to assume more of their own defense burden so that the United States could redirect more of its military resources to the Persian Gulf and Indian Ocean.

As the 1980 presidential election neared an end, there were persistent rumors in Washington that should Carter be reelected, there would be a postelection fight over the roles of Muskie and Brzezinski in the second term. According to the National Security Advisor, Vice President Mondale was being pressured by "left-liberal segments of the Democratic Party gunning for [him]," to join with Muskie in the showdown that was to take place. Whether there would have been such a postelection struggle cannot be known for certain since Carter lost the election to RONALD REAGAN. But there is no doubt about the enmity that Muskie felt for Brzezinski, two leaders of Polish ethnicity who had joked at their first meeting that they would "not be Poles apart," but who political observers often joked were just that.

Trying to act as a mediator between the two rivals was future secretary of state MADELEINE ALBRIGHT, who had been given her first salaried position by Muskie but had been hired in 1978 by her former Columbia University professor, Brzezinski, to handle congressional relations for the National Security Council. Albright, however, was never able to bridge the relationship between two men she regarded as her mentors. "I used to tell myself," she later wrote in her memoirs, "that as much as I liked Muskie and Brzezinski, I was not sure I could survive a second term with the two of them."

On January 16, 1981, Muskie was awarded the Presidential Medal of Freedom by President Carter. After leaving office, he practiced law in Washington, D.C. In 1986, he was appointed to a three-member presidential commission (the Tower Commission) investigating the Reagan administration's actions in the notorious Iran-contra affair. The next year, the commission delivered a report highly critical of the president. Muskie also led a delegation to Vietnam in April 1993 to explore lifting the embargo against that country and chaired the Center for National Policy, a Democratic think tank.

Edmund Muskie died on March 18, 1996, of a heart attack following an operation to clear a blocked artery in his right leg. At his funeral, former president Jimmy Carter remarked that he had "never known any American leader who was more highly qualified to be president."

Nelson, Gaylord Anton
(1916–2005) *member of the Senate*

The father of Earth Day and one of the leading environmentalists on Capitol Hill, Democratic senator Gaylord Nelson of Wisconsin was one of the members of the liberal wing on Capitol Hill who worked most closely with President Carter. Not only did he share with Carter a common interest on environmental issues, which always remained his highest priority, but Nelson was more willing to follow the president's lead on such matters as hospital cost containment and Social Security than other liberals in the Senate.

The son of a rural physician and a nurse, Nelson was born on June 4, 1916, in Clear Lake, Wisconsin, a tiny town of about 700 in northwest Wisconsin. He later traced his concern with the environment to his rural upbringing, but he would also remind his audiences that rats in an urban slum were also an environmental problem. Both his parents identified themselves as LaFollette Republicans, meaning that they considered themselves within the tradition of the Progressive Party founded by Robert M. La Follette but merged into the Republican Party in 1946.

Although raised in rural Wisconsin, Nelson did his undergraduate work in economics at San Jose State College in California (B.A., 1939). After graduating, he returned to Wisconsin, where he received his law degree (LL. B., 1942). During World War II, he served in the U.S. Army, commanding an all-black company in the quartermaster corps and serving overseas in the Okinawa campaign, where he reconnected with an army nurse, Carrie Lee Dotson, whom he had met earlier; they married in 1947. The story of their romance was later recounted by the reporter and author Tom Brokaw in his best seller *The Greatest Generation* (2001)

After the war, Nelson returned to his native Polk County, set up a law practice, and ran unsuccessfully for the state assembly as a Republican. Following his defeat, he moved to Madison, joined the Democratic Party (after the Republican Party was taken over by conservatives), and was elected in 1958 to the state senate. He served three terms in the senate, eventually becoming the Democratic floor leader. In 1958, he was elected as Wisconsin's first Democratic governor in 25 years. As governor, he created the Outdoor Recreation Acquisitions Program, which levied a one-cent tax on each package of cigarettes sold in Wisconsin. The proceeds were used to purchase wetlands, parklands, and open spaces, with the eventual goal of acquiring 1 million acres of public lands.

In 1962, Nelson ran successfully for the U.S. Senate, defeating the four-term Republican incumbent, Alexander Wiley. He was reelected in 1968 and 1974 by comfortable margins. Almost immediately, he established his credentials as a national spokesman for the environment. His maiden speech on the Senate floor was in support of a ban on polluting detergents. He also tried unsuccessfully to persuade President John F. Kennedy of the enormity of the environmental crisis. According to Nelson, the president never fully appreciated the extent of the problem. Nevertheless, during the Kennedy and Lyndon B. Johnson administrations, Nelson was responsible for a number of environmental and conservation measures, including legislation to preserve the 2,100-mile Appalachian Trail and creation of a national hiking trails system. He also introduced legislation to ban the insecticide DDT, to require the restoration of land that had been strip-mined, and to designate the Department of Interior rather than the Office of Science and Technology as the primary agency for ecological research. In 1968, he helped establish the St. Croix Wild and Scenic Riverway.

As a liberal, Nelson was a a strong supporter of the New Frontier and Great Society programs and a leading proponent of the Civil Rights Act of 1964 and the Voting Rights Act of 1965. He was particularly proud of the National Teachers Corps, which he and Senator EDWARD KENNEDY (Mass.) cosponsored in an effort to alleviate the shortage of teachers in poverty areas. But although he was persuaded by Senate Foreign Relations Committee chairperson J. William Fulbright to vote for the 1964 Gulf of Tonkin Resolution, authorizing the use of military action in Vietnam, he soon regretted his vote and by early 1966 was speaking out against the use of combat troops in Vietnam.

During RICHARD NIXON's administration, Nelson opposed his prolongation of the war in Vietnam even as he continued his own efforts on behalf of the environment. In 1969, he helped gain a temporary ban on the use of DDT and other dangerous pesticides in the United States, which was later upheld by the Supreme Court and then formally prohibited by the recently established Environmental Protection Agency (EPA). In 1970, he helped establish the Apostle Islands National Lakeshore. That same year, the Wisconsin senator captured world headlines by launching the first Earth Day. Seeking to emulate the success of college "teach-ins" to discuss the Vietnam War, Nelson proposed to devote a day in April to hold similar discussions about the endangered planet. Unexpectedly tapping into the world's growing concern with environmental issues, the first Earth Day, held on April 22, drew 20 million participants. *American Heritage* magazine called the event "one of the most remarkable happenings in the history of democracy." At Nelson's urging, Earth Day has since become Earth Week, an annual event in which hundreds of millions of persons throughout the globe participate in environmentally related matters, including planting trees, picking up litter, recycling, and holding teach-ins on the environment.

Nelson often locked horns with the White House in attempting to maintain most of the antipoverty programs established in the 1960s. He was able to gain a three-year extension of the Office of Economic Opportunity (OEO), and he won approval of legislation creating the Community Services Administration, which gave some of the poverty programs the status of a permanent independent federal agency. But President Nixon was able to effectively dismantle the OEO and cut back or eliminate many of the programs of the Great Society. Nelson's ongoing opposition to Nixon's domestic programs and the war in Vietnam, including supporting the Cooper-Church amendment prohibiting the funding of military operations in Cambodia and opposing the 1971 draft-extension bill, won him a place on the infamous Nixon "hit list."

Interestingly, while Nelson became one of Nixon's most committed foes in the Senate and opposed the Vietnam War, one of his closest personal friends in Washington was Melvin Laird, a nine-term Republican congressman from Wisconsin and the president's first secretary of defense, whom Nelson had known from the time when they both served in the Wisconsin senate in the 1940s. They spent many evenings together discussing personal and political matters well into the night. "There was no closer political friendship and love between two opposite party members," Laird later recalled. Nelson also had a good working relationship with President GERALD FORD, whom he knew from the House, but with whom, like Laird, he disagreed on most issues of substance. "Republicans, Democrats, Progressives actually socialized as friendly adversaries. They did not consider one another as enemies," Nelson remarked at a law school reunion in 2000.

More than most liberals on Capitol Hill, Nelson also worked reasonably well with President Carter. He was one of about 40 members of the Democratic power structure who were invited to meet with Carter as a group at the home of columnist Clayton Fritchey in March 1976, when the former Georgia governor was just beginning to be recognized as a leading candidate for the nomination. Nelson was also a close friend of WALTER MONDALE of neighboring Minnesota and welcomed his nomination to be Carter's running mate.

During Carter's first months as president, he worked hard to defeat a drive by industry and labor to weaken the 1970 Clean Air Act, a measure that Nelson had vigorously supported, by weakening controls on automobile exhaust fumes and lessening protection of pure air over national parks. Nelson was pleased not only by the effort the president made to defeat this drive but, paradoxically, also by his willingness to allow a special amendment giving American Motors, a major employer in Wisconsin with special problems, additional time to comply with the emissions rules. Nelson also supported Carter's efforts to kill a number of pork-barrel water projects, most notably the Tennessee-Tombigbee Waterway project, which the Wisconsin senator later called "the biggest pork barrel boondoggle of them all." Even though construction began on the project and 25 percent was complete by 1979, Nelson introduced legislation to kill the project and to limit the Army Corps of Engineers' authority to justify billions of dollars' worth of water projects. The senator even charged that the Corps of Engineers had "deliberately misled" Congress on the project's costs.

Unlike many liberal Democrats opposed to the deregulation of natural-gas prices, Nelson backed the administration's efforts to break a Senate filibuster against gas deregulation led by South Dakota senator JAMES ABOUREZK (D). In November 1979, he offered an amendment, supported by the White House, to levy a windfall-profits tax on newly discovered oil, a move that would increase federal revenues by $71 billion over the 1980–90 decade. The oil was exempted altogether by the Senate Finance Committee. The next month, following threats by the oil-producing countries to reduce or cut off supplies of oil to the United States, amounting to 4.3 million barrels a day in a worst-case scenario, Nelson urged Carter to impose gasoline rationing immediately as a measure of self-defense.

As chair of the Senate Subcommittee on Social Security, Nelson also sought unsuccessfully to find a back-door method of transferring Treasury funds to the Social Security system during times of high unemployment as part of a White House plan for curing deficits in the system. He also worked repeatedly with the White House from 1977 to 1979 in unsuccessful efforts to require mandatory hospital cost-containment measures rather than the voluntary measures that the full Finance Committee, led by RUSSELL LONG (La.), favored. In February 1978, Nelson warned that if hospitals failed to cut costs for basic services to Medicare and Medicaid patients, "they will simply make this up by extending costs to private patients." He even engineered a proposal in 1978 that left the extent of cost cutting to the hospitals as long as they met certain goals, which became the basis for the administration's proposal in 1979. But he lost out repeatedly to a coalition of Senate Republicans and southern conservatives who preferred higher increases in scheduled Social Security taxes (the maximum tax increasing from $965 in 1977 to $2,854 in 1986) and voluntary hospital cost-containment guidelines.

Carrying on his activities on behalf of the environment, Nelson continued a campaign he had begun in 1970 against the herbicide 2,4,5-T, which was widely used by the United States Forest Service, utility companies protecting power lines, and farmers, but had been shown to be toxic even in diluted mixtures. In 1978, the EPA stopped the use of 2,4,5-T pending the outcome of an administrative mechanism called Rebuttable Presumption Against Registration. First instituted in 1975, this mechanism allowed the agency, in case of a highly suspect compound, to ban its sale pending a review procedure that shifted the burden of proof of the safety of the compound onto the producer. Nelson also worked unsuccessfully to abrogate an exemption of large land corporations in California from a limit of 1,280 acres on the amount of irrigated land that a farm operator might own or lease. After two days of debate in 1979 on the first major attempt in 40 years to modernize the Reclamation Act of 1902, which had seldom been enforced, the status quo generally went undisturbed.

In 1980, Nelson announced that he would be seeking reelection to a fourth term in the Senate. Most political observers did not expect that he would have a difficult time in this campaign. A popular senator, he had won both his earlier bids for reelection by well over 60 percent. As chair of the Senate Small Business Subcommittee, he had worked to preserve family farms and protect the shaky incomes of Wisconsin's dairy farmers. In one state poll, conducted as late as October 7, he was leading his Republican opponent, Robert W. Kasten, Jr. by a margin of 51 percent to 30 percent. But Nelson was one of a number of Democratic liberals against whom conservative groups had targeted considerable resources. He was also vulnerable to charges from his youthful opponent that, with unemployment reaching as high as 15 percent in some areas of the state, Nelson had outlived his usefulness in the Senate. Further, Kasten labeled Nelson as a "big spender," a conservative message that resonated with voters. In the Reagan landslide of 1980, Nelson narrowly lost by 17,000 votes out of more than 1.28 million ballots cast.

After leaving the Senate, Nelson became a counselor for the Wilderness Society. In his 14 years with the society, he was involved with a wide range of land-preservation issues, including elimination of logging subsidies and expansion of the National Wilderness Preservation System. He received the Environmental Leadership Award of the United Nations in 1992 and, on September 29, 1995, the Presidential Medal of Freedom, the nation's highest civilian award, for his work on behalf of the environment. In a speech in 2001 at the University of Wisconsin–Madison, where the Institute for Environmental Studies was being renamed the Gaylord Nelson Institute for Environmental Studies, he blasted President George W. Bush for his indifference to environmental issues.

A resident of Kensington, Maryland, in his final years, Nelson died of cardiovascular failure on July 3, 2005. He was 89 years old.

Nixon, Richard Milhous

(1913–1994) *thirty-seventh president of the United States*

During Jimmy Carter's presidency, Richard Milhous Nixon came out of the self-imposed exile he had been in since his forced resignation as president in August 1974 as a result of the Watergate scandal. He published his memoirs, made his first public appearances since leaving office, and even returned to the White House for a state dinner. Although at first supportive of Carter's foreign policy, the area of greatest interest to Nixon, the former president became increasingly harsh in his views of Carter's human rights policy, the SALT II treaty, and especially the administration's treatment of the former shah of Iran, MOHAMMAD REZA PAHLAVI, which he regarded as unforgivable.

Born in Yorba Linda, California, on January 9, 1913, Nixon was raised in Whittier, California. From a poor family, he worked his way through college and graduated with honors both from Whittier College (B.A., 1934) and from Duke University Law School (LL.B., 1937). From 1937 to 1943, Nixon practiced law in Whittier. During World War II, he joined the U.S. Navy and saw action in the South Pacific. After the war, he decided to enter politics, and in the Republican sweep of 1946, he was elected to the U.S. House of Representatives. As a member of the House Un-American Activities Committee (HUAC), he spearheaded the investigation of Alger Hiss, a former State Department official who was later found guilty of perjury for denying under oath that he had been a communist. In 1950, Nixon ran successfully for the Senate in a campaign tainted by his "red-baiting" attacks against his Democratic opponent, Helen Gahagan Douglas.

In 1952, Dwight D. Eisenhower, seeking to balance the ticket and mollify the right wing of the Republican Party, selected Nixon as his running mate. After Eisenhower was elected, Nixon served dutifully as his vice president for the next eight years, When Nixon narrowly lost to John F. Kennedy in the 1960 presidential election and then ran unsuccessfully for governor of California two years later, it seemed that his political career was finished. Instead, he kept his name in the limelight by speaking out on foreign affairs and government policies. He also spent the next six years quietly cultivating the support of Republican leaders. In 1968, he was rewarded for his efforts with the Republican presidential nomination. In the November election, he defeated his Democratic opponent, Vice President HUBERT HUMPHREY, by less than 500,000 votes.

During the campaign, Nixon had indicated that he had a secret plan for getting the United States out of the Vietnam War. In fact, he had no plan, but, sensing the growing antiwar tide in the United States, he began a phased withdrawal of American forces from the country. Although he coupled the withdrawal with an escalation of the bombing campaign—including secretly bombing Cambodia—and increasing military aid to the South Vietnamese army in a policy known as Vietnamization, he was able to quell the antiwar movement in the United States.

Meanwhile, Nixon surprised many of his liberal critics by taking an advanced position on a number of important domestic issues. For example, he lobbied for the establishment of an Environmental Protection Agency and a Department of Natural Resources. He also supported a proposal that would have guaranteed a family of four an annual income of $1,600 plus $800 in food stamps; adopted the Philadelphia Plan, which set aide jobs for minorities in the construction industry; strengthened the

Equal Employment Opportunity Commission; and supported the Equal Rights Amendment to the Constitution.

Nixon's main interest, however, was foreign affairs. In 1971, he surprised much of the world by sending his brilliant National Security Advisor, HENRY KISSINGER, to Beijing to lay the groundwork for a presidential visit to China early the next year. During that 1972 visit, taking advantage of a growing split between China and the Soviet Union, he agreed to move toward normalization of Sino-American relations. In May 1972, he went to Moscow, where he and Soviet leader LEONID BREZHNEV signed the first Strategic Arms Limitation Talks treaty (SALT I).

Midway through his first term in office, Nixon had to deal with a renewed antiwar movement after he decided to send troops into Cambodia in April 1970. Protests raised the country's tension level and led to the killing of four students by members of the Ohio National Guard during a demonstration at Kent State University. He also had difficulty controlling inflation and reducing unemployment. For the most part, however, Americans were satisfied with Nixon's performance as president. On the eve of the November 1972 presidential election, the White House even announced that peace was at hand in Vietnam. Consequently, American voters saw no reason to vote Nixon out of office, and he won an overwhelming victory over Senator GEORGE MCGOVERN (S.Dak.) by a margin of 61 percent to 38 percent. In casting their ballots, most Americans ignored news stories of White House involvement in the arrest of five persons linked to the Committee to Re-elect the President (CREEP) for burglarizing the Democratic National Committee headquarters in Washington's Watergate complex.

In January 1973, Nixon was able to announce that after the heaviest bombing of North Vietnam yet, the Hanoi government had agreed to a cease-fire, thus allowing the United States to withdraw its remaining forces from Vietnam on the basis of "peace with honor." Unfortunately for Nixon, this was the last time he would be able to win public favor. Soon thereafter, his administration began to unravel. This was partly due to the sharp turn he took toward the political right, even dismantling the Office of Economic Opportunity. New economic problems, including balance of payments deficits, the weakening of the dollar—which led the United States to go off the gold standard—and rising gasoline prices as a result of an Arab oil embargo imposed on the United States after it resupplied military equipment to Israel during the Yom Kippur War of October 1973, all resulted in a skyrocketing inflation rate, a stagnant economy, and a dramatic decline in the stock market.

What really led to Nixon's undoing as president, however, was the so-called Watergate affair, having to do with the involvement of White House staff in the break-in of Democratic headquarters at the Watergate complex in 1972 and the president's subsequent false denials of any knowledge of the break-in. After a long ordeal—including the Senate's establishment of a special committee to investigate presidential campaign activities; the hiring and firing of one special prosecutor, Archibald Cox, and the hiring of another, Leon Jaworski, to look into the events surrounding the Watergate burglary; and the refusal of the president to hand over to Jaworski secret tape recordings of meetings in the Oval Office that might implicate Nixon in a cover-up—on July 27, 1974, the House Judiciary Committee voted out articles of impeachment. Under pressure from the Republican leadership, which had learned of a tape of a June 23, 1972, meeting in the White House establishing clearly that Nixon had tried to use the CIA to cover up the Watergate break-in (the so-called smoking gun), Nixon announced on August 8, 1974, that he would resign the next day, thereby becoming the first American president ever to leave office voluntarily before the end of his term.

Following Nixon's resignation, the former president went into a deep depression and virtual seclusion. By 1976, however, he began to become more visible and active. Taking an interest in the forthcoming presidential election, he predicted after Jimmy Carter appeared to be the likely Democratic nominee that he would choose Senator WALTER MONDALE of Minnesota as his vice-presidential candidate. "It has to be Mondale," he said. "He's a liberal. He's from the Midwest. He looks good on the tube." As for Carter, Nixon thought he "might be good on defense" since he had been in the navy.

With respect to the Republicans, Nixon thought President GERALD FORD had made a political mistake by not being more visible in the nation's bicentennial celebrations. He also tried to use his influence with party leaders to get Ford to select his former Treasury secretary, John Connally of Texas, as his running mate. "Without a man of Connally's forceful personality, political skill and vote-getting ability to offset Jimmy Carter's strength among Southern voters," he told a reporter from the *New York Times*, "Ford could not win." He even tried to telephone Ford to give him the same message, but the president would not accept his call.

Throughout the campaign, Nixon continued to send advice to Ford, including how the president should conduct himself during his debates with Carter. "Remember, Carter scares the hell out of me," he advised Ford. "Scare the hell out of the American people about Carter's foreign policies; bear down on it. He'll come close to making us a number two power." He also suggested that an "international incident" could be useful to Ford, so that if one blew up he should "dramatize it." Finally, he took Secretary of State Henry Kissinger to task for talking so much about Africa, and he advised against appearing too pro-Israeli. "The Democrats have the Negroes and the Jews, and let them have them—in fact, tie them around their necks," he remarked. Ford took some of Nixon's advice but rejected other suggestions.

Once Carter was elected, Nixon was generally supportive of the president's foreign policy. He backed the Panama Canal Treaties and had high praise for the Camp David accords of September 1978 between Prime Minister MENACHEM BEGIN of Israel and President ANWAR SADAT of Egypt. As a result of the agreements, Nixon predicted peace in the Middle East. In 1978, he returned to the White House for the first time since resigning the presidency to attend a state dinner for Chinese deputy prime minister DENG XIAOPING, who conferred with him at length and arranged for Nixon to visit China the following year.

President Carter, however, held Nixon in low esteem as a result of the Watergate affair, and he wanted to distance himself from Nixon as much as possible. "As an American," Carter later remarked, "I had been embarrassed by the Watergate scandal and the forced resignation of the President. I realized that my own election had been aided by a deep desire among the people for open government, based on a new and fresh commitment to changing some of the Washington habits which had made it possible for the American people to be misled." He also had been frustrated and angered, while he was governor of Georgia and Nixon was president, by the absence of even minimal cooperation between the Nixon White House and state and local leaders. As a result, when Nixon visited Washington in 1978 to attend the funeral of former vice president Hubert Humphrey, Carter refused to accord him the courtesy, normally given to former presidents visiting the nation's capitol, of staying at the government's guesthouse on Lafayette Square. He had his picture taken with former presidents Nixon and Ford, but the two men hardly

President Carter, Gerald Ford, and Richard Nixon at the White House for the funeral for Hubert Humphrey, 1978 *(Jimmy Carter Library)*

exchanged formal courtesies. Although Carter invited Nixon to the state dinner for Deng Xiaoping, he did so only because the Chinese had insisted he be invited.

During the last two years of Carter's presidency, Nixon became more critical of the president's foreign policy. Adopting a harder line toward the Soviet Union, he criticized Carter for "trying to preserve détente at almost any cost," even though that had been Nixon's policy as president and Carter was moving toward adopting his own, tougher policy toward Moscow. Strongly opposed to the SALT II agreement that Carter negotiated with the Soviet Union in 1979, he declined the president's invitation to be briefed on the agreement. He also spoke out against what he considered to be the president's indiscriminate application of his human rights policy to friends as well as foes of the United States, and he took issue with the White House's pressure on Nicaragua's dictator, ANASTASIO SOMOZA DEBAYLE, to resign. "I think it is crucial that every possible step be taken to make sure that a Castro-type does not come to power in Nicaragua because that would be a threat to every free nation in the Western hemisphere," he remarked.

Like former secretary of state Kissinger, however, Nixon saved his heaviest salvos against the administration for what he regarded as its shabby treatment of the shah of Iran, Mohammad Reza Pahlavi, in particular its refusal to admit the shah into the United States after he fled Iran in January 1979. On July 13 that year, the former president visited the former Iranian leader in exile in Cuernavaca, Mexico, to let him know "that "millions of Americans in the United States are still his friends." After the shah expressed his bitterness at Carter for refusing to admit him into the United States, Nixon told him to keep on fighting. When the shah died of cancer in Egypt on July 17, 1980, Nixon was outraged by the White House's almost indifferent response to news of his death and by its refusal to send an official delegation to attend his funeral. The former president therefore flew to Egypt on a commercial jet in order to attend the ceremonial burial of the former Iranian leader. He denounced the Carter administration's treatment of the shah as "one of the black pages of American foreign policy."

In 1980, Nixon published his first book on U.S. foreign policy, *The Real War*, a strident warning about the danger from the Soviet Union; it was a best seller on both sides of the Atlantic. While promoting the book, following the failed April 1980 attempt by the White House to rescue the American hostages being held by Iran, Nixon told Barbara Walters in an interview on ABC that he thought President Carter was making a mistake in placing so much emphasis on trying to free the American hostages. "They are important," he said, but the moment their lives and safety become one's only concern, "you are inviting blackmail. [The Iranians] know you'll pay any price in order to save those lives and we could never do that."

During the 1980 presidential campaign, Nixon served as a commentator on NBC's *Today* show. He found Carter to be "very tough, very shrewd" with a "ruthless" staff that would use the full power of the presidency to win the election. But Nixon thought that the Republican nominee, RONALD REAGAN, would win. The president's weakness was "his record, his deeds." Nixon also correctly predicted the exact states Reagan would carry.

Once Reagan won the election, Nixon offered—and, indeed, he expected—to be an unofficial adviser to the new president. But while Reagan was courteous and occasionally called upon the former president for advice, Nixon spent most of the rest of his life working on a series of books on American foreign policy. Although he was never able to put the Watergate affair and the ignoble end to his presidency behind him, he was able, through his writings and public comments, to establish a personal reputation of considerable renown. As a result, when he died on April 24, 1994, of a stroke, his death was widely mourned as the passing of an international statesman of the first rank who, unfortunately, could not overcome personality flaws that went back to his childhood. All the former living presidents, including Jimmy Carter, attended his funeral. At the time of his death, Nixon was 81 years old.

Nunn, Sam

(Samuel Augustus Nunn)
(1938–) *member of the Senate*

Although just completing his first term as a U.S. senator from Georgia when Jimmy Carter became president in 1977, Sam Nunn was already widely respected on Capitol Hill as an expert on national defense and arms control, a reputation that would continue to grow over his remaining three terms in the Senate. Even though he often disagreed with the administration on defense issues, he was, for the most part, the president's reliable and dependable ally in Washington, just as he had been when Carter was governor of Georgia and Nunn was one of his trusted lieutenants on the floor of the Georgia House of Representatives.

Born on September 8, 1938, in Perry, a small town in central Georgia, Nunn came from a prominent family that was also well-connected politically. His great-uncle was Carl Vinson, one of the lions of Capitol Hill, who served for 51 years in the House of Representatives, much of that time as chair of the House Armed Services Committee. His father was a lawyer, banker, and farmer as well as the town's mayor. As a result, young Sam had opportunities to meet many of Georgia's most prominent political figures, including the state's two U.S. senators, Richard Russell and Walter George.

A star basketball player in high school, Nunn attended Georgia Tech University (1956–59) but decided to join the U.S. Coast Guard before completing his degree. After active duty (1959–60), he served for six years in the U.S. Coast Guard reserves. He completed his undergraduate and law degrees with honors at Emory University (B.A., 1960; LL.B., 1962). After working on the staff of the House Armed Services Committee, he returned to Perry and was elected to the state legislature in 1968. In 1970, he served as a district manager for Jimmy Carter's second campaign for governor.

When Carter was elected governor, he appointed Nunn to preside over the Goals for Georgia program, which the governor had established as one of his first acts as the state's chief executive. Modeled on an earlier Goals for Dallas program, Goals for Georgia was intended as a nonpartisan vehicle for mobilizing public support on behalf of such projects as government reorganization and regional development. In the State House, Nunn also became one of the few lawmakers that the governor could rely on regularly for support. He was therefore bitterly disappointed, when, following the death of Richard Russell in 1971, Governor Carter named David Gambrell, one of his largest campaign contributors, rather than Nunn, to fill out the remainder of Russell's Senate term. Nunn even charged that Gambrell had bought the seat from Carter with his campaign contributions, leading to a temporary rift in their relationship.

Carter, however, soured on Gambrell. When Nunn told him that he was planning to challenge Gambrell in 1972 for a full term to the U.S. Senate, the governor gave him his tacit support by refusing to endorse Gambrell. Nunn was still given little chance of winning. "I was only 33 then, a junior legislator," he later recalled. "Even Uncle Carl [Vinson] said I couldn't win, but I felt I had to try." The newcomer surprised everyone by defeating Gambrell in a runoff primary. In November, Nunn defeated his Republican opponent, Fletcher Thomas, with 54 percent of the vote despite Thomas's effort to link Nunn to Democratic presidential candidate GEORGE MCGOVERN, whose liberal views and opposition to the war in Vietnam were unpopular in Georgia.

Even though he was a freshman senator, Nunn came to Washington already assured a seat on the prestigious Armed Service Committee, the assignment he most wanted. Before the election, his uncle had arranged for him to meet some of the most important members of the committee, including HENRY JACKSON (D-Wash.) and JOHN STENNIS (D-Miss.). Both Jackson and Stennis were impressed by the fact that, at a time of growing antiwar sentiment, especially among Democrats, Nunn believed in a strong defense and wanted to serve on their committee; they told him he would be given a seat on Armed Services if he were elected. Throughout his career, Nunn forged a strong alliance with Jackson.

Beyond his belief in a strong defense and his interest in issues of national security, Nunn impressed his colleagues by his deference, caution, cerebral approach to problems, and mastery of issues. Nunn considered himself a southern centrist, but in most respects, he was a conservative. Except for his commitment to major increases in defense spending, he sought to limit government spending. While he had accepted the civil-rights gains of blacks over the previous 20 years, he was not a social liberal and did not look to Washington for social justice. During the 1972 campaign, he had met with Alabama governor GEORGE WALLACE, and as he remarked in an interview 15 years later, he "frankly admired Wallace, not because of his racial views, but because of his willingness to stand up and shake a fist at Washington occasionally."

By the time Nunn took his seat in the U.S. Senate, Carter had decided to run for president. As part of his strategy to win the Democratic nomination in 1976, he was told by his aide and political strategist, HAMILTON JORDAN, to pretend that he was preparing to run for the Senate, but to make it clear to both Nunn and Georgia's other U.S. senator, HERMAN TALMADGE, that he did not intend to seek a Senate seat. Although Nunn greatly admired Carter's rival for the Democratic nomination, Henry Jackson, he backed Carter for the nomination.

Once Carter took office as president, Nunn became one of his strongest allies in the Senate. A practicing Methodist, he also participated in the congressional prayer group that met every Monday at the White House. But there were a number of issues having to do with national security and military defense with which he disagreed with the president.

The first of these concerned the Panama Canal Treaties that the Carter administration negotiated with Panama in 1977. Eventually Nunn voted for the treaties, but it was one of his most difficult decisions since coming to Washington. Like other opponents of the treaties, he believed Panama could not guarantee U.S. access through the Panama Canal, which he considered vital to the nation's security. Only after the administration accepted a reservation giving the United States the right, under certain limited conditions acceptable to Panama, to send troops into Panama after the year 2000 to protect the canal, did Nunn agree to support the agreements.

Although Nunn finally gave his support to the Panama Canal Treaties, he firmly opposed Carter's decision, which the president announced at a press conference on January 26, 1977, to carry out his campaign pledge to withdraw the United States's 32,000 ground combat troops in South Korea. (Some 16,000 airmen and army logistical forces would remain indefinitely.) While the president supported a buildup of American ground forces in Europe, where Soviet troops outnumbered NATO forces, he saw no useful military purpose for American troops in Korea, which he believed could be better defended with U.S. air and logistical support.

In contrast, Nunn believed that the withdrawal of most of the United States' forces from Korea invited a North Korean attack. He was not the only lawmaker to share this view. The outcry against the president's decision was so strong on Capitol Hill that Carter was forced to cut back the planned withdrawal drastically. In 1978, 3,400 troops were withdrawn; another 2,600 were scheduled to leave in 1979. But even this cut in troop levels concerned Nunn. Together with three other senators who toured East Asia in February 1979, he warned the president about the growing military imbalance on the Korean peninsula. He and the other senators estimated that North Korea had an army of 600,000 men with 2,600 tanks, compared to South Korea's 560,000 troops and 800 tanks. They also estimated that North Korea had a two-to-one disadvantage in tactical aircraft and a four-to-one advantage in warships.

The president assured the lawmakers that he would adjust his policy "should circumstances affecting the balance [on the Korean peninsula] change significantly." After he left the White House, however, Nunn told reporters that, if necessary, Congress could block funds for the pullout. "We haven't made any legislative threat, but I don't foreclose that possibility," the Georgia senator remarked.

Another matter on which Nunn opposed the president concerned Carter's decision in 1978 to cancel development of an enriched-radiation weapon (ERW), commonly known as the neutron bomb, which had been designed to deter a Soviet attack in Europe by enabling Western forces to destroy enemy tank personnel without ravaging nearby population centers. The concept of a weapon that killed people but did not destroy property deeply troubled Carter as it did many other Americans. Critics of the weapon also maintained that deployment of ERWs would increase the chances of war since it implied an ability to wage, win, and recover from a nuclear attack.

After much hesitation, President Carter announced on April 7, 1978, that he was deferring production of the bomb. His decision created a political tempest in the United States and throughout Western Europe. Americans and Europeans alike accused him of vacillation. On Capitol Hill, House and Senate leaders were flooded with angry telegrams from proponents of the bomb. Nunn warned that cancellation of the ERW program would "place in the minds of the Soviets the image of a timid and hesitant America which lacks the courage to confront the difficult choices ahead."

The most significant issue on which the Georgia senator disagreed with the president, however, was over ratification of the Strategic Arms Limitation Talks treaty (SALT II) signed at Vienna in June 1979 by President Carter and Soviet leader LEONID BREZHNEV. Had the president decided not to withdraw the agreement from the Senate following the Soviet invasion of Afghanistan, it is doubtful that senators would have ratified the agreement. Most of those who opposed the treaty thought it was not verifiable and made too many concessions to the Soviets. A smaller number were against it because they believed it did nothing to stop the arms race.

Nunn had different reasons for opposing the agreement. Like the treaty's hard-line opponents, he thought the agreement made the treaty more vulnerable to Soviet attack, but not irredeemably so. Instead, he took the position that he could support the agreement provided the White House consented to an increase in real defense spending. What he wanted was not the 3 percent increase the administration found acceptable but a 5 percent increase after inflation for the next five years. He held his vote on the agreement hostage to a 5 percent increase, and he warned National Security Advisor ZBIGNIEW BRZEZINSKI that SALT II would not be ratified without major increases in defense spending.

Having angered Nunn and Jackson in September 1979 by vetoing a resolution calling for a 5 percent rather a 3 percent increase in defense spending, the president announced on December 12 that his 1981 defense budget would be 5.6 percent higher in real terms than his request for the 1980 budget. Although Jackson dismissed his pledge entirely, Nunn softened his position, announcing that he would not oppose SALT outright although he wanted additional assurances that the White House would keep its promises. At the time the president decided to withdraw the SALT treaty from consideration, it was not clear how Nunn was planning to vote on the agreement. Most likely, he would have supported it if assured of increased defense spending of 5 percent or more.

Although Nunn often found himself at odds with the president on national security and defense issues, on most other matters he remained a dependable ally. He joined Carter in opposing the development of the B-1 bomber on grounds that it could not accomplish its intended mission of penetrating Soviet defenses and striking at targets within the Soviet Union. He also supported the president on such important domestic legislation as his energy program, welfare reform, and reform of the Social Security system.

Nunn was among BERT LANCE's strongest defenders on Capitol Hill during the so-called Lance affair, in which questions were raised about the Office of Management and Budget (OMB) director's banking practices as president of the Calhoun National Bank and National Bank of Georgia; he found the case against Lance "woefully weak." In 1978, Nunn deftly undermined the highly publicized Kemp-Roth amendment to tax legislation, which would have slashed the income-tax rate by one-third. As an alternative, Nunn proposed what became known as the "son of Kemp-Roth," which would cut taxes by $164.5 billion by 1983 but would go into effect only if specified decreases in federal spending and the budget deficit were achieved.

By the time that Carter was defeated for reelection by RONALD REAGAN in 1980, Nunn was widely recognized by Republicans and Democrats as one of the nation's leading authorities on defense and national security matters. He was even widely touted as a potential presidential candidate in 1988, although he showed only passive interest in a presidential run. In 1984 and 1990, he was easily reelected to the Senate.

During the Reagan administration, Nunn achieved what he considered his most important legislative accomplishment. In 1986, he cosponsored, with Senator BARRY GOLDWATER (R-Ariz.), the Defense Reorganization Act, which strengthened the role of the chairperson of the Joint Chiefs of Staff (JCS) by making that person the president's principal military adviser and, for the first time, subordinating the other chiefs of staff to the chair. The measure also established a direct chain of command between the secretary of defense, the JCS chairperson, and the commanders in the 10 world area commands. Finally, the legislation more effectively coordinated joint military command in the field. In addition, Nunn coauthored, with Senator Richard Lugar (R-Ind.), the Nunn-Lugar Cooperative Threat Reduction Program, whose purpose was to assist Russia and the former Soviet republics in destroying their excess weapons of mass destruction.

In 1986, Nunn helped establish the Democratic Leadership Council, intended as a centrist organization to aid the Democratic Party in recapturing the White House in 1988. Although there continued to be speculation over Nunn's own interest in the presidency, he decided in 1996 to leave politics entirely and take a position as partner with the Atlanta law firm of King and Spalding. Since returning to private life, Nunn has assumed the role of elder statesman who is frequently called on by government officials and the media to give them his expertise on national security issues. He has also become cochairman and chief executive officer of the Nuclear Threat Initiative, an organization whose purpose is to reduce the global threat of nuclear and other weapons of mass destruction. Having retired from King and Spalding, Nunn is currently a distinguished professor at the Sam Nunn School of International Relations at Georgia Tech and chairman of the board of the Center for Strategic and International Studies in Washington, D.C.

Obey, David Ross
(1938–) *member of the House of Representatives*

A liberal Democrat from Wisconsin's Seventh Congressional District, David Obey was elected to the House of Representatives in 1969 to replace Republican Melvin Laird, chosen by President RICHARD NIXON as his secretary of defense. As the newest member of the House, Obey joined forces with other liberal Democrats to force major changes in the way business was conducted in the lower chamber. By the time Jimmy Carter became president in 1977, Obey was recognized as one of the rising stars on Capitol Hill and within the Democratic Party. But he also became one of the president's many liberal critics on Capitol Hill, mainly because of Carter's conservative fiscal policies and his failure, in Obey's view, to consult with congressional leaders on important legislative priorities.

Born in Omulgee, Oklahoma, on October 3, 1938, Obey grew up in Wausau, Wisconsin. Both he and his future wife, Joan Lelpinski, attended Catholic parochial schools and Wausau East High School before attending the University of Wisconsin–Madison, where Obey majored in Soviet studies (B.S., 1960). He then pursued graduate work in Soviet studies at Madison under a three-year National Defense Education Act fellowship (M.A., 1962), fully expecting to teach Russian and Chinese studies.

Obey's boyhood experiences shaped his later political priorities. Although he did not realize it at the time, his father's floor-covering business exposed both his father and him to asbestos and later made Obey a leading advocate of protecting workers' health and safety. An illness his father sustained, in which his arm was paralyzed for a number of months, made Obey realize the importance of some form of guaranteed medical health insurance to all Americans. The fact that his father's illness also nearly kept him from completing his undergraduate work at Wisconsin convinced Obey of the need to provide access to all qualified college students regardless of their families' resources.

In 1963, the same year he was married, Obey ran successfully as a Democrat for the Wisconsin State Assembly, where he played a key role in creating Wisconsin's Technical College Districts and the state's public broadcasting network. Rising to the position of assistant Democratic leader, he sponsored Wisconsin's pioneering Homestead Tax Relief Act for seniors and served on the state commission that established the state's first Medicaid law.

He also became a protégé and disciple of U.S. senator GAYLORD NELSON (D-Wis.).

In 1969, Obey ran successfully in a special election to fill the House seat being vacated by newly appointed secretary of defense Melvin Laird. Once in the House, Obey threw his efforts behind a reform effort being led by PHILLIP BURTON (Calif.) and other liberal Democrats to democratize the rules of the House. The reformers sought to liberalize the seniority system by which chairs of committees and subcommittees were appointed in order to give greater power to the younger members of the House. They also promoted changes in the House rules that made it easier to get legislation out of committee and onto the floor for consideration by the full House.

While working with Burton to reform the House rules, Obey developed serious reservations about the California lawmaker, whom he found arrogant, abrasive, and overbearing. "Obey fears Burton might use the [caucus] chairmanship for his own purposes, for the pure joy of exercising power," wrote the *Chicago Tribune*. One of Obey's concerns about Burton had to do with funding the war in Indochina. Although he opposed further military aid to Indochina at a time when North Vietnam was on the verge of toppling the Saigon government, Obey objected to Burton's use of the Democratic Caucus to stop the funding even before the House Appropriations Committee had met.

In contrast to Burton, Obey regarded another congressional reformer, RICHARD BOLLING (D-Mo.), whose distaste for Burton was reciprocated by the California lawmaker, with great respect. He later referred to Bolling as the "greatest member of the House in modern history who never became Speaker." In 1976, he supported Bolling for House majority leader against Burton. When Bolling came in third to JIM WRIGHT (Tex.) in a preliminary round of voting, Obey backed Wright over Burton, who lost by one vote. Obey then tied his own fortunes to the leadership of House Speaker TIP O'NEILL and Majority Leader Wright.

Following O'Neill's election as Speaker, he asked Obey, who had been heading a commission to study House rules on ethics, to prepare a set of recommendations with an eye toward reform. Among the matters that the Obey Commission proposed were measures limiting the sources of outside income lawmakers could earn; mandating detailed disclosure of their personal finances; and restricting speaking fees, gifts from lobbyists, and personal use of campaign funds. With O'Neill's backing, the House approved the strongest ethics bill in the country's history in exchange for not repealing an automatic pay raise provided by earlier legislation. Opposition to the ethics bill, however, was so strong that a few years later, Obey was narrowly defeated in the Democratic Caucus for chairman of the Budget Committee, a position that O'Neil later wrote "he should have easily won."

Although close to O'Neill and Wright, the reform-minded Obey frequently clashed with one of O'Neill's lieutenants, Majority Whip DANIEL ROSTENKOWSKI of Chicago, who strongly resisted Obey's efforts to challenge the House rules on ethics. "If David Obey goes home and makes a town meeting, maybe he will have a beer," Rostenkowski complained. "If I go home, I have to go visit two or three restaurants, shake hands with people, let them know I am in town." After the rules were approved, Rostenkowski complained, "Why do I have to live and abide by the rules that [Obey is] writing for Wausau?"

In 1979, Obey and other reformers tried to win House approval for the appointment of an administrator and a system of internal audits that would help the Speaker manage the House bureaucracy and eliminate much of the spoils system that still remained in the lower chamber. Had such an administrative structure been in place, the House might have avoided the banking scandal that took place in the early 1990s. But this last effort at reform was too much for the lawmakers, who defeated it.

This internal conflict, even within the House leadership during the 1970s, compounded President Carter's problems in dealing with Congress, making it difficult for the Speaker to set an agenda or impose discipline on often-warring parties among Democratic lawmakers. Even reformers like Obey, however, shared a common disregard for Carter because of what they considered his own distaste of Congress, his lack of consultation with lawmakers, his more general lack of political skills, and his failure to support the traditional Democratic social agenda and entitlement programs.

In 1976, Obey and another liberal Democrat from Wisconsin, HENRY REUSS, had been instrumental in persuading the liberal congressman from Arizona, MORRIS UDALL, to seek the Democratic presidential nomination. Obey had campaigned actively on Udall's behalf and was keenly disappointed when he lost to Jimmy Carter. He attributed Udall's narrow loss in Michigan to remarks made by the black civil rights leader and supporter of Carter, ANDREW YOUNG, concerning Udall's Mormon heritage. Young said that while Carter had tried to open the front doors of his church to blacks, Udall's church "won't even let you in the back door." Although Young later apologized for those remarks, Obey never forgave him or Carter.

Years later, Obey expressed his belief to Reuss that had Udall won the election, he could have changed for the better the history of the last quarter of the 20th century. "[Udall] understood," he said in 1991, "that political death is not when you lose an election; political death is when you have the power to do something and don't do it." In contrast to Udall, President Carter had committed "political death" in Obey's view.

During the Carter administration, when Obey met with officials from the White House or conservative Democrats from the Senate seeking to maintain defense spending at the expense of social programs, he would often lose his temper. One such incident occurred in budget discussions following the Soviet Union's invasion of Afghanistan in December 1979. Although Obey agreed reluctantly to cuts in social spending in the 1981 budget in order to fight double-digit inflation, he was incensed by the insistence of Senator Ernest "Fritz" Hollings of South Carolina that further cuts were needed in order to increase military spending. The chairman of the Council of Economic Advisers, CHARLES SCHULTZE, described what took place: "About three quarters of the way through this process Fritz Hollings of South Carolina came in and just starts making a big spiel, 'well you can't cut defense,' and he just went on spieling numbers off for twenty minutes while Dave Obey got madder and madder and madder. ... Dave started to really rant and go on."

Obey was also upset by President Carter's decision in July 1979 to fire Secretary of Health, Education and Welfare (HEW) JOSEPH CALIFANO for disloyalty. "[I]t is inconceivable," he stated publicly, "that they should dismiss the only effective Secretary of HEW I have seen in my ten years in Congress while retaining second- and third-raters like [Office of Management and Budget director JAMES] MCINTYRE and [White House chief of staff HAMILTON] JORDAN."

After Carter's defeat in 1980, Obey worked closely with House Speaker O'Neill and such rising stars of the Democratic Party as Congressman Richard Gephardt of Missouri. As a senior member of the House Appropriations Committee and, for two years, its chair, he still remains one of the most powerful Democrats in Congress and a leader of old-style liberals in the House. He has been a strong critic of President George W. Bush's conduct of the war in Iraq and policy of homeland security in the United States, which, he maintains, has been inadequately funded.

In the presidential campaign of 2004, Obey supported Gephardt for the Democratic presidential nomination. That same year, he was reelected to his 18th full term in the House of Representatives. In 2005, he introduced legislation to put Congress on record against "coercive and abusive religious proselytizing" at the U.S. Air Force Academy. He also introduced an amendment to a spending bill that was later approved, restoring $100 million for Public Broadcasting that had been cut by the House Appropriations Committee.

O'Neill, Tip

(Thomas Phillip O'Neill, Jr.)
(1912–1994) *speaker of the House of Representatives*

Speaker of the House Thomas "Tip" O'Neill, 1978 *(Jimmy Carter Library)*

Thomas "Tip" O'Neill was Speaker of the House of Representatives during and after Jimmy Carter's term as president. When he became Speaker in 1977, he was delighted to have a Democrat in the White House. It quickly became apparent, however, that Carter was not the Democrat he had in mind. O'Neill's and Carter's personalities, values, and even physical appearances were totally opposite. In contrast to Carter's unassuming manner and appearance, O'Neill was a large man both in height and girth, with a bulbous nose and wavy white hair, deep voice, and reddish complexion, whose dress was dapper and whose presence filled a room. A product of an urban political culture, central to which were the neighborhood and the ward, where reciprocal favors were the currency of political activity and deals were transacted with the shake of a hand, O'Neill believed, as he was often quoted as saying, that all politics were local.

Carter, in contrast, was a product of rural Georgia. He also won his first elected office by successfully challenging in court a local political boss who had tried to rig the election. He won the presidency with little political obligation to the traditional Democratic political establishment. In sharp distinction to O'Neill, Carter had minimal tolerance for cloakroom politics or for most of the other premises on which the Speaker based his approach to conducting the nation's business. Although the Speaker backed most of the president's legislative agenda and proved to be a reliable ally of the White House on Capitol Hill, privately he had little regard for the president and even less for the Georgians whom Carter brought with him to Washington.

Born in Cambridge, Massachusetts, on December 9, 1912, O'Neill grew up in a middle-class Irish-Catholic family. He was given his nickname as a child, after the baseball player James "Tip" O'Neill (who was not related). His father worked in the brickyards before becoming an elected city councilor and then superintendent of sewers for the city of Cambridge. During the Great Depression, the senior O'Neill found jobs for the unemployed and brought coal to employees who did not have money to keep their families warm. The Depression and the New Deal that followed had a great impact on Tip O'Neill's later political thinking. Together, they convinced him of the munificence of government as an instrument of economic recovery and social reform, making him a lifelong believer in New Deal liberalism and an active foe of political and social conservatism.

In the same year that O'Neill graduated from Boston College (B.A., 1936), he ran successfully for the Massachusetts State House of Representatives. Winning reelection every two years, he was elected in 1949 as Speaker of the House, at age 36 the second-youngest person and the first Democrat and Irish-Catholic to hold that position. When Congressman John F. Kennedy gave up his safe seat in the U.S. House of Representatives to run for the U.S. Senate in 1952, O'Neill won a strongly contested election to replace him. He was reelected 16 times, usually with little or no competition, until he retired from Congress in 1986.

In contrast to his rapid rise to leadership in the state legislature, longevity on Capitol Hill and the rules of seniority were such that O'Neill did not attain the political prize he wanted so much, Speaker of the House, until 1977, when he was 64 years old. Prior to that time, he had served as Democratic Party whip (1971–73) and majority leader (1974–76). A backslapper and gifted storyteller, a bridge between the more liberal wing and the old guard of congressional Democrats, sometimes garrulous but almost always gracious, and a person for whom loyalty was the linchpin of leadership and deal-making the stuff of politics rather than the foe of effective governance, he was also a talented political infighter who had to overcome major challenges in his rise to leadership. When House Speaker Carl Albert of Oklahoma decided to retire in 1976, O'Neill succeeded him, having already dispatched his most serious rival, PHILLIP BURTON (Calif.), who had strong support among the liberal freshman class of 1974.

Even before Jimmy Carter took the oath of office on January 20, 1977, he and his staff had locked horns with O'Neill. In December 1976, the president-elect paid a courtesy call on the lawmaker. In a private conversation with Carter, O'Neill emphasized to him the need to set aside the anti-Washington rhetoric of his campaign in order to work closely with the Congress. Rather than agreeing with O'Neill, the president-elect stated that he intended to run his office the same way he had functioned as governor of Georgia and that he would take his case to the people if Congress tried to block his programs. He later gave the same message to a group of lawmakers. "Carter didn't seem to understand," O'Neill later wrote.

The speaker was also offended by an entirely different matter involving the issue of tickets to a preinaugural celebration at the Kennedy Center. O'Neill and his wife Millie had excellent seats in the presidential box, but the Speaker complained later that other seats he had requested from Carter's chief aide, HAMILTON JORDAN, for his family and friends were in the last row of the second balcony rather than down in front in a special section reserved for members of Congress. Worse, he accused Jordan of doing this purposely to slight him. Jordan denied these accusations, later writing that he had to scurry to get even the balcony seats. Nevertheless, O'Neill remained permanently alienated from Jordan, whom he claimed to have seen only three or four other times during Carter's entire presidency and whom he referred to as "Hannibal Jerken."

O'Neill was also turned off by what he regarded as Carter's lack of style—his insistence on carrying his own luggage, his elimination of chauffeurs and limousines for the White House staff, his orders to the U.S. Marine band not to play "Hail to the Chief" at his public appearances, and his decision to get rid of the presidential yacht *Sequoia*. While O'Neill thought it was admirable for the president and his wife, ROSALYNN CARTER, to appear as "just plain folks," he also believed strongly that the American public preferred a magisterial air in the White House and some pomp in their presidents, and that the *Sequoia* had provided an opportunity for previous presidents to mix with lawmakers and conduct business in a friendly and impressive environment.

Far more serious to O'Neill, however, was the fight Carter picked with Congress in February 1977, shortly after taking office, over the elimination of a number of water projects that had strong support on Capitol Hill but which the president regarded as unnecessary and wasteful. His action arose from a campaign pledge he had made to remove pork-barrel projects from the federal budget. Unlike other lawmakers on Capitol Hill, O'Neill was hardly affected by the president's hit list of projects to eliminate. What bothered the Speaker, though, as it did other lawmakers, was that Carter's action seemed to be just one of several examples of presidential indifference to Congress. Even the president acknowledged that his new administration had sometimes "inadvertently" given Congress cause for complaint by not conferring with the congressional leadership.

Despite his qualms about Carter and the White House staff, O'Neill felt bound by party loyalty to support the president as much as possible. In particular, he was instrumental in shepherding the administration's fiendishly complex energy proposal, at the heart of which was a tax on all domestic oil production and a standby gasoline tax to cut back on energy consumption, through the House of Representatives. He realized that the massive measure, with its many sections, would never make its way through the House if it were parceled out to the different committees that had jurisdiction over its different parts. Accordingly, he won a change in the House rules allowing him to appoint a special ad hoc committee to consider and report out the measure in its entirety. Then he set a firm deadline for a final report and made sure to include on the committee influential members from the authorization committees who might otherwise feel left out of the legislative process but were now wedded to the legislation. In this manner, O'Neill was able to get the bill, largely intact, through the House in August 1977. By any measurement, it was an outstanding achievement on the Speaker's part. Unfortunately for the White House, the legislation met an entirely different reception in the Senate, where it was largely gutted.

Publicly, O'Neill continued to support the president, even on such unpopular decisions on Capitol Hill as the one in June 1977 to kill the B-1 bomber program. The Speaker remarked that Carter was "the only President who doesn't have to rely on the Pentagon to make his military decisions." Realizing that the Social Security Trust Fund would be bankrupt if the payroll tax was not increased, as the White House was asking, O'Neill resorted to his earlier strategy with the energy bill of appointing an inclusive Social Security Task Force, headed by first-term representative Richard Gephardt (D-Mo.) to help win in December the largest increase in payroll taxes in history.

Even privately, O'Neill was touched by the president's efforts to reach out to him, such as when he was taken on Air Force One to Notre Dame University, where Carter delivered a commencement address in 1977 and both men received honorary doctorate degrees, or when he and his wife were invited to dinner in the private residence. He found the president to be gracious and a good listener, even when he did not agree with him. He considered Carter one of the most intelligent persons he had ever met, with an amazing knowledge and grasp of all the many matters that crossed his desk every day. O'Neill also developed a deep respect for the president's domestic adviser, STUART EIZENSTAT.

Yet throughout Carter's four years in office, there always remained an unbridgeable gap between the Speaker and the president. Their differences were fundamental. O'Neill loved the give-and-take of politics, Carter did not much care for politics at all. O'Neill was always focused on the plight of the poor, the unemployed, and the socially neglected. In the tradition of the New Deal, his solutions for dealing with these problems were extensions of existing entitlement programs and the addition of new ones such as universal health coverage. Although sharing O'Neill's concerns, Carter was focused on governmental efficiency, fighting inflation, and balancing the budget. O'Neill's concerns invariably meant increased governmental expenditures, Carter's meant lower levels of spending even if that required cutting back on existing programs and eliminating or delaying new ones such as health coverage.

O'Neill objected, therefore, to the president's decision less than three months after taking office to forego, on the grounds of fighting inflation, a $50 tax rebate for every American as a way of stimulating the economy. Not only did he regard this sudden reversal of policy an indication of the White House's political ineptness and an embarrassment to lawmakers who had pushed for the measure on the president's behalf just a few days earlier, it also indicated that the president's highest priority would be to deal with inflation and balance the budget irrespective of other economic or social concerns. Similarly, the Speaker was disturbed that the president seemed to be taking much of his economic advice from ARTHUR BURNS, the conservative Republican chair of the Federal Reserve Board.

Furthermore, O'Neill grew unhappy with Carter's increased concern with foreign policy to the neglect, in his view, of the nagging problems at home. "Unemployment was rising, inflation was soaring, and interest rates were going crazy," he later wrote about the president's regular breakfast meetings with legislative leaders, "but the president preferred to discuss Angola, Rhodesia, the Middle East, and just about every other place under the sun."

Mostly, though, O'Neill's major complaints about the president remained Carter's domestic priorities and the White House's political ineptitude. Prime examples of these problems, in his view, were Carter's address to the nation on July 15, 1979, and his firing two days later of several cabinet members. By this time, a lack of confidence in the administration was taking hold throughout the country, caused by rising inflation, growing unemployment, and rapidly increasing energy prices. After canceling a planned address to the nation on the energy crisis and then spending 11 days at Camp David meeting with leading Americans from all walks of life, the president delivered a nationally televised speech in which he talked about a "crisis of spirit" in America. Although he never used the term *malaise*, it rapidly became the catchword for his message. Two days later, the president accepted the resignations of five members of his cabinet.

O'Neill, who had attended several of the sessions Carter held at Camp David, thought that the address and the president's subsequent shake-up up of his cabinet were the height of political folly. "The responsibility of leadership isn't to dwell on the negative, but to offer a positive way out of the morass," he later commented. The president blundered again when he purged his cabinet instead of his staff. The Speaker was particularly angered by Carter's dismissal of Secretary of Health, Education and Welfare JOSEPH CALIFANO, who was personally and ideologically close to O'Neill; indeed, Califano regarded the Speaker as something of a father figure. O'Neill was aggrieved, moreover, that the president had acted without keeping him informed.

Although the immediate public response to the president's July 15 speech was generally favorable, the response to his cabinet shakeup was disastrous. Carter fell so low in the polls that many political observers thought it unlikely that he would even win renomination in 1980. Ready to replace him at the head of the Democratic ticket was Massachusetts senator EDWARD KENNEDY, whose decision to seek the Democratic nomination in 1980 placed O'Neill in awkward position. Both men shared similar political ideologies, opposed the president's own set of priorities, and came from the same state. But they were not close political allies. O'Neill's career owed much to former House Speaker John McCormack, an inveterate opponent of the Kennedy family in Massachusetts politics whose nephew, former attorney general Edward McCormack, had been denied the Democrat nomination for the Senate seat held by Kennedy since 1963 because of the family's financial muscle and political influence. O'Neill also felt a sense of party obligation to the president, and he did not think Kennedy could be elected in 1980 because of the lingering scandal surrounding the accidental drowning in 1969 of Mary Jo Kopechne after a car driven by Kennedy, in which she was a passenger, went off a bridge while they were driving home from a party in Chappaquiddick, Cape Cod.

The Speaker was therefore torn by Kennedy's candidacy for president and finessed the problem by remaining neutral in the contest between the president and the senator. At the Democratic convention in 1980, however, he played a backstage role in getting a very reluctant Kennedy to endorse the president for reelection in exchange for some concessions in the party platform by the Carter-controlled convention.

O'Neill had political problems of his own during the Carter administration, largely having to do with accepting favors and gifts from a wealthy South Korean lobbyist and intelligence agent, Tongsun Park. In 1973 and 1974, he had also allowed Park to give lavish birthday parties in his honor that were attended by some of Washington's most influential luminaries and political figures. Although a number of other lawmakers also accepted gifts and favors from Park, and the controversial events had happened before the Carter administration took office, the scandal, dubbed Koreagate by *New York Times* columnist WILLIAM SAFIRE, broke in 1977. The Justice Department appointed a special counsel, Leon Jaworski, the special prosecutor during the Watergate affair, to investigate the charges; the House Ethics Committee conducted its own investigation. In both cases, O'Neill was acquitted of the charges against him, but they caused him considerable embarrassment.

In 1980, after Carter was defeated in his bid for reelection by RONALD REAGAN and the Republicans captured the Senate, O'Neill became the most powerful Democrat to hold office. The Republicans ridiculed him as a cigar-chomping wheeler-dealer, backroom politician, and free-spending New Deal liberal. Accepting his role as the nation's leading Democrat, O'Neill responded by accusing the White House of serving the interests of the rich and powerful at the expense of the nation's powerless through tax and budget cuts that drove up the national debt and threatened such popular programs as Social Security and Medicare and Medicaid. Although he was able to preserve most of the entitlement programs enacted over the last half-century of Democratic dominance of government and even to increase Democratic control of the House in 1982, he was not able to hold back the conservative tide that became the Reagan revolution.

In 1986, O'Neill decided to retire from politics and the job he loved so much, having served as Speaker of the House longer than any of his predecessors. In 1994, he died of cancer at the age of 81.

Percy, Charles Harting
(1919–) *member of the Senate*

Charles Harting Percy was in his second term as U.S. senator from Illinois when Jimmy Carter was elected president in 1976. He was regarded highly enough nationally to be considered a potential candidate for the presidency. A liberal Republican who often found himself on opposite sides of issues from most other members of his own party, he frequently supported the president's legislative agenda. During the Carter administration, however, he was best known as one of the senators who helped bring about the resignation of BERT LANCE as director of the Office of Management and Budget (OMB).

Percy was born on September 27, 1919, in Pensacola, Florida, and his family moved to Chicago, Illinois, soon thereafter. While still a young man, he impressed his Sunday school teacher, Joseph McNabb, the president of Bell and Howell, at that time a small manufacturer of cameras. After Percy graduated from the University of Chicago (B.A., 1941), McNabb offered him a position with Bell and Howell, and Percy accepted. After serving in the navy for three years (1942–45), he returned to the company, and he was its president by 1949. During his presidency, sales skyrocketed, sales grew 32-fold, and the company went public on the New York Stock Exchange.

Percy's interest in politics began in the 1950s when President Dwight D. Eisenhower encouraged him to seek a political career. During the mid-1950s, he worked as a fund-raiser for the Illinois Republican Party; he also wrote an impressive proposal for the long-range goals of the National Republican Party. This led to his appointment as chair of the platform committee of the 1960 National Republican Convention.

In 1964, Percy ran unsuccessfully for governor of Illinois against the incumbent, Otto Kerner. Two years later, he ran for the U.S. Senate, upsetting the highly respected Democratic incumbent, Paul Douglas, who had taught him economics when he was a student at the University of Chicago. During the campaign, Percy suffered a personal tragedy when one of his twin daughters, Valerie, was murdered in the family's home.

On Capitol Hill, Percy quickly distinguished himself s a senator who spoke openly on a variety of issues and as a Republican who voted for such programs as increased federal aid to education, expansion of the food-stamp program, and the establishment of a Consumer Protection Agency. As a member of the Senate's Special Committee on Aging, he took a particular interest in providing for the elderly. He worked to include provisions for the elderly in social welfare legislation, and he helped gain approval in 1972 of a measure that tied Social Security benefits to cost-of-living increases. In 1974, he outlined his views on the elderly in a book, *Growing Old in the Country.*

Percy's liberal views on domestic issues put him at odds with members of his own party, including, after 1969, President RICHARD NIXON. In the five-and-a-half years that Nixon was president, relations between him and Percy grew increasingly strained. Not only did Percy take a more liberal position than Nixon on many issues, he opposed the president's nomination of Clement Haynsworth and G. Harrold Carswell to the U.S. Supreme Court. An early and vocal opponent of the Vietnam War, he disapproved of President Nixon's handling of the war. In 1970, he voted for the Cooper-Church Amendment to cut off funds for combat operations in Cambodia. The following year, he voted against extension of the draft, and in 1972 he voted to cut off funds for combat operations by the end of the year. In 1973, he cosponsored the War Powers Act, which limited the ability of the president to engage U.S. troops in combat without the consent of Congress. Percy was also one of the earliest Republicans to break with Nixon over his handling of the Watergate affair. He drafted the resolution that called for the appointment of a special Watergate prosecutor, and he was one of the first Republican senators to state that Nixon should resign his office for the good of the country.

Regarded as one of the rising new stars of the Republican Party, Percy considered running for the Republican presidential nomination in 1976 but decided against it. During the Carter administration, he supported much of the White House's legislative program. In 1977, he was one of the few Republican senators to speak out in favor of the president's energy program. "It's the greatest challenge any peacetime President ever gave the nation," Percy commented after Carter spoke to the country about the energy crisis. He also supported the administration's proposal for fair housing legislation, voted in favor the Panama Canal Treaties, backed the White House's efforts at nuclear nonproliferation, and endorsed the sale of F-15 fighters to Saudi Arabia. At the same time, he criticized his own party for not being sensitive enough to the needs of the poor and the underprivileged. "We have to get the party out of the country clubs, out of a Caucasian atmosphere," he said. "As long as the Republican Party takes a Neanderthal point of view, I don't see why it deserves to win."

As the ranking minority member of the Senate's Governmental Affairs Committee, however, he helped bring about the resignation of OMB director Bert Lance, Carter's closest friend in the administration. The Lance affair, which dominated the headlines for much of the summer of 1977, involved allegations of inappropriate business and banking practices by Lance while he was president of the Calhoun National Bank and the National Bank of Georgia (NBG). The charges included permitting sizable overdrafts on the personal accounts of bank officers and their families, arranging loans for himself with correspondent banks at unusually low interest rates, and improperly using a corporate airplane for his private use.

The Lance affair began innocently enough when President Carter asked the Government Affairs Committee to allow Lance a delay in selling stock he owned in the NBG beyond the date by which the OMB director had promised to sell the stock. The president had earlier directed that all his appointees divest themselves of any asset that might lead to a conflict of interest. Because of unusual circumstances, Carter said, Lance would otherwise be faced with a huge financial loss. The columnist WILLIAM SAFIRE subsequently accused Lance of peddling his influence to secure a loan with deferred interest from the First National Bank of Chicago, and the *Washington Post* claimed the loan was made in return for a $200,000 deposit of NBG funds in a noninterest-bearing account. As a result, the chairperson of the Governmental Affairs Committee, ABRAHAM RIBICOFF (D-Conn.), asked Lance to appear before the committee for an explanation. After Lance testified that he was paying a respectable interest on the loan, the senators appeared satisfied—except for Percy, who wanted to probe further. The committee nevertheless granted Lance the extension he sought.

Over the following weeks, matters began to unravel for Lance. On August 18 the Comptroller's Office issued a blistering report accusing Lance of having engaged in inappropriate patterns of borrowing, then informed the White House that it was referring Lance's private use of the NBG airplane to the Justice Department and the Internal Revenue Service for investigation. Almost overnight, national attention was focused on the allegations against Lance. Over the next four weeks, demands grew for the OMB director's resignation. On Labor Day, Ribicoff and Percy met with the president to urge that Lance be asked either to resign or take a leave of absence; the president turned down their request. Appearing on the White House lawn afterward, the two senators charged that Lance might have embezzled funds from the Calhoun Bank. Their accusation was based on testimony by a former vice president of the bank who had earlier pleaded guilty to embezzling $1 million from the institution and who said that Lance had been an accomplice to the crime. Later, Percy charged that Lance might have backdated three checks totaling $196,000 for the purpose of taking an improper tax deduction. Percy also expressed outrage at the revelation that Lance had used a corporate plane for private purposes.

On September 15, 1977, Lance appeared before the Ribicoff committee to answer the charges made against him. In an opening statement and then in three days of testimony, he accused members of the committee and others of defaming his character without consideration of due process or fair play. The OMB director proved to be an effective witness, and after his appearance, many observers thought he might be able to keep his job. By the time Lance testified, however, sentiment against him had become so strong that Senate Majority Leader ROBERT BYRD (D-W.Va.) went to the White House to tell the president that for the good of his own administration, Lance had to resign. Carter had little choice other than to coax his close friend into tendering his resignation on September 21, 1977.

The Lance affair left an indelible mark on the Carter administration. It brought into question President Carter's promise as a candidate to be worthy of the trust of the American people. But it also left Percy in the unsavory position of appearing as "chief prosecutor" of Lance. No other senator, including Ribicoff, had been so dogged in his determination to go after the OMB director. Indeed, Press Secretary JODY POWELL was so angry at Percy's accusations concerning Lance's improper use of a corporate plane that he leaked a story that, as president of Bell and Howell, Percy had regularly flown on a corporate jet. As it turned out, the jet did not exist, and Powell immediately apologized for his attempt to discredit Percy. But the Illinois senator, who had built a reputation as a man of conscience and high character, appeared meanspirited, partisan, and suspect in his conduct during the Lance affair.

As a result, Percy found himself in serious political trouble as he sought reelection to a third term as senator in 1978. At one point in the summer, he had enjoyed a 20 percent lead in the polls over his Democratic opponent, Alex Seith, a wealthy Chicago lawyer who had never run for political office before. By October, Seith was leading Percy in the polls by 6 percent. Intensely disliked by conservatives within his own party, Percy had alienated moderates and liberals by his conduct during the Lance affair. His vote in favor of selling jets to Saudi Arabia also hurt him with the influential Jewish vote in Illinois. Yet he was able to turn the election around and win a third term with a last-minute television appeal to the voters in which he promised to hew a more conservative line if reelected, including cuts in spending and taxes.

In 1981, Percy became chair of the Foreign Relations Committee. In that capacity, he took a special interest in the Middle East and became a harsh critic of Israeli policy in the Arab-Israeli dispute. "Many Israeli acts seriously harm our relations with Israeli's Arab neighbors," he told the Senate in 1982, "yet a strong American position throughout the Middle East is in Israel's interest as well."

Notwithstanding his promises to the electorate, Percy remained within the moderate wing of the Republican Party. At the 1980 Republican National Convention, he clashed with conservatives over the Republican platform plank that urged the appointment of judges "who respect traditional family values and the sanctity of human life." At a convention dominated by right-wingers intent on nominating RONALD REAGAN for president, he was mocked for opposing the plank, even by members of his own Illinois delegation. To their cheers and laughter, conservative congressman Henry Hyde wondered, "who could be against traditional family values."

In 1984, Percy ran for a fourth term as a conservative Reaganite. Nevertheless, he was without a political base since the conservatives were unforgiving of past "heresies" and actually worked against his reelection. At the same time, his opponent was Congressman Paul Simon, a prolabor Democrat who won the vote of liberals who had supported Percy in the past.

After his defeat in the election, Percy established a Washington, D.C.–based trade and technology investment consulting firm, Charles Percy & Associates, Inc. He also continued to be a harsh critic of Israeli policy toward the Palestinians and of the American Israel Public Affairs Committee, a pro-Israeli lobby in Washington, which, he strongly suggested, had contributed to his defeat in 1984.

Peterson, Esther Eggertson

(1906–1997) *special assistant to the president for consumer affairs*

Esther Peterson led a long life that defied convention even though she was not defiant by nature. A practicing Mormon whose religious upbringing had emphasized the role of a woman as wife and homemaker, she was a career women who raised four children. A union organizer and consumer advocate, she was hired as a vice president for consumer affairs by a large food chain in an industry that was often the target of union and consumer activity. A determined advocate, she practiced the velvet glove rather than the iron fist. Highly successful in most everything she sought to achieve, as special assistant to the president for consumer affairs, she failed to gain what she most desired from the Carter administration: a Consumer Protection Agency.

The daughter of Danish immigrants, Esther Eggertson was born in Provo, Utah, still a frontier community, on December 9, 1906. Although her father was a superintendent of schools, family life revolved around farming. Helping with the farm in a frontier community and growing up as a Mormon taught Esther the value of hard work and personal responsibility. "'Do what is right: let the consequences follow' was the theme that was deep in me," she recalled in an interview she gave two years before she died.

After graduating from Brigham Young University with a degree in physical education (B.A., 1927), Eggertson earned a graduate degree at Columbia University (M.Ed., 1930), where she met her future husband, Oliver Peterson, a political activist who encouraged her interest in social activism. After graduating, she began teaching at a private girls' school in Boston and volunteered to teach physical education and gymnastics to garment workers at a local YMCA in the evening. While there, she became outraged to learn that her students had stopped coming in the evening because they were having to spend more time sewing a new model of dress at no additional pay per garment. She therefore organized a strike of the seamstresses, but, resorting to the tactic of the velvet glove, she got upper-middle-class women to demonstrate in front of police who were mounted on horses and escorting strikebreakers. "I had fancy women come down with their furs and fancy coats, and, boy, those horses did not come up on them," she later remarked.

The strike became a turning point in Esther Peterson's life. During the 1930s, she taught in the Summer School for Women's Workers at Bryn Mawr College in a program that she described as combining "socialism and Shakespeare" for low-income women workers. In 1938, she became a union organizer for the American Federation of Teachers. The next year, she moved to New York City to work for the Amalgamated Clothing Workers of America (ACWA). During World War II, she codirected the ACWA Committee on War Activities and sought to organize other nonunion workers, especially African-American women, into the union. She also sought to raise the minimum wage and campaigned for both Franklin D. Roosevelt and Harry S. Truman in presidential elections.

After the war, Peterson accompanied her husband to Sweden, where he was labor attaché at the U.S. embassy. This gave her the opportunity to work with European women trade leaders. She also was able to spend time with Eleanor Roosevelt, serving as the former first lady's personal escort when she visited Sweden. Her meeting with Roosevelt was, according to Peterson, another defining moment of her life. "Oh, we drove all over the place," she recounted. "And I fell in love with her, just absolutely in love with her." From her experience in Sweden, Peterson developed a working relationship with Roosevelt that lasted until the first lady's death in 1962.

Returning to the United States in 1957, Peterson continued her organizing activities, working for the International Ladies' Garment Workers Union (ILGWU) and the Amalgamated Clothing Workers of America. By 1961, she had gained sufficient prominence within the trade-union movement that President John F. Kennedy appointed her assistant secretary of labor and director of the Women's Bureau responsible for administering labor laws concerning women. At Peterson's urging, Kennedy created the Presidential Commission on the Status of Women and put her in charge of running it. To chair the commission, she selected Mrs. Roosevelt. Also at Peterson's urging, and with Vice President Lyndon Johnson's lobbying efforts on Capitol Hill, Kennedy pushed through Congress the Equal Pay Act of 1963, making it illegal to pay women less than men for the same work.

After becoming president following Kennedy's assassination in 1963, Johnson established the White House Office of Consumer Affairs. To run the new office, he appointed Peterson, whom he also made his special assistant for consumer affairs. Peterson had great admiration for Johnson's public stance on women's issues and his support of the consumer. She particularly appreciated his backing of the proposed Equal Rights Amendment and his effort to bring more women into government. But she objected to his risqué jokes, often based on the female anatomy. She also noted that his propensity for locker-room language created discomfort for women around him.

Out of government after Johnson left office, Peterson, 65, accepted a position as vice president for consumer affairs at Giant Food Inc., the largest supermarket chain in the Washington, D.C.–Baltimore area. This upset a number of consumer groups who had come to identify her as the voice of the consumer because of her work in the Johnson administration; they wondered how she could work for a business and represent consumers at the same time. But throughout her career, Peterson had relied heavily on listening—asking for an opinion on a proposal, for instance—and persuasion rather than confrontation to achieve her ends. This was the policy she pursued at Giant Food. Agreeing to leave her position after six months if her policies hurt the company financially, she was able to persuade the food chain, before they were required by federal law, to enact product-expiration dates, unit pricing, ingredient labeling, and nutritional labeling. The policies proved so popular that other supermarket chains began to emulate Giant. At times featured in Giant's advertisements, she became a familiar figure at its stores because of her grandmotherly appearance, complete with grey, braided hair pinned on top of her head.

Both as governor of Georgia and as a candidate for president, Jimmy Carter had spoken out on the need to protect the rights of consumers. Although he had not campaigned explicitly for the establishment of a Consumer Protection Agency (CPA), he allied himself during the campaign with the nation's leading spokesman on behalf of the consumer, Ralph Nader, whom he had invited to his home in Plains after receiving the Democratic nomination. As president, Carter made the establishment of a CPA one of his early goals. On Nader's recommendation, and because her name had also become synonymous with consumer activism, the president invited Peterson to become his special assistant for consumer affairs, the same position she had held during the Johnson administration. Explaining to her his plans to establish a CPA, Carter added that he wanted "the federal government to think like the consumer would think." Although she was already 70 years old, Peterson agreed to accept the position.

Much to Peterson's regret, Congress failed to pass legislation establishing a CPA. Business interests launched an intense and well-funded attack against the measure, leading Peterson to remark at one time that she was "frightened for [her] country after seeing this demonstration of corporate power." Opponents of the CPA were able to argue successfully that the establishment of such an agency would merely add another layer of federal regulation to the Washington bureaucracy.

In an interview in 1981, Peterson blamed herself for not using her authority as special assistant to the president to push harder for the CPA, especially with the congressional liaison office headed by FRANK MOORE. "I would have been on the Hill lots more, lobbying what I felt," she remarked. "I was a little reluctant to do that because Frank Moore and I didn't get along too well. ... I didn't want them to think that I was sticking my nose in their affairs." With Moore's office unenthusiastic about the legislative prospects for a CPA, the president decided not to expend the energy necessary to win its approval.

Instead, Carter did by executive order what he was not able to do by legislative fiat. He made Peterson head of a newly created Consumer Affairs Council and gave her authority to oversee new consumer-advocacy programs with 43 federal agencies. She was also given input into all administration proposals that affected consumers. With this mandate, she worked in specific and practical ways to protect and enhance the rights of consumers and to make government at all levels more responsive to consumer needs. She provided consumers with information on a wide range of matters, from how to save on food and energy bills to how to form neighborhood co-ops. She represented consumer interests at public utility hearings, and she appealed to grocery stores not to raise prices during times of inflation. She also convinced Carter to sign an executive order, later repealed by RONALD REAGAN, banning the export of products considered unsafe in the United States.

The president and Peterson developed a special fondness for each other. According to PETER BOURNE, the president's special assistant for health issues and, later, biographer, Carter formed a closer attachment to Peterson than he did to any of his other non-Georgian appointees. In 1981, just before leaving office, he presented her with the nation's highest civilian award, the Presidential Medal of Freedom. In 1988, he asked her to represent the administration at the Democratic National Convention, remarking that she represented the best of what his administration stood for. As for Peterson, she later remarked that she "could not underscore strongly enough [her] belief in this man."

After leaving the White House, although she was then approaching her mid-70s, Peterson took a position with the National Association of Professional Insurance Agents as its consumer adviser, concentrating on the problems of the elderly. At the same time, she continued to serve on the board of Consumers Union, one of the nation's leading consumer-advocacy groups. Also a lobbyist for the International Organization of Consumers Unions, she helped win—over the objections of the U.S. delegation—approval by the United Nations General Assembly of a measure that called for making public a list of all products the United States had banned, withdrawn, or restricted in American markets.

Peterson ended her public career when she was appointed by President Bill Clinton in 1993 to serve in a largely honorary role as a member of the U.S. delegation to the United Nations. She died on December 20, 1997, at the age of 91.

Powell, Jody

(Joseph Lester Powell, Jr.)
(1943–) *press secretary*

Press secretary to President Jimmy Carter and one of his most trusted advisers, Jody Powell was also one of the most controversial figures within the administration. His loyalty to the president was unquestioned, but his relationship with the Washington press corps was frequently turbulent. Critics of the administration often pointed to Powell as an example of the harm to the president caused by his over-reliance on a small group of young, and mostly inexperienced, fellow Georgians who had been with him for all or most of his political career.

Born Joseph Lester Powell, Jr., in Cordele, Georgia, on September 30, 1943, the young Jody grew up in nearby Vienna, about 25 miles northeast of Plains. A bright student, he was accepted into the U.S. Air Force Academy, but, one semester before graduation, he was expelled for cheating. He then attended Georgia State University from which he graduated in 1966, and Emory University, where he worked on a Master's degree in political science.

Powell met Jimmy Carter through the future president's uncle, Senator Hugh Carter. In 1969, he became one of group of students who volunteered to work in Carter's second gubernatorial campaign. Traveling the state as the candidate's driver and personal assistant and a few years older than most of the other volunteers, Powell became close to Carter, who was impressed by his knowledge of politics. Both men also came from similar backgrounds and were churchgoing Baptists. Carter became a father figure to Powell; Powell became Carter's alter ego. As Carter emerged as one of the leading contenders for the governorship and the state's media assigned more reporters to the campaign, Powell's responsibilities shifted more and more to those of a press secretary, briefing reporters and issuing statements on Carter's behalf. Not surprisingly, after being elected governor, Carter appointed Powell as his press secretary. Even more than that, Powell became one of his most trusted advisers.

Yet Powell's advice was not always the best. For example, he urged the governor during the 1972 Democratic convention to nominate Alabama's racist governor, GEORGE WALLACE, for president, something Carter refused to do and something that almost certainly would have haunted him had he still chosen to run for president in 1976. Powell also expressed serious reservations when Carter began to meet with his other close advisers in October 1972 to consider running for president. He was mainly concerned that the governor's political enemies in the state, especially Lieutenant Governor LESTER MADDOX, would ridicule Carter for his presumption that he should be president.

Once the governor made the decision to run, however, Powell became one of the team,

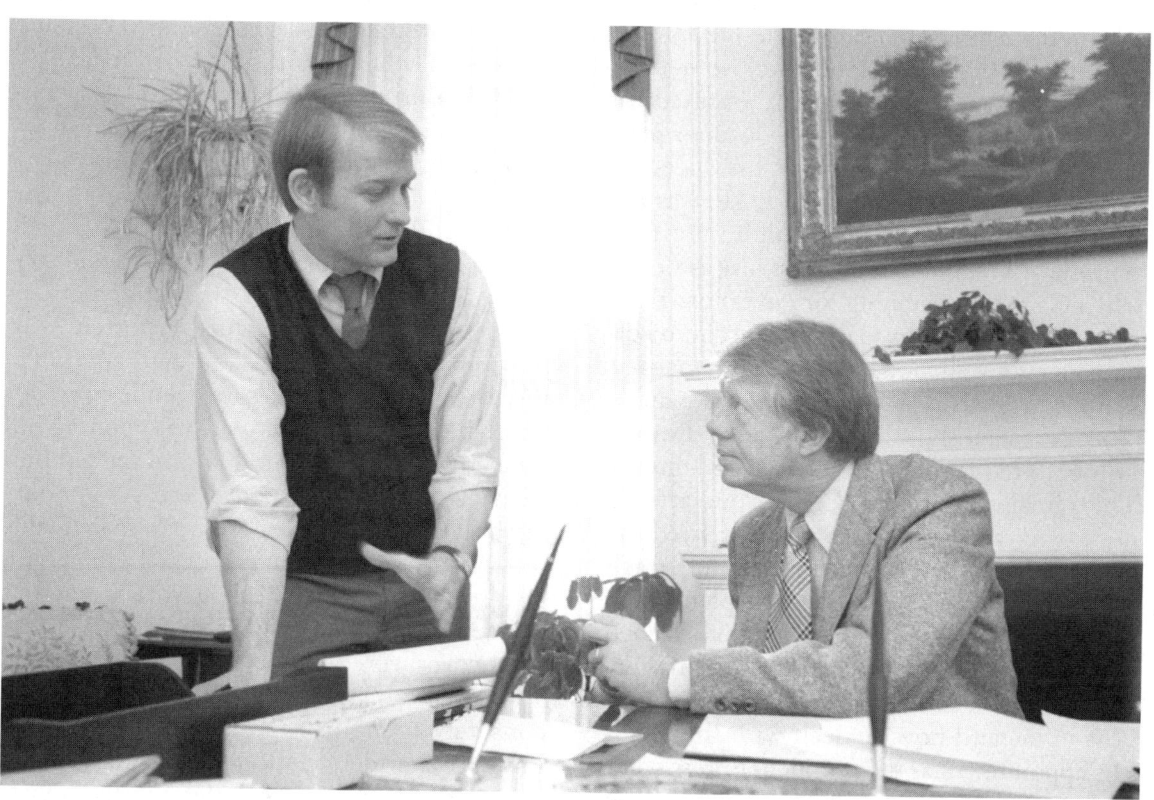

Press Secretary Jody Powell confers with President Carter, 1977. *(Jimmy Carter Library)*

headed by HAMILTON JORDAN, that laid the foundation for Carter's campaign. Unlike Jordan, who resigned his position as executive secretary to the governor in 1973 to become staff director of the Democratic National Campaign Committee, Powell remained in Atlanta as a member of the governor's staff. Like other staff members, he became involved in Carter's effort to reorganize state government, handling press coverage and serving as liaison between the governor's office and the Public Awareness Advisory Committee, a public-interest group whose purpose was to sell the reorganization plan to the state's voters. But increasingly Powell turned his interest to the presidential campaign.

Starting in 1975, after Carter began his campaign in earnest, Powell assumed much the same responsibilities he had during Carter's 1970 gubernatorial campaign. He traveled with the presidential candidate, sometimes in a small plane, other times in a rented car. Sometimes Powell acted as an events planner, other times as a critic of his speeches, yet at other times as a strategist. He was also Carter's spokesperson, with full authority to represent the candidate's views, just as he had when Carter was running for governor. There was no one closer to Carter on a day-to-day basis than Powell, not even campaign manager Hamilton Jordan. As Carter later explained, "Jody was almost always at my side." Powell's loyalty to the candidate was fierce and intense. This remained so even as Carter's quest for the presidency appeared less quixotic, rented cars were replaced by busloads of reporters tracking the candidate, and one-engine planes were replaced by Carter's own commercial-size jet.

Following Carter's election as the nation's 39th president in 1976, Powell's fidelity to his boss influenced how he dealt with the media. His appointment as the president's press secretary was never much in doubt, given his closeness to Carter and the role he had played in the campaign. In fact, his was one of the first appointments the president-elect made. As press secretary, though, Powell's relationship with reporters was stormy. In a book he wrote after leaving office, *The Other Side of the Story* (1984), Powell argued that throughout Carter's four years in office, the press had treated the administration unfairly and inaccurately. He accused reporters of being elitists scornful of the fact that a southern governor from a rural background whose closest advisers were young southerners like himself, supposedly unsophisticated in the ways of Washington, could capture the White House and lead the nation effectively. Among the journalists for whom he had particular contempt were the syndicated columnists JACK ANDERSON and Joseph Kraft. But he also accused such other notables as Leslie Stahl of CBS News and Sam Donaldson of ABC News of conducting themselves inappropriately or, in the case of Donaldson, of fabricating stories out of whole cloth. More generally, he used such terms as *brats* and *dilettantes* to describe the White House press corps.

Yet as Powell himself later acknowledged, he was a chain smoker with a nervous disposition and a fiery temper that he sometimes failed to control. He assailed reporters with frequent tongue-lashings and pejoratives. He was even inclined at times to juvenile antics for which he later apologized, such as phoning Bill Lynch of NBC News at 3:00 A.M. to "tell him what a lowlife degenerate he was" or pouring a glass of wine over ABC's Sam Donaldson. According to correspondent Leslie Stahl, he also had difficulty dealing with women at a time when only a few of the White House press corps were female.

Despite his personal faults and what he considered unfair reporting by the press, Powell was widely respected by White House reporters. He gave daily briefings and sometimes ad hoc sessions. He was witty, humorous, and generally candid with the press. Because he was a part of the president's inner circle—something that had not always been the case with former press secretaries—they also tended to place greater value on his briefings than they might have with someone else. Although Powell later acknowledged that on at least two occasions he had lied to reporters—during the 1978 Camp David negotiations between Israeli prime minister MENACHEM BEGIN and Egyptian president ANWAR SADAT when it appeared that Sadat was about to break off the talks and return home, and then again in 1980 when he knew, but denied knowledge of, a plan to rescue the American hostages seized in Iran—the press did not make a major issue of these lies.

Furthermore, as an unknown presidential candidate prior to the caucus and primary season of 1976, Carter had cultivated the national press. He continued to do so after entering the Oval Office, even though he grew increasingly disenchanted with the media and reporters came to dislike him. The president and Powell adopted the policy of having two televised news conference each month (a policy that they both came to regret and later modified). At his press conferences, Carter was well prepared, articulate, and responsive to questions. Powell also promised the press an "open presidency," including opening up some cabinet sessions to press coverage and making the president's full daily appointments schedule public. While some of these promises proved impractical, the more important ones were kept.

In a survey conducted by Robert Pierpoint of CBS News and published in *Parade Magazine* in 1982, veteran White House reporters rated the nation's seven presidents from Dwight D. Eisenhower through RONALD REAGAN. Both Powell and Carter earned the second-highest ratings behind only President Kennedy in terms of their dealings with the press. They were evaluated in such categories as candor, informative value, and press-conference skills.

Powell's importance within the Carter administration extended beyond his position as press secretary. Having direct access to the Oval Office, he participated in most of the major policy discussions at the White House. Having been so close to Carter during most of his political career, Powell could also be unabashedly forthright with the president, letting him know when he was going astray, trying to do too much, or causing himself and his administration political harm. Yet while Powell was not afraid to express his views on matters of substance or presidential behavior, he refrained from getting overly involved in the decision-making process because, as he later explained, taking sides could pose obstacles to the type of internal news gathering that he needed in order to do his job effectively and might even raise questions about his own credibility when he was on the losing side of a policy decision.

After leaving the White House following Carter's defeat for reelection in 1980, Powell became a syndicated columnist for the *Dallas Times Herald*, the Los Angeles Times Syndicate, and ABC News. He also joined the lecture circuit and was a frequent commentator on news shows. In his columns and appearances, he remained critical of the press, stating that it was overly sensitive to criticism and failed to police itself for inaccurate and false reporting. In 1987, he went to work in the Washington, D.C., office of an advertising agency. Three years later, he cofounded Powell-Tate, now one of Washington's most successful public relations and lobbying firms.

Powell, Lewis Franklin, Jr.

(1907–1998) *associate justice, U.S. Supreme Court*

Variously described as "the quintessential southern aristocratic," "the quintessential establishment lawyer," and "the paradigm of a lawyer turned justice," Louis F. Powell, Jr., came to the Supreme Court after a long career as a corporate lawyer, community leader, and pillar of the American legal profession. The one black mark in his otherwise distinguished career was during the 1950s and 1960s when, as chairman of the Richmond (Virginia) School Board and then as a member of the Virginia State Board of Education, he did nothing to implement the integration of the Richmond and Virginia schools following the historic Supreme Court decision in *Brown v. Board of Education of Topeka.* The irony was that as a member of the Court in 1978, his was the decisive vote in the landmark case affirming the principle of affirmative action in civil rights cases, *Regents of the University of California v. Bakke.*

Powell was born on September 19, 1907, in Suffolk, Virginia, but was raised in Richmond, where his father was owner of a manufacturing firm. He received both his undergraduate and law degrees from Washington and Lee University (B.A., 1929; LL.B., 1931), serving as student body president and a member of Phi Beta Kappa as an undergraduate and graduating first in his class as a law student. Following a year of graduate work studying under Felix Frankfurter at the Harvard Law School (LL. M., 1932), he worked for a small law firm in Richmond before joining the prestigious firm of Hunton, William, Gay, Powell & Gibson.

During World War II, Powell served as an intelligence officer in the Army Air Force, rising in rank from lieutenant to colonel and working in a top-secret capacity decoding German war messages. After being discharged from the service in 1946, he returned to his law firm, where he spent the rest of his career until his appointment to the Supreme Court. He built up a lucrative practice as a corporate lawyer and served on the board of 11 major corporations.

Powell also became a civic leader, serving as chairman of the Richmond School Board (1952–61) and then as a member of the Virginia State Board of Education (1961–69). Unlike other office holders and community leaders in Virginia, he did not oppose the mandate of the Supreme Court following the 1954 *Brown* decision. But he also did nothing to hasten the integration of Virginia's schools, and not until 1960 did African-American students begin to attend Richmond's hitherto all-white schools. Powell claimed that the Richmond School Board lacked the authority to reassign students to different schools, but the board failed to exercise the power it did have to prohibit dual-attendance areas—zones which were designated either white or colored. Furthermore, as a member of the Virginia State Board of Education, he supported its decision to leave control of student placement to local school boards, and he endorsed its recommendation against "any general or unnecessary reallocation or reassignment of students" currently in the system. As a result, until the Supreme Court ruled in *Green v. County School Board of New Kent County* (1968) that local school boards needed to integrate immediately, a number of school districts in the state remained segregated.

Powell's ineffectiveness in helping to bring about the integration of schools in Virginia was one reason why the Black Caucus, a group of African-American members of the House of Representatives established in 1969, in Congress refused to support his nomination to the Supreme Court in 1971. But because he did not openly oppose school integration and, in fact, urged compliance with the Supreme Court's decision at a time when much of the South was locked in a campaign of resistance against the Court, he gained a reputation among those who knew him as a political moderate. This image was further enhanced by his activities within the legal profession. Long active in the American Bar Association (ABA), he served as president of the ABA (1964–65), as president of the

American College of Trial Lawyers (1968–70), and as president of the American Bar Foundation (1969–71). In these capacities, he was a strong advocate of providing legal services to the poor, making a key decision to cooperate with the federal government's Legal Services Program and serving as vice president of the National Legal Aid and Defender Society.

In 1969, the White House approached Powell about being a nominee for a seat on the U.S. Supreme Court, as President RICHARD NIXON anticipated he would be tough on crime. At first, Powell declined consideration, being content in his law practice, not wanting to go through the confirmation process, and believing he was already too old to begin a new career as an associate justice of the Court. But after Nixon appealed to him personally in 1971, he accepted the position being vacated by Justice Hugo Black. He was easily confirmed by the Senate in December 1971.

As a jurist, Powell believed in judicial restraint, separation of powers, state and local jurisdiction, and broad corporate discretion. In *San Antonio Independent School District v. Rodriguez* (1973), he spoke for the majority of the Court in ruling that it was not unconstitutional for Texas to base the financing of education on local property taxes, even though school districts with lower property values would receive less financial support per student than those with higher property values. "It is not the province of the Court," he wrote, "to create substantive constitutional rights in the name of guaranteeing equal protection of the laws." He also emphasized that the Court lacked expertise in matters involving fiscal educational policy. In *National Labor Relations Board v. Bell Aerospace Co.* (1974), a case involving the right of purchasing agents for the company to unionize, he sided with Bell in ruling that they were managerial employees and therefore outside the jurisdiction of the National Labor Relations Board. In *Warth v. Seldin* (1975), he spoke for the majority on the Court in denying standing to a group of low-income plaintiffs and others who challenged the zoning ordinance of the New York town of Penfield, claiming that it excluded poor people from the town. In his ruling, Powell contended that the low-income plaintiffs lacked standing because they could not identify housing they could afford if they won their lawsuit.

In other cases, Powell tended to favor business in antitrust suits and voted against advocates in cases involving environmental and consumer protection. In most criminal cases, he sided with law-enforcement officials and tended to narrow the Fifth Amendment's guarantees against self-incrimination. In First Amendment cases, he weighed rights of free speech against societal interests, upholding in one case the First Amendment rights of California inmates against a mail-censorship system except when necessary to ensure prison security and discipline, but finding in another case in favor of property owners over the free-speech rights of antiwar protesters.

Yet Powell's record as a jurist was not consistently conservative in any area of the law, and in two of the defining cases of the 1970s, *Roe v. Wade* (1974) and *Regents of the University of California v. Bakke* (1978), he voted with the Court's more moderate and liberal jurists. Powell was not a member of the Court when the *Roe* case, involving the legal right of a woman to have an abortion, was first heard in 1971. Over the strong objections of Justice William Douglas, he voted to rehear the case in 1972. To the surprise of many, when the Court rendered its verdict in January 1973, Powell voted with the majority in a ruling that invalidated states' laws prohibiting abortions while acknowledging the legitimate interest of a state in protecting both a pregnant women's health and "potential life." Furthermore, while Justice HARRY BLACKMUN, who wrote the majority opinion, would have limited the ruling to the first trimester of a pregnancy (before life became viable, in his view), Powell argued, along with Justice WILLIAM BRENNAN, that all previability abortions should be free of state regulation, without defining when life became viable.

In subsequent cases, Powell steadfastly opposed virtually all restrictions on abortions, and he joined with pro-choice forces to strike down restrictions on second-trimester abortions. But he joined with pro-life forces in upholding the constitutional right of state and federal governments to withhold funding for abortions, arguing that the government could constitutionally favor childbirth over abortion.

Powell's best-known decision came in the *Bakke* case, involving a special admissions program for minorities at the University of California–Davis School of Medicine that included racial quotas. In his decision, he upheld the principle of affirmative action while rejecting the use of quotas. The case was the most divisive to face the Court during Powell's tenure on the bench. He once described the Court as nine independent law firms, and this never appeared truer than in the case of *Bakke.* At no time was there a majority of the justices who fully agreed with each other on the case. Four of the justices supported affirmative-action programs; four were opposed to any program that favored one race over another. Even those who supported the principle of affirmative action were divided as to the constitutional grounds on which such programs should be based and the extent to which the principle of affirmative action should be applied.

Prior to *Bakke,* Powell had often spoken about the merits of Harvard College's admissions process, which used race as one of a number of factors in reaching decisions on whom to admit to its freshman class. In his view, racial classifications had to be "precisely tailored to serve a compelling governmental interest." But while he believed with the majority on the Court that racial quotas were inherently unconstitutional, he also maintained that the aim of a diverse student body met this strict scrutiny test. His opinion in the *Bakke* case, therefore, contained two parts. First, racial quotas were unconstitutional per se because they violated the equal-protection clause of the Fourteenth Amendment. Second, race could be one of many factors taken into consideration by a college's or graduate school's admissions committee.

Powell's opinion stood alone. Justices Brennan and THURGOOD MARSHALL, for example, could not accept his strict accountability standard. They joined Justices BYRON WHITE and Harry Blackmun in agreeing on the constitutionality of affirmative-action programs, yet disagreeing with much of his rationale and language. But Powell was the key vote in deciding the *Bakke* case. This galled Marshall, who later commented that he "owed his victory to the Court's lone southerner, a former segregationist and consistent foe of forced busing." But as Marshall also commented, without Powell's opinion, "*Bakke* would probably have been the death knoll of all voluntary affirmative action programs."

In other cases decided during the Carter presidency, Powell wrote the majority opinion in *Ingraham v. Wright* (1977), stating that notice and hearing were not constitutionally required before imposition of corporal punishment in public schools and remarking that the courts were "too deep already into schools." He also voted with the majority in invalidating an Illinois law allowing illegitimate children to inherit only from their mothers in cases where there was not a will (*Trimble v. Gordon,* 1977); voted with the majority in *Foley v. Connelie* (1978), upholding a New York law requiring state police to be U.S. citizens; voted in the minority in *Houchins v. KQED* (1978), upholding the constitutional right of access to information on the part of the press; and voted with the majority in *Gannett Co. v. DePasquale* (1979) that the public could be barred from pretrial proceedings to minimize the effects of prejudicial pretrial publicity. In *Goldwater v. Carter* (1979), an important case involving foreign policy, Powell voted with the majority in upholding the President Carter's right to abrogate a mutual-defense treaty with Taiwan without first obtaining the consent of Congress.

Powell retired from the Court in 1987, citing age and health problems. Although often ill, he remained active by delivering lectures; working on various legal projects, including chairing a committee appointed by Chief Justice WILLIAM REHNQUIST on habeas corpus in capital cases; and serving regularly as an appeals court judge in Richmond. He died of pneumonia on April 25, 1998.

Precht, Henry

(1932–) *director of Iranian affairs, Department of State*

Henry Precht was the Department of State's leading expert on Iran during the Iranian revolution of 1978–79. Because most high-level State officials were preoccupied with other matters during the first months of the revolution, he was largely responsible for dealing with the crisis. In his mind, the key political failure of the United States before and during the revolution was not to recognize Iran as a country with politics of its own.

Precht was born in Savannah, Georgia, on June 15, 1932. After attending Emory University (B.A., 1953), he joined the navy and then worked for the Department of Labor before becoming a foreign service officer in 1961. He spent the next 17 years mainly in Middle East, including four years in Iran (1972–76), before becoming the State Department's director of Iranian affairs in June 1978. Around this time, mass demonstrations against the shah's rule were beginning to grow in number and strength. Because the department's higher echelons—including Secretary of State CYRUS VANCE, Deputy Secretary of State WARREN CHRISTOPHER, and Assistant Secretary of State for Near East and South Asian Affairs Harold Saunders—were involved with other matters, such as normalization of relations with China, ratification of the Strategic Arms and Limitation Talks agreement (SALT II), and the Arab-Israeli dispute, Precht was left largely alone to deal with Iran.

During the four years Precht had spent in Iran, he had been struck by both the process of westernization taking place in the country and the lack of political freedom. Iran seemed to him a society with a growing middle class willing to trade political rights for prosperity. But it was a society that also attributed the oppression of the shah's rule to the United States, which had restored the shah to power in 1953 and had continued to support him for the next 25 years. While Precht was impressed more by the apparent quiescence of Iranian society than the potential of revolution, once the revolution began, he became convinced that the shah's days were numbered. He recommended, therefore, that the United States abandon the shah in favor of a more moderate government, a position shared by the U.S. ambassador to Iran, WILLIAM SULLIVAN, but strongly opposed by Brzezinski. In December 1978, Precht wrote a letter to Sullivan highly critical of Brzezinski's reliance on the shah's ambassador to the United States, Ardeshir Zahedi, whom he regarded as self-serving and undependable, and asking advice on how to deal with the opposition to the shah. "I believe his counsel has been one of the strongest factors working on opinion in the White House," he told Sulllivan.

Ironically, no one had greater influence on Brzezinski than GARY SICK, a member of the National Security Council (NSC) staff responsible for Iranian affairs. Sick had known Precht since the 1960s and had considered him a close friend, but the two men broke over Iran. "[T]he near breakdown of communications [that followed with Precht and the State Department] was personally painful to me," Sick later wrote. "[I]t closed a potentially useful channel of policy dialogue just at the moment when it could have been most valuable."

Precht had his own frustrations. Although Secretary of State Vance had recommended making contact with the AYATOLLAH RUHOLLA KHOMEINI, the exiled leader of the dissident Iranians, it was not until after the shah fled the country on January 17, 1979, that he proposed trying to reach some kind of accommodation with the leaders of the revolution, including the formation of a coalition government. By this time, however, Khomeini had begun the process of consolidating his power in the country.

Precht was himself hardly blameless for the events that followed between January and the following November, when militant Iranians claiming to be students seized the American embassy in Tehran. During this time, he continued to emphasize the growing influence of moderate elements in Iran led by Prime Minister Mehdi Barzagan. Although he recognized the serious problems facing the Barzagan regime, he also thought that the Iranians, fatigued by the turmoil of the previous year and concerned by the threat of the Soviet Union, would seek to reconcile their differences with the United States. Even Sullivan rejected that notion, believing that things were getting worse in Iran, not better.

Events revealed how much Precht had underestimated the power of the militants. At the time that Khomeini came to power in early 1979, the United States' biggest embassy was in Iran, with over 1,400 people. In the months that followed, the embassy was virtually abandoned and the ambassador replaced by a chargé d'affairs, BRUCE LAINGEN. Precht was once more left virtually in charge of Iranian affairs as the State Department and White House became preoccupied again with other matters. Relations with Iran also appeared to stabilize, seeming to validate Precht's analysis of developments there.

At the end of October, however, President Carter agreed to let the shah, who had been in Mexico, come to the United States for medical treatment. On November 4, 1979, the embassy was seized by militant Iranians claiming to be students. Americans at the embassy were taken as hostages, and for the next 444 days—until the day Carter left office—the Iranian hostage crisis became the president's overriding concern.

Precht had only recently returned from a two-week visit to Iran when he heard about the seizure of the embassy. According to the diplomat, he had been concerned during his visit to Iran by demonstrations outside the embassy and had even met with Prime Minister Barzagan to get his assurance that the American compound would not be seized. Precht had feared the Iranians would perceive the president's decision to allow the shah into the United States as the first step toward trying to restore him to power, just as the American government had done 25 years earlier. In his view, the president's decision to keep the embassy open and at the same time let the shah into the United States was a "fatal mistake."

Yet there is no indication that Precht ever recommended closing the embassy or even advised destroying the large quantity of classified documents that fell into the hands of the Iranians when it was taken. According to most accounts of the embassy's seizure, moreover, Precht and Laingen had met with Barzagan and Iranian foreign minister Ibrahim Yazdi, on instructions from Washington, to inform them that the shah was coming to New York for medical reasons and to ask them for protection of American citizens in Iran. During the meeting, they were assured by Iranian officials that they would do their best to protect the embassy. Precht was taken aback, therefore, when he learned on his way back from New York to Washington that the embassy had been seized on November 4 and American hostages taken by the Iranians. For the rest of Carter's administration, he worked with the White House in trying to gain the hostages' release.

This was not an easy task, because Precht was dogged by the bureaucratic antipathy that had developed between members of the NSC staff and the State Department over Iranian policy. For his part, the diplomat did not believe the White House understood Iranian society, and he thought that some of the president's actions, such as his decision to attempt a military rescue mission in April 1980, were motivated at least in part by the intense pressure from the American public to do something. According to Precht, the logistical problems of getting a rescue mission to Tehran and then rescuing the hostages from the huge American compound and the Foreign Ministry doomed it from the start. But, frustrated at not being able to get the hostages released by diplomatic avenues and under pressure from Brzezinski for a rescue mission and the need to do something for political reasons, the president approved the mission. "The longer the hostage crisis went on, the worse shape he was going to be in for reelection," Precht remarked.

When the hostages were finally released on January 20, 1981, just a few minutes after RONALD REAGAN was sworn in as the nation's new president, Precht flew with Carter to Wiesbaden, West Germany, to greet them. He found the former president's mood on the trip to be one of great relief rather than one of disappointment at having suffered a humiliating defeat in November. A number of hostages, however, blamed Precht for essentially having allowed them to be taken captive in 1979.

Precht remained in the foreign service until 1987, when he retired after Republican Senator JESSE HELMS of North Carolina blocked his assignment as an ambassador. Following his retirement, he served as president of the World Affairs Council in Cleveland and taught international affairs at Case Western Reserve University. He has written articles for the *Christian Science Monitor* and other publications in which he has been highly critical of the United States for what he regards as its "heavy Israel bias" and Israel's illegal settlements in the Gaza Strip and West Bank. In 2004, he published *A Diplomat's Progress: Ten Tales of Diplomatic Adventure In and Around the Middle East*, a fictionalized account of Precht's own assignments while in the foreign service. Precht divides his time between Bethesda, Maryland, and Bridgton, Maine.

Proxmire, William Edward

(1915–) *member of the Senate*

Chair of the Senate Banking Committee during the Carter administration, William Proxmire, a Democrat, was one of the most independent-minded and unpredictable members of the Senate. An iconoclast, he was best known for his monthly Golden Fleece Awards, in which he identified what he considered the most useless waste of taxpayer's money. Throughout his career in the Senate, he emphasized personal accountability, budgetary restraint, and consumer protection.

Proxmire was an unlikely Democrat. Born on November 11, 1915, in the wealthy Chicago suburb of Lake Forest, Illinois, he was the son of a prominent surgeon, who was chief of staff at Lake Forest Hospital and a die-hard Republican. His education and early career were those of the American gentry: private school at Hill Preparatory in Pottsville, Pennsylvania; an undergraduate degree in English from Yale

University (B.A., 1938); graduate work at the Harvard School of Business (M.B.A., 1940); and a position with the investment firm of J. P. Morgan & Co.

During World War II, Proxmire served as a counterintelligence officer with the U.S. Army. After the war, his career took a new direction when he became interested in public policy and politics. Much to his father's chagrin, he also became a Democrat. After taking a second degree from Harvard's Graduate School of Public Administration (M.P.A., 1948), he moved to Madison, Wisconsin, intent on a political career. Although he worked briefly as a reporter for the *Capital Times*, he ran successfully in 1950 for a seat in the state assembly and, almost immediately, began planning his race for governor in 1952.

Proxmire ran for governor of Wisconsin in 1952, 1954, and 1956 and lost each time. But in both 1954 and 1956, he received about 48 percent of the vote, first against the incumbent governor, Walter Kohler, Jr., who had easily defeated him two years earlier, and then against the incumbent attorney general, Vernon Thompson. More important, he raised face-to-face campaigning to a new level.

In his private high school, Proxmire had been named "most energetic and biggest grind" of his class, and these were characteristics he displayed throughout his entire political career. He was intense, focused, and driven. A health freak whose daily regimen consisted of miles of running and a Spartan diet, he had an inexhaustible fountain of energy. In each of his campaigns, he traveled the state relentlessly, foregoing set speeches and shaking as many hands as possible. As a result, when Senator Joseph McCarthy suddenly died in 1957, Proxmire was known throughout Wisconsin. In the special election to replace McCarthy, he beat off a primary challenge and then, running as the underdog, decisively defeated Walter Kohler, Jr., who had twice beaten him for governor. A year later, he won the general election with 57 percent of the vote, the first of five successive elections.

In the Senate, Proxmire quickly established his reputation as a maverick. As a new senator, he challenged the tight control of the upper chamber by Majority Leader Lyndon Johnson, which he referred to as "unwholesome and arbitrary" and called for more frequent Democratic caucuses. In the first few days of the Kennedy administration, he opposed several of Kennedy's appointments, including that of John Connally as secretary of the navy because, he said, Connally's association with Texas oil interests amounted to a conflict of interest. He was the only senator to vote against Connally's confirmation.

During the 1960s, Proxmire also opposed much of the legislation of the New Frontier and Great Society because of their high costs. Committed to balancing the budget and reducing federal spending, he targeted the Pentagon, which he accused of mismanagement. But as a fiscal conservative who was also a social liberal, he voted for school aid and Medicare and was a strong voice in support of civil rights legislation. He orchestrated a filibuster against a constitutional amendment to supersede the "one man-one vote" decision of the Supreme Court, and he was the chief sponsor in 1968 of a "truth-in-lending" law requiring lending institutions to disclose the actual amount of interest charged to borrowers. An early supporter of the war in Vietnam, he later came to be a critic of the war and voted against a tax increase to pay for its cost. In 1967, he began the practice, which he continued for 19 years, of giving daily speeches on the need to ratify the Convention on the Prevention and Punishment of the Crime of Genocide.

Proxmire's fiscal conservatism and social liberalism continued during the RICHARD NIXON and GERALD FORD administrations. He voted against such proposals as funds for construction of a supersonic transport airplane (SST) and a bailout of Lockheed Aircraft. He also introduced legislation that would prohibit U.S. corporations from engaging in bribery and political payoffs abroad. In 1970 and 1972, he published, respectively, *Wasteland: America's Military Industrial Complex* and *Uncle Sam: The Last of the Bigtime Spenders*, whose titles were self-explanatory. In 1975, he began the practice of his monthly Golden Fleece Awards. He also attacked Nixon's economic stabilization program, including wage and price controls, which he termed unworkable and inequitable.

As the ranking member and, after 1974, chairperson of the Banking, Housing, and Urban Affairs Committee, Proxmire took a particular interest in protection of consumer interests in lending practices. In 1970, he sponsored the Fair Credit Reporting Act, which gave consumers the right to check and correct personal credit files maintained by credit agencies. In 1976, he won approval of the Home Mortgage Disclosure Act, making redlining in real-estate lending practices more difficult. (Redlining is the practice of refusing mortgages or insurance in areas that are deemed to be deteriorating.)

Throughout President Jimmy Carter's administration, Proxmire remained a gadfly. He wrote to Carter before the president-elect even took office, suggesting that after Carter was inaugurated, he walk part of the way from the Capitol to the White House as a means of promoting physical fitness. Although Carter thought the proposal was "rather silly" and initially dismissed it, he decided to walk the last 1.2 miles to the White House as a symbolic way of reducing "the imperial status of the Presidency and his family."

During Senate hearings and confirmations on Carter's cabinet appointments, Proxmire questioned the president's nominee for secretary of housing and urban development, PATRICIA HARRIS, as to her qualifications to represent the poor because of her economic and social status. He was also the only senator to vote against the confirmation of BERT LANCE as director of the Office of Management and Budget (OMB) on the grounds that Lance lacked administrative and economic policy experience.

Proxmire was also one of the first senators to call for Lance's resignation as OMB director after questions began to be raised about his banking practices as president of the Calhoun National Bank and the National Bank of Georgia (NBG). In June 1977, the senator clashed with the OMB director over a letter Lance had signed opposing the Community Reinvestment Act (CRA), which Proxmire had pushed through the Senate as a new title to a larger housing and community development bill. An antiredlining measure, the CRA directed banking regulators to consider an institution's record of meeting the credit needs of "its entire community, including low- and moderate-income neighborhoods" when evaluating the institution's application to open a new branch. The OMB opposed the measure as being cumbersome. Proxmire termed the letter "a direct violation" of Lance's written commitment to the Senate to recuse himself in matters involving banking regulations.

Already at odds with Lance about his qualifications to be director of the OMB, Proxmire was convinced that the letter incident and revelations that Lance might have acted improperly as president of the NBG meant he should resign or be fired from his position. In September 1977, the Senate Banking Committee began an investigation into Lance's banking practices. Under heat from several other quarters, Lance announced his resignation a few weeks later.

As chairperson of the Banking Committee, Proxmire used it to promote his maverick agenda. He cosponsored legislation with ALAN CRANSTON (D-Calif.) that aimed at helping small depositors at financial institutions by authorizing interest-bearing checking accounts. The measure also lowered from $10,000 to $1,000 the minimum amount required to purchase money-market certificates. Believing that government bailouts rewarded fiscal irresponsibility or malfeasance, he opposed a federal guarantee of New York City bonds but allowed the legislation to pass through his committee after Senator DANIEL PATRICK MOYNIHAN (D-N.Y.) persuaded him that it was necessary for the city's economic recovery. But he opposed a financial bailout of Chrysler Motor Corporation in 1979 even though it was strongly backed by the White House and the United Auto Workers. Although a bankruptcy of Chrysler, which employed 137,000 workers, would have had major national economic consequences. Proxmire called the proposal "a massive giveaway for the taxpayers, and a massive windfall for the banks, stockholders and others who have the main stake in a Chrysler bailout." He vowed to make any aid terms "as tough as possible."

Proxmire's contempt of big business was reflected in his treatment in 1978 of Carter's nominee, G. WILLIAM MILLER, to replace ARTHUR BURNS as chair of the Federal Reserve Board (Fed). At issue was Miller's personal integrity as chair of the giant conglomerate Textron. Hearings on Miller's nomination were delayed for five weeks until an investigation could be conducted into accusations by Proxmire that Textron's Bell Helicopter division had bribed an Iranian official, presumably with Miller's knowledge, to win a contract for its helicopters in the mid-1960s. The investigation failed to substantiate Proxmire's charges, and Miller made his own strong defense when he testified before the committee. Nevertheless, the Banking Committee chair refused to relent and so badgered the former head of Textron that his own committee voted to confirm Miller by a vote of 14 to 1, with Proxmire casting the only dissenting vote.

Proxmire may have had disdain for big business and big banking, but unlike many liberal Democrats in Congress, he became one of the Fed's strongest defenders on Capitol Hill. In particular, he had great admiration for PAUL VOLCKER, whom Carter named in 1979 to replace Miller as chair of the Fed following his appointment of Miller as secretary of the Treasury. Carter had appointed Volcker with some reluctance because of his reputation for independence and the president's preference for the sort of team player that Miller had been. It was precisely Volcker's reputation as a gadfly that appealed to Proxmire.

As he did with most nominees before his Banking Committee, Proxmire put Volcker through grueling questioning. But even before the hearing, the senator referred to Volcker as "a man of great intellect and proven leadership ability," unusual praise from the usually staid chairperson. Once Volcker took the helm of the Fed and began to attack inflation by hiking interest rates to unprecedented levels through highly restrictive monetary policies, Proxmire defended the Fed and its chairperson against charges that they were driving the country into recession. "This policy is going to cause some pain," he acknowledged in the Senate. "Anybody who says we can do it without more unemployment or more recession is just deceiving you or is deceiving himself." When an odd coalition of liberal Democrats and conservative Republicans threatened to strip the Fed of some of its authority in the 1980s, Proxmire made it clear that he would oppose such action.

Although Proxmire was concerned mostly with domestic issues during Carter's administration, he was also a sharp critic of the second Strategic Arms Limitation Talks treaty with the Soviet Union, SALT II, which the president signed in June 1979. The treaty, however, was never voted on by the Senate because of the Soviet invasion of Afghanistan in December that year. Unlike most senators who opposed the agreement because they thought it made too many concessions to the Soviets or did not provide enough verification, Proxmire joined a smaller group of senators, including GEORGE MCGOVERN (D-S.Dak.), in opposing the agreement because they believed it did not go far enough toward slowing the arms race.

Because Proxmire was never identified with any political wing, he easily survived the Reagan landslide of 1980. In Wisconsin, he was so popular among voters that in his last two campaigns for reelection in 1976 and 1982, he refused to accept any campaign funds and expended only a few hundred dollars on the campaigns. Citing his age, however, he announced in 1987 that he would not seek a sixth term in the Senate.

After leaving the Senate, Proxmire wrote a twice-weekly syndicated column focusing on national and international economic issues. He also continued to make his monthly Golden Fleece Awards. In March 1998, he announced that he had Alzheimer's disease and was, therefore, discontinuing his column. "As brilliant as my husband was," his wife Ellen said in an interview in 2003, "nothing he says now makes sense anymore." He lived in a long-term facility in Sykesville, Maryland until his death on December 15, 2005.

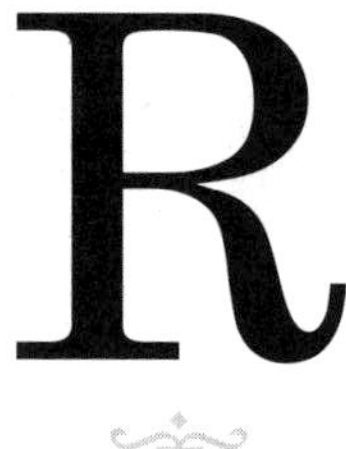

Rafshoon, Gerald

(1934–) *staff assistant in charge of communications*

Brought into the White House in 1978 to improve the public's perception of the president, Gerald Rafshoon had worked as a media consultant for Jimmy Carter since the latter's first campaign for governor in 1966. In his role as staff assistant in charge of communications for the president, he made considerable strides in improving the Carter's image with the public. But the president's own actions undermined his efforts, and Rafshoon was unable to keep Carter from being defeated in his campaign for reelection in 1980.

The son of a career air force officer, Rafshoon was born in Brooklyn, New York, on January 11, 1934. In 1955, he graduated from the University of Texas with a degree in journalism. After a job writing advertising copy for an Austin radio station owned by Lyndon Johnson and then serving four years in the navy, he became national advertising manager for Twentieth Century Fox in 1963. Three years later, he opened his own advertising firm in Atlanta, Georgia.

Rafshoon first became acquainted with Carter during the future president's campaign for governor in 1966. Rafshoon had developed a sophisticated media campaign for Georgia commissioner of insurance Jimmy Bentley, who was considering running for governor. Deciding to run for reelection instead, Bentley encouraged Rafshoon to approach Carter with his campaign proposal. Struck by the poor quality of Carter's own media effort, Rafshoon arranged a meeting with the candidate. The two men took an immediate liking to each other, and Carter asked Rafshoon to run his media campaign.

In 1970, when Carter decided to run for governor again, he turned once more to Rafshoon, who ran a brilliant, if not always high-minded, campaign. Adopting the peanut as Carter's symbol and emphasizing image over issues, he portrayed Carter as a God-fearing, hard-working, conservative-populist peanut farmer from Plains running against former governor Carl Sanders, the candidate of the high-living, ultraliberal, urban-secular elite. In contrasting the two candidates this way, Rafshoon made a not-too-subtle appeal to supporters of Alabama's racist governor, GEORGE WALLACE, who by 1970 had developed a sizeable national following.

Although Rafshoon could have had a top position in the new administration following Carter's victory, he decided to remain in the private sector. He continued to advise the governor on media affairs, however, and in 1971 he undertook a massive public-relations campaign in support of the governor's plan for reorganization of state government. In 1972, he was one of a small group of Georgians who tried to get the presumptive Democratic candidate for president, GEORGE MCGOVERN, to choose Carter as his running mate. Later that year, when it appeared almost certain that McGovern would lose by a wide margin, Rafshoon was among the few who met with Carter to persuade him to run for president in 1976.

Once the Georgia governor decided, by the end of December 1972, to seek the Democratic nomination, Rafshoon assumed responsibility for public relations. During the primary season, he relied heavily and effectively on media advertisements to introduce the largely unknown candidate in places like Iowa, New Hampshire, and southern Florida. Victory in the Iowa caucuses and New Hampshire primary made Carter a serious contender for the Democratic nomination. Victory over George Wallace in the Florida primary all but assured he would be nominated.

Through the primaries and then the general election that followed, Rafshoon pursued much the same script he had in 1970, stressing themes and images over issues and substance and portraying Carter as a hardworking, honest, progressive leader, untainted by the Washington crowd; a southern governor who had made history by tearing down the walls of segregation and opening his administration to black office seekers; and a president who promised to be the voice of the American people, giving them new hope by restoring honesty, decency, and fiscal prudence to the conduct of the nation's business.

Following Carter's election as president in November 1976, Rafshoon chose once more not to take a position in the new administration but to serve instead as an unofficial consultant and adviser to the president and to assist in various media events such as fireside chats and press conferences. But as Carter's approval ratings in the polls tumbled to 38 percent by July 1978 due to rising inflation, disaffection with the president among liberal Democrats, and a growing perception that he was incapable of governing, the president persuaded Rafshoon to accept a position as his staff assistant in charge of communications. Press Secretary JODY POWELL would remain responsible for daily briefings and other day-to-day communication problems; he would also continue to serve as one of the president's closest advisers. But Rafshoon would be responsible for developing overarching themes for the administration and changing public perceptions of the president.

Rafshoon was ideally suited for these tasks. In the months that followed, he put together a tight schedule of highly visible public appearances by the president. He even arranged for a televised "town meeting" from Berlin during Carter's visit to Germany in July 1978. He also coached the president on how to be consistent in his remarks and to stay always on target with whatever message the White House was trying to convey. As another part of his responsibilities, Rafshoon took control of the speechwriting staff, serving as a conduit between the writers and the Oval Office. This arrangement was far from perfect. The lack of linkage between making and articulating policy would continue to plague the Carter administration just as it had the presidency of GERALD FORD before it. The problem was exacerbated by the fact that Carter liked to write his own speeches and rarely gave the staff a sense of his own priorities or of his long-term vision for his administration. Nevertheless, the president stayed on message most of the time, and his approval ratings began to climb. Lawmakers returning from an August recess reported continuing goodwill for Carter among their constituencies. Rafshoon was given considerable credit for this.

Nothing annoyed Rafshoon more, however, than to be told he was just an image maker. What he did, as he later corrected his critics, was to sharpen the president's image, not to predetermine one for him, something that would have impugned on the president's motives and been unacceptable to him. Rafshoon was deeply annoyed, for example, when the *Wall Street Journal* ran a story stating that Carter had vetoed the construction of a nuclear carrier because Rafshoon wanted the president to look tough against Congress. The newspaper even referred to the president's veto of the carrier as "Rafshoon's veto." The president, Rafshoon said in response, had consistently opposed the construction of the carrier and would have had a difficult time trying to justify what he was doing if he had signed the measure.

Still, the distinction Rafshoon drew between image and image maker was never as sharp as he believed. One of the president's most effective addresses to the nation was his one on energy on July 15, 1979, a speech that Carter had planned to make on July 5 but had postponed for 11 days while consulting at Camp David with Americans from all walks of life. In the speech, the president commented on a sense of crisis that seemed to be sapping the American will; it has since been ridiculed as "the malaise speech" although Carter never used the word *malaise* in his address. At the time he delivered it, however, it was well received. Following Rafshoon's recommendations, the president had purposefully used short, crisp sentences, seemed to make sense out of complex issues, appeared candid and sincere, spoke with passion and eloquence, and inflected his voice for dramatic effect better than he had at any time before. Finally, and most important, Carter appeared strong, decisive, and ready to take on the enemies of the consumer—the oil industry and the OPEC cartel. For a short time, at least, Rafshoon had, indeed, made over the president's image and won plaudits for it. Unfortunately, the president undermined his effort a few days later when he asked for and accepted the resignations of five members of his cabinet.

Rafshoon left the White House a few months later to return to his company, Rafshoon's Communications. During the 1980 election, he was again in charge of media communications and public relations for the Carter reelection campaign. Following the president's defeat, he became increasingly involved in the production of films, something he had been interested in doing since the time he had worked for Twentieth Century Fox. He has produced or coproduced a number of films for television and national distribution, including *Running Mates*, a political film starring Tom Selleck for Turner Home Entertainment, which was released in 2002. He has also been in negotiations to produce a talk show on a cable news network to be hosted by Howard Dean, the former governor of Vermont and candidate for the Democratic presidential nomination in 2004. Toward the end of 2005, Rafshoon suggested that President George W. Bush would help himself if he sought, in private conversations, candid advice from his most inveterate opponents. Even important individuals who were "outspoken in their criticism" of the president "would turn into sycophants" once they crossed the threshold.

Reagan, Ronald Wilson

(1911–2004) *Republican Party presidential nominee*

A successful B-movie actor until he entered politics in the 1960s, Ronald Reagan was always underestimated both by political pundits and by his potential political opponents until they ran against him. This was no less true when the former California governor began his race for the presidency in 1980. Considered the underdog against President Carter even after he won the Republican presidential nomination, he became known as the Great Communicator, skillfully taking advantage of the national conservative tide he helped create and disarming Americans worried about his fitness to be president, the most serious charge levied against him by his Democratic opponent.

Reagan was born in Tampico, Illinois, on February 6, 1911, but considered Dixon, Illinois, to be his hometown. Although his father, a shoe salesman, was an alcoholic, the young Ronald had a generally happy childhood growing up in small-town mid-America. He attended Eureka College, where he played football and joined the dramatic society. After graduating from Eureka (B.A., 1932), he worked as a radio announcer and sports broadcaster in Iowa before signing an acting contract with Warner Brothers in 1937. During this time, he studied the speaking style of President Franklin Roosevelt, a man he much admired.

As an actor, Reagan played in more than 50 low-budget movies over the next 25 years. In 1940, Reagan met his first wife, actress Jane Wyman, while they were making a movie together. Following the outbreak of World War II, he served as a captain in the U.S. Army, making more than 400 training movies for the War Department. After his discharge from the army in 1945, he returned to his acting career in Hollywood. In 1949, he and Wyman divorced, and he married actress Nancy Davis three years later. From 1947 to 1952, and then again from 1959 to 1960, he served as president of the Screen Actors Guild. A New Deal Democrat, he also campaigned for Harry Truman in 1948.

In the 1950s, Reagan became a corporate spokesman for General Electric (GE). Around this time, his politics also began to change. Influenced by his new wife and the business executives with whom he frequently came into contact through his activities for GE, he became increasingly conservative and more politically active. Although still a Democrat, he campaigned for Dwight D. Eisenhower in 1952 and 1956 and RICHARD NIXON in 1960. In 1962, he officially switched parties, becoming a registered Republican. In 1964, he delivered a nationally televised speech in support of BARRY GOLDWATER, which made Reagan a rising political star among conservatives. Although he was still not taken seriously by the mainstream political press or by the more moderate Republicans who continued to dominate the Republican Party, he became the new hope of the party's conservative wing after Goldwater's defeat in November 1964.

Reagan's own political career began in 1966 when he ran for governor of California against the two-term liberal incumbent, Pat Brown. Although Democrats welcomed Reagan's candidacy, regarding the actor-turned-politician as a political lightweight, he shocked Democrats, and most political analysts, when he defeated Brown by 1 million votes.

Reagan served two terms as governor, during which he became widely regarded as the nation's leading conservative spokesman. Having campaigned on lowering taxes, he was forced to raise them as governor, but he was able to blame his large budget and tax increases on his predecessor. He also shifted the tax burden from property taxes to sales and income taxes and levies on banks and corporations, which made them more palatable to voters. By the time he left office in 1975, moreover, he could take credit for providing significant tax-relief funds to local governments, providing credits of 20–35 percent on state income taxes and leaving a sizeable budget surplus. He had, in addition, reformed the welfare system, cutting welfare rolls by 400,000, increasing benefits for those still receiving assistance, and requiring all able-bodied recipients to take public service jobs. Although earlier critics of Reagan remained hostile to him because of his attacks on big government and what they considered his simplistic solutions to the nation's pressing economic and social programs, his success as governor confirmed the validity of conservatism for those sharing that point of view.

In 1968, Reagan made a last-minute bid for the Republican presidential nomination but then threw his support behind Richard Nixon and campaigned for him actively both in 1968 and in his landslide reelection victory in 1972. After leaving the California governorship in 1975, Reagan became a full-time candidate for the Republican presidential nomination in 1976. Having already proven his ability on the stump, he undertook a heavy speaking schedule in which he expanded on his conservative philosophy. He also wrote a weekly syndicated news column and did a daily radio broadcast. Although he was once more considered the underdog against President GERALD FORD, he became so popular within Republican circles by campaigning in opposition to the return of the Panama Canal and Canal Zone to the Panamanians that he nearly defeated Ford for the nomination.

Following Ford's defeat by Jimmy Carter, Reagan prepared to run for president in 1980, becoming the Republican Party's leading critic of the Carter administration over the next four years. He spent much of this time using his heavy load of speeches and media appearances to assail the administration's domestic and foreign policies. Early in the administration he made the Panama Canal Treaties, negotiated by the Carter administration in 1977, the target of his attacks. Following the negotiation of the agreements, he called them a "giveaway" of property rightfully owned by the United States. During the 1980 primaries, he remarked that the United States had built and paid for the canal and so "we should tell [the Panamanian government of General [OMAR] TORRIJOS and Company that we are going to keep it."

Reagan also promoted his theme of across-the-board tax cuts to stimulate the economy, spoke out against the administration's failure to reform the nation's welfare system, condemned its support of affirmative-action programs, criticized its proposals on bilingual education, and opposed expansion of the Comprehensive Employment and Training Act (CETA) and other jobs programs. In addition, the former California governor preached a type of messianic anticommunism that manifested itself in opposition to lifting the embargo against Cuba, advocacy of a harder U.S. stand against Cuban forces in Angola and the Horn of Africa, criticism of the president's human rights policy when it affected right-wing anticommunist governments in Latin American and Africa, and opposition to the 1979 Strategic Arms Limitation Talks agreement (SALT II).

Reagan's criticism of the Carter presidency, however, was merely the prelude to his own 1980 campaign for the White House. Although a number of candidates announced for the Republican nomination, Reagan was clearly the front-runner among Republicans. In trial heats in December 1979, President Carter enjoyed comfortable leads, including a 14-point edge over Reagan, his closest rival in the polls. But by April 1980, Reagan was proving to be a much more formidable candidate than the president's campaign staff had anticipated. In addition, the president still had to fend off a major challenge within his own party from Edward Kennedy (Mass.), and a third-party challenge from Representative JOHN ANDERSON (R-Ill.) inserted a discomforting wild card into the race.

In May 1980, Reagan called for an across-the-board 10 percent cut in personal income taxes; Republican lawmakers on Capitol Hill seconded the idea. So popular was the proposal for a tax cut that Democratic leaders in the Senate offered a preemptive bill of their own despite Carter's plea for fiscal austerity and a balanced budget for fiscal 1981.

On July 16, 1980, Ronald Reagan received the Republican nomination for president, and selected GEORGE HERBERT WALKER BUSH, his most formidable rival during the primary season prior to the Republican convention, as his running mate. Because of a series of factors—in particular, rising inflation, high gasoline prices, high unemployment, and the failed mission in April 1980 to rescue the hostages who had been seized at the American embassy in Tehran the previous November—Reagan jumped into a 28 percent lead over Carter in public-opinion polls. In August, Democrats nominated Carter for a second term without much excitement and with real doubts as to whether he could beat Reagan in November.

As the campaign went into full swing in the fall, however, the president began to cut into Reagan's lead and then draw even with or slightly ahead of him in the polls. Well before the Democratic convention, HAMILTON JORDAN, the president's chief political strategist who had given up his position as White House chief of staff in order to join the campaign full-time, decided to focus on Reagan himself rather than Carter's position on the major issues. The president had anticipated as early as October 1979 that he would be running against Reagan, and he agreed that Reagan's qualifications should dominate the Democratic campaign strategy in 1980.

For most of the campaign, it appeared that Jordan and Carter's strategy might work. Following the convention, the president kicked off his bid for reelection on September 1, 1980, with a huge rally at Tuscumbia, Alabama. At the event were about 20 robed members of the Ku Klux Klan, whom the president denounced as cowards who "counsel[ed] fear and hatred." Nevertheless, Reagan insinuated the next day that Carter was seeking the support of racists. Reagan realized immediately that the comment was a mistake: "I shouldn't have said it because the minute after I said it, I knew that this was what would be remembered."

The Republican candidate's remark was only the latest in a series of gaffes on his part. Earlier he had called the Vietnam War a "noble cause," expressed personal doubts about the theory of evolution, remarked that the New Deal was patterned after Benito Mussolini's state socialism, proposed making Social Security voluntary, and voiced pro-Taiwan views that threatened relations with the Beijing government. "If Reagan keeps putting his foot in his mouth for another week or so we can close down campaign headquarters," gloated PAT CADDELL, Carter's pollster, after one of Reagan's blunders.

Even the economy seemed to be coming around to Carter's advantage. The economic signals were mixed and indicated at best a slow recovery, but by the beginning of October, there were a number of signs that the recession was bottoming out. Housing starts were up, businesses were borrowing more to expand production and increase inventories, and the Department of Commerce was estimating that the gross national product (GNP), which had been falling since the first quarter, would rise in the fourth quarter and continue to grow slowly through the second quarter of 1981.

As a result of these occurrences, Reagan's lead over Carter nearly disappeared. A *Newsweek* poll taken at the end of September showed the Republican challenger leading the president by a margin of only 4 percent, with 12 percent of the voters surveyed still undecided. According to the president's own polls, in states like Connecticut, where Carter had been trailing Reagan by more than a two-to-one margin in the middle of July, or in Iowa, where he had been behind by almost a three-to-one margin, he had pulled even or close to even by the middle of September.

After much deliberation, however, Carter made the decision not to engage in a three-way debate with Reagan and independent candidate John Anderson. The president was anxious to debate the Republican candidate one-on-one; he did not want to strengthen Anderson's campaign by appearing with him or allowing both Reagan and Anderson to gang up on him. As a result, Reagan, who had insisted on a three-way meeting, and Anderson debated without the president. Afterward, Hamilton Jordan acknowledged that Carter had been hurt by not participating. "When it was over," he remarked, "I didn't feel very good. Reagan had not made any big mistakes."

Another source of concern for the Carter campaign was the so-called meanness issue. After Reagan had accused him of seeking the votes of racist elements in the South, the president retaliated by suggesting strongly that Reagan was himself a racist. Carter also delivered a series of hard-hitting speeches in which he portrayed the choice between the Republican candidate and himself as one between war and peace. His attacks on Reagan culminated in an address in Chicago on October 6 in which he said that Reagan's election would divide the nation, "black from white, Jew from Christian, North from South, rural from urban," and could well "lead our country toward war."

The president's comments were ill-advised. By attacking Reagan in this way, Carter damaged one of his most valuable campaign assets, the still-popular perception of him as a decent and honorable person—especially since his mudslinging was directed against an opponent who, like himself, was widely regarded as a good and fair-minded individual. Reagan played on his own "nice guy" image by responding to Carter's remarks with expressions of "sorrow" and "regret" rather than by lunging for the jugular as the president seemed to be doing.

During October, the momentum of the campaign shifted back and forth between Reagan and Carter, depending on reports from Iran on the state of negotiations to free the American hostages still being held by the Iranians, news on the state of the economy, and blunders on the campaign trail by the two candidates, although Reagan seemed to make decidedly more of these. Sensing, however, that the campaign was slipping out of their grasp, Reagan and his advisers decided to debate the president without John Anderson. Surveys of public opinion indicated that the voters were turning to Carter in part because of concerns that the Republican nominee was not very smart. There was, however, no groundswell of enthusiasm for the president. If Reagan could dispel his image as a warmongering zealot lacking the intellect to be president, he stood a good chance of breaking Carter's toehold. The best way to achieve this was to debate Carter one-on-one.

Strategically, Reagan's decision to debate Carter was the crucial move of the campaign and probably won him the election. The debate was held in Cleveland at the end of October, just one week before election day. During his 90 minute session with Reagan, Carter handled himself well. In terms of style and image, however, Reagan was the clear winner. Appearing relaxed, reasonable, and informed, and avoiding any obvious mistakes, he effectively undermined the single concern that that had propelled Carter into a virtual tie with him in the polls—that he lacked presidential timber. He also came across as warmer than the president and more intimate with the voters, often fending off Carter's jabs with a sorrowful shake of the head, followed by "aw shucks" or "there you go again."

But the masterful stroke of the debate came at the end when Reagan turned to the two issues—the economy and America's position in the world—that had surfaced in the polls more than any others save Reagan's own fitness to be president. "Are you better off than you were four years ago?" he asked. With that penultimate question, he sealed the election. In all the polls taken after the debate, Reagan was the victor. Reagan's senior adviser, JAMES BAKER, had predicted that all the Republican candidate had to do to win the debate was to stay even with the president. But he had done more than that. With seven days remaining in the campaign, he had made the election once more a referendum on the Carter presidency.

The results of the referendum were a landslide for Reagan that gave him 51 percent of the vote to Carter's 41 percent and John Anderson's 7 percent. In terms of electoral votes, Reagan's victory was even more clear-cut. He lost in the District of Columbia but carried every state except Rhode Island, West Virginia, Georgia, Minnesota, and Maryland for a total of 489 electoral votes to Carter's 49. According to an ABC postelection analysis, more than one out of every four voters settled on a candidate during the last week of the campaign. Out of this group, 44 percent voted for Reagan and 38 percent for Carter.

The 1980 elections were also part of a conservative tide that Reagan had helped create, beginning with the defeat of Barry Goldwater in 1964, and that gave the Republicans control of the Senate for the first time in 24 years. More than a half-dozen of the leading liberal Democrats went down to defeat in the Senate. Democrats remained in control of the House, but leading liberal House members were also defeated, and the size of the Democratic majority was vastly reduced.

The way was prepared, in other words, for what became known as the Reagan Revolution, bringing into office for two terms the most popular president since Franklin D. Roosevelt and a change in the view of the role of government and its responsibilities that many political experts believe was as sweeping as the New Deal of the 1930s.

After leaving office in 1989, Reagan went on the lecture circuit, more popular than ever. In 1994, however, he was diagnosed with Alzheimer's disease. He lived, mostly in seclusion at his ranch in Los Angeles, until June 5, 2004, when he succumbed to pneumonia. He was 93 years old.

Rehnquist, William Hubbs

(1924–2005) *associate justice, U.S. Supreme Court*

In a Supreme Court characterized as much by the idiosyncratic as by the ideological approach of its nine justices to the law and the Constitution, William Rehnquist was its most ideologically consistent member. In almost every case he decided, he was guided by his conservative values—primarily states' rights and convictions of criminals. He was often the lone dissenter in Court decisions, yet he believed in judicial restraint and was not a strict constructionalist. And while he was a political conservative, he was not a cultural conservative. One of his abiding talents, moreover, was to get along well with his ideological opponents. Together with his irreverent wit and sheer brilliance, this made him stand out during Jimmy Carter's term as president.

Born on October 1, 1924, (the same day as Carter) in Minneapolis, Wisconsin, Rehnquist grew up in a comfortable, staunchly Republican, middle-class family. His parents espoused conservative and patriotic values, which he fully shared even as a youth. After briefly attending Kenyon College on a scholarship, he joined the Army Air Corps and spent three years (1943–46) serving as a weather observer in North Africa. After returning from Africa, he used the G. I. Bill to attend Stanford University, where he majored in political science and graduated Phi Beta Kappa (B.A. and M.A., 1948). He then got a second master's degree in government from Harvard (M.A., 1949), intending to become a professor of government. A change in career interests, however, took him back to Stanford Law School, where he graduated (LL.B., 1952) at the top of his class, which included another future Supreme Court justice, Sandra Day O'Connor.

Following law school, Rehnquist clerked for Supreme Court justice Robert Jackson. As Jackson's clerk, Rehnquist wrote highly controversial memorandums on two civil rights cases that would later be used against him during his confirmation hearings for associate justice and then chief justice of the Supreme Court. In the first of these, on the historic *Brown v. Board of Education of Topeka* case (1954), Rehnquist argued that the doctrine of separate but equal was constitutionally valid. In the second, *Terry v. Adams* (1953), he maintained that exclusion of blacks from preprimary selection of Texas Democrats was also constitutionally appropriate. Rehnquist later claimed that he was expressing these views at Jackson's request, a claim that Jackson's secretary and a number of legal scholars have disputed. Whether Rehnquist was speaking for Jackson or himself, the two memorandums reflected a central point of his own judicial philosophy—judicial deference to the majority will.

After clerking for Jackson, Rehnquist moved in 1953 to Phoenix, Arizona, where he practiced law and became active in the Republican Party, which had been revitalized by newly elected senator BARRY GOLDWATER. Through his activities in Republican Party politics, he met Richard Kleindienst, whom President RICHARD NIXON named deputy assistant attorney general in 1969 and who recommended Rehnquist for a position in the Justice Department. Rehnquist was appointed assistant attorney general in charge of legal counsel. Very quickly, Rehnquist proved to be a brilliant lawyer who caught Nixon's attention by his defense of executive power, including the president's withholding of information from Congress, his secret use of wiretapping and electronic surveillance, no-knock entry, pretrial detention, and mass arrest of antiwar demonstrators in Washington. In a speech to the Kiwanis Club in 1969, Rehnquist said the nation had to devote all its energies to countering "the dangers posed by the new barbarians." In 1971, he told a Senate subcommittee that the Justice Department opposed any legislation hindering the government's ability to collect information on citizens and that surveillance of demonstrators did not violate the free-speech rights of the First Amendment.

Rehnquist's views on the law and the Constitution resonated with the president. When two positions became available on the Supreme Court following the retirements of Justices Hugo Black and John Marshall Harlan in 1971, Nixon nominated Rehnquist and LEWIS POWELL to fill their seats. Civil rights and liberal groups strongly opposed Rehnquist's nomination. At his confirmation hearings, the questions focused on whether he had lied in his account of the prosegregationist memorandums for Justice Jackson and whether his conservative views made him too strong an ideologue to sit on the Supreme Court. He was also questioned about a statement he had made in 1964 opposing a local public-accommodations law. But he said he had changed his mind since then, not having understood how strongly minorities felt about protecting their rights. Despite the controversy surrounding his nomination, the Senate confirmed him by a vote of 68 to 26.

Very quickly, Rehnquist established himself as one of the most brilliant and conservative of the nine Court justices. He advanced a narrow conception of judicial review and held to the position that policy making was the function of the legislature and not the courts. He almost invariably deferred to the states on matters involving individual rights. In *Roe v. Wade* (1973), upholding the constitutional right of women to choose an abortion, he was only one of two justices to dissent, the other being Justice BYRON WHITE. In contrast to

White, who wrote a blistering dissent, analyzing the case as one involving the convenience of the mother over the existence of the life or potential life of the fetus, Rehnquist interpreted the case as one of the rights of the states and the majority of its citizens to legislate on abortions. "[T]he fact that a majority of the States," Rehnquist wrote, "reflecting after all the majority sentiment in those States, has had restrictions on abortion for at least a century is a strong indication, it seems to me, that the asserted right to an abortion is not 'so rooted in the traditions and conscience of our people as to be ranked as fundamental.'"

Similarly, in the case of *National League of Cites v. Usery* (1976), a case involving the government's ability to apply the minimum wage to state and local government employees, Rehnquist wrote the majority opinion, maintaining that the Tenth Amendment prevented Congress from acting in a way that "impairs the States' integrity or their ability to function effectively in a federal system." In criminal cases, he generally voted to sustain government power over individual rights, upholding police searches and seizures and ruling that a policeman could stop and frisk a suspect for weapons on the basis of a informant's tip and could then proceed to search the suspect's car without a warrant. In First Amendment cases, such as those involving pornography, he generally ruled that societal interests trumped individual rights.

The most important—and divisive—Supreme Court case heard during the Carter presidency, *Regents of the University of California v. Bakke* (1978), involved a special admissions program for minorities at the University of California–Davis School of Medicine that included quotas. The Court had to decide whether to render its opinion on statutory or constitutional grounds. It also had to decide two separate issues, the permissibility of racial quotas and that of affirmative-action programs that excluded explicit quotas but allowed race to be one of several factors in making decisions on admissions. The two most liberal justices on the court, THURGOOD MARSHALL and WILLIAM BRENNAN, believed racial quotas were constitutionally valid; the other justices did not. On the questions of whether affirmative-action programs without racial quotas might be constitutional, there was sharp division among the more moderate justices. The difficulty centered on finding the appropriate language to rule against racial quotas but allow or disallow affirmative-action programs.

For Rehnquist, though, *Bakke* did not cause much soul-searching. After the Court heard oral arguments on the case, Chief Justice WARREN BURGER, Justice POTTER STEWART, and Rehnquist wanted to find the Davis program unconstitutional without any provision for affirmative-action programs. Burger and Justice JOHN PAUL STEVENS argued that the program was barred by Title VI of the Civil Rights Act of 1964, prohibiting discrimination on the basis of race, and that the case could be decided, therefore, as an interpretation of a federal statute rather than of the Constitution. Rehnquist and Stewart had trouble even with this procedure. "I take it as a postulate that difference in treatment of individuals based on their race or ethnic origin is at the bulls-eye of the target at which the Fourteenth Amendment's Equal Protection Clause was aimed," wrote Rehnquist. When the case was finally decided, Justice Powell wrote the majority opinion striking down racial quotas but permitting affirmative-action programs on constitutional grounds.

Despite his concerns expressed earlier about deciding the case only on statutory grounds, Rehnquist went along with Stevens's opinion that there was no need to consider the constitutional merits of the case. As a result, only the majority opinion spoke of the Fourteenth Amendment's equal-protection clause.

In subsequent cases, however, Rehnquist made clear his conclusion that all racial classifications imposed by the government for whatever purpose were in violation of that clause.

In other Supreme Court cases decided during the Carter presidency, Rehnquist voted with the majority that a notice and a hearing were not constitutionally necessary before corporal punishment could be administered in public schools (*Ingraham v. Wright*, 1977). He also dissented in a case that struck down an Illinois law allowing illegitimate children to inherit only from their mothers in cases where there was no will (intestate) (*Trimble v. Gordon*, 1977). In a similar case (*Lalli v. Lalli*, 1978), he voted with the majority in upholding a New York law that allowed illegitimate children to inherit from their father intestate only if a court of competent jurisdiction had, while the father was alive, entered an order declaring paternity.

In cases during the Carter administration involving the First Amendment right of free speech, Rehnquist continued to adhere to the maxim that societal needs prevailed over free expression. The first of these cases, *Wooley v. Maynard* (1977), involved a New Hampshire law requiring motor vehicles to bear license plates with the state motto "Live Free or Die." Maynard and his wife, both Jehovah's Witnesses, found the motto repugnant and taped it over on their plates; they were fined for violating state law. In contrast to the majority of the Court, which found in Maynard's favor, Rehnquist refused to recognize Maynard's conduct as symbolic speech covered by the First Amendment, remarking that there was no protected "symbolic speech" in the case.

In *Houchins v. KQED* (1977), Rehnquist voted in the majority against the constitutional rights of access to information on the part of the press beyond that of the public generally. He took a similar position in a third case (*Gannett Co. v. DePasquale*, 1979) that involved both the First and Sixth Amendments (the right to a speedy and public trial). In this case, Rehnquist voted with the majority to affirm a lower-court ruling that the press could be excluded, at the request of the defendants in a murder case, from a pretrial hearing on a motion to suppress a confession and a murder weapon. "The Sixth Amendment," said Rehnquist, "means for me only protection for the rights of the accused. . . . The Framers didn't give the public a right to access."

In *Zablocki v. Redhail* (1978), Rehnquist was the lone dissenter in a case where the Court struck down a state law prohibiting residents with minor children not in their custody from marrying without court permission, which could be given only if the minor children were receiving support and were not likely to become public charges. The law's real purpose was to ensure the enforcement of support orders. Even Rehnquist believed the measure was "screwy," but he was the only member of the Court to believe that the equal-protection clause had not been violated.

In an important case involving foreign policy (*Goldwater v. Carter*, 1979), in which Senator Barry Goldwater, one of Rehnquist's political heroes, challenged President Carter's right to abrogate a mutual-defense treaty with Taiwan without the consent of Congress, the justice played a decisive role in framing the majority ruling that termination of a treaty is a nonjusticiable political question.

Until RONALD REAGAN came to office in 1981, Rehnquist was clearly the most conservative member of the Supreme Court. But as the Court became increasingly more conservative, he found himself voting increasingly with the majority. His deference to states' rights and to providing greater scope to law-enforcement agencies, so prevalent throughout his career, are now widely shared on the Court. Yet he became less strident and far less of a cultural conservative than later additions to the

Court, Antonin Scalia and Clarence Thomas. Appointed chief justice of the Court in 1986, he proved, in sharp contrast to his predecessor, Warren Burger, to be a highly efficient and effective administrator. Also in contrast to Burger, he was well-liked and highly respected for his political acumen and judicial mind, even by those ideologically apart from him.

In 2004, Rehnquist was diagnosed with thyroid cancer, and there was growing talk that he was planning to resign from the Court. His long absence from the Court's 2004–05 term added to that speculation. He remained as chief justice, however, until his death on September 4, 2005, at age 80.

Reuss, Henry Schoellkopf

(1912–2002) *member of the House of Representatives*

Henry Reuss was chair of the House Banking and Currency Committee during the Carter administration. More than that, he was one of the most influential and respected legislators on Capitol Hill, known for his cerebral approach to legislation. An expert on matters having to do with the domestic and international economies, he played a decisive role in the establishment of organizations as diverse as the Peace Corps and the Ice Age National Scenic Trail. A liberal Democrat from Wisconsin, he was highly critical of the administration's economic policies, which he blamed for the recession that began in the waning days of the Carter presidency. At the same time, he shepherded through Congress a number of measures intended to strengthen the Federal Reserve System and make it more responsible to Congress.

Reuss was born on February 22, 1912, in Milwaukee, Wisconsin. A graduate of Cornell University (B.A., 1933), where he majored in history and government, and of Harvard Law School (LL.B., 1936), where he was elected in his first year to the *Harvard Law Review*, Reuss later traced his fascination with public policy to his undergraduate years at Cornell. His commitment to liberal social programs came about through his analysis of New Deal programs as the legislation editor of the *Law Review*. At the same time, he acknowledged that he was a conservative before he embraced liberalism and a Republican before he became a Democrat. Of German descent, he described himself as coming from "a long line of conservative-industrial-financial Republicans." Both his grandfather and father were successful local bankers.

Reuss began his law practice with Quarles, Spence and Quarles, a distinguished corporate law firm in Milwaukee. In 1939, he decided to take a position as Milwaukee County Corporation counsel (1939–40) and then served as counsel for the U.S. Office of Price Administration (OPA, 1941–42). In the first of these two positions, he had an insider's look into what he later described as "two shipwrecked segments of society—the mentally ill and the unemployed," the latter numbering about 25 percent of Wisconsin's labor force during the depression. At the OPA, he met the liberal economist John Kenneth Galbraith, whom he described as his lifelong mentor. By the time he volunteered for the army in 1943, he was committed to political liberalism and social activism.

Reuss served as an infantry officer in the army from 1943 to 1945 and was awarded the Bronze Star. After the war ended, he remained in Europe, where he served in the military government as chief of price control for Germany until he was shipped home at the end of 1945. Over the next several years, he became active in liberal political circles in Milwaukee. In 1948, he ran for mayor of Milwaukee, came in second in the primary in a crowded field, but lost the general election. He then served for 14 months in Paris as acting general counsel for the Economic Cooperation Administration (the Marshall Plan). Coupled with his experience in World War II, his work with the Marshall Plan made him an internationalist as well as a social activist.

In 1950, Reuss ran as the Democratic candidate for Wisconsin state attorney after he had helped lead a successful coup of progressives against the old-line Democratic leadership that had dominated the party, but he was defeated by his Republican opponent in November. Two years later, he made another failed bid for the Senate seat occupied by the demagogic red-baiter, Joseph McCarthy. Scaling back his political ambitions, he ran successfully for the Milwaukee School Board. Together with the political base he had developed over the previous six years, the position provided enough of a springboard to get him elected to Congress in 1954, defeating the McCarthyite incumbent, Charles J. Kersten. He was reelected 13 times before deciding not to seek reelection in 1982. The only other election he lost was in 1960, when he again ran unsuccessfully for mayor of Milwaukee.

Almost from the time Reuss arrived on Capitol Hill, he made his mark in the House. Together with a number of other freshman representatives, he conducted a debate on the country's foreign policy in which he spoke out in support of an independent Central European community that would include a unified and independent Germany, provided the Soviet Union withdrew to its historic borders. For most of the remainder of the 1950s, Reuss continued to refine his concept of disengagement from Eastern Europe and to deal with the difficult question of when American military intervention abroad was appropriate. In his view, it was justified only when it was done on behalf of a country that was humane, had the support of that country's citizens and the United States' allies, and a vital U.S. interest was at stake.

This philosophical template led Reuss to have serious reservations in the 1960s with respect to the U.S. intervention in Vietnam, which he later described as "surely the saddest chapter in the history of our country during my congressional years." Even though he voted in 1964 for the Gulf of Tonkin Resolution, authorizing President Lyndon Johnson to send troops to Vietnam, and was a strong supporter of Johnson's Great Society programs, he supported Minnesota senator Eugene McCarthy's quixotic candidacy for the Democratic presidential nomination in 1968.

Perhaps Reuss's most significant accomplishment in foreign policy as a young congressman was assisting in the establishment of the Peace Corps in 1961. The idea for the Peace Corps had come to him in 1957 during a visit to Cambodia when he realized the assistance that such a group could offer to the poor countries of the Third World. "Too often we seem to emphasize military alliances with corrupt or reactionary regimes," he wrote in an article in *Commonweal* in May 1960. "Would we not be further along," he asked, "if we relied more heavily on a group of some thousands of young Americans willing to help with an irrigation project, digging a village well, or setting up a rural school?" Later he helped the Bonn government in West Germany establish its own version of a Peace Corps.

In addition to his other interests, Reuss was a passionate environmentalist. Soon after coming to Congress, he joined in a campaign, led by Supreme Court justice William A. Douglas, to protect the Potomac River from highway and dam construction and to establish the Chesapeake and Ohio National Scenic Trail that runs along the river. In 1955, he sponsored legislation prohibiting the secretary of the interior from draining national wildlife refuges without the approval of Congress. In 1962, he won a two-year fight to protect wildlife from federally subsidized drainage of wetlands. In 1964, he gained passage of the National Scientific Reserve to protect northern Wisconsin's Ice Age heritage. A 90-mile Ice Age Trail was later established on the reserve. In 1971, he resurrected the Refuse Act of 1899, which prohibited anyone from polluting a lake or stream without obtaining a permit from the Army Corps of Engineers. He used that act to successfully sue four major polluters in Wisconsin, forcing them to pay heavy fines.

By the early 1970s, Reuss was already one of the most widely respected members of the House, especially among such other diehard liberals as TIP O'NEILL (D-Mass.) and MORRIS UDALL (D-Ariz.). In his sophomore term in the House, Reuss had helped put together the Democratic Study Group (DSG), which sought to challenge the southern minority that controlled most of the House's major committees. In the years that followed, the DSG came to include about 80 liberal-to-moderate congressmen, a number of whom, like O'Neill and Udall, were already making their own marks on Capitol Hill. In addition, Reuss was acquiring seniority on the House Banking and Currency Committee, where he had served since coming to Capitol Hill in 1955, and on the Joint Economic Committee, on which he had served since 1958.

As a member of the Banking and Currency Committee, Reuss had made himself an expert on international monetary and trade issues. He was one of the first congressmen in the 1960s to express concern about the outflow of gold from the United States and the development of the Eurodollar market as a result of the country's declining trade balance and growing military spending and capital investments overseas. He also became a member of the Bellagio Group, whose members included some of the world's leading experts on international money. Even before President RICHARD NIXON decided to take the dollar off the gold standard and float it against other currencies, effectively killing off the Bretton Woods system of fixed exchange rates that had been in existence since 1944, Reuss had called for the closing of the gold window and the establishment of a new post-Bretton Woods regime that might include a new international monetary unit (like the euro now being used in daily trade by members of the European Union). At the risk of alienating his support among union workers, Reuss also always remained a strong advocate of free trade.

In 1972, Reuss supported Senator EDMUND MUSKIE (Maine) for the Democratic presidential nomination, because he both opposed the war in Vietnam and was an environmentalist. After Muskie lost to GEORGE MCGOVERN (S.Dak.) and McGovern was then badly defeated by Nixon, Reuss approached his close friend in the House, Morris Udall, about running for president in 1976. In 1974, he and his colleague in the House, DAVID OBEY (D-Wis.), circulated a petition among House members urging Udall to consider running for president, something he was already contemplating. Reuss was disappointed when Udall was defeated by Carter for the Democratic nomination. "I still believe that had Udall won," he later wrote, "he could have ... changed for the better the history of the twentieth century's last quarter."

Reuss was badly disappointed by the Carter presidency. Except for their common interest in the environment and urban reform, the liberal congressman from Milwaukee, who had been in Washington for more than 20 years, and the conservative president from Plains, who had run on an anti-Washington platform and seemed to disdain Congress, had little in common. Even on the need for a new energy program, on which they both agreed, they had fundamental differences. In contrast to the president, who wanted to conserve energy by making it more expensive, Reuss wanted to conserve energy by rationing gasoline to its most essential users. Accordingly, he regarded Carter's comprehensive energy program "as containing everything but the one element that could have made it work."

Reuss welcomed the president's interest in urban reform, in which he also took an abiding interest. In 1977, the same year Carter was inaugurated, Reuss had written *To Save a City: What Needs to Be Done*, in which he called for a national urban policy that included such ideas as neighborhood redevelopment, restrictions on automobile use in central districts, and a greater role for the states in urban redevelopment. But while he felt the Carter administration was doing more for the city than any earlier administration, including increasing the number of public-service jobs and signing into law a $12.5 billion urban-aid bill targeted at the nation's most distressed areas, he believed it did not go far enough. In particular, he was distressed when the White House rejected the recommendations of the Urban and Regional Policy Group (URPG), headed by Secretary of Housing and Urban Development PATRICIA HARRIS, which called for adding $8–12 billion to the $50 billion in aid that cities and towns already received, and when Carter did not include any urban initiatives in his fiscal 1979 budget. More generally, Reuss thought the president was "ill-advised" in holding down spending at the expense of social welfare and other entitlement programs. He later commented that Carter was the first Democratic president since Thomas Jefferson "to create a recession."

During the Carter administration, Reuss also served as chair of the Banking and Currency Committee. He had wrested that position in 1975 from Wright Patman of Texas in a power coup in which he had the backing of a group of liberal congressmen elected in 1974 who were able to change the seniority rules that still governed the election of committee chairpersons. Reuss used his powerful position to make the Federal Reserve System (Fed), widely recognized as the most independent regulatory agency in Washington, more accountable to Congress. In 1975, he got Congress to approve a congressional resolution requiring the Fed chair to testify semiannually before the Banking and Currency Committee on financial conditions in the country and its monetary policies, a practice that was instituted into law in 1978. In 1977, Reuss also helped push through Congress measures outlawing redlining (mortgage and insurance discrimination) in low-income neighborhoods, extending conflict-of-interest laws to the Fed, requiring the 12 Fed regional banks to include women and blacks on the boards of directors, and requiring foreign banks operating in the United States to adhere to the same standards as domestic banks.

At the same time, Reuss sought to strengthen the Fed by pushing through Congress the Monetary Control Act of 1980, which required banks that were not part of the Federal Reserve System to maintain noninterest-bearing reserves with the system. The legislation was in response to a decline in the Fed's membership and to complaints by its members that they were increasingly unable to compete against nonmember banks because of the noninterest-bearing reserves they had to maintain with the Fed. Reuss supported the legislation after opposing another measure to pay interest on these reserves. The bill also lowered reserve requirements and extended the clearing facilities of the Fed to nonmember banks.

Although Reuss was later critical of the Fed for paying too much attention to its statutory responsibility of minimum inflation and not enough attention to its other statutory duty of maximum employment, he was far more interested during the Carter administration in having the Fed wrestle with inflation than with employment. In 1979, he strongly supported the appointment as Fed chair of

PAUL VOLCKER, who was committed to dealing with inflation by cranking up interest rates to unprecedented levels through highly restrictive monetary policies. Only after the country was plunged into recession in the last year of the Carter presidency and the first two years of RONALD REAGAN's administration did Reuss begin to criticize Volcker.

In Reuss's view, however, Volcker's monetary policy "pale[d] against the fiscal and regulatory sins of both the Carter and Reagan administrations." In 1980, he supported Massachusetts senator EDWARD KENNEDY's failed attempt to capture the Democratic nomination from Carter. Reuss subsequently became an outspoken critic of President Reagan's economic programs as favoring the rich, even swapping his Banking and Currency Committee chair for that of the Joint Economic Committee, on which he had also served since 1958, in order to put him in a stronger position in 1982 to fight Reagan's tax and budget cuts.

That same year, however, Reuss decided not to seek reelection. He had grown frustrated by what he regarded as the growing contentiousness and lack of collegiality in Congress. After leaving the House, he practiced law in Washington and was active in various nonprofit organizations. In 1995, he moved to the San Francisco Bay area, where he died of congestive heart failure on January 12, 2002, at the age of 89.

Rhodes, John Jacob

(1916–2003) *member of the House of Representatives, House minority leader*

House minority leader during the Carter presidency, John J. Rhodes was a conservative Republican, who, along with his friend and colleague, BARRY GOLDWATER, had helped establish the modern Republican Party in Arizona. Increasingly critical of President Carter, he worked hard, and generally successfully, to maintain Republican unity in the House. Despite political and ideological differences with Speaker of the House TIP O'NEILL (Mass.), he got along well with O'Neill and other Democratic leaders in the lower chamber and was widely respected among Washington insiders.

The youngest son of a local businessman and Kansas state treasurer, Rhodes was born on September 18, 1916, in Council Grove, a small farming community along the old Santa Fe Trail in northeast Kansas. A graduate of Kansas State University (B.S., 1928) and Harvard Law School (LL.B., 1941), Rhodes served during World War II in the Army Air Corps and was stationed in Arizona. After the war, he opened a law practice in Mesa, Arizona, and helped start a firm that became the Farm and Home Life Insurance Company. He also became good friends with Barry Goldwater, who was president of a family-owned chain of department stores and was trying to shape the Republican Party to reflect his own conservative thinking in a state that had always been a Democratic stronghold. Generally sharing Goldwater's conservative views, Rhodes joined him in managing the successful 1950 campaign of Howard Pyle, the first Republican to be elected governor of the state. At Goldwater's persuasion, Rhodes ran for attorney general that same year. Although he was narrowly defeated, he ran successfully for Congress two years later, riding on the coattails of Dwight D. Eisenhower's presidential victory and becoming the first Republican to be elected to the House of Representatives from Arizona. He was returned to the House for the next 30 years.

Rhodes became an important figure in the House in the 1960s when he participated in a rebellion of "young Turks" against the staid Republican leadership of minority leader Charles Halleck (Ind.), who was replaced by

GERALD FORD (Mich.) in 1965. At the same time, Rhodes was chosen to be chair of the House Republican Policy Committee. When Ford was selected by President RICHARD NIXON in 1973 as his vice president to replace Spiro Agnew, who had resigned after pleading no contest to tax-evasion charges, Rhodes moved up to the position of minority leader.

Throughout his legislative career, Rhodes voted mainly along conservative lines, opposing most of President Lyndon Johnson's Great Society programs, although he supported the Voting Rights Act of 1965. During both the Johnson and Nixon administrations, he was also a strong supporter of the Vietnam War. Of particular importance to his constituents, in 1968 he played a key role in winning congressional approval of the Central Arizona Project, which, by diverting the waters of the Colorado River to the arid areas around Phoenix and Tucson, made possible their rapid growth in size and population.

Rhodes became the House's Republican leader at the beginning of the historic effort to impeach Richard Nixon and remove him from office because of the Watergate cover-up. Although Rhodes had been a strong supporter of the president, on May 9, 1974, the same day the House Judiciary Committee opened hearings on Nixon's impeachment, he broke ranks with the rest of the Republican leadership by suggesting publicly that Nixon should resign from office. As it became apparent by August that Nixon would be impeached by the House, Reuss asked the Democratic majority leader, Tip O'Neill, whether it would be possible to work out an arrangement whereby the House would censure rather than impeach the president. But O'Neill said it was too late for a compromise and that unless Nixon resigned, he would be impeached by the House, found guilty by the Senate, and sent to prison. After the release of a tape on August 5 revealing the full extent of the president's involvement in the Watergate cover-up, Rhodes went to the White House with Senator Barry Goldwater and Senate minority leader Hugh Scott (Pa.) to tell the president he needed to resign. The president asked if he had any options. Rhodes responded, "I want to tell the people outside that we didn't discuss any options." On August 7, Rhodes informed O'Neill that Nixon would resign on August 9.

Although Rhodes had worked closely with Gerald Ford as part of the minority leadership in the House and was on the president's short list to replace him as vice president, once Ford became president, according to the Arizona lawmaker, "an invisible curtain seemed to come down, diminishing the easy access formerly available to many of his old friends." Rhodes was also dismayed when he learned that the new president was going to grant Nixon a pardon. He let Ford know that it would cost Republicans a number of seats in the forthcoming congressional elections. As Rhodes predicted, the Republicans suffered major losses in the November 1974 elections.

Following Jimmy Carter's victory in the 1976 presidential election, Rhodes urged the Democrats to work in unity with the Republicans at a time when the country was still trying to recover from the aftermath of Nixon's resignation. This did not keep him from being the leader of the loyal opposition. He was generally successful in maintaining party unity as Republicans developed their own legislative agenda. Also, he came to have real reservations about Carter's ability to lead the nation, even describing him later as "a man of considerable meanness and tactlessness."

Rhodes was particularly upset by the president's decision to cut what Carter regarded as pork-barrel water projects, including the $1.6 billion Central Arizona Project, which Rhodes regarded as his most significant legislative accomplishment and which would become his most important legacy. Such a decision, on what was the largest Bureau of Reclamations project, Rhodes said, "would be in direct conflict with the president's proposals for creating more jobs." He also warned the president that Congress would override any veto of the public-works bill containing the water projects. House Speaker O'Neill also urged the president to avoid a confrontation with Congress over the matter.

Chastened by the political reaction to his plan to cut water projects, the president decided to remove the Central Arizona Project from his targeted list of cuts, along with the $1.4 billion Tennessee-Tombigbee Waterway. This did not do much, however, to mollify Rhodes, who, like Senate minority leader HOWARD BAKER (Tenn.), had already proven to be a formidable foe of the White House. Working in concert, the two men were able to keep the conservative and liberal wings of their party together while successfully opposing the president's $50 tax-rebate plan and a proposal for common situs picketing (picketing by a labor union of an entire construction project as a result of a grievance against a single subcontractor). They also helped to kill the president's proposals for election reform, including election-day registration. Even though he had initially supported the concept of universal registration, Rhodes reversed his position, arguing that it would lead to voter fraud.

Over the next several months, Rhodes took umbrage at a series of Carter's legislative proposals, including his energy plan, which the House minority leader criticized for putting too much emphasis on conservation and "leaving supply up to chance," and his proposal for welfare reform, which Rhodes said might add as much as $6 billion to the current welfare tab. In September 1977, the Arizona congressman joined a growing number of Republicans and Democrats in urging the president to fire BERT LANCE, the director of the Office of Management and Budget (OMB) and Carter's closest friend within the administration, for alleged improprieties when Lance had been president of the Calhoun National Bank and the National Bank of Georgia. The president "came into this office with campaign promises about how pure this Administration was going to be and I think it is up to him to decide whether or not [the Lance affair] meets with that purity," Rhodes remarked.

On foreign policy, Rhodes was critical of what he regarded as the president's lack of judgment in dealing with the Soviet Union, first attacking the Soviets for violating human rights and then proposing a plan in Moscow for comprehensive arms reductions that the Soviets would never accept. The president, he said, "cannot substitute a play to the gallery and ploys for the media for skill, patience, timing, and firmness expressed through action. His actions to date have damaged, not helped, the cause of human rights around the globe."

In a speech to the California Club of California in October 1977, which was reprinted by the *New York Times*, the House minority leader delivered a blistering attack on President Carter. "[E]ight months of the Carter administration," he remarked, "reveal a pattern of uncertainty and ineptitude, compounded by a moral blindness and a lack of understanding of the very processes of government that bode no good for the nation's economic health or for the state of its defenses." He also accused Carter of lacking a political backbone, saying the president had "taken a series of initiatives and then publicly retreated as soon as these initiatives came under fire."

In contrast to his attitude toward the White House, Rhodes—who was generally regarded by his colleagues and Washington reporters who covered him as being low-key, straightforward, and generally good-natured—maintained good relations with the Democratic leadership in the House, especially Speaker O'Neill, with whom he disagreed on most issues. On one occasion in 1977, during a debate on the establishment of the House Permanent Select Committee on Intelligence, O'Neill shouted at Rhodes for allegedly changing his mind on the establishment of the committee. "I wish the minority leader could lead instead of always following his followers around here," O'Neill said. But this outburst was not characteristic of their relationship. "We would fight on the House floor if we had to and then go play golf together," Rhodes explained. "I've got to believe the country was better off because we didn't hate each other."

The minority leader's relationship with the White House remained polite but nevertheless strained for the remainder of Carter's administration, as Rhodes continued to attack the president on such matters as high federal taxes, rising inflation, and deficit spending. In July 1978, he announced that a tax-cut bill introduced by Representative Jack Kemp (R-N.Y.) and Senator William Roth (R-Del.) that would slice federal income taxes by $113.4 billion over three years had become the Republican Party's official policy. This was in contrast to the administration proposal for a tax cut of $15 billion. The Republican bill, Rhodes, said, would actually increase federal tax collections because it would generate increased economic activity.

In 1979, Rhodes fought against the Carter administration's proposal for the deregulation of domestic oil prices and a windfall-profits tax. He would support a windfall-profits tax, he said, but only if the revenues were used to increase oil production. He also assailed the Camp David discussions of July 1979 between the president and a cross section of prominent Americans, which were followed by a nationally televised speech in which Carter spoke of a "crisis of spirit" in the nation and proposed additional measures for dealing with the nation's energy crisis. Among the measures the president proposed were a limit on oil imports and the establishment of an Energy Security Corporation to help finance the development of synthetic fuels. Remarking that he was "incredulous" that House Republicans had been excluded from the Camp David meetings, Rhodes assailed the latest energy proposals for relying too heavily on conservation and not enough on increasing oil supplies. He said the Republicans would have been more prepared to support some of the president's ideas if Carter had accepted some of their own. In contrast to most of the Republican leadership, however, Rhodes opposed a 1979 Republican proposal for a constitutional amendment to limit federal spending, calling the balanced budget amendment a "gimmick" that would not work.

In terms of foreign policy, Rhodes was equally critical on most issues. Although he broke with Senator Goldwater and most other conservative Republicans in supporting the normalization of relations with the People's Republic of China in 1979—he had led an American delegation to China in 1975—as well as the abrogation of the United States' mutual-defense treaty with Taiwan, he remained critical of the administration on such matters as the sale of F-15 jets to Saudi Arabia and its handling of the Iranian hostage crisis. He also had a negative response to the State of the Union address of January 23, 1980, in which the president announced the so-called Carter Doctrine, warning the Soviets, who had invaded Afghanistan the previous month, that any Soviet move toward the Persian Gulf would be regarded as a threat to the vital interests of the United States and would be repelled by any means necessary. Rhodes wryly commented, "There was a little of saber rattling but not much in the saber," and added in a televised response to Carter's address: "We do not have the means of defending the Persian Gulf at this time."

By this time, Rhodes had decided to step down as House minority leader following the end of the 96th Congress. Although a critic of President Carter, he was frustrated by the growing partisanship on Capitol Hill and by what he regarded as a breakdown in the machinery of government. In 1976, he had published a book, *The Futile System: How to Unchain Congress and Make the System Work Again*, in which he spelled out these concerns. He was also interested in becoming secretary of the interior should a Republican be elected president in 1980, which seemed a real possibility. That he was not offered the position following RONALD REAGAN's election was due mainly to the opposition of Senator Paul Laxalt (R-Nev.), a close friend of the president-elect who was delegated responsibility for selecting the person to fill the position and was one of the few Republicans in Washington who did not get along well with Rhodes.

Even though he relinquished his leadership position, Rhodes remained in Congress until 1992, when he decided to retire. Filling his position as minority leader was Robert H. Michel (R-Ill.), a consensus builder whose leadership style was similar to that of Rhodes. In 1988, Rhodes was prepared to run for governor of Arizona if then-Governor Evan Mecham was recalled in a special election. The state Supreme Court, however, cancelled the election.

After retiring from office, Rhodes practiced law with the firm of Hunton and Williams until 1997. He also traveled extensively with his wife Betty and wrote (with Dean Smith) his memoirs, *John Rhodes: I Was There* (1995). In 2002, he received the first Congressional Distinguished Service Award. By then suffering from a virulent form of cancer that had caused the amputation of an arm and left him in a wheelchair, he died on August 24, 2003, in Mesa, Arizona. He was 86 years old.

Ribicoff, Abraham Alexander

(1910–1998) *member of the Senate*

Reelected in 1974 to his third term as U.S. senator from Connecticut, Democrat Abraham Ribicoff had a long record of public service and was one of the most powerful members of the Senate at the time that Jimmy Carter entered the White House in 1977. A liberal, he had major disagreements with the legislative priorities of the Carter administration, but he became best known for the role he played in forcing BERT LANCE, President Carter's close friend and the director of the Office of Management and Budget (OMB), to resign in 1977 amid scandal about his banking practices.

Ribicoff was born into poverty in New Britain, Connecticut, on April 9, 1910, the son of Jewish immigrants from Poland; his father was a peddler and factory worker. Raised in a tenement, he worked in a zipper-and-buckle factory and then as a salesman while attending New York University. When his company transferred him to manage sales in its Chicago office, he was able to attend classes at the University of Chicago, where he was admitted to its law school and earned his law degree cum laude (LL.B., 1933) without completing an undergraduate degree.

Ribicoff combined a law practice with elective politics, serving two terms in the Connecticut legislature from 1938 to 1942 and then as a judge of the Hartford Police Court from 1941 to 1943 and from 1945 to 1947. In 1948, he was elected overwhelmingly to the U.S. House of Representatives and then reelected by an even wider margin in 1950. In 1952, however, he was narrowly defeated for a vacant seat in the U.S. Senate by Republican Prescott S. Bush, father of future president GEORGE HERBERT WALKER BUSH. After briefly returning to his law practice, Ribicoff ran successfully for governor of Connecticut, defeating John Davis Lodge. As governor, he became known for his rigid enforcement of highway-safety laws, earning Connecticut the reputation as the safest state to drive in the nation.

A close friend of Senator John F. Kennedy (D-Mass.), Ribicoff urged Kennedy to run for president in 1960. Later he commented on how he, a Jew, had to persuade Catholic Irish advisers of the Kennedy family that a Catholic could be elected president of the United States. Ribicoff was rewarded for his efforts on behalf of Kennedy's presidential campaign when the president-elect appointed him secretary of health, education, and welfare (HEW). Rumors circulated that Kennedy had even offered Ribicoff the position of attorney general, but the Connecticut governor had advised him to give the position to his brother Robert.

Ribicoff hated the 16 months he spent as HEW secretary. "I wasn't happy in the Cabinet," he later told an interviewer. "I found myself advocating positions I did not believe in. When you go into the Cabinet you're the president's man. I'd been used to being my own man." As secretary of HEW, he worked unsuccessfully for passage of health insurance for the elderly.

Returning to Connecticut in 1962, Ribicoff ran successfully for the U.S. Senate, defeating the Republican candidate, Representative Horace Seely-Brown, Jr. In the Senate, he attracted considerable attention as one of its strongest champions of the New Frontier and Great Society programs. He played a key role in passing such key legislation as Medicare and federal funding for education. In contrast to his friend, Senator EDWARD KENNEDY (D-Mass.), he opposed universal health care as too expensive. Instead, he and Senator RUSSELL LONG (D-La.) cosponsored legislation to provide insurance for only catastrophic illnesses. He also championed civil rights legislation that sought to eliminate the distinction between de jure (based on law) and de facto (based on actuality) segregation.

At the same time, Ribicoff became an outspoken opponent of the war in Vietnam. At the Democratic presidential convention in Chicago in 1968, he drew national attention, when, from the podium, he denounced Mayor Richard Daley for engaging in "Gestapo tactics" in using police and tear gas to put down antiwar protesters in the streets. Daley could be seen on national television responding to the Connecticut senator by mouthing the foulest four-letter epithets.

Four years later, Ribicoff helped lead South Dakota senator GEORGE MCGOVERN's successful bid for the Democratic presidential nomination. After McGovern's running mate, Thomas Eagleton, bowed out of the race because of questions about his mental health, Ribicoff's name was floated as a possible replacement for Eagleton on the Democratic ticket. Although McGovern was roundly defeated by RICHARD NIXON, Ribicoff was reelected for a second term to the Senate and was appointed chair of the Governmental Affairs Committee. Four years later, in 1976, he was briefly considered again for the second spot on the Democrat ticket by the party's presumptive nominee for president, Jimmy Carter.

In the Senate, Ribicoff continued to press for a program of limited national health insurance and the creation of a consumer protection agency, both of which had the support of the White House. As a former secretary of HEW, the Connecticut senator also favored merging HEW's educational programs with programs from other agencies to form a new Department of Education, another measure the Carter administration favored. Despite serious reservations about the trustworthiness of the Soviet Union, in part a result of the heavy-handed treatment he had received from the Kremlin while visiting Moscow, Ribicoff also agreed to lobby in support of the Strategic Arms Limitation Talks treaty (SALT II) with Moscow. Notwithstanding being a Jew and a strong supporter of Israel, he also backed an arms agreement negotiated by the administration with Saudi Arabia, believing that fighter planes should be sold to Saudi Arabia and Egypt as well as to Israel.

At the same time, Ribicoff was often scornful of the Carter administration. He helped lead the fight in the Senate against the White House's energy bill recently passed by the House of Representatives, which he labeled "a shambles." He was also derisive of the president's insistence on comprehensive welfare reform without additional cost to the government. "With all due respect for the administration," he remarked during a press conference, "they don't know what the hell they are doing with welfare reform. They're changing their minds every day."

It was as chair of the Governmental Affairs Committee, however, that Ribicoff locked horns with the Carter administration during the so-called Lance affair. Before taking the position of director of the OMB, Bert Lance had agreed to the president's request that he sell his considerable assets in the National Bank of Georgia (NBG). Because of a sudden drop in the NBG's stock, Lance's assets, much of which were used as collateral for personal loans, were cut in half. In response, President Carter wrote to Ribicoff as chair of the Governmental Affairs Committee, asking if Lance could have an extension to the end of the year in order to sell his shares. After Lance appeared before the Government Operations Committee in July to answer accusations made by WILLIAM SAFIRE of the *New York Times* that he was guilty of banking improprieties and had been peddling his office for a "sweetheart loan" from the First National Bank of Chicago, the Ribicoff committee granted Lance the extension the president had requested. "You have been smeared," Ribicoff even told Lance after his testimony.

A fireball of controversy over Lance's banking practices developed shortly afterward, however, when the comptroller of the currency, John Heimann, issued a report strongly critical of the OMB director, including his practice of permitting sizeable overdrafts on the personal accounts of the NBG's officers and relatives and using the NBG's private airplane for personal use. Heimann even told the president that he was referring Lance's use of the NBG plane to the Justice Department and the Internal Revenue Service for investigation.

In response to the accusations against Lance, Ribicoff opened hearings into his activities as a private banker. As the testimony continued, they brought into question Lance's qualifications to be OMB director. Although the OMB director delivered a spirited defense of his actions in a second appearance before the committee on September 15, demands grew for his resignation even among Democrats, who understood the damage that the charges surrounding Lance were causing the president. Responding to this pressure, Carter convinced his friend that it would be in everyone's best interest if he tendered his resignation, which Lance did on September 19, 1977.

No Democrat was more vigorous in calling for Lance's resignation than Ribicoff. Although he had been supportive of the OMB director when he made his first appearance before his Governmental Affairs Committee, the Connecticut senator's attitude changed dramatically as questions mounted about the ethics of Lance's banking practices. He became outraged when he received information that Lance might have been embezzling funds from his own bank. On September 3, 1977, he and Senator CHARLES PERCY (Ill.), the ranking minority leader on the Governmental Affairs Committee, sent the president a memorandum outlining a number of matters concerning Lance that had not been covered in the comptroller's report. "Information has been brought to our attention," they told Carter, "which would appear to substantiate allegations that the Justice Department acted improperly in failing to fully investigate potential criminal violations of Federal banking law growing out of the Lance for Governor campaign [Lance had run for governor of Georgia in 1974] and Mr. Lance's personal affairs during that time."

Subsequent to Lance's resignation, William Safire won the Pulitzer Prize for breaking the story on Lance. Ribicoff wrote Safire a short note to congratulate him on winning the Pulitzer. "You deserved it. … Your perceptions on Bert Lance were early and correct. Mine were not," the senator wrote.

Although Ribicoff could probably have won a fourth term to the Senate, he decided not to seek reelection in 1980. "There is a time to stay and a time to go," he stated in announcing his decision to retire after nearly 50 years of public service. Instead, he took a position with Kaye, Scholer, Fierman, Hays & Handler, a large New York law firm, and remained largely out of the political limelight. "I loved every day I was in politics," he later explained. "But I got out at the right time. I never miss it." In his retirement, however, he commented on the "meanness" that he believed had crept into politics.

Darkly handsome, self-confident, and an elegant dresser for most of his life, Ribicoff died on February 22, 1998, in New York after suffering from Alzheimer's disease. He was 87 years old.

Rickover, Hyman George

(1900–1986) *admiral, United States Navy*

Often referred to as the father of the nuclear-powered navy, Admiral Hyman G. Rickover may have had more influence on the adult Jimmy Carter—who had worked for him—than anyone else. In the admiral, the future president found a father figure, a man he idolized for his intelligence, work ethic, attention to detail, and demand for perfection. When Carter, then in the navy, interviewed with Rickover for a position, the admiral asked him, "Why not the best?" The question stuck in Carter's mind, became the title of his campaign biography, and was one of the guiding principles of his presidency. As for Rickover, he was given a degree of access to the Oval Office unheard of for any officer not in the highest echelons of the Pentagon.

Born in the Jewish ghetto of Makow in Russian-occupied Poland on January 27, 1900, Rickover was six when he and his parents immigrated to the United States, where the family settled in Chicago. Although a good and hard-working student, he did not stand out as exceptional among his peers. He was able, however, to secure an appointment to the U.S. Naval Academy at Annapolis, Maryland, in 1918. At the academy, he began to develop a reputation that would follow him for the rest of his life as a bookworm and loner who cared little for socializing or engaging in sports and was not afraid to break the rules or speak his mind. The fact that he was Jewish may also have set him apart from the rest of the midshipmen and made him an object of frequent hazing.

Graduating from Annapolis 107th out of a class of 540 in 1922, Rickover had an uneventful career over the next 15 years, spending much of his time on sea duty and rising in the ranks at regular intervals. Although he received good to outstanding evaluations from his commanding officers, he gained a reputation among his fellow officers as unfriendly and an introvert who preferred studying engineering mathematics to socializing with his peers. Anxious to pursue his education as an engineer, he was able to secure an appointment to the Naval Postgraduate School in Annapolis in 1927 and then to obtain a graduate degree in electrical engineering from Columbia University (M.S., 1929).

The next eight years were seminal for Rickover. He was appointed to the naval submarine school at New London, Connecticut, and then spent the next three years aboard submarines. This experience convinced him that the submarine represented a fundamental change in the nature of warfare and deserved a greater role in the overall order of battle. It also left him disdainful of his fellow officers, whom he characterized as lacking in initiative, anti-intellectual, petty in their treatment of enlisted men, and concerned mainly with advancing their own careers. Following his submarine duty, Rickover was reassigned first to shore duty, then to service on the battleship *New Mexico*, and, finally, to command of an old minesweeper being used to tow gunnery targets. He was then reassigned at his request to EDO (engineering duty only). In contrast to line officers, who were trained to command ships, EDOs were responsible only for designing, repairing, and maintaining ships.

Rickover would distinguish himself not as a line officer and commander of ships, but as an EDO officer and as the nation's most prominent promoter of nuclear submarines. His biggest break came in 1939 when he was assigned to the Bureau of Ships in Washington. As head of the Bureau's electrical section at a time when the fleet was rapidly expanding to meet wartime needs, he was in a key position to design and improve its electrical systems. Driven, compulsive, and an iconoclast, he made major improvements to the fleet, designing shockproof electric equipment on ships, improving equipment to make it more compact and lighter, reducing noise on submarines, developing underwater detectors and infrared signaling devices, and inventing an antimagnetic mine device.

Following Japan's attack on Pearl Harbor on December 7, 1941, Rickover's section assumed responsibility for repairing the electrical and propulsion systems of two battleships that had been seriously damaged but not destroyed by the Japanese. Typically, he clashed with his superiors and civilian engineers from General Electric over the best way to proceed with repairing the two ships. Though he usually got his way, he added to his reputation as a brilliant and meticulous engineer who got things done but who was nevertheless self-righteous, vain, irascible, often insubordinate, and almost always insufferable. In his last fitness report for 1945, he was given low marks on his ability to command, his use of suggestions given by others, and his unwillingness to effectively delegate responsibility. Because of this, his chances of promotion from his present rank of captain to flag rank were compromised severely.

Rickover's experience on submarines and his work at the Bureau of Ships, however, put him in an excellent position to parlay his background into an appointment to the atomic submarine project at Oak Ridge National Laboratory after the war. Still, his reputation for single-mindedness and not being a team player almost prevented this appointment, and when it was offered to him, it was made clear that he was to be part of the navy team and not its leader.

As early as 1933, Rickover had expressed concern about the world's supply of energy because of increased industrialization that was, in his view, coincident with the introduction of oil. Noting that scientists were already "attempting to obtain sub-atomic energy," he remarked, "I sincerely hope they fail in this. It reminds me of Pandora's Box, where a great deal of misery was let loose by learning too much." Except for this offhand remark made in a letter to his wife, Ruth D. Masters, whom he had married in 1931, it does not appear that Rickover gave much additional thought to the potential use of nuclear power either for wartime or peacetime uses. Like most Americans, he believed the use of the atomic bomb against Hiroshima and Nagasaki in August 1945 was justified. Beyond that, he did not say much.

Once he went to Oak Ridge in 1946, however, Rickover studied the naval files on nuclear power and very quickly became the champion of nuclear-powered submarines, even though the navy was more interested after the war in nuclear-powered aircraft carriers. Rickover also became the de facto head of the navy development team, notwithstanding his orders to the contrary. The engineering and bureaucratic obstacles he needed to overcome before gaining authorization for a nuclear-propelled submarine were enormous, not the least of which were that a civilian agency, the Atomic Energy Commission (AEC), made the final decisions on the military and peaceful uses of nuclear energy. The navy's own chain of command also did not support a nuclear-powered submarine. It took enormous skill, technological acumen, and dogged perseverance over a period of six years—including Rickover's willingness to risk his career by going around the chain of command and appealing directly to the chief of naval operations, Admiral Chester A. Nimitz, a submariner himself—before the navy approved plans for two nuclear-powered submarines, the *Nautilus* and the *Sea Wolf.* In the process, Rickover added to his list of enemies both in the navy and among two of the major contractors for the project, General Electric and Westinghouse.

Rickover also amassed enormous power, which he was not shy in using to promote his vision of a nuclear-powered navy. Specifically, he was given joint assignments as head of the Nuclear Power Branch of the Bureau of Ships and chief of the Naval Research Branch of the AEC. In this way, he gained great autonomy in establishing the direction of the navy's nuclear-propulsion program.

Invariably, Rickover clashed with his naval and civilian superiors at the Pentagon over such questions as classes and numbers of nuclear-powered ships to be built (submarines versus surface ships, for example, and nuclear-propelled versus diesel-propelled aircraft carriers) and the needed number of reactors for each ship (ranging from one to as many as eight for aircraft carriers). So strong was the animosity toward Rickover among his fellow officers that in 1951 and 1952, he was passed over for promotion from captain to rear admiral despite his impressive record in heading up the nuclear navy. Nonetheless, as a skillful political infighter and a self-promoter, he had developed such strong support on Capitol Hill that his case for promotion was reconsidered in 1953, and he was advanced to rear admiral.

Once construction of the first of the nuclear-powered submarines got underway, Rickover assumed absolute control over the selection of naval officers to be trained to operate and command nuclear-powered ships. One of the first officers he chose was Lieutenant Jimmy Carter, whose selection was to affect the young officer more than he could ever have imagined. In 1970, when Rickover received an invitation to Carter's inauguration as Georgia's new governor, he had to ask one of his aides who Carter was. But Carter remembered well his experience as one of Rickover's junior officers. "Admiral Rickover had a profound effect on my life—perhaps more than anyone except my own parents," the future president later wrote.

There were, of course, differences between the two men. Rickover was more of a conceptualizer and visionary than Carter. While they both read extensively and deeply, Rickover read more broadly. Oddly, the career officer was also a better political infighter than the future politician and president. But their similarities far outweighed their differences. They were both loners who never cared much for the navy's social life. They were hardworking. They approached problem solving through a mastery of detail. They were self-righteous and not prone to compromise. They needed to be in charge. They demanded excellence. They micromanaged. They believed that self-fulfillment meant something more than material gain and that they served some singular purpose other than their own ambitions. Accord-

First lady Rosalynn Carter, President Carter, and Admiral Hyman Rickover (far right) aboard the nuclear submarine USS *Los Angeles,* 1977 *(Jimmy Carter Library)*

ingly, they were prepared to skirt ordinary chains of command or conventional political processes. They were, in brief, soul mates.

Rickover reached the height of his influence in government with Carter's election as president. Although the admiral did not attend the Georgia governor's inauguration in 1970, the two men struck up an ongoing conversation during Carter's term in the state office. Besides his interest in a nuclear propulsion, Rickover had taken a keen interest in what he regarded as a totally inadequate system of public education that promoted mediocrity and failed to provide the competence needed in the new age of technology. In the late 1950s and early 1960s, Rickover published three books describing what he believed to be the woeful state of American education and calling for the training of more engineers and scientists. The Georgia governor read the books and expressed his admiration for them.

During his campaign for the White House in 1976, Carter wrote to Rickover that if he were elected president and it was "within the bounds of military/political propriety," he would like to have the admiral's views on a number of matters, including the structure of the Defense Department, the method of awarding contracts, and the emphasis to place on nuclear power. As president, Carter also made clear to his staff that he was to see any letters or memorandums sent to him by Rickover and to make sure that he responded to his telephone calls.

In the course of Carter's presidency, Rickover commented extensively on all three matters Carter raised, but in early 1977, one of them vexed him in particular—the overcharges he believed defense contractors were billing the government and which he regarded as being so inflated as to be fraudulent. This bitterly fought battle had begun in 1969 when the navy settled an overcharge with the Todd Shipbuilding Corporation. Other large contractors with the navy then filed their own claims, which at one point amounted to more than $1.72 billion. Although the issues involved were extremely complex, for Rickover they came down to one simple question: did the ship contractors exist for the navy, or did the navy exist for the contractors? In his view, no ground for compromise existed. The fact that he could maintain this position and delay efforts at compromise, even by the secretary of the navy, merely underscored the extraordinary power Rickover wielded within the Defense Department. Even the strong-willed secretary of defense under President GERALD FORD, Donald H. Rumsfeld, had been reluctant to take him on, turning down the recommendation of his deputy defense secretary, William Clements, who had dealt directly with Rickover, that the admiral be fired.

After Carter took office, Rickover brought up again what he believed to be fraudulent overcharges on which the naval contractors were trying to collect. As part of his campaign against the contractors, he also raised issues having to do with the government's patent policy, which, he claimed, resulted in large companies getting the lion's share of government contracts and then using them to establish monopolies at government expense.

Carter was instinctively sympathetic to Rickover's accusation. A fiscal conservative himself, committed to eliminating wasteful spending and balancing the budget, yet sharing some of the populist bias of one who grew up in the rural South against large corporate interests, he asked his special assistant for domestic affairs, STUART EIZENSTAT, to look into the charges Rickover was making with respect to awarding patents to big-business interests. Later he reminded Eizenstat that his own orientation was toward government ownership of patents. Similarly, he expressed much interest in Rickover's extended comments on how the Defense Department could be restructured to make it more efficient at less cost.

On numerous other issues, the president received solicited and unsolicited comments from the admiral, covering a wide range of topics. Rickover applauded Carter's stance on human rights, for example, and also gave him the suggestion to describe the energy crisis in an April 1977 speech as "the moral equivalent of war," whose acronym, MEOW, was widely ridiculed. Secretary of Health, Education and Welfare JOSEPH CALIFANO bristled when, at a meeting with Rickover suggested by the president in August 1977, the admiral called the Office of Education "incompetent and unproductive [and] the last people you should listen to." After the Soviet Union invaded Afghanistan in December 1979, Rickover recommended to Secretary of State CYRUS VANCE that the United States send as much as a battalion of men into Afghanistan in response to the attack.

Carter showed his deep respect and esteem for Rickover, who had remarried two years after the death of his first wife in 1972, by occasionally having him and his wife to dinner in the White House residence. On at least one occasion in 1979, the Rickovers reciprocated by having the Carters to dinner at their home. Yet Carter never let his respect for the admiral interfere with his own judgment on policy and issues. Notwithstanding Rickover's strong support for another nuclear aircraft carrier and nuclear cruiser, for example, the president did not include them in his 1979 budget, believing they were too expensive and not needed. When Congress included them anyway in the Defense Authorization Bill, the president vetoed the bill, which was later upheld in the House. In 1979, however, the president signed legislation that included funds for the construction of another nuclear-propelled carrier, the *Theodore Roosevelt.*

To his credit, Rickover promised the president that he would never try to influence budget matters or act as a spokesman for the navy. He kept that promise. Appearing on the television news show *Face the Nation* just as Congress was scheduled to vote on overriding the president's veto of the Defense Authorization Bill, Rickover repeatedly refused to state his position on the nuclear carrier, stating that he had agreed to appear on the program only to discuss education.

Because Rickover was regarded as an expert on nuclear energy, he played an important role in responding in March 1979 to an accident at the nuclear power plant on Three Mile Island, about 10 miles south of Harrisburg, Pennsylvania. The plant's reactor core had overheated and for days threatened to send lethal radioactive gases into the atmosphere. Although that worse-case scenario did not happen, the accident undermined claims endorsing the safety of nuclear energy. Rickover was asked by the media and by an investigating commission established by Carter (the Kenneny Commission) to comment on the incident. The admiral used the opportunity to emphasize the safety of nuclear reactors but also to stress the need for highly trained personnel, like those officers he selected for the navy's nuclear vessels, to run the reactors.

Following the Three Mile Island incident, Rickover began to rethink his views on nuclear power. At a celebration of his retirement in 1982, he remarked that both nuclear weapons and nuclear power should be outlawed. "I'm not proud of the part I played," he remarked. In 1986, the admiral's daughter-in-law, Jane Rickover, claimed she had been told by her father-in-law that the full report of the Kenneny Commission had not been made public because it showed that the accident at Three Mile Island was much more serious than what the public had been told. She also stated that the admiral told her he had used his influence with the president to have a sanitized version of the report published, but that he had come to regret his action. There is no evidence, however, that Rickover ever interceded with Carter to prevent the release of the Kenneny Commission report. If Rickover began to have reservations about nuclear power, moreover, they were not grave enough to keep him from taking a position as a lobbyist for the operator of Three Mile Island, the General Public Utilities Nuclear Corporation, which sought to open a second undamaged unit that he had inspected and deemed safe to operate. It resumed operations in October 1985.

By this time, Rickover's long career in the navy was over. No longer having the support of the White House, he was retired from active duty in 1982. In 1984, congressional investigators revealed that Rickover had received an unusually large fee from General Public Utilities as well as a number of gifts, including jewelry for his wife, from contractors with whom he had done business. The next year, Secretary of the Navy John Lehman censured him for accepting gratuities from the General Dynamics Corporation.

Two years later, on July 8, 1986, Rickover died. Former president Carter was among a thousand persons, but the only living president, who attended the funeral service at the National Cathedral. In his eulogy of his former superior, Carter repeated what he had said and written a number of times: "Second only to my own father, Hyman Rickover made my life."

Rockefeller, David

(1915–) *banker, financier*

Grandson of the famed industrialist John D. Rockefeller and chairman of the Chase Manhattan Bank during the Carter administration,

David Rockefeller was also an internationalist and an acquaintance of the shah of Iran, MOHAMMAD REZA PAHLAVI. As an internationalist, he was a founder of the Trilateral Commission, a body intended to promote cooperation among the world's leading industrial nations. The commission's membership included President Carter, Vice President WALTER MONDALE, Secretary of State CYRUS VANCE, Secretary of Defense HAROLD BROWN, Secretary of the Treasury W. MICHAEL BLUMENTHAL, and National Security Advisor ZBIGNIEW BRZEZINSKI. As an acquaintance of the shah of Iran, Rockefeller helped lobby successfully in 1979 to gain admission of the deposed Iranian monarch into the United States for emergency medical treatment, which led to the Iranian hostage crisis of 1979–81.

The fifth and youngest son of John D. Rockefeller, Jr., David Rockefeller was born in New York City on June 12, 1915. As a member of one of the nation's wealthiest families, he enjoyed all the privileges that accompany families of great fortunes. He lived in the largest private residence in New York City (a nine-story home that included a play area on the roof and even its own infirmary) and roller-skated up Fifth Avenue accompanied by a limousine to pick him up when he became tired. He spent weekends at the family estate in Pocantico Hills, Westchester County, where he developed his interest in collecting species of beetles, and summers in Maine at the Eyrie in Seal Harbor.

There was, though, another side to Rockefeller's upbringing. His father was rigid and aloof and, like his grandfather, a stern Baptist who required his children to learn and recite passages from the Bible every morning in his study. John Rockefeller often communicated with his children by formal letters, frequently with moral admonitions. He suffered for a sense of inadequacy and went through a bout of depression that kept him at home for more than a year. However, he also infused his children with a sense of civic duty and commitment to philanthropy and, along with David's mother, Abby Aldrich Rockefeller, a lifelong love of the arts.

David Rockefeller attended the Lincoln School of Columbia University's Teacher's College and Harvard University, where he majored in history and literature (B.A., 1936). He then did graduate work in economics at Harvard and the London School of Economics before receiving his doctorate in economics from the University of Chicago (Ph.D., 1940), which his grandfather had founded in the 1890s. After receiving his Ph.D., Rockefeller served as an unpaid intern in the office of Mayor Fiorello H. La Guardia and then worked briefly for the state of New York before enlisting as a private in the army following the United States' entry into World War II. During the war, he became a military intelligence officer serving in North Africa and France, including six months as a military attaché in Paris. He was awarded the Italian, French, and U.S. Legions of Honor.

After the war, Rockefeller began his lifelong career with the Chase Manhattan Bank, beginning as assistant manager in the foreign department and rising steadily in the ranks until becoming its chairman in 1961. During this time, he was also actively involved in the redevelopment of lower Manhattan and was influential in Chase's decision to build its new headquarters, Chase Plaza, in the area.

Throughout his career, Rockefeller had an abiding interest in international affairs. He traced this interest back to his father, who had been a staunch supporter of the League of Nations and an active participant in the worldwide Protestant ecumenical movement, and to his experience during World War II. "Like many in my generation," he later wrote, "I returned from World War II believing a new international architecture had to be erected and that the United States had a moral obligation to provide leadership in that effort."

Through his family connections and his responsibilities with the Chase Bank, Rockefeller met many of the world's financial and political leaders. In 1949, he was elected to the board of directors of the Council on Foreign Relations. He served on the board for 36 years and became its chairperson in 1970. Beginning in 1954, he also participated regularly in the secret Bilderberg conferences, an annual three-day meeting of some of Europe's and North America's most influential bankers, economists, politicians, and government officials. The group's name was taken from the Bilderberg Hotel in Oosterbeek, Netherlands, where the conference was initiated by Prince Bernhard of the Netherlands in 1954 to discuss issues of common interest to the Atlantic community.

Rockefeller also participated in other international forums and was active in the formation of a number of organizations with an international orientation. Among these was the International Executive Service Corps (IESC), which he helped establish in 1963 with SOL LINOWITZ, the chief executive officer of Xerox Corporation. The IESC's purpose was to provide technical advice and managerial assistance in developing countries.

The most prominent organization Rockefeller helped establish, however, was the Trilateral Commission, which he formed in 1973 in order to promote closer ties between the United States, Europe, and Japan. "The idea for an organization including representatives from North America, Europe, and Japan—the three centers of democratic capitalism—resulted from my realization in the early 1970s that power relationships in the world had fundamentally changed," he later explained. Rockefeller wanted a forum along the lines of the Bilderberg conferences, but one that also included Japan, which had been excluded from the Bilderberg meetings. He decided to organize the Trilateral Commission after conferring with Zbigniew Brzezinski, Robert Bowie of the Center for International Studies at Harvard, Henry Owen of the Brookings Institution, and McGeorge Bundy of the Ford Foundation. The commission would examine such matters as trade and investment, environmental problems, population control, and assistance to developing nations. To head the group, Rockefeller appointed Brzezinski, who was then teaching at Columbia University and had published a book, *Between Two Ages: America in the Technetronic Era* (1970), much along the lines of Rockefeller's thinking. The two had met at the 1972 Bilderberg meeting.

The Trilateral Commission invited some of the brightest and most influential minds from each of the three regions represented in the organization. Wanting to have "a forward looking" Democratic governor from the South on the commission, and having learned of newly elected Georgia governor Jimmy Carter's interest in promoting trade relations among Georgia, the Common Market, and Japan, Brzezinski invited Carter to serve on the commission. Having decided to run for president and seeking to gain international exposure, the governor gladly accepted the invitation. Yet despite Brzezinski's endorsement, Rockefeller had reservations about Carter, whom he later described as "an obscure Democratic governor of Georgia [whose] campaign was subtly anti-Washington and antiestablishment [sic]." He was surprised, therefore, when President-elect Carter appointed 15 members of the Trilateral Commission to positions in his administration, including all his key foreign policy advisers.

Following Carter's election in 1976, Rockefeller met with the president, Secretary of State Vance, and National Security Advisor Brzezinski to discuss an impending visit he was about to make to the People's Republic of China to discuss Chase's correspondent banking relationship with the Bank of China. (The relationship had been established after President RICHARD NIXON's visit to China in 1972.) According to Rockefeller, the White House gave him its permission to discuss its interest in moving toward normalizing relations with the Beijing government. Aside from this meeting, there is no indication that Rockefeller tried to influence administration policy directly or through the Trilateral Commission prior to 1979. Following the Iranian revolution and the flight of the shah from Iran that year, however, Rockefeller joined with former secretary of state HENRY KISSINGER and former Chase Manhattan Bank chair John McCloy in lobbying the administration to allow the shah into the United States.

Prior to the 1970s, Rockefeller had visited the former Iranian leader only twice. In the 1970s, the two men met more often, but mainly to discuss matters involving Chase investments in Iran. Rockefeller found the shah arrogant, remarking that he "seemed to think that because he believed something, it was automatically a fact." Having grown increasingly pessimistic about Iran's future, Rockefeller was not entirely surprised by the events of early 1979 and assumed the overthrown leader would come directly to the United States. As he later noted, though, he "did not give much thought to [the shah's] movement because I was more concerned about the Iranian revolution's impact on Chase."

In March 1979, however, Undersecretary of State David Newsom contacted Rockefeller, asking if he would fly to Morocco, where the shah had moved but was no longer welcomed, to inform the exiled leader that he would not be allowed to come to the United States out of fear that Iran might seize Americans as hostages. Newsom had made a similar request to Kissinger, who had known the shah since he was National Security Advisor in the Nixon administration. Like Kissinger, Rockefeller was taken aback by the request, which he rejected.

A week after receiving Newsom's request, Rockefeller was approached by the shah's twin sister, Princess Ashraf, whom he had met earlier when she represented Iran on the United Nations' Women's Rights Commission. The princess asked him to intervene with the president on her brother's behalf. That same evening, Rockefeller met with Kissinger and with Happy Rockefeller, the widow of his recently deceased brother Nelson. Mrs. Rockefeller had a close relationship with the shah and had offered him a place to live in the United States when it became clear that he would probably have to leave Iran. Believing with Kissinger that it would be dishonorable to deny a former close ally asylum in the United States, David Rockefeller decided to join the former secretary of state in asking the White House to allow the shah into the country. In April, he met with the president; clearly irritated, Carter turned him down. Over the next several months, Rockefeller and Kissinger tried to find another country that would accept the shah, who had now settled temporarily in the Bahamas. Finally, Kissinger was able to persuade Mexican president José López Portillo to grant the former Iranian leader a visa to live in Cuernavaca.

Although Kissinger and McCloy continued to lobby the White House on the shah's behalf, Rockefeller did nothing else until the end of September 1979, when he told Newsom that the shah, who had been secretly diagnosed with lymphoma in 1973, might have to come to the United States for medical treatment. After Rockefeller was told a few weeks later by a physician, whom he had twice sent to Mexico to examine the shah, that the former monarch needed emergency medical treatment available only in New York, he joined Kissinger and McCloy in urging the president to allow the shah into the United States. When Vance joined Brzezinski, who had always favored providing asylum, in agreeing that the shah should be permitted to enter the country on humanitarian grounds, Carter reluctantly gave his consent. On October 23, 1979, the shah arrived in New York to begin his treatment.

On November 4, Iranians seized 60 Americans as hostages at the U.S. embassy in Tehran. On November 15, Rockefeller informed the president that the shah was ready to leave the United States and asked to see either Vance or the president's counselor, LLOYD CUTLER. Carter responded that he was against such a meeting because he did not want to have anything to do with the shah's decision to leave. That was, according to the New York banker, the last of his involvement with the administration on the shah's behalf.

Rockefeller has continued to believe that the Carter administration acted shamefully in its treatment of the shah. "When it comes to principle," he has written, "nations must stand for something; they must keep their word. We failed to do this with the Shah, who, despite his imperfections as a ruler, deserved more honorable treatment from the most powerful nation in the world." As chair of the Chase Manhattan Bank, however, he was relieved, when, following the seizure of the American hostages, the president froze Iranian assets in the United States and then, as part of a comprehensive deal freeing the hostages in 1981, allowed the bank to use monies from those assets to pay off loans that Chase had declared insolvent in 1979.

In 1981, Rockefeller retired as Chase's chair, although he remained chair of the bank's international advisory board. In the 1990s, he fought successfully to preserve his family ties to the Rockefeller Center, which his father had built during the Great Depression. In 1989, the family had sold 80 percent of the Center to Japan's Mitsubishi Estate Corporation. When, a few years later, Mitsubishi was about to take it into bankruptcy, Rockefeller joined with a group of investors, including Goldman Sachs & Co., to buy back a 50 percent share. Rockefeller Center has since gone through extensive renovation and has begun to thrive again as a major New York City business and entertainment center and tourist attraction.

Rockefeller has also continued the family tradition of philanthropy. In 2005, he made two major gifts of $100 million each, the first to Rockefeller University, founded by his grandfather, and the second to New York's Museum of Modern Art, established by his mother. In 1995, he was awarded the Presidential Medal of Freedom by President Bill Clinton. He has published *David Rockefeller: Memoirs* (2003), the only member of the extended Rockefeller family to publish his memoirs. He continues to spend his time managing the family's investment firm and collecting beetles.

Rostenkowski, Daniel David

(1928–) *member of the House of Representatives*

Daniel Rostenkowski was a senior member of the House Ways and Means Committee and Democratic deputy whip during the Carter administration. A machine politician who was a strong believer in deal making, he developed an uncanny ability for accurate nose counts on key Capitol Hill issues. Because he differed with the administration on a number of issues, his relationship with the White House remained strained throughout the Carter presidency.

Born on January 2, 1928, in Chicago, Illinois, Rostenkowski grew up versed in machine politics. His grandfather and father were Chicago aldermen, Democratic ward committeemen, and leaders of Chicago's huge Polish community at a time when all politics were still truly local. As a boy, young Daniel used to pack clothes for the poor, deliver food baskets on holidays, and watch his father take care of his constituents. Joseph Rostenkowski found them jobs, extended them credit through a credit union he operated from his home, paid their utility bills, and turned vacant lots into playgrounds for local youth.

After graduating from a private military school in 1946, Daniel Rostenkowski served for 18 months in the U.S. Army (1946–48). He then enrolled part-time at Loyola University in downtown Chicago. Instead of finishing a degree, though, he opted to begin his political career. As a member of the Cook County political machine that came to be headed by Mayor Richard Daley and dominated state politics, his father was able, with the machine's backing, to get Daniel elected to the Illinois General Assembly (1952) and, three years later to the Illinois Senate (1954). During this time, Daley became Rostenkowski's political mentor while the lawmaker became the mayor's reliable lieutenant in Springfield, the state's capital.

In 1958, Rostenkowski was rewarded for his service when the congressman for his district, Thomas Gordon, one of his father's loyal allies, decided to retire after serving in Congress since 1942. With the support of the Democratic organization, Rostenkowski was elected to the vacant seat with virtually no opposition. For the next 35 years, he scarcely had to worry about being reelected.

As a product of machine politics, Rostenkowski spent his early years in the House learning the ropes rather than seeking national attention. He spent most of his weekends in Chicago building his local organization and attending to the business of his constituents, whose problems ranged from federal legislation to parking tickets. He also met frequently with Mayor Daley. His relationship with Daley and his party loyalty paid dividends in Washington, where, as a House freshman, he got a choice assignment on the Interstate and Foreign Commerce Committee. In 1964, he was able to move over to the Ways and Means Committee, the House's most powerful committee, controlled by Wilbur Mills (Ark.), one of its most savvy legislators.

Rostenkowski also mingled readily with House leaders. In 1967, House Speaker John McCormack of Massachusetts handpicked him to be chair of the Democratic Caucus, which made him part of the House leadership. In that position, he made friends with urban machine politicians like himself and southern Democrats who still controlled most of the major House committees. Gradually, Rostenkowski focused his attention more on being a team player on Capitol Hill rather than Daley's lieutenant in Washington, although he never forgot his roots or Chicago's city hall.

Rostenkowski had less contact with a growing number of stalwart northern liberals who were more independent and less loyal than he to the party and House leadership. In the 1960s and early 1970s, they coalesced into the Democratic Study Group (DSG), which had been established in 1959 by a small band of freshman lawmakers to organize liberal forces in the House. They were opposed to the type of machine politics that Rostenkowski represented and did not much care for his gruff style.

Rostenkowski also alienated the new Speaker of the House, Carl Albert (Okla.), by claiming that, at the tumultuous 1968 Democratic convention in Chicago, he had been instructed by President Lyndon Johnson to take the gavel from Albert, who at the time was House majority leader. Maintaining that he gave the gavel ceremoniously to a lawmaker from the convention's host city, Albert called Rostenkowski a liar.

When Albert became Speaker in 1970, he helped to defeat Rostenkowski for reelection as chair of the Democratic Caucus. He then chose TIP O'NEILL (Mass.) as majority whip over the Chicago congressman, who had vied for the position and had the support of Majority Leader Hale Boggs (La.). Observers said that Rostenkowski, no longer part of the House leadership, wept at his defeat.

Rostenkowski's return to power in the House was abetted curiously enough by many of the same liberal members of the DSG who disliked the kind of politics he represented. Between 1970 and 1976, they helped to engineer major changes in the House rules that reduced the power of committee chairs, removed three of the most conservative southerners from powerful positions as chairs, and gave junior members of the House greater power, including choice committee assignments. At the same time, Wilbur Mills was forced to step down as chair of the Ways and Means Committee and then to retire from the House because of his drunken escapades with a burlesque dancer. The result of these changes was that Rostenkowski advanced in seniority and authority on the Ways and Means Committee, which had been a particular target of the DSG. He also assumed the position of chair of the Subcommittee on Health, an issue that became increasingly important in the following two decades.

In 1976, Rostenkowski was able to use his well-developed political skills during a spirited contest for majority leader. The position opened after Tip O'Neill, who had become majority leader following the accidental death of Hale Boggs in 1974, was picked to be Speaker of the House following Carl Albert's retirement from Congress in 1976. The leader of the DSG, PHILLIP BURTON, an abrasive but brilliant political strategist and ultraliberal from San Francisco, was favored to be elected majority leader. He was challenged for the position, however, by RICHARD BOLLING (Mo.), a leader of the House reform movement who was respected for his intelligence but widely disliked for his arrogance, and JIM WRIGHT (Tex.), a moderate who was the underdog in the race but had the quiet support of Tip O'Neill. By first working with Burton against Bolling, whom Rostenkowski hated and who was eliminated from the race in a second round of balloting, and then quietly working the House floor in support of Wright, Rostenkowski proved to be decisive in getting Wright elected over Burton as majority leader by a single vote. In return, Rostenkowski won the support of O'Neill and Wright to become majority deputy whip. (The majority whip's position had already been promised to JOHN BRADEMAS [Ind.].)

Through his position as a senior member of the Ways and Means Committee, still one of the most powerful House committees. Rostenkowski was once more a major powerbroker in Congress, enjoying the support of both the House Speaker and the majority leader. Because of Rostenkowski's importance in the House, President Carter tried to cultivate good relations with the Chicago lawmaker. The president's liaison for congressional affairs, FRANK MOORE, told the president in 1978 that Rostenkowski had been flattered by Carter's agreement to have his picture taken with the congressman's daughters and subsequently indicated a willingness to help the president in his fight against several water projects being pushed by other lawmakers.

Nevertheless, the results of the president's efforts were generally disappointing to Rostenkowski. In the first place, the Illinois representative remained a machine politician, and try as hard as he might, the president did not like political machines. "To Jimmy Carter," wrote Martin Tolchin of the *New York Times*, "political machines meant sleepy southern court houses, corrupt organizations, the sort of thing that almost stole his first election." Second, relations between the White House and the Chicago lawmaker got off to a bad start when the president turned down an invitation from Rostenkowski to address the annual Cook

County Democratic Dinner. Third, Rostenkowski had little regard for Frank Moore and the president's chief aide, HAMILTON JORDAN. Finally, he did not believe that Chicago's Democrats were getting their fair share of patronage from Carter's staff.

As a member of the Ways and Means Committee who did not share the liberal views of many of his colleagues, Rostenkowski joined with the chairperson of the Ways and Means Committee, AL ULLMAN (Oreg.), in opposing the White House's frontal assault on major tax breaks for businesses without first consulting the committee, which was responsible for tax legislation. Instead, they supported a measure that reduced the maximum tax rate on capital gains from 49 percent to 35 percent. Although the president signed the 1978 tax measure, he was bitterly disappointed by it. Following a meeting with Ullman and Rostenkowski, he wrote, "I found through bitter experience that *any* tax proposal … attracted to Capitol Hill a pack of powerful and ravenous wolves, determined to secure for themselves additional benefits at the expense of other Americans." Tip O'Neill was also disappointed by the final tax legislation, although he blamed it more on Ullman, whom he distrusted, than Rostenkowski. In contrast, most other House liberals blamed the measure on Rostenkowski, a politician they never liked.

Another issue important to the White House that had to go through Rostenkowski's Health Subcommittee, hospital cost containment, also fared poorly insofar as the administration was concerned. Rostenkowski initially supported the proposal, although he warned that it would be extremely difficult for hospitals to keep within the 11–12 percent limit in cost increases proposed by the president. Increasingly, however, he was persuaded by health and hospital lobbyists and by other members of his subcommittee that too many changes would have to be made for the measure to work, such as exemptions for smaller hospitals and a more generous formula for determining hospital revenues than currently contained in the legislation. Even labor leaders opposed to the measure believed that cost containment would come at the expense of wages for hospital workers. Rather than a mandatory containment bill, the measure the Health Subcommittee finally agreed upon was a voluntary cost-containment program approved by the hospital industry itself.

The president was deeply annoyed with Rostenkowski, calling him to the White House for a meeting with Secretary of Health, Education and Welfare JOSEPH CALIFANO and several of his aides. "They were busting my buns for saying that the plan could only be voluntary," Rostenkowski later recounted. But he insisted that he lacked the votes for anything more than a voluntary program, and he refused even to bring the measure out for a vote by the full Ways and Means Committee. In retaliation, the president left Rostenkowski off the official U.S. delegation to the installation of the first Polish head of the Catholic Church, Pope John Paul II, until Tip O'Neill interceded on Rostenkowski's behalf.

The Chicago lawmaker was correct that the votes were not there for something more stringent than a voluntary program. But as a deal maker who believed in the give-and-take of politics, he was convinced that if the president had provided better leadership, sought to reach some kind of accommodation with committee members, understood the pressures they were under from the powerful medical lobby, and met them halfway on such matters as exemptions for some hospitals and more flexibility on spending limits, a more satisfactory measure on cost containment could have come out of the committee.

Rostenkowski was convinced that the president's refusal to reach out to members of Congress in these ways doomed not only a meaningful cost-containment measure but most of the president's legislative agenda. Halfway into the administration, he expressed his concern to House Speaker O'Neill. "The problem between the White House staff and ourselves is getting out of hand," he told O'Neill. Out of a sense of frustration with Carter and his own subcommittee, Rostenkowski moved in 1979 from being Health Subcommittee chair to chairing the Select Revenue Measures Subcommittee. Not until he made this move was an anemic cost-containment measure brought to the floor in 1980. Even then it died in the Senate.

Rostenkowski's influence in the House actually grew after President Carter was defeated for reelection in 1980 by RONALD REAGAN. In 1981, he became chair of the full House Ways and Means Committee, in which position he helped secure legislation in 1983 to keep the Social Security system solvent. In 1986, he played a decisive role in passing one of the most sweeping overhauls of the federal tax system in the nation's history. He was also deeply involved in developing the nation's trade policy, including the 1993 North American Free Trade Agreement (NAFTA). Furthermore, he put together complex budget packages, including President Bill Clinton's important deficit-cutting legislation in his first year in office (1993). Democratic liberals continued to complain about Rostenkowski's "back-room" deals, but by granting local favors or making small changes in legislation, he was able to move broad legislation through the House. Although never having the power or authority of Wilbur Mills, he became the most influential chairperson of the Ways and Means Committee since Mills.

On Capitol Hill, however, Rostenkowski was as much feared as respected by his colleagues, and he had powerful enemies even within his own party. Practices common to machine politics or even in Congress a generation earlier, such as using public funds to pay employees who did little or no work and to buy personal gifts, were no longer acceptable by the 1980s. Yet Rostenkowski continued to engage in them, including converting over $20,000 of postage stamps to cash in the House Post Office over seven years. These practices led to his downfall. In 1994, he was indicted on 17 counts of corruption and was forced to step down as chair of the Ways and Means Committee. Although he ran for reelection that year, he was defeated by a Republican.

In 1996, Rostenkowski pleaded guilty to two counts of mail fraud. He served 15 months in a minimum-security prison and paid a $100,000 fine. While in prison, he refused to allow any of his family or friends to visit him because of the humiliation it would cause him. He continued to believe he had been unfairly singled out by his enemies and was a victim of shifting rules. In 2000, President Clinton pardoned him. Since leaving prison, Rostenkowski has worked as a consultant and commentator, appearing frequently on television.

S

Sadat, Anwar el-
(Muhammad Anwar el-Sadat)
(1918–1981) *president of Egypt*

Admired by Jimmy Carter more than any other world leader and widely considered a martyr for peace by the Western world, Anwar el-Sadat was president of Egypt from 1970 until his assassination in 1981. Having won an important moral victory in the Yom Kippur War of 1973 by showing that Egypt and its Arab allies could inflict serious military damage on Israel, he turned peacemaker in November 1977 by traveling to Israel as a first step toward making peace with Egypt's historic foe. He was the first Arab leader to officially visit Israel and speak before the Knesset (parliament) in Jerusalem.

Sadat's visit to Israel began a process that led in September 1978 to the signing of the Camp David accords, the crowning achievement of the Carter presidency, and the signing the following March of the Egyptian-Israeli peace agreement ending more than 30 years of hostility between the two countries. Although the Camp David agreement proved not to be the end of the Arab-Israeli dispute, it changed forever the calculus of Middle East politics and made another Arab-Israeli war highly unlikely. But Sadat's decision to make peace with Israel without resolving the Palestinian question or the Israeli occupation of territories seized during the 1967 war angered other Arab states, who ostracized the Egyptian leader.

Sadat was born on December 25, 1918, in the poor Nile delta village of Mit Abul-Kum, 40 miles north of Cairo. One of 13 children, he would always return to his village's peasant life as a way of reestablishing his ties with the Egyptian people and Egyptian history. Although Sadat struggled with his education, he managed to join the Royal Military Academy in 1936. As a child, he had developed great admiration for Mustafa Kemal Ataturk, the father of modern Turkey. At the Royal Military Academy, he learned self-discipline and became increasingly committed to ridding Egypt of British colonial rule. He also met Gamal Abdel Nasser (1918–70), whose future closely resembled to his own. After graduation, he engaged in secret anti-British meetings and, with Nasser, helped form the nationalist Free Officers' Organization.

During World War II, Sadat continued to engage in anti-British activity and even worked with Nazi Germany in an effort to rid Egypt of British control which was completed in 1956. He also admired such diverse figures as Mahatma Gandhi for his anti-British views and Adolf Hitler for his nationalist fervor.

Several times during and after the war, Sadat was thrown in jail on charges that included espionage and even murder. Each time, he was acquitted for lack of evidence and returned to the army at a higher rank.

In 1952, Sadat plotted with Nasser and other members of the Free Officers' Organization to bring about the bloodless overthrow of Egypt's corrupt, narcissistic leader, King Farouk, who was allowed to go into exile. Following the coup, Sadat worked closely with President Nasser and became his most trusted lieutenant over time. In 1969, the Egyptian leader named him vice president. When Nasser died suddenly of a heart attack the following year, Sadat succeeded him.

At the time that Sadat became president of Egypt, few observers thought he would remain in power long, much less become one of Egypt's most important and charismatic leaders. Other military leaders ridiculed him as a peasant and one of Nasser's cronies who merely carried out his commander's orders. Sadat was allowed to become vice president in 1969 by other members of Nasser's inner circle only because they believed he would be easy to control. In no way was he regarded as a strong figure in his own right. Nasser had himself become weak and indecisive following Egypt's overwhelming defeat by the Israelis in the 1967 war, a defeat from which he never fully recovered.

President of Egypt Anwar el-Sadat, President Jimmy Carter, and Israeli prime minister Menachem Begin at the Camp David accords signing ceremony, 1978 *(Jimmy Carter Library)*

Sadat, however, realized the serious military, economic, and political situation that Egypt faced. In the last few years of Nasser's life, the country had become increasingly isolated within the Arab world. Attacked as pusillanimous by the Palestinians, Egypt was ridiculed by such radical Arab states as Syria, Iraq, and Libya for not being more aggressive in the struggle against Israel. Sadat had also become increasingly distrustful of the Soviet Union, which had been Egypt's main supplier of arms but which began cutting back on the military and economic assistance it had been giving Cairo. In 1972, Sadat ordered the immediate withdrawal of the Soviet Union's 5,000 military advisers, to be followed by 15,000 air combat personnel.

Before he could deal with the other pressing problems, Sadat realized he would have to change the equation of Middle Eastern politics and reassert Egypt's own leadership in the Arab world by inflicting a military defeat on Israel and regaining the occupied territories. Whether he actually sought a peace agreement with Israel at this point and believed that the road to peace was through war is uncertain. But he did believe that without some kind of military victory over Israel, any change in the unacceptable status quo in the Middle East could not be achieved. Accordingly, he secretly planned with Syria a war with Israel, which began on October 6, 1973, as Israelis were observing Yom Kippur, the holiest day for Jews.

The war took the Israelis completely by surprise. In the first week, the Egyptians, attacking across the Suez Canal, and the Syrians, moving down the Golan Heights into northern Israel, inflicted enormous casualties on Israeli forces, destroying hundreds of tanks. Egyptian SAM (surface-to-air) missiles brought down about 60 Israeli aircraft in the first three days of the war; Syrian air defense brought down another 30 Israeli planes. Not until the United States provided a major resupply effort were the Israelis able to turn the war around, moving back across the Sinai and, for a time, surrounding and threatening to destroy Egypt's entire Second and Third Armies. In the north, the Israelis retook the Golan Heights and even began to move toward Damascus.

Rather than being regarded as another humiliating Arab defeat by the Israelis, however, the Yom Kippur War had the effect Sadat wanted. It revealed that Israel was not an impenetrable military colossus and instilled fear in the Israelis, who had never come so close to being destroyed militarily as they did in the fall of 1973. It also enhanced pride in the Arab world, reestablished Egypt's role as leader of the Arab countries, and put to rest any doubts about Sadat as Nasser's rightful heir.

The truce ending the war was brokered by U.S. secretary of state HENRY KISSINGER. Although the Soviet Union had once more come to Egypt's assistance during the war, Sadat became convinced that good relations with Washington served Egypt's interest better than ties to Moscow. Accordingly, in 1976 he abrogated the treaty of friendship that Egypt still had with the Soviet Union. By the end that year, he had also reached the conclusion that it was time to end the state of hostilities that had existed between Egypt and Israel since Israel's establishment in 1948. Quietly, he made it known to Israel's new prime minister, MENACHEM BEGIN, that he would like to be invited to Israel.

In one of the most dramatic and courageous steps ever taken by an Arab leader, Sadat made an historic three-day trip to Israel, beginning on November 17, 1977. His visit to Jerusalem and address to the Knesset (Israel's parliament) drew worldwide attention. Thousands of Israelis, many waving Egyptian flags, turned out to welcome their former enemy. In his hour-long speech to the Knesset, Sadat captured the poignancy of the moment when he said he had come to Israel not to sign a peace treaty but to break down "the barriers of suspicion, fear, illusion, and misrepresentation" that for so many years had kept his country and Israel from even talking about peace.

Although Sadat's visit to Israel and Begin's return visit to Egypt were widely hailed as first steps toward resolving the Arab-Israeli conflict, such optimism quickly gave way to pessimism. In the first place, the Egyptian president incurred the wrath of much of the Arab world just for going to Israel. Returning home, the Egyptian president invited "all the parties to the [Mideast] conflict" to Cairo in order to prepare for a Geneva conference on the Middle East. But not one of the Arab states came. Instead, representatives from such anti-Sadat nations as Iraq, Algeria, and Libya gathered in Tripoli, where they formed a "rejectionist" front and condemned the Egyptian leader.

The peace process begun by Sadat also floundered on Prime Minister Begin's unwillingness to stop Israeli settlements in the occupied territories or to agree to the establishment of a Palestinian state. Israel wanted security; Egypt wanted the Sinai and justice for the more than 1 million Palestinians living under Jewish rule. But Begin found no room for compromise on these issues. Fundamental differences in personality also separated the two leaders. Sadat was gregarious, pragmatic, and a generalist, little interested in the specific details of extended negotiations. Begin was introverted and cautious, with a lawyerly concern about precision and specifics. Sadat was also dapper, embracing, and conciliatory. Begin was courtly, standoffish, and intractable. In personal meetings, there was a lack of chemistry between the two leaders; they simply did not get along well together.

In contrast, President Carter took an immediate liking to Sadat, whom he first met in Washington on April 4, 1977, as one of a series of meetings he was then holding with leaders from the Middle East. He found the Egyptian leader charming, bold, and willing to take chances for peace. Although insisting on a return of the territories seized by Israel during the 1967 war and resolving the Palestinian question, Sadat indicated a surprising degree of flexibility for an Arab leader. On the occupied territories, for example, he stated that "some minimal deviation from the 1967 borders might be acceptable." On the ending of the Arab boycott against Israel, he affirmed it could be terminated with a peace agreement. On military sales to Egypt, he remarked that he would rather do without certain needed weapons like the F-5e fighter plane "in order not to endanger the possibilities of a Middle East settlement this year."

Carter had never been as impressed by any leader as he was by Sadat. "There was an easy and natural friendship between us from the first moment I knew Anwar Sadat," he later remarked. "We trusted each other." Their meeting took place, moreover, before Sadat made his journey to Jerusalem in November 1977. The president did not even learn that Sadat was planning to go to Israel until the second week of November, when the Egyptian president informed him about it. Like much of the non-Arab world, he was astonished—and delighted—by Sadat's visit and his address to the Knesset, which Carter termed "among the most dramatic events of modern history."

Despite the lack of progress that followed Sadat's visit to Israel, therefore, Carter was all the more determined to capitalize on the worldwide thrill that gesture had generated by bringing an end to the Arab-Israeli dispute, something he had wanted to do since becoming president. In February 1978, he again met with Sadat in Washington. In his discussions with Carter, the Egyptian leader stated categorically that the Israeli prime minister did not want peace. Sadat also expressed his disappointment that Washington was not playing a more instrumental role as mediator. Convinced his initiative would collapse unless the United States pressured Israel into making concessions, he wanted Washington to resume its central role in negotiating a Mideast peace.

Over the next six months, the White House tried several strategies, based on close collaboration with Sadat and separate negotiations with Begin, to get the peace process back on track. But nothing worked. In a last-ditch effort to prevent the total collapse of the peace effort and the possibility of renewed conflict in the Mideast, President Carter decided to invite the Egyptian and Israeli leaders to Camp David on September 5, 1978, for what turned out to be 13 days of negotiations. During this time, the president attempted to mediate between the two men, who did not even meet with each other after the first day of the summit. But no progress was made until September 12, when Carter presented Sadat with a four-page proposal for an Egyptian-Israeli peace treaty, the key sentence of which provided for restoration of "full Egyptian sovereignty ... in the Sinai." The Egyptian leader considered the draft largely acceptable, but the next day, Begin flatly rejected it, stating that he would never agree to the removal of Israeli settlements from the Sinai.

The critical moment in the summit had arrived. Sadat announced that he was preparing to leave immediately for Egypt. Informed that the Egyptian delegation was already packing its bags, Carter hurried to Sadat's cottage and warned him that the American people would hold the Egyptian leader responsible for the failure of the summit. Relations would deteriorate, peacekeeping efforts would end, and his own administration would be discredited. Shaken by the force of Carter's arguments, Sadat agreed to continue the negotiations.

Events then moved swiftly. Under tremendous pressure from the president, Begin relented on the Sinai in exchange for the promise of a peace agreement with Egypt. Sadat and Begin then consented to a two-part agreement. The first provided for a framework for peace between Egypt and Israel (although even that was the subject of more bitter differences between Begin and Sadat requiring further personal intervention by Carter before a peace agreement was signed at the White House at the end of March 1979). The second established an ambiguous "framework for peace for the Middle East" that was supposed to resolve the Palestinian problem and the question of the occupied territories in stages over the next five years.

For their accomplishment, Sadat and Begin were jointly awarded the Nobel Peace Prize for 1978. Even so, the promise of Camp David was never totally fulfilled. The resolve to tackle the Palestinian issue fell apart soon after Begin and Sadat returned home. Notwithstanding Camp David, Israel remained recalcitrant on the establishment of a Palestinian state and the return of the occupied territories (other than the Sinai). Begin also insisted that the framework for peace in the Middle East agreed to at Camp David only obligated Israel to talk about an agreement on a Palestinian state. Sadat had hoped that Jordan and other more moderate states would eventually join the peace process established at Camp David, but even Jordan refused to come to the bargaining table.

Sadat continued to work for peace in the Middle East, but he was clearly disappointed by the results of Camp David. A hero and object of respect in the Western world, he was regarded as a pariah among more radical elements in the Arab world. His Western mannerisms and dress only fueled hatred of the Egyptian leader among Islamic fundamentalists. Soon after the Camp David agreements, moreover, he began to impose a more oppressive regime in Egypt, jailing his opponents and virtually eliminating any open resistance to his regime.

On October 6, 1981, during a massive military parade in Cairo celebrating the 1973

Yom Kippur War against Israel, Sadat was assassinated by army members of the Egyptian Islamic Jihad organization. The West mourned his death with an outpouring of grief and eulogies, but there was dancing in the streets in some Arab capitals. In Cairo, there was a discernible quiet, in distinct contrast to the wails that could be heard throughout the city upon the news of Nasser's death 11 years earlier.

For former president Jimmy Carter, Sadat's death was a personal loss. Asked by President RONALD REAGAN to lead the official U.S. delegation to Sadat's funeral, along with former presidents RICHARD NIXON and GERALD FORD, Carter even considered declining. He would have preferred to attend the funeral as a private citizen mourning the loss of one of his dearest friends.

Safire, William

(William Safir)

(1929–) *syndicated columnist*

William Safire has had a storied and varied career as a newspaper reporter, radio and television correspondent and producer, public-relations executive, small-business owner, speechwriter for President RICHARD NIXON, novelist, and etymologist. He is best known, however, as a conservative political columnist for the *New York Times* and frequent guest commentator on television news shows. In 1978, he won the Pulitzer Prize for his 1977 columns on the banking practices of President Carter's close friend BERT LANCE, who was forced to resign in September 1977 as director of the Office of Management and Budget (OMB).

Safire was born William Safir in New York City on December 17, 1929. (His name was later changed legally to correspond to the way it was pronounced.) His father died in 1933 when Safire was only four years old. Raised by his mother, Ida, he graduated from the Bronx High School of Science and then attended Syracuse University (1947–49). He dropped out after two years in order to work for Tex McCrary, a well-known celebrity columnist for the *New York Herald Tribune* who also had his own radio show and was active in Republican Party politics. In 1951, Safire accepted a position as a correspondent in Europe and the Middle East. The next year he joined the army.

After leaving military service in 1954, Safire produced a radio and television show featuring McCrary and his wife. In 1955, McCray named him vice president of his public-relations firm, a position Safire held until 1961 when he opened his own public-relations business. Meanwhile, he became increasingly active in the Republican Party. In 1960, he was chief of special projects in Vice President Richard Nixon's campaign for president, and in 1964 he headed public relations for Governor Nelson Rockefeller's unsuccessful presidential bid. The next year, he volunteered as an unpaid speechwriter for Nixon during the former vice president's comeback from political anonymity. In 1968, Safire wrote Nixon's victory speech following his election as president.

In 1969, Safire sold his firm in order to join Nixon's White House staff as a special assistant and speechwriter. Of the president's three major speechwriters—Patrick Buchanan, Ray Price, and himself—Safire was widely perceived in Washington as a political moderate, someone less doctrinaire than Buchanan but more conservative than Price. He was also known for his satirical wit and ability to turn a phrase, including making clever use of alliteration—for example, the memorable "nattering nabobs of negativism" to describe the liberal media in a speech he wrote in 1970 for Vice President Spiro Agnew.

In spring 1973, just before the Watergate scandal broke, Safire left the White House to accept a position as political columnist for the *New York Times*. Other *Times* journalists were critical of his appointment because they regarded Safire as a lightweight public-relations person and staunch Nixon loyalist rather than an accomplished reporter. Even Safire acknowledged that his first columns for the *Times*, in which he strongly defended President Nixon against charges of involvement in the Watergate cover-up, were written without much hard reporting on his part.

As the evidence against the president mounted, however, and as Safire discovered that his telephone had been tapped, he ceased to defend Nixon. Referring to himself as a "libertarian conservative" who spoke out against unrestrained government and in support of basic liberties, including the right of privacy, he concluded that the president had been complicit in the cover-up of the Watergate break-in. Yet he never stopped admiring Nixon. Indeed, his enormous respect for the former president's accomplishments and for his unrealized promise of greatness made his cover-up all the more inexplicable to Safire.

The journalist's admiration for Nixon may also have affected his reporting of what became known during the Carter administration as the Lance affair but which Safire referred to as "Lancegate" or the "Lance cover-up." In attacking Bert Lance for his banking practices and alleged influence-peddling as director of the OMB, such as his allegation that Lance peddled his political influence to obtain a $3.5 million loan with deferral interest from the First National Bank of Chicago, Safire may have been seeking retribution for what he regarded as the shoddy treatment of the former president by the liberal press. In earlier columns, he had accused the Kennedy and Johnson administrations of engaging in the same corrupt practices—or worse—as those leveled against Nixon, but without public disclosure of these activities or provisions for legal redress. He continued to make abuse of power by persons of authority a recurring theme in his later columns.

In attacking Lance, Safire and other conservative Republicans may also have wanted to keep the OMB director from replacing ARTHUR BURNS as chair of the Federal Reserve Board. According to Lance, who struck up a correspondence with Safire in the 1980s, this was the explanation the columnist gave him. But Safire was also led into attacking Lance by what he considered the sanctimonious religiosity and ethical hypocrisy of President Carter and his alleged "cronies." In a book Safire published in 1980, he acknowledged that Carter's "self-righteousness turned him off" and that the lock his administration thought it had on purity "stimulated a certain polemical passion" in the columnist's writing.

In 1978, Safire won the Pulitzer Prize for his investigation of Lance. For the remainder of the Carter administration, he continued to write columns critical of the president and his circle of advisers, referring to them, in one column, as "the Magnolio Mafia." He also accused the president's chief of staff, HAMILTON JORDAN, of interceding with Carter in 1979 on behalf of the fugitive financier, Robert Vesco, in return for a $10,000 bribe to one of Jordan's cronies. However, his most serious accusations against the president—ones that had been aired earlier in the media but which Safire resurrected in 1979—had to do with alleged financial shenanigans during Carter's 1976 campaign. These involved, according to Safire, an uncollateralized loan to the Carter family peanut business by Bert Lance's National Bank of Georgia and the improper extension of credit to the Carter campaign using the advertising agency of GERALD RAFSHOON, the candidate's media consultant, as a conduit.

Following a seven-month grand-jury investigation of the charges made by Safire

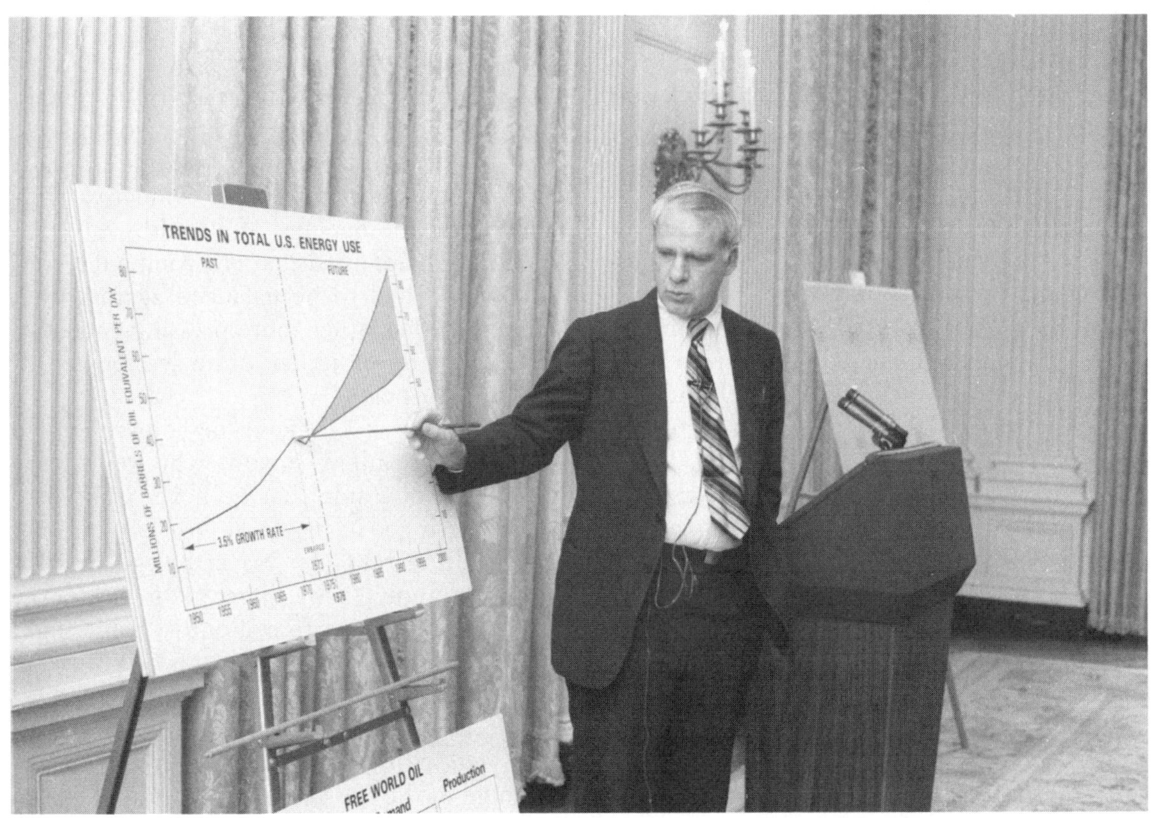

Secretary of Energy James R. Schlesinger presenting a briefing on energy, 1977 *(Jimmy Carter Library)*

Carter, Rafshoon, and ROBERT LIPSHUTZ, the president's counsel and Carter's national campaign treasurer in 1976, were exonerated. Nevertheless, Safire continued to accuse the president of "ethical corner-cutting."

Carter and his circle of advisers have not been the only targets of Safire's pen. In the years since the Carter presidency, he has also lashed out at the alleged ethical hypocrisy of other political figures from both parties and continued to speak out against the double standard he believes the media has applied in reporting the news. Although he appears to have modified his rhetoric in recent years, Safire has retained his sharp wit, ironic and self-effacing sense of humor, and core conservative values. Unabashed in his support of both the Gulf War of 1991 and the war in Iraq begun in 2003, he has, at the same time, spoken out against the USA PATRIOT Act of 2002 because of the threat he believes it poses to civil liberties. Safire lives in Chevy Chase, Maryland, and continues to write occasionally for the *New York Times.*

Schlesinger, James Rodney

(1929–) *assistant to the president, secretary of energy*

A former assistant director of the Bureau of the Budget, chair of the Atomic Energy Commission, director of the Central Intelligence Agency (CIA), and secretary of defense, James

Schlesinger added to his long portfolio of government service by serving as assistant to President Carter, with responsibility for developing a comprehensive energy plan, and by being the first secretary of the newly established Department of Energy. Known for his brilliance as well as his austere and acerbic personality, he alienated both members of the Carter administration and lawmakers on Capitol Hill.

Born in New York City on February 15, 1929, Schlesinger graduated summa cum laude from Harvard University (B.A., 1950) and subsequently received his doctorate in economics from Harvard (M.A., 1952; Ph.D., 1956). A member of the faculty at the University of Virginia (1955–63), he left academia to accept a position with the RAND Corporation, first as a staff member (1963–67) and then as director of strategic studies (1967–69). During this period, he also served as a consultant to the Board of Governors of the Federal Reserve System and to the U.S. Bureau of the Budget. Schlesinger's experiences as a student at Harvard and during the first decade of the cold war were formative. Touring Europe as a student, he adopted a hard-line attitude toward the Kremlin to which he adhered throughout the remainder of the cold war. Even after the Soviet Union's demise, he stressed the importance of a strong nuclear capability and had little patience for those he regarded as soft on defense issues.

Schlesinger began his career in government service in 1969 when he accepted a position as assistant director of the Bureau of the Budget (later the Office of Management and Budget). Two years later, President RICHARD NIXON appointed him chair of the Atomic Energy Commission (AEC). Oddly enough in light of subsequent circumstances, Schlesinger won a reputation during these three years for cutting defense spending by $6 billion and for being an environmentalist; the latter figured into his appointment as head of the AEC and subsequently as energy secretary. He remained committed to the proposition that the United States needed to maintain military supremacy over the Soviet Union, but he also believed that this did not preclude looking critically at existing weapons systems. Similarly, while advocating the benefits of a healthy environment, he maintained that environmental considerations had to be balanced against what he regarded as other more pressing concerns, such as the development of nuclear power for peaceful purposes.

Schlesinger's abrasive personality tolled even on President Nixon, who reportedly instructed one aide that he never wanted to see Schlesinger in the Oval Office because of his insulting remarks. Nevertheless, in 1973 Nixon promoted Schlesinger to director of the CIA. Over the next four months, Schlesinger fired 6 percent of the staff, making him, in the words of one official, the "most unpopular director in the C.I.A.'s history." This went over well with Nixon, who viewed the CIA as a refuge of the Ivy League intellectuals whom he despised.

Five months after appointing Schlesinger to the CIA, Nixon named him secretary of defense as part of a cabinet reshuffle. During the Yom Kippur War of 1973, according to Nixon and his secretary of state, HENRY KISSINGER, Defense Secretary Schlesinger opposed allowing El Al aircraft or U.S. military aircraft to resupply the beleaguered Israeli forces with military equipment because he did not want to offend the Arab states, but he was overruled by the president. Most writers, however, attribute the delay in resupplying Israeli forces to Kissinger, who had wanted to make it clear to the Israelis that they could not exist without the United States.

As defense secretary, Schlesinger also took a hard line against any new Strategic Arms Limitation Talks agreement (SALT II) that did not give the United States an overwhelming advantage over the Soviet Union. According to Nixon, he even remarked at a meeting of the National Security Council that the president would be able to persuade Soviet leader LEONID BREZHNEV to accept such an agreement because Brezhnev had been impressed by Nixon's "forensic ability." Later, the president wrote that Schlesinger's comments "were really an insult to everybody's intelligence and particularly to mine."

As the Watergate affair took its toll on the administration by the end of 1973, Schlesinger came to believe that Nixon had become paranoid. Furthermore, he continued to oppose a SALT II agreement, even publishing a letter in which he disassociated the Department of Defense from the White House's position regarding imposition of a freeze on existing multiple independently targeted reentry vehicles (MIRVs). In fact, in January 1974, he proposed a new nuclear targeting doctrine, NSDM-242, that served to undermine a SALT II agreement by calling for the development of counterforce capabilities, specifically selective targeting against Soviet hardened missile sites.

Despite his differences with President Nixon, Schlesinger remained in the cabinet. When GERALD FORD became president in August 1974, following Nixon's resignation because of the Watergate scandal, he also kept Schlesinger at the Pentagon, where the defense secretary continued to urge a hard line against the Soviet Union. Emphasizing a growing Soviet military threat and raising concern in 1975 about a Soviet naval missile-storage facility in Somalia, he also pointed to a Soviet buildup of a counterforce strategic missile capability.

Although Ford had retained Schlesinger as defense secretary, the president disliked him intensely, finding him patronizing and imperious. Schlesinger's hard line toward the Soviet Union also clashed with the policy of détente being pursued by Secretary of State Kissinger. Furthermore, Ford resented the defense secretary's efforts at courting a favorable press, sometimes at the expense of the administration. That he did not dismiss Schlesinger in his first few weeks as president was due solely to the fact that the defense secretary had become the darling of the strong anti-détente forces within the Republican Party whose support Ford still needed. Rumors that Schlesinger was backing RONALD REAGAN for the 1976 Republican nomination, however, were too much for the president. On November 2, 1975, he asked for Schlesinger's resignation. Afterward, Reagan charged that Ford had fired Schlesinger because he was "afraid to tell the American people the truth about our military status."

Schlesinger's career as a high-level government official was not over, however. After Reagan lost his bid for the Republican nomination, the former defense secretary joined forces with the Democratic nominee, Jimmy Carter, who was impressed by his sheer brilliance and breadth of government experience. Anxious also to underscore the importance he attached to a comprehensive energy plan by a show of bipartisanship, Carter appointed Schlesinger as his special assistant responsible for developing a comprehensive national energy policy within 90 days and with several specific objectives in mind. Conservation and a more efficient use of energy resources were to be the plan's cornerstone. Reduction of oil imports, balancing energy needs with environmental stewardship, and making the public aware of the true value of energy by raising the domestic price of oil to world levels were to be the other major features of the plan.

Working with only a small staff and in deep secrecy, Schlesinger met the deadline Carter had imposed, presenting to the president a complex energy proposal containing 113 separate provisions, the most important of which were a multitiered system of oil and gas prices, a wellhead tax intended to force consumers to conserve energy by raising oil prices to world prices, and a standby gasoline tax to cut back on energy consumption. The program also imposed a "gas guzzler" tax on automobiles with low fuel efficiency, penalized heavy industrial users of oil and natural gas, and instituted tax credits and other incentives to encourage energy conservation. In April 1977, Carter went on national television to promote his new energy program, calling it the "moral equivalent of war." To get the program through the House of Representatives, Speaker TIP O'NEILL (Mass.), established a special ad hoc committee to consider the measure in its entirety rather than having sections of the proposal parceled out among different committees.

Although O'Neill was able in this way to get the bill through the House largely intact by August, it met an entirely different reception in the Senate, where it was divided into six separate measures, each considered by a different committee. The final bill, which was not approved until October 1978, contained none of the tax provisions intended to conserve energy. Its single most important provision was the extension of federal control over intrastate as well as interstate sales of natural gas, thereby establishing one national pricing system for natural gas, and the gradual deregulation of natural gas prices. Instead of a measure based on the principle of conservation through taxation, the legislation that Carter signed into law in October emphasized deregulation and tax credits, the former intended to increase domestic production and the latter to provide incentives for expanded use of nonfossil fuels.

Even before Carter first presented his energy bill to Congress in 1977, he had asked lawmakers to create a new Department of Energy. In contrast to his energy program, Congress responded expeditiously, establishing the new department on August 3. The next day, the president signed the bill into law, and the following day he named Schlesinger to head the department, which brought under one roof a number of different agencies with about 20,000 employees and a budget of $10.4 billion.

The legislation establishing the new department provided for an organization built around function (for example, research, resource applications, conservation) rather than around fuel types (for example, fossil, nuclear, solar), reflecting the administration's commitment to a comprehensive energy plan rather than to fuel management, as had been the emphasis of government policy in the past. Bringing under one roof sometimes-conflicting agencies and imposing a new organizational structure on them was an enormously difficult task for Schlesinger, who also had responsibility for promoting the administration's energy plan. A year after the new department was established, the energy secretary defended his record, remarking that in comparison to other large departments established after World War II, his "look[ed] pretty good." *Time* magazine, however, commented in January 1979, that the agency appeared to be "sinking into a bureaucratic stupor." Critics on Capitol Hill made similar comments.

Yet it was Schlesinger's advocacy of his original energy plan, which even its backers acknowledged had serious flaws resulting from the speed and secrecy in which it had been put together, and his peremptory and dismissive style that created the most difficulty for him. Even within the administration, Schlesinger irritated a number of the president's senior aides and other members of the cabinet. Carter's special assistant for domestic affairs, STUART EIZENSTAT, who was widely respected in Washington's political circles, was disturbed by Schlesinger's insistence on secrecy in developing the energy plan as well as his unwillingness to submit it to scrutiny by his staff until the essential decisions about the plan were made.

Eizenstat also quarreled with Schlesinger over the plan's complexity and his failure to decontrol natural-gas prices, something the president had pledged to do during the campaign. Secretary of the Treasury W. MICHAEL BLUMENTHAL was similarly angry that he had not been properly consulted when the energy program was being drawn up, despite its implication for his department. On a related matter, Secretary of the Interior CECIL ANDRUS, who had opposed the establishment of a Department of Energy, took umbrage at Schlesinger's opposition to limiting oil drilling in what became the Arctic National Wildlife Refuge.

On Capitol Hill, where Schlesinger still had to deal with bruised egos from his previous government service, his hard sell of the energy plan exacerbated his relations with lawmakers. "He was always careful to assume full responsibility for the most unpopular proposals," Carter later explained, "and many of the members would therefore blame [him] for their dissatisfaction." Environmentalists, who once numbered Schlesinger among their own, were also taken aback by a number of positions Schlesinger took as energy secretary, such as his support of the Clinch River breeder reactor, his minimization of the danger resulting from an accident in 1979 at the Three Mile Island nuclear reactor in Pennsylvania (which at one point raised the horror of a nuclear meltdown), and his support of oil drilling in the Alaskan wilderness.

Isolated and frustrated by the criticism that surrounded him. Schlesinger, who had earlier offered to resign, decided in 1979 to step down as energy secretary. The president, who had previously asked him to stay on, now agreed that he should leave the administration, though Carter still had great respect for him. Because of the hard-line positions Schlesinger continued to take toward the Soviet Union and a SALT II agreement with the Kremlin, he also had the strong support of National Security Advisor ZBIGNIEW BRZEZINSKI and Secretary of Defense HAROLD BROWN. The president understood, however, the enmity being directed against his energy secretary. "Everyone believed that Jim Schlesinger had exhausted his usefulness during the long and bitter struggles with Congress over the energy legislation," Carter later wrote about his decision to accept Schlesinger's resignation. As part of a cabinet shake-up that Carter instituted in July 1979, therefore, he announced that Schlesinger would be leaving his cabinet along with Secretary of Health, Education and Welfare JOSEPH CALIFANO, Treasury Secretary Blumenthal, Attorney General GRIFFIN BELL, and Secretary of Transportation BROCK ADAMS.

After leaving the Carter administration, Schlesinger took a position as senior adviser to Lehman Brothers, Kuhn Loeb, Inc., in New York City. From 1982 to 1983, he also served on the President's Commission on Strategic Forces and was vice chairman of the president's blue-ribbon task force on nuclear weapons program management. In the 1990s, he served as a member of the Commission on National Security for the 21st Century. In 2004, he cochaired a task force on Iraq for the Council on Foreign Relations. Schlesinger also headed an independent commission to look into the torture of detainees at Iraq's Abu Ghraib prison and the treatment of those held in Guantánamo Bay, Cuba. In its report, which was made public in August, the commission concluded that the blame for Abu Ghraib lay mainly with the American soldiers who ran the prison, but it also faulted senior commanders and top-level Pentagon officials for failed leadership and oversight.

As a private citizen, Schlesinger continued to speak out against any policy he deemed would weaken the United States in its struggle with the Soviet Union. Even after the demise of the USSR, he supported an ongoing program of testing and updating the United States' nuclear deterrence capability. During congressional hearings in 1999, he spoke out against a comprehensive test-ban treaty. "In the absence of testing," he remarked, "confidence in the reliability of the [American nuclear] stockpile will inevitably, ineluctably decline." In the task force's report, he called for American and coalition forces to remain indefinitely in Iraq. "Disengagement now would be tantamount now to American failure," he commented in defending the report's conclusions.

Schmidt, Helmut Heinrich

(1918–) *West German chancellor*

Helmut Heinrich Schmidt served as chancellor of the Federal Republic of Germany (West Germany) from 1974 to 1983. Of the leaders of Western Europe, he was the most inveterate foe of the Carter administration. Known for his sharp tongue and quick thinking, he considered President Carter inexperienced politically, lacking in statesmanship, irresolute, and indifferent to the security concerns of the United States' allies.

Schmidt was born on December 23, 1918, in Barbeck, a working-class district of Hamburg, Germany. Both his parents were schoolteachers. His father taught his son toughness and self-discipline; from his mother he gained an appreciation of music and the visual arts. After graduating in 1937 from the Lichtwark-Schule, a school that encouraged critical thinking and self-reliance, Schmidt was drafted into the German army. He fought during World War II on both the eastern and western fronts and spent the last six months of the war in a British prisoner-of-war (POW) camp. It was as a POW, talking with other German prisoners and trying to understand what happened in Germany under the Nazis, that Schmidt became committed to establishing a social democracy in Germany.

Following the war, Schmidt renewed his education at the University of Hamburg. During this time, he became active in the German Socialist Students Federation (SDS), which he headed from 1947 to 1949. He also joined the Social Democratic Party (SPD) when it was reconstituted in 1946. Although believing in democratic socialism, Schmidt was more a realist and pragmatist than an ideologue. As head of the SDS, he criticized his fellow students for being content to accuse the university of being "reactionary" without offering any program for reform.

Schmidt's ambition was to be an architect, but since there were no courses in architecture at Hamburg, he studied economics and political science. His senior thesis, written in 1949, was a comparison of Japanese and German currency reform. After obtaining his degree, he became an economist for the city of Hamburg. He also remained active in the SPD. Because of his reputation for being a clear thinker and an excellent speaker, he began to get invitations to speak at party rallies throughout northern Germany. In 1953, he ran for the Bundestag (West Germany's lower house of parliament) but lost to his Christian Democratic Union (CDU) opponent. Under Germany's complicated election process, however, he was able to get an SPD appointment to the Bundestag. In 1957, he was elected to a second term.

As a member of the Bundestag, Schmidt gained considerable notoriety by denouncing West Germany's bid for nuclear weapons, which he referred to as "German nationalist megalomania." He also developed an enviable reputation for his verbal jousting with the opposition. Tired of being a member of the perennial opposition in a legislative body dominated by the CDU, Schmidt returned to city politics, serving as Hamburg's senator for interior affairs. His skillful leadership of a rescue mission following one of the worst storms ever to hit Hamburg garnered him more national visibility and respect.

In 1965, Schmidt decided to seek national office once more. Reelected to the Bundestag that year, he became SPD floor leader in 1966 and deputy chairman of the party in 1968. The next year, he helped bring the SPD into a coalition government with the CDU and Christian Social Union (CSU), headed by Berlin's former mayor, Willy Brandt. The new West German chancellor gave Schmidt his first cabinet appointment, naming him defense minister in October 1969. In 1972, from July to November, Schmidt served both as minister for economics and minister of finance. From December 1972 until May 1974, he served as minister of finance.

As defense minister, Schmidt was one of the architects and principal proponents of Brandt's Policy of *ostpolitik* (normalizing relations with West Germany's eastern neighbors). As early as 1966, he had favored renunciation of the Hallstein Doctrine of 1955, by which West Germany refused to grant diplomatic recognition to any country that had relations with the German Democratic Republic (East Germany). Schmidt nonetheless became increasingly unhappy at what he regarded as the chancellor's lax leadership and even considered retiring from politics. But when Brandt was forced to step down as chancellor in May 1974 because of a spy scandal, Schmidt was the logical person to replace him, as there was no one else more experienced in finance, defense, or diplomacy.

One of Schmidt's principal foreign policy aims as he assumed his new office was to get the United States to give greater consideration to

President Jimmy Carter and West German chancellor Helmut Schmidt, 1978 *(Jimmy Carter Library)*

Germany's needs in formulating its foreign and defense policies. What disturbed him was his conviction that Washington rarely consulted with Bonn or other European governments on foreign and military matters despite the fact that they frequently involved Germany's own security interests. The issue became an especially galling one for him after Jimmy Carter entered the White House.

During the 1976 U.S. election, Schmidt had taken the unusual step of openly supporting the reelection of President GERALD FORD. On election day, he compounded his impolitic action by congratulating Ford on his victory before later returns showed that Carter had won the election. The German chancellor simply did not believe that a peanut farmer and one-term governor had the knowledge and experience necessary to be a world leader. "A former governor of Georgia, he came [to the Oval Office] bereft of any experience in international affairs," Schmidt later commented. Based on statements Carter had made during the campaign, moreover, he feared that the new administration would deviate from the Nixon-Ford-Kissinger strategy of détente with Moscow, which, he thought, would be a grave mistake. "The European governments had no need of a new beginning in Washington," he also stated. Rather, "they had high hopes for a confirmation of America's overall strategy and its consistency in pursuing it."

Schmidt was upset, therefore, by Carter's human-rights campaign against the Soviet Union. He was convinced the campaign would make it all the more difficult for the Soviets to negotiate a second strategic Arms Limitation Talks agreement (SALT II) with the United States, something that Schmidt had long advocated and believed was essential to West Germany's own security. He became even angrier when the president tried to get Moscow to agree to a comprehensive arms-limitation treaty that would have been unacceptable to the Soviets even absent the president's human-rights campaign. He warned Secretary of State CYRUS VANCE that the Soviets "would be dismayed [by] Carter's way of thinking, which could not help but remain mysterious to them [and] would lead them to suspect intentions they could not decipher." The failure of Vance's mission to Moscow in March 1977 to begin negotiations on a SALT II agreement only confirmed for Schmidt how naïve the new administration was with respect to the Soviet Union.

Other issues also developed between the German chancellor and the American president. Schmidt was irate because the Carter administration, committed to nuclear nonproliferation, was attempting to undercut a $4.7 billion sale by West Germany to Brazil of a complete nuclear-fuel facility to develop its own nuclear-weapons capability. Similarly, Schmidt was annoyed that the Pentagon appeared ready to renege on an agreement to buy German Leopard II battle tanks because of their alleged inferiority to American tanks. He also resented the administration's pressure on him to stimulate the German economy as part of a coordinated effort with the United States and Japan to prevent a global recession.

At the beginning of May 1977, Carter traveled to London, where he participated in a summit meeting with Schmidt and the other leaders of Western Europe, Canada, and Japan. Much of the summit was spent considering ways to deal with the worldwide economic problems of high inflation and unemployment and the rising global trend toward protectionism. At the conference, Carter seemed to get along famously with Schmidt. Still, the German chancellor continued to bicker with the president over his policy toward Moscow and his human-rights advocacy. After talks were resumed in May between the United States and the Soviet Union over an arms agreement, Schmidt reproached the White House for not consulting its NATO partners in negotiating with Moscow.

Schmidt's differences with Carter reached crisis proportions after the president decided not to go forward with the development of an enriched-radiation weapon (ERW), commonly known as the neutron bomb. The weapon was intended to deter a Soviet attack in Europe by enabling Western forces to destroy enemy tank concentrations without ravaging nearby population centers. For West Germany, with its high concentration of urban dwellers and long borders with countries of the Warsaw Pact, the neutron bomb could be an especially useful weapon. For that reason, Schmidt had encouraged the United States to develop the bomb.

On April 7, 1978, however, President Carter announced that he was deferring production of the weapon. The morality of a nuclear device that killed people but preserved property weighed heavily on the president's mind, as it did for opponents of the weapon throughout the United States and Europe. For that reason, none of the European countries, including West Germany, were willing to have such a weapon on their soil. This was another reason why Carter decided not to go forward with its development. Nevertheless, his announcement created a political tempest in the United States and throughout Western Europe. Schmidt charged the president with betrayal, and the rift that had developed between the two leaders was by now palpable and irreparable.

In June 1979, Schmidt and Carter attended the G-7 economic summit in Tokyo. The major issue at the summit was the huge increases in oil prices by the Organization of Petroleum Exporting Countries (OPEC) that were sending the world into a major recession. President Carter hoped that the United States and its trading partners would stand together against the oil cartel. Instead, the meeting underscored significant differences among the world's strongest industrial powers and OPEC's largest customers. Although the seven leaders in Tokyo ratified an American proposal to set specific country-by-country ceilings on oil imports, they did so only after a bitter exchange between Carter and Schmidt. According to the president, "Schmidt got personally abusive," claiming that Washington's interference in the Middle East was responsible for the oil crisis.

At the end of 1979, Carter and Schmidt got into another tangle after the Soviet Union invaded Afghanistan. In response to the invasion, the president instituted a series of measures against the Soviets that included a grain embargo, postponement of consideration of the SALT II agreement signed in Vienna during the summer, and a call for an international boycott of the 1980 Summer Olympics in Moscow. In Europe, NATO allies were deeply troubled by the U.S. response. Although they condemned the Soviet action, they refused to become involved, arguing that the attack did not necessarily mean aggressive designs on other nations outside the Soviet orbit. Once again, Schmidt was harshly critical of the president, complaining that Carter conducted foreign policy without considering its impact on Western Europe. For his part, the president viewed Schmidt as unstable, unreliable, and egotistical.

A final problem that developed between the two leaders in 1980 concerned the placement of additional weapons in Europe. In many ways, this was the capstone to the relationship between the two leaders. At issue was the Soviet Union's superior capability in medium-range nuclear missiles capable of hitting much of Western Europe, but not the United States, and the need for a Western response. The SALT II agreement did not take account of the Euro-strategic weapons problem. Schmidt had wanted the issue discussed during the SALT negotiations and was already angry that the United States had apparently not done so.

To deal with the problem, Schmidt sought to begin a new round of negotiations with Moscow over arms control while at the same time getting President Carter to agree to place intermediate-range ballistic missiles and ground-launched cruise missiles in Europe as a counterweight to the Soviet Union's missiles. But he insisted that West Germany's European allies share the new weapons rather than having them exclusively on German territory since that would make West Germany, which already had the largest concentration of nuclear weapons in western Europe, still more clearly the prime Soviet target in case of a future war. At a meeting of NATO foreign and defense ministers in Brussels on December 12, 1979, the NATO allies agreed to go forward with the deployment of 572 Pershing 2 and ground-launched cruise missiles while calling upon Moscow to begin a new round of arms negotiations to deal with the Euro-strategic weapons issue.

In contravention to what had been agreed upon in Brussels, Schmidt was quoted by the press, while campaigning for reelection in 1980, as calling for a three-year moratorium on the disposition of new missiles. In a telephone call to President Carter, Schmidt said he had been misquoted. But after a time, more stories began to circulate in which the German chancellor was again reported as favoring a suspension of new missiles. In response, Carter sent Schmidt a communiqué expressing concern about the confusion his statements were creating. The message became public and Schmidt, convinced the president was trying to undermine efforts at arms control, became furious.

Some of the differences between Carter and Schmidt were papered over once more at the G-7 summit of June 1980 in Venice. Before the start of the gathering, the president met with Schmidt to try to settle their conflicts. In a stormy session, Schmidt claimed that he had been insulted by Carter's last message to him and that West Germany was not the United States' 51st state. After Carter agreed to make a public statement expressing confidence in Schmidt and noting their concurrence on theater nuclear forces, matters quieted down. In Venice, at the summit itself, the American president was able to get the seven leaders to agree to a final communiqué condemning the Soviet Union for endangering world peace as a result of its invasion of Afghanistan in December 1979. In return, the president agreed to shelve his demands for further punitive measures against the Soviets and to consider the possibility of negotiations with Moscow at some later date.

Carter and Schmidt remained disdainful of each other, however. The president feared that the West German chancellor would make concessions to Moscow on arms control even though he promised at Venice not to break ranks with the allies. The German leader retained his own suspicions about Carter, joining Europe's other leaders in wondering whether an Atlantic alliance, predicated on American economic and military dominance after World War II and crafted for the recovery of Europe and the defense of the North Atlantic, was still sustainable or even desirable.

At home, Schmidt's administration came under growing attack. Although he was able to beat off his conservative challenger, Franz Joseph Strauss, in the 1980 elections, the coalition that supported him started to unravel shortly thereafter. The left wing of the SPD was rebellious, and his junior partner in the coalition, the Free Democrats, defected. In 1982, he lost a vote of no confidence in the Bundestag and was succeeded as chancellor by Helmut Kohl.

Out of office, Schmidt joined the national newsmagazine *Die Zeit* as coeditor in 1983, becoming managing editor in 1985. In 1987, he published his memoirs, *Men and Powers:*

A Political Retrospective. He has also played an active role in the formation of the European Monetary System. He remained an outspoken critic of the Kohl government until its defeat in 1998.

Schultze, Charles Louis

(1924–) *chair, Council of Economic Advisers*

As a highly respected economist who had served as director of the Bureau of the Budget during Lyndon Johnson's presidency and then as a senior fellow at the liberal Brookings Institution, Charles L. Schultze was widely perceived as a neo-Keynesian, one who looked to administrative policies rather than the marketplace to regulate the economy. He was certainly predisposed that way as chairman of President Carter's Council of Economic Advisers, especially during the president's first year in office. But even before becoming a member of the Carter administration, he had come to modify his views. As the White House's emphasis changed from one of stimulating the economy to dealing with inflation, he depended increasingly on market mechanisms as the solution to the nation's economic and societal woes. It was no coincidence, therefore, that the most conservative of the president's economic advisers, JAMES MCINTYRE, the director of the Office of Management and Budget (OMB), came to regard Schultze as one of his closest allies in the White House.

Schultze was born in Alexandria, Virginia, on December 12, 1924, and grew up just across the Potomac River from the nation's capital. He entered Fordham University in New York City in 1942 but left after a year to enter the army, seeing combat in Europe during World War II. After the war, he attended Georgetown University, where he completed his undergraduate degree (B.A., 1948) and then did a master's degree in economics (M.A., 1950). From 1949 to 1951, he taught at the College of St. Thomas in Minnesota before taking a position for a year as an economist with the Office of Price Stabilization in Washington. He then spent six years as a staff economist on the Council of Economic Advisers while completing his doctorate in economics at the University of Maryland (Ph.D., 1960). After teaching at Indiana University and the University of Maryland, he joined the Bureau of the Budget (BOB) as an assistant director in 1962.

In 1965, President Lyndon Johnson appointed Schultze as head of the BOB. In that position, he applied the systems analysis procedures pioneered by Secretary of Defense Robert McNamara, utilizing experts to evaluate how well government agencies were using their appropriations and to suggest better alternatives in carrying out their responsibilities. The new method, known as the planning-programming-budgeting system, was first used in preparing the fiscal 1968 budget. *Forbes* magazine praised the new budget as "the first attempt of the U.S. government to figure out in detail what it really is spending the tax dollar for."

At this point in his career, Schultze was very much a proponent of the Keynesian "new economics," which emphasized an active fiscal policy on the part of the federal government as the key to economic growth and stability. In 1968, he served as an adviser to HUBERT HUMPHREY during the latter's unsuccessful campaign for the presidency. Following Humphrey's defeat, he became a senior fellow and head of economic policy at the Brookings Institution and wrote several works analyzing the federal budget during the RICHARD NIXON administration.

By 1976, Schultze was widely considered to be the Democratic Party's preeminent economist. Although he did not really get to know Jimmy Carter or have much to do with him during the presidential campaign, once Carter was elected president, he offered

Schultze the position of chair of the Council of Economic Advisers (CEA). The Brookings economist would have preferred to head the Office of Management and Budget (OMB) because he thought it would have more clout, but that position had already been reserved for the president-elect's close friend, BERT LANCE. Schultze agreed to accept the CEA position only on condition that there would be no special assistant to the president for economic affairs. As he later explained, he saw no purpose in having a CEA chair if there was going to be a "person of stature" between the chair and the president. "The whole point precisely is to be almost the personal economic adviser with enough of an institutional staff that you can do more than lick the back of an envelope," he added. Carter agreed to his terms.

About the same time that Schultze assumed his new duties as CEA chair in January 1977, he published an important new book, *In the Public Use of Private Interest*, in which he made clear some of the evolution that had taken place in his economic thinking since his days in the Johnson administration. There had been too much of a tendency, he wrote, to rely on command-and-control government in American society. Government, he said, should renounce old progressive orthodoxies and substitute for administrative methods the much-greater efficiency of the market, which, he added, was "an efficient instrument for society." Government still had the responsibility to take "corrective action to create efficient markets." But with diminishing resources, it needed to look increasingly to the noncoercive discipline of the market to meet societal needs.

One of the initial problems Schultze faced was working out his relationship with the president's two other leading economic advisers, Bert Lance and Secretary of the Treasury W. MICHAEL BLUMENTHAL. Together, the three officials formed the administration's Economic Policy Group (EPG), a single cabinet-level committee with a small staff, which was to meet weekly with senior deputies from other agencies involved with the EPG to discuss major issues. Very quickly, the EPG became an unwieldy body whose membership came to include several cabinet members, Vice President WALTER MONDALE, and domestic policy staff director STUART EIZENSTAT. Some of its meetings were attended by as many as 40 people. Instead of helping to coordinate the administration's economic policy, it had the opposite effect. The EPG often submitted memorandums to the president with too many options and discordant views.

At first, the EPG and its executive committee were chaired by Blumenthal and Schultze, but after six months Schultze stepped down as cochair because he wanted to retain his identity as an independent voice with the president. An additional advantage he had over the president's other economic advisers was that none of them had his experience in dealing with macroeconomic issues, such as the unusual economic recession the Carter White House had inherited from the Ford administration: unusual in the sense that it combined high inflation with high unemployment, thereby adding a new term, *stagflation*, to the lexicon.

Focusing on the problem of unemployment rather than inflation, Schultze recommended a modest economic-stimulus program that included increases in federal jobs programs; increased spending for public works; small, permanent tax reductions; and a $50 tax rebate to every taxpayer. Although Schultze defended the program in traditional Keynesian terms as a way to boost spending during a period of insufficient consumer demand, the program was modest compared to similar programs during the Kennedy and Johnson administrations and to spending levels being urged by Democrats in Congress. It became even more modest following the president's decision to forego the tax rebate once it became apparent that the economy was already beginning to recover without the stimulus package.

Notwithstanding the modest nature of the stimulus package, Schultze expressed regret later that, in helping to devise the program, he had paid too much attention to the rate of unemployment and not enough to inflation, which at the time Carter took office was approaching nearly double-digit levels as a result of rapidly rising increases in food and fuel. In addition to the stimulus program, increases in the minimum wage and in agricultural price supports, agreed to reluctantly by a president more worried about inflation than even his economic advisers, stoked the flames of inflation.

Schultze believed that his support for the stimulus program, especially the $50 tax rebate, diminished his influence with the president. Carter and other White House officials denied this emphatically. Regardless, beginning with a nationally televised speech Carter made in October 1978 and continuing for the remainder of the Carter administration, inflation replaced unemployment as the White House's greatest economic concern. Cutting the federal budget, instituting voluntary wage-and-price controls, limiting pay raises for federal workers, and raising interest rates, even at the expense of higher unemployment, became the major White House strategy for beating inflation. Secondarily, but also of great importance, was promoting market efficiencies through economic deregulation.

This was the program Schultze recommended and fully supported. His allies included McIntyre; ALFRED KAHN, who was appointed in October as the president's adviser on inflation and head of the Council on Wage and Price Stability (COWPS); and Blumenthal, although both Schultze and Kahn had personal and tactical differences with the Treasury secretary, whom they found abrasive and unimaginative. The administration, however, never articulated the program as coherently as it might have or resisted countervailing forces, such as the opposition of organized labor and other interest groups within the Democratic Party. These were represented by Vice President Mondale; Secretary of Labor RAY MARSHALL; Secretary of Health, Education and Welfare JOSEPH CALIFANO; and, on a more irregular basis, Domestic Policy Director Eizenstat. According to Schultze, Mondale in particular but liberals in general did not understand the new reality of fiscal restraint.

The Iranian revolution, beginning in late 1978, cut off a major spigot of the world's oil supplies and led to panic buying in the United States. This resulted in huge jumps in gasoline prices that exacerbated inflation and further undermined the administration's latest inflation program. Carter responded by proposing major new budget cuts, temporary controls on consumer credit, an increase in gasoline taxes, and stepped-up monitoring of wage-and-price controls. Again, these were proposals that had Schultze's full support.

More troublesome was the decision by PAUL VOLCKER, the chair of the Federal Reserve Board (Fed), to fight inflation by drastically curtailing the money supply through open-market sales of Treasury securities, which meant drastically higher interest rates and lower economic growth in an already sluggish economy. By allowing the market instead of the Fed to set rates even as he pushed them higher by tightening the money supply, Volcker also shielded the Federal Reserve System from political pressure.

Schultze was greatly disturbed by Volcker's action because of its obvious impact on the administration's battle against inflation. Although believing, as a general proposition, in the societal efficiency of the market, he also recognized that it was not without costs as well as benefits and that government still had the responsibility to reconcile the two.

When he first learned of Volcker's intentions, therefore, he attempted to get the president to intervene. He was joined in this effort by G. WILLIAM MILLER, who had replaced Michael Blumenthal as Treasury secretary following a cabinet shake-up in July 1979. In meetings and phone calls, Schultze also tried to get Volcker to reconsider his decision. In October 1979, the president made a speech in which he referred to Volcker's emphasis on the money supply as a way of containing inflation as "ill advised." In the end, however, Carter felt he had no choice other than to support the person he had appointed as Fed chairman, especially given the president's own commitment to taming inflation.

By the time the full impact of Volcker's draconian Fed program—both its costs and its benefits—was felt, Carter had been defeated for reelection and RONALD REAGAN was president. Following Carter's defeat, Schultze taught at Stanford University and returned to the Brookings Institution as a senior fellow in its economics program. In 1984, he also served as president of the American Economics Association.

During the 1980s and early 1990s, Schultze became an outspoken critic of President Reagan's conservative economics and of the national industrial policy (NIP) being promoted by such liberal economists as MIT's Lester Thurow and Harvard's Robert Reich. Among other things, NIP emphasized the long-term decline of the United States and maintained that the government should be directly involved in establishing national industrial goals. While accepting the argument that certain old-line heavy industries, like steel and automobiles, had structural problems, Schultze maintained that the United States still had a dynamic economy able to make a gradual transition from older industries to newer ones in the forefront of the global technological revolution.

In the 1990s, Schultze also became a regular commentator on NBC's *Nightly Business Report*, in which he excoriated the large tax cuts and federal borrowing being proposed by both parties. "Only when both sides give up their tax cuts and also make some gradual reductions in Social Security spending, can this country get on a realistic path to budget balance," he remarked, for example, on December 26, 1995.

In 1997, Schultze was named as the first recipient of the John C. and Nancy D. Whitehead Chair at the Brookings Institution, where he is presently a senior fellow emeritus.

Sick, Gary Gordon

(1935–) *staff member, National Security Council*

Gary Sick served on the National Security Council (NSC) as an expert on the Middle East under Presidents GERALD FORD, Jimmy Carter, and RONALD REAGAN. He was the principal White House aid for Iran during the Iranian revolution and hostage crisis of 1978–81. In 1985, he wrote a nationally acclaimed book, *All Fall Down: America's Tragic Encounter with Iran*, in which he was extremely critical of the Carter administration's response to the revolution and the subsequent seizure of American hostages. In 1991, he published a second, highly controversial work, *October Surprise: America's Hostages and the Election of Ronald Reagan*, in which he accused the leaders of Ronald Reagan's campaign for president in 1980 of conspiring with Iran to delay the release of the American hostages until after the election in November in order to prevent President Carter's reelection. In return, Iran would receive arms from Israel. Sick's accusations led to a congressional investigation that turned into a political brouhaha between Republicans and Democrats.

Born on April 4, 1935, in Beloit, Kansas, Sick was a graduate of the University of Kansas (B.A., 1957). A career naval officer, he attended the U.S. Naval War College (1969–70) and received a master's degree from George Washington University (M.S., 1970) as well as a doctorate in political science from Columbia University (Ph.D., 1973). Prior to joining the NSC staff in 1976, he served in the Persian Gulf, North Africa, and the Mediterranean. He was also an assistant naval attaché at the American embassy in Cairo (1965–67) and country director for the Persian Gulf sheikhdoms and Indian Ocean area in the Office of the Assistant Secretary of Defense for International Security Affairs (1973–76).

According to Sick, he never started out to become an authority on Iran and the Persian Gulf. When President Ford asked him to join the NSC staff, though, he was an intelligence officer who was knowledgeable about weapons systems and had extensive service in the Mediterranean and Middle East at a time when the United States was building up the military forces of the shah of Iran, MOHAMMAD REZA PAHLAVI. After Carter defeated Ford in the presidential election later in 1976, Sick was invited by the new president to remain on the NSC staff with a new mission of reducing the shah's military purchases.

Sick made a favorable impression on Carter's National Security Advisor, ZBIGNIEW BRZEZINSKI, who appointed him the NSC officer responsible for Iranian affairs. On several occasions in 1978, Sick warned Brzezinski that political conditions in Iran were unraveling and that the shah was in danger of being toppled from power by Islamic zealots hostile to the United States. Most intelligence, however, did not pick up on Sick's warnings, and not until the autumn did the U.S. ambassador to Iran, WILLIAM SULLIVAN, realize that the shah was in trouble. Then he recommended that the United States "think the unthinkable" and open communication with various opposition groups in case the shah was ousted from power. In November 1978, he wrote a long letter to the State Department recommending that the United States prepare for the transfer of power from the shah to a coalition government led by the spiritual leader of Iran's 32 million Shi'ite Muslims, AYATOLLAH RUHOLLA KHOMEINI.

What followed was the basis for later accusations and counteraccusations over who was responsible for the series of events that led to the overthrow of the shah, Khomeini's ascension to power and the hostage crisis that consumed President Carter throughout the remainder of his administration. A central question has been whether stronger U.S. support for the shah, including backing his use of military force to suppress the opposition to his rule, might have kept him in power or whether his regime was doomed and overtures to the opposition, as Sullivan had advised, was the only realistic option available to the administration. Brzezinski rejected Sullivan's recommendation and dismissed as a form of appeasement the formation of a coalition government after the shah fled the country in January 1979, preferring instead a military regime.

According to Brzezinski, no one had greater influence on his own thinking or was more involved on a daily basis with the Iranian crisis than Sick. Certainly no one was louder in his criticism of Sullivan than Sick, who accused the ambassador of misleading the White House by his optimistic reporting on Iran and of undermining the shah's will to resist when he should have been encouraging the monarch to take a firm stand against the militants. Yet in *All Fall Down*, Sick emphasizes how surprised everyone in the administration was by the opposition to the shah and how unprepared it was for dealing with the crisis that followed. Furthermore, he faults the NSC as well as the State Department for compounding the problem because of the ongoing rivalry between Brzezinski and Secretary of State CYRUS VANCE, which led each agency to seek its own sources of information (and disinformation).

Sick continued to serve on the NSC staff even after Carter was defeated for reelection in 1980. In 1982, he retired from the navy with the rank of captain. From 1982 to 1987, he was the deputy director for international affairs at the Ford Foundation, where he was responsible for programs relating to foreign policy. He then took a position as senior research scholar and adjunct professor of international relations at Columbia University.

In *October Surprise*, Sick comments on how he became increasingly struck during the 1980s by what he considered the coincidence of circumstances surrounding the delayed release of the Iranian hostages until after President Carter left office. In 1988, he met with Martin Kilian, Washington correspondent for *Der Spiegel*, German's weekly newsmagazine, who was independently pursuing the same track as Sick and who, according to Sick, had uncovered his own evidence of a secret deal over the Iranian hostages. His conversations with Kilian persuaded Sick to pursue the evidence that he had already uncovered. Employing computer analyses of data banks, chronological files, and other information gathered from interviews and conversations, he came up with what seemed to him inconvertible evidence of a deal between the Reagan campaign and Iran over the American hostages.

Most startling, in Sick's view, were alleged secret meetings in Spain in July and August 1980 and in Paris in October that year between Iranian officials and Ronald Reagan's campaign manager, William Casey, a former spymaster during World War II. Significantly, Israel made a massive shipment of arms to Iran during the last weeks of the presidential campaign and after Reagan took office. "The deal to delay the release of the hostages," Sick wrote in *October Surprise*, "may well have been the first act in a drama that was ultimately to conclude with the Iran-Contra Affair." Making matters even worse according to Sick was the fact that President GEORGE HERBERT WALKER BUSH, Reagan's running mate in 1980, had been present at the October meeting and knew about the secret negotiations.

Sick's charges, together with the revelations of the Iran-contra scandal that shook the last years of the Reagan administration, resulted in a House congressional investigation into the allegations that ran into the 1992 presidential elections. The committee, led by Representative Lee Hamilton (D-Ind.), found no evidence that Bush had been present at the October 1980 meeting in Paris, as Sick had charged. Nor was it able independently to confirm Sick's other accusations. Republicans seized on the investigation to accuse the Democrats of attempting to cover Bush with a coat of scandal in order to prevent his reelection in November. They also called the investigation a "witch hunt" and depicted Sick as a cynical Democratic liberal and President Carter's "foreign policy director," whose chief witnesses were a South African arms dealer and the 1960s radical, Abbie Hoffman.

Since 1991, when *October Surprise* was published, Sick has remained at Columbia University, where he is cochair of its Seminar on the Middle East and the executive director of Gulf/2000, an international research project on political, economic, and security developments in the Persian Gulf sponsored by Columbia. He is also a member of the International Institute of Strategic Studies (London) and the Council on Foreign Relations as well as a member of the board of Human Rights Watch in New York and cochair of the advisory committee of Human Rights Watch/Middle East. In recent years, he has begun to speak out in favor of improving U.S. relations with Iran. He resides in New York.

Somoza Debayle, Anastasio
(1925–1980) *president of Nicaragua*

In 1937, Anastasio Somoza Garcia used his command of the National Guard (a combined army and national police force) to gain absolute control of the government of Nicaragua. From then until the 1970s, the Somoza family maintained their dictatorial rule of Nicaragua as caudillos—leaders who use military power to govern. Under pressure, however, from the Carter administration, which attacked the Somoza regime for its human rights violations, the heir of the Somoza dynasty, Anastasio Somoza Debayle, was forced in 1979 to give up his rule and flee the small Central American country.

The younger son of Anastasio Somoza Garcia, Somoza Debayle (also frequently called Tachito) was born on December 5, 1925, in Leon, Nicaragua, but moved with his family to Managua as his father rose through the ranks of the National Guard before seizing power in the 1930s. After attending Saint Leo Preparatory College in Tampa, Florida, and La Salle Academy in Long Island, New York, with his older brother Luis, Tachito entered the United States Military Academy at West Point (B.S., 1946). Unlike Luis, who was more interested in civilian life, Anastasio tied his career to the military. By the time he returned to Nicaragua from West Point, he was already a major in the National Guard. Soon he was promoted to lieutenant colonel and, at age 21, to chief of staff. Over the next decade, he effectively ran the Guard on his father's behalf. One writer has quipped that he was only graduate of West Point to be given an army as a graduation present.

In 1956, Tachito was promoted to colonel and made commander of the Guard. That same year, his father, who was preparing to run for president in elections he controlled, was assassinated, and Luis Somoza Debayle was installed as president. Responding to pressure from Washington to loosen the family's control over the country, Luis picked a loyal supporter, Rene Shick, for his successor as president in 1963, rather than his brother Tachito, who had promoted himself to major general and wanted to maintain the family's control over Nicaragua. Just before Luis died in 1967 of a heart attack, though, Tachito, who had made himself a five-star general in 1964, had himself elected president.

In contrast to his brother, Anastasio Somoza Debayle tightened his family's control over Nicaragua by appointing relatives to key positions in government. He also increased the family's fortunes by taking greater control over the economy and brutally suppressed rising opposition to his rule, led by a Marxist guerrilla group known as the Sandinista National Liberation Front (FSLN). Following a catastrophic earthquake in 1972 that destroyed much of the nation's capital of Managua and killed 10,000 people, the Somoza family lined its own pockets with much of the relief money that flowed into the country. Even the Roman Catholic Church became critical of the regime.

Because of its strong stand against communism, however, the Somoza regime enjoyed the support of the United States, especially after Somoza agreed to the establishment in 1974 of a three-member junta, including a member of the opposition. Nevertheless, with the support of the U.S. ambassador, Somoza even brushed aside the junta. In 1974, he had himself elected to a six-year presidential term. When the FSLN guerrillas responded by seizing prominent Nicaraguan officials, the regime was forced to release political prisoners and pay a large ransom. In 1977, the FSLN seized the entire National Congress and held it captive, forcing Somoza to release more political prisoners. Humiliated, he responded by instituting a state of siege, imposing press censorship, and applying brutal force in his attempt to suppress the rebels. In 1978, the leader of the opposition, a popular journalist named Pedro Joaquin Chamorro, was assassinated, leading to massive demonstrations and a business-sponsored national strike against the Somoza regime. With Cuban support, the Sandinista movement continued to grow, notwithstanding Somoza's efforts to smother it.

Shocked by developments in Nicaragua and the growing opposition to Somoza, the Carter administration followed a zigzag course—criticizing Somoza's human-rights violations, deploring even more the Sandinistas' Marxist leanings and Cuban support, but advocating a mediated end to the war. At the same time, the president's inconsistency alienated both the Nicaraguan dictator and the opposition.

As Nicaragua drifted toward civil war, the White House applied more pressure on Somoza to give up the reins of powers. The U.S. ambassador to Nicaragua, Lawrence Pezzulo, privately called Somoza "a corrupt, greedy, and ultimately brutal man." Within the United States, however, strong opposition among the conservative right wing of the Republican Party, led by Senator JESSE HELMS (N.C.), assailed the administration for not backing the anticommunist Somoza regime. Even conservative Democrats, like HERMAN TALMADGE (S.C.), while regarding Somoza as a "free lance thug," thought it was mistake to replace him by "even more dangerous fanatics" like the Sandinistas.

Believing that Somoza's continued presence increased the chances of a radical takeover, the White House finally terminated military aid and most economic assistance to Nicaragua and reduced the size of the U.S. embassy in Managua. Still, President Carter continued to vacillate; there was even a report in the *Washington Post* that the administration was considering a resumption of some aid to Nicaragua. Although this did not happen, the White House was clearly having considerable difficulty coming up with a firm policy in response to a deteriorating situation into the United States' own backyard.

Complicating matters for Carter were conflicting pressures he was receiving from foes and friends of the Somoza regime. Opposition to the dictator mounted after a correspondent for ABC News, Bill Stewart, was forced to lie down with his face on the ground and then was shot in the back of the head by a member of Somoza's National Guard. The execution, shown on national television, shocked and infuriated the American public. Thousands of letters and telegrams poured into the White House demanding immediate reprisals of some sort.

Somoza, however, continued to have his own American backers who argued that the Sandinistas were Marxists and that their victory would create another Cuba near the United States. In the House, opponents of the Panama Canal Treaties, who were trying to block funds for their implementation, tied their opposition to Somoza, seeing an opportunity to trade Panama treaty votes for support of Somoza's troubled regime. Others tried to block the treaties by claiming that the Panamanians were providing aid to Somoza's opponents. On June 13, 1979, more than 120 members of the House signed a letter urging the president to stop the reported flow of arms from Cuba and Panama to the Sandinistas. Former president RICHARD NIXON deplored Carter's call for Somoza's resignation. "I think it is crucial," he told the *New York Times* in July 1979, "that every possible step be taken to make sure that a Castro-type government does not come to power in Nicaragua because that would be a threat to every free nation in the Western Hemisphere."

The White House was also worried about the leftist leanings of the Sandinistas and their ties to Cuba. In order to prevent the Sandinistas from simply seizing power after toppling Somoza, the State Department proposed to establish an Organization of American States (OAS) peacekeeping force and an interim government of national reconciliation. On June 21, Secretary of State CYRUS VANCE outlined this plan to the OAS, but the idea was doomed from the start. Neither the Sandinistas nor the other OAS members were prepared to accept a proposal that did not recognize the Sandinistas' right to install a temporary government.

By this time, it was apparent that Somoza's days as Nicaragua's strongman were numbered. At the end of May 1979, the Sandinistas had launched their "final offensive," seizing Leon, the country's second-largest city, and capturing a string of towns both north and south of the capital. They had also established a five-member junta to serve as head of a provisional government. By July, all of Nicaragua was under Sandinista control except Managua.

On July 17, 1979, Somoza fled the country. Although President Carter agreed to allow him to fly to Miami, the president made it clear that Somoza was not welcome to remain in the United States. As a result, he was forced about a month later to flee to Asuncion, Paraguay. "I spit on the help of Carter, the traitor," he remarked soon afterward. On September 17, 1980, Somoza was assassinated when his car was hit by bazooka and machine-gun fire, reportedly by Argentine guerrillas. A few months earlier, he had published his memoir, *Nicaragua Betrayed*, in which he blamed the Carter administration for his downfall. He was 54 years old at the time of his death.

Sorensen, Theodore Chaikin

(1928–) *nominee for director of the CIA*

Nominated by President Carter to be director of the Central Intelligence Agency (CIA), Theodore Sorensen became the center of a storm of controversy over his suitability for the position, leading him to withdraw his name from consideration just as Senate confirmation hearings on his nomination were beginning. What made the scuttling of his nomination so significant was that it amounted to a personal rebuke of the president. It also raised serious questions on Capitol Hill and among political observers about the competence of the White House staff.

Few doubted Sorensen's intellectual brilliance and many political talents. The son of a liberal Republican lawyer who later became Nebraska's attorney general, he was born in Lincoln, Nebraska, on May 8, 1928. After receiving both his undergraduate and law degrees from the University of Nebraska (B.S., 1949; J.D., 1951), where he had been first in his class as an undergraduate and editor in chief of the *Law Review*, he worked as an attorney for the Federal Security Agency (1951–52) and then as a staff member for the U.S. Senate Joint Committee on Railway Retirement. In 1953, he joined the staff of Senator John F. Kennedy (D-Mass.).

Over the next 11 years, Sorensen went from being Kennedy's speechwriter to being his intellectual alter ego and one of his closest advisers. A gifted writer who was a master in using alliteration, pungent phrasings, and inspirational themes, he most likely ghost-authored Kennedy's Pulitzer Prize–winning *Profiles of Courage* (1956), although that remains a matter of controversy. Special counsel to the president after Kennedy moved to the White House in 1961, Sorensen continued to write the president's major speeches, including his famous inaugural address. He also figured prominently as Kennedy's policy adviser and legal counsel on matters ranging from civil rights legislation to the Cuban Missile Crisis. He refined the president's pragmatism and sense of irony with his own liberalism and progressivism. Long before Kennedy was assassinated in November

1963, their views on most matters had become almost indistinguishable.

Following Kennedy's assassination, Sorensen left the White House and spent the next 18 months writing *Kennedy* (1965), a paean to the martyred president. He also took a position as a partner with the New York law firm of Paul, Weiss, Rifkin, Wharton, & Garrison. In 1970, he ran unsuccessfully for the U.S. Senate from New York. After that, he seemed to disappear from the political radar screen.

This made President-elect Carter's nomination of Sorensen to be director of the CIA all the more surprising and baffling to lawmakers and political observers. As they began to scrutinize his background, they raised serious questions about the appointment. In the first place, Sorensen seemed to lack the managerial and administrative experience necessary to run such a behemoth as the CIA. It was his brain, not his talent as an administrator, which had always made Sorensen stand out. One of the president-elect's well-known requirements for each cabinet-level position was that the person he named be an experienced manager. In appointing as his CIA director someone who had no experience running a large institution, the president appeared to be violating his own rules.

More important, Sorensen had registered during the Korean War as a conscientious objector, reflecting his mother's pacifistic influence. Given the nature of some of the CIA's covert operations, this made a number of lawmakers wonder about his suitability to carry out the agency's mission or to work with the military at the CIA or at other intelligence agencies. Even Kenneth O'Donnell, a Boston businessman who had been one of the Sorensen's colleagues in the Kennedy administration, warned the incoming administration against making the appointment. When he heard that the president might name Sorensen to head the CIA, O'Donnell called Greg Schneiders, a Carter assistant working at the transition headquarter in Americus, Georgia. "They're not going to stand for this," he remarked with respect to the military. "I don't want to see Carter get hurt by this."

After leaving the White House in 1963, Sorensen had taken with him a number of boxes of classified materials in order to write his book on Kennedy. When he later donated these and other nonclassified materials to the John F. Kennedy Library, he took an $87,000 tax deduction. In removing the materials and taking the tax deduction, Sorensen had violated no criminal statute. Another of his colleagues from the Kennedy White House, Arthur Schlesinger, Jr., had used classified materials to write his own account of the Kennedy presidency. Nevertheless, a number of lawmakers questioned the ethics of what Sorensen had done and raised the issue of how much he could be trusted with classified materials.

Other issues with respect to Sorensen's appointment developed as well. Many conservative Republicans thought he was too liberal to serve at the CIA. Others were concerned about his strong connections to the Kennedy family, wondering aloud whether he would be serving Senator EDWARD KENNEDY (Mass.) or Jimmy Carter. Finally, he lacked any experience in intelligence work and had even urged a cutback in the CIA's use of covert operations, matters that deeply concerned retired and former intelligence officers, who lobbied actively against his appointment.

By the time of Sorensen's confirmation hearing before the Senate Intelligence Committee, opposition to his appointment had become so great as to put it in doubt. Senator BARRY GOLDWATER (R-Ariz.) refused even to grant Sorensen the customary courtesy call given to nominees. After sampling sentiment among Republicans, Senator ROBERT DOLE (Kans.) urged the president to withdraw the nomination. Nor was the opposition limited to Republicans. Even the highly respected head of the Intelligence Committee, Senator Daniel Inouye (D-Hawaii), a much-decorated veteran who had lost his right arm during World War II, had serious reservations about the nomination and once advised Carter to withdraw it.

What really turned the tide against Sorensen, however, was an affidavit he gave during the 1973 trial of Daniel Ellsberg in which he defended Ellsberg's copying of the Pentagon's classified materials relating to the Vietnam War; these were later published as *United States–Vietnam Relations, 1945–1967: A Study Prepared by the Department of Defense*, better known as the Pentagon Papers. In defending his own removal of classified materials from the White House, Sorensen had stated in the affidavit that the government had a tendency to overuse its prerogative to classify documents even when there was no actual threat to national security. Sorensen's comment infuriated conservative Republicans and supporters of the Vietnam War who believed that Ellsberg had given aid and comfort to the enemy by publishing the Pentagon Papers. The affidavit was not widely circulated, though, until Senator JOSEPH BIDEN (D-Del.) found a copy of it and handed it to Inouye. Once it became public, the outcry was immediate. Sorensen's "actions with the classified material and his support of Ellsberg," one Democratic member of the committee remarked, "would have raised doubts with sources around the world about the reliability of the [CIA] director."

Sorensen was blindsided by the reaction to his nomination. Although he had helped raise money for Carter during the presidential campaign and had worked actively for him, he had been as surprised as anyone by the president-elect's nomination of him as CIA director. Given his previous status as a conscientious objector, he had his own doubts about his suitability for the position, but he had accepted it on the assumption that the president's staff had already checked into his background fully. A few days later, however, the president-elect's chief aid, HAMILTON JORDAN, asked Sorensen whether he had been a conscientious objector during the Korean War. After he explained that he had received classification as a noncombatant but had never tried to avoid military service and suggested other matters that could give rise to Senate concerns, Jordan told him that was not necessary. On this basis, Sorensen assumed the incoming administration had enough confidence in his nomination that he had no cause for further concern.

Taken aback by the uproar over his nomination, Sorensen tried to save it by walking the halls of Congress and looking to the incoming president for assistance. But what he found on Capitol Hill, even among Democrats, was dwindling support and a growing sense that it would be in everyone's best interest if he withdrew his name from consideration. Senator Adlai Stevenson, Jr. (D-Ill.) told him that the president should have known about the affidavit that had been released earlier, adding, "If you didn't tell him, it reflects badly on your judgment, and if he didn't ask you it makes me wonder about his judgment."

As for Carter, while he told Sorensen that he would stand behind him, he also made clear that he would not be disappointed if Sorensen withdrew his name. A head count of the Intelligence Committee showed that Sorensen had only five committee votes, while nine were against him. On January 17, 1977, the day of his confirmation hearing, Sorensen appeared before the Intelligence Committee. Instead of giving testimony, however, he read a 10-page rebuttle of what he called "scurrilous and personal attacks" on him and then announced that he was withdrawing his name from consideration as CIA director. Carter subsequently nominated STANSFIELD TURNER.

As Adlai Stevenson had made clear to Sorensen earlier, the failure of his nomination was as much a reflection of the Carter administration's poor judgment as it was a rejection of the candidate. Despite the months of extensive examination the incoming president and his aides had expended in the selection process for cabinet and senior-level positions in his administration, they had failed to give due diligence to the selection of the CIA director.

Humiliated by the experience he had undergone, Sorensen returned to New York, where he continued to practice law, focusing on international law, and to write. In 1984, he published *A Different Kind of Presidency: A Proposal for Breaking the Political Deadlock.* This was been followed by *The Kennedy Legacy* (1993), *Why I Am a Democrat* (1996), and *Decision-Making in the White House: The Olive Branch or the Arrow* (2005). In these works, Sorensen argues the ongoing importance of the presidency, notwithstanding the growing power of the other branches of government. He makes clear the reverence he still has for John F. Kennedy and the Kennedy White House, which remains a benchmark for him in evaluating other presidencies. He also underscores his commitment to liberal and progressive values, which he continues to identify with the Democratic Party. "Only the Democratic Party," he has written, "has the history, philosophy, diversity and constituency to become again the Party of Conscience."

Sorensen has been a faculty member at the Progressive Century Institute and has lectured widely in the United States and abroad. He has been active in promoting nuclear nonproliferation and has appeared on PBS's *NewsHour.*

Stennis, John Cornelius

(1901–1995) *member of the Senate*

One of the last of the southern barons of the Senate and chair of the powerful Senate Armed Services Committee, John Stennis (D-Miss.) believed in following the lead of the president, regardless of party, on issues related to matters of national defense. He also believed in increased defense spending. These were the positions he followed during the Carter administration. The president was unable, however, to persuade him to support the Panama Canal Treaties. Stennis also had serious reservations about the Strategic Arms Limitation Talks agreement of 1979 (SALT II). Owing his power on Capitol Hill to his longevity as Mississippi's senior senator and the rewards of the seniority system, he was, nevertheless, respected and trusted on both sides of the aisle, which added to the influence he was able to bear on Capitol Hill. He was also known as the personification of southern courtliness and gentility.

Stennis was born on August 3, 1901, in the small town of DeKalb in the red-clay hills of east-central Mississippi. He came from a prominent family of doctors, lawyers, farmers, teachers, and legislators. A graduate of Mississippi State University (B.S., 1923), where he was a member of Phi Beta Kappa, he received his law degree from the University of Virginia (LL.B., 1928). A year out of law school, he was elected to the Mississippi House of Representatives and established a law practice in DeKalb. In 1932, he was elected prosecuting attorney in Mississippi's 16th judicial district. After serving in that position for five years, he was elected as a circuit judge of the same district.

In 1947, Stennis decided to run as a Democrat for the U.S. Senate seat vacated by the death of the arch-segregationist Theodore G. Bilbo. In an election without a runoff, Stennis defeated five opponents, including two sitting U.S. congressmen. Although fully committed to the southern system of segregation, he purposely avoided the volatile racial issue that Bilbo had exploited for many years. Instead, he adopted a message that could easily be understood by rural Mississippians: "I want to plow a straight furrow right down to the end of the row. This is my political religion, and I have lived by it too long to abandon it now." In 1952, he was elected to a full term in the U.S. Senate. Until his last campaign, he was never seriously challenged for reelection. (In 1982, a 34-year old Republican, Haley Barbour, launched a viable challenge, making Stennis's advanced age his major issue. Still, the senior senator defeated his young challenger by a margin of about two to one.)

Almost as soon as he took office, Stennis had to confront the southern revolt against the civil rights program of the Truman administration; his maiden speech in the Senate was a strong anti–civil rights statement. In February 1948, some 4,000 political leaders from throughout Mississippi adopted a resolution calling for the South to withhold, if necessary, its electoral votes in the presidential election. Stennis urged that the fight be kept within the Democratic Party, but he was politely ignored. Throughout the 1950s and 1960s, Stennis joined other southern leaders in resisting the Civil Rights movement taking place in the South, but he generally sought to be a voice of reason. In 1956, he was one of the signers of the Southern Manifesto condemning the Supreme Court decision in *Brown v. Board of Education of Topeka* (1954), which had declared segregation to be unconstitutional. But he had helped tone down an earlier draft of the manifesto that endorsed the concept of interposition and condemned "the illegal and unconstitutional decision of the Court."

During the 1960s, Stennis generally opposed the programs of the New Frontier and Great Society, although he did support health programs such as medical research. He also remained an unalloyed advocate of "preserving the southern way of life," voting against every civil rights bill and trying to undermine support for racial integration by ending the distinction between de jure (based on law) and de facto (based on fact) segregation. Toward this end, in 1970 he submitted the Elementary and Secondary Education Amendment, whose aim was to ensure that federal desegregation pressure would "be applied uniformly in all regions of the United States." Stennis never played the role of racial demagogue, however, and he had little use for people who tried to build their political careers around the racial issue. He condemned violent actions by the Ku Klux Klan and other hate groups, and he did not drink, smoke, swear in public, or use racial epithets. As a result, he won the respect of such liberals as Paul Douglas (D-Ill.), one of the early Senate leaders promoting civil rights legislation, who, during one battle over a civil rights measure, declared, "If I were ever to have to go on trial, I would want John Stennis to be my judge." Other liberals who expressed great admiration for Stennis even though they parted with him on civil rights and other legislation included GAYLORD NELSON (D-Minn.) and HENRY JACKSON (D-Wash.).

Because of his reputation for fairness, Stennis was often called upon to head political inquiries. As early as 1954, he was appointed as a member of a committee investigating charges against the red-baiting senator from Wisconsin, Joseph McCarthy, after being the first Democrat to call for his public censure. To ignore McCarthy's actions, he stated on the Senate floor, would mean that "something big and fine has gone out of this chamber and something of a wrong character, something representing a wrong course, a wrong approach will have entered." In 1962, he investigated accusations that the State Department and Pentagon were trying to muzzle military officers who wanted to speak out against communism, During the Watergate scandal of the early 1970s, President RICHARD NIXON took advantage of Stennis's reputation for integrity by proposing that instead of turning over the infamous Watergate tapes to a special prosecutor, he allow Stennis to listen to them and validate summaries prepared by the White House. Stennis also wrote the first code of ethics for the Senate and was the first chair of the Senate Ethics Committee.

Stennis was best known, however, for his service on the Senate Armed Services Committee, first under the iconic Richard Russell of Georgia and then as chair of the committee. In 1961, he supported an increase of $500 million over the budget request of President John F. Kennedy for the building of long-range bombers. During the 1960s, he fought against troop reductions in Europe. In 1966, he joined two other members of the Armed Services committee, Henry Jackson and John Tower (R-Tex.), in a major campaign to pressure the administration to deploy the United States' Anti-Ballistic Missile System.

Stennis had initial misgivings about the escalation of U.S. military involvement in Vietnam. In 1968, he spoke out against increasing American troop levels in the Vietnam War above 350,000. He also refused to join other senators in chastising the antiwar movement as procommunist and un-American. Having expressed as early as the 1960s his concern that the war in Vietnam might set a precedent for American entry into later wars without congressional approval, he was one of the sponsors of the War Powers Act of 1973, limiting the power of the president to engage in an extended military conflict without prior congressional approval. Believing that the U.S. commitment in Vietnam had to be honored, however, he became a hawk in defending the American policy in Vietnam, including the increased use of air power. In 1968, he spoke out against a proposal by Senator WILLIAM PROXMIRE (D-Wis.) to reduce appropriations for a buildup of B-52 bomber operations in Vietnam. In 1972, he opposed the Case-Church amendment that mandated a deadline to cut off all funding for U.S. military involvement in Indochina subject to the release of U.S. prisoners of war. Approval of the Case-Church proposal, he said, would force the United States out of Vietnam "like a whipped dog." Yet Stennis always believed that his and Richard Russell's opposition to President Lyndon Johnson's war policy in Vietnam was a key factor in Johnson's decision not to seek reelection in 1968.

In January 1973, Stennis was nearly killed when he was shot while interrupting a robbery after returning to his home in Washington. Although the assailants were apprehended and he made a full recovery, he had to have surgery and go through an extended period of recuperation before he was able to return to the Senate.

In 1976, Stennis supported Senator Lloyd Bentsen of Texas for the Democratic presidential nomination. Early in Jimmy Carter's administration, he attacked the president for proposing to cut funding for the $1.6 billion Tennessee-Tombigbee waterway project intended to link the Tennessee and Tombigbee Rivers by a canal, thereby providing a direct outlet to the Gulf of Mexico for all the barge traffic in the Ohio River Basin and southern Appalachia. Although work had been begun on the project in 1972, less than 25 percent of it was complete when Carter took office. The waterway was originally on the list of water projects that the new president proposed to cut back or eliminate soon after he took office. Using his influence on Capitol Hill, however, Stennis engaged in considerable logrolling to save the project. "The other Senators would tell me how important their project was," he recalled, "and I would them about Tenn-Tom." The project was completed in 1985.

Recognizing Stennis's influence on Capitol Hill, especially among conservatives, Carter was anxious to win his support for the Panama Canal Treaties, which the president had successfully negotiated in 1977. The White House regarded Stennis as among the five or six most important Democrats in the Senate whose votes on the agreements, which would turn the canal over to Panama by the year 2000, could determine their outcome. As part of his lobbying effort on behalf of the treaties, he provided Stennis and a small group of other senators with a special briefing on the day the signing ceremonies took place in September 1977. But Stennis remained opposed to the agreements, maintaining that transfer of the canal would cost the United States more than $1 billion. In fact, he allowed his Armed Services Committee to be used as a forum for forces opposed to the treaties to present their arguments. On March 13, 1978, just days before the first vote on the treaties, the president had Stennis to lunch at the White House in a final effort to try to get him to change his mind. But the senator respectfully told Carter that he could not vote for the agreements.

The Mississippi senator also expressed serious reservations about the SALT II treaty negotiated with the Soviet Union in 1979. In September, he announced that his Armed Services Committee wanted to interrogate Secretary of State CYRUS VANCE and CIA director STANSFIELD TURNER about the existence of a Soviet combat brigade in Cuba. Opponents of the SALT II agreement hoped to use the issue of the combat brigade in Cuba, the existence of which had only recently been disclosed by Senator FRANK CHURCH (D-Idaho), in order to underscore their point that the Soviets could not be trusted to abide by the provisions of an arms-limitation agreement such as SALT II.

Stennis also continued to advocate a stronger military and more spending for defense. When the army failed to meet its annual quota in the last quarter of 1978 for enlistees into the regular army and the reserves, he called for reviving some form of the draft, stating that an all-volunteer force was a failure. He also called in 1980 for the United States to "seriously explore" alternatives to the liquid-fuel Titan missiles, which had been part of the nuclear arsenal since 1963 and were supposed to have been replaced in 1971. Although the Titans were not scheduled to be phased out until the Air Force began deploying the MX missiles, perhaps in another decade, Stennis was concerned by the recent explosion of a Titan missile, indicating that they were no longer reliable.

For the most part, however, Stennis tried to accommodate President Carter, even when the White House rejected some of the Pentagon's spending requests, just as he had tried to accommodate occupants of the White House before him. Years later, he said in an interview that he never tried to second-guess presidents on foreign policy and military matters.

During the Carter administration, Stennis found himself turning over more of the responsibilities for running the Armed Services Committee to his younger colleague, Henry Jackson, who shared his views on a strong defense and assumed a much harsher position against the administration than the more courtly and unassuming committee chair. Increasingly, Stennis perceived his role to be that of a teacher of younger senators. Although he rarely missed a day away from Capitol Hill when Congress was in session, he felt able, with lawmakers like Jackson and SAM NUNN (D-Ga.) on the Armed Services Committee, to give them more responsibility.

In 1984, Stennis had to have his left leg amputated because of cancer; he had bars constructed on his desk in the Senate chamber so that he could still pull himself out of his wheelchair and stand whenever he spoke. But the loss of his leg and advancing age began to take their toll on him. Having lost his wife of more than 50 years in 1983, he also suffered from loneliness. In 1988, he announced that he would retire after his term ended that year.

After leaving the Senate, Stennis retired to Starkville, the home of Mississippi State University and the John C. Stennis Institute of Government and John C. Stennis Center for

Public Service, created by Congress to train young leaders. In failing health, he spent the last years of his life in a nursing home near Jackson, Mississippi. He died on April 23, 1995, at the age of 93.

Stevens, John Paul
(1920–) *associate justice, U.S. Supreme Court*

In making appointments to the Supreme Court, presidents have historically nominated individuals whose views on constitutional law reflect their own political ideology. Given the unusual circumstances by which he became president, however, GERALD FORD was intent on avoiding a political battle over the replacement in 1975 for retiring Supreme Court justice William O. Douglas. Discounting ideological considerations, he relied on the advice of Attorney General Edward Levi, who recommended Judge John Paul Stevens of the U.S. Seventh Court of Appeals. Since then, Stevens has proven to be the most difficult member of the Supreme Court to classify in terms of his judicial philosophy among several justices known for their ideological inconsistency.

From a prominent and wealthy family, Stevens was born in Chicago, Illinois, on April 20, 1920. He attended the University of Chicago, from which he graduated magna cum laude and Phi Beta Kappa (B.A., 1941), and Northwestern University Law School (J.D., 1947), where he was editor in chief of the school's law review and received the highest grades in the school's history. During World War II, he served as an intelligence officer in the navy and was awarded the Bronze Star. After receiving his law degree, he clerked for Supreme Court justice Wiley Rutledge and then went into private practice with the prestigious Chicago law firm of Poppenhusen, Johnston, Thompson and Raymond.

In 1952, Stevens left the firm to start his own law practice specializing in antitrust law. His expertise as an antitrust litigator was enhanced by his service as associate counsel to the House Antitrust Subcommittee on the study of monopoly power (1951–52) and as a member of the Attorney General's National Committee to Study Antitrust Laws (1953–55). He also served as a lecturer in the schools of law at Northwestern (1950–54) and the University of Chicago (1955–58).

In 1970, President RICHARD NIXON appointed Stevens, a Republican, to the Seventh Circuit Court of Appeals. During his five years on the appellate bench, Stevens earned an excellent reputation for his intelligence and judicial craftsmanship. He was considered a moderate with a nonideological approach to the cases before him. President Ford's nomination of Stevens to the Supreme Court in November 1975 was therefore widely endorsed. The American Bar Association and a team of Harvard law professors found his opinions "well-written, highly analytical, closely researched and meticulously prepared." The only opposition to the appointment came from a few women's groups who were angry that Ford had not appointed a woman to the Court and who claimed that Stevens was insensitive to women's rights. In the Senate, his appointment was confirmed by a vote of 98 to 0. He took his seat on the Court on December 19, 1975.

Many observers had expected Stevens to play a leadership role in molding the Court's jurisprudence. Very much an individualist, he proved, instead, to be a maverick and a loner. He defied the Court's unwritten conservative dress code by wearing a bowtie beneath his robes, which one legal scholar commented gave him "a perpetual sophomoric appearance." Instead of hiring four law clerks, as he was allowed, he hired only two. On his first day on the bench, he heard a case involving the constitutionality of a Civil Service Commission regulation prohibiting resident aliens from holding most federal positions (*Hampton v. Mow Sun Wong*, 1976). At conference, he took a singular position, stating that discrimination against aliens was unconstitutional if it were based on a Civil Service Commission regulation, but it could be constitutional if it were predicated on an act of Congress or a presidential directive. Although Stevens was assigned to write the majority opinion in this case, he preferred to make his own decisions rather than align himself with other justices. Nor did he try to persuade them to his point of view. In his first full term on the Court, he wrote 17 separate concurrences and 27 dissents, more than any other Justice.

The most important—and divisive—case before the Court during Carter's administration was *Regents of the University of California v. Bakke* (1978), involving a special admissions program for minorities at the University of California–Davis School of Medicine that included racial quotas. In its ruling on *Bakke*, the Court upheld the principle of affirmative action (race could be one of several factors in making decisions in admissions cases) while rejecting the use of quotas. In his dissenting opinion, Stevens found that there was no need to consider the constitutional merits of the case. In his view, racial quotas and affirmative-action programs violated Title VI of the 1964 Civil Rights Act, which prohibited discrimination based on race. The case could be decided, therefore, as an interpretation of a federal statute rather than of the Constitution. "Affirmative action programs have performed a fine service," Stevens told his colleagues on the Court before preparing his dissent, "but they ought to be temporary—[however] I can't believe the day would come when the two-track admission system would be unnecessary. If we can duck the constitutional holding we should." In the case of *Fullilove v. Klutznick* (1980), involving the constitutionality of a federal statute to set aside at least 10 percent of public-works grants for minority business enterprises, Stevens also voted in the minority against the principle of affirmative action.

In other cases decided during the Carter presidency, Stevens voted against a majority ruling that notice and a hearing were not constitutionally necessary before corporal punishment could be administered in public schools (*Ingraham v. Wright*, 1977). In *Trimble v. Gordon* (1977), he sided with the majority in striking down an Illinois law that allowed illegitimate children to inherit only from their mothers in cases where there was not a will (intestate). In a similar case, he dissented in a ruling upholding a New York law that allowed illegitimate children, in intestate cases, to inherit from the father only if a court of competent jurisdiction had, while the father was alive, entered an order declaring paternity (*Lalli v. Lalli*, 1978).

In a case involving the First Amendment right of free expression (*Houchins v. KQED*, 1978), Stevens voted in the minority to uphold the constitutional right of access to information on the part of the press. "[I]nformation gathering is entitled to some measure of constitutional protection," he wrote. In another First Amendment case (*Gannett Co. v. DePasquale*, 1979), however, Stevens voted with the majority to affirm a lower-court ruling that the press could be excluded, at the request of the defendants in a murder case, from a pretrial hearing. He also dissented in a majority ruling upholding a New York law requiring state police to be U.S. citizens (*Foley v. Connelie*, 1978).

In *Zablocki v. Redhail* (1978), Stevens sided with the majority in striking down a state law prohibiting residents with minor children not in their custody from marrying without court permission, which could be given only if the minor children were receiving support and were not likely to become public charges. The law's real purpose was to ensure the enforcement of support orders. It was, said Stevens, "too questionable that this kind of collection device is permissible."

In an important case involving foreign policy (*Goldwater v. Carter*, 1980), Stevens voted with the majority in upholding President Carter's right to abrogate a mutual-defense treaty with Taiwan without first obtaining the consent of Congress. At first, he wanted to deny that the petitioners even had standing in the Court, but the other justices were not ready to maintain that a congressman (or a group of them) could not bring an issue to the Court concerning the exercise of their official duties. The result of the decision was to recognize the right of the president to terminate treaties while immunizing him from judicial review.

In the years since Carter was defeated by RONALD REAGAN in 1980, Stevens has remained among the Supreme Court's most unpredictable justices. In the 1983–84 term, he disagreed with the majority in 50 of the 91 divided opinions. He has also continued to find it difficult to join with a majority or dissenting opinion without adding his own comment or looking at a case from his own distinct perspective. As the Court has become more conservative, he has grown increasingly more liberal in his interpretation of the law. He has, for example, altered his views on affirmative action, most recently voting to uphold the affirmative-action programs challenged at the University of Michigan (*Grutter v. Bollinger and Gratz v. Bollinger*, 2003). He has also voted in the minority against a ruling allowing the Boy Scouts to exclude gay scoutmasters (*Boy Scouts of America v. Dale*, 2000), and in the majority in favor of abortion rights (*Planned Parenthood v. Casey*, 1992). Although often viewed as a gadfly on the Court, he remains respected for the elegance and thoughtfulness of his decisions. In addition to his duties on the Court, Stevens has also been a contributor of numerous articles to law journals and reviews.

Stewart, Potter

(1915–1985) *associate justice, U.S. Supreme Court*

Nominated to the U.S. Supreme Court as an associate justice by President Dwight D. Eisenhower in 1958 at the relatively young age of 43, Potter Stewart served on the Court for the next 23 years before retiring at the comparatively young age of 66. Typical of the direct style and pithy language that characterized his many opinions as a justice and of his wit and humor was the comment he made in explaining his decision to retire: "It's better to go too soon than to stay too late." Widely regarded as either a progressive conservative or a moderate liberal, he was more a pragmatist than an ideologue. Some Court historians have maintained that Stewart was a conservative force in the liberal Earl Warren Court and a liberal force in the conservative WARREN BURGER Court. When asked if he was a liberal or a conservative, he replied, "I am a lawyer." One description of him, which may have been the most accurate but still missed the mark, was that he was "tough on crime, strong on civil rights, and flexible on just about everything else."

In fact, in his attitude toward the law, Stewart was closest to his colleague for many years, Justice BYRON WHITE, whose approach was to make his decisions on a case-by-case basis and to blend a certain degree of common sense with his interpretation of the law and the Constitution. Stewart also favored narrow rulings limited to those issues necessary to decide a case rather than broad constitutional questions. The cases Stewart found most interesting had to do with the First Amendment (free speech), the Fourth Amendment (security against unreasonable searches and seizures) and the equal-protection clause of the Fourteenth Amendment. Court historians have generally regarded Stewart as an above-average jurist, pointing to his tightly reasoned, well-written, and lucid opinions.

Stewart was raised in a family of privilege that later suffered severe financial loss in the Great Depression. As a result, he had to rely on his own talents to put himself through college. Born on January 23, 1915, in Jackson, Michigan, he grew up in Cincinnati, Ohio, where his father, James Garfield Stewart, was mayor before being appointed to the Ohio Supreme Court. His mother, Harriet Loomis Potter, was a leader of the League of Voters and the Cincinnati Reform Movement. After attending the exclusive Hotchkiss School in Connecticut (the last years on a scholarship), Stewart entered Yale University on a scholarship, graduating cum laude and Phi Beta Kappa (B.A., 1937). Following Yale, he studied international law at Cambridge University on a fellowship before returning to the Yale Law School, where he received his law degree cum laude (LL.B., 1941).

After working for less than a year at a Wall Street law firm, Stewart joined the navy, serving during World War II as an officer on an oil tanker in the Atlantic and Mediterranean. Discharged from the navy in 1945, he returned to Wall Street briefly before accepting a position at a distinguished Cincinnati law firm. A Republican in a predominantly Republican city, he became active in municipal politics and served two terms on the city council, once as vice mayor. Although a close friend of Senator Robert Taft, Jr., he supported Dwight D. Eisenhower for the Republican nomination in 1952. In 1954, President Eisenhower appointed him to the Sixth Circuit Court of Appeals, making Stewart, at age 39, the nation's youngest federal judge. Four years later, after Stewart had developed a reputation as one of the best circuit judges because of the simple but precise language in his opinions, Eisenhower nominated him to the Supreme Court. Following a bitter seven-month fight against his nomination, led by Richard Russell of Georgia, because of Stewart's decision on a civil-rights case, he was confirmed by the Senate on May 5, 1959, by a vote of 70 to 17.

During the Warren Court, especially before it achieved a liberal majority after the retirement of Felix Frankfurter in 1962, Stewart was considered a swing vote along with Byron White, who was appointed to the Court in 1962. To some Court observers, there seemed no consistency in Stewart's decisions on such matters as free speech and the powers of the government. While he was sensitive to the First Amendment right of free speech and opposed broad delegations of government authority, he believed in balancing individual rights against government needs. He denied, for example, that free speech was an absolute right, and he upheld the power of the House Un-American Activities Committee to question individuals about their alleged prior membership in the Communist Party. In *Shelton v. Tucker* (1960), however, he wrote the majority ruling that an Arkansas law requiring teachers to list organizations to which they belonged was an invalid interference with associational freedom. In *Rideau v. Louisiana* (1963), he also ruled a murder conviction invalid because he found that the televised broadcast of the murder confession amounted to "kangaroo court proceedings."

Stewart also dissented in a case in which the Court upheld state laws requiring that businesses be closed on Sundays, arguing that by forcing orthodox Jews to choose between religion and economic gain, the laws violated the free-exercise clause of the First Amendment. In what was to be his most memorable comment, he wrote a concurring opinion on the unconstitutionality of criminal laws against most forms of free expression, other than hard pornography, which, he admitted, he could not define. But "I know it when I see it," he also said.

In the last half of the 1960s, Stewart dissented in the *Miranda v. Arizona* ruling of 1966 requiring the police to read defendants their rights, but the next year he wrote a majority opinion overturning a 39-year-old precedent by declaring as unconstitutional unreasonable searches and seizures and the use of electronic eavesdropping devices without a judicial warrant. In 1967, he also wrote the majority opinion in a case upholding the contempt-of-court convictions of Martin Luther King, Jr., and seven other black leaders resulting from 1963 demonstrations in Birmingham, Alabama. In a 1968 ruling, however, he held that an 1866 federal law prohibited racial discrimination in the sale or rental of property and sustained the law's constitutionality on the basis of the Thirteenth Amendment.

In 1969, after Earl Warren retired as chief justice, President RICHARD NIXON considered Stewart to replace Warren until Stewart asked to have his name removed from consideration because he thought it would be wiser to choose someone from outside the Court. Nixon chose Warren Burger. On the Burger Court, Stewart continued his nonideological approach to the law, although he also continued to be guided by such convictions as a reverence for free speech, a belief in the need to balance societal needs with individual rights, and a dedication to protecting the individual from an unnecessarily intrusive government. His written opinions also continued to be characterized by their craftsmanship.

In 1971, the Court decided the famous Pentagon Papers case, *New York Times Co. v. United States*, concerning the right of the *New York Times* and the *Washington Post* to publish the hitherto top-secret Pentagon Papers, a 47-volume history of U.S. involvement in Vietnam, which the government had sought to prevent from being published on the grounds of the harm it would cause to national defense and security. In this case, Stewart voted with the majority, asserting the principle against prior restraint of the press, but he did not base his opinion on an absolutist view of that principle. In another landmark case, *Roe v. Wade* (1974), Stewart voted with the majority to uphold the constitutional right of a woman to a legal abortion, even though he had difficulty in dealing with issues of contraception and abortion. He termed a Connecticut law prohibiting the use of contraceptives "uncommonly silly," but he nonetheless found it constitutional because of his doubts about the existence of an inherent right of privacy. In *Roe v. Wade*, he also wondered whether the majority was making "policy judgments [that were] more legislative than judicial." In *United States v. Nixon* (1974), involving the Watergate special prosecutor's demand for tapes recorded in the Oval Office, Stewart played a pivotal role in arriving at a decision acceptable to the justices that denied President Nixon's claims of presidential privilege and separation of powers in keeping the tapes from the special prosecutor.

During the Carter administration, Stewart voted with the minority against the principle of affirmative action both in the landmark *Regents of the University of California v. Bakke* (1977) and in *Fullilove v. Klutznick* (1980), which involved the constitutionality of a federal statute to set aside at least 10 percent of public-works grants for minority business enterprises. In his discussion of the *Bakke* case, Supreme Court justice THURGOOD MARSHALL framed the question of affirmative action by remarking that for some persons it was a way of letting people in; for others it was a way of keeping people out. Although *Klutznick* was not, strictly speaking, an affirmative-action case, the principle still involved one of inclusion or exclusion on the basis of race. In Stewart's view, exclusion of whites because of their race was just as wrong as exclusion of blacks for the same reason. "Under the Constitution as I understand it," he wrote, "the Fifth and Fourteenth

[Amendments] must mean you can't predicate exclusion on race. It's per se invidious, however loftily motivated."

In *Foley v. Connelie* (1978), Stewart sided with the majority in upholding a New York law requiring state police to be U.S. citizens despite the claim that the law unconstitutionally excluded aliens. "The Fourteenth Amendment suggests that citizenship has a superior status," Stewart wrote, "yet we use the Fourteenth to give aliens special consideration." In a case involving the First Amendment, *Wooley v. Maynard* (1977), Stewart sided with proponents of free speech—but with an important qualification. The case involved a New Hampshire law requiring motor vehicles to bear license plates with the state motto "Live Free or Die." George Maynard and his wife, both members of Jehovah's Witnesses, found the motto repugnant and taped it over on their plates. As a result, they were found guilty of violating the statute. Stewart sided with the majority on the Court in finding in favor of Maynard, stating that covering up the motto was his nonverbal way of communicating his disagreement with the motto. But the justice also remarked that "sometimes interests in free expression must be subordinated to strong societal policies."

Similarly, in *Houchins v. KQED* (1978), which involved the right of the California television station KQED to visit part of a county jail where a suicide had taken place, Stewart made clear that the station had no inalienable right to film in the jail. He took the same position in a majority opinion that he wrote in still another First Amendment case, *Gannett Co. v. DePasquale* (1979), which excluded both the public and the press from a pretrial hearing in a murder case.

As a jurist, Stewart was outspoken in the courtroom, asking pointed questions of lawyers during argument. Like other members of the Burger Court, he also frequently disagreed with the legal arguments of the chief justice even when he agreed with his opinion, as in the Pentagon Papers and *Nixon* cases. In a number of instances, he wrote sharp memorandums to the chief justice to get him to rewrite his draft opinions.

Although he was only 66 in 1981, Stewart surprised everyone by deciding to retire from the Court for no reasons other than to spend more time with his family and because he believed that some previous justices had remained on the bench too long, even when suffering from poor health or senility. He said later that he had thought about leaving the bench in 1980 but delayed his decision in order to avoid an election-year confirmation fight over his successor. At a press conference, shortly after he announced his decision to retire, he was asked how he wanted to be remembered. He answered: "As a good lawyer who did his best."

After Stewart retired, he continued to take on assignments on lower courts. He also appeared with television news producer Fred W. Friendly in a PBS series on the Constitution. He died on December 7, 1985, in Hanover, New Hampshire, five days after suffering a stroke. He was 70 years old.

Strauss, Robert Schwartz

(1918–) *special trade representative, special counselor on inflation, Middle East envoy, Carter reelection campaign committee chair*

The consummate political insider, Robert Strauss has never held public office, but even before Jimmy Carter became president, he was recognized as a powerbroker and troubleshooter, a person who could get things done and resolve problems. A founding partner of one of Texas's largest and most prestigious law firms, he served as Carter's special trade representative and roving ambassador in the Middle

East. He was, however, more of a shaker and a doer, someone who was able to bridge the gap in the Democratic Party between traditional Democratic liberals, yet who felt neglected by the Carter White House, and the Carter loyalists from Georgia. For that reason, Carter asked Strauss to head his reelection committee in 1980.

Fundamentally a pragmatist rather than an ideologue, Strauss was also known for his ability to work in a bipartisan way with the Republican leadership in Washington. His skill in arbitrating successfully between individuals of different persuasions may be attributed in part to the fact that he was of the Jewish faith and had been raised in the small town of Stamford, West Texas, where his father, Charles Strauss—a trained concert pianist who had been a piano salesman—eked out a living by running a dry-goods store with his wife Edith. As Strauss later remarked, "A poor Jewish kid from West Texas learns early how to survive."

Born on October 19, 1918, in Lockhart, Texas, Strauss attended the University of Texas. While there, he clerked at the state capitol, where he had his grounding in state politics. He also became friends with John B. Connally, a future governor of Texas, and worked on the congressional campaign committee of future president Lyndon Johnson, becoming one of his political cronies. After graduating from the University of Texas Law School (LL.B., 1941), Strauss joined the FBI. In 1946, he established his own law practice with a college friend, Richard Gump, in Dallas, Texas: today it is the prestigious worldwide law firm of Akin, Gump, Strauss, Hauer & Feld (known generally as Akin & Gump). He also invested successfully in real estate and broadcasting, making him a wealthy man and giving him the time to engage in nonelective Democratic politics. When Connally ran successfully for governor in 1962, Strauss was one of his largest fundraisers. In return, Connally appointed him chair of the Texas State Baking Commission. In 1968, Connally named Strauss to the Democratic National Committee. By the 1970s, Strauss had become one of the highest-paid powerbrokers and lobbyists in Washington, well known for his inflated ego, down-home storytelling, political connections, and ability to seal a deal.

In 1972, Strauss became treasurer of the National Democratic Party, in which role he was successful in eliminating the debt left over from the 1968 presidential campaign. Regarded as too conservative, however, he was ousted as party treasurer by followers of Democratic presidential nominee GEORGE MCGOVERN and subsequently devoted his efforts to raising money for congressional candidates. He promised the current chair of the Democratic Congressional Campaign Committee, future Speaker of the House TIP O'NEILL (Mass.), to raise $1 million in 1972. To O'Neill's astonishment, Strauss delivered on his pledge by holding a series of cocktail parties in New York, Chicago, Dallas, and Los Angeles. Following McGovern's overwhelming defeat in the presidential election a few months later, Strauss was elected chair of the Democratic Party. In the months that followed, he used his well-known skills as a mediator to restore a semblance of unity to the badly divided party.

Strauss became acquainted with Georgia governor Jimmy Carter in 1973 when Carter, who had supported the Texan's election as party chair, invited him to Atlanta to speak at the Jefferson-Jackson Day dinner. After the dinner, Carter invited Strauss to the executive mansion, where they discussed fund-raising for Democratic congressional candidates. Later, Strauss invited Carter to cochair (along with Terry Sanford of North Carolina) the Committee to Elect Democrats in 1974. Usually an honorific appointment, Carter used it to travel the country in support of congressional candidates. In the process, he built political capital, learned the rules of the Democratic Party inside out, and laid the groundwork for his successful bid for the Democratic presidential nomination in 1976.

Although Strauss preferred someone like Senator HENRY JACKSON (Wash.) to be the party's nominee and was galled that a newcomer like Carter could seize his party's nomination on an antiestablishment platform, he showed, as he had in the past, that he was a master fundraiser. He introduced the Democratic nominee to wealthy businessmen, members of the Hollywood establishment, and other contributors, a number of whom the candidate disliked personally but whose campaign contributions fattened the campaign treasury. Carter also had no special liking for Strauss, whom he thought was too ambitious and vain.

Nevertheless, after being elected president, Carter rewarded Strauss by appointing him as the nation's special trade representative (STR), a cabinet-level position with the rank of ambassador in charge of negotiating all trade agreements under the Tariff Act of 1930. Strauss remained special trade representative from 1977 to 1979, during which time he negotiated the Tokyo Round of trade talks. With the assistance of his deputy, ALONZO MCDONALD, he pressed the Japanese, who ran a huge trade surplus with the United States, to open more of its markets to American producers while persuading the American people not to view the Japanese as hostile to American interests. In 1979, he successfully concluded the Tokyo Round, which many observers had predicted was doomed to failure, and then helped direct the approval of the trade agreement through Congress. For his accomplishment, he was widely hailed in the press as a brilliant negotiator, the best trade representative the United States had ever had.

Over time, Strauss gained the confidence of Carter, who felt culturally more attuned with the folksy Texan than with other pillars of the Washington establishment. The president also came to appreciate Strauss's commonsense approach to problems, his wide network of acquaintances, and, above all, his loyalty to the administration and his effectiveness. Other top officials in the White House who knew Strauss felt the same way. They were willing to overlook his enormous ego because he knew how to play the game of Washington politics effectively. As Carter's closest adviser and chief of staff, HAMILTON JORDAN, later commented, what made Strauss "unusual and attractive in a community of political and social climbers was that he made no attempt to disguise his own considerable ego and freely admitted to both playing the game and enjoying it." It was also important for Jordan and the president to hear what Strauss had to say because he was able to measure Washington's pulse with great acumen, and he was candid in reporting his views to the White House, warning the president at a cabinet meeting in March 1978, for example, that "no one" was for the administration, "not business, not labor, not politicians, not big unions."

In April 1978, the president announced his appointment of Strauss as special counselor on inflation even though he continued to serve as the nation's STR. Although Strauss had doubts about the credibility of the administration's anti-inflation program, he went on to use his considerable talents as a wheeler-dealer to jawbone business and labor into maintaining the voluntary guidelines on wages and prices that the president had instituted three months earlier.

Following the Camp David accords between Egyptian president ANWAR SADAT and Israeli prime minister MENACHEM BEGIN in September 1978, Carter made Strauss his special envoy to the Middle East to deal with the Palestinian autonomy negotiations with Israel. At first, Strauss was excited by the appointment, seeing it as an opportunity to gain stature for himself as a diplomat and even to make a major impact on history if he could help achieve a lasting agreement between Israeli and Palestinian authorities. But over time he became discouraged by the lack of progress and was glad to get out of the assignment a year later to work on Carter's reelection campaign. His appointment had furthermore deeply distressed Secretary of State CYRUS VANCE, who thought the president was turning him (Vance) into a figurehead with little authority in foreign affairs. Both Vance and National Security Advisor ZBIGNIEW BRZEZINSKI also objected to Strauss's increasing assertiveness on foreign-policy issues.

In 1980, Carter looked to Strauss once more, this time to chair his reelection committee. Strauss's primary functions were fundraising and dealing with the press, party, and congressional leaders, while Hamilton Jordan handled the campaign's strategy and nuts and bolts. Very early in 1980, as the hostage crisis in Iran was still developing, the Texan seemed to realize that the president's chances of winning reelection were not good. "Poor bastard," he wrote of Carter, "he used up all of his luck in getting here. We've had our share of victories and defeats, but we've not had a single piece of good luck in the past three years." In March, the United States voted in favor of a UN resolution rebuking Israel for establishing settlements in Jerusalem and the West Bank, a vote that helped Senator EDWARD KENNEDY (Mass.) to defeat Carter in the New York State primary. Strauss blamed the State Department for the vote, remarking that "there are some goddamn Arabists over there and they ought to be fired." Believing that the president could handle himself well in a debate with Kennedy, he tried in June, along with other members of Carter's campaign team, to persuade him to debate the senator as a way of finally ending the nearly defunct Kennedy challenge, but the president refused.

Although Carter lost his bid for reelection, Strauss remained the consummate Washington insider, with friends and acquaintances reaching across party lines. On January 16, 1981, just before leaving office, President Carter awarded him the Presidential Medal of Freedom, citing his accomplishments as the nation's special trade representative. After the Republicans took office, Strauss dined at the White House with the new president, RONALD REAGAN, and became good friends with Vice President GEORGE HERBERT WALKER BUSH, who had been his opposite in 1974 as chair of the Republican National Committee. In 1991, President Bush appointed Strauss ambassador to Moscow, where he watched over the dissolution of the Soviet Union and the establishment of the Russian Federation.

In 1992, Strauss resigned as ambassador to rejoin his law firm of Akin & Gump. Among his partners was the former executive director of the National Urban League during the Carter administration, VERNON JORDAN. Strauss had hired Jordan in 1980 when other major law firms were still reluctant to take on a controversial black leader as a senior partner. Strauss continues to retain law offices in Washington, D.C., and Dallas and remains active in both the Washington and Dallas social scenes.

Sullivan, William Healy

(1922–) *U.S. ambassador to Iran*

William H. Sullivan was the United States's controversial ambassador to Iran during the events preceding the Iranian revolution. A lifelong foreign service officer, he had a number of increasingly responsible positions before being appointed ambassador to Iran in 1977. During the Iranian revolution, he was attacked by National Security Advisor ZBIGNIEW BRZEZINSKI for not providing the shah of Iran, MOHAMMAD REZA PAHLAVI, with sufficient

American support to bolster his regime. In his defense, Sullivan argued that he was trying to deal with the reality of the unfurling political situation in Iran.

Sullivan was born the son of a dentist in Cranston, Rhode Island, on October 12, 1922. He had a privileged background and had never met an African American until he went to New York by steamship with his mother and brother and was met at the port by his uncle's black chauffeur. After graduating summa cum laude from Brown University (B.A., 1942), he enlisted in the navy and served during World War II on minesweepers and destroyers in the Atlantic, Mediterranean, and Pacific theaters.

Following the end of World War II, Sullivan graduated from Tufts University's Fletcher School of Law (M.A., 1947) and entered the foreign service immediately after graduation. Over the next 20 years, his career took him to Bangkok, Calcutta, Tokyo, Naples, The Hague, and Geneva. In 1964, he was appointed ambassador to Laos. After serving in Laos during the buildup of the war in Vietnam, he participated in the negotiations in Washington and Saigon that led to an end to American involvement in Vietnam. In 1973, he was appointed to the Philippines, where he served for four years before he was reassigned as ambassador to Iran in 1977.

Sullivan's tenure as ambassador to Tehran was—and remains—extremely controversial. On the one hand, his critics—led by National Security Advisor Brzezinski and the National Security Council's chief expert on Iran, GARY SICK—have accused the ambassador of misleading the White House by his optimistic reporting on Iran and of undermining the shah of Iran's will to resist when he should have been encouraging the monarch to take a firm stand against the militants. On several occasions in 1978, Sick warned the administration that political conditions in Iran were unraveling and that the shah was in danger of being toppled from power by Islamic zealots hostile to the United States led by AYATOLLAH RUHOLLA KHOMEINI. But Sullivan did not realize that the shah was in trouble until the autumn.

As late as October 28, 1978, Sullivan wrote the State Department a cable in which he remarked that "the Shah is the unique element which can, on the one hand, restrain the military and, on the other hand, lead a controlled transition." He added: "I would strongly oppose any overture to Khomeini." On November 9, however, he wrote a long telegram to the State Department pressing the government "to think the unthinkable," to act as if the revolution would succeed, and to prepare for the transfer of power from the shah to a coalition government of Khomeini's followers and the military. After the shah was overthrown by Islamic militants loyal to Khomeini, but before the Ayatollah consolidated his power, Sullivan recommended trying to reach an understanding between the military and Khomeini loyalists.

With the support of President Carter, who took most of his advice on Iran from Brzezinski and General Robert Huyser, the deputy commander of U.S. forces in Europe whom he and Secretary of Defense HAROLD BROWN had sent to Iran to strengthen the resolve of its military forces, Brzezinski rejected Sullivan's recommendation. He dismissed the formation of a coalition government as a form of appeasement, preferring a military regime even after the shah fled the country in January 1979. Later, President Carter was highly critical of Sullivan and the State Department for resisting the White House's directives: "My instructions had been to do everything possible to strengthen the Shah, but during these days [just before the shah fled the country] I became increasingly troubled by the attitude of Ambassador Sullivan, who seemed obsessed with the need for the Shah to abdicate without further delay."

In fairness to Sullivan, however, most intelligence did not pick up the warnings that Sick had been making until the autumn, and even then there had been a clutter of reports about the shah's situation that made it difficult to evaluate precisely how precarious it was. Even Sick emphasized how surprised everyone in the administration was by the opposition to the shah and how unprepared it was for dealing with the crisis that followed. Furthermore, Sick faults the National Security Council as well as the State Department for compounding the problem because of the ongoing rivalry between Brzezinski and Secretary of State CYRUS VANCE, which led each agency to seek its own sources of information (and disinformation).

By late autumn 1978, moreover, when it became apparent to almost everyone in Washington that the shah's regime was in trouble, it was by no means certain that it could have been salvaged by giving him more support. Secretary of the Treasury W. MICHAEL BLUMENTHAL was shocked by the ruler's situation when he visited Tehran in November 1978. Former undersecretary of state GEORGE BALL, who had been asked by the president to study the situation in Iran, also concluded in December that the shah was about to collapse and that the United States should arrange for the appointment of a Council of Notables, consisting of elder Iranian statesmen not tainted by previous subservience to the monarch who would preside over a transitional government, with the shah remaining on the throne. But by the time that Ball issued his report, it is doubtful that the shah could have remained as even the titular head of a government. The monarch himself shied away from using military force to confront his subjects in the streets.

Notwithstanding the president's criticism of Sullivan, furthermore, once the shah fled the country in January 1979, it was extremely unlikely that a military regime could have been established that would have kept Khomeini from seizing power. Indeed, the officer corps had begun secretly to make its peace with the opposition weeks before the shah fell. "It became apparent," Sullivan later wrote about negotiations with the military in December 1978, "that a significant number of senior officers in various strategic positions within the military-command structure were not only sympathetic with the aims of the liberation movement but also closely in touch with its leaders on a regular basis." To the surprise of almost every official concerned with Iran, in the 12 days after the shah fled Iran, Iranian military forces ceased opposing the revolution. Twenty-six American military advisers in Iran were trapped under fire and had to be saved through the intervention of two of Khomeini's closest aides.

By the time the shah fled Iran, in other words, no political person or force existed to challenge Khomeini. The Iranian revolution had taken on an ineluctable momentum that would have been impossible to stop short of some kind of outside intervention by the United States. Brzezinski continued to hold out hope of a coup, but Sullivan thought the idea was preposterous. When asked by telephone from Washington about the feasibility of a coup, the ambassador suggested indelicately to Undersecretary of State David Newsom what the National Security Advisor could do with the idea. "That is not very helpful," said Newsom, to which Sullivan responded, "Do you want me to translate it into Polish?" In expressing such sarcasm about a coup, Sullivan appears to have been on solid ground.

In March 1979, after Khomeini's rise to power, Sullivan was recalled to the United States. Because of his sharp differences with the Carter White House over its handling of events in Iran, he resigned from the State

Department in June 1979. Since leaving the foreign service, Sullivan has served as president of the American Assembly. He has also written two books: *Mission to Iran* (1981), a defense of his actions as ambassador to Iran; and *Obbligato: Notes on a Foreign Service Career* (1984), whose title speaks for itself. Sullivan lives in New York City.

T

Talmadge, Herman Eugene

(1913–2002) *member of the Senate*

Serving in his fourth term as U.S. senator from Georgia when Jimmy Carter was elected president in 1976, Herman Talmadge voted in favor of the Panama Canal Treaties, which was crucial in winning Senate approval of the agreements. For the most part, he also supported the administration's foreign policy. But as a political conservative, he had quietly opposed Carter when he was governor of Georgia and was generally critical of Carter as president. During the last two years of the administration, Talmadge endured personal tragedies and a political scandal that contributed to his narrow defeat for reelection in 1980.

The son of Eugene Talmadge, the flamboyant champion of Georgia's redneck rural population who created one of the state's great political dynasties, Herman Eugene Talmadge was born on August 13, 1913, on a farm near McRae, Georgia. Until his senior year of high school, when the family moved to Atlanta, he attended McRae's public schools. After receiving his law degree from the University of Georgia (LL.B., 1936), he joined his father's law firm and ran his campaigns for governor. In 1941, Talmadge volunteered for service in the U.S. Navy, seeing extensive action in the Pacific Theater during World War II. By the time of his discharge in 1945, he had attained the rank of lieutenant commander.

In 1946, Talmadge's father was elected to what would have been his fourth term as governor, but before he could take office, he died. Because Eugene had been ill, a small group of his supporters had started a write-in campaign for Herman, who received several hundred write-in votes during the election. On this basis, he persuaded the Georgia legislature to choose him as the state's new governor, a decision that was challenged by the incumbent governor, Ellis Arnall, who refused to surrender his office, and the lieutenant governor-elect, M. E. Thompson. For a time, there was a real chance of violence breaking out between those supporting Arnall, who refused to surrender his office, and those backing Talmadge, who even branded a .38 Smith & Wesson in his belt for protection. But after Talmadge had served only 67 days, the state Supreme Court ruled that Thompson should serve as governor until a special election could be held in September 1948. When the election took place, Talmadge trounced Thompson to become the state's governor. He was elected to a full term in 1950.

As governor, Talmadge was fully committed to the system of segregation that ruled the

South. When the Supreme Court made its historic *Brown v. Board of Education of Topeka* decision in 1954, declaring the doctrine of "separate but equal" invalid, he was the first southern governor to declare that he would not abide by the decision. He even went so far as to remark that the state's public schools would have to be closed because Georgia's state constitution made it unconstitutional to fund integrated schools. At the same time, he insisted on paying African-American schoolteachers the same salaries as white teachers in accordance with the doctrine of "separate but equal." He also pushed through a 3 percent sales tax to fund public education in Georgia, although his administration allocated twice as much for white schools as for black schools. In 1953, moreover, he blocked African-American student Horace Ward from entering the University of Georgia Law School.

One of the Talmadge family's strongest backers was Jimmy Carter's father, Earl. In 1952, Earl Carter ran successfully for the state legislature with the backing of Governor Talmadge. The next year, he persuaded the governor to make the commencement address at Plains High School and to spend the night at the Carter family home. When Earl died in 1954, the governor offered Earl's seat to his wife, Lillian, notwithstanding her longstanding sympathy for blacks. When Lillian declined, Talmadge supported one of Earl's closest friends for the seat, Thad Jones, who was reelected to the legislature without opposition several times.

Talmadage and Jimmy Carter later became political opponents. In 1956, Talmadge ran for the U.S. Senate after persuading the venerable incumbent, Walter George, not to seek reelection. In the Democratic primary, he once again defeated former governor M. E. Thompson. As soon as he took office, he joined other southern senators in opposing civil rights legislation. "I never read a civil rights bill," he remarked, "that didn't destroy more constitutional rights than it purported to give any group."

An opponent of most of the New Frontier and Great Society programs of John F. Kennedy and Lyndon Johnson, including the Voting Rights Act of 1965, Talmadge was, nevertheless, the author of the school-lunch program and helped to develop the food-stamp program. He also supported work-incentive programs and coauthored the Rural Development Act of 1972, designed to encourage economic development in rural areas. He was best known, however, for his thoughtful questioning of witnesses as a member of the Senate Select Committee looking into the unfolding Watergate break-in and cover-up. In 1974, he was voted in public polls as one of the country's most-admired senators.

During the 1960s, Talmadge became increasingly concerned about the state senator from Plains, Jimmy Carter. Although he did not take a position on Carter's first race for governor in 1966, he briefly considered running for governor himself but was persuaded that he was more valuable to Georgia on Capitol Hill. He began to moderate his views on race, even promising a group at the predominantly black Hungry Club of Atlanta, when he was thinking about running for governor, that he would appoint blacks to high places if he were elected and pledging no more race-baiting campaigns in Georgia. But he later acknowledged that the person in the contest he most admired was the Atlanta businessman and arch-segregationist, LESTER MADDOX, who had been willing to close his successful restaurant rather than yield to federal law requiring him to serve African Americans. This action, according to Talmadge, showed how principled Maddox was.

Following Carter's successful race for governor in 1970, Talmadge and his followers were concerned that Carter, who could not succeed himself as governor, would challenge

Talmadge for the U.S. Senate in 1974. Accordingly, his supporters at the state house in Atlanta, who wielded considerable power both within the legislature and as the heads of state agencies, used their influence to try to limit or defeat the governor's highest priority—the reorganization of state government. Although Carter thought he would have trouble beating Talmadge in a race for the Senate, the senator was nonetheless relieved when Carter informed him privately that he intended to run for president rather than for the senator's seat. In response, Talmadge told Carter that he thought his chances of winning the presidency were a long shot but that he would help the governor in the race.

Nevertheless, like most of the Georgia congressional delegation and state party leadership, Talmadge did not throw his support behind Carter for the Democratic nomination until after the former Georgia governor beat Alabama governor GEORGE WALLACE in the Florida primary, thereby solidifying his position as the candidate of the South. But the senator never warmed up to his fellow Georgian, later remarking that Carter "kind of slipped into the Democratic nomination and the presidency itself by seeming to be all things to all people."

Two weeks after Carter was elected president, Talmadge hosted a group of congressional leaders at his estate in Lovejoy to make plans for the incoming administration. Once Carter took office, Talmadge agreed to support the Panama Canal Treaties even though they were unpopular in Georgia and he was convinced that the United States should maintain control of the Canal. His decision to support the agreements may have persuaded Georgia's other highly respected senator, SAM NUNN, to alter his vote as well. Instead of insisting on an amendment to the first of the two treaties, the Neutrality Treaty, which would have given the United States the right to station troops in Panama after 1999 in order to keep the canal open, Nunn and Talmadge agreed to a toned-down reservation, negotiated by Nunn, which allowed the United States to station forces in Panama in situations where the two governments considered it "necessary and appropriate."

Given the fact that the agreement was approved by one vote more than the necessary two-thirds required for ratification, Talmadge's and Nunn's votes were decisive to the outcome. The president was especially grateful for Talmadge's support on the Panama Canal Treaties. "Although he never mentioned it to me," he wrote in his memoirs, "I will always believe that he did it out of respect for me as a fellow Georgian, whom he saw to be quite vulnerable to serious embarrassment and loss of prestige if the treaties were rejected."

Talmadge also supported the Camp David accords of 1978, Carter's normalization of relations with China in 1979, his negotiation of the Strategic Arms Limitation Talks treaty of 1979 (SALT II), and his handling of the Iranian hostage crisis in 1980. "Although I disagreed with Jimmy [Carter] on a good number of issues," Talmadge later remarked, "I can't help but think that he got too much blame for his failures and too little credit for his successes. This is particularly true of his foreign policy."

Yet Talmadge's general view of the Carter presidency was one of disdain. In his view, Carter "pretty much became a captive of the left-wingers rather than the strong leader necessary to move the party in another direction." He also thought the administration was incompetent and termed Carter's 1977 farm bill, which raised price supports on a number of crops, "silly." As head of the Senate's Subcommittee on Health, Talmadge favored a program of catastrophic health insurance and handing over the operation of the Medicaid program from the states to the federal government, with a single national set of guidelines. But he thought it would be "foolhardy" to have a broader program of health insurance, as the White House advocated, until the country could better manage its existing Medicare program. He supported the administration's proposals for hospital cost containment, but he preferred a weaker, voluntary program rather than the stronger, compulsory one the White House wanted. He also successfully opposed the administration's effort to borrow from the Social Security program's healthy Hospital Insurance Trust Fund to help the Disability Trust Fund over its critical 1979–80 shortfall. He feared this could be the beginning of financing the Medicare program from general revenues.

Even in the area of foreign policy, Talmadge was critical of the administration and ridiculed the president's human-rights policy. Noting the downfall of the shah of Iran, MOHAMMAD REZA PAHLAVI, and the dictator of Nicaragua, ANASTASIO SOMOZA DEBAYLE, in part because of their violations of human rights, he thought Carter's emphasis on this score missed the forest for the trees. "A foreign policy dedicated to world peace and human rights produced less of both because our leaders acted as if they believed an 'inordinate fear of Communism' was worse than Communism itself," he later said. Talmadge was particularly disapproving of the president's ambassador to the United Nations, ANDREW YOUNG, whom he took to task for supporting leftist regimes in Africa and for too often putting his foot in his mouth, as, for example, when he apparently supported the Palestine Liberation Organization at the United Nations. Talmadge referred to Young as "one of the most embarrassing figures in a generally inept administration."

For the Georgia senator, however, much of the Carter presidency years was characterized by personal and political tragedy. In 1975, Talmadge's son Robert drowned in a swimming accident at age 29. Another son, Eugene, was divorced, and in 1977, Talmadge's own wife of 35 years, Betty, divorced him, claiming "cruel treatment and habitual intoxication." Already a heavy drinker, Talmadge increased his drinking even more. In 1978, he admitted himself into an alcoholic treatment program at the naval hospital in Long Beach, California. After successfully completing the program, he returned to Washington, where he became embroiled in a financial scandal when an aide, Daniel Minchew, claimed he had diverted—on Talmadge's orders—$37,000 in campaign funds to a secret account. Although the senator denied the claims, his former wife produced 77 hundred-dollar bills, which, she said, she had found in his overcoat. During the divorce proceedings, she had also reported finding wads of cash stuffed in her husband's coat pockets. A Senate Ethics Committee, conducting hearings into Talmadge's financial dealings, found him guilty of misappropriating funds. In the Senate, he was denounced by his colleagues for "reprehensible conduct."

Still denying wrongdoing, although admitting negligence "in overseeing certain aspects of the operation of my office," Talmadge paid the Senate $43,435 and announced his candidacy for a fifth term in 1980. Although he won the Democratic primary against Lieutenant Governor Zell Miller and appeared to have won the general election in November against his Republican opponent, Mack Mattingly, late results from Cobb County, an Atlanta suburb, gave Mattingly a narrow 25,000-vote victory.

Talmadge lost the election for a number of reasons, including his problems in Washington. In a broader sense, however, he was defeated because of a new political age in the South, characterized by a shift in power from the region's poor rural areas, which had been the base of the Talmadge dynasty, to the increasingly Republican urban areas like the suburbs of Atlanta.

Following his defeat, Talmadge retired to his 2,500-acre tree farm in Henry County. In

1984, he married Lynda Cowart Pierce, a home economist 25 years his junior. They lived in a modest home on Lake Talmadge. In 1987, the former senator published *Talmadge: A Political Legacy, a Politician's Life*, a frank and highly readable memoir written in the style of a good southern storyteller. He lived out his remaining years quietly enjoying his favorite hobby of fishing until his death of throat cancer on March 22, 2002, at the age of 88.

Thurmond, Strom

(James Strom Thurmond)
(1902–2003) *member of the Senate*

The longest-serving senator at the time of his retirement in 2003, Strom Thurmond had been a segregationist governor of South Carolina, the presidential candidate of the Dixiecrat Party in the 1948 elections, and one of the Senate's staunchest opponents of the Civil Rights movement in the 1950s and 1960s. He was also the first major southern politician to switch from the Democratic to the Republican Party. Much of his past, especially his views on segregation, was forgiven by his colleagues as Thurmond, beginning in the 1970s, accepted the legacy of the Civil Rights movement and the new political realities of the South, where the black vote became increasingly important. By the time of his retirement in 2003, he was even being lionized on Capitol Hill for his years of public service and the accommodation he had made to the end of overt racial politics.

President Jimmy Carter, however, had little patience for his fellow southerner—and the feeling was mutual. If Thurmond no longer championed racial politics, he remained a staunch southern conservative, an ultranationalist in foreign policy, and a Republican partisan. To the greatest extent possible, he used his authority as a ranking member of the Senate to oppose the Carter administration.

James Strom Thurmond was born on December 5, 1902, in Edgefield, South Carolina, home of several South Carolina governors, including the race-baiting Benjamin R. Tillman, who knew his father. After graduating from Clemson College (now Clemson University) with a degree in horticulture (B.S., 1923), Thurmond taught and was a physical education coach in the Edgefield schools before becoming the local superintendent of education (1929–33). He also took correspondence courses in law and passed the South Carolina bar in December 1929. After serving as both city and county attorney, he was elected to the state senate in 1933, resigning in 1938 to become South Carolina's youngest state circuit judge at the age of 35. Although a segregationist, he called upon a grand jury in Greenville in 1940 to be prepared to take action against the Ku Klux Klan, which, he said, represented "the most abominable type of lawlessness."

During World War II, Thurmond served with distinction in the army's 82nd Airborne Division in Europe, dropping behind enemy lines during the Normandy invasion. After Germany surrendered in 1945, he served briefly in the Pacific Theater. He received numerous military decorations, including the Bronze Star and the French Croix de Guerre, for his service and returned to civilian life as a lieutenant colonel. As an army reservist, he rose to the rank of major general.

While overseas, Thurmond had been reelected circuit judge. A war hero and indefatigable campaigner, he resigned his seat in 1946 in order to run successfully for governor. As South Carolina's governor, he brought in a tough prosecutor to try a white mob who had lynched a black man. He also sought additional funding to improve black schools. In 1948, however, he captured national headlines when, at the Democratic National Convention, he led a walkout of southern delegates in protest over its civil rights plank and then formed the

States' Rights Democratic Party, better known as the Dixiecrat Party, which nominated him as president. In November, he received more than 1 million votes, carried four southern states (South Carolina, Alabama, Mississippi, and Louisiana), and received 39 electoral votes. "All the laws of Washington and all of the bayonets of the Army cannot force the Negro into our homes, into our schools, our churches and our places of recreation and amusement," he remarked. He later defended his position on segregation as one based not on racial bias but on a defense of states' rights against federal intrusion.

Limited to one term as governor, Thurmond ran unsuccessfully for the U.S. Senate in 1950, losing in a close race to the incumbent, Olin T. Johnston. After opening up his own law firm in Aiken, he ran again for the Senate in 1954 following the death of the incumbent, Burnet R. Mayfield. When the State Democratic Committee nominated a local state senator to replace Mayfield (normally tantamount to election), Thurmond challenged Mayfield as a write-in candidate, decisively beating him and becoming the only U.S. senator ever to be elected in a write-in ballot.

As a new senator, Thurmond received national attention in 1957 when he spoke for 24 hours on the Senate floor in a vain attempt to defeat the first significant, albeit limited, legislative attack on the edifice of southern segregation. Throughout his long senatorial career, however, Thurmond became known more for his success in bringing pork barrel back to his state and for supporting the army as a member of the Armed Services Committee than for authoring any major legislative measure. For the most part, he remained an obstructionist, opposing the "modern Republicanism" of Dwight Eisenhower and the programs of the New Frontier and Great Society. A strident cold warrior and anticommunist who suggested communists ("silent socialists," as he called them) had infiltrated the government, he was a strong defender of the war in Vietnam.

In 1964, Thurmond became the first major southern leader to break his ties to the Democratic Party, becoming a Republican and supporting the presidential candidacy of BARRY GOLDWATER. "The party of our fathers is dead," he remarked in explaining his decision to change political parties. As the Civil Rights movement gained momentum, however, and black voting power became an important factor in the South as a result of the Voting Rights Act of 1965, the South Carolina senator accepted the new realities of politics. He was one of the first southern senators to hire an African American for his staff in 1971, and he began to court black elected officials. Unlike Governor GEORGE WALLACE OF Alabama, however, he never apologized for having been a segregationist firebrand.

In 1968, Thurmond helped RICHARD NIXON carry out his "southern strategy" by gaining him the support of southern delegates, many of whom had been leaning toward California governor RONALD REAGAN for the Republican nomination. In the election, he campaigned heavily for Nixon against his most serious challenger in the South, the third-party candidacy of George Wallace. In return, he gained Nixon's pledge to support an antiballistic missile system, slow down school desegregation, choose a southerner as his running mate, and nominate only strict constructionists to the Supreme Court.

During the Nixon administration Thurmond continued to oppose most social-welfare legislation, although he supported housing and welfare funds for his state. He also supported an increase in Social Security benefits, voted for the Rural Development Act, and cosponsored the Equal Rights Amendment (ERA), remarking that it represented a "genuine reflection of the needs of many people."

In 1972, Thurmond was easily reelected to the Senate for a fourth term, appealing to black leaders for the first time on the basis of what he could deliver to the state as a senior member of the Senate. In 1978, when he ran for a fifth term, he faced the strongest challenge of his Senate career from an ex-Wall Street investment banker, Charles "Pug" Ravenel, Jr., who attacked Thurmond for being ineffective in the Senate despite his seniority. Ravenel also charged that Thurmond had been largely negative in his approach to legislation and that only seven of his 185 proposals had become law.

In November 1978, Thurmond was elected by a smaller margin than six years earlier (56 percent as opposed to 64 percent in 1972), but he still won comfortably. Ravenel was correct that the South Carolina senator's record was characterized more by what he voted against than what he supported. But it was precisely his opposition to such measures as the Panama Canal Treaties and the Senate version of the Labor Law Reform bill during the Carter administration that won rather than cost him votes in 1978.

Throughout the Carter presidency, in fact, Thurmond almost always opposed the White House, and he was outraged when the president nominated THEODORE SORENSEN for director of the Central Intelligence Agency (CIA). A New Frontiersman from the Kennedy adimistration Sorensen was a conscientious objector during the Korean War whose appointment was widely opposed in the intelligence community. His critics, inlcuding Thurmond, raised questions about his suitability to carry out the agency's mission or to work with the military at the CIA or other intelligence agencies.

Despite strong appeals by some of the Republicans' most respected leaders, including former president GERALD FORD, Thurmond vigorously opposed ratification of the Panama Canal Treaties. He and several other Republican opponents of the agreements flew to the Panama Canal Zone to listen to complaints of Americans living there. Along with Senator JESSE HELMS (R-N.C.), Thurmond also flaunted a poll conducted in August 1977 by the Opinion Research Corporation showing that 78 percent of American favored keeping the canal, while only 14 percent were willing to cede it to Panama. "We paid for it, we built it," Thurmond remarked with respect to the canal. President Carter was so frustrated by the opposition of Thurmond and Helms to the canal agreements that in his diary he referred to them as "nuts."

The next year, Thurmond helped lead the fight in the Senate against a labor-reform bill that would amend the 1935 National Labor Relations Act by making it easier for unions to organize workers. Specifically, the bill, which had already passed the House and had the backing of more than 50 senators, would empower the National Labor Relations Board (NRLB) to set wages for newly unionized workers if the NRLB determined that an employer had not bargained in good faith. It would also give workers fired for union organizing activities time and a half in back pay and reduce the legal organizing period from 45 to 30 days so as to give management less time to fight unionization. "We will fight this bill," declared Thurmond, "and fight it to the last." Despite having the support of a majority of the senators, a threatened filibuster by opponents of the measure, who argued that it would be hugely inflationary and bankrupt many small nonunion firms, was enough to derail the legislation before it could be approved and sent to Carter for his signature.

On other matters, Thurmond joined conservative senators in an effort to lift sanctions against the import of chrome from Rhodesia before it agreed to fair elections that would replace the minority white government of Ian

Smith with a representative and proportional black government. Viewing the antigovernment movement in Rhodesia as part of a larger series of guerrilla movements in Africa "armed and guided by the Soviet Union, China, Cuba and other Communist states," he stated, "[w]e must not give aid or comfort to guerrillas who would overthrow a democratic government and install a Marxist government." He also opposed the Internal Revenue Service's lifting of the nonprofit tax exemption for segregated private academies in the South. "There is not a shred of authority for such an action," he said.

In 1980, Thurmond joined other Democrats and Republicans in opposing the Strategic Arms Limitation Talks agreement (SALT II) that the president had negotiated with Soviet leader LEONID BREZHNEV in Vienna in 1979. Instead, according to Thurmond, "it was imperative that the United States undertake to increase defense spending at an annual rate of 10–20 percent," figures that were totally unrealistic. That same year, when the president's brother, BILLY CARTER, was being investigated by the Justice Department for failing to register as a lobbyist for the Libyan government, Thurmond attacked Attorney General BENJAMIN CIVILETTI for not pursuing the investigation with more vigor.

Attuned to the interests of his constituents in South Carolina, however, Thurmond did, on occasion, side with the administration or his more liberal colleagues in the Senate. In 1977, for example, he backed a supplemental appropriation to the Small Business Administration's disaster-relief program to provide aid to farmers suffering from a two-year drought. In 1978, in an apparent effort to influence black voters in his tough reelection battle with Pug Ravenel, Jr., he even joined with Senator EDWARD KENNEDY (D-Mass.) in supporting a constitutional amendment that would give the District of Columbia two senators and one or two representatives, depending on the outcome of 1980 census. After Kennedy became chair of the Judiciary Committee in 1979, he and Thurmond developed a good working relationship, agreeing on a compromise, for example, on the testy question of whether nominees for federal judgeships should be required to resign from all-white private clubs.

With the defeat of President Carter and the capture of the Senate by the Republicans in the 1980 elections, Strom Thurmond became president pro tem of the Senate and chair of the Judiciary Committee, something that Democrats had talked about, and feared, since even before Thurmond's reelection in 1978. But as chair of the committee from 1981 to 1987 (when he became chair of the Armed Services Committee), he supported the appointment of a number of African Americans for federal judgeships. In 1982, he voted for renewal of the Voting Rights Act, and by 1983, he was supporting a federal holiday for Martin Luther King, Jr. In 1991, he also voted for legislation that made it easier to prove employer discrimination in the workplace. He also favored highly controversial fetal-tissue research.

A ladies' man whose first wife had died of cancer in 1960, Thurmond married the 22-year-old Miss South Carolina in 1968, when he was 68; together, they had four children. Also known as a fitness buff since he had been a physical education coach as a young teacher, Thurmond engaged in a daily regimen of physical exercises, rarely drank alcohol, and refused tea or coffee. Even though he grew deaf and became increasingly infirm as age caught up with him, he refused to wear hearing aids or be seen in a wheelchair. As a result, his aides had to help him into the Senate chamber and shout into his ear on how he should vote. Yet voters returned him to an eighth term in 1996. By the time he decided to retire in 2002, he had become the longest-serving and longest-living member of the upper chamber in its history.

Thurmond died on June 26, 2003, in his home town of Edgefield. He was 100 years old.

Torrijos, Omar

(1929–1981) *political leader of Panama*

Widely regarded as one of Panama's best-known leaders, Omar Torrijos negotiated with President Carter the Panama Canal Treaties of 1977, ceding the Panama Canal and the Panama Canal Zone. It was his proudest and most notable achievement but it did not end Panamanian resentment against the United States for what Panamanians regarded as illegal U.S. control of Panama's most vital resource and violation of Panama's national sovereignty.

The son of schoolteachers, Torrijos was born on February 13, 1929, in Santiago, Panama, located about 100 miles southwest of Panama City. He came from the country's small but ultranationalist and antiforeign middle class. After attending the local Juan Demostenes Arosemana school, he won a scholarship at age 17 to the military academy in San Salvador. Graduating with a commission as a second lieutenant, he joined the 9,000-strong Panamanian army (the National Guard), considered one of the most effective military forces in Latin America. Promoted to captain in 1956, he studied at the School of the Americas at Fort Benning, Georgia, where highly selected Latin American military officers often trained. As a young officer, he won distinction in fighting guerrilla movements in Panama's interior provinces. By 1966, Torrijos had attained the rank of lieutenant colonel in the Panamanian army. Two years later, with the aid of Colonel Boris Martinez, he led a revolution that overthrew the elected government of Aernulfo Arias, who had been removed twice before in his long and controversial career. In 1969, Torrijos deported Martinez and made himself brigadier general and the head of government.

The majority of Panamanians could relate to Torrijos since, unlike the white-skinned elite who spoke English and ruled the country, he had been poor, was dark-skinned, and spoke Spanish like them. By 1972, he had seized absolute control of the country. He closed the independent media, dissolved the various political parties and legislature, and took control of the judiciary. He did not allow any opposition to his government.

No issue was more critical for Torrijos than gaining control of the Panama Canal and Canal Zone. The Hay-Bunau-Varilla Treaty of 1903 had given the United States the right to build and own a canal through Panama in perpetuity. Returning the canal to Panama had been the nation's most pressing issue for most of the century. In 1955, the Eisenhower administration had concluded a new treaty with the Panamanians that had made a number of concessions to them, including increasing the annual annuity the United States paid to Panama for the canal. But this hardly mollified the Panamanians because of the sovereignty issue.

During the Kennedy administration, the United States made another concession to the Panamanians, allowing their flag to fly beside the U.S. flag in civilian installations in the Canal Zone. On January 9, 1964, however, a group of American students and their parents at the Canal Zone's Balboa High School took down the Panamanian flag. Panamanian students responded by marching into the zone in protest. A riot broke out and then escalated. By the time fighting ended four days later, it had spread into the interior and left four American soldiers and 20 Panamanians killed, as well as 85 North Americans and more than 200 Panamanians wounded. President Johnson responded to the violence with concern that it had been started by communists seeking to

President Jimmy Carter, Organization of American States general secretary Alejandro Orfila, and Panamanian leader General Omar Torrijos sign the Panama Canal Treaty, 1977. *(Jimmy Carter Library)*

overthrow the government of Roberto Chiari and with the conviction that the United States needed to be more responsive to Panamanian nationalism. Following a high-level meeting of his foreign-policy team, he undertook negotiations with Panama. In December 1964, he offered a new treaty with Panama that would recognize Panamanian sovereignty and do away with the "in perpetuity" clause of the Hay-Bunau-Varilla Treaty. Negotiations for a new treaty began the next year. In June 1967, negotiators concluded a series of agreements that recognized Panamanian sovereignty over all its territory, including the Canal Zone, and provided for Panamanian participation in the administration and operation of the canal, although ultimate authority over it would remain with the United States.

Because the agreement still kept the Panama Canal and Canal Zone under the control of the United States, it remained so unpopular in Panama that it was never sent to the National Assembly for its approval. When the junta headed by General Omar Torrijos came to power in 1968, it rejected the agreement outright. In 1973, Torrijos focused world attention on the situation in Panama by persuading the UN General Assembly to hold a meeting in Panama City instead of New York. One result of the meeting was that 13 of the Security Council's members adopted a resolution accepting the Panamanian view of the canal problem.

Although the United States vetoed the resolution, Washington agreed to replace the 1903 treaty with a new agreement replacing the "in perpetuity" clause of the 1903 treaty with a fixed termination of American ownership of the canal and Canal Zone, although giving the United States the right to operate and defend the Canal during the life of the treaty. This became the basis of the Panama Canal Treaties that Torrijos and President Carter signed on September 7, 1977, giving Panama total control of the canal effective in 2000.

In 1997, General Manuel Noriega revealed in his book *America's Prisoner* that had the Senate not ratified the agreement, Torrijos planned to sabotage the canal. According to Noriega, Panamanian explosive experts and frogmen had infiltrated the U.S. security cordon around the canal, living for two months as peasants and fishermen. If Torrijos gave the signal, they were instructed to destroy the Panama-Colon railway with explosives and rocket launchers and to assault and seize the canal. The signal was to be given in a radio broadcast, but that was cancelled after the treaty was signed.

The Panama Canal Treaties were just as unpopular in Panama as they were in the United States. Panamanians objected especially to the 20-year transition period before the canal was turned over to them. Torrijos was depicted as a stooge of Washington by critics in his country. Although more than 90 percent of Panamanians voted on the treaties and more than two-thirds of them approved the agreements, the evidence indicates the elections were fraudulent.

In 1978, Torrijos revealed that he would not extend his position as chief of government. Instead, he made one of his followers, Aristides Royo, president, but this was in name only; Torrijos effectively remained in charge. A 1978 report of the Inter-American Commission on Human Rights found that while the human-rights situation in Panama had improved since 1972, there were still numerous violations of human rights taking place under Torrijos's rule, including restrictions on the freedoms of assembly, expression, and association, and interference in the judicial process by government officials.

Although Torrijos had often spoken out against the United States since taking power and had even seemed to identify with Fidel Castro against Washington on occasion, he had always been an ardent nationalist rather than an ideologue and had proven to be a generally reliable friend of the United States. He was trusted by the U.S. military and foreign bankers, and he proved amenable to reservations added to the Panama Canal Treaties in order to assure their approval by the Senate, including one that permitted the United States to intervene militarily in Panama after the turn of the century if the canal should be closed down for any reason. Furthermore, he allowed the shah of Iran, MOHAMMAD REZA PAHLAVI, to stay in Panama after he was treated for cancer in the United States in 1979 when most other countries were unwilling to accept the former Iranian leader. Torrijos continued his control of the Panamanian military until July 31, 1981, when he died in a plane crash at the age of 52.

Turner, Stansfield

(1923–) *director of the Central Intelligence Agency*

A classmate of Jimmy Carter at the U.S. Naval Academy, a Rhodes scholar, and a career naval officer for 31 years, Admiral Stansfield Turner served as director of the Central Intelligence Agency (CIA) from 1977 to 1981. In this role, he made major changes in the agency's operations, modernizing the agency's management operations, improving relations with Congress, and integrating the various intelligence organizations more closely. At the same time, he placed less emphasis on espionage and more on technology for gathering intelligence information. Following the tragic events of September 11, 2001, he was charged by the *Los Angeles Times* and others of bearing some of the responsibility for these events by weakening the CIA's ability to uncover terrorist activities through covert operations. He was also accused of being taken to task by President Carter for failing to foresee the Muslim revolution in Iran in 1979. Turner has denied these charges. He has also called for the establishment of a powerful director of national intelligence able to coordinate the disparate agencies responsible for intelligence gathering.

The future CIA director was born in Highland Park, Illinois, on December 1, 1923. After spending two years at Amherst College (1941–42), he transferred to the U.S. Naval Academy at Annapolis, Maryland, where he graduated first in his class (1946) and obtained a Rhodes scholarship to study philosophy, politics, and economics at Oxford University. In 1966, he studied at the Harvard School of Business. Turner's 31-year record of naval service was one of increasingly responsible commands and steady promotions. During his service, he commanded a minesweeper, a destroyer, a guided-missile cruiser, a carrier task group, and a fleet. He was promoted in 1966 to captain and to rear admiral in 1970. From 1968 to 1970, he served as assistant to naval secretaries Paul Ignatius and John Chafee. In 1972, he was named president of the U.S. Naval War College in Newport, Rhode Island, and was promoted to vice admiral. While president of the Naval War College, he changed its curriculum from an emphasis on lecturing to one involving student reading, writing, and critical analysis. After serving from 1974 to 1975 as commander of the navy's Second Fleet and NATO's Striking Fleet in the Atlantic Ocean, he was promoted to admiral. In 1975, he was given command of allied forces in southern Europe, but he became bored by his job and felt he had little chance for further advancement since he was now working for NATO and not the U.S. Navy. Ready to turn in his uniform, he was delighted when, in February 1977, President Carter offered him the CIA directorship.

In his memoirs, Carter fails to explain why he offered Turner the position at the CIA. Turner is unsure himself; although he had discussed military affairs with Carter while he was governor of Georgia, he had no memory of Carter as a midshipman. As a naval officer, he had worked closely with intelligence operations, but he was not an experienced intelligence professional.

It is clear, however, that Carter chose Turner to head the CIA after his first choice, Theodore Sorensen, decided to withdraw his name, amid controversy over his nomination, because he greatly admired his former classmate since his days at Annapolis, where Turner had been an impressive athlete, student leader, and brigade commander, and where almost every midshipman expected that he would one day be an admiral or perhaps even chief of naval operations. Carter also wanted someone who would restore the CIA's morale and reputation, which had become badly tarnished as a result of revelations of unethical and illegal activities uncovered over the past few years by a Senate investigation. Led by Senator FRANK CHURCH (D-Idaho), the investigation's discoveries had included plots to assassinate such world leaders as Cuba's Fidel Castro and Chile's Marxist president, Salvador Allende. Turner's distinguished and unblemished record of leadership made him an ideal candidate to carry out the task of clearing up the CIA. The president also wanted a director who would be in charge of coordinating the entire intelligence community, which encompassed far more than the CIA. The admiral insisted on having this overreaching authority before agreeing to accept the position. Subsequently, the president signed an executive order giving the Director of Central Intelligence (DCI) control of such intelligence groups as the National Security Agency (NSA) and the foreign intelligence arms of the Federal Bureau of Investigation and the State Department.

During his tenure as DCI, Turner worked to make the CIA more accountable and efficient. Even before he was confirmed as CIA director, he was taken aback by the fact that the acting director, Henry Knoche, who would serve as his subordinate after Turner's confirmation, refused his request to accompany him to meetings with congressional leaders. He found the briefings books given to him by the CIA's major agencies long and lacking in rigorous analysis. At dinner meetings with senior officials, he was unpleasantly surprised by the lack of clarity in their answers to his questions. After the second meeting, he canceled the remaining dinners that had already been scheduled. "Overall," he later wrote, "my first encounters with the C.I.A. did not convey either a feeling of warm welcome or a sense of great competence."

Turner also came to the CIA convinced that technological information gathering could be even more effective than human intelligence. This did not mean that he regarded covert operations and other forms of field espionage as unimportant; he just did not think that they were necessarily the most effective way of gathering intelligence. He also had real quarrels with some of the legal and ethical practices of field agents and their operatives. He had no tolerance for what he considered criminal or unethical activities, even in clandestine operations.

In what came to be known in the annals of the CIA as the "Halloween Massacre," Turner shook up the agency in fall 1977 by cutting its covert personnel from more than 1,200 to fewer than 400, including dismissing many operatives with years of field experience. Disturbed by the bureaucratic inertia that seemed, in his view, to pervade the agency, he also fired, or forced into early retirement, a number of senior officials, some with checkered pasts and a few who would be involved in later scandals. Turner's purge of the CIA came back to haunt him during the Iranian revolution and hostage crisis of 1979.

Turner's effort to take charge of the entire intelligence community proved a greater challenge for him than the scandal and bureaucratic inertia he faced at the CIA. The NSA proved particularly resistant to his efforts. Once a branch of the CIA, this highly secret agency, whose main purpose was to obtain secrets by eavesdropping on and deciphering all forms of communication, had been created in 1952 to be the CIA's eyes and ears. By the 1970s, it had morphed into a large, independent, and powerful organization. Although its original purpose had been to collect and share information, it was also analyzing and hoarding the information it obtained.

Turner attributed the United States' failure to understand the background and purpose of a Soviet "combat" brigade in Cuba during the 1970s—a failure that he considered the most serious of his tenure at the CIA—to the NSA's unwillingness to cooperate with other agencies in sharing and analyzing the information it had on the brigade. In response to a review of Soviet military activities in Cuba ordered by National Security Advisor ZBIGNIEW BRZEZINSKI in 1979, the NSA revealed what it had known since the end of the missile crisis in 1964: that the Soviet Union had maintained a military force of 2,000–3,000 personnel in Cuba. In revealing this information, however, the NSA referred to the Soviet force as a "combat brigade," and Senator Frank Church, now seeking reelection in 1980, made it appear that the brigade was a new military unit with a combat mission that posed a serious threat to the United States.

Until President Carter was able to diffuse this issue with a speech in October 1980, it alarmed the American people and threatened to explode into a major crisis. In Turner's view, the whole incident could have been avoided had the NSA been more responsible in sharing its information with other intelligence agencies. "The fundamental mistake," he later wrote with respect to the brigade, "was in the NSA's doing its own analysis." While the NSA had excellent analysts to do its processing, it lacked "the range of analytic talent needed for responsible analysis, nor [did it have] all the relevant data from the other collecting agencies needed for a comprehensive job. … In this case, it meant that the NSA was not sensitive to how the policy-makers would interpret the term 'combat.'"

Later, after Turner had left the CIA, he acknowledged that he had had only limited success at DCI in managing what he referred to as the great "octopus" of intelligence collection by the United States. This was a matter that he would discuss in greater detail in the media and before Congress following the events of September 11, 2001.

The most serious event to confront Turner as CIA director, however, was the Iranian revolution and the seizure of American hostages in Tehran in November 1979. In recounting the events of the revolution, Turner acknowledged an intelligence failure over Iran. The CIA, he admitted, should have had a better understanding of the opposition building against the shah, MOHAMMAD REZA PAHLAVI, by Islamic religious fundamentalists opposed to the secularization of Iranian society, by secular aspirants for political power, and by Iran's merchant class, who expected a larger share of the nation's growing economic prosperity. He also acknowledged a letter he received from President Carter on November 11, 1978, in which Carter expressed his dissatisfaction to him "with the quality of our political intelligence" with respect to Iran.

In his defense, however, Turner pointed to the fact that neither his predecessors in the RICHARD NIXON or GERALD FORD administrations had any accurate information about the imminent collapse of the shah's regime in Iran—nor, for that matter, did experts on the area from outside the intelligence community. "[T]here is little evidence," he remarked, "that Middle East scholars and reporters were more attuned to the trends in Iran than was the CIA." He also commented: "U.S. policy in that region was so dependent on the shah that it was all too easy for us to assume that he would do what was necessary to play the role we had in mind for him." Finally, Turner emphasized that the quantity of covert intelligence about developments in Iran was so diffuse as to make it nearly impossible to forecast long-term developments in the country. In his view, ground intelligence—while still important—was not as important as sophisticated technical information gathering. "It [was] not a question of down-grading espionage," he later wrote, "but of recognizing that all the branches contribute to the final product."

Regardless of the degree to which Turner was responsible for the way in which the intelligence community was caught off guard by the Iranian revolution and the overthrow of the shah, the U.S. "intelligence failure" exploded into a major public issue. Those who had been scarred by the Halloween Massacre of 1977 and a number of others who had doubts about Turner's management of the CIA placed the failure squarely on the DCI's shoulders. The president's letter of November 1978 expressing dissatisfaction with intelligence reports about Iran, which was leaked to the press less than two weeks later and was reported by *New York Times* columnist William Safire on November

23, poured fuel on the flames and led to calls on Capitol Hill for Turner's dismissal.

Yet Carter retained confidence in his DCI. The leaked letter may, in fact, have been a ploy on the part of National Security Advisor Zbigniew Brzezinski to make Turner the "fall guy" for the events that were to occur in Iran. Notwithstanding Brzezinski's later statements to the contrary, he and Turner did not like or trust each other much. In the first place, the National Security Council (NSC) adviser wanted to maintain strict control over the CIA, while Turner favored more open access to the agency, including even the release of unclassified CIA materials. Second, Brzezinski was a much greater believer in covert operations than the CIA director, who believed the NSC adviser "held unrealistic expectations of what could be achieved by covert action." Finally, Turner thought that Brzezinski was overly ambitious and zealous in promoting his own political agenda.

Turner believed, therefore, that the National Security Advisor had put Carter up to writing his letter of November 1978. In fact, the letter, was predicated on two memoranda that GARY SICK, the NSC staff member concerned with Iran, had written to Brzezinski commenting on the "astonishing lack of hard information" on developments taking place in Iran and recommending an overhauling of operations in Tehran. Sick also prepared a directive to this effect to be signed by Secretary of State CYRUS VANCE and Turner. Instead, the NSC adviser sent Sick's briefing papers and draft directive to the president with a complaint about the poor quality of intelligence on Iran. It was this information that prompted Carter to write his letter. Furthermore, Brzezinski later acknowledged that he had purposely leaked the letter to the press.

Whatever Turner's responsibility for the intelligence breakdown, he kept Carter closely informed of the events that followed the accession to power of AYATOLLAH RUHOLLA KHOMEINI, often supplementing his regularly scheduled meetings with the president with additional briefings. As events unfolded over the next two years, he adopted a middle-of-the-road set of recommendations. He had earlier supported the State Department against Brzezinski in opposing a military government to suppress the revolution before the overthrow of the shah. After the shah left Iran in January 1979 but before Khomeini actually took power, Turner remarked that Khomeini's support was so strong that it would defeat the military even if the military controlled key points in the country. After the American embassy was seized in Tehran in November 1979, Turner made it clear to a crisis management group that Khomeini had given permission for the attack on the embassy, it had been well-organized, chances of negotiating with the militants were not good, and any military effort to free the hostages could well result in their deaths.

As months passed, and the White House gave increasing attention to military options, Turner acknowledged the erosion of the American position in Iran but continued to speak out against any military action, believing it would not succeed. In April 1980, however, he agreed to support a mission to rescue the hostages "because we had run out of [other] alternatives." When the mission failed, he faulted virtually every aspect of it from Brzezinski's insistence on it in the first place to the mission's preparations and execution. In Turner's view, the rescue effort was one of a number of examples of botched responses to terrorism resulting in part from public impetuosity when faced with complex problems involving extended negotiations. He also raised disturbing questions about the legitimacy of placing the welfare of American hostages before vital U.S. policy interests.

As DCI, Turner was involved in the final negotiations leading to the hostages' release just as the Carter administration was coming to a close. He also took part in all other important security matters during the Carter presidency, including the June 1979 Strategic Arms Limitation Talks agreement (SALT II) with the Soviet Union and the Soviet invasion of Afghanistan the following December. In the months after the signing of the SALT II treaty, it seemed its fate might hinge on Turner's testimony to the Senate on the verifiability of Soviet compliance with the agreement. Near the end of the negotiations on the treaty, he had raised serious questions about Washington's ability to verify Soviet compliance because of the highly technical question of telemetry encryption (the encoding of important missile measuring data in order to monitor and verify a missile's performance in flight). Turner had wanted a total ban on Soviet encryption, but the Soviets agreed to only a limited ban. Although Turner testified that the SALT II agreement was verifiable in the sense that wholesale cheating was unlikely, the White House had not been absolutely certain about what he would say until he testified.

As for the Soviet invasion of Afghanistan in December 1979, while there is some dispute as to whether Turner can be faulted for another "intelligence gap," the evidence seems to suggest that he can. An interagency intelligence study, *The Soviet Invasion of Afghanistan: Implications for Warning*, prepared in October 1980 at the NSC's request, concluded that "the U.S. intelligence collection system proved equal to the task of providing analysts with sufficiently detailed, accurate, and timely data to allow them to reach essentially correct conclusions about the military activities in the Soviet Union with respect to Afghanistan."

In a more recent study, *Predicting the Soviet Invasion of Afghanistan: The Intelligence Community Record* (2001), Douglas MacEachin, a high-level official who had served for 32 years at the CIA and was its well-respected deputy director for intelligence from 1993 to 1995, takes issue with this view. Instead, he reveals a pattern during the six months prior to the Soviet invasion in which the CIA, while cognizant of a Soviet military buildup along its frontier with Afghanistan and not ruling out the possibility of Soviet military intervention, nevertheless discounted the likelihood of a major Soviet incursion. This was also despite the growing Muslim insurgency against the communist-controlled government in Kabul. A memorandum from Turner to the president and other senior officials on September 14, 1979, for example, warned that the "Soviet leaders may be on the threshold of a decision to commit their own forces to prevent the collapse of the regime and to protect their sizeable stakes in Afghanistan." But the DCI also said that Moscow was fully aware of the open-sided military and political costs that could result from such an action and that if they were to increase their military stake in Afghanistan, they would do so only incrementally. Analysts continued to hold to this view, believing that the Soviets were interested primarily in bolstering Afghan forces against the Muslim insurgents.

A new element of uncertainty about Afghanistan was also added to intelligence reports after the November 1979 seizure of the U.S. embassy in Iran. Some reports, noting the improved readiness of Soviet forces, attributed it to unease about U.S. reaction to the seizure of the embassy. By December, the CIA and other intelligence agencies were reporting on increased Soviet activity in Afghanistan, including airborne flights into Kabul and the arrival of motorized rifle battalions with equipment for combat operations. The *National Intelligence Daily* and the *Defense Intelligence Daily* said that the deployment could be "indicative of a decision by the Soviets to increase their forces substantially." But they also stated that it was "not certain that Moscow has embarked" on implementing a much-larger force in Afghanistan.

Not until December 19, 1979, did Turner inform Carter and his senior advisers that the Soviets "had crossed a significant threshold in their growing military involvement in Afghanistan." Even then, analysts continued to disagree over the size and significance of the military force likely to be involved. With few exceptions, the general expectation remained that the introduction of Soviet forces would be incremental to augment security for Soviet personnel and help the Kabul regime maintain its authority. The massive Soviet invasion of Afghanistan in the last week of December therefore came as a surprise to the U.S. intelligence community at large and to Turner in particular. Yet the president continued to maintain his confidence in the admiral, and he remained at the CIA until the end of the Carter presidency.

After leaving the CIA, Turner authored the following books: *Secrecy and Democracy* (1985); *Terrorism and Democracy* (1991); *Caging the Nuclear Genie—An American Challenge for Global Security* (1997); and *Caging the Genies—A Workable Solution for Nuclear, Chemical, and Biological Weapons* (1999). In these books, he recounted his service as CIA director; advocated the use of technological information gathering; recounted the United States's experience in making deals with terrorists, including his own experience in the Iran hostage crisis; called for nuclear disarmament; and wrote about the ongoing dangers of nuclear, chemical, and biological proliferation. Turner has also taught at Yale University and the University of Maryland, where he is a member of the public affairs faculty. A frequent commentator and contributor to *Foreign Affairs*, the *New York Times Magazine*, and the *Christian Science Monitor*, he joined with other former CIA directors after the terror attacks of September 11, 2001, in urging congressional passage of legislation giving a newly established intelligence director near-cabinet rank authority over 14 separate intelligence agencies. He has criticized the war in Iraq and Vice President Dick Cheney for lobbying against a bill that would have prevented the CIA from using torture against suspected terrorists. He is the author of *Burn Before Reading: Presidents, CIA Directors, and Secret Intelligence* (2005) and a senior research scholar at the University of Maryland's School of Public Policy.

Udall, Morris King

(Mo Udall)
(1922–1998) *member of the House of Representatives, Democratic presidential nomination candidate*

Morris "Mo" Udall of Arizona served in the House of Representatives from 1961 to 1991. In 1976, he was one of a group of liberal lawmakers who sought the Democratic nomination for president. Throughout the long primary process, he presented the most lasting challenge to Jimmy Carter despite the fact that, like the former Georgia governor, he was among the least-known of the candidates seeking the nomination. Although he ran and was defeated in 22 primaries, he placed second in a number of them and would most likely have won several of those, including Wisconsin, Michigan, and, perhaps even New Hampshire, had the liberal vote not been so divided. It was Carter's ability to take advantage of the split among liberal voters by appealing to more moderate Democrats that helped the Georgian to win the Democratic nomination.

Although not well-known nationally until 1976, Udall was already one of the most influential members of Congress. After 1976, he built on that reputation, becoming increasingly respected on Capitol Hill for his honesty, decency, self-deprecating wit, and humanity and as a champion of such causes as the rights of Native Americans, congressional reform, campaign-finance reform, and health-related issues. Most of all, he was singled out by other lawmakers and by the environmental movement as one of the leading congressional advocates of protecting the environment.

Udall was born in St. Johns, Arizona, on June 15, 1922, the fourth of six children. At age six, he lost his right eye in an accident while playing with another boy; a year later, he nearly died of spinal meningitis. Nevertheless, he became a star athlete in both basketball and football. In 1940, he enrolled at the University of Arizona on a basketball scholarship. In 1942, he was drafted, and after graduating from Officers Candidate School, he was assigned to noncombat service. After the war, he returned to the University of Arizona, where he received his law degree with distinction (LL.B., 1949). While at Arizona, he served as student body president, obtained his pilot's license, and played professional basketball during the 1948–49 season.

Upon graduation, Udall passed his bar exams with the highest average in the state. After practicing law for a brief time in Tucson and while serving as the county attorney for Pima County, he opened a practice in Tucson with his brother Stewart, who was elected to Congress in 1954. While Stewart Udall served in Washington, Mo maintained the practice and lectured on labor law at the University of Arizona. In 1961, he served as vice president of the State Bar Association. That same year, he won a special election to fill his brother's seat after Stewart was appointed by President John F. Kennedy as secretary of the interior. A liberal in a highly conservative state and district, Morris Udall was reelected to the House 15 times; among his campaign contributors in his last election was the conservative icon BARRY GOLDWATER, who remarked that Udall had done more for Arizona than any other lawmaker.

During Udall's first years in office, he busied himself, like all new lawmakers, by attending mostly to the needs of his constituency, which comprised all of Arizona outside of Phoenix and its surrounding area. By 1967, he had already begun to develop a reputation as a liberal maverick opposed to the seniority system by which the House operated. That year, he successfully led an effort to strip New York's Adam Clayton Powell of his position as chair of the House Committee on Education and Labor. Udall also broke with the House leadership and risked his own political career by delivering a speech opposing the war in Vietnam. Because he was one of the first lawmakers to break with President Lyndon Johnson over the war, his address made headlines nationwide. In 1968, he published *The Job of the Congressman*, which for many years was widely regarded as required reading for all new lawmakers. Following the November 1968 election of RICHARD NIXON as president, Udall led an unsuccessful effort by House liberals to unseat Speaker of the House John W. McCormack, Jr. (D-Mass.), with himself as the Speaker's replacement. Two years later he lost in a similar effort against Majority Leader Hale Boggs (D-La.).

Although defeated in his challenges to McCormack and Boggs, Udall's efforts were not entirely wasted. One result was to get the House leadership to agree to monthly meetings of the Democratic caucus and to review the entire issue of seniority. Another was to make Udall a leader among insurgent forces within the Democratic Party, whose numbers swelled in 1974 when 71 new Democrats were elected to the House. By this time, Udall had also become a key proponent of campaign-finance reform, helping to get through Congress legislation making lawmakers accountable for their fund-raising and expenditures and providing for the public funding of presidential elections. He had also developed his reputation as a leading environmentalist. In 1973, he sponsored legislation to put aside more than 100 million acres of federal land in Alaska for national parks, national forests, and wildlife refuges. That same year, he was named legislator of the year by the National Wildlife Federation.

In November 1974, Udall announced in New Hampshire that he would be a candidate for the Democratic nomination for president. Few expected that he had much chance to win, but the same constellation of political forces that worked in Jimmy Carter's favor (qualities of character and the attraction by voters to someone relatively unknown and judged as outside the mainstream of Democratic leadership) worked to a lesser degree in Udall's favor as well. There was also considerable attraction for a liberal congressman from a conservative state who had overcome serious obstacles throughout his life. Standing six feet, five inches tall, with a self-effacing wit, he even appeared Lincolnesque to many American voters. Commenting on his wit, the conservative columnist James K. Kilpatrick said he was "too funny to be president," a remark that later became the title of the congressman's 1988 autobiography. In the New Hampshire primary, Udall came in second to Carter, receiving 22.7 percent of the vote to Carter's 28.4 percent. In both Massachusetts and New York, the Arizona lawmaker actually finished ahead of the former Georgia governor but behind Senator HENRY JACKSON (Wash.). In Wisconsin, Udall lost to Carter by fewer than 8,000 votes and in Michigan by fewer than 2,000 votes, even though Carter had the support of the United Auto Workers. Udall thought he might have a chance to win in Ohio going one-on-one with the president, but the decision by Senator FRANK CHURCH (Idaho), a latecomer to the presidential race, to enter the Ohio primary despite what the Arizona lawmaker thought was an agreement to stay out of the state, assured a Carter victory there as well. In the final tally of state primaries, Udall was unable to win a single one. Characteristically, he took to calling himself "second-place Mo." After losing the Ohio primary in June, he bowed out of the race.

Yet it was after the 1976 election that Udall reached the pinnacle of his political career. In 1977, he became chair of the Committee on Interior and Insular Affairs, an important position for any lawmaker from the West. Being committee chair allowed him over the next quarter of a century to write much of the nation's most important environmental legislation, including strip-mining legislation in 1977 that led to the reclamation of 1.5 million acres of strip-mined coal land by 1987; numerous measures setting aside endangered public land for preservation as wilderness; a measure authorizing the secretary of the interior to engage in feasibility studies of certain water-resource developments; and the Alaska Land Bill of 1980, which set aside more than 100 million acres of wilderness, protecting it from commercial development. He also sought to protect the rights and heritage of Native Americans by sponsoring the Indian Child Welfare Act of 1978, which established guidelines for placing Indian children in foster or adoptive homes. In 1979, he gained approval of the Archaeological Resources Protection Act, setting up a system for safeguarding Indian artifacts and other archaeological resources from vandalism and theft from the public lands.

During the Carter administration, Udall was active in a number of other fronts as well. He spoke out, for example, on the need for a program of national health insurance and played a major role in the passage of Carter's civil-service reforms. In 1980, he was rewarded for his efforts by being chosen to deliver the keynote address at the Democratic National Convention.

During the administration of RONALD REAGAN, Udall was an outspoken opponent of Secretary of the Interior James G. Watt, one of the most controversial and ill-suited figures ever to hold that office, who was known for his efforts to open the public lands to private development. In both the Reagan administration and that of his successor, GEORGE HERBERT WALKER BUSH, Udall continued to work in support of the environment, shepherding through Congress several measures setting aside millions of acres of land to protect the Grand Canyon, ending huge federal subsidies to two pulp mills that were cutting down the ancient forest in southeast Alaska, and developing a nuclear waste-management policy. In 1987, the Sierra Club named him legislator of the year.

In 1984, Udall considered running again for president, but five years previously he had been diagnosed as having Parkinson's disease. He concluded that his candidacy would be a forum over the illness rather than one on his qualifications to be president. Meanwhile, his commitment to public service and his workaholic schedule had told on his personal life. A nonpracticing Mormon with six children, he was married three times and had a shaky family life. His first wife divorced him to escape the demands of a politician's wife, and his second, an alcoholic, committed suicide. Several of his children grew up feeling neglected and alienated, although one of them, Mark, would later serve as a member of Congress.

In January 1991, Udall fell down a flight of stairs, badly hurting himself. The accident forced him to resign from Congress and move to a nursing home for the rest of his life. In recognition of his work on behalf of the environment, Congress established a highly competitive and prestigious national program of undergraduate scholarships named after him. In 1996, President Bill Clinton presented him with the Presidential Medal of Freedom. Udall died of Parkinson's disease on December 12, 1998, at the age of 76.

Ullman, Al

(Albert Conrad Ullman)
(1914–1986) *member of the House of Representatives, chair of the House Ways and Means Committee*

Al Ullman (D-Oreg.) was a member of the House of Representatives for 24 years and chair of the powerful House Ways and Means Committee from 1975 to 1980, when he was defeated for reelection by Republican Denny Smith as part of the Reagan landslide that year. At one time regarded as a liberal in his political views, he became increasingly conservative as a result of his experience on the Ways and Means Committee. As the committee's chair, he is best known for his advocacy of a form of national sales tax along the lines of the European value-added tax (VAT).

Ullman was born on March 9, 1914, in Great Falls, Montana, but grew up in eastern Oregon. He studied political science at Whitman College in Walla Walla, Washington (B.A., 1935). After teaching history and government for two years at Port Angeles High School in Washington State, he moved to New York, where he did graduate work in public law at Columbia University (M.A., 1939). During World War II, he served as a navy communications officer in the South Pacific. After the war, he became a builder and real-estate developer in Baker, Oregon. In 1956, he ran successfully for Congress from Oregon's Second Congressional District, which covered the two-thirds of the state east of the Cascade Mountains. What made his election notable was that he was a Democrat from a rural, conservative area who was able to defeat the Republican incumbent, Samuel Coon, despite President Dwight D. Eisenhower's landslide victory that year.

Until January 1975, when he became chair of the Ways and Means Committee following the resignation in disgrace of Wilbur D. Mills of Arkansas, Ullman had been widely regarded as an amiable but rather obscure and ineffectual member of the House whose conservative views were out of step with most Democrats. In contrast, Mills was recognized by many lawmakers as the single most powerful member of the House, known for ruling his committee though a combination of persuasion and fear.

Ullman became chair of the Ways and Means Committee at a time when fundamental reforms were taking place in the House, the result of which was to increase the committee's size and put more reform-minded lawmakers on it. The reforms also increased the number of subcommittees to accommodate the new members, created new subcommittee chairs and stripped the committee of its authority for making committee assignments. These changes were the result of an ongoing effort to break the long-standing control of the House by southern Democrats as a result of the seniority system by which committee and subcommittee chairs were appointed and of the election in 1974 of a large class of independent-minded liberal Democrats. Because of the unusual power that Mills had exerted as chair of Ways and Means as well as the clubby nature of that committee, where all tax legislation originated, it had been targeted for change by the Democratic caucus led by PHILLIP BURTON (Calif.).

Even before Mills resigned as chair of Ways and Means, Ullman had sought to take control of the new subcommittees by naming the nonmembers of the full committee. However, Burton and another reformer, DAVID OBEY (D-Wis.), went to Majority Leader TIP O'NEILL (Mass.), who forced Ullman to back off from his plan. Reporting on what had transpired on the Ways and Means Committee, the columnists Rowland Evans and Robert Novak remarked, "Burton is the true successor to Mills as the uncrowned king of the House."

Certainly Ullman never wielded the power that Mills had enjoyed as chair of the Ways and Means Committee. Even if he had had the disposition of his predecessor, the changes in the composition and rules of the House would have made that impossible. But the way Ullman chose to run the committee made his task all the more difficult. Rather than trying to steer the committee toward consensus, through a combination of accommodation and intimidation in the manner of Mills, Ullman preferred a more hands-off approach. In fact, he went out of his way to contrast his differences in style from Mills. "I see my role as altogether different than chairmen used to see theirs," he remarked in obvious reference to Mills. "They were worried about image and not losing any bills and not bringing a bill to the floor unless they had all the votes in their pocket. ... I see my role as one of leadership and trying to expand the thinking of Congress in new directions in order to meet the long-term needs of the country."

As a result both of changes in the House and of his own leadership style, Ullman proved to be a weaker and less-influential chair of the Ways and Means Committee than his predecessor Wilbur Mills as well as his successor, DANIEL ROSTENKOWSKI (D-Ill.), and his counterpart on the Senate Finance Committee, RUSSELL LONG (D-La.). When, for example, Ullman failed to touch the oil industry's treasured oil and gas depletion allowance as part of a tax-cutting measure in 1975, House Democrats forced inclusion of a depletion-allowance repeal to the tax measure, something they would never have attempted when Mills was Ways and Means chair. Furthermore, the Senate expanded the tax cuts in the House measure from \$20 billion to \$27 billion. In the conference committee that followed, Long outfoxed Ullman, inserting into the measure incentives for employee stock-ownership plans, known as ESOPs (a modern version of his father Huey's "Share the Wealth" scheme), an earned-income credit, a home-buying credit, and partial restoration of the depletion allowance. Although the size of the tax cut, \$20.9 billion, the largest in the nation's history, was closer to the House bill than the Senate version, it was the other provisions that had most interested Long. "Ullman had managed to pare down the cost of the tax bill," observed *New York* magazine reporter Aaron Latham, "but Long had retained all of the amendments about which he really cared. If you looked at the price tag, then Ullman had won the conference. If you looked only at the provisions, then Long had won."

That said, it would be wrong to conclude that Ullman was a pushover as chair of the Ways and Means Committee. He could rightfully claim that, as a freshman chair, he had gone head-to-head with one of Capitol Hill's shrewdest legislative tacticians (Long). He had also come out of conference committee with a compromise measure, which both houses approved by wide margins and which President GERALD FORD, known for his use of the veto pen, signed even though it exceeded the tax cut he had wanted by almost \$5 billion.

Like other more liberal Democratic leaders, Ullman often found himself at odds with President Carter. After Carter took office in

1977, one of his highest priorities was legislation to stimulate the nation's sagging economy, basic to which was a $50 tax rebate to all taxpayers. Although the president failed to consult any of the key members of Congress about his stimulus program and most of them, including Ullman, thought the rebate was wasteful and would not serve its intended purpose, he was able to get the measure approved by Ways and Means and the House. But before the Senate could act on the tax rebate, Carter pulled the plug on it, explaining that an improving economy made the rebate no longer necessary. Like other leaders who had deferred to the president even though they thought he was proposing bad legislation, Ullman was angry. "It was a little less than fair to those of us who supported [the rebate] against our better judgment and worked hard to get it passed," he complained to the White House after it notified him about the president's change of mind with respect to the tax rebate. No longer would he trust the White House.

Because of Ullman's leadership style and views that were more conservative than those of more liberal Democrats, his relationship with Speaker of the House Tip O'Neill was also strained. O'Neill, in fact, was more accommodating to the president than Ullman. In contrast to the Speaker, who sought to gain quick passage of the president's legislative agenda, especially his energy bill, Ullman was more selective in supporting the president's proposals and objected to the tight schedule that O'Neill wanted to follow. This created problems for the Speaker. Despite the addition of more reform-minded members to the Ways and Means Committee, it remained a bastion of conservatism, with 10 of its 25 Democratic members still southern conservatives. As a result, O'Neill had to depend on his majority whip and the ranking Democratic member of the Ways and Means Committee, Dan Rostenkowski, to act as his agent on the committee. "Tip interpreted Ways and Means as too conservative" when Ullman was chair, explained Rostenkowski. One reason that O'Neill created a special ad hoc committee on energy to push Carter's complex energy program through the House in 1977 was to circumvent the Ways and Means Committee. A few months later, he followed a similar strategy by creating an ad hoc panel from three House committees in effort to get the president's welfare proposals through the House. But Ullman's strong opposition to the administration's welfare program was enough to kill the legislation. Ullman was also effective in blocking the administration proposals for a phased-in national health plan and tax reform, although in the latter case the opposition came mostly from liberal members of the committee who objected to efforts by its conservative members to drastically reduce the tax on capital gains.

After Ullman, joined by Rostenkowski, urged Carter to abandon his tax-reform plan, the frustrated president wrote in his diary that he "found through bitter experience that *any* tax proposal—including our welfare and tax reform packages—attracted to Capitol Hill a pack of powerful and ravenous wolves, determined to secure for themselves additional benefits at the expense of other Americans. ... We were never successful in focusing sufficient attention on them to implement this important reform." Although Congress ultimately passed a tax-reform measure that the president signed, it catered to higher-income taxpayers by reducing the capital gains tax from 49 to 35 percent and eliminating most of the reforms the president had proposed when he first sent his tax program to Congress in January 1978.

As chair of the Ways and Means Committee, Ullman is best remembered for his proposal for a national sales tax akin to the VAT used throughout Europe, as part of the Tax Restructuring Act of 1980. Many economists and commentators regarded VAT as a regressive tax; as a result, it never received much consideration in 1980. Nevertheless, the proposal had its supporters among those who argued that because it taxed consumption, it would encourage savings and reduce inflation. Even President Bill Clinton raised the possibility of a VAT in 1993 as part of an overhaul of the nation's tax structure. But as *Time* magazine remarked in 1989, "nearly a decade [after Ullman proposed a VAT] a Congressman cannot even discuss the possibility of that kind of tax increase without being warned 'Remember what happened to Ullman.'"

As *Time* suggested, Ullman's support of the value-added tax may have cost him his reelection in 1980. His opponent, Denny Smith, who had never run for political office before, tagged him "Sales Tax Ullman." The Oregon congressman attributed his defeat, however, to the Reagan landslide of 1980 and to the fact that Carter's concession speech, before the polls closed in Oregon, kept many Democrats who might have voted for him from going to the polls. For Ullman—as for other Democrats—this was only the latest of a long list of mistakes that Carter had made as president.

Following his defeat in 1980, Ullman formed a consulting firm in Washington, D.C. He was, however, already suffering from prostate cancer, and he died in Bethesda, Maryland, on October 11, 1986. He was 72 years old.

Vance, Cyrus Robert
(1917–2002) *secretary of state*

Secretary of state for most of Jimmy Carter's presidency, Cyrus Vance resigned on April 28, 1980, following Carter's ill-fated effort to rescue 52 Americans being held hostage in Iran. This made Vance only the third person holding that office ever to resign publicly over a foreign-policy dispute with the president. More was involved in his decision to leave office, however, than the failed rescue attempt. Throughout the three years he served in the Carter administration, Vance had been in conflict with Carter's flamboyant and aggressive National Security Advisor, ZBIGNIEW BRZEZINSKI, over the formulation and conduct of foreign policy. By the time of the rescue effort, it had become clear to him, as it had to most political observers in Washington, that Brzezinski had won the upper hand as the president adopted an increasingly hard line toward the Soviet Union, one that Brzezinski advocated and Vance opposed. Thus, the attempt to rescue the American hostages, which Vance thought was ill-advised, was only the last in a series of developments that persuaded him he could no longer serve in the Carter administration.

Vance was born in Clarksburg, West Virginia, on March 27, 1917. In 1918, his family moved to Bronxville, New York, where he was raised. His father, from a well-established West Virginia family, died when Cyrus was just five years old. His mother was from a wealthy Philadelphia family, and his uncle was John W. Davis, the Democratic nominee for president in 1924. Growing exceptionally close to his nephew and serving as his mentor, Davis instilled in Cyrus his interest in the law and a sense of patrician civic responsibility. The young Vance would often spend Sunday afternoons being drilled on the leading cases of the day.

A graduate of Yale University (B.A., 1939) and Yale Law School with honors (LL.B., 1942), Vance served as a naval gunnery officer in the Pacific during World War II and was discharged in March 1946 with the rank of lieutenant senior grade. After the war, he became a highly respected corporate lawyer with a thriving international practice. He also became an active member of the Council on Foreign Relations. In 1957, Senate Majority Leader Lyndon Johnson asked him to come to Washington to serve as special counsel to the Senate Preparedness Investigation Committee. During the three years he served as counsel (1957–60), Vance developed a close working relationship with Johnson and helped draft the bill establishing the National Aeronautics and Space Administration (NASA), one of Johnson's highest priorities. As vice president, Johnson persuaded President John F. Kennedy to appoint Vance as general counsel to the Department of Defense (1961–62) and then as secretary of the army (1962–64). In 1964, President Johnson appointed him deputy secretary of defense (1964–67). While at the Pentagon, Vance worked closely with Secretary of Defense Robert McNamara, who put him in charge of a new Office of Management Planning and Organization Studies responsible for reorganizing the Pentagon and developing new personnel and weapons policies. He also served on troubleshooting missions to Panama, the Dominican Republic, Cyprus, and Korea. Although he left government service in 1967 because of ill health, he was a negotiator at the Paris Peace Conference on Vietnam (1968–69).

A quiet, unassuming, and meticulous person known for his patience, hard work, integrity, and skill as a negotiator, Vance had become, by the time Carter won the Democratic nomination for president in July 1976, the front-runner for the office of secretary of state. Carter had wanted someone for the position who would be a good diplomat and

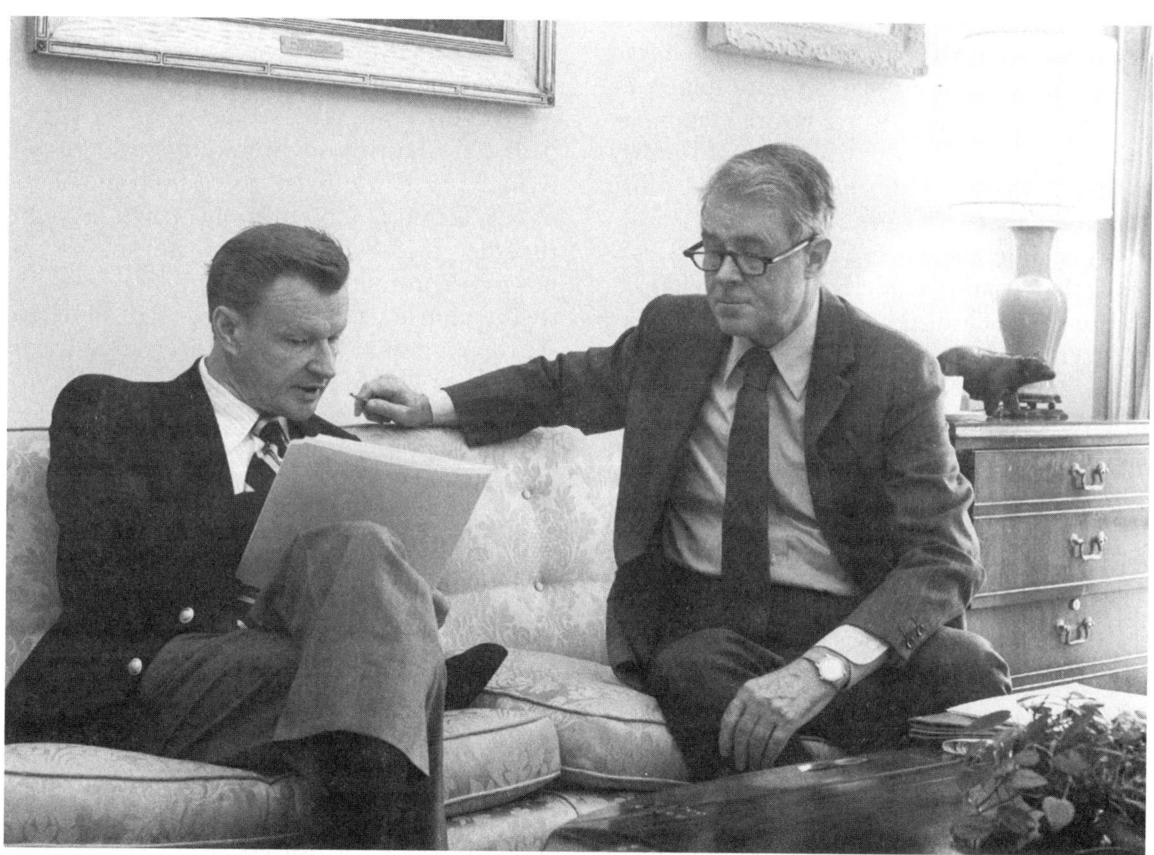

National Security Advisor Zbigniew Brzezinski and Secretary of State Cyrus Vance, 1977 *(Jimmy Carter Library)*

able administrator rather than an innovator in foreign policy. Vance seemed to fit that job description perfectly. The president-elect's decision to appoint Vance to the highest cabinet position was widely hailed in the United States and abroad.

In appointing Vance as his secretary of state, however, Carter chose someone who was not only the polar opposite in style from his brash and opinionated National Security Advisor but a person who also had fundamental differences with Brzezinski on substance. Most important, Vance favored a less-confrontational policy toward the Soviet Union than Brzezinski, who tended to see the world in a more bipolar manner. Vance also believed it was counterproductive to use military power as a negotiating tool, while Brzezinski believed it should continue to play an important role in diplomacy. Finally, Vance favored taking an incremental approach to major foreign-policy matters, whereas Brzezinski preferred more comprehensive strategies.

The differences between Vance and Brzezinski that would characterize their relationship over much of the next three years were apparent early in the Carter administration when the White House took the initiative in resuming negotiations with the Soviet Union for a new Strategic Arms Limitation Talks treaty (SALT II) to replace the SALT I agreement that was to expire in October. Although both Vance and Brzezinski were anxious to resume negotiations, which had been stalled for almost a year because of the presidential campaign, Brzezinski wanted a comprehensive proposal. Vance shared the same goal, but he did not think Moscow would accept the broader approach without protracted and difficult negotiations. Accordingly, he preferred a more limited initiative predicated on an agreement between former U.S. president GERALD FORD and Soviet president LEONID BREZHNEV at Vladivostok, Russia, in 1974, one that could be concluded before the SALT I agreement expired.

Brzezinski prevailed. The comprehensive proposal that Vance took with him to Moscow in March 1977 set limits on both the United States and the Soviet Union of 2,400 missile launchers, with a ceiling of 1,320 for multiple, independently targeted reentry vehicle warheads (MIRVs). The Soviets, who were already angry at Washington over administration attacks on Moscow's human-rights record, were furious. Almost all the major cutbacks being proposed by the administration for a SALT II agreement were in weapons categories favoring the United States over the Soviet Union. Brezhnev responded by rejecting the American proposal out of hand and breaking off further discussions. Vance returned to Washington empty-handed.

At this point, the secretary of state and National Security Advisor were still on good terms. The two officials were both members of the Trilateral Commission, which brought together leaders from the major industrial powers to promote closer cooperation between their countries. Vance had supported Brzezinski's appointment as National Security Advisor and, along with Secretary of Defense HAROLD BROWN, they met at least once a week for lunch. Their goals did not seem all that different even if their approaches for achieving them did. Although the Soviet refusal in March 1977 to even discuss the American proposal for a SALT II agreement and a stern lecture that Vance received from Brezhnev denouncing the American proposal were humiliating to the secretary of state, he was satisfied when the Soviets agreed to resume discussions in early May in Geneva. Following the Moscow debacle, moreover, the White House seemed more amenable to Vance's more moderate approach to dealing with the Soviets.

The secretary of state and the National Security Advisor also cooperated on such other matters as the treaties returning ownership and control of the Panama Canal to Panama (1977), and the Camp David accords (1978) returning the Sinai Peninsula to Egypt in return for Egypt's recognition of the State of Israel and the establishment of a framework for ending the Arab-Israeli dispute. These agreements were widely recognized as two of the most significant accomplishments of the Carter administration. In his memoirs, *Power and Principle* (1983), Brzezinski acknowledged the major role that Vance had played in achieving them.

That said, Vance became increasingly concerned by Brzezinski's growing influence over the formulation of foreign policy, which he attributed in part to the way in which decision-making on national security and foreign policy issues was structured at the White House. As he later recounted in his own memoirs, *Hard Choices* (1983), Vance had agreed reluctantly to a procedure Brzezinski had put forth before the new administration took office by which there would be two committees of the National Security Council (NSC): a Policy Review Committee, usually chaired by the secretary of state, and a Special Coordinating Committee (SCC), normally chaired by the National Security Advisor, who would also have responsibility for preparing summaries of both these meetings. When one of the committees had a recommendation for the president, it would be sent to him as a presidential directive (PD) for his signature. Although heads of departments could come to the White House to review the summaries, they would normally be forwarded without further consideration.

It was this lack of vetting that Vance came to regret. As he later recounted, "The summaries quite often did not reflect adequately the complexity of the discussion or the full range of participants' views." Often there were discrepancies in the summaries that he caught only when the president chose to forward the documents to the State Department. When he left office in 1980, Vance urged his successor, Senator EDMUND MUSKIE (D-Maine) to insist on the right to review the NSC-prepared summaries.

Although Vance had played a crucial role in the events leading to the Panama Canal Treaties and Camp David accords, by the end of 1978 his influence in the administration had begun to wane as Brzezinski's grew. Being in the West Wing of the White House and seeing the president virtually every day gave the determined National Security Advisor an advantage over the secretary of state in influencing the president. From the very beginning of his administration, moreover, Carter had been dubious about what he regarded as the State Department's lethargic bureaucracy. Notwithstanding assurances he had given to Vance to the contrary, he always expected Brzezinski to be the administration's idea man, thinking in broad geopolitical terms and providing him with a comprehensive overview of international developments. Foreign policy would originate in the White House and not the State Department; Vance would be the diplomat transacting the nation's business abroad.

Vance was also out-schemed and outmaneuvered by Brzezinski. In addition to the Panama Canal Treaties and the Camp David accords, another one of the major accomplishments of the Carter administration was the normalization of relations with the People's Republic of China (PRC) in 1978. While both Brzezinski and Vance favored the idea in principle, Brzezinski seized the initiative, proposing to the president that he (Brzezinski) go to China to discuss a strategic relationship directed against the Soviet Union. Having already met with Chinese leaders the previous August, Vance opposed the National Security Advisor's proposal, arguing that it would raise questions about who spoke for the United States on foreign policy. He also believed the trip was premature, that courting China would offend the Soviet Union and delay a SALT II agreement with Moscow, and that the United States needed to develop a more calibrated approach toward normalization of relations done in close consultation with Congress.

By the time Brzezinski made his proposal to go to China, however. President Carter's position toward the Soviet Union had hardened considerably. Soviet involvement in the Somali-Ethiopian War in the Horn of Africa, including its airlift of 12,000 Cuban troops to the Horn, predisposed him toward Brzezinski's argument that Soviet behavior in the Horn should be linked to completion of a SALT II agreement. The president was also concerned by the military buildup of the Soviets' Warsaw Pact allies and angered by the Soviet arrest of three well-known dissidents, Yuri Orlov, Alexander Ginsburg, and Anatoly Sharansky.

Over Vance's objections, therefore, Carter approved Brzezinski's plan to go to Beijing. After the National Security Advisor returned from China, Vance warned the president against "trying to play off China against the Soviets," predicting correctly that Washington's overtures to China would harm, not hasten, negotiations in Geneva for a SALT II agreement. But the president was now committed to restoring normal relations with the Beijing government by year's end. He had also come to share Brzezinski's bipolar perception of international affairs.

Vance was aware of his diminishing influence with the president and the fact that the State Department was being increasingly relegated to the sidelines. He also resented Brzezinski's public posture, including hiring his own press spokesman, holding frequent press briefings, and appearing often on television interview shows, all of which conflicted with the confidential and deliberate manner in which the secretary of state thought diplomacy should be conducted.

Throughout the Iranian revolution, beginning with the overthrow of the shah of Iran, MOHAMMAD REZA PAHLAVI, in January 1979, Vance and Brzezinski fought a type of guerrilla war over the policy the administration should pursue toward Iran. While Vance had previously proposed making contact with AYATOLLAH RUHOLLA KHOMEINI, the exiled leader of the dissident Iranians, Brzezinski had recommended strong support of the shah. After the shah was overthrown by Islamic militants loyal to Khomeini, but before the Ayatollah consolidated his power, Vance proposed trying to reach an understanding between the military and Khomeini loyalists, while Brzezinski urged the establishment of a military government that would suppress the militants. Later in the year, Vance recommended, before news was learned of the shah's terminal illness, against letting him into the United States because of the backlash it would create in Iran, but Brzezinski urged that he be allowed into the country.

Vance also had serious differences with Brzezinski and the president over the policy that the United States should pursue toward Moscow following the Soviet Union's invasion of Afghanistan at the end of 1979. In contrast to Vance, who proposed to the president that the United States offer to neutralize Iran and Pakistan in exchange for a Soviet withdrawal from Afghanistan, Brzezinski wanted harsh measures imposed against the Soviet Union and aid provided to the Afghan resistence. The president sided with his National Security Advisor and adopted a number of measures that included the imposition of a grain embargo against the Soviets, a boycott of the Summer Olympics in Moscow in 1980, and deferment of the Senate's consideration of the SALT II agreement that he and Brezhnev had signed in Vienna in June 1979. He also announced what became the Carter Doctrine, a warning to Moscow that any move against the Persian

Gulf region would be repelled by the United States, even if this meant using military force.

Although Vance did not object to any of these measures and agreed with the White House that the Soviet invasion of Afghanistan necessitated a strong response from the United States, he also believed that it had come about as a result of a number of local and global pressures, including what he referred to as "the downward spiral in U.S.-Soviet relations [that] released the brakes on Soviet international behavior." He thought further that the United States needed to pursue a more balanced policy toward Moscow that "should avoid violent swings between trust and hysteria."

No longer did Vance think it was possible to contain the sharp differences within the administration that prevented a coherent foreign policy. The fact that the president decided to break off relations with Iran on April 7, 1980, and impose new sanctions against Iran even though the secretary of state had advised against that policy, arguing that it was easier to sever ties with a nation than restore them, was, for him, further evidence of this fact.

What finally persuaded Vance to resign, however, was Carter's decision four days later to try a military rescue of the 52 American hostages being held captive by Iran. The secretary of state believed strongly that the mission would endanger lives, threaten the negotiations already taking place for release of the hostages, and ultimately fail. What disturbed Vance as much as the decision itself, however, was the fact that it was made at a meeting of the NSC while he was on vacation in Florida. Although Vance informed President Carter of his decision to resign before the hapless rescue was launched, at the president's request he kept it secret until after the mission had been attempted and failed.

Following his resignation, Vance resumed his law practice and wrote his memoirs. In subsequent years, the United Nations called upon him for a number of peacemaking missions, including helping to negotiate a cease-fire in Croatia in 1991 and, together with David Owen of the European Union, a tenuous peace plan for Bosnia in 1992. Vance died on January 12, 2002, in New York at the age of 84 after suffering from Alzheimer's disease.

Volcker, Paul Adolph

(1927–) *chair, Federal Reserve Board*

Paul Volcker was chair of the Federal Reserve Board (Fed) during the last two years of the Carter administration. In an effort to deal with the problem of rising inflation, which he and just about every other economist and banker had identified as the most serious economic problem facing the United States both at home and in international monetary markets, he developed new strategies for squeezing inflation out of the economy. He ruthlessly cut back on the nation's money supply, thereby leading to rapidly rising interest rates and an economic slowdown that turned into the worst recession since the Great Depression of the 1930s. Although he was widely vilified for the human cost of the recession he had helped to create and came under pressure from the Carter White House to modify his policy in an election year, he refused to deviate from his policy of tight money and high interest rates. After 1983, the economy turned around and began a period of rapid growth sustained by the throttling of inflation. By this time, Carter had been out of office for more than two years. Instead of being vilified, Volcker was widely hailed as an economic genius and one of the truly outstanding leaders of the Fed. Even among his remaining critics, who believed he could have turned the economy around with less cost, he was widely respected for his strength, integrity, and commitment to public service.

Lanky, dressed in rumpled suits that he might have picked off a sales rack, and for most of his adult life a smoker of cheap cigars, Volcker hardly fitted the stereotype of a successful banker and financier, even one who spent much of his career as a public servant. Yet at six feet, seven inches, he towered over most of those around him, physically as well as intellectually. Born on September 5, 1927, in Cape May, New Jersey, but raised in the residential community of Teaneck, across the Hudson River from New York City, Volcker was taught by his stern and somewhat aloof father, who was city manager of Teaneck, the virtues of frugal living, personal conviction, and public service. After graduating summa cum laude from Princeton University (B.A., 1949), he attended the Graduate School of Public Administration at Harvard University, where he received a master's degree in public economy and government (M.A., 1951) and completed the course work for a Ph.D. The following year, he went to the London School of Economics as a Rotary Fellow with the intention of writing his dissertation, but he spent much of his time traveling throughout Europe. Although he never finished his Ph.D., banking and monetary policy became his central interest, and he wrote a 250-page manuscript, "The Problems of Federal Reserve Policy since World War II."

In 1952, Volcker took a position as an economist at the Federal Reserve Bank in New York, where he had worked during the summers. Over the next 20 years, he divided much of his time between the public and private sectors. In 1957, he left the Bank in order to accept a position as a financial economist with Chase Manhattan Bank. While he was at Chase, he developed a close relationship with the bank's chairperson, DAVID ROCKEFELLER, who recruited him as his special assistant on a congressional commission on money and credit in America and then on an advisory commission to the U.S. Treasury Department.

In 1962, Volcker took a considerable cut in pay to join the Treasury Department as director of financial analysis. While there, he attracted the attention of Secretary of the Treasury C. Douglas Dillon, in private life one of Wall Street's leading investment bankers. He had been recruited by Robert Roosa, undersecretary of the treasury for monetary affairs in the Kennedy administration and one of the country's most prominent experts on international monetary policy. The next year, Dillon promoted Volcker to deputy undersecretary for monetary affairs.

Although Volcker returned to the Chase Manhattan Bank in 1965, this time as vice president in charge of planning, his primary interest remained public policy. When, in 1969, President RICHARD NIXON offered him the position of undersecretary of the Treasury for monetary affairs, he accepted. In that position, Volcker figured prominently in Nixon's historic decision in 1971 to bring an end to the Bretton Woods system of fixed exchange rates, in existence since 1944, by ending the linkage of the dollar to gold. He was also the official who negotiated lower price levels for the dollar against other major currencies in order to bring down the nation's lumbering trade deficit. Volcker valued his years in the Treasury Department and enjoyed the influence and power he had as the department's third-ranking official. He relished even more being at the center of historic changes in international financial and monetary markets and applying his considerable talents to public service. Nevertheless, he was twice passed over by Nixon to replace John B. Connally as Treasury secretary, with the job going first to George P. Schultz and then to William E. Simon. By 1974, he had also become disturbed by the obvious corruption of the Nixon presidency; accordingly, he submitted his resignation early that year.

Instead of returning to Wall Street, Volcker took a position as a senior fellow at Princeton University's Woodrow Wilson School of Public and International Affairs. The next year, he accepted an offer by the Federal Reserve Board chair, ARTHUR BURNS, to become president of the Federal Reserve Bank of New York, the most influential of the 12 privately owned regional banks that comprised the Federal Reserve System.

Volcker and Burns had important differences over Fed policy. In particular, Volcker felt that the Fed chair had not done enough to curb inflation by curtailing the money supply. Burns believed the Treasury Department could have done more to persuade its major trading partners to raise the value of their currencies (effectively devaluing the dollar) without the United States having to take the draconian step of decoupling the dollar from gold. Despite these differences, Burns had met with Volcker and other Treasury officials over lunch at least twice a week while Volcker was at the Treasury Department. Burns developed great respect for Volcker, and he wanted someone at the New York bank with precisely his background and experience in banking and monetary policy.

Although not affording Volcker the same opportunity to influence national policy as his earlier position at Treasury, being president of the New York Fed was still a coveted position. Not only did the New York bank carry out monetary policy for the entire Federal Reserve System through its Open Market Desk, which bought and sold U.S. Treasury securities, its president was a permanent member of the Fed's Open Market Committee, which set that policy. Servicing the center of financial power in the United States, it also provided the nation's biggest private banks with the hundreds of millions and even billions of dollars of short-term funds they needed each day to meet shortages in reserve requirements. Although not having the independence and authority of the legendary Benjamin Strong in the 1920s, a strong and assertive New York Fed president could still wield considerable influence, both among private bankers and within the Federal Reserve System. Sensing that opportunity, Volcker had accepted the position Burns offered him.

What neither man anticipated was President Carter's decision in 1978 to replace Burns with G. WILLIAM MILLER, the chief executive of Textron Inc. Although Burns had wanted his position renewed for a third four-year term in 1978, his public criticism of the administration for its failure to reduce budget deficits, which he regarded as the primary cause of inflation, rankled the White House and led the president to find a new Fed chairman.

Although a director of the Federal Reserve Board of Boston, Miller was neither a banker nor an economist and lacked Burns's credentials as an inflation fighter. Carter's appointment of him as the new Fed chairman, therefore, rattled already shaky financial markets. Matters only grew worse as the Organization of Petroleum Exporting Countries (OPEC) doubled the price of oil through 1978 and 1979, and as Miller resisted pressures to raise interest rates in order to counter inflation and prop up the sinking dollar in world money markets. By mid-1979, inflation was running at an annual rate of more than 12 percent. In the view of Wall Street investors and of Europe's central bankers, neither of whom the White House could ignore any longer, Miller needed to be replaced by someone who had the experience, the fortitude, and the independence to tackle inflation regardless of political consequence. The overwhelming consensus within financial circles was that Paul Volcker, who by this time had gained an international reputation as a brilliant monetary technician and diplomat, best met those qualifications.

The White House was not enamored of Volcker, whose reputation for independence was in marked contrast to Miller's as a team player and who was an undesirable reminder of his strong-minded predecessor at the Fed, Arthur Burns. But needing to replace Miller and also to find a successor for the recently fired Treasury secretary, W. MICHAEL BLUMENTHAL, Carter moved Miller over to the Treasury in August 1979 and nominated Volcker to succeed him at the Fed, even though Volcker had made clear to the president his determination to be independent.

Volcker proved to be a nightmare for the administration. His solution for inflation was to allow money markets to determine interest rates by drastically tightening the money supply through open-market sales of Treasury securities instead of manipulating rates themselves through periodic increases (or decreases) in the discount rate (the rate at which banks could borrow from the Fed). This meant drastically higher interest rates and lower economic growth in an already sluggish economy. By allowing the market instead of the Fed to set rates even as he pushed rates higher by tightening the money supply, Volcker also shielded the Fed from political pressure; in effect, the administration's future became mortgaged to the will of the Fed.

The White House understood this. As Carter's chairperson of the Council of Economic Advisers, CHARLES SCHULTZE, later commented, the Federal Reserve became "the only game in town." As the effect of Volcker's tight money policy began to take hold in 1980 and the nation slid into a recession during an election year, the president signaled his dissatisfaction with Volcker's tight-money policy. First, he ordered restrictions removed on consumer credit that the Fed had imposed in March. More important, he stated in a speech in October that he believed Volcker's emphasis on the money supply as a way of containing inflation was "ill-advised." Other administration members, including Schultze, Treasury Secretary Miller, and Press Secretary JODY POWELL, made similar comments.

Even this measured attempt to influence Fed policy, however, was short-lived. In the first place, the president's speech created a backlash. Arthur Burns called the president's comments "regrettable," while another former Fed chairperson, William McChesney Martin, termed them "deplorable." The RONALD REAGAN presidential campaign suggested that Carter was attempting to deflect the administration's responsibility for its own failed economic policies from itself to the Fed.

Volcker's aim of achieving price stability by crushing inflation also accorded with the president's own priorities. Even if he were so inclined, it would have been difficult for Carter to have launched a sustained attack against the Fed, since his appointment of Volcker had been an endorsement of its independence; by nominating Volcker as Fed chair, in other words, the president had effectively forfeited whatever chance he had of getting the Fed to coordinate its monetary policy more closely with the White House's fiscal policy.

Accordingly, the president had little choice other than to support Volcker publicly, notwithstanding the fact that by spring 1980 the unemployment rate had risen to 7 percent, the prime interest rate was over 18 percent, and the price of gold (a hedge against inflation) had reached $850 an ounce. Whether a different Fed chairperson might have staved off a recession or whether that, in turn, might have kept Carter in office for a second term is impossible to determine. What is certain is that the recession continued into the Reagan administration and almost certainly was on voters' minds when they cast their ballots in November 1980.

By December, the prime interest rate had peaked at 21.5 percent, and the United States fell into its worst recession in 40 years. Beginning sometime in fall 1982, however, after the inflation rate had begun to decline and Volcker began to loosen his grip on the money supply, the economy began a long and sustained rebound. The formerly maligned Fed chairperson was then widely hailed as the knight-errant who had killed the inflation dragon and restored the nation's economic well-being.

Volcker remained as the Fed chair until 1987, when he left the Fed under considerable pressure from within the Reagan administration and among its allies, who resented Volcker's independence and his public statements against the administration's huge budget deficits and its efforts at bank deregulation. A number of administration officials, including Treasury Secretary Donald T. Regan and Chief of Staff JAMES BAKER, campaigned privately against Volcker's reappointment for a second term in 1982 and even after Volcker was reappointed. Their opposition came to include the Federal Reserve Board itself, where Reagan appointees, favoring looser controls on the money supply, controlled a majority by 1986.

Thus, rather than seek a third term as Fed chair in 1987 and face the possibility of not being reappointed by Reagan, Volcker decided instead to return to the private sector and build up his nearly empty personal savings, but not before agreeing to serve as the unpaid chair of the National Commission on the Public Service, a private group working on behalf of the nation's civil servants. Instead of taking a position with one of the largest banks or financial institutions, he chose to become chair of James D. Wolfensohn, Inc., a small but highly successful investment-banking firm, where he would be closely involved with his clients. His decision proved to be a mutually profitable one. When Wolfensohn was bought out by BankAmerica Corp. in 1996, Volcker made an estimated $15 million from the sale. For the first time in his life, Volcker had become a wealthy man, although his lifestyle remained relatively frugal.

Since leaving the Fed and then investment banking, Volcker has remained extremely active. He was a major participant in the 1998 $1.25 billion settlement with Swiss banks which had held the savings of Holocaust victims during World War II. He also headed the in-house investigation into the business practices of the accounting firm of Arthur Andersen and Co. in a futile effort to save that firm from going out of business following the Enron debacle of 2002 in which Andersen was implicated for its illicit accounting practices. Volcker has been a member of the blue-ribbon commission investigating accounting procedures for stock options paid out to attract and keep corporate leaders and other employees. Finally, he has led an investigation into the scandal-ridden United Nations' Iraq Oil for Food program. He continues to reside in New York City.

Wallace, George Corley

(1919–1998) *governor of Alabama, presidential candidate*

A racist and segregationist, George Wallace was a four-term governor of Alabama and four-time candidate for president. What made him such an important national political figure in the 1960s and 1970s was that he was able to tap into a national backlash against big government and the Civil Rights movement among large blocks of blue-collar workers, suburbanites, Catholics, and ethnic groups in the North who felt their jobs, neighborhoods, and even way of life threatened by the federal government and what they considered its coddling of blacks, criminals, and welfare cheaters (who were often the same groups in their minds). Wallace's attraction among southern Democrats posed one of the biggest obstacles to Carter's campaign for the Democratic nomination for president in 1976. Carter's defeat of Wallace and Senator HENRY JACKSON (Wash.) in the crucial Florida state primary that year went a long way toward assuring his victory.

Wallace was born in the southeast Alabama cotton town of Clio on August 25, 1919. Although his grandfather was a popular local physician, his father was a gruff redneck farmer who barely eked out a living that was supplemented by the small earnings of Wallace's mother, who gave occasional piano lessons. Ambitious and pugnacious like his father, Wallace was baptized into politics at an early age when, as a 15-year-old teenager, he was able to secure a position as a legislative page at the state capitol in Montgomery. He loved the hurly-burly of state politics, revered the spot at the state capitol where Jefferson Davis had been sworn in as president of the Confederacy, and became determined even then to become governor of the state. Small of stature at five feet, six inches and never weighing more than 120 pounds, but a natural athlete, Wallace played football and took up boxing in high school, twice becoming Alabama bantamweight Golden Gloves champion. He was also a talented salesman, traveling through much of the South in 1937 selling magazine subscriptions by telling potential customers in rural shacks that the federal government required everyone to have reading materials.

In 1937, Wallace entered the University of Alabama at Tuscaloosa wearing the same shiny suit he had worn as a page. Keenly aware of his own impoverished background, he developed a deep resentment of the wealthier students who joined fraternities and dominated student government and the university's social life. As a freshman, Wallace was able to organize a coalition of independent and unpledged freshmen to win election as his class president. Although he never held another student office, his campaign gave him a taste of underdog politics, which he carried throughout the rest of his career. He also distanced himself over time from his family and in later life rarely spoke about his father.

Waiting tables, driving a taxi, boxing professionally, and borrowing books, Wallace was able to put himself through the three-year prelaw curriculum and two years in law school. After receiving his law degree (LL.B., 1942) and being admitted to the bar, he joined the U.S. Army Air Force. In 1943, he married Lurleen Burns, a 16-year-old dime-store clerk. During the war, he served in the Pacific theater, flying as an engineer on nine missions before the war ended. When he refused to fly a 10th mission after the war, he was given a medical discharge with a 10 percent disability for war fatigue.

Even during the war, Wallace had prepared for his political career by sending hundreds of notes to potential voters back home, most of who had never heard of him. Back in Alabama, he took a position as an assistant attorney general for the state. In 1947, he won election to the state legislature and aligned himself with Alabama's racially moderate, populist governor, "Big Jim" Folsom. Wallace established a liberal voting record in the 1950s, supporting an increase in the number of the state's trade schools and other measures to promote industry in the state and trying to shift more of the state's tax burden to corporate interests and the wealthy. He also got Folsom to name him as a trustee of the all-black Tuskegee Institute. In 1948, he attended the Democratic Party convention. Instead of walking out of the convention with segregationist "Dixiecrats," he remained loyal to the party. Members of the press named him one of the state's best legislators.

In 1953, Wallace campaigned successfully for district judge of Barbour County, but his goal was still to become governor of Alabama. In 1954, he helped lead Folsom's second successful campaign for governor. Since by state law Folsom could not serve two consecutive terms, Wallace spent the following four years preparing for his own gubernatorial campaign.

The 1958 gubernatorial election was a milestone in Wallace's political career. Although he had always been a segregationist, he had never run a blatantly racist campaign. Because of his association with Folsom, he had been widely perceived in the state as a moderate Democrat. But in 1958, Wallace's principal opponent for governor, Alabama attorney general John Patterson, trounced him by running as a racist. In response, Wallace, who had started the campaign as a dark-horse candidate, vowed that no one would "ever out out-nigger me again." As Wallace prepared to run again in 1962, he aligned himself with some of the most extreme groups and individuals in the state, including members of the White Citizens' Councils and Ku Klux Klan (KKK). In the campaign itself, he won overwhelmingly by promising to stop integration from taking place in Alabama. In his inaugural address as governor, he made a statement that would haunt him throughout his political career: "Segregation now, segregation tomorrow, segregation forever."

If Wallace had fulfilled his lifelong ambition by being elected governor of Alabama in 1962, developments in the state quickly propelled him onto the national stage. He first gained national notoriety through such histrionics as standing at the doorway to block two black students from entering the University of Alabama in June 1963 and then moving aside when confronted by Assistant Attorney General Burke Marshall. He also forced the delay of school integration in several Alabama cities and may have been indirectly responsible, because of his outspoken opposition to integration and his association with some of the worst fringe elements in the state, for the dynamiting in September 1963 of a black church in Birmingham that killed four young girls.

Following these developments in Alabama, Wallace was besieged by invitations to appear on Sunday news shows and speak on college campuses. Instead of the redneck governor that many had expected to see, he came across as a polite, thoughtful, and even humorous public official who couched his defense of segregation not in terms of racism but of defending states' rights against intrusive government. He sought to protect the rights of the common man against the dictates of a court system gone amuck and abetted by a left-wing government out of touch with the wishes of the people it purported to represent. Encouraged to run for president in 1964, Wallace entered the Wisconsin, Indiana, and Maryland Democratic primaries and did surprising well. Attacking the civil rights bill of 1964 that would integrate public accommodations, he gained nearly a quarter of the vote in Wisconsin and a third of the vote in Indiana, and he almost won the primary in Maryland. After this, though, he had nowhere to go, and he bowed out of the presidential race after Senator BARRY GOLDWATER (Ariz.), who also opposed the 1964 Civil Rights Act and whose message was not that different from Wallace's, received the Republican nomination.

Two years later, when the state legislature refused his request to change Alabama's constitution to allow him to run for reelection as governor, Wallace had his wife Lurleen, who had recently been diagnosed with cancer, run in his place; the clear understanding was that he would remain governor in fact. She won by a landslide but died of cancer in 1968 and was succeeded by Albert Brewer. Meanwhile, Wallace's performance in the 1964 primaries had stoked his presidential ambitions. The tumult of the 1960s increased the appeal of his message among disaffected whites alienated by the activism and civil disorder of the decade. Forming his own American Independent Party and choosing General Curtis LeMay as his running mate, Wallace made a strong showing as a third-party presidential candidate in the 1968 election, gaining 13 percent of the national vote and carrying five states in the South, with 46 electoral votes.

In 1970, Wallace again ran for governor. It was his most flagrantly racist campaign, even employing the KKK to circulate fliers accusing the family of his opponent, incumbent governor Albert Brewer, of sexual perversions and miscegenation. After the election, Wallace managed to get the state law changed so that he could run again (successfully) in 1974. Nevertheless, his national ambitions remained unchanged, and in 1972 he geared up to run for president a third time, this time as a Democrat. The move struck fear within the Democratic Party, which had no clearly strong candidate to oppose President RICHARD NIXON's bid for reelection (after Massachusetts senator EDWARD KENNEDY decided against running) and was in a state of disarray. Even Nixon had been concerned enough about a Wallace candidacy in 1972 that he had provided $400,000 to Brewer's reelection bid in 1970.

In the early primaries in 1972, Wallace ran even stronger than he had four years earlier, finishing second in Wisconsin and winning the primaries in Maryland and Michigan on May 16. However, an attempted assassination in Laurel, Maryland, by Arthur Bremer, while Wallace was still campaigning rendered him paralyzed below the waist and left him struggling for the rest of his life with pain and various other illnesses. It also took him out of the 1972 race and cleared the way for the eventual nomination of South Dakota senator GEORGE MCGOVERN and Nixon's landslide victory in November.

Permanently disabled and confined to a wheelchair, Wallace would never be the fiery campaigner he had been in the past. By 1976, moreover, much of the discord that had characterized the 1960s had dissipated. The social conservatism with which Wallace first identified would flourish as a political movement, helping to bring about the election of RONALD REAGAN in 1980, but it would be embedded in a politics of hope and optimism rather than in the politics of resentment and fear-mongering espoused by the Alabama governor. In this sense, time had eclipsed Wallace.

In 1976, however, Wallace still remained an important national political figure and making a fourth bid for the presidency. While few political observers believed he could win the Democratic nomination, he posed a significant political threat to the other southern candidate, former Georgia governor Jimmy Carter. Running for governor in 1970 in a campaign that many of his followers later regretted, Carter had tried to identify himself with Wallace in an obvious appeal to segregationist voters in the state. But after becoming governor, he had distanced himself from Wallace's racist and segregationist views, becoming the leading symbol of the new, racially integrated, tolerant South.

In 1976, Carter faced Wallace in the Florida primary. All the other candidates for the Democratic nomination, except Washington senator Henry Jackson, had sat out the primary, believing the state was Wallace country. Victory in Florida was crucial, however, to Carter's presidential chances. Following the Iowa caucus in January and the New Hampshire primary in February 1976, he had emerged as a major contender for the Democratic nomination in July. Between New Hampshire and Florida, though, the Georgian had suffered a major defeat in Massachusetts, where he had finished a poor fourth in the state's primary. If he lost in Florida, he would probably be through as a serious candidate. But if he beat Wallace in the South, his claim to be the moderate southern alternative to the Alabama governor would stay viable, and his strategy of running as a centrist candidate acceptable to the mainstream of the Democratic Party would be justified. Conversely, if Wallace won, his victory would be a reaffirmation of his own regional strength in the South.

Unfortunately for the Alabama governor, Carter's strategy worked brilliantly. He finished with 34.3 percent of the primary vote in Florida compared with Wallace's 30.6 percent and Henry Jackson's 23.9 percent. As *Time* reported, Carter "dominated the center on the issues, had the best organization and had the broadest appeal of all the candidates." He won large majorities among voters under age 25, blue-collar workers, and Democrats identifying themselves as liberals. In the weeks that followed, Carter also won easily over Wallace in Illinois and North Carolina. No longer a dominant national political figure, Wallace ended up endorsing Carter for the Democratic nomination when it became clear that the choice was between the Georgian and his more liberal challengers.

Yet Wallace remained the dominant political figure in Alabama. After stepping down as governor in 1979, he won an unprecedented fourth term in 1982. With his health clearly deteriorating, he decided to retire when his term ended in January 1987.

George Wallace's four terms as governor were characterized by corruption and cronyism involving his brother Gerald, who accepted graft and built businesses based on lucrative state contracts. Wallace also left a legacy of trade schools, junior colleges, and small four-year colleges throughout the state that were often redundant and an educational waste while ignoring the state's two flagship schools, Auburn University and the University of Alabama. On the more positive side, he sponsored a constitutional amendment establishing an oil and gas trust fund to support noneducational segments of state government and promoted a $310 million educational bond issue. He also boosted salaries of teachers and state employees and poured funds into highway and road construction.

After 1979, Wallace tried to rewrite history and reinvent his persona, denying that he had ever felt racial hatred for black people and maintaining that his advocacy of segregation had been predicated on a defense of states' rights against the federal courts and his reading of the Bible and Constitution rather than on racism. He also took responsibility for the phenomenon that became known as Reaganism.

Wallace also sought forgiveness from the black citizens who had been the target of his demagogic defense of segregation. He championed black voting rights, appointed black officials to state offices, attended meetings of the NAACP, spoke at African-American churches, and telephoned black leaders throughout the country asking forgiveness. Many African Americans did, in fact, forgive Wallace for his past behavior, even voting for him in large numbers in 1982.

After leaving public office, Wallace accepted a position with Troy State University in Montgomery. He died of respiratory and cardiac arrest on September 14, 1998, at the age of 79.

Warnke, Paul Culliton

(1920–2001) *director, Arms Control and Disarmament Agency*

As President Carter's chief arms-control negotiator and director of the Arms Control and Disarmament Agency (ACDA), Paul Warnke was one of the first government officials to strongly support the idea of reductions in the nuclear arsenals of the world's superpowers. His nomination as chief negotiator to the second round of the Strategic Arms Limitation Talks (SALT II) revealed the depth of the opposition in the United States to any agreement seeming to be disadvantageous to the United States. A close friend of Secretary of State CYRUS VANCE, Warnke was widely regarded in Washington as a dove on arms control, and his critics feared that he would make too many concessions to the Soviets. Although the president managed to get Warnke confirmed, the closeness of the vote (58-40) indicated the difficulty he would have in getting the two-thirds majority needed in the Senate for ratification of a new SALT agreement.

Warnke was born on January 31, 1920, in Webster, Massachusetts, and raised in Malborough, Massachusetts. After graduating from Yale University (B.A., 1941), he enlisted in the Coast Guard and served in both the South Pacific and Atlantic during World War II. Following his discharge in 1946, he attended Columbia University Law School after being denied admission to its School of Journalism. Although he had, by his own admission, a mediocre career at Yale, he was editor of Columbia's law review and graduated at the top of his class (LL.B., 1948). After graduation, he joined the prestigious Washington law firm of Covington and Burling. He remained at Covington and Burling, where he did antitrust work for such companies as Continental Banking and Procter and Gamble, until 1966, when Secretary of Defense Robert McNamara persuaded him to become general counsel for the Department of Defense, overseeing the work of 4,000 lawyers.

In August 1967, President Lyndon Johnson appointed Warnke as assistant secretary of defense for international security affairs, the third-highest civilian position at the Pentagon. He was also the highest Pentagon official to openly question the United States' conduct in the Vietnam War. He played an important role in pushing for deescalation of the conflict and in persuading McNamara and his successor, Clark Clifford, with whom he developed close working relationships, to oppose the United States' continued involvement in the war. He also had supervisory responsibility for the 47-volume study known as the Pentagon Papers, a documentary history of America's growing involvement in the war that was secretly released to the press by Daniel Ellsberg, a defense-policy analyst at the Pentagon. Opponents of the conflict used the Pentagon Papers as evidence of the mistaken U.S. policy with respect to Vietnam.

In 1969, Warnke left the Pentagon to establish his own law firm with Clark Clifford. In 1972, he served as national security adviser to Senator EDMUND MUSKIE (Maine) in his bid for the Democratic presidential nomination and then as GEORGE MCGOVERN's chief foreign policy adviser in his unsuccessful bid for the presidency. In 1975, he published a landmark article in *Foreign Policy*, "Apes on a Treadmill," which encapsulated his view on arms control. Regarding the arms race as a primary cause, rather than a symptom, of political conflict, he urged a unilateral policy of restraint on the part of the United States, which, he anticipated, would lead the Soviet Union to adopt a similar policy of restraint. "The Soviet Union," he remarked, "has only one superpower model to follow. To date, the superpower aping has meant the antithesis of restraint. ... It is time, I think, for us to present a worthier model. ... We can be the first off the treadmill." Following Jimmy Carter's election as president in 1976, Warnke was one of only three contenders, along with Cyrus Vance and former undersecretary of state GEORGE BALL, for the position of secretary of state. On the recommendation of Vance, who later described Warnke as a "tough and skillful negotiator and an expert in arms control matters," Carter nominated him to be director of the ACDA and chief negotiator for the SALT II talks with the Soviet Union.

Although the nomination easily passed the dovish Senate Foreign Relations Committee, it created a storm of protest among cold-war hawks who feared that Warnke would make too many concessions in negotiating arms control with the Soviets. Among those opposed to the nomination were former deputy secretary of defense Paul Nitze and Senator HENRY JACKSON (D-Wash.), who headed the Armed Services Subcommittee on Arms Control.

At one time, Nitze and Warnke had been close friends and colleagues at the Pentagon, but they were polar opposites in their views on negotiations with the Soviet Union. Author of NSC-68, the famous 1950 national security directive that described the Soviet threat as primarily military, and cochair of the hawkish Committee on the Present Danger (CPD), Nitze had been a member of the SALT I negotiating team. He had also been critical of Secretary of State HENRY KISSINGER for his apparent lack of concern about the Soviet nuclear advantage. In testimony before the Foreign Relations Committee, he called Warnke's views on arms control "absolutely asinine" and "a screwball, arbitrary, fictitious kind of viewpoint that is not going to help the security of the country."

Leading the fight in the Senate against Warnke's appointment, however, was Henry Jackson. A cold war liberal and defense hawk, Jackson had opposed President RICHARD NIXON's policy of détente with the Soviets and in 1972 had helped establish the Coalition for a Democratic Majority, a union of Democrats favoring a strong military to counter the Soviet threat. In 1974, he had also opposed the SALT I agreement until an amendment was inserted into the pact guaranteeing U.S. parity with the Soviets in land-based missiles in future negotiations.

In Jackson's view, Warnke represented the flaccid underbelly of U.S. foreign policy, a diplomat who blamed the arms race on the United States and not the Soviet Union and who dismissed nuclear superiority as not all that consequential as long as either superpower maintained a minimal nuclear deterrent. In close and exhaustive questioning of Warnke, in which he referred to the nominee's own works and public comments, Jackson forced him to acknowledge inconsistencies between his prior positions and his testimony before the Foreign Relations Committee in which he appeared to hoe a tougher line with respect to arms control. The senator also assembled a group of experts on arms control, including Nitze and other members of the CPD, to lobby against Warnke's confirmation as chief arms negotiator and director of the ACDA.

Although Jackson was unable to prevent the Senate from confirming Warnke, he and his cohorts continued to criticize the ACDA director's views on arms control as being too simplistic. Within the administration, Warnke also encountered an increasingly stiffer position with respect to the SALT talks as the hard-line views of National Security Advisor ZBIGNIEW BRZEZINSKI and Secretary of Defense HAROLD BROWN prevailed over those of himself and Secretary of State Vance. In January 1978, Brown warned against any undue haste or one-sided concessions to the Soviets in the arms negotiations. Any agreement that was negotiated, he said, had to be such that it could be sold to the American public. In April, Brzezinski wrote a memorandum to the president in which he remarked that it was "clearly in the Soviet interest, and part of Soviet strategy, to focus attention on SALT and to proclaim the agreement to be evidence of general improvement in U.S.-Soviet relations." This, he continued, would leave "the Soviets free to pursue their political objectives elsewhere and by other means."

In June 1978, Warnke was instructed by the White House to tell Soviet ambassador Anatoly Dobrynin that nothing in the proposed treaty should prevent the United States from deploying an intercontinental mobile missile system (the MX) during the term of the agreement; this was in contradistinction to a decision made just a few weeks earlier to adopt Vance's view that a SALT II agreement needed to be negotiated as quickly as possible. Warnke later described Brzezinski's position on the MX missile in caustic terms: "The bigger, the uglier, the nastier the weapon—the better." At meetings on SALT, Warnke and Brown engaged in head-to-head exchanges on such esoteric matters as encryption of missile-test telemetry, missile diameters, and cruise-missile range-definitional issues.

In the wake of the grilling he had been put through during his confirmation, the close vote by which he had been confirmed, the unremitting drumfire he had had to endure from opponents of the SALT II process, and the increasing ascendancy of the hard-liners within the administration, Warnke found his dual position as ACDA director and chief arms negotiator increasingly untenable. In November 1978, he resigned his position to return to his private law practice just as negotiations on a SALT II agreement appeared to be reaching a conclusion. "I'm sure there will be those who will be able to contain their regret," he stated in tending his resignation. The White House was, in fact, relieved that Warnke's presence would not be another obstacle to overcome in what already promised to be a Herculean fight over ratification of the treaty.

As a private citizen, Warnke continued to speak out in favor of arms control. When the administration of RONALD REAGAN announced in 1986 that it no longer felt bound by the SALT II treaty, he remarked, "The nuts have won." Warnke also served as a member of the Council on Foreign Relations and on President Bill Clinton's arms control and nonproliferation advisory board. His later years were marred by the 1991 collapse of the Clifford law firm he had helped establish as a result of Clark Clifford's involvement in the Bank of

Credit and Commerce International (BCCI) scandal and by a dispute over his new firm's handling of the estate of the diplomat Averell Harriman. Warnke died of a pulmonary embolism on October 31, 2001, at his home in Washington, D.C. He was 81 years old.

Watson, Jack Hearn, Jr.
(1938–) *special assistant to the president, White House chief of staff*

Jack H. Watson, Jr., headed the Carter-Mondale Policy Planning Group and then the transition team during the change in government from President GERALD FORD to President-elect Jimmy Carter. After the 1976 election, he lost a battle with Carter's chief aide, HAMILTON JORDAN, over who would control the appointments process for the new administration. As special assistant to the president, he had the dual responsibility of serving as cabinet secretary and assistant to the president for intergovernmental affairs. In 1980, the president appointed Watson chief of staff. But although he was part of Carter's senior staff and played an important role, especially in terms of trying to develop new relationships between the White House and state and local officials, Watson never exerted the same influence with the president as other members of the senior staff.

Special Assistant to the President Jack H. Watson, Jr., 1977 *(Jimmy Carter Library)*

Watson was born the son of a navy enlisted man on October 24, 1938, in El Paso, Texas, but lived in Pine Bluff, Arkansas, as a child and student. A Phi Beta Kappa graduate of Vanderbilt University (B.S., 1960), he joined the U.S. Marines immediately upon graduation and served for two years, setting two permanent obstacle-course records at the Quantico base, where he became an officer. After being discharged from the marines in 1963, he attended Harvard Law School (LL.B., 1966). In 1966, he came to Atlanta to work for CHARLES KIRBO's law firm, King and Spalding, where he was made a partner in 1972. He had met Jimmy Carter through Kirbo in 1966 when Watson spent a day in Plains talking with the gubernatorial candidate. Following Carter's defeat, the two men met occasionally when the Plains politician was in Atlanta. Watson was deeply impressed with Carter, later remarking: "I was fascinated with him, with his intellect, with his voracious appetite for reading and learning … by his singleness of purpose. There were many things about him that utterly intrigued me."

During Carter's second, successful campaign for governor in 1970, Watson joined a number of other young Atlanta professionals who served as volunteer workers in the campaign. He was rewarded when Governor

Carter appointed him to the Board of Human Resources, along with another Atlanta lawyer who would later serve in the White House as President Carter's legal counsel, ROBERT LIPSHUTZ. As the board's pro bono vice chairperson and then chair, Watson had responsibility for the oversight of what was the largest agency in Georgia's reorganized state government, combining the functions of the former health and welfare departments.

By 1974, Watson had joined a small group of Georgians who helped plan Governor Carter's presidential campaign. During the campaign, he served as chair of the Georgia finance committee, proving himself to be an adept organizer and skilled fund-raiser. Until after the critical Pennsylvania presidential primary in April 1976, most of the money for the campaign came from Georgia. During the Pennsylvania primary, when the campaign was particularly strapped for funds, Watson helped mobilize an all-out effort to raise the money needed to carry the state.

With Carter's selection as the Democratic presidential nominee almost locked up, Watson suggested to the candidate that he establish a policy-planning organization to prepare for his transition from candidate to president. The idea of a candidate planning a presidential transition before he had even received his party's nomination might have seemed presumptuous to Carter (and may have been part of the reason why he harbored reservations about Watson as an opportunist). But the former Georgia governor was confident enough about becoming president in November that he committed $150,000 in scarce campaign funds to what became the Carter-Mondale Policy Planning Group. With this support, Watson gathered together in Atlanta a small group of less than 50 young professionals like himself to do planning on issues that included national security, national health insurance, the environment, and tax reform.

When Carter won the election in November 1976, Watson presented him with a series of briefing books and policy papers as well as recommendations for staffing. The Watson involvement in the staffing process provided early insight into a recurring problem of the Carter presidency: weak or conflicting delegation of authority. Although the group reviewed thousands of résumés on potential Carter appointees, the president-elect never gave it exclusive responsibility for staffing. As a result, much of its work was duplicated in a separate operation at the Democratic National Committee. Making matters worse, Hamilton Jordan wanted to be in charge of White House personnel. When Watson submitted a transition budget giving him only one staff member, Jordan exploded, accusing Watson of trying to undercut him.

The president-elect was finally forced to intervene. Close to Jordan and having reservations about Watson, he sided with Jordan. Despite strong urgings from Carter's close friend and adviser Kirbo, who regarded his law partner as far more mature and able than Jordan and thought that Watson should be appointed chief of staff, the president-elect announced on November 15 that Jordan would assume primary responsibility for presidential appointments, in effect stripping Watson of much of his power.

Still intending for Watson to play an important role in the administration, Carter named him as cabinet secretary and special assistant to the president for intergovernmental affairs. Neither of these roles had existed before. Although President Dwight D. Eisenhower had created the position of secretary of the cabinet and subsequent administrations had staff secretaries for the cabinet, their roles were essentially to prepare the agenda and maintain the minutes of cabinet meetings. In contrast, Carter intended Watson's role to be more one of coordination and follow-up. As he explained to his special assistant, he was to be a manager of the cabinet who would act and work on the president's behalf in executing foreign and domestic policy. As Watson later acknowledged, it soon became apparent that the National Security Council (NSC) would be responsible for coordinating and executing foreign policy.

Watson's more interesting responsibility was that of special assistant for intergovernmental affairs. Previous administrations had established similar positions, but although the president never articulated his intention clearly until after he left the presidency, he sought to establish a new type of federalism involving close collaboration between federal, state, and local officials in resolving problems and carrying out programs. In this regard, Carter was influenced by his experience as governor of Georgia when, on several occasions, he was unable to talk to the president or to an assistant to the president. "He saw a serious weakness in the placement of the people who had previously worked on intergovernmental affairs," Watson later remarked about Carter. "They had no authority to speak and act on behalf of the president, and so were unable to coordinate or get things done very effectively." Watson was given that authority. In fact, the president viewed Watson's two responsibilities as cabinet secretary and special assistant for intergovernmental affairs as interrelated. As he remarked in an interview after he left the White House, he wanted "one man to relate to all the Cabinet officers who were responsible for domestic policy and also for the same person to relate to all the Governors and mayors and let them know that anytime they called day and night they could reach Jack Watson, and anytime they wanted to they could reach me."

Watson was by no means satisfied with his new responsibilities or the overall staffing at the White House. For one thing, he had been effectively blindsided by Jordan. For another, the administration started off, in his opinion, with too many people having too much distributed authority for separate responsibilities. He thought the president should have appointed someone with more stature and respect on Capitol Hill than an unknown like FRANK MOORE, whom the president named to be his liaison with Congress. He believed that National Security Advisor ZBIGNIEW BRZEZINSKI should have played a less-visible role in the administration. He was also persuaded that the administration emphasized issues of government reorganization and process too much and issues of substance not enough.

Worse, in Watson's view, was the lack of clarity as to Jordan's role in the new administration—"the first among purported equals" is how he described Jordan. In Watson's view, somebody had to be in charge "unquestionably, unmistakably in charge." But Jordan had neither the interest nor the temperament to be that person, and Carter did not want someone cutting off the flow of paper and information to him. The lack of a chief of staff, Watson believed, was "a central, and in many respects a fatal, flaw." Sharing this view, Charles Kirbo later regretted that he not pushed the president-elect harder after the election to name Watson as his chief of staff.

Responsible for intergovernmental affairs, Watson tried to find synergies between that role and his other role as cabinet secretary. In 1978, for example, in his capacity as cabinet secretary, he decided to participate in the formulation of urban policy, organizing an Interagency Coordinating Council (IACC) whose responsibility was to expedite major domestic policy initiatives, beginning with urban policy. In his capacity as assistant for intergovernmental affairs, he assigned his deputy, Bruce Kirschenbaum, the lead responsibility for implementing and coordinating urban policy as well as a small community and rural counterpart. In both instances, he was to work closely with state and local officials.

Watson had limited success, however, in his effort to bring about interagency coordination or implementation of urban policy. On a case-by-case basis, he was able to respond in an expeditious manner to requests from governors, mayors, and other state and local officials. But he had far less success in bringing about interagency cooperation in the development of an urban policy. That was being done on the cabinet level, in the Oval Office, and by the domestic policy staff led by STUART EIZENSTAT. It was also being handled by another coordinating body, the Interagency Urban Policy Research Group (URPG), which the president had created to be the primary vehicle for coordination of federal reform efforts. In the end, the UPRG proved a failure, and in 1978 the president announced a new urban policy that rang hollow. Although it emphasized partnerships at all levels of government and between the public and private sectors, Carter provided no funds to implement the changes being recommended. He even lost interest in the implementation process.

At a minimum, Watson would have liked to mesh the implementation with the formulation of an urban policy. But he simply lacked the access to the president that Eizenstat, Jordan, or Press Secretary JODY POWELL enjoyed. Eizenstat was in charge of domestic policy, and he ignored questions of implementation because he was not concerned with them. This categorization of the staff was firm in Carter's mind; in Watson's view, the president simply did not understand how things worked in real operations.

Yet Watson remained in the White House with increased responsibilities. In summer 1979, as part of a reorganization of the administration, President Carter asked Hamilton Jordan to be chief of staff and Watson to assume responsibility for presidential appointments. By this time, even Jordan recognized the need for the president to have a buffer between the Oval Office and the senior staff who could coordinate and advise the president with respect to the stream of sometimes conflicting views that came to the Oval Office. As for Watson, he took charge of the Presidential Personnel Office and was responsible for vetting all presidential appointments, including cabinet and subcabinet positions. After Jordan went over to the Carter reelection campaign the next year, the president replaced him with Watson, giving him the position that he had always desired. The overwhelming consensus within the White House staff was that the high point of organizational effectiveness during the Carter presidency occurred in its last months during Watson's tenure as chief of staff.

Following Carter's defeat in 1980, Watson directed the transition of government from President Carter to President RONALD REAGAN. He then returned to his law firm of King and Spalding. In 1986, he consulted with senior members of the Brazilian government on the revision of Brazil's constitution. Six years later, he consulted with the president of Zambia on the constitutional and governmental organization issues facing the new, democratically elected Zambian government. The next year, he was part of a five-person U.S. delegation under the sponsorship of the National Committee for U.S.–China Relations. He has also served as the chief legal strategist for Monsanto (1998–2000). He resides in Atlanta.

Weddington, Sarah Ragle

(1945–) *special assistant for women's affairs, assistant to the president*

Best known as the attorney who argued the landmark abortion case of *Roe v. Wade* before the U.S. Supreme Court (1973), Sarah Weddington was President Jimmy Carter's special assistant for women's issues. After 1979, she also took on additional political responsibilities, reflected in a change in her title from special assistant to assistant and making her one of the president's senior staff.

Weddington was born Sarah Ragle on February 5, 1945, in Abilene, Texas. Her father was a Methodist minister serving several west Texas towns. After skipping two grades, she enrolled at age 16 in McMurry College, a small, Methodist-affiliated college in Abilene from which she graduated magna cum laude (B.A., 1965). Although she was discouraged by her dean from pursuing a law degree because, he said, it was not a "woman's profession," she applied to the University of Texas School of Law and was one of only five women to enroll in her class. Completing her degree in 27 months (J.D., 1967), she was unable to find a position with a law firm because most firms were not yet ready to accept women lawyers. Instead, she took a position with a former professor preparing a code of professional conduct for lawyers, which was eventually adopted by most bar associations.

Weddington also became active in various women's causes. When a group of her colleagues decided to file a lawsuit contesting the rights of states to prohibit the dissemination of information concerning birth control and abortions, they asked her to take the case because she was the only attorney who would do it for free. Weddington had had an illegal abortion in Mexico to end an unplanned pregnancy in 1967 so that she could finish law school and support her future husband, who was also a law student at Texas. Accepting the case, she filed a class-action suit on behalf of Jane Roe, a pseudonym for Norma McCorvey, a woman who had become pregnant as a result of an alleged rape and had sought an abortion. (In the 1990s, McCorvey recanted her story that she had been raped and came out against legalized abortions.) The case was filed against Henry Wade, the district attorney of Dallas County, for enforcing the law against abortions. Before *Roe v. Wade*, Weddington had never argued a case in a court of law. Her legal practice had been limited mainly to uncontested divorces and preparation of wills.

To Weddington's surprise, the Supreme Court agreed to hear the case. On January 22, 1973, the same day that former president Lyndon Johnson died, the Court overturned antiabortion statutes in Texas and throughout the country by a vote of seven to two. *Roe v. Wade* has since become one of the most well-known and hotly debated Court decisions in the nation's history. In a book Weddington

Assistant to the President Sarah Ragle Weddington, 1978 *(Jimmy Carter Library)*

later wrote about the case, *A Question of Choice* (1992), and in various discussions, she has stressed the point that in arguing *Roe v. Wade*, she was not championing abortion but arguing the principle that women—and not government—were the appropriate persons to make decisions about reproduction.

Roe v. Wade elevated Weddington into the national limelight and into state politics. Two years earlier, she had joined a coalition of other women to form the Texas Women's Political Caucus to elect more women to public office. Because law was a traditional route into politics and she was still one of a relatively few women to have a law degree, she was encouraged to run for office. In 1973, after a difficult primary contest, she was elected to the Texas state legislature. As a state legislator, she won approval of a number of measures intended to provide legal guarantees to women, including their right to apply for credit without their husbands' approval, prohibiting lawyers in rape cases from questioning rape victims about their prior sex lives, and preventing the dismissal of female teachers when they became pregnant.

In 1977, Weddington left Texas for Washington after she was offered the position of general counsel for the U.S. Department of Agriculture (USDA) by John White, a friend and prior state commissioner of agriculture whom Carter had appointed to be the number-two person at the Agriculture Department. She accepted the position even though she had some reservations about Carter because he opposed the federal funding of abortions. Only 32 years old, she was the first woman and youngest person to serve as general counsel of the USDA. She was in charge of more than 200 lawyers working for the agency, and the cases she handled ranged from those having to do with the environment to food safety issues.

In 1978, President Carter asked Weddington to come to the White House to serve as his special assistant for women's affairs. Although the president had hired a number of women to high positions, including three members of his cabinet, he was in trouble with his female constituency. Former congresswoman BELLA ABZUG, whom he had appointed as chair of the National Advisory Commission on the observance of International Women's year and later as cochair of the National Advisory Committee on Women, had become outspoken in her criticism of what she regarded as the "white-male dominated" White House. Abzug also reviled against the administration's opposition to funding abortions except when a women's life was threatened or a pregnancy was the result of rape or incest. More importantly, Carter had forced out of the White House MIDGE COSTANZA, who had been his special assistant for public liaison but had also been responsible for women's affairs. Her lopsided advocacy of liberal causes and groups had caused an uproar among the very groups Carter had sought to embrace.

The president had named ANNE WEXLER to be in charge of public liaison but wanted someone to be in charge of women's issues. The White House therefore solicited recommendations from various women's groups, who overwhelmingly recommended Weddington. President Carter offered her the position after she was interviewed by ROSALYNN CARTER and HAMILTON JORDAN.

As special assistant for women's affairs, Weddington devoted a considerable part of her time working to win approval of the Equal Rights Amendment, which Congress had passed in 1972 but which still had to be ratified by four more states. Her responsibilities, however, covered a wide spectrum of issues. She helped obtain federal funding, for example, for the first domestic violence center and made sure that women's special health needs were taken into account in formulating health-care policies. She participated in expanding opportunities for women in the military and in appointing women to a number of high-level positions, including future Supreme Court justice Ruth Bader Ginsburg to the federal district bench. She supervised the Inter-departmental Task Force on Women, which the president had established by executive order, and was responsible for getting federal agencies to coordinate their efforts on problems and issues concerning women. She also worked closely with Anne Wexler's office in arranging White House briefings for women's groups on matters than included not only women's issues but other matters such as the Strategic Arms Limitation Talks agreement (SALT II) and environmental and energy policy. In contrast to her predecessor, Midge Costanza, Weddington purposefully soft-pedaled the abortion issue, stating that her primary loyalty was to the president and that she supported his efforts to "push contraceptive availability and research." At the same time, she was embarrassed when Carter refused to let her testify at a congressional hearing on women's issues.

In 1979, when TIM KRAFT, one of the president's senior staff, was moved over to the Carter-Mondale Reelection Campaign, Weddington's position was elevated to assistant to the president, and she took over Kraft's role as liaison to the Democratic National Committee. Her additional duties involved such matters as assuming responsibility for briefings, correspondence, and referrals for state and local party leaders and activists, in addition to taking charge of the White House's Speaker's Bureau. As a member of the president's senior staff, she often met with the president in the Oval Office and traveled with him on Air Force One. As the 1980 campaign moved into high gear, she spent an increasing amount of personal leave time to work for the campaign, although women's issues continued to take up the major part of her time.

Following Carter's defeat in 1980, Weddington held a number of positions, including teaching at Wheaton College in Norton, Massachusetts (1981–83), and at the University of New Mexico School of Law (1982–83), and serving in Washington as a lobbyist for the state of Texas (1983–85). She lectures widely and maintains a law practice in Austin, Texas, where she is also an adjunct professor at the University of Texas–Austin's Center for Women's Studies.

Wexler, Anne Levy

(1930–) deputy undersecretary of commerce; head, Office of Public Liaison

In May 1978, Anne Wexler was named to head the Office of Public Liaison. In this role, she worked to involve interest groups and individuals in the making and implementation of policy and to develop and stimulate efforts to support presidential priorities. Her grassroots approach to winning nationwide support for the administration became a model for subsequent presidential administrations and made her one of the most widely respected members of the Carter administration. After leaving the White House, she went on to become one of the most powerful political lobbyists in Washington.

Wexler was born in New York City on February 10, 1930. A graduate of Skidmore College (B.A., 1951) and a person with a long career of helping to organize liberal causes, she figured prominently in Minnesota senator Eugene McCarthy's 1968 presidential campaign. She then went to work for the public advocacy organization Common Cause (1973–76) before accepting a position as Washington bureau chief and associate publisher of the magazine *Rolling Stone* during its muckraking heyday. In 1972, she was one of the top advisers to Senator GEORGE MCGOVERN in his campaign for the presidency. By 1974, she was being described in the media as "the most influential woman in American politics." That year, presidential candidate Jimmy Carter was able to recruit her for his campaign during the Democratic Party miniconvention in Kansas City. After Carter was elected president, Wexler accepted a position as deputy undersecretary of commerce. Her major responsibilities were to coordinate the department's programs and field operations and to direct the department's Office of State and Local Governments.

In 1978, Wexler moved over to the White House to head the Office of Public Liaison (OPL), replacing MIDGE COSTANZA, who had upset business groups because of her lack of tact and her liberal stance on most issues. Although Wexler was also one of the more liberal members of the administration, she had a long reputation of being able to bring disparate interests together; she had persuaded construction unions, for example, to support antiwar Democrats during the war in Vietnam.

Wexler took a different approach to her job than Costanza. In the first place, she focused the OPL almost exclusively on those policy issues before Congress that were of high priority for the president. Then she established outreach programs involving citizens at the grassroots level rather than appealing to Washington's institutional structure of congressional aides, lobbyists, influential power brokers, and prominent party spokesmen. She sought not only to activate key constituents but to convert or neutralize opponents to the administration's point of view. She practiced two basic maxims of politics: (1) deputize your supporters and (2) citizens appreciate access.

Instead of lawmakers objecting to interference on their turfs, they generally welcomed Wexler's intercession because, among other things, she involved them in her operations. She asked them for names of persons from their districts to invite to the outreach programs, thereby allowing them to demonstrate their access to the White House and to reward their constituents. Lawmakers also had a way of gauging and responding to opinion before having to make their own commitments. Because federal law prohibited the use of federal funds for lobbying purposes, the outreach programs were always presented as educational in purpose, adding a cloak of legitimacy, for both lawmakers and the White House, to what might otherwise have been regarded as simple advocacy.

Wexler avoided becoming liaison for certain special groups or a single point of view. At the same time, she made certain in her outreach sessions to involve administration officials who could make the strongest arguments in support of the White House's position. She engaged National Security Advisor ZBIGNIEW BREZINZSKI, for example, to make the argument in support of the Strategic Arms Limitation Talks treaty (SALT II) precisely because she knew his reputation as a hard-liner toward the Soviet Union would make his advocacy of an arms-limitation agreement with the Kremlin all the more compelling to those who believed the SALT agreement might weaken the United States.

In addition to her other responsibilities, Wexler organized special events for the White House, such as the state dinner for Chinese leader DENG XIAOPING during his visit at the end of January 1979. Most political observers agreed that Wexler enjoyed considerable success in doing what the president had promised to do before taking office but had failed to do well in his first year as president—take his case to the American public. Yet she did so without the threat of going over the head of Congress, as Carter had told Speaker of the House TIP O'NEILL he would do if necessary.

Wexler was not immune, however, to the criticism that developed against the administration in the last two years of the Carter presidency. Many Christian fundamentalists, who felt betrayed by the administration, focused their attention on Wexler, whom they labeled "a pro-abortionist feminist." Her small staff and lack of clearly defined responsibilities also limited the effectiveness of her office. After Carter reshuffled his cabinet in 1979 following his so-called malaise speech of July 1979, her responsibilities were more clearly defined and she was given an increased range of responsibilities. Still, she was never satisfied that she had the president's ear or that she was achieving her purpose within the administration. Reflecting in 2003 about what had gone wrong in the Carter administration, she remarked that the president "never re-established the rapport he had with the American people in 1976. ... I think he didn't listen, and he really didn't get it."

After leaving the White House in 1981, Wexler established her own lobbying firm, the Wexler Group. Over the next two decades, she was able to build it into one of the most successful firms in Washington. In 2004, it was purchased by WPP Group PLC, a publicly traded advertising and public-relations company. In 1992, Wexler also served as a member of President-elect Clinton's transition team. In 1998, *Washington* magazine named her as one of the city's most influential lobbyists in a world, it remarked, "still dominated by men." In 2004, Wexler was again listed in a survey conducted by *The Hill* as among the top lobbyists in Washington. She was also instrumental in promoting a free-trade agreement with Australia, for which she was made an honorary member of the Order of Australia in 2002.

Wexler serves as a director of several investment and financial firms and is a member of the Council of Foreign Relations. She is married to Dr. Joseph Duffey, also a well-known and respected figure in Washington circles.

White, Byron Raymond

(1917–2002) *associate justice, U.S. Supreme Court*

Nominated to the U.S. Supreme Court by President John F. Kennedy in 1962, Byron White epitomized the appellation of "the best and the brightest" often given to Kennedy appointees. A junior member of Phi Beta Kappa and a Rhodes Scholar, a star college athlete and outstanding professional football player, first in his class at Yale Law School and the first law clerk of the Supreme Court to be appointed a justice, White was always modest, diffident, and private. Though he was one of the youngest members ever appointed to the Supreme Court and had no judicial experience, his appointment was greeted enthusiastically in the press and on Capitol Hill. Many commentators expected that his decisions would reflect the generally liberal views of the Warren Court. Others anticipated that he would become one of the Court's great justices alongside Oliver Wendell Holmes, Louis Brandeis, Benjamin Cardozo, and Felix Frankfurter.

When White retired from the court in 1993, though, the consensus was that he had not achieved the greatness expected of him at the time of his appointment. His decisions seemed ideologically inconsistent, and his written opinions were unexceptional, His defenders argued that this was because he was pragmatic, abjured legal theory, believed in judicial restraint, and insisted on attention to the historical context of the cases on which he had to render a decision. Certainly this seemed to be applicable to the cases on which he rendered verdicts during the Carter presidency.

White was born on June 8, 1917, in Fort Collins, Colorado, but grew up in Wellington, a small farming town in northern Colorado where he spent summers working in the region's sugar-beet fields. Although neither of his parents had graduated from high school, White excelled academically and athletically, winning an academic scholarship to the University of Colorado, where he made all-American on the football field, starred in basketball and baseball, and graduated with one of the highest academic averages in the university's history. He was also given the nickname Whizzer (which he hated) by a sportswriter because of his speed on the field. When he graduated from Colorado with a bachelor's degree in economics (B.S., 1938), he had to choose between a Rhodes scholarship to attend Oxford University or playing professional football for the Pittsburgh Pirates (later Steelers). He chose the latter, receiving the highest salary ever paid to a National Football League (NFL) player at the time.

White was able to defer the Rhodes scholarship to spring 1939 while he played professional football, leading the National Football League in rushing. At Oxford, he studied law and met John F. Kennedy, whose father was then U.S. ambassador to Great Britain. With the outbreak of war in Europe in 1939, White's studies at Oxford were cut short. Returning to the United States, he attended Yale Law School, won the Edgar Cullen Award for receiving the highest grades of the freshman class, and was offered a coveted position on the *Law Review*. But he declined it in order to play two more seasons with the Detroit Lions.

After the Japanese bombing of Pearl Harbor in December 1941, White gave up his football career and delayed finishing law school to enlist in the navy, where he served as an intelligence officer in the South Pacific, winning two bronze stars for bravery. He also prepared the recommendation for a commendation for P-T boat commander John F. Kennedy.

Following the war, White returned to Yale Law School, graduating magna cum laude (LL. B., 1946), and then accepted a clerkship with Supreme Court justice Fred Vinson. He was also approached by the Colorado State Democratic Party about the possibility of running for governor of Colorado. He turned down those who approached him, stating that he did not think being a professional football player qualified him to be governor.

While clerking for Vinson in Washington, White became reacquainted with Congressman Kennedy. Instead of taking a lucrative position with a Washington law firm after completing his clerkship at the Supreme Court, he returned to Denver to open his own law practice specializing in antitrust, bankruptcy, and litigation. In 1959, after Kennedy announced his candidacy for the presidency, White delivered most of the Colorado delegation for Kennedy at the Democratic Convention and then led the National Citizens for Kennedy campaign. He was rewarded for his effort by being appointed deputy attorney general, the second ranking spot in the Department of Justice. As deputy attorney general, he personally took charge of 400 federal marshals sent to Alabama to protect the Freedom Riders whose lives had been endangered in May 1961 by opponents of the Civil Rights movement. In Alabama, he remained steely while listening to a 45-minute diatribe against the Kennedy administration by the state's governor, John Patterson.

When a vacancy was created in the Supreme Court in early 1962 by the resignation of Justice Charles Whittaker, Kennedy nominated White to fill the seat, notwithstanding White's lack of judicial experience. At age 44, White was the youngest man to date to be named to the Supreme Court. Widely expected to be another strong liberal voice on the Warren Court, he instead became a frequent dissenter. Essentially he adopted a liberal view on issues having to do with race but a distinctly conservative one on matters having to do with criminal procedures. Guiding his decisions was a belief that the Court needed to protect the constitutional rights of those persons or groups unable to protect themselves (such as African Americans in the South). This was coupled, however, with the conviction that laws protecting the rights of citizens should trump laws protecting the rights of criminals. Police behavior should, for example, be evaluated in terms of practical considerations rather than on the basis of dogmatic presumptions.

In the famous case of *Miranda v. Arizona* (1966), White wrote a blistering dissent attacking the majority view that the police had violated the rights of the plaintiff by not warning him of his legal rights before interrogating him. "The real concern," he wrote in his dissent, "is not the unfortunate consequences of this new decision on the criminal law as an abstract, disembodied series of authoritative proscriptions, but the impact on those who rely on the public authority for protection and who without it can only engage in violent self-help." Fundamental to this approach to the law was an analytical bent of mind, a strong sense of pragmatism, a lack of interest in abstract theory, and a preference for statutory authority over judicial interpretation.

In First Amendment cases, White also tended to favor societal interests over freedom of the press and argued for judicial deferment to statutory authority. A celebrity most of his adult life who sought to protect his privacy, he distrusted the power of the media and was leery of journalistic privilege. Although he voted with the majority in 1971 to deny a government request for an injunction to halt newspaper publication of the Pentagon Papers, he also wrote a majority decision the same year denying the First Amendment right of journalists to withhold testimony from a grand jury obtained from confidential sources.

In 1969, Earl Warren resigned as chief justice of the Supreme Court, and in the 1970s a more conservative Court emerged, headed by WARREN BURGER, whom President RICHARD NIXON had appointed as chief justice. In the Burger Court, White often found himself in the position of swing vote in close decisions, siding frequently with the more conservative rather than with the more liberal justices. In the Court's first landmark case, *Roe v. Wade* (1973), involving the legal right of women to have abortions, White was only one of two dissenters opposing the right of abortion, a position he held in subsequent cases. "I find nothing in the language or history of the Constitution to support the Court's judgment [in favor of the right of women to have abortions]," he wrote. "This issue, for the most part, should be left with the people and to the political processes the people have devised to govern their affairs." He had confidence in the democratic process and in elected public officials.

In what legal scholars believe to have been the most important Supreme Court case decided during the Carter presidency, *Regents of the University of California v. Bakke* (1978), involving the issues of racial quotas and affirmative action in admitting students to the University of California–Davis School of Medicine, White went so far as to approve racial quotas in the admissions process. In doing so, however, he showed again his preference for legislative and administrative authority and skirted almost entirely the constitutional issues involved in the case. "Davis may set this quota and fill it with qualified Negroes," he wrote. "I'll rely on the legislative and executive view of what's permissible under the Fourteenth Amendment."

In a series of cases on the environment that came before the Supreme Court during the Carter administration, White continued to rely heavily on statutory authority rather than constitutional interpretation in making his decisions. But he found himself, for the most part, siding with environmentalists. In almost all cases involving land policy, he favored federal over state authority, including decisions on submerged lands, school land, and mining on federal land. In *United States v. New Mexico*

(1978), he joined the dissenters in opposing the Court's rejection of federal water claims to sustain fish and wild animals in national forests. In *California v. United States* (1978), he wrote a spirited dissent against the Court's decision supporting states' rights in a Reclamation Act conflict.

In two First Amendment cases during the Carter presidency, White reasserted his reservations about journalistic privilege. In *Zurcher v. Stanford Daily* (1978), he argued for the majority that the First Amendment did not protect the press against search warrants. In *Herbert v. Lando* (1979), he stated again for the majority that the First Amendment did not protect journalists against wide-ranging discovery demands. The ruling on *Zurcher* led to the enactment of a 1980 federal law restricting, but not eliminating, the exercise of search warrants on news organizations.

White served on the Supreme Court for 12 more years after Jimmy Carter left office in 1981, not retiring until 1993, after having been on the Court for 31 years. During that period, he wrote an opinion upholding Georgia's antisodomy law; took a middle course on the death penalty, narrowly circumscribing the circumstances under which capital punishment could be administered; remained a consistent opponent of a woman's right to abortions; took a more narrow view of affirmative action that he had in the *Bakke* case; and dissented strongly from decisions upholding presidential immunity and Congress's legislative veto. Although he never attracted much of a following among either conservatives or liberals in having a grand ideological vision for the Court, he remained true to his belief in judicial restraint. Judges, he observed, had "an exaggerated view of their roles in [the nation's] polity." He also believed that cases before him had to be considered on their own merits rather than on some abstract theory of the law. Each case before the Court, he argued, presented another "moment when you stand face to face with doing."

By the time White stepped down from the Court, he had written more opinions than any justice in Supreme Court history. In character with his modesty and desire for privacy, he gave up his offices in the Court even though it was common practice for retired justices to retain their offices. He died on April 15, 2002, in Denver of complications from pneumonia at age 84.

Woodcock, Leonard Freel

(1911–2001) *chief of U.S. liaison office in Beijing, U.S. ambassador to the People's Republic of China*

The first U.S. ambassador to the People's Republic of China (PRC, or Communist China) since the end of the Chinese Revolution in 1949, Leonard Woodcock had been a labor leader and president of the United Auto Workers (UAW) before becoming a diplomat during the Carter administration. Without any diplomatic training or experience, he was an unusual choice to be U.S. representative to one of the world's great powers and largest nation in terms of population. Yet his experience in the labor movement and his ability as a negotiator prepared him well for his new assignment. By most accounts, he carried out his responsibilities in the PRC with great skill.

The son of a machine worker who was a British citizen, Woodcock was born in Providence, Rhode Island, on February 15, 1911. In 1914, his family moved to Germany where his father, Ernest, installed machinery for his Rhode Island employer. When World War I broke out a few months later, Ernest was interned in Germany as a British citizen, although Leonard and rest of his family were allowed to flee to England. They remained there for a few years after Ernest was reunited with the family. Returning to the United States in 1926, they settled in Detroit, Michigan, where Ernest became active in the Mechanical Educational Society of America, the predecessor to the UAW. Because of his union activities, he was blacklisted during the 1930s.

Although Leonard Woodcock attended Detroit City College (now Wayne State University) for two years, he had to leave to work during the Depression. While working 12 hours a day, seven days a week, earning 35 cents an hour assembling machines, Woodcock began his career as a labor organizer, helping to unionize the workers in his plant as part of the American Federation of Labor (AFL). He also met Walter Reuther, the legendary leader of the UAW.

Intelligent, ambitious, and hard-working, Woodcock worked his way up through union ranks as Reuther's protégé. In 1938, he joined the UAW as a staff organizer. After Reuther became president of the UAW in 1946, he appointed Woodcock his administrative assistant. In 1955, Woodcock was elected an international vice president of the union in charge of its General Motors and aerospace departments; however, his career remained at a standstill until 1970, when Reuther died in a plane crash. Following a brief but fierce campaign, the UAW's executive board chose Woodcock over Douglas Fraser, the head of the Chrysler and skilled trades division, as the UAW's new president by a vote of 13 to 12. Woodcock now headed the nation's second largest union, with 1.5 million members.

Shortly after becoming UAW president, Woodcock led his workers in a bitter 67-day strike against General Motors. He proved to be an adept and tough negotiator. When the strike ended, he had secured one of the richest contracts in the history of organized labor, including substantial wage increases, automatic cost-of-living adjustments without any ceiling, a dental plan, and a provision for a monthly pension of $500 after 30 years of service (at first beginning at age 58 but changed in a subsequent contract to "30-and-out" regardless of age).

Although Woodcock approached the strike as a militant unionist, he had moderated his views considerably since the 1930s, when he and Reuther had been members of the Socialist Party. Like other labor leaders, he became part of the mainstream of American politics, participating in the civil rights marches of the 1960s and working actively on behalf of the Democratic Party. During the 1972 presidential campaign, the UAW initially supported Maine senator EDMUND MUSKIE for the Democratic presidential nomination but then backed South Dakota senator GEORGE MCGOVERN at the party's national convention. During the campaign, Woodcock, who had been briefly considered by McGovern as his possible running mate, criticized AFL-CIO President GEORGE MEANY for calling McGovern "an apologist for the Communist world."

Embarrassed that Alabama governor GEORGE WALLACE had won the 1972 Michigan primary, the UAW decided to back Georgia's moderate former governor, Jimmy Carter, in the 1976 campaign as a way of keeping down Wallace's primary vote, even though Carter was from a "right-to-work" state. Woodcock also knew Carter as a fellow member of the Trilateral Commission, which banker DAVID ROCKEFELLER had established in 1973 to bring together highly influential figures from North America, Europe, and Japan to promote closer cooperation among the world's major industrial powers.

UAW locals in Iowa campaigned on behalf of Carter in the Iowa caucuses, helping him to carry the caucuses and giving him his first national exposure as a serious candidate for the Democratic nomination. In February 1976, Woodcock helped dissuade one of Carter's liberal challengers, Representative MORRIS

UDALL, from entering the March Florida primary by informing the Arizona congressman that his union intended to back Carter in that state in order to beat Wallace. Woodcock, whose support of Carter had become as much personal as organizational, spent a day campaigning with the former Georgia governor in Florida. In May, he formally endorsed Carter, giving him badly needed liberal credentials. Woodcock was embarrassed, however, when, despite his endorsement Carter barely beat Udall, in the Michigan primary, receiving only 44 percent to Udall's 43 percent.

Following Carter's nomination and election, Woodcock reported to the UAW in early 1977 that "we are moving from a period of depression, despair and despondency into a time of renewed hope." Shortly thereafter, he announced his intention not to seek a new term as president of the UAW. About the same time, President Carter asked him to lead a mission to Vietnam and Laos in order in order to determine the fate of Americans declared missing in action (MIA) during the Vietnam War and to return the recently recovered remains of 12 MIAs. In May 1977, Carter named Woodcock to be the chief of the United States Liaison Office in Beijing, succeeding GEORGE HERBERT WALKER BUSH. "They'll probably throw me out after six months," Woodcock told a friend, referring to his lack of experience.

Woodcock's strong support for Carter when he was just beginning his seemingly quixotic race for the White House was undoubtedly an important reason why the president appointed him to his new position (and career). Carter, however, offered other, equally valid, reasons: "I admired Leonard personally, and knew him to be quiet but forceful, a man whose age, experience, and demeanor would be an advantage in dealing with the Chinese leaders. Further, my choice of a person of his stature in the American community was a clear signal to the Chinese that we wanted closer relations."

Before Woodcock left for Beijing in July, the president met with him and Secretary of State CYRUS VANCE at the White House. Carter told Woodcock that while he wanted to normalize relations with the PRC, he was not yet ready to go that far. The United States, he said, could not abandon its commitment to Taiwan, with whom it had a mutual-defense treaty. This, however, was the rub. Although the Beijing government was anxious to establish formal diplomatic relations, it insisted as preconditions that the United States nullify its defense treaty with Taiwan, stop selling arms to that country, and withdraw its forces from the island. As a matter of principle and for domestic political reasons, the president was unwilling to stop the sale of defensive weapons or all trade to Taiwan. He was prepared to abrogate the mutual-defense treaty, but only after giving one year's notice, as the agreement provided. He furthermore insisted that the dispute between mainland China and Taiwan be resolved peacefully.

Anticipating the issues the Beijing government would raise before agreeing to normalization of relations and realizing that he would face considerable domestic opposition over the future status of Taiwan, Carter instructed Woodcock to proceed incrementally, resolving one problem before proceeding to the next. But Woodcock found the process exasperatingly slow, a fact confirmed by Secretary of State Vance when he visited China in August. For a time, negotiations even came to a complete standstill. Although the former union leader sent signals to the Chinese that the United States wanted to proceed with talks, they responded with silence.

It took developments in southeast Asia—including China's determination to prevent Vietnam's conquest of Kampuchea (Cambodia) and growing concern about the Soviet military threat along the Amur River bordering China and the Soviet Union—to end the impasse in the talks. This was followed by long months of intense discussions, a trip to China in May 1978 by National Security Advisor ZBIGNIEW BRZEZINSKI (which Woodcock had opposed), and a series of presentations by Woodcock on the American position on normalization, until an agreement was finally reached, reestablishing relations between Beijing and Washington. In December 1978, the president was able to announce the resumption of full diplomatic ties between the two countries and the forthcoming visit of China's deputy prime minister, DENG XIAOPING, to the United States. Furthermore, China had accepted the administration's insistence on giving one year's notice before abrogating its defense pact with Taiwan and on the continuation of some military sales to the Taiwanese government after the treaty expired.

In his memoirs, Secretary of State Vance gave high marks to Woodcock for his skill as a negotiator with the Chinese: "The decision to use Woodcock as negotiator instead of undertaking highly publicized shuttle diplomacy proved a sound one. [He] proved an instinctive and brilliant diplomat. He had a photographic memory, discretion, and a verbal precision critical in these negotiations. We all came to rely on his wisdom."

When Carter appointed Woodcock to head the U.S. liaison office in Beijing, he said he also wanted him to be the nation's first ambassador to the PRC. In January 1979, the president sent his nomination of Woodcock to the Senate, which easily passed by a vote of 82 to 9. As ambassador, Woodcock negotiated a series of agreements with China that nourished the new relationship between Beijing and Washington. Among them were a civil-aviation agreement that established direct flights between China and the United States, a maritime agreement that opened the ports of both to the ships of the other, and a consular agreement that increased the number of American consulates in China from two to five.

In 1981, following the accession of RONALD REAGAN as president, Woodcock resigned as ambassador to China and began teaching political science at the University of Michigan at Ann Arbor as an adjunct professor. Continuing his involvement in U.S.–China relations for the next 20 years, he played the role of educator, teaching both sides the realities and complexities of their two very different societies and political systems. In 1989, just five months after the Chinese army's massacre of student protestors in Tiananmen Square, Woodcock traveled to Beijing in a successful effort to obtain an exit visa for the human-rights leader Fang Lizhi, who had taken sanctuary at the U.S. embassy. He also worked throughout the 1990s to obtain most-favored nation (MFN) status for China. In 1992, he helped arrange the first sale of U.S. automobiles and trucks to China.

Woodcock died at his home in Ann Arbor, Michigan on January 16, 2001, of pulmonary complications. He was 89 years old.

Wright, Jim

(James Claude Wright, Jr.)
(1922–) *member of the House of Representatives, House majority leader*

Majority leader during Jimmy Carter's presidency, Jim Wright of Texas was elected to that position in 1976 over two other more liberal Democrats, PHILLIP BURTON (Calif.) and RICHARD BOLLING (Mo.) in a race in which Wright was the decided underdog. His modest demeanor, charm, and moderate voting record helped to get him elected to the leadership post and then to succeed Speaker of the House TIP O'NEILL following the Speaker's retirement from Congress in 1986. But they also masked a hot temper and driving ambition that proved his undoing just three years later. Like other House and Senate leaders, Wright had serious differences with the Carter administration. He later blamed what he considered the failure of the Carter presidency on the fact that the president "thought too small." But his differences with Jimmy Carter went deeper than that.

Born James Claude Wright, Jr., in Fort Worth, Texas, on December 22, 1922, Wright attended Weatherford College and the University of Texas, where he became embroiled in defending free speech and helping to organize a group of young liberals. A bright student who had skipped several grades before entering college, he never completed a degree. On December 8, 1941, the day after the Japanese attack on Pearl Harbor, he enlisted in the U.S. Army Air Corps; he was commissioned an officer in 1942. During the war, he flew as a navigator on a bomber in the South Pacific and earned a Distinguished Flying Cross.

After the war, Wright made his home in Weatherford, Texas, near Fort Worth, and bought into a successful family business that his father had started, organizing trade shows and exhibits for small-town businessmen. But he had a passion for politics. Even as a boy, Wright thought seriously of becoming president of the United States; his high school yearbook predicted that he would be a member of Congress in 1955. He referred later to politics as a way of achieving what he deemed his "messianic impulse." He was also influenced by his father, a traveling salesman who was an egalitarian and economic populist. In one of several towns in Texas and Oklahoma where Wright lived while growing up, his father even argued that all schoolchildren should be made to wear jeans since poorer children would not feel inferior to their wealthier classmates who wore better clothes. For Wright, therefore, politics was a means of achieving economic and social goals as well as satisfying personal ambition.

As a member of the state legislature (1947–49), Wright became part of a group of Democrats whose liberal leanings earned them the derisive label "the Russian Embassy." Yet although a liberal by southern standards, Wright was hardly a liberal by national standards. In 1948, when he realized he might lose his race for reelection, he appealed to the voters along traditional segregationist lines. "I believe in the Southern tradition of segregation and have strongly resisted any and all efforts to destroy it," he stated in an advertisement in a local newspaper. He lost the election anyway. After his defeat in 1948, he became cautious in his public positions and zealously sensitive to the needs of his former constituents.

In 1950, Wright was elected mayor of Weatherford, a position he held until 1954, when he won election to the U.S. House of Representatives, defeating a reactionary Democratic incumbent, Wingate Lucas, who had been a burr to Speaker of the House Sam Rayburn. Anxious to please his constituents and his elders on the Texas delegation, Wright took a position on the Public Works Committee, where he remained for the next 22 years. During this time, he became known for his ability to funnel federal dollars to his home town. (A 1979 study found that his district got the highest "return" per tax dollar of any in the country.)

Balancing his moderate views on most national political issues with the need to win reelection at home, Wright was one of only a few southerners who refused to sign the Southern Manifesto denouncing the 1954 Supreme Court decision on integration. Nevertheless, he still held that segregation could be maintained without discrimination. In the 1950s, he voted for President Dwight Eisenhower's national highway program. In the 1960s, he supported most of the programs of John F. Kennedy's New Frontier and Lyndon Johnson's Great Society, but he voted against the landmark Civil Rights Act of 1964. In 1968, he traveled the country on behalf of HUBERT HUMPHREY's campaign for president. In a district that was home to some of the nation's largest defense contractors, though, he remained a staunch supporter of the war in Vietnam. Not until the 1970s, when he became majority leader, did he back civil rights initiatives, and as late as 1973, he was in the minority when he voted against a resolution to end the bombing in Indochina.

Ambitious for power, Wright ran unsuccessfully in 1961 for the Senate seat formerly held by Vice President Lyndon Johnson. When he failed to obtain the cabinet position or ambassadorship that he had requested from Johnson, he thought about retiring from politics. In 1966, he again considered running for the Senate but decided he would not be able to raise enough money to run an effective campaign. Abandoning his presidential ambitions, Wright devoted himself to building his power in the House, where he was widely known for his passionate and compelling oratory. According to the syndicated columnist JACK ANDERSON, he had the ability to "charm the indignation out of the most righteous." As a result, he was frequently asked to speak at fund-raising and campaign events by his colleagues and other office seekers. He made it policy to accept as many of these invitations as possible. He also seized an opportunity in 1969 to be one of four deputy whips in the House.

In 1976, when the Democrats had to choose a new majority leader to replace Tip O'Neill, Wright saw an opportunity to elevate himself to the second leadership position in the House. A cagey politician, he allowed himself to be "drafted" for the position by those Democrats who were not keen on either of the two major contenders for the position, Phil Burton of California or Dick Bolling of Missouri. The two liberals were primarily responsible for changes in the House rules that had democratized much of the previous seniority system in the House. They also enjoyed stronger constituencies in the House than Wright, whose past voting record on the war and civil rights still made him suspect among liberals. Burton and Bolling, however, were archenemies whose arrogance and abrasiveness had rubbed many lawmakers the wrong way. Through a voting process that eliminated the candidate with the least votes after each ballot, Wright was able to get more votes than Bolling and then, with the quiet support of O'Neill, who did not want Burton as his chief aide, to defeat Burton by one vote for the position of majority leader. Analysis of the election later showed that Wright had won because lawmakers liked him personally, and he had courted his colleagues over the years by helping to fund their pet projects through his seniority on the Public Works Committee. Further, he was the only candidate from the South, and since 1931 there had always been at least one southerner in the House's top leadership positions.

Once Wright was elected, he named DANIEL ROSTENKOWSKI (Ill.), who had played a decisive role in rounding up votes for him, as his chief deputy whip. He also began building bridges with those who had opposed him. He knew that Burton was considering challenging him for majority leader in 1978, and he was also preparing for the time when O'Neill, who was 10 years older than he, would retire from Congress.

Throughout the Carter administration, Wright's relations with the president were strained. As soon as Carter took office, Wright clashed with him over a number of water projects that the president wanted cut from the budget. For Carter, these projects amounted to wasteful pork; for Wright, they represented an investment in America's future (as well as political power for himself). The president wanted to balance the budget; the majority leader supported that goal more than House Speaker O'Neill or other Democratic leaders, but not at the expense of projects and programs he wanted. "I was talking about balancing the budget," Carter recalled about a meeting he had with the Democratic leadership in Plains after the election to deal with economic issues. "I mean it was anathema to them to be talking about balancing the budget. That wasn't something that a Democratic president was supposed to do."

The president's opposition to water projects and other public works Wright favored continued to be a bone of contention between the two men throughout Carter's presidency. In 1978, Wright even joined forces with Tip O'Neill in an ultimately unsuccessful attempt to override the president's veto of a water-projects measure Congress had passed. The veto was intended by the White House to be a message to Congress that Carter was still a strong president prepared to do battle with the House and Senate to cut spending. It was uncommon, but not extraordinary, for a president to veto a measure that the majority of his own party supported. It was extraordinary for the party's house leadership to try to override that veto. The White House also angered Wright when it gave him only one part-time position with which to reward his supporters when he asked for three positions.

Wright's position with respect to the president was by no means entirely one-sided. At the meeting in Plains between the president and the Democratic leadership after the election, Wright played a prominent role in trying to develop an economic-stimulus program that did not overstimulate the economy. Despite the fact that he was beholden politically to the oil and gas industry in Texas, he worked closely with Speaker O'Neill in 1977 to get an energy program through Congress that would decrease the nation's dependence on foreign oil. He also played a key role in the development of the president's second energy program in 1979, in particular the proposal to establish a Synthetic Fuel Corporation with authority to spend up to $88 billion over the next 10 years developing alternative energy sources. He voted in favor of the Panama Canal Treaties and against the B-1 bomber even though these were unpopular positions in his district, assuring the toughest reelection fight of his congressional career in 1980.

Generally, though, Wright found Carter arrogant and self-righteous and a person with whom it was difficult to work. "You know, even when you are working together on a project, he makes you feel somehow or another that everything you are doing is dirty," he remarked about the president to his colleagues. Like other Democratic leaders who had regular Tuesday breakfasts with the president, he also resented the fact that Carter overwhelmed them with a list of his priorities while seeming to forget that Congress had its own agenda. As Carter's close friend and former director of the Office of Management and Budget, BERT LANCE, later wrote, "Jimmy was working on what was important to him, but he was unwilling to concede that Congress was going to work on what was important to Congress."

In 1980, Wright joined with several other congressional leaders, including O'Neill, House Majority Whip JOHN BRADEMAS (Ind.), and Senate Majority Whip ALAN CRANSTON (Calif.) in refusing to endorse Carter for the Democratic presidential nomination in 1980. Instead, they took the position that they would support whoever was the Democratic nominee. This left open the possibility (unlikely in Wright's case) that they might support EDWARD KENNEDY (Mass.) for the Democratic nomination.

Wright remained majority leader until 1986, when Tip O'Neill decided to retire from Congress, and he was easily chosen to replace O'Neill as Speaker of the House. To make certain that he would be selected for the position, he moved to the left on a few key issues during RONALD REAGAN's presidency, such as voting against the MX missile, a balanced-budget amendment, aid to the contras fighting the Sandinistas in Nicaragua, and a measure to block federal funding for abortions in the District of Columbia. He also provided funds from his personal political action committee to his colleagues and campaigned heavily on their behalf. Furthermore, he led the floor debate on the major budget and tax fights of the previous five years. But he still remained more conservative than most members of his party, often voting with a coalition of Republicans and southern conservative Democrats. Several polls taken in 1981 indicated that Wright voted more than 60 percent of the time with this coalition.

Wright was generally considered an effective House Speaker who expanded the traditional role of that position by engaging, at President Reagan's request, in a peace-seeking effort in Central America that carried into the presidency of GEORGE HERBERT WALKER BUSH. In 1988, however, he became the target of a House Ethics Committee probe after he published a short book, *Reflections of a Public Man*. The book was sold only in bulk to special interests, such as the Teamsters Union and the National Association of Realtors. Wright received royalties of 55 percent of the book's cover price of $5.95, far more than the 10 percent common to authors in the publishing industry. Even before the book's publication, charges had also been made against him by Republicans, led by Newt Gingrich (Ga.), that Wright had used his office for personal gain and exerted improper influence on behalf of his constituents.

In early 1989, the House Ethics Committee found that sales of *Reflections of a Public Man*, which had been put together by one of Wright's aids and was largely a compilation of views the speaker had expressed in print earlier, was an attempt on Wright's part to earn speaking fees in excess of the allowed maximum. The committee also found that Wright's wife Betty had been put on a padded payroll to avoid limits on gifts. Faced with these findings, Wright stepped down as Speaker of the House in June 1989 and resigned from Congress at the end of the month.

After leaving the House, Wright went to work as a senior political consultant to American Income Life Insurance Company. He also served as a distinguished lecturer at Texas Christian University, where he taught a course on "Congress and the Presidents." He lives in Fort Worth, Texas.

Young, Andrew Jackson, Jr.
(1932–) *ambassador to the United Nations*

A leader of the Civil Rights movement in the 1960s and a congressman in the 1970s, Andrew Jackson Young, Jr., was the most prominent African American in the Carter administration. His appointment as U.S. ambassador to the United Nations was popular in the United States and abroad. He became increasingly controversial, however, particularly among right-wing groups in the United States, as a result of his outspoken views on human rights, racism, and national self-determination.

Born on March 12, 1932, Young grew up in a middle-class African-American home in New Orleans. His mother was a schoolteacher and his father a dentist who hoped his son would follow in his profession. Unlike most southern blacks, Young's parents were practicing Congregationalists rather than Southern Baptists. This opened more opportunities for Andrew to interact with northern whites than most others of his race in the South, and it was one reason why he proved so valuable in the Civil Rights movement as an intermediary between blacks and whites.

After a year at Dillard University in New Orleans, Young decided to transfer to Howard University in Washington, D.C., where he graduated with a major in biology (B.S., 1951). While a student, he attended a summer conference sponsored by the Congregationalist Church at Kings Mountain, North Carolina. There he began to think seriously about spiritual matters and his relationship with God. A short time later, he attended another retreat sponsored by the National Council of Churches, where he became interested in the nonviolent teachings of Mohandas Gandhi and reflected further on his spiritual beliefs. Only one of two African Americans at the retreat, he later remarked that he had "never before met any white people whose personal faith made a difference in their actions on the question of race." Over the objections of his father, Young decided to become a minister. After graduating from Hartford Theological Seminary in Connecticut (B.D., 1955), he was ordained a minister in the United Church of Christ.

Young's ministry took him to several black churches in the South, but in 1957 he moved to New York City, where he worked for the National Council of Churches (NCC) as associate director of its Youth Department. As part of his responsibilities, Young was involved with the international missions of the NCC's constituent churches, including a program to combat international racism and to aid the liberation movements in Zimbabwe and South

Andrew Jackson Young is sworn in as U.S. ambassador to the United Nations, 1977. *(Jimmy Carter Library)*

Africa. He even attended occasional briefing meetings between NCC staffers and Secretary of State John Foster Dulles. His experience with the NCC may have influenced his later conviction as a diplomat that religion and diplomacy were entwined. "I learned to transcend my southern roots and prejudices," he later remarked, "and see religion as a global force."

Andrew and his wife Jean, whom he had married in 1954, loved the excitement and cosmopolitanism of the city, but they were drawn back to their roots by the developing nonviolent Civil Rights movement in the South, led by Dr. Martin Luther King, Jr. They moved to Atlanta in 1961, just as sit-in demonstrations at all-white lunch counters throughout the South by mostly black college students touched off a half-dozen years of often bloody confrontations between civil rights workers seeking the end of segregation in the South and white southerners trying to hold onto a racially separatist and decidedly unequal society. In Atlanta, Young headed a black voter-registration effort sponsored by the United Church of Christ and shortly thereafter went to work for the Southern Christian Leadership Conference (SCLC) headed by King.

Although Young had met the civil rights leader in Ghana in 1957, when both men had attended the new country's independence celebration, King later confessed to having no recollection of that meeting. Nevertheless, Young quickly became one of King's closest lieutenants, serving as an intermediary between the SCLC leader and the white power structure in such places as Albany, Georgia, in 1962; Birmingham, Alabama, in 1963; and Selma, Alabama, in 1965. He also helped to organize and lead demonstrations in these major battle grounds of the Civil Rights movement. In 1964, King appointed Young as the new executive director of the SCLC. That same year, Young was beaten by segregationists in the historic city of St. Augustine while taking part in demonstrations to desegregate the city.

In the four years that followed, Young joined King in extending the Civil Rights movement to include opposition to the war in Vietnam and support for racial, political, and economic justice worldwide. On April 4, 1968, Young was with King in Memphis, Tennessee, when the civil rights leader was assassinated by James Earl Ray. Afterward, Young helped organize and lead the ill-fated Poor People's Campaign that took place in Washington, D.C., in the summer of 1968. But without King, Young believed the SCLC was powerless to affect significant change because the Civil Rights movement had to work within the limits imposed on it by a racist society. He was also convinced that it took a special kind of person, like King (and perhaps himself), who could mediate between blacks and whites and break through racial barriers by holding the United States morally accountable for how it treated people of color.

In 1970, Young began a new phase in his life when he decided to run for Congress. Although he lost that year, he was successful two years later and was reelected twice, winning in a district where the majority of voters were white and becoming the first black person from Georgia to win a congressional seat since Reconstruction. As a congressman, he fought against cuts in social programs and increases in the military budget. Among the causes he championed were increases in the minimum wage, day care, and national health insurance. He also applied his lifelong skills in mediating to his work with the Congressional Black Caucus, established in 1969. He gained considerable national attention for his stand in support of affirmative action at home, peace in Vietnam, and racial and social justice around the world, including independence for the Portuguese colonies of Angola and Mozambique in Africa and the end of apartheid in Southern Rhodesia and South Africa.

It was Young's stand in support of human rights in Africa that led to President-elect Jimmy Carter's decision to appoint him as U.S. ambassador to the United Nations. Young first met Carter in 1970 when Carter was campaigning a second time for governor and Young was running for Congress for the first time. Two years later, the Georgia governor endorsed Young for Congress. At the Democratic convention in July 1972, he asked Young to put his name forward as a candidate for the vice-presidential nomination.

Afterward, two of Carter's earliest and most influential campaign workers in his presidential bid, STUART EIZENSTAT and JACK WATSON, supported Young in his congressional campaign. Although at first dubious about the chances of a white southerner being elected president, Young became the first major black political figure to back the Georgia governor for president. He was impressed by Carter's stand on racial issues and the large number of blacks he had appointed to important positions within his administration as governor. He also was attracted to Carter by his commitment to human rights, his religious convictions, and his apparent honesty and sincerity.

Once Carter announced his candidacy in 1974, Young helped to introduce him to influential black leaders and liberal groups. At the Democratic convention in New York in July 1976, he seconded Carter's nomination. Once Carter won the nomination, Young campaigned extensively with him throughout the country, noting his special relationship with African Americans. To the surprise of very few political observers, then, President-elect Carter appointed Young to be ambassador to the United Nations, even though Young had said earlier that he expected no position within the new administration and was content to remain in Congress. The appointment underscored Carter's commitment both to placing African Americans in high places in government and to human rights. It also reflected his own deeply religious belief in the moral imperative of sharing more of the world's material wealth with peoples of color in developing countries. Both Carter and Young believed that poverty was not only unnecessary but immoral.

Young's appointment was popular not only among African Americans but people of color in developing countries because of his stand on racial and economic equality and on ending apartheid. As he later commented, he saw "members of liberation movements in Africa, the Middle East and Latin America ... not as enemies to be destroyed but as brothers and sisters to be redeemed." As UN ambassador, he played an important role in winning repeal of the 1973 Byrd Amendment that had permitted the sale of chrome from southern Rhodesia. By repealing the sale of the chrome, one of Rhodesia's most important exports, the White House hoped to pressure that country into ending its apartheid practices. Hitherto the United States had been only one of two nations (the other being Portugal) that had violated the sanctions against Rhodesia imposed on it since it had declared its independence from Great Britain in 1966. Later Young helped to bridge the gap between Rhodesia's white minority government headed by Ian Smith and the militant black Patriotic Front (PF) led by Robert Mugabe and Joshua Nkomo; this led in 1980 to the peaceful transition of Rhodesia to the nation of Zimbabwe under black majority rule.

Young also helped to improve relations with oil-rich Nigeria, which became the leading exporter of oil to the United States, and he was instrumental in persuading President Carter to visit Nigeria and Liberia, the first American president to visit sub-Saharan Africa. More generally, he was instrumental in focusing U.S. attention on Africa and the problems of poor developing nations.

Yet almost from the moment that Young became UN ambassador, he was the center of controversy. If the first rule for any diplomat is to be diplomatic, Young violated that basic principle from the start. Indeed, in accepting his new position, he made clear that his style was always to be independent, and he quickly became famous for his outspokenness. Commenting, for example, on the presence of Cuban troops in Angola just one day after he took office, he remarked that the Cubans had at least brought stability and order to Angola. A few months later, while in London, he remarked that the "old colonial mentality" was still strong in Britain and that the Russians and Swedes were racists. Referring in 1978 to the trial of Soviet human rights dissident Anataloy Shcharansky, Young said there were "hundreds—perhaps even thousands—of people [in American prisons] whom I would call political prisoners." In response, Carter was forced to issue a release remarking that statements on U.S. foreign policy came from the president and secretary of state and that Young's remarks did not represent the position of the United States. But Young continued to make remarks attacking racism and human rights violations in the United States.

Within a year after Young assumed his position, therefore, calls began to develop in the United States for his dismissal. These were led by North Carolina's Republican senator JESSE HELMS but included other conservative Republicans and even some Democrats. Finally, in 1979, Young was forced to resign after it was revealed in the press that he had met secretly with Zehdi Labib Terzi, the UN observer for the PLO despite explicit State Department regulations prohibiting official contact with that organization. President Carter accepted Young's resignation on August 15, 1979.

In 1981, just before leaving office, President Carter awarded Young the Presidential Medal of Freedom. That same year, at the urging of Coretta Scott King and other black leaders, Young ran successfully for mayor of Atlanta. As mayor, he attracted considerable new business to Atlanta and worked to bridge the racial gap between blacks and whites. Reelected in 1985, he helped bring the 1996 Olympic Games to Atlanta. Limited to two terms, he ran unsuccessfully for governor of Georgia in 1990. Following his defeat in the Democratic primary, he cochaired the Atlanta Organizing Committee for the Olympics. In 1991, President Bill Clinton appointed him to chair the newly established $100 million Southern African Enterprise Development Fund.

Young is currently chair of Good Works International, a consulting group based in Atlanta that advises corporations and governments operating in the global economy. He also holds a public-affairs professorship at Georgia State University's Andrew Young School of Political Studies. In 2000–01, he served as president of the National Council of Churches. He continues to speak out on issues of racism and poverty although he now regards the latter as the more important of the two problems. He regards racism as "one of the symptoms of poverty and insecurity"

Young, Coleman Alexander
(1918–1997) *mayor of Detroit*

Mayor of Detroit from 1974 to 1994, Coleman Young was one of the first black mayors of a major northern city. He was also one of the first national black leaders to endorse Jimmy Carter's candidacy for president in 1976. As a result of his early support for Carter, he enjoyed strong influence within the Carter administration and was able to obtain considerable federal aid for his city.

Young was born in Tuscaloosa, Alabama, on May 14, 1918, but his family moved to Detroit when he was five years old. He grew up in the city's multiethnic area known as the Black Bottom. Although he graduated from high school with honors in 1935 and hoped to attend college, he was forced to go to work for Ford Motor Company after he was unable to win a scholarship to the University of Michigan. In the early 1940s, he took a job on the assembly line at Ford and began to engage in union and civil rights activities, but he was fired after a fistfight over racial slurs made against him. He worked briefly for the Post Office before being drafted into the army in 1942. During the war, he became one of the famous Tuskegee Airmen and reached the rank of lieutenant as a bombardier-navigator.

The 20 years after the war were turbulent ones for Young. Hired as a union organizer by the Congress of Industrial Organizations (CIO) but feisty and combative, he was fired after clashing with union leader Walter Reuther. During the McCarthy era of the early 1950s, he was suspected of being a communist sympathizer because he was cofounder and executive secretary of the leftist-leaning National Negro Labor Council and had engaged in Progressive Party politics. Asked by the House Un-American Activities Committee in 1952 to inform on his union colleagues, he responded, "You have me mixed up with a stool pigeon." Shunned by organized labor and unable to find steady employment, he was forced to work in different jobs, including running his own cleaning business, driving a taxi, and selling insurance.

Young's fortunes started to change at the end of the 1950s when his insurance business began to grow and he decided to enter politics. In 1961, he served as a delegate to the Michigan Constitutional Convention. Three years later, he ran for and won a seat in Michigan's state senate. He served in the senate for the next nine years and became Democratic floor leader. In 1968, he also became the first African-American member of the Democratic Party National Committee.

In 1973, Young decided to run for mayor of Detroit, which had still not recovered from the race riots of 1967 and was faced with white flight to the suburbs, a high crime rate, and job losses in the automobile industry. In a city that was about 50 percent African-American, Young received 92 percent of the black vote, while his white opponent, Detroit police chief John F. Nichols, who ran on a law-and-order platform, received 91 percent of the white vote in the bitterly contested election. But the overwhelming black support for Young—who accused Detroit's police force, especially its tactical crime unit, STRESS, of being racist—was enough to give him a narrow victory, making him the first African-American mayor of Detroit.

Young, Tom Bradley of Los Angeles, and MAYNARD JACKSON of Atlanta were also the first African-Americans elected as mayors of major U.S. cities. Accordingly, Young attracted considerable national attention. His penchant for profanity and one-liners made his story all the more colorful. But as a person of considerable substance and a consummate politician, the new mayor intended to transform city government, especially the police department, to better reflect the city's racial makeup. He did this through the application of affirmative-action programs, including even the use of quotas. He also suspended police officers living outside the city.

Young intended to work with the business community to diversify the economy and bring economic redevelopment to downtown Detroit. But he had only limited success in this regard. Following his inauguration, the new mayor bought together the city's leading employers and labor leaders and persuaded them to construct the $350 million Renaissance Center, a complex of four cylindrical office towers and a hotel along the Detroit River. He also developed a five-year economic plan for Detroit, which he presented to President GERALD FORD.

Unfortunately, the Renaissance Center, which opened in 1977, suffered from a number of problems, the most important being that it was cut off from the rest of the city by man-made barriers and was built at a time when the real-estate market was wary of investing in downtown. Architecturally, the cylindrical shape of its buildings and poor signage confused visitors and discouraged them from returning to the center. In 1996, General Motors bought the complex for about $80 million, or less than a quarter of what it had cost to build it 20 years earlier. As for Young's economic plan for Detroit, after the mayor presented it to Ford, the president paid little attention to it.

Despite these setbacks, both General Motors and Ford Motor Company built new plants in Detroit. Other companies also undertook major construction projects, including the Millender Center apartment-hotel and retail complex. Plans were begun for a downtown monorail system that opened to the public in 1987. Young also had the city build the Joe Louis Arena in downtown Detroit. He adopted a no-tolerance policy toward drug dealers. "I issue an open warning to all dope pushers, to all rip-off artists, to all muggers," Young stated. "It's time to leave Detroit." Although a staunch Democrat, he succeeded in luring the Republican National Convention to Detroit in 1980.

Young attracted the attention of Jimmy Carter when he became one of the first black leaders to endorse the future president's candidacy. Young's early endorsement of Carter in 1976 was doubly important. As the columnist David Broder pointed out, not only was the black constituency important in its own right, but black support made a candidate more acceptable to white liberal activists. Young also supported Carter during some of the direst times in his primary campaign. In April 1976, the presidential candidate talked of maintaining the "purity" of ethnic neighborhoods and preventing "alien intrusion." In response, Young remarked that Carter's comments were "as American as apple pie" and added, "Blacks have a kind of radar about white folks and somewhere along the line Jimmy passed the test." When the candidate later apologized for his comments, Young said Carter's apology was "satisfactory" and that the whole matter had been a "phony issue."

In May 1976, Young's effort in support of Carter was critical to the Georgia governor's narrow victory in Michigan over Congressman MORRIS UDALL (Ariz.) by a majority of 43.5 to 43.2 percent. A defeat in Michigan at the same time that California governor JERRY BROWN was crushing Carter, 49 to 37 percent in the Maryland primary, could have put Carter's candidacy in jeopardy.

After Carter was elected president, he offered Young a cabinet-level position. The mayor declined, preferring to remain in Detroit, but he wielded considerable influence within the administration. From 1977 to 1981, Detroit was put on the fast track for millions of dollars in federal funds. During this time, Young also served as vice chairperson of the Democratic National Committee and chair of the platform committee at the 1980 Democratic Convention that renominated President Carter. He also headed the United State Conference of Mayors from 1982 to 1983 and was president of the Democratic Conference of Mayors from 1986 to 1993.

Having been easily reelected in 1977 and then again in 1981, Young's third term was marred by two federal investigations into his efforts to direct municipal business to black firms. He was never brought to trial, though, and was reelected to fourth and fifth terms in 1985 and 1989. In 1993, his administration was wracked by scandal, including accusations that he had used campaign funds for his own slush fund. Further, his police chief was indicted for stealing $2 million of the department's money, and two white policemen were charged with the beating death in 1992 of a black man. Faced with this scandal and with his health deteriorating as a result of emphysema, Young decided not to seek reelection.

After leaving politics, Young served as an adjunct professor at Wayne State University and wrote his autobiography, *Hardstuff* (1994). He also invested in building a casino in Detroit. He died on November 29, 1997, of respiratory failure at the age of 79.

CHRONOLOGY

1977

January 20—President Carter delivers first inaugural address.

January 21—President Carter urges 65 degrees as maximum heat in homes to ease energy crisis.
—President Carter pardons draft resisters.

February 2—President Carter gives televised "fireside chat" from the White House wearing cardigan sweater.
—President Carter signs Emergency Natural Gas Act.

February 20—President Carter sends letter of support to dissident Soviet physicist Andrei Sakharov.

March 6—Israeli premier Yitzhak Rabin arrives in Washington, D.C., for talks with President Carter.

March 9—President Carter announces intention to withdraw U.S. forces from South Korea in four or five years.

March 12—Egyptian president Anwar el-Sadat says Egypt must have all Israeli-occupied Arab territory back.

March 15—The United States sends arms to Zaire to help repel invading forces from Angola.

March 16—President Carter holds a televised "town meeting" in Clinton, Massachusetts.

March 30—Arms talks between Secretary of State Cyrus Vance and Soviet leader Leonid Brezhnev break down.

April 3—Egyptian president Anwar el-Sadat arrives in Washington, D.C., for talks with President Carter on peace terms in the Middle East.

April 6—White House announces the United States will halt work on nuclear breeder reactor.
—President Carter signs Reorganization Act.

April 14—President Carter announces unexpectedly that he is rescinding his administration's proposal for a $50 tax rebate.

April 18—President Carter addresses the nation on the energy crisis. He warns of a national crisis unless the United States responds with a "moral equivalent of war" to diminishing energy supplies.

April 25—Jordan's King Hussein arrives in Washington, D.C., to discuss admitting the Palestine Liberation Organization to Geneva Conference on Middle East.

April 28—The Department of Health, Education and Welfare bans discrimination against 35 million disabled Americans.

May 5—Congress passes $20.1 billion measure to increase employment through various jobs programs.

May 7–8—President Carter meets in London with leaders from the United Kingdom, Canada, Germany, France, Italy, and Japan to discuss global recession.

May 17—Menachem Begin becomes Israel's presumptive new premier after his Likud Party defeats the hitherto dominant Labor Party.

May 24—Crown Prince Fahd of Saudi Arabia praises President Carter for supporting the idea of a Palestinian homeland.

May 25—The United States says Cuba has military advisers in Ethiopia.

May 30—Rosalynn Carter begins tour of seven Caribbean and Latin American nations.

June 16—Leonid Brezhnev is named first Soviet presdent.

June 30—President Carter declares opposition to development of B-1 bomber.

July 19—Israeli prime minister Menachem Begin arrives in Washington, D.C., for meetings with President Carter.

August 4—Department of Energy established.

August 5—U.S. House of Representatives passes President Carter's energy program.

August 6—President Carter proposes new welfare system with emphasis on work.

August 10—The United States and Panama agree on basic provisions of treaty for transfer of control of Panama Canal.

August 18—Comptroller John Heinmann releases his agency's report on the banking practices of Bert Lance, director of the Office of Management and Budget (OMB).

August 25—Former California governor Ronald Reagan urges Senate to reject Panama Canal Treaties.

August 31—Grand jury in Washington, D.C., indicts Tongsun Park in South Korean influence peddling.
—Rhodesian prime minister Ian Smith reelected with 80 percent majority. Only 15,000 of 6.2 million blacks vote.

September 5—Senators Charles Percy (R-Ill.) and Abraham Ribicoff (D-Conn.) urge that OMB director Bert Lance resign.

September 7—The United States and Panama sign Panama Canal Treaties, transferring ownership of the Panama Canal to Panama after 1999.

September 15—U.S. House of Representatives approves hikes in minimum wage, rejects lower wage for youth.
—OMB director Bert Lance testifies before Senate Governmental Affairs Committee.

September 18—Israeli foreign minister Moshe Dayan arrives in Washington, D.C., for new round of talks on the Middle East.

September 21—President Carter accepts resignation of OMB director Bert Lance.

September 25—Israeli cabinet approves U.S. plan for single Arab delegation at Geneva Conference on the Middle East.

September 26—Israel announces cease-fire on border with Lebanon.

October 1—The United States issues joint communiqué with Soviet Union calling for a new Geneva Conference on the Middle East.

October 5—President Carter signs International Covenant on Human Rights.

October 13—President Carter attacks U.S. oil industry for opposing energy plan.

October 21—President Carter sends letter to Egyptian president Anwar el-Sadat asking for his support for a Middle East peace effort.

October 27—President Carter announces that the United States will support a UN arms embargo on South Africa.

November 1—President Carter signs minimum-wage increase from $2.30 to $3.35 an hour by 1981.

November 2—Egyptian president Anwar el-Sadat proposes to President Carter a conference in East Jerusalem attended by Israel, Egypt, and permanent members of the UN Security Council.

November 7—President Carter postpones trip abroad in order to seek enactment of his energy program.

November 13—Somalia orders all advisers out of country and breaks relations with Cuba.

November 14—Egyptian president Anwar el-Sadat announces that he is ready to address the Israeli Knesset.

November 15—Shah of Iran is disturbed by tear gas used to quell protests during his speech at White House.

—Israeli premier Menachem Begin invites Egyptian president Anwar el-Sadat to address the Knesset.

November 20—In his speech to the Israeli Knesset, Egyptian president Anwar el-Sadat offers "peace with justice." Sadat also pledges "no more war" but emphasizes that Israel will have to recognize the rights of Palestinians and withdraw from the occupied territories.

November 24—Rhodesia's prime minister, Ian Smith, states that he is prepared to concede the principle of full voting rights for Rhodesia's black majority.

November 26—Black nationalist leader Bishop Abel Muzorewa agrees to hold talks with Rhodesian prime minister Ian Smith based on universal suffrage.

December 5—Hard-line Arab nations fail to unite against Egypt's President Anwar el-Sadat's peace initiative with Israel.

December 6—Some 165,000 members of the United Mine Workers walk off the job.

December 16—Israeli prime minister Menachem Begin agrees to return Sinai to Egypt.

December 21—Egyptian president Anwar el-Sadat bars Israeli military presence on West Bank of Jordan.
—OPEC decides to freeze price of a barrel of oil at $12.70.

December 29—President Carter travels to Europe and the Middle East.

December 31—Cambodia breaks relations with Vietnam.

1978

January 3—Vietnamese troops are reported to occupy 400 square miles of Cambodia.

January 9—Sixty Iranians are killed in rally for Ayatollah Ruholla Khomeini in holy city of Qom.

January 10—Pedro Joaquim Chamorro, editor of *La Prensa* and critic of Nicaraguan dictator Anastasio Somoza, is murdered.

January 11—Riots erupt in Nicaragua after funeral of dissident editor Pedro Joaquim Chamorro.

January 13—The United States and Japan reach accord on easing trade tensions.

January 26—President Carter announces his intention to withdraw U.S. troops from South Korea.

February 2—U.S. Jewish leaders decide against meeting with Egyptian president Anwar el-Sadat.

February 3—Egyptian president Anwar el-Sadat arrives in the United States for talks with President Carter.

February 8—President Carter tells American Jewish leaders that Israel is biggest obstacle to a Mideast peace.

February 10—Somalia mobilizes its armed forces and prepares to dispatch them into the Ogaden region of Ethiopia.

February 18—Troops in Iran break up protests against the shah in Tabriz.

February 23—Deadly clash takes place between troops and protesters in Nicaraguan capital of Managua.

February 26—Israeli cabinet decides to expand settlements in Sinai despite U.S. opposition.

March 3—Rhodesian leaders sign pact providing for majority rule.

March 6—President Carter invokes Taft-Hartley Act in an effort to get coal miners back to work.

March 8—Somali troops agree to leave Ogaden.

March 9—Nicaraguan National Guard chief General Reinaldo Pérez-Vega is assassinated.

March 14—Israeli force of 22,000 invades southern Lebanon, attacking PLO bases.

March 16—Senate approves first of two treaties with Panama (the neutrality treaty) on the Panama Canal after turning back a series of "killer amendments."

March 18—President Carter delivers a major speech at Wake Forest University in which he warns against Soviet military aggression.

March 20—Israeli prime minister Menachem Begin arrives in the United States for talks with President Carter.

March 21—In Rhodesia, the first steps are taken toward majority rule when three black nationalists are sworn in as joint leaders of the nation's new interim government.

March 24—United Mine Workers agree to contract, ending strike of 109 days.

March 29—Under pressure from Congress, President Carter proposes to increase farm subsidies in return for land diversion. Farm bloc in Congress indicates that it will push for still more aid.

April 3—The White House announces that president Carter will veto development of neutron bomb.

April 11—In a speech before the American Society of Newspaper Editors, President Carter states that he will take the lead in breaking the spiraling rate of inflation by limiting pay raises to 5.5 percent for federal employees and freezing the salaries of political appointees.

April 18—By a vote of 68 to 32, the Senate votes to turn over the Panama Canal to Panama on December 31, 1999.

April 27—Afghanistan's president, Mohammad Daud, is killed in a military coup. The Democratic Republic of Afghanistan is established; Nur Mohammad Taraki, a member of the Afghan Communist Party, is appointed prime minister.

April 30—Israeli prime minister Menachem Begin arrives in the United States for discussions with President Carter.

May 11—In Iran, after four days of rioting, Islamic leaders ask an end to the shah's program of modernization and return of mosque lands seized for land reform.

May 16—Shah Mohammad Reza Pahlavi responds to mounting opposition to his regime by stating his intention to continue his policies of modernization.

June 6—Californians vote in favor of Proposition 13, cutting property taxes by $7 billion.

June 7—President Carter tells Soviets that they can choose between cooperation and confrontation. Kremlin responds by reaffirming policy of détente and calling the president's remarks "strange."

June 13—Israelis withdraw last of invading forces in south Lebanon.

June 28—In the case of *Regents of the University of California v. Bakke*, the Supreme Court votes 5 to 4 in support of affirmative action in college admissions programs.

July 14—Anatoly Sharansky and two other Soviet dissidents receive long jail terms.

July 16–17—President Carter meets with world leaders at Bonn Economic Summit. Carter urges its trading partners to do more to stimulate their economies.

July 23—Israeli prime minister Menachem Begin rejects Egyptian request to turn over El Arish and Mount Sinai.

August 4—First families begin leaving Love Canal, Niagara Falls, New York, after learning their homes had been built over a former chemical dump.

August 30—Nicaraguan rebels seize National Palace, taking hundreds of hostages. Crisis is resolved after the government of Anastasio Somoza accedes to guerrilla demands for ransom money and release of political prisoners.

September 8—Martial law sparks riots in Iran; police open fire. Opposition claims 2,000 victims.

September 15—Nicaraguan dictator Anastasio Somoza mobilizes National Guard to fight rebels in seven cities.

September 17—After meeting at Camp David for 13 days, in talks brokered by President Carter, Israeli prime minister Menachem Begin and Egyptian president Anwar el-Sadat reach Camp David accords providing for a

"Framework for Peace in the Middle East" and a "Framework for the Conclusion of a Peace Treaty between Egypt and Israel."

September 20—Jordan states that it will not be bound by the Camp David accords.

September 27—President Carter ends three-year ban on arms sales to Turkey.

October 6—U.S. Senate extends deadline for approval of Equal Rights Amendment.
—France grants asylum to Ayatollah Ruholla Khomeini after he is expelled from Iraq.

October 12—Egyptian-Israeli peace talks begin.

October 14—President Carter signs first major revision of U.S. civil-service laws in 20th century.
—Nicaraguan dictator Anastasio Somoza extends martial law for six months.

October 19—President Carter orders production of elements for neutron bomb.

October 21—Middle East peace talks come to an end.

October 24—President Carter calls for voluntary wage and price controls to bring down inflation.

October 30—Thousands of Iranians clash with police in nationwide oil strike.

November 5—Arab League calls on Egypt to renounce accord with Israel.

November 6—Shah of Iran puts his country under military control in an effort to end two days of revolutionary chaos.

November 9—President Carter signs watered-down energy bill.

November 13—Oil workers in Iran end two-week strike after being threatened with dismissal.

December 5—Soviets sign 20-year friendship pact with Afghanistan.

December 10—Israeli prime minister Menachem Begin and Egyptian president Anwar el-Sadat jointly win Nobel Peace Prize.

December 11—Millions march in Tehran in opposition to the shah.

December 15—President Carter delivers television speech in which he announces his decision to grant full diplomatic status to the People's Republic of China. He also announces the forthcoming visit of China's deputy prime minister, Deng Xiaoping.

December 18—Senator Barry Goldwater (R-Ariz.) questions constitutionality of President Carter's decision to end mutual-defense pact with Taiwan.

1979

January 1—The United States and the People's Republic of China formally resume relations.

January 4—President Carter meets with leaders of France, Great Britain, and Germany at Guadeloupe Summit.

January 6—Shah of Iran names Shahpour Bakhtiar, an outspoken critic of the shah's regime, to head new civilian government.

January 7—Vietnamese troops seize Cambodian capital of Phnom Penh.

January 13—Twenty-three members of the National Advisory Committee of Women

resign to protest President Carter's dismissal of Bella Abzug as cochair of the committee.
—Ayatollah Ruholla Khomeini says he has formed a council to assume the duties of the shah of Iran.

January 16—The Shah of Iran leaves Iran for Egypt.

January 22—In a budget message to Congress, President Carter calls for total expenditures of $532 billion, which includes a projected deficit of $29 billion, or $12 billion less than the 1979 deficit. The budget is a firm indication of Carter's commitment to fiscal austerity.
—Having returned in September from a trip to Libya, President Carter's brother, Billy, is widely quoted in newsmagazines as having made anti-Semitic remarks about Jews in the United States.

January 28—Chinese deputy prime minister Deng Xiaoping arrives in the United States for a state visit.

January 30—Whites in Rhodesia vote to accept limited rule by black majority.

February 1—Millions greet Ayatollah Ruholla Khomeini on arrival in Iran.

February 5—Three thousand farmers use tractors to clog traffic in Washington, D.C., to demand higher price supports.

February 8—More than 1 million march in Tehran to demand the resignation of Premier Shahpour Bakhtiar.
—Washington breaks military ties with Nicaragua after President Anastasio Somoza rejects three-nation proposal for ending the civil strife in his country.

February 11—In Iran, premier Shahpour Bakhtiar resigns as the military withdraws supports.

February 14—U.S. ambassador to Afghanistan Adolph Dubs is killed in Kabul.
—Armed insurgents attack U.S. embassy in Tehran.

February 17—Chinese troops move across border into Vietnam.

February 24—Border war breaks out between North and South Yemen.

February 25—President Carter disavows seemingly anti-Semitic remarks by his brother, Billy Carter.

March 7—The United States sends arms and advisers to North Yemen.

March 15—According to an AP poll, only 29 percent of the American people approve Carter's handling of the presidency.

March 20—Israeli prime minister Menachem Begin bars establishment of Palestinian state in occupied areas.

March 23—Beijing announces it will withdraw its forces from Vietnam.

March 26—Israeli prime minister Menachem Begin and Egyptian president Anwar el-Sadat sign formal treaty ending 30 years of war as President Carter watches at White House.

March 27—Arab League agrees on steps against Egypt for signing peace treaty with Israel.

March 28—In Britain, the labor government of James L. Callaghan falls after losing vote of no confidence in House of Commons.
—An accident at Three Mile Island near Harrisburg, Pennsylvania, poses threat of nuclear meltdown.

March 30—Iranians vote overwhelmingly in favor of establishing an Islamic republic.

April 2—Menachem Begin becomes the first Israeli prime minister to visit Egypt.

April 20—Egyptian president Anwar el-Sadat wins landslide vote for peace treaty.

April 23—Billy Carter vows not to drink again.
—President Carter's pollster warns the president that if he cannot deal effectively with inflation and restore the confidence of the American people, he will lose the election in 1980.

April 24—Bishop Abel Muzorewa's United African National Council will control 51 of 100 seats in Rhodesia's first biracial Parliament.

April 26—Israel and Palestine Liberation Organization agree to UN truce in Lebanon.

May 1—George H. W. Bush announces candidacy for Republican presidential nomination.
—In an article in *Atlantic Monthly*, President Carter's former speechwriter, James Fallows, delivers a scathing attack against Carter, accusing him of being ignorant of how power could or should be exercised.

May 3—Margaret Thatcher becomes Europe's first woman prime minister as her Conservative Party wins victory in Great Britain.

May 5—President Carter orders gradual decontrol of oil prices.

May 23—Former director of Office of Management and Budget Bert Lance and three others are indicted in bank conspiracy.

June 2—Sandinistas open long-awaited offensive in Nicaragua.

June 6—Nicaraguan president Anastasio Somoza declares state of siege.

June 7—President Carter approves MX missile program.
—President Carter announces that he will continue to impose sanctions against Rhodesia indefinitely despite April election of Rhodesia's first black prime minister, Bishop Abel Muzorewa.

June 9—President Carter's approval rating hits all-time low of 30 percent in polls.

June 17—Nicaraguan rebels form provisional government.

June 18—President Carter and Soviet leader Leonid Brezhnev sign SALT II Treaty in Vienna.

June 23—Organization of American States calls for ouster of Nicaragua's president Anastasio Somoza.

June 28—OPEC raises oil prices 16 percent, now up 50 percent in last year.
—President Carter attends Tokyo Economic Summit.

July 4—President Carter cancels a planned vacation in order to prepare an address to Congress calling for a "bold, forceful" energy program.

July 6–10—President Carter engages in consultations with leaders from all walks of life.

July 9—Ayatollah Ruholla Khomeini declares general amnesty for crimes committed when the shah of Iran was in power.

July 15—President Carter delivers "crisis of confidence" speech.

July 17—Anastasio Somoza resigns as president of Nicaragua and flees to the United States.

July 17–20—President Carter accepts resignation of Secretary of Health, Education and Welfare Joseph Califano, Secretary of the Treasury W. Michael Blumenthal, Attorney General Griffin B. Bell, Secretary of Energy James Schlesinger, and Secretary of Transportation Brock Adams.

July 22—An AP/NBC poll, taken after the resignations, finds that only 23 percent of Americans give President Carter a "good to excellent" rating, which is two points lower than at the time of his address to the nation on July 15.

July 26—UN ambassador Andrew Young holds unauthorized meeting with Labib Terzi, a representative of the Palestine Liberation Organization.

July 31—Chrysler Corporation asks the U.S. government for $1 billion to keep the company afloat.

August 8—Twenty-one Iraqi officials are executed for plotting revolt against Ayatollah Ruholla Khomeini.

August 15—Andrew Young resigns as ambassador to the United Nations after being reprimanded for holding an unauthorized meeting with members of the Palestine Liberation Organization.

August 16—Afghanistan's president Taraki killed in coup; Premier Hafizullah Amin takes over.

August 24—President Carter's chief aide, Hamilton Jordan, denies taking cocaine at Studio 54 in New York.

August 26—Woman who said Hamilton Jordan used cocaine changes story.

August 31—Soviet combat troops reported in Cuba.

September 7—President Carter announces plan to deploy 200 MX missiles.

October 1—President Carter delivers speech in which he calls the presence of a Soviet brigade in Cuba "a political challenge to the United States" and announces that he is increasing American surveillance over Cuba and strengthening the American presence in Caribbean.

October 6—Soviet leader Leonid Brezhnev says Soviets will pull 20,000 troops out of East Germany.
—Pope Paul John II becomes the first pope to be received at White House.

October 15—A coup in El Salvador led by military deposes president Carlos Romero and establishes a civilian-military junta in his place.

October 17—President Carter signs bill establishing new Department of Education.

October 22—Deposed shah of Iran Mohammad Reza Pahlavi is allowed into the United States for medical treatment.

November 4—Sixty-three Americans taken hostage at U.S. embassy in Tehran.
—Democratic candidate for president Edward Kennedy of Massachusetts makes unfavorable impression in taped interview with Roger Mudd of CBS.

November 7—Edward Kennedy formally announces his candidacy for the Democratic presidential nomination.
—Civilian government in Iran is ousted, yielding power to Ayatollah Ruholla Khomeini. Marchers in Iran chant "death to Americans."

November 12—Former California governor Ronald Reagan announces his candidacy for the Republican presidential nomination.

November 14—President Carter freezes Iranian assets in the United States.

November 17—Ayatollah Ruholla Khomeini orders release of black and female American hostages.

December 2—NATO countries, France and Greece dissenting, agree to take 572 U.S. cruise missiles.

December 4—President Carter officially announces his campaign for reelection as president.

December 12—NATO agrees to deploy theater nuclear weapons.

December 15—Former shah Mohammad Reza Pahlavi leaves the United States for exile in Panama.
—After the British worked out a successful compromise between warring factions in Rhodesia, promising genuine black-majority rule in the country, the United States withdraws sanctions against Rhodesia (renamed Zimbabwe Rhodesia).

December 20—Following the House's lead the day before, the Senate approves $1.5 billion in federal loan guarantees to save the Chrysler Corporation from bankruptcy.

December 21—Robert Mugabe, Joshua Nkomo, and Bishop Abel Muzorewa sign agreements ending Rhodesia's seven-year civil war.

December 27—The Soviet Union invades Afghanistan.

1980

January 3—President Jimmy Carter asks the Senate to delay SALT II ratification in response to Soviet action in Afghanistan.

January 4—The United States retaliates against the Soviet invasion of Afghanistan with a grain embargo.

January 21—President Carter beats Senator Edward Kennedy decisively in Iowa caucuses.

January 23—In his toughest attack on the Soviet Union since taking office, President Carter delivers his State of the Union address, in which he announces what became known as the Carter Doctrine.

January 24—In rebuff to the Soviets, the United States will sell arms to China.

January 25—Abolhassan Bani-Sadr is named prime minister of Iran.

January 29—Six Americans hiding in Tehran escape from Iran by posing as Canadian diplomats.

February 17—Israeli diplomats arrive in Cairo to open first embassy in Arab world.

March 3—Prime rate for most banks increased to 16.75 percent.

March 6—In Iran, Islamic militants say they will turn over hostages to Revolutionary Council.

March 10—Ayatollah Ruholla Khomeini lends support to militants holding U.S. hostages.

March 14—Pointing to escalating inflation, President Carter announces that he will cut federal spending by $13 billion in order to achieve a balanced budget by next year.

March 21—President Carter informs athletes at White House the United States will not take part in the Moscow Olympics.

March 23—Deposed shah of Iran leaves Panama for Cairo one day before Iran was to request his extradition.

March 25—Senator Edward Kennedy wins primary victories in New York and Connecticut. Polls, however, show Kennedy losing support in the rest of the country, particularly in the South and Midwest.

March 26—Stuart Eizenstat, head of the president's domestic policy staff, tells Carter that the United States is on verge of a severe economic crisis.

March 31—President Carter deregulates the banking industry.

April 1—Iranian president Abolhassan Bani-Sadr announces that control over American hostages will be transferred to the Iranian government.

April 2—President Carter approves U.S. windfall profits tax on oil industry.

April 7—The United States breaks diplomatic ties with Iran, imposing sanctions for Khomeini's backing of captors.

April 9—Iranian militants declare that American hostages will die if the United States tries even the smallest military action.

April 17—Illinois representative John Anderson announces that he is prepared to run for president on independent ticket.

April 18—Zimbabwe Rhodesia's name changed to Zimbabwe.

April 21—Secretary of State Cyrus Vance submits resignation.

April 24—Military attempt to rescue American hostages in Tehran fails, with eight killed and five wounded.

April 30—Former OMB director Bert Lance is cleared on nine counts of fraud.

May 1—U.S. jobless rate hits 7 percent, largest in three years.

May 6—President Carter defeats Edward Kennedy by overwhelming margins in Indiana, Tennessee, and North Carolina. Kennedy beats Carter in District of Columbia.

May 16—The Environmental Protection Agency finds evidence of chromosome damage in residents of Love Canal.

May 24—The World Court orders release of all U.S. hostages held in Iran.

May 29—Great Britain imposes sanctions on Iran after long holdout.

June 3—Edward Kennedy wins California primary for Democratic presidential nomination.

June 10—OPEC hikes oil prices up to $32 per barrel.

June 20—U.S. Congress deregulates trucking industry.

June 22—Soviets announce partial withdrawal of troops in Afghanistan.

June 23—President Carter and leaders of other industrial countries hold summit meeting in Venice. They disagree sharply about international politics.

June 29—Full-scale release of krypton gas begins at Three Mile Island.

June 30—President Carter signs Energy Security Act.

July 2—President Carter signs bill for draft registration of American men at age 18.

July 14—Billy Carter registers as agent of Libyan government. He discloses that he has received $200,000 in payments from Libya.

July 16–17—Republicans nominate Ronald Reagan for president and George H. W. Bush for vice president.

July 22—The White House issues a statement asserting that at no time had there been any conduct between the Justice Department and the White House concerning the investigation into Billy Carter's financial dealings.

July 27—Deposed shah of Iran dies in Egyptian exile.

August 5—President Carter announces nuclear strategy shift from civilian to military targets.

August 13–14—Democrats nominate President Carter and Vice President Walter Mondale for reelection.

August 21–22—Billy Carter testifies for nine hours before Senate committee looking into his financial dealings with Libya.

August 29—The United States marks 300th day of captivity for hostages in Iran.

September 7—Hua Kuo-feng resigns as premier of China. He is replaced by Zhao Ziyang.

September 10—Libya and Syria announce they are a "unified state." They invite other Arab nations to join.

September 17—Former Nicaraguan dictator Anastasio Somoza Debayle is assassinated in Asuncion, Paraguay.

September 20—Tehran calls up military reserves to fight Iraq.

September 26—Iraq halts oil exports.

October 2—Senate investigation acquits Billy Carter of any illegal behavior.

October 14—North Korea's Communist Party names Kim Jong Il to succeed his father, Kim Il Sung, as president.

October 19—Iraqi troops surround oil city of Abadan.

October 28—President Carter and Ronald Reagan meet in presidential debate.

November 2—Iranian parliament approves conditions for hostage release; demands $24 billion.

November 4—Ronald Reagan elected president.

November 10—The United States sends delegation to Algeria to respond to Iranian conditions on hostages.

November 12—Congress approves the Alaskan Lands Bill.

December 7—President Carter warns Soviets against military intervention in Poland.

December 11—President Carter approves Superfund to control toxic waters.

December 21—The United States rejects $24 billion as condition for release of hostages in Iran.

1981

January 19—The United States and Iran sign accord on release of American hostages.

January 20—Ronald Reagan sworn in as 40th president of the United States.

—Iran releases U.S. hostages. At President Reagan's request, former President Carter travels to West Germany to greet them.

Principal U.S. Government Officials of the Carter Years

Supreme Court

Warren Burger, Chief Justice, 1969–86
William J. Brennan, Jr., 1956–90
Potter Stewart, 1958–81
Byron R. White, 1962–93
Thurgood Marshall, 1965–91
Harry A. Blackmun, 1970–94
Lewis F. Powell, Jr., 1972–87
William Hubbs Rehnquist, 1972–2005
John Paul Stevens, 1975–

Executive Departments

Department of Agriculture
Secretary of Agriculture
Robert S. Bergland, 1977–81

Department of Commerce
Secretary of Commerce
Juanita M. Kreps, 1977–79
Philip M. Klutznick, 1979–81

Department of Defense
Secretary of Defense
Harold Brown, 1977–81

Department of Education
Secretary of Education
Shirley M. Hufstedler, 1979–81

Department of Energy
Secretary of Energy
James R. Schlesinger, 1977–79
Charles W. Duncan, 1979–81

Department of Health, Education and Welfare
Secretary of Health, Education and Welfare
Joseph A. Califano, Jr., 1977–79
Patricia R. Harris, 1979–80

Deparment of Health and Human Services
Secretary of Health and Human Services
Patricia R. Harris, 1980–81

Department of Housing and Urban Development
Secretary of Housing and Urban Development
Patricia R. Harris, 1977–79
Moon Landrieu, 1979–81

Department of the Interior
Secretary of the Interior
Cecil D. Andrus, 1977–81

Department of Justice
Attorney General
Griffin B. Bell, 1977–79
Benjamin R. Civiletti, 1979–81

Department of Labor
Secretary of Labor
Ray Marshall, 1977–81

Department of State
Secretary of State
Cyrus R. Vance, 1977–80
Edmund S. Muskie, 1980–81

Department of Transportation
Secretary of Transportation
Brock Adams, 1977–79
Neil E. Goldschmidt, 1979–81

Department of the Treasury
Secretary of the Treasury
W. Michael Blumenthal, 1977–79
G. William Miller, 1979–81

Regulatory Commissions and Independent Agencies

Central Intelligence Agency
Director of Central Intelligence
Stansfield Turner, 1977–81

Environmental Protection Agency
Administrator
Douglas Costle, 1977–81

Federal Emergency Management Agency (FEMA)
Director
James K. Hafer, May 1975–April 1979
Gordon Vickery (acting), April 1979–July 1979
Thomas Casey (acting), July 1979
John Macy, August 1979–January 1981

Federal Reserve System
Chair
Arthur F. Burns, 1970–78
Paul A. Volcker, 1979–87

National Endowment for the Arts
Chair
Nancy Hanks, 1969–78
Livingston L. Biddle, Jr., 1978–81

National Aeronautics and Space Administration (NASA)
Administrator
Robert Frosch, 1977–81

Securities and Exchange Commission
Chair
Harold M. Williams, 1977–81
Roberta S. Karmel, 1977–80
Stephen J. Friedman, 1980–81
Barbara S. Thomas, 1980–83

UNITED STATES HOUSE OF REPRESENTATIVES

95th Congress (1977–79)
Speaker of the House
Tip O'Neill (D-Massachusetts)

Majority Leader
Jim Wright (D-Texas)

Minority Leader
John J. Rhodes (R-Arizona)

Majority Whip
John W. Brademas (D-Indiana)

Minority Whip
Robert H. Michel (R-Illinois)

96th Congress (1979–81)
Speaker of the House
Tip O'Neill (D-Massachusetts)

Majority Leader
Jim Wright (D-Texas)

Minority Leader
John J. Rhodes (R-Arizona)

Majority Whip
John W. Brademas (D-Indiana)

Minority Whip
Robert H. Michel (R-Illinois)

UNITED STATES SENATE

95th Congress (1977–79)
President
Walter F. Mondale (D)

President Pro Tempore
James O. Eastland (Mississippi)

Majority Leader
Robert C. Byrd (D-West Virginia)

Minority Leader
Howard H. Baker, Jr. (R-Tennessee)

Majority Whip
Alan M. Cranston (D-California)

Minority Whip
Ted Stevens (R-Arkansas)

96th Congress (1979–81)
President
Walter F. Mondale (D)

President Pro Tempore
James O. Eastland (Mississippi)

Majority Leader
Robert C. Byrd (D-West Virginia)

Minority Leader
Howard H. Baker, Jr. (R-Tennessee)

Majority Whip
Alan M. Cranston (D-California)

Minority Whip
Ted Stevens (R-Arkansas)

SELECTED PRIMARY DOCUMENTS

1. Inaugural Address, January 20, 1977
2. Address to the General Assembly of the United Nations, March 17, 1977
3. Address to the Nation on the Energy Problem, April 18, 1977
4. Remarks at the United Automobile Workers Convention in Los Angeles, May 17, 1977
5. Address at Wake Forest University, North Carolina, March 17, 1978
6. Address at the United States Naval Academy Commencement Exercises, June 7, 1978
7. Address to the Nation on Energy and National Goals ("Crisis of Confidence" Speech), July 15, 1979
8. State of the Union Address, January 23, 1980
9. Message to Congress on Environmental Priorities and Programs, August 2, 1979
10. Rescue Attempt for American Hostages in Iran, Address to the Nation, April 25, 1980
11. Farewell Address to the Nation, January 14, 1981

1. Inaugural Address January 20, 1977

Public Papers of the Presidents of the United States: Jimmy Carter. 9 vols. Washington, D.C.: Government Printing Office, 1997–1982.

For myself and for our Nation, I want to thank my predecessor for all he has done to heal our land.

In this outward and physical ceremony, we attest once again to the inner and spiritual strength of our Nation. As my high school teacher, Miss Julia Coleman, used to say, "We must adjust to changing times and still hold to unchanging principles."

Here before me is the Bible used in the inauguration of our first President, in 1789, and I have just taken the oath of office on the Bible my mother gave me just a few years ago, opened to a timeless admonition from the ancient prophet Micah: "He hath showed thee, O man, what is good; and what doth the Lord require of thee, but to do justly, and to love mercy, and to walk humbly with thy God."

This inauguration ceremony marks a new beginning, a new dedication within our Government, and a new spirit among us all. A President may sense and proclaim that new spirit, but only a people can provide it.

Two centuries ago, our Nation's birth was a milestone in the long quest for freedom. But the bold and brilliant dream which excited the founders of this Nation still awaits its consummation. I have no new dream to set forth today, but rather urge a fresh faith in the old dream.

Ours was the first society openly to define itself in terms of both spirituality and human liberty. It is that unique self-definition which has given us an exceptional appeal, but it also imposes on us a special obligation to take on those moral duties which, when assumed, seem invariably to be in our own best interests.

You have given me a great responsibility—to stay close to you, to be worthy of you, and to exemplify what you are. Let us create together a new national spirit of unity and trust. Your strength can compensate for my weakness, and your wisdom can help to minimize my mistakes.

Let us learn together and laugh together and work together and pray together, confident that in the end we will triumph together in the right.

The American dream endures. We must once again have full faith in our country—and in one another. I believe America can be better. We can be even stronger than before.

Let our recent mistakes bring a resurgent commitment to the basic principles of our Nation, for we know that if we despise our own government, we have no future. We recall in special times when we have stood briefly, but magnificently, united. In those times no prize was beyond our grasp.

But we cannot dwell upon remembered glory. We cannot afford to drift. We reject the prospect of failure or mediocrity or an inferior quality of life for any person. Our Government must at the same time be both competent and compassionate.

We have already found a high degree of personal liberty, and we are now struggling to enhance equality of opportunity. Our commitment to human rights must be absolute, our laws fair, our national beauty preserved; the powerful must not persecute the weak, and human dignity must be enhanced.

We have learned that more is not necessarily better, that even our great Nation has its recognized limits, and that we can neither answer all questions nor solve all problems. We cannot afford to do everything, nor can we afford to lack boldness as we meet the future. So, together, in a spirit of individual sacrifice for the common good, we must simply do our best.

Our Nation can be strong abroad only if it is strong at home. And we know that the best way to enhance freedom in other lands is to demonstrate here that our democratic system is worthy of emulation.

To be true to ourselves, we must be true to others. We will not behave in foreign places so as to violate our rules and standards here at home, for we know that the trust which our Nation earns is essential to our strength.

The world itself is now dominated by a new spirit. Peoples more numerous and more politically aware are craving, and now demanding, their place in the sun—not just for the benefit of their own physical condition, but for basic human rights.

The passion for freedom is on the rise. Tapping this new spirit, there can be no nobler nor more ambitious task for America to undertake on this day of a new beginning than to help shape a just and peaceful world that is truly humane.

We are a strong nation, and we will maintain strength so sufficient that it need not be proven in combat—a quiet strength based not merely on the size of an arsenal but on the nobility of ideas.

We will be ever vigilant and never vulnerable, and we will fight our wars against poverty, ignorance, and injustice, for those are the enemies against which our forces can be honorably marshaled.

We are a proudly idealistic nation, but let no one confuse our idealism with weakness. Because we are free, we can never be indifferent to the fate of freedom elsewhere. Our moral sense dictates a clear-cut preference for those societies which share with us an abiding respect for individual human rights. We do not seek to intimidate, but it is clear that a world which others can dominate with impunity would be inhospitable to decency and a threat to the well-being of all people.

The world is still engaged in a massive armaments race designed to ensure continuing equivalent strength among potential adversaries. We pledge perseverance and wisdom in our efforts to limit the world's armaments to those necessary for each nation's own domestic safety. And we will move this year a step toward our ultimate goal—the elimination of all nuclear weapons from this Earth. We urge all other people to join us, for success can mean life instead of death.

Within us, the people of the United States, there is evident a serious and purposeful rekindling of confidence. And I join in the hope that when my time as your President has ended, people might say this about our Nation:

—that we had remembered the words of Micah and renewed our search for humility, mercy, and justice;

—that we had torn down the barriers that separated those of different race and region and religion, and where there had been mistrust, built unity, with a respect for diversity;

—that we had found productive work for those able to perform it;

—that we had strengthened the American family, which is the basis of our society;

—that we had ensured respect for the law and equal treatment under the law, for the weak and the powerful, for the rich and the poor; and

—that we had enabled our people to be proud of their own Government once again.

I would hope that the nations of the world might say that we had built a lasting peace, based not on weapons of war but on international policies which reflect our own most precious values.

These are not just my goals—and they will not be my accomplishments—but the affirmation of our Nation's continuing moral strength and our belief in an undiminished, ever-expanding American dream.

Thank you very much.

2. Address to the General Assembly of the United Nations March 17, 1977

Public Papers of the Presidents of the United States: Jimmy Carter. 9 vols. Washington, D.C.: Government Printing Office, 1997–1982.

Thank you, Mr. Secretary General.

Last night I was in Clinton, Massachusetts, at a Town Hall meeting where people of that small town decide their political and economic future.

Tonight I speak to a similar meeting where people representing nations all over the world come here to decide their political and economic future.

I am proud to be with you tonight in this house where the shared hopes of the world can find a voice. I have come here to express my own support and the continuing support of my country for the ideals of the United Nations.

We are proud that for the 32 years since its creation, the United Nations has met on American soil. And we share with you the commitments of freedom, self-government, human dignity, mutual toleration, and the peaceful resolution of disputes—which the founding principles of the United Nations and also Secretary General Kurt Waldheim so well represent.

No one nation by itself can build a world which reflects all these fine values. But the United States, my own country, has a reservoir of strength—economic strength, which we are willing to share; military strength, which we hope never to use again; and the strength of ideals, which are determined fully to maintain the backbone of our own foreign policy.

It is now eight weeks since I became President. I have brought to office a firm commitment to a more open foreign policy. And I believe that the American people expect me to speak frankly about the policies that we intend to pursue, and it is in that spirit that I speak to you tonight about our own hopes for the future.

I see a hopeful world, a world dominated by increasing demands for basic freedoms, for fundamental rights, for higher standards of human existence. We are eager to take part in the shaping of that world.

But in seeking such a better world, we are not blind to the reality of disagreement, nor to the persisting dangers that confront us all. Every headline reminds us of bitter divisions, of national hostilities, of territorial conflicts, of ideological competition.

In the Middle East, peace is a quarter of a century overdue. A gathering racial conflict threatens southern Africa; new tensions are rising in the Horn of Africa. Disputes in the eastern Mediterranean remain to be resolved.

Perhaps even more ominous is the staggering arms race. The Soviet Union and the United States have accumulated thousands of nuclear weapons. Our two nations now have five times more missile warheads today than we had just 8 years ago. But we are not five times more secure. On the contrary, the arms race has only increased the risk of conflict.

We can only improve this world if we are realistic about its complexities. The disagreements that we face are deeply rooted, and they often raise difficult philosophical as well as territorial issues. They will not be solved easily. They will not be solved quickly. The arms race is now embedded in the very fabric of international affairs and can only be contained with the greatest difficulty. Poverty and inequality are of such monumental scope that it will take decades of deliberate and determined effort even to improve the situation substantially.

I stress these dangers and these difficulties because I want all of us to dedicate ourselves to a prolonged and persistent effort designed first to maintain peace and to reduce the arms race; second, to build a better and a more cooperative international economic system; and third, to work with potential adversaries as well as our close friends to advance the cause of human rights.

In seeking these goals, I realize that the United States cannot solve the problems of the world. We can sometimes help others resolve their differences, but we cannot do so by imposing our own particular solutions.

In the coming months, there is important work for all of us in advancing international cooperation and economic progress in the cause of peace.

Later this spring, the leaders of several industrial nations of Europe, North America, and Japan will confer at a summit meeting in London on a broad range of issues. We must promote the health of the industrial economies. We must seek to restrain inflation and bring ways of managing our own domestic economies for the benefit of the global economy. We must move forward with multilateral trade negotiations in Geneva.

The United States will support the efforts of our friends to strengthen the democratic institutions in Europe, and particularly in Portugal and Spain.

We will work closely with our European friends on the forthcoming Review Conference on Security and Cooperation in Europe. We want to make certain that the provisions of the Helsinki agreement are fully implemented and that progress is made to further East-West cooperation.

In the Middle East we are doing our best to clarify areas of disagreement, to surface underlying consensus, and to help to develop mutually acceptable principles that can form a flexible framework for a just and a permanent settlement.

In southern Africa, we will work to help attain majority rule through peaceful means. We believe that such fundamental transformation can be achieved, to the advantage of both the blacks and whites who live in that region of the world. Anything less than that may bring a protracted racial war, with devastating consequences to all.

This week the Government of the United States took action to bring our country into full compliance with United Nations sanctions against the illegal regime in Rhodesia. And I will sign that bill Friday in Washington.

We will put our relations with Latin America on a more constructive footing, recognizing the global character of the region's problems.

We are also working to resolve in amicable negotiations the future of the Panama Canal.

We will continue our efforts to develop further our relationships with the People's Republic of China. We recognize our parallel strategic interests in maintaining stability in Asia, and we will act in the spirit of the Shanghai Communiqué.

In Southeast Asia and in the Pacific, we will strengthen our association with our traditional friends, and we will seek to improve relations with our former adversaries.

We have a mission now in Vietnam seeking peaceful resolution of the differences that have separated us for so long.

Throughout the world, we are ready to normalize our relationships and to seek reconciliation with all states which are ready to work with us in promoting global progress and global peace.

Above all, the search for peace requires a much more deliberate effort to contain the global arms race. Let me speak in this context, first, of the U.S.–Soviet Union relationship, and then of the wider need to contain the proliferation of arms throughout the global community.

I intend to pursue the strategic arms limitation talks between the United States and the Soviet Union with determination and with energy. Our Secretary of State will visit Moscow in just a few days.

SALT is extraordinarily complicated. But the basic fact is that while negotiations remain deadlocked, the arms race goes on; the security of both countries and the entire world is threatened.

My preference would be for strict controls or even a freeze on new types and new generations of weaponry and with a deep reduction in the strategic arms of both sides. Such a major step towards not only arms limitation but arms reduction would be welcomed by mankind as a giant step towards peace.

Alternatively, and perhaps much more easily, we could conclude a limited agreement based on those elements of the Vladivostok accord on which we can find complete consensus, and set aside for prompt consideration and subsequent negotiations the more contentious issues and also the deeper reductions in nuclear weapons which I favor.

We will also explore the possibility of a total cessation of nuclear testing. While our ultimate goal is for all nuclear powers to end testing, we do not regard this as a prerequisite for the suspension of tests by the two principal nuclear powers, the Soviet Union and the United States.

We should, however, also pursue a broad, permanent multilateral agreement on this issue.

We will also seek to establish Soviet willingness to reach agreement with us on mutual military restraint in the Indian Ocean, as well as on such matters as arms exports to the troubled areas of the world.

In proposing such accommodations I remain fully aware that American-Soviet relations will continue to be highly competitive—but I believe that our competition must be balanced by cooperation in preserving peace, and thus our mutual survival.

I will seek such cooperation with the Soviet Union—earnestly, constantly, and sincerely.

However, the effort to contain the arms race is not a matter just for the United States and Soviet Union alone. There must be a wider effort to reduce the flow of weapons to all the troubled spots of this globe.

Accordingly, we will try to reach broader agreements among producer and consumer nations to limit the export of conventional arms, and we, ourselves, will take the initiative on our own because the United States has become one of the major arms suppliers of the world.

We are deeply committed to halting the proliferation of nuclear weapons. And we will undertake a new effort to reach multilateral agreements designed to provide legitimate supplies of nuclear fuels for the production of energy, while controlling the poisonous and dangerous atomic wastes.

Working with other nations represented here, we hope to advance the cause of peace. We will make a strong and a positive contribution at the upcoming Special Session on Disarmament which I understand will commence next year.

But the search for peace also means the search for justice. One of the greatest challenges before us as a nation, and therefore one of our greatest opportunities, is to participate in molding a global economic system which will bring greater prosperity to all the people of all countries.

I come from a part of the United States which is largely agrarian and which for many years did not have the advantages of adequate transportation or capital or management skills or education which were available in the industrial States of our country.

So, I can sympathize with the leaders of the developing nations, and I want them to know that we will do our part.

To this end, the United States will be advancing proposals aimed at meeting the basic human needs of the developing world and helping them to increase their productive capacity. I have asked Congress to provide $7½ billion of foreign assistance in the coming year, and I will work to ensure sustained American assistance as the process of global economic development continues. I am also urging the Congress of our country to increase our contributions to the United Nations Development Program and meet in full our pledges to multilateral lending institutions, especially the International Development Association of the World Bank.

We remain committed to an open international trading system, one which does not ignore domestic concerns in the United States. We have extended duty-free treatment to many products from the developing countries. In the multilateral trade agreements in Geneva we have offered substantial trade concessions on the goods of primary interest to developing countries. And in accordance with the Tokyo Declaration, we are also examining ways to provide additional consideration for the special needs of developing countries.

The United States is willing to consider, with a positive and open attitude, the negotiation on agreements to stabilize commodity prices, including the establishment of a common funding arrangement for financing buffer stocks where they are a part of individual negotiated agreements.

I also believe that the developing countries must acquire fuller participation in the global economic decision-making process. Some progress has already been made in this regard by expanding participation of developing countries in the International Monetary Fund.

We must use our collective natural resources wisely and constructively. We've not always done so. Today our oceans are being plundered and defiled. With a renewed spirit of cooperation and hope, we join in the Conference of the Law of the Sea in order to correct past mistakes of generations gone by and to ensure that all nations can share the bounties of the eternal oceans in the future.

We must also recognize that the world is facing serious shortages of energy. This is truly a global problem. For our part, we are determined to reduce waste and to work with others toward a fair and proper sharing of the benefits and costs of energy resources.

The search for peace and justice also means respect for human dignity. All the signatories of the U.N. Charter have pledged themselves to observe and to respect basic human rights. Thus, no member of the United Nations can claim that mistreatment of its citizens is solely its own business. Equally, no member can avoid its responsibilities to review and to speak when torture or unwarranted deprivation occurs in any part of the world.

The basic thrust of human affairs points toward a more universal demand for fundamental human rights. The United States has a historical birthright to be associated with this process.

We in the United States accept this responsibility in the fullest and the most constructive sense. Ours is a commitment, and not just a political posture. I know perhaps as well as anyone that our own ideals in the area of human rights have not always been attained in the United States, but the American people have an abiding commitment to the full realization of these ideals. And we are determined, therefore, to deal with our deficiencies quickly and openly. We have nothing to conceal.

To demonstrate this commitment, I will seek congressional approval and sign the U.N. covenants on economic, social, and cultural rights, and the covenants on civil and political rights. And I will work closely with our own Congress in seeking to support the ratification not only of these two instruments but the United Nations Genocide Convention and the Treaty for the Elimination of All Forms of Racial Discrimination, as well. I have just removed all restrictions on American travel abroad, and we are moving now to liberalize almost completely travel opportunities to America.

The United Nations is a global forum dedicated to the peace and well-being of every individual—no matter how weak, no matter how poor. But we have allowed its human rights machinery to be ignored and sometimes politicized. There is much that can be done to strengthen it.

The Human Rights Commission should be prepared to meet more often. And all nations should be prepared to offer its fullest cooperation to the Human Rights Commission, to welcome its investigations, to work with its officials, and to act on its reports.

I would like to see the entire United Nations Human Rights Division moved back here to the central headquarters, where its activities will be in the forefront of our attention and where the attention of the press corps can stimulate us to deal honestly with this sensitive issue. The proposal made 12 years ago by the Government of Costa Rica, to establish a U.N. High Commission[er] for Human Rights, also deserves our renewed attention and our support.

Strengthened international machinery will help us to close the gap between promise and performance in protecting human rights. When gross or widespread violation takes place—contrary to international commitments—it is of concern to all. The solemn commitments of the United Nations Charter, of the United Nations Universal Declaration for Human Rights, of the Helsinki Accords, and of many other international instruments must be taken just as seriously as commercial or security agreements.

This issue is important in itself. It should not block progress on other important matters affecting the security and well-being of our people and of world peace. It is obvious that the reduction of tension, the control of nuclear arms, the achievement of harmony in the troubled areas of the world, and the provision of food, good health, and education will independently contribute to advancing the human condition.

In our relationships with other countries, these mutual concerns will be reflected in our political, our cultural, and our economic attitudes.

These then are our basic priorities as we work with other members to strengthen and to improve the United Nations.

First, we will strive for peace in the troubled areas of the world; second, we will aggressively seek to control the weaponry of war; third, we will promote a new system of international economic progress and cooperation; and fourth, we will be steadfast in our dedication to the dignity and well-being of people throughout the world.

I believe that this is a foreign policy that is consistent with my own Nation's historic values and commitments. And I believe that it is a foreign policy that is consonant with the ideals of the United Nations.

Thank you very much.

3. Address to the Nation on the Energy Problem April 18, 1977

Public Papers of the Presidents of the United States: Jimmy Carter. 9 vols. Washington, D.C.: Government Printing Office, 1997–1982.

Good evening.

Tonight I want to have an unpleasant talk with you about a problem that is unprecedented in our history. With the exception of preventing war, this is the greatest challenge that our country will face during our lifetime.

The energy crisis has not yet overwhelmed us, but it will if we do not act quickly. It's a problem that we will not be able to solve in the next few years, and it's likely to get progressively worse through the rest of this century.

We must not be selfish or timid if we hope to have a decent world for our children and our grandchildren. We simply must balance our demand for energy with our rapidly shrinking resources. By acting now we can control our future instead of letting the future control us.

Two days from now, I will present to the Congress my energy proposals. Its Members will be my partners, and they have already given me a great deal of valuable advice.

Many of these proposals will be unpopular. Some will cause you to put up with inconveniences and to make sacrifices. The most important thing about these proposals is that the alternative may be a national catastrophe. Further delay can affect our strength and our power as a nation.

Our decision about energy will test the character of the American people and the ability of the President and the Congress to govern this Nation. This difficult effort will be the "moral equivalent of war," except that we will be uniting our efforts to build and not to destroy.

Now, I know that some of you may doubt that we face real energy shortages. The 1973 gas lines are gone, and with this springtime weather, our homes are warm again. But our energy problem is worse tonight than it was in 1973 or a few weeks ago in the dead of winter. It's worse because more waste has occurred and more time has passed by without our planning for the future. And it will get worse every day until we act.

The oil and natural gas that we rely on for 75 percent of our energy are simply running out. In spite of increased effort, domestic production has been dropping steadily at about 6 percent a year. Imports have doubled in the last 5 years. Our Nation's economic and political independence is becoming increasingly vulnerable. Unless profound changes are made to lower oil consumption, we now believe that early in the 1980's the world will be demanding more oil than it can produce.

The world now uses about 60 million barrels of oil a day, and demand increases each year about 5 percent. This means that just to stay even we need the production of a new Texas every year, an Alaskan North Slope every 9 months, or a new Saudi Arabia every 3 years. Obviously, this cannot continue.

We must look back into history to understand our energy problem. Twice in the last several hundred years, there has been a transition in the way people use energy. The first was about 200 years ago, when we changed away from wood—which had provided about 90 percent of all fuel—to coal, which was much more efficient. This change became the basis of the Industrial Revolution.

The second change took place in this century, with the growing use of oil and natural gas. They were more convenient and cheaper than coal, and the supply seemed to be almost without limit. They made possible the age of automobile and airplane travel. Nearly everyone who is alive today grew up during this period, and we have never known anything different.

Because we are now running out of gas and oil, we must prepare quickly for a third change—to strict conservation and to the renewed use of coal and to permanent renewable energy sources like solar power.

The world has not prepared for the future. During the 1950s, people used twice as much oil as during the 1940s. During the 1960s, we used twice as much as during the 1950s. And in each of those decades, more oil was consumed than in all of man's previous history combined.

World consumption of oil is still going up. If it were possible to keep it rising during the 1970s and 1980s by 5 percent a year, as it has in the past, we could use up all the proven reserves of oil in the entire world by the end of the next decade.

I know that many of you have suspected that some supplies of oil and gas are being withheld from the market. You may be right, but suspicions about the oil companies cannot change the fact that we are running out of petroleum.

All of us have heard about the large oil fields on Alaska's North Slope. In a few years, when the North Slope is producing fully, its total output will be just about equal to 2 years' increase in our own Nation's energy demand.

Each new inventory of world oil reserves has been more disturbing than the last. World oil production can probably keep going up for another 6 or 8 years. But sometime in the 1980s, it can't go up any more. Demand will overtake production. We have no choice about that.

But we do have a choice about how we will spend the next few years. Each American uses the energy equivalent of 60 barrels of oil per person each year. Ours is the most wasteful nation on Earth. We waste more energy than we import. With about the same standard of living, we use twice as much energy per person as do other countries like Germany, Japan, and Sweden.

One choice, of course, is to continue doing what we've been doing before. We can drift along for a few more years.

Our consumption of oil would keep going up every year. Our cars would continue to be too large and inefficient. Three-quarters of them would carry only one person—the driver—while our public transportation system continues to decline. We can delay insulating our homes, and they will continue to lose about 50 percent of their heat in waste. We can continue using scarce oil and natural gas to generate electricity and continue wasting two-thirds of their fuel value in the process.

If we do not act, then by 1985 we will be using 33 percent more energy than we use today.

We can't substantially increase our domestic production, so we would need to import twice as much oil as we do now. Supplies will be uncertain. The cost will keep going up. Six years ago, we paid $3.7 billion for imported oil. Last year we spent $36 billion for imported oil—nearly 10 times as much. And this year we may spend $45 billion.

Unless we act, we will spend more than $550 billion for imported oil by 1985—more than $2,500 for every man, woman, and child in America. Along with that money that we transport overseas, we will continue losing American jobs and become increasingly vulnerable to supply interruptions.

Now we have a choice. But if we wait, we will constantly live in fear of embargoes. We could endanger our freedom as a sovereign nation to act in foreign affairs. Within 10 years, we would not be able to import enough oil from any country, at any acceptable price.

If we wait and do not act, then our factories will not be able to keep our people on the job with reduced supplies of fuel.

Too few of our utility companies will have switched to coal, which is our most abundant energy source. We will not be ready to keep our transportation system running with smaller and more efficient cars and a better network of buses, trains, and public transportation.

We will feel mounting pressure to plunder the environment. We will have to have a crash program to build more nuclear plants, strip mine and burn more coal, and drill more offshore wells than if we begin to conserve right now.

Inflation will soar; production will go down; people will lose their jobs. Intense competition for oil will build up among nations and also among the different regions within our own country. This has already started.

If we fail to act soon, we will face an economic, social, and political crisis that will threaten our free institutions. But we still have another choice. We can begin to prepare right now. We can decide to act while there is still time. That is the concept of the energy policy that we will present on Wednesday.

Our national energy plan is based on 10 fundamental principles. The first principle is that we can have an effective and comprehensive energy policy only if the Government takes responsibility for it and if the people understand the seriousness of the challenge and are willing to make sacrifices.

The second principle is that healthy economic growth must continue. Only by saving energy can we maintain our standard of living and keep our people at work. An effective conservation program will create hundreds of thousands of new jobs.

The third principle is that we must protect the environment. Our energy problems have the same cause as our environmental problems—wasteful use of resources. Conservation helps us solve both problems at once.

The fourth principle is that we must reduce our vulnerability to potentially devastating embargoes. We can protect ourselves from uncertain supplies by reducing our demand for oil, by making the most of our abundant resources such as coal, and by developing a strategic petroleum reserve.

The fifth principle is that we must be fair. Our solutions must ask equal sacrifices from every region, every class of people, and every interest group. Industry will have to do its part to conserve just as consumers will. The energy producers deserve fair treatment, but we will not let the oil companies profiteer.

The sixth principle, and the cornerstone of our policy, is to reduce demand through conservation. Our emphasis on conservation is a clear difference between this plan and others which merely encouraged crash production efforts. Conservation is the quickest, cheapest, most practical source of energy. Conservation is the only way that we can buy a barrel of oil for about $2. It costs about $13 to waste it.

The seventh principle is that prices should generally reflect the true replacement cost of energy. We are only cheating ourselves if we make energy artificially cheap and use more than we can really afford.

The eighth principle is that Government policies must be predictable and certain. Both consumers and producers need policies they can count on so they can plan ahead. This is one reason that I'm working with the Congress to create a new Department of Energy to replace more than 50 different agencies that now have some control over energy.

The ninth principle is that we must conserve the fuels that are scarcest and make the most of those that are plentiful. We can't continue to use oil and gas for 75 percent of our consumption, as we do now, when they only make up 7 percent of our domestic reserves. We need to shift to plentiful coal, while taking care to protect the environment, and to apply stricter safety standards to nuclear energy.

The tenth and last principle is that we must start now to develop the new, unconventional sources of energy that we will rely on in the next century.

Now, these 10 principles have guided the development of the policy that I will describe to you and the Congress on Wednesday night.

Our energy plan will also include a number of specific goals to measure our progress toward a stable energy system. These are the goals that we set for 1985:

—to reduce the annual growth rate in our energy demand to less than 2 percent;

—to reduce gasoline consumption by 10 percent below its current level;

—to cut in half the portion of U.S. oil which is imported—from a potential level of 16 million barrels to 6 million barrels a day;

—to establish a strategic petroleum reserve of one billion barrels, more than a 6-months supply;

—to increase our coal production by about two-thirds to more than one billion tons a year;

—to insulate 90 percent of American homes and all new buildings;

—to use solar energy in more than 2½ million houses.

We will monitor our progress toward these goals year by year. Our plan will call for strict conservation measures if we fall behind. I can't tell you that these measures will be easy, nor will they be popular. But I think most of you realize that a policy which does not ask for changes or sacrifices would not be an effective policy at this late date.

This plan is essential to protect our jobs, our environment, our standard of living, and our future. Whether this plan truly makes a difference will not be decided now here in Washington but in every town and every factory, in every home and on every highway and every farm.

I believe that this can be a positive challenge. There is something especially American in the kinds of changes that we have to make. We've always been proud, through our history, of being efficient people. We've always been proud of our ingenuity, our skill at answering questions. Now we need efficiency and ingenuity more than ever.

We've always been proud of our leadership in the world. And now we have a chance again to give the world a positive example.

We've always been proud of our vision of the future. We've always wanted to give our children and our grandchildren a world richer in possibilities than we have had ourselves. They are the ones that we must provide for now. They are the ones who will suffer most if we don't act.

I've given you some of the principles of the plan. I'm sure that each of you will find something you don't like about the specifics of our proposal. It will demand that we make sacrifices and changes in every life. To some degree, the sacrifices will be painful—but so is any meaningful sacrifice. It will lead to some higher costs and to some greater inconvenience for everyone. But the sacrifices can be gradual, realistic, and they are necessary. Above all, they will be fair. No one will gain an unfair advantage through this plan. No one will be asked to bear an unfair burden.

We will monitor the accuracy of data from the oil and natural gas companies for the first time, so that we will always know their true production, supplies, reserves, and profits. Those citizens who insist on driving large, unnecessarily powerful cars must expect to pay more for that luxury.

We can be sure that all the special interest groups in the country will attack the part of this plan that affects them directly. They will say that sacrifice is fine as long as other people do it, but that their sacrifice is unreasonable or unfair or harmful to the country. If they succeed with this approach, then the burden on the ordinary citizen, who is not organized into an interest group, would be crushing.

There should be only one test for this program—whether it will help our country. Other generations of Americans have faced and mastered great challenges. I have faith that meeting this challenge will make our own lives even richer. If you will join me so that we can work together with patriotism and courage, we will again prove that our great Nation can lead the world into an age of peace, independence, and freedom.

Thank you very much, and good night.

4. Remarks at the United Automobile Workers Convention in Los Angeles May 17, 1977

Public Papers of the Presidents of the United States: Jimmy Carter. 9 vols. Washington, D.C.: Government Printing Office, 1997–1982.

Thank you very much, President Woodcock, distinguished members of the UAW who have come here from all over the Nation to reconfirm what you stand for, to my good friend Doug Fraser and to many people in the audience and behind me, who throughout the last 2 years stood in factory shift lines in the cold and in the rain so that I could become better informed about what a President ought to be, about what our Nation is, and what our future might hold:

It's a very rare occasion that I have a chance to come to a convention. I haven't been to one since I've been President. I may not go to another one this year. But I particularly wanted to come and be with you.

Ordinarily Vice President Mondale is the one who chooses to go and make a speech at the conventions. I had to send him to Yugoslavia to have this chance today. He'll be coming back to our country in about a week, having been to Portugal—a brand-new democracy; to Spain—a brand-new democracy; having visited the President of South Africa to try to work out some solution to the difficult problems in that continent; having met with Marshal Tito in Yugoslavia to reconfirm their independence of the Big Bear to the north of them; and then having come back through England to discuss the common basis on which we approach the future.

So, I'm glad to have a chance to be with you today. I've been talking a lot about conservation, lately, and efficiency in automobiles. When I got off the plane, I was greeted and rode in one of your finest products—a very large, very black Cadillac limousine. [Laughter] So, I've enjoyed my visit so far, and I'm looking forward to the rest of it and to speak to you. Later, I'll be on a 90-minute call-in television show, and then I'm going to visit some of the farmlands around Fresno.

It's no accident that I've chosen the UAW convention to make this speech and to make this appearance. Your union was born in struggle, and you've won many victories. But you've never retreated into complacency or narrow selfishness.

The UAW is still fighting, because this union has always understood that it cannot stand alone. And above every other trade union I know in the world, you've always seen that your membership and your leadership were part of a larger society and a larger world. Very few institutions anywhere have been so fortunate as to have the kind of superb leadership that has always been a mark of the UAW.

For 31 years, this union has been led by men whose vision and sense of responsibility extended far beyond the walls of Solidarity House—men who have demanded decency and a better life not just for the UAW membership but for all the people.

The next president of the UAW has big shoes to fill. I won't predict who's going to win your election tomorrow, although I noticed that Doug Fraser doesn't look too worried.

Seven years ago, when Walter Reuther's life was so tragically cut short, there were predictions that this union would turn inward and would abandon its role as defender of social justice. Leonard Woodcock showed how wrong these predictions were. He's left his mark of support for the poor and the oppressed as clearly as for his own members at the bargaining table.

Recently, as you know, I asked him to undertake an extremely sensitive assignment in Vietnam. Leonard Woodcock did a superb job. And although he is retiring as president of this international union, he will continue to serve his country in a new, international role. I will soon submit his name to the Senate to be Chief of the U.S. Liaison Office in China, with the rank of Ambassador.

I don't believe anyone in the world who's familiar with international relations would doubt the importance of this assignment. Now some people may wonder why I'm sending a labor leader instead of a professional diplomat to handle such important negotiations. But I think there are some executives at Ford and

General Motors and Chrysler and American Motors who might be able to answer that question very well.

We want a tough negotiator. We want someone who understands human sensitivities. We want someone who has the personal integrity to build up trust where doubt now exists. And I know that Leonard Woodcock will fill this role as competently and with as much grace as he has the important job of being president of the UAW.

I have complete confidence in him. And if he'll just help me with a few sensitive things in the Congress, I'm going to even send a translator to China with him to help him out with the language. [Laughter]

Today, I want to talk to you briefly about some domestic problems which prey on my mind and rest on my shoulders as your President.

The domestic problems which we do face as Americans are difficult, indeed, but we have the courage and the ingenuity and the greatness of spirit to meet these challenges. I believe that we can build an America in which our day-to-day practices live up to our democratic ideals, in which the family life, mine and yours, is strong and stable, in which the neighborhoods of our cities are vital and safe, in which work is available and is justly rewarded, in which opportunity is not limited by color or sex or religion or economic or educational background, in which there is schooling and employment for the young and dignity and security for the old.

We must work together to control inflation and to get our economy moving again. We must come to terms with the growing shortage of energy which, if ignored, will gravely damage the very fabric of our society. We must safeguard the integrity of our social security system. We must totally reform our tax and our welfare systems. We must ensure the health of the American people. And we must develop a government which is open enough to earn the trust and support of the people in addressing these and other crucial issues, and efficient enough and competent enough to ensure that our efforts will bear fruit.

The achievement of all our goals depends on the first one that I mentioned—a strong and a growing economy.

At the beginning of this administration, less than 4 months ago, our economy was still floundering from the worst recession in 40 years. The well-being of our people was squeezed between the twin pressures of high unemployment and inflation.

That picture has already improved because we have restored the confidence of consumers and business. Last month, the number of Americans with jobs in the private sector of our economy went over 90 million for the first time in our country's history. Eight hundred thousand people have gone off the unemployment rolls since December. Half a million found jobs in April alone. Private surveys have shown that business investment plans for 1977 are up significantly, more than 15 percent, compared to 1976.

Unemployment now stands at the lowest level in 29 months—down a full 1 percent since last November. But of course, you know and I know that a 7 percent unemployment rate is still completely unacceptable. We still have a long way to go.

The equally dangerous threat of inflation is building. Consumer prices reflecting the drought and last winter's cold weather have been going up at an annual rate of about 10 percent in the last 3 months, and the basic inflation rate, under everything else, has been running 6 or 6½ percent.

These inflation figures are too high for comfort. And as you know, also, inflation falls most heavily on people with modest means and people who've worked all their lives for a little security and who then find that security threatened. Inflation robs us of our confidence in the future.

However, it's interesting to point out, at the recent London summit conference, the single issue of most concern to the seven heads of state assembled there was unemployment among young people. In the ideological struggle with the Eastern Socialist and Communist countries, this is our one major vulnerability. We have got to provide in our country an economic system that's healthy enough and an education system that's competent enough so that when our young people reach the age of 18 or 19 years old, they can find a way to use the talent and ability and opportunities that God gave them and not enter adult life discouraged and excluded from society. This ought to be number one in all our efforts in the future.

Experience has shown us and all economists that we must attack inflation and unemployment together. To get our economy moving again, in the short 4 months that I've been in office, we proposed both direct creation of jobs and permanent tax reduction for the low-income and middle-income taxpayers.

Last week I signed a bill, public works, which will provide both necessary community improvements where you live, plus about 600,000 jobs concentrated in areas of high unemployment.

We have proposed more than doubling the existing jobs program for the long-term unemployed and the young. And Congress has already appropriated the money that we requested to increase public service jobs from 310,000 to 725,000.

I've also proposed—and I believe the Congress will rapidly approve—a major initiative to train our young people and to put them to work in productive jobs in our cities, rural areas, national parks and forests. And in addition to this, above and beyond what I've just described, we will provide work this summer for about 1.1 million young people, more than ever before.

To help our hard-pressed cities, which quite often in the past have not gotten a fair share of governmental opportunity, we've supported—and Congress just passed yesterday—a major expansion of countercyclical revenue sharing, which means that the money goes to the areas that are most in need.

We've also proposed a renewed community block grant program with changes that will stimulate private investment, in particular housing and other developments, and put more of the money into the cities again which need it most.

We support extending the earned-income tax credit for working people and a general, personal tax credit, which together add up to $6.8 billion annually in individual tax relief, mostly for low- and middle-income families, including those families too poor to owe any income tax.

And also, I will sign into law within the next few days—Congress has already passed—a permanent $4 billion tax cut through increases in the standard deductions. Eighty-eight percent of this tax relief will go to families with incomes of less than $15,000 a year, and 3.3 million low-income taxpayers who now, pay taxes will not have to pay any Federal income taxes at all.

Now, this new law will obviously save people money, and it will also create jobs because consumers will have more of their paycheck to keep and to spend for goods that we produce. It's also going to save a lot of headaches next April, because 75 percent of all taxpayers will be able to take a standard deduction and compute their taxes on one side of one sheet of paper in one step.

So, the multiple goals of economic strategy reinforce one another, they work together. The strategy is designed to cut unemployment to below 5 percent by 1981; to work with business and labor, together, to knock 2 percentage points off the inflation rate by the end of

1979; and by the higher revenues that growing employment will bring, to achieve a balanced budget in fiscal year 1981.

Again, I want to stress two points about our economic policies because it's important for you and all Americans to understand. One point is that we aim to balance the budget in 1981 in a strong and healthy economy, with the revenues that come into the Government when people are employed and our industrial capacity is being used.

It's not legitimate spending on human needs that causes Federal deficits. It's principally the inadequate revenues that come in from a sluggish economy that create those deficits. Understanding that is a very good move in the right direction. Cutting back programs that really help people is not the way to balance the budget. But even with adequate revenues, we'll still have to make some hard choices about how we spend the taxpayers' money. We can't afford to do everything.

The other important point I want to make about the economy is that I'm inalterably opposed to fighting inflation by keeping unemployment high and factories idle. This has been done too much in the past. That approach has been proved in the last 8 years to be economically ineffective and morally bankrupt. If the economy should falter during the years ahead, I will not hesitate to propose the economic and budgetary measures needed to get the economy going again. And you can depend on that.

Now, the second major challenge I want to discuss with you this morning is energy. The energy crisis is the greatest domestic challenge that our country will face in our lifetime. I still find it almost incredible that our country has no coherent plan for dealing with it until this year. We have now proposed such a plan to the Congress and also proposed a new department to deal with the energy question.

This plan is based on three inescapable realities. There's no way to get around them. The first is that we are simply running out of oil. The second is that oil will, nevertheless, have to remain our primary source of energy for many years and must not be wasted. And the third principle is that unless we begin soon to prepare for the transition to other sources of energy, the consequences on our society and our way of life will be very severe.

We could face massive unemployment, crippling inflation, social and political instability, and threats to our freedom of action in international affairs. We cannot just rely on increased production. While finding more oil is important, we would have to discover a new Alaskan oil field every year just to keep pace with the annual growth in world consumption. No matter how strong the financial incentives, that is simply not going to happen. We must save oil and gas for uses where there is no good substitute. One obvious example is moving vehicles. We must shift to other sources when possible, and we must develop new sources, such as solar energy.

There are no workers in America whose future jobs depend more than yours on a good energy program based on strict conservation. Now, you know and I know that meeting our energy goals is not going to be easy. It will require sacrifice from everyone in the country.

We cannot use the fuel crisis as an excuse for not cleaning up our air. I have proposed tough but fair air pollution standards. We've got to improve the efficiency of our cars, and that's why I proposed a gas-guzzler tax.

Now you and I have honest differences of opinion over some aspects of my proposals. But I don't hesitate to call on you for help, because I know what you've done in the past. You've never lost sight of the broader interests of our Nation. Walter Reuther helped to make possible the Clean Air Act as it was originally passed. And your members are already building cars highly efficient, getting more than 30 miles per gallon.

It's absolutely inevitable, no matter who's the President of the United States, that we will have to shift to more efficient automobiles with a clean exhaust. This past quarter, unfortunately, a larger percentage of Americans bought foreign-made cars than ever before. Now, I know that you agree that the solution is not to erect trade barriers to keep out foreign competition because it only leads to trade wars, to retaliation, and added inflation. The solution lies in using our great American ingenuity to design and produce the right cars for the future.

I can think of no more disastrous assumption for the American automobile industry to make than that we cannot successfully compete with foreign companies that produce and sell such cars. We can compete, and we will compete successfully.

Now I want to discuss something that's important to you and me both—our social security system. This is a problem for all Western democracies. Social security, which is probably the greatest legacy left over for us from the New Deal, has served us now for 40 years. But since 1975, social security has been paying out more than it's been taking in. Unless we take action now, the Disability Insurance Fund's reserves will be gone in 2 years, and the retirement reserves will be gone 4 years from then.

Some have proposed a simple solution for this: to tax the American worker to the hilt. Well, we are not going to do that. Too many people are already paying more payroll taxes than they do income taxes, and we are not going to go this route to save the social security system. And we are not going to let social security go broke.

We're going to keep faith with the 33 million Americans who already enjoy social security benefits and with the 104 million of us, who are paying into the social security system with the expectation that we will receive benefits when we retire, or when we become disabled, or those that are necessary to take care of our families if something happens to us.

Now, there's no easy answer, but the changes that I have already submitted to the Congress will make social security financially sound for the rest of the century and will correct most of the problems for the next 75 years—and without a higher tax rate than already scheduled by law for the average wage earner. I'm going to need your help in Congress to get this bill passed, and I hope you'll help me with it.

Our fourth major goal, I want to mention briefly, is our welfare system and our tax system. In both of these cases, tinkering is not going to be enough. They must be thoroughly redesigned. Our present welfare system robs the taxpayers who support it, discourages the people who administer it, and sometimes degrades the people who really do need help. It's an extraordinarily complex and difficult problem, even more so than I had expected.

Two weeks ago I outlined the principles that must underlie the reform of the system, and we will have legislative proposals ready by the end of this summer. We've already begun to move in this direction by simplifying the food stamp program—eliminating the purchase requirement and reforming the eligibility rules.

As for our tax system, it, too, must be reformed through and through. Our tax system was once relatively simple, fair, and progressive. It isn't any more, because it's been changed so much over the years—often for the benefit of those who are rich enough to hire their own lobbyists in Washington. The process of redesign is well underway, and we intend to submit legislation to the Congress for a fair and simple income tax system this year.

Our fifth major concern is the health of our people. On the airplane coming here from Washington early this morning, I had a chance to talk at length with Congressman Jim Corman about the future of our national health program. Good health for every American is one of my primary concerns, and I know it's one of yours. Again, it's a complicated question. If it weren't complicated, the problem would have been solved many years ago.

We must deal with the cause of illness. This means promoting a cleaner environment and safer and healthier workplaces. And we will be submitting these proposals in about a week. It means helping our children avoid preventable diseases—as was the case when I was a child and, perhaps, when many of you were young—some 5½ million children will be immunized over the next 30 months.

Also, under our proposed Child Health Assessment Program now before the Congress, 10 million young children will be screened annually by 1982. This is five times more than are presently examined at this time to see what childhood diseases might be prevented as they approach adulthood as students.

In order to make medical care available in inner cities and rural areas, we proposed legislation already that will make nurse practitioners and physicians' assistants available to help fill the gap.

And finally, I'm committed to the phasing-in of a workable national health insurance system. [Applause] It's certainly not difficult to guess which union has made national health insurance a national issue. Beginning many months ago, Leonard Woodcock has given me an education about the need and the possible ways for meeting it. He's a member of the advisory committee that will help design the whole system and will hold its first meeting later on this week. And we are aiming to submit legislative proposals early next year.

We must move immediately to start bringing health care costs under control. If we don't—and I want you to listen carefully to this—if we don't bring the health care costs, particularly hospitals, under control, no matter what kind of health system we have in our country, the cost will double every 5 years. Now, we can't afford that. We can't afford that. Hospital costs now take 40 cents of every health dollar, and they've gone up an incredible 1,000 percent since 1950.

I proposed hospital cost containment legislation that would put the brakes on these increases. Sixty other nations have managed to come up with national health programs that meet the needs of our people—of their people. It's not beyond our own ingenuity to do the same, and I want this program to be established during my time in office.

There's a lot that we can do as consumers. In many instances, medical doctors, hospitals, and others, have been very careless about how much health care actually costs.

Late last month, my wife was found to have a tumor on her breast. She went to Bethesda Hospital about 2 o'clock in the afternoon. She had a long incision made, 4 or 5 inches long, and the tumor was removed. She was back home at 5 o'clock.

Quite often, if doctors and hospitals want to hold down the time we spend in intensive care and the extraordinary cost of medical care, they can do it. But we, as consumers, need to help.

The sixth major need is for an open and efficient Government. Now I've done the best I could to open up the Presidency. I've talked publicly about foreign policy matters that were formerly considered too secret and too complicated for the ears of the American people. I've had frequent press conferences, and I've had direct encounters with people who don't normally get to work—get to talk to a President.

When I leave here this morning, I'll go to one of the Los Angeles television stations and for an hour and a half, I will receive calls from people throughout this part of California asking me questions, unscreened, on any subject they choose.

I feel that it's important for the American people to know what's going on. But I also feel it's important for a President to learn from the people of this country. And I want you to know what the options are and what the problems are and what the possibilities are in complicated matters like the control of the nuclear weapons, the resolution of problems in southern Africa, the Middle East, and also in domestic questions which I've discussed with you today. I want you to be a partner with me in making our Government be effective and efficient.

There are many other ways that we can build more openness and responsiveness into our system of government. We can make the activities of government officials devote themselves exclusively to the public interest. I've asked the Congress to impose strict financial disclosure requirements for more than 13,000 top Federal Government executives.

This will make it very difficult for high Government officials to have interests which conflict with those of the public. And we should insist on the same high standards for private institutions. That's why I proposed to Congress making foreign bribery by American companies and officials a crime.

I want to mention now a subject that's important to me and to you. I've worked with many of your members trying to overcome the very great difficulties of simply getting free American people registered to vote. We need to open up our electoral system to greater participation. Many working people don't vote because they don't have the time to go through lengthy and needless registration procedures.

Vice President Mondale and I have worked out legislation that would let people register at the polls on the day of a Federal election. There are some powerful, special interests, including the Republican Party, who are trying to kill the electoral reform bill because they don't want working people to register and to vote. I need you to help me get this bill passed through Congress.

And we need to create an agency for consumer protection. Now in Government, many of the regulatory agencies that were designed originally to protect consumers have been seduced, and now they protect the industry that's supposed to be regulated. This needs to be changed.

This bill would consolidate consumer advocacy programs that are now scattered ineffectively throughout the maze of Federal agencies. It would just give consumers a voice in Government offices where, too often, the only voices heard have been those of lobbyists for the wealthy and powerful. Now, there are enormous pressures to kill this legislation creating this new consumer agency. I want to make sure that they don't get away with it.

The UAW has long supported the consumer agency and easy registration procedures to vote. Together, I believe we can get both these measures passed this year.

We must also make government more efficient, because we don't have the money to waste on inefficiency, on duplication, or to give handouts to those who can take care of themselves. Waste robs us all. It prevents the realization of our hopes and dreams.

An efficient government means spending money only where it will actually benefit our people. We've proposed a $350 million increase in the Title I education funds for poor and deprived little children. We've proposed raising the basic opportunity grants from $1,400 to $1,800 a year, to help families put their children through college.

But when spending is wasteful—when spending is wasteful—we've moved vigorously to cut it out. We found $4 billion in water projects that simply couldn't be justified or were more expensive or elaborate than they needed to be.

We are moving to get rid of some of the more than 1,100 advisory commissions in the Federal Government. We are instituting zero-based budgeting, and we are supporting sunset legislation to help us get rid of programs that have outlived their usefulness.

The more money that we can save that's now being wasted, the more money we'll have without increasing taxes to meet the needs of our people.

We've also begun a complete reorganization of the executive branch, and we are starting at home in the Executive Office of the President.

Now, I believe that we can be fiscally responsible and still satisfy the needs of our people. And I believe that we cannot satisfy our needs unless we are competent and efficient. We can cut both unemployment and inflation. And I believe that our policies will help us reach both goals.

In closing let me say this: We can do these things if we remember that nothing good comes quickly or easily. Every one of these programs that I've outlined to you this morning has been too long ignored.

When I became President, I could see very clearly, as can you, that 4, 8, 12, 20 years ago, these difficult problems should have been addressed. We must make hard choices about how to use our resources, and we must realize that only a lean and efficient government can translate good intentions into actions that will improve the lives of our people.

That's the kind of government I'm determined to have. And I'm going to stick to that determination in spite of whatever criticism may come. And I need you to be partners with me in the next 4 years. [Applause]

Just remain standing. And I want to say one other thing. I've just got one final comment to make.

In his final report to this convention, President Leonard Woodcock wrote: "In the United States, we are moving from a period of depression, despair and despondency into a time of renewed hope."

If we work together in our free Nation, that hope will never fade.

Thank you very much. God bless you all.

5. Address at Wake Forest University, North Carolina March 17, 1978

Public Papers of the Presidents of the United States: Jimmy Carter. 9 vols. Washington, D.C.: Government Printing Office, 1997–1982.

As someone who comes from a great tobacco-producing State, it's an honor for me to be here in the capital of the greatest tobacco State in the world. What you do here means a lot to Georgia. And we have always found that the people in the Winston-Salem area and throughout North Carolina share with us common purposes, a common heritage, and a common future. You've always received me with open arms. You expressed your confidence in me during the campaign for President. And I'm indeed honored to come here to Wake Forest, to Winston-Salem, and to North Carolina, our neighbor State, to make a speech of major importance.

It's a pleasure to be with your great Senator, Bob Morgan, who cast a courageous vote yesterday, and who is extremely knowledgeable about the subject that I will talk about. He's on the Armed Forces Committee, as you know—the Armed Services Committee, responsible for our Nation's defense. He's on the special committee, a highly selective committee on our Nation's intelligence, and he has been one of the staunch protectors of our Nation and is a great man and a great statesman. Bob, I'm very glad to be with you.

It's also good to renew my friendship with your great Governor, Jim Hunt. I first met him before he was Governor and before I was President. We formed an instant personal friendship, and his leadership of your State has brought credit to you and the admiration of the rest of the Nation.

And I'm particularly grateful to be here with Steve Neal. The first time I came here was to join with him in his campaign in 1974, when the prospects were not very bright. But because of the confidence in him, expressed by the people of the Fifth District, he was successful.

He's now assumed a leadership position in the Congress. He's a man, also, who believes in the strong defense of our country. His voting record proves this. In addition, he's on the Science and Technology Committee, which is responsible for advancing our purposes in the future. And he is honored by being the chairman of that portion of the Banking and Finance Committee responsible for international trade. This means a great deal to us, because the exporting of our products and the protection of our textile industry, our tobacco industry, our farm products, is very crucial, and Steve has now worked himself up to a seniority position so he can be exceptionally effective, now and in the future.

I'd like to also acknowledge the presence of two members of my Cabinet, Secretary of Defense Harold Brown, and your own Juanita Kreps, Secretary of Commerce.

To Georgia and to North Carolina, the most important, perhaps, Member in the Congress is the chairman of the Senate Agriculture Committee. He takes care of tobacco farmers; he takes care of peanut farmers, important to both Georgia and North Carolina. And I'm very honored today to have with us my own United States Senator, Herman Talmadge.

I won't acknowledge the presence of every distinguished guest here today, but I would like to say that I'm pleased that several of North Carolina's great Members of Congress have chosen to come to honor me by their presence—Charlie Whitly, Richardson Preyer, Bill Hefner, Lamar Gudger. Would you stand up, please, gentlemen? Please stand up. Thank you very much.

Charlie, I believe that you and Bob Morgan are alumni of Wake Forest. Is that not correct? I know the Wake Forest people are glad to have you back.

Well, I'd like to say that this is a remarkably great honor for me. This is a great college, and it's a time in our Nation's history when we need to stop and assess our past, our present, and our future.

I've noticed the statistics in North Carolina that shows that under my own administration—because of your work, not mine—there's been remarkable economic progress.

In the State of North Carolina, the unemployment rate, for instance, last year, dropped 2.3 percent. You now have an extraordinarily low unemployment rate of only 4½ percent. This shows not only that our Nation is strong but the North Carolina people want to work. And when they are given a chance, they do work. And I thank you for that.

A hundred and ninety-eight years ago, in the southern part of your State, 400 North Carolina militiamen took up arms in our own War of Independence. Against a force of 1,300 British soldiers, the North Carolinians prevailed, and their battle at Ramsour's Mill became a step on the road to victory at Yorktown 1 year later.

Your ancestors in North Carolina and mine in Georgia and their neighbors throughout the Thirteen Colonies earned our freedom in combat. That is a sacrifice which Americans have had to make time and time again in our Nation's history. We've learned that strength is the final protector of liberty.

This is a commitment and a sacrifice that I understand well, for the tradition of military service has been running deep for generations in my own family. My first ancestor to live in Georgia, James Carter, who moved there from North Carolina, fought in the Revolution. My father was a first lieutenant in World War I. My oldest son volunteered to go to Vietnam. And I spent 11 years of my life as a professional military officer in the United States Navy. This is typical of American families.

Down through the generations, the purposes of our Armed Forces have always been the same, no matter what generation it was: to defend our security when it's threatened and, through demonstrated strength, to reduce the chances that we will have to fight again.

These words of John Kennedy will still guide our actions, and I quote him, "The purpose of our arms is peace, not war—to make certain that they will never have to be used."

That purpose is unchanged. But the world has been changing, and our responses as a nation must change with it.

This morning I would like to talk to you about our national security—where we now stand, what new circumstances we face, and what we are going to do in the future.

Let me deal at the beginning with some myths. One myth is that this country somehow is pulling back from protecting its interests and its friends around the world. That is not the case, as will be explained in this speech and demonstrated in our actions as a nation.

Another myth is that our defense budget is too burdensome and consumes an undue part of our Federal revenues. National defense is, of course, a large and important item of expenditure, but it represents only about 5 percent of our gross national product and about a quarter of our current Federal budget.

It also is a mistake to believe that our country's defense spending is mainly for intercontinental missiles or nuclear weapons. Only about 10 percent of our defense budget goes for strategic forces or for nuclear deterrence. More than 50 percent is simply to pay for and support the services of the men and women in our Armed Forces.

Finally, some believe that because we do possess nuclear weapons of great destructive power, that we need do nothing more to guarantee our Nation's security. Unfortunately, it's not that simple.

Our potential adversaries have now built up massive forces armed with conventional weapons—tanks, aircraft, infantry, mechanized units. These forces could be used for political blackmail, and they could threaten our vital interests unless we and our allies and friends have our own military strength and conventional forces as a counterbalance.

Of course, our national security rests on more than just military power. It depends partly on the productive capacity of our factories and our farms, on an adequate supply of natural resources with which God has blessed us, on an economic system which values human freedom above centralized control, on the creative ideas of our best minds, on the hard work, cohesion, moral strength, and determination of the American people, and on the friendship of our neighbors to the north and south.

Our security depends on strong bonds with our allies and on whether other nations seek to live in peace and refrain from trying to dominate those who live around them. But adequate and capable military forces are still an essential element of our national security. We, like our ancestors, have the obligation to maintain strength equal to the challenges of the world in which we live, and we Americans will continue to do so.

Let us review briefly how national security issues have changed over the past decade or two.

The world has grown both more complex and more interdependent. There is now a division among the Communist powers. The old colonial empires have fallen, and many new nations have risen in their place. Old ideological labels have lost some of their meaning.

There have also been changes in the military balance among nations. Over the past 20 years, the military forces of the Soviets have grown substantially, both in absolute numbers and relative to our own. There also has been an ominous inclination on the part of the Soviet Union to use its military power—to intervene in local conflicts, with advisers, with equipment, and with full logistical support and encouragement for mercenaries from other Communist countries, as we can observe today in Africa.

This increase in Soviet military power has been going on for a long time. Discounting inflation, since 1960 Soviet military spending has doubled, rising steadily in real terms by 3 or 4 percent a year, while our own military budget is actually lower now than it was in 1960.

The Soviets, who traditionally were not a significant naval power, now rank number two in world naval forces.

In its balanced strategic nuclear capability, the United States retains important advantages. But over the past decade, the steady Soviet buildup has achieved functional equivalence in strategic forces with the United States.

These changes demand that we maintain adequate responses—diplomatic, military, and economic—and we will.

As President and as Commander in Chief, I am responsible, along with the Congress, for modernizing, expanding, and improving our Armed Forces whenever our security requires it. We've recently completed a major reassessment of our national defense strategy. And out of this process have come some overall principles designed to preserve our national security during the years ahead.

We will match, together with our allies and friends, any threatening power through a combination of military forces, political efforts, and economic programs. We will not allow any other nation to gain military superiority over us.

We shall seek the cooperation of the Soviet Union and other nations in reducing areas of tension. We do not desire to intervene militarily in the internal domestic affairs of other countries, nor to aggravate regional conflicts. And we shall oppose intervention by others.

While assuring our own military capabilities, we shall seek security through dependable, verifiable arms control agreements wherever possible.

We shall use our great economic, technological, and diplomatic advantages to defend our interests and to promote American values. We are prepared, for instance, to cooperate with the Soviet Union toward common social, scientific, and economic goals. But if they fail to demonstrate restraint in missile programs and other force levels or in the projection of Soviet or proxy forces into other lands and continents, then popular support in the United States for such cooperation with the Soviets will certainly erode.

These principles mean that, even as we search for agreement in arms control, we will continue to modernize our strategic systems and to revitalize our conventional forces. And I have no doubt that the Congress shares my commitment in this respect.

We shall implement this policy that I've outlined so briefly in three different ways: by maintaining strategic nuclear balance; by working closely with our NATO allies to strengthen and modernize our defenses in Europe; and by maintaining and developing forces to counter any threats to our allies and friends in our vital interests in Asia, the Middle East, and other regions of the world.

Let me take up each of these three in turn.

Our first and most fundamental concern is to prevent nuclear war. The horrors of nuclear conflict and our desire to reduce the world's arsenals of fearsome nuclear weapons do not free us from the need to analyze the situation objectively and to make sensible choices about our purposes and means.

Our strategic forces must be—and must be known to be—a match for the capabilities of the Soviets. They will never be able to use their nuclear forces to threaten, to coerce, or to blackmail us or our friends.

Our continuing major effort in the SALT talks taking place every day in Geneva are one means toward a goal of strategic nuclear stability.

We and the Soviets have already reached agreement on some basic points, although still others remain to be resolved. We are making good progress. We are not looking for a one-sided advantage. But before I sign any SALT agreement on behalf of the United States, I will make sure that it preserves the strategic balance, that we can independently verify Soviet compliance, and that we will be at least as strong, relative to the Soviet Union, as we would be without any agreement.

But in addition to the limits and reductions of a SALT II agreement, we must make other steps to protect the strategic balance. During the next decade, improvements in Soviet missiles can make our land-based missile forces in silos increasingly vulnerable to a Soviet first strike. Such an attack would amount to national suicide for the Soviet Union. But however remote, it is a threat against which we must constantly be on guard.

We have a superb submarine fleet, which is relatively invulnerable to attack when it's at sea, and we have under construction new Trident submarines and missiles which give our submarine ballistic missile force even greater range and security.

I have ordered rapid development and deployment of cruise missiles to reinforce the strategic value of our bombers. We are working on the MX intercontinental ballistic missile and a Trident II submarine-launched ballistic missile to give us more options to respond to Soviet strategic deployments. If it becomes necessary to guarantee the clear invulnerability of our strategic deterrent, I shall not hesitate to take action for full-scale deployment and development of these systems.

Our strategic defense forces, our nuclear forces, are a triad—land-based missiles, sea-based missiles, and air-breathing missiles, such as bombers and cruise missiles. Through the plans I've described, all three legs of this triad will be modernized and improved. Each will retain the ability, on its own, to impose devastating retaliation upon an aggressor.

For 30 years and more we've been committed to the defense of Europe, bound by the knowledge that Western Europe's security is vital to our own. We continue to cooperate with our NATO Allies in a strategy for flexible response, combining conventional forces and nuclear forces so that no aggressor can threaten the territory of Europe or its freedom, which in the past we have fought together to defend.

For several years we and our allies have been trying to negotiate mutual and balanced reduction in military forces in Europe with the Soviets and with the Warsaw Pact nations who are their allies. But in the meantime, the Soviets have continued to increase and to modernize their forces beyond a level necessary for defense. In the face of this excessive Soviet buildup, we and our NATO Allies have had to take important steps to cope with short-term vulnerabilities and to respond to long-term threats. We are significantly strengthening U.S. forces stationed in Western Europe and improving our ability to speed additional ground and air forces to the defense of Europe in a time of crisis.

Our European allies, who supply the major portion of NATO's conventional combat strength, are also improving their readiness and their reinforcement capabilities and their antitank defenses. The heads of the NATO governments will be here in our country attending a summit meeting in May, where we will address our long-term defense program which will expand and integrate more closely allied defense plans.

For many years, the United States has been a major world power. Our longstanding concerns encompass our own security interests and those of our allies and friends far beyond our own shores and Europe.

We have important historical responsibilities to enhance peace in East Asia, in the Middle East, in the Persian Gulf, and throughout our own hemisphere. Our preference in all these areas is to turn first to international agreements that reduce the overall level of arms and minimize the threat of conflict. But we have the will, and we will also maintain the capacity, to honor our commitments and to protect our interests in those critical areas.

In the Pacific, our effective security is enhanced by mutual defense treaties with our allies and by our friendship and cooperation with other Pacific nations.

Japan and South Korea, closely linked with the United States, are located geographically where vital interests of great powers converge. It is imperative that Northeast Asia remain stable. We will maintain and even enhance our military strength in this area, improving our air strength and reducing our ground forces, as the South Korean army continues to modernize and to increase its own capabilities.

In the Middle East and the region of the Indian Ocean, we seek permanent peace and stability. The economic health and well-being of the United States, Western Europe, Japan, depend upon continued access to the oil from the Persian Gulf area.

In all these situations, the primary responsibility for preserving peace and military stability rests with the countries of the region. But we shall continue to work with our friends and allies to strengthen their ability to prevent threats to their interests and to ours.

In addition, however, we will maintain forces of our own which can be called upon, if necessary, to support mutual defense efforts. The Secretary of Defense, at my direction, is improving and will maintain quickly deployable forces—air, land, and sea—to defend our interests throughout the world.

Arms control agreements are a major goal as instruments of our national security, but this will be possible only if we maintain appropriate military force levels. Reaching balanced, verifiable agreements with our adversaries can limit the cost of security and reduce the risk of war. But even then, we must—and we will—proceed efficiently with whatever arms programs our own security requires.

When I leave this auditorium, I shall be going to visit with the crew aboard one of our most modern nuclear-powered aircraft carriers in the Atlantic Ocean. The men and women of our Armed Forces remain committed, as able professionals and as patriotic Americans, to our common defense. They must stand constantly ready to fight, in the hope that through strength, combat will be prevented. We as Americans will always support them in their courageous vigil.

This has been a serious and a sober talk, but there is no cause for pessimism. We face a challenge, and we will do whatever is necessary to meet it. We will preserve and protect our country and continue to promote and to maintain peace around the world. This means that we shall have to continue to support strong and efficient military forces.

For most of human history, people have wished vainly that freedom and the flowering of the human spirit, which freedom nourishes, did not finally have to depend upon the force of arms. We, like our forebears, live in a time when those who would destroy liberty are restrained less by their respect for freedom itself than by their knowledge that those of us who cherish freedom are strong.

We are a great nation made up of talented people. We can readily afford the necessary costs of our military forces, as well as an increased level, if needed, to prevent any adversary from destabilizing the peace of the world. The money we spend on defense is not wasted any more than is the cost of maintaining a police force in a local community to keep the peace. This investment purchases our freedom to fulfill the worthy goals of our Nation.

Southerners, whose ancestors a hundred years ago knew the horrors of a homeland devastated by war, are particularly determined that war shall never come to us again. All Americans understand the basic lesson of history: that we need to be resolute and able to protect ourselves, to prevent threats and domination by others.

No matter how peaceful and secure and easy the circumstances of our lives now seem, we have no guarantee that the blessings will endure. That is why we will always maintain the strength which, God willing, we shall never need to use.

Thank you very much.

6. Address at the United States Naval Academy Commencement Exercises June 7, 1978

Public Papers of the Presidents of the United States: Jimmy Carter. 9 vols. Washington, D.C.: Government Printing Office, 1997–1982.

Admiral McKee, Governor Lee, distinguished guests, members of the graduating class, and friends:

We do have many distinguished guests here today. I invited my old boss, Admiral Hyman Rickover, to come and join us. He sent word back that he would, of course, comply with my orders as Commander in Chief, but he thought his work for the Navy in Washington was more important than listening to my speech. [Laughter] And I was not surprised. [Laughter]

I am glad to be back for a Naval Academy graduation, although I return with a different rank. I remember that 32 years ago I had the same experience that most of you are sharing today. I was not a midshipman officer. Most of you are not officers. I was thinking more about leave and marriage than I was about world events or a distant future. I would guess there are some among you who feel the same. [Laughter]

I was quite disappointed with my first appointment. We drew lots for assignments, and I had requested a new destroyer in the Pacific. I was assigned to the oldest ship in the Atlantic [laughter]—the U.S.S. Wyoming, which was so dilapidated that because of safety purposes it was not permitted to come into Norfolk to tie up alongside the pier, but had to anchor in isolation in Hampton Roads. [Laughter]

We had a distinguished speaker, Admiral Chester Nimitz. As will be the case with you, I don't remember a word he said. [Laughter] My one hope was that the graduation services would be brief. As will be the case with you, I was disappointed. [Laughter]

And I have to confess with you in confidence that at the time I did not expect to come back here later as President of the United States.

Seven years later, I reluctantly left the Navy. But I can say in retrospect that the Naval Academy and my service in the U.S. Navy was good preparation for the career which I eventually chose.

I congratulate the members of the Class of 1978. Although your education from the perspective of an older person has just begun, you have laid the foundation for a career that can be as rewarding and as challenging as any in the world.

As officers in the modern Navy, you will be actors in a worldwide political and military drama. You will be called upon not only to master the technicalities of military science and military leadership but also to have a sensitive understanding of the international community within which the Navy operates.

Today I want to discuss one of the most important aspects of that international context—the relationship between the world's two greatest powers, the United States of America and the Soviet Union.

We must realize that for a very long time our relationship with the Soviet Union will be competitive. That competition is to be constructive if we are successful. Instead it could be dangerous and politically disastrous. Then our relationship must be cooperative as well.

We must avoid excessive swings in the public mood in our country—from euphoria when things are going well, to despair when they are not; from an exaggerated sense of compatibility with the Soviet Union, to open expressions of hostility.

Détente between our two countries is central to world peace. It's important for the world, for the American public, and for you as future leaders of the Navy to understand the complex and sensitive nature.

The word "détente" can be simplistically defined as "the easing of tension between nations." The word is in practice however, further defined by experience, as those nations evolve new means by which they can live with each other in peace.

To be stable, to be supported by the American people, and to be a basis for widening the scope of cooperation, then detente must be broadly defined and truly reciprocal. Both nations must exercise restraint in troubled areas and in troubled times. Both must honor meticulously those agreements which have already been reached to widen cooperation, naturally and mutually limit nuclear arms production, permit the free movement of people and the expression of ideas, and to protect human rights.

Neither of us should entertain the notion that military supremacy can be attained, or that transient military advantage can be politically exploited.

Our principal goal is to help shape a world which is more responsive to the desire of people everywhere for economic well-being, social justice, political self-determination, and basic human rights.

We seek a world of peace. But such a world must accommodate diversity—social, political, and ideological. Only then can there be a genuine cooperation among nations and among cultures.

We desire to dominate no one. We will continue to widen our cooperation with the positive new forces in the world.

We want to increase our collaboration with the Soviet Union, but also with the emerging nations, with the nations of Eastern Europe, and with the People's Republic of China. We are particularly dedicated to genuine self-determination and majority rule in those areas of the world where these goals have not yet been attained.

Our long-term objective must be to convince the Soviet Union of the advantages of cooperation and of the costs of disruptive behavior.

We remember that the United States and the Soviet Union were allies in the Second World War. One of the great historical accomplishments of the U.S. Navy was to guide and protect the tremendous shipments of armaments and supplies from our country to Murmansk and to other Soviet ports in support of a joint effort to meet the Nazi threat.

In the agony of that massive conflict, 20 million Soviet lives were lost. Millions more who live in the Soviet Union still recall the horror and the hunger of that time.

I'm convinced that the people of the Soviet Union want peace. I cannot believe that they could possibly want war.

Through the years, our Nation has sought accommodation with the Soviet Union, as demonstrated by the Austrian Peace Treaty, the Quadripartite Agreement concerning Berlin, the termination of nuclear testing in the atmosphere, joint scientific explorations in space, trade agreements, the antiballistic missile treaty, the interim agreement on strategic offensive armaments, and the limited test ban agreement.

Efforts still continue with negotiations toward a SALT II agreement, a comprehensive test ban against nuclear explosives, reductions in conventional arms transfers to other countries, the prohibition against attacks on satellites in space, an agreement to stabilize the level of force deployment in the Indian Ocean, and increased trade and scientific and cultural exchange. We must be willing to explore such avenues of cooperation despite the basic issues which divide us. The risks of nuclear war alone propel us in this direction.

The numbers and destructive potential of nuclear weapons has been increasing at an alarming rate. That is why a SALT agreement which enhances the security of both nations is of fundamental importance. We and the Soviet Union are negotiating in good faith almost every day, because we both know that a failure to succeed would precipitate a resumption of a massive nuclear arms race.

I'm glad to report to you today that the prospects for a SALT II agreement are good.

Beyond this major effort, improved trade and technological and cultural exchange are among the immediate benefits of cooperation between our two countries. However, these efforts to cooperate do not erase the significant differences between us. What are these differences?

To the Soviet Union, détente seems to mean a continuing aggressive struggle for political advantage and increased influence in a variety of ways. The Soviet Union apparently sees military power and military assistance as the best means of expanding their influence abroad. Obviously, areas of instability in the world provide a tempting target for this effort, and all too often they seem ready to exploit any such opportunity.

As became apparent in Korea, in Angola, and also, as you know, in Ethiopia more recently, the Soviets prefer to use proxy forces to achieve their purposes.

To other nations throughout the world, the Soviet military buildup appears to be excessive, far beyond any legitimate requirement to defend themselves or to defend their allies. For more than 15 years, they have maintained this program of military growth, investing almost 15 percent of their total gross national product in armaments, and this sustained growth continues.

The abuse of basic human rights in their own country, in violation of the agreement which was reached at Helsinki, has earned them the condemnation of people everywhere who love freedom. By their actions, they've demonstrated that the Soviet system cannot tolerate freely expressed ideas or notions of loyal opposition and the free movement of peoples.

The Soviet Union attempts to export a totalitarian and repressive form of government, resulting in a closed society. Some of these characteristics and goals create problems for the Soviet Union.

Outside a tightly controlled bloc, the Soviet Union has difficult political relations with other nations. Their cultural bonds with others are few and frayed. Their form of government is becoming increasingly unattractive to other nations, so that even Marxist-Leninist groups no longer look on the Soviet Union as a model to be imitated.

Many countries are becoming very concerned that the nonaligned movement is being subverted by Cuba, which is obviously closely aligned with the Soviet Union and dependent upon the Soviets for economic sustenance and for military and political guidance and direction.

Although the Soviet Union has the second largest economic system in the world, its growth is slowing greatly, and its standard of living does not compare favorably with that of other nations at the same equivalent stage of economic development.

Agricultural production still remains a serious problem for the Soviet Union, so that in times of average or certainly adverse conditions for crop production, they must turn to us or turn to other nations for food supplies.

We in our country are in a much more favorable position. Our industrial base and our productivity are unmatched. Our scientific and technological capability is superior to all others. Our alliances with other free nations are strong and growing stronger, and our military capability is now and will be second to none.

In contrast to the Soviet Union, we are surrounded by friendly neighbors and wide seas. Our societal structure is stable and cohesive, and our foreign policy enjoys bipartisan public support, which gives it continuity.

We are also strong because of what we stand for as a nation: the realistic chance for every person to build a better life; protection by both law and custom from arbitrary exercise of government power; the right of every individual to speak out, to participate fully in government, and to share political power. Our philosophy is based on personal freedom, the most powerful of all ideas, and our democratic way of life warrants the admiration and emulation by other people throughout the world.

Our work for human rights makes us part of an international tide, growing in force. We are strengthened by being part of it.

Our growing economic strength is also a major political factor, potential influence for the benefit of others. Our gross national product exceeds that of all nine nations combined in the European Economic Community and is twice as great as that of the Soviet Union. Additionally, we are now learning how to use our resources more wisely, creating a new harmony between our people and our environment.

Our analysis of American military strength also furnishes a basis for confidence. We know that neither the United States nor the Soviet Union can launch a nuclear assault on the other without suffering a devastating counterattack which could destroy the aggressor nation. Although the Soviet Union has more missile launchers, greater throw-weight, and more continental air defense capabilities, the United States has more warheads, generally greater accuracy, more heavy bombers, a more balanced nuclear force, better missile submarines, and superior antisubmarine warfare capability.

A successful SALT II agreement will give both nations equal but lower ceilings on missile launchers and also on missiles with multiple warheads. We envision in SALT III an even greater mutual reduction in nuclear weapons.

With essential nuclear equivalence, relative conventional force strength has now become more important. The fact is that the military capability of the United States and its allies is adequate to meet any foreseeable threat.

It is possible that each side tends to exaggerate the military capability of the other. Accurate analyses are important as a basis for making decisions for the future. False or excessive estimates of Soviet strength or American weakness contributes to the effectiveness of the Soviet propaganda effort.

For example, recently alarming news reports of the military budget proposals for the U.S. Navy ignored the fact that we have the highest defense budget in history and that the largest portion of this will go to the Navy.

You men are joining a long tradition of superior leadership, seamanship, tactics, and ship design. And I'm confident that the U.S. Navy has no peer, no equal, on the high seas today, and that you, I, and others will always keep the Navy strong.

Let there be no doubt about our present and future strength. This brief assessment which

I've just made shows that we need not be overly concerned about our ability to compete and to compete successfully. Certainly there is no cause for alarm. The healthy self-criticism and the free debate which are essential in a democracy should never be confused with weakness or despair or lack of purpose.

What are the principal elements of American foreign policy to the Soviet Union? Let me outline them very briefly.

We will continue to maintain equivalent nuclear strength, because we believe that in the absence of worldwide nuclear disarmament, such equivalency is the least threatening and the most stable situation for the world.

We will maintain a prudent and sustained level of military spending, keyed to a stronger NATO, more mobile forces, and undiminished presence in the Pacific. We and our allies must and will be able to meet any foreseeable challenge to our security from either strategic nuclear forces or from conventional forces. America has the capability to honor this commitment without excessive sacrifice on the part of our citizens, and that commitment to military strength will be honored.

Looking beyond our alliances, we will support worldwide and regional organizations which are dedicated to enhancing international peace, like the United Nations, the Organization of American States, and the Organization for African Unity.

In Africa we and our African friends want to see a continent that is free of the dominance of outside powers, free of the bitterness of racial injustice, free of conflict, and free of the burdens of poverty and hunger and disease. We are convinced that the best way to work toward these objectives is through affirmative policies that recognize African realities and that recognize aspirations.

The persistent and increasing military involvement of the Soviet Union and Cuba in Africa could deny this hopeful vision. We are deeply concerned about the threat to regional peace and to the autonomy of countries within which these foreign troops seem permanently to be stationed. That is why I've spoken up on this subject today. And this is why I and the American people will support African efforts to contain such intrusion, as we have done recently in Zaire.

I urge again that all other powers join us in emphasizing works of peace rather than the weapons of war. In their assistance to Africa, let the Soviet Union now join us in seeking a peaceful and a speedy transition to majority rule in Rhodesia and in Namibia. Let us see efforts to resolve peacefully the disputes in Eritrea and in Angola. Let us all work, not to divide and to seek domination in Africa, but to help those nations to fulfill their great potential.

We will seek peace, better communication and understanding, cultural and scientific exchange, and increased trade with the Soviet Union and with other nations.

We will attempt to prevent the proliferation of nuclear weapons among those nations not now having this capability.

We will continue to negotiate constructively and persistently for a fair strategic arms limitation agreement. We know that no ideological victories can be won by either side by the use of nuclear weapons.

We have no desire to link this negotiation for a SALT agreement with other competitive relationships nor to impose other special conditions on the process. In a democratic society, however, where public opinion is an integral factor in the shaping and implementation of foreign policy, we do recognize that tensions, sharp disputes, or threats to peace will complicate the quest for a successful agreement. This is not a matter of our preference but a simple recognition of fact.

The Soviet Union can choose either confrontation or cooperation. The United States is adequately prepared to meet either choice.

We would prefer cooperation through a détente that increasingly involves similar restraint for both sides; similar readiness to resolve disputes by negotiations, and not by violence; similar willingness to compete peacefully, and not militarily. Anything less than that is likely to undermine détente. And this is why I hope that no one will underestimate the concerns which I have expressed today.

A competition without restraint and without shared rules will escalate into graver tensions, and our relationship as a whole with the Soviet Union will suffer. I do not wish this to happen, and I do not believe that Mr. Brezhnev desires it. And this is why it is time for us to speak frankly and to face the problems squarely.

By a combination of adequate American strength, of quiet self-restraint in the use of it, of a refusal to believe in the inevitability of war, and of a patient and persistent development of all the peaceful alternatives, we hope eventually to lead international society into a more stable, more peaceful, and a more hopeful future.

You and I leave here today to do our common duty—protecting our Nation's vital interests by peaceful means if possible, by resolute action if necessary. We go forth sobered by these responsibilities, but confident of our strength. We go forth knowing that our Nation's goals—peace, security, liberty for ourselves and for others—will determine our future and that together we can prevail.

To attain these goals, our Nation will require exactly those qualities of courage, self-sacrifice, idealism, and self-discipline which you as midshipmen have learned here at Annapolis so well. That is why your Nation expects so much of you, and that is why you have so much to give.

I leave you now with my congratulations and with a prayer to God that both you and I will prove worthy of the task that is before us and the Nation which we have sworn to serve.

Thank you very much.

7. Address to the Nation on Energy and National Goals ("Crisis of Confidence" Speech) July 15, 1979

Public Papers of the Presidents of the United States: Jimmy Carter. 9 vols. Washington, D.C.: Government Printing Office, 1997–1982.

Good evening.

This is a special night for me. Exactly 3 years ago, on July 15, 1976, I accepted the nomination of my party to run for President of the United States. I promised you a President who is not isolated from the people, who feels your pain, and who shares your dreams and who draws his strength and his wisdom from you.

During the past 3 years I've spoken to you on many occasions about national concerns, the energy crisis, reorganizing the Government, our Nation's economy, and issues of war and especially peace. But over those years the subjects of the speeches, the talks, and the press conferences have become increasingly narrow, focused more and more on what the isolated world of Washington thinks is important. Gradually, you've heard more and more about what the Government thinks or what the Government should be doing and less and less about our Nation's hopes, our dreams, and our vision of the future.

Ten days ago I had planned to speak to you again about a very important subject—energy. For the fifth time I would have described the urgency of the problem and laid out a series of legislative recommendations to the Congress. But as I was preparing to speak, I began to ask myself the same question that I now know has been troubling many of you. Why have we not been able to get together as a nation to resolve our serious energy problem?

It's clear that the true problems of our Nation are much deeper—deeper than gasoline lines or energy shortages, deeper even than inflation or recession. And I realize more than ever that as President I need your help. So, I decided to reach out and listen to the voices of America.

I invited to Camp David people from almost every segment of our society—business and labor, teachers and preachers, Governors, mayors, and private citizens. And then I left Camp David to listen to other Americans, men and women like you. It has been an extraordinary 10 days, and I want to share with you what I've heard.

First of all, I got a lot of personal advice. Let me quote a few of the typical comments that I wrote down.

This from a southern Governor: "Mr. President, you are not leading this Nation—you're just managing the Government."

"You don't see the people enough any more."

"Some of your Cabinet members don't seem loyal. There is not enough discipline among your disciples."

"Don't talk to us about politics or the mechanics of government, but about an understanding of our common good."

"Mr. President, we're in trouble. Talk to us about blood and sweat and tears."

"If you lead, Mr. President, we will follow."

Many people talked about themselves and about the condition of our Nation. This from a young woman in Pennsylvania: "I feel so far from government. I feel like ordinary people are excluded from political power."

And this from a young Chicano: "Some of us have suffered from recession all our lives."

"Some people have wasted energy, but others haven't had anything to waste."

And this from a religious leader: "No material shortage can touch the important things like God's love for us or our love for one another."

And I like this one particularly from a black woman who happens to be the mayor of a small Mississippi town: "The big-shots are not the only ones who are important. Remember, you can't sell anything on Wall Street unless someone digs it up somewhere else first."

This kind of summarized a lot of other statements: "Mr. President, we are confronted with a moral and a spiritual crisis."

Several of our discussions were on energy, and I have a notebook full of comments and advice. I'll read just a few.

"We can't go on consuming 40 percent more energy than we produce. When we import oil we are also importing inflation plus unemployment."

"We've got to use what we have. The Middle East has only 5 percent of the world's energy, but the United States has 24 percent."

And this is one of the most vivid statements: "Our neck is stretched over the fence and OPEC has a knife."

"There will be other cartels and other shortages. American wisdom and courage right now can set a path to follow in the future."

This was a good one: "Be bold, Mr. President. We may make mistakes, but we are ready to experiment."

And this one from a labor leader got to the heart of it: "The real issue is freedom. We must deal with the energy problem on a war footing."

And the last that I'll read: "When we enter the moral equivalent of war, Mr. President, don't issue us BB guns."

These 10 days confirmed my belief in the decency and the strength and the wisdom of the American people, but it also bore out some of my longstanding concerns about our Nation's underlying problems.

I know, of course, being President, that government actions and legislation can be very important. That's why I've worked hard to put my campaign promises into law—and I have to admit, with just mixed success. But after listening to the American people I have been reminded again that all the legislation in the world can't fix what's wrong with America. So, I want to speak to you first tonight about a subject even more serious than energy or inflation. I want to talk to you right now about a fundamental threat to American democracy.

I do not mean our political and civil liberties. They will endure. And I do not refer to the outward strength of America, a nation that is at peace tonight everywhere in the world, with unmatched economic power and military might.

The threat is nearly invisible in ordinary ways. It is a crisis of confidence. It is a crisis that strikes at the very heart and soul and spirit of our national will. We can see this crisis in the growing doubt about the meaning of our own lives and in the loss of a unity of purpose for our Nation.

The erosion of our confidence in the future is threatening to destroy the social and the political fabric of America.

The confidence that we have always had as a people is not simply some romantic dream or a proverb in a dusty book that we read just on the Fourth of July. It is the idea which founded our Nation and has guided our development as a people. Confidence in the future has supported everything else—public institutions and private enterprise, our own families, and the very Constitution of the United States. Confidence has defined our course and has served as a link between generations. We've always believed in something called progress. We've always had a faith that the days of our children would be better than our own.

Our people are losing that faith, not only in government itself but in the ability as citizens to serve as the ultimate rulers and shapers of our democracy. As a people we know our past and we are proud of it. Our progress has been part of the living history of America, even the world. We always believed that we were part of a great movement of humanity itself called democracy, involved in the search for freedom, and that belief has always strengthened us in our purpose. But just as we are losing our confidence in the future, we are also beginning to close the door on our past.

In a nation that was proud of hard work, strong families, close-knit communities, and our faith in God, too many of us now tend to worship self-indulgence and consumption. Human identity is no longer defined by what one does, but by what one owns. But we've discovered that owning things and consuming things does not satisfy our longing for meaning. We've learned that piling up material goods cannot fill the emptiness of lives which have no confidence or purpose.

The symptoms of this crisis of the American spirit are all around us. For the first time in the history of our country a majority of our people believe that the next 5 years will be worse than the past 5 years. Two-thirds of our people do not even vote. The productivity of American workers is actually dropping, and the willingness of Americans to save for the future has fallen below that of all other people in the Western world.

As you know, there is a growing disrespect for government and for churches and for schools, the news media, and other institutions. This is not a message of happiness or reassurance, but it is the truth and it is a warning.

These changes did not happen overnight. They've come upon us gradually over the last generation, years that were filled with shocks and tragedy.

We were sure that ours was a nation of the ballot, not the bullet, until the murders of John Kennedy and Robert Kennedy and Martin Luther King, Jr. We were taught that our armies were always invincible and our causes were always just, only to suffer the agony of Vietnam. We respected the Presidency as a place of honor until the shock of Watergate.

We remember when the phrase "sound as a dollar" was an expression of absolute dependability, until 10 years of inflation began to shrink our dollar and our savings. We believed that our Nation's resources were limitless until 1973, when we had to face a growing dependence on foreign oil.

These wounds are still very deep. They have never been healed.

Looking for a way out of this crisis, our people have turned to the Federal Government and found it isolated from the mainstream of our Nation's life. Washington, D.C., has become an island. The gap between our citizens and our Government has never been so wide. The people are looking for honest answers, not easy answers; clear leadership, not false claims and evasiveness and politics as usual.

What you see too often in Washington and elsewhere around the country is a system of government that seems incapable of action. You see a Congress twisted and pulled in every direction by hundreds of well-financed and powerful special interests. You see every extreme position defended to the last vote, almost to the last breath by one unyielding group or another. You often see a balanced and a fair approach that demands sacrifice, a little sacrifice from everyone, abandoned like an orphan without support and without friends.

Often you see paralysis and stagnation and drift. You don't like it, and neither do I. What can we do?

First of all, we must face the truth, and then we can change our course. We simply must have faith in each other, faith in our ability to govern ourselves, and faith in the future of this Nation. Restoring that faith and that confidence to America is now the most important task we face. It is a true challenge of this generation of Americans.

One of the visitors to Camp David last week put it this way: "We've got to stop crying and start sweating, stop talking and start walking, stop cursing and start praying. The strength we need will not come from the White House, but from every house in America."

We know the strength of America. We are strong. We can regain our unity. We can regain our confidence. We are the heirs of generations who survived threats much more powerful and awesome than those that challenge us now. Our fathers and mothers were strong men and women who shaped a new society during the Great Depression, who fought world wars, and who carved out a new charter of peace for the world.

We ourselves are the same Americans who just 10 years ago put a man on the Moon. We are the generation that dedicated our society to the pursuit of human rights and equality. And we are the generation that will win the war on the energy problem and in that process rebuild the unity and confidence of America.

We are at a turning point in our history. There are two paths to choose. One is a path I've warned about tonight, the path that leads to fragmentation and self-interest. Down that road lies a mistaken idea of freedom, the right to grasp for ourselves some advantage over others. That path would be one of constant conflict between narrow interests ending in chaos and immobility. It is a certain route to failure.

All the traditions of our past, all the lessons of our heritage, all the promises of our future point to another path, the path of common purpose and the restoration of American values. That path leads to true freedom for our Nation and ourselves. We can take the first steps down that path as we begin to solve our energy problem.

Energy will be the immediate test of our ability to unite this Nation, and it can also be the standard around which we rally. On the battlefield of energy we can win for our Nation a new confidence, and we can seize control again of our common destiny.

In little more than two decades we've gone from a position of energy independence to one in which almost half the oil we use comes from foreign countries, at prices that are going through the roof. Our excessive dependence on OPEC has already taken a tremendous toll on our economy and our people. This is the direct cause of the long lines which have made millions of you spend aggravating hours waiting for gasoline. It's a cause of the increased inflation and unemployment that we now face. This intolerable dependence on foreign oil threatens our economic independence and the very security of our Nation.

The energy crisis is real. It is worldwide. It is a clear and present danger to our Nation. These are facts and we simply must face them.

What I have to say to you now about energy is simple and vitally important.

Point one: I am tonight setting a clear goal for the energy policy of the United States. Beginning this moment, this Nation will never use more foreign oil than we did in 1977—never. From now on, every new addition to our demand for energy will be met from our own production and our own conservation. The generation-long growth in our dependence on foreign oil will be stopped dead in its tracks right now and then reversed as we move through the 1980's, for I am tonight setting the further goal of cutting our dependence on foreign oil by one-half by the end of the next decade—a saving of over 4½ million barrels of imported oil per day.

Point two: To ensure that we meet these targets, I will use my Presidential authority to set import quotas. I'm announcing tonight that for 1979 and 1980, I will forbid the entry into this country of one drop of foreign oil more than these goals allow. These quotas will ensure a reduction in imports even below the ambitious levels we set at the recent Tokyo summit.

Point three: To give us energy security, I am asking for the most massive peacetime commitment of funds and resources in our Nation's history to develop America's own alternative sources of fuel—from coal, from oil shale, from plant products for gasohol, from unconventional gas, from the Sun.

I propose the creation of an energy security corporation to lead this effort to replace 2½ million barrels of imported oil per day by 1990. The corporation will issue up to $5 billion in energy bonds, and I especially want them to be in small denominations so that average Americans can invest directly in America's energy security.

Just as a similar synthetic rubber corporation helped us win World War II, so will we mobilize American determination and ability to win the energy war. Moreover, I will soon submit legislation to Congress calling for the creation of this Nation's first solar bank, which will help us achieve the crucial goal of 20 percent of our energy coming from solar power by the year 2000.

These efforts will cost money, a lot of money, and that is why Congress must enact the windfall profits tax without delay. It will be money well spent. Unlike the billions of dollars that we ship to foreign countries to pay for foreign oil, these funds will be paid by Americans to Americans. These funds will go to fight, not to increase, inflation and unemployment.

Point four: I'm asking Congress to mandate, to require as a matter of law, that our Nation's utility companies cut their massive use of oil by 50 percent within the next decade and switch to other fuels, especially coal, our most abundant energy source.

Point five: To make absolutely certain that nothing stands in the way of achieving these goals, I will urge Congress to create an energy mobilization board which, like the War Production Board in World War II, will have the responsibility and authority to cut through the red tape, the delays, and the endless roadblocks to completing key energy projects.

We will protect our environment. But when this Nation critically needs a refinery or a pipeline, we will build it.

Point six: I'm proposing a bold conservation program to involve every State, county, and city and every average American in our energy battle. This effort will permit you to build conservation into your homes and your lives at a cost you can afford.

I ask Congress to give me authority for mandatory conservation and for standby gasoline rationing. To further conserve energy, I'm proposing tonight an extra $10 billion over the next decade to strengthen our public transportation systems. And I'm asking you for your good and for your Nation's security to take no unnecessary trips, to use carpools or public transportation whenever you can, to park your car one extra day per week, to obey the speed limit, and to set your thermostats to save fuel. Every act of energy conservation like this is more than just common sense—I tell you it is an act of patriotism.

Our Nation must be fair to the poorest among us, so we will increase aid to needy Americans to cope with rising energy prices. We often think of conservation only in terms of sacrifice. In fact, it is the most painless and immediate way of rebuilding our Nation's strength. Every gallon of oil each one of us saves is a new form of production. It gives us more freedom, more confidence, that much more control over our own lives.

So, the solution of our energy crisis can also help us to conquer the crisis of the spirit in our country. It can rekindle our sense of unity, our confidence in the future, and give our Nation and all of us individually a new sense of purpose.

You know we can do it. We have the natural resources. We have more oil in our shale alone than several Saudi Arabias. We have more coal than any nation on Earth. We have the world's highest level of technology. We have the most skilled work force, with innovative genius, and I firmly believe that we have the national will to win this war.

I do not promise you that this struggle for freedom will be easy. I do not promise a quick way out of our Nation's problems, when the truth is that the only way out is an all-out effort. What I do promise you is that I will lead our fight, and I will enforce fairness in our struggle, and I will ensure honesty. And above all, I will act.

We can manage the short-term shortages more effectively and we will, but there are no short-term solutions to our long-range problems. There is simply no way to avoid sacrifice.

Twelve hours from now I will speak again in Kansas City, to expand and to explain further our energy program. Just as the search for solutions to our energy shortages has now led us to a new awareness of our Nation's deeper problems, so our willingness to work for those solutions in energy can strengthen us to attack those deeper problems.

I will continue to travel this country, to hear the people of America. You can help me to develop a national agenda for the 1980s. I will listen and I will act. We will act together. These were the promises I made 3 years ago, and I intend to keep them.

Little by little we can and we must rebuild our confidence. We can spend until we empty our treasuries, and we may summon all the wonders of science. But we can succeed only if we tap our greatest resources—America's people, America's values, and America's confidence.

I have seen the strength of America in the inexhaustible resources of our people. In the days to come, let us renew that strength in the struggle for an energy secure nation.

In closing, let me say this: I will do my best, but I will not do it alone. Let your voice be heard. Whenever you have a chance, say something good about our country. With God's help and for the sake of our Nation, it is time for us to join hands in America. Let us commit ourselves together to a rebirth of the American spirit. Working together with our common faith we cannot fail.

Thank you and good night.

8. State of the Union Address January 23, 1980

Public Papers of the Presidents of the United States: Jimmy Carter. 9 vols. Washington, D.C.: Government Printing Office, 1997–1982.

Mr. President, Mr. Speaker, Members of the 96th Congress, fellow citizens:

This last few months has not been an easy time for any of us. As we meet tonight, it has never been more clear that the state of our Union depends on the state of the world. And tonight, as throughout our own generation, freedom and peace in the world depend on the state of our Union.

The 1980s have been born in turmoil, strife, and change. This is a time of challenge to our interests and our values and it's a time that tests our wisdom and our skills.

At this time in Iran, 50 Americans are still held captive, innocent victims of terrorism and anarchy. Also at this moment, massive Soviet troops are attempting to subjugate the fiercely independent and deeply religious people of Afghanistan. These two acts—one of international terrorism and one of military aggression—present a serious challenge to the United States of America and indeed to all the nations of the world. Together, we will meet these threats to peace.

I'm determined that the United States will remain the strongest of all nations, but our power will never be used to initiate a threat to the security of any nation or to the rights of any human being. We seek to be and to remain secure—a nation at peace in a stable world. But to be secure we must face the world as it is.

Three basic developments have helped to shape our challenges: the steady growth and increased projection of Soviet military power beyond its own borders; the overwhelming dependence of the Western democracies on oil supplies from the Middle East; and the press of social and religious and economic and political change in the many nations of the developing world, exemplified by the revolution in Iran.

Each of these factors is important in its own right. Each interacts with the others. All must be faced together, squarely and courageously. We will face these challenges, and we will meet them with the best that is in us. And we will not fail.

In response to the abhorrent act in Iran, our Nation has never been aroused and unified so greatly in peacetime. Our position is clear. The United States will not yield to blackmail.

We continue to pursue these specific goals: first, to protect the present and long-range interests of the United States; secondly, to preserve the lives of the American hostages and to secure, as quickly as possible, their safe release, if possible, to avoid bloodshed which might further endanger the lives of our fellow citizens; to enlist the help of other nations in condemning this act of violence, which is shocking and violates the moral and the legal standards of a civilized world; and also to convince and to persuade the Iranian leaders that the real danger to their nation lies in the north, in the Soviet Union and from the Soviet troops now in Afghanistan, and that the unwarranted Iranian quarrel with the United States hampers their response to this far greater danger to them.

If the American hostages are harmed, a severe price will be paid. We will never rest until every one of the American hostages are released.

But now we face a broader and more fundamental challenge in this region because of the recent military action of the Soviet Union.

Now, as during the last 3½ decades, the relationship between our country, the United States of America, and the Soviet Union is the most critical factor in determining whether the world will live at peace or be engulfed in global conflict.

Since the end of the Second World War, America has led other nations in meeting the challenge of mounting Soviet power. This has not been a simple or a static relationship. Between us there has been cooperation, there has been competition, and at times there has been confrontation.

In the 1940s we took the lead in creating the Atlantic Alliance in response to the Soviet Union's suppression and then consolidation of its East European empire and the resulting threat of the Warsaw Pact to Western Europe.

In the 1950s we helped to contain further Soviet challenges in Korea and in the Middle East, and we rearmed to assure the continuation of that containment.

In the 1960s we met the Soviet challenges in Berlin, and we faced the Cuban missile crisis. And we sought to engage the Soviet Union in the important task of moving beyond the cold war and away from confrontation.

And in the 1970s three American Presidents negotiated with the Soviet leaders in attempts to halt the growth of the nuclear arms race. We sought to establish rules of behavior that would reduce the risks of conflict, and we searched for areas of cooperation that could make our relations reciprocal and productive, not only for the sake of our two nations but for the security and peace of the entire world.

In all these actions, we have maintained two commitments: to be ready to meet any challenge by Soviet military power, and to develop ways to resolve disputes and to keep the peace.

Preventing nuclear war is the foremost responsibility of the two superpowers. That's why we've negotiated the strategic arms limitation treaties—SALT I and SALT II. Especially now, in a time of great tension, observing the mutual constraints imposed by the terms of these treaties will be in the best interest of both countries and will help to preserve world peace. I will consult very closely with the Congress on this matter as we strive to control nuclear weapons. That effort to control nuclear weapons will not be abandoned.

We superpowers also have the responsibility to exercise restraint in the use of our great military force. The integrity and the independence of weaker nations must not be threatened. They must know that in our presence they are secure.

But now the Soviet Union has taken a radical and an aggressive new step. It's using its great military power against a relatively defenseless nation. The implications of the Soviet invasion of Afghanistan could pose the most serious threat to the peace since the Second World War.

The vast majority of nations on Earth have condemned this latest Soviet attempt to extend its colonial domination of others and have demanded the immediate withdrawal of Soviet troops. The Moslem world is especially and justifiably outraged by this aggression against an Islamic people. No action of a world power has ever been so quickly and so overwhelmingly condemned. But verbal condemnation is not enough. The Soviet Union must pay a concrete price for their aggression.

While this invasion continues, we and the other nations of the world cannot conduct business as usual with the Soviet Union. That's why the United States has imposed stiff economic penalties on the Soviet Union. I will not issue any permits for Soviet ships to fish in the coastal waters of the United States. I've cut Soviet access to high-technology equipment and to agricultural products. I've limited other commerce with the Soviet Union, and

I've asked our allies and friends to join with us in restraining their own trade with the Soviets and not to replace our own embargoed items. And I have notified the Olympic Committee that with Soviet invading forces in Afghanistan, neither the American people nor I will support sending an Olympic team to Moscow.

The Soviet Union is going to have to answer some basic questions: Will it help promote a more stable international environment in which its own legitimate, peaceful concerns can be pursued? Or will it continue to expand its military power far beyond its genuine security needs, and use that power for colonial conquest? The Soviet Union must realize that its decision to use military force in Afghanistan will be costly to every political and economic relationship it values.

The region which is now threatened by Soviet troops in Afghanistan is of great strategic importance: It contains more than two-thirds of the world's exportable oil. The Soviet effort to dominate Afghanistan has brought Soviet military forces to within 300 miles of the Indian Ocean and close to the Straits of Hormuz, a waterway through which most of the world's oil must flow. The Soviet Union is now attempting to consolidate a strategic position, therefore, that poses a grave threat to the free movement of Middle East oil.

This situation demands careful thought, steady nerves, and resolute action, not only for this year but for many years to come. It demands collective efforts to meet this new threat to security in the Persian Gulf and in Southwest Asia. It demands the participation of all those who rely on oil from the Middle East and who are concerned with global peace and stability. And it demands consultation and close cooperation with countries in the area which might be threatened.

Meeting this challenge will take national will, diplomatic and political wisdom, economic sacrifice, and, of course, military capability. We must call on the best that is in us to preserve the security of this crucial region.

Let our position be absolutely clear: An attempt by any outside force to gain control of the Persian Gulf region will be regarded as an assault on the vital interests of the United States of America, and such an assault will be repelled by any means necessary, including military force.

During the past 3 years, you have joined with me to improve our own security and the prospects for peace, not only in the vital oil-producing area of the Persian Gulf region but around the world. We've increased annually our real commitment for defense, and we will sustain this increase of effort throughout the Five Year Defense Program. It's imperative that Congress approve this strong defense budget for 1981, encompassing a 5-percent real growth in authorizations, without any reduction.

We are also improving our capability to deploy U.S. military forces rapidly to distant areas. We've helped to strengthen NATO and our other alliances, and recently we and other NATO members have decided to develop and to deploy modernized, intermediate-range nuclear forces to meet an unwarranted and increased threat from the nuclear weapons of the Soviet Union.

We are working with our allies to prevent conflict in the Middle East. The peace treaty between Egypt and Israel is a notable achievement which represents a strategic asset for America and which also enhances prospects for regional and world peace. We are now engaged in further negotiations to provide full autonomy for the people of the West Bank and Gaza, to resolve the Palestinian issue in all its aspects, and to preserve the peace and security of Israel. Let no one doubt our commitment to the security of Israel. In a few days we will observe an historic event when Israel makes another major withdrawal from the Sinai and when Ambassadors will be exchanged between Israel and Egypt.

We've also expanded our own sphere of friendship. Our deep commitment to human rights and to meeting human needs has improved our relationship with much of the Third World. Our decision to normalize relations with the People's Republic of China will help to preserve peace and stability in Asia and in the Western Pacific.

We've increased and strengthened our naval presence in the Indian Ocean, and we are now making arrangements for key naval and air facilities to be used by our forces in the region of northeast Africa and the Persian Gulf.

We've reconfirmed our 1959 agreement to help Pakistan preserve its independence and its integrity. The United States will take action consistent with our own laws to assist Pakistan in resisting any outside aggression. And I'm asking the Congress specifically to reaffirm this agreement. I'm also working, along with the leaders of other nations, to provide additional military and economic aid for Pakistan. That request will come to you in just a few days.

In the weeks ahead, we will further strengthen political and military ties with other nations in the region. We believe that there are no irreconcilable differences between us and any Islamic nation. We respect the faith of Islam, and we are ready to cooperate with all Moslem countries.

Finally, we are prepared to work with other countries in the region to share a cooperative security framework that respects differing values and political beliefs, yet which enhances the independence, security, and prosperity of all.

All these efforts combined emphasize our dedication to defend and preserve the vital interests of the region and of the nation which we represent and those of our allies—in Europe and the Pacific, and also in the parts of the world which have such great strategic importance to us, stretching especially through the Middle East and Southwest Asia. With your help, I will pursue these efforts with vigor and with determination. You and I will act as necessary to protect and to preserve our Nation's security.

The men and women of America's Armed Forces are on duty tonight in many parts of the world. I'm proud of the job they are doing, and I know you share that pride. I believe that our volunteer forces are adequate for current defense needs, and I hope that it will not become necessary to impose a draft. However, we must be prepared for that possibility. For this reason, I have determined that the Selective Service System must now be revitalized. I will send legislation and budget proposals to the Congress next month so that we can begin registration and then meet future mobilization needs rapidly if they arise.

We also need clear and quick passage of a new charter to define the legal authority and accountability of our intelligence agencies. We will guarantee that abuses do not recur, but we must tighten our controls on sensitive intelligence information, and we need to remove unwarranted restraints on America's ability to collect intelligence.

The decade ahead will be a time of rapid change, as nations everywhere seek to deal with new problems and age-old tensions. But America need have no fear. We can thrive in a world of change if we remain true to our values and actively engaged in promoting world peace. We will continue to work as we have for peace in the Middle East and southern Africa. We will continue to build our ties with developing nations, respecting and helping to strengthen their national independence which they have struggled so hard to achieve. And we will continue to support the growth of democracy and the protection of human rights.

In repressive regimes, popular frustrations often have no outlet except through violence.

But when peoples and their governments can approach their problems together through open, democratic methods, the basis for stability and peace is far more solid and far more enduring. That is why our support for human rights in other countries is in our own national interest as well as part of our own national character.

Peace—a peace that preserves freedom—remains America's first goal. In the coming years, as a mighty nation we will continue to pursue peace. But to be strong abroad we must be strong at home. And in order to be strong, we must continue to face up to the difficult issues that confront us as a nation today.

The crises in Iran and Afghanistan have dramatized a very important lesson: Our excessive dependence on foreign oil is a clear and present danger to our Nation's security. The need has never been more urgent. At long last, we must have a clear, comprehensive energy policy for the United States.

As you well know, I have been working with the Congress in a concentrated and persistent way over the past 3 years to meet this need. We have made progress together. But Congress must act promptly now to complete final action on this vital energy legislation. Our Nation will then have a major conservation effort, important initiatives to develop solar power, realistic pricing based on the true value of oil, strong incentives for the production of coal and other fossil fuels in the United States, and our Nation's most massive peacetime investment in the development of synthetic fuels.

The American people are making progress in energy conservation. Last year we reduced overall petroleum consumption by 8 percent and gasoline consumption by 5 percent below what it was the year before. Now we must do more.

After consultation with the Governors, we will set gasoline conservation goals for each of the 50 States, and I will make them mandatory if these goals are not met.

I've established an import ceiling for 1980 of 8.2 million barrels a day—well below the level of foreign oil purchases in 1977. I expect our imports to be much lower than this, but the ceiling will be enforced by an oil import fee if necessary. I'm prepared to lower these imports still further if the other oil-consuming countries will join us in a fair and mutual reduction. If we have a serious shortage, I will not hesitate to impose mandatory gasoline rationing immediately.

The single biggest factor in the inflation rate last year, the increase in the inflation rate last year, was from one cause: the skyrocketing prices of OPEC oil. We must take whatever actions are necessary to reduce our dependence on foreign oil—and at the same time reduce inflation.

As individuals and as families, few of us can produce energy by ourselves. But all of us can conserve energy—every one of us, every day of our lives. Tonight I call on you—in fact, all the people of America—to help our Nation. Conserve energy. Eliminate waste. Make 1980 indeed a year of energy conservation.

Of course, we must take other actions to strengthen our Nation's economy.

First, we will continue to reduce the deficit and then to balance the Federal budget.

Second, as we continue to work with business to hold down prices, we'll build also on the historic national accord with organized labor to restrain pay increases in a fair fight against inflation.

Third, we will continue our successful efforts to cut paperwork and to dismantle unnecessary Government regulation.

Fourth, we will continue our progress in providing jobs for America, concentrating on a major new program to provide training and work for our young people, especially minority youth. It has been said that "a mind is a terrible thing to waste." We will give our young people new hope for jobs and a better life in the 1980's.

And fifth, we must use the decade of the 1980s to attack the basic structural weaknesses and problems in our economy through measures to increase productivity, savings, and investment.

With these energy and economic policies, we will make America even stronger at home in this decade—just as our foreign and defense policies will make us stronger and safer throughout the world. We will never abandon our struggle for a just and a decent society here at home. That's the heart of America—and it's the source of our ability to inspire other people to defend their own rights abroad.

Our material resources, great as they are, are limited. Our problems are too complex for simple slogans or for quick solutions. We cannot solve them without effort and sacrifice. Walter Lippmann once reminded us, "You took the good things for granted. Now you must earn them again. For every right that you cherish, you have a duty which you must fulfill. For every good which you wish to preserve, you will have to sacrifice your comfort and your ease. There is nothing for nothing any longer."

Our challenges are formidable. But there's a new spirit of unity and resolve in our country. We move into the 1980's with confidence and hope and a bright vision of the America we want: an America strong and free, an America at peace, an America with equal rights for all citizens—and for women, guaranteed in the United States Constitution—an America with jobs and good health and good education for every citizen, an America with a clean and bountiful life in our cities and on our farms, an America that helps to feed the world, an America secure in filling its own energy needs, an America of justice, tolerance, and compassion. For this vision to come true, we must sacrifice, but this national commitment will be an exciting enterprise that will unify our people.

Together as one people, let us work to build our strength at home, and together as one indivisible union, let us seek peace and security throughout the world.

Together let us make of this time of challenge and danger a decade of national resolve and of brave achievement.

Thank you very much.

9. Message to Congress on Environmental Priorities and Programs August 2, 1979

Public Papers of the Presidents of the United States: Jimmy Carter. 9 vols. Washington, D.C.: Government Printing Office, 1997–1982.

To the Congress of the United States:

Four months after I took office, I presented to the Congress a comprehensive Message on the Environment, a charter for the first years of my Administration. Building on the record of the Congress in the 1970's, I sought both to protect our national heritage and to meet the competing demands on our natural resources.

Certain basic ideas remain the foundation of American environmental policy. Our great natural heritage should be protected for the use and enjoyment of all citizens. The bounty of nature—our farmlands and forests, our water, wildlife and fisheries, our renewable energy sources—are the basis of our present and future material well-being. They must be carefully managed and conserved. The quality of our environment must be nurtured by wise decisions and protected from hasty or unplanned actions. Clean air and water remain essential goals, and we intend to achieve them in the most efficient and effective ways possible. And we have a serious responsibility to help protect the long-term health of the global environment we share with all humanity.

I am proud of the achievements of this period. The program I offer today emphasizes continuity, but it also reflects a keener awareness of certain serious emerging problems—such as disposition of the toxic wastes our highly technological society produces.

Accomplishments Since 1977

We have made great strides together since I took office. With my strong support, the Congress enacted and I signed into law:

- the 1977 Amendments to our two fundamental laws for cleaning up pollution, the Clean Air and Clean Water Acts, including strict but enforceable standards and a strong wetlands protection program;
- the 1977 Surface Mining Reclamation Act, which established the first federal environmental standards for coal mining, and under which regulations were developed with strong public involvement;
- the 1977 Federal Mine Safety and Health Act, which established the Mine Safety and Health Administration in the Department of Labor to promulgate and enforce health and safety standards in all mines;
- the 1977 Nuclear Non-Proliferation Act, which sets conditions on U.S. nuclear exports to deter the spread of nuclear weapons, and offers other countries incentives to cooperate with our safeguards against proliferation;
- indefinite deferral of other activities which might lead to weapons proliferation, particularly nuclear fuel reprocessing and commercialization of the breeder reactor;
- the 1978 National Energy Act, with specific policies and programs emphasizing energy conservation;
- the 1978 Federal Environmental Pesticide Control Act, which provided for generic registration and control of pesticides;
- reauthorization, in 1978, of the Endangered Species Act, including new procedures for resolving conflicts under the Act;
- enactment of the National Parks and Recreation Act of 1978 and other legislation to preserve nationally significant areas, adding 45 million acres to the National Park System, 13 new Wild and Scenic Rivers and National Trails, and protecting more than 4.5 million additional acres of wilderness.

In addition, I issued Executive Orders in 1977 and 1978 directing federal agencies to improve their implementation of the National Environmental Policy Act under new regulations, which were issued in 1978; examine the environmental effects of federal actions abroad; preserve and restore natural values of wetlands and floodplains; protect our public lands from damage caused by off-road vehicles; and analyze the impacts of new federal policies on urban areas. These directives are being implemented.

Environmental Program

With these accomplishments behind us, we can turn our attention to new issues and to other key issues that are still unresolved.

In the decade ahead, we will face difficult decisions as we confront the necessity of reducing dangerous dependence on foreign oil. The leaders of the major industrial democracies met in Tokyo last month to chart a course that would help cut the use of imported oil from uncertain foreign suppliers. Each nation committed itself to a specific reduction in imports, to be accomplished in a way appropriate to its particular needs and resources.

For the past two and one-half years, conservation and energy from the sun have been major thrusts of my energy program. Solar energy funding has been tripled during that period and the Congress in 1978 enacted the National Energy Act which will save 2.5 million barrels of imported oil per day. Much of these savings will be accomplished with conservation initiatives. In addition, another 1.5

million barrels of imported oil will be saved as a result of my April energy message and June solar energy package.

To build on these major savings, I have proposed an expanded effort to put this nation on a sound energy footing, with clear goals for the next decade. That effort is based on a bold program to increase domestic energy production and on additional energy conservation initiatives. Overall, this program will reduce our dependence on foreign oil by 4.5 million barrels per day by 1990.

Some of the measures I have proposed will simultaneously serve the goals of reducing oil imports and enhancing our environment. I proposed establishing a major new residential and commercial conservation program designed to save at least 500,000 barrels of oil a day by 1990. I further proposed a total of $16.5 billion over the coming decade for improvements in the nation's public transportation system and in transportation fuel efficiency. A major solar energy program will help us to meet our goal of 20 percent solar energy by the year 2000.

We must also embark on a major energy production effort through a new Energy Security Corporation that will have broad responsibility for developing 2.5 million barrels a day of replacement fuels by 1990. That Corporation will be specifically authorized to develop not only synthetic fuels but also sources of energy which could have significant environmental benefits, such as natural gas and biomass. I do not pretend that all new replacement sources of energy will be environmentally innocuous. Some of the new technologies we will need to develop pose environmental risks, not all of which are yet fully understood. I will work to ensure that environmental protections are built into the process of developing these technologies, and that when tradeoffs must be made, they will be made fairly, equitably, and in the light of informed public scrutiny. We will examine not only the impact of new energy technologies on land and water and the effects of toxic chemicals, but also the longer term implications of increasing carbon dioxide concentration in the atmosphere.

I am pledged to be sensitive. both to energy needs and to environmental considerations. There is no excuse for unnecessary red tape, which has plagued construction of some needed energy projects. I have proposed the creation of an Energy Mobilization Board to accelerate decision-making on critical energy facilities. This will cut out excessive delay, but I will not allow it to undermine protection of our nation's environment. I intend, for instance, to make the environmental impact statement process fit the decision schedule set by the Energy Mobilization Board so that waivers of these statements will be rare.

Only in exceptional cases will alternative procedures be necessary for the orderly completion of a critical energy facility. With the exception of new requirements imposed when construction of a critical facility is underway, the Board could not waive substantive environmental standards. The President will retain the right to override decisions of the Board on any waiver issue, and Board waiver decisions would be subject to judicial review.

Solving the nation's energy problem is essential to our economy and our security. We will not lose sight of our other goals but we must not fail in ending the energy crisis. This Administration's basic commitment to clean air, clean water and the overall protection of the environment remains strong.

Alaska Lands

The highest environmental priority of my Administration is the passage of adequate legislation designating National Parks, Wildlife Refuges, Wilderness Areas, National Forests, and Wild and Scenic Rivers in Alaska.

To protect these magnificent Alaskan lands, I took several actions after the 95th Congress failed to provide protection against exploitation of certain areas in Alaska. By executive action, I designated 17 areas as National Monuments, covering 56 million acres. Additional areas were set aside by the Secretaries of Interior and Agriculture. These areas should be promptly and permanently protected by legislation.

The legislation I support not only protects Alaska's natural and cultural heritage but also accommodates the need for balanced development of Alaska's natural resources. Under the Alaska Statehood Act and Native Claims Settlement Act, federal land comprising an area nearly as large as Texas will soon be in state, native and private ownership. My proposals leave most of Alaska's mineral and timber wealth available for development, both on federal and nonfederal lands. In particular, all of the off-shore and 95 percent of the onshore areas in Alaska with favorable potential for oil and gas would be open to exploration and development.

The only area with significant potential for oil and gas reserves that would be foreclosed from exploration and development is the Arctic Wildlife Refuge, the calving grounds of the largest remaining caribou herd in the world and an important part of the herd's migratory route. Because of our responsibility to protect this extraordinary remnant of our continent's original wildlife, and because oil and gas are plentifully available elsewhere in Alaska, I firmly believe that the Arctic Wildlife Refuge deserves the full protection the House bill would provide.

There are other Alaskan areas where disagreements and conflicts exist over proper management. The Administration's proposals strike a balance that offers future generations of all Americans—especially Alaskans—broad opportunities for prosperity and enjoyment without the mistakes in land management we have seen elsewhere in the country.

I applaud the recent passage by the House of Representatives, by a margin of 300 votes, of a strong and fair bill which will protect Alaska's wildlife and wild areas, while providing for America's future economic needs. I urge the Senate to act with equal foresight this session.

Hazardous Waste

In August 1978, I declared Love Canal in Niagara Falls, New York, a national disaster, thus authorizing the use of federal disaster relief aid. The tragedy of Love Canal exemplifies the legacy of past improper hazardous waste disposal.

Last month I submitted to Congress a legislative proposal designed to prevent future disasters like the one at Love Canal. My proposed legislation—the Oil, Hazardous Substances and Hazardous Waste Response, Liability and Compensation Act—will provide the first comprehensive program to address releases of oil and hazardous substances from spills and from inactive and abandoned sites into navigable waters, ground waters, land and air. The legislation builds on present authority and fills gaps where present authority is inadequate to protect the human environment.

We do not yet know all of the problems associated with the disposal of hazardous wastes, but we must take further steps immediately. A report done for the Environmental Protection Agency estimates that there are 33,000–50,000 dumpsites which may contain some hazardous wastes. Of these, EPA estimates that 1,200 to 2,000 may present potentially significant problems, and 500 to 800 of them may have to be abandoned. Other accounts of improper disposal describe shallow burial in steel drums which leak after years in the ground, dumping in open lagoons, and clandestine dumping in sewers and along our highways. These abuses have caused serious damage to human health and economic welfare, pollution of ground and drinking water, and degradation of residential and recreation areas. The cost of cleaning up these sites runs into the billions of dollars. But the costs of ignoring the problem would be far higher.

Timely action by the Congress on my program will enable the Federal government, in cooperation with State and local governments and industry, to:

- identify abandoned hazardous dump sites across the nation;
- establish a uniform system of reporting spills and releases;
- provide emergency government response and containment to clean up and mitigate pollution without delay in cases where those responsible do not respond adequately or cannot be quickly identified;
- provide vigorous investigation of releases of oil, hazardous substances or hazardous waste from spills or abandoned and inactive sites;
- provide stronger authority to compel the responsible parties to clean up dangerous sites wherever possible;
- provide compensation for damages to property and for some other economic losses resulting from spills; and
- provide financing for these actions through a national fund of appropriations and a fee on the oil and chemical industries, and State cost-sharing over certain limits.

Solar Energy

My Solar Energy Message, submitted to the Congress on June 20, 1979, calls for a national commitment to the use of solar energy. That message and the program it lays out came from a 13-month effort by my Administration and the public, begun on Sun Day—May 3, 1978.

Solar energy is renewable and secure. It is clean and safe. In the long run, solar and other renewable sources of energy provide a hedge against inflation. Unlike the costs of depletable resources, which rise at increasing rates as reserves are consumed, the cost of energy from the sun will go down as we develop better and cheaper ways of applying it to everyday needs. For everyone in our society—especially our low-income or fixed-income families—solar energy will provide an important way to avoid rising fuel costs in the future. No foreign cartel can embargo the sun or set the price of the energy we harness from it.

I have set a national goal of achieving 20 percent of the Nation's energy from the sun and other renewable resources by the year 2000. To do this we must commit ourselves to several major new initiatives which will hasten the introduction of solar technologies. I am proposing a variety of solar programs to be funded from my proposed Energy Security Trust Fund, including a Solar Bank to help finance solar installations in homes and commercial buildings; tax credits for new buildings that use solar energy and for using the sun's heat for industrial and agricultural processes; and stronger efforts to remove institutional, financial, and information barriers that currently inhibit the use of solar energy by citizens. These proposals are in addition to the expanded research, development and demonstration program I included in my budget for fiscal year 1980.

Nuclear Waste Management and Safety

I will soon announce a national nuclear waste management policy that will be designed to deal effectively with nuclear wastes from all sources, including commercial, defense, medical, and research activities. This nuclear waste management policy will be based primarily on recommendations presented to me by the Interagency Review Group on Nuclear Waste Management. Some of the important findings of that Report include the following:

- Existing and future nuclear waste from military and civilian activities, including discarded spent fuel from the once-through nuclear fuel cycle, should be isolated from the biosphere so that it does not pose a significant threat to public health and safety.
- The responsibility for establishing a waste program should not be deferred to future generations.
- A broader research and development program for waste disposal, particularly geologic isolation, should begin promptly.
- Public participation should be developed and strengthened for all aspects of nuclear waste management programs.

I also look forward to receiving the recommendations on reactor safety from the Kemeny Commission in the aftermath of the Three Mile Island accident so that we can assure that nuclear reactors are as safe as the public expects them to be.

Water Resources Policy

I remain firmly committed to the water resources policy reforms I announced in my Message to Congress one year ago. The revised criteria used by the Administration in reviewing proposed water projects have already shown their worth. They are producing environmental benefits and reducing wasteful government spending. In 1979, for the first time in four years, the Executive branch proposed funding new water projects, using the more systematic and objective evaluation procedures I have instituted. With the help of Congress and State and local governments, the Administration has prepared legislation to make further reforms in water resources management, including cost-sharing and assistance to states for comprehensive water resources planning. I look forward to cooperation with the 96th Congress in this area.

National Heritage Policy Act

I strongly support the establishment of a comprehensive Federal program to identify and protect significant natural areas and historic places. I will soon propose a National Heritage Policy Act which would help Federal agencies, State and local governments, Indian tribes and citizens identify potential heritage areas; establish a new National Register of Natural Areas to supplement the existing National Register of Historic Places; and protect areas listed on either Register, or eligible for listing, from adverse federal actions. This important legislation would support the Heritage Conservation program already established by the Secretary of the Interior in 1977.

Saving the Whales

With U.S. leadership, the nations of the world are making encouraging progress toward protecting the great whales. At the July 1979 meeting of the International Whaling Commission (IWC), proposals by the United States and other countries for a moratorium on commercial whaling led to dramatic improvements. By the necessary three-fourths majority, IWC members voted to:

- End whaling from factory ships on the high seas (except for hunting of the relatively numerous minks) and allow whaling only from coastal stations;
- Reduce killing of the commercially valuable but jeopardized sperm whales by more than three-quarters, with world quotas down from 9,360 sperm whales to 2,203;
- Establish a whale sanctuary in most of the Indian Ocean where no hunting of any of the great whales will be allowed for 10 years.

I am wholeheartedly committed to strong action to guarantee the survival of the great whales. The progress made in this year's IWC meeting shows that many other nations share the American commitment. I will continue to press for better scientific understanding of these magnificent and highly intelligent creatures and will maintain the effort to halt commercial whaling.

Implementation of 1978 National Parks and Recreation Act

Following passage of the National Parks and Recreation Act of 1978, the Administration has sought to speed the acquisition of new park land before it is spoiled or priced out of reach. We shall continue to do that.

Among the most significant and imaginative actions included in the 1978 legislation is the program to establish a million-acre Pinelands National Reserve in New Jersey. The Department of the Interior will support local and State efforts to protect the Pinelands and its unique scenic and natural resources while maintaining private ownership and a sound local tax base. The Administration strongly supports this new Federal, State and local partnership in the Pinelands, and will work hard to see that federal agencies cooperate with State and local governments to ensure its success.

Pollution Control

Making the Clean Air and Clean Water Acts work is an important commitment of my Administration. We will continue the progress we have made in the past two years in promulgating fair standards and regulations, and we will continue to encourage new approaches to control of pollution, such as alternative and innovative waste water treatment projects. The Environmental Protection Agency has taken a number of steps in the right direction. For example, the "bubble concept," "offset" policy, and permit consolidation are intended to simplify pollution controls.

I will seek the reauthorization of the Safe Drinking Water Act, which expires next year. This law protects our citizens from newly-discovered toxic pollutants within drinking water, as well as imposing standards for conventional contaminants. For toxic substances which may enter the environment in a multitude of ways, my Administration is committed to the reauthorization and vigorous enforcement of the comprehensive Toxic Substances Control Act.

Oil Pollution of the Oceans

The recent collision in the Caribbean of two supertanker behemoths, each carrying more than 1.4 million barrels of oil, underscores the importance of effective national and international programs to reduce oil spills. At the outset of my Presidency, I proposed a comprehensive program to reduce the threat of oil pollution from tankers in United States waters, and to win international agreement to higher standards of tanker safety and pollution prevention.

Responding to the U.S. initiative, maritime nations of the world agreed in 1978 to tighten inspection requirements and significantly raise world standards for tanker construction and equipment. The Department of Transportation is completing new rules, based on the international agreement, to require improved features on both U.S. ships and foreign tankers entering our ports, including: segregated ballast, protective location of ballast space, crude oil washing, inert gas systems, and improved emergency steering systems. Dual radars and other aids to navigation are already required.

In addition, for the past two and one-half years, the Coast Guard has boarded and examined at least once a year every foreign-flag tanker entering our ports, recorded any deficiencies, and required repairs if necessary.

The Secretary of Transportation will promptly add to this program requirements for:

- improved construction of tank barges;
- safe conduct of lightering (ship to ship transfer of oil);
- improved U.S. standards for tanker crews and pilots; and
- pollution prevention features for older, smaller tankers not covered by the international standards.

Requirements for collision avoidance aids will also be added; international agreement is near on standards for these important tanker safety devices.

The United States will continue to urge other nations to put into effect promptly the requirements of the 1978 international agreements on tanker safety and pollution prevention. I also urge the prompt adoption by all nations of the new international standards for training and certification of seafarers, agreed upon in 1978.

The proposed Oil, Hazardous Substances and Hazardous Waste Response, Liability and Compensation Act, submitted to the Congress by the Administration, provides for swift cleanup of oil spills, strict liability of spillers, and compensation for victims of oil spill damage.

I expect the Coast Guard to report to me promptly on the results of its study of devices to improve tanker maneuverability and stopping. In addition, the Coast Guard is undertaking a study of past accidents to evaluate further the usefulness of double bottoms and side protection in reducing oil spills. The Department of Transportation will continue to evaluate promising ideas to preserve the oceans and its resources from pollution by oil.

Regulatory Reform

Improving government regulations is important to my effort to make government more efficient and private-sector responses more cost-effective. Environmental protection can and should benefit. I intend to improve the regulatory process in a way that does not weaken our commitment to environmental quality.

If there are better methods to achieve our environmental goals, we should use them. Agencies should seek and adopt innovative alternatives to government regulations which reduce burdens on private citizens or businesses. The Environmental Protection Agency has become a leader among federal agencies in examining new approaches and has made several moves to streamline its regulatory process. In addition to the permit consolidation, bubble concept, and offset policy mentioned above, EPA is doing an effective job of implementing my Executive order on regulatory reform and published the first agenda of regulations issued by any federal agency. A regulatory calendar is now prepared and published on a governmentwide basis by the Regulatory Council I recently established.

Since 1977 the Occupational Health and Safety Administration has gotten rid of hundreds of unnecessary standards, and has reorganized its program to devote 95 percent of its resources to the most serious workplace hazards. In addition, regulatory agencies have begun to work together to coordinate their activities and use their resources more efficiently. I expect such progress to continue and I intend that it reinforce—not diminish—our environmental improvement efforts.

Pending Legislation and Reauthorizations

I have proposed and will continue to support reauthorization of important environmental statutes, including the Endangered Species Act, the Toxic Substances Control Act, the Safe Drinking Water Act, and the Resource Conservation and Recovery Act. I also continue to support a nongame wildlife program, and a wide range of wilderness proposals.

The Environmental Program I am outlining today expands upon the efforts we have already begun with a series of new initiatives in land and resource management, agricultural conservation, urban quality, and improving the global environment.

New Initiatives

I. Land and Resource Management

America's land and natural resources have nourished our civilization. Because our original heritage was so abundant, we sometimes take these resources for granted. We can no longer do so. Our land and natural resources do have limits, and our demands upon them are growing at increasing rates. Renewable resources—farmlands, fisheries, and forests—can be depleted through overuse and misuse. We must build into our decisions the understanding that unwise actions affecting our lands and resources are difficult and costly, if not impossible, to correct.

Conservation of resources takes care and planning, and requires a partnership between various levels of government, and public and private actions. The following initiatives for protection and wise management of our coastal resources, public lands, wildlife and rivers and trails reflect this understanding.

National Coastal Protection

America's coast lines are extraordinarily varied, productive and beautiful. Congress recognized the need for special protection in the Coastal Zone Management Act of 1972, which established a voluntary Federal-State partnership for the conservation and management of coastal resources. Under this partnership, many states have already made notable progress. They have passed comprehensive coastal management laws; adopted new measures to protect wetlands, barrier islands, mineral resources, historic sites and other important coastal resources; worked out better management of hazardous areas; and streamlined Federal, State and local actions affecting the coast. By the end of 1979, 75 percent of the U.S. shoreline will be covered by Federally approved state coastal zone management programs.

The coastal zone is subject to unusual pressures, both from natural causes and human activities. The land and water resources which support the environments and economies of coastal communities are in danger of depletion. The opportunity for our citizens to enjoy beaches, bays, and marshes is often threatened. I support efforts to improve our understanding of these coastal issues, and I heartily endorse the designation by conservation organizations of the year 1980 as the "Year of the Coast."

To help achieve the balanced, comprehensive and wise management intended by the Coastal Zone Management Act, I am announcing three initiatives to continue and improve our resource protection policy.

First, I will submit to Congress legislation to reauthorize Federal assistance to state coastal zone management programs under the Coastal Zone Management Act. Under this extension, each state would be guaranteed a total of five years of federal assistance at current levels after a state management program is approved and before federal support is gradually phased down. This will help ensure that recently developed state and local coastal zone management efforts become fully established and accepted functions of government.

Second, I will recommend enactment of new amendments to the Coastal Zone Management Act that will establish a national coastal protection policy. Working through the states, the goals of this policy will be:

- to protect significant natural resources such as wetlands, estuaries, beaches, dunes, barrier islands, coral reefs, and fish and wildlife;

- to manage coastal development to minimize loss of life and property from floods, erosion, saltwater intrusion and subsidence;
- to provide predictable siting processes for major defense, energy, recreation and transportation facilities;
- to increase public access to the coast for recreation purposes;
- to preserve and restore historic, cultural and aesthetic coastal resources; and
- to coordinate and simplify government decision-making to ensure proper and expedited management of the coastal zone.

Third, I am directing the Secretary of Commerce to conduct a systematic review of federal programs that significantly affect coastal resources. This review, to be conducted by the National Oceanic and Atmospheric Administration, will provide the basis for specific recommendations to improve federal actions affecting the coastal zone and to develop any additional legislation needed to achieve our national coastal management goals.

Public Land Resources

Among the many natural resource issues facing the Nation, few are more important than the management, protection and use of the 417 million acres of public land owned by all Americans and administered by the Secretary of the Interior through the Bureau of Land Management.

The public lands include vast tracts of the arid rangelands of the West which were once lands that no one wanted. Now, some of these lands are highly valued for their energy and other valuable resources, and they have come to be appreciated for their scenic and natural values. My Administration is committed to purposeful management of the public lands and resources administered by the Bureau of Land Management in an environmentally sound and cost-effective manner.

Therefore, I am directing the Secretary of the Interior to manage the public lands administered by BLM in accordance with these principles:

- The Federal Government will be a good steward of the land, seeking to find the best balance of uses to assure that resources are available to meet the Nation's needs and that environmental values are carefully protected.
- The Federal Government will be a good neighbor, providing full opportunities for those affected by our management decisions to be involved in making them, with a special concern for the people and institutions of the Western States that are most directly affected.
- The Federal Government will make cost-effective investments in protecting and enhancing these lands within the constraints of fiscal responsibility.
- The Federal Government will seek to resolve conflicts among competing uses in a spirit of cooperation and trust, and will make—not avoid—tough decisions on the allocation of the valued resources of public lands.

We have already made significant progress in bringing these lands under effective management. A concerted federal effort is now underway to reverse the declining productivity of the 174 million acres of rangeland ecosystems managed by the Bureau of Land Management for livestock, wildlife, soil and moisture conservation, and other beneficial purposes. We have developed a comprehensive on-the-ground planning process for each unit of BLM-managed land which involves the public and assesses the environmental impacts of alternative actions. On June 4, 1979, the Secretary of the Interior announced our new federal coal management program, which establishes a balanced and efficient process for determining coal leasing and management on federal lands.

Much more remains to be done. I am therefore directing that the following actions be taken:

- The Secretary of the Interior will establish a comprehensive "program development process" for managing all the lands under BLM stewardship, which will, for the first time, set long range goals to ensure balanced protection and use of the resources and develop and analyze alternative programs and investment strategies to meet the goals. Each alternative program will be designed to achieve environmentally sound, fiscally responsible, and economically efficient investment, development, protection, and resource use. This new program planning process will supplement BLM's current unit-by-unit planning. It will invite State and local governments and interested citizens to participate in making better informed choices among the alternative programs.
- The Secretary will give special attention to protecting areas of BLM-administered lands with nationally significant wildlife, natural, scientific, cultural, or scenic resources. An example is the Birds of Prey area, located along the Snake River in the Idaho desert, that has North America's richest concentration of birds of prey, including dense nesting populations of falcons, eagles, and other raptors.
- Finally, I am directing the Secretary of the Interior and the Secretary of Agriculture to work together to coordinate their Departments' natural resource policies and programs, particularly those of the Bureau of Land Management and the Forest Service. I am requesting the two Secretaries to develop within six months a detailed statement of coordination objectives and a process and timetable for achieving them.

Wildlife Law Enforcement

A massive illegal trade in wild animals, wild animal parts and products, and wild plants has been uncovered in the last year through investigations by the Department of Justice, the Fish and Wildlife Service, the Customs Service and the Departments of Agriculture and Commerce.

This illegal trade in wildlife and plants has several very serious consequences. It can introduce exotic diseases, threatening agriculture. It creates a market for thousands of species of wildlife and plants taken in violation of the laws of foreign nations, ultimately threatening the survival of these species. It is a danger to the survival of hundreds of species listed on the Convention on International Trade in Endangered Species, to which the U.S. is a signatory nation.

I am therefore submitting to Congress a bill to overcome obstacles inhibiting enforcement efforts.

In addition, I am directing the Departments of Agriculture, Commerce, Interior, Justice, and Treasury to investigate this trade aggressively and to prosecute violators of the law. I am directing the Department of the Interior to coordinate this effort, through an interagency Wildlife Law Enforcement Coordinating Committee which will review enforcement experiences, priorities and problems. I am also directing the Department of Agriculture to chair a task force to investigate the illegal trade in plants and to prosecute where appropriate.

I am further directing that the following specific steps be taken: The Treasury and Commerce Departments will raise the priority of wildlife enforcement cases; the Agriculture Department will place greater emphasis on coordinating its wildlife enforcement program with its disease quarantine program, and will begin hiring special agents to investigate the illegal plant trade; and the Department of Justice will establish a Wildlife Section which will be staffed principally by attorneys trained as wildlife law enforcement specialists.

Wild and Scenic Rivers

Our Nation's river corridors are a rich concentration of natural ecosystems, scenic beauty, and historic and recreational values. Since my Environmental Message of May 1977, eight rivers totalling 695 miles have been added to the National Wild and Scenic Rivers System, and nine new rivers have been recommended for study. As part of the Administration's Alaska proposals, 33 additional rivers have been proposed for National Wild and Scenic Rivers designation.

Development along the banks of our rivers continues to outpace our ability to protect those rivers that might qualify for designation. This problem is particularly acute near urban areas, where there are greater demands for recreational opportunities which can partly be met by river protection.

We need to speed up the process for studying Wild and Scenic Rivers for designation and to consider the protection of rivers or parts of rivers which can protect important natural ecosystems. Moreover, the Federal government should set an example of sound management for state, local, and private landowners by taking an aggressive role in protecting possible Wild and Scenic Rivers which flow through our public lands. Accordingly, I am directing the following actions be taken:

- federal land management agencies shall assess whether rivers located on their lands and identified in the National Inventory prepared by the Heritage Conservation and Recreation Service are suitable for inclusion in the Wild and Scenic Rivers System; if so, these agencies shall take prompt action to protect the rivers either by preparing recommendations for their designation or by taking immediate action to protect them;
- all federal agencies shall avoid or mitigate adverse effects on rivers identified in the National Inventory; and
- the Secretary of Agriculture and the Secretary of the Interior shall jointly revise their Guidelines for evaluating wild, scenic, and recreational rivers to ensure consideration of river ecosystems and to shorten the time currently used to study rivers for designation.

In addition to the new policy initiatives, I am reaffirming my support for four river segments proposed in my last Environmental Message and recommending four new river segments which will add a total of 930 miles to the Wild and Scenic Rivers System:

- Gunnison River, Colorado (new)
- Encampment River, Colorado (new)
- Priest River, Idaho (new)
- Illinois River, Oregon (new)
- Bruneau River, Idaho (1977 Message)
- Dolores River, Colorado (1977 Message)
- Upper Mississippi River, Minnesota (1977 Message)
- Salmon River, Idaho (1977 Message)

I am also directing the Secretary of the Interior to develop, through the National Park Service and with full public participation, a conceptual master plan for the Upper Mississippi River in Minnesota. I expect this planning process to determine the specific requirements for protecting the river corridor and providing public access, campgrounds and other recreational facilities on the lands now in private ownership. The conceptual master plan for this important national resource will be developed in cooperation with the Minnesota Department of Natural Resources, affected Indian tribes, and the public. It will be completed by April 1980.

In my last Environmental Message, I proposed 20 river segments for study as potential additions to the National Wild and Scenic Rivers System. Several of those rivers have already been designated. Except for rivers where subsequent development has affected the river's qualifications for designation, I will continue to seek study authorizations for these rivers. In addition, I am submitting legislation to add the North Umpqua River in Oregon to the list of those rivers to be studied.

I am also forwarding to Congress reports on several rivers which, after thorough study, were found to qualify for inclusion in the National System. However, because of the interest of the states or local governments in protecting their natural values, the reports recommend that the rivers be protected and managed by state and/or local action. I am greatly encouraged by the efforts which all levels of government are taking to protect valued natural resources. I am particularly pleased to note that in the case of the Housatonic and Shepaug Rivers in Connecticut, local governmental agencies are taking the lead in developing management plans to protect these significant river resources. I am transmitting reports on:

- Pine Creek, Pennsylvania
- Buffalo River, Tennessee
- Youghiogheny River, Pennsylvania-Maryland
- Shepaug River, Connecticut
- Kettle River, Minnesota
- Lower Wisconsin River, Wisconsin
- Housatonic River, Connecticut
- Illinois River, Oklahoma

National Trails

More than 61 million of the Nation's people go nature walking and more than 28 million people hike or backpack at least five times a year. To meet the growing needs of these and other trail users, Congress enacted the 1968 National Trails System Act and directed that a National Trails System be established. Since the establishment of the National Trails System, 257 National Recreation Trails have been designated, including 21 trails for those using wheelchairs and 13 trails designed for the use of blind people, with interpretive signs in braille.

The National Trails System is still in its fledgling stage and should grow to meet widespread public interest. National trails near urban areas can serve an energy-conscious nation by providing recreation close to home for the majority of our citizens and, in some cases, by providing commuter routes for bicyclists, walkers, and joggers.

To meet these objectives, under my direction, the U.S. Forest Service will establish 145 additional National Recreation Trails by January 1980, achieving a goal of two National Recreation Trails in each National Forest System unit. I am directing each Federal land management agency to follow the example set by the Forest Service and by January 1980 announce a goal for the number of National Recreation Trails each agency will establish during 1980 on the public lands administered by the agency. I am also directing that, by the end of 1980, a minimum of 75 new National Recreation Trails shall be designated on public land other than National Forests by the Federal land management agencies.

I am directing the Secretary of the Interior, through the Interagency Trails Council, to assist other Federal agencies in surveying existing trails on federal lands to determine which of those can be made part of our National Trails System and to initiate a grassroots effort in every region of the country to assess our nationwide trails needs. In addition, I am directing the Secretary of the Interior, the Secretary of Agriculture, the Secretary of Defense and the Chairman of the Tennessee Valley Authority to encourage states, localities, Indian tribes, and private landholders to designate trails on their lands.

Finally, I will submit legislation to the Congress which will designate the 513-mile Natchez Trace National Trail through Tennessee, Alabama and Mississippi. I will resubmit legislation to establish the Potomac Heritage Trail through Pennsylvania, Maryland, West Virginia, Virginia and Washington, D.C. And I am reaffirming my support for the 3,200-mile North Country Trail, extending from the State of New York to North Dakota, which has already passed the House of Representatives.

I am also reaffirming the Administration's commitment to assuring the protection of the Appalachian Trail, one of America's best known and most popular recreation trails. The 2,000-mile Appalalachian Trail winds through 14 states and is readily accessible to nearly half of the population of the U.S. It has been created by a volunteer movement without parallel in the history of outdoor recreation in America. In 1978 this Administration supported and I signed into law a bill to protect threatened portions of the right-of-way which are located on private lands. I expect this goal to be substantially achieved by September 30, 1981. This is a prompt but realistic timetable for the acquisition program.

II. Agricultural Conservation

From our beginnings as a nation we have sustained ourselves and others on abundant yields from our farmlands. In this century, scientific and technological advances have increased our agricultural production to unsurpassed levels.

But in emphasizing ever-increasing production we have sometimes neglected to maintain the soil, water, and biological resources upon which the long-term stability and productivity of our agriculture depends. These resources are being degraded in many areas of the country. Our farm and land management practices have led to excessive soil erosion, we have overused chemical fertilizers and pesticides, and some of our most productive farmlands are being converted to nonagricultural uses. The agricultural conservation initiatives that I am announcing today address these issues.

Soil Conservation Incentives

Over the past half century we have invested more than $20 billion of federal funds in efforts to conserve soil. These funds have been used for cost sharing, technical assistance, resource management, loans, research, and education. Yet in that same half century wind and water erosion have removed half the fertile topsoil from nearly one-third of the Nation's potentially usable croplands. The cost of replacing just the plant nutrients lost to erosion has been estimated at $18 billion a year. Moreover, agricultural runoff adversely affects two-thirds of the Nation's streams.

Our soil protection programs have undoubtedly prevented even worse soil loss, but we must do better to maintain the long-term productivity of the soil.

The Department of Agriculture is now making an important appraisal of soil and water conservation policies under the Soil and Water Resources Conservation Act of 1977. The first Appraisal, Program and Policy reports required by the Resources Conservation Act (RCA) are due in January 1980. These documents will analyze conservation problems nationwide, set conservation targets and propose ways to solve the problems. They will provide an essential first step in the wise management of agricultural lands, and will guide my Administration's overall soil and water conservation recommendations to the Congress. Reports will be updated every 5 years and I will receive annual reports of progress and program effectiveness.

I am directing the Secretary of Agriculture, in consultation with the Chairman of the Council on Environmental Quality, to build on the RCA process and to undertake a further detailed and systematic study of possible conservation incentives. The study will search for ways to modify or coordinate agricultural assistance programs already in existence in order to reduce soil erosion. Moreover, it will also look for conflicts or inconsistencies between farm income programs and soil conservation programs and will recommend measures to eliminate these conflicts where possible.

The results of this study will be submitted to me in January 1981. This report will provide me with specific administrative and legislative recommendations to reduce soil erosion and to improve soil stewardship in order to maintain the Nation's long-term agricultural productivity, building on the policy recommendations contained in the RCA 1980 program.

A second critical land issue for America's farmers and consumers is the availability of agricultural lands—particularly prime farmlands—and their conversion to other uses. In June, the Administration initiated an important new effort to address this issue. The Secretary of Agriculture and the Chairman of the Council on Environmental Quality are co-chairing an interagency study of factors affecting the availability of land for agricultural uses. The study will evaluate the economic, environmental, and social effects of the conversion or retention of agricultural lands and will make recommendations for consideration by federal, state, and local governments by January 1981.

Many members of Congress are particularly interested in these two critical issues affecting the stewardship of our nation's agricultural lands. I hope that the Administration and the Congress will work together to develop and implement appropriate actions, based on the results of these studies.

Integrated Pest Management

For all their benefits, chemical pesticides can cause unintended damage to human health and the environment. Many pests have developed resistance to chemical pesticides, escalating the cost of pest control by conventional methods. This resistence to pesticides has also decreased our ability to control some pests, which has reduced agricultural yields from what they would otherwise be.

Integrated pest management (IPM) has evolved in recent years as a comprehensive pest control strategy which has important health, economic, and environmental benefits. IPM uses a systems approach to reduce pest damage to tolerable levels through a variety of techniques, including natural predators and parasites, genetically resistant hosts, environmental modifications and, when necessary and appropriate, chemical pesticides. IPM strategies generally rely first upon biological defenses against pests before chemically altering the environment.

The Federal government—which spends more than $200 million a year on pest control research and implementation programs—should encourage the development and use of integrated pest management in agriculture, forestry, public health, and urban pest control. As a result of a governmentwide review initiated by my 1977 Environmental Message, I am now directing the appropriate federal agencies to modify as soon as possible their existing pest management research, control, education, and assistance programs and to support and adopt IPM strategies wherever practicable. I am also directing federal agencies to report on actions taken or underway to implement IPM programs, and to coordinate their efforts through an interagency group.

III. Urban Quality

Our cities give us diversity and enjoyment, occupations and avocations, shopping and services, recreation and culture. By strengthening the health of our urban environment, we broaden the range of opportunities open to all of our citizens, as I emphasized in my National Urban Policy Message last year. The investments we make in maintaining and improving urban quality—particularly those involving federal taxpayer dollars—can be designed to meet environmental objectives, such as safe, convenient, well-planned public transportation, quieter communities, and assistance in mediating potential conflicts between healthy urban economies and environments. The initiatives I am proposing today will help to achieve these goals.

Transportation Policy

Our transportation systems can greatly affect the Nation's environment, for better or worse, especially in our cities. For many years, our energy and other resources were so plentiful that the Federal government encouraged the rapid expansion of a transportation system based on the private automobile without fully considering the profound effects on our resources, our urban environments, and our way of life. Although we have developed an extraordinary transportation system, we have missed opportunities in the past to improve transportation and at the same time to achieve these other national objectives.

The United States has built the most extensive and complex transportation system in the world. Federal transportation expenditures exceed $17 billion annually, including $12 billion in grants to state and local agencies. Transportation consumes approximately 53 percent of all petroleum used in the U.S. The energy and cost advantages of using this system more efficiently—for example, by greater use of carpools, vanpools and mass transit—are now obvious. Better design and use of transportation systems will also help to save and strengthen our cities and their amenities and to reduce air and noise pollution. Thus transportation decisions can help to conserve limited resources, and to further our energy, fiscal, and urban environmental goals.

Federal transportation decisions cannot escape difficult choices among competing objectives, but they must be guided by new transportation policies which I am establishing for my Administration. Urban transportation programs and projects should be reoriented to meet environmental, energy and urban revitalization goals. I am therefore directing the Department to take immediate actions to assure that:

- federal transportation funds are used to promote energy conservation, for example through special lanes for carpools, vanpools and transit vehicles;
- encouragement is given to using federal funds for public transportation projects;
- a careful review is made of any transportation proposals which would encourage urban sprawl (a major cause of high energy consumption) or which would tend to draw jobs away from urban centers;
- consideration is given to improving and rehabilitating existing facilities, or using non-construction methods such as better traffic management to improve transportation systems, as alternatives to constructing new facilities;
- major transportation projects are used to help improve the urban economy and to attract jobs to the urban cores; and
- firm actions are taken to mitigate adverse effects of transportation projects on the natural and urban environment and to carry out the environmental commitments that are made in planning and approving transportation projects.

We have done a great deal to make our transportation policies and actions more sensitive to our national environmental and energy goals. We can do a great deal more with cooperation of state and local governments as our partners in the national transportation system. The steps I have outlined will move us in that direction.

Economic Assistance Program

Most Americans benefit directly from the healthier and more agreeable environment that results from our air, water and other pollution control programs. Although economic data indicate that environmental programs are a strong positive factor in providing employment, there is continued concern about their possible adverse impact on individual firms, communities, or groups of workers. The fact that there have not been a large number of such economic dislocations does not suggest that those that do occur are unimportant. Furthermore, in some instances they can be avoided, or at least significantly mitigated, by appropriate government action.

In 1977 I established an Economic Assistance Task Force, chaired by the Council on Environmental Quality, to investigate whether we needed to improve federal assistance for those cases when jobs are lost partly as a result of actions taken to reduce pollution, and to recommend initiatives we might take. The Task Force concluded that existing federal assistance programs should be adequate, but that we need to take practical steps to let people know about the programs and to make sure help is delivered swiftly when it is needed.

I am therefore directing the Administrator of the Environmental Protection Agency to create an Economic Assistance Program in his agency and to designate Economic Assistance Officers both in headquarters and in the field, who will help the public understand and use the programs, and to make sure that eligible people receive assistance promptly. I am also directing all federal agencies with programs in this area to publicize and coordinate closely their programs. A booklet describing and locating available federal assistance programs will be released soon by the Council on Environmental Quality and the Environmental Protection Agency.

Urban Noise Program

A certain level of urban noise is tolerable or even agreeable, reflecting the multitude of activities that make a city thrive. However, most of our cities suffer from too much noise. Excessive noise is a serious disturbance in city dwellers' lives, and degrades the urban environment.

Most noise abatement actions are taken by state and local governments, but there is an important role for the Federal government. I am initiating today a program to reduce urban noise by directing the Departments of Commerce, Defense, Energy, Housing and Urban Development, Transportation, and the Environmental Protection Agency and General Services Administration, in consultation with other federal agencies, to take a number of actions to improve existing noise abatement programs, including:

- programs to achieve soundproofing and weatherization of noise sensitive buildings, such as schools and hospitals;
- use of quiet-design features in transportation projects affecting urban areas;
- measures to encourage the location of housing developments away from major noise sources;
- purchase of quiet equipment and products—such as typewriters and lawn mowers which have been designed to reduce noise—and assistance to state and local agencies to do likewise; and
- support for neighborhood efforts to deal with noise problems.

IV. Global Environment

Efforts to improve the environment cannot be confined to our national boundaries. Ten years ago, at the dawn of the environmental decade, we landed on the moon. For the first time people could stand on the surface of another world and look at the whole earth. The sight of earthrise was awesome. It was also sobering. From that moment we could no longer avoid understanding that all life must share this one small planet and its limited resources. The interdependence of nations is plain, and so is the responsibility of each to avoid actions which harm other nations or the world's environment. I am announcing today two initiatives which address global environmental problems of the greatest importance.

World Forests

The world's forests and woodlands are disappearing at alarming rates. Some estimates suggest that world forests could decline by about

20 percent by 2000. More than 40 percent of the closed forests of South Asia, Southeast Asia, Pacific, and Latin America could be lost.

Nearly all the world's forest loss is occurring in or near the tropics. In these areas, environmental damage from deforestation can be severe—even irreversible-and the human costs extremely high. For example, denudation of Himalayan slopes has led to severe soil erosion, silting of rivers, loss of groundwater, and intensified, catastrophic flooding downstream. Many tropical forests, once cut, will not regrow because soils, rainfall, temperature, or terrain are too unfavorable; nor will the land support crops or pasture for more than a few years. Another serious possible consequence of tropical forest loss is accelerating extinction of species. Tropical forests provide habitat for literally millions of plant and animal species—a genetic reservoir unmatched anywhere else in the world. Equally serious is the possibility that forest loss may adversely alter the global climate through production of carbon dioxide. These changes and their effects are not well understood and are being studied by scientists, but the possibilities are disturbing and warrant caution.

The United States and other nations are just beginning to appreciate fully the scope and seriousness of the problem and to assess the effects of development projects on world forests. There is much more to be done. I am therefore directing all relevant federal agencies to place greater emphasis on world forest issues in their budget and program planning. An interagency task force established last fall and chaired by the State Department will report to me in November 1979 on specific goals, strategies, and programs that the United States should undertake. On the basis of these recommendations, I will direct federal agencies to carry out an integrated set of actions to help toward protection and wise management of world forests.

In the international arena, the Governing Council of the United Nations Environment Programme has just adopted a resolution—introduced by the United States—calling for a meeting of experts to develop proposals for an integrated international program for conservation and wise utilization of tropical forests, and to report to the next Governing Council meeting in April 1980. I am asking the Departments of State and Agriculture, the Council on Environmental Quality, and other federal agencies to give this program full support and assistance and to encourage and support high-level multinational conferences on forest problems in regions where forest losses are severe.

To help protect the earth's natural resource base, I issued an Executive Order earlier this year, which directs federal agencies to review carefully in advance the effects of many federal activities abroad. I am directing the Council on Environmental Quality and the Department of State to report to me within six months on the best ways to designate the globally important resources to which the order applies.

Acid Rain

Acid rain has caused serious environmental damage in many parts of the world including Scandinavia, Northern Europe, Japan, Canada and the Northeastern part of the United States. Over the past 25 years the acidity of rainfall has increased as much as fifty-fold in parts of the Eastern half of the United States. In the Adirondacks in New York, many mountain lakes have become devoid of fish partly because of increasing acidification. Adverse effects on crops and forests are suspected; steel and stone buildings and art works may suffer as well.

Acid rain is produced when rain removes sulfur dioxide and nitrogen dioxide from the air, forming sulfuric and nitric acid. Sulfur and nitrogen oxides are emitted in all forms of fossil fuel combustion. Power plants, smelters, steel mills, home furnaces, automobiles—all may contribute to acid rain.

To improve our understanding of acid rain, I am establishing a ten year comprehensive Federal Acid Rain Assessment Program to be planned and managed by a standing Acid Rain Coordination Committee. The assessment program will include applied and basic research on acid rain effects, trends monitoring, transport and fate of pollutants, and control measures. The Committee will establish links with industry to promote cooperative research wherever appropriate. The Committee will also play a role in future research cooperation with Canada, Mexico, and other nations and international organizations. The Committee will prepare a comprehensive 10-year plan for review by the end of the year. In its first full year of operation, the program will have $10 million in reprogrammed research funds available, double the current amount for acid rain research.

It is important to emphasize that such a long-time acid rain research program will not delay application of necessary pollution control measures to meet the mandate of the Clean Air Act. In addition, interim results from the acid rain research program will be made available to the public, to states, to industry and to the federal government agencies responsible for developing measures to reduce air pollution.

Continued and Cooperative Efforts

The preservation of our environment has needed to become a special concern to our country at least since the ending of the Western frontier. A former President put it clearly: "The conservation of our natural resources and their proper use constitute the fundamental problem which underlies almost every other problem of our National life. We must maintain for our civilization the adequate material basis without which that civilization cannot exist. We must show foresight, we must look ahead. The reward of foresight of this nation is great and easily foretold. But there must be the look ahead, there must be a realization of the fact that to waste, to destroy, our natural resources, to skin and exhaust the land instead of using it so as to increase its usefulness, will result in undermining in the days of our children the very prosperity which we ought by right to hand down to them amplified and developed."

That was President Theodore Roosevelt speaking in a State of the Union Message more than 70 years ago.

That message needs to be repeated and heard just as clearly today. Above all—it needs to be delivered.

My Administration will continue to lead in conserving our resources and reducing risks to the environment through sound and efficient management. But all our citizens must join the effort by contributing energies and ideas.

Only with your cooperation can we maintain our advance towards protecting our environment. Only together can we hope to secure our world for the life to come.

10. Rescue Attempt for American Hostages in Iran Address to the Nation April 25, 1980

Public Papers of the Presidents of the United States: Jimmy Carter. 9 vols. Washington, D.C.: Government Printing Office, 1997–1982.

Late yesterday, I cancelled a carefully planned operation which was underway in Iran to position our rescue team for later withdrawal of American hostages, who have been held captive there since November 4. Equipment failure in the rescue helicopters made it necessary to end the mission.

As our team was withdrawing, after my order to do so, two of our American aircraft collided on the ground following a refueling operation in a remote desert location in Iran. Other information about this rescue mission will be made available to the American people when it is appropriate to do so.

There was no fighting; there was no combat. But to my deep regret, eight of the crewmen of the two aircraft which collided were killed, and several other Americans were hurt in the accident. Our people were immediately airlifted from Iran. Those who were injured have gotten medical treatment, and all of them are expected to recover.

No knowledge of this operation by any Iranian officials or authorities was evident to us until several hours after all Americans were withdrawn from Iran.

Our rescue team knew and I knew that the operation was certain to be difficult and it was certain to be dangerous. We were all convinced that if and when the rescue operation had been commenced that it had an excellent chance of success. They were all volunteers; they were all highly trained. I met with their leaders before they went on this operation. They knew then what hopes of mine and of all Americans they carried with them.

To the families of those who died and who were wounded, I want to express the admiration I feel for the courage of their loved ones and the sorrow that I feel personally for their sacrifice.

The mission on which they were embarked was a humanitarian mission. It was not directed against Iran; it was not directed against the people of Iran. It was not undertaken with any feeling of hostility toward Iran or its people. It has caused no Iranian casualties.

Planning for this rescue effort began shortly after our Embassy was seized, but for a number of reasons, I waited until now to put those rescue plans into effect. To be feasible, this complex operation had to be the product of intensive planning and intensive training and repeated rehearsal. However, a resolution of this crisis through negotiations and with voluntary action on the part of the Iranian officials was obviously then, has been, and will be preferable.

This rescue attempt had to await my judgment that the Iranian authorities could not or would not resolve this crisis on their own initiative. With the steady unraveling of authority in Iran and the mounting dangers that were posed to the safety of the hostages themselves and the growing realization that their early release was highly unlikely, I made a decision to commence the rescue operations plans.

This attempt became a necessity and a duty. The readiness of our team to undertake the rescue made it completely practicable. Accordingly, I made the decision to set our long-developed plans into operation. I ordered this rescue mission prepared in order to safeguard American lives, to protect America's national interests, and to reduce the tensions in the world that have been caused among many nations as this crisis has continued.

It was my decision to attempt the rescue operation. It was my decision to cancel it when problems developed in the placement of our rescue team for a future rescue operation. The responsibility is fully my own.

In the aftermath of the attempt, we continue to hold the Government of Iran responsible for the safety and for the early release of the American hostages, who have been held so long. The United States remains determined to bring about their safe release at the earliest date possible.

As President, I know that our entire Nation feels the deep gratitude I feel for the brave men who were prepared to rescue their fellow Americans from captivity. And as President, I also know that the Nation shares not only my disappointment that the rescue effort could not be mounted, because of mechanical difficulties, but also my determination to persevere and to bring all of our hostages home to freedom.

We have been disappointed before. We will not give up in our efforts. Throughout this extraordinarily difficult period, we have pursued and will continue to pursue every possible avenue to secure the release of the hostages. In these efforts, the support of the American people and of our friends throughout the world has been a most crucial element. That support of other nations is even more important now.

We will seek to continue, along with other nations and with the officials of Iran, a prompt resolution of the crisis without any loss of life and through peaceful and diplomatic means.

Thank you very much.

11. Farewell Address to the Nation January 14, 1981

Public Papers of the Presidents of the United States: Jimmy Carter. 9 vols. Washington, D.C.: Government Printing Office, 1997–1982.

Good evening.

In a few days I will lay down my official responsibilities in this office, to take up once more the only title in our democracy superior to that of President, the title of citizen.

Of Vice President Mondale, my Cabinet, and the hundreds of others who have served with me during the last 4 years, I wish to say now publicly what I have said in private: I thank them for the dedication and competence they've brought to the service of our country. But I owe my deepest thanks to you, to the American people, because you gave me this extraordinary opportunity to serve.

We've faced great challenges together, and we know that future problems will also be difficult. But I'm now more convinced than ever that the United States, better than any other country, can meet successfully whatever the future might bring. These last 4 years have made me more certain than ever of the inner strength of our country, the unchanging value of our principles and ideals, the stability of our political system, the ingenuity and the decency of our people.

Tonight I would like first to say a few words about this most special office, the Presidency of the United States. This is at once the most powerful office in the world and among the most severely constrained by law and custom. The President is given a broad responsibility to lead but cannot do so without the support and consent of the people, expressed formally through the Congress and informally in many ways through a whole range of public and private institutions. This is as it should be.

Within our system of government every American has a right and a duty to help shape the future course of the United States. Thoughtful criticism and close scrutiny of all government officials by the press and the public are an important part of our democratic society. Now, as in the past, only the understanding and involvement of the people through full and open debate can help to avoid serious mistakes and assure the continued dignity and safety of the Nation.

Today we are asking our political system to do things of which the Founding Fathers never dreamed. The government they designed for a few hundred thousand people now serves a nation of almost 230 million people. Their small coastal republic now spans beyond a continent, and we also now have the responsibility to help lead much of the world through difficult times to a secure and prosperous future.

Today, as people have become ever more doubtful of the ability of the Government to deal with our problems, we are increasingly drawn to single-issue groups and special interest organizations to ensure that whatever else happens, our own personal views and our own private interests are protected. This is a disturbing factor in American political life. It tends to distort our purposes, because the national interest is not always the sum of all our single or special interests. We are all Americans together, and we must not forget that the common good is our common interest and our individual responsibility.

Because of the fragmented pressures of these special interests, it's very important that the office of the President be a strong one and that its constitutional authority be preserved. The President is the only elected official charged with the primary responsibility of representing all the people. In the moments of decision, after the different and conflicting views have all been aired, it's the President who then must speak to the Nation and for the Nation.

I understand after 4 years in this office, as few others can, how formidable is the task the new President-elect is about to undertake, and to the very limits of conscience and conviction, I pledge to support him in that task. I wish him success, and Godspeed.

I know from experience that Presidents have to face major issues that are controversial, broad in scope, and which do not arouse the natural support of a political majority. For a few minutes now, I want to lay aside my role as leader of one nation, and speak to you as a fellow citizen of the world about three issues, three difficult issues: the threat of nuclear destruction, our stewardship of the physical resources of our planet, and the preeminence of the basic rights of human beings.

It's now been 35 years since the first atomic bomb fell on Hiroshima. The great majority of the world's people cannot remember a time when the nuclear shadow did not hang over the Earth. Our minds have adjusted to it, as after a time our eyes adjust to the dark. Yet the risk of a nuclear conflagration has not lessened. It has not happened yet, thank God, but that can give us little comfort, for it only has to happen once.

The danger is becoming greater. As the arsenals of the superpowers grow in size and sophistication and as other governments, perhaps even in the future dozens of governments, acquire these weapons, it may only be a matter of time before madness, desperation, greed, or miscalculation lets loose this terrible force.

In an all-out nuclear war, more destructive power than in all of World War II would be unleashed every second during the long afternoon it would take for all the missiles and bombs to fall. A World War II every second—more people killed in the first few hours than in all the wars of history put together. The survivors, if any, would live in despair amid the poisoned ruins of a civilization that had committed suicide.

National weakness, real or perceived, can tempt aggression and thus cause war. That's why the United States can never neglect its military strength. We must and we will remain strong. But with equal determination, the United States and all countries must find ways to control and to reduce the horrifying danger that is posed by the enormous world stockpiles of nuclear arms.

This has been a concern of every American President since the moment we first saw what these weapons could do. Our leaders will require our understanding and our support as they grapple with this difficult but crucial challenge. There is no disagreement on the goals or the basic approach to controlling this enormous destructive force. The answer lies not just in the attitudes or the actions of world leaders but in the concern and the demands of all of us as we continue our struggle to preserve the peace.

Nuclear weapons are an expression of one side of our human character. But there's another side. The same rocket technology that delivers nuclear warheads has also taken us peacefully into space. From that perspective, we see our Earth as it really is—a small and fragile and beautiful blue globe, the only home we have. We see no barriers of race or religion or country. We see the essential unity of our species and our planet. And with faith and common sense, that bright vision will ultimately prevail.

Another major challenge, therefore, is to protect the quality of this world within which we live. The shadows that fall across the future are cast not only by the kinds of weapons we've built, but by the kind of world we will either nourish or neglect. There are real and growing dangers to our simple and our most precious possessions: the air we breathe, the water we drink, and the land which sustains us. The rapid depletion of irreplaceable minerals, the erosion of topsoil, the destruction of beauty, the blight of pollution, the demands of increasing billions of people, all combine to create problems which are easy to observe and predict, but difficult to resolve. If we do not act, the world of the year 2000 will be much less able to sustain life than it is now.

But there is no reason for despair. Acknowledging the physical realities of our planet does not mean a dismal future of endless sacrifice. In fact, acknowledging these realities is the first step in dealing with them. We can meet the resource problems of the world—water, food, minerals, farmlands, forests, overpopulation, pollution if we tackle them with courage and foresight.

I've just been talking about forces of potential destruction that mankind has developed and how we might control them. It's equally important that we remember the beneficial forces that we have evolved over the ages and how to hold fast to them. One of those constructive forces is the enhancement of individual human freedoms through the strengthening of democracy and the fight against deprivation, torture, terrorism, and the persecution of people throughout the world. The struggle for human rights overrides all differences of color or nation or language. Those who hunger for freedom, who thirst for human dignity, and who suffer for the sake of justice, they are the patriots of this cause.

I believe with all my heart that America must always stand for these basic human rights at home and abroad. That is both our history and our destiny.

America did not invent human rights. In a very real sense, it's the other way around. Human rights invented America. Ours was the first nation in the history of the world to be founded explicitly on such an idea. Our social and political progress has been based on one fundamental principle: the value and importance of the individual. The fundamental force that unites us is not kinship or place of origin or religious preference. The love of liberty is the common blood that flows in our American veins.

The battle for human rights, at home and abroad, is far from over. We should never be surprised nor discouraged, because the impact of our efforts has had and will always have varied results. Rather, we should take pride that the ideals which gave birth to our Nation still inspire the hopes of oppressed people around the world. We have no cause for self-righteousness or complacency, but we have every reason to persevere, both within our own country and beyond our borders.

If we are to serve as a beacon for human rights, we must continue to perfect here at home the rights and the values which we espouse around the world: a decent education for our children, adequate medical care for all Americans, an end to discrimination against minorities and women, a job for all those able to work, and freedom from injustice and religious intolerance.

We live in a time of transition, an uneasy era which is likely to endure for the rest of this century. It will be a period of tensions, both within nations and between nations, of competition for scarce resources, of social, political, and economic stresses and strains. During this period we may be tempted to abandon some of the time-honored principles and commitments which have been proven during the difficult times of past generations. We must never yield to this temptation. Our American values are not luxuries, but necessities—not the salt in our bread, but the bread itself. Our common vision of a free and just society is our greatest source of cohesion at home and strength abroad, greater even than the bounty of our material blessings.

Remember these words: "We hold these truths to be self-evident, that all men are created equal, that they are endowed by their Creator with certain inalienable Rights, that among these are Life, Liberty and the pursuit of Happiness."

This vision still grips the imagination of the world. But we know that democracy is always an unfinished creation. Each generation must renew its foundations. Each generation must rediscover the meaning of this hallowed vision in the light of its own modern challenges. For this generation, ours, life is nuclear survival; liberty is human rights; the pursuit of happiness is a planet whose resources are devoted to the physical and spiritual nourishment of its inhabitants.

During the next few days I will work hard to make sure that the transition from myself to the next President is a good one, that the American people are served well. And I will continue, as I have the last 14 months, to work hard and to pray for the lives and the well-being of the American hostages held in Iran. I can't predict yet what will happen, but I hope you will join me in my constant prayer for their freedom.

As I return home to the South, where I was born and raised, I look forward to the opportunity to reflect and further to assess, I hope with accuracy, the circumstances of our times. I intend to give our new President my support, and I intend to work as a citizen, as I've worked here in this office as President, for the values this Nation was founded to secure.

Again, from the bottom of my heart, I want to express to you the gratitude I feel. Thank you, fellow citizens, and farewell.

SELECTED BIBLIOGRAPHY

Abernathy, M. Glenn, Dilys Hill, and Phil Williams, eds. *The Carter Years: The President and Policymaking*. New York: St. Martin's Press, 1984.

Albright, Madeleine, with Bill Woodward. *Madam Secretary: A Memoir.* New York: Hyperion, 2003.

Anderson, Jack, with Daryl Gibson. *Peace, War, and Politics: An Eyewitness Account.* New York: Tom Doherty Associates, 1999.

Anderson, Pat. *Electing Jimmy Carter: The Campaign of 1976.* Baton Rouge: Louisiana State University Press, 1994.

Andrianopoulos, Gerry Argyris. *Kissinger and Brzezinski: The NSC and the Struggle for Control of U.S. National Security Policy.* New York: St. Martin's Press, 1991.

Andrus, Cecil, and Joel Connelly. *Cecil Andrus: Politics Western Style.* Seattle: Sasquatch Books, 1998.

Ashby, LeRoy, and Rod Gramer. *Fighting the Odds: The Life of Senator Frank Church.* Pullman: Washington State University Press, 1994.

Ball, Howard. *The Bakke Case: Race, Education, and Affirmative Action.* Lawrence: University Press of Kansas, 2000.

Barry, John M. *The Ambition and the Power.* New York: Viking, 1989.

Bass, Jack, and Marilyn W. Thompson. *Ol' Strom: An Unauthorized Biography.* Marietta, Ga.: Longstreet Press, Inc., 1998.

Beckman, Robert L. *Nuclear Non-Proliferation: Congress and the Control of Peaceful Nuclear Activities.* Boulder, Colo.: Westview Press, 1985.

Beckwith, Charlie, and Donald Knox. *Delta Force.* New York: Harcourt Brace and Jovanovich, 1983.

Bell, Griffin B., with Ronald J. Ostrow. *Taking Care of the Law.* New York: William Morrow, 1982.

Berman, Larry. *The Office of Management and Budget and the Presidency, 1921–1979.* Princeton, N.J.: Princeton University Press, 1979.

Biggs, Jeffrey R., and Thomas Foley. *Honor in the House: Speaker Tom Foley.* Pullman: Washington State University Press, 1999.

Bill, James A. *The Eagle and the Lion: The Tragedy of American-Iranian Relations.* New Haven, Conn.: Yale University Press, 1988.

———. *George Ball: Behind the Scenes in U.S. Foreign Policy.* New Haven, Conn.: Yale University Press, 1997.

Blumenthal, W. Michael. *The Invisible Wall: Germans and Jews, a Personal Exploration.* New York: Counterpoint, 1998.

Bourne, Peter. *Jimmy Carter: A Comprehensive Biography from Plains to Post-Presidency.* New York: Scribner, 1997.

Brademas, John. *The Politics of Education: Conflict and Consensus on Capitol Hill.* Norman: University of Oklahoma Press, 1987.

Brands, H. W. *Into the Labyrinth: The United States and the Middle East, 1945–1993.* New York: McGraw Hill, 1994.

Brauer, Carl M. *Presidential Transitions: Eisenhower through Reagan.* New York: Oxford University Press, 1986.

Brinkley, Douglas. *The Unfinished Presidency: Jimmy Carter's Journal Beyond the White House.* New York: Penguin, 1998.

Brown, Harold. *Thinking about National Security: Defense and Foreign Policy in a Dangerous World.* Boulder, Colo.: Westview Press, 1983.

Brzezinski, Zbigniew. *Between Two Ages: America's Role in the Technetronic Era.* New York: Viking Press, 1970.

———. *Power and Principle: Memoirs of the National Security Adviser, 1977–1981.* New York: Farrar, Strauss, Giroux, 1983.

Califano, Joseph A., Jr. *Governing America: An Insider's Report from the White House and the Cabinet.* New York: Simon and Schuster, 1981.

———. *Inside: A Public and Private Life.* New York: PublicAffairs, 2004.

Campbell, Colin. *Managing the Presidency: Carter, Reagan, and the Search for Executive Order.* Pittsburgh, Pa.: University of Pittsburgh Press, 1986.

Cannon, James. *Time and Chance: Gerald Ford's Appointment with History.* New York: HarperCollins, 1994.

Cannon, Lou. *President Reagan: The Role of a Lifetime.* New York: Simon and Schuster, 1991.

Carr, Jonathan. *Helmut Schmidt: Helmsman of Germany.* New York: St. Martin's, 1985.

Carroll, Peter N. *It Seemed Like Nothing Happened: The Tragedy and Promise of the 1970s.* New York: Holt, Rinehart, and Winston, 1982.

Carter, Dan T. *The Politics of Rage: George Wallace, the Origins of the New Conservatism, and the Transformation of American Politics.* New York: Simon and Schuster, 1995.

Carter, Hugh. *Cousin Beedie and Cousin Hot: My Life with the Carter Family of Plains, Georgia.* Englewood Cliffs, N.J.: Prentice Hall, 1978.

Carter, Jimmy. *Always a Reckoning and Other Poems.* New York: Times Books, 1994.

———. *The Blood of Abraham: Insights Into the Middle East.* Houghton Mifflin Company, 1985.

———. *Campaign Promises, 1976.* Transition Planning Group, 1976.

———. *A Government as Good as Its People.* New York: Pocket Books, 1977.

———. *An Hour Before Daylight: Memories of a Rural Boyhood.* New York: Touchstone, 2001.

———. *Keeping Faith: Memoirs of a President.* New York: Bantam Books, 1982.

———. *Living Faith.* New York: Times Books, 1996.

———. *An Outdoor Journal: Adventures and Reflections.* New York: Bantam Books, 1988.

———. *Turning Point: A Candidate, a State, and a Nation Come of Age.* New York: Times Books, 1992.

———. *Why Not the Best?* Nashville, Tenn.: Broadman, 1977.

Carter, Jimmy, and Rosalynn Carter. *Everything to Gain: Making the Most of the Rest of Your Life.* New York: Random House, 1987.

Carter, Lillian, and Gloria Carter Spann. *Away from Home: Letters to My Family.* New York: Simon and Schuster, 1977.

Carter, Rosalynn. *First Lady from Plains.* Boston: Houghton Mifflin Company, 1984.

Chellany, Brahma. *Nuclear Proliferation: The U.S.-Indian Conflict.* New Delhi: Orient Longman, 1993.

Christison, Kathleen. *Perceptions of Palestine: Their Influence on U.S. Middle East Policy.* Berkeley: University of California Press, 1999.

Christofferson, Bill. *The Man from Clear Lake: Earth Day Founder Senator Gaylord Nelson.* Madison: University of Wisconsin Press, 2004.

Christopher, Warren. *Chances of a Lifetime: A Memoir.* New York: Scribner, 2001.

Clymer, Adam. *Edward M. Kennedy: A Biography.* New York: HarperCollins, 1999.

Clymer, Kenton. *The United States and Cambodia, 1969–2000: A Troubled Relationship.* New York: Routledge, 2004.

Clymer, Kenton, et al. *American Hostages in Iran: The Conduct of a Crisis.* New Haven, Conn.: Yale University Press, 1985.

Cohen, Richard E. *The Pursuit of Power and the End of the Old Politics.* Chicago: Ivan R. Dee, 1999.

Cramer, Richard Ben. *Bob Dole.* New York: Random House, 1995.

Cynkin, Thomas M. *Soviet and American Signalling in the Polish Crisis.* New York: St. Martin's Press, 1988.

Dallek, Robert T. *Hail to the Chief: The Making and Unmaking of American Presidents.* New York: Hyperion, 1996.

Dayan, Moshe. *Breakthrough: A Personal Account of the Egypt-Israel Peace Negotiations.* New York: Alfred A. Knopf, 1981.

DeRoche, Andrew J. *Andrew Young: Civil Rights Ambassador.* Wilmington, Del.: Scholarly Resources Inc., 2003.

Dionne, E. J., Jr. *Why Americans Hate Politics.* New York: Simon and Schuster, 1991.

Dobbs, Michael. *Madeleine Albright.* New York: Henry Holt and Company, 1999.

Dobrynin, Anatoly. *In Confidence: Moscow's Ambassador to America's Six Cold War Presidents (1962–1986).* New York: Times Books, 1996.

Donovan, Hedley. *Roosevelt to Reagan: A Reporter's Encounter with Nine Presidents.* New York: Harper and Row, 1985.

Drew, Elizabeth. *American Journal: The Events of 1976.* New York: Random House, 1977.

Dumbrell, John. *The Carter Presidency: A Re-Evaluation.* Manchester: Manchester University Press, 1993.

Duncan, Francis. *Rickover: The Struggle for Excellence.* Annapolis Md.: Naval Institute Press, 2001.

Eisler, Kim Isaac. *A Justice for All: William J. Brennan, Jr. and the Decisions that Transformed America.* New York: Simon and Schuster, 1993.

Eizenstat, Stuart E. *Imperfect Justice: Looted Assets, Slave Labor, and the Unfinished Business of World War II.* New York: PublicAffairs, 2003.

Farber, Tom. *Taken Hostage: The Iran Hostage Crisis and America's First Encounter with Radical Islam.* Princeton, N.J.: Princeton University Press, 2005.

Ferguson, Thomas, and Joel Rogers. *The Decline of the Democrats and the Future of American Politics.* New York: Hill and Wang, 1986.

———. *The Hidden Election: Politics and Economics in the 1980 Presidential Campaign.* New York: Pantheon Books, 1981.

Fink, Gary M., and Hugh Davis Graham, eds. *The Carter Presidency: Policy Choices in the Post-New Deal Era.* Lawrence: University Press of Kansas, 1998.

Frady, Marshall. *Wallace.* Random House, 1996.

Freeman, Robert O. *The Soviet Union and the Carter Administration.* Pittsburgh, Pa.: University of Pittsburgh Center for Russian and European Studies, 1987.

Garrison, Jean. *Games Advisors Play: Foreign Policy in the Nixon and Carter Administrations.* College Station: Texas A&M University Press, 1999.

Garthoff, Raymond L. *Détente and Confrontation: American-Soviet Relations from Nixon to Reagan.* Washington, D.C.: Brookings Institution, 1994.

Gates, Robert M. *From the Shadows: The Ultimate Insider's Story of Five Presidents and How They Won the Cold War.* New York: Simon and Schuster, 1996.

Germond, Jack W., and Jules Witcover. *Blue Smoke and Mirrors: How Reagan Won and Why Carter Lost the Election of 1980.* New York: Viking, 1981.

Gibbons, Francis M. *Jack Anderson: Mormon Crusader in Gomorrah.* Lincoln, Nebr.: Writers Club Press, 2003.

Gillon, Steven M. *The Democrats' Dilemma: Walter F. Mondale and the Liberal Legacy.* New York: Columbia University Press, 1992.

Glad, Betty. *Jimmy Carter: In Search of the Great White House.* New York: W. W. Norton, 1980.

Goldberg, Robert Alan. *Barry Goldwater.* New Haven, Conn.: Yale University Press, 1995.

Grasselli, Gabriella. *British and American Responses to the Soviet Invasion of Afghanistan.* Brookfield, Vt.: Dartmouth, 1996.

Greene, John Robert. *The Presidency of Gerald R. Ford.* Lawrence: University Press of Kansas, 1995.

Greider, William. *Secrets of the Temple: How the Federal Reserve Runs the Country.* New York: Touchstone, 1987.

Griffith, Ernest S. *The American Presidency: The Dilemmas of Shared Power and Divided Government.* New York: New York University Press, 1976.

Harding, Harry. *A Fragile Relationship: The United States and China Since 1972.* Washington, D.C.: Brookings Institution, 1992.

Hargrove, Edwin C. *Jimmy Carter as President: Leadership and the Politics of the Public Good.* Baton Rouge: Louisiana State University Press, 1988.

Harris, David. *The Crisis: The President, the Prophet, and the Shah—1979 and the Coming of Militant Islam.* New York: Little, Brown and Company, 2004.

Harwood, Richard, ed. *The Pursuit of the Presidency 1980.* New York: Berkley Publishing Co., 1980.

Hayward, Steven F. *The Real Jimmy Carter: How Our Worst Ex-President Undermines American Foreign Policy, Coddles Dictators and Created the Party of Clinton and Kerry.* Washington, D.C.: Regnery, 2004.

Hess, Stephen. *Organizing the Presidency.* Washington, D.C.: Brookings Institution, 1976.

Hodgson, Godfrey. *The Gentleman from New York: Daniel Patrick Moynihan: A Biography.* Boston: Houghton Mifflin Co., 2000.

Hogan, J. Michael. *The Panama Canal in American Politics.* Carbondale: Southern Illinois University Press, 1986.

Horowitz, Daniel. *Jimmy Carter and the Energy Crisis of the 1970s: The 'Crisis of Confidence' Speech of July 15, 1979: A Brief History with Documents.* Boston: Bedford/St. Martin's, 2005.

Hurst, Steven. *The Carter Administration and Vietnam.* New York: St. Martin's Press, 1996.

Huyser, Robert E. *Mission to Iran.* New York: Harper and Row, 1986.

Jacobs, John. *A Rage for Justice: The Passion and Politics of Phillip Burton.* Berkeley: University of California Press, 1995.

Javits, Jacob K., with Rafael Steinberg. *Javits: The Autobiography of a Public Man.* Boston: Houghton Mifflin Company, 1981.

Jeffries, John C., Jr. *Justice Lewis F. Powell, Jr.* New York: Charles Scribner's Sons, 1994.

Johnson, Haynes. *In the Absence of Power: Governing America.* New York: Putnam, 1982.

Jones, Charles O. *The Trusteeship Presidency: Jimmy Carter and the United States Congress.* Baton Rouge: Louisiana State University Press, 1988.

Jordan, Hamilton. *Crisis: The Last Year of the Carter Presidency.* New York: Putnam, 1982.

———. *No Such Thing as a Bad Day: A Memoir.* Atlanta: Longstreet Press, 2000.

Jordan, Vernon E., Jr., with Annette Gordon-Reed. *Vernon Can Read: A Memoir.* New York: PublicAffairs, 2001.

Jorden, William J. *Panama Odyssey.* Austin: University of Texas Press, 1984.

Kagan, Robert. *A Twilight Struggle: American Power and Nicaragua, 1977–1990.* New York: Free Press, 1996.

Kaufman, Burton I., and Scott Kaufman. *The Presidency of James Earl Carter, Jr.* 2d ed. Lawrence: University Press of Kansas, 2006.

Kaufman, Robert G. *Henry Jackson: A Life in Politics.* Seattle: University of Washington Press, 2000.

Kellerman, Barbara. *The Political Presidency: Practice of Leadership from Kennedy through Reagan.* New York: Oxford University Press, 1984.

Klutznick, Philip M., with Sidney Hyman. *Angles of Vision: A Memoir of My Lives.* Chicago: Ivan R. Dee, 1991.

Kotz, Nick. *Wild Blue Yonder: Money, Politics, and the B-1 Bomber.* New York: Pantheon Books, 1988.

Kraus, Sidney, ed. *The Great Debates, Carter vs. Ford, 1976.* Bloomington: Indiana University Press, 1979.

Kucharsky, David. *The Man from Plains: The Mind and Spirit of Jimmy Carter.* New York: Harper and Row, 1976.

LaFeber, Walter. *The Panama Canal: The Crisis in Historical Perspective.* New York: Oxford University Press, 1990.

Laidi, Zaki. *The Superpowers and Africa: The Constraints of a Rivalry, 1960–1990.* Chicago: Chicago University Press, 1990.

Laingen, Bruce. *Yellow Ribbon: The Secret Journal of Bruce Laingen.* Washington, D.C.: Brassey's, 1992.

Lake, Anthony. *Somoza Falling: A Case Study of Washington at Work.* Amherst: University of Massachusetts Press, 1989.

Lance, Bert, with Bill Gilber. *The Truth of the Matter: My Life In and Out of Politics.* New York: Summit Books, 1991.

Lawson, Steven F. *In Pursuit of Power: Southern Blacks and Electoral Politics, 1965–1982.* New York: Columbia University Press, 1985.

Leuchtenburg, William E. *In the Shadow of FDR: From Harry Truman to Ronald Reagan.* New York: Oxford University Press, 1984.

Light, Paul Charles. *The President's Agenda: Domestic Policy Choices from Kennedy to Carter (with Notes on Ronald Reagan).* Baltimore: Johns Hopkins University Press, 1982.

Linowitz, Sol. M. *The Making of a Public Man: A Memoir.* Boston: Little, Brown and Co., 1985.

Lynn, Laurence E., Jr., and D. F. Whitman. *The President as Policymaker: Jimmy Carter and Welfare Reform.* Philadelphia: Temple University Press, 1982.

McCraw, Thomas K. *Prophets of Regulation. Charles Francis Adams, Louis D. Brandeis, James M. Landis, Alfred E. Kahn.* Cambridge, Mass.: Harvard University Press, 1984.

McLellan, David S. *Cyrus Vance.* Totowa, N.J.: Rowan & Allanheld, 1985.

Maltz, Earl M. *The Chief Justiceship of Warren Burger, 1969–1986.* Columbia: University of South Carolina Press, 2000.

Mann, James. *About Face: A History of America's Curious Relationship with China, From Nixon to Clinton.* New York: Vintage Press, 2000.

Mann, Robert. *Legacy to Power: Senator Russell Long of Louisiana.* New York: Paragon House, 1992.

Mazlish, Bruce, and Edwin Diamond. *Jimmy Carter: A Character Portrait.* New York: Simon and Schuster, 1979.

Merriner, James L. *Mr. Chairman: Power in Dan Rostenkowski's America.* Carbondale: Southern Illinois University Press, 1999.

Miller, William Lee. *Yankee from Georgia: The Emergence of Jimmy Carter.* New York: Times Books, 1978.

Mohammad Reza Pahlavi. *Answer to History.* New York: Stein and Day, 1980.

Mollenhoff, Clark. *The President Who Failed: Carter Out of Control.* New York: Macmillan, 1980.

Moore, David. *The Super Pollsters: How They Measure and Manipulate Public Opinion in*

America. New York: Four Walls Eight Windows, 1992.

Morley, Morris H. *Washington, Somoza, and the Sandinistas: State and Regime in U.S. Policy toward Nicaragua, 1969–1981*. New York: Cambridge University Press, 1994.

Morris, Kenneth E. *Jimmy Carter: American Moralist*. Athens: University of Georgia Press, 1996.

Mower, A. Glenn. *Human Rights and American Foreign Policy: The Carter and Reagan Experiences*. Westport, Conn.: Greenwood Press, 1987.

Muravchick, Joshua. *The Uncertain Crusade: Jimmy Carter and the Dilemmas of Human Rights*. New York: Hamilton Press, 1986.

Neuringer, Sheldon Morris. *The Carter Administration and Vietnam*. New York: St. Martin's Press, 1996.

Neustadt, Richard E. *Presidential Power: The Politics of Leadership from FDR to Carter*. New York: John Wiley and Sons, 1980.

Newsom, David. *The Soviet Brigade in Cuba: A Study of Political Diplomacy*. Bloomington: Indiana University Press, 1987.

Nielsen, Niels C. *The Religion of President Carter*. Nashville, Tenn.: Thomas Nelson, 1977.

Norton, Howard and Bob Slosser. *The Miracle of Jimmy Carter*. Plainfield, N.J.: Logos International, 1976.

O'Neill, Thomas P., with William Novak. *Man of the House: The Life and Political Memoirs of Speaker Tip O'Neill*. New York: Random House, 1987.

Pastor, Robert. *Condemned to Repetition: The United States and Nicaragua*. Princeton, N.J.: Princeton University Press, 1987.

———. *Whirlpool: U.S. Foreign Policy toward Latin America and the Caribbean*. Princeton, N.J.: Princeton University Press, 1992.

Peterson, Mark A. *Legislating Together: The White House and Capitol Hill from Eisenhower to Reagan*. Cambridge, Mass.: Harvard University Press, 1990.

Pippert, Wesley G. *The Spiritual Journal of Jimmy Carter: In His Own Words*. New York: Macmillan, 1978.

Polsby, Nelson W. *Consequences of Party Reform*. New York: Oxford University Press, 1983.

Powell, Jody. *The Other Side of the Story*. New York: William Morrow, 1982.

Quandt, William B. *Camp David: Peacemaking and Politics*. Washington, D.C.: Brookings Institution, 1986.

Reuss, Henry S. *When Government Was Good: Memories of a Life in Politics*. Madison: University of Wisconsin Press, 1999.

Rhodes, John, with Dean Smith. *John Rhodes: "I Was There."* Salt Lake City, Utah: Northwest Publishing Inc., 1995.

Robinson, Archie. *George Meany and His Time*. New York: Simon and Schuster, 1981.

Rockefeller, David. *Memoirs*. New York: Random House, 2003.

Rosati, Jerel. *The Carter Administration's Quest for Global Community: Beliefs and Their Impact on Behavior*. Columbia: University of South Carolina Press, 1987.

Rosenbaum, Herbert D., and Alexej Ugrinsky, eds. *Jimmy Carter: Foreign Policy and Post-Presidential Years*. Westport, Conn.: Greenwood Press, 1994.

———, eds. *The Presidency and Domestic Policies of Jimmy Carter*. Westport, Conn.: Greenwood Press, 1994.

Rosenkranz, E. Joshua, and Bernard Schwartz, eds. *Reason and Passion: Justice Brennan's Enduring Influence*. New York: W. W. Norton and Co., 1997.

Ross, Robert S. *Negotiating Cooperation: The United States and China, 1969–1989*. Stanford, Calif.: Stanford University Press, 1995.

Rozell, Mark J. *The Press and the Carter Presidency*. Boulder, Colo.: Westview Press, 1989.

Rubin, Barry. *Paved with Good Intentions: The American Experience in Iran*. New York: Oxford University Press, 1980.

Ryan, Paul B. *The Iranian Rescue Mission and Why It Failed.* Annapolis, Md.: Naval Institute Press, 1986.

Safire, William. *Safire's Washington.* New York: Times Books, 1980.

Sanders, Jerry W. *Peddlers of Crisis: The Committee on the Present Danger and the Politics of Containment.* Boston: South End Press, 1983.

Sarkesian, S., ed. *Defense Policy and the Presidency: Carter's First Years.* Boulder, Colo.: Westview Press, 1979.

Savranskaya, Svetlana, and David A. Welch. *Global Competition and the Deterioration of U.S.-Soviet Relations, 1977–1980.* Providence, R.I.: Center for Foreign Policy Development, 1995.

Schieffer, Bob, and Gary Paul Gates. *The Acting President.* New York: E. P. Dutton, 1989.

Schmidt, Helmut. *Men and Power: A Political Perspective.* New York: Random House, 1989.

Schoultz, Lars. *Human Rights and U.S. Policy towards Latin America.* Princeton, N.J.: Princeton University Press, 1981.

Schram, Martin. *Running for President, 1976: The Carter Campaign.* New York: Stein and Day, 1977.

Schulman, Bruce J. *The Seventies: The Great Shift in American Culture, Society and Politics.* New York: Da Capo Press, 2001.

Schultze, Charles L. *Other Times, Other Places.* Washington, D.C.: Brookings Institution, 1986.

Schwartz, Bernard. *The Ascent of Pragmatism: The Burger Court in Action.* Reading, Mass.: Addison-Wesley Publishing Co., 1990.

Seliktar, Ofira. *Failing the Crystal Ball Test: The Carter Administration and the Fundamentalist Revolution in Iran.* Westport, Conn.: Praeger, 2000.

Shogan, Robert. *Promises to Keep: Carter's First Hundred Days.* New York: Thomas Y. Crowell, 1977.

Shoup, Laurence H. *The Carter Presidency and Beyond: Power and Politics in the 1980s.* Palo Alto, Calif.: Ramparts Press, 1980.

Sick, Gary. *All Fall Down: America's Tragic Encounter with Iran.* New York: Random House, 1985.

———. *October Surprise: America's Hostages in Iran and the Election of Ronald Reagan.* New York: Times Books, 1991.

Skidmore, David. *Reversing Course: Carter's Foreign Policy, Domestic Politics, and the Failure of Reform.* Nashville, Tenn.: Vanderbilt University Press, 1996.

Skowronek, Stephen. *The Politics Presidents Make: Leadership from John Adams to George Bush.* Cambridge, Mass.: Harvard University Press, 1993.

Smith, Gaddis. *Morality, Reason and Power.* New York: Hill and Wang, 1986.

Smith, Hedrick. *The Power Game: How Washington Works.* Ballantine Books, 1988.

Spiegel, Steven L. *The Other Arab-Israeli Conflict: Making America's Middle East Policy, from Truman to Reagan.* Chicago: University of Chicago Press, 1985.

Stivers, William. *America's Confrontation with Revolutionary Change in the Middle East, 1948–83.* New York: St. Martin's Press, 1986.

Strong, Robert A. *Working in the World: Jimmy Carter and the Making of American Foreign Policy.* Baton Rouge: Louisiana State University Press, 2000.

Stroud, Kandy. *How Jimmy Won: The Victory Campaign from Plains to the White House.* New York: William Morrow, 1977.

Sullivan, William H. *Mission to Iran.* New York: W. W. Norton, 1981.

———. *Obbligato, 1939–1979: Notes on a Foreign Service Career.* New York: W. W. Norton and Company, 1984.

Talbott, Strobe. *Endgame: The Inside Story of SALT II.* New York: Harper and Row, 1979.

Talmadge, Herman E., with Mark Royden Winchell. *Talmadge: A Political Legacy, A Politician's Life: A Memoir.* Atlanta: Peachtree Publishers, Ltd., 1987.

Tebbell, John William, and Sarah Miles Watts. *The Press and the Presidency: From George Washington to Ronald Reagan.* New York: Oxford University Press, 1985.

Thompson, Kenneth W., ed. *The Carter Presidency: Fourteen Intimate Perspectives of Jimmy Carter.* New York: University Press of America, 1990.

Thornton, Richard C. *The Carter Years: Toward a New Global Order.* New York: Paragon House, 1991.

Timmerman, Kenneth R. *Shakedown: Exposing the Real Jesse Jackson.* Washington, D.C.: Regnery Publishing, Inc., 2002.

Treaster, Joseph B. *Paul Volcker: The Making of a Financial Legend.* Hoboken, N.J.: John Wiley and Sons, Inc., 2004.

Turner, Stansfield. *Secrecy and Democracy: The CIA in Transition.* Boston: Houghton Mifflin, 1985.

———. *Terrorism and Democracy.* Boston: Houghton Mifflin Company, 1991.

Tyler, Patrick. *A Great Wall: Six Presidents and China.* New York: PublicAffairs, 2000.

Udall, Morris K., with Bob Neuman and Randy Udall. *Too Funny to be President.* New York: Henry Holt and Company, 1988.

Vance, Cyrus. *Hard Choices: Critical Years in America's Foreign Policy.* New York: Simon and Schuster, 1983.

Vogelsang, Sandy. *American Dream, Global Nightmare: The Dilemma of U.S. Human Rights Policy.* New York: W. W. Norton, 1980.

Wasserman, Sherri. *The Neutron Bomb Controversy: A Study in Alliance Politics.* New York: Praeger, 1983.

Weddington, Sarah. *A Question of Choice.* New York: Penguin Books, 1993.

Witcover, Jules. *Marathon: The Pursuit of the Presidency, 1972–1976.* New York: Viking Press, 1977.

Woodward, Bob. *Shadow: Five Presidents and the Legacy of Watergate.* New York: Simon and Schuster, 1999.

Wooten, James. *Dasher: The Roots and the Rising of Jimmy Carter.* New York: Summit Books, 1978.

Wright, Jim. *Balance of Power: Presidents and Congress from the Era of McCarthy to the Age of Gingrich.* Turner Publishing Inc., 1996.

Young, Andrew. *Andrew Young: An Easy Burden: The Civil Rights Movement and the Transformation of America.* New York: HarperCollins, 1996.

INDEX

Boldface page numbers indicate primary discussions. *Italic* page numbers indicate illustrations.

F

O